P9-DMS-989

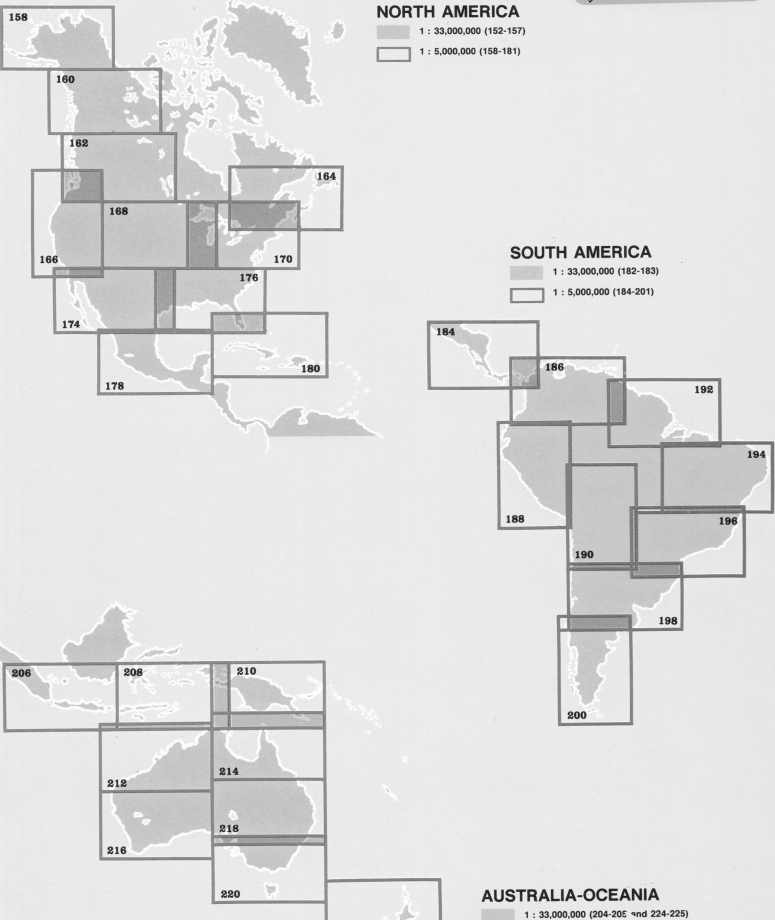

## NORTH AMERICA

1 : 33,000,000 (152-157)

1 : 5,000,000 (158-181)

158
160
162
164
168
166
170
176
174
180
178

## SOUTH AMERICA

1 : 33,000,000 (182-183)

1 : 5,000,000 (184-201)

184
186
192
194
188
196
190
198
200

206
208
210
212
214
216
218
220
222

## AUSTRALIA-OCEANIA

1 : 33,000,000 (204-205 and 224-225)

1 : 5,000,000 (206-228)

# WEBSTER'S
# NEW WORLD
# ATLAS

# WEBSTER'S
# NEW WORLD
# ATLAS

PRENTICE HALL PRESS
NEW YORK

GREENLAND
(DENMARK)

ICELAND

REYKJAVIK

Arctic circle
66° 33'

60°

ALASKA (U.S.)

C A N A D A

Vancouver

Quebec
OTTAWA • Montreal
Toronto
Chicago • Detroit • Boston
New York
WASHINGTON

ATLANTIC

DUBLIN
IRELAND

PORTUGAL
LISBON

OCEAN

RABAT

40°

San Francisco

U N I T E D   S T A T E S

Los Angeles

PACIFIC

Houston
New Orleans
Miami
BAHAMAS
NASSAU
HAVANA
CUBA

MOROCCO

WESTERN SAHARA

Tropic of Cancer
23° 27'
20°

MEXICO

MEXICO
CITY

Belmopan
BELIZE
GUATEMALA
GUATEMALA
EL SALVADOR
SAN SALVADOR

KINGSTON
JAMAICA
HONDURAS
TEGUCIGALPA
NICARAGUA
MANAGUA

HAITI SANTO DOMINGO
PORT-
AU-PRINCE
DOMINICAN
REPUBLIC

Nouadhibou
NOUAKCHOTT
MAURITANIA

St-Louis
PRAIA
CAPE VERDE
ISLANDS
DAKAR
GAMBIA
BANJUL
BISSAU
GUINEA BISSAU
SENEGAL
BAMAKO
CONAKRY
SIERRA LEONE
FREETOWN
LIBERIA
MONROVIA

OUAG

GUINEA

COSTA RICA
SAN JOSE
PANAMA
PANAMA

CARACAS
VENEZUELA
BOGOTA
COLOMBIA

GEORGETOWN
GUYANA PARAMARIBO
SURINAM

IVORY
COAST
SAC
ET P

TARAWA
0°

KIRIBATI

QUITO
ECUADOR

PERU

Equator

OCEAN

TUVALU
FUNAFUTI
WESTERN
SAMOA
APIA

BRAZIL

Recife

ATLANTIC

LIMA

FIJI SUVA TONGA
20°

BRASILIA

LA PAZ
BOLIVIA

Tropic of Capricorn
23° 27'

NUKU'ALOFA

PARAGUAY

Rio de Janeiro

ASUNCION
São Paulo

ARGENTINA
URUGUAY

NEW
WELLINGTON
ZEALAND

SANTIAGO
CHILE
BUENOS AIRES

MONTEVIDEO

OCEAN

San Juan
PUERTO RICO
(U.S.)

(U.K.)
VIRGIN ISLANDS
(U.S.)
NETHERLANDS
ANTILLES
ST-CHRISTOPHER
AND NEVIS

ANGUILLA (U.K.)
ST-MARTIN (F. and Neth.)
ST-BARTHELEMY (F.)

BASSE-
TERRE
ANTIGUA
BARBUDA
ST-JOHN'S

MONTSERRAT
(U.K.)

GUADELOUPE (F.)

Caribbean

Sea

DOMINICA
ROSEAU

MARTINIQUE (F.)

ST-LUCIA
CASTRIES

BARBADOS
BRIDGETOWN

60°

SAINT-VINCENT
AND THE
GRENADINES
KINGSTOWN

GRENADA
ST-GEORGE'S

0   100   200 km

Antarctic circle
66° 33'

PORT OF SPAIN
TRINIDAD
AND TOBAGO

VENEZUELA

ANTARCTIC

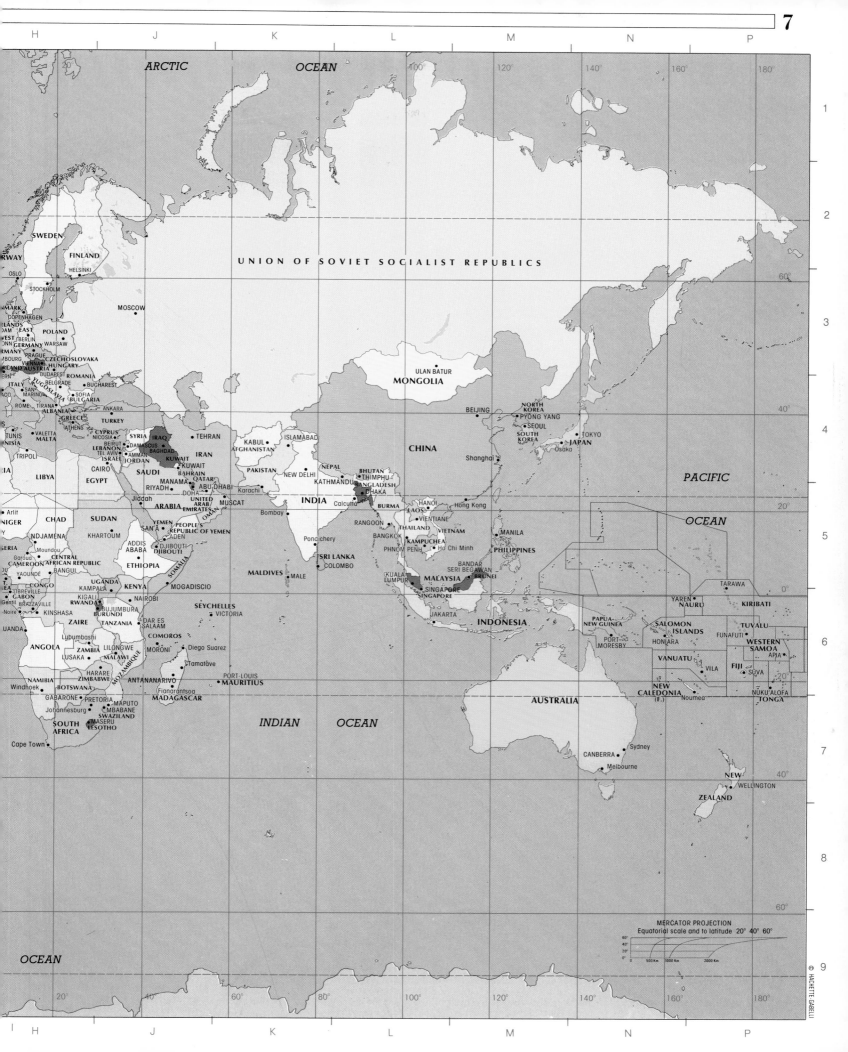

## DEVELOPMENT OF CARTOGRAPHY

### The Early Days

There are cartographic documents dating back to the Mesopotamian period, but cartography proper was invented by the Greeks. Eratosthenes (ca. 276-194 B.C.) measured the meridian at Syene (Aswan) and devised a right-angle grid of intersecting East-West parallels and North-South meridians on which territory could be drawn. The earliest known world map is Ptolemy's (A.D. 130).

### The Ascent of Cartography

Only with the Age of Exploration and the invention of printing (1440) did cartography make real progress. The Romans had produced little, and for religious reasons the cartographer monks of the Middle Ages considered the earth to be a flat surface surrounded by water, with its center at Jerusalem. Yet there are two famous medieval maps: one by Sanuto, a 12th-century Venetian, and the Catalan Map. The real breakthrough was made by two Flemish geographers: Mercator, the father of modern cartography, and Ortelius, whose principal works appeared in 1569 and 1570 respectively.

### The First Exact Depictions of the Earth

Two 17th-century Frenchmen, Sanson and Delisle, produced the first globes. Only with progress in mathematics and astronomy and with Picard and Cassini's measurement of the arc of the meridian did cartography become a true science. John Harrison's 18th-century invention of the marine chronometer made it possible to measure longitude; that period produced the first complete and exact world maps.

### The Contribution of New Technology

In the first half of the 19th century, cartography became a virtual preserve of the military, who codified conventional signs and adopted the use of shading to indicate relief. In 1875, after geodesic and cartographic studies, 20 countries opted to standardize measurements of length with the metric system.

New possibilities emerged early in our century with advances in aviation and printing. Photogrammetry replaced conventional topography, and shading gave way to contour lines, more suited to the varied needs of users. Thematic mapping became widespread. Progress continues with such new technologies as data processing and remote sensing (satellite photography).

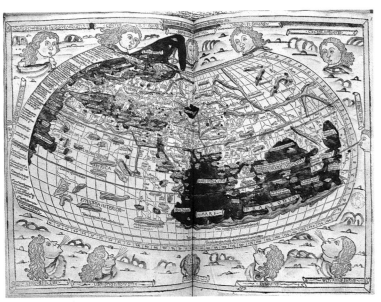

Ptolemy's map of the world, as printed in Ulm in 1482. Note the contrast between the relative precision of the Mediterranean Sea and the depiction of the Indian Ocean (south of which, from Africa down, lay terra incognita: parts unknown). The elongation of Europe and Asia left no room for undiscovered America. These errors survived into the 16th century. Photograph: Bibliotheque Nationale, Paris.

## PROJECTIONS, FROM MERCATOR TO THE PRESENT

The main problem for the map-maker is representing a curved surface on a flat sheet. The distortion and inaccuracy inherent in that process can be minimized by the use of various systems of projection.

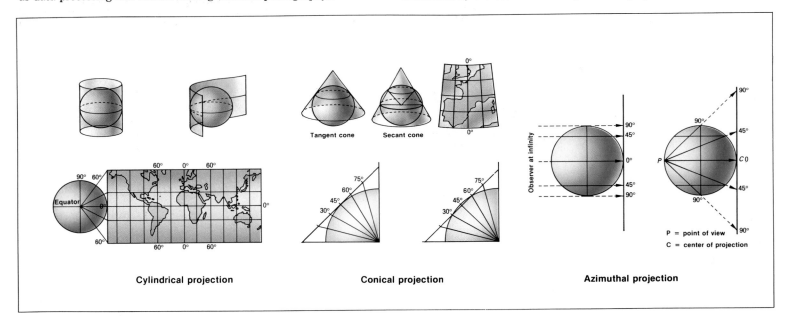

Tangent cone    Secant cone

Observer at infinity

P = point of view
C = center of projection

Cylindrical projection    Conical projection    Azimuthal projection

### Cylindrical Projection

In Mercator's projection, the Earth's surface is projected onto a cylinder tangent to the equator. When unrolled, the cylinder becomes a plane surface with a right-angle grid of meridians and parallels. The drawback is that this exaggerates the size of high-latitude areas. Greenland, half the size of India, appears much larger. But coastlines and angles are correctly represented. This is known as a conformal projection, and it is used in particular for planispheres, marine charts and maps of low-latitude regions.

### Conic Projection

This system, devised by Lambert, is used for large-scale maps and the middle latitudes. The Earth is projected onto a cone whose vertex coincides with the polar axis, either tangent or secant to the globe along a parallel.

### Azimuthal Projections

These are of two kinds: orthographic and stereographic. The first is a projection of the Earth as seen by an observer an infinite distance away; points are projected perpendicular to the plane of projection. Any point on the globe may be defined as a pole and will then serve as the center of the area to be mapped. This is how the sun and other planets are represented.

In stereographic projection the point of view is that of a point on the surface of the Earth opposite the center of the projection. Angles remain true, but distances and surfaces are magnified as they become more distant from the center of projection. It is used for polar and celestial maps, and globes.

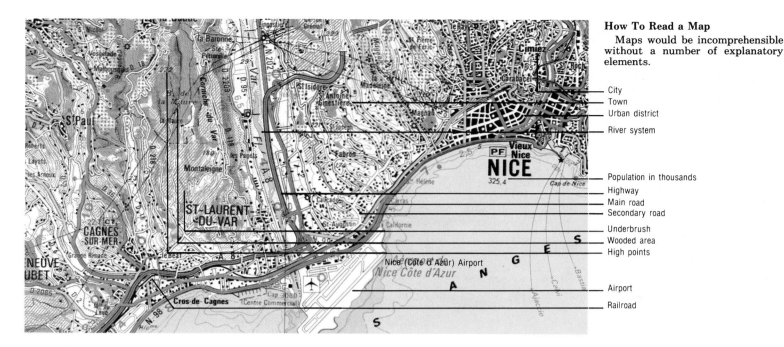

### How To Read a Map

Maps would be incomprehensible without a number of explanatory elements.

City
Town
Urban district
River system

Population in thousands
Highway
Main road
Secondary road
Underbrush
Wooded area
High points

Airport
Railroad

### Scale and Legend

The first is SCALE: the relationship between true distances and those of the map. On maps at 1:10,000 and 1:25,000 scale 1″ represents 833 ft. and 2083 ft., respectively.

The LEGEND is the second element needed to understand a map. It explains the meaning of the symbols used.

### Representation of Relief and Water

On topographical maps relief is indicated by linear signs such as contour lines or dashed or dotted lines, or by altitude figures. Water systems are shown in blue.

### Land Use

This is indicated by areas of color or shading. Road and rail systems are indicated by continuous lines, with colors signifying varying size or importance.

### Conventional Signs

The size of a place is indicated by the size of the typeface used. On thematic maps, symbols such as squares, rectangles or circles can indicate various features. Areas and points of color are also used. In general, maps are most graphic when the relationship among the most important features is clear.

The SPOT satellite, orbiting the Earth at an altitude of 500 miles, transmits black and white and color photographs at resolutions of 33 ft and 66 ft. respectively.

A bend in the River Seine photographed from 13,000 ft. from an aircraft flying back and forth over a fixed area to obtain parallel bands of data.

The Cotentin peninsula: Infrared satellite picture. Source: IGN, France.

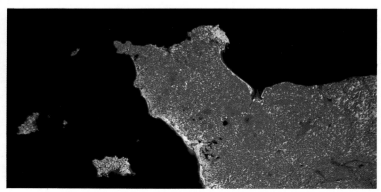

## THE SURFACE OF THE EARTH

The Earth is a sphere revolving on its polar axis. Its surface is irregular, with plateaus, hills and mountains. The average altitude of the continents is 2700 ft.; the average depth of the seas, 29,000 ft.

The Earth's highest peak is Mt. Everest, in the Himalayas (29,021 ft. above sea level). Ocean trenches can be as deep as the tallest mountains are high, and even deeper in the Marianas Trench, which reaches 36,080 ft. below sea level. This 12 mile range between the two extremes is a mere 1/135 of the Earth's radius.

## PLATE TECTONICS

Continental and ocean-floor relief takes the shape of mountain ranges (such as the Alps, the Himalayas, the Rockies and the Andes) or ocean ridges (the largest being the mid-Atlantic ridge, whose visible portions form Iceland, the Azores and St. Helena).

The solid part of the Earth's crust, the lithosphere, is subjected to forces caused by magma welling up from the asthenosphere. The lithosphere is split into shifting plates. The submarine crust takes the form of ocean ridges: Magma rises and the plates it creates rupture under the force of the new material welling up. These movements used to be called continental drift.

Points of contact between plates are generally marked by volcanic and seismic activity. The 'belt of fire' in the Pacific is where a vast oceanic plate meets the surrounding continents. In California two plates abut along the San Andreas fault; this caused the 1905 San Francisco earthquake. Along the Andes, such contact has buried the oceanic crust, creating a marine trench parallel to the coast.

Mountains are formed when the continental crust fractures and crumples under the force of colliding plates. The massive Himalayas are the result of the collision of the Deccan plate and the Eurasian plate.

Plate tectonics permits a consistent interpretation of the Earth's features.

## CONTINENTAL DRIFT

The continents are changing in shape and position; 200 million years ago there was a single vast continent, Pangea, which covered about 40% of the Earth's surface. About 80 million years later, the effects of continental drift split it in two, producing Laurasia in the north and Gondwana in the south, separated by the Sea of Tethys. Some 60 million years after that, Laurasia broke up into North America and Eurasia, and Gondwana into South America, Africa, Australia and Antarctica: the continents we know today.

The continental drift theory is comparatively recent, having been expounded by the German, Alfred Wegener, in 1915.

## AN OCEAN PLANET

Seven tenths of our planet is covered by water, divided into four main areas: the Pacific, Atlantic, Indian and Arctic Oceans. The Pacific alone covers 350 times the area of France, or 69 sq. miles. Smaller seas surrounded by land penetrate deep into the continents. For example, the Mediterranean Sea meets the Atlantic Ocean and, with the Black and Azov Seas, extends into the very heart of Eurasia. Some geographers and scientists hold that the Southern (Antarctic) Ocean constitutes a fifth ocean.

## EARTH'S DIMENSIONS

Earth is the third planet from the sun, after Mercury and Venus, and before Mars, Jupiter, Saturn, Uranus, Neptune and Pluto. Its single satellite, the Moon, is about one fiftieth its size. A distinguishing feature of Earth is its relatively dense atmosphere, which protects it from solar radiation and provides the gasses necessary for life and enabling it to sustain its own resources through photosynthesis (ordchlorophyll assimilation). The atmosphere is in layers, their thickness varying with distance from the equator. Since the layers differ in altitude and temperature we can distinguish between the troposphere, the stratosphere, the mesosphere and the thermosphere.

The Earth's surface is varied as well. The oceans occupy a vast area, descending to depths unmatched by the height of any of the continents. Less is known about the internal composition of the Earth than about the atmosphere. The planet has several layers, varying in density and thickness. The crust is thin and subject to tectonic plate movements, decisive in determining continental and undersea relief. The mantle is more stable and appears to be immune to faulting. In the true center of the earth, the core matter is fluid, owing to the intense heat. This is the seat of the electrical and magnetic forces that cause such phenomena as terrestrial magnetism.

Mean radius: 3,956 miles
Equatorial diameter: 7,921 miles
Polar diameter: 7,894 miles
Flattening: 0.0034
Equatorial circumference: 24,887 miles
Polar circumference: 24,845 miles
Mean density: 5.53
Approx. mass: $13.16 \times 10^{24}$ lbs, or 13183.5 billion billion tons
Area: 196,898,989 sq. miles
Gravitational acceleration at the equator: 32 ft/second
Escape velocity: 7 miles/second
Period of sidereal rotation: 23 hr, 56 min, 4 sec
Equatorial inclination to orbital plane: 23°26'
Albedo: 0.33
Strength of magnetic field: $5 \times 10^{-5}$ tesla (average at Earth's surface)
Semimajor axis of orbit: 93,067,760 miles (= 1 astronomical unit)
Maximum distance from sun: 94,454,100 miles
Minimum distance from sun: 91,349,100 miles
Eccentricity: 0.0167
Inclination of the ecliptic: 0 by definition
Period of sidereal revolution: 365 days, 6 hr, 9 min, 5 sec.
Mean orbital speed: 18.50 miles/ "per" second
Volume: 259,972,000 cubic miles

## CONTINENTS AND ISLANDS

Dry land is divided into six major masses: Eurasia, Africa, North America, South America, Antarctica and Australia. Other land areas, such as Greenland, New Guinea, Borneo and Madagascar, count as islands.

Tens of millions of smaller islands are found on the fringes of the continents or grouped in archipelagos or strings of islands in mid-ocean.

The hemispheres are not symmetrical. The South is basically oceanic with a continent at the pole, while the North is more continental, with an ocean at its pole.

*A silent world. Only in this century have we begun to unlock the secrets of the ocean depths. One feature dominates these discoveries: the Rift, a vast fissure 37,260 miles long intersected by precipitous valleys.*
*Map: Tanguy de Rmur's map of the seabed. Mercator projection. (Scale at the equator, 1:48,000,000)*

## CLIMATIC FACTORS

The lowest layer of the atmosphere (the troposphere) is the site of the atmospheric phenomena causing the weather that makes up the Earth's varied climates. Climate is influenced by such factors as distribution of land and sea, relief and latitude.

### Solar Radiation

The spherical shape of the Earth means that solar radiation decreases from the equator to the poles, although the heavy cloud layer between the Tropics mitigates the theoretical effects of days of sunlight per year, which near 100% in the arid tropics (97% in the Sahara); the North Pole sees 186 sunless winter days. Between the Tropics of Cancer and Capricorn the sun is directly overhead at noon once a year. The Arctic and Antarctic Circles mark latitudes above which 24-hour darkness reigns when the sun is at its zenith in the Tropic of the opposite hemisphere.

### Temperature

The heating and cooling of air masses causes the formation of anticyclones (high pressure) and depressions (low pressure), producing energy transfer in the form of heat (temperature) and water vapor (cloud). Altitude influences temperature, which decreases 32.27°F/328 ft. Latitude is another factor.

A basic temperature is 32°F, at which water changes from a liquid to solid ice or snow. Sea water freezes at 28.4°F. Freezing point helps define regions where there is no frost (tropical or intertropical), those where it is rare or seasonal (medium latitudes) and those with frequent or perpetual frost (polar and high mountain regions).

### Precipitation

Precipitation (solid or liquid) is as essential a climatic element as temperature. Quantity, type, seasonal distribution and regularity of precipitation are crucial to human societies, and especially to farmers. Equatorial countries get abundant rainfall (more than 39") distributed throughout the year. Further from the equator there is less precipitation, and it tends to be concentrated in the summer. Only the monsoon— centered on southeastern Asia and parts of Africa— brings substantial rainfall (up to 512" in India).

In tropical latitudes mean annual rainfall drops below 11.8"; this is typical of desert areas, the largest of which is the Sahara. Beyond 32°N and 32°S, precipitation again rises, particularly in the cold season in Mediterranean climates, then more regularly in temperate climates, with snow in winter. In still higher latitudes, the proportion of snow increases, covering the ground for several months a year.

The cold is intense and permanent in the Polar regions. The sparse precipitation takes the form of snow. Evaporation is slight, helping keep the land masses relatively stable. The angle of incidence minimizes the sun's rays and the short or nonexistent summer prevents snow and ice from melting; this explains the formation of the Greenland and Antarctic ice sheets.

## TYPES OF CLIMATE

Different combinations of geographic and meteorological factors yield different types of climate.

The **EQUATORIAL CLIMATE** is hot and humid. Temperatures are high (78.8° to 82.4°F) all year round,

the air is constantly saturated, and rain is frequent and heavy in all seasons (59" to 394" along the mountainous coasts).

Temperatures are high in **TROPICAL CLIMATES** too, but with seasonal variations. It is dry in winter and spring; the rainy season is in summer and autumn. The length of the dry season and the heaviness of the rain vary with latitude: Further from the equator, rainfall is less and the dry season longer (59" and 3-5 months near the equator; 20" and 6-9 months nearer arid regions). The seasonal cycle is the same in tropical monsoon climates, but rainfall is much higher.

**DESERT CLIMATES**, marked by heat and drought (higher than 86°F with .984" of rain), are found in tropical and subtropical latitudes. Temperature can vary by as much as 86° in a day. Semidesert climates, which get slightly more rain, mark the transition to tropical climates.

The range of temperatures in **OCEAN CLIMATES** is narrow, the seasons ill-defined and rainfall distributed throughout the year (7.87" to 9.84", with the maximum in winter). Temperatures are mild and winters moderate.

**CONTINENTAL CLIMATES** are little affected by the oceans. Temperatures are high in summer and low in winter. Thunderstorms are common in the hot season but annual precipitation is low. Temperatures can drop as low as −40°F in the 4-5 months of winter. Continental climates have their desert regions, generally in sheltered areas or very far from the sea.

The **MEDITERRANEAN CLIMATE** is not widespread. Temperatures (59-68°F), and rainfall uneven (11.8" to 39.37"). Summers are hot and dry, winters wet and mild.

In **POLAR CLIMATES** temperatures are always very low, and the meager precipitation is always in solid form.

## THE WATER CYCLE

The range of temperatures is limited by the oceans and their huge mass of water, comprising 97% of the hydrosphere, or $792 \times 10^6$ cubic miles. The remaining 3% is made up of ice sheets and glaciers (2.09%), underground deposits (0.6%), lakes and rivers (0.01362%), the atmosphere (0.00094%) and the biosphere (0.00004%).

Each year 15,185 trillion cubic ft. of water evaporate from the oceans and 2,472 trillion cubic ft. from the land; 13,772 trillion cubic ft. fall into the oceans and 3,884 trillion cubic ft. onto the land. Water evaporates from the land, runs off at the surface in rivers, or seeps down to replenish the water table which feeds the springs. Waterways then return the water to the seas and oceans.

**The Water Cycle**

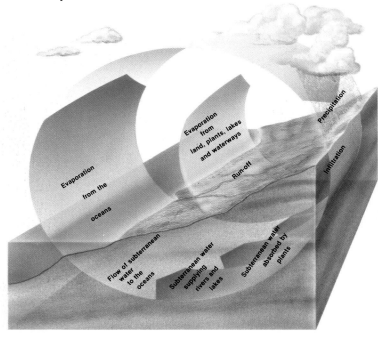

Evaporation from the oceans

Evaporation from land, plants, lakes and waterways

Precipitation

Run-off

Infiltration

Flow of subterranean water to the oceans

Subterranean water supplying rivers and lakes

Subterranean water absorbed by plants

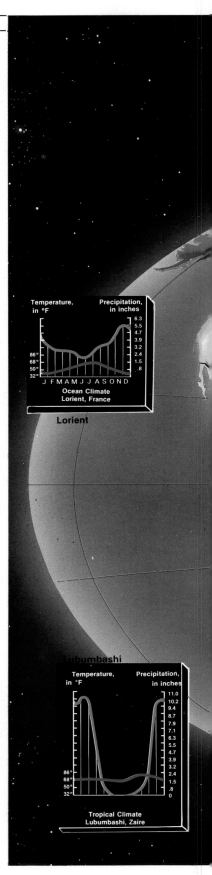

Temperature, in °F    Precipitation, in inches

6.3
5.5
4.7
3.9
3.2
2.4
1.5
.8

86°
68°
50°
32°

J F M A M J J A S O N D

Ocean Climate
Lorient, France

Lorient

Lubumbashi

Temperature, in °F    Precipitation, in inches

11.0
10.2
9.4
8.7
7.9
7.1
6.3
5.5
4.7
3.9
3.2
2.4
1.5
.8
0

86°
68°
50°
32°

Tropical Climate
Lubumbashi, Zaire

**The Earth's Climates**

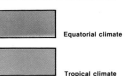

Equatorial climate

Tropical climate

**Temperature, in °F** **Precipitation, in inches**

Polar Climate
Thule, Greenland

Thule

Thule

Kiev

Lorient

Calcutta

El Fasher

Singapore

Lubumbashi

Adelaide

Kiev

**Temperature, in °F** **Precipitation, in inches**

86°
68°
50°
32°
14°

3.9
3.2
2.4
1.5
.8
0

J F M A M J J A S O N D

Continental Climate
Kiev, USSR

Calcutta

**Temperature, in °F** **Precipitation, in inches**

86°
68°
50°
32°

11.8
11.0
10.2
9.4
8.7
7.9
7.1
6.3
5.5
4.7
3.9
3.2
2.4
1.5
.8
0

J F M A M J J A S O N D

Tropical Monsoon Climate
Calcutta, India

Singapore

**Temperature, in °F** **Precipitation, in inches**

104°
86°
68°
50°
32°

11.0
10.2
9.4
8.7
7.9
7.1
6.3
5.5
4.7
3.9
3.2
2.4
1.5
.8
0

J F M A M J J A S O N D

Equatorial Climate
Singapore

El Fasher

**Temperature, in °F** **Precipitation, in inches**

86°
68°
50°
32°

5.5
4.7
3.9
3.2
2.4
1.5
.8
0

J F M A M J J A S O N D

SemiArid Tropical Climate
El-Fasher, Sudan

Adelaide

**Temperature, in °F** **Precipitation, in inches**

86°
68°
50°
32°

3.9
3.2
2.4
1.5
.8

J F M A M J J A S O N D

Mediterranean Climate
Adelaide, Australia

Subtropical climate,
Eastern portion of a continent

Arid continental climate

Mediterranean climate

Ocean climate

Continental climate

Cold continental climate

Mountain climate

Polar climate

## CLIMAX VEGETATION AND EXISTING VEGETATION

Various factors can change the parallel relationship between climate and plant life. Microclimates can be very localized, and human intervention has often changed the landscape. Thus, we must differentiate between climax vegetation (adapted to climatic conditions) and existing vegetation. Forests are one of the main vegetable environments, covering 15 million sq. miles, nearly one third of our planet's dry land.

## HOT REGIONS

### A Green World

The **EQUATORIAL FOREST** lies within a few degrees of the equator, in hot, humid climates. Forest species are stratified in four or five stories, the highest reaching 164 ft., which makes the forest dark, dense and stifling. Leaves are green all year round.

### Adaptation to Drought

The **TROPICAL FOREST** lies between the two Tropics and varies with the length of the dry season, which can range from three to six months. In deciduous forests, the trees lose their leaves in the rainy season. There are many bamboos in the monsoon forest of Southeast Asia. Progressing toward the savanna lies the **OPEN FOREST**, where the vegetation is homogeneous but scattered and low. The dominant species is the baobab. In coastal and marshy areas we find the **MANGROVE SWAMP**; the mangrove, its characteristic tree, has both underwater and overhead roots.

The tropical forest alone covers 2.8 billion acres.

### A World of Drought

The **SAVANNA** is adapted to a 6 to 9-month dry season and is found at the edge of desert areas. Grasses 3 to 9 ft. in height dominate. With sufficient rainfall it can become a treed savanna with isolated trees and shrubs, a park savanna where scattered trees are grouped in groves, or a river bank gallery forest.

In **DESERTS**, vegetation is nearly absent. They are located in arid or semiarid climates where precipitation never exceeds 16 inches. This lack of water is combined with very high temperatures. Deserts at the western ends of the various continents lie between the 15th and 30th parallels. Further to the east in the heart of Eurasia, they range from the Tropic of Cancer to 45°N.

Human activity, such as intensive sheep raising or exploitation of forest

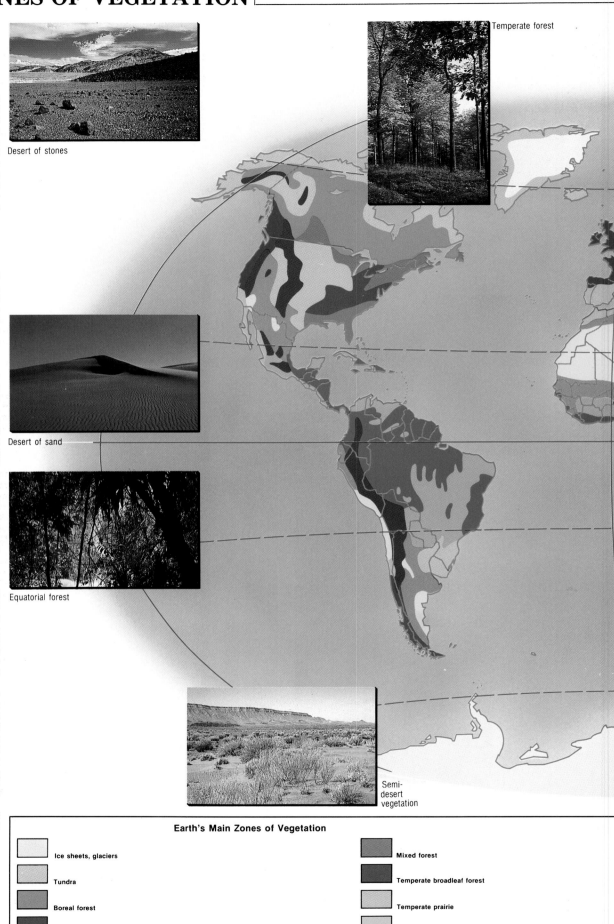

Temperate forest

Desert of stones

Desert of sand

Equatorial forest

Semi-desert vegetation

**Earth's Main Zones of Vegetation**

Ice sheets, glaciers

Tundra

Boreal forest

Oceanic conifer forest

Mixed forest

Temperate broadleaf forest

Temperate prairie

Mediterranean vegetation

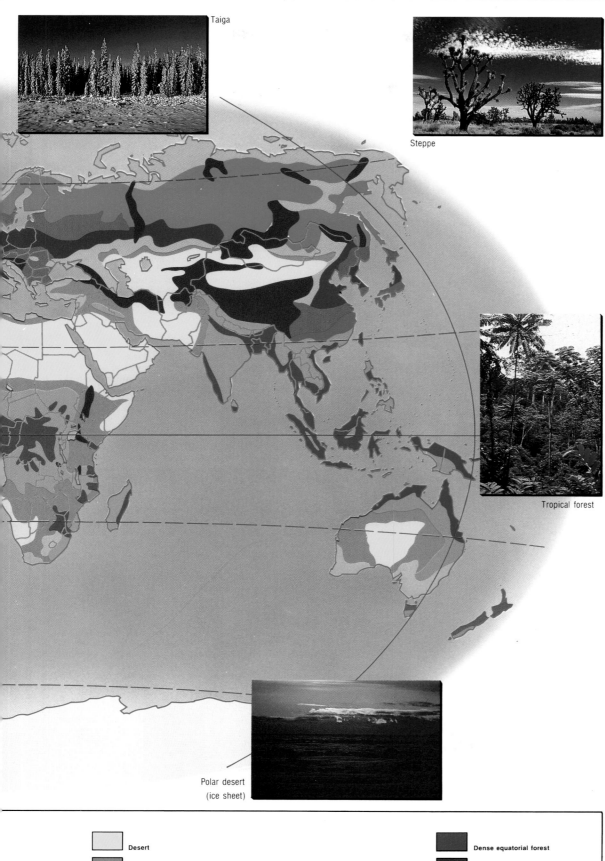

Taiga

Steppe

Tropical forest

Polar desert
(ice sheet)

land in semiarid zones, is causing desert creep, at the estimated rate of 12–14 million acres per year worldwide. This is not irreversible: In areas protected from animals a spontaneous regrowth of savanna vegetation has been observed.

## TEMPERATE AND COLD REGIONS

### A Changing Environment

In temperate continental climates (cold in winter, hot and dry in summer) the equivalent of the savanna is the **STEPPE**. Covered in dried vegetation in the dry season, it blooms with plants and colorful flowers at the first rains.

### In the Grip of the Cold

The boreal forest, or **TAIGA**, is composed of resinous trees, either evergreen conifers or broadleafed. It forms an unbroken belt of forest land 621 to 1,552 miles wide between the Arctic Circle and 50°N.

The **TUNDRA** is virtually treeless; apart from a few dwarf trees it is a land of marshes and peat bogs.

These two zones are found in rough, cold climates, where temperatures can drop below −58°F. The scanty precipitation (15.7″ to 19.6″) is often in the form of snow.

### A World of Variety

The **TEMPERATE FOREST** is found in warm and humid temperate climates such as in the Mediterranean, Africa, southern Australia, southern United States and South America, and in cooler humid temperate areas such as Europe, Canada and central Asia.

The natural vegetation in Mediterranean climates is open forest, with evergreen trees. The main species are the holm oak, the cork oak, conifers and a few broadleaf types.

Temperate forests have been damaged by over-exploitation, and have been replaced by **HEATH** and **SCRUBLAND**. The first is found on chalky soil, and is patchily covered with a few aromatic plants and small trees such as the kermes oak. In the second we find dense growth of shrubs such as juniper and briar in siliceous soil.

In cooler temperate climates, the forest varies with latitude. Oceanic environments favor the growth of broadleaf forests (oaks and beeches). The Pacific coast of North America is a land of conifers, such as the sequoia, which can grow to enormous height. Mixed forests are composed of both conifers and broadleafs, and are found in the eastern portions of the various continents.

Desert

Steppe and shrub vegetation

Savanna and open forest

Humid subtropical forest

Dense equatorial forest

High mountain vegetation

# 16 □ POPULATION AND SOCIETIES

## POPULATION DENSITY

The world's population has always been unevenly distributed. Primitive man sought areas rich in game and water; later the decisive factor was the fertility of the soil, and later still its energy and mineral potential. While natural environment still plays an important role in some parts of the world (such as Africa and Asia), this tends to diminish in more developed areas. Cities, the centers of political and economic activity, exercise a considerable pull. In economically weak countries that pull is felt also by those who cannot support themselves in the countryside.

### Uneven Distribution

The world's population is 5 billion, but density varies greatly from one inhabited area to another, and within countries. Asia alone contains about half the population of the Earth, with density as high as 964/sq. mile in Bangladesh; the USSR accounts for only 6%.

The most densely populated continent is Europe. Even though density is only 256/sq. mile, this is three times the world average of 78/sq. mile and higher than Asia's 241/sq. mile, excluding the USSR). The range of densities in Europe is enormous, from 1106/sq. mile in the Netherlands to 5/sq. mile in Iceland.

### The Influence of the Environment

It is clear from these examples that regions with the harshest climates have the lowest population densities (e.g., Iceland, with its vast expanses of swamps, peat bogs and tundra). Similarly, African countries which are mostly desert approach or equal Iceland: Chad with 10/sq. mile and Libya and Mauritania with 5/sq. mile. Tropical areas such as hot, humid, unhealthy forest basins are no more conducive to settlement, and density is low: Congo has only 13/sq. mile and Brazil 41/sq. mile. Most of Brazil's population is concentrated near the coast; the Amazon forest is nearly uninhabited.

There are two types of high-density regions: those where population is very high and evenly spread (density in Java's fertile plains can be as high as 2591/sq. mile, and the great deltas of Asia, such as the Ganges Delta, can have more than 1295/sq. mile; and those with zones of high density, such as major cities or urbanized areas, interspersed with countryside, as one finds throughout Europe.

Of course, climate is not the only influence on a country's population density, although it is often the overriding factor determining its historical, social and political development, as in the case of the great mercantile cities.

## LANGUAGE

### Interchange or Isolation

Language is another element in this diversity. It is generally associated with the concept of nationhood. A shared language can bring nations together, just as misunderstandings can arise among peoples speaking different languages. In India, linguistic differences have sufficed to create tensions among groups.

An estimated 2,500 to 3,000 languages are spoken today. Some have overflowed their original borders thanks to trade and colonization; this has led to some countries adopting new languages. It is estimated that in the year 2000 4.3% of the world's population will speak French. Spanish is now used by 290 million people and Portuguese by 137 million. English is spoken in India, the United States, Canada, South Africa, etc., by 470 million people in all.

### Classification of Languages

Several groups of languages have been identified on the basis of typological criteria (rational structure and basic concepts) and genetic criteria (surmised linguistic kinships): Indo-European (Europe and southeastern Asia); Afro-Asiatic (Middle East and North Africa); black African (Sudan, Guinea and West Africa, and the Bantu languages); Khoisan (southern Africa); Dravidian (India); Austroasian (Cambodia, Viet Nam); Uralic (East Europe and northwestern Asia); Turkic; Mongolic (northeastern Asia); and Sino-Tibetan (Far East).

## RELIGION

Religions know no geographic or linguistic boundaries. The major faiths have spread far beyond their countries of origin. Several of today's major religions or philosophical systems appeared in the first millennium B.C. or A.D. among the ancient Middle and Far Eastern civilizations and were spread by land or by sea.

### Four and a Half Billion Believers

**Buddhism** (249 million followers) began in India, where it was replaced by **Hinduism** (437 million), and spread to most of southeastern Asia, China and Japan. **Confucianism** (168 million) remains linked to China. **Islam,** originally a faith of nomads and merchants, conquered the ancient world's steppes and deserts and neighboring areas. It spread to the East Indies and its influence is felt throughout black Africa. Its following is almost 548 million. **Christianity** has become essentially European owing to the spread of Islam. After the Age of Exploration it was carried by major seafaring nations to the Americas and Oceania, where it prevails, and to Africa, in whose animist areas missionaries have been successful for a century. It is divided into several often conflicting branches, the main ones being Catholicism (600 million), Protestantism (353 million) and the Orthodox Church (68 million). These in turn are subdivided: Both Lutherans and Calvinists are Protestants. In total there are one billion Christians. **Judaism** is the oldest of the monotheistic religions and the first to have given rise to a modern nation, Israel. Its 17 million followers are found throughout the world, and include 3 million in Israel.

## SOCIAL AND POLITICAL SYSTEMS

Modern societies and even some political systems have been defined by geographical and ecological conditions, religion and history. India and the Islamic world are examples of societies heavily influenced by religion. The teachings of Islam emphasize commerce over agriculture; Moslem cities, centered around mosques, are true centers of civilization, and urban societies therefore predominate in the Islamic world.

Although prohibited by political leaders, the caste system remains deeply ingrained in India, producing the ultimate rigid society, where everyone belongs to the caste of his parents. Each caste corresponds to certain trades or professions. Economic change is obviously difficult in such a system.

Some political systems too bear the stamp of religion. South Africa's *apartheid* (the 'separate development' of races) is largely based on Afrikaner interpretation of the Bible. Anti-religious reaction in the USSR helped establish socialist political structures. In black Africa, the ecology, political structures and religion are sometimes closely linked, particularly in non-Europeanized areas where indigenous societies dominate: Throughout the savanna the same varieties of sorghum and millet are grown and political organization is along tribal lines.

Rural and urbanized societies are very different, and the transition from one to the other can cause a group of people to lose its identity and can standardize social behavior. There is talk of a 'Europeanized' society. If no cultural movements arise to resist this, all differences between peoples could disappear, resulting in a new, politically and socially levelled civilization. The tendency is fostered by economic factors which tend to outweigh a country's natural balance. Consider the frequently poor use of raw materials in the third world.

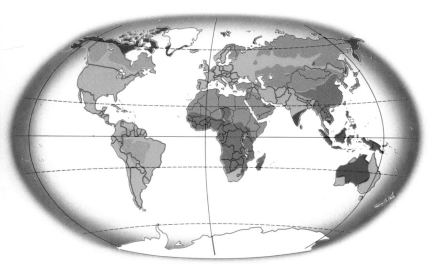

**The World's Main Languages**

 Indo-European

 Sino-Tibetan

 Ural-Altaic

Sudanic-Bantu

Afro-Asiatic

Amerindian

 Austroasian

Other

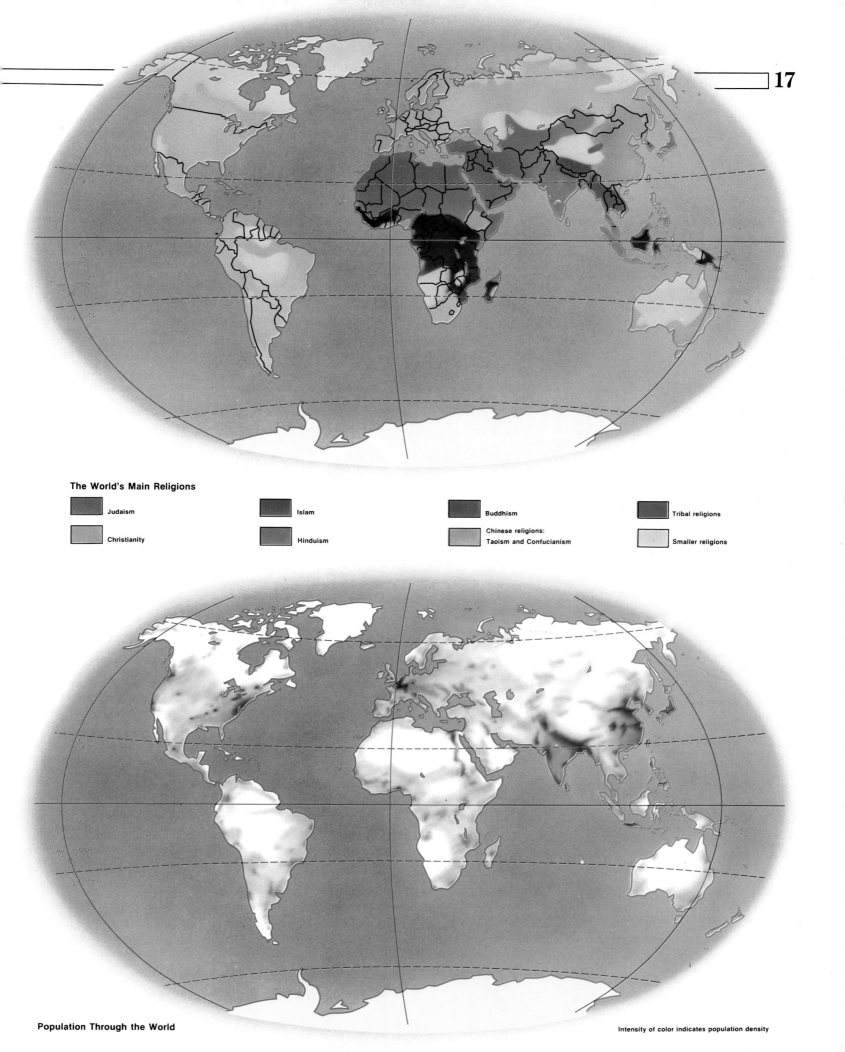

## The World's Main Religions

Judaism

Christianity

Islam

Hinduism

Buddhism

Chinese religions:
Taoism and Confucianism

Tribal religions

Smaller religions

**Population Through the World**

Intensity of color indicates population density

## DEMOGRAPHIC IMBALANCE

Since the appearance of mankind, an estimated 80 billion people have lived on Earth, barely 20 times the present world population. Growth began slowly, but has accelerated. The 1 billion mark was reached in 1820, 2 billion 105 years later in 1925, 3 billion in 1960 (35 years later) and 4 billion 15 years later, in 1975. World population in 1985 was more than 4.85 billion.

### Demographic Balance in Traditional Societies

Population growth is a function of birth rate and death rate. For thousands of years, throughout the world, birth and death were essentially balanced, with birth rate slightly higher, which resulted in slow net growth.

In 16th and 17th century Europe, for example, the birth rate ranged from 40 to 45 per thousand, while the death rate was 35 to 45 per thousand. Catastrophes such as wars and epidemics could cause sudden major drops in population, another factor for slow increase.

In pre-colonial Africa, Asia and America, death and birth rates were both high, and the patterns of growth were similar.

## TODAY'S SHARP CONTRASTS

Today, demography is no longer uniform. There are vast differences between industrialized countries and the third world. These differences exist in birth rate, infant mortality (deaths before age one per 1,000 live births), and fertility rate (births per year per 1,000 women aged 15 to 49).

### The Developed Countries: The Problem of an Aging Population

In rich countries low birth rates are causing an aging population and, consequently, near-zero growth. There is no guarantee in Europe, North America and Australia that the generations are replacing themselves. In West Germany the birth rate is 9.5 per thousand, while the death rate is 11.3.

Between 1962 and 1984, the birth rate in France dropped from 17.7 per thousand to 13.8, in Switzerland from 18.7 to 11.5 and in Belgium from 16.8 to 11.7. This is all the more serious as fertility is very low: 1.98 children per woman in those four countries, compared with 4.09 in the developing world.

Despite low infant mortality (less than 17 per thousand) and long life expectancy (an average of 73 years), mortality still often exceeds 10 per thousand. This is explained by age: With an older population, deaths are more frequent.

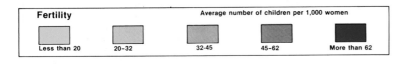

**Fertility** — Average number of children per 1,000 women

Less than 20 | 20–32 | 32-45 | 45–62 | More than 62

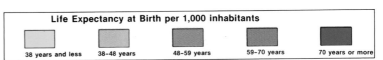

**Life Expectancy at Birth per 1,000 inhabitants**

38 years and less | 38–48 years | 48–59 years | 59–70 years | 70 years or more

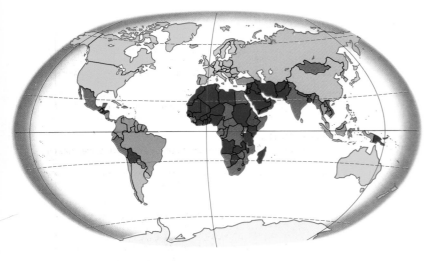

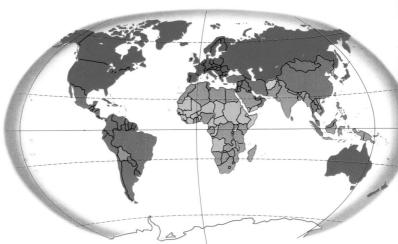

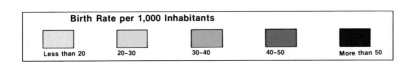

**Birth Rate per 1,000 Inhabitants**

Less than 20 | 20–30 | 30–40 | 40–50 | More than 50

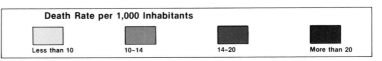

**Death Rate per 1,000 Inhabitants**

Less than 10 | 10–14 | 14–20 | More than 20

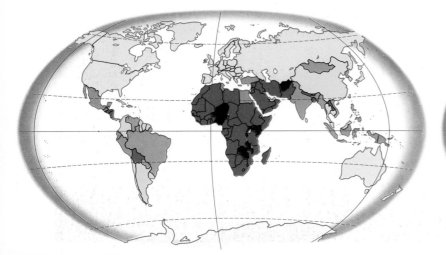

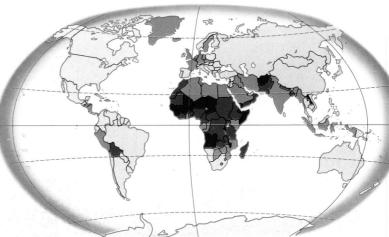

## Changes in Population, by continent

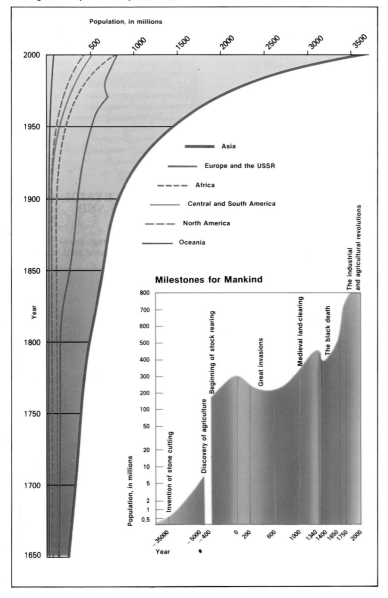

Population, in millions

500 1000 1500 2000 2500 3000 3500

Asia

Europe and the USSR

Africa

Central and South America

North America

Oceania

### Milestones for Mankind

Population, in millions

800 700 600 500 400 300 200 100 50 20 10 5 2 1 0,5

Invention of stone cutting

Discovery of agriculture

Beginning of stock rearing

Great invasions

Medieval land-clearing

The black death

The industrial and agricultural revolutions

−35000  −5000  −400  0  200  600  1000  1340  1400  1650  1750  2000

Year

### The Population Explosion in the Third World

Although infant mortality still exceeds 150 per thousand in many developing countries, population growth remains very rapid. Birth rate is high (45 to 50 per thousand in Africa and Islamic countries) and the population is young. In India, Africa and South America, more than half the population is under 20, which makes for very high fertility rates. Death rates have diminished greatly thanks to imported Western medical practices, but growth is slowed by low life expectancy at birth: 53 years in central Africa and 56 years in India and North Africa.

### Factors in this Variation

Physiological and socio-cultural factors explain these differences; one of the most important is higher standard of living. In South Africa, records are kept for two population groups: Birth rate for blacks is 46.1 per thousand, but only 22.8 for whites.

Improved living conditions lead to changes in social behavior and outlook that work against population growth. Among the sociological factors that promote lower birth rates are: women working outside the home; contraception and abortion; higher age at marriage; fewer marriages; more divorce; and urbanization. Children therefore remain dependent for longer.

Better sanitation and food and medical progress are physiological reasons for lower mortality. In the least developed countries, despite the introduction of Western medicine (which has rapidly lowered death rates by 50% in the second half of the 20th century), most of the population still does not live in a modern society. Behavior and outlook are slow to change.

The inhabitants marry young (in India, at 14 1/2 for women and 20 for men). Women rarely work outside the home. Birth control has made a tangible impact in southeastern Asia and South America, but a very small one in Africa and the Islamic world.

## DEMOGRAPHY IN TRANSITION

Demographic change is directly linked to economic development. For every country there are five phases: traditional society; transition to economic advancement; economic advancement; progress toward maturity; and the period of mass consumption.

Traditional society is marked by high birth and death rates; the age pyramid is very narrow at the top. The pyramid in some consumer societies, on the other hand, is narrow at its base, broader in the middle, and tapered at the top.

### Lower Mortality, Fewer Births

The first signs of economic development are accompanied by lower death rates. In the developed countries this began in the late 18th century with the industrial revolution, improved food and agricultural production and, above all, progress in medicine. France was among the first to begin the transition; the rest of Europe followed in the first half of the 19th century.

It was only in 1945 that death rates in the developing countries plummeted. The fall was speedy because of the advent of modern mass medicine (vaccination, antibiotics, etc.). In some areas such as central Africa, birth rates have hardly fallen, but in others the change is marked. Cuba's rate of growth has fallen by 47%. The average birth rate is no greater than 35 per thousand in Central America and 32 per thousand in southeastern Asia.

### The Future

The present worldwide rate of population increase is 2% a year. There are about 400,000 births a day and 165,000 deaths. At that rate the world's population will be more than 6 billion by the year 2000: 1.212 billion will live in China and 976 million in India. In 2075 those countries will have populations of 1.297 billion and 1.798 billion respectively, since India's rate of growth is higher. But if in its economic evolution the developing world follows the pattern of the industrialized countries, world population should stabilize in the second half of the 21st century.

Of the world's population, 15% is found in Europe, the USSR, North America and Australia; the rest, in South America, Africa and Asia.

## The Age Pyramid

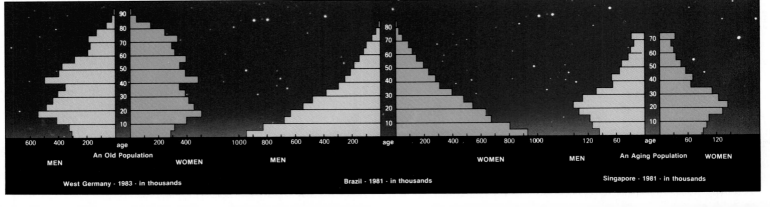

600 400 200 age 200 400

MEN   An Old Population   WOMEN

West Germany · 1983 · in thousands

1000 800 600 400 200 age 200 400 600 800 1000

MEN   WOMEN

Brazil · 1981 · in thousands

120 60 age 60 120

MEN   An Aging Population   WOMEN

Singapore · 1981 · in thousands

## ECONOMIC INEQUALITIES

The world is marked not only by physical, meteorological and human diversity but also by varying economic and developmental levels, as reflected in standards of living and in each country's role in world production.

### Per Capita GNP

Per capita GNP (Gross National Product) is the total value of goods and services a country produces in one year, divided by the number of inhabitants. It is the best indicator of a country's average standard of living, and huge contrasts exist world wide. The four main GNP blocs are: North America and Europe in the North; Australia and New Zealand in the South-East; Latin America in the South-West; and Africa and Asia in the center.

Of the 29 countries in the first bloc, 25 are considered rich, three (Portugal, Rumania and Yugoslavia) moderately rich, and one (Albania) very poor. The United States ranks sixth in the world, with a per capita GNP of $14,490, and France sixteenth with $10,390. Australia and New Zealand, rich countries of the South-East, rank fourteenth and twenty-sixth respectively. As for the South-West, the majority of Latin American countries are moderately rich, with Argentina wealthier ($2,070) and Guyana, Peru and the Central American countries poorer.

The differences in Africa and Asia are greater because of dependency on oil; some oil-producing countries have an extremely high standard of living. Economically, the United Arab Emirates, Qatar and Kuwait rank first, second and fourth, with Saudi Arabia tenth. Libya is thirty-sixth; it is the only African country whose income equals that of a developed country. With very few exceptions, all other African and Asian countries are poor or very poor, the poorest of all being Bhutan, a small country on India's north-east border where per capita income is a mere $83.

### Standard of Living and GNP

Birthplace (whether in a poor or a rich country) has a decisive impact on standard of living. From conception to death, those born in wealthier countries will enjoy sanitary conditions and health care that will increase their chances of survival and promote longevity. Schooling will be provided to age 16 at least, and to 18 in most cases. They will have enough to eat and their food will supply all essential nutrients. In addition to these advantages (which ought to be commonly available throughout the world), income will be sufficient to buy goods such as cars, washing machines and high fidelity equipment.

By contrast, those born in poor or very poor countries will experience hunger, poverty and illiteracy, with educational opportunities restricted to a tiny, privileged minority. Without skills or land to farm, they will be unemployed and unable to feed their own numerous children, who will tread the same path as their parents.

## WORLD PRODUCTION

Economic analysis distinguishes between countries not only on the basis of per capita GNP, but also according to the structure of their economies.

### Groups of Countries

The world's powerful countries are divided among capitalist and socialist states. North America, Western Europe, Japan, Australia, New Zealand and South Africa have free economies, while the Eastern bloc countries have opted for economies planned by the government. Among developing countries too there are capitalist states (e.g. Brazil, Indonesia, and the Philippines) and socialist states (e.g. China, Viet Nam, Cuba and Algeria), although their development level depends on whether or not they possess oil deposits.

### Each Group's Share of World Production

The industrialized countries of North America, Europe and Japan clearly dominate the world economic scene, accounting for the bulk of world industrial and agricultural production. They use their own resources or import third-world raw materials which they process either at home or, increasingly, in the developing country of origin, where labor is cheaper.

But there is a difference: Service-sector production in market-economy industrialized countries is 16 times higher than in planned-economy industrialized countries, and industrial production is 13 times higher. The percentage of GNP generated by industry is greater in socialist countries (56.1%) than in capitalist countries (35%).

The contrast is even more striking in high-income oil-exporting developing countries, where industry—essentially the energy sector—accounts for 65% of GNP, whereas the world wide figure is only 11.9%. On the other hand, the agricultural sector is virtually (or even totally, as in Kuwait) nonexistent.

In the poor third-world countries the agricultural sector is highly developed, although it does not play a major world role. Agriculture often accounts for the highest percentage of GNP (59% in Nepal and 58% in Burundi). But per capita production is very low, and the figures reflect the high proportion of the population taking part (93% in Nepal and 75% in Burundi).

Generally, the three sectors are balanced in third-world countries, apart from high-income oil-exporters. But unemployment has led to the proliferation of subsidiary minor service trades, which can account for 30–40% of real wealth produced. The third world partly depends on this underground economy.

Yet these economic concepts should be treated with caution. For example, the 1973–74 oil crisis was followed barely 12 years later by a drop in prices, ending the euphoria in producer countries, caused by the seeming dependency of the rich countries.

Ultimately, the main factors remain a country's level of industrialization and the diversification of its economy, which in the medium and long term guarantee a stable GNP. The fragility of the developing countries is very real. They are prey to fluctuations in the financial markets: Think of the crisis caused in Brazil by the drop in coffee prices, the problems in Chile resulting from the collapse in copper prices, and, more recently, the case of Mexico, now the second most indebted country in the world (after Brazil), owing in part to the drop in the price of oil.

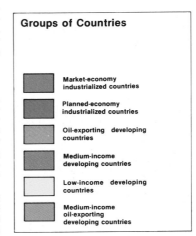

**Groups of Countries**

- Market-economy industrialized countries
- Planned-economy industrialized countries
- Oil-exporting developing countries
- Medium-income developing countries
- Low-income developing countries
- Medium-income oil-exporting developing countries

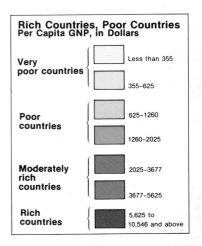

**Rich Countries, Poor Countries**
Per Capita GNP, in Dollars

|  |  |
|---|---|
| Very poor countries | Less than 355 |
| | 355–625 |
| Poor countries | 625–1260 |
| | 1260–2025 |
| Moderately rich countries | 2025–3677 |
| | 3677–5625 |
| Rich countries | 5,625 to 10,546 and above |

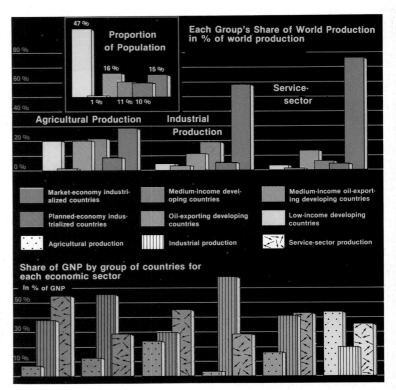

Proportion of Population

47% 16% 15% 1% 11% 10%

Each Group's Share of World Production
in % of world production

Agricultural Production — Industrial Production — Service-sector

- Market-economy industrialized countries
- Planned-economy industrialized countries
- Medium-income developing countries
- Oil-exporting developing countries
- Medium-income oil-exporting developing countries
- Low-income developing countries
- Agricultural production
- Industrial production
- Service-sector production

Share of GNP by group of countries for each economic sector
In % of GNP

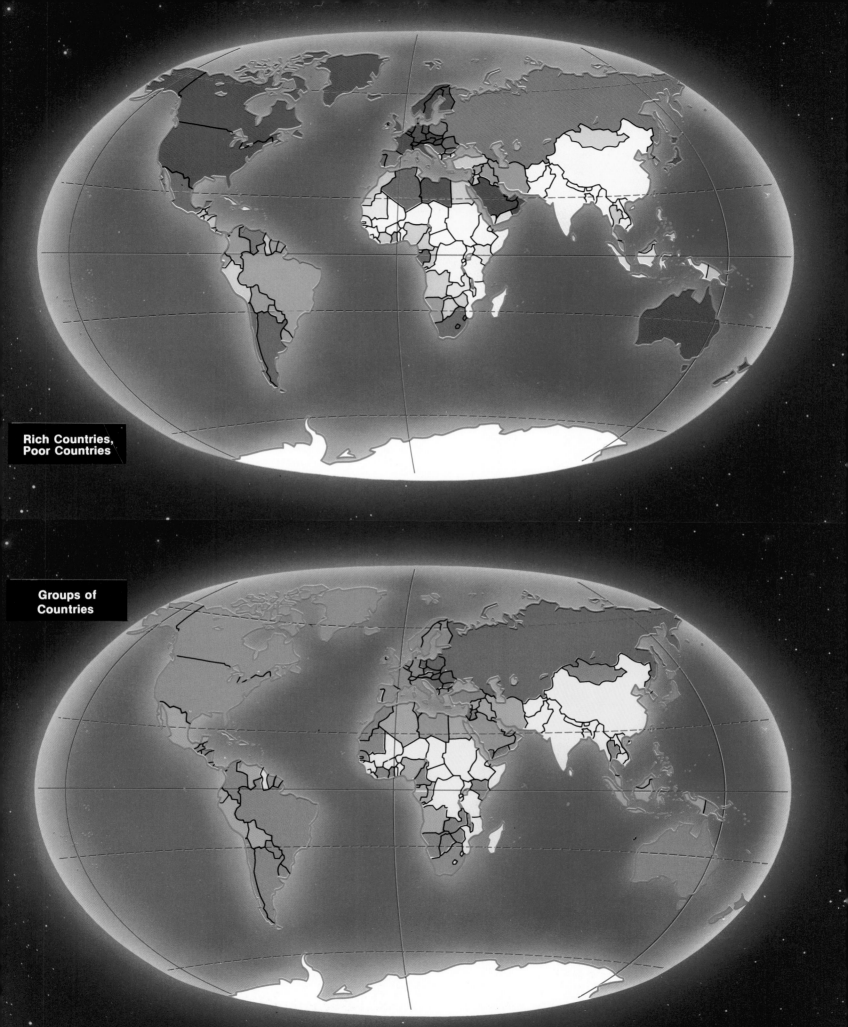

Rich Countries,
Poor Countries

Groups of
Countries

## WORKING AGRICULTURAL POPULATION

### Controlling the Environment

Wherever man has tamed nature—through selecting plants and animals, improving the soil, creating artificial climates (such as greenhouses), or through mechanization—the percentage of the population actively engaged in agriculture has dropped. Progress in each of those areas has led to a significant reduction in that percentage world wide; in just over a century it has fallen from 84% to 44%.

### Underdeveloped Countries

In underdeveloped regions, agricultural output is lower than in industrialized countries. The majority of the population works the land. In Africa, 64% are farmers, yet they hardly manage to feed the continent. In Asia, especially in rice-growing areas, production is higher, but this leads to greater population density: The fertile plains of Java support 2,600 inhabitants per square mile, and 55% of the working population is engaged in agriculture.

### Developed Countries

In the developed countries, personnel requirements have been reduced by intensive farming methods, systematic fertilizer use, regular watering, industrialized stock rearing, improved food preservation and domestic and foreign shipping capabilities. In North America basic food production is carried out by a mere 2% of the work force. Although few in number, farmers in the developed world often produce enough for export; France exports wheat and the United States soy beans and grain. Imports make up for any shortages.

## WORLD HUNGER

### The Undernourished

Undernourishment now affects a third of mankind, mainly (and paradoxically) concentrated in areas with the largest working agricultural populations. In underdeveloped countries the situation has been magnified by the drop in mortality rates: Great population growth has not been paralleled by increased agricultural production.

The highest percentages of undernourishment are found in Africa: 48% in Mauritania and 47% in Niger. In South America the contrasts are greater: 45% in Bolivia vs. 13% in Brazil. The figure for India and Bangladesh is 30%.

This is due in part to low soil productivity, but national food policies also contribute. The most severely undernourished countries are also the most heavily indebted, and must often grow crops for export, which increases dependence.

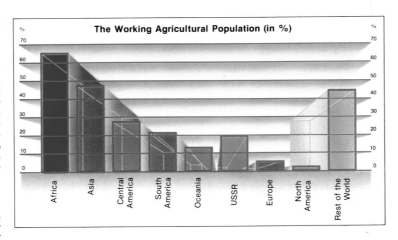

**The Working Agricultural Population (in %)**

### Diet

To function properly, the body at rest requires 2,000 to 2,400 calories per day. Below that level, undernourishment sets in, often accompanied by malnutrition caused by a lack of nutrients, such as proteins, iron, minerals and vitamins, which are found in three food types: cereals and oils; meat and dairy products; and fruit and vegetables.

In underdeveloped countries, diet is often limited to cereals, for economic or religious reasons. Some Indian religions, for example, prohibit all meat consumption. The main cereal crop in Asia is rice and in Africa millet and sorghum.

The problem of scarce and low-quality food is not equally severe all over the world. In southeastern Asia, West Africa and India, daily per capita intake is between 1,700 and 2,047 calories, and available animal protein comes to .194 ounces. North of the Tropic of Cancer, however, the body's needs are largely met: consumption exceeds 3,300 calories per day, and protein intake averages 3.7 ounces, 75% of it animal protein.

But not all countries south of the Tropic of Cancer suffer from undernourishment, just as not all northern lands enjoy plenty: there is enough to eat in Argentina, while in Afghanistan 50% are undernourished.

The key to good nutrition, of course, is having both enough to eat and a varied diet. Important though they be, climate and natural disasters do not create malnutrition. Economic management and political problems are still the main causes of this scourge.

### Percentage of Proteins in the Diet

Ideally, the body should daily absorb .028 ounces of proteins per pound of body weight. An average man should thus consume 2.11 ounces of proteins as part of a daily intake of 3,000 calories. There are no good or bad proteins; they are one among the ingredients the body needs.

## WORLD CEREAL PRODUCTION

Cereals and potatoes remain the world's primary food resource. Wheat predominates in temperate lands, with yield averaging 3,563 lbs per acre. It is also grown in winter in countries with monsoon climates. The USSR is both the biggest producer and the biggest importer of wheat, the United States being the biggest exporter.

Rice is found mainly in Asia, where output is very high, around 5,344 lbs per acre. It is the dietary staple of half the world's population. China and India are the major producers. The main importers are Indonesia and Viet Nam, and the United States is the leading exporter.

Millet and sorghum are eaten mainly in Africa, where they are the staple diet, but also in India and China. Barley and oats are grown largely for animal feed, and principally in temperate climates. Rye is cultivated for human consumption, but is on the decline.

**DAILY FOOD INTAKE PER PERSON**

*Daily per capita caloric and animal protein intake are indicators of food consumption. The two curves show the imbalances among the various continents. In countries afflicted by malnutrition, the proteins the body needs are consumed in small quantities.*

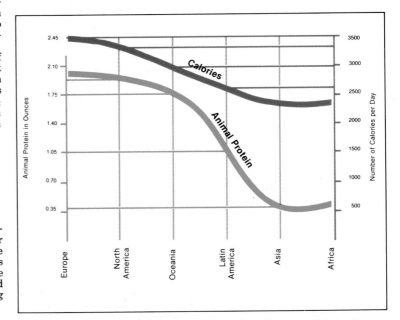

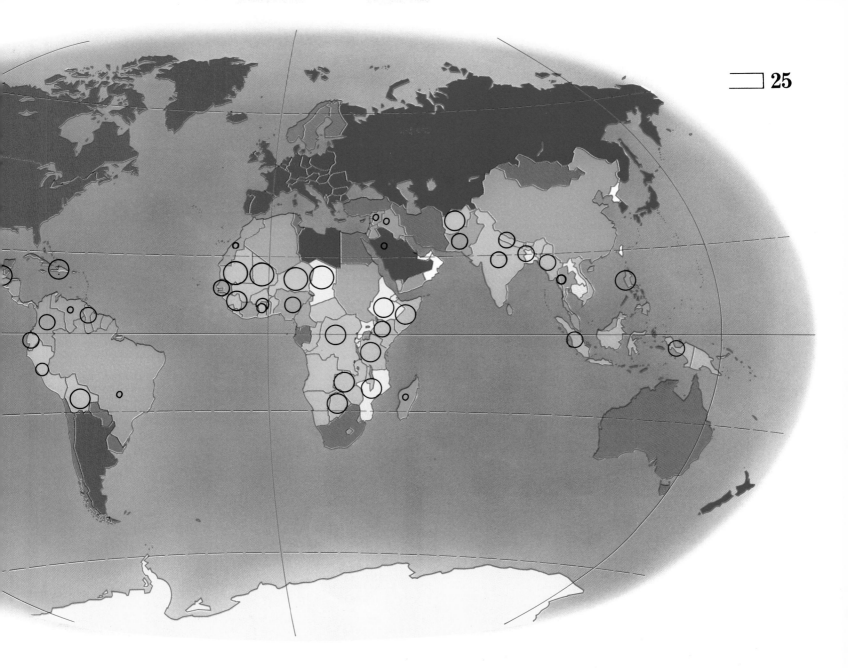

**Daily Per Capita Intake of Calories**

| | | |
|---|---|---|
| 1,700–1,900 | 2,700–3,100 | |
| 1,900–2,300 | 3,100–3,300 | |
| 2,300–2,700 | Greater than 3,300 | No statistics available |

Percentage of population undernourished

| Greater than 45% | 30–45% | 25–30% | 23–25% | 20–23% | Less than 20% |
|---|---|---|---|---|---|

**World Cereals Production in 1984**

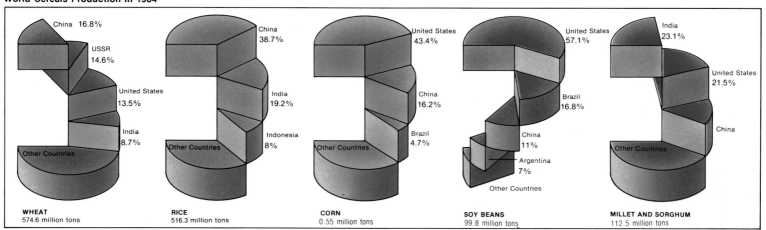

WHEAT
574.6 million tons

China 16.8%
USSR 14.6%
United States 13.5%
India 8.7%
Other Countries

RICE
516.3 million tons

China 38.7%
India 19.2%
Indonesia 8%
Other Countries

CORN
0.55 million tons

United States 43.4%
China 16.2%
Brazil 4.7%
Other Countries

SOY BEANS
99.8 million tons

United States 57.1%
Brazil 16.8%
China 11%
Argentina 7%
Other Countries

MILLET AND SORGHUM
112.5 million tons

India 23.1%
United States 21.5%
China
Other Countries

## HEALTH: AN ECONOMIC ISSUE

Development, malnutrition, undernourishment, availability of doctors, and life expectancy: Throughout the world all these factors are closely linked. Standard of living depends largely on the level of medical care, which depends in turn on education and average income.

### Unequal in the Face of Death

A country's economic health determines the life expectancy of its people. In areas with very low standards of living—much of Africa (central, east and west), Asia (India, Bangladesh and Nepal) and Latin America (Peru, Bolivia, Guatemala and El Salvador)—people rarely live beyond age 65. Reaching that age implies a decent standard of living, as in Brazil, Mexico or Iran. The higher the standard of living, the greater the life expectancy. Where this is very high, as in Europe and North America, the threshold is 78 years. Longevity greatly exceeding that average is still the exception, the record being held by a Japanese who died in 1986, aged over 120 years.

Yet there are exceptions to the rule, the most striking being Saudi Arabia and Oman. While per capita GNP is very high ($10,240 and $6,170 respectively), life expectancy is low (60 years for Saudi Arabia and 49 for Oman). Economic growth is very recent and agricultural level remains low: that explains the anomaly. It was only in 1965–1970 that they began, thanks to oil, to grow rich; and while living standards have risen considerably, agriculture remains poorly developed. Only 0.5% of Saudi Arabia's land is under cultivation and 0.2% of Oman's. Grain yield is low: 792 lbs and 2,578 lbs per acre respectively. Moreover, social-service and medical training is virtually nonexistent despite recent efforts.

### Main Causes of Death

Birthplace often determines cause of death. Climate, sanitation and resistance to viruses and other microbes vary greatly. In developed countries cardiovascular diseases—caused by tobacco and alcohol abuse, over-rich food and stress—are more common, while physicians can effectively treat infectious diseases such as influenza, measles and scarlet fever. A better-fed body is more resistant to infection, and the death of a child or an adult under age 60 is a rare event, often caused by congenital defects in children and by accidents in adults: 9% of deaths in France and 10% in Canada result from accidents. The inhabitants of rich countries, better protected against illness, die of old age and its consequences.

It is different in underdeveloped countries. Life is short and there are few geriatric diseases. Death can come at any age, but especially in infancy. Infectious and parasitical diseases are the main culprits: A weak body is less germ-resistant, and most people, particularly children, are undernourished. Infant mortality rates are very high in many third-world countries: more than 200 per 1,000 in Cambodia, Gambia and Sierra Leone and 8,090 in Brazil, despite great progress. The average infant mortality rate in developed countries is 14 per 1,000, but the figure is 40 per 1,000 in the USSR and 6.5 in Finland. The rates in some third-world countries, such as Singapore (10.8), Cuba (18.5) and Puerto Rico (18.6), are lower than in most socialist countries, such as Poland (21) and Yugoslavia (31).

Hunger-related diseases take various forms, including marasmus, kwashiorkor, beriberi, scurvy and rickets. Parasitic diseases are fostered by poor hygiene, common in underdeveloped countries. Malaria and sleeping sickness are the most widespread. They are transmitted by insects, the first by the mosquito and the second by the tsetse fly, and could be effectively

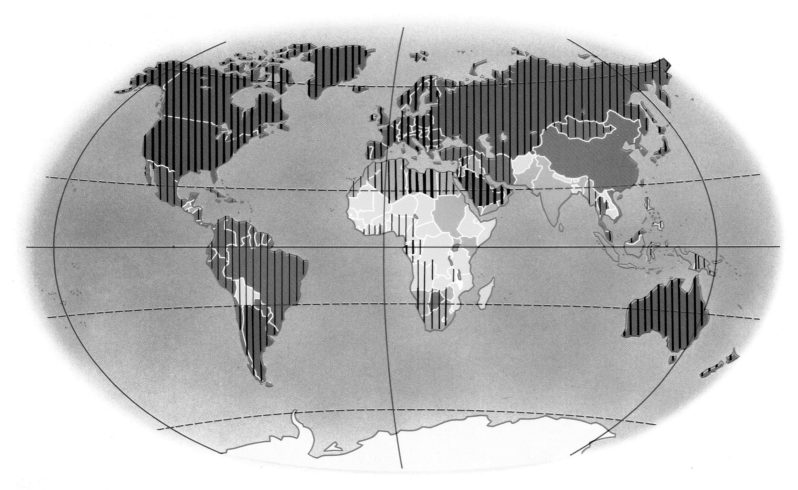

**Life Expectancy at Birth and Level of Development (on the basis of per capita GNP, in dollars)**

Life expectancy at birth

- 38-48 years
- 48-55 years
- 55-66 years
- 66-78 years and greater

Per capita GNP in dollars

- Very poor countries: $83-468
- Poor countries: $526-1,474
- Moderately rich countries: $1,564-4,960
- Rich countries: More than $5,000

combatted by taking proper action: Early in this century malaria totally disappeared from infested parts of southern Italy.

## Inequalities in Medical Treatment

Here too there are stark differences between developed and developing countries. There are several geographic zones. In the first there are many physicians (irrespective of specialty), at least 2 for each 1,000 inhabitants: North America, Argentina, Australia, all of Europe, and North and southern Africa. The second category is composed of areas with fewer, but not inadequate, medical personnel: Asia, Mexico and South America. Then there is the zone between the two Tropics—including the rest of Africa, Indonesia, Thailand and Cambodia—where doctors are sometimes lacking. Indonesia has one doctor per 11,000 inhabitants, and some African countries have only one per 40,000, as in Niger, Burundi, Burkina Faso and Ethiopia. The concentration of physicians and facilities in urban areas makes the situation worse. Rural people must travel many miles for treatment. To remedy this situation some countries train medical officers specializing in the treatment of the single disease most prevalent in their area, but totally helpless when faced with a different illness. Other countries train people to provide only basic health care, such as China's "barefoot" doctors.

Serious shortages of hospital facilities and poor hygiene, sometimes accompanied by a total lack of drugs and by malnutrition, take a considerable toll. Long-term solutions obviously demand greater industrialization and education in the countries concerned.

*His mother's bony arms can scarcely lift him. His belly is swollen and he lacks the strength to cry. In the eyes of his mother we see the tragedy of a people afflicted by famine.*

*After a few weeks of a balanced diet under medical supervision, this Ethiopian woman and her baby are now smiling and confident.*

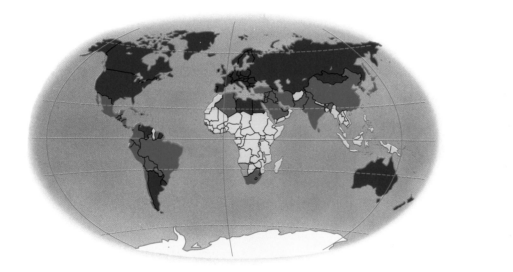

[Legend of little world map]
**Number of Physicians per 10,000 Population**

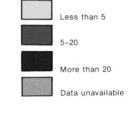

Less than 5

5–20

More than 20

Data unavailable

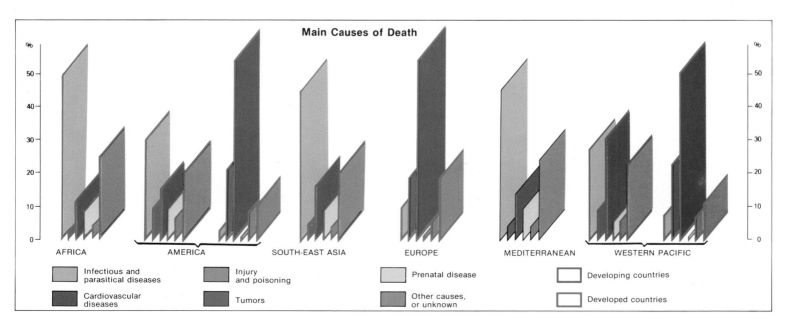

**Main Causes of Death**

AFRICA | AMERICA | SOUTH-EAST ASIA | EUROPE | MEDITERRANEAN | WESTERN PACIFIC

Infectious and parasitical diseases

Cardiovascular diseases

Injury and poisoning

Tumors

Prenatal disease

Other causes, or unknown

Developing countries

Developed countries

## EDUCATION AROUND THE WORLD

### Literacy

In most countries education is compulsory, on average between the ages of 6 and 15, although this varies from place to place: The ages in the USSR are 7 to 17, in Togo 6 to 12 and in the United Kingdom 5 to 16.

In 1980, 33% of the world's population was in school. As an effect of decreasing birth rates, this will fall to 29% by the year 2000.

In many countries the main concern is having enough classrooms. Yet such efforts seem pointless when schools are miles from pupils' homes, which is why there are no compulsory education laws in certain underdeveloped countries, including some in Africa and Asia. While schooling is compulsory in others, many children do not attend because their parents need their help. It is easy to see why illiteracy is common in most of the third world. The literacy rate is about 40% in Africa and 60% in Asia.

The existence of illiteracy in a country does not necessarily mean economic problems or a lack of schools: 46% of Europe's population cannot read or write (46% in the Netherlands, 2% in the United Kingdom and 1% in France). Often these are elderly people or young adults who attended poor schools.

Literacy rates vary according to age and sex, but especially to economic development and the percentage of GNP invested in education. In Morocco, 81.4% of those over 65 and 60.2% of those aged 10 to 14 are illiterate. In Martinique, 42% of those over 65 are illiterate, but only 2% of young people aged 15 to 19; the figures for Greece are similar. The statistics closely reflect each country's progress.

Illiteracy is generally more common among females, especially in underdeveloped countries. The comparison in the Central African Republic, for example, is 80.8% vs. 51.7% and in Morocco 90.2% vs. 66.4%. Although Greece is considered a developed country, 23.7% of its women are illiterate compared with 6.7% of its men. In those countries, it is thought that a woman's job is to cook, till the soil and care for the children, and that reading and writing are not needed for such tasks.

Financial concerns can also play a part. A low-income family is more willing to make sacrifices for a boy, who will have more contact with the world beyond the family, than for a girl.

## GNP AND EDUCATION BUDGETS

We have seen the close link between economic development and literacy. Obviously, a country's ability to invest in education depends on its wealth. It is obvious too that spending on education will be low where there is no compulsory schooling. For example, in Uganda in 1980 it was only 1.8% of GNP.

Thus, educational spending varies greatly, and the gap between developed and developing countries is very wide. On average, the former spend $14.9 billion on education, and the latter $1.96 billion. The difference is even greater given that industrialized countries have fewer children and already have facilities in place. But some third-world countries are making a great effort to catch up. Algeria is spending an annual average of more than $3 billion on education. Switzerland spends $4.7 billion. Note that, while those two sums are not very different, there are 7 million Swiss and 21 million Algerians.

The battle for literacy is not always seen as a high priority, particularly by third-world political leaders, even though that battle could lead to a victory over world hunger.

**Education Spending as a Percentage of GNP**

- Less than 3%
- 3%–4%
- 4–5%
- 5–6%
- 6–7%
- 7–8%
- More than 8%
- Data unavailable or incomplete

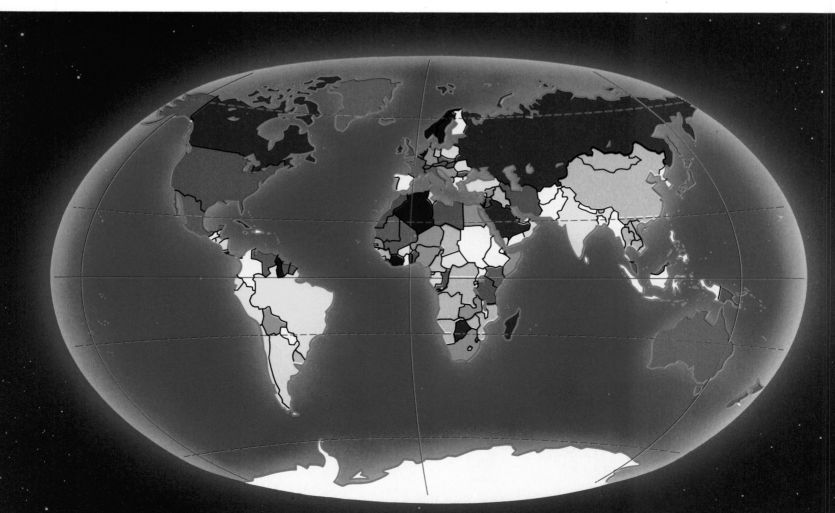

## LEVEL OF EDUCATION

There are students at all levels from nursery school through elementary and high school to university. The proportion of attendance at each level relates directly to the age pyramid and to economic development. In developing countries with many children, elementary schooling is the priority, and college is for a small minority. Nursery schools and kindergartens too are rare, since women do not usually hold jobs outside the home and look after young children themselves. Thus, in Angola there are 46 nursery schools attended by 0.5% of all pupils; in France, 2- to 5-year-olds make up 9% of the school population.

It is in the Ivory Coast that the greatest portion of GNP is spent on education; 84.9% of the school population is in elementary school, compared with 41.3% in the United States. At high school level the figure is 13.8%, while it remains steadier in the United States at 31.7%.

At college level, the percentages in developing countries drop close to those for nursery schools. In Ivory Coast, college students are a mere 0.9%, compared with 18.1% in the United States.

Third-world countries frequently send their students to the developing world. Out of 6,000 Ivory Coast college students, 61% are studying abroad (44% in France). Of the 528,751 students in Egyptian universities only 4.1% are foreigners.

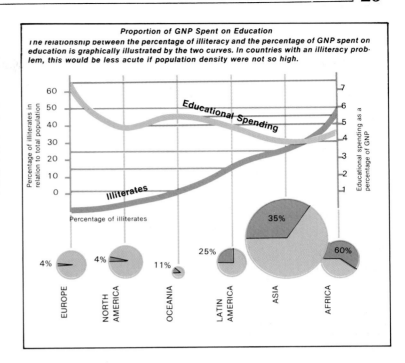

**Proportion of GNP Spent on Education**
The relationship between the percentage of illiteracy and the percentage of GNP spent on education is graphically illustrated by the two curves. In countries with an illiteracy problem, this would be less acute if population density were not so high.

**Rates of Illiteracy**

| | | |
|---|---|---|
| Less than 10% | 25–45% | Greater than 75% | Data unavailable or incomplete |
| 10–25% | 45–75% | | |

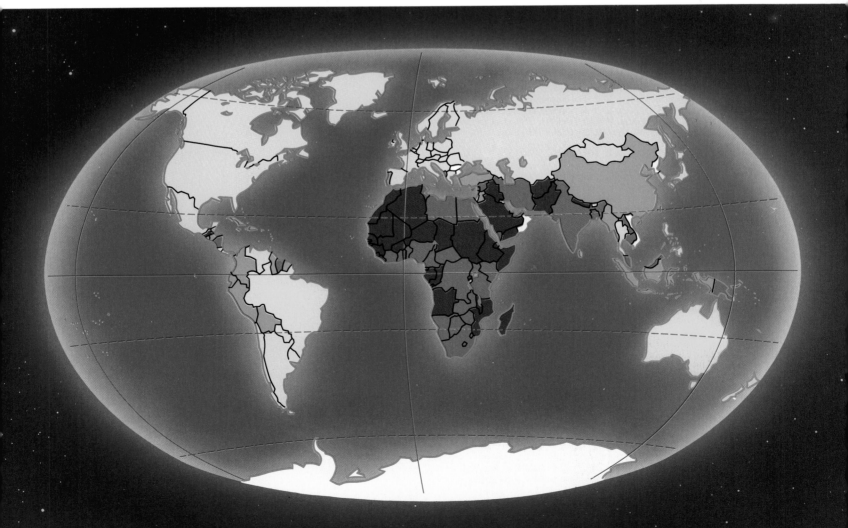

## CULTURAL INFLUENCE AND CULTURAL EXPANSION

The United Nations has six official languages—Chinese (spoken by more than one billion people but limited in use by its ideographic script), Arabic, Spanish, Russian, French and English—but uses only the last two as its working languages.

### English: A World Language

English was spread world wide with British colonization and is used everywhere: from the United States to Oceania; in Asia and in Africa. Two thirds of scientific and technical publications are in English; it is the language of business and serves as a common tongue in countries lacking linguistic unity, such as India and many African States.

### French: A Distinguished Past

While still an international language, French has declined since its high prestige in the courts of 18th-century Europe. Before 1919, when it came to share its role with English, it was the sole official language of diplomacy. It overflows the borders of France: 60 million Europeans speak French, and in 24 African countries it is the official language, sometimes alongside others, such as English in Cameroon or Arabic in the Maghreb. About 150 million Africans speak or understand French. In the Americas, there are 7.4 million French-speaking Canadians (86% of them in Quebec); in Louisiana it is understood by 800,000 people and it is the official language of Haiti. French has declined in Asia, but is used by 60% of the population of Lebanon.

### Spanish: A Language on the Increase

Because of Spain's expansion in the 1500s, Latin America speaks Spanish, apart from Brazil (Portuguese), the Guyanas and a few Caribbean islands. Spanish ranks third among world languages, with 275 million speakers in 1984. Its role in Europe is secondary; even in Spain other languages and dialects are still used. It is virtually non-existent in Africa and Asia, and suffers from the fact that no technologically advanced country uses it.

### Russian: Language of an Empire

Since 1923 Russian has been the official language of the USSR and is now the mother tongue of 143 million people. Yet 270 million Soviet citizens speak it alongside their local languages, Russification being incomplete in some provinces.

### Arabic: Language of a Religion

A Semitic language spoken originally by a few nomadic Arabian tribes, Arabic spread with the expansion of Islam in the seventh century. At its peak it made its mark from Spain to Iran and was known as far away as Java, but it declined in the 1200s. A 19th-century nationalist revival helped reassert the language. Today 16 African and Middle Eastern States accounting for 166 million people have adopted it as their official language.

## COMMUNICATIONS AND THE PRESS

In the 19th century reading and writing began to be available to the masses, not just to an elite. This is reflected in a proliferation of newspapers, some with circulations in the millions. In 1984 six countries published more than 10 million copies of their daily papers: the USSR, Japan, the United States, West Germany, the United Kingdom and France. The Japanese are the largest consumers, with 575 copies per 1,000 inhabitants. At the other extreme, Spain publishes a mere 79 per 1,000.

### Motion Pictures and Television

Along with the written word (and at its expense), movies and TV have become major media. India is the top film producer (737 in 1981). While the audience for American films is greater than that for Japanese or French movies, those two countries produce more (332 in Japan, 231 in France and 226 in the United States in 1981). Soviet citizens see three times as many films as Americans.

Television made its appearance in the United States in the 1940s, and a decade later in Europe. In the developed countries, the number of TV sets has grown fast, often exceeding 68 sets per 100 homes, as in Monaco. The figure in the United States is 63.1 per 100 inhabitants; in Spain it is 24.1 and in Morocco fewer than 4. Thus, television is a phenomenon of the developed world.

### Radio

Radios are found in both the developed and the developing world. In the Maghreb there are 17 radios per 100 people. In some developed countries there are hardly more radios than there are televisions (in West Germany, 34.8 radios per 100 vs. 38.3 televisions). In poor countries with few televisions or telephones, radio is the main communications medium.

Country where one or more of the six languages is used

Other languages used

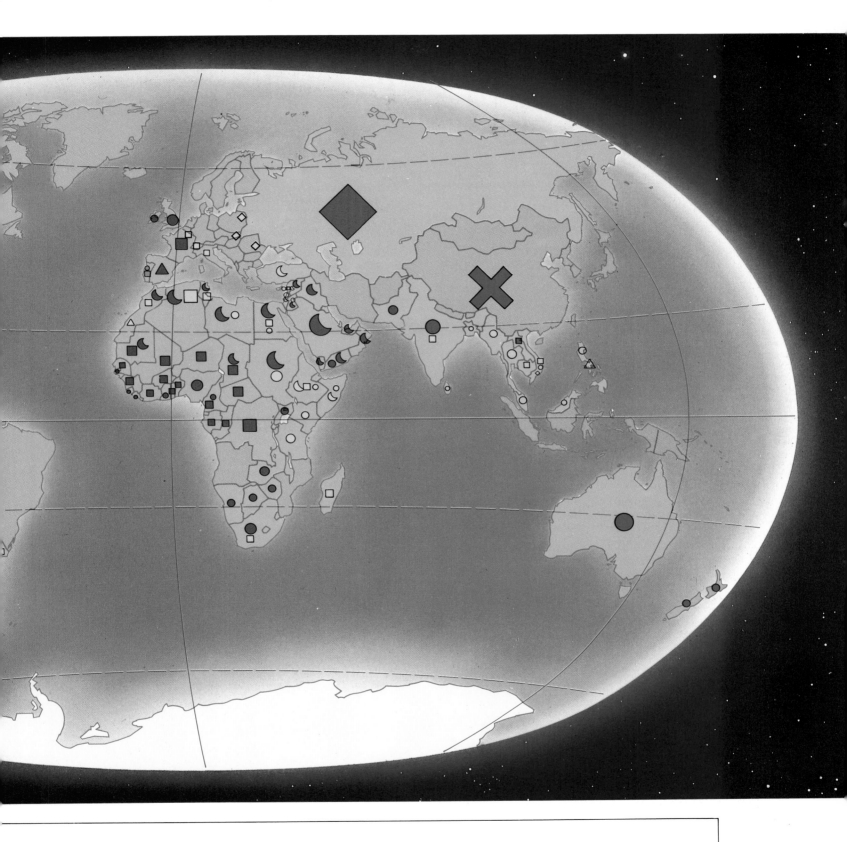

**Cultural Influence of Six Principal Languages**

English | French | Spanish | Arabic | Russian | Chinese

| | |
|---|---|
| ● English | |
| ○ English | |
| ■ French | |
| ▢ French | |
| ▲ Spanish | |
| △ Spanish | |
| ☾ Arabic | |
| ☾ Arabic | |
| ◆ Russian | |
| ◇ Russian | |
| ✖ Chinese | |
| ✖ Chinese | |

Official language spoken alongside other languages or dialects

Unofficial language, but spoken by a portion of the population

## TRANSPORT

Communications are of overriding importance in today's world and national economies. The quality of a communications network is a good indicator of a country's state of development. The industrialized countries have dense and varied networks carrying people and goods throughout their territory. In most third-world countries only urban areas are served; places with natural obstacles or scattered population are neglected. North America has the greatest railroad mileage, but Europe is more densely served.

Since being eclipsed by the railroad in the last century, road travel has been revitalized with the spread of the private car.

## THE AUTOMOBILE

In the industrialized world, the automobile appeared at the end of the 19th century, but it took some 50 years to become widely available. Today, the third world is in the position of turn-of-the-century Europe, hence the marked contrast in car ownership between developed and developing countries. In industrialized countries there is an average of 276 private cars per 1,000 inhabitants, although the difference between market-economy (324 per thousand) and socialist (81 per thousand) countries is marked; in the United States there is one car for every 1.9 people and in the USSR one for every 26.

In Asia there are 55.5 cars per 1,000 people, although industrialized Japan has 214.9, and Kuwait 247; India and Pakistan have only 1.6 to 2. Apart from South Africa (with 101 per thousand), the average in Africa is no more than 14.

## AIR TRANSPORT

The airplane is the latest arrival on the transport scene; it is here that the most spectacular progress has been made in a dozen years. In 1971, passenger-miles totaled 306.7 billion miles; by 1983 this had nearly quadrupled. Freight now totals 198,904 billion tons per mile worldwide, of which 23.6% is air freight and 2.7% air mail. This efficiency has resulted from the ever increasing capacity of cargo and passenger aircraft.

Airports have had to be adapted to this trend. Runways must be long and wide enough to accommodate large planes. A major international airport today requires 500 times more space than 50 years ago. Despite a few sensational disasters, this is still the safest means of transport.

## MARITIME TRANSPORT

Despite the headway made by air transport, shipping still plays an essential role for certain kinds of goods—especially oil (which accounts for 40% of world tonnage), but also gas, coal and iron and other ores. Ships too have adapted in a very impressive way. Maximum gross capacity was 66,138,000 tons in 1953, but has been increased to 1,102,300,000 tons. But the age of these monsters is ending, and one by one they are being decommissioned. More and more general cargo is being shipped aboard container carriers.

National ownership is giving way to 'flags of convenience'. Several third-world countries (e.g. Liberia, Panama, Cyprus, Singapore, Somalia and Oman) have attracted foreign shipowners: 31.7% of their vessels belong to the United States, 20.7% to Greece, 16.9% to Hong Kong and 9.7% to Japan.

Today there is traffic on all the world's oceans, with the heaviest on the Atlantic. Oil leaves the Middle East and Africa bound for North America and Europe. Via the Pacific Ocean, the Middle East also supplies Australia, India and Japan. North-South routes also make use of the Atlantic ports of North America and Straits of Dover, Hormuz and Malacca and the Suez and Panama Canals play a strategic role in shipping.

Despite a drop in the oil trade, marine transport should continue to develop, thanks to the use of multipurpose ships able to carry ores, liquids and general cargo.

## TOURISM

Although tourism began its rise in the 18th century, it involved only the leisured classes of the developed countries. Paid vacations were instituted only at the beginning of this century, and became common only between 1930 and 1950. Prosperity and longer vacations have created an economic sector employing several million. It is the main economic activity in a number of countries, including Greece and Mauritius. It promotes shipbuilding, construction and clothing manufacture and even influences the appearance of some regions.

Depending on their income, tourists have a wide choice of accommodations, from camp sites, clubs, inns and hotels to private vacation homes. Travel continues to focus on the same spots: the seashore, the countryside and the mountains. With the recent wider accessibility of air travel, a new international tourism has emerged, sending travelers world wide in search of the exotic. Between 1950 and 1982 the number of international tourists rose from 25 million to more than 290 million, and today in excess of $90 billion is generated by this sector, 40 times as much as in the 1960s.

Europe and North America are the most popular continents (228 million and 33 million visitors in 1982), but each year Africa, Asia and Oceania also attract many tourists from wealthy countries: 8 million for Africa, 15 million for Asia and 4 million for Oceania.

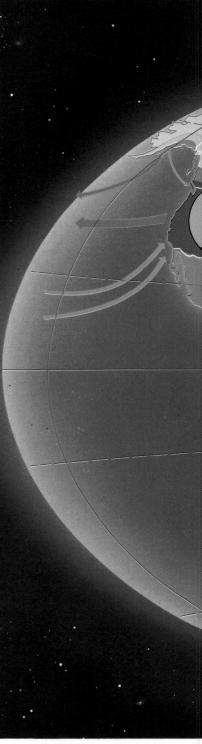

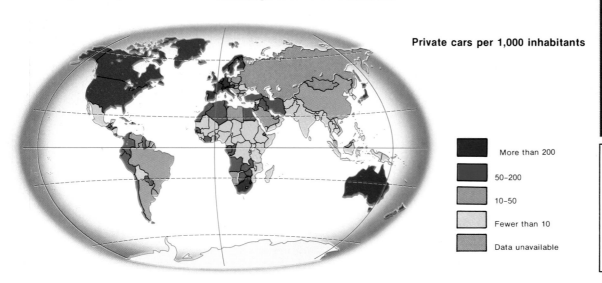

**Private cars per 1,000 inhabitants**

- More than 200
- 50–200
- 10–50
- Fewer than 10
- Data unavailable

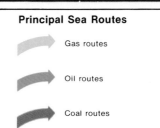

**Principal Sea Routes**

- Gas routes
- Oil routes
- Coal routes

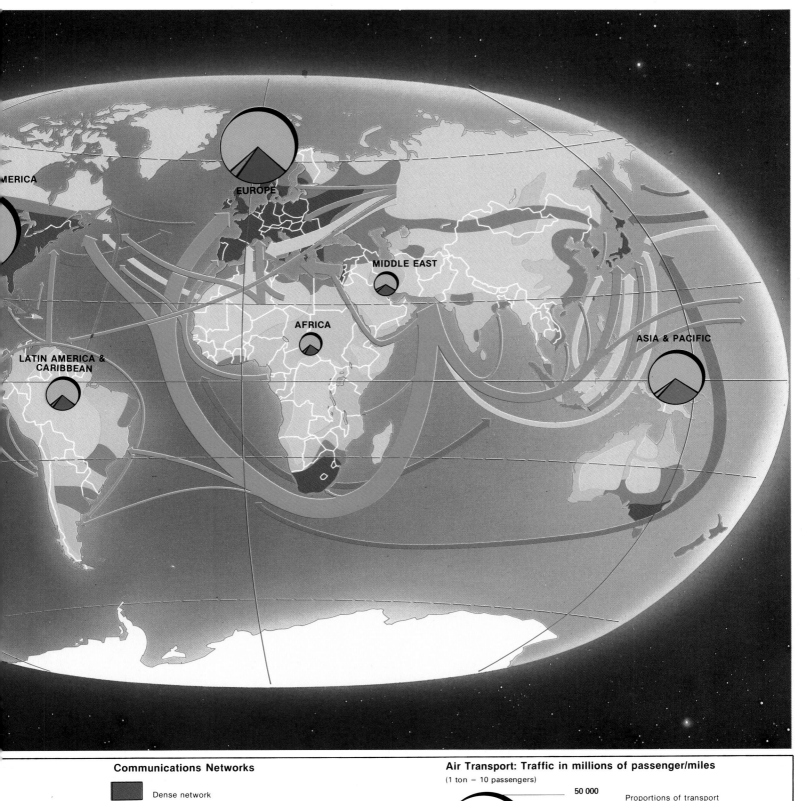

EUROPE

MIDDLE EAST

AFRICA

ASIA & PACIFIC

AMERICA

LATIN AMERICA &
CARIBBEAN

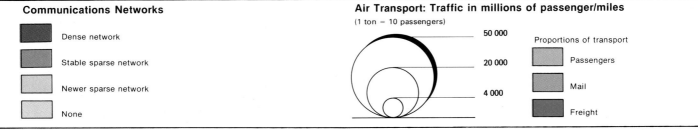

**Communications Networks**

Dense network

Stable sparse network

Newer sparse network

None

**Air Transport: Traffic in millions of passenger/miles**

(1 ton = 10 passengers)

50 000

20 000

4 000

Proportions of transport

Passengers

Mail

Freight

## CONSUMPTION

### Levels of Consumption

Today's energy needs are 115 times those of primitive man. "Technological" man uses 230 kilojoules a day. Average worldwide oil consumption totals 507,058 tons, but is uneven: The energy needs of an African are 17 times those of an Asian, and 1/15 those of an American. Americans use 1.6 times as much as Europeans and 1.2 times as much as Soviets.

### Changing Energy Consumption

Per capita energy use remained stable for centuries, but since the industrial revolution and the advent of oil, consumption has become more widespread, and it increased by 4% to 5% a year through 1973 (3% between 1870 and the First World War).

The 1973 and 1979 oil crises reduced consumption and slowed the growth of world energy use, which fell 15% between 1975 and 1984. Most affected were the industrialized countries. In the Soviet Union, consumption rose only 13% (as against 34% for the period 1965-75). In Japan the figures were 2.2% (as against 45.3%) and in France 5% (23.7%). In the United Kingdom and the United States consumption actually fell 4%.

Ten years ago, energy use in the year 2000 was projected as 50% higher than today's. Importer countries are saving energy to minimize their dependence on producers. The change was spurred by high oil prices, but also by growing awareness that oil reserves were not infinite.

## NON-RENEWABLE RESOURCES

### Hydrocarbons

Through 1970 oil consumption grew considerably; oil was gradually replacing coal, which is harder to handle and more expensive to extract. The Middle East, America, southeastern Asia and Africa possessed major reserves. The OPEC countries were the main suppliers, with production of 1,673,004.8 million tons; with the discovery of deposits in the North Sea and in Mexico they reduced their production by 30% to avert a drop in prices. World reserves are estimated at 211,641.6 tons, but that seems to be the limit, for new discoveries are increasingly rare. For some years these just about kept pace with production, but at the present rate they cannot last more than 33 years.

Natural gas reserves amount to 40% of oil reserves (3,390 billion cubic feet), but major discoveries are still possible. While exploitation is growing, only a little more than 6.56 billion ft. have been exploited, mainly in Siberia, the Orient and North America. The USSR and the United States account for 72% of world production and possess 47% of reserves; Iran holds 13%. Reserves are estimated to last 48 years.

### Coal

Much used early in the century, coal has gradually been replaced by oil. It is shunned in industrialized countries but at present rates of consumption reserves—which total more than 22,046 trillion tons—could last 4,000 years.

### Nuclear Energy

Nuclear energy is obtained from fissionable isotopes of the heavy element uranium (U-235 and U-238). Exploration is recent, and known reserves are comparatively small. But discoveries outpace consumption. Known deposits are found in Canada, the United States, South Africa, Australia, Namibia, Niger, France, Gabon and Brazil. Nuclear energy production is dominated by a few industrialized countries: the United States (343.6 Terawatts/hour); France (191.2); Japan (126.8) and the USSR (131). They account for 64% of world production.

## RENEWABLE RESOURCES

Since the oil crisis all countries have tried to develop renewable energy sources. But some were already widely used and others are expensive and not yet practical.

### Hydraulic Energy

Water has long been used as an energy source, but hydroelectric power dates only from 1869. While industrial countries have taken advantage of most usable sites, there remains great potential in the developing world. In 1983 Brazil and Paraguay built a 12,000 megawatt electricity plant, the largest in the world. If all possible sites in the third world were used, they would account for 48% of world resources. In the year 2000 an estimated 8% of our energy will come from hydraulic power.

### Geothermal Energy

Great hopes are pinned on geothermal energy, a power source which, while not yet mastered, is inexhaustible since it makes use of the heat of the Earth's core. It can be exploited in all regions near the edges of tectonic plates: 10% of the surface of the Earth. In both domestic and industrial use, by the year 2000 geothermal electricity production should equal today's output of hydroelectric power. In 1983 it accounted for 3,653 megawatts. The largest producer is the United States (39% of world output), followed by Italy (20%), the Philippines (16%), New Zealand (9%) and Japan and Mexico (7%).

### Additional Energy Sources

The sun, the tides, biomass and the wind are other new sources of energy now under study. They constitute an inexhaustible reserve that must not be ignored.

Direct solar energy is the most widespread, but low yield and storage problems confine it mainly to domestic use. Indirect solar energy (the sea, wind and biomass) supplies gas and electricity. Good sites for tidal power plants are rare, and at present there are only two in use: in France and in the USSR.

Biomass comes from the decomposition or combustion of vegetable or other organic materials, and in certain countries supplies an appreciable percentage of total energy. Major development efforts are underway in the United States, Brazil, France and India. It is the most sensitive of renewable resources: While it lets us employ what were considered unusable materials, environmental concerns must be addressed.

## Energy Production and Consumption

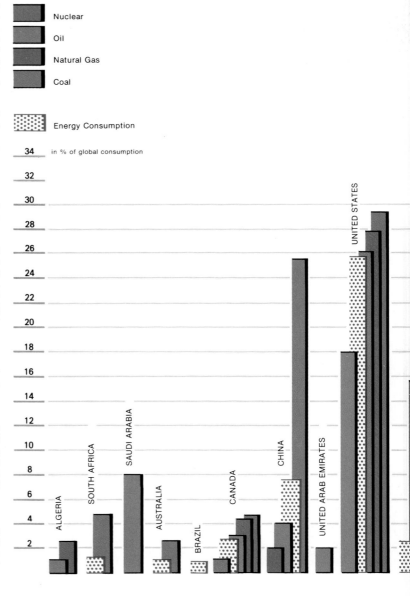

Nuclear

Oil

Natural Gas

Coal

Energy Consumption

in % of global consumption

## Renewable Energy

$\dot{\leq}$ Main Hydroelectric Plants

✳ Main Solar Energy Plants

Possible Tidal Energy Sites

Good Areas for Geothermal Energy

Annual sunlight

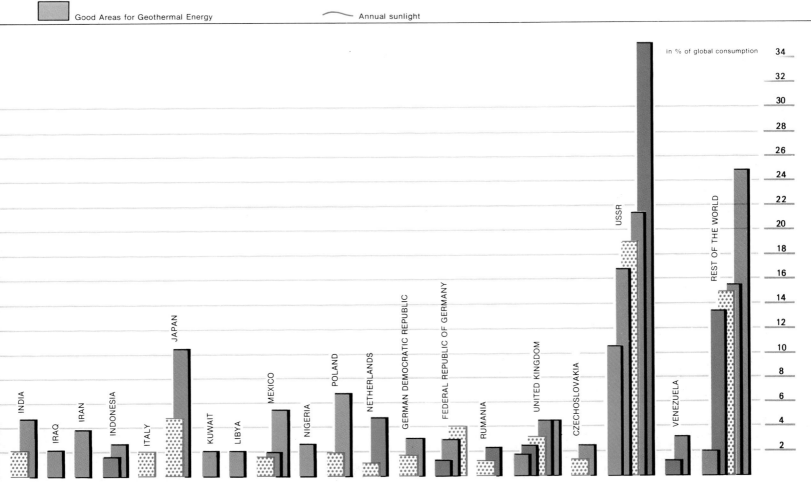

in % of global consumption

INDIA
IRAQ
IRAN
INDONESIA
ITALY
JAPAN
KUWAIT
LIBYA
MEXICO
NIGERIA
POLAND
NETHERLANDS
GERMAN DEMOCRATIC REPUBLIC
FEDERAL REPUBLIC OF GERMANY
RUMANIA
UNITED KINGDOM
CZECHOSLOVAKIA
USSR
VENEZUELA
REST OF THE WORLD

34
32
30
28
26
24
22
20
18
16
14
12
10
8
6
4
2

## LIMITED RESERVES

Mineral resources make up a mere 1% of the lithosphere. Some have been exploited for thousands of years, but in no great quantity. Only since the industrial revolution has there been a threat to known reserves. At present rates of consumption, gold will last only 28 years, uranium 49, copper 56 and silver 15. The threat to iron is not so great: reserves could last 440 years.

### Vast Inaccessible Reserves

The problem is not the quantity of ore: It is our limited ability to exploit it. It could take 1.5 billion years to use all the Earth's bauxite, but accessible reserves will last only 300 years. As for iron, total deposits could supply our needs for 25 million years, 104,167 times longer than accessible reserves.

For some minerals, such as uranium, molybdenum and cobalt, the problem is compounded by their concentration in a handful of countries, which must supply the entire world. Similar monopolies exist for agricultural raw materials such as rubber, linen and cotton, but the problem of reserves is not the same. These materials are inexhaustible, so long as we care for our natural heritage.

## NON-RENEWABLE AND RENEWABLE RESOURCES

### Iron and the Modern Steel Industry

Iron has been used since antiquity for weapons, tools and containers, and it now forms the basis of the steel industry. It is too soft to be used in pure form. Cast iron is too high in carbon and is brittle, but at very high temperatures it loses some of its carbon, producing steel.

Steel is often alloyed with other metals to give it various properties. Chromium, cobalt and nickel make it resistant to corrosion. Molybdenum makes it ductile, so it can be stretched without breaking. Cobalt makes it

## THE INTERDEPENDENCE OF CONSUMERS AND PRODUCERS

### Mining: The Great Powers

While a few industrialized countries are well endowed with mineral wealth (the USSR supplies 17.4% of the world's lead and 14% of its copper, the United States 34.3% of its phosphates and 15.2% of its uranium and Canada 25.6% of its uranium and 17.9% of its zinc) developing countries hold the bulk of the world's raw materials.

### The Third World: Mainly Exports

Malaysia is the top producer of tin and rubber; Bolivia leads in antimony and Chile in copper. But the third world as a whole consumes only 6% of

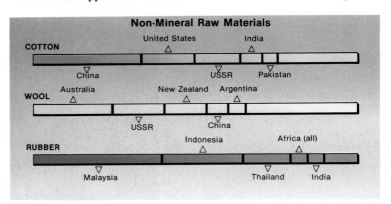

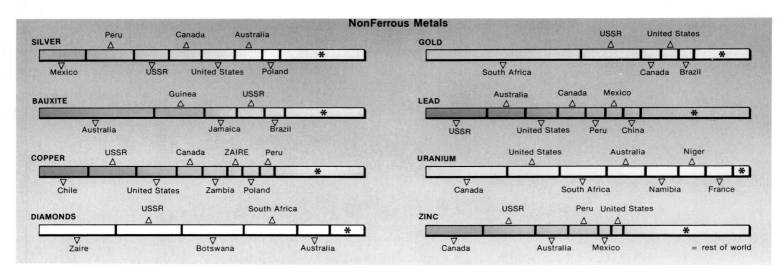

magnetic. Vanadium and tungsten strengthen it, and manganese gives it tensile strength.

### Uneven Distribution of Minerals

Forty countries mine iron ore, but four account for 63.2% of world production: the USSR, Brazil, China and Australia. Deposits of alloy metals are even less evenly distributed, although different countries are rich in different ores (apart from the USSR, which is a veritable treasure house of minerals). China and the USSR supply 44.5% of our tungsten; Australia, Canada and the USSR 58.2% of the nickel; South Africa, Brazil and the USSR 73.2% of the manganese; and the USSR, Zaire and Zambia 74.7% of the cobalt.

### Other Raw Materials

Apart from rare metals, mineral fertilizers, precious metals and rubber, raw materials are generally more evenly distributed, although monopolies exist here too. Australia, Guinea and Jamaica mine 59.6% of the bauxite from which aluminum is made; the USSR, Morocco and the United States 68.2% of phosphates for fertilizer; and South Africa and the USSR 67% of our gold. Nearly 54% of the world's wool is produced in Australia, New Zealand and the USSR. Natural rubber and uranium are rare. There are six main rubber producers; Malaysia, Indonesia and Thailand account for 78.5%.

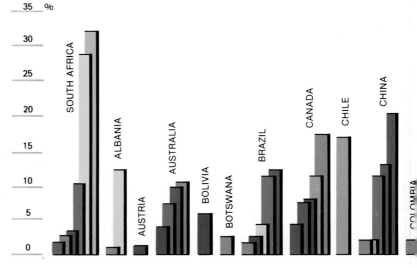

production while generating 30% of our mineral raw materials. Market-economy countries produce 45% while consuming 69%. Only planned-economy countries strike a balance between production and consumption (25% each). Thus, processing takes place far from where ores are extracted. For instance, although the United States produces 6.8% of the world's iron, it imports vast quantities for its steel industry, supplying 11.8% of the world's steel.

**Dependent Industrialized Countries**

With their nearly nonexistent or exhausted resources, Japan and Europe are even more dependent. Yet Japan is the third largest steel producer after the USSR and the United States.

The big industrial countries wish to exploit seabed resources. Polymetallic nodules would release them from their dependence on producer countries. But developing countries bitterly oppose this, seeking the internationalization of the use these nodules with a view to sharing in the profits. Use of poly-metallic nodules would result in disastrous loss of income for certain countries: mining accounts for 53.2% of Chile's income, and iron for 85% of Mauritania's and 70% of Liberia's. Zambia and Zaire depend on copper for 95% and 70% of their respective incomes.

**A More Balanced Distribution of Income**

Developing countries are very much aware of the threat posed by the present system, and want to process their own ores. A steel industry has been established in India, Egypt, Algeria and Iran, and Chile has nationalized its existing processing industry. Some time in the future, such industrialization and the general exhaustion of accessible reserves will probably make for greater balance in raw materials income.

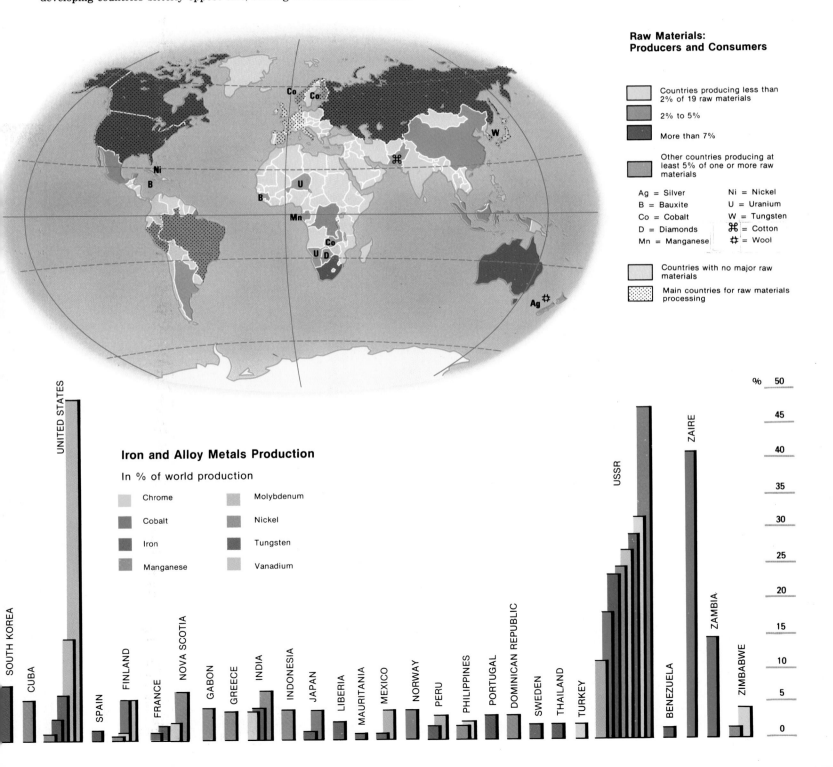

## AN ECONOMIC TURNING-POINT

In the last 15 years the world economy has changed. The industrial West underwent a serious economic upheaval connected in part with the oil crises of 1973 and 1979. Unemployment and inflation are up, and investments down.

During the same period some third world countries, such as those of southeastern Asia and the oil producers, have emerged from economic paralysis to challenge Western dominance in many fields. But the 1985-1986 drop in oil prices created problems in the oil-producing states, without solving those of the non-producers.

## THE ECONOMIC CRISIS

### Industry in Decline

The economic crisis that began in the 1960s affected the whole world, but the countries at the extremes of the economic scale were hardest hit. The effect on poor countries was devastating, and their already weak economies further declined, giving rise to an economic "fourth world," composed of almost all the African countries, and some in the Middle East and South-East Asia. Poor balance of payments has created a dire economic situation, where modernization is impossible.

The rich countries—both market and planned economy—experienced a large decline in industrial growth: greater than 50% in Western Europe and 25% in North America and Eastern Europe. Growth in these regions is now slower than in much of the third world.

### Unemployment

Unemployment is a prime symptom of this decline. Nearly everywhere it exceeds 7% and it is on the increase, especially in older coal, steel and textile producing regions. Only the USSR appears to have escaped, although unemployment is not officially acknowledged there: There is overstaffing, and part of the workforce is underpaid.

The new industrial countries fall between these two extremes. Unemployment in China and in South Korea is less than 3%, and it is on the decline in the Middle East.

## THE RISE OF THE THIRD WORLD

### The Growth of Investment

There is a stark contrast between the Western economic Powers and the new industrial countries of the Pacific, the Middle East and South America. In 10 years, investment in the former has grown by a rate of barely 3%, and has actually declined in Scandinavia, Switzerland and the Netherlands. But in the South the rate has exceeded 3%, surpassing 10% for oil-producing countries. Developed countries continue to invest more heavily than others, but the gap is narrowing.

Third-world countries have benefitted in several ways. The population explosion has provided young, cheap labor; India, China and Brazil have thus been able to diversify their industries. Foreign capital invested through multinational corporations has given fresh life to small southeastern Asian States like Hong Kong, Singapore and Taiwan. At present, investment in South Korea equals that in Belgium and amounts to 80% of that in the Netherlands. Thanks to higher oil prices, the OPEC countries have amassed

**The Worldwide Economic Crisis**

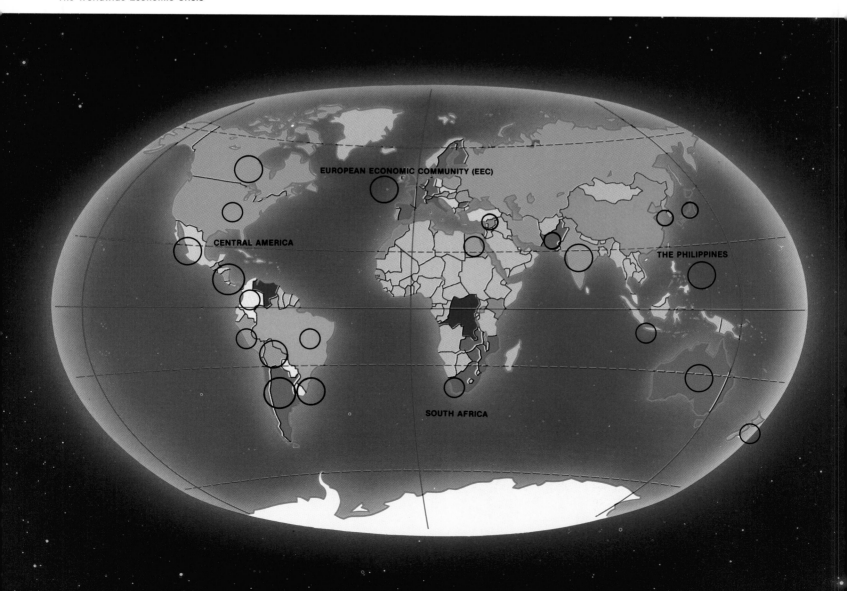

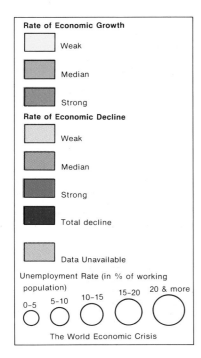

**Rate of Economic Growth**

Weak

Median

Strong

**Rate of Economic Decline**

Weak

Median

Strong

Total decline

Data Unavailable

Unemployment Rate (in % of working population)

0–5   5–10   10–15   15–20   20 & more

The World Economic Crisis

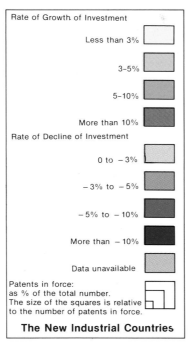

Rate of Growth of Investment

Less than 3%

3–5%

5–10%

More than 10%

Rate of Decline of Investment

0 to −3%

−3% to −5%

−5% to −10%

More than −10%

Data unavailable

Patents in force: as % of the total number. The size of the squares is relative to the number of patents in force.

**The New Industrial Countries**

capital enabling them to create a technologically advanced industry. The industrial strength of India and Brazil has increased: Between 1965 and 1985 India's export income from industrial products grew by 27%, and Brazil's by more than 500%.

**Technology on the Move**

Competition and the development race compel businesses to invest more and more in research. The developed world is still ahead, but some third-world countries have made great efforts. South Korea has nearly six times as many researchers as France.

The developing countries benefit from technology transfers, but suffer from the flow of their researchers to the industrialized world. Industrialized countries do send technicians to the third world, but mostly to set up the plants they sell there. Investment in research over the past decade has been enormous, and it is still increasing.

The crisis in the West affects this area too. One of the first industrialized States, the United Kingdom, has also been one of the first to lose its vigor. Its investment in research steadily dropped between 1961 and 1975, and, despite small improvements since 1975, remains inadequate.

The breakthrough of the third world is exemplified by South Korea. Since 1965 financing for research and development has increased greatly and continuously. It has grown from 0.3% of total investment in that year to 0.4% in 1975 and 0.9% in 1984.

India is a special case in the third world and in the world of science. Its influence remains small, but it is a true scientific power in all spheres: medicine and medical research, as well as biochemistry, physics, chemistry and physical chemistry.

The diverse potential of developing countries could lead the economic world into a new era.

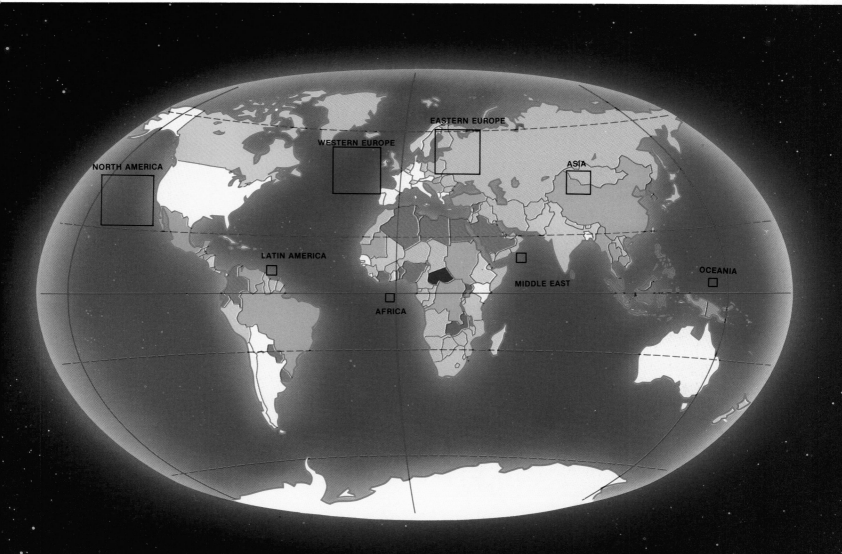

## POLITICAL PRESSURE

To exert pressure a weapon is needed. Energy and food are effective political weapons, for they can bring about the economic subordination of dependent countries.

## INTERNATIONAL TRADE

Thanks to improved transport and reduced customs duties, international trade has expanded considerably over the past 40 years. The main beneficiaries have been the industrialized countries, since they conduct most of this trade. They produce or import many raw materials, and their capital resources enable them to process and export those materials in the form of valuable manufactured goods. Their agricultural surpluses let them sell to others or provide aid to third-world countries, sometimes in exchange for a say in their production policies. Third-world countries often export only one product, and their economies depend on market prices which they themselves rarely set.

## DEPENDENCE IN ENERGY

The world's main energy resources are coal, oil and gas, with which industrialized countries have thus far been unable to dispense, despite the contribution of alternative sources. Japan is the most dependent, importing almost 661,380 million tons. It ranks first in imports of coal, second in oil and third in natural gas. Europe too is highly dependent, although it has developed alternative sources. The main suppliers of Europe, Japan and the other importing countries are the United States, the USSR, Australia, South Africa and the OPEC countries, joined in recent years by new producers. Gas, generally a byproduct of oil production, also comes from the Middle East, and Indonesia is another fairly large exporter.

## BLACK GOLD

Until some two decades ago, all the economic pressure was exerted by the industrial countries on the developing world. Now the world economy has taken a new turn and in some areas certain developing countries can compete with the industrial Powers.

The most graphic example of this reversal is oil. Until 1973 oil prices were set by the industrial countries, at a fairly low level. When OPEC was established, its member countries quadrupled prices, a sudden increase that let them exert enormous pressure on the importers: principally the industrialized world. The pressure was all the greater since the industrial countries, accustomed to this major source of cheap energy, had neglected their coal mining industries and had few nuclear power plants.

Prices stopped skyrocketing in 1980, and between 1980 and 1986 they dropped from $40 a barrel to less than $15. But the enormous wealth accumulated by OPEC members had made possible rapid industrialization or investment in other countries.

## FOOD AS A WEAPON

The demand for grain is enormous, yet it is met by a handful of countries. North America accounts for 54.3% of the world wheat trade. France, the granary of Europe, ranks third, followed by Australia and Argentina. Surprisingly, the bulk of the exports goes not to the needy countries of Africa and Asia, but to the USSR. The small quantities exported to the third world are in the form of food aid, principally rice.

But demand in the developed countries is always growing, both for human and animal consumption. Increasing quantities of soy beans, wheat and corn are used for stock rearing. The European Community imports 80% of world soy bean production. Until 1973 the United States had a virtual monopoly on soy bean production and trade, but the economic embargo imposed by President Richard Nixon meant a search for new suppliers. Brazil is now the second exporter, after the United States.

Food is difficult to wield as a weapon: if governments block exports, stocks can pile up, bringing prices down and angering the farmers. Consider the case of the United States and the USSR. In times of tension, the United States embargoes exports to the Soviet Union, inevitably arousing the ire of American farmers.

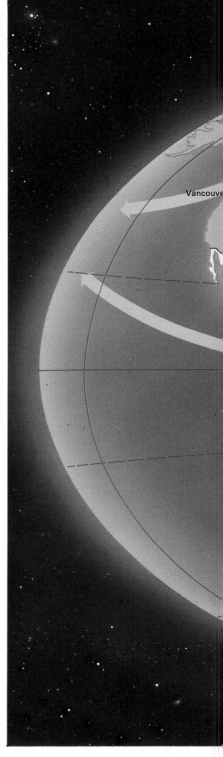
Vancouver

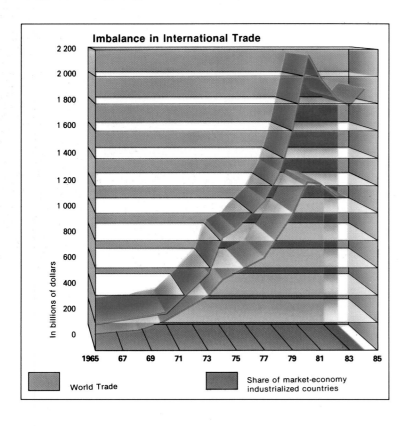

**Imbalance in International Trade**

In billions of dollars

2 200 — 2 000 — 1 800 — 1 600 — 1 400 — 1 200 — 1 000 — 800 — 600 — 400 — 200 — 0

1965 67 69 71 73 75 77 79 81 83 85

◼ World Trade
◼ Share of market-economy industrialized countries

**Grain Trade**

Imports
in % of national production

☐ 0–33.2

▨ 33.2–66.5

▨ Greater than 66.5

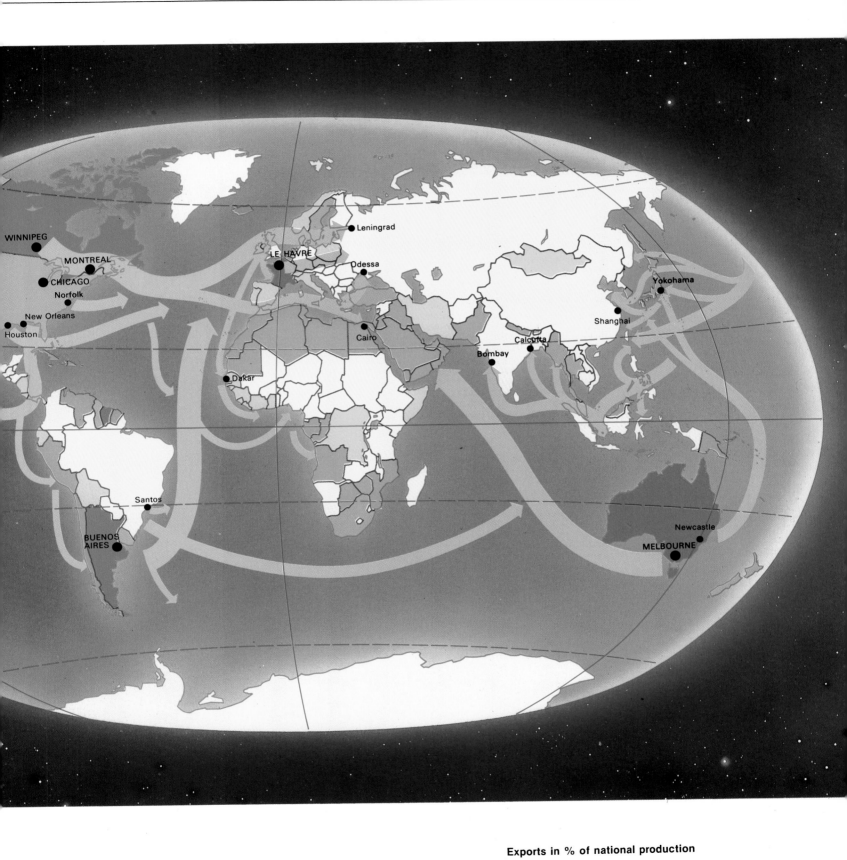

WINNIPEG

MONTREAL

CHICAGO

Norfolk

New Orleans

Houston

Leningrad

LE HAVRE

Odessa

Yokohama

Shanghai

Cairo

Calcutta

Bombay

Dakar

Santos

BUENOS AIRES

Newcastle

MELBOURNE

Main wheat markets

Major flows of wheat exports

**Exports in % of national production**

Greater than 40

20–40

0–20

## GEOGRAPHY AND THE DEVELOPMENT OF GEOSTRATEGY

The location of oceans, deserts, mountains and rivers has a great affect on political and military strategy. Views differ on the main features of this strategy.

The first is based on the concept of a pivotal 'heartland' in European Russia constituting the center of the 'world island' of the Old World. Thanks to its location, this region is destined to be the focal point of a continental power which will attempt to control the 'rimland' comprising the States of Europe and Asia.

The second theory has it that the basis of power is the sea, placing the United States at its center because that country alone can oppose the expansion of the continental power. That is why the USSR seeks greater access to the oceans, for despite its size it has only one ocean port that is ice-free all year round: Murmansk. The rest of its coast is blocked by ice for part of the year or lies on inland seas whose straits are controlled by 'rimland' countries.

### Economic Unions and Military Alliances

Since the end of the Second World War, the two super-powers have been the centers of the East and West geopolitical blocs. Militarily, this economic and ideological split is reflected in treaty alliances: NATO (North Atlantic Treaty Organization), ANZUS (Australia-New Zealand-United States) and ASEAN (Association of South-East Asian Nations) in the West, and the Warsaw Pact in the East. In the face of this East-West split, some countries have sought non-alignment, mainly third-world nations wishing to redefine the relationship between the underdeveloped South and the developed North. The rift is bound to be military as well as economic. Each power has a historical sphere of influence: The Americas are the preserve of the United States; Africa is the special partner of Western Europe; the Far East looks basically to Japan. Australia is trying to create an economic bulwark with the proliferation of island micro-nations.

### Weapons

The balance of power has been altered by the atomic bomb, the Second World War and decolonization. The two big powers possess nuclear arsenals capable of destroying each other's vital centers. The risks have grown with new members joining the nuclear club: the United Kingdom in 1952, France in 1960, China in 1966 and India in 1977 (Israel and South Africa too are suspected of possessing nuclear weapons). The Treaty on the Non-Proliferation of Nuclear Weapons was an attempt to stem transfer of this technology. But even conventional weapons, possessed by all governments, are destructive, and the threat persists.

Arsenals provide a means of pressure, deterrence and self-assertion; many underdeveloped countries therefore devote a large portion of their GNP to armaments.

### Areas of Conflict

Many countries are at peace within their own borders, but because of treaty alliances only a few have avoided all military conflict over the past 12 years. Between 1973 and 1983 only 25 countries did not participate in an armed conflict. Ten supported distant states, and the rest were involved in widespread conflicts, border wars or civil wars.

Today, the third world is the site of the most acute tensions. In the Far East there is confrontation between China and the Soviet Union; Iran, Iraq, Afghanistan and Pakistan are beset by widespread conflict, border wars and regional civil wars; there is civil war in Lebanon, exacerbated by the Arab-Israel conflict that began in 1947. The borders of South Africa have seen many armed attacks. Some Central American countries have been destabilized by guerrillas. So it is no surprise that the third world imports many weapons.

Industrialized countries are heavily involved in these confrontations. The United States has sent troops to Lebanon and France to Chad, and the United Kingdom fought Argentina in the Falklands War.

### Terrorism

Terrorism is another form of pressure, generally used by the weak. It is carried out by small groups often financed and trained by governments and takes many forms, depending on its goals: bomb attacks, hostage taking, hijacking, and assassination. As a rule terrorist violence results in casualties and death. In 1985, 21 people were wounded in France, and in 1984 airlines of several countries were the targets of 28 hijacking attempts, 15 of them successful. The Middle East is the source of most terrorists, although they come also from Ireland, Corsica and Belgium. Each group (such as the CCC in Belgium, the PLO in Palestine, the Baader-Meinhof gang in Germany and the IRA in Ireland) claims responsibility for its acts.

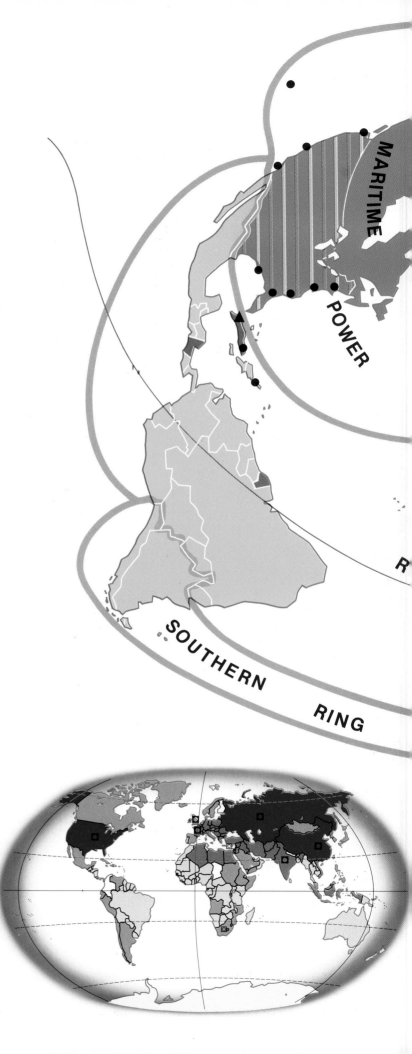

## Weapons

**Number of tanks or other armored vehicles**

|   | |
|---|---|
| ⬜ | Less than 100 |
| ▨ | 100–1,000 |
| ▦ | 1,000–10,000 |
| ▩ | More than 10,000 |
| ⬛ | Data unavailable |
| ▣ | Countries possessing nuclear weapons |
| ▢ | Countries suspected of possessing nuclear weapons |

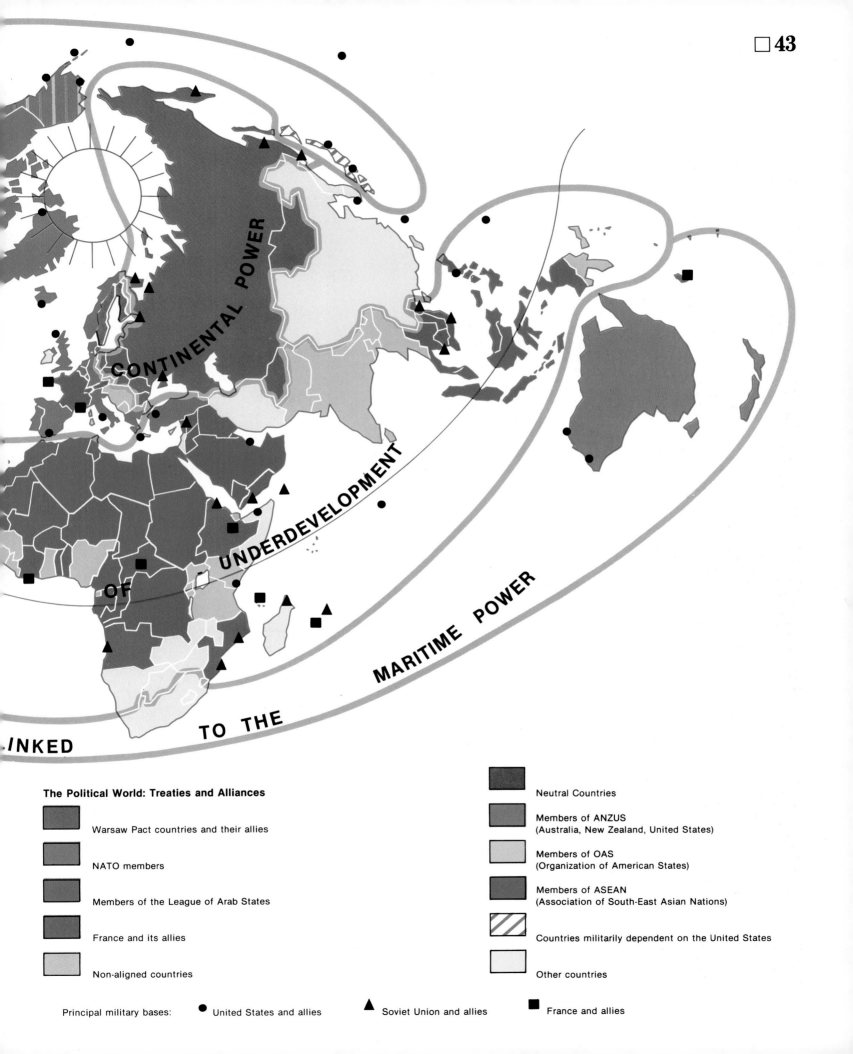

CONTINENTAL POWER

UNDERDEVELOPMENT

OF

MARITIME POWER

TO THE

INKED

**The Political World: Treaties and Alliances**

Warsaw Pact countries and their allies

NATO members

Members of the League of Arab States

France and its allies

Non-aligned countries

Neutral Countries

Members of ANZUS
(Australia, New Zealand, United States)

Members of OAS
(Organization of American States)

Members of ASEAN
(Association of South-East Asian Nations)

Countries militarily dependent on the United States

Other countries

Principal military bases: ● United States and allies   ▲ Soviet Union and allies   ■ France and allies

| COUNTRY | OFFICIAL LANGUAGE(S) | AREA in sq mi | POPULATION | POPULATION DENSITY pop/sq mi | GNP in billions of $ (1982) | WORLD RANK | PER CAPITA Income (1982 dollars) | WORLD RANK | CAPITOL | POPULATION | PER CAPITA ELEC. CONSUMPTION in millions of kwh | No. of VEHICLES per 1,000 inhabitants | No. of DOCTORS per 1,000 inhabitants | % POPULATION less than 15 years of age |
|---|---|---|---|---|---|---|---|---|---|---|---|---|---|---|
| ALBANIA | albanian | 11,112 | 2,900,000 | 261 | 1.80 | 116 | 630 | 144 | TIRANA | 250,000 | 783 | — | 1.39 | 37.3 |
| ANDORRA | catalan | 175 | 34,000 | 194 | 0.270 | 161 | 6,800 | 39 | ANDORRA LA V. | 5,500 | — | — | — | 22 |
| AUSTRIA | german | 32,378 | 7,555,000 | 233 | 67.40 | 27 | 8,860 | 26 | VIENNA | 1,525,000 | 5,223 | 320 | 2.27 | 22.8 |
| BELGIUM | french, dutch | 11,783 | 9,860,000 | 837 | 81.50 | 23 | 8,265 | 31 | BRUSSELS | 997,000 | 5,306 | 331 | 2.5 | 21.8 |
| BULGARIA | bulgarian | 42,827 | 8,970,000 | 210 | 68.50 | 39 | 4,760 | 52 | SOFIA | 200,000 | 4,910 | 94 | 3.29 | 22.3 |
| CYPRUS | greek, turkish | 3,572 | 66,000 | 185 | 2.14 | 111 | 3,240 | 65 | NICOSIA | 120,000 | 1,876 | 207.7 | 0.94 | 24.7 |
| CZECHOSLOVAKIA | czech, slovak | 49,379 | 15,500,000 | 313 | 94.86 | 20 | 6,140 | 43 | PRAGUE | 1,250,000 | 5,065 | 129.4 | 3.5 | 24.3 |
| DENMARK | danish | 16,631 | 5,110,000 | 307 | 56 | 30 | 10,940 | 15 | COPENHAGEN | 1,200,000 | 5,136 | 272 | 2 | 22.4 |
| EAST GERMANY | german | 41,772 | 16,700,000 | 400 | 657.70 | 4 | 8,600 | 30 | BERLIN | 1,150,000 | 6,373 | 143.2 | 2 | 19.5 |
| FINLAND | finnish | 130,132 | 4,880,000 | 38 | 47.80 | 36 | 9,855 | 20 | HELSINKI | 750,000 | 9,293 | 290 | 1.97 | 21.7 |
| FRANCE | french | 211,228 | 54,900,000 | 259 | 514.90 | 5 | 9,450 | 24 | PARIS | 8,708,000 | 4,971 | 177 | 2 | 21.8 |
| GREECE | greek | 50,949 | 9,910,000 | 194 | 36.40 | 42 | 3,695 | 60 | ATHENS | 3,200,000 | 2,454 | 107.6 | 2.55 | 22.4 |
| HUNGARY | hungarian | 35,922 | 10,600,000 | 295 | 21.01 | 55 | 1,960 | 85 | BUDAPEST | 2,000,000 | 3,235 | 110.4 | 3 | 23.1 |
| ICELAND | icelandic | 39,772 | 240,000 | 6 | 2.30 | 110 | 9,705 | 22 | REYKJAVIK | 130,000 | 15,954 | 403 | 2.14 | 27.5 |
| IRELAND (REP.) | english | 27,138 | 3,540,000 | 131 | 17.70 | 57 | 5,030 | 51 | DUBLIN | 920,000 | 3,179 | 205 | 1.29 | 30.6 |
| ITALY | italian | 116,314 | 57,000,000 | 489 | 355.10 | 7 | 6,255 | 41 | ROME | 3,000,000 | 3,428 | 346 | 2.9 | 23.7 |
| LIECHTENSTEIN | german | 61 | 26,000 | 43 | 0.470 | 156 | 16,621 | 5 | VADUZ | 4,600 | — | — | — | 22.3 |
| LUXEMBOURG | luxembourgeois | 999 | 366,000 | 366 | 3.20 | 99 | 8,740 | 28 | LUXEMBOURG | 81,000 | 11,269 | 385 | 1.14 | 18.5 |
| MALTA | maltese | 122 | 38,000 | 3,114 | 1.21 | 129 | 3,410 | 64 | VALLETTA | 14,000 | 1,790 | 1,968.4 | 1.27 | 24.6 |
| MONACO | french | .70 | 27,000 | 38,631 | 0.280 | 160 | 11,340 | 13 | MONACO | 1,234 | — | 604 | 2.23 | 11.9 |
| NETHERLANDS | dutch | 15,771 | 14,430,000 | 914 | 133.30 | 17 | 9,280 | 25 | AMSTERDAM | 994,062 | 4,463 | 330 | 1.72 | 21.8 |
| NORWAY | norwegian | 125,194 | 4,140,000 | 33 | 55 | 31 | 13,330 | 9 | OSLO | 642,954 | 22,485 | 335 | 2.03 | 23.5 |
| POLAND | polish | 120,736 | 37,100,000 | 308 | 150.51 | 13 | 4,124 | 54 | WARSAW | 1,500,000 | 3,327 | 86.5 | 2.4 | 23.9 |
| PORTUGAL | portuguese | 35,556 | 10,190,000 | 287 | 20.50 | 56 | 2,030 | 83 | LISBON | 2,000,000 | 1,960 | 136.5 | 1.42 | 27.9 |
| RUMANIA | rumanian | 91,708 | 22,560,000 | 246 | 51.28 | 33 | 2,245 | 78 | BUCHAREST | 1,959,000 | 3,185 | — | 1.97 | 25.4 |
| SAN MARINO | italian | 24 | 22,000 | 935 | 0.235 | 162 | 8,760 | 27 | SAN MARINO | 5,000 | — | — | — | 20.6 |
| SPAIN | spanish | 194,915 | 38,500,000 | 198 | 159.40 | 12 | 4,170 | 53 | MADRID | 1,500,000 | 2,935 | 228.7 | 2.6 | 27.6 |
| SWEDEN | swedish | 173,747 | 8,340,000 | 48 | 91.60 | 21 | 10,995 | 14 | STOCKHOLM | 1,550,000 | 13,829 | 361 | 2.2 | 20.6 |
| SWITZERLAND | french, german, italian, romansch | 15,943 | 6,540,000 | 410 | 98.20 | 16 | 15,110 | 7 | BERNE | 290,000 | 6,701 | 392 | 2.45 | 21 |
| UNITED KINGDOM | english | 94,235 | 56,400,000 | 597 | 449.20 | 6 | 8,020 | 33 | LONDON | 8,000,000 | 4,949 | 289 | 1.7 | 22.9 |
| USSR | russian | 8,650,340 | 276,500,000 | 32 | 1,378 | 2 | 5,100 | 49 | MOSCOW | 8,400,000 | 5,072 | 38 | 4 | 27.4 |
| VATICAN | italian | .17 | 1,000 | 5,886 | — | — | — | — | VATICAN | 1,000 | — | — | — | |
| WEST GERMANY | german | 95,819 | 61,200,000 | 636 | 146 | 15 | 10,680 | 17 | BONN | 300,000 | 6,265 | 401 | 2.30 | 20.3 |
| YUGOSLAVIA | serbo-croatian, macedonian | 98,776 | 22,860,000 | 230 | 45.71 | 38 | 2,000 | 84 | BELGRADE | 1,500,000 | 3,177 | 119 | 1.49 | 24.4 |

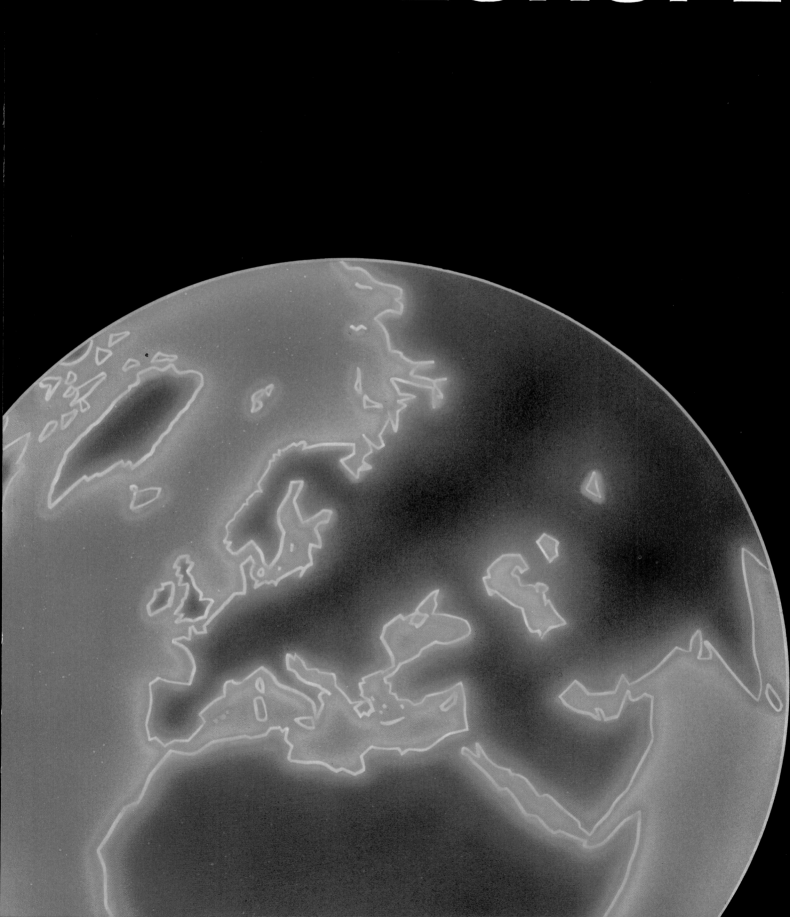

Scale 1 : 33,000,000

WANDEL SEA

ARCTIC OCEAN

K. Bridgman
K. E. Rasmussen
Kronbrins Christians Land
Nordostrundingen
4038
Fj. Danmark
Fredbenk Vill. land
Kong
Hovgaards Ø
GREENLAND
I. de France
Germania Land
Store Koldewey
Shannon
Clavering Ø
Fj. du Roi Oscar
Baie Foste

GREENLAND SEA

Spitsbergen
Nordaustlandet
Kvitøya
54
Kong Karls Land
Newtontoppen 1713
Longyearbyen
Vestspitsbergen
Edgeøya

BARENTS SEA

O. Rudol'fa
Greem Bell
Zeml'a Aleksandry
Franz Josef Land
O. Zeml'a Georga
Zeml'a Yil'čeka
O. Sal'm.
590

Novaya Zemlya

Bear I.
548
69
70°

K Brewster
Denmark Strait
2284

NORWEGIAN SEA
4014

Grimsey
Arctic Circle
882 · Faeroe Is.
Shetland 450
53

Magerøya North Cape
Varangerfjord
Sørøya
Hammerfest
Kvaløy
Senja
Vesteralen
Lofoten
Narvik 2117
Kebnekaise
LAPLAND
Murmansk
191 Kola
Peninsula
Kanin Pen.
O. Moržovec
303
TUNDRA
Timansky Mts 463

Donna 1703
Vikna
Hitra
Trondheim
Otrøy
Vågsøy
SCANDINAVIAN MTS
2470 Jotunheimen
1933
Oslo

WHITE SEA
Arkhangelsk
KARELIA
384
310
Solovečkije O-va
L. Onega
293
North Hills
331

2000 Iceland
1446
Hekla 1448 2116 Hvannadalshnukur
Reykjavik

FINNISH LAKES
Helsinki
Ahvenanmaa
Tampere
Åland
Gulf of Bothnia
L. Ladoga
L. Onega

Orkney Is.
Hébrides
SCOTLAND
Ben Nevis 1345
Grampian Mts
Edinburgh
Cheviot Hills
106
Rockall
Shetland

Stockholm
Gotland
Öland
Khiuma
Sarema
Estonia
Leningrad
L. Rybinsk
Valdajskaja vozvyšennost'
Moscow
Moskova
CENTRAL RUSSIAN UPLANDS
Gor'kij
Kazan

NORTH SEA
Ireland
Dublin
Snowdon 1085
WALES
Kerry Mts
1041
London
C. Land's End

Great Britain
Pennines
ENGLAND
Copenhagen
Sjælland
Bornholm
LITHUANIA
Niemen
Belorussian Uplands

BALTIC SEA
POMERANIA
GERMAN-POLISH PLAIN
Berlin
Warta
Oder
Warsaw
Pinsk Marshes
Podol'skaja Vozv.
UKRAINIAN PLAIN
Donskaja Ravnina
Donbass
Volga Plateau

NETHERLANDS
Amsterdam
Brussels
Flanders
Ardenne
Harz 1147
Erzgebirge 1244
Sudety
Praha 1453
Bohemian Forest
Moravia
Kijev
Dniepr
Don
Volgograd

ATLANTIC OCEAN
Channel Is.
English Channel
Hills of Brittany
BASSIN PARISIEN
Paris
Loire
BASSIN
Puy de Sancy 1885
MASSIF CENTRAL
Vosges
Jura
Black Forest
Bern
L. Leman
Vienna
Budapest
L. Balaton
Great Hungarian Plain
Transylvania
Bihor 1848
Moldavia
Bucharest
Crimea
SEA OF AZOV
Kuban

Bay of Biscay
5665
C. Finisterre
Cantabrian Mts 2648
Iberic Mts
2419
AQUITAIN
PYRÉNÉES
P. d'Aneto 3404
CASTILA
Madrid 2469
ALPS
Mt. Blanc 4808
Mte. Rosa 4652
TIROL 3797
3841 Viso
APENNINES
Tuscany
Roma
DINARIC ALPS
Belgrad
Iron Gate
BALKAN MTS
Sofija
Rhodopa 2925
GREAT CAUCASUS 5633
ELBRUS
Georgia 5047
Tbilisi
Azerbaijan
Kazbek

Lisbon
Tage
Sierra Morena
Sierra Nevada
Mulhacen 3478
Barcelona 3069
Balearic Is.
Ibiza
Majorca
Minorca
Sardinia
3730
TYRRHENIAN SEA
Corsica
Mt Cinto 2710
Gr. Sasso 2914
Vesuvius 1277
Mt. Olympus 2911
AEGEAN
Istanbul
Pontic Mountains 2600
Ankara
Sakarya
ANATOLIA
Erciyas 3916
Aladaglar 3734
TAURUS
Little Caucasus
Aragac 4490
Armenia
Bü Agri D. 5185
4821
KURDISTAN

MEDITERRANEAN SEA
C. St. Vicente
Strait of Gibraltar
Algiers 2308
Kabylie
Aures 2328
ATLAS
Rif 2456
Quarsenis
Atlas Saharien
Etna
Sicily
Malta
Calabria
IONIAN SEA
Peloponnesos
Sporades
Crete 2456
Rhodos 3590
Cyprus
JEZIREH
Aleppo
SYRIAN DESERT
Damascus
Baghdad

Madeira 1861
Canary Is. 3718
Anti Atlas
J. Toubkal 4165
Hamada du Draa
Great Western Erg
Great Eastern Erg
Jabal Nafusah 968
Tripoli
Gulf of Sidra
Benghazi 876
J. Akhdar
CYRENAICA
Qattara Depression
Nile
Sina 2642
Dead Sea
J. Duruz 1800
Négev
AN NEFUD

© HACHETTE-IGN

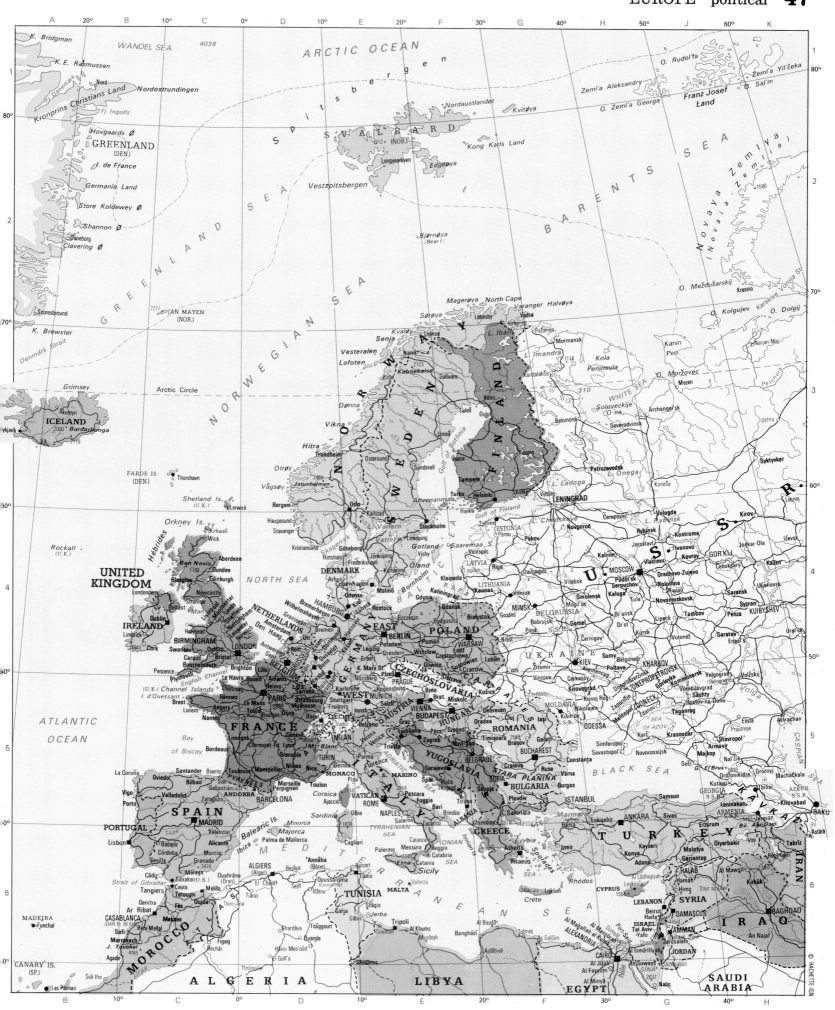

Scale 1 : 5,000,000

U.S.S.R.

BARENTS SEA

MURMANSK

Severomorsk
Monchegorsk
Kandalaksha
Kirovsk
Kola
Murmaši

FINLAND

OULU
Oulu
Kemi
Rovaniemi
Tornio
Haparanda
Kalix

LAPLAND

LAPPLAND

FINNMARK

North Cape
Magerøya
Hammerfest
Honningsvåg
Nordkinn
Gamvik
Berlevåg
Båtsfjord
Vardø
Vadsø
Varanger
Kirkenes
Nikel
Boris Gleb

TROMS

Tromsø
Senja
Sørøya
Seiland
Kvaløya
Hasvik
Øksfjord
Alta
Kautokeino
Karasjok
Karigasniemi

Kiruna
Gällivare
NORRBOTTEN

Narvik
Svolvær
Lofoten
Vesterålen
Andøya
Langøya
Hadseløya
Hinnøya
Bodø

VÄSTERBOTTEN
Skellefteå
Piteå
Luleå
Boden

NORWAY

Mosjøen
Mo
Rana
Nesna

NORWEGIAN SEA

Arctic Circle

Mo i Rana

### Iceland inset

ICELAND

Reykjavík
Akureyri
Keflavík
Húsavík
Vopnafjörður
Seyðisfjörður
Egilsstaðir
Höfn
Selfoss
Hekla
Vatnajökull
Mýrdalsjökull
Langjökull
Hofsjökull
Vík
Grímsey
Arctic Circle
Ísafjörður
Breiðafjörður
Faxaflói
Snæfell
Hvannadalshnúkur
Borgarnes
Akranes
Vestmannaeyjar

### Faroe Islands inset

FAROE IS.
(Den.)

Tórshavn
Østerø
Strømø
Vágø
Suderø
Nordoyar
Viderø
Sandø

NORGE

NORWAY

0 50 100 Kilomètres
0 50 Statute Miles

**SWEDEN**

**DENMARK**

**POLAND**

**ESTONIA**

**LATVIA**

**LITHUANIA**

**U.S.S.R.**

**BYELORUSSIA**

**R.S.F.S.R.**

**G.D.R.**

**F.R.G.**

**NETHERLANDS**

HELSINKI
TURKU
TAMPERE
PORI
HÄMEENLINNA
LAHTI

STOCKHOLM
UPPSALA
SÖDERTÄLJE
NORRKÖPING
LINKÖPING
ÖREBRO
VÄSTERÅS
GÄVLE
GÖTEBORG
JÖNKÖPING
KALMAR
KARLSKRONA
HELSINGBORG
MALMÖ
LUND

OSLO
BERGEN
STAVANGER
KRISTIANSAND

COPENHAGEN
ÅLBORG
ÅRHUS
ODENSE
ESBJERG

TALLINN
TARTU
PSKOV
RIGA
JELGAVA
LIEPAJA
VENTSPILS
KLAIPĖDA
(MEMEL)
ŠIAULIAI
PANEVEŽYS
KAUNAS
(KOVNO)
VILNIUS
KALININGRAD
DAUGAVPILS
BIAŁYSTOK

GDAŃSK
GDYNIA
SZCZECIN

HAMBURG
LÜBECK
KIEL
ROSTOCK
BREMERHAVEN
WILHELMSHAVEN

GULF OF BOTHNIA

BALTIC SEA

NORTH SEA

KATTEGAT

SKAGERRAK

GULF OF FINLAND

GOTLAND

ÖLAND

BORNHOLM (Den.)

© HACHETTE-IGN

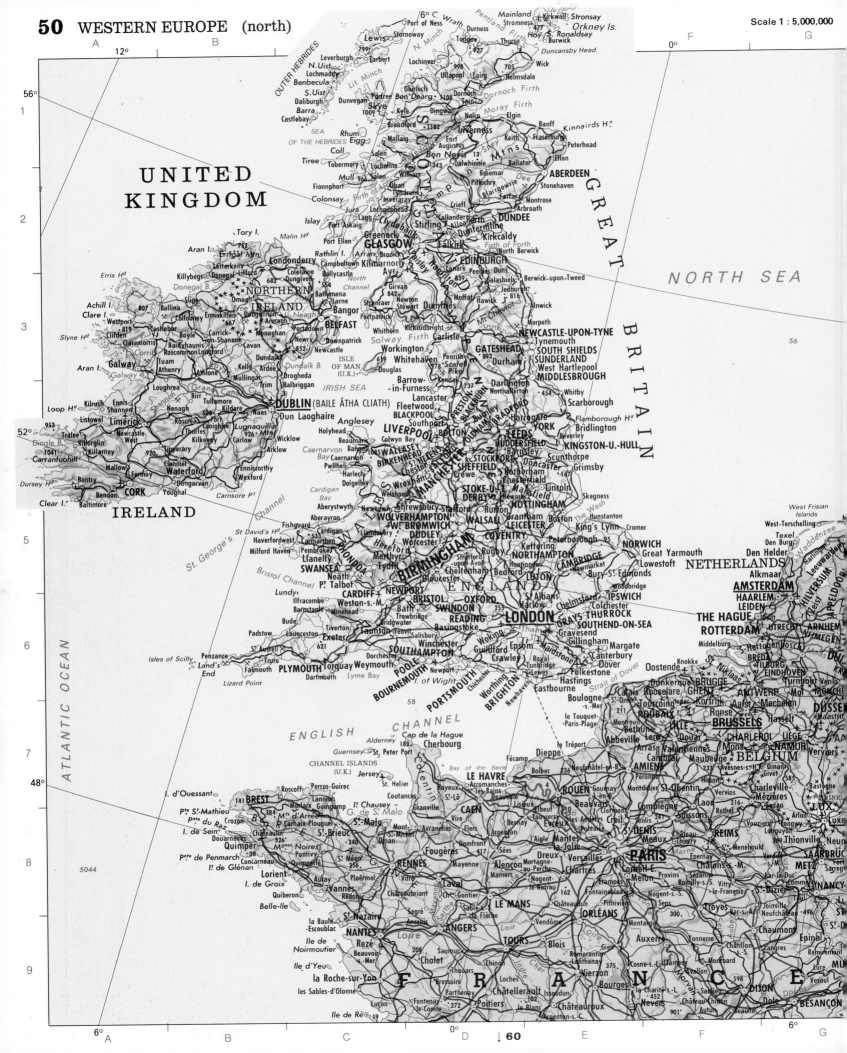

Scale 1 : 5,000,000

UNITED
KINGDOM

GREAT BRITAIN

NORTH SEA

IRELAND

NETHERLANDS

AMSTERDAM
HAARLEM
LEIDEN
THE HAGUE
ROTTERDAM

ATLANTIC OCEAN

ENGLAND

LONDON

ENGLISH CHANNEL

CHANNEL ISLANDS (U.K.)

BELGIUM
BRUSSELS

FRANCE

PARIS

50 100 Kilomètres
50 Statute Miles

↑ 49

NORWAY

SWEDEN

ESTONIA

LATVIA

LITHUANIA

DENMARK

SKAGERRAK

KATTEGAT

BALTIC SEA

Gulf of Riga

TALLINN

RIGA

STOCKHOLM

UPPSALA

VÄSTERÅS

ÖREBRO

LINKÖPING

NORRKÖPING

JÖNKÖPING

GÖTEBORG

VÄRMLAND

SKARABORG

SÖDERMANLAND

BLEKINGE

HELSINGBORG

COPENHAGEN

MALMÖ

ODENSE

ÅLBORG

ÅRHUS

KIEL

LÜBECK

HAMBURG

BREMEN

BREMERHAVEN

OLDENBURG

HANOVER

BRAUNSCHWEIG

MAGDEBURG

BERLIN

POTSDAM

ROSTOCK

STRALSUND

SCHLESWIG-HOLSTEIN

NIEDERSACHSEN

GERMAN DEMOCRATIC REPUBLIC

LEIPZIG

DRESDEN

KARL-MARX-STADT

ZWICKAU

GERA

ERFURT

HALLE

KASSEL

GÖTTINGEN

DORTMUND

MÜNSTER

BIELEFELD

OSNABRÜCK

REP. OF GERMANY

FRANKFURT-A.-M.

OFFENBACH

DARMSTADT

MANNHEIM

HEIDELBERG

KARLSRUHE

STUTTGART

WÜRTTEMBERG

WÜRZBURG

NÜRNBERG

REGENSBURG

BAVARIA

MUNICH

AUGSBURG

SWITZERLAND

AUSTRIA

VIENNA

SALZBURG

LINZ

PRAGUE

PLZEŇ

ČESKOSLOVAKIA

BRNO

BRATISLAVA

POLAND

WARSAW

POZNAN

ŁÓDŹ

WROCŁAW

KRAKÓW

KATOWICE

GDAŃSK

GDYNIA

SZCZECIN

BYDGOSZCZ

TORUŃ

BIAŁYSTOK

LUBLIN

RADOM

KIELCE

CZĘSTOCHOWA

OSTRAVA

U.S.S.R.

KALININGRAD

KLAIPĖDA (MEMEL)

KAUNAS (KOVNO)

ŠIAULIAI

LIEPAJA (Libau)

VENTSPILS (Windau)

JELGAVA (Mitau)

R.S.F.S.R.

HUNGARY

BUDAPEST

DEBRECEN

MISKOLC

NYIREGYHAZA

KOŠICE

BORNHOLM

ÖLAND

GOTLAND

RÜGEN

JYLLAND

© HACHETTE-IGN

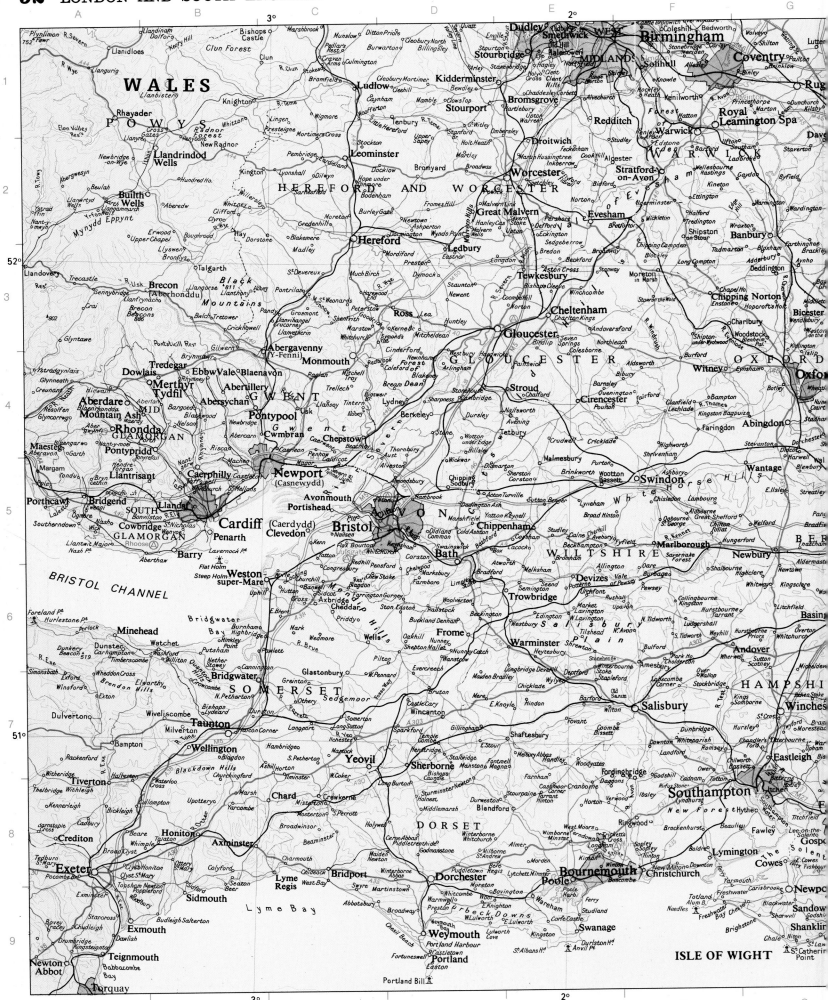

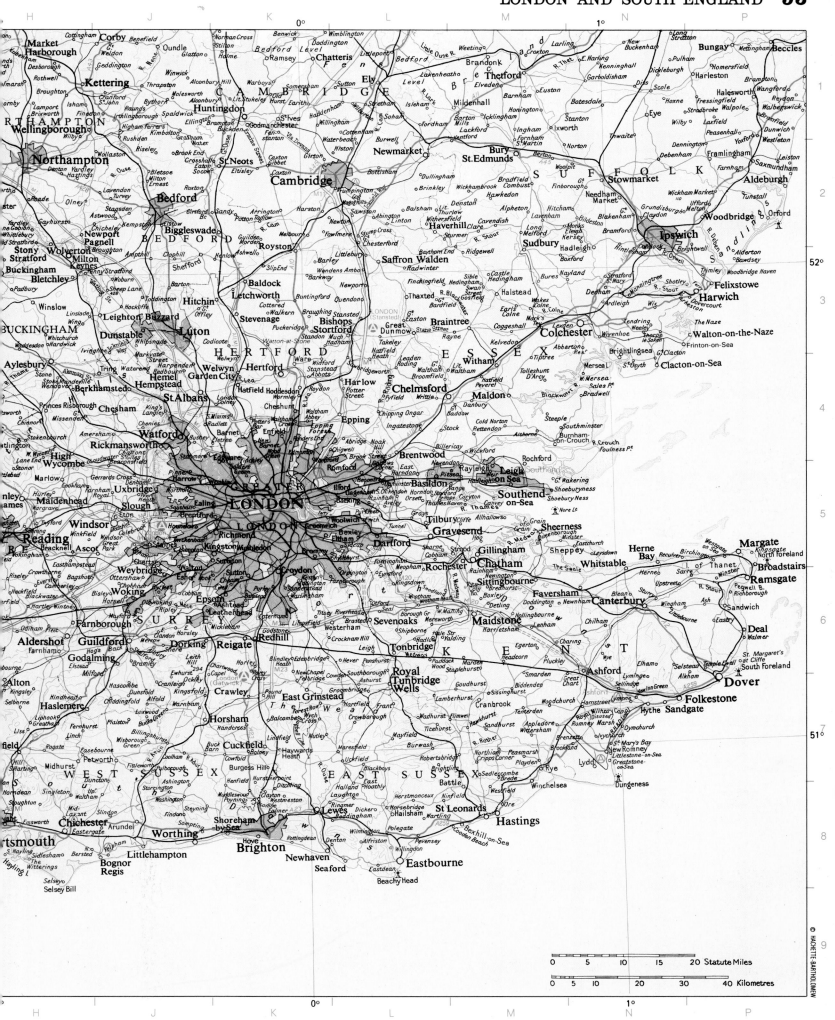

0 5 10 15 20 Statute Miles

0 5 10 20 30 40 Kilometres

© HACHETTE-BARTHOLOMEW

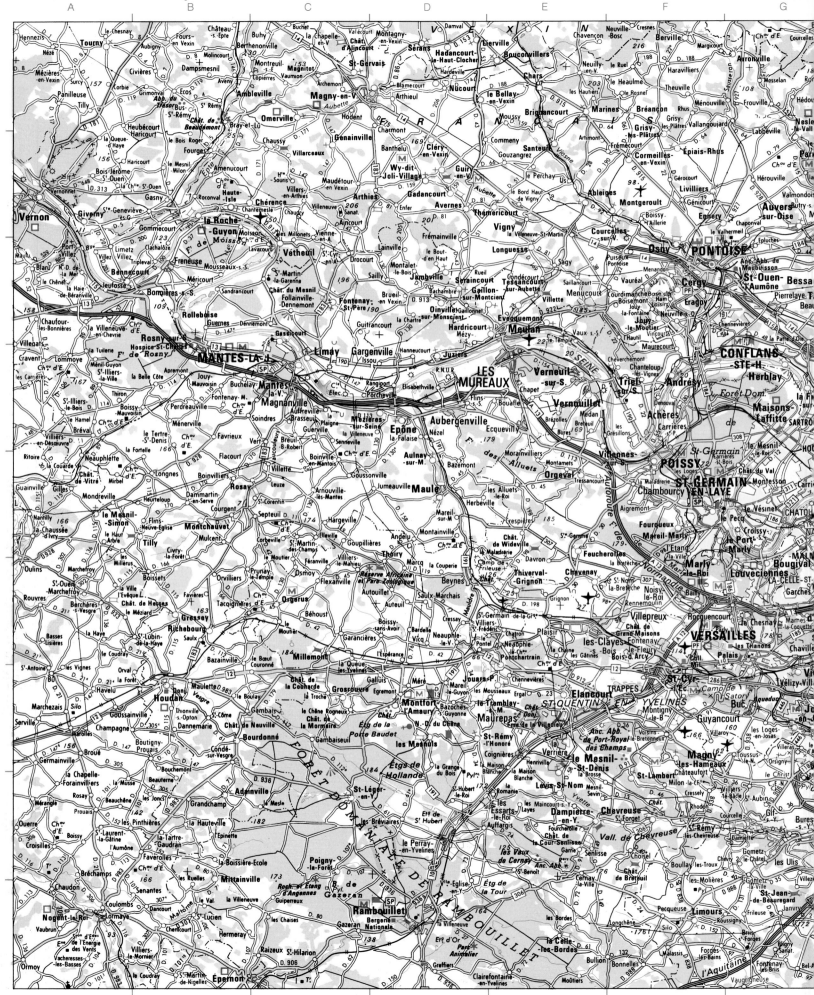

0 2,5 5 Kilomètres

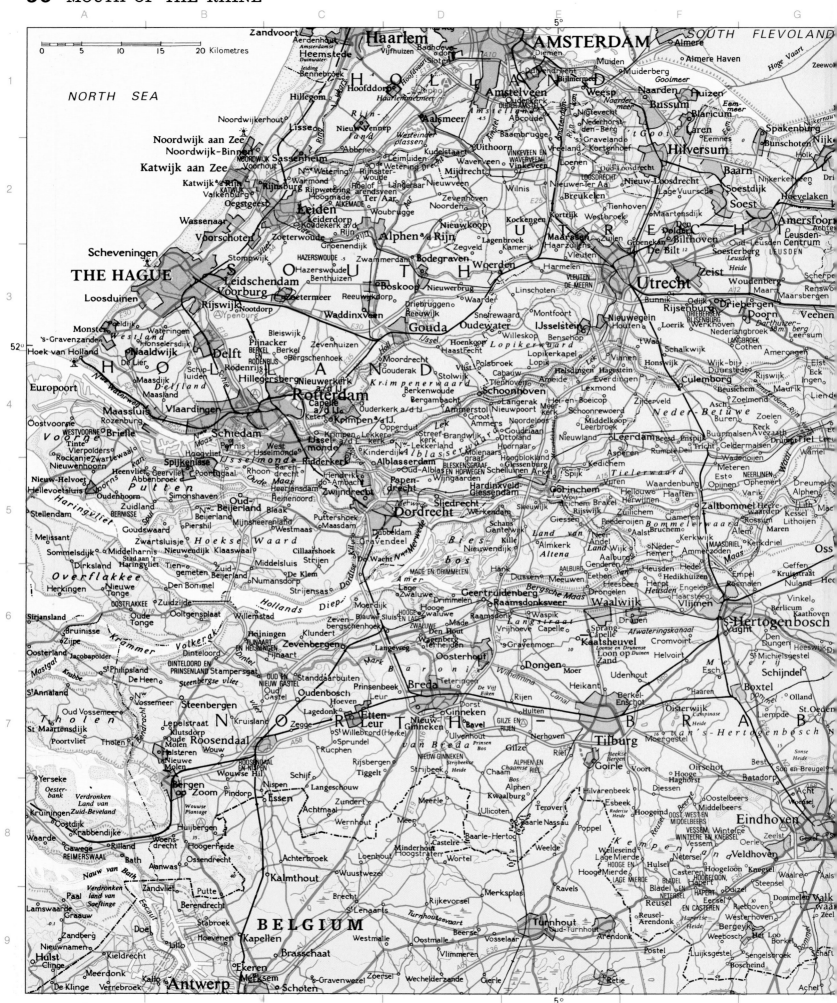

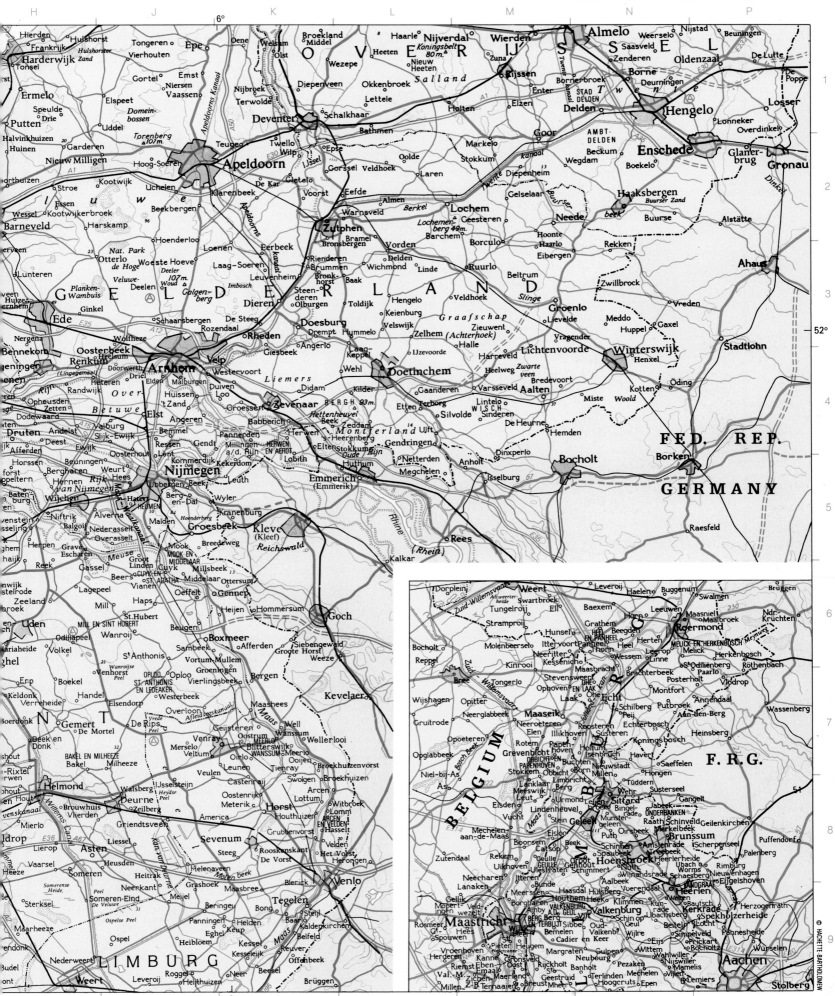

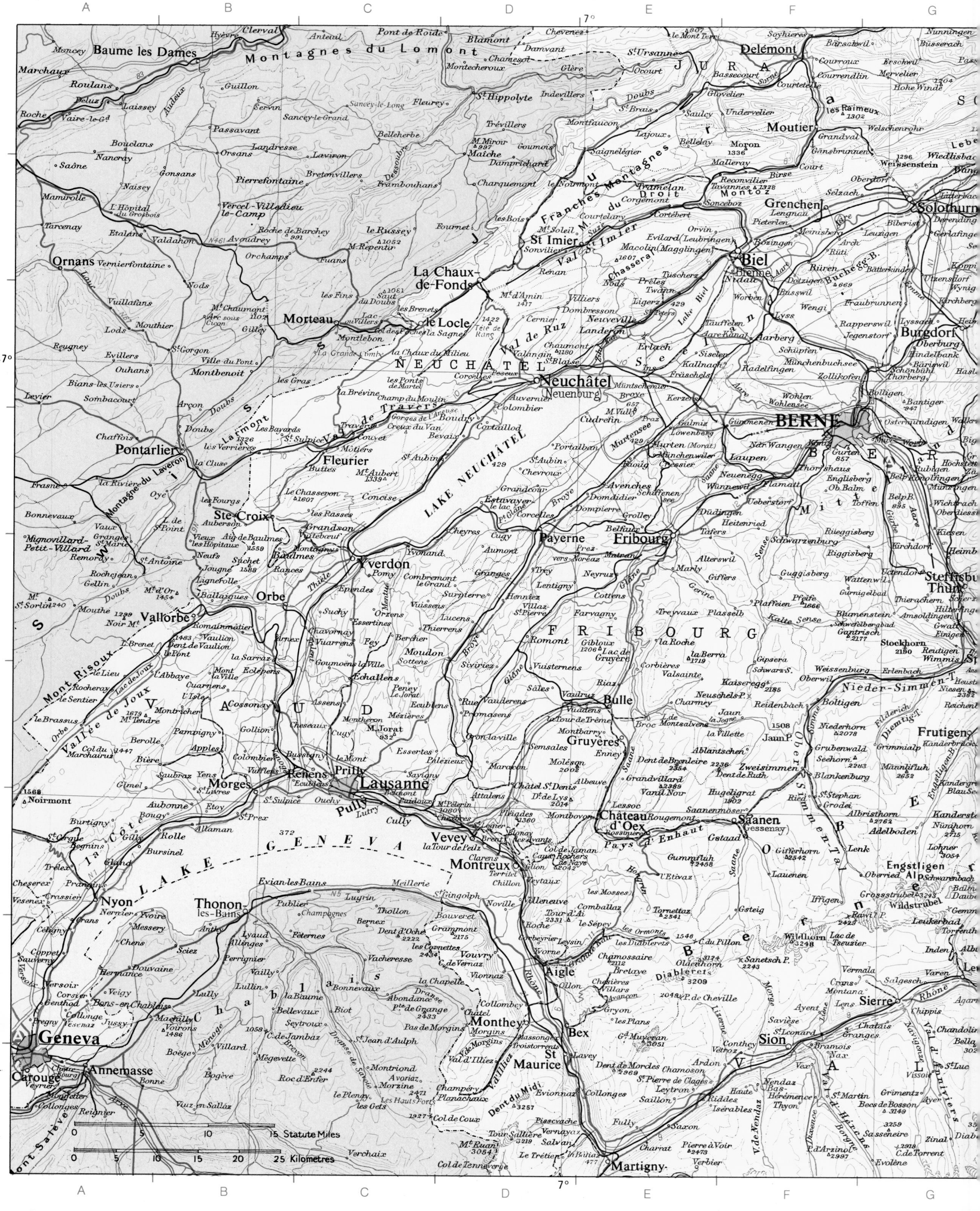

Montagnes du Lomont

JURA

Delémont
Moutier
Grenchen
Solothurn
Biel
Burgdorf

St Imier
La Chaux-de-Fonds
le Locle
NEUCHÂTEL
Neuchâtel (Neuenburg)
Val de Ruz
Val de Travers

BERNE

Baume les Dames
Ornans
Pontarlier
Morteau
Fleurier
Yverdon
Orbe
Ste Croix
Vallorbe

LAKE NEUCHÂTEL

Payerne
Fribourg
Avenches
Murten (Morat)
Laupen

FRIBOURG

Bulle
Gruyères
Château d'Oex
Saanen
Zweisimmen
Frutigen

Lausanne
Renens
Prilly
Pully
Morges
Cossonay
Moudon
Romont

Vevey
Montreux
la Tour de Peilz
Villeneuve
Aigle
Bex
St Maurice
Monthey

LAKE GENEVA

Nyon
Rolle
Thonon-les-Bains
Evian-les-Bains

Geneva
Carouge
Annemasse

Sion
Sierre
Martigny

Chablais

Pays d'Enhaut

Nieder-Simmen-tal

Thun
Steffisburg
Stockhorn
Wimmis

Statute Miles
0     5     10     15
Kilometres
0   5   10   15   20   25

7°     47°

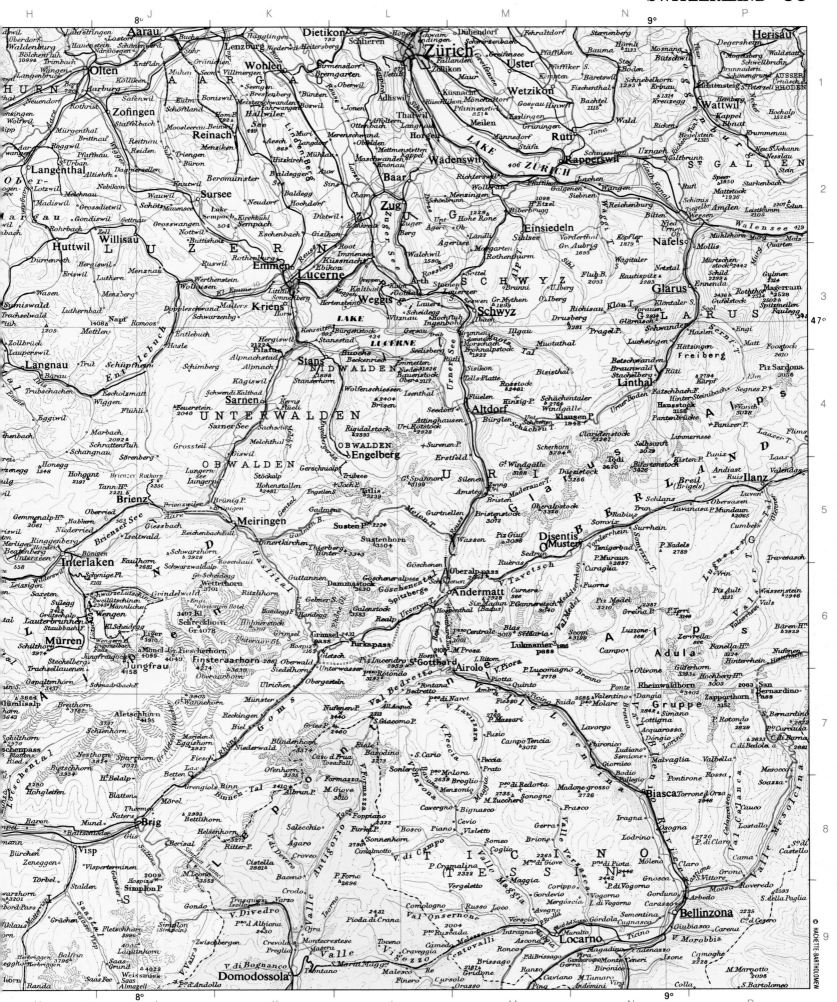

ATLANTIC OCEAN

Bay of Biscay

FRANCE

SPAIN

PORTUGAL

MOROCCO

ALGERIA

ATLANTIC OCEAN

BALEARIC ISLANDS

Strait of Gibraltar

**Major cities and places:**

LA CORUÑA · El Ferrol del Caudillo · GIJÓN · OVIEDO · SANTANDER · BILBAO · BARACALDO · SAN SEBASTIAN · BAYONNE · BIARRITZ · PAMPLONA · VITORIA · LOGROÑO · BURGOS · LEÓN · VALLADOLID · ZAMORA · SALAMANCA · SEGOVIA · ÁVILA · MADRID · ZARAGOZA · HUESCA · LERIDA · ANDORRA · TARRASA · SABADELL · BARCELONA · TARRAGONA · REUS · VALENCIA · CASTELLON DE LA PLANA · ALBACETE · ALICANTE · ELCHE · MURCIA · CARTAGENA · ALMERIA · GRANADA · MALAGA · CÓRDOBA · JAÉN · SEVILLE · HUELVA · CÁDIZ · JEREZ DE LA FRONTERA · ALGECIRAS · Gibraltar (U.K.) · TOLEDO · CUENCA · CIUDAD REAL · BADAJOZ · MÉRIDA · CÁCERES · EXTREMADURA

PORTO · Vila Nova de Gaia · Matosinhos · VIGO · PONTEVEDRA · Braga · COIMBRA · LISBON · Setúbal · Évora · Faro

TANGIER · TÉTOUAN · Ceuta (Spain) · Melilla (Spain) · Larache · KENITRA · RABAT · SALÉ · CASABLANCA · MEKNÈS · FÈS · OUJDA

ORAN · MOSTAGANEM · CHLEF (Orléansville) · BLIDA · MEDEA · ALGIERS · BOUFARIK · Tlemcen · Mascara

BORDEAUX · la Rochelle · Rochefort · Saintes · Cognac · Angoulême · Périgueux · Bergerac · Agen · Montauban · TOULOUSE · Tarbes · PYRENEES

Mountain ranges: CORDILLERA CANTABRICA · CORDILLERA CENTRAL · CORDILLERA IBERICA · CORDILLERA BETICA · SIERRA MORENA · SIERRA NEVADA · CORDILLERA CARPETO-VETONICA · Montes de Toledo · ANDALUCIA · CASTILLA LA NUEVA · NAVARRA · CATALONIA · ATLAS MTS

Elevation points: 3478 (Sª Nevada) · 3404 · 3335 · P. de Aneto · 2648 (P. de Europa) · 2744 · 2417 · 2188 · 2265 · 2469 (Sª de Guadarrama) · 2592 · 2294 (Sª de Gredos) · 1991 (Sª da Estrela)

Coordinate grid markings: 44° · 40° · 36° · 6° · 50 · 78

50 100 Kilomètres
50 Statute Miles

↑ 51

6° 12°

**MUNICH**

**VIENNA**

**SALZBURG**

**INNSBRUCK**

48°

DIJON BESANÇON BASEL SCHAFFHAUSEN

ZÜRICH

BERN LAUSANNE

SWITZERLAND LIECHTENSTEIN AUSTRIA

GENEVA

LYON GRENOBLE TURIN MILAN BERGAMO BRESCIA VICENZA VERONA PADUA VENICE TRIESTE RIJEKA (Fiume)

ZAGREB

NOVARA PAVIA Cremona Mantova Rovigo Chioggia

ALESSANDRIA PIACENZA PARMA REGGIO N. MODENA FERRARA

GENOA BOLOGNA RAVENNA

SLOVENIA

CROATIA

YUGOSLAVIA

MARSEILLE TOULON NICE MONACO S. Remo Imperia

LA SPEZIA Massa-Carrara Viareggio LUCCA PISTOIA PRATO FLORENCE S. MARINO RIMINI

LIVORNO PISA Siena AREZZO Perugia ANCONA

44°

MAR LIGURE (LIGURIAN SEA)

C. Corse Capraia

Bastia I. d'Elba

CORSICA

Ajaccio

Grosseto Orbetello

TERNI Teramo PESCARA Chieti

ABRUZZI

VITERBO Rieti L'Aquila

Civitavecchia VATICAN CITY ROME Tivoli Avezzano Sulmona Vasto

SARDINIA

SASSARI NUORO

ORISTANO

CAGLIARI

Lido di Ostia Ostia Latina Frosinone

Terracina Gaeta Formia CASERTA BENEVENTO Avellino

NAPLES Pozzuoli Pompei

SALERNO

MEDITERRANEAN SEA

MAR TIRRENO (TYRRHENIAN SEA)

FOGGIA Manfredonia

BARI

POTENZA MATERA

BASILICATA TARENTO

G. di Taranto

40°

COSENZA

CATANZARO

Isole Lipari o Eolie Stromboli

SICILY

PALERMO MESSINA REGGIO DI CALABRIA

Trapani Marsala CALTANISSETTA CATANIA

Agrigento Gela SYRACUSE

TUNIS

BEJAIA SKIKDA ANNABA

CONSTANTINE

TUNISIA SOUSSE

BATNA

MALTA

36°

6° 12°

↓ 79

0 50 100 Kilomètres
0 50 Statute Miles

↑ 67 →

**U.S.S.R.**

BLACK SEA
(CORNOJE MORE)   (KARA DENIZ)

CRIMEA

Nov. Zburjevka
Skadovsk
M. Tarchankut
Černomorskoje
Yevpatoriya
Saki
SIMFEROPOL'
Bachčisaraj
SEVASTOPOL'
M. Chersonesskij
Foros
Alupka
Yalta
G. Raman-Koš
M. Meganom
Sudak
Alušta
St. Krym
Feodosiya
Dzhankoy
Krasnoperekopsk
Razdol'noje
Belogorsk
Krasnogvardejskoje
Nižnegorskij
Gvardejskoje

M. Kazantip
KERCH
Temr'uk
Taman
Anapa
Krymsk
Gelendžik
NOVOROSSIYSK
Tuapse

Slav'ansk-na-Kubani
Krasnoarmejskaja
Păskovskij
Belorečensk
KRASNODAR
Afipskij
Jablonovskij
APŠERONSK
MAYKOP
Labinsk
Otradnaja
Mostovskoj

Kurganinsk
Mineral'nyje Vody
Zelenovodsk
Georgievsk
Mozdok
Prochladnyj
Cherkessk
Pyatigorsk
Kislovodsk
Jessentoki
Baksan
Majskij
NAL'ČIK
EL'BRUS

CAUCASUS

GEORGIA
SOCHI
Gagra
Sukhumi
Gudauta
Nkvarcheli
Poti
Kobuleti
BATUMI
Hopa
Artvin

KUTAISI
Zugdidi
Chiatura
Zestafoni

ARMENIA

TRABZON
Rize
Çayeli
Ardeşen
Findikli
Akçaabat
Sürmene
Of

Kars
Sarikamiş
ERZURUM
Pasinler
Horasan
Aşkale
Erzincan
Kemah
Tunceli
Bingöl
Muş
Varto
Hinis
Bulanik
Malazgirt

İnebolu
Cide
İnce Bur.
Sinop
Ayancik
Gerze
Bafra Bur.
Bafra
SAMSUN
Çarşamba
Ünye
Fatsa
Ordu
Giresun
Tirebolu
Gümüşhane
Bayburt

Kurucaşile
Bartin
Kastamonu
Taşköprü
Boyabat
Vezirköprü
Havza
Merzifon
Amasya
Erbaa
Niksar
Koyulhisar
Suşehri
Zara
Divriği

ZONGULDAK
Kozlu
Ereğli
Karabük
Safranbolu
Tosya
Osmancik
İskilip
Çorum
Zile
Turhal
Tokat
SİVAS
Hafik
Kangal
Gürün
Darende

Karasu
Akçakoca
Düzce
Bolu
Gerede
Çerkeş
Çankiri
Yapraklı
Kalecik
Alaca
Sungurlu
Boğazköy
Yozgat
Sorgun
Akdağmadeni
Şarkışla
MALATYA
ELAZIG
Keban
Baskil

ADAPAZARI
Sapanca
Göynük
Beypazari
Güdül
Elmadağ
ANKARA
KIRIKKALE
Keskin
Bala
Yerköy
Boğazliyan
Sarioğlan
Akçadağ
Hekimhan

ESKİŞEHİR
Sivrihisar
Polatli
Haymana
Kirşehir
Kaman
Mucur
Hacibektaş
Bünyan
Pinarbaşi
Gürün
DIYARBAKIR
Çermik
Siverek
URFA

TAURUS MTS.

KONYA
Karapinar
Ereğli
Ulukişla
Niğde
Bor
Aladağlar
Feke
Kozan
Kadirli
Osmaniye
GAZIANTEP
Nizip
Birecik
Suruç
Akçakale

KAYSERI
Develi
Yahyali
K. MARAS
Pazarcik
Besni
Adiyaman
Mardin
Nusaybin

ANTALYA
Side
Manavgat
Alanya
Gazipaşa
Anamur
Silifke
MERSIN
TARSUS
ADANA
Ceyhan
Dörtyol
İskenderun
Kilis
ALEPPO
Al Bab

CYPRUS
NICOSIA
Kyrenia
Famagusta
Larnaca
DHEKELIA (U.K.)
Tróodos Oros
Páfos
AKROTIRI (U.K.)
Limassol

LATAKIA
HAMAH
HOMS
TRIPOLI (TRABLOS)
Baalbeck
BEIRUT
LEBANON
DAMASCUS
DŪMĀ

EUPHRATES
Dayr az Zawr
Al Mayādīn
Ar Raqqah
Al Qāmishli
Al Ḩasakah

IRAQ

→ 72

30°   36°   42°

↓ 82

© HACHETTE-IGN

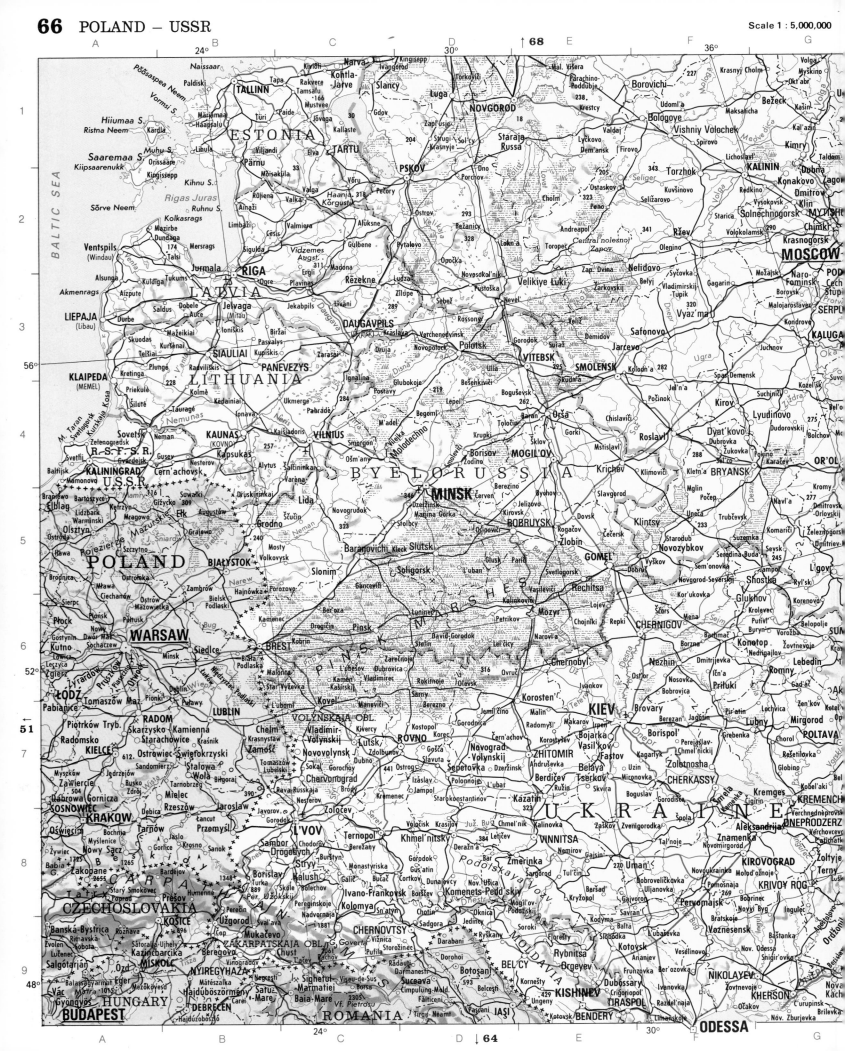

100 Kilomètres
50 Statute Miles

42°   ↑69   48°   M   P   54°

Nerekhta
ROSLAV  Furmanov  Vičuga  Putč  Katúnki  Gorodec  CUVASH  Urmary  Kamskoje-Ustje  Šenta  Abdulino
um  IVANOVO  Šuja  Zavolžje  Pravdinsk  Bor  Kstovo  Vorotynec  Jadrin  Civil'sk  Kujbyšev  Nurlat  Pohvistnevo  Bugurslan
Teykovo  Kochma  DZERZHINSK  Lyskovo  Shumerlya  Kanash  Novočeremšansk  Sernovodsk  .317  Ponomar'ovka
rostov  Kochma  Volodarsk  GORKY  Pil'na  Sergač  Batyrevo  Buinsk  A.S.S.R.  Čerdakly  Timaševo  Borskij  Kinel' Čerkasy  Gračovka
Nerl'  KOVROV  V'azniki  Bogorodsk  Gorochovec  Pjana  Alatyr'  Kir'a  Dimitrovgrad  .305  Aleksandrovka
ROSTOKROSTAL  VLADIMIR  Vorsma  Perevoz  Ardatov  Kem'l'a  UL'YANOVSK  Jelchovka  Otradnyy  Kinel'  Sorochinsk
Kameškovo  Navašina  Pavlovo  Sura  Sengilej  Majna  KUIBYSHEV  .273  Samara
OREKHOVO-ZUYEVO  Murom  T'oša  Kulebaki  Arzamas  Lukojanov  Surskoje  .334  TOGLIATTI  Zigutevsk  NOVOKUYBYSHEVSK  Aleksejevka  .297
Gus'Khrustal nyy  Satki  .235  Saransk  .375  Teren'ga  Okt'abr'sk  Chapayevsk  Osinki  Tašla  Burli
Rosal'  Melenki  Vyksa  Ardatov  Pervomajsk  Kem'l'a  Vešķajma  Kuzovatovo  Bezenčuk  Morša  Sobolev
Satura  Temnikov  SARANSK  Inza  SYZRAN'  .187
KOLOMNA  Kasimov  Jermiš  Krasnoslobodsk  MORDVINIAN  Ružaevka  Nikol'sk  Radiščevo  Pugachev  URALSK
Oz'ory  Spas-Klepiki  Kadom  Kovylkino  .289  Lulinsk  Insar  Gorodišče  Kuznetsk  .351  Vol'sk  Gornyj  .259  Algabas
Zarajsk  Rybnoje  Sasovo  Zubova Pol'ana  Mokšan  PENZA  Sursk  .332  Chvalynsk  Balakovo  Dergači  Oz. Šalkar
RYAZAN  Spassk-R'azanskij  Šilovo  Para  Mekša  Uza  .370  Sennoj  Ozinki  Kamenka  Budarino
Kašira  Michajlov  NOVOMOSKOVSK  Pačelma  Niž. Lomov  Kamenka  Svobodnyj  Jeršov  .228  Čiža 2-ja
Skopin  Korablino  Sarai  Zemetčino  .292  Bašmakovo  Belinskij  Petrovsk  Marx  KRASNYJ KUT
TULA  Ryazhsk  Morshansk  Kolyšlej  Serdobsk  SARATOV  ENGELS  Novouzensk
Miloslavskoje  Tamala  Jekaterinovka  Puškino  P'atimar
RUSSIA  Kirsanov  .330  Privolžskij  Krasnoarmejsk  Furmanovo
Caplygin  Kočetovka  TAMBOV  Rasskazovo  Rtishchevo  Atkarsk  Krasnyj Kut  Aleksandrov Gaj  Kaztalovka
Dankov  Michurinsk  Kotovsk  Turki  Arkadak  Lysyje Gory  Kamenskij  .63  Mal. Uzen
Lebed'an'  .219  Inžavino  Kalininsk  Novouzensk
Yeffremov  LIPETSK  Gryazi  Uvarovo  Romanovka  .259  Zirnovsk  Rudn'a  Pallasovka
Yelets  Syrskij  .234  Usman  Žerdevka  Gribanovskij  Jelan'  .358  Oz. Aralsor
Verchovje  Ertil'  Balashov  Buzuluk
Livny  Ramon  Voronežskij Zapov.  Anna  Novochop'orsk  Borisoglebsk  Povorino  Klotovo  Petrov Val  Nov. Kazanka
VORONEZH  Krasnolesnyj  Novonikolajevskij  Kamyshin  El'ton
Semiluki  Davydovka  Bobrov  Talovaja  .239  Uryupinsk  Novoanninskij  Nikolajevskij  Oz. El'ton  Urda
Staryy Oskol  Georghiu-Dej  Buturlinovka  Mikhaylovka  Bykovo  Sajchin
Gubkin  .276  Ostrogozhsk  Kalač  Frolovo  Primorsk
Koroča  Aleksejevka  Pavlovsk  Serafimovič  Ilovl'a  Dubovka  VOLZHSKIY  Kapustin Jar  Oz. Baskunčak  Košalak
Novyj Oskol  Rossosh  Bogučar  Vešenskaja  Kletskaja  .250  Lenjinsk  Akhtubinsk  .21  Verch. Baskunčak
BELGOROD  Volokonovka  Valujki  VOLGOGRAD  Sr. Achtuba  Čornyj Jar  DEPRESSION
Šebekino  Volčansk  Kalač-na-Donu  Krasnoslobodsk
KHARKOV  Kup'ansk  Čertkovo  Sovetskaja  Surovikino  Svetlyj Jar  Sasykoli  Charabali
Čuguev  Kup'ansk  Belovodsk  Millerovo  .164  Nikol'skoje
Mereta  Svatovo  Starobel'sk  Černyškovskij  Okt'abr'skij  Caca  CASPIAN
Zmijev  Balakleya  Krasnyj Liman  Rubežnoje  Kamensk-Shakhtinskiy  Belaja Kalitva  Sadovoje  Kr. Jar
Andrejevka  Iz'um  LISICHANSK  Morozovsk  Kaliva  Kotel'nikovo  Sarpa  ASTRAKHAN
Lozovaya  SLAVYANSK  KADIEVKA  KOMMUNARSK  VOROSHILOVGRAD  Glubokij  KALMYTSKAYA  Kr. Barrikady
Jurjevka  KRAMATORSK  KONSTANTINOVKA  Debal cevo  KRASNYJ LUČ  Kr. Sulin  Konstantinovskij  Volgodonsk  Zimovniki  Utta  Kirovskij
Sachnovščina  Dobropolje  GORLOVKA  Jenakijevo  SHAKHTY  A.S.S.R.  Trudfront
JEPROPETROVSK  Krasnoarmejsk  MAKEYEVKA  Sverdlovsk  .170  Orlovskij  Elista  Jaškul'  Kaspijskij
Pavlograd  Selidovo  DONECK  Chartcyk  Anträci  Matvejev-Kurgan  .221  Grada  Prijutnoje
ZAPOROZH'YE  Vasil'kovka  Jasinovataja  NOVOCHERKASSK  Proletarskaja  Komsomol'skij
rganeč  Orechov  Gul'aipole  TAGANROG  ROSTOV-NA-DONU  Zernograd  .115  Mary. Gudilo  Divnoje  Južno-Suchokumsk
POL'  Tokmak  Novoazovsk  Batajsk  AZOV  Gigant  Sal'sk  .192  Arzgir
MELITOPOL'  Pologi  Rózovka  Priazovskaja  .324  ZHDANOV  Kuščevskaja  Belaja Glina  Ipatovo  Prikumsk  Ačikulak  KIZL'AR
Moločansk  Černigov  BERD'ANSK  Yeysk  Leningradskaja  Novopokrovskaja  Krasnogvardejskoje  Zelenokumsk  Terekli-Mektet
kseje ka  Primorsko-Akhtarsk  Dolžanskaja  Pavlovskaja  STAVROPOLSKAYA  Svetlograd  Neftekumsk
O. Bir'učij  Obitočnaja Kosa  Tikhoretsk  Novoaleksandrovskaja  Izobil'nyj  Blagodarnoje  Spakovskoje
AZOVSKOJE MORE  Kanevskaja  Kropotkin  Gul'keviči  STAVROPOL'  .831  Aleksandrovskoje  Chasavjurt
SEA OF AZOV  Bručoveckaja  Vyselki  Novokubansk  ARMAVIR  KRAJ  Georgijevsk
Geničesk  Timaševsk  Tbilisskaja  Usť-Labinsk  STAVROPOL'  Nevinnomyssk  Mineral'nyje Vody
KRASNODAR  Laba  Kurganinsk

36°  ↓65  42°  44°

Scale 1 : 5,000,000

36° 42° 48° 54°

*BARENCEVO MORE*
*(BARENTS SEA)*

O. Kolguyev
166
Bugrino
Pomorskii Proliv
Tobseda
Koregavka

NORWAY
Båtsfjord
Vardø
637
Vadsø
Kirkenes
Pečenga
Zapolyarnyj
Nikel
631

Tsyp Navolok
P-ov Rybačij
O. Kil'din
Teriberka
Rynda
Vostočnaja Lica

M. Lajdennyj
M. Sv'atoj Nos
Indiga
Ledkovo
Novyj Bor
Narjan-Mar
Oksino
Velikovisočnoje
Ust'-Cil'ma

Kanin Nos
242
Poluostrov Kanin
M. Mikulkin
Šojna
Čeśskaja Guba
303
Trusovo

MURMANSK
Severomorsk
Pol'arnyj
Kola
Murmaši
636
Varzino
Jenozero
Gremicha
Lumbovka
M. Sv'atoj Nos
Čiža
Oma
Nes'
Niž. Mgla

Sokosti 718
Monchegorsk
1114
Chibiny 1191
Kirovsk 151
Apatity
Olenogorsk
397
Ponoj
O. Moržovec
M. Voronov
Kojda
Dolgoščelje
Mezen
142
Koz'mogorodskoje
Kojnas

KOLSKIY P-ov
Kandalaksha 635
Afrikanda
Nivskij 785
Kovdor
Kuttusvaara

Terskij Bereg
Kanevka
Sosnovka
256
Oz. Sergozero
Kuzomen
Tetrino

Belomorsko-
Kuloiskoje Plato
210
208
Ruči
Kuškušara

ARCHANGEL'SKAJA

FINLAND
OULU

BELOJE MORE
(WHITE SEA)

Dvinskaja Guba
O. Mugjugskij
ARKHANGEL'SK
SEVERODVINSK
Pervomajskij
Cholmogory

Letnij Navolok
Letn'aja Zolotica
Lopšen'ga
Onežskij P-ov
Nenoksa

Belomorsk
Sorovec
L'amca
Purnema
K'anda
Cholmogorskaja
Kodino
Samoded
Oboz'orskij
Jemeck
Bereznik

Onega
Mudjuga
Maloš'ika

PETROZAVODSK
Kondopoga
Medvež'egorsk

Plesetsk
Nyandoma
Konosha
VOLOGDA
CHEREPOVETS

HELSINKI
LENINGRAD
Kronštadt
Vyborg
Priozersk
Sortavala

LADŻSKOJE OZERO
(L. LADOGA)
ONEŽSKOJE OZERO
(L. ONEGA)

SUOMEN LAHTI
(Gulf of Finland)

RYBINSK
KOSTROMA

30° 36° 42°
↓ 66

Scale 1 : 5,000,000

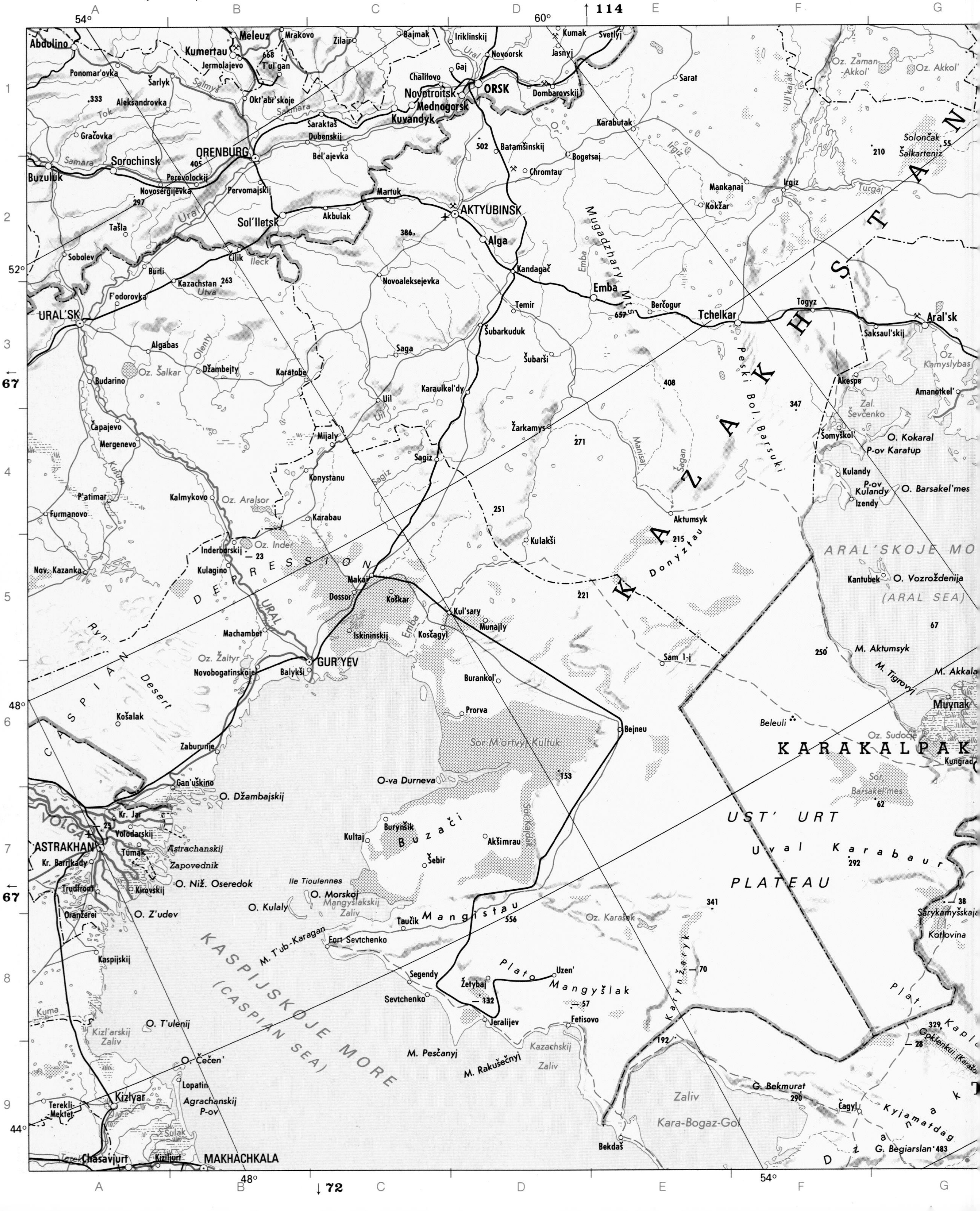

↑ **114**

54° A | B | C | D 60° | E | F | G

**1**

Abdulino
Ponomar'ovka
Kumertau
668
Meleuz
Mrakovo
Zilair
T'ul'gan
Jermolajevo
Bajmak
Iriklinskij
Novoorsk
Svetlyj
Kumak
Jasnyj
Gaj
Chalilovo
Ural
Novotroitsk
ORSK
Dombarovskij
Sarat
Šarlyk
Okt'abr'skoje
Sakmara
Mednogorsk
Kuvandyk
Karabutak
.333
Gračovka
Aleksandrovka
Tok
Salmyš
502
Batamšinskij
Bogetsaj
Oz. Zaman-Akkol'
Oz. Akkol'
Solončak
55
Šalkarteniz
210

**2**

Buzuluk
Sorochinsk
Samara
QRENBURG
405
Perevolockij
Bel'ajevka
Chromtau
Ural
Novosergijevka
297
Pervomajskij
Martuk
AKTYUBINSK
Mankanaj
Kokžar
Irgiz
Tašla
Sol'Iletsk
Akbulak
Alga
Irgiz
Sobolev
Burli
Cilik
Ileck
386.
Kandagač
Emba
Berčogur
Tchelkar
Togyz
Aral'sk
F'odorovka
Kazachstan 263
Utva
Novoaleksejevka
Temir
657
Emba
Saksaul'skij

**3**

52°
URAL'SK
Algabas
Olenty
Džambejty
Karatobe
Saga
Subarkuduk
Šubarši
408
347
Akespe
Oz. Kamyslybas
O. Kokaral
P-ov Karatup
Amanotkel'
Budarino
Oz. Salkar
Uil
Karaulkel'dy
271
215
Somyškol
Zal. Ševčenko
Čapajevo
Uil
Žarkamys
Kulandy
P-ov Kulandy
O. Barsakel'mes
Izendy

**4**

67
P'atimar
Mergenevo
Kalmykovo
Oz. Aralsor
Mijaly
Sagiz
Konystanu
251
Aktumsyk
ARAL'SKOJE MO
Furmanovo
Karabau
Kulakši
Donyztau
Nov. Kazanka
Inderborskij
23
DEPRESSION
Makat
221
Kantubek
O. Vozroždenija
(ARAL SEA)
Kulagino
Dossor
Koškar
Kul'sary
Sam 1-j
250
M. Aktumsyk
M. Tigrovyj
M. Akkala

**5**

URAL
Machambet
Iskininskij
Emba
Kosčagyl
Munajly
67
Muynak
Oz. Žaltyr
Novobogatinskoje
Balykši
GUR'YEV
Burankol'
250
Beleuli
Oz. Sudočje
KARAKALPAK

**6**

48°
Košalak
Zaburunje
Prorva
Bejneu
Sor M'ortvyj Kultuk
KARAKALPAK
Kungrad
UST' URT
Uval Karabaur
PLATEAU

**7**

Gan'uškino
O. Džambajskij
O-va Durneva
153
Sor
Barsakel'mes
62
ASTRAKHAN
Kr. Jar
25
Volodarskij
Astrachanskij
Kultaj
Burynšik
Buzači
Akšimrau
Sor Kajdak
292
Kr. Barrikady
Tumak
Zapovednik
Šebir
341
VOLGA
Kirovskij
O. Niž. Oseredok
Ile Tioulennes
O. Morskoj
Taučik
556
38
Sarykamyšskaja

**8**

67
Trudfront
Mangyšlakskij Zaliv
Segendy
Plato Mangyšlak
Uzen'
70
Kotlovina
Oranzerei
O. Z'udev
O. Kulaly
Taučik
Žetybaj
57
Kaspijskij
M. T'ub-Karagan
Fort Sevtchenko
132
Fetisovo
Kavynžaryk
KASPIJSKOJE MORE
(CASPIAN SEA)
Sevtchenko
Jeralijev
329
Kaplen
28

**9**

44°
Kizl'arskij Zaliv
O. T'ulenij
Lopatin
Kyma
O. Čečen'
Agrachanskij P-ov
M. Pesčanyj
M. Rakušečnyj
Kazachskij Zaliv
192
G. Bekmurat
290
Čagyl
Kyjamatdag
Terekli-Mektet
Kizlyar
Zaliv Kara-Bogaz-Gol
Bekdaš
G. Begiarslan 483
Chasavjurt
Kizljurt
MAKHACHKALA
Sulak
Terek

A | B 48° | ↓ **72** C | D | E 54° | F | G

CASPIAN Desert

Ryn

K A Z A K H S T A N

Peski Bol. Barsuki

Mugadzhary Mts.

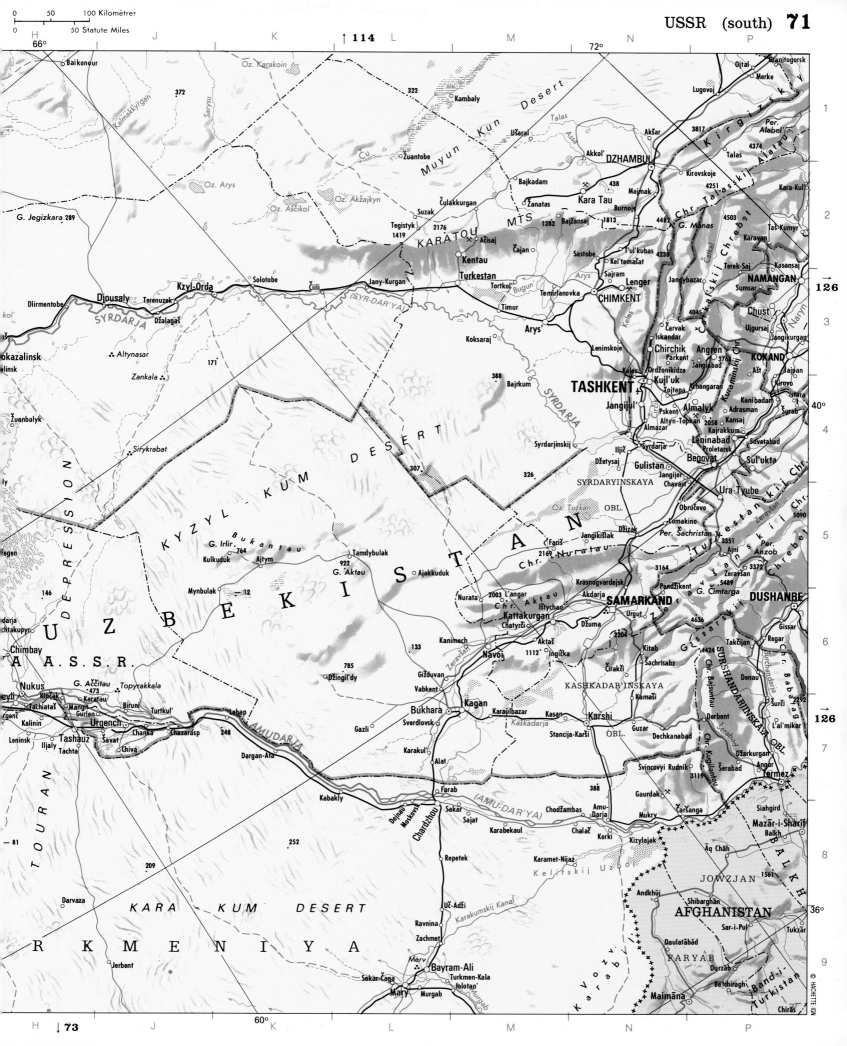

0  50  100 Kilomètres
0  50 Statute Miles

66° H

↑ **114**

72°

J  K  L  M  N  P

Baïkonour

*Oz. Karakoin*

372

*Sarysu*

322

Kambaly

MUYUN KUN Desert

*Talas*

Ušaral

Akšar

Lugovoj

Ojtal

Granitogorsk

Merke

Per. Alabel'

3817

KIRGIZSKIJ

*Cu*

Žuantobe

Bajkadam

Zanatas

Akkol'

**DZHAMBUL**

Majmak

Kirovskoje

Talas

4374

4251

Kara-Kul

*Oz. Arys*

*Oz. Ašikol'*

*Oz. Akžajkyn*

Suzak

Čulakkurgan

Kara Tau

438

Burnoje

**G. Manas**

4503

Taš-Kumyr

G. Jegizkara 289

KARATOU

2176

Ačisaj

1282

Bajžansaj

1813

Sastobe

4482

Kel'temašat

4238

T'ul'kubas

Karavan

Kasansaj

Tegistyk

1419

Kentau

Turkestan

Tortkol'

Sajram

Jangybazar

Terek-Saj

**NAMANGAN**

Solotobe

Kzyl-Orda

Čiili

Jany-Kurgan

(SYR-DAR'JA)

*Arys'*

Temirlanovka

Lenger

Sumsar

Ujgursaj

Chust

Djousaly

Terenuzek

Džalagaš

SYRDARJA

Timur

**CHIMKENT**

Čarvak

4045

Jangikurgan

Dlirmentobe

kol'

Arys'

Leninskoje

Iskandar

Angren

3768

Ašt

**KOKAND**

kazalinsk

171

Koksaraj

Chirchik

Parkent

Jangiabad

Kirovo

Altynasar

Zankala

388

Bajrkum

SYRDARJA

**TASHKENT**

Keles

Ordžonikidze

Kuil'uk

Tojtepa

Achangaran

Istara

Kani badam

Surab

Žuanbalyk

Sirykrabat

KYZYL - KUM DESERT

307

326

Syrdarjinskij

Jangijul'

Pskent

**Almalyk**

Altyn-Topkan

2058

Adrasman

Kansaj

40°

DEPRESSION

Syrdarja

Almazar

Kajrakkum

darja

chtakupyr

Iljič

Leninabad

Sovetabad

U Z B E K I S T A N

Džetysaj

Gulistan

Syrdarja

Proletarsk

Benovat

Sul'ukta

G. Irlir

764

Bukantau

Tamdybulak

Krasnogvardejsk

SYRDARYINSKAYA

Jangijier

Chavast

Ura-Tyube

5090

Kulkuduk

Ajtym

922

G. Aktau

Ajakkuduk

OBL.

Obručevo

Lomakino

Per. Sachristan

3351

Per. Anzob

Mynbulak

12

146

Nurata

2003

L'angar

Ištyčan

Džizak

Fariš

2169

Chr. Nuratau

3164

Pendžikent

Ajni

Zeravšan

3372

5489

G. Čimtarga

**DUSHANBE**

Chr. Aktau

Akdarja

**SAMARKAND**

Krasnogvardejsk

Kattakurgan

Džuma

Urgut

4636

Gissar

133

Kanimech

Čatyrči

Aktaš

Ingička

2204

Kitab

Sachrisabz

4424

Regar

292

785

Džingil'dy

Zeravšan

Navoi

1112

Čirakči

Denau

Surči

Chimbay

G. Ačcitau

473

Topyrakkala

Gizduvan

KASHKADAR'INSKAYA

Kamaši

SURSHANDARIINSKAYA OBL.

Nukus

Karafau

Biruni

Vabkent

Derbent

Džarkurgan

Šerabad

eylli

Kinčak

Gurlen

Turtkul'

Lebap

Bukhara

Kagan

Karaúlbazar

Kasan

Karshi

Guzar

L'al'mikar

tachiatas

Mangit

Gazli

Sverdlovsk

OBL.

3119

Angor

**Termez**

Urgench

Chanka

Chazarasp

248

AMUDARJA

Karakul'

Alat

Stancija-Karši

Dechkanabad

Svincovyj Rudnik

Čaršanga

Kalinin

Šavat

Chiva

Kaškadarja

**Mazār-i-Sharīf**

Leninsk

Tashauz

Iljaly

Tachta

Dargan-Ata

Karabekaul

388

Gaurdak

Mukry

Siahgird

Balkh

Kabakly

Farab

Chodžambas

Amu-Darja

Chalač

Kerki

Kizylajak

Āq Čāh

81

TOURAN

Dejnau

Moskovskij

Sakar

Sajat

Čardzhou

(AMU-DAR'JA)

BALKH

209

252

Repetek

Karamet-Nijaz

JOWZJAN

1561

KARA - KUM DESERT

Uč-Adži

Karakumskij Kanal

Andkhŭi

Shibarghān

**AFGHANISTAN**

36°

Darvaza

Ravnina

Zachmet

Daulatābād

Sar-i-Pul

Tukzār

Jerbent

Merv

*Murgab*

Vozv.

Karab.

FARYAB

R K M E N I Y A

Sakar-Čaga

Turkmen-Kala

Iolotan'

Maimana

Belchiragh

Bandi-i-Turkistan

**Mary**

Murgab

**Bayram-Ali**

Durzab

Chirās

H ↓ **73**

60°

↓ **73**

© HACHETTE-IGN

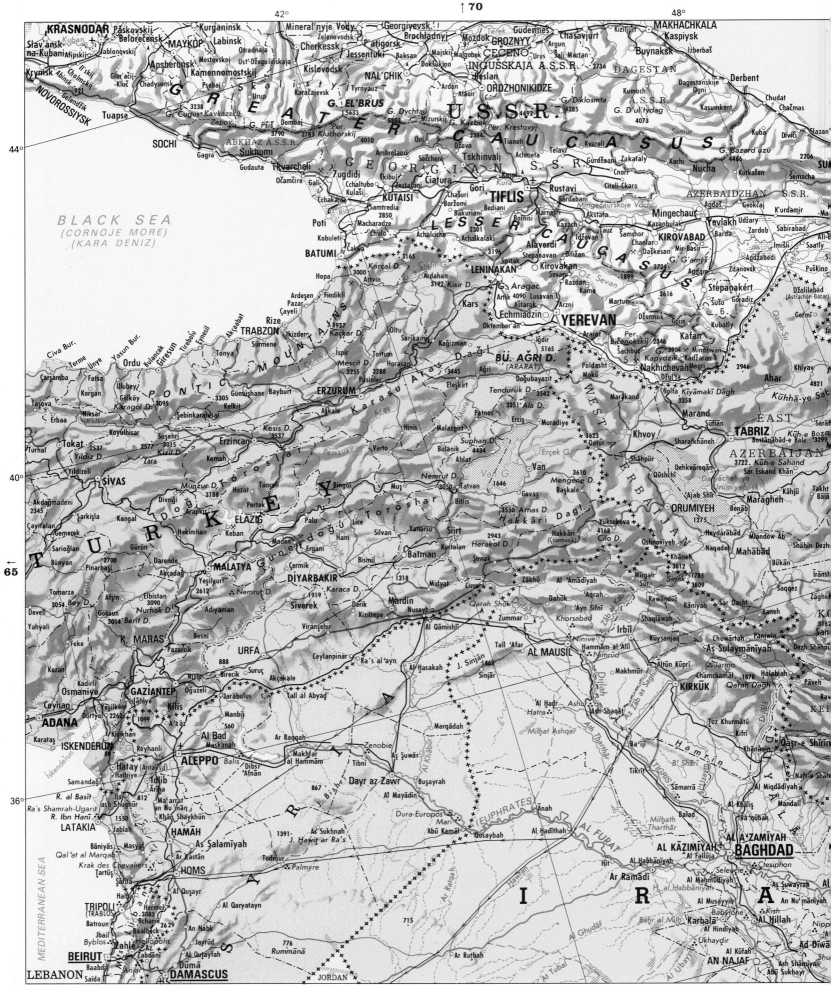

0   50   100 Kilomètres
0   50 Statute Miles

↑ **71**

54°

→ **126**

U.S.S.R.

Bachardok   Bachardok   Kirovsk

Krasnovodskoje   Oglanly   Kazandžik   Kizyl-Arvat   Bami   Bacharden   Geok-Tepe   Bezmein   ASHKHABAD   Artyk   Dušak   Tedzhen

Pr. Kara-Bogaz-Gol   · 26   Plato   · 308   Chr. Bol. Balchan   Nebit-Dag   1880   1005   Fir'uza   Kaachka
Kuuli-Majak   Ožanga   Džebel   Kum-Dag   2246   2942   Kūh-e Rīzeh   Darreh Gaz   Kabūd Gonbad
Krasnovodsk   Koturdepe   Im. 26 Bakinskich Komissarov   Kara-Kala   Gifān   Kūh-e Hazār Masjed   3117
Art'om-Ostrov   Neft'anye Kamni   Čeleken   P-ov Čeleken   Šarlauk   Shīrvān   Qūchān   Chanāran   MTS.
O. Žiloj   M. T'ulenij   Karagel   Messerian   Bojnūrd   MESHED
Stepan Razin   Okarem   Marāveh Tappeh   Kūh-e Shāh Jahān   Kūh-e Ālādāgh   Bām   Kūh-e Bīnālūd   3211
BAKU   Turkmenskij   Zaliv   3060   Mīānābād   Neyshābūr   Kafar Qal'eh
Bakinskii Archipelag   O. Ogurčinskij   2972   Miānābād   36°
26 Bakinskich Komissarov   Kizyl-Atrek   Dasht   Jājarm   Hokmābād   Soltānābād   Sabzevār
Zapov. im. Kirova   1023   Gazan-Kuli   2577   Nardin   Kūh-e Jogbatāy   Kūh-e Sorkh
enkoran'   Wall of Alexandre   Gonbad-e Kāvūs   2995   Mazinān   3020
Astārā   · 21   Tureng Tepe   Mayāmey   Tūrān   Kāshmar
Bandar-e Shah   Gorgān   Bastām   Bīārjmand   Ma'dan   Kondor
Kord Kuy   3910   Shāhrūd   Dorūneh
Behshahr   Dāmghān   KHURASAN
Hashtpar   Bābol Sar   Sārī   Fūlād Mahalleh   Ferdows
Bandar-Anzali   Lāhījan   Bābol   Shāhī   Torūd   Naginfeh
3209   Langarūd   Rūd Sar   Ramsar   Shahsavār   Chālūs   Now Shahr   Āmol   3729   Boshrūyeh
RASHT   3689   3582   Gardaneh-ye Gadūk   SEMNĀN
Fowman   4805   MOUNTAINS   2235   Semnān
Rūdbār   Gach Sar   QOLLEH-YE DAMAVAND   5604   Firūzkūh   Lāsjerd   Tabas
Qahab   Manjil   Qareh Tekān   SHEMIRAMAT   Damavand   Kūh-e Gūgerd   SALT   DESERT   Deyhūk
Zanjān   Qazvin   1533   Tajrīsh   TEHRAN   2845   Kūh-e Marghūb
Soltānīyeh   Gardaneh-ye Kuhin   Ziārān   Karaj   REY   Eyvānakī   Garmsār
Abhar   Tākestān   Soltānābād   Yārامīn   Robāt-e Khān
Yengī Kand   Khar Rūd   Ja'farābād   Jandaq   Khvor
Bijārd   2356   Āveh   Zarand   Daryācheh-ye Namak   Biābānak   Posht-e Bādām
HAMADĀN   Gardaneh-ye Āveh   Sāveh   Manzariyeh   Anarak   1490   Kūh-e Sorkh
Qorveh   Razan   Nowbarān   QOM   Naṣrābād   Zarrīn
Row'an   2993   Tarkhowrān   Rāhjerd   Kūh-e Aliābād   Ardestān
HAMADĀN   Qareh Su   Kāshān   3356   Nā'īn   Ardakān   Kūh-e Khowrnag   Kūhbonān
Ecbatane   Mahallat   Natanz   3896   Āqdā   Meybod   Yazd   Bāfq   32°
Asadābād   3571   Kūh-e Alvand   Tūysarkān   Arāk   3334   Kūh-e Karkas   Meymeh   Kūh-e Marshīnān   Kūhpāyeh   3197
Kangāvar   Malāyer   Tūreh   Qeydū   Golpāyegān   Mūrcheh Khvort   ISFAHAN   Ardakān   Sar-e Yazd   Kermānshāhān
Nahāvand   Borūjerd   Khvonsar   Najafābād   Gāv Khūnī   Shīr Kūh   4075
Bisotūn   Dow Rūd   Alīgūdarz   Dārān   Khār Kūh   3511   Shams
KERMANSHAH   Oshtorān Kūh   Esfandārān   Deh-e Shīr   Anār   Namaki
Khorramābād   4070   Shahr Kord   Shahrezā   Rafsanjān
Kūhdasht   Dūl Gap   Sar Kūl   Qīyād   BAKHTĪARĪ   Borūjen   Yazd-e Khvāst   Abarqū   3600   Kūh-e Madvār
Shirvan   Malavi   Jelow Gīr   Zard Kūh   4548   Shalamzār   Kūh-e Alījūd   3723   Ābādeh   KERMĀN
2800   Shelār   3715   Izeh   Dehdez   Semirom   Eqlīd   Kūh-e Būl   Deh Bīd   Bavānāt   3510   Tājābād
Abdānān   Naṣrīan-e Pā'īn   Andimeshk   Lālī   Semīrom   3660   Kūh-e Khātūn   Sa'īdābād
Dizful   3162   Kūh-e Karūn   Jasuj   Kūh-e Dīnār   Aspās   Morghāb   Pasargades   (Sirjan)
Shūsh   Shūshtar   Masjed Soleymān   Haft Gel   4431   Marvast
Qal'at Ṣāliḥ   Naft-e Safīd   Rāmhormoz   Tal-e Khosravī   Sivand   Arsenjān   3090
Al 'Amārah   Aghā Jārī   Kūh-e Khāīz   Bāsht   Dow Gonbadān   Persepolis   Daryācheh-ye Tashk
Ar Rifā'ī   Behbahān   3189   BOYER AHMADĪ-YE   Ardakān   Daryācheh-ye Bakhtegān   Meydān-e Gel
Lagash   Al Qurnah   Pāzanān   Kūh-e Tābask   Marv Dasht   Neyrīz
Shatrah   Bandar-e Ma'shūr   3218   Gach Sārān   Zohreh   SHĪRAZ   FARS   Eṣtahbānāt   3166

48°   ↓ **83**   54°

© HACHETTE-IGN

Scale 1 : 33,000,000

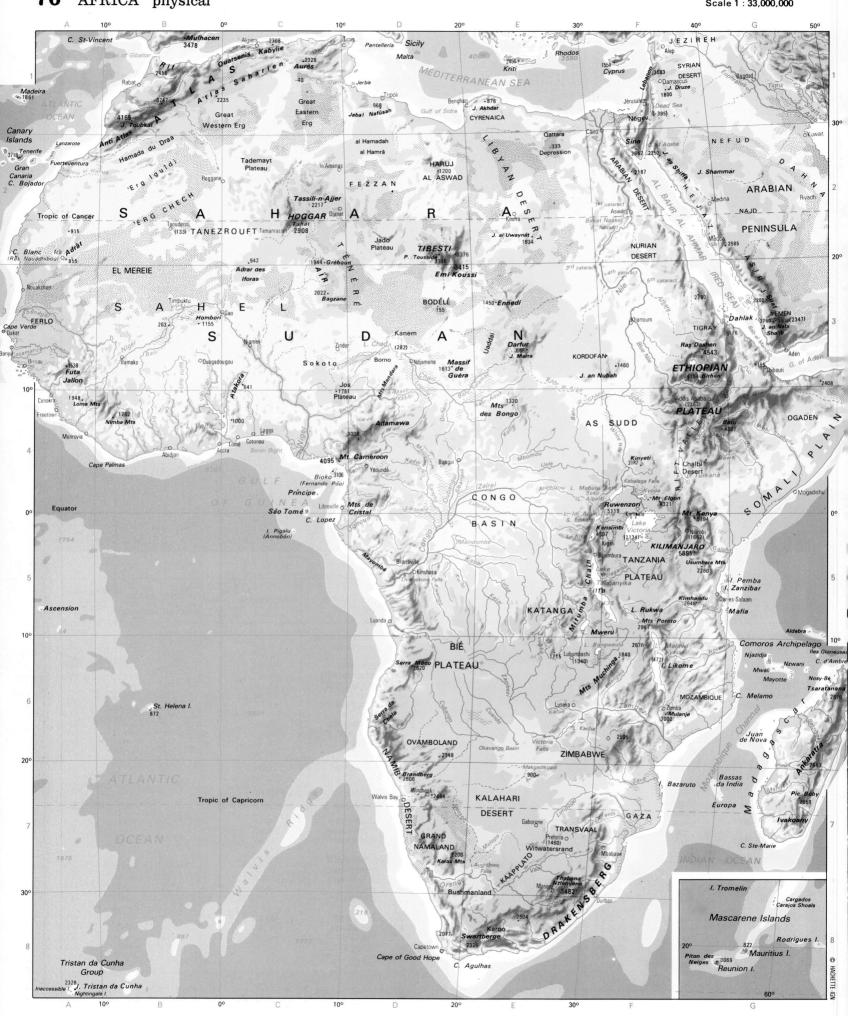

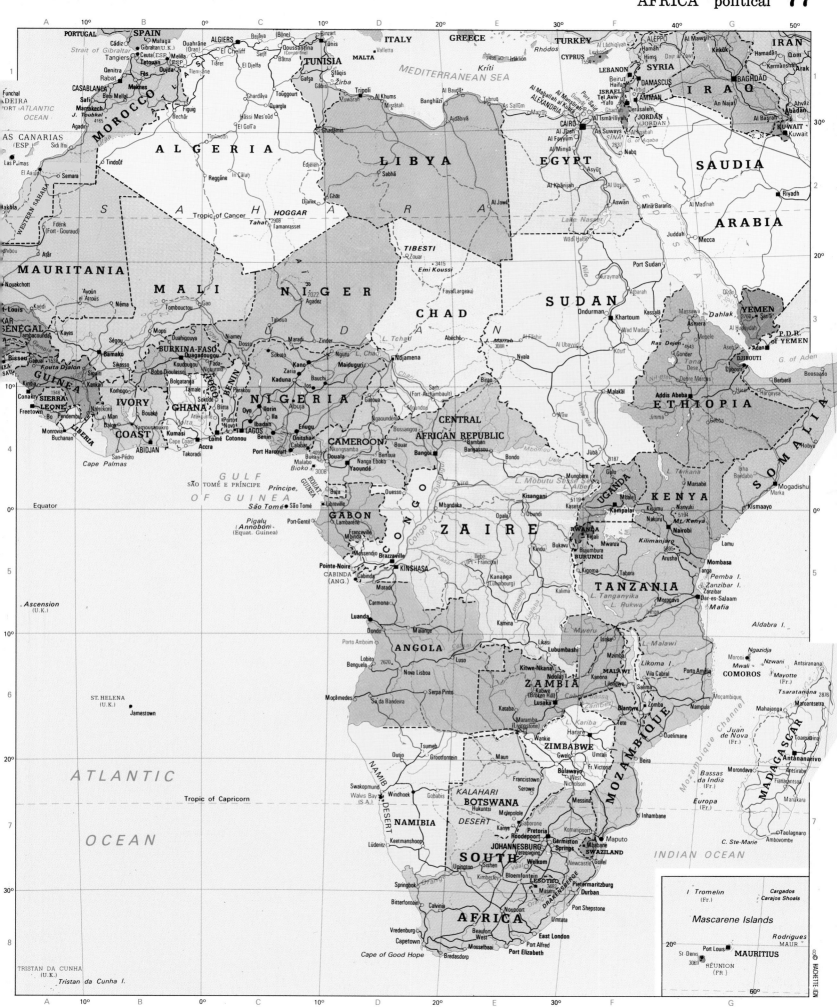

Scale 1 : 5,000,000

↑ 60

**MADEIRA**
(Portugal)

MADEIRA ARCHIPELAGO

P.to Moniz
S. Vicente
.1861
Madeira
P. Ruivo Funchal
Porto Santo
Porto Santo
Chão
Deserta Grande
Bugio
Desertas

ATLANTIC
OCEAN

SPAIN

Sanlúcar de Barrameda
El Puerto de Santa María
CÁDIZ
S. Fernando
C. Trafalgar
S. Roque
Algeciras
C. Spartel
TANGIER
Asilah
Larache
Moulay
Bou Selham
Arbaoua
St.-el-Arba-du-R.

JEREZ DE LA
FRONTERA
Ronda
.1919
Marbella
La Linea
Gibraltar
(U.K.)
P.te Almina
Ceuta (Spain)
TÉTOUAN
O. Laou
Ksar el Kebir
Chechaouén
Ouezzane
Tidirhine
GRANADA
S.a Nevada .3478
Torremolinos
MÁLAGA
C. Sacratif
Alborán
(Spain)
ALBORAN SEA
Peñón de Vélez
de la Gomera (Spain)
I.t Alhucemas (Spain)
Al-Hoceima
C. Quilatès
Targuist
Midar
.2066
.2322
.2168
ALMERÍA
G. de
Almería
C. de Gata
C. des Trois
Fourches
Melilla (Spain)
I.t Chafarinas (Spain)
Nador
Selouane
Zaïo
C. Figalo
Beni Saf
Saïdia
Ghazaouet
TLEMCEN

KENITRA
Mehdiya
S.t Bouknadel
RABAT
SALÉ
Bouznika
MOHAMMEDIA
CASABLANCA
El-Jadida (Mazagan) [DAR EL BEIDA]
El Jorf-Lasfar
(Cap Blanc)
Azemmour
Oualidia
C. Beddouza
(Cap Cantin)
Doukkala
SAFI
S.t Smail
Khemis des-Zemamra
S.t Bennour
SETTAT
Boulaouane
Imfout
El Gara
Benahmed
Berrechid
Médiouna
Bouskoura
Ben-Slimane
Rommani
Ezzhiliga
S.t-Slimane
S.t-Kacem
Volubilis
M.y Idriss
FÈS
MEKNÈS
El-Hajeb
Ifrane
Azrou
Qulmès
Sefrou
Imouzzer-du-Kandar
Boulemane
Tahala
Taza
Guercif
Berkine
Debdou
Aïn
Benimathar
El-Aricha
Sebdou
M.ts de Tlemcen .1843
OUJDA
Taourirt
Jerada
Berkane
Ahfir
Maghnia
Msoun
Moulouya

Khemisset
Temara
Bou Regreg
Khouribga
El-Borouj
Oued-Zem
Boujâd
Aït
Isehak
Khénifra
Itzer
Missour
.3340
J. Bou Nâceur
Outat-Oulad-
el-Haj
Tendrara
Charef
Chott Rharbi

MARRAKECH
Chichaoua
Tleta Oulad Dlim
El-Kelaâ-
des-Srerhna
El-Ksiba
Kasba-
Tadla
Beni-Mellal
Ouaouizarht
.3277 J. Ayachi
.3747
Imilchil
Midelt
.2571
Rich
Plaine de Tamelt
.2120
Talsinnt
Bouârfa
.2083
Figuig .2160
Aïn-Sefra
HAUT
MONTS

AGADIR
Inezgane
Aït-Melloul
Taroudannt
Ouled Dlim
.3555
J. Erdouz .3575
.2094
Tizi n'Test
J. Toubkal .4165
Asni
Oukaïmeden .2260
Tizi n'Tichka
.4071
J. Ighil Mgoun
HAUT ATLAS
Boumalne
Tinerhir
Goulmima
Boudenib
Kenadsa
Béchar
Abadla
Taghit

ANTI ATLAS
Tiznit
Sidi Ifni
Cap Noun
Bou-Izakarn
Goulimime
Tafraoute
2359
2531
Tata
Tissinnt
Akka
Foum-
Zguid
Bou-Azzer
Agdz
Nekob
Zagora
Alnif
Erfoud
Rissani
Kelaâ des Mgouna .2712
Jbel Sarhro
Ouarzazate
Amerzgane
Taliouine
3304 J. Sirova
Tazenakht
Rheris
Tafilalt
Taouz
Taghit
Hamada du Guir
Hamaguir
Iglì
Beni Abbès

Jbel Bani
Tagounite
Mhamid
HAMADA DU DRAÂ
Drâa
581
673
1097
Jbel Ouarkziz

GRAND
Erg er Raoui
Hamada de la Daoura
Tabelbala
.836
Kerzaz
Timoudi
ERG IABES
Bou Bernous
(Bordj Fly S.te Marie)
.391
ERG EL KREBS
Adrar .263
TOUAT
Règgan

**ATLANTIC OCEAN**

Pitones
Selvagen Grande
Salvage Islands
(Portugal)

CANARY ISLANDS
(Spain)

San Andrés y Sauces
2423
Los Llanos de Aridane
S.ta Cruz de la Palma
La Palma
LA PALMA

Tenerife
La Orotava
S. Cristóbal de la Laguna
SANTA CRUZ DE TENERIFE
Hermigua
Garajonay
S. Sebastián de la G.
1487
La Gomera
Valverde
1501
Hierro
Pico de Teide 3718
El Escobonal
Granadilla de Abona
Guía de Gran Canaria
P. de las Nieves
S. Nicolás 1949
Telde
LAS PALMAS DE GRAN CANARIA
Gran Canaria
807

Montaña Clara
Alegranza
Graciosa
Lanzarote
Haría
670
Yaisa
Arrecife
Lobo
La Oliva
Fuerteventura
724
Puerto del Rosario
Tuineje
Gran Tarajal

Cap Juby
Tarfaya
MOROCCO

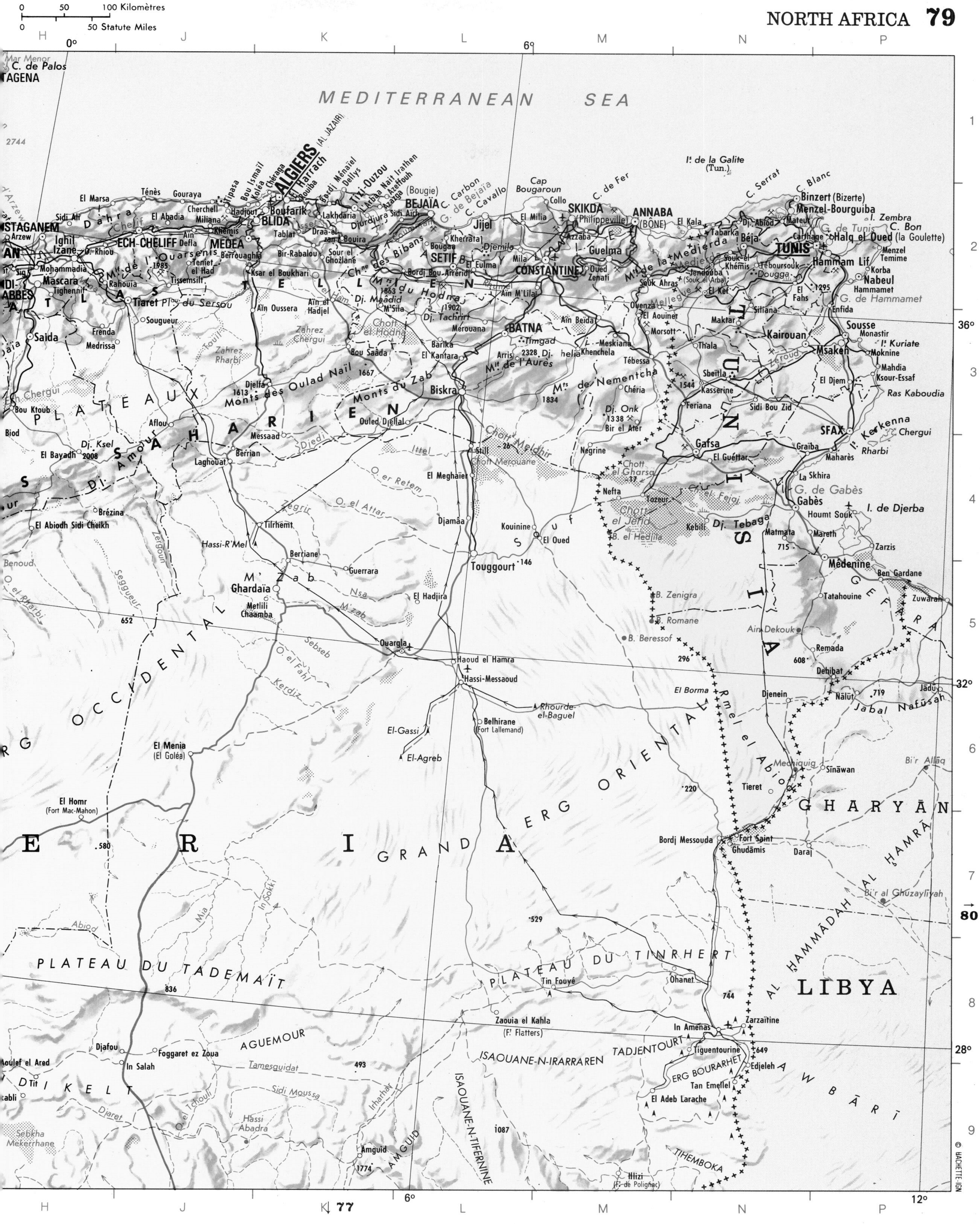

0 50 100 Kilomètres
0 50 Statute Miles

MEDITERRANEAN SEA

C. de Palos
Mar Menor
CARTAGENA

ALGIERS (AL JAZAIR)
El Harrach
Bou Ismail
Koléa Chéraga
Tipasa
Cherchell
Miliana
Hadjout
BLIDA
Boufarik
El Marsa
Ténès
Gouraya
Sidi Ali
El Abadia
Khemis
Ain Defla
MEDEA
ECH-CHELIFF
Berrouaghia
Tablat
MOSTAGANEM
Ighil Izane
O. Rhiou
Mohammadia
Mascara
SIDI BEL ABBES
Tighennif
Saida
Frenda
Medrissa
Sougueur
Tiaret
Aïn Oussera
Aïn el Hadjel
Ksar el Boukhari
Bordj Bou Arréridj
Bir-Rabalou
Sour el Ghozlane
Bou Saâda
M'Sila
Barika
El Kantara
Djelfa
Monts des Oulad Nail
Aflou
Amour
Messaad
Berriane
Laghouat
Tilrhemt
Hassi-R'Mel
Berriane
Guerrara
Ghardaïa
Metlili Chaamba
El Hadjira
Ouargla
Haoud el Hamra
Hassi-Messaoud
El-Gassi
Belhirane (Fort Lallemand)
El-Agreb
Rhourde el-Baguel
El Borma
El Menia (El Goléa)
El Homr (Fort Mac-Mahon)
GRAND ERG OCCIDENTAL
GRAND ERG ORIENTAL
PLATEAU DU TADEMAÏT
AGUEMOUR
In Salah
Djafou
Foggaret ez Zoua
Zaouia el Kahla (F. Flatters)
ISAOUANE-N-IRARRAREN
ISAOUANE-N-TIFERNINE
PLATEAU DU TINRHERT
Tin Fouyé
Ohanet
In Amenas
Tiguentourine
Edjeleh
Zarzaïtine
El Adeb Larache
Amguid
Illizi (F. de Polignac)
TIHEMBOKA

TIZI-OUZOU
Dellys
Bordj Ménaïel
Azazga
Beni Aïssi
Dra-el-Mizan
Lakhdaria
Bouira
BEJAÏA (Bougie)
Djidjelli Sidi Aïch
Jijel
El Milia
Collo
SKIKDA (Philippeville)
Mila
Djemila
SETIF
CONSTANTINE
Oued Zenati
El Eulma
Bou Taleb
Mérouana
BATNA
Arris
Mt de l'Aurès
Timgad
Khenchela
Aïn Beïda
Tébessa
Biskra
Ouled Djellal
El Meghaïer
Djamâa
Touggourt
Kouinine
El Oued
Negrine
Feriana
Gafsa
El Guéttar
Nefta
Tozeur
Chott el Jérid
Kebili
Dj. Tebaga
Matmata
Mareth
Gabès
Houmt Souk
I. de Djerba
Zarzis
Médenine
Ben Gardane
Tatahouine
Remada
Dehibat
Nalut
Jadu
Jabal Nafusah
Ghudamis
Daraj
Bordj Messouda
Fort Saint
GHARYAN
AL HAMMADAH AL HAMRA
AL HAMMADAH AL HAMRA
LIBYA

ANNABA (BONE)
Guelma
El Kala
Tabarka
Béja
Jendouba
Souk Ahras
El Kef
Siliana
Maktar
Kairouan
Thala
Kasserine
Sbeïtla
Sidi Bou Zid
SFAX
Graïba
Maharès
La Skhira
G. de Gabès

BINZERT (Bizerte)
MENZEL-BOURGUIBA
Mateur
TUNIS
Carthage
Halq el Oued (la Goulette)
Hammam Lif
Nabeul
Korba
Hammamet
Enfida
Sousse
Monastir
Moknine
Mahdia
Ksour-Essaf
El Djem
Ras Kaboudia
I. Kerkenna
Chergui

TUNISIA

C. de Fer
C. Serrat
C. Blanc
C. Bon
G. de Tunis
G. de Hammamet
I. de la Galite (Tun.)
I. Zembra
I. Kuriate

ATLAS TELLIEN
PLATEAUX DU SAHARIEN
Monts du Zab
Chott el Hodna
Chott Melrhir
Chott el Gharsa

GEFARA

Scale 1 : 5,000,000

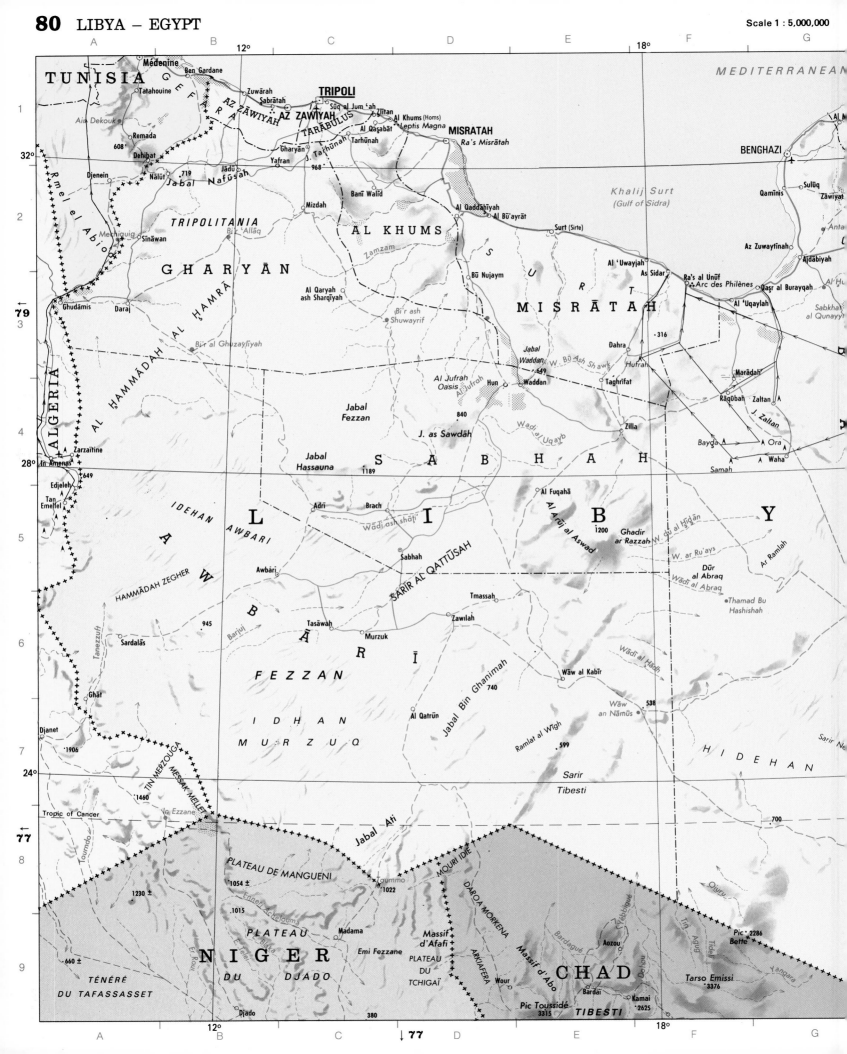

TUNISIA

Médenine
Ben Gardane
Tatahouine
Zuwārah
Şabrātah
TRIPOLI
Sūq al Jum'ah
AZ ZĀWIYAH
AZ ZAWIYAH
Zlītan
Al Khums (Homs)
Leptis Magna
MISRATAH
Ra's Misrātah
Aïn Dekouk
Remada
Dehibat
Gharyān
Tarhūnah
J. Tarhūnah
Yafran
608
Djenein
Nālūt
Jādū
719
Jabal Nafūsah
968
BENGHAZI
Qamīnis
Sulūq
Zāwiyat

MEDITERRANEAN

TRIPOLITANIA
Mizdah
Banī Walīd
Al Qaddāhīyah
Al Bū'ayrāt
AL KHUMS
Surt (Sirte)
Az Zuwaytīnah
Ajdābiyah
Mechiguig
Sīnāwan
Bi'r 'Allāq
Zamzam
Bū Nujaym

Khalīj Surt
(Gulf of Sidra)

Rmel el Abio

GHARYĀN
Al Qaryah
ash Sharqīyah
Bi'r ash
Shuwayrif
Al 'Uwayjah
As Sidar
Ra's al Unūf
Arc des Philènes
Al 'Uqaylah
Qaşr al Burayqah

Ghudāmis
Daraj
Bi'r al Ghuzaylīyah

SURT

MISRĀTAH

Sabkhat
al Qunayy

ALGERIA

Jabal
Fezzan
J. as Sawdāh
840
Jabal
Hassauna
1189
Al Jufrah
Oasis
Al Jufrah
Hun
Waddan
Jabal
Waddan
649
W. Bū Ash Shawk
Taghrīfat
Dahra
316
Hufrah
Marādah
Rāqūbah
Zaltan
J. Zaltan
Bayda Δ
Ora
Waha
Samah
Zilla

AL ḤAMMĀDAH AL ḤAMRĀ

In Amenas
28°
Zarzaïtine
649
Edjeleh
Tan
Emellel

SABHAH

LIBYA

IDEHAN
AWBARI
Adrī
Brach
Al Fuqahā
Al 'Arūl al Aswad
1200
Ghadir
ar Razzah
W. du al Ḥiḍān
W. ar Ru'ays
Dūr
al Abraq
Wādī al Abraq
Ar Ramlah
Wādī ash shāṭi
Sabhah
SARĪR AL QATTŪSAH

HAMMĀDAH ZEGHER
AWBARI
945
Barjuj
Tasāwah
Murzuk
Tmassah
Zawīlah
Thamad Bu
Hashishah

Sardalās
Ghāt

AWBĀRĪ

FEZZAN
Jabal Bin Ghanimah
740
Wāw al Kabīr
Wādī al Ḥadh
538
Waw
an Nāmūs

Djanet
1906
IDHAN
MURZUQ
Al Qatrūn
Ramlat al Wīgh
599
HIDEHAN
Sirir Ne

Sarir
Tibesti

Tropic of Cancer
77
Tin Merzouga
1460
MESSAK MELLET
In Ezzane
Jabal Atı
700

PLATEAU DE MANGUENI
1054 ±
Toummo
1022
MOURI IDIE
DAROA MORKENA

Er Rouı
Enneri Achelouma
1015
Madama
Qijru

1230 ±

PLATEAU
Emi Fezzane
Massif
d'Afafi
Aozou
Pic 2286
Bette

NIGER
660 ±
DU DJADO
PLATEAU
DU
TCHIGAÏ
Massif d'Abo
Wour
ARKIAFERA
CHAD
Tarso Emissi
3376

TÉNÉRÉ
DU TAFASSASSET
Djado
380
Pic Toussidé
3315
Bardai
Kamai
2625
TIBESTI

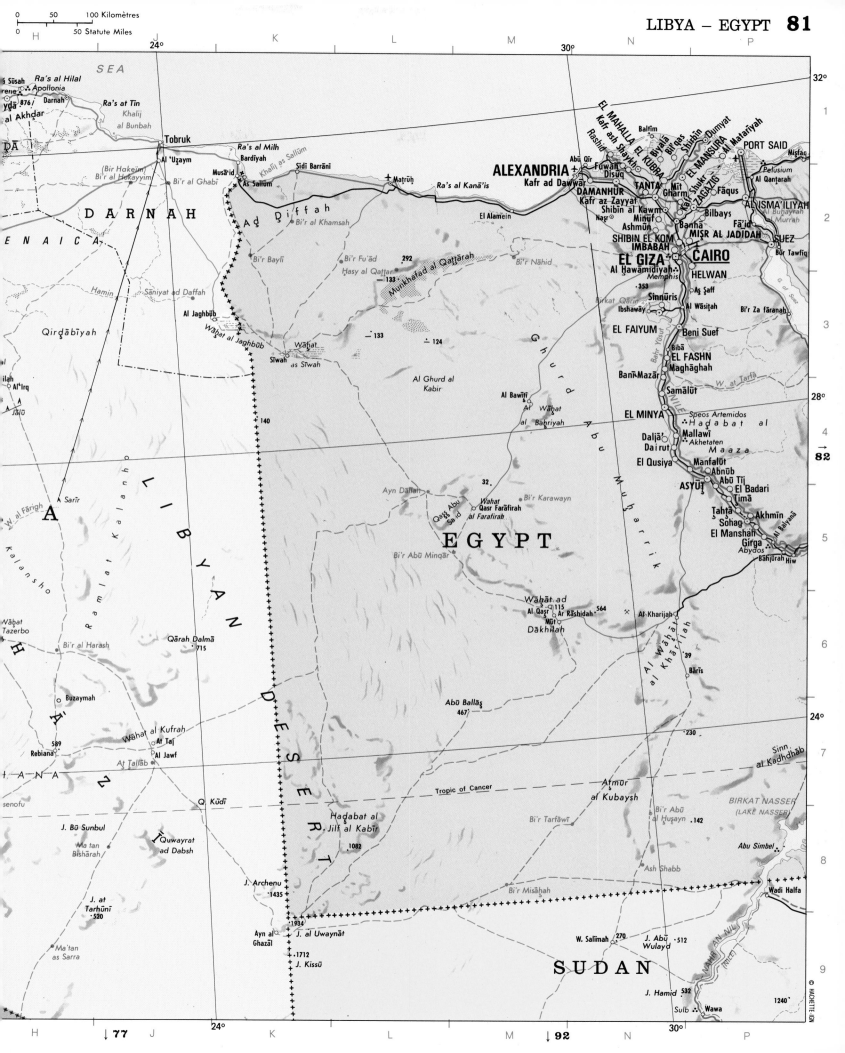

SEA

Ra's al Hilal
Apollonia
Ra's at Tin
Darnah

876
al Akhdar
(Bir Hakeïm)
Bi'r al Hukayyim

Tobruk
Al 'Uzaym
Bardiyah
Ra's al Milh
Khalij as Sallūm
Sīdī Barrānī

Musā'id
As Sallūm
Bi'r al Ghabī

**DARNAH**

Aḍ Ḍiffah

Matrūh

Ra's al Kanā'is

**CYRENAICA**

Bi'r al Khamsah

El Alamein

Bi'r Baylī

Bi'r Fu'ād
292

Munkhafad al Qattārah

Bi'r Nāhid

133

133

Hamin

Sāniyat ad Daffah

Qirḍabīyah

Al Jaghbūb
Wāḥat al Jaghbūb

133
124

Wāḥat
as Sīwah
Sīwah

Al Ghurd al
Kabir

Al Bawītī
Al Wāḥat
al Bahriyah

**ALEXANDRIA**
Kafr ad Dawwār
Abū Qīr
Fuwah
Disūq
Rashīd

**EL MAHALLA EL KUBRA**
Kafr ash Shaykh
Balṭīm
Biyala
Bi'l qas
Shibīn
Dumyat
Al Matarīyah

**EL MANSURA**

**PORT SAID**
Mişfaq
Pelusium
Al Qantarah

**DAMANHŪR**
Kafr az Zayyat
**TANTA**
Mīt Gharm
Kafr Shukr
**ZAGAZIG**
Fāqus

**AL ISMA'ILIYAH**
Al Buhayrah
al Murrah

Naşr
Shibīn al Kawm
Ashmūn
Minūf

Bilbays
Fā'id

**SHIBIN EL KOM**
**IMBABAH**
Banha
**MIŞR AL JADIDAH**

**SUEZ**
Būr Tawfīq

**EL GIZA**
Al Hawamidiyah
Memphis
**CAIRO**

**HELWAN**

353

Aş Şaff

Birkat Qārūn
Sinnūris
Ibshaway

Al Wāsitah

Bi'r Za farānah

**EL FAIYUM**

Beni Suef

Bibā
**EL FASHN**
Maghāghah

Banī Mazār

Samālūt

W. at Tarfā

Ghurd

Abū Muḥarrik

**EL MINYA**

Speos Artemidos

**H a d a b a t a l**

**M a a z a**

Mallawī
Akhetaten
Dairūt

Daljā

El Qusiya

Manfalūt
Abnūb
Abū Tij
**ASYŪT**
El Badari
Timā

Tahtā
Akhmīn
Sohag
El Manshah
Girga
Abydos

Al Balyana

Bahjūrah
Hiw

82

32

Ayn Dāllah

Wahat
Qasr Farāfirah
al Farafirah

Qaşş Abu
Sa'id

Bi'r Karawayn

**EGYPT**

Bi'r Abū Minqār

**L I B Y A N   D E S E R T**

Wāḥat ad
Al Qaşr
115
Mūt
**Dākhilah**

Ar Rāshidah
564

Al-Kharijah

Al Wāḥāt al Kharijah

39

Bāris

**R a m l a t   K a l a n h**

Qārah Dalmā
715

Wāḥat
Tazerbo

Bi'r al Harash

Buzaymah

Abū Ballāş
467

230

**D E S E R T**

Wāḥat al Kufrah
At Taj
589
Rebiana
Al Jawf
At Tallāb

Q. Kūdī

Tropic of Cancer

Atmūr
al Kubaysh

Sinn
al Kadhdhāb

**BIRKAT NASSER**
**(LAKE NASSER)**

senofu

J. Bū Sunbul

Ma'tan
Bishārah

Quwayrat
ad Dabsh

Hadabat al
Jilf al Kabir
1082

Bi'r Tarfāwī

Bi'r Abū
al Ḥuşayn
142

Abu Simbel

J. at
Tarhūnī
520

Ma'tan
as Sarra

J. Archenu
1435

Ash Shabb

1934
Ayn al
Ghazāl

Bi'r Misāḥah

Wadi Halfa

J. al Uwaynāt

1712
J. Kissū

W. Salimah
270
J. Abū
Wulayd
512

**SUDAN**

J. Hamid
532

Sulb
Wawa

1240

© HACHETTE-IGN

MEDITERRANEAN SEA

BEIRUT
LEBANON
DAMASCUS
SYRIA
SYRIAN DESERT

Ar Ruṭbah
Rummāna
Al Qutayfah
Az Zabdānī
Dūmā
Baabda
Anjar
Sour Tyr
Saïda
Sidon
Marjayoun
Banīyas
El Qunatirah
Zefat
'Akko
Tiberias
Sea of Galilee
As Suwaydā'
J. ād Durūz
Salkhad
1800
HAIFA
209
Dar'a
Atlit
Nazareth
IRBID
Ar Ramthā
Al Mafraq
Caesarea
Janin
J. Umm ad Darāj
1247
Hadera
Tūl Karm
Jarash
Netanya
Nablus
As Salt
ZARQA
RAMAT GAN
TEL AVIV YAFO
PETAH-TIQWA
AMMAN
HOLON
Ramla
Jericho
Rehovot
JERUSALEM
ISRAEL
Ashdod
Bethlehem
Ashqelon
Hebron
Ascalon
Qiryat Gat
Gaza
Lakhish
Mezad
Al Karak
Khān Yūnis
Haluza
Sedom
Dimona
Aṭ Ṣāfiyah
BE'ER SHEVA
Avedat
Oron
Aṭ Ṭafīlah
Negev
Al Jair
Har Ramon
1035
Ma'an
1736
Petra 1727
J. Mabrak
Ra's an Naqb

J. Unayzah
940
Khabrat Abū al Ḥusayn
Al Ubayyid
Jūdayyidat-'Ar'ar
Aṭ Ṭurayf
Badanah
Al Jalāmīd
Qalamat umm Khansur
Al Ḥadīthah
Liss
1128
1070
1215
J. al 'Āmūd
Sakākā
Al Jawf
Al Qārah
Al Jauf
Al Isawīyah
Bāyir
Al Qurayyāt
Al Hadithah

JORDAN
Wādī as Sirhān

PORT SAID
El Arish
Pelusium
Al Qantarah
Mişfaq
Al Isma'iliyah
El Mansura
Dumyat
Bir Qas
Shidin
Al Mataariyah
Shukr
ZAGAZIG
Kafr Shaykh
Fāqus
Benha
Bilbays
Fā'id
MIŞR AL JADĪDAH
Suez
CAIRO
EL GIZA
Bur Tawfiq
Sinnuris
As Saff
Al Wāsiṭah
EL FAIYUM
Bi'r Za faranah
Beni Suef
Biba
El Fashn
Maghāghah
Bani Mazār
Samālūt
EL MINYA
Speos Artemidos
Hadabat al
Maaza
Mallawi
Akhetaten
Dairut
El Qusiya
Manfalūt
Abnūb
ASYUT
Abū Tīj
El Badari
Tima
Tahta
Sūhag
Akhmin
El Manshah
El Balyanā
Girga
Dishnā
Abydos
Naqadah
Dandara
Bahjūrah
Hiw
Thebes
Qus
Armant
Karnak
Luxor
Matūlī
EGYPT
Isnā
610
Hieraconpolis
Idfu
(Apollinopolis Magna)
Salwā Baḥrī
An Nasser
Kawm Umbu
Ombos
ASWAN
Sadd al Aswan
Philae
Kalabsha
Sadd al 'Ālī
BIRKAT NASSER
(LAKE NASSER)
As Sibū
Amada
Qasr Ibrim
Abu Simbel
Bāris
230
142
39

SINAI
PENINSULA
Al Junaynah
Abū Zanīmah
1626 al Muzayyinah
J. Katrīnah
2637
Abū Darbah
Aṭ Ṭūr
Dhahad
Ras Ghārib
1751
J. Ghārib
Naqb
Nabq
Sharm
Aṭ Ṭawīlah
Jamsah
Jazīrat Shadwān
Al Ghudaqah
(Hurgada)
Jiftūn al Kabīr
J. Shā'ib al Banāt
2187
Bur Safajah
J. Safajah
ARABIAN
DESERT
Al Qusayr
Qina
J. as Sibā'ī
1477
Marsá al 'Alam
1504
Wādī Jimal
J. Nuqruş
Al Kharijah
Wādī Kharīt
Shāṭī
J. Hamāṭah
1977
Mīnā' Baranīs
J. Zabarjad
Ra's Banās
Foul Bay
B. Shalatayn
J. Natiṭyāy
1165
J. Niqrub al Fawqāni
1078
1419
J. Jarf
Siyal
Ra's Abū Dārah
Halā'ib al Kabīrah
Halā'ib
Ra's al Ḥadāribah
J. Eigat
1606
Marsa al Mar'ūb
J. Muqsim
839
1851
SUDAN

An Nakhl
El Tih
Ra's Abū Qurūn
1086
Al Buḥayrah al Murrah
Khalīj as Suways (Gulf of Suez)
Gulf of Aqaba
Elat
Al 'Aqabah
Haql
J. Mazḥafah
1900
Al Quṣaymah
Al Mudawwarah
Ḥallat 'Ammār
Bi'r Ibn Hirmās
Al Quwayrah
Tabūk
2578 J. al Lawz
Aynūnah
2350
Tarīm
Zibā
J. Dabbāgh
Madyan
Wādī Shifā'
Harrat al 'Uwayriḍ
Ra's Muḥammad
J. Tiran
Tiran
Madīq Jūbāl
AL BAHR AL AHMAR (RED SEA)

AL JAWF
Al 'Urayq
Al Hūj
1007
Al Hufrah
An NAFŪ
Jubbah
Mawqaq
Jabal Aja
Al Mustajid
HĀ'IL
Taymā'
Qal'at al Akhḍar
AL HĀ'IL
Mada' in Sālih
Al 'Ula
Ṣafājah
Ḥ. Ithnayn
Jabal
Ṣah
As Sufan
Hulayt
AL MADĪNAH
Al Wajh
R. Karkūmā
J. Umm Urūmah
1200
Al Mudarraj
Hadīyah
Tubjah
Khaybar
Harrat Khaybar
Bi'r al Kwrayzīyah
J. Mashābih
Hanak
J. Shaybārā
Um Lajj
2313
J. al Hassānī
R. Abū Madd
Bi'r al Amir
Wādī al
Bi'r Nasīf
639
MEDINA
Sūq Suwayq
R. Baridi
Yanbu
Al Musayjīd
Al Ḥamra
Al Far'ah
Badr Hunayn
Ḥarrat Rahat
Umm al Birak
Ar Rubad
Mastūrah
Rābigh
Qadīmah
Khulays
Tuwwal
Wādī Ḥammā
Dahabān
Usfan
As Sayl
631
Ash Shuyūkh
Zaymah
MĀ
JIDDAH
MECCA
Haddā
Mīnā

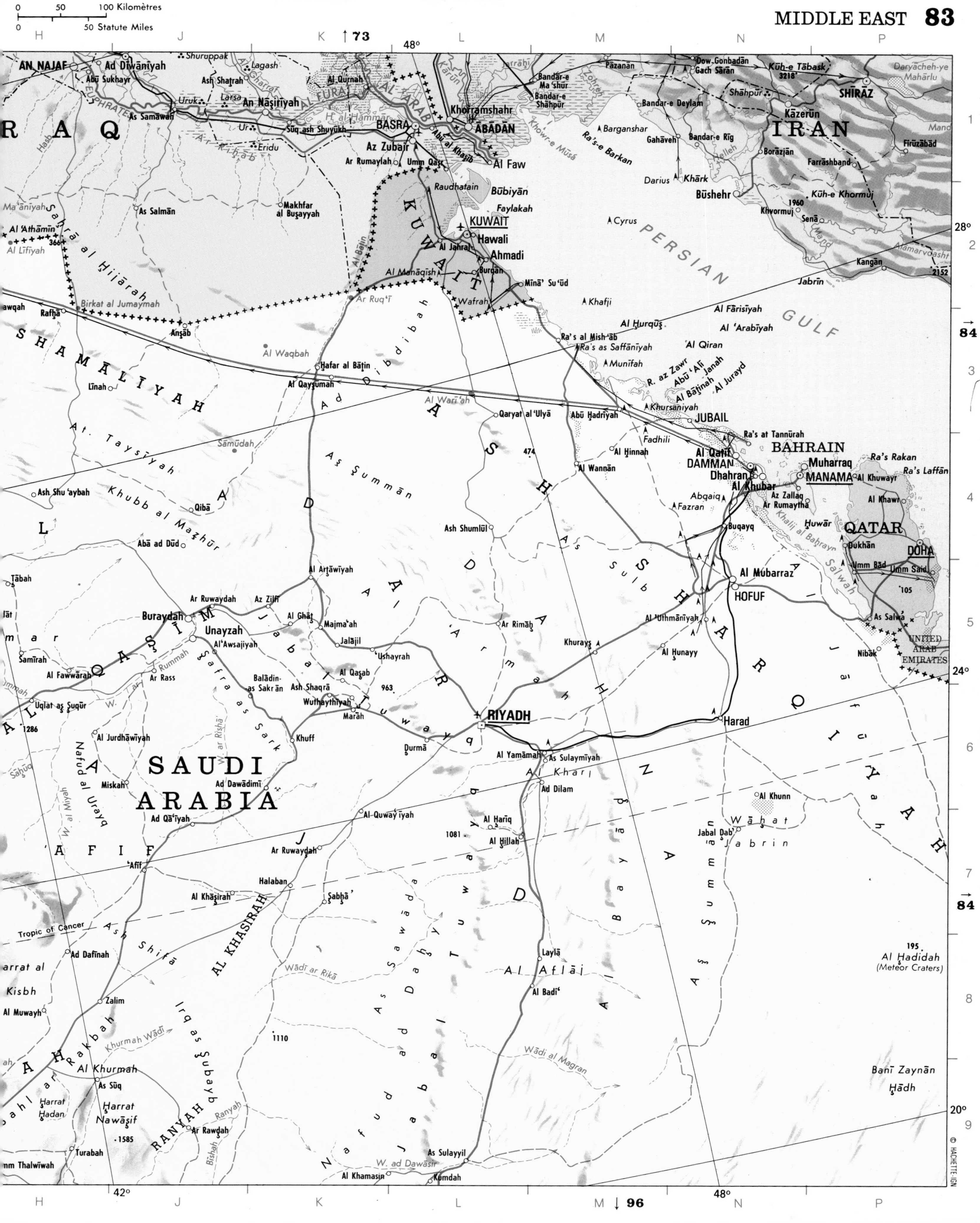

0 50 100 Kilomètres
0 50 Statute Miles

↑73

48°

**I R A Q**

AN NAJAF
Ad Dīwānīyah
Abū Sukhayr
Shuruppak
Lagash
Ash Shatrah
An Nāṣirīyah
Al Qurnah
Uruk
Larsa
As Samāwah
Sūq ash Shuyūkh
Ur
Eridu
BASRA
Khorramshahr
ABĀDĀN
Az Zubair
Abū al Khaṣīb
Al Faw
Ar Rumaylah
Umm Qaṣr
Al Jarrāḥi
Bandar-e Ma'shūr
Bandar-e Deylam
Pāzanan
Dow Gonbadān
Gach Sārān
Kūh-e Tābask
3218
Daryācheh-ye Maharlu
SHIRAZ
Kāzerūn
Bandar-e Rīg
Gahāveh
Shāhpūr
Barganshar
Ras-e Barkan
IRAN
Firūzābād
Borāzjān
Farrāshband
Khārk
Darius
BŪSHEHR
Kūh-e Khormūj
1960
Kūh-e Khormūj
Khvormūj
Senā
Kangān
2152
Hāmarvdasht
Mano

Ma'anīyah
Al Athāmīn
360
Al Līfīyah
As Salmān
Makhfar al Buṣayyah
Raudhatain
Būbiyān
Faylakah
KUWAIT
Hawali
Ahmadi
Burgān
Mīnā' Su'ūd
Khafji
PERSIAN
Cyrus
Jabrīn
28°

awqah
Rafḥā
Birkat al Jumaymah
Anṣāb
Al Manāqīsh
Ar Ruq'ī
Wafrah
Ra's al Mish'āb
Ra's as Saffānīyah
Al Hurqūṣ
Al Fārisīyah
Al 'Arabīyah
Al Qirān
Munīfah
GULF
→ 84

**SHAMĀLĪYAH**
At. Taysīyah
Līnah
Al Waqbah
Ḥafar al Bāṭin
Al Qayṣūmah
Al Wari'ah
Sāmūdah
A S H
Aṣ Ṣummān
Qaryat al 'Ulyā
Abū Ḥadrīyah
Khursanīyah
R. az Zawr
Abū 'Alī
Janah
Al Bāṭinah
Al Jurayd
JUBAIL
Fadhili
Ra's at Tannūrah
BAHRAIN
Muharraq
Ra's Rakan
Ra's Laffān

**A L  Q A S I M**
Buraydah
Unayzah
Al'Awsajīyah
Az Zilfī
Ar Ruwaydah
Al Ghāṭ
Majma'ah
Jalājil
Ushayrah
Al Qaṣab
963
Ash Shaqrā
Balādin-as-Sakrān
Wuthaythīyah
Marāḥ
Durmā
RIYADH
Al Yamāmah
As Sulaymīyah
Ar Rimāḥ
Ash Shumlūl
474
Al Wannān
Al Ḥinnah
Al Qaṭīf
DAMMAN
Dhahran
Al Khubar
MANAMA
Al Khuwayr
Al Khawr
Abqaiq
Fazran
Az Zallaq
Ar Rumaythā
Huwār
QATAR
Dukhān
DOHA
105
Umm Bāb
Umm Saīd
As Salwā
Buqayq
Al Mubarraz
HOFUF
Al 'Uthmānīyah
Khuf
Samīrah
Al Fawwārah
Ar Rass
Uqlat aṣ Ṣuqūr
1286
Al Jurdhāwīyah
Miskah
Ad Dawādimī
Ad Qā'īyah
Khuff
Al Khārj
Ad Dilam
24°

**SAUDI ARABIA**
'AFIF
'Afif
Ar Ruwaydah
Halaban
Al Khāṣirah
Ṣabḥā'
Al Hāriq
1081
Al Hillah
Al Quway'īyah
Khurays
Al Hunayy
Nibāk
UNITED ARAB EMIRATES
→ 84

Tropic of Cancer
Ash Shitā'
AL KHASIRAH
Wādī ar Rikā
Jabal Dab'
Wāhat al Jabrin
Layla
Al Aflāj
Al Badi'
195
Al Hadidah
(Meteor Craters)

Kisbh
Al Muwayh
Zalim
Irq aṣ Ṣubayb
1110
Wādī al Magran

A Ḥrakbah
Al Khurmah
As Sūq
Harrat Hadan
Harrat Nawāṣif
Ar Rawdah
RANYAH
Turabah
m Thalwīwah
Bishah Wādī
Ranyah
1585
As Sulayyil
Al Khamāsin
W. ad Dawāsir
Komdah
Banī Zaynān Ḥādh
20°

42°        48°
↓96

© HACHETTE-IGN

H   J   K   L   M   N   P

Scale 1 : 5,000,000

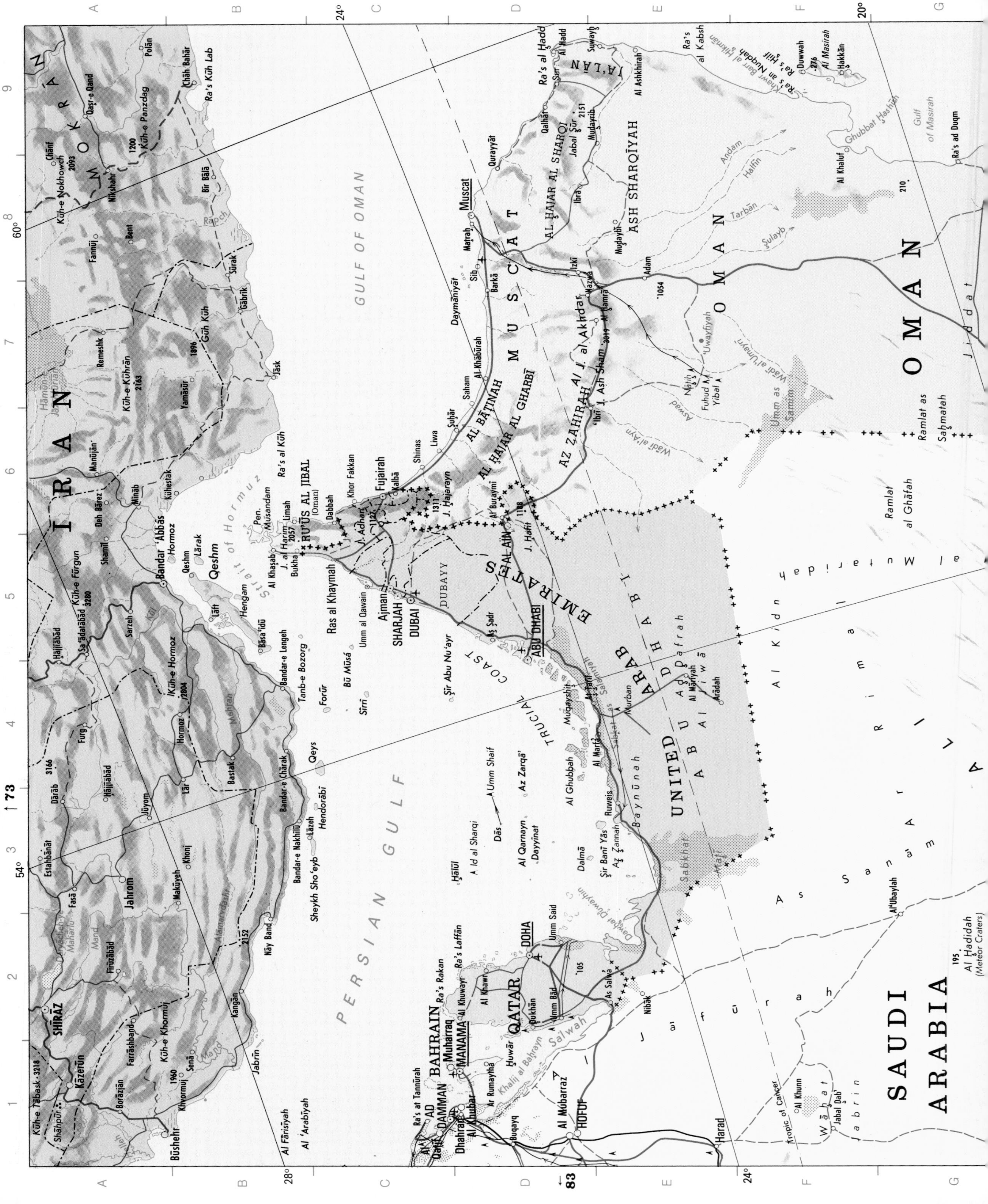

IRAN

SAUDI ARABIA

OMAN

MUSCAT

UNITED ARAB EMIRATES

ABU DHABI

QATAR

BAHRAIN

DUBAI

SHARJAH

PERSIAN GULF

GULF OF OMAN

Gulf of Masirah

Strait of Hormuz

TRUCIAL COAST

AL BĀTINAH

AL HAJAR AL GHARBĪ

AL HAJAR AL SHARQĪ

ASH SHARQĪYAH

AZ ZAHIRAH

RUŪS AL JIBAL (Oman)

Pen. Musandam

AL BĀTINAH

Muscat
Maṭraḥ
Sīb
Barkā
Suḥār
Shinas
Liwā
Al Khābūrah
Qurayyāt
Ra's al Hadd
Al Hadd
Sūr
Qalhāt
Mudayrib
Ibrā
Izki
Nazwā
Adam
Al Ashkhirah
Al Khaluf
Ra's ad Duqm

Khor Fakkan
Fujairah
Kalbā
Dabbah
Limah
Bukha
Al Khaṣab
Dibā
J. al Harim
Ra's al Kūh

Ras al Khaymah
Umm al Qawain
Ajman
Umm al Dawain
Al 'Ain
Al Buraymi
J. Ḥajarayn
J. Hafīt

Abu Dhabi
Aṣ Ṣadr
Al Marfa'
Muqayshit
Ṣīr Banī Yās
Murban
Ḍas
Dalmā
Az Zannah
Ruweis
Umm Said
As Salwā
Nibāk

DOHA
Manama
Muharraq
Al Khuwayr
Dukhān
Umm Bāb
Al Khawr
Al Mubarraz

AD DAMMAN
Al Khubar
Dhahran
Al Hofuf
Harad
Al Khunn
Jabal Dāb
Al 'Ubaylah
Al Hadidah (Meteor Craters)

Ramlat al Ghāfah
Al Kidn
el Mutaridah
Ramlat as Saḥmatah
Wādī al 'Ayn

SHIRAZ
Kāzerūn
Būshehr
Jahrom
Lār
Bastak
Bandar 'Abbās
Bandar-e Lengeh
Qeshm
Hormoz
Lārak
Bandar-e Charak
Qeys
Jāsk
Bent
Fannūj

Tropic of Cancer

PERSIAN GULF

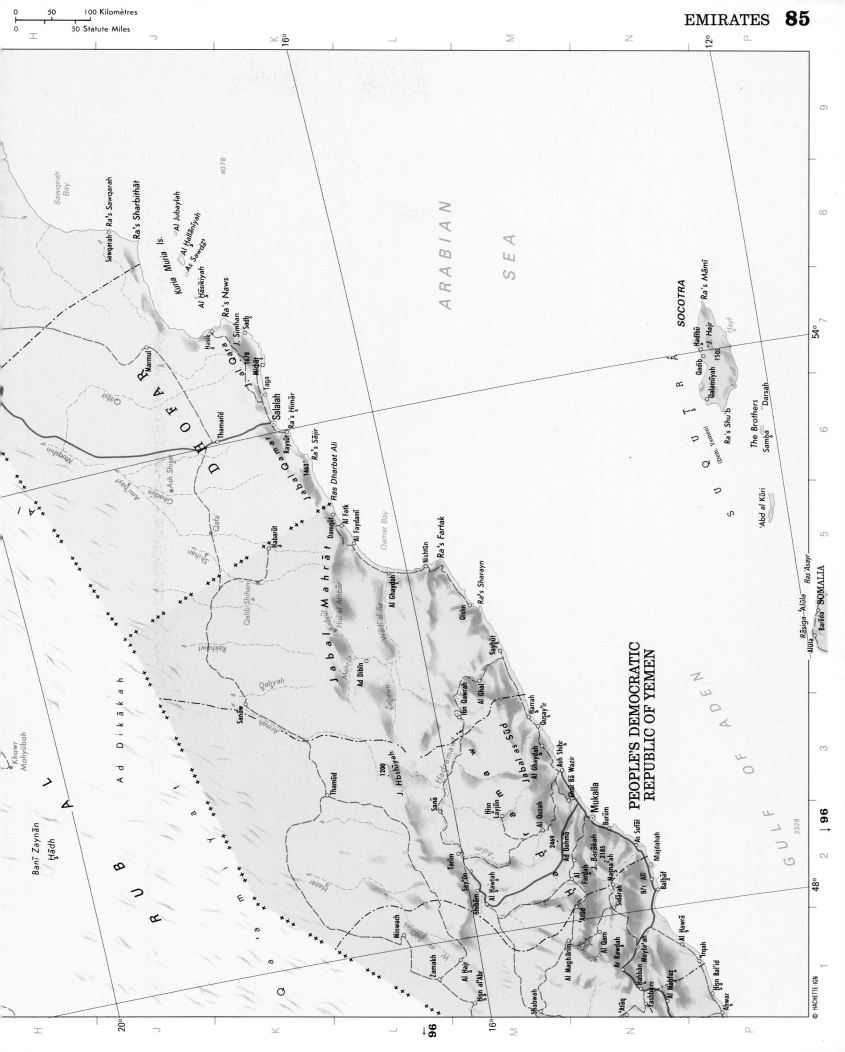

Scale 1 : 5,000,000

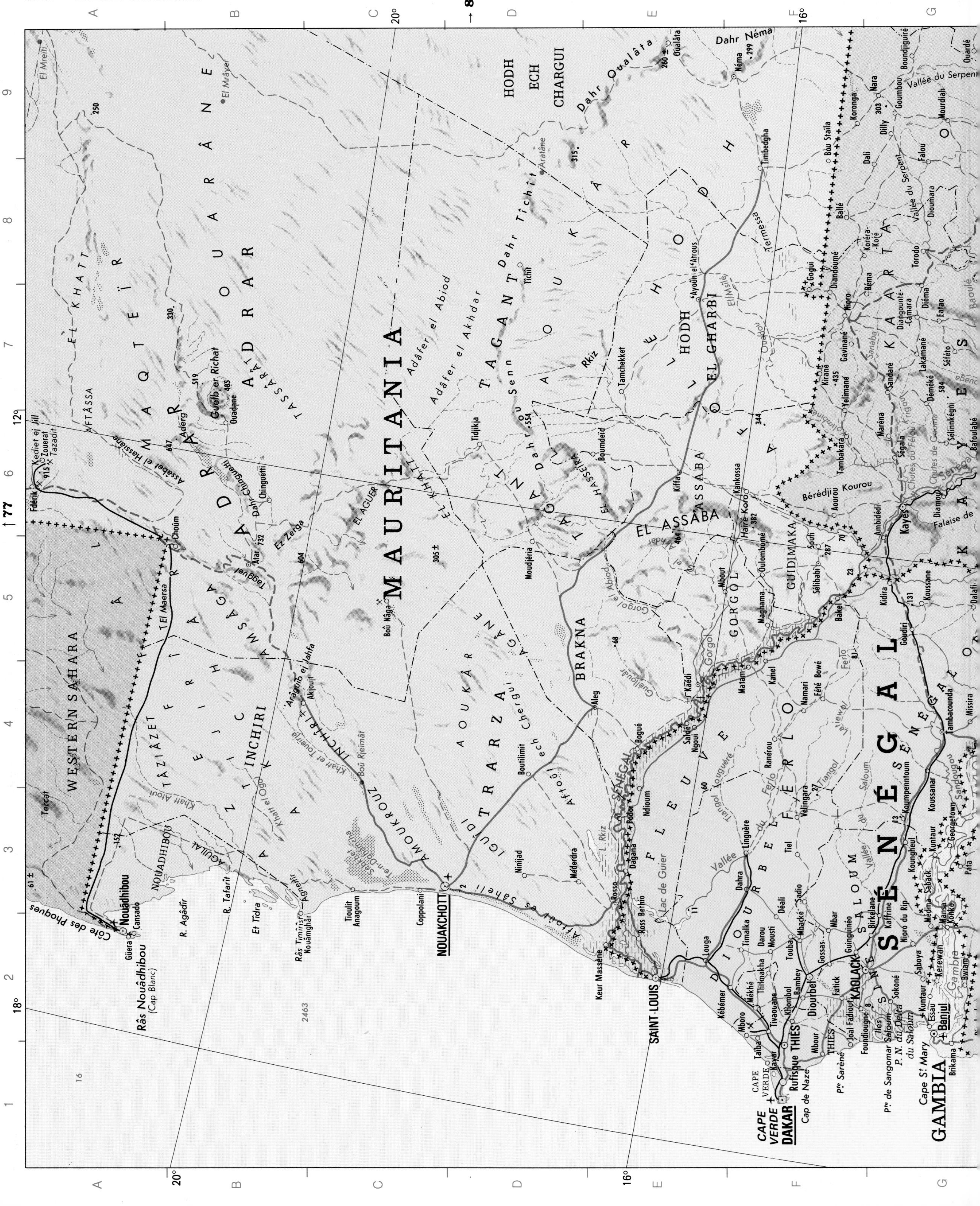

WESTERN SAHARA

MAURITANIA

SÉNÉGAL

GAMBIA

HODH ECH CHARGUI

HODH EL GHARBI

EL ASSABA

BRAKNA

TRARZA

INCHIRI

ADRAR

TAGANT

GUIDIMAKA

GORGOL

KAARTA

NOUAKCHOTT

DAKAR

SAINT-LOUIS

THIÈS

KAOLACK

Banjul

Nouâdhibou

Râs Nouâdhibou (Cap Blanc)

Atâr

Chinguetti

Tidjikja

Tichit

Néma

Oualâta

Kayes

Bakel

Matam

Kaédi

Rosso

Aleg

Boghé

Podor

Dagana

Louga

CAPE VERDE

Cap de Naze

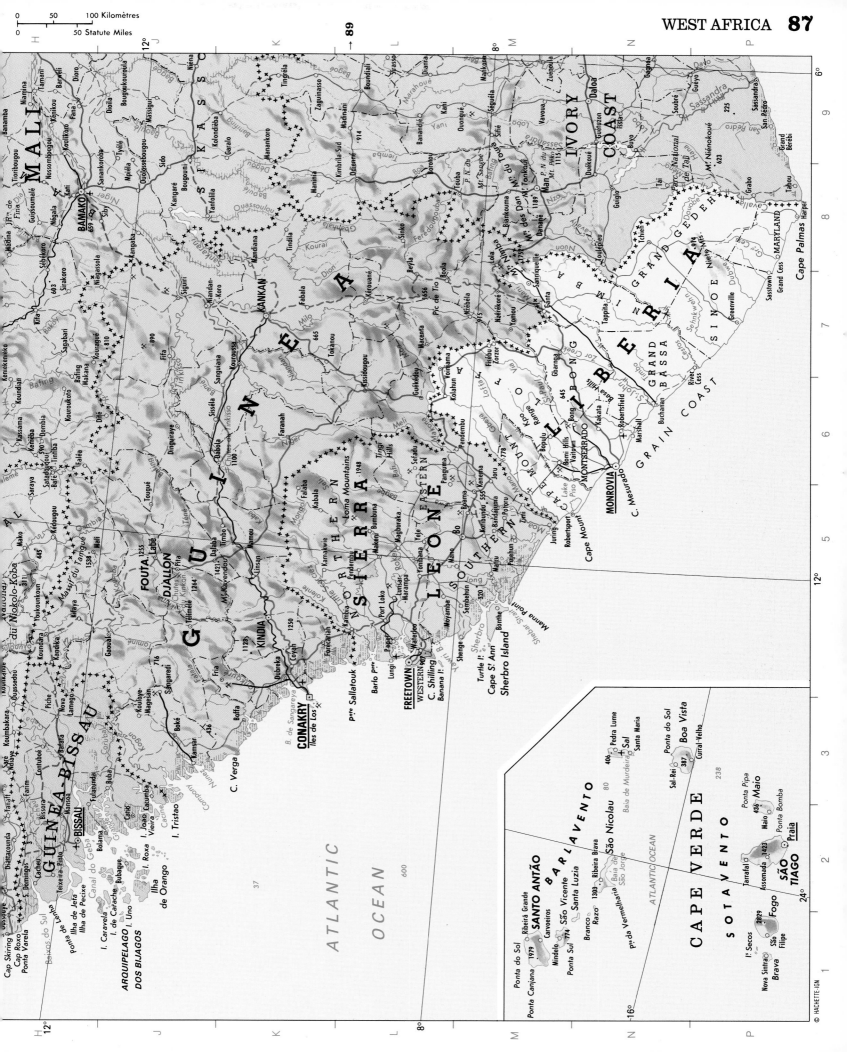

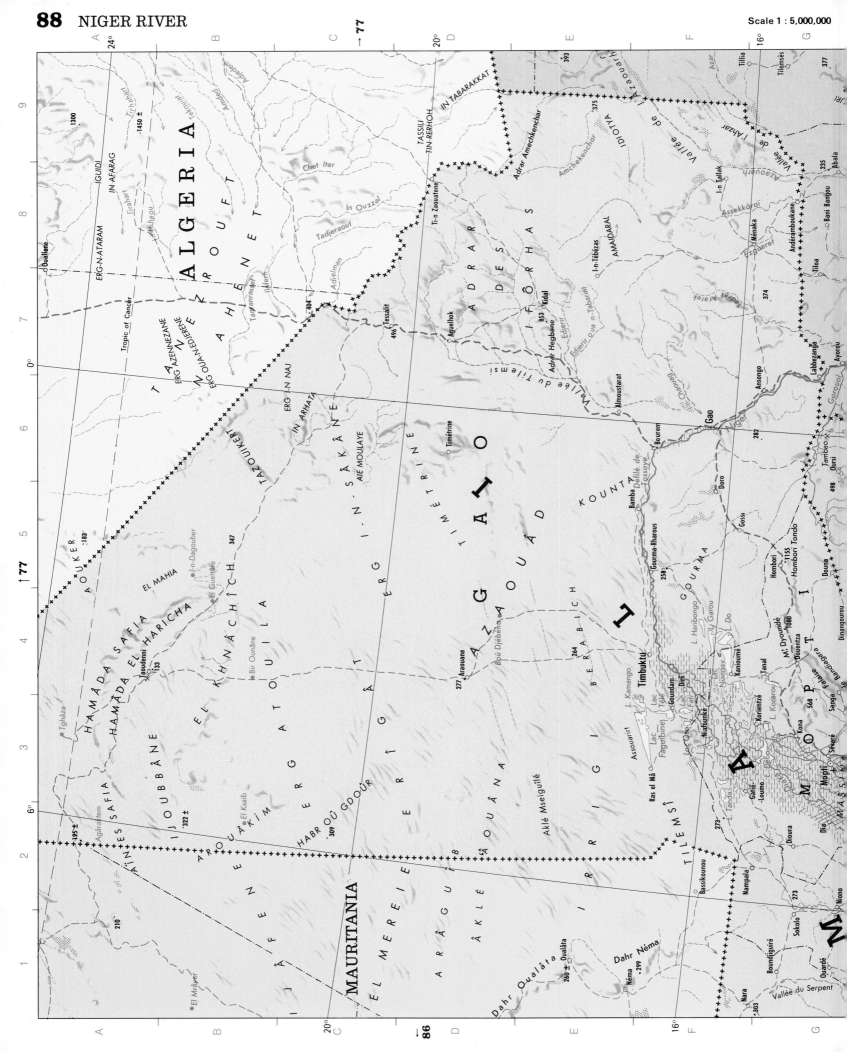

100 Kilomètres
50 Statute Miles

NIGERIA

BENIN

TOGO

GHANA

BURKINA-FASO

IVORY COAST

GULF OF GUINEA

Bight of Benin

NIAMEY

OUAGADOUGOU

ACCRA

LAGOS

IBADAN

ABIDJAN

LOMÉ

COTONOU

PORTO NOVO

BOBO-DIOULASSO

© HACHETTE, IGN

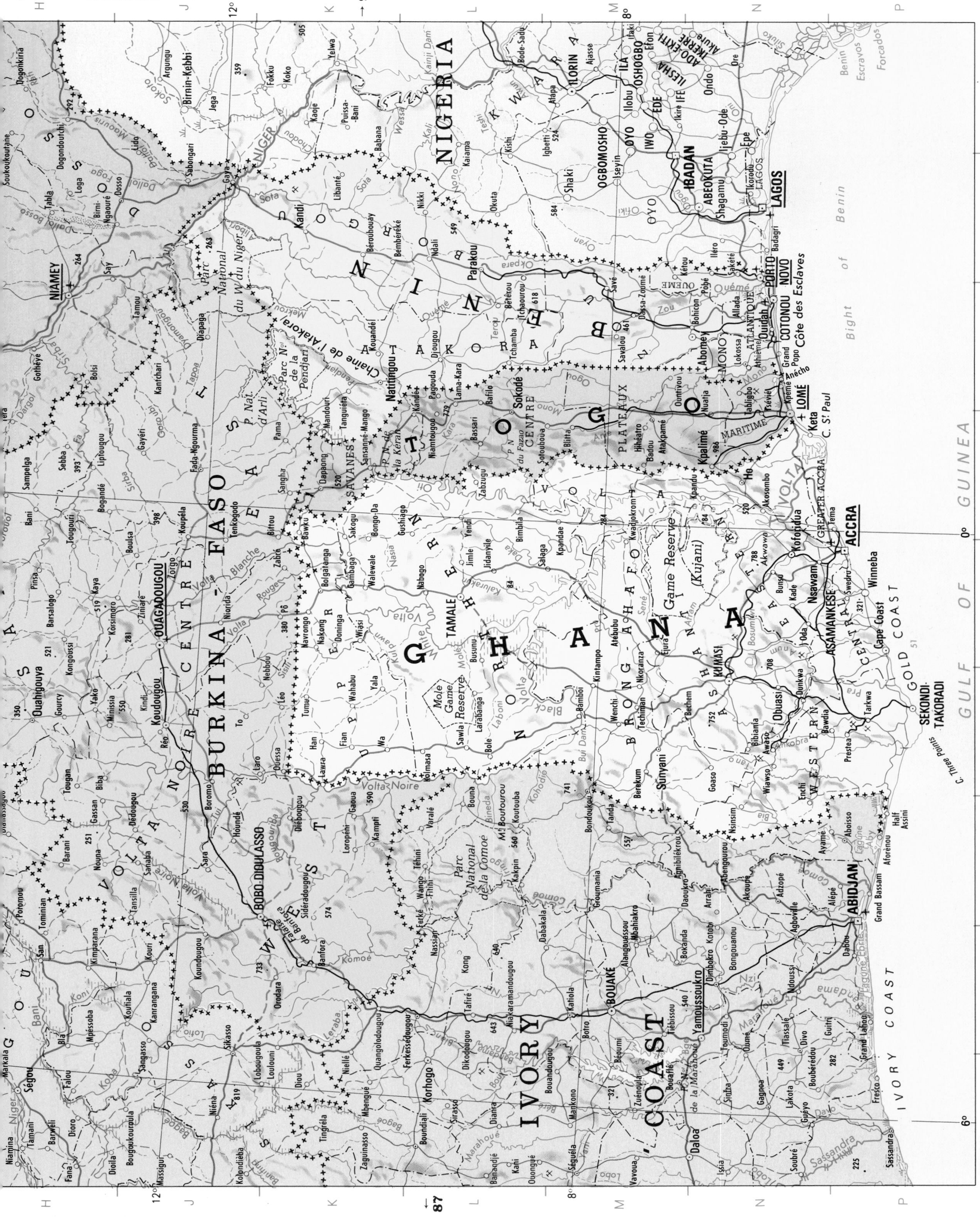

NIGER

MOUNIO

Birni-Nkonni   Dabnou   Madaoua   Koukouta
Dogueraoua   Vallée du Goulbin Kaba   Tessaoua   Damagaram-Takaya   Dellakori
Rima   MARADI   Gazaoua   Zinder   Guidimouni   Gouré
Marnona   Maradi   519   Takiéta   Mirria 661   Guidiguir   458   Goudoumaria   Nguig   Rig-Rig
Sokoto   350   Katsina   Daura   Matamèye   Maïné-Soroa   Diffa   Bosso
538   Jibiya   Magaria   Burum Gana   Komadugu Yobé   Baga   287

SOKOTO   Gummi   Zurmi   Kaura Namoda   Sankara   Gumel   Hadejia   Nguru   Gashua   Geidam   Mongonu   Marte   Dje

Zuru   Wasagu   Gusau   Zamfara   Malumfashi   KANO   Wudil   Azare   Potiskum   Damaturu   Gubio   Dikwa   BORNO
505   Kirto   Sakaba   KANO   742   Funtua   Birnin-Kudu   586   Kari   MAIDUGURI   Bama
Yelwa   Bunsuru   ZARIA   Darazo   Buni   Biu   Yerwa   Ndjigui   Parc Nat. de Waza
Kontagora   686   Birna-Gwari   Panbeguwa   Bauchi   Gombe   Bu   Mora   1442   Méri   Bogo   Mokolo   MAROUA
NIGER   KADUNA   KADUNA   920   Kachia   Jos   1693   BAUCHI   Bauchi   Biliri   Gombi   1350   Mubi   Bourrah   Guider   Kaélé   Mindif
Tegina   Mt Giggan   Kafanchan   Yankari Game Reserve   862   Peské   Bori   Guider 1000   Léré   Mayo Kebi   234
420   Minna   Lapai 611   Abuja   Wamba   Pankshim 1586   Shendam   Zurak   Numan   Garoua   Palar
Bode-Sadu   330   Bida   Pategi   Baro   Keffi   Nasarawa   945   Lafia   PLATEAU   Ankwé   Kam   Yola   P. Nat. de la Bénoué   197   Rey Bouba   Tchollire-Djarendi
Lafiagi   Ajasse   Egbe   683   Benue   Wukari   Ataraba   1500   Kontcha   Mbé   1605   P. Nat. de Bouba-Njida
ILA   Ifaki   Lokoja   Kabba   Okene   Ayangba   Makurdi   Ndoro Hills   Wonka Hills   1676   Réserve du Faro   1960   Moungel   Vina   1923
ADO-EKITI   Ikare   Oka   Echau   Otukpo   Gboko   BENUE   Takum   Wanga   Gotel Mountains   1799   ADAMAWA   Tignere   Ngaoundéré
ILESHA   IKERRE   Akure   Owo   Ifon   Idah   Otukpa   Ombi   Obudu   1152   Mts   1610   2460   Galim   Tibati   1327   Bagodo   Meiganga
Ondo   Ore   Ubiaja   Nsukka   Ogoja   Obudu   Nkambé   Banyo   Martap
BENIN CITY   ENUGU   526   ANAMBRA   Abakaliki   Ikom   NORD OUEST   Wum   Njinikom   Banso   Mayo Darlé   Garoua Boulai   Baboua
Agbor   Asaba   Afikpo   Obubra   Oban   2034   Bamenda   2335   Foumban   Bétaré Oya
Sapele   Kwale   ONITSHA   Ihiala   Ikot   Oban 1067 Hills   Mamfé   Monts Bamboutos 2740   Mbouda   Foumbot   Yoko   Belabo   Batouri
Warri   Borutu   IMO   Owerri   Umuahia   Ekpene   Itu   SUD OUEST 1117   Dschang   Bafoussam   Bafang   Bangangté 1585   Bafia   Nanga-Eboko   Minta   Bertoua   Nguélémendouka   Doumé
RIVERS   ABA   Calabar   Mt Rumpi   Manengouba   2396   Nkongsamba   Loum   Ndikiniméki   Bokito   Ntui   1023   Essé
PORT-HARCOURT   Elele   Buan   Oron   Mt Mbanga   Ekoundou   Titi   Kumba   Yabassi   Ngambé   Ndom   Monatélé   Saa   Nanga-Eboko   Abong Mbang
Yenagoa   Nembe   Opobo   Eket   Cameroun 4070   Buéa   Tiko   DOUALA   1295   YAOUNDÉ   Ayos   Akonolinga   Méssaména   Yokadoum
Bonny   31   Limbe (Victoria)   Edéa   Eséka   Mbalmayo   Okola   Obala   Doumé
Mouths of the River Niger   MALABO   Pic de Basile 3106   Riaba   Rio de Douala-Edéa   Lolodorf   Nyong   Réserve du Dja   Lomié
BIOKO (FERNANDO POO)   Luba   Baie Panavia   Kribi   Kienke   Ebolowa   Mengong   Sangmélima   Bek
GULF OF GUINEA   Bight of Biafra   EQUATORIAL   Rio de Campo   Ntem   Ambam   Djoum   464
GUINEA   RIO MUNI   Bata   Niefang   Ebébiyin   Bitam   GABON   Minvoul   Souanké
Campo   Ntem   Oveng   Ayina

CAMEROON

NIGERIA

100 Kilomètres
50
0
50 Statute Miles
0

18°  24°

**CHAD**

NEM  M
BATHA  OUADDAÏ  DARFUR

Am Zoèr  Kutum
Plat. de  J. Gurgei  Mellit
Moussoro  Guélafara  2397  El Fasher
Ngouri  Haraz  Abéché  Kernoya  Kabkabiyah
Massakori  Ifénat  Id el Gara  Geneina  J. Marrah
Ngoura  Djedaa  Am Guérèda  Adré  Hilléket  Zalingei  3088  Jadïd Ra's al Fil
Terset  Yao  Oum Hadjer  Am Dam  Adé  Duju  Garsila  1512  Dibs  Menawashei
AMENA  Am Djéména  761  Saraf  Makokou  1133  **SUDAN**
Moyto  290°  L. Fitri  Mangalmé  Goz Beïda  Mongororo  Kubbum  Nyala  Beringil
Kamé  Bokoro  Mongo  Gabassour  1053  12°
Massaguet  Arboutchatak  Bitkine  1506  Miélé  792  Tedji  Hajar Banga  Idd al Ghanam
Bili  Massalassef  Mt. de Guéra  Abou Déia  El Kouk  Seïfou  705  Rahad al Bardï  Tullus
Massénya  Badanga  1613  Djébren  Zakouma  Am Timan  Fongoro  Rajaj
Mousgougou  Melfi  1124  Bédi  SALAMAT  Koubo Abou Gara  Goz Sassoulko  Am Dafok  Buram
Bousso  1091  Lairi  Daguéla  Koungouri  Djouna  Mangueigne  Birao  Al Fifi
Ba Ili  Tari  Karo  Zann  708  Tiéou  Manôvo  VAKAGA  Hufrat an Nahas
Bongor  Ngam  Korbol  Ataouay  387  Takalaou  Boromara  Kokab  Delembé  Said Bundas
Dik  Niellim  L. Iro  Singako  Harazé Mangueigne  Reserve  Mélé  1227  J. Manda
TANDJILÉ  Goundi  Tarangara  Kyabé  Gondey  P.N. St. Floris  Gordil  Tiroungoulou  Ngono
Lai  Guidari  Gayam  Bahr Keita  Garba  Koumbala  Ouandjia  Mt. des Bongo  1330  Toussoro
Kélo  Dono-Manga  Koumra  Sarh  Akoursoulbak  Ouanda-Djallé  Boro
Bénoye  Balkabra  Doba  Moussafoyo  Golongosso  Miaméré  Poto-Poto  1055
Moundou  627  Bam  Maro  Gribingui  Ndélé  Penndé  Ouadda  1039  Bolanda
Baïbokoum  Moïssala  380  Mbo  Bamingui-Bangoran  Krakoma  M. Ngouo
Goré  Kabo  Parc National  Yambala  HAUTE-KOTTO
Paoua  Bolia  621  Ouandago  de Bamingui  Bamingui  Mouka  Adelayé  HAUT
Markounda  Kouki  Batangafo  Bangoran  Madonguéré  Boulouba  Reserve
OUHAM  Bébora III  Kambakota  GRIBINGUI  Yalinga  MBOMOU
PENDÉ  1113  Taley  Crampel  Balakété  Ippy  Bria  de Zémongo
Bozoum  Dékoa  562  Mbrès  Bakala  Ira-Banda  Bakouma  Djéma
Bossangoa  Bouca  KEMO-  Afongo-Bakari  Yakosi  Banangi
**CENTRAL  AFRICAN  REPUBLIC**
Bossentélé  Bodoupa  GRIBINGUI  Grimari  Bambari  Matibika  Banima  Kitesa
Bouar  Bogangolo  Sibut  Transafricaine  Kandjia  BASSE-  Mingala  Dembia
Bossembélé  Yao Malikidza  KOTTO  Bangassou  Rafai  Zemio
OMBELLA-  Yaloké  Possel  Ngadza  691  Alindao  Gambo  Adama
TANBÉRÉ  Gadzi  Korpélé  MPOKO  Sidi  Kouango  Bianga  Kongbo  Ndu  Simango  Baykumbala
Carnot  805  Boali  725  Damara  Pandu  Bavula  Mbada  Kembé  Ouango  Biaketé
Bimbo  714  BANGUI  Zongo  Bokada  Mobaye  Satema  Yakoma  Monga  Bili
LOBAYE  Bodoupa  Bosobolo  Mobayi-  Dondo  Matundu  Senza  Ihgasu
Bouar  Boda  Bodjokole  Mbongo  Mogwaka  4°
berati  Bambio  Mbaïki  Bomotu  700  Yengazewe  Uele  Bondo  Mbuma
Nola  Zinga  Bodjaki  Businga  Abumonbazi  Muma  Angu
SANGHA  Mandoukou  Libengé  700  Bodalangi  Likati  Kumu  Wamani
Salo  Mongoumba  Bodebe  Karawa  Gumba  Titulé
Bayanga  Enyélé  Mawuya  Gemena  Bongado  Balabala  **ZAIRE**  Dulia
komo  Dongo  Budjala  Likimi  Liboko  Bumba  Köle
Imese  Biduni  Dapere  Modjamboli  Ibembo  Paipal
Mokolo Moniangi  Bomboma  Akula  Molanda  Wolikombo  Aketi
**CONGO**  Bokala  Kungu  Lisala  ZAIRE  Bumba  Lolo
Dongou  Gwalangu  Bombamo  Gundji  Roby  Yaolumbu  Bolama  Tokele

18°  **99**  24°

© HACHETTE-IGN

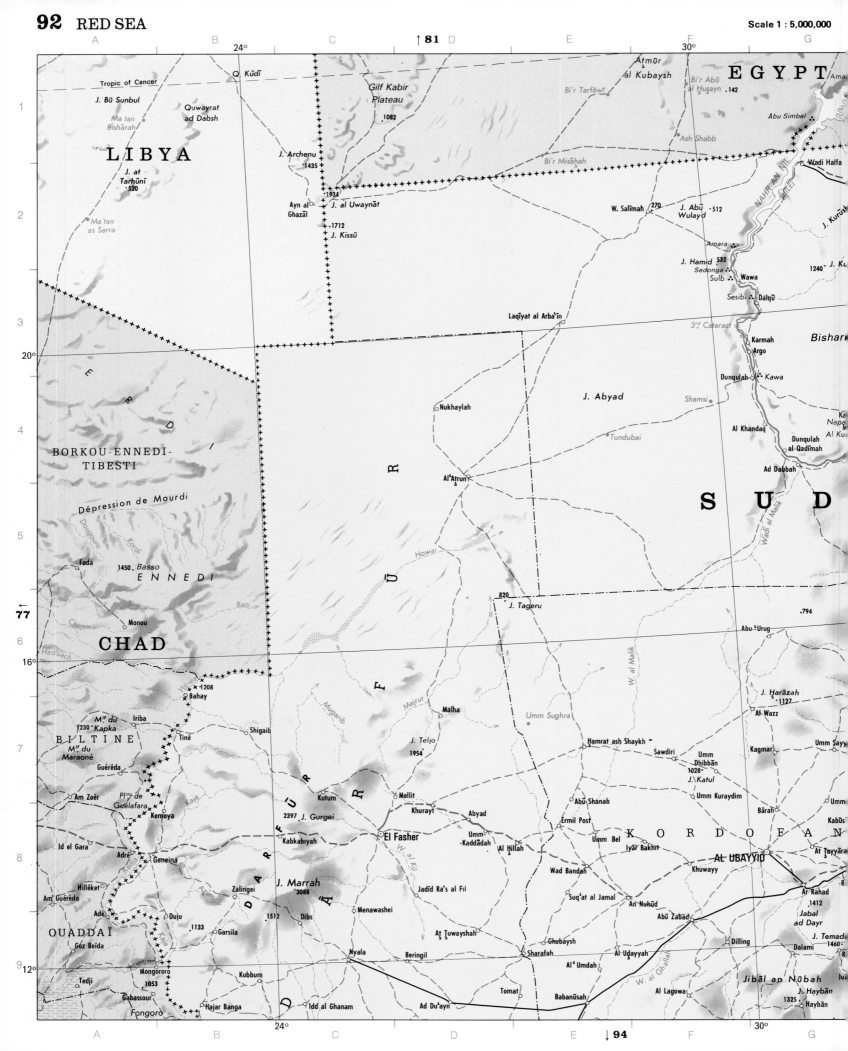

Scale 1 : 5,000,000

Tropic of Cancer

Q. Kūdī

Gilf Kabir
Plateau

Aṭmūr
al Kubaysh

Bi'r Abū
al Ḩuşayn .142

EGYPT

J. Bū Sunbul

Ma tan
Bishārah

Quwayrat
ad Dabsh

Bi'r Tarfāwī

Ash Shabb

Abu Simbel

**LIBYA**

1082

Bi'r Misāhah

Wadi Halfa

J. at
Tarhūnī
.520

J. Archenu
.1435

Ma'tan
as Sarra

.1934

W. Salīmah  270

J. Abū  .512
Wulayd

J. Kurūsh

Ayn al
Ghazāl

J. al Uwaynāt

.1712
J. Kissū

J. Hamid  532
Sedonga
Sulb    Wawa

1240  J. Ku

Amara

Sesibi  Dalqū

Laqīyat al Arba'īn

3rd Cataract

Karmah
Argo

Bishar

J. Abyad

Shamsi

Dunqulah  Kawa

Nukhaylah

BORKOU-ENNEDI-
TIBESTI

Al Khandaq

Napa
Al Ku

Dépression de Mourdi

Tundubai

Dunqulah
al Qadīmah

Douguera
Kordi

Al ʿAṭrun

Ad Dabbah

**S U D**

Fada

1450  Basso

ENNEDI

Wādi al Malik

Sinī

Bao

Howar

820

J. Tageru

.794

Monou

Chiri

Abu Urug

**CHAD**

Haouach

W. al Malik

Howar

.1208
Bahay

Majrur

Malha

Umm Sughra

J. Harāzah
.1127

Mª du
Kapka
1230

Iriba

Shigaib

Al Wazz

**BILTINE**

Tiné

Mugarib

Mª du
Maraoné

Guéréda

J. Teljo
1954

Hamrat ash Shaykh

Sawdiri

Umm
Dhibbān
1028

Kagmar

Umm Sayy

Am Zoèr

Plªu de
Guélafara

Kutum

Mellit

J. Katul

Umm Kuraydim

Umm

Kernoya

Kaja

2397  J. Gurgei

Khurayt

Abyad

Abū Shanab

**KORDOFAN**

Bārah

Id el Gara

Adré

Geneina

Kabkabiyah

**El Fasher**

Umm
-Kaddādah

Al Hillah

Umm Bel

Iyāl Bakhīt

Ermil Post

Kabūs

Aṭ Ṭayyāra

Milléket

J. Marrah
.3088

Wad Bandah

**AL UBAYYIḌ**

Am Guéréda
Balha

Zalingei

Jadīd Ra's al Fīl

Suq'at al Jamal

An Nuhūd

Khuwayy

Ar Rahad
.1412

Umm

Adé

Duju

.1512

Dibs

Menawashei

Ghubaysh

Abū Zabad

Jabal
ad Dayr

**OUADDAĬ**

Goz Beïda

.1133

Garsila

Aṭ Ṭuwayshah

Sharafah

Al Uḍayyah

Dilling

J. Temad

Dalami

1460

Tedji

Mongororo
1053

Kubbum

Nyala

Beringil

Al ʿUmdah

Jibāl an Nūbah

J. Haybān

Gabassour

Hajar Banga

Idd al Ghanam

Ad Du'ayn

Tomat

Babanūsah

Al Lagowa

W. al Ghallah

1325

Haybān

Fongoro

50 100 Kilomètres
0 50 Statute Miles

↑ 82

36° K  L  M  42° N  P

**SAUDI ARABIA**

JIDDAH
MECCA
AT TA'IF
BALJARSHI

NUBIAN DESERT

PORT SUDAN
Suakin
Erkowit
Trinkitat
Tawkav

AL BAHR AL AHMAR (RED SEA)

Jaza'ir Sawakin

Farasan Is.
Zufaf
Marrak

BAIYUDA DESERT

Atbara
Ad Damir

N

Mérōe
Kabūshiyah

KHARTOUM
Khartoum North
OURMAN

KASSALA
Kashm el Girba

ERITREA

Mitsiwa
Keren
ASMERA
Adoulis

Al Qadarif

WAD MEDANI

Sennar
Kusti

Gonder

**ETHIOPIA**

L. Tana
Bahir Dar
Debre Tabor

TIGRAY

Mekele

Dese

GOJAM
Choke

Dindar Nat Park

© HACHETTE-IGN

↓ 95 36°

↑ **92**

A | B | C | 30° | D | **92** | E | F | G

**12°** 1

At Ṭuwayshah
Ghubaysh
Beringil
Sharafah
Al ᶜUmdah
Al Udayyah
Dilling
Dalami
Rashād
J. Temading 1460
Geigar
Ad Damazin
Ar Ruṣayriṣ

Tomat
Babanūsah
Al Lagowa
Jibāl an Nūbah
J. Haybān 1325
Haybān
Abū Jubeyhah
Al Qurdūd
Aworo Kit
Bangjang
Idris
Bobuk
Bikori
Qeissan

Ad Duᶜayn
Abū Jābirah
Al Muglad
Talawdī
Tungaru
Kodok (Fashoda)
Gwa
Malūt
Paloich
Ban Donige
Kayli
Kurmuk
Shali-al Arab
Belfodio

2

Abū Maṭariq
Gabras
Al Malamm
Qurdūd
Riangnom
Fagwir
Tonga
Malakāl
Doleib Hill
Abwong
Wunagak
Yelgu
Mortesoro
Asosa
Bombashi

As Sumayḥ
Abyei
Bentiu
Fangak
Kan
Kigille
Daga Post
Ghemi 2085
Gidami
3301
Tulu Wa

**91** 3

Nyamlell
Madol
Wun Rog
Mashra'ar Raqq
Ler
Adok
Mogogh
Ayod
Wa'th
Nyerol
Nāsir
Jekaw
Itang
Dembidolo
Gambela

Uwayl
Chak Chak
Gogrial
Jur
Kyango
Ayom
Madeir
Maper
Duk Fadiat
Fathai
Faddoi
Akobo
Tori
Abodo
Komaton

**8°** 4

J. Bolanda 1039
Daym Zubayr
Wāw
Tonj
Toni
Gel
Shambe
Duk Faiwil
Kongor
Pibor Post
Lopaye
Gurra

Cheibet
Bo River
Gnap
Rumbek
Akot
Yirol
Jonglei
Baidit
Veveno Khawr
Kangen
Towot 1740
Nelichu

5

M! Dangoura 910
Djéma
Mvolo
Akeu
Papiu
Bor
Tali Post
Tindalo
Jummayzah
J. Kathangor 1063

CENTRAL AFRICAN REPUBLIC
Banangi
Tambura
J. Angeleri 838
Amadi
Terakeka
Medi
J. Lado 1006

6

Kitesa
Mboki
Obo
Nzara
Ibba
Maridī
Baka
J. Odo 1020
Mongalla
Juba
Kapoeta

Gwane
Doruma
Yambio
P. Nat. de la Garamba
Tori
J. Gumbiri 1708
Loka
Rejaf
Ngangala
Torit
Nagichot
Lokichoggio

Digba
Banda
Bangadi
M! Genze 1067
Yakuluku
Yei
J. Lotuke 2795
Kidepo Nat. Park

**4°** 
Pia
Ango
Faradje
Aba 1591
Kajo Kaji
Kinyeti 3187
Napass

7

Ar Uele
Bambili
Amadi
Niangara
Wando
Moyo
Nimule
Madi Opei
Kakamari

Bima
Titule
Bambesa
Dili
Dungu
Tora
Koboko
Yumbe
Laropi
Adjomani
Kitgum
Kitgum Matidi
Loyoro

Kumu
Wamani
Makongo
Gabu
Tapili
Rungu
Ambarau
Watsa
Adranga
Ovujo
Arua
Atiak
Pabo
Pajule
Adilang
Kotido

Zobia
Poko
Tely
M! Tena 1480
Gao
Moto
Arebi
Aru
Rhino Camp
Gulu
Paranga
Moroto

**91** 
Niapu
Viadana
Nekalagba
Mungbere
Gombari
Baku 1365
Nioka
Okolo
Anaka
Lira
Kangole
M! Moroto 3083

8

Y Kole
Medje
Vube
Andulu
Mahagi
War
Pakwach
Nat. Park Murchinson Falls
Azura
Koroto
Orungo
Katakwi

ZAIRE
Sese
Babonde
Wamba
Batsumoni
Mongbwalu
Nizi
Djugu
Mahagi-Port
Butiaba
Masindi
Masindi Port
Keberamaido
Molitar
Namasale
Soroti
Kumi
Ngora

Panga
Bafwazio
Nia-Nia
Nduye
Irumu
Bunia
L. Mobutu Sese Seko (L. Albert)
Hoima
Nakasongola
Bugondo
Kyere
Bukedea

Banalia
Kondolole
Bomili
Adusa
Epini
Komanda
Kasenyi
Gety
2619
1442
Kiboga
1612
Kidera
Pallisa
Busiu

Bengamisa
Mambasa
Nabilatuk
SEBEI M! Elgon 4321

9

KISANGANI (STANLEYVILLE)
Abakwasimbo
Bela
Hoyshá
Bundibugyo
Fort Portal
Kyenjojo
MUBENDE
Mubende
Bombo
KAMPALA
JINJA
WESTERN

Madula
Wanie-Rukula
Manguredjipa
Beni 5119
RUWENZORI
TORO
Kyegegwa
Kahunge
Jeza
Kabulasoke
Mpigi
Lugazi
Mukono
Busia
Tororo

**0°**
Biaro
Opienge
Butembo 2413
Kasindi
Kasese
Ntusi
Entebbe
Nianzi
L. VICTORIA
Port Victoria
Butere

↓ **100** 30°

A | B | C | D | E | F | G

0 50 100 Kilomètres
0 50 Statute Miles

↑ 93

36° H J K L M 42° N P

Gulf of Aden

**Mendi**
Ismala-Giyorgis
Zege
Bahir Dar
Tis Abay
Wichale
Meli
Abe
DJIBOUTI
Eali-Sabih
As Ela
Dikhil
Daouenle
Berbera

1

Beleye
3131
Dangla
Debra Mai
Magdala
Bâti
Aŷsha
Abdal Qadr
Bawn
Bullahâr
Balas
Mota
Keramo
Emba Farit
Dese
Kembolcha
Tareina
Adi Gala
SOMALIA
Booraama
Daba Jog
Issuuugan
1988
Daarburuk

Koko
438
Injibara
Bure
Jiga
Choke
Talo
4154
Mertola-Maryam
3975
Were Ilu
4305
Rike
Abaymeda
Harrawa
1945
Nabadid
Gebile
Bedewanak
Adâdle
Odwêyne

Cherari
Mabil
Debre Markos
Bichena
Molale
12102
Ayelu
Gewani
Dire Dawa
Gota
Alem Maya
Harer
Jijiga
HARGEYSA

2

Vasi
Abay (Blue Nile)
Alibo
Dejen
Tullumilki
Fiche
Deneba
Robi
Debre Birhan
Ankober
Miesso
Deder
3384
Gara Muleta
Asbe Teferi
Bedessa
Gelemso

Ghimbi
3109
Asendabo
Shembu
Gedo
Ketama
Sheno
Sendefa
Megezez
3878
Awash
Eror
Dakata
Fafen

Nekemte
Tuka
Sire
Tibbe
Hiywet
3403
Sabata
Genet Alem
Sululta
ADDIS ABABA
Metehara
Awash
Ramis
Mojo
Fik
Degeh Bur

Argio
Bilo
Debre-Zeit
Borshoto
Awarech

97 →

Metu Yamba
Dembi
Bedele
Koma
Wolisò
Gurage
3719
Nazret
Arba Gugu
Mechara
Gunâ
Dunkata
Mana
Dega Medo
Sasabeneh

8° 3

Agaro
Kossa
Asendabo
Welkite
Butajira
Zwai
Baddaa
Robi
Sirê
Gelolcha
Skek Husen
Segag
1122

Jima
Sambo
3390
Maigudo
Hosaina
Shala
Adami Tulu
Asela
4133
Ticho
Bekoji
Guri
Surur
Auatu
2119
Kololo
Hamaro Hadad

4

2729
Shewa Gimira
Waka
Sodo
Kolito
Shashemenne
Awasa
Hako
4307
Batu
Goba
Megalo
Hara Buri
Imi
Kugno
Omein
Kebri Dehar

Teferi
Bonga
Bole
Yirga Alem
Dodola
Meslo
Tullù Michire
Mendebo
Hara Bonel
Derka Dur
Ididole
Danan
Korahe

Maji
Bulki
Bako
Borodda
Chencha
4200
Gughe
Arba Minch
Delo
3600
Dila
Agere Maryam
Ara Fana
El Mendo
El Kere
Shilabe

5

Weka
Kere
Gidole
Jarso
Negele
Filtu
1690
El Dere
Kelafo
583
Mustahil

Kelam
Hamer Koke
Yabelo
Arero
Malka Guba
Mogu
Dawa Parma
Alamashindo
Yêd
698
Ted 'Eidâr Dabole

1725
Namuruputh
Todenyang
Chew Bahir
Gamud
2486
Mega
El Niabo
Bogbol Manyo
Dôlow
Huddur Hadama
Tayêgle

4° 6

Lokitaung
Illeret
Dukana
Moiale
Ramu
Mandera
Lûq
Wâjid
566
Tôtias

Sogo Hills
Huri Hills
Moyale
784
Garbaharrey
ALTO GIUBA
Isha Baydabo

7

Lodwar
North Horr
1222
El Wak
El Shama
Bûr Hakkaba
600
Madamarodi

Lokicharr
Marsabit
1705
Dobel
SOMALIA
Dinsôr
Saranley

97 →

M! Nyiru
2805
South Horr
Wajir
Salagle
Bârdere
623
Korioley

8

Kalossia
Baragoi
Laisamis
Domadare
Dujûma
Banta
Habay

RIFT VALLEY
Barsaloi
EASTERN
NORTH-EASTERN
Dif
Shabêlle
Ganâne
Barâwe

Cherangani M!
425
Maralal
Wamba
2688
Merti
Habaswein
Muddo Gashi
Lac Bissigh
Afmedow
35
Jilib
Jamâme

9

Edama-Ravine
Kabarnet
Solai
Archer's Post
Lare
Garda-Tula
Isiolo
Meru
Timau
KENYA
BASSO-GIUBA
INDIAN OCEAN

36° H J K L ↓ 101 M 42° N P

© HACHETTE-IGN

PEOPLE'S DEMOCRATIC
REPUBLIC OF YEMEN

SAUDI ARABIA

RUB' AL KHALI

AL HUDAYDAH

SAN'A

TA'IZZ

ADEN

MADINAT
ASH-SHA'B

DJIBOUTI

SOCOTRA
(Dem. Yemen)

RED SEA

GULF OF ADEN

Al Mukalla

Ash Shihr

Shibam

Tarim

Say'un

Ra's Fartak

Nishtun

Qishn

Sayhut

Ma'rib

Sa'dah

Najran

Zahran

Abha

Qizan

Kamaran

Perim
(Dem. Yemen)

Bab al Mandab

Hanish Is.

Farasan Is.

Jabal as Sirat

Ramlat as Sab'atayn

Ramlat Dahm

Hadramawt

Jabal al Qamar

Jabal Mahrat

Bani Ma'arib

NAJRAN

'ASIR

TIHAMAT 'ASIR

Bab al Mandab

Obock

Tadjoura

DJIBOUTI

Assab

Bosaso

Qandala

Alula

'Asayr

Handa

Bargal

Hafun Bay

Ras Hafun

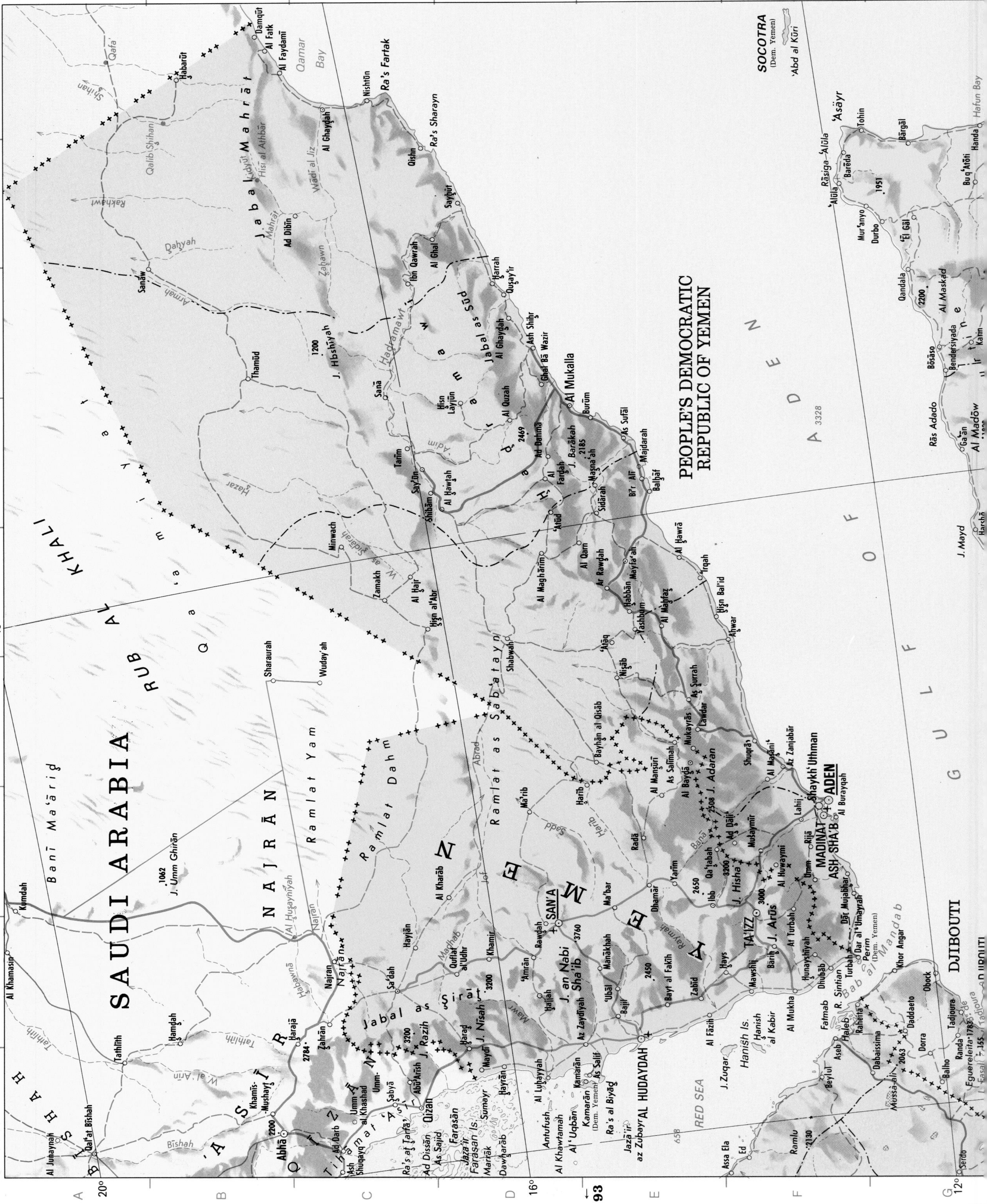

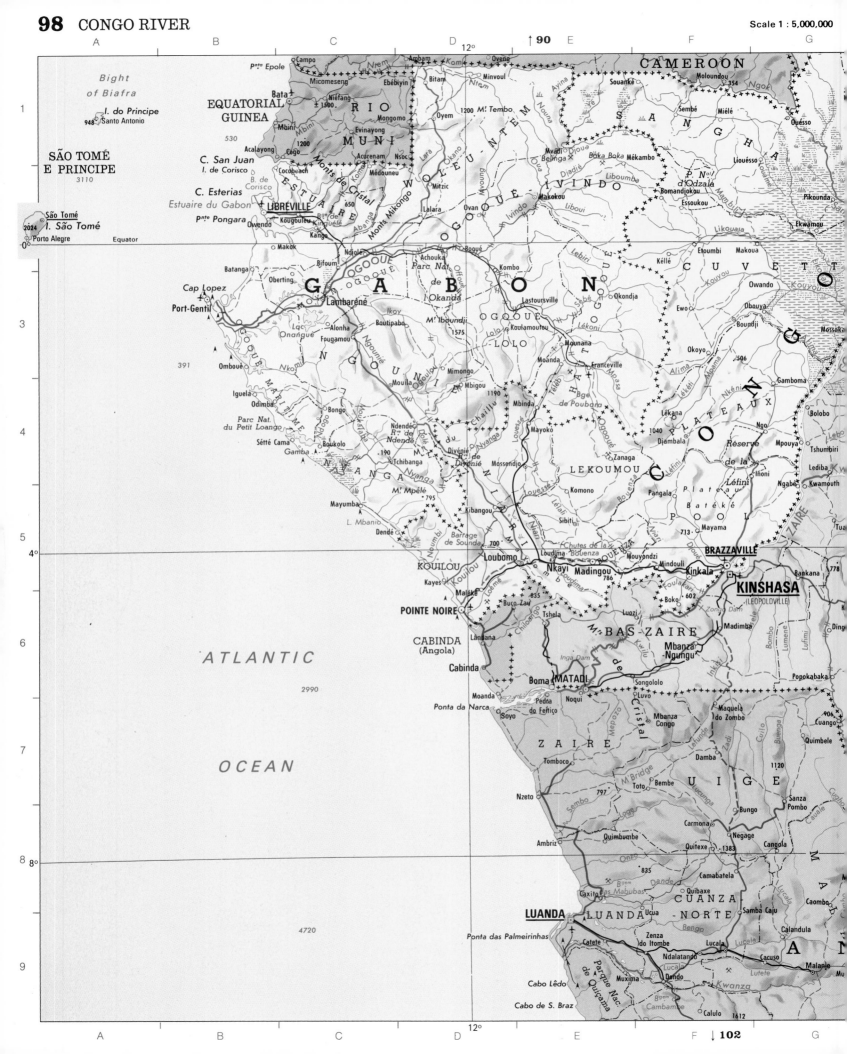

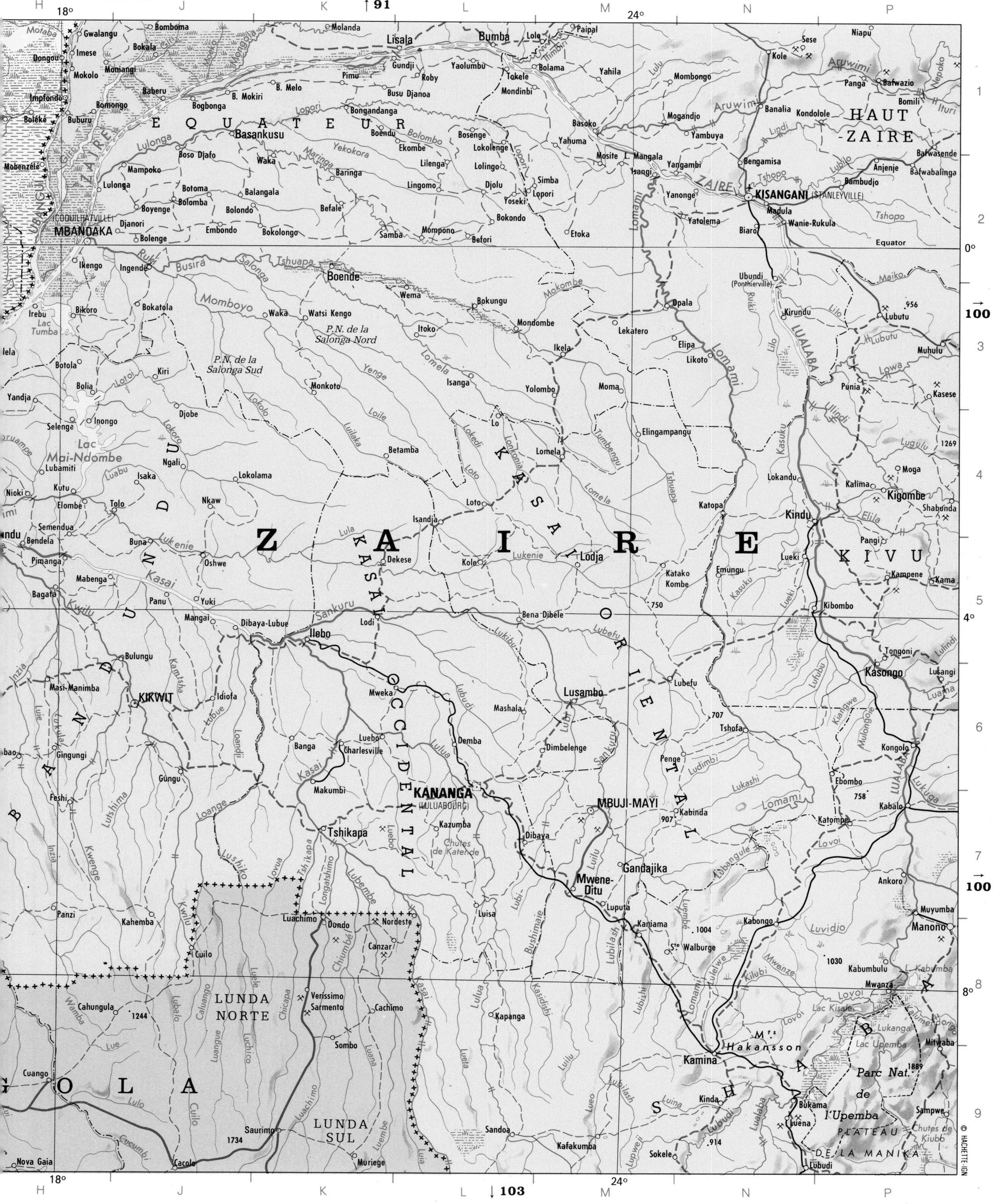

0 50 100 Kilomètres
0 50 Statute Miles

↑ 91

18° H J K 24° L M N P

**EQUATEUR**

**HAUT-ZAIRE**

Lisala Bumba
Basankusu
MBANDAKA
Boende
KISANGANI (STANLEYVILLE)

P.N. de la Salonga Nord
P.N. de la Salonga Sud

Lac Mai-Ndombe
Lac Tumba

**Z A I R E**

**KASAI ORIENTAL**

**KASAI OCCIDENTAL**

**KIVU**

Kindu
Kasongo
Kongolo
Kabalo

KIKWIT
KANANGA (LULUABOURG)
Tshikapa
MBUJI-MAYI
Mwene-Ditu
Gandajika
Kamina
Manono
Mwanza

**B A N D U N D U**

**LUNDA NORTE**

**LUNDA SUL**

**A N G O L A**

Parc Nat. de l'Upemba
PLATEAU DE LA MANIKA
Chutes de Kiubb

↓ 103

→ 100

© HACHETTE-IGN

30° ↑ 94 36°

A | B | C | D | E | F | G

**UGANDA**

**ZAIRE**

**RWANDA**

**BURUNDI**

**TANZANIA**

**ZAMBIA**

**KENYA**

Babonde, Wamba, Batsumoni, N'Gayu, Nduye, Mongbwalu, Nizi, Mahagi, Mahagi Port, Butiaba, Nat. Park, Murchison Falls, Lira, Orungo, Kafakwi, Nabilatuk, Amudat, Kalossia

Bafwazio, Bomili, Nia-Nia, Adusa, Epini, Irumu, Bunia, Kasenyi, L. Mobutu Sese Seko (L. Albert), Masindi, Masindi Port, Molitar, Namasale, Soroti, Ngora, Kumi, Kapchorwa, Kunyao, 3325

Avakubi, Bafwasende, Mambasa, Komanda, Gety, Hoima, Nakasongola, Kidera, Kyere, Bukedea, M' Elgon 4321, Kitale, Cherangani M

Bafwabalinga, Abakwasimbo, Manguredjipa, Bela, Hoysha, Bundibugyo, Fort Portal, Kyenjojo, Kiboga, Bombo, Kayunga, Iganga, Busembatia, Tororo, Broderick Falls, Kabarnet, Tambach

Opienge, Equator, Angumu, Beni, Butembo, Mutwanga, Kasese, Kyegegwa, Mubende, Jeza, KAMPALA, Lugazi, JINJA, Busia, WESTERN, Eldoret, Edama-Ravine, Solai, NAKU

5119, RUWENZORI, TORO, Kahunge, Kabulasoke, Mpigi, Mukono, Butere, Kakamega, Kapsabet

2413, Kasindi, Katwe, Ibanda, Ntusi, Nianzi, Magyo, Port-Victoria, KISUMU

P.N. de Maiko, Lubutu, Lubero, Queen Elizabeth Nat. Park, ANKOLE, Kabula, Bukakata, Kome I., Lolui I., NYANZA, Kendu, Kericho

Muhulu, Lutunguru, Luofu, L. Edward 912, Bushenyi, Mbarara, Masaka, Sese Islands, Mfwanganu I., Homa Bay, Kisii, Mau Escarpment 3098, Nai

Kasese, Walikale, Rwindi, KIGEZI, Rutshuru, Lwasamaire, Sanje, Kagera, Kyaka, Bukoba, LAKE VICTORIA 1134, Muhoro, Kinesi, Tarime, Masai Mara Reserve, Subugo 2683, Narok

956, Lowa, Masisi, Karisimbi 4507, Kisoro, Kabale, Kakitumba, Parc de la Kagera, Byumba, Gabiro, Bumbiri I., Ukara I., Musoma, Ikoma, Loliondo, Mag

Kabunga, Sake, Goma 1460, Gisenyi, Ruhengeri, 1713, Ukerewe I., Nansio, MARA

1269, Lac Kivu, Idjwi, RWANDA, Gitarama, KIGALI, Kibungo, Rubondo I., Kome I., Nyahanga, Serengeti Nat. Park

Kigombe, Shabunda, Kabare, BUKAVU, Kamanyola, Cyangugu, 2767, Nyanza, Gikongoro, Butare, Muhinga, Biharamulo, MWANZA, Ilemera, Nyakabindi, 3648, Loolmalasin

Ikosi, Kamituga, Mwenga, Bubanza, Ngozi, Lusahanga, Geita 1690, Mabuki, Bariadi, Ngorongoro Crater, Oldeani, Manyara Nat. Park

Pangi, Itula, Uvira 3267, Muramvya, Gitega, Ruyigi, Kibondo, MWANZA, Malampaka, Nyalikungu, L. Eyasi, L. Manyara

Kampene, Kama, BUJUMBURA, 2468, Bururi, Rutana 2492, Kahama, Shinyanga, Jomu, Shinyanga, 2417, Leya, Babati

Kasongo, Lusangi, Kabambare, Luhimba 2259, Nyanza, Kasalu, Kibondo, Nzega, Sekenke, L. Kitangiri 1905, Hanang 3418, Kondoa

Tongoni, Kabale, Nyunzu, Niemba, 2575, 773, Kigoma, Ujiji, Uvinza, 1385, Tabora, Singida, Meia Meia

Kongolo, Kalemie, Katumbi 2373, Makari Mtns, Kalya, Mpanda, RUKWA, Karema, Manyoni, Bahi, Gulwe

Ankoro, Muyumba, Manono, Kiambi, Masanga, Moba (Baudouinville) 2460, Zongwe, Kipili, 2351, Inyonga, Rungwa, Ruaha Nat. Park, 2357, Rudi

Kabumbulu, Kabumba, Lake Tanganyika, Kalumbi, Moliro, Sumbawanga, MBEYA, Kipembawe, Selegu 2454, Iringa

Sampwe, Parc Nat. de l'Upemba 1889, Mitwaba, Kilwa, Chiengi, Mweru Marsh, Sumbu Game Res., Kalambo Falls 2068, Mbala, Momba, Chunya, 2142, Sao Hill, Makumbako, Njombe

Kilwa I., Lusenga Plain Game Res., Mporokoso, Mpulungu, Nakonde, Tunduma, 2037, Tukuyu, Mwaya, Chitipa, Ruhudji

Kawamba, **ZAMBIA**

↓ 106

0 50 100 Kilomètres
0 50 Statute Miles

↑ 95

42°

**SOMALIA**

Awdegle

Salagle

Koriòley

MARKA

Shalanbod

Domadare

Dujuma

Habay

Brava

Banta

Shabelle

Mogadishu

South Horr

Baragoi

Laisamis

Wajir

Barsaloi

Merti

Habaswein

Muddo Gashi

Dif

Lac Bissigh

Wamba

·2688

Samburu Game

Uaso Nyiro

Chandler's Falls

Archer's Post

Isiolo

Lare

Garda-Tula

Lak Dera

Afmadow

·35

Jilib

NORTH-EASTERN

NYERI

Nanyuki

Timau

Meru

Meru Game

Equator

0°

BASSO

GIUBA

Jamáme

KENYA

5194

Chuka

Ishiara

Tana

Embu

Garissa

Kindaruma Dam

hika

Fort Hall

Tula

Kismaayo

NTRAL

rdare Nat. P.

Hiraman

Bura

Kolbio

NAIROBI

2123

Kitui

Machakos

Yatta Plateau

Mutha

Ijara

Bur Gabo

Thowa

Konza

ajiado

1500

Jumbo

Ras Jumbo

asai boseli serve

Emali

Kibwesi

Tiva

Wangi

Kwaihu I.

Amboseli

Garsen

Witu

Lamu

Patta I.

KILIMANJARO

5895

Tsavo

Tsavo Nat. Park

Kipini

Lamu I.

Moshi

Himo

Taveta

Voi

Lugard's Falls

Formosa Bay

Arusha

Chini

Bura

Galana

Ras Ngomeni

4005

Nyumba

Mungu Dam

1643

Mackinnon Road

Voi

Mambrui

Malindi

PARE

Same

Kilifi

Takaungu

2612

Mkomazi Game Res.

Kihurio

Rabai

Kwale

460

MOMBASA

Kihuro

2280

Umba

Kilindini

Mkomazi

Usambara Mtns

Kwale

4°

Mombo

Chale Point

INDIAN

Shimoni

Wasin I.

TANGA

Wete

Ras Kiuyu

Korogwe

1129

Muheza

Pemba I.

Handeni

Pangani

Chake Chake

OCEAN

Mkoani

Nziha

PEMBA

Ras Nungwi

Mvomero

Sadani

Mkokotoni

Koani

ZANZIBAR I.

Nguru

2112

ZANZIBAR

Chwaka

Bagamoyo

Ras Kazim Kazi

Morogoro

Ngerengere

Ruvu

Kilosa

DAR ES SALAAM

Kisarawe

2646

Kimhandu

Msanga

Ras Pembamnasi

kumi

eserve

432

Kisiju

Mikumi

Kisaki

Kwale I.

Koma I.

Ras Mkumbi

1590

Kirongwe

Kilindoni

Mafia I.

Madaba

2312

2600

Songo Songo I.

Kilwa Kivinje

·785

Kilwa Masoko

Kilwa Kisiwani I.

4090

42°

© HACHETTE-IGN

Scale 1 : 5,000,000

A · B · C ↑ **98** · D · 18° E · F · G

**ATLANTIC**

**OCEAN**

1360

Porto Amboim
Gabela
.2081
Quibala
Ngunza
Quibala
Mussende
Calucinga
.1690
Andulo
Nharea
1374 Sautar

CUANZA SUL

MALANJE

LUNDA SUL

Cucumbi
Chassengue
Muconda
Dala
Luacano
.1160
Parque Na
da Caméia
Lumege

Cubal
2479
Bimbe

A N G O L

Lobito
Bocoio
Balombo
2620
HUAMBO
Bailundo
Kuito
Camacupa
Cuemba
Umpulo
Munhango
1264

Benguela
Serra do Môco
Chingoar
Vila Nova
Kwanza

BENGUELA
Cuma
Huambo
Coolo
Lumai

Cubal
2286
Lepi
BIÉ
.1553
Cassamba
Luconha

Ganda
1818
Luio

Cuio
Chongoroi
Caconda
Chitembo
Alto Cuito
Cangamba
.1230

2490 Serra da Neve
2418.
Caluquembo
Mumbué
Lumbala
N'Guimbo

Lucira
Quilengues
Cangombe

Cabo de Sta Maria

Cabo de Sta Marta

1921

Bibala
Paiva Couceiro
Matala
Capelongo
Cuchi
Menongue
Chiume

Lubango
Folgares
Colui
Cuito Cuanavale
Chiume

2306
Joao de Almeida
Cassinga

Namibe
HUILA
Cunene
Cuchi
.1214
Mavinga
1119

Giraul
Chibemba
Caiundo
Lomba
Cubia

Ponta Albina
Chiange
Rio da Mupa
1340
Baixo Longa
1260

Porto Alexandre
Serra da Chela
Caculuvar
Evale
Pôcô
CUBANGO
Cuande

Baia dos Tigres
1589
Roçadas
Tandaué
Cuito

Foz do Cunene
Nat. Park of Iona
Cunene
Ngiva
Cubango

Quedas do Ruacana
Kunene
Cuangar
Marunga

Kuring Kuru
Dwase
Okavango
Dirico
Mucusso

Ondangua
Rupfu
Andara

Ohopoho
OVAMBOLAND
Shakawe

Kaap Frio
1783
Ovambo Omuramba
Khaudun
1805

Etosha Game Reserve
Etoshapan
Namutoni
Karakuwisa

Okaukuejo
Tsumeb
Nurugas
Reserve

Kamanjab
Otavi
.2148
Grootfontein

Otjikondo
Okomukandi

Outjo
NGA

1685
Waterberg

Otjiwarongo
1340

2606
Kalkfeld
Sukses

Brandberg
2289
NAMIBIA

Omaruru
Omatako
(SOUTH WEST AFRICA)

Kaapkruis
Steinhausen
Orlogsende

2350
Karibib
Rietfontein
1190
Ghanzi

Hentiesbaai
Erongoberg
Usakos
Wilhelmstal
Okahandja
Sandfontein
Mamuno
Kalkfontein

Swakopmund
DAMARALAND
Brakwater
Omitara
Witvlei
Gobabis

Windhoek
Kapps
1538

WALVIS BAY
(South Africa)
2484

Walvis Bay

0 50 100 Kilomètres
0 50 Statute Miles

H 24° J ↑99 K L M 30° N P

**ZAIRE**

**NORTHERN**

Malonga · Kasaji · Kanzenze · Tenke · Guba · B⁰ de Nzilo · Chutes de la Lofoi · Kienge · Kasenga · Luwingu · Kasama · Chinsali

1088 · KOLWEZI · Kambove · 1718 · Kamangombe · Kalungwishi · Lukulu · Kalungu

LIKASI (JADOTVILLE) · Minga · 1715 · Wiswila · Mansa · Mbawala I. · Isangano Game Res. · Mpika

Mutshatsha · Dilolo · Luashi · Lovua · Mwinilunga · Kipushi · LUBUMBASHI (ELISABETHVILLE) · Sakania · Kabunda · Kampolombo · L. Chaya · 1840 · Lufila

Cazombo · 1614 · Solwezi · Mwenda · Samfya · Lake Bangweulu · Kasanka Game Res. · 1795 · Lavushi Manda Game Res. · Lukusuzi Game Res.

1470 · Macondo · Lunga Game Res. · Chililabombwe (Bancroft) · 1468 · Mokambo · Kabwe · Nsefu · Chipata (Fort-Jameson)

Zambezi · Kabompo · CHINGOLA · MUFULIRA · Chambishi · Kalulushi · KITWE · NDOLA · Mumbwa · Serenje · Kanona · Petauke · Sinde

Lukulu · Kasempa · 1637 · **COPPERBELT** · LUANSHYA · Kapiri Mposhi · 1122 · Luangwa · Nkasanga

**ZAMBIA**

**WESTERN** · Busanga Swamp · Kafue · Nat. Park · KABWE · Old Mkushi · Chisamba · Rufunsa · Zambué · 1448 · Vila Vasco da Gama · Fingoè · 1539

Mongu · 1150 · Kaoma · Mumbwa · Lukanga Swamp · Mulungushi Dam · Lusemfwa · **LUSAKA** · 1280 · Kafue · Miruro · Zumbo · **MOZAMBIQUE** · **TETE**

Senanga · Namwala · Mazabuka · Kafue · ZAMBEZI · Feira · Mâgoé · Caborra Bassa Dam

Kataba · Ngoma · Monze · Chirundu · Angwa · Mecumbura · 872 · Chioco

Silumbu · Masese · Kalomo · Choma · Pemba · Kariba · Mangula Mine · Sipolilo · Mt Darwin

Luiana · 1242 · Zongwe · L. Kariba · 1389 · Karoi · Chinhoyi · Kildonan · Bindura · Shamva

**SOUTHERN** · Sinazongwe · 1432 · **MASHONALAND** · Zawi · Glendale · **NORTH** · Mutoko

Seshcke · Katima Mulilo · Kazungula · MARAMBA (Livingstone) · Binga · Copper Queen · Darwendale · 1656 · **HARARE** (SALISBURY) · Mrewa

Kongola · Kasane · Victoria Falls · Matetsi · Sebungwe · Chakari · Chegutu · **HARARE** · Macheke · Inyanga · 2595

Kachikau · 1108 · Wankie · Dekai · Mlibizi · **MIDLANDS** · Kadoma · Umtali · Beatrice · Marondera · Rusape · Mutare

Panda ma Tenga · Wankie Nat. Park · Dett · Kennedy · Lupane · Gokwe · Kwekwe · Mangwendi · Vila de Manica

**CHOBE** · Ngamo · Gwai · **ZIMBABWE** · Lonely Mine · 1422 · Gweru · Enkeldoorn · 1585 · Mvuma · Chatsworth · Gutu

Maun · Kanyu · Basuto · Nata · Igusi · Queens Mine · Bembezi · Somabula · Selukwe · Mashaba · Masvingo · 2439 · Melsetter · 1292

Makalamabedi · 930 · Makarikari · **BULAWAYO** · Essexvale · Zvishavane · Kyle Dam · 1568 · Zimbabwe · Zaka · Chipinga

Mopipi · Lake Dow · Orapa · 900 · Figtree · 1554 · Matopos Nat. Park · Filabusi · Birchenough Bridge · Espungabera

Khomo · Lothlakane · Francistown · Plumtree · Matopo Hills · Antelope · Gwanda · West Nicholson · Rutenga · Machaze

**BOTSWANA** · **ZINGWATO** · Seruli · Serowe · Selebi-Phikwe · Bobonong · Beit Bridge · Massangena · **MOZAMBIQUE**

© HACHETTE-IGN

H 24° J ↓105 K L M 30° N P

Scale 1 : 5,000,000

ATLANTIC

OCEAN

**BOTSW**

**KALAHAR**

**NAMIBIA**
(SOUTH WEST AFRICA)

**G R O O T   N A M A L A N D**

**D E S E R**

**K G A L A G A D I**

Kalahari
Gemsbok
Nat. Park

**BOPHUTHATSWAN**

Swakopmund
Walvisbaai
Pelicanpunt
**WALVIS BAY**
(South Africa)
Sandvisbaai

Brakwater
Windhoek
Kapps
2484
2421
Dordabis
Rehoboth

Witvlei
Gobabis
1538

Ramoshwani

Pretorius

KHOMAS HOCHLAND

Tsumis Park

Massering

Tropic of Capricorn

Conceptionbaai

Kuiseb

Lidfontein
Aranos
Kalkrand
Stampriet
Mariental

Kang

Hukuntsi
Tshane

Dutlhe

**KWI**

Hollams
Voëleiland

1705

Maltahöhe

Gibeon

Gochas

1130

Kukong

Kakia

**NGWAKE**

Sint Francisbaai

Schwarzrand

Tses

Koes

Werda

Terra Firma
Pomfret

Helmeringhausen

1868
Gr Tiras

Bethanie

Keetmanshoop

Tshabong

Molopo

Hottentotsbaai

Lüderitz

Elisabethbaai

Aus  .1804

Goageb

Seeheim

Narubis

Aroab
Rietfontein

Kuruman

Aansluit

Moshaveng

**Vryburg**

Konkiep

2202

Askham

Lower
Dikgatlhong

Kuruman

Possession I.

839

Holoog

Grünau

Bokhara

Olifantshoek

Sishen

Kuruman-Heuwells

1855

Pudimoe

Bogenfels
Kaap Dernburg

Witputs

Groot Karasberge

HUIB HOCHPLATEAU

Danielskuil

Warrenton
Koopmansfonte

Karasburg

Ariamsvlei

Upington

Postmasburg
**GRIQUALAND
WEST**

Griquatown

Ulco

**Kimberle**

Oranjemond
Alexander Bay

ORANGE
1378
Gamka

Warmbad

Augrabies Falls

Lutzputs

Keimoes

Groblershoop

Douglas

Ritchie

Mo

Steinkopf

Goodhouse

Onseepkans
Kakamas

Niekerkshoop

Koffiefonte
Kalkfonte

Port Nolloth

**NAMAQUALAND**

Pofadder

Kaimoepslaagte

Kenhardt

Marydale
1083

Pieska

Belmont

Hopetown

Okiep

Springbok

1075

Stridenburg

Sodium

Phil
Philipstown

Kleinsee

**C A P E**

Groot Vloer
Verneukpa

Brandvlei

Vanwyksvlei

Britstown

De Aar

Colesberg

Kondeklipbaai

Kamieskroon
1708

Garies

HOË  KAROO

**S O U T H**

Vosburg

Mynfontein

Kom

Swart Doring

Sakrivier

Carnarvon

Merriman

Hanover

No

2600

Bitterfontein

Loeriesfontein

1482

Pampoenpoort

Williston

Loxton

Victoria
West

Richmond

Middelburg

73

Nieuwoudtville

Kootjieskolk

Kompasberg

.2504

Vredendal
Klawer

Vanrhynsdorp

Calvinia

1672

Fraserburg

Three Sisters

1966

Murraysburg

Nieu-
Bethesda

2430

Lambertsbaai

Clanwilliam

Roggeveldberge

Nuweveldreeks

**P R O V I N C E**

Graaff Reinet

Cape St. Martin

Paleisheuvel
Velddrif

Citrusdal

Sutherland
1922

1721

Beaufort West

Luttig

Aberdeen

Vredenburg
Saldanha
Langebaan

Piketberg
Hopefield

Porterville

Laingsburg

Kruidfontein

**G R E A T**

Klipplaat
Jansenville

Baroe

185

Dasseneiland

Darling
Malmesbury

Ceres  Matroosberg
2251

Touwsrivier

Komsberge

Prince Albert

**K A R O O**

Somer

Steytlerville

4600

Robbeneiland
Wellington
Bellville

Paarl
1647
Stellenbosch
Strand

Worcester

Robertson
Villiersdorp  Swellendam
Caledon

Ladismith
2326
Calitzdorp

**SWARTBERGE**

De Rust

Oudtshoorn

Willowmore

Avontuur
1765
Uniondale

Kougaberge

Kpega

Patensie

**CAPETOWN**
(KAAPSTAD)
Simonstown
CAPE OF GOOD HOPE

Hermanus
Walker
Bay

Gansbaai
Bredasdorp
Arniston
C. Agulhas

**LANGEBERGE**

KLEIN KAROO

Riversdale

Witsand
St. Sebastian Bay

Outeniekwaberge
George

Mosselbaai
Kaap St Blaize

Knysna

Humansdorp

Sealpunt

**P.**
**ELIZA**

**Uiten**

St. Francis

50 100 Kilomètres
50 Statute Miles

↑ 103
→ 107

**ZIMBABWE**

**MOZAMBIQUE**

**INHAMBANE**

**TRANSVAAL**

VENDA

GAZA

Kruger National Park

Limpopo

Seruli · Selebi-Phikwe · Bobonong
Serowe · Palapye
Shoshong · Mahalapye · Machaneng
Lephepe
Molepolole · Mochudi
**Gaborone**
Lobatse

Massangena · Save · Inhassoro
I. do Bazaruto
Chicualacuala · Maxaila · Mabote · Benguérua
Vilanculos · Ponta S. Sebastião
Mapai · Mapinhane

Beit Bridge
Messina
Waterpoort · Vivo · Thohoyandou
2046 · 1743 · Soutpansberge · Pafuri
Louis Trichardt · Bandelierkop
Soekmekaar
**Pietersburg** · Tzaneen · Leydsdorp
Duiwelskloof · Letaba
Massingir · Mabalane · Chigubo · Funhalouro
Ponta da Barra Falsa · 132

Tropic of Capricorn · Massinga
Morrumbene
Homoine · Panda
Maxixe · **Inhambane** · Ponta da Barra
Baia de Inhambane

Tom Burke
2085 · Thabazimbi · Potgietersrus · Zebediela
Vaalwater · Naboomspruit · Roedtan · Steelpoort
Middelwit · Northam · Warmbad · Marble Hall · Groblersdal
Nylstroom · Tuinplaas · Ohrigstad · Graskop
Beestekraal · Pienaarsrivier · Lydenburg · Stoffberg
2286 · Skukuza
402 · Magude · Xinavane · Guija · Chokwe
Chibuto · Macia · Xai-Xai · Chidenguele · Quissico
Inharrime · Chicomo · Manjacaze
92 · Mau-é-ele

T542 · Zeerust · Swartruggens · **Rustenburg** · Brits · **PRETORIA**
1853 · Silverton · Bronkhorstspruit · Middelburg · Belfast · Machadodorp
Koster · Nelspruit · Kaapmuiden · Komatipoort
**JOHANNESBURG** · KRUGERSDORP · ROODEPOORT · SOWETO · BENONI · SPRINGS
Witbank · Ogies · Barberton · 1902 · Havelock · Pigg's Peak
Lichtenburg · Coligny · VENTERSDORP · GERMISTON · Brakpan
CARLETONVILLE · Meyerton · Nigel · Heidelberg · Leslie
Delareyville · Ottosdal · Potchefstroom · Lochville · 1917 · Balfour · Bethal · Carolina · Breyten · Lothair
Klerksdorp · Vanderbijlpark · **VEREENIGING** · Villiers · Standerton · Ermelo · Amsterdam
Wolmaransstad · Vierfontein · Vredefort · Parys · Sasolburg · Frankfort · Piet Retief
Makwassie · Bothaville · Heilbron · Vrede · Volksrust · Wakkerstroom
Wesselbron · **WELKOM** · Odendaalsrus · Kroonstad · Petrus Steyn · Lindley · Reitz · Warden · Witkoppies · Newcastle · Utrecht
Brandfort · Theunissen · Ventersburg · Kestell · Harrismith · Dannhauser · Vryheid
Bultfontein · 1418 · Senekal · Bethlehem · Fouriesburg · Glencoe · Dundee · 1448
Winburg · Ladybrand · Ficksburg · Clocolan · Butha-Buthe · Bergville · Ladysmith · Nondweni

**SWAZILAND**
Oshoek · Mbabane · Manzini · Stegi · Góba · Moamba · Marracuene
Hlatikulu · Golel · Gollel · Namaacha
Bela Vista · Catuane · Zitundo

**MAPUTO** (LOURENÇO MARQUES)
Inhaca Island
Cabo de Sta Maria
Inhaca

**ORANGE** · FREE · STATE
**BLOEMFONTEIN** · Dewetsdorp · Reddersburg · Edenburg
Thaba Nchu · Wepener · Maseru · Mafeteng
**LESOTHO**
Maluti Mtts · Central Range · Thabana Ntlenyana · 3482
Mont aux Sources · 3280
**DRAKENSBERGE**
Teyateyaneng · Leribe · Sekakes · Qachas Nek
Mohales Hoek · Quthing · Matatiele · 3002
Smithfield · Zastron · Rouxville · Aliwal N · Lady Grey

Ixopo · Kokstad · Harding · Bizana
Mooirivier · New Hanover · Howick · Richmond · Mid Illovo
Underberg · Glenside · Tongaat · Stanger
Estcourt · **PIETERMARITZBURG** · Pinetown · **DURBAN**
Weenen · Kranskop · Greytown · Amatikulu · Amanzimtoti
Nkwalini · Eshowe · Scottburgh
Melmoth · Empangeni · Richards Bay · Port Shepstone
Mtubatuba · Kaap St Lucia · Margate · Port Edward

Louwsburg · Nongoma · Mkuze
Games Reserves · Hluhluwe
Umfolozi · Sibayameer · Sint Luciameer

**INDIAN OCEAN**

Tarkastad · Whittlesea · 2370 · Winterberge · Cathcart · 2019
Molteno · Dordrecht · Elliot · Maclear · Engcobo · Umtata · Port St Johns
Queenstown · Qamata · Idutywa · Bashee
Adelaide · Seymour · Stutterheim · Butterworth
Fort Beaufort · King William's Town
Grahamstown · Peddie · **EAST-LONDON** (OOS LONDEN) · 2936
Alicedale · Alexandria · Port Alfred

CISKEI · TRANSKEI · Lusikisiki

146 · 3621 · 1472 · 1591 · 40 · 351 · 1472

30° · 36° · 24° · 28° · 32°

© HACHETTE-IGN

INDIAN OCEAN

DAR ES SALAAM

TANZANIA

ZAMBIA

NORTHERN

MOZAMBIQUE

MALAWI

NYASSA

CABO DELGADO

LINDI

MTWARA

RUVUMA

NAMPULA

LAKE NYASSA

L. Tanganyika

Selous Game Reserve

Luwegu Game Reserve

Ruaha Nat. Park

Livingstone Mtns

Kipengere Range

ZAIRE
(Baudouinville)

Morogoro · Kisaka · Kilosa · Mikumi · Ifakara · Mahenge · Kilombero · Iringa · Mbeya · Tukuyu · Karonga · Rumpi · Mzimba · Lilongwe · Dedza · Salima · Zomba · BLANTYRE · Chikwawa · Tete · Cahora Bassa Dam

Mtwara · Lindi · Mikindani · Masasi · Newala · Palma · Mocimboa da Praia · Pemba · Chiure Novo · Macomia · Montepuez · Namuno · Marrupa · Lichinga · Cuamba · Gurue · Mocambique · Mossuril · Angoche · Nampula · Meconta · Monapo · Memba · Nacala

Rovuma · Lugenda · Lurio · Shire · Zambezi · Luangwa · Chambeshi

Lake Bangweulu · Mpika · Serenje · Kanona

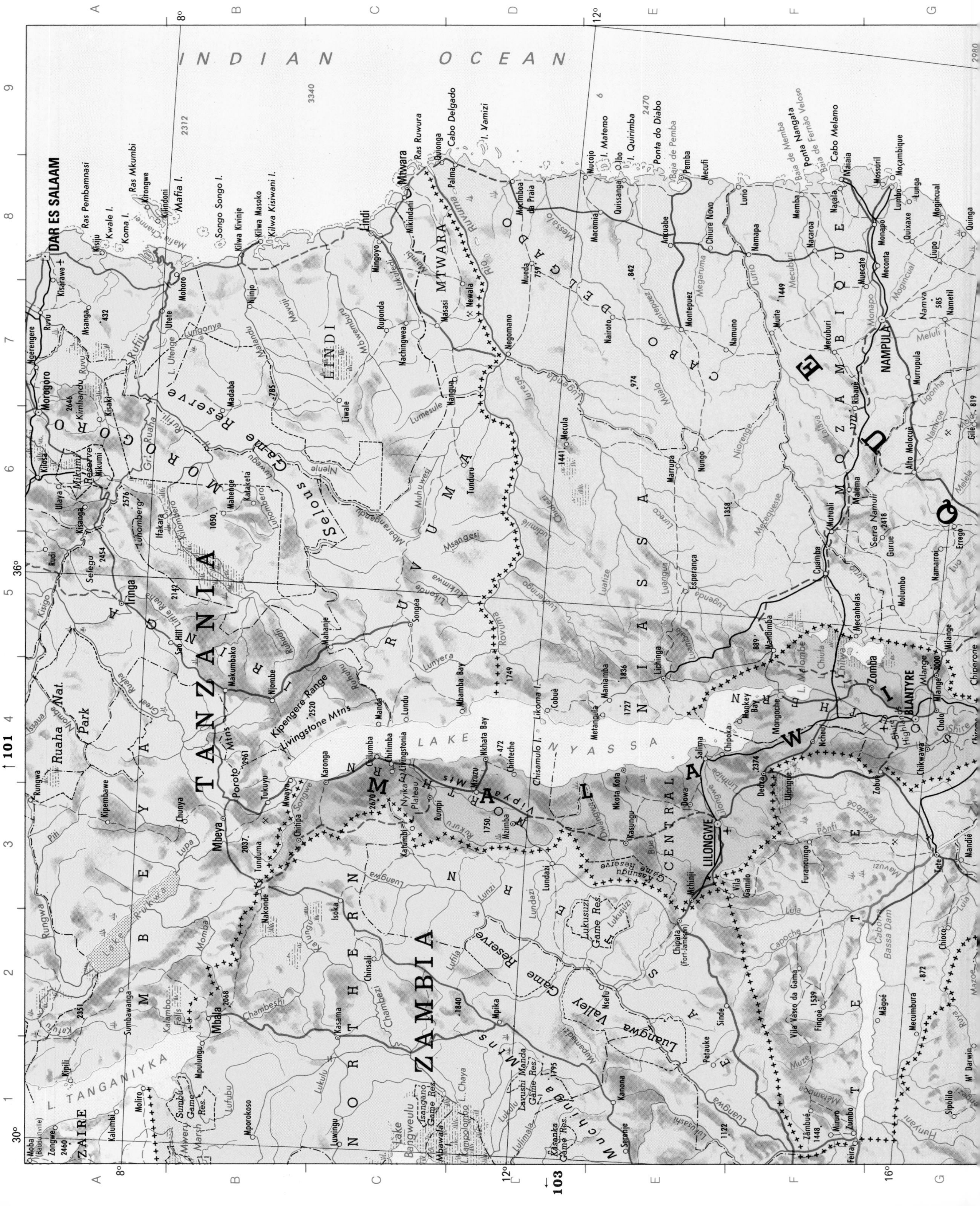

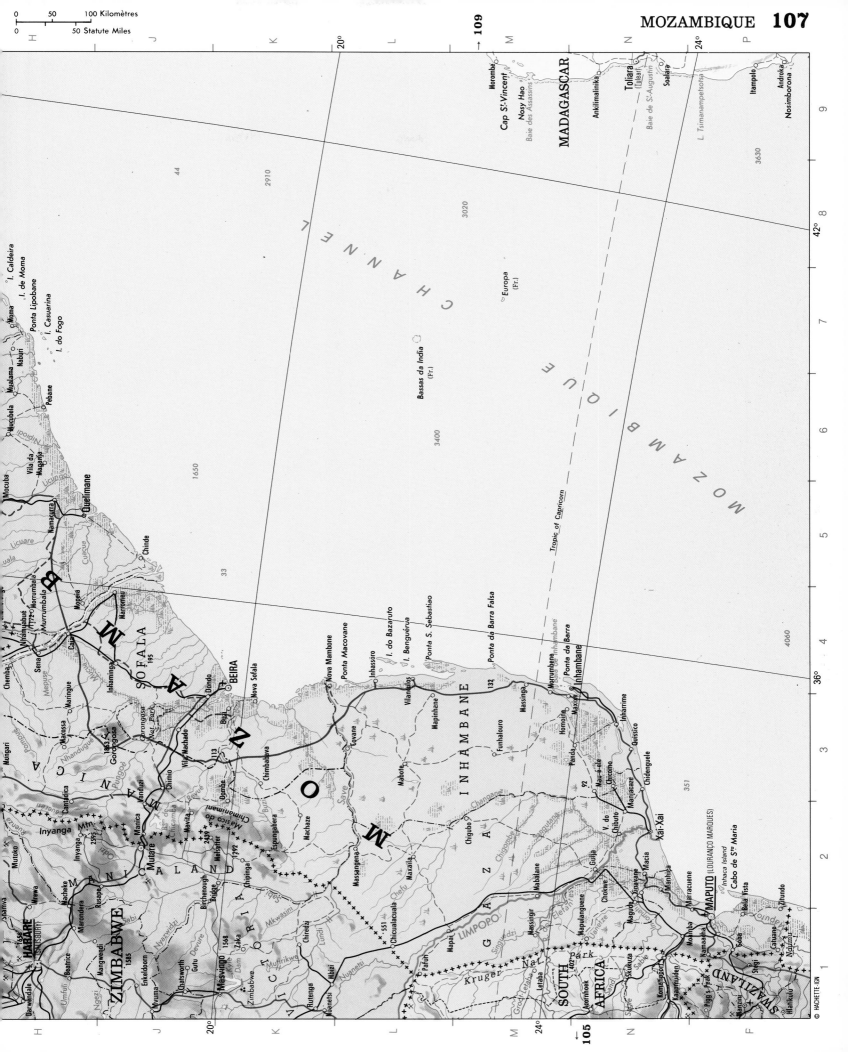

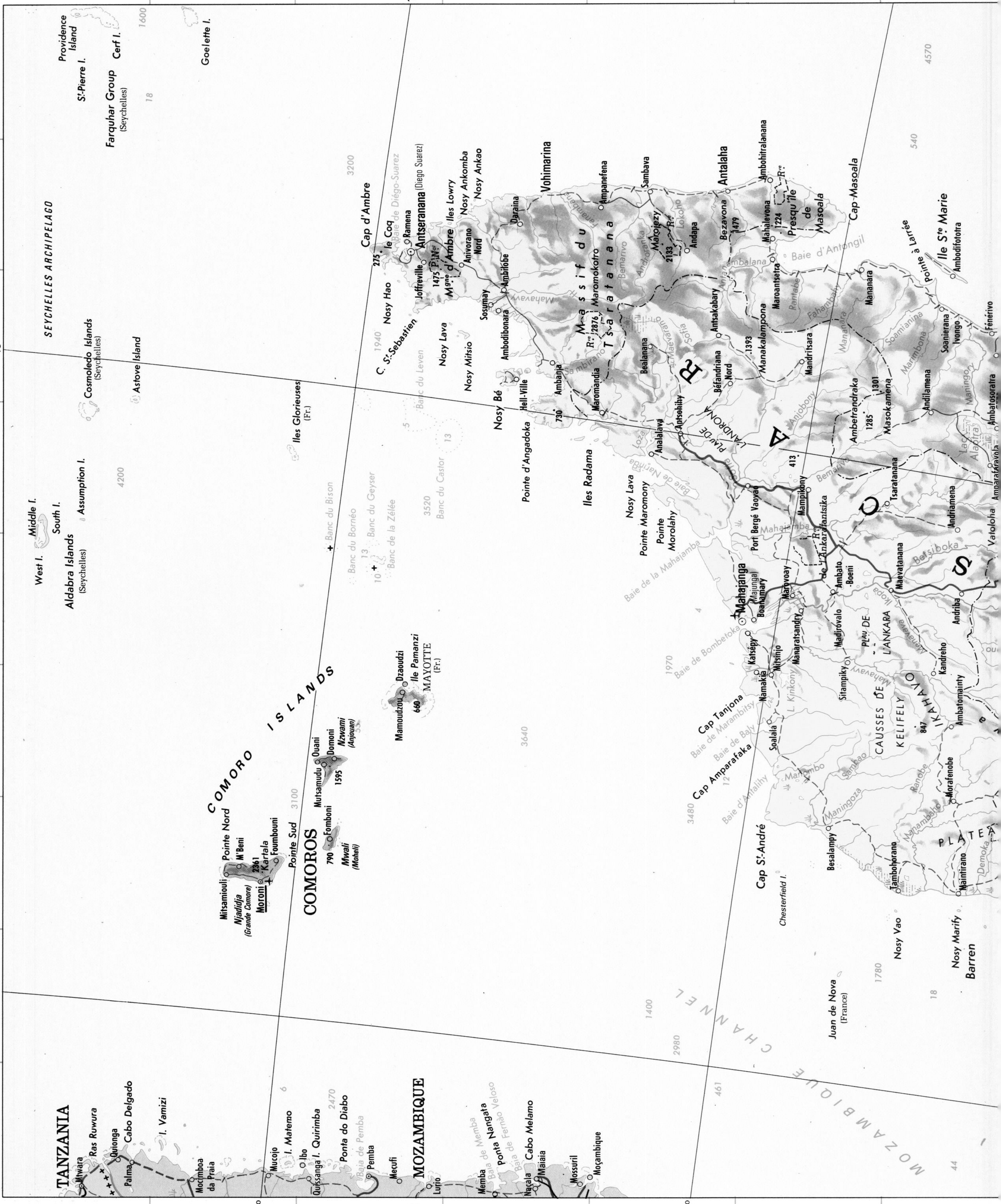

SEYCHELLES ARCHIPELAGO

Providence Island
St-Pierre I.
Cerf I.
Farquhar Group (Seychelles)
Goelette I.

Cosmoledo Islands (Seychelles)
Astove Island
C. St-Sebastien

West I.
Middle I.
South I.
Aldabra Islands (Seychelles)
Assumption I.
Iles Glorieuses (Fr.)

Banc du Bison
Banc du Bornéo
Banc du Geyser
Banc de la Zélée
Banc du Castor

COMORO ISLANDS

Pointe Nord
Mitsamiouli
Njadidja (Grande Comore)
M'Beni
Moroni
Kartala 2361
Foumbouni
Pointe Sud

Mutsamudu Ouani
Domoni
Nzwami (Anjouan) 1595
Fomboni 790
Mwali (Mohéli)

COMOROS

Mamoudzou
Dzaoudzi
Ile Pamanzi
MAYOTTE (Fr.) 660

TANZANIA
Ras Ruwura
Mtwara
Quionga
Palma
Cabo Delgado
I. Vamizi
I. Matemo
Mucojo
I. Ibo
Quissanga I. Quirimba
Ponta do Diabo
Mocimboa da Praia
Pemba
Baia de Pemba
Mecufi

MOZAMBIQUE
Lurio
Memba
Baía de Memba
Nangata
Ponta de Fernão Veloso
Naçala
Cabo Melamo
Maiaia
Mossuril
Moçambique

MOZAMBIQUE CHANNEL

Cap d'Ambre
Ile Coq
Ramena
Antseranana (Diego Suarez)
Baie de Diégo-Suarez
Iles Lowry
Joffreville
P.N.
Mgne d'Ambre 1475
Anivorano Nord
Sosumay
Ambilobe
Ambodibonara
Ambanja
Nosy Hao 275
Nosy Lava
Nosy Mitsio
Nosy Bé
Hell-Ville 730
Nosy Faly

Daraina
Ampanefena
Vohimarina
Sambava
Bezavona 1479
Antalaha
Ambohitralanana
Cap Masoala
Pesqu'île de Masoala 1224
Mahalevona
Andapa
Maromokotro 2876
Massif du Tsaratanana
Bemarivo
R 2133

Ile Ste Marie
Pointe à Larrée
Ambatosoratra
Ambodifototra
Nosy Ankao
Nosy Ankomba

Baie d'Antongil
Maroantsetra
Mananara
Antsakabary
Antsohihy
Befandriana Nord 1393
Maromandia
Bealanana

Ambanja
Analalava
PLD DE MANDRONA 413
Maroantsetra

Manakalampona
Mandritsara
Ambodiamontana
Ametrandraka 1301
Masokamena 1285

Andilamena
Andriamena
Imerivo

Pointe d'Angadoka
Iles Radama
Nosy Lava
Pointe Maromony
Pointe Morolahy

Port Bergé Vaovao
Mampikony
Tsaratanana

Mahajanga
Majunga
Boahamary
Marovoay
Ambato-Boeni
Maevatanana

Andriba
Kandreho

Baie de Bombetoka
Katsepy
Mitsinjo
Manaratsandry
Madirovalo
PLU DE LANKARA

Besalampy
Maintirano

Cap Tanjona
Baie de Marambitsy
Baie de Baly
Soalala
Namakia
Sitampiky
L. Kinkony
L. Ihotry

Cap Amparafaka
Baie d'Antsalhy
Mambo

Cap St-André

CAUSSES DE KELIFELY
IKAHAO 847

Ambatomainty
Morafenobe

Chesterfield I.
Tambohorano
Maintirano

PLATE

Juan de Nova (France)

Nosy Vao
Nosy Marify
Barren

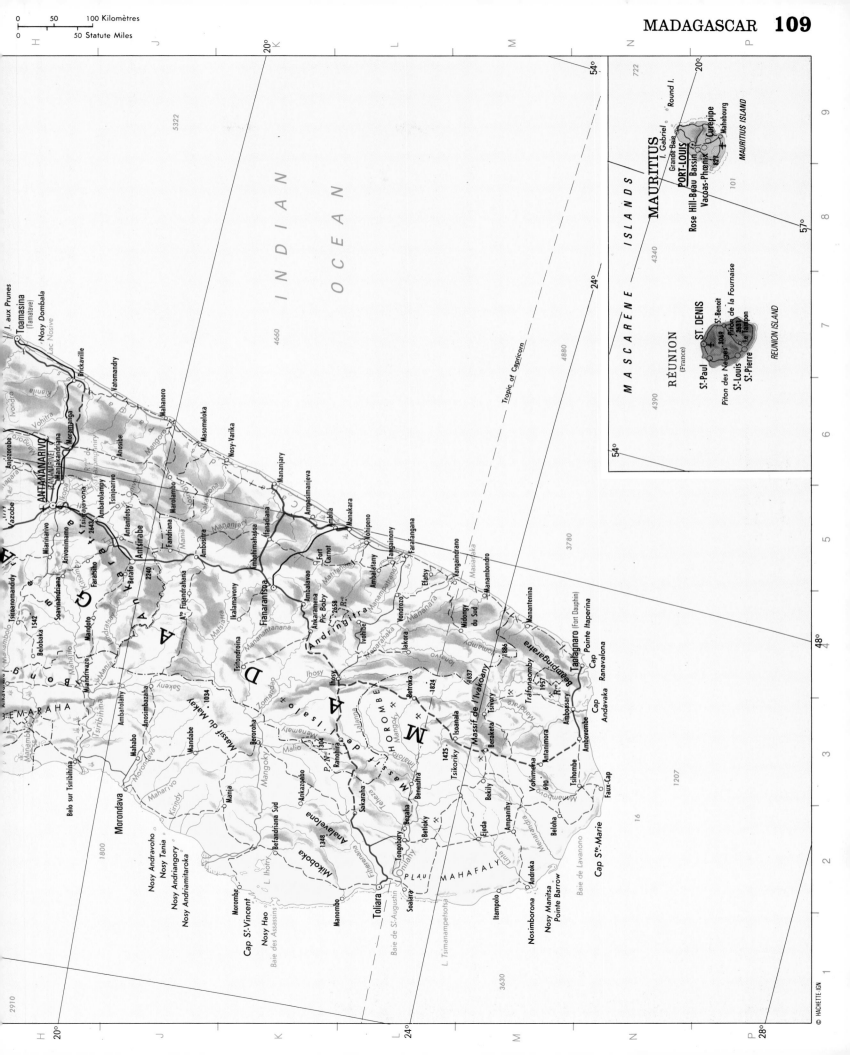

0    50    100 Kilomètres
0    50 Statute Miles

**INDIAN OCEAN**

**MASCARENE ISLANDS**

**MAURITIUS**

I. Gabriel · Round I.
Grande Baie
Curepipe
PORT-LOUIS
Rose Hill-Beau Bassin
Vacoas-Phénix · Mahebourg
873
101
*MAURITIUS ISLAND*

722

**RÉUNION**
(France)
ST. DENIS · St-Benoît
St.-Paul
Piton des Neiges · Piton de la Fournaise
3069 · 2631
St.-Louis · Le Tampon
St.-Pierre
*REUNION ISLAND*

4340
4390

Tropic of Capricorn

4660
4880
3780
5322
2910
3630
1207
16
1800

I. aux Prunes
Toamasina
[Tamatave]
Nosy Dombala
Lac Nosive
Brickaville
Vatomandry
Anjozorobe
Manjakandriana
Moramanga
Anosibe
Mahanoro
Masomeloka
Nosy-Varika
Antananarivo
[TANANARIVE]
Manjakandriana
Mananjary
Tsiroanomandidy
Miarinarivo
Arivonimamo
Antsirabe
Tsinjoarivo
Ambatolampy
Ampasimanjeva
Fandriana
Antanifotsy
Ambositra
Ifanadiana
Ambohimahasoa
Fianarantsoa
Ambia
Manakara
Vohipeno
Farafangana
Ampasimanjeva
Tangainony
Vohitrafy
1542
Soavinandriana
Faratsiho
Betafo
2643
2240
Ambalavao
Ambodiamontana
Fort Carnot
Ikalamavony
A° Fianarahana
Ikalalao
Ambalavao
Ankaramena · Pic Boby 2658
Ihosy
Andringitra
Vangaindrano
L. Masianaka
Manambondro
Efaty
Ambalatany
Vondrozo
Midongy du Sud
Manantenina
686
1037
1957
Tsivory
Betroka
1824
Massif de l'Ivakoany
Betroka
1425
Isoanala
Isoanala
Trafonaomby
Tsikoriky
Berenty
Ber10ky
Ambosary
Cap Andavaka
Ranavalona
Taolagnaro [Fort Dauphin]
Cap Pointe Itaperina
Bekily
Ampanihy
Antanimora
Vohimena
690
Tsihombe
Faux-Cap
1207
Ranohira
P.-N.° 1304
Tsivory
Vangaindrano
Midongy du Sud
Manambondro
Bedimpingaratra

HACHETTE-IGN

Morondava
Nosy Andravoho
Nosy Tania
Nosy Andriangory
Nosy Andriamifaroka
Cap St.-Vincent
Nosy Hao
Pointe Barrow
Moromba
Morondava
Belo sur Tsiribihina
Ambatolahy
Anosimbazaha
Mahabo
Beroroha
Mandabe
Manja
Ankazoabo
Befandriana Sud
Tongobory
Betioky
Bezaha
Sakaraha
Ejeda
Ampanihy
Androka
Itampolo
Nosimborona
Nosy Maritsa
Pointe Barrow
Toliara
Soalara
Manombo
L. Tsimanampetsotsa
Baie de Lavanono
Cap Ste.-Marie
**MAHAFALY**
**PLAU**
Manamena
1348
Analavelona
Mikoboka
1034
1542
**ME-M-A-R-A-H-A**
**HOROMBE**
Massif du Makay
Analavelona
Andringitra

| COUNTRY | OFFICIAL LANGUAGE(S) | AREA in sq mi | POPULATION | POPULATION DENSITY pop/sq mi | GNP in billions of $ (1982) | WORLD RANK | PER CAPITA Income (1982 dollars) | WORLD RANK | CAPITOL | POPULATION | PER CAPITA ELEC. CONSUMPTION in millions of kwh | No. of VEHICLES per 1,000 inhabitants | No. of DOCTORS per 1,000 inhabitants | % POPULATION less than 15 years of age |
|---|---|---|---|---|---|---|---|---|---|---|---|---|---|---|
| AFGHANISTAN | persian | 250,023 | 17,670,000 | 71 | 2.96 | 101 | 172 | 192 | KABUL | 1,300,000 | 72 | — | 0.07 | 45 |
| BAHREIN | arabic | 240 | 415,000 | 1730 | 4.20 | 91 | 10,680 | 17 | MANAMA | 110,000 | 5,103 | 99.3 | 1 | 44.6 |
| BANGLADESH | bengali | 55,603 | 96,730,000 | 1740 | 11.10 | 64 | 122 | 200 | DACCA | 3,500,000 | 39 | 0.6 | 0.1 | 43.2 |
| BHUTAN | tibetan | 18,148 | 1,390,000 | 76 | 0.170 | 167 | 142 | 198 | THIMPHU | 20,000 | 19 | — | — | 40.4 |
| BRUNEI | malay | 2,228 | 260,000 | 117 | 4.20 | 92 | 16,150 | 6 | BANDAR S.B. | 60,000 | 2,800 | 167.7 | 0.40 | 38 |
| BURMA | burmese | 261,242 | 36,390,000 | 139 | 6.12 | 78 | 171 | 193 | RANGOON | 3,500,000 | 50 | 1.4 | 9.2 | 40.5 |
| CHINA | chinese | 3,705,751 | 1,036,000,000 | 284 | 275.30 | 9 | 267 | 180 | BEIJING | 12,900,000 | 344 | 29.4 | 0.52 | 36.9 |
| INDIA | hindi, english | 1,269,463 | 732,300,000 | 578 | 182.50 | 11 | 252 | 184 | NEW DEHLI | 5,700,000 | 202 | 1.6 | 0.4 | 40.8 |
| INDONESIA | indonesian | 782,735 | 162,400,000 | 221 | 74.98 | 26 | 482 | 155 | JAKARTA | 7,500,000 | 96 | 4.9 | 0.06 | 50 |
| IRAN | persian | 636,355 | 42,800,000 | 67 | 90 | 22 | 2,140 | 80 | TEHRAN | 4,600,000 | 703 | 21.8 | 0.37 | 44.4 |
| IRAQ | arabic | 167,941 | 5,200,000 | 90 | 23 | 53 | 1,600 | 96 | BAGHDAD | 3,200,000 | 935 | 15.09 | 0.56 | 48.3 |
| ISRAEL | hebrew, arabic | 8,020 | 4,200,000 | 500 | 24.10 | 50 | 5,900 | 45 | JERUSALEM | 420,000 | 3,482 | 115 | 2.5 | 38.3 |
| JAPAN | japanese | 143,764 | 120,500,000 | 839 | 1,157 | 3 | 9,705 | 23 | TOKYO | 8,400,000 | 5,067 | 220.6 | 1.3 | 22.5 |
| JORDAN | arabic | 37,741 | 3,360,000 | 89 | 6.65 | 76 | 2,050 | 82 | AMMAN | 1,000,000 | 591 | 44.8 | 0.58 | 51.5 |
| KAMPUCHEA | khmer | 69,904 | 7,060,000 | 101 | 0.795 | 145 | 117 | 202 | PHNOM PENH | 500,000 | 20 | — | 0.05 | 44.9 |
| KUWAIT | arabic | 6,880 | 1,760,000 | 259 | 32.84 | 44 | 19,900 | 3 | KUWAIT | 220,000 | 7,925 | 306 | 1.47 | 44.4 |
| LAOS | laotian | 91,437 | 4,130,000 | 45 | 1.27 | 127 | 325 | 172 | VIENTIANE | 200,000 | 119 | — | 0.05 | 43.4 |
| LEBANON | arabic | 4,016 | 2,620,000 | 654 | 4.77 | 87 | 1,800 | 90 | BEIRUT | 900,000 | 478 | 175.7 | 0.75 | 42.6 |
| MALAYSIA | malay | 127,329 | 15,200,000 | 119 | 27.52 | 47 | 1,835 | 88 | KUALA LUMPUR | 800,000 | 820 | 4.1 | 0.31 | 41.5 |
| MALDIVES | maldivian | 115 | 170,000 | 1507 | 0.070 | 184 | 412 | 159 | MALE | 36,593 | 60 | — | 0.05 | 43.9 |
| MONGOLIA | kazakh | 604,306 | 1,850,000 | 3 | 1.91 | 115 | 1,061 | 115 | ULAAN BATAAR | 465,000 | 1,317 | — | 2.27 | 43 |
| NEPAL | nepali | 54,367 | 15,740,000 | 290 | 2.62 | 107 | 168 | 260 | KATHMANDU | 800,000 | 21 | 0.8 | 0.04 | 43.5 |
| NORTH KOREA | korean | 46,544 | 19,660,000 | 422 | 26.50 | 48 | 1,390 | 100 | PYONGYANG | 1,000,000 | 2,137 | — | — | 40 |
| NORTH YEMEN | arabic | 75,297 | 8,540,000 | 113.4 | 4.01 | 94 | 647 | 143 | SAN'A | 300,000 | 139 | 11.4 | 0.16 | 49.4 |
| OMAN | arabic | 82,038 | 1,190,000 | 15 | 6.97 | 74 | 6,170 | 42 | MASQAT | 60,000 | 1,240 | — | 0.67 | 44 |
| PAKISTAN | urdu | 310,433 | 91,800,000 | 296 | 31.57 | 45 | 352 | 167 | ISLAMABAD | 200,000 | 204 | 2.2 | 0.3 | 45.2 |
| PHILIPPINES | tagalog | 115,841 | 53,300,000 | 460 | 33.96 | 43 | 655 | 142 | QUEZON CITY | 8,000,000 | 399 | 5.9 | 0.15 | 42.9 |
| QATAR | arabic | 4,248 | 294,000 | 69 | 6.01 | 80 | 21,460 | 1 | DOHA | 180,000 | 11,050 | 312.5 | 0.75 | 32.3 |
| SAUDI ARABIA | arabic | 830,077 | 10,850,000 | 13 | 111.10 | 18 | 10,240 | 19 | RIYADH | 400,000 | 3,071 | 242.7 | 0.37 | 43.3 |
| SINGAPORE | malay, tamil, chinese, english, mandarin | 239 | 2,530,000 | 10,602 | 16.32 | 61 | 6,530 | 40 | SINGAPORE | 2,300,000 | 3,417 | 71.1 | 0.91 | 24.4 |
| SRI LANKA | sinhalese | 25,335 | 15,600,000 | 616 | 5.06 | 86 | 328 | 171 | COLOMBO | 1,500,000 | 134 | 8.09 | 0.13 | 39 |
| SOUTH KOREA | korean | 38,415 | 40,600,000 | 1067 | 75.38 | 25 | 1,885 | 87 | SEOUL | 8,900,000 | 1,334 | — | 0.7 | 38.1 |
| SOUTH YEMEN | arabic | 128,572 | 2,220,000 | 17.4 | 1.07 | 135 | 498 | 153 | ADEN | 290,000 | 46 | — | 0.13 | 45.7 |
| SYRIA | arabic | 71,505 | 9,930,000 | 139 | 16.77 | 59 | 1,745 | 91 | DAMASCUS | 950,000 | 615 | 4.6 | 0.4 | 35.3 |
| TAIWAN | chinese | 13,893 | 19,010,000 | 1368 | 49.78 | 34 | 2,650 | 70 | TAIPEI | 2,442,884 | — | — | — | 34.3 |
| THAILAND | thai | 198,475 | 50,500,000 | 254 | 39.24 | 40 | 793 | 130 | BANGKOK | 4,800,000 | 396 | 9.4 | 0.15 | 38.6 |
| TURKEY | turkish | 301,410 | 43,300,000 | 160 | 53.30 | 32 | 1,115 | 111 | ANKARA | 2,500,000 | 620 | 9.8 | 0.6 | 38.5 |
| UNITED ARAB EMIRATES | arabic | 32,281 | 1,210,000 | 37 | 23.72 | 52 | 20,000 | 2 | ABU DHABI | 350,000 | 6,605 | 882.3 | 1.97 | 26.3 |
| VIETNAM | vietnamese | 127,262 | 58,380,000 | 458.4 | 10.81 | 65 | 188 | 190 | HANOI | 1,500,000 | 73 | — | 0.25 | 41.8 |

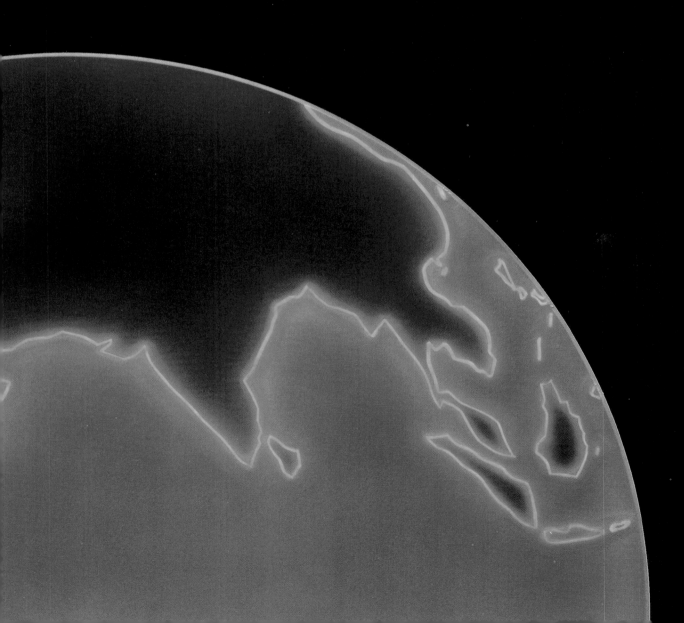

ASIA

Scale 1 : 33,000,000

Scale 1 : 33,000,000

Sichote-Alin
Khabarovsk
2640
2071
2004
2541
2522
gyeongsanm
244
Tatar Strait
Sakhalin I.
1609
C. Aniva
La Pérouse Strait
3328
Rebun Tō
Risiri Tō
C. Siretok
Asahi
2290
Sapporo
Hokkaido
Kunasir
Sikotan
Sibotu
1855
Vladivostok
Chan
KURYL TRENCH
Kuryl Islands
Shiashkotan
Matua
Rasshua
Simushir
Urup
Iturup

SEA
OF JAPAN

Korea
Taebaeg Sanmaeg
1708
1915
Seoul
2522

JAPAN
Honshu
Sado
Mts Etigo
2678
Mts Hida
3190
Tokyo
3776
Mt. Fuji
Osaka
1915
Mts Tyugoku
1981
Shikoku
1786

JAPAN TRENCH
7916

NORTH PACIFIC

Ulreong

Jeju-do

EAST CHINA
SEA
zinghai
angzhoi
Bay

Kyushu
Miyake
Nanpo
Tori-Sima
Sofu-Gano
Syotō
Tagena
Yaku
Amami

Izu-Shichito
IZU-BONIN TRENCH

Mukosima-Retto
Titisima-Retto
Hahasima-Retto
Ogasawara
Islands
(Bonin Islands)

324

JAPAN OCEAN

4953

Kure  Midway

Lisianski

6209

Okinawa
Ryukyu Islands
Minami
Daito Is.
Okino

Kita-io-si
Kazan Is.
Iwo jima
969
Minami-io-si
8660

VOLCANO TRENCH

8400

Minami-Tori-Sima
(I. Marcus)

Tropic of Cancer

Taipei
Sakishima
T'aiwan
Yushan
3997
(Formosa)
Chutiyangsha6rmo

PHILIPPINES

Okino Tori Sima
(Parece Vela)

Farallon de Pajaros
Maug
Asuncion
Agrihan 881
Pagan

Wake

Batan
Babuyan Is.

SEA

Mariana Is.
Sarigan
Anatahan
Farallon de Medinilla

MARIANA TRENCH

Pulog
2933
Luzon
Sierra Madre

Saipan
Rota
Guam
405

Taongi

6370

Manila

Catanduanes
Halcon
2582
Mindoro
Mayon
2462
Masbate
Calamian
Panay
Cebu
Leyte
Samar

MICRONESIA

Bikar

Bikini
Rongerik
Eniwetok
Rongelap
Utirik'
Ailuk
Wotho
Jemo
Likiep
Wotje
Ujelang
Kwajalein
Ujae
Lae
Kaven
Maloelap
Namu
Aur

Marshall Islands

Negros
1185
Kaatoan
2937
Mindanao
Davao
2953
Apo
Banggi

Ulithi

172 Yap

Ngulu
Sorol
Palau
233
Kayangel
Babelthuap
Urukthapel
Angaur

Falaurep
O. Fayu
Pikelot
Olimarao
Puluwat
Lamotrek
Pulusuk

Hall

Truk
Nama

Senyavin Is.
Ponape
Mokil
Pingelap

Ailinglapalap
Majuro
Jaluit
Kusaie
Ebon
Arno
Mili
Knox

Mt Kinabalu
4100
Basilan
Tawitawi
Sulu Arch.
Kepulauan Talaud

SULU
SEA

Nomoi

Sonsorol

Caroline Islands

Nukuoro

Butaritari

Sangi

Tobi  Helen

Kapingamarangi

Abaiang  Marakei

CELEBES
SEA
Ogoamas
3000
Katopasa
3505
Sulawesi
(Celebes)
Rantekombola
3440
Sula Obi
Klabat
1994
Morotai
1636
Kep.
HALMAHERA
SEA
1730
Asia
Ajoe
2111
Boo
Waigeo
2581
Tamrau
Misool

Halmahera

Gilbert
Aranuka  Maiana  Abenama
Islands

Equator
Nauru
Ocean I.
Nonouti
Tabiteuea
Nukunau

Mekongga
2790
Buru
273B
Ceram
3027
Binaija

Japen

Gr. Ninigo
Kaniet
Hermit
Admiralty Is.
Manus
Purdy
Lavongai
St. Matthias Group

Butung
Kabaena
BANDA
SEA
Maluku
7440
Kep. Kai
Kep. Aru
5800

Puntjak Djaja
5030
4130
Trikora
Maoke
Mt. Wilhelm
4694
New
Guinea
Long
Rooke

Schouten
Manam
Karkar
Bismarck Arch.
New
Ireland
Mt Sinewit
2398
New
Britain
2438
Mt Balbi
2743
Bougainville

Lihir Gr.
Tanga
Feni

Nukumanu

Ontong Java

Arorae

Nanumea

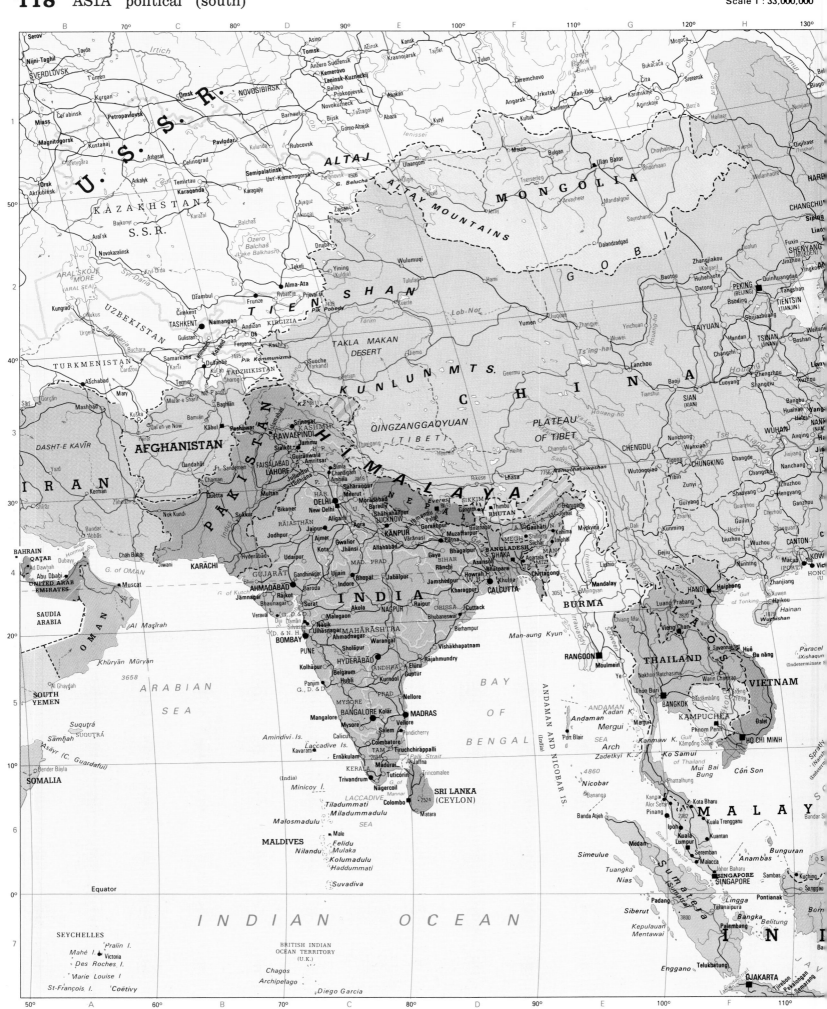

140°  K  150°  L  160°  M  170°  N  180°  P  170°

Amur
Komsomol'sk-na-Amure
Tymovskoje
Sakhalin
Siaskotan
gdomyn
Birobidžan
Poronajsk
Matua
Sovetskaja Gavan
Rassua
Chabarovsk
Simušir
40°

Ussurijsk
La Pérouse Strait
Urup
Tet'uche-Pristan
Iturup
International Dateline

Vladivostok
Rebun Tō
Siretoko M.
Kunašir
Nachodka
Risiri Tō
Šikotan

Cheongjin
Asahikawa
Asahi 3290
Zel'onyj
SAPPORO
Hokkaidō
Kuširo

SEA
Hakodate

30°

OF JAPAN
Tsugaru Str.
Aomori

NORTH PACIFIC

NORTH KOREA
Akita
Morioka
Hamheung
Yamagata
Sendai
PYONGYANG
Niigata
Hukusima
KOREA
Nagano
eong
SEOUL
Toyama
Takasaki
Incheon
Kanazawa
Mito
SOUTH
Hukui
TOKYO
OW
KYŌTO
Itinomya
Chiba
YOKOHAMA
KOREA
Tottori
3776
Daejeon
Matue
Hirosima
Husi San
Daegu
NAGOYA
Miyake
Gwangju
KŌBE
Okayama Wakayama
BUSAN
OSAKA
30°

A
Simonoseki
Takamatu
Mogpo
Hirosima
Shikoku
OCEAN

KITA-KYŪSYŪ
Kōti
Bennu
Jeju-do
Hukuoka
Kyushu
Tori Sima

Nagasaki
J
Miyazaki

Kumamoto
Kagosima

GZHOU
Tanega Sima
Sōhu-Gan
HANGHAI
Yaku Sa.

king
Amami Ō Sa.
Mukozima Rettō

Ningbo
EAST CHINA
Ogasawara Guntō
Titizima Rettō

ai
Ogasawara Gunto
(Bonin Islands)
Hahazima Rettō
Tropic of Cancer

Wenzhou
(NIP.)

SEA
Minami-Tori Sima
(NIP.)

chow
Okinawa Tō
Kita-iō Za.

Strait
Naha
Minami-daitō Za.

T'AIPEI
Daitō Zima (NIP.)
Kazan Rettō
(Volcano Is.) 'Iō Za.

Yushan 3950
Okino-daitō Za.
Minami-iō-Za.

Chiai
Ryukyu Islands
20°

TAIWAN
(FORMOSA)

PHILIPPINES
Farallon de Pajaros
WAKE

Okino Tori
Maug
ISLAND
(U.S.A.)

Sima
Asuncion

Batan Is.
Agrihan

Babuyan Is.
Pagan
SEA

Laoag
NORTHERN

Pulog 2933
Mariana Islands
Sarigan
MARIANAS
ISLANDS
Taongi

San Carlos
Luzon
Anatahan
(U.S.)

Caloocan
Quezón City
Farallon de Medinilla

Batangas
MANILA
Garapan
TRUST TERRITORY
MARSHALL
Bikar

Saipan
Rota
ISLANDS

Mindoro
Catanduanes
(U.S.)
Bikini

Naga
GUAM
Agaña
OF THE PACIFIC ISLANDS
Eniwetok
Rongerik

Calamian Gr.
(U.S.A.)
Wotho
Rongelap
Utirik

Masbate
Calbayo
Ujelang
Jemo
Ailuk

Panay
Samar
M
I
C
R
O
Kwajalein
Likiep
Wotje

Iloilo
Cebu
Leyte
Ulithi
(U.S.)
Ujae
Lae
Kaven
Maloelap

Bacolod
Cebu
Yap
N
Namu
Aur

SULU
Ngulu
Falaurep
O. Fayu
Pikelot
Hall
E
Ailinglapalap

SEA
Palau
Sorol
S
Majuro
Arno

Negros
Kayangel Babelthuap
Olimarao
Puluwat
Truk
Senyavin Is.
Ponape
I
Jaluit
Mili

Mindanao
Uruktapel
Koror
Lamotrek
Pulusuk
Nama
A
Knox

Banggi
Angaur
Eauripik
Mokil
Kusaie

Zamboanga
Davao
Sonsorol
Nomoi
Pingelap

Basilan
FEDERATED STATES OF MICRONESIA
Kolonia

Kinabalu (Jesselton)
Apo
(U.S.)

Tawi Tawi Gr.
Sulu Arch.
Kepulauan Talaud
Tobi
Helen Is.
BELAU
(U.S.)
C
a
r
o
l
i
n
e
I
s
l
a
n
d
s
Nukuoro

wan
CELEBES
Kep. Sangihe
SEA
Morotai
Kapingamarangi
Equator
Butaritari

Manado
Tobelo
HALMAHERA
Abaiang
Marakei

Waigeo
Kaniet
Tarawa

Gorontalo
Halmahera
SEA
Kep. Aju
Ninigo Gr.
Admiralty Is.
St. Matthias Group
Nauru Yaren
Tarawa
Maiana Gilbert Is.

Sulawesi
(Célèbes)
Sula Obi
Kep.
Boo
Misool
Japen
Hermit
Manus
Lavongai
Kavieng
NAURU
Aranuka
Abemama

Buru
Tifu
Seram
Napan
Purdy Is.
Bismarck
Lihir Gr.
Banaba (Ocean)
Nonouti

Butung
Ambon
Irian
Sukarnapura
Schouten Is.
New Ireland
Tanga
KIRIBATI
Tabiteuea
Nukunau

Kabaena
Moluccas
Sonobo
Manam
Arch.
Feni
Arorae

BANDA
Kokenau
Bougainville
New Britain
Nukumanu

Duala
Puntjak Djaja
New Guinea
Mt. Wilhelm 4694
Long
Karkar
Rabaul
Sohano
Ontong Java
TUVALU
Nanumea

Pandang
Kep. Kai
PAPUA-NEW GUINEA
Taku Is.
SOLOMON IS.

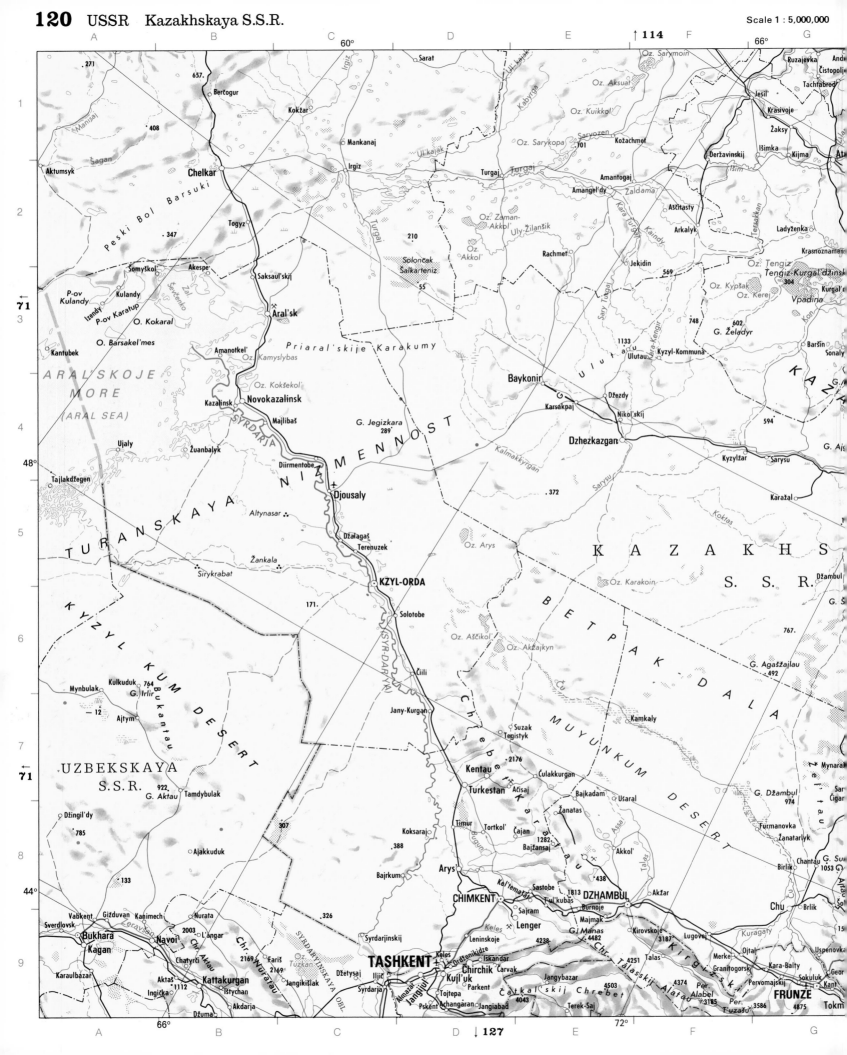

**Scale:** 0 — 50 — 100 Kilomètres / 0 — 50 Statute Miles

**OMSK**

**NOVOSIBIRSK**

**BARNAUL**

**BIYSK**

**TSELINOGRAD**

**KARAGANDA**

**SEMIPALATINSK**

**UST'KAMENOGORSK**

**VOSTOCHNO**

**ALMA-ATA**

**Balkhash** (Lake Balkhash) / Oz. Balchaš

**CHINA**

**DZUNGARIAN BASIN**

**KAZAKHSTANSKAYA OBL.**

Selected place names and features:

Kokchetav, Shchuchinsk, Zerenda, Borovoje, Krasnoarmejsk, Im. Molodogvardejcev, Alekseevka, Čkalovo, Vol'noje, Poltavka, Serbakul', Jur'evo, Niž Omka, Ust'-Tarka, Sipicyno, Severnoje, Panyčevo, Bakčar, Plotnikovo, Markelovo

Makinsk, Stepn'ak, Aksu, Bogembaj, Kzyltu, Teke, Tavričeskoje, Odesskoje, Pavlogradka, Bobrinka, Novovaršavka, Čerlak, Čistooz'ornoje, Tatarsk, Čany, Kujbyšev, Čumakovo, Martemjanovskij, Koževnikovo

Voznesenka, Žuravl'ovka, Žaltyr, Akbeit, Šortandy, Sofijevka, Žolymbet, Turgaj, Jermentau, Bestobe, Novoalekseevka, Krasnokutskoje, Kačiry, Kupino, Barabinsk, Zdvinsk, Jarki, Kargat, Čulym, Kolyvan', Vjuny, Bolotnoje

Tselinograd, Roždestvenka, Višn'ovka, Anar, Kijevka, Kalkaman, Leninskij, Pavlodar, Ščerbakty, Tavolžan, Slavgorod, Znamenka, Kamen'-na-Obi, Suzun, Čerepanovo, Masl'anino

Temirtau, Aktau, Tokarevka, Osakarovka, Uljanovskoje, Ekibastuz, Jermak, Majkain, Kulunda, Blagoreščenka, Zavjalovo, Mamontovo, Pavlovsk, Novoaltajsk, Barnaul, Zarinskaja

Karaganda, Saran, Novodolinskij, Sachtinsk, Abaj, Karabas, Spasskij-Zavod, Kornejevka, Semizbugy, Bajanaul, Karakabak, Majskoje, Semijarka, Molgary, Michajlovka, Volčicha, Šipunovo, Pospelicha, Alejsk, Kalmanka, Troickoje, Borovl'anka, Sorokino, Biysk

Darjinskij, G. Burkit, Žaryk, Aksu-Ajuly, Karkaralinsk, Jegindybulak, Karagajly, Sarybulak, Aktas, Sarytau, Novopokrovka, Bol. Vladimirovka, Dolon', Belagaš, Rubtsovsk, Gorn'ak, Zmeinogorsk, Tretjakovo, Čaryšskoje, Taurak, Gorno-Altajsk

Aktau, Aktogaj, G. Aksoran, Kajnar, G. Karakus, G. Ordatas, Karaul, Kaskabulak, Suykbulak, Čarsk, Glubokoje, Belousovka, Ul'ba, Leninogorsk, Verchubinka, Abaj, Ongudaj

Kyzylespe, G. Bektauata, Karašengel, Kounradskij, Balkhash, Baršatas, G. Kosoba, Žarma, Kokpekty, Samarskoje, Zyr'anovsk, Bol'šenarymskoje, G. Belukha

Gul' Šad, Tomar, Kr. Okt' abr', Sajak, Majkamys, Im. Frunze, Aktogaj, Ajaguz, G. Sagymžal, Šingoža, Aksuat, Prioz' ornyj, Akžar, Buran, Kurčum, Kalguty, Alekseevka, Habahe

Majtan, Karaoj, O. Tasaral, Bakanas, Lepsy, Mataj, Žarsuat, Taskesken, Urdžar, G. Tastau, Makanti, Tacheng (Chuguchak), Emin, Zajsan, Jimunai, Buerjin

Bajtajlak, Akkol', Aktogaj, Mulaly, Užaral, Andrejevka, Kyzylagaš, Oz. Alakol', Yumin, Wuergasaershan, Muz Tau, Saur, Wulunguhu, Fuhai

Ushtobe, Koksu, Taldy-Kurgan, Karabulak, Sarkand, Lepsinsk, Antonovka, Džansugurov, Tekeli, G. Besbaskan, Rudničnyj, Khrebet Dzhungarskiy Altau, Wenquan, Bole, Qiershankou, Kelamayi (Karamai)

Alma-Ata, Kaskelen, Talgar, Im. Panfilova, Ili, Saryozek, Konyrolen, Panfilov, Huocheng, Santai, Taluokenskankou, Duoheyan, Sailimuhu, Ajbihu, Manasihu

Mountain/spot heights: 947, 28, 64, 105, 135, 166, 234, 313, 897, 503, 100, 1027, 1049, 1055, 1085, 351, 606, 621, 1187, 1559, 1565, 1366, 1064, 1090, 1035, 1162, 1146, 1608, 2776, 2599, 2820, 3036, 4506, 3373, 2645, 1449, 3871, 3083, 2779, 2507, 2992, 2335, 2053, 2598, 3816, 2540, 342, 328, 756, 347, 343, 1549, 1446, 3908, 4464, 3959, 4359, 2073, 2150, 2923, 2550, 1848, 189, 259, 468, 1587, 1215

**Kyzyltas Mts.**, **Chr. Čingiz-Tau**, **Khrebet Tarbagatay**, **Chr. Manrak**, **Altayskiy Kray**, **Vostochno**, **Kulundinskaya Step'**, **Baraba Step'**, **Steppes**, **Sary Isikotrau**, **Taukum**, **Priobskoje Plato**

Lakes: Oz. Ul'ken-Karoj, Oz. Seleteniz, Oz. Tengiz, Oz. Čany, Oz. Kulundinskoje, Oz. Bol. Azbulat, Oz. Zalauly, Oz. Kučukskoje, Oz. Sasykkol', Oz. Alakol', Oz. Zajsan, Oz. Markakol'

Rivers: Irtyš (Irtyš), Ob', Išim, Nura, Ajaguz, Aksu, Lepsy, Ili, Čaryš, Bija, Katun'

© HACHETTE-IGN

Scale 1 : 5,000,000

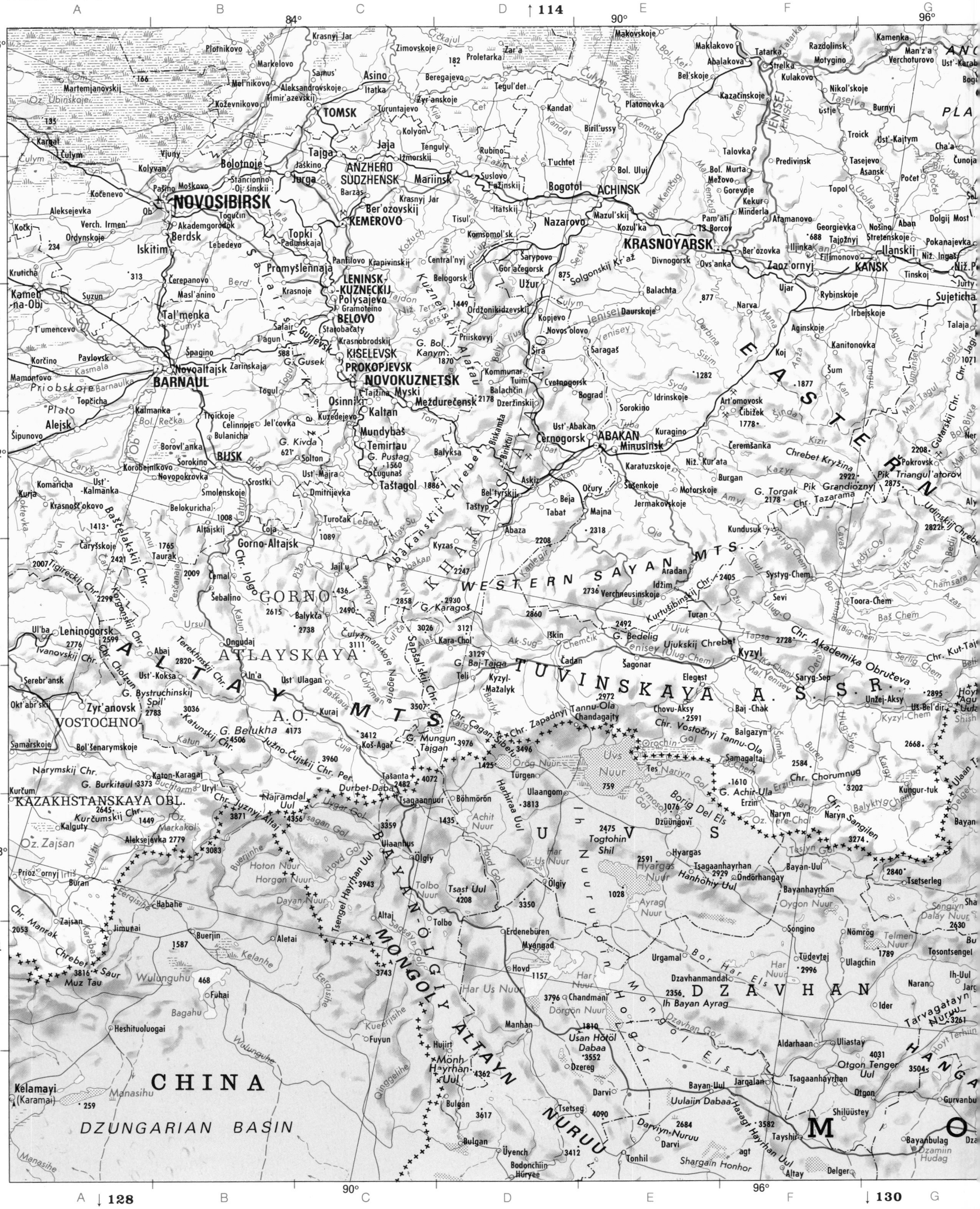

↑ **114**

56°

84° C 90° D E F G 96°

1

TOMSK

NOVOSIBIRSK
KEMEROVO
ACHINSK
KRASNOYARSK
KANSK

ANZHERO-SUDZHENSK
Mariinsk

← 121

LENINSK-KUZNECKIJ
BELOVO
KISELEVSK
PROKOPJEVSK
NOVOKUZNECK

BARNAUL

BIJSK

52°

Cernogorsk
ABAKAN
Minusinsk

EASTERN

Gorno-Altajsk

GORNO-
ALTAYSKAYA
A.O.

KHAKASS A.O.

WESTERN SAYAN MTS

TUVINSKAYA A.S.S.R.

Kyzyl

ALTAY MTS

Leninogorsk

VOSTOCHNO-

G. Belukha 4173

KAZAKHSTANSKAYA OBL.

← 121

48°

U V S

MONGOLY ALTAYN NURUU

DZAVHAN

HANGA

CHINA

M O

9

DZUNGARIAN BASIN

Kelamayi
(Karama)

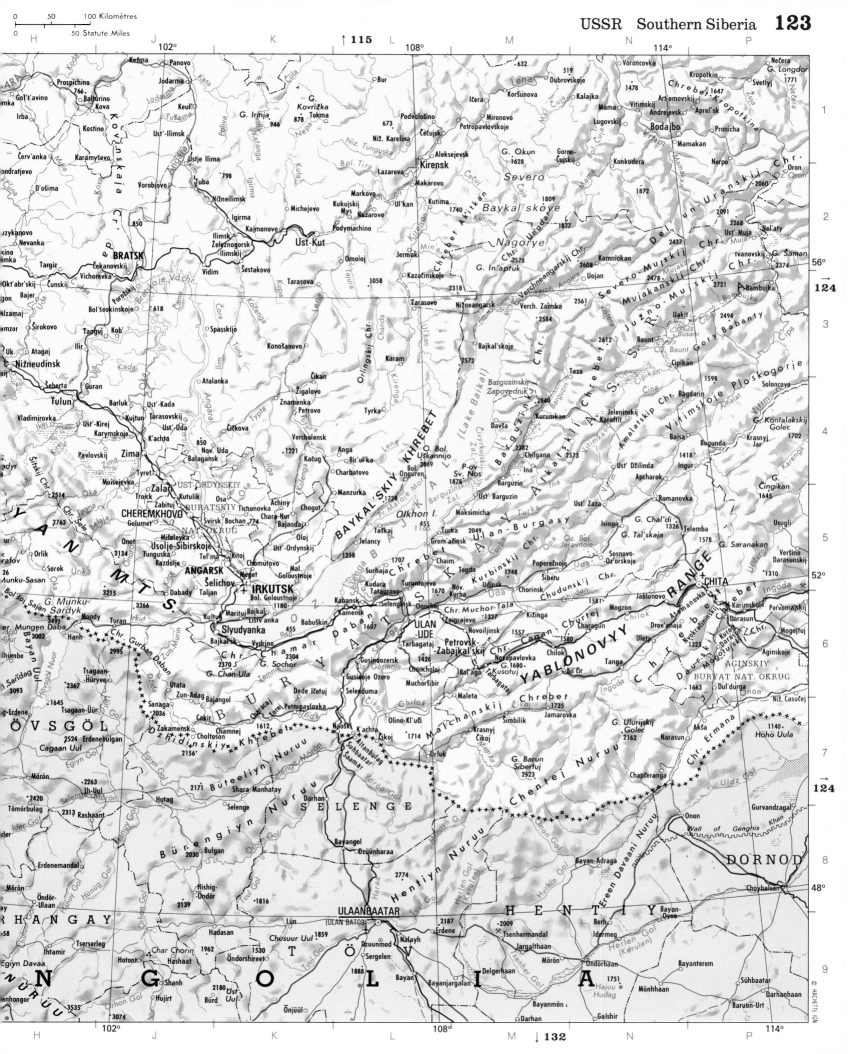

120°    126°   ↑ **115**    132°

**STANOVOY KHREBET**

**U.**   **S.**   **S.**

Oron
2406
2602
Čara
Naminga
2515
2004
2467
Chr. Udokan
Kabaktan
Taluma
Berkakit
Čul'man
1854
Zolotinka
Sutamo Gonamskij Chr.
1772
1644
1959 2412 G. Skalistyj Golec 2312
1802 Chr. Džugdyr
2107
Majsk

2219
Ust'-N'ukža
1612
1669
Nagornyj
1622
1073
Vladimirovskij
Kupuri
Bomnak
Ust'unja

Ivanovskij
G. Saman
2374
Sr. Kalar
Chr. Jankan
El'gakan
Ust'-Urkima
Lapri
Tyndinskij
Nikolajevskij
Dambuki
Inarogda
1018
Sovetskij
1589
1593
Khr. Dzhagdy

**56°**

Bambujka
Kalakan
Sr. Ol'okma
1227
Chr. Černyševa
G. Lukinda 1572
Ves'olyj
Dželtulak
Belen'kaja
Khr. Tukuringra
1442
1470
Khr. Sokťachan
Norsk

**123**

Soloncovo
Ust'-Karenga
G. Černyšova
1668
Gul'a
Tupik
Orogžan
1600
Amutkači
Kirovskij
Solovjevsk
Kirovskij
1606
Dožalivyj
Zolotaja-Gora
Jubilejnyj
Novojampol
Gogolevka
Ust' Tygda
Kuchterin
Lug
Byssa

G. Kontalakskij Golec 1702
Tungirskij Chrebet 1808
1432
Čičatka
1058 Amazar
Perofej Pavlovič
Tachtamygda
Uruša
Skovorodino
Never
Taldan
Daktuj
Magdagači
Tolbuzino
Tygda
Ovs'anka
Jasnyj 904
Okt'abr'skij
Glubokij
Selemdž

**3**

Zel'onoje Ozero
Mogoča
Amazar
Ignašino
Džalinda
Albazino
Bejtonovo
Čern'ajevo
Sivaki
Kuznecovo
Múchino
AMURSKO - ZEJSKOJE
PLATO
OBLAST

Davenda
Kl'učevskij
Karagan
Pokrovka
Amazar
Mohe
Kaikukang
Novovoskresenovka
Simanovsk
Novogeorgijevka
Niž. Buzuli
Novokijevskij Uval
Zejsko-Bureinskaja

Ksenjevka
Gorbica
Silka
Fergunahe
Humaerwojishan 1451
Guqigu
Dalahan
Ušakovo
Huma
Svobodnyj
Krasnojarovo
Ravnina

Čingikan
1645
Nerčinsko-Kuengskij Chr.
1432
Aks'onovo
Žilovskoje
Ust'-Karsk
Boty
1501
Wuma
Emuershan
Xinganlingzhan
Hutongzhen
Kumara
Busse
Belogorsk
Seryševo
Romny
Jekaterinoslavka

Usugli
Čer skogo
Veršino Darasunskij
Ukrejskij
Kokuj
Sretensk
1298
Nalimsk
Ust'-Urov
1557
 Seryševo
Zavitinsk

**52°**

1310
Arbagar
Nerčinsk
Dunajeno
Kurlejá
1372
Gazimurskij Chr.
Xilalin
Jinhe
1339
Deerbuer
1150
Eergunaqi
1257
Yaozhan
Aihun
Tamboyka
Blagovechtchensk
Rajčichinsk

Cholbon
Silka
Priiskvyj
Šelopugino
Gazimurskij Zavod
Gornyj Zerentuj
Nerčinskij Zavod
Nanuteshan
Vitulihe
Alihe
Huolongmen
782
Aihucun
Xiaoxinganlingshanmo
Xunke
Kuerbin
Wuyun

Pervomajskij
Balej
1412
Veršino-Sachtaminskij
1448
Kadaja
Zapokrovskij
Byrka
Sanhe
Shangkuli
Duobukuershan
Yian
Huolongmen
Sunwu
Xunhe

Mogojtuj
Bukuka
Aleksandrovskij Zavod
Klička
Priargunsk
Xiaohezi
Xiguitugi
Mianduhe
Boketu
1149
Nenjiang
Longzhen
Dedu
Namoer
Beian

Kalanguj
Oloy'annaja
Mirnaja
Okt'abr'skij
HEILONGJIANG
Yalu
Gannan
Fuyu
Nahe
Laha
Keshan
Kedong
Songjia
Haibei
Hailun

Serlovaja Gora
Niž. Casučej
Borz'a
Charanor
Daurija
1139
Zabajkal'sk
Manzhouli
Zhalainuoer
Cuogang
HAILAR
DAXINGANLINGSHANMO (GREATER KHINGAN R.)
Butehaqi
Langfeng
Gannan
Yian
Baiquan
Suileng
Tieli
Xiaob

**6**

Gurvandzagal
Genghis
of
Wall
Hulunchi
Hoh Nur
Khan
Ganzhuermiao
Jiangjunmiao
Nianzishan
Longjiang
QIQIHAR
Angangxi
Fulaerji
Lindian
Zhenxiang
Wangkui
Minsgshui
Haifeng
280
Qingang
Suihua
Xinglongzhen
Dongxing

**123**

Choybalsan
Buyr Nuur
Haihing R.
1344
Jingxing
Duerbote (Taikang)
Saertu
Renmin
Anda
Lanxi
Shenjia
Xindia
Bayan
Mulan

**48°**

DORNOD
Menengiyn Tal
1034
Tamsagbulag
Yiershi
1748
Marakaton
Tazicheng
Tailai
Zhaodong
Hulan
HARBIN
Acheng

Büridein Hudag
Suolun
Dashizhai
Dongping
Tailai
Datong
Zhaozhou
Zhaoyuan
Wuzhan
Shuaugcheng
Lalin
Maqershan
Binxian

MONGOLIA
Matad
Wulanhaote
Zhenlai
Anguang
Maoxing
DONGBEIPINGYUAN (MANCHURIAN PLAIN)
Dalai
Fuyu
Changchunling
Wuchang

**SÜHBAATAR**
Darhanhaan
1359
1367
Heshimiao
Nuonayimiao
1394
Liuhucun
Tuliemaodu
Tuquan
Taoan
BAICHENG
Qianguoerluosi
Qianguerluosi
Sanhecher
Yushu
Shanhe

Erdenetsagaan
Dongwuzhumuqinqi
1350
278 Tongyu
Fulongquan
Nongan
Dehui
Hongqi
Shulan

114°    ↓ **132**    120°    126°

A B C D ↑ **71** E F G

TURKMENSKAYA S.S.R.

U.

Tūrān · Sabzevār · Solţānābād · Kūh-e · 3117 Hazar Masjed · Kaachka · Kirovsk · Tedžen · Chardzho

Repetek

Ma'dan · Neyshābur · Chanārān · Kabud Gonbad · Dušak · Sakar-Čaga · Mary · Merv · Uč-Adži · Ravnina · Karabe

Dorūneh · Kūh-e Binālūd · MASHHAD · Chauz-Chan · Murgab · Bajram-Ali · Zachmet

Kondor · Kāfar Qal'eh · Sang Bast · Čaača · Tedženstroj · Turkmen-Kala Iolotan

Kūh-e Sorkh · 3020 · Kāshmar · Sarakhs · Serachs · Krasnoje Znam'a · Sandykači

Nagineh · Kavīr-e Namak · Farīmān · Baghbaghū · Taškepri

Robāţ-e Khān · Ţabas · Boshrūyeh · Ferdows · Jūymand · Gonābād · Shahr-e Now · Torbat-e Jām · Kalai-Mor · Tachta-Bazar · Vozv. Andk

Torbat-e Heydarīyeh · 1267 · Kuška · Dowlat

K H O R A S A N · Kūh-e Kalāt · 2850 · Khvāf · 980 · F A R Y Ā

Deyhūk · 2845 · Qāyen · Bohnābād · Sangān · Kūhestān · Golrān · Koshk-e Kohneh · Bālā Morghāb · Qeyşār · Meymaneh

I R A N · Farrokhī · Tir Pol · Ghūrīān · Qal'eh-ye Now · Qādes · Belcheragh · Darz ab

D A S H T-E · Kūh-e Nāy Band · 2992 · Khūr · Shāhrakht · Yazdān · 2110 Kūh-e Do Shākh · HERĀT · Karokh · 3588 · Qal'eh-ye Niaz · 3497 · Bandar-e Mollāha · Naleng · Chirās

Nāy Band · Khūsf · Birjand · 2877 Kūh-e Āhangārān · Peshīn Jān · Pahreh · Ribat · Seh Darakht · Chesht-e Sharīf · Selseleh-ye Safīd Kūh · Āhangārān · Dahan Kās

Chehel Pāyeh · 2599 · Sarbīsheh · 2783 · Tabas · Mandel · Kārīz-e Dasht · Daryā-ye Adraskan · Adraskan · Farsi · Tūlak · Kūh-e Wāla · Shahrak · Shotor Khūn

Kūh-e 2438 Darband · Feyzābād · Dasht-e Nāomīd · Anār Darreh · Shīndand · Azīzābād · Jijah · 2143 Mil Kūh · Khush · Titān · Selseleh-ye Sīāh Kūh · 3923 · Dowlat Yār

Bālā Howz · Sahlābād · Dūruh · 2561 · Dasht-e Barang · Farāh · Zar Mardān · Por Chaman · Teyvareh · Kūh-e Sangān · 3699 Qal'eh-ye Sang-e Takht

2729 Shāh Kūh · Shūsf · Kūh-e Estand · 2488 · Nehbandān · Siah Band · 2560 Khormāleq · Tavesk · 4148 · Kūh-e Qeyşār · 4101 Timran · Sharan

Pashū'īyeh · 2061 · Bandān · Lāsh-e Joveyn · Pishavaran · Jehīl-e Pūzak · Delārām · Vāshīr · Baghrān · Khowleh · Gīzāb · 3986 Koh-i-Khurd

K E R M A N · Noşratābād · Kūh-e Malūsān · 2565 · Zābol · Chakhānsūr · Arērē · Khash · Posht-e Rūd · Langara · Now Zād · Shāhidān · Mūsá Qal'eh · Hazar Qadam

E L Ū T · Hormak · Ramrud · Tarakun · Sekūheh · Zaranj · Gonbadeh · Gereshk · Sangīn · Kajakī · 3787 Kāfar Jār Ghar · Towkhi · Meydan Kalay

Fahraj · Gorg · Kūh-e Malek Sīāh · Qual'eh-ye Fath · Sarutara · Dasht-e Mārgow · Qal'eh-ye Best · Khūgīānī · Ziārat-e Shah Maqsūd · Qalāt-i-Ghilzai

Zāhedān · 1645 · Gydar-i-Shah · Chahār Borjak · Daryā-ye Helmand · Küchnay Darvīshān · Dand · Pomazai · 2857 Jaldak

N Ī M R Ū Z · 2341 · Rūdbar · Palālak · Dehshū · Landay · Şaffār Kalay · QANDAHAR (KANDAHAR) · Khūgīānī · Z Ā B O L

Nāzil · Saindak · Mīrjāveh · Lādīz · 4042 · 2332 Sultan · Manzil · 2462 · Malik Nāro · Kanuk · R ī g e s t ā n · 1824 · Spin Būldak · Ma'rūf · Qal'eh-ye Rashīd

Shandak · Kūh-e Taftān · Mashki Chāh · Kanuk · Chaman · Khojak · Gulistān · Towrzi · Toba K · 3086 · Murgha Faqīrzai · Hindubagh

2547 · Kūh-e Bazmān · Bazmān · Khāsh · Chāh Sandan · Nok Kundi · Chāgai · Hāmūn-i-Lora · Pishin Lora · Nushki · QUETTA · 3593 · Ziārat · Khost

3485 · Kārevāndar · Dālbandīn · Ahmad Wāl · Mastung · Mach · Harnai

Bampūr · Iranshahr · 2743 Kūh-e Bīrag · Paskūh · 2620 · Qila Lādgasht · Shahestān · Yakmach · Rās Koh · 3007 · Khārān · Kalāt · Koh-i-Mārān · 3277 · Johan · Dādhar · 1604 · Sibi · Chakar · P

Chānf · 2093 · Kūh-e Nokhowch · Zābolī

A B C ↓ **138** D E 66° F G

← **73** ← **114** 32° 28°

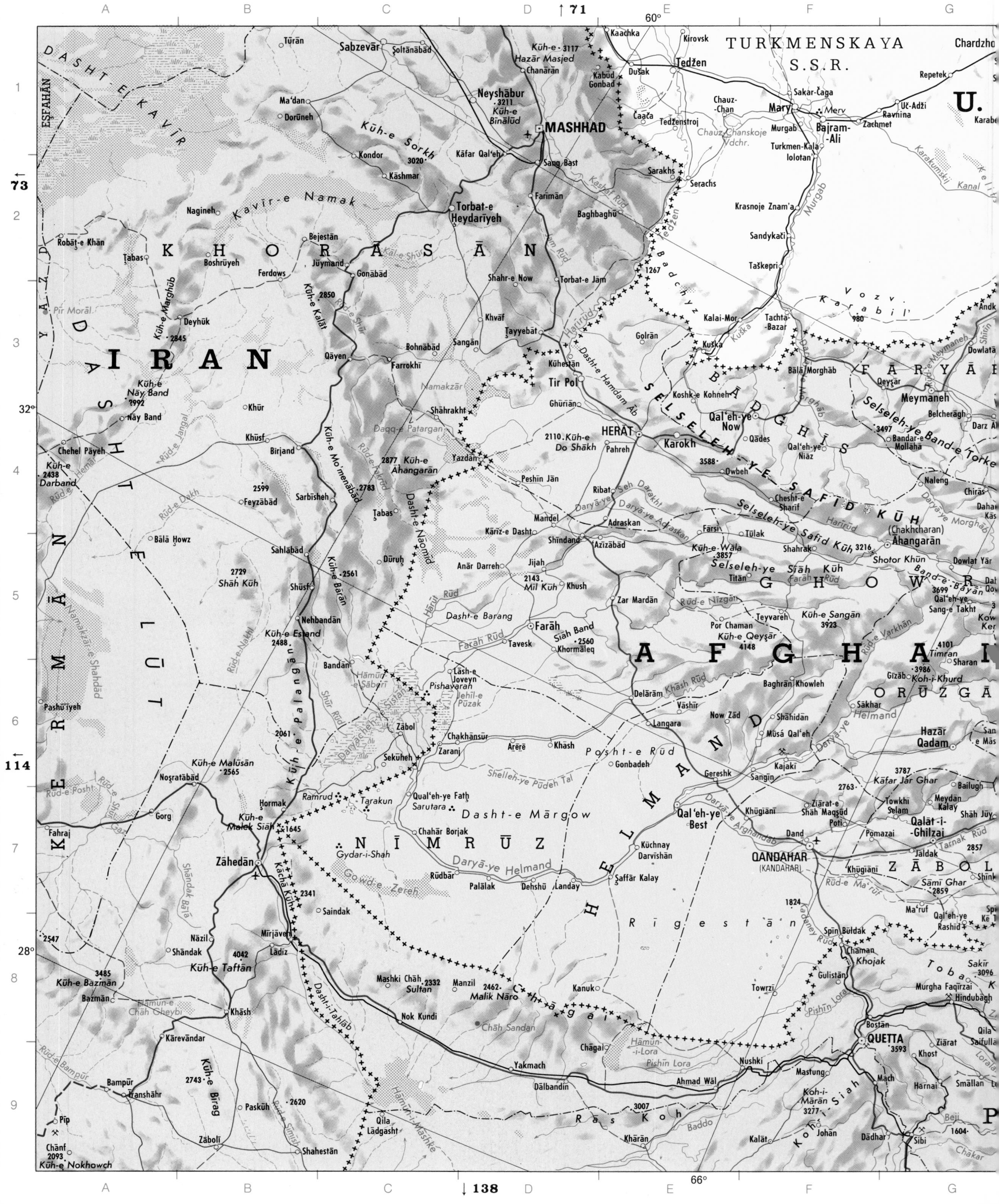

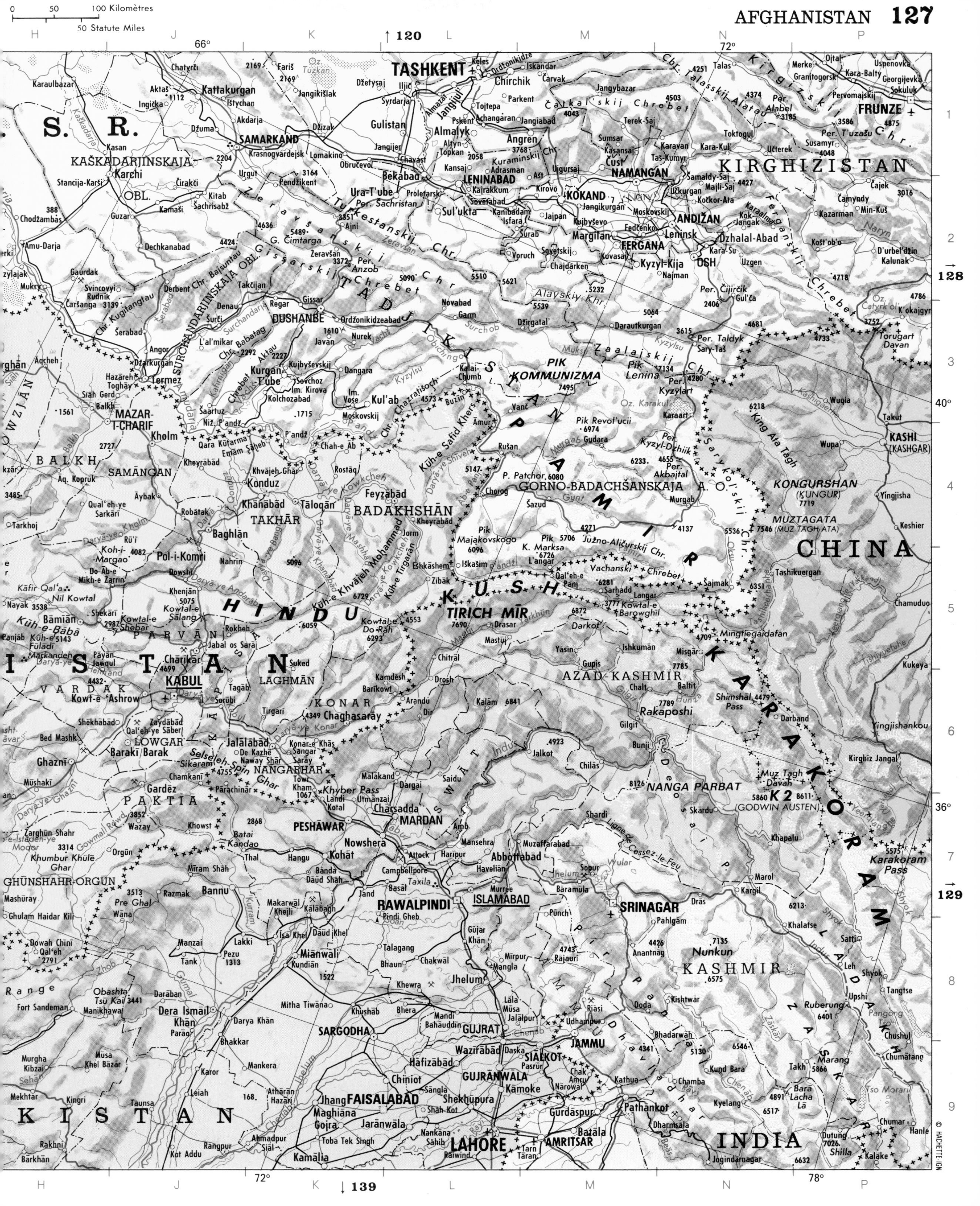

0 50 100 Kilomètres
50 Statute Miles

**S.S.R.**

**KIRGHIZISTAN**

**TASHKENT**
**SAMARKAND**
KAŠKADARJINSKAJA OBL.
**LENINABAD**
**NAMANGAN**
**KOKAND**
**ANDIŽAN**
**FERGANA**
**OSH**
**FRUNZE**

**DUSHANBE**
TADŽIKISTAN

**PIK KOMMUNIZMA** 7495
Pik Lenina 7134

**MAZAR-I-CHARIF**
BALKH
SAMANGAN
**BADAKHSHAN**
TAKHĀR

GORNO-BADACHŠANSKAJA A.O.

**CHINA**

**KASHI (KASHGAR)**

KONGURSHAN (KUNGUR) 7719
MUZTAGATA (MUZ TAGH ATA) 7546

PAMIR

**Baghlān**
Pol-i-Komri
**Bāmiān**
Kūh-e-Bābā

HINDU KUSH
TIRICH MĪR 7690

PARVĀN
VARDĀK
**KABUL**
LAGHMĀN
KONAR
NANGARHAR
Jalālābād
Khyber Pass
Chaghasarāy

AZAD-KASHMIR
Rakaposhi 7789
Gilgit
Skardu

**K2 (GODWIN AUSTEN)** 8611

NANGA PARBAT 8126

KARAKORAM
Karakoram Pass

PAKTIA
Ghaznī
Gardez
LOWGAR
**PESHĀWAR**
**MARDAN**
Nowshera
Kohāt
**RAWALPINDI**
**ISLAMABAD**
**SRINAGAR**

KASHMIR
Nunkun 7135
Leh
**JAMMU**
Udhampur
**SIALKOT**
**GUJRAT**
Wazirabad

**SARGODHA**
Jhelum
Mianwali
Dera Ismail Khan
**GUJRĀNWALA**
**FAISALABAD**
**LAHORE**
**AMRITSAR**

**INDIA**

KISTAN

Fort Sandeman

↑120  ↓139  →128  →129
© HACHETTE-IGN

Scale 1 : 5,000,000

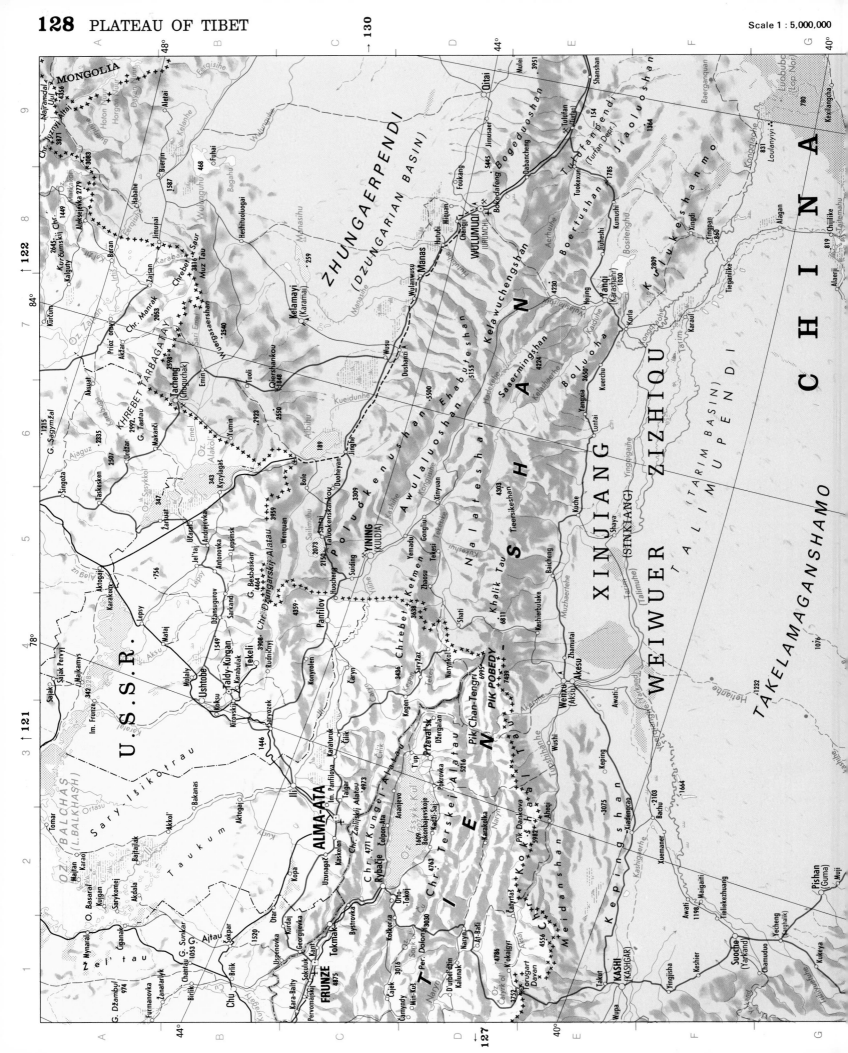

MONGOLIA

ZHUNGAERPENDI
(DZUNGARIAN BASIN)

KHREBET TARBAGATAY

U.S.S.R.

OZ. BALCHAS
(L.BALKHASH)

ALMA-ATA

FRUNZE

WULUMUQI
(URUMCHI)

TIAN SHAN

XINJIANG
(SINKIANG)

WEIWUER ZIZHIQU

TALIM (TARIM BASIN) UPENDI

TAKELAMAGANSHAMO

KASHI
(KASHGAR)

Suoche
(Yarkand)

CHINA

Pishan
(Guma)

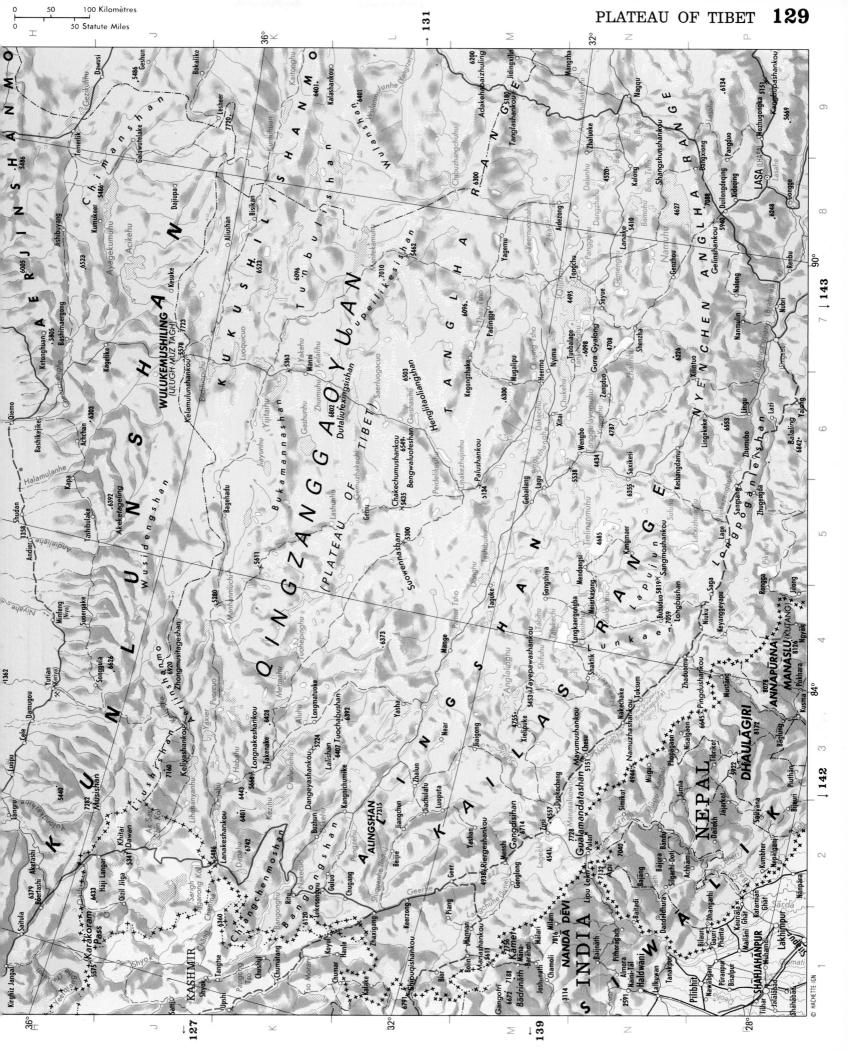

GOBI DESERT

DUNDGOVĬ

ÖMNÖGOVĬ

ÖVÖRHANGAY

HANGAY

ARHANGAY

HÖVSGÖL

TÖV

DZAVHAN

MONGOL ALTAYN NURUU

GOVĬ ALTAYN NURUU

GOVĬ-ALTAY

BAYAN-ÖLGIY

U.S.S.R.

BEISHAN

GASHUNSHAMO

Nuomingminggenshamo

Wall of Genghis Khan

DZUNGAERPENDI (DZUNGARIA)

Tsengel Hayrhan Uul

Altayn Ömnöh Govi

Edrengiyn Nuruu

Suluxing Tagh

Keerleikeshan

Mazongshan

Luóbubo (Lop Nor)

Darhan
Selenge
Bulgan
Hutag
Mörön
Tsetserleg
Tariat
Hangay
Bayanhongor
Altay
Hovd
Bulgan
Ulaanhus
Ölgiy
Delgerhangay
Dalandzadgad
Mandal-Ovoo
Hami
Shanshan
Tulufan (Turfan)
Jitai
Aletai
Mulei
Anxi
Daquan

GOBI DESERT

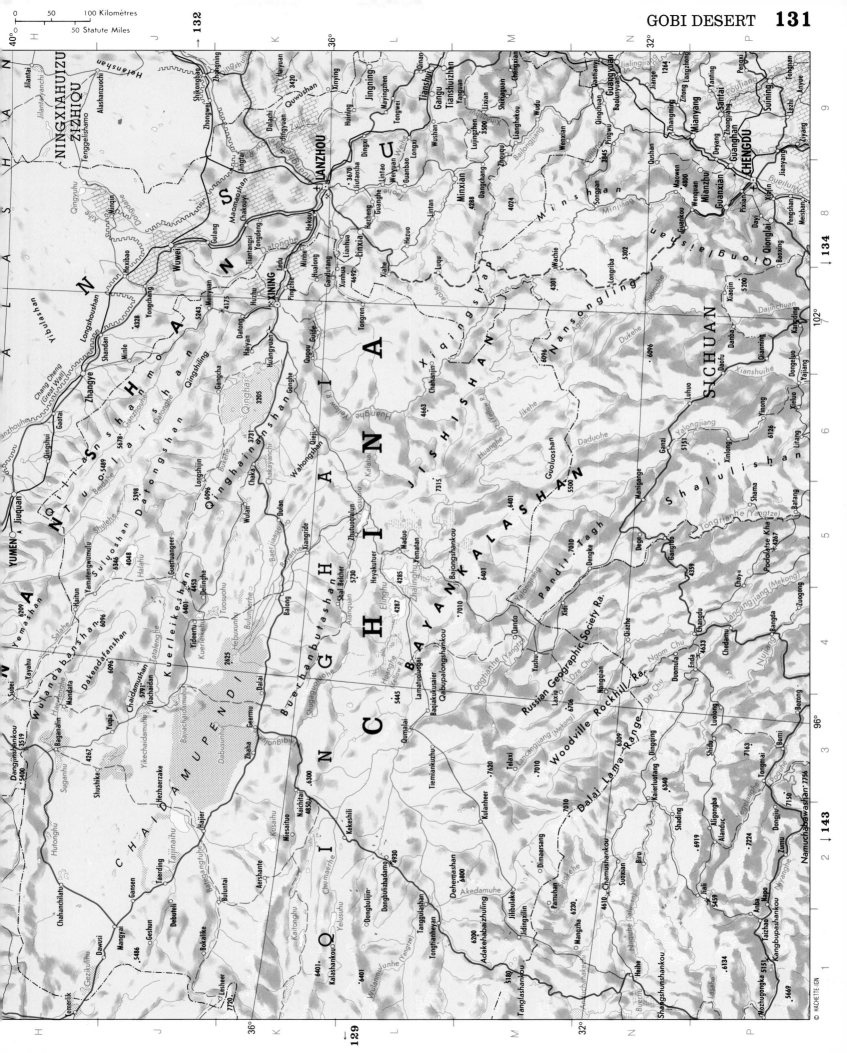

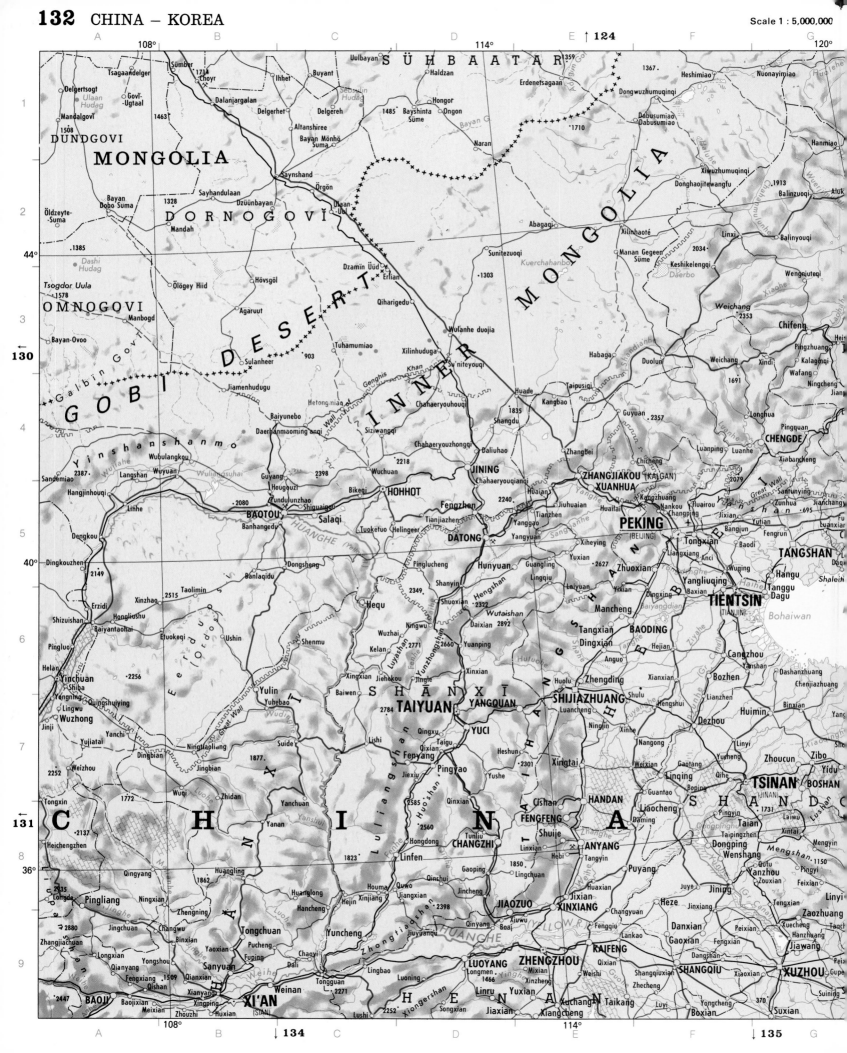

0 50 100 Kilomètres
0 50 Statute Miles

126° ↑ 125 132°

**MANCHURIAN PLAIN**

Taoan
Tuquan
Tongyu
Dehui
Honggi
Taolaizhad
Shanhetun
Laoheishan
Razdol'npje
Art'om
Smol'aninovo
Sučan

Nongan
Shulan
Jiangmifeng
Xinzhan
Emusuo
Jingbohi
1071
Vol'no
Nadeždinskoje
Uglovoje
Sokolovka

Balahushi
-278
Fengku
Fulongguan
-231
Changling
Jiutai
Jiuzhan
Jiaohe
Huangnihe
Guandiru
1225
1498
Panling
Chunhua
Baraba
**VLADIVOSTOK**
Bol. Kamen'
**NAKHODKA**

Zhanyu
Fengku
Yinmahe
**JILIN**
Dunhua
Dashitou
1126
1498
Panling
Slav'anka
Tromyslovka
Dunai
Zaliv America

**CHANGCHUN**
-594
Huaide
Yitong
Panshi
Huadian
Antu
Yanji
Honchun
Kraskino
Posjet
**U.S.S.R.**

Keerginzuozhongqi
Shuangshan
1236
Longjing
1341
Kaishantun
Sanhe
Aozi
Seosura
Zaliv Petra Velikogo

Kailu
Shebaitu
Tongliao
**SIPING**
**LIAOYUAN (SIAN)**
Huinan
Jingyu
Helong
1487
Musan
**Ungigi**
Gomusan
**Najin**
Ungigi-man

iyefu
Bamiancheng
Dongfeng
Hailong
Meihekou
Shanchengzhen
Dayangcha
Samjiyeon
2744
Gyeongseong
Nanam
2541
**CHONGJIN**

Naimanqi
Kulungi
-549
Xifeng
1287
Fusong
Changbaishan
2435
Nampotae-san
Gyeongseong-man
Eorang-dan

Kangping
Tongjiangkou
Laocheng
Quingyuan
Linjiang
2150
Changbai
Bocheonbo
Baegam
Yeongan

**FUXIN**
Faku
Tieling
1094
Xinbin
1335
Yayuan
Hyesan
Singalpajin
Gilju
Musu-dan

Beipiao
819
Heishan
Xinlitun
1367
Huanren
Jian
Manpo
Huchang
Gabsan
Yongyang
Honggun
**KIMCHAEK**

**SHENYANG (MOUKDEN)**
**FUSHUN**
1359
Jianchang
Ganggye
Dongmungeori
Pungsan
2522
Danchon

Beizhen
Dahushan
Goubangzi
Saima
Guanshui
Kuandian
1470
Chosan
Unsong
Jangjin
Hoban
**NORTH KOREA**

**LIAOYANG**
**ANSHAN**
**BENXI**
Tengaobao
Tongyuanbao
2184
Heuicheon
Iwon
Bugcheong
Sinchang

**JINZHOU**
Panshan
Niuzhuang
Haicheng
Fengcheng
1452
Baeg-san
Hongweon

Jinxi
Xingcheng
**YINGKOU**
Yingkouxian
Gaiping
**DANDONG**
**SINUIJI**
Guseong
Guiang
Jangsang
Yongheung
**HAMHUNG**
**HEUNGNAM**

Suizhong
Fuzhou
Xiuyan
750
Seoncheon
Jeongju
Sinanju
Gaecheon
Oro
Goweon
**DONGHAN-MAN**

**LIAODONGBANDAO**
1132
Gushan
Ga-do
Sinmi-do
Seohan-man
Sunan
Sainjang
Yangdeog
Majeon
**WONSAN**
Tongcheon

Changxingdao
1050
Xinin
Dachangshandao
Sanig
1530
Gosan
Goseong

**LUDA (DAIREN)**
Chengzituan
**PYONGYANG**
-man
Songrim
Sepo
Changdo
Naegeumgang
Ganseong
**KOREA**

**LUSHUN (PORT ARTHUR)**
401
Jinxian
Guangludao
Changshanquando
**NAMPO**
Hwangju
Singye
Gimhwa
1708
Ullung-do

Bohai Haixia
**KOREA BAY**
Cho-do
954
**Sariwon**
Pyeongsan
Cheolweon
**CHUNCHON**
Gangreung
984

Daxiaoqindao
Tuojidao
Jangyeon
Joeryeong
846
Tosan
Yeoncheon
1577
Gyebang-san
Samcheog

Zhangshandao
Penglai
**YANTAI**
Weihai
Chengshanjiao
Sanggouwan
945
**KAESONG**
**Eujjeongbu**
Hongcheon
Samcheog

Huangxian
805
Wendeng
Baegyeong-do
Daecheong-do
Ongjin
Yeonan
Ganghwa
**SEOUL**
**WONJU**
Yeongweol
Uljin
**SOUTH KOREA**

**SHANDONGBANDAO**
Rushan
Wuleidaowan
**HAEJU**
Sunwi-do
**INCH'ON**
Yeongdeungpo
Teoju
Janghoweon
Jecheon
1219
Irweol-san
1201

Yexian
**YELLOW SEA**
**GYEONGGI-MAN**
Deogjeog-gundo
**SUWEON**
Pyeongtaeg
Anseong
Chungju
Andong
Yeongdeog

Pingdu
1158
Laiyang
Shidao
Anheung
Hongseong
Gongju
**CHONGJU**
Sangju
Euiseong
Pohang
36°

Cangkou
Anmyeon-do
Seosan
790
Cheonan
Yeongdong
Seonsan
Gimcheon
Yeongcheon

Jiaoxian
**TSINGTAO (QINGDAO)**
Oyeon-do
Daecheon
**TAEJON**
Nonsan
1594
**TAEGU**
Milyang
Gyeongju
137

Zhucheng
-740
Shuilingshandao
Janghang
Iri
Geochang
Jinyeong
**ULSAN**

Ganyu
Linhongkou
Wi-do
Buan
**KUNSAN**
**CHONJU**
1915
Namweon
**MASAN**
Jinhae
Dongrae
**PUSAN**

Lianyungang
625
Beobseongpo
Jeongeub
Damyang
Goseong
Kami-Tusima

**XINHAILIAN**
Donghai
Songjeong
Hampyeong
Naju
Boseong
**KWANGJU**
Hadong
Jinju
Chungmu
Geoje-do

Jioaxian
Bunam-gundo
Naju-gundo
**YOSU**
Suncheon
Namhae
Changseon-do
Okino Sa.
Tusima

Zhuchen
Hong-do
Heugsan-jedo
Daeheugsan-do
**MOKPO**
808
Haenam
Jindo
Geum-o-do
558
Izuhara
Tutu

Linhongkou
Soheugsan-do
Chuja-do
Wando
Bo-gildo
Goheung
Donaro-do
Hirado
**HUKUOKA**

**JAPAN**

Binhai
Funing
Yancheng
Jeju
Hanra-san
Hanrin
1950
Seoguipo
Daejeong
**Cheju-do**
Goto Retto
**NAGASAKI**
32°

120° 126°
© HACHETTE-IGN

Scale 1 : 5,000,000

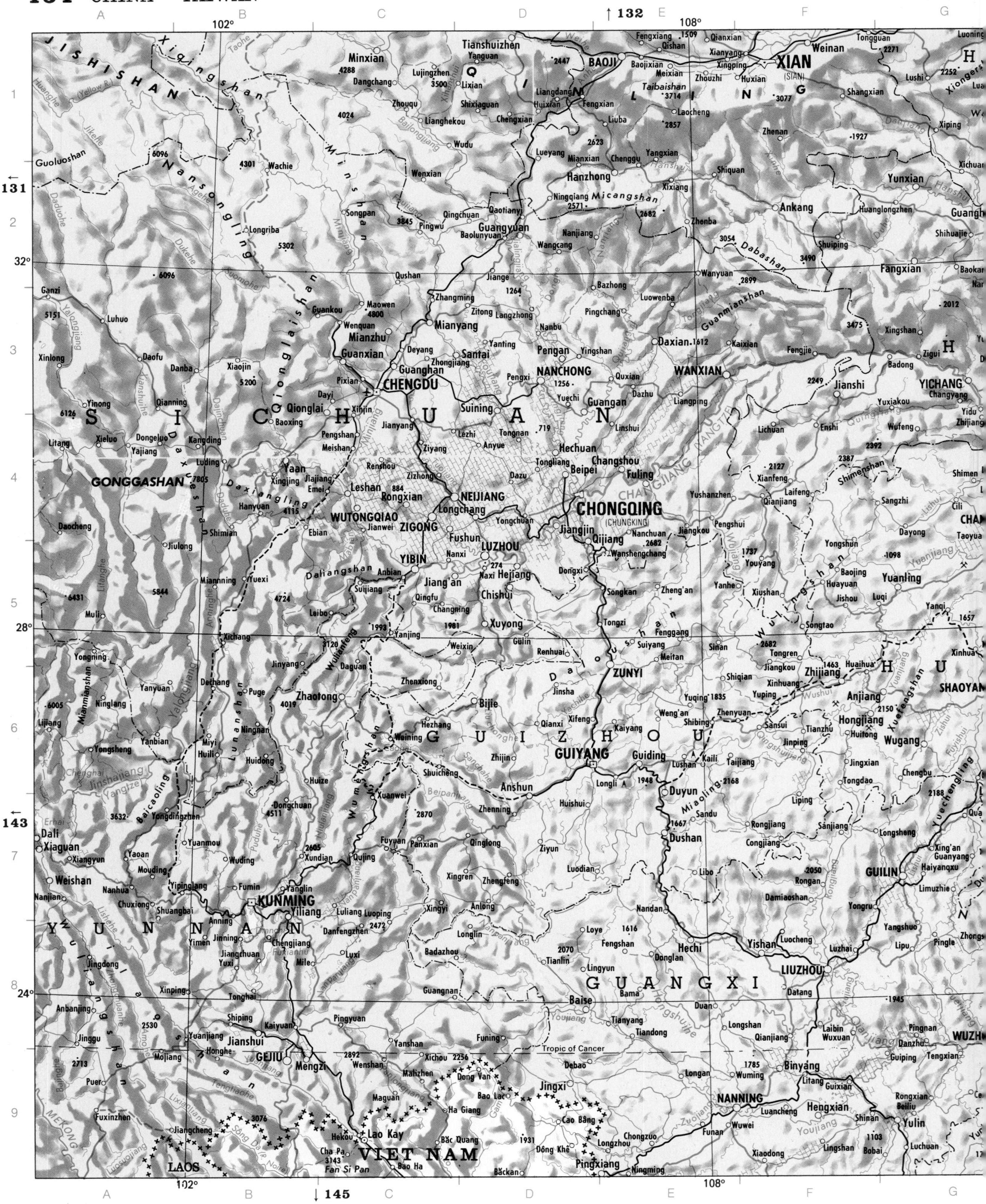

102° ↑ 132 108°

JISHISHAN
Xiqingshan
Nansongling
Minshan
Qionglaishan
Daxiangling
Daliangshan
Wumengshan
Miaoling
Xuefengshan
Wulingshan

**SICHUAN**
**YUNNAN**
**GUIZHOU**
**GUANGXI**

Huanghe (Yellow R.)
Guoluoshan 6096
Guloushan
Ganzi 5151
Xinlong
Yinong 6126
Litang
Daocheng
Jiulong
Muli 6431
Lijiang
Ninglang
Yanyuan
Yanbian
Yongsheng
Miyi
Huili
Huidong
Dali Xiaguan
Xiangyun
Weishan
Nanjian
Chuxiong
Shuangbai
**KUNMING** Yiliang
Anning
Yimen
Jinning
Jiangchuan Yuxi
Tonghai
Jianshui
Honghe
**GEJIU**
Mengzi
Pingyuan
Yanshan
Wenshan
Malizhen
Xichou 2256
Maguan

Minxian 4288
Dangchang
Zhouqu
Songpan
Longriba 5302
Wachie 4301
Wenquan
Guanxian
Mianzhu
Guanghan
Pixian
**CHENGDU**
Qionglai
Dayi
Baoxing
Xinjin
Jianyang
Pengshan
Meishan
Yaan
Xingjing
Jiajiang
Emei
Leshan
Rongxian
**ZIGONG**
**WUTONGQIAO**
Jianwei
**YIBIN**
Anbian
Suijiang
Leibo
Yuexi
Miannning
Xichang
Dechang
Huize
Dongchuan 4511
Xuanwei
Qujing
Wuding
Xundian
Mile
Luxi

Tianshuizhen
Yanguan
Lixiaguan
Lujingzhen 3500
Liangdang
**BAOJI**
Baojixian
Meixian
Xianyang
Xingping
**XIAN** (SIAN)
Weinan
Tongguan
Luoning
Xichuan
Lushi
Shangxian
Zhenan
Fengxiang 1509
Qianxian
Huxian
Zhouzhi
Taibaishan 3714
Laocheng
Liuba
Fengxian
Lueyang
Mianxian
Chenggu
Yangxian
**Hanzhong**
Ningqiang Micangshan 2571
Zhenba
Ankang
Shuiping
Fangxian 3490
Dabashan
Wanyuan 2899
Daxian 1612
**WANXIAN**
Kaixian
Fengjie
Badong
**YICHANG**
Changyang
Enshi
Wufeng
Jianshi
Lichuan
Qianjiang
Xiushan
Yongshun
Dayong
Cili

Qingchuan
Pingwu
Baolunyuan
**Guangyuan**
Jiange 1264
Zhangming
Zitong
Langzhong
Nanbu
Pengan
Yingshan
**NANCHONG**
Pengxi
Yuechi
Guangan
Dazhu
Liangping
Wangcang
Nanjiang
Pingchang
Bazhong
Luowenba

Mianyang
Deyang
Zhongjiang
Santai
Yanting
Suining
Tongnan
Lezhi
Anyue
Ziyang
Renshou
Zizhong
**NEIJIANG**
Longchang
Yongchuan
Fushun
Nanxi
Jiang'an
Qingfu
Changning 1981
Xuyong
Gulin
Naxi Hejiang
Chishui
**LUZHOU** 274
Dongxi
Songkan
Zheng'an
Tongzi
Renhuai
Fenggang
Suiyang
Meitan
**ZUNYI**
Jinsha
Xifeng
Kaiyang
Weng'an
Guiding
Longli 1948
**GUIYANG**
Qianxi
Zhijin
Bijie
Hezhang
Weining
Shuicheng
Anshun
Zhenning
Huishui
Ziyun
Luodian
Libo
Dushan 1667
Duyun 2168
Sandu
Rongjiang
Congjiang

Tongliang
Changshou
Beipei
Fuling
**CHONGQING** (CHUNGKING)
Jiangjin
Qijiang 2682
Nanchuan
Wanshengchang
Hechuan
Dazu
Yongchuan
Dongxi

Jiangkou
Xinhuang
Zhijiang 1463 Huaihua
Yuping
Anjiang
Hongjiang 2150
Huitong
Wugang
Jingxian
Tongdao
Chengbu
Liping 2188
Longsheng
Sanjiang
**GUILIN**
Xing'an
Guanyang
Haiyangxu
Limuzhe
Yongfu
Yangshuo
Lipu
Pingle
Lingchuan
Yishan
Luocheng
Luzhai
**LIUZHOU**
Datang
Xincheng
Laibin
Wuxuan
Guiping
Tengxian
**WUZHOU**
Pingnan
Danzhu
Rongxian
Beiliu
**NANNING**
Luancheng
Hengxian
Wuming
Binyang
Shinan
**Yulin**
Bobai
Xiaodong

Dongan
Hechi
Nandan
Loye 1616
Fengshan
Tianlin
Lingyun
Tiandong
Tianyang
Baise
Bama
Longan
Longzhou
Pingxiang
Ningming
Fusui
Chongzuo
Funan

**VIET NAM**
**LAOS**
Mekong
Lao Kay
Hekou
Cha Pa 3143
Fan Si Pan
Bao Ha
Bắc Quang
Ha Giang
Dong Van
Bao Lac
Cao Bằng
Đông Khê
Bắckan
Tropic of Cancer

**GONGGASHAN**
Kangding
Luding
Danba
Xiaojin 5200
Hanyuan
Shimian
Ebian
Qianning
Daofu
Luhuo
Xieluo
Yajiang
Dongeluo
Xinlong

32°
28°
24°
131
143
145

↑ **133**

0 50 100 Kilomètres
0 50 Statute Miles

114° 120°

EAST CHINA SEA

SOUTH CHINA SEA

FORMOSA STRAIT

**HENAN** · **ANHUI** · **JIANGSU** · **HUBEI** · **ZHEJIANG** · **JIANGXI** · **FUJIAN** · **HUNAN** · **GUANGDONG**

**TAIWAN (FORMOSA)**

Major cities: **HUAINAN**, **HEFEI**, **NANJING (NANKING)**, **ZHENJIANG**, **YANGZHOU**, **TAIZHOU**, **NANTONG**, **CHANGZHOU**, **CHANGSHU**, **WUXI**, **SUZHOU**, **SHANGHAI**, **HUZHOU**, **JIAXING**, **HANGZHOU**, **SHAOXING**, **NINGBO**, **WUHU**, **WUHAN**, **HUANGSHI**, **ANQING**, **JINGDEZHEN**, **NANCHANG**, **CHANGSHA**, **XIANGTAN**, **ZHUZHOU**, **WENZHOU**, **FUZHOU**, **NANPING**, **QUANZHOU**, **XIAMEN (AMOY)**, **ZHANGZHOU**, **SHANTOU**, **GANZHOU**, **MEIXIAN**, **CHAOAN**, **GUANGZHOU**, **FOSHAN**, **MACAO (Portugal)**, **KOWLOON**, **HONG KONG (United Kingdom)**, **VICTORIA**, **TSUN WAN**, **JIANGMEN**

Taiwan: **T'AIPEI**, **CHILUNG**, **SANCHUNG**, **HSINCHU**, **T'AICHUNG**, **CHIAI**, **T'AINAN**, **KAOHSIUNG**, **P'INGTUNG**, **T'aitung**, **Hualien**

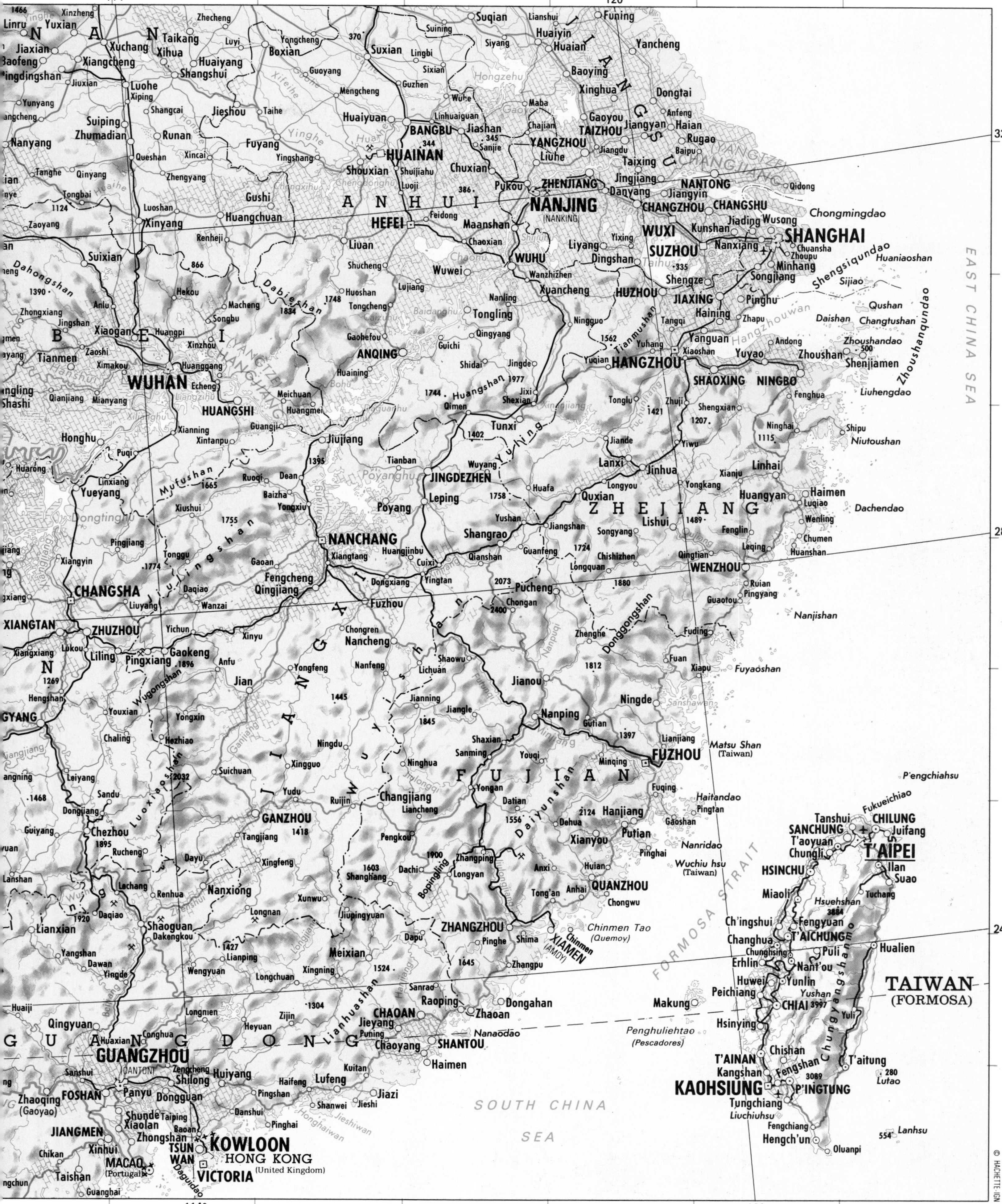

Chinmen Tao (Quemoy), Matsu Shan (Taiwan), Penghuliehtao (Pescadores), Makung, Lutao, Lanhsu, Oluanpi, Hengch'un

Dongtinghu, Poyanghu, Taihu, Hongzehu

32° 28° 24°

© HACHETTE-IGN

HONSHU

HOKKAIDO

U.S.S.R.

CHINA

J A P A N

O F

U.S.S.R.

P R I M O R S K I J   K R A J

VLADIVOSTOK

USSURIJSK

NAKHODKA

SAPPORO

OTARU

MURORAN

TOMAKOMAI

HAKODATE

ASAHIKAWA

OBIHIRO

KUSHIRO

AOMORI

HIROSAKI

HATINOHE

MORIOKA

AKITA

YAMAGATA

SENDAI

ISONOMAKI

FUKUSIMA

KORIYAMA

AIZU-WAKAMATU

IWAKI

HITATI

NIIGATA

NAGAOKA

KASIWAZAKI

Wakkanai

Nemuro

Siretoko Mi.

Sōya Mi.

La Pérouse Strait

Kunasir

Sikotan

O. Polonskogo

O. Zel'onyi

O. Tanfiljera

Malaya Kuril'skaja Gr'ada

Zaliv Petra Velikogo

Sado

Ōsima

Okusiri Tō

Rebun Tō

Risiri Tō

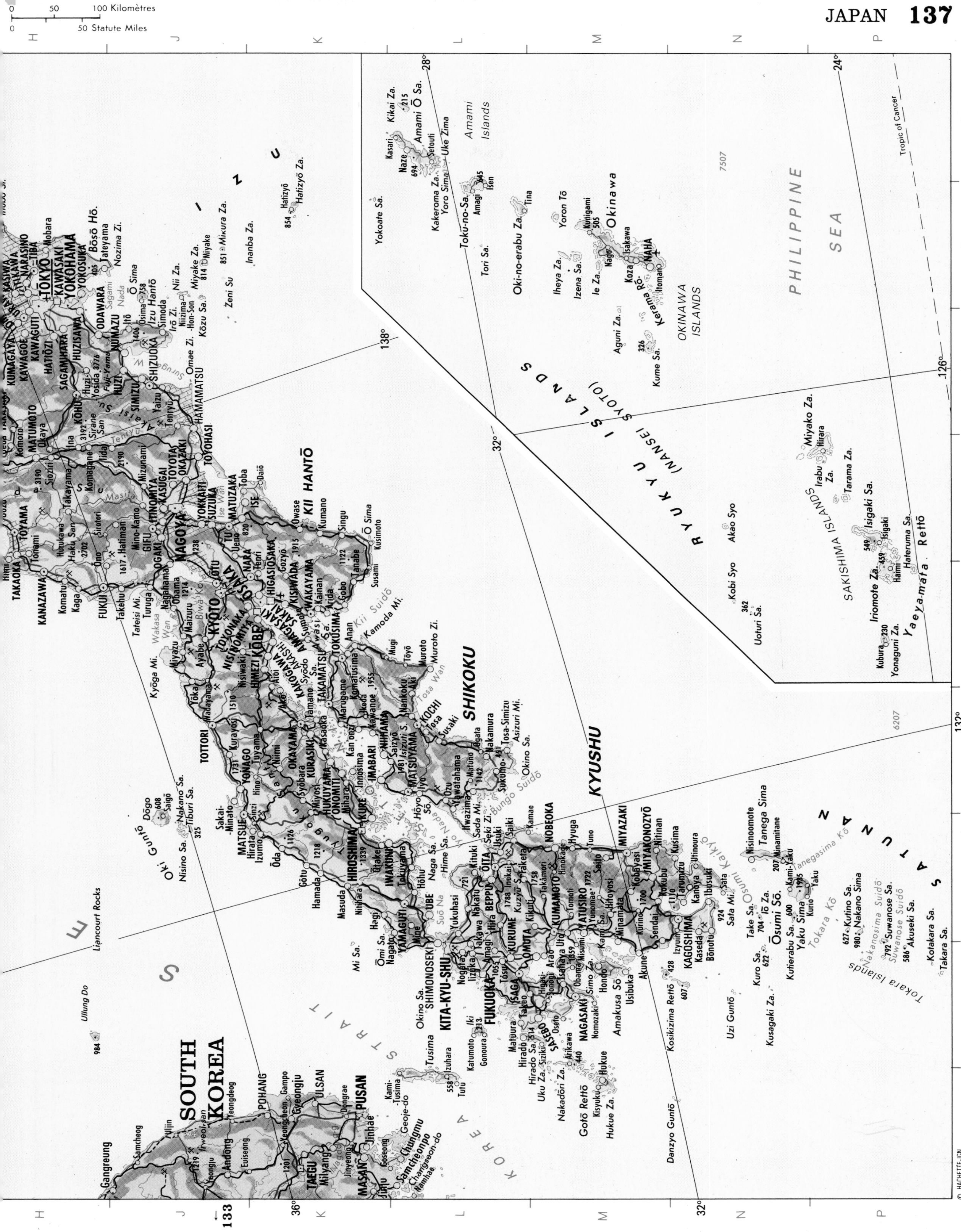

0 50 100 Kilomètres
0 50 Statute Miles

PHILIPPINE SEA

Tropic of Cancer

RYUKYU ISLANDS (NANSEI SYOTO)

Amami Islands

Kasari · Kikai Za. · 215
Naze · Amami Ō Sa. · Setouti
694 · Yoro Sima · Uke Zima
Yokoate Sa. · Toku-no-Sa. · 445 · Amagi
· Isen
Tori Sa. · Oki-no-erabu Za. · Tina
Kakeroma Za. · 894
Iheya Za. · Yoron Tō
Izena Sa. · Ie Za. · Kunigami
Nago · Isikawa · 505
Aguni Za. · Koza · Okinawa
Kerama Rô · NAHA
326 · Itoman
Kume Sa. · OKINAWA ISLANDS

SAKISHIMA ISLANDS
Miyako Za. · Hirara
Irabu Za. · Tarama Za.
549 · Isigaki Sa.
Kobi Syo · Akao Syo · 459 · Isigaki
362 · Iriomote Za. · Haim · Haterma Sa.
Uotuvi Sa. · Kubura · 230 · Yaeyama · Haterma Rettō
Yonaguni · 132°

7507

SATUNAN

PHILIPPINE

IZU

TOKYO · KAWASAKI · YOKOHAMA · YOKOSUKA
KUMAGAYA · KAWAGOE · NARASINO · TIBA
Mobara · Bōsō Hō.
ODAWARA · NUMAZU · Nozima Zi.
SAGAMIHARA · HUZISAWA · Tateyama
HATIŌZI · SIMIZU · SHIZUOKA
Huzi · Fuji-Yama 3776
KOHU · Yoshida · Katsui San
MATUMOTO · Hamamatsu · HAMAMATSU
Ō Sima · Izu Hantō
Simoda · Irō Zi.
Niizima · Hon-Son
Kōzu Sa. · Miyake Za.
Zeni Su · 814 Miyake
851 · Mikura Za.
854 · Hatiyō · Hatizyō Za.
Inanba Za.

SHIKOKU
KOCHI · Tosa
Muroto Zi. · Muroto Mi.
TOKUSIMA · Komatusima
TAKAMATSU · Naruto
MATSUYAMA · NIHAMA · IMABARI
Iyo · Saizyo
Sukumo · Okino Sa. · Asizuri Mi.
Nakamura · Tosa-Simizu

KYUSHU
MIYAZAKI · MIYAKONOZYŌ
NOBEOKA · Hyuga
OITA · BEPPU · Usuki · Saiki
KUMAMOTO · YATUSIRO
KURUME · ŌMUTA
SAGA · FUKUOKA · KITA-KYU-SHU
SHIMONOSEKI · UBE · YAMAGUTI
NAGASAKI · SASEBO
KAGOSHIMA · Sendai
Ibusuki · Kanoya
Tanega Sima · Yaku Sima
Nisinoomote · 1935
Kuro Sa. · Ō Sumi Sō
Kuchierabu Sa. · Tokara Islands
Uzi Guntō · Kosikizima Rettō
Danzyo Guntō

SOUTH KOREA
PUSAN · MASAN · ULSAN
TAEGU · Miryang · Jinhae
Gangreung · Pohang · Gyeongju
Tusima · KOREA STRAIT

NAGOYA · KYOTO · OSAKA · KOBE
GIFU · YOKKAITI · SUZUKA
NARA · WAKAYAMA · KII HANTŌ
HIGASIŌSAKA · SAKAI · AMAGASAKI
NISINOMIYA · HIMEZI
KANAZAWA · FUKUI · TOYAMA
TAKAOKA · TOTTORI · TOYOOKA
OKAYAMA · KURASIKI · FUKUYAMA
HIROSHIMA · IWAKUNI · Kure
YONAGO · MATSUE · Izumo
Oki Guntō · Dōgo · Nisino Sa.
Liancourt Rocks
Ullung Do

TOYOHASI · OKAZAKI · TOYOTA
ITINOMIYA · KASUGAI · Ō Sima
SUZUKA · ISE · Toba · Daiō
MATUZAKA · Owase · Kumano
Singu · Kusimoto

© HACHETTE-IGN

Scale 1 : 5,000,000

↑ 126

AFGHANISTAN

QUETTA
3593

IRAN

BALUCHISTAN

MAKRAN

PAKISTAN

Kārevāndar
Bampūr
Īranshāhr
Kūh-e Birag
2743
Paskūh
2620
Nok Kundi
Chāh Sandan
Yakmach
Chāgai
Hāmūn-i-Lora
Pishīn Lora
Nushki
Mastung
Ziārat
Khost
Pīp
Qila Lādgasht
Dālbandin
Ahmad Wāl
3007
Ras Koh
Baddo
Koh-i-Mārān
3277
Dādhar
Sibi
1604
Mach
Harnai
Smallan
Chānf
2093
Kūh-e Nokhowch
Zāboli
Shahestān
Qasr-e Qand
Sarbāz
2147
Hāmūn-i-Mashkel
Rūd-e Mashkid
1622
Siāhān Range
2065
Nāg
Shireza
2480
Khuzdār
Johān
Sūrāb
Anjira
Gandāva
Jhal
Nuttal
Dera
Kah

Kowr-e Kolā
Dashtiāri
Polān
Rūd-e Nahang
Rakhshān
Panjgūr
Sāka Kalāt
2282
Iebri
Central Makrān Range
Nāl
2353
Wad
Karkh
Garhi Khairo
Shāhdādkot
Ghaibidero
Kambar
Ratodero
Kandhkot
Shikarpur
Jacobābad
Thul

Dāsht
Suntsar
Kohak
Turbat
Hoshab
Labach
Mashkai
Gidar Dhor
2171
Mohenjodaro
Mehar
Lārkāna
Khairpur
Rohri
SUKKUR

Gwātar B.
Gwadar
Jīwani
Rās Pīshukān
Gwādar West B.
Rās Nūh
Makrān Coast Range
1453
Jhal Jaho
1517
Kotiro
Dadu
Moro
Rānipur
Kandiāro
Naushahro Firoz
Sorāh
Kot Diji
Miāno

Rās Jaddi
Astola I.
Khor Kalmat
Pasni
Ormāra
Hinglāj
1580
Bela
Johi
Sehwan
Mānchhar Lake

Rās Ormāra
Ras Malān
Uthal
Dureji
Nawābshāh
Sākrand
Khadro
Shāhdādpur
Hāla
Brāhmanābad
Sanghar
Khipro
Surtanāl
91

Tropic of Cancer
Sonmiāni
Hab
Thāno Bula Khān
Kotri
Tando Ādam
HYDERABAD
Mirpur Khās
Munābā
Naya Chor

Hab Nadi Chowki
KARACHI
Kālu
Jungshāhi
Tando Allāhyār
Tando Muhammad Khān
Matli
Digri
Umarkot
Naokot
Mithi

Korangi
Gharo
Mirpur Sakro
Tatta
Kinjhar Dhand
Badin
SIND
Islāmkot
Vāk

Kotri Allāhrakhio
Sujāwal
Jāti
Shāhbandar
Rahim Ki Bāzar
Diplo
4
Rann of Kutch

ARABIAN
SEA

Mouths of the Indus
INDUS
Kori Creek
Lakhpat
Khāvda
KACHCHH (Kutch)
Rāpa
217
Li

2643
Jakhau
Bhuj
434
Mandvi
Anjār
Kandla
Navlakhi
Mundra
Gulf of Kutch
Okha
Bedi Bandar
Jodiya
Morw
Dwārka
Salāya
JĀMNAGAR
Wānk
Khambhāliya
GUJ
Miāni
Jām Jodhpur
RĀJKOT
KATHIA
Porbandar
627
Upleta
Dhorāji
Jetpur
Gondal
Jas
Bāntva
Junāgadh
117 Gorakhnath
Visāvadar
Am
Keshod
Māngrol
Dhāri
648
Gir
Verāval
Kodinār
Delvāda
Diu
(G., D. & D.)

50 100 Kilomètres
50 Statute Miles

**States / Regions:** HIMACHAL PRADESH · PUNJAB · HARYANA · RAJASTHAN · UTTAR PRADESH · MADHYA PRADESH · GUJARAT · ZHONGGUO (CHINA) · NEPAL

**Major cities:** LAHORE · AMRITSAR · MULTAN · FAISALABAD · GUJRANWALA · SIALKOT · JAMMU · LUDHIANA · CHANDIGARH · DEHRA DUN · SAHARANPUR · DELHI · NEW DELHI · MEERUT · MORADABAD · RAMPUR · BAREILLY · ALIGARH · AGRA · JAIPUR · JODHPUR · AJMER · BIKANER · UDAIPUR · KOTA · GWALIOR · JHANSI · KANPUR · AHMADABAD · VADODARA (BADORA) · SURAT · INDORE · UJJAIN · BHOPAL · SAGAR · JABALPUR · RATLAM · FIROZABAD · FARRUKHABAD · SHAHJAHANPUR

**Regions / Physical features:** THAR · MARŪBHUMI · (GREAT INDIAN DESERT) · ARAVALLI · MALWĀ PATHAR · RĪWA PATHAR · VINDHYA · SATPURA · MAIDAN · INDUS · SUTLEJ · Panjnad · Chenab · Beas · Ravi · Ghaggar · Yamuna · Chambal · Betwa · Narmada · Tapti · Lūni · Banas · Gandhi Sāgar · Dhebar L.

**Other towns:** Sargodha · Gujrat · Jalalpur · Bhadarwāh · Bhakkar · Wazirabad · Daska · Pasrūr · Chamba · Kyelang · Marang · Chushul · Chumatang · Hafizabad · Kamoke · Narowal · Kathua · Pathankot · Dharmsala · Kund Bara · Takh · Hanle · Chiniot · Sangla · Shekhūpura · Gurdaspur · Batala · Jogindarnagar · Mandi · Dutung · Shilla · Kalake · Jhang · Maghiana · Gojra · Jaranwala · Toba Tek Singh · Nankana Sahib · Raiwind · Tarn Taran · Kapurthala · Hoshiarpur · Una · Bilaspur · Rampur · Chini · Bolin · Khanewal · Mandi Burewala · Okara · Kasur · Firozpur · Faridkot · Jullundur · Phagwara · Nawashahr · Bassi · Simla · Chitkul · Montgomery · Pakpattan · Haveli · Chunian · Moga · Jagraon · Rupar · Kasauli · Nahan · Bahawalnagar · Fazilka · Muktsar · Abohar · Malaut · Kot Kapura · Bhatinda · Maler Kotla · Nabha · Patiala · Ambala · Bahawalpur · Chishtian Mandi · Karanpur · Ganganagar · Hārūnabad · Fort Abbas · Sangrur · Mansa · Samana · Yamunanagar · Jagadhri · Kaithal · Thanesar · Uttarkashi · Gangotri · Badrinath · Māna · Anupgarh · Sirsa · Tohana · Fatehabad · Narwana · Jind · Karnal · Roorkee · Deoband · Shamli · Hardwar · Pauri · Rishikesh · Joshimath · Chamoli · Kishangarh · Pūgal · Birsilpur · Lunkaransar · Mahajan · Nohar · Hissar · Hānsi · Panipat · Kairana · Muzaffarnagar · Bijnor · Najibabad · Nagina · Kotdwara · Ramnagar · Almora · Naini-Tal · Haldwani · Baijnath · Rāmgarh · Sri Mohangarh · Deshnoke · Kolayat · Sardarshahr · Rajgarh · Churu · Bhiwani · Rohtak · Sonepat · Loharu · Dādri · Jhajjar · Ghaziabad · Hāpur · Chandpur · Baraut · Amroha · Kashipur · 2591 · Bāp · Nagaur · Ratangarh · Fatehpur · Jhunjhunu · Chirāwa · Mahendragarh · Rewari · Gurgaon · Bulandshahr · Sambhal · Anupshahr · Khurja · Chandausi · Nawābganj · Pilibhit · Pūranpur · Bisalpur · Pokaran · Phalodi · Dechu · Sikar · 1052 · Nawalgarh · Nārnaul · Faridabad · Palwal · Mathura · Hathras · Kasganj · Etah · Budaun · Sahaswan · Mailani · Jaisalmer · Devikot · Didwāna · Makrana · Degana · Sambhar · Chomu · Alwar · Kāman · Kosi · Dig · Bharatpur · Etāwa · Shahabad · Sitāpur · Merta Road · Merta · Pipār · Kishangarh · Nasirabad · Daosa · Bayāna · Hindaun · Gangapur · Karauli · Sir Muttra · Dholpur · Bāri · Morena · Ambāh · Mainpuri · Hardoi · Sāndi · Sandila · Bilara · Pāli · Beawar · Sojat · Mālpura · Lālsot · Deogarh · Toda Rai Singh · Tonk · Deoli · 518 · Sawai Madhopur · Jora · Bhind · Auraiya · Bilhaur · Unnāo · Barmer · Bālotra · Jālor · Sirohi · Raniwāra · Pindwāra · Guru Sikhar · Abu Road · Kankroli · Maoli · Mandalgarh · Bhilwāra · Shāhpura · Būndi · Lakheri · Sheopur · Pohri · Shivpuri · Datia · Gwalior · Lahar · Kūnch · Jhansi · Jālaun · Orai · Kālpi · Hamirpur · Rāth · Fatehpur · Mahoba · Bānda · Tharād · Sānchor · Deesa · Diodār · Pālanpur · Sidhpur · Tharanga Hill · Khed Brahma · Himatnagar · Dūngarpur · Partabgarh · Nimbahera · Bari Sādri · Chitorgarh · 624 · Bhanpura · Jhalawar · Chhabra · Guna · Ashoknagar · Chanderi · Lalitpur · Mahroni · Tikamgarh · Chhatarpur · Ajaigarh · Panna · Nagod · Satna · Rewa · Maihar · Visnagar · Kherwāra · Parsad · Nimach · Rāmpura · Suwāsra · Aklera · 503 · Rajgarh · Sironj · Bina · Khurai · Banda · Shāhgarh · Deogarh · Bans 606 · Patan · Viramgam · Ahmadabad · Mehsana · Kalol · Nadiad · Kapadvanj · Lūnāvada · Modasa · Mandsaur · Jaora · Gangdhār · Biaora · Narsinghgarh · Vidisha · Sanchi · Damoh · Hatta · Murwāra · Beohari · Shahdol · Surendranagar · Dholka · Petlad · Dakor · 206 · Godhra · Dohad · Jhabua · Ratlam · 594 · Dewās · Shujālpur · Sehore · Raisen · Gādarwāra · Khariā · Cambay · Anand · Borsad · Bhadran · 829 · Sirdārpore · Dhār · Mhow · Ujjain · Ashta · Bhopal · Ubaidullāganj · Udaipura · Hoshangabad · Itarsi · Narsinghpur · Nainpur · Mandla · Vadodara (Badora) · Dabhoi · Chhota Udaipur · Ali Rajpur · Bāgh · Mandu · Singarchori 881 · Kannod · Harda · Piparia · Pachmarhi · Lakhnadon · Surat · Navsāri · Navapur · Nandurbar · Shirpur · Khargon · Khandwa · Betul · Narmada · Tapti

Scale 1 : 5,000,000

↑ 139

→ 142

↑ 138

**MADHYA PRADESH**

**MAHARASHTRA**

**ANDHRA PRADESH**

**KARNATAKA**

**GUJARAT**

ARABIAN SEA

G. of Cambay

Gir

Konkan

Malabar Coast

JABALPUR

BHILAI

Durg RAIPUR

NAGPUR

AMRĀVATI

AKOLA

NĀNDER

JALGAON

DHŪLIA

MĀLEGAON

NĀSIK

AHMADNAGAR

POONA (PUNE)

KIRKEE

BOMBAY

BĀNDRA

THĀNA

ULHĀSNAGAR

KALYĀN

KOLHĀPUR

SHOLĀPUR

GULBARGA

BIJĀPUR

BELGAUM

HUBLI

DĀVANGERE

SHIMOGA

BHADRĀVATI

BELLARY

KURNOOL

HYDERĀBAD

SECUNDERĀBAD

NIZĀMĀBAD

WARANGAL

VIJAYAWĀDA

GUNTŪR

ELURU

RĀJAHMUNDRY

KĀKINĀDA

MACHILIPATNAM (BANDAR)

NELLORE

SURAT

BROACH

BHĀVNAGAR

CHANDRAPUR

GODAVARI

KRISHNA

NARMADA

TĀPTI

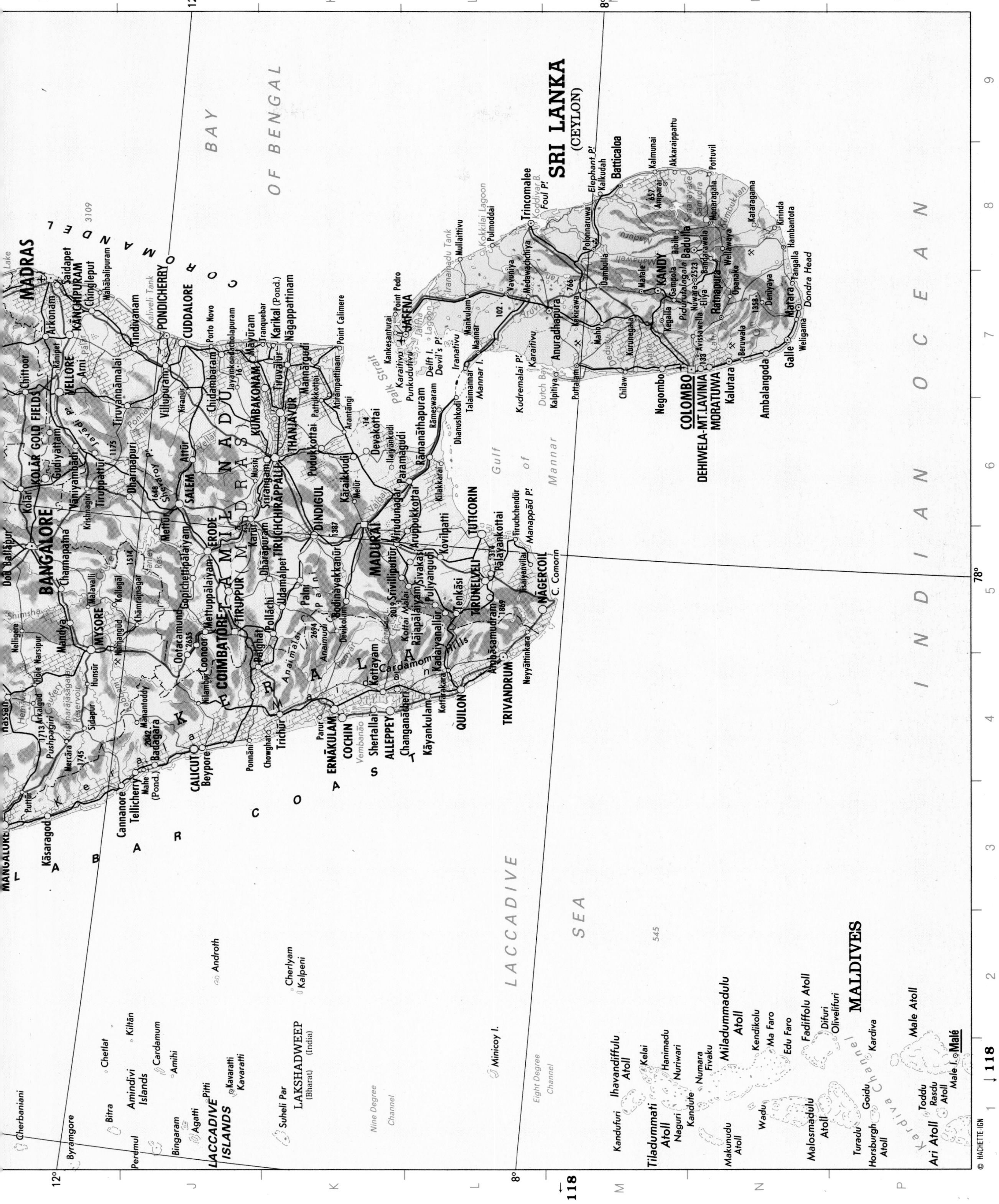

0 50 100 Kilomètres
0 50 Statute Miles

**BAY OF BENGAL**

**SRI LANKA (CEYLON)**

**MADRAS**
Lake
Saidapet
Chittoor
KANCHIPURAM
Arkonam
Ranipet
VELLORE
Arni
Chingleput
Mahabalipuram
Tindivanam
PONDICHERRY
CUDDALORE
Tiruvannamalai
Villupuram
Kilaiyur
Porto Novo
Chidambaram
Mayuram
Tranquebar
Karikal (Pond.)
Nagappattinam
Point Calimere
Krishnagiri
Dharmapuri
Attur
SALEM
KUMBAKONAM
Tiruvalur
THANJAVUR
Pudukkottai
Karaikkudi
Devakottai
KOLAR GOLD FIELDS
Kolar
Gudiyattam
Tiruppattur
Namakkal
TIRUCHCHIRAPPALI
Srirangam
Karur
DINDIGUL
Melur
BANGALORE
Hosur
Krishnagiri
Dod Ballapur
MYSORE
Mandya
Chamrajnagar
ERODE
TIRUPPUR
COIMBATORE
Ootacamund
Coonoor
Mettuppalaiyam
Pollachi
Palni
Udamalpet
Dharapuram
Madukkarai
Palladam
MADURAI
Srivilliputtur
Sivakasi
Rajapalaiyam
Puliyangudi
Sankaranayinar
TENKASI
TIRUNELVELI
TUTICORIN
Kovilpatti
Kayalpatti
Tiruchchendur
Manappad Pt.
PALAYANKOTTAI
NAGERCOIL
C. Comorin
TRIVANDRUM
QUILON
Kayankulam
ALLEPPEY
Shertallai
Changanacheri
Kottayam
ERNAKULAM
COCHIN
Trichur
Ponnani
CALICUT
Beypore
Tellicherry
Mahe (Pond.)
Cannanore
Kasaragod
MANGALORE

**K E R A L A**
**M A D R A S**
**T A M I L N A D U**
**M Y S O R E**

Cardamom Hills
Anaimudi
Anaimalai
Palni Hills

**KOROMANDEL**
**COROMANDEL**

Palk Strait
Jaffna
JAFFNA
Point Pedro
Kankesanturai
Elephant Pt.
Foul Pt.
TRINCOMALEE
Kokkilai Lagoon
Pulmoddai
Mullaittivu
Iranamadu Tank
Vavuniya
Medawachchiya
Mankulam
Mannar I.
Talaimannar
Karaitivu
Delft I.
Devil's Pt.
Rameswaram
Dhanushkodi
Pamban
Mandapam
Ramanathapuram
Paramagudi
Kilakkarai
Kalpitiya
Puttalam
Chilaw
Kudremali Pt.
ANURADHAPURA
Maho
Kekirawa
Kurunegala
Polonnaruwa
Dambulla
Matale
Bibile
Kegalla
Gampola
KANDY
Pidurutalagala 2523
Nuwara Eliya
NEGOMBO
COLOMBO
DEHIWELA-MT. LAVINIA
MORATUWA
Kalutara
Ambalangoda
Avissawella
Ratnapura
Galle
Weligama
Matara
Dondra Head
Tangalla
Hambantota
Kirinda
Katharagama
Kumbukkan
Monaragala
Wellawaya
Badulla
BATTICALOA
Kalmunai
Akkaraipattu
Pottuvil
Amparai

**I N D I A N   O C E A N**

**L A C C A D I V E   S E A**

**LACCADIVE ISLANDS**
Cherbaniani
Byramgore
Bitra
Peremul
Bingaram
Agatti
Kavaratti
Amindivi Islands
Chetlat
Kiltan
Kadamat
Amini
Andrott
Kalpeni
Cheriyam
Suheli Par
Pitti
LAKSHADWEEP (Bharat)
Minicoy I.

Nine Degree Channel
Eight Degree Channel

**MALDIVES**
Ihavandiffulu Atoll
Tiladummati Atoll
Miladummadulu Atoll
Fadiffolu Atoll
Male Atoll
Ari Atoll
Malé
Nine Degree Channel

© HACHETTE-IGN

↑ 129
← 139
← 140

**UTTAR PR.**
**NEPAL**
**SIKKIM**
**MADHYA PRADESH**
**CHHATTISGARH**
**ORISSA**
**BIHAR**
**WEST BENGAL**
**INDIA (BHARAT)**
**BANG**

Mt EVEREST (ZHUMULANGMAFENG) 8848
MAKALU 8474
KANCHENJUNGA 8597
Cho Oyu 8153
Gosainthan 8045

**LUCKNOW (LAKHNAU)**
**KANPUR**
**ALLAHABAD**
**VARANASI (BENARES)**
**MIRZAPUR**
**PATNA**
**GAYA**
**MONGHYR**
**BHAGALPUR**
**JABALPUR**
**RANCHI**
**JAMSHEDPUR**
**ROURKELA**
**BILASPUR**
**RAIPUR**
**BHILAI**
**DURG**
**SAMBALPUR**
**CUTTACK**
**BHUBANESWAR**
**BERHAMPUR**
**VISHAKHAPATNAM**
**RAJAHMUNDRY**
**KAKINADA**
**ELURU**
**MACHILIPATNAM**
**HOWRAH**
**CALCUTTA**
**KHARAGPUR**
**BURDWAN**
**ASANSOL**
**KHULNA**
**BARANAGAR**
**BHATPARA**
**SERAMPORE**
**CHINSURA**
**RAJSHAHI**
**DARBHANGA**
**MUZAFFARPUR**
**GORAKHPUR**
**FAIZABAD**

KATHMANDU
Bhadgaon
Patan (Lalitpur)
Darjeeling
Kalimpong
Gangtok
Siliguri
Jalpaiguri

Mainpuri · Hardoi · Sandi · Biswan · Bahraich · Balrampur
Etawah · Kannauj · Nawabganj · Gonda · Bhairawa
Auraiya · Unnao · Jhawani
Kalpi · Orai · Rae Bareli · Sultanpur
Hamirpur · Fatehpur · Akbarpur · Tanda · Deoria · Gopalganj · Motihari · Sitamarhi
Banda · Jaunpur · Mau · Ghazipur · Ballia · Chapra · Hajipur · Samastipur
Mahoba · Bhadohi · Chunar · Buxar · Arrah · Danapur · Begusarai · Purnea
Chhatarpur · Ajaigarh · Panna · Satna · Rewa · Sidhi · Robertsganj · Sasaram · Dehri · Aurangabad · Nawada · Jamui · Banka
Maihar · Beohari · Daltonganj · Hazaribagh · Giridih · Deoghar · Dumka
Murwara · Khamaria · Shahdol · Manendragarh · Chirmiri · Ambikapur · Latehar · Chatra · Barhi
Mandla · Nainpur · Balaghat · Dharmjaygarh · Korba · Jashpurnagar · Gumla · Khunti · Purulia · Bankura · Bishnupur
Gondia · Khairagarh · Raigarh · Champa · Sundargarh · Simdega · Chakradharpur · Chaibasa · Saraikela · Jhargram · Midnapore
Raj Nandgaon · Dhamtari · Nawapara · Patnagarh · Bolangir · Sonepur · Balasore · Bhadrakh
Kanker · Balod · Tilagarh · Baudh · Athmallik · Angul · Dhenkanal · Jajpur
Paralkote · Kondagaon · Dharmgarh · Bhawanipatna · Nayagarh · Khurda · Puri · Konarak
Bijapur · Jagdalpur · Nowrangapur · Rayagada · Russellkonda · Ballipadar · Chilka Lake
Sukma · Tulasi · Jeypore · Koraput · Parvatipuram · Gunupur · Parlakimidi · Chatrapur
Konta · Malakanagiri · Salur · Ichchapuram · Tekkali · Srikakulam
Devadi Munda · Vizianagaram · Anakapalle · Narsipatnam
Gudivada · Bhimavaram · Amalapuram · Narasapur · Divi

GANGES
BAY OF BENGAL
MOUTHS OF THE GANGES
SUNDARBANS
Chilka Lake
Hiratud Dam
Tropic of Cancer
24°
20°
16°
84°
90°
BAGHELKHAND
CHHOTA NAGPUR
GODAVARI

0 50 100 Kilomètres
0 50 Statute Miles

**Countries / Regions:** CHINA · BURMA · THAILAND · LAOS · ARUNACHAL PRADESH · ASSAM · NAGALAND · MANIPUR · MIZORAM · TRIPURA · MEGHALAYA · DESH · CHIN · SAGAING · KACHIN · YUNNAN · SHAN · KAYAH · KAREN · ARAKAN · PEGU

**Selected place names:**

Naidong · Yangzhuyonghu · Zhegu · Kartotra La · 4862 · Kongmo La · 5340 · Zhuosamu · 6037 · Motuo · Singing · 4755 · 4359 · 6736 · Sudun · Ningjing · Baiyunding

Long · Luozha · Lagangzong · Kula Gangri · 7620 · Longzi · San'anzhuling · Mirl P · Subansiri · Mara · 3983 · Along · 5230 · Chayu · 5881 · Hkakabo Razi · 6005 · 6110 · 5151 · Derong · Xiangcheng · Daocheng · Muli

Tongsa Dzong · Bomdila · 4523 · Takum · 3776 · Hāpoli · Murkong Selek · Sadiya · Saikhoa Ghāt · Chameliang · 5304 · Gongshan · Zhongdian · Yongning · Yanbian

Tashigang · Nowgong · Tezpur · Jorhāt · Sibsāgar · Dibrugarh · Tinsukia · Digboi · 4578 · Putao · Fugong · Weixi · 6005 · Ninglang

GAUHĀTI · Mangaldai · Rangia · Silghat · Golāghāt · Khela · Patkoi P · 1219 · Pangsau Pass · Tarung · 2432 · Shingbwiyang · Sumprabum · 4389 · 4755 · 4938 · Lijiang

Shillong · 1965 · Nongpoh · Diphu · Mokokchūng · Tuensang · 2638 · 2692 · Bumhpa Bum · 3410 · Htawgaw · 3803 · Bijiang · Yunlong · Haoqing · Yongsheng

Cherrapunji · Muphlang · Rajbāri · NAGALAND · 3826 · Saramati · Singkaling Hkāmti · Kamaing · 2569 · Mogaung · Sadon · 3403 · Tengchong · Baoshan · XIAGUAN · Dali

Jāria · Sunāmganj · Chhatak · Lumding · Kohīma · 3014 · Homalin · Taungthonlon · 1708 · Hopin · Myitkyinā · Lianghe · Longling · 4133 · Taihezhen · Weishan

Sylhet · Hailākāndi · Silchar · MANIPUR · IMPHAL · Thoubāl · Mansi · Mohnyin · 2392 · Yingjiang · Changning · Luxi · 3217 · Yunxian · Jingdong

Agartala · TRIPURA · Aizwal · 2140 · Tamu · Banmauk · Indaw · Shwegu · Bhamo · Ruili · Zhenkang · Gengma · Shuangjiang · Jinggu

CHITTAGONG · Rāngāmāti · Kaptai · Haka · Falam · Kalewa · Kyunhla · Tigyaing · Katha · Si-u · 2350 · Namhkàm · Mu-se · 2948 · Menglang · Lincang · Anbanjing · 2530

Cox's Bāzār · Lungleh · Tiddim · 2703 · Kalemyo · Taze · Thabeikkyin · Mōng Mit · 2299 · Bawdwin · Namtu · Hsenwi · Ho-pang · 2640 · Cangyuan · 2713 · Puer

MIZORAM · Mingin · Ye-u · Shwebo · Mogok · Namhsan · Lashio · Mān Panglao · 2675 · 2490 · Kunlong

Paletwa · Gangaw · Kani · Budalin · Ayadaw · Monywa · Madaya · Mōng Yai · Hsipaw · Ximeng · Lancang · Fuxinzhen

BURMA · 1329 · Pale · Myinmu · MANDALAY · Maymyo · Kyawkku · Kē-hsi · Mānsan · Mōng Hsu · Menglian · Mandun · Yunjinghong · Menghai · 2380 · Mengban

Teknāf · Maungdaw · M.t Victoria · 3200 · Kanpetlet · Saw · Pagan · Myaing · Pauk · Pakokku · MYINGYAN · Myittha · Sagaing · Kyaukse · Mōng Küng · Mōng Nawng · Mōng Yang · Keng Tung · 2380 · Loi Mwe · Mōng Yawng · Muang Sing · Louang Namtha

Myohaung · Minbya · Seikpyu · Chauk · Popa · 1518 · Kyaukpadaung · Thazi · Wundwin · Taungtha · Lawksawk · 2363 · Pangtara · Ta-kawl · 2563 · Mōng Hpayak · 2058

SITTWE (AKYAB) · Sidoktaya · Salin · Yenangyaung · Myothit · Yamethin · MEIKTILA · Kalaw · Kyong · 2518 · Taunggyi · Mōng Sit · Keng Tawng · Mōng Nai · Mōng Pan · HOUAKHONG · LAOS

Kyauktaw · Minbu · Magwe · Pyawbwe · Pintaung · Mawkmai · Mōng Ton · Mae Sai · Chiang Khong · Muang Paktha · 144

Ramree I. · Kyaukpyu · Pauksa Ngape · 1708 · Yenanma · Taungdwingyi · Sa-koi · 1890 · Fang · Chiang Rai · Muang Pakbeng · Nameo · 20°

Cheduba I. · Taungup · Mindon · Lewe · Thayetmyo · 611 · Loi-kaw · 2163 · Pai · 1727 · Mae Hong Son · Phrao · Thoeng · Phan · Muang Rôngsa

PROME · Paukkaung · Toungoo · KAYAH · Bawlake · Mawchi · 2623 · Nattaung · Mae Taeng · 2030 · Pua · Xaignabouri

Paungde · Pyu · Kyaukkyi · Doi Inthanon · 2600 · Chom Thong · CHIENG-MAI · Lamphun · Lampang · Pak-Lay

Myanaung · Nantha K. · PEGU · Nyaunglebin · Tharrawaddy · Shwegyin · Mae Sariang · Hang Dong · Ban Hong · Phrae · 1727 · Muang Pak-Lay

HENZADA · PEGU · Danubyu · Taikkyi · Waw · Kyaiklo · Om Koi · Den Chai · Tha Pla · Si Satchahalai · Sop Prap · Uttaradit · Loei · M. Boten

THAILAND

↑ **143**

**CHITTAGONG**
**BANGLADESH**

Kutubdia I.
Maiskhāl I.
Cox's Bāzār
Elephant Pt
Teknāf
Maungdaw
Saint-Martins Islands
Rathedaung
Myohaung
Minbya
Oyster I.
**SITTWE**
(AKYAB)

Dohāzari
INDIA
Paletwa
Kyauktaw

CHIN
Rong Klang
Mozo
Gangaw
Myaing
Yesagyo
Pakokku
Pauk
Saw
Seikpyu
Chauk
Kyaukpadaung
Sidoktaya
Salin
Pagan

BURMA
Kani
Budalin
Ayadaw
Monywa
Myinmu
Sagaing
MANDALAY
Madaya
Maymyo
Shwebo
Singu
Myingyan
Myittha
Kyaukse
Wundwin
Thazi
MEIKTILA
Pyawbwe
Yamethin
Kalaw
Inle

Hsipaw
Mān Panglao 2675
Ximeng
Lancang
Fuxinzhen
Mong Yai
Pāng Yāng 2608
Menglian
Mandun
Yunjinghong
Kē-hsi
Mānsān
Mong Küng
Mong Hsu
Mong Nawng
Mong Yang
Menghai 2380
Ta-kaw
Keng Tung 2380
Loi Mwe 2563
Mong Yawng
Muang Sing
Louang Namt 2058

SHAN

Sun. 1989
M! Victoria 3200 Kanpetlet
Popa 1518
Taungtha
Yenangyaung
Myothit
Zawgyi

**20°**

Pauksa
Ngape 1708
Minbu
Magwe
Yenanma
Mindon
Kyaukpyu
Ramree I.
Ramree
Cheduba
Cheduba I.
Ye Kyun
Unguan I.
Sandoway
Taungup Pass
Nantha K.

Khadaungnge 1328
PROME
Taungup
1286
Myanaung
Ingabu
Gwa
HENZADA
Ngathainggyaung

Thayetmyo 611
Binhon Taung
Yedashe
Thandaung
Mawchi
Nattaung 2623
Paukkaung
Toungoo
Paungde 820
Pyu
Kyaukkyi
Nyaunglebin
Letpadan
Tharrawaddy
Waw
PEGU
Taikkyi

KAYAH
Loi-kaw 2163
Bawlake 1727
1890
Fang
Chiang Rai
Mae Sai
Chiang Khong
Muang Paktha
Muang Pakbeng

HOUAKHONG

Khun Yuam
Mae Hong Son
Pai
Phrao
Phan
Thoeng
Ban Pakkhop

Doi Inthanon 2600
Hang Dong
CHIENG MAI
Lamphun
Mae Taeng 2030
Ngao
Phayao
Pong
Pua 2079
Nan
Xaignal

Mae Chaem
Ban Hong
Lampang
Rong Kwang 1727
Phrae
Xaignabu

Chom Thong
Hot
Om Koi
Li
Thoen
Sop Prap
Den Chai
Tha Pla
Muang
Kenthao
M! Boten 2300
Muang
Muang
Tha

SALWEEN
Papun
Shwegyin
Kadaingti
Kyaikto
Bilin
Hlaingbwe
Pa-an
2080
Tha Song Yang
Mae Ramat
Tak
Sawankhalok
Sukhothai
Phitsanulok
Si Satchanalai
Uttaradit
Nam Pat
Dan Sai 1819
Lom Sak

BASSEIN
Myaungwya 427
Moulmeingyun
Danubyu
Kyaunggon
Pantanaw
Ma-ubin
Insein
**RANGOON**
Syriam
Kyauktan
Kungyangon
Thongwa

IRRAWADDY
Labutta
Pyapon
Ngayok Aw

**16°**

Paya Maw
Thamihla K.
Purian Pt
Kadonkani

Chaungzon
Bilugyun K.
Gulf of Martaban
MOULMEIN
Martaban
Kawkareik
Amherst

THAI

Kamphaeng Phet
Khlong Khlung
Phichit
Taphan Hin
Phetchabun
Sri Thep
Nong Phai

Kya-in
Seikkyi
Umphang 1980
Khao Mokochu
Lat Yao 772
Nakhon Sawan
Uthai Thani
Nong Bua
Chum Saeng
Wichian Buri
Phai Salt
Khon

BAY
OF
BENGAL

Thanbyuzayat
Kalegauk I.
Ye 1298
1819
Phra Chedi Sam Ong
Sangkhla
Ban Rai
Chainat
Ta Khli
Khok 551 Samrong
Si Khiu

Preparis Island

16

Heinze Chaung
Si Sawat
Ban Kao 1015
Doem Bang Nang Buat
Sing Buri
Lop Buri
Suphan Buri

Coco Channel
Coco Islands
Landfall I.
Clough Pass.
C. Price
Smith I.
Blair Bay
North Andaman
North Reef I.
Saddle Peak 732
Interview I.
Sound I.
Karen
Anderson I.
M! Diavolo
Flat I. 511
Middle Andaman
Spike I.
Baratang
Outram I.
H. Lawrence I.
Barren I.
Defence I.
J. Lawrence I.
South Andaman
Havelock I.
Neill I.
Herbertābād
North Sentinel I.
Tarmugli I. 460
Port Blair
Rutland I.
Cinque I.
South Sentinel I.
Palālānkwe
Chetamāle
West B. 190
Hut B.
Ignoitijala
Little Andaman

Narcondam I.

3308

ANDAMAN

SEA

3072

ANDAMAN
and NICOBAR
(Bharat) (India)

Moscos Kyunzu
**TAVOY**
Launglon
Thayetchaung
Tavoy Maw

Mali K.
Palaw
Kadan K. (King) 766
Thayawthadangyi Kyun
Daung K.
Saganthit Kyun
Bentinck I.
Letsôk-Aw K. (Domet)
**MERGUI** 1534
Tenasserim

MERGUI ARCHIPELAGO
Kanmaw Kyun
Maw Daung Pass
Clara I.
Lanbi K.
Kau-Ye K.
Namnoi K. 755
Pathiu

TENASSERIM
2073
Myinmoletkat Taung
642
Hua Hin
Pran Buri
Prachuap Khiri Khan 1251
Thap Sakae
905
Bang Saphan
Bokpyin
Chumphon

Kanchanaburi
Sai Yok
Tha Yang
Phet Buri
Rat Buri
Nakhon Pathom
Nakhon Nay
**BANGKOK**
**THON BURI**
Samut Prakan
Samut Sakhon
Songkhram
Chon Buri
Si Racha

Pathum Thani
Nonthaburi
Phra Nakhon Si Ayutthaya 1350
Khao Lae
Prachin Buri
Kabin
Chachoengsao
Ang Thong
Sara Buri
Sara Buri

Ko Kram Yai
Ko Samet
Sattahip
Rayong
Klaenc
Si Khiu

Gulf
of Thailand

↓ **146**

100 Kilomètres  
50 Statute Miles

↑ **134**

**CHINA**

**NANNING**

Nanning · Hengxian · Luancheng · Rongxian · Beiliu · Cenqi · Luodian
Wuwei · Shinan · Yulin · Luchuan · Yangchun · Guanghai · Chikan
Funan · Lingshan · Bobai · Taishan

Maguan · Ha Giang · Bao Lac · Cao Bằng

3076 · Hekou · Lao Kay · Bắc Quang · 1931 · Đông Khê · Longzhou · Qinzhou · Hepu · Beihai
Cha Pa · 3143 · Fan Si Pan · Na Sầm · Pingxiang · Ningming · Fangcheng · 1382
Lai Châu · Than Uyên · Tuyên Quang · Lạng Sơn · Dinh Lập · Jiangping · Mongcai
Muang Khoa · 2984 · Phú Thọ · Vĩnh Yên · B. Lam · Tiên Yên · ZHANJIANG

Phong Sali · 1842 · Điện Biên Phủ · Sơn La · **HANOI** · Bắc Ninh · Quang Yên · Hon Gai
Muang Khoa · Muang Ngoy · Mộc Châu · 1969 · Hòa Bình · 1198 · **HAIPHONG**
Muang Nambak · Muang Xiangkho · Xam Nua · Hưng Yên · Nam Định

**L A O S** · **VIETNAM**

**Luang Prabang** · 2212 · Col Barthélémy · Thanh Hóa · Sầm Sơn
Plateau de Xieng Khoang · Xiangkhoang · 2710 · Phủ Quì
**BORIKHAN** · Muang Borikhan · Khê Bô · Câu Giat
P. Bia 2818 · Muang Thathôm · Phú Diễn Châu

**VIENTIANE** · Vinh · Linh Cam · Hà Tĩnh · Ky Anh · Mui Ron
Tha Bo · Nong Khai · Tuyên Hóa · Ba Đôn
Udon Thani · Pak-Hinboun · Đông Hoi · Lê Thuy
Nakhon Phanom · Khammouan (Thakhek) · 1623 · Vĩnh Linh
Sakon Nakhon · That Phanom · Muang Mahaxai · Quang Tri
**KHON-KAEN** · Savannakhet · Xêpôn · Huong Hoa · Phong Điền · **HUÉ**
Kalasin · Mukdahan · Muang Phin · **ĐÀ NẴNG** · Cù Lao Cham
Maha Sarakham · Muang Songkhon · Ralao 2066 · Hội An · Tam Ky

**THAILAND** · Saravane · Ban Buang Nam · 2193 · **K H O S A W A I**
At Samat · M. Lakhonpheng · Plateau des Laôngam · Tong Ha · Cu Lao Re
Ubon Ratchathani · Khôngxêdôn · 1716 · Ngoc Linh 2600 · Quang Ngai
Rasi Salai · **Pakxe** · Pakxong · Dak Sut · Mui Ba Lang An
Sisaket · M. Phônthong 1408 · Attapu · Dak To · Sa Huynh
Surin · Champasak · M. Pathoumphon · Muang Kao · Ba To · Hoai Nhon
Sangkha · Ban Hans Phya Bac · Kontum 1747 · Phu My
**Korat** · **Phanom Dongrak** · 696 · Prasat · M. Mounlapamôk · 1547 · Siempang · Pleiku · An Tuc · **QUI NHON**
Khon Buri · **PREĂH VIHÉAR** · Virôchey · Lê Thanh · Sông Câu
**ÔTDAR MÉANCHEY** · Chông Kal · Khsant · Phu Nhon · Hậu Bôn · Tuy Hòa
Sisophôn · Tŏek Chou · Kulên · Phnôm Tbêng · **RÔTÂNÔKIRI** · Lumphăt · Buôn Blech · Mui Kê Ga
Battambang · Banteay Srei · Angkor · Siĕmréab · Roviang Tbong · Srêpôk · Buôn Dôn · Ban Mê Thuột
Pailin · Bœng Tônlé Sab · Spóng Stœng · Trêng · M'Drak 2059 · Ninh Hòa
**KAMPUCHEA** · Môung Roessei · Kâmpóng Thum · **MÔNDÔL KIRI** · 2442 · Chu Yang Sin · **NHA TRANG**
Trat · Pouthĭsăt · Kâmpóng Chhnang · Senmonorom · Đục Lập · Bi Doup 2289 · Hon Tre
**Kâmpóng Cham** · Srê Khtŭm 982 · **DA LAT** · Cam Lâm
Kâmpóng Thum · Snuôl · Gia Nghĩa · 1982 · Đục Trong · Phan Rang

**PHNOM PENH** · **KANDAL** · Prey Vêng · Lôc Ninh · An Lôc · Bao Lôc · Di Linh · Phan Rang
Takêv · Svay Riĕng · Tây Ninh · 1642 · Phan Thiết
**KAOH KŎNG** · Kâmpóng Spœ · Hiếu Thiện · Vo Đat
Kompong-Som · Kâmpôt · Phsar · Ap Tuyền Bình · Khiêm-Cuong · Mui Ke Ga
Kaôh Kŏng · Chrouy Yéay Sên · Bok Kou · **HO CHI MINH** (SAIGON) · Ham Tân · Tuy Phong
Chrouy Samĭt · Kaôh Rŭng 330 · Châu Phu · Biên Hòa · Phước Lê · Phan Ly Cham
Phu Qui Dao (Cecir de Mer)

**GULF OF TONKIN**

Dao Bach Long Vi (I. Nightingale)

**HAIKOU** · Lingao · Wenchang
**HAINANDAO** · Xinzhou · Chengmai
Changjiang · Danxian (Nada) · Tunchang · Qionghai
Dongfang · Baisha · 1892 · Qiongzhong · Wanning
Ledong · Wuzhishan · Lingshui
Huangliu · Yaichengzhen · Yulin

Weizhoudao · Qiongzhouhaixia · Donghaidao · Naozhoudao
Leizhoudbandao · Haikang (Leizhou) · Hailingdao
Xuwen

**SOUTH CHINA SEA**

Zongjiandao

Xishaqundao (Paracel Is.) · Beijiao · Xuandequndao
Yunglequndao · Yongxingdao

↓ **147**

↑ 144

**ANDAMAN SEA**

**MERGUI ARCHIPELAGO**

**BURMA**

Thayawthadangyi Kyun
Daung K.
Hattras Passage
Mergui
Tenasserim
1534
Pran Buri
Ko Samet
Chanthaburi
923
Peam Prus
Pouthisat
Pouthisat
Chuŏi Phnum
1749
Tuŏl Khpos
1450
Baray
Kámpóng Chhnang
**KAMP**
**PHNOM-PENH**
Ŏdóng
Takh

Bentinck I.
Saganthit Kyun
Maw Daung Pass
Prachuap Khiri Khan
Laem Ngop
Trat
Krŏng Kaôh
Kámpóng Spoe
Chumnum
**KAÔH KÔNG**
Kámpóng
Kâmpót

Letsôk-Aw (Domet)
Clara I.
Kanmaw Kyun
1251
Thap Sakae
Ko Mak
Ko Chang
743
Khlong Yai
Kaôh Kŏng
Chrouy Yéay Sên
Srê Âmbêl
422
Phumi Kus
Tani

Kau-Ye K.
905
Bang Saphan
Ko Kut
Chrouy Samit
Kaôh Rŭng
330
Phsar Réam
540
Bok Koŭ
Kâmpôt

Lanbi K.
Bokpyin
Namnoi
755
Chumphon
**Gulf of Thailand**
Kompong-Som
Kaôh Tang
Kaôh Chrâluh
Ha-Tiên
Phu Quôc
Hon Chŏng

Zadetkale K.
673
Isthmus of Kra
Kra Buri
70
Poulo Wai
Dao Phu Quôc
Rach Gia

Zadetkyi K.
Kawthaung
Ranong
Ao Sawi
Laem Pracham Hiang
Ko Tao
Hon Nam Du
Hon Rai
Vung Rach Gia

Than K.
**THAILAND**
Lang Suan
Ko Phaluai
635
Ko Samui
Hon Thô Châu
Quan Lo
Dam

Ko Chan
Kapoe
1395
Chaiya
Ao Ban Don
Ko Samui
Hon Chuôi
Hon Buông
Mui Ba Quan
Nam

Ko Phra Thong
Takua Pa
Surat Thani
Ko Phangan
Hon Thô Châu
Pointe de Ca Mau (Mui Bai Bung)
Hon Kh

Bon Ko
Ban Kapong
Khiri Rat/Nikhom
Phun Phin
Si Chon
78

Phangnga
1350
Ban Na San
**Nakhon Si Thammarat**
1835
Laem Talumphuk

Thalang
Ko Yao Noi
Krabi
Thung Song
Pak Phanang
Ko Losin

**Ko Phuket**
529
Ko Yao Yai
Khlong Thom
Ban Ron Phibun
Hua Sai

**Phuket**
Ko Phi-Phi
Ko Pu
Huai Yot
Phatthalung
Ranot
Thale Luang

Ko Racha Yai
Ko Muk
Kantang
Trang
1322
Palian
Rattaphum
**MALAY PENINSULA**

Ko Racha Noi
Ko Lanta
Ko Talibong
Ko Sukon
Songkhla
Laem Pho
73

99
Ko Tarutao
Langu
Satun
**Hat-Yai**
Thepha
Pattani
Sai Buri
Kampong Raja
347 P. Redang

Batong Group
Sadao
Na Thawi
Yala
Narathiwat
Kampong Raja

P. Langkawi
880
Kangar
Kuala Nerang
Bannang Sata
Rangae
Tumpat
**KOTA BHARU**

P. Perak
**PERLIS**
Alor Setar
1452
Sungai Kolok
G. Lawit 1517
**KUALA TERENGGANU**

**KEDAH**
Ygn
1862
Betong
Krohi
Kuala Krai
P. Tenggol

Sungei Patani
Grik
Temengor
**KELANTAN**
**TERENGGANU**

**PINANG (GEORGETOWN)**
G. Bintang
G. Chamah 2170
Gua Musang
Bukit Besi 1478
G. Mandi Angin
Kuala Dungun

Butterworth
Nibong Tebal
Taiping
Port Weld
Kuala Kangsar
1656
2182
Menggiri
2190
G. Tahan
632
Kertch
**MALAYSIA**

**IPOH**
Trough
Tanah Rata
Batu Puteh
1511
Tanj. Gelang

Lumut
Tapah
2130
Kuala Lipis
Benta
**PAHANG**

Telok Anson
Bagan Datoh
1932
G. Benom
Jerantut
Tapis
**KUANTAN**

P. Jarak
Selim
2108
Raub
Bentong
Maran
Pekari

P. Berhala
Kuala Kubu Bahru
Batang Berjuntai
Temerloh
Triang
Rompin

**SELANGOR**
G. Nuang 1496
Shah Alam
Kuala Klawang
P. Tioman

**KUALA LUMPUR**
Port Kelang
Kelang
Kuala Pilah
1038

**Banda-Aceh**
Sigli
Meureudu
Tg Djambuair
Kuala Selangor
Banfing
**NEGERI**
Gemas
P. Aur

P. Weh
Sabang
2140
Lhokseumawe
Banting
**SEREMBAN**
**SEMBILAN**
Segamat
P. Pemanggil

P. Breueh
2309
G. Peuetsagoe 2801
Bireuen
Tampin
1276
1035 G. Besar
Mersing
521

Semp. Maláka
Meureudu
G. Geureudong 2855
Peureulak
L. Tawar
Labis
G. Ophir
**JOHOR**

Lammeulo
Takingeun
Langsa
Kualalangsa
Malacca
Muar
1009 G. Blumut
Jemaluang

Tjalang
G. Lembu
Tel. Langsa
Uwak 2961
Kluang
634
Sedili Besar

Geumpang
3044
Tel. Aru
Pangkalansusu
Batu Pahat
652
Tg Berah

Meulaboh
Blangkedjeren
Pangkalanberandan
Kulai
**JOHOR BAHARU**

Kutanibong
3465 G. Leuser
Tandjungpura
**SINGAPORE**

**ATJEH**
Peg. Serbeulangi 3012
Belawan
Kukup
Str. of Singapore
P. Bin

Kep. Kokos
U. Radja
Bindjai
**MEDAN**
P. Berhala
P. Rangsang
P. Batam
Tg Berah

U. Dewa
Tapaktuan
Kuala
2451
Tebingtinggi
Sel. Pandjang
348 P. Bin

P. Simeulue
Balangpidie
Kabandjahe
Bangunpurba
Tandjungbalai
P. Rupat
Dumai
Tanjungpinar

**INDONESIA**
Bakungan
Merek
2591
Kisaran
Tg Pertandangan
P. Bengkalis
P. Kundur

566 Sinabang
Sidikalang
Panguuran 899
Labuhanbilik
Bagansiapiapi
P. Mendol

P. Lasia
P. Babi
2157
Prapat 1707
P. Samosir
Port Dickson
Pekanbaru

Kep. Banjak
313 P. Tuangku
Singkilbaru
Balige
2330
P. Alang Besar
Minas
P. Temiang
P. Sebang

P. Bangkaru
Barus
Tarutung
Rantauprapat
Kotapinang
Perawang
Buatan
P. Bakung

**SUMATERA**
Sibolga
2008 G. Tampulon Andjing
Dumai
Siaksriinderapura

P. Musala
Gunungtua
**PEMATANGSIANTAR**
Danau Toba
Sintong
Kukup

5348
Lahewa
Gunungsitoli
Padangsidimpuan
**UTARA**
Kotatengah

P. Nias 885
Telukdalam
2145 G. Sorikmerapi
Hutanopan
Pasirpengaraian
Bangkinang
Sungaiguntung

Kep. Hinako
Tabujung
2912 G. Talakmau
Natal
Airbangis
Lubuksikaping
**PEKANBARU**

P. Pini
U. Tuan
Kep. Batu
**SUMATERA BARAT**
Airbangis

Equator
96°
102°
↓ 206

**ANDAMAN and NICOBAR (Bharat) (India)**

Car Nicobar I.
89 Kakana
94°
4360

Batti Malv I.
**NICOBAR ISLANDS**

Chaura I.
Tillanchong I.
273 Bompoka I.
Chanumla
Koihoa
Camorta I.
Teressa I.
Trinkat I.
239 Nancowry I.
Mohean
Katchall I.

Sombrero Channel
Enfok 3135
Little Nicobar
Murray P!

Mt Thuillier 642
Great Nicobar
Dakoänk

Henhoaha
Bananga
Parsons P!

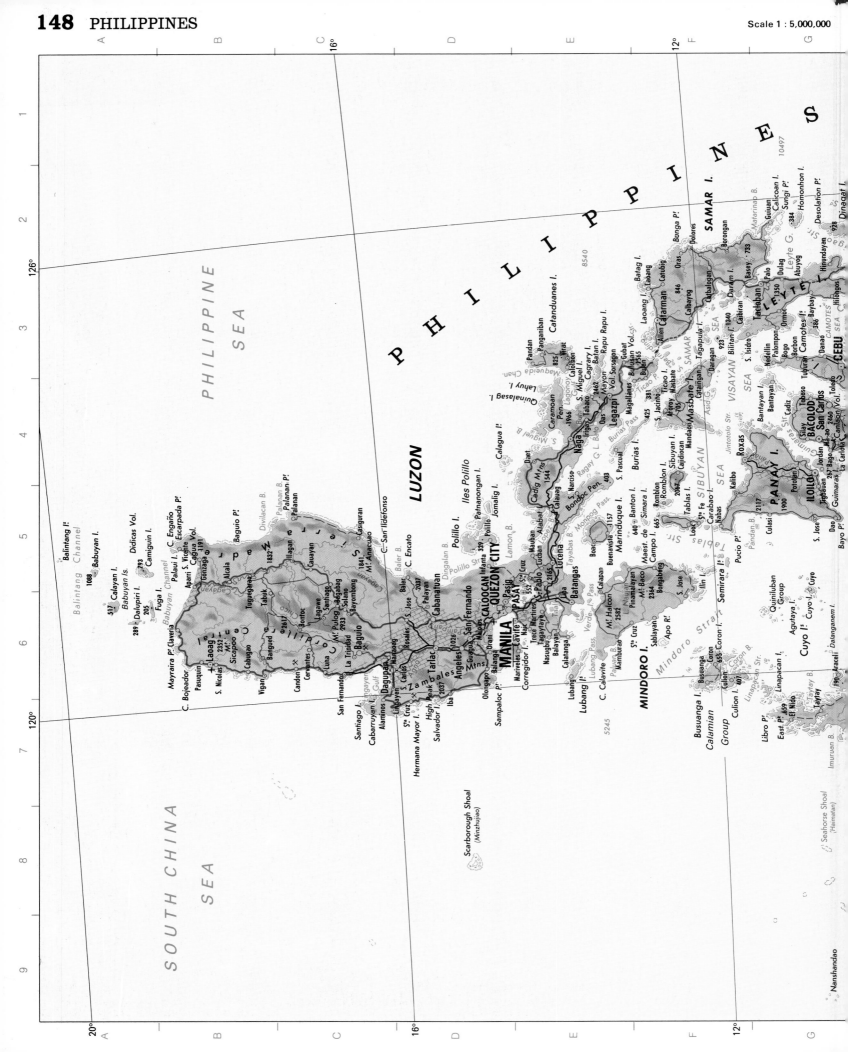

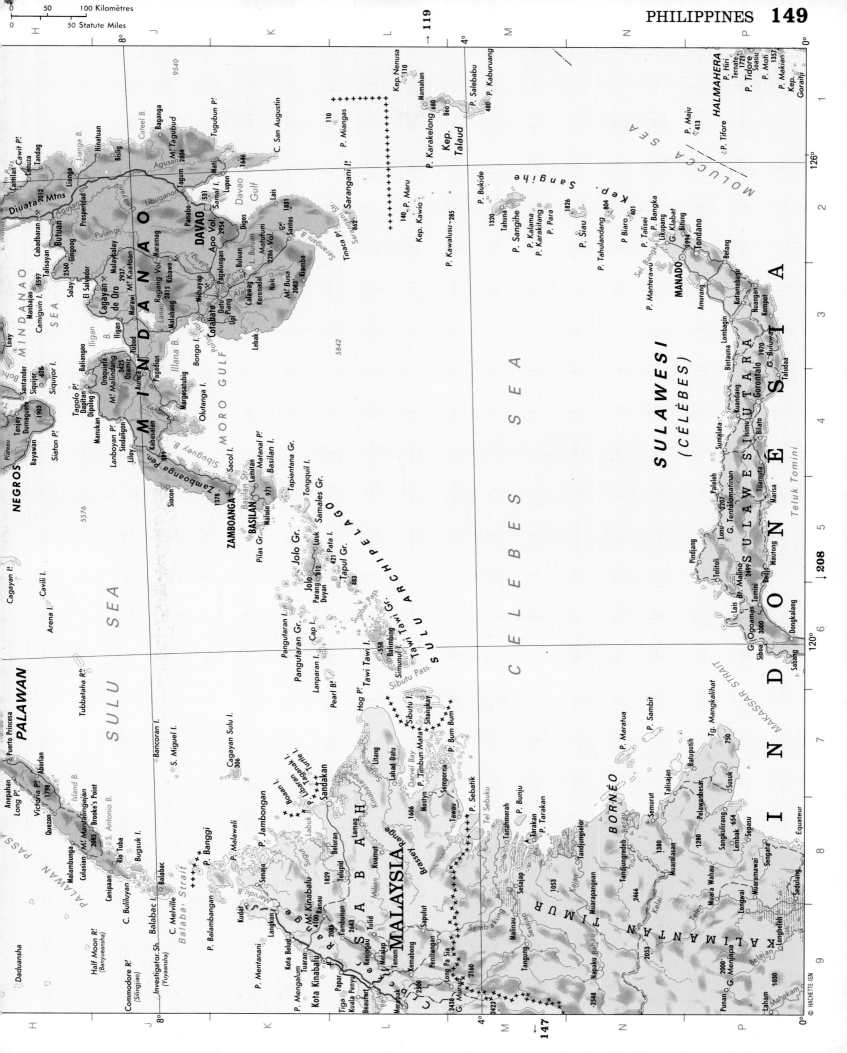

| COUNTRY | OFFICIAL LANGUAGE(S) | AREA in sq mi | POPULATION | POPULATION DENSITY pop/sq mi | GNP in billions of $ (1982) | WORLD RANK | PER CAPITA Income (1982 dollars) | WORLD RANK | CAPITOL | POPULATION | PER CAPITA ELEC. CONSUMPTION in millions of kwh | No. of VEHICLES per 1,000 inhabitants | No. of DOCTORS per 1,000 inhabitants | % POPULATION less than 15 years of age |
|---|---|---|---|---|---|---|---|---|---|---|---|---|---|---|
| ANTIGUA/BARBUDA | english | 171 | 79,000 | 464 | 0.130 | 174 | 1,625 | 94 | ST. JOHN'S | — | 808 | — | 0.5 | — |
| ARGENTINA | spanish | 1,068,401 | 30,100,000 | 28 | 61.66 | 29 | 2,070 | 81 | BUENOS AIRES | 9,000,000 | 1,451 | 78.8 | 1.9 | 30.4 |
| BAHAMAS | english | 5,379 | 230,000 | 42 | 0.90 | 141 | 4,090 | 55 | NASSAU | 140,000 | 4,220 | 289.1 | 0.82 | 38.1 |
| BARBADOS | english | 166 | 253,000 | 1520 | 0.760 | 147 | 2,920 | 68 | BRIDGETOWN | 30,000 | 1,423 | 97.3 | 0.67 | 30.7 |
| BELIZE | english | 8,866 | 160,000 | 18 | 0.110 | 166 | 1,110 | 112 | BELMOPAN | 8,000 | 379 | 46.8 | 0.30 | 46.1 |
| BOLIVIA | spanish | 424,204 | 6,250,000 | 15 | 6.53 | 77 | 1,106 | 113 | LA PAZ | 916,000 | 282 | 8.1 | 0.5 | 41.9 |
| BRAZIL | portuguese | 3,286,793 | 132,600,000 | 40 | 209.70 | 10 | 1,610 | 95 | BRASILIA | 450,000 | 1,246 | 78.4 | 0.7 | 37.29 |
| CANADA | english, french | 3,852,165 | 25,200,000 | 6 | 326.90 | 8 | 13,100 | 10 | OTTAWA | 600,000 | 14,896 | 430 | 1.9 | 23.0 |
| CHILE | spanish | 292,306 | 11,900,000 | 41 | 17.40 | 58 | 1,490 | 98 | SANTIAGO | 4,200,000 | 1,081 | 53.1 | 0.88 | 34.4 |
| COLOMBIA | spanish | 439,778 | 27,520,000 | 63 | 37.00 | 41 | 1,345 | 102 | BOGOTA | 4,500,000 | 984 | 18.9 | 0.51 | 44.6 |
| COSTA RICA | spanish | 19,577 | 2,500,000 | 128 | 2.63 | 106 | 1,120 | 110 | SAN JOSE | 600,000 | 1,093 | 39.8 | 0.7 | 44.0 |
| CUBA | spanish | 42,808 | 10,000,000 | 234 | 7.63 | 72 | 780 | 132 | HAVANA | 1,900,000 | 1,166 | 18.3 | 2.06 | 29.7 |
| DOMINICA | english | 170 | 77,000 | 267 | 0.080 | 181 | 1,025 | 118 | ROSEAU | 12,000 | 237 | — | 0.23 | — |
| DOMINICAN REPUBLIC | spanish | 18,817 | 6,150,000 | 326 | 8.24 | 70 | 1,400 | 99 | SANTO DOMINGO | 1,900,000 | 570 | 21 | 0.6 | 47.5 |
| ECUADOR | spanish | 109,494 | 9,570,000 | 88 | 10.07 | 66 | 1,100 | 114 | QUITO | 1,000,000 | 489 | 24 | 0.62 | 44.5 |
| EL SALVADOR | spanish | 8,124 | 5,040,000 | 14 | 3.64 | 96 | 713 | 136 | SAN SALVADOR | 900,000 | 308 | 14.3 | 0.31 | 46.2 |
| GRENADA | english | 133 | 111,000 | 836 | 0.095 | 179 | 860 | 127 | ST GEORGE'S | 7,500 | 227 | — | 0.3 | — |
| GUATEMALA | spanish | 42,047 | 8,170,000 | 194 | 8.96 | 67 | 1,135 | 109 | GUATEMALA | 710,000 | 214 | 11.1 | 0.3 | 45.1 |
| GUYANA | english | 83,008 | 936,000 | 11 | 0.520 | 154 | 565 | 149 | GEORGETOWN | 170,000 | 474 | 34.8 | 0.1 | 39.4 |
| HAITI | french | 10,715 | 5,050,000 | 471 | 1.75 | 117 | 330 | 170 | PORT-AU-PRINCE | 800,000 | 60 | 3.5 | 0.11 | 41.2 |
| HONDURAS | spanish | 43,282 | 4,240,000 | 98 | 2.84 | 103 | 690 | 138 | TEGUCIGALPA | 500,000 | 280 | 23.3 | 0.32 | 47.7 |
| JAMAICA | english | 4,244 | 2,290,000 | 539 | 3.50 | 97 | 1,535 | 97 | KINGSTON | 700,000 | 1,041 | — | 0.35 | 45.9 |
| MEXICO | spanish | 759,604 | 76,800,000 | 101 | 135.83 | 16 | 1,810 | 89 | MEXICO CITY | 15,000,000 | 1,095 | 67.9 | 0.8 | 46.5 |
| NICARAGUA | spanish | 50,198 | 3,170,000 | 63 | 3.49 | 98 | 1,163 | 108 | MANAGUA | 650,000 | 355 | 7.8 | 0.45 | 48.1 |
| PANAMA | spanish | 29,764 | 2,130,000 | 72 | 3.96 | 95 | 1,895 | 86 | PANAMA | 500,000 | 1,072 | 54.5 | 0.99 | 43.4 |
| PARAGUAY | spanish | 157,062 | 3,580,000 | 23 | 4.06 | 93 | 1,170 | 107 | ASUNCION | 470,000 | 244 | 11.0 | 0.55 | 43.0 |
| PERU | quechua | 496,271 | 19,210,000 | 39 | 16.54 | 60 | 885 | 126 | LIMA | 5,000,000 | 499 | 15.7 | 0.69 | 44.2 |
| ST. KITTS AND NEVIS | english | 101 | 50,000 | 496 | 0.041 | 188 | 1,025 | 119 | BASSETERRE | — | 660 | 66.0 | 0.2 | 49.6 |
| ST. LUCIA | english | 239 | 127,000 | 533 | 0.130 | 175 | 1,000 | 122 | CASTRIES | 5,000 | 544 | 38.6 | 0.3 | 42.6 |
| ST. VINCENT | english | 150 | 102,000 | 681 | 0.090 | 180 | 900 | 124 | KINGSTOWN | 12,000 | 284 | 47.1 | 0.23 | — |
| SURINAM | dutch | 63,045 | 351,000 | 6 | 1.28 | 126 | 3,660 | 62 | PARAMARIBO | 200,000 | 3,704 | 108.9 | 0.54 | 46.4 |
| TRINIDAD AND TOBAGO | english | 1,951 | 1,170,000 | 590 | 8.32 | 69 | 7,235 | 35 | PORT OF SPAIN | 350,000 | 2,106 | 171 | 0.69 | 35.9 |
| UNITED STATES | english | 3,615,457 | 236,600,000 | 65 | 3,281.60 | 1 | 13,995 | 8 | WASHINGTON | 2,900,000 | 10,280 | 530.7 | 1.8 | 22.2 |
| URUGUAY | spanish | 68,043 | 2,999,000 | 44 | 5.07 | 85 | 1,707 | 92 | MONTEVIDEO | 1,240,000 | 1,262 | 101 | 0.69 | 27.0 |
| VENEZUELA | spanish | 352,177 | 16,890,000 | 48 | 48.78 | 35 | 3,090 | 66 | CARACAS | 3,000,000 | 2,417 | 98 | 1.0 | 42.5 |

# AMERICAS

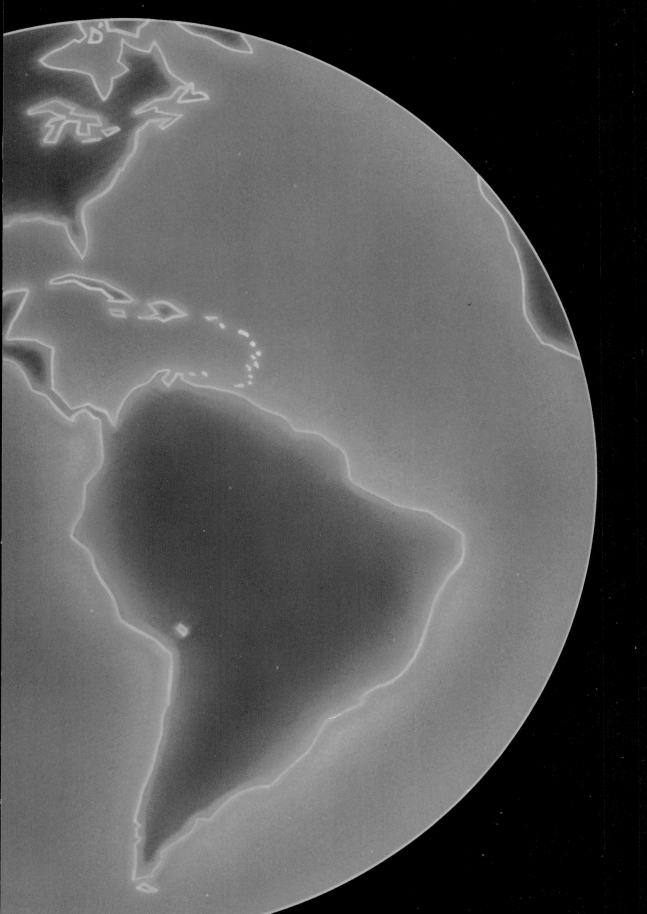

Scale 1 : 33,000,000

IZABETH ISLANDS

ARCTIC OCEAN

Meighen I.

Sverdrup Islands

Axel Heiberg I.

Amund Ringnes I.

Ellef Ringnes I.

Magnetic
+ 1884

Bay Group

Cornwallis I.

Devon I.

Somerset I.

Boothia

Melville Peninsula

Prince Charles Island

Air Force

Penny Highland

Cumberland Pen.

C. Mercy

Half Pen.

Baffin Island

Brodeur Pen.

Prince Regent Inlet

Bylot I.

Mt Thule

K. York

Melville Bugt

Swartenhuk Halvø

Disko

Nugssuaq

United States Range

Ellesmere

Nares Strait

Greely Fd

Graham I.

Jones Sound

Lancaster Sound

Barrow Strait

Ward Hunt I.

C. Hecla

LINCOLN SEA

J. Murray Ø

C. Morris Jesup

Peary Land

K. Bridgman

K. E. Rasmussen

Knud Rasmussen Land

Ingelfield Land

Thule

Fj. Independence

Fj. Danmark

Kronprins Christians Land

Hovgaards Ø

I. de France

Germania Land

Store Koldewey Ø

Shannon Ø

Clavering Ø

King Christian X Land

Fj. du Roi Oscar

Scoresby Sund

K. Brewster

Nordostrundingen

WANDEL SEA

Mc KINLEY SEA

GREENLAND

2000

2100

2560

2050

2000

2900

3200

3000

2399

1250

1061

G R E E N L A N D

GREENLAND SEA

BAFFIN BAY

Davis Strait

Arctic Circle

King Frederik IX Land

King Christian IX Land

Mt Fore

Gunbjørns Fjeld
3700

I. Grimsey

Reykjavik

Hekla

Hvannadalshnukur

Iceland

Denmark Strait

542

Godthåb

King Frederik VI Land

Kap Farvel

LABRADOR SEA

Ungava

Peninsula

Ungava Bay

Akpatok I.

C. Chidley

Resolution I.

Torngat Mts 1677

LABRADOR

Hope Mts

Mealy Mts

Mts Otish 1128

Mansel I.

Belcher I.

Coats I.

Nottingham I.

Salisbury I.

Southampton

Foxe Basin

Meta Incognita Pen.

PLATEAU

Laurentides 1190

Québec

Mt Washington 1916

Adirondack Mts

Nova Scotia

Cape Breton I.

Prince Edward Island

Newfoundland

Avalon Pen.

Is. St-Pierre et Miquelon

Gulf of St. Lawrence

I. Anticosti

Gaspésie

Str. of Belle-Isle

Gulf of Maine

Long Island

New York

C. Cod

ATLANTIC OCEAN

Rockall

Ireland

Cork

C. Finisterre

Azores

I. Flores

I. Terceira

I. Pico

I. S. Miguel

I. Santa Maria

Lisboa

C. St-Vincent

4300

5665

953

© HACHETTE-IGN

ARCTIC OCEAN

EEN ELIZABETH ISLANDS

Meighen I.
Sverdrup Islands
Ward Hunt I.
C. Hecla
LINCOLN SEA
J. Murray Ø
MAC KINLEY HAV
K. Bridgman
Nordostrundingen

Peary Channel
Ellef Ringnes
Axel-Heiberg I.
United States Range
Alert
Peary Land
K. E. Rasmussen
Nord

A. Ringnes I.
Eureka
E. Hyde F.
Nansen Sd.
Graham I.
Eureka Strait
Knud Rasmussen Land
Kronprins Christians Land
Ingolfs Fj.

Pôle Nord magnétique
Belcher Chan.
Inglefield Land
Thule
2000
Independence Fj.
Danmarks Fj.
Hovgaards Ø

Cornwallis I.
Devon I.
Jones Sound
K. Parry
80°
I. de France

Somerset I.
Barrow Strait
Lancaster Sound
Dundas
2100
2560
2050
Germania Land
Store Koldewey Ø

Brodeur Pen.
Prince Regent Inlet
K. York
Melville Bugt
Shannon Ø

Pond Inlet
Bylot I.
GREENLAND
Daneborg
Clavering Ø

Melville Peninsula
BAFFIN B.
(DEN.)
2900
2

Repulse Bay
Prince Charles Island
Air Force Island
Koch I.
Clyde
Upernavik
Swartenhuk Halvø
3200
King Christian X Land
Joseph F. Foster Bugt
Scoresbysund

Wager Bay
Foxe Basin
Home B.
Nugssuaq
Umanak
3000
Kong Oscars Fj.

RITORIES
Southampton I.
Coral Harbour
Nettilling
Amadjuak
2134
Pangnirtung
Qutdligssat
Disko
Godhavn
Jakobshavn
Christianshåb
Scoresby Sund
K. Brewster

D
Coats I.
Nottingham I.
Salisbury I.
Hudson Strait
C. Mercy
Holsteinborg
Søndre Strømfjord
Arctic Circle
King Christian IX Land
Gunnbjørns Fjeld
3700
70°

Ivugivik
Mansel I.
Frobisher Bay
Sukkertoppen
King Frederik VI Kyst
Mt Forel 3360
Grimsey
Ísafjörður

A
Saglouc
Lake Harbour
Godthåb
King Frederik VI Kyst
Angmagssalik
Akureyri
Bårdarbunga
2000

Ungava Peninsula
Akpatok I.
Resolution I.
LABRADOR
Frederikshåb
Ivigtut
Narssarsuaq
Denmark Strait
Reykjavík
2119
ICELAND

Ottawa I.
Puvirnituq
Bellin
Ungava B.
C. Chidley
SEA
Julianehåb
Nanortalik
Vestmannaeyjar
Vík

Inoucdjouac
Belcher
Nastapoka I.
Kap Farvel
60°

Poste-de-la-Baleine
LABRADOR
Nain
Rockall (U.K.)

Ft-George
Ft-Chimo
Hebron

Akimiski I.
Schefferville
NEWFOUNDLAND
L. Bienville

Ft-Rupert
L. Manicouagan
Churchill Falls
Cartwright
4

QUEBEC
Goose B.
IRELAND

Chibougamau
B. Comeau
Battle Harbour
Limerick
Cork

Dolbeau
Sept-Îles
Lac Alfard
Cooks Harbour

Jean
Lawrence
Natashquan

Chicoutoumi
1311
Matane
Gaspé
I. Anticosti
Island of Newfoundland

Québec
Rimouski
G. of St. Lawrence
Windsor
Corner Brook
Gander
50°

Trois-Rivières
NEW BRUNSWICK
814
St-Pierre
Bonavista

MONTRÉAL
Fredericton
PRINCE EDWARD ISLAND
Pt-aux-Basques
St-Pierre
St. John's

Hull
Ottawa
1806
Charlottetown
ST-PIERRE ET MIQUELON (FR.)

Sherbrooke
MAINE
Moncton
Cape Breton I.

Bangor
Saint John
Sydney

Augusta
Bay of Fundy
Halifax
Dartmouth

Montpelier
Lewiston
NOVA SCOTIA
Sable Island (CAN.)

Concord
Worcester
Boston
ATLANTIC

New Bedford
C. Cod

Hartford
Providence
New Haven
Stamford
OCEAN

NEW YORK
Newark
SPAIN

PHILADELPHIA
La Coruña

Trenton
AZORES (PORT.)
Vigo
Porto

1 NEW HAMPSHIRE
2 VERMONT
3 MASSACHUSETTS
4 RHODE ISLAND
5 CONNECTICUT
6 NEW JERSEY
7 DELAWARE
8 MARYLAND
Flores
PORTUGAL
Lisboa

Horta
Terceira
Angra do Heroísmo

Pico
2320
São Miguel

Ponta Delgada
Santa Maria

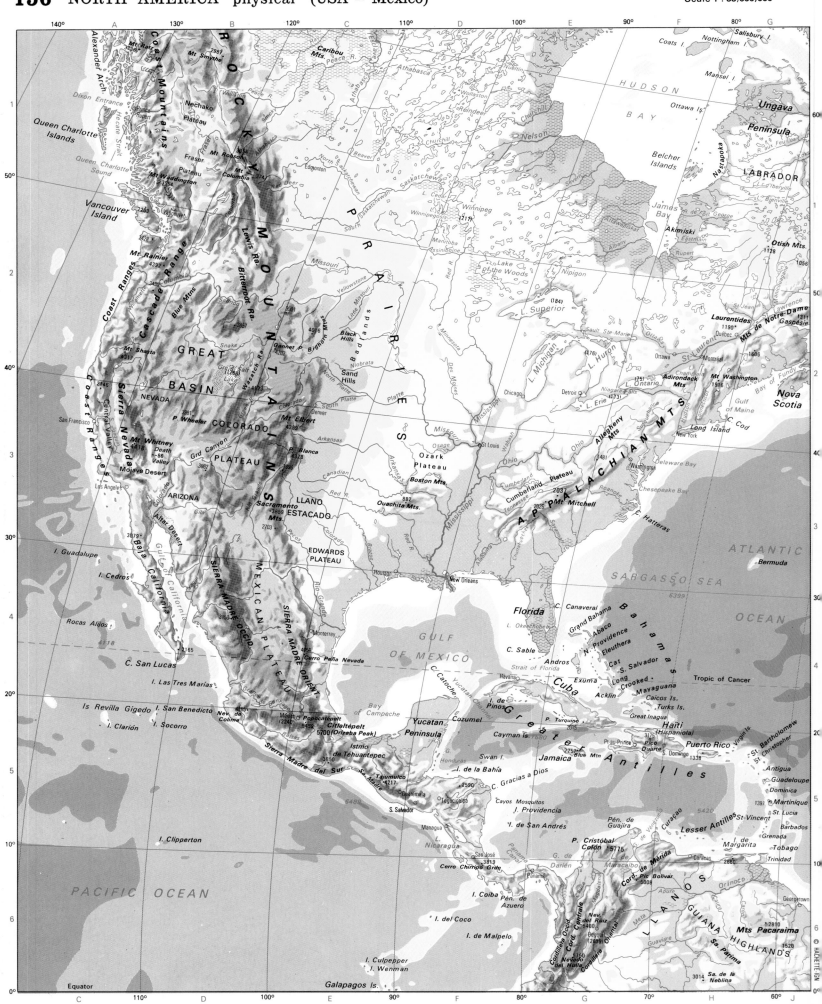

Scale 1 : 5,000,000

BERING SEA

PACIFIC OCEAN

Gambell
Southwest C. · Northwest C.
St. Lawrence Island
673 · Savoonga
Kookooligit Mt.
Southeast C. · Sooghmeghat
Punuk I? · Kulowiyi
Northeast C.

St. Matthew I.
(U.S.A.)
459
C. Upright

203
St. Paul · St. Paul I.
Pribilof Islands
St. George I. · 309
St. George

C. Mohican
Nash Harbor
Nunivak Island
Mekoryok
C. Etolin
Kwigamiut · C. Vancouver
C. Mendenhall · 510 · Roberts Mtn
Tununak
Nelson I.

C. Romanzof
Hooper Bay
720 · Scammon Bay
Sheldon
Alakanuk
Kwigut
New Fort Hamilton
Pastolik
Nok
Mountain Village
Marshall · 853
Russian Mission
Anvik
Bonasila Dome · 610
Phillips
Okriagamut · Holy Cross

Kipnuk
Anogok
Kiwigillingok
Kulvagavik
Napaiskak · Kwethluk · Akiachak
Eek
Quinhagak
Bethel

Kuskokwim Bay

C. Newenham
Platinum
Goodnews
C. Peirce
543
Hagemeister I.
Warlus I?
Togiak
Hagemeister Str.

M? Hamilton · 1111
1387
Kilbuck Mtns
Napamute · Horn Mtns
1143
Kiokluk Mtns
Barometer Mtn · 776
Sleetmute
Taylor Mtns · 1091

KUSKOKWIM

1266
Holitna

C. Sarichef
Pogromni Vol. · 2001
C. Mordvinof
Unimak
Shishaldin Vol. · 2857
False Pass
C. Lazaref
C. Pankof
Unimak Island
Amak I.
Bechevin B.
1762
King Cove
Fort Randall
Deer I.
530 · Pauloff Hbr · 792
Sanak I? · Belkofski
Caton I.
Dolgoi I.
Pavlof B.
Pavlof I?

C. Leontovitch
C. Lieskof
2517 Pavlof Vol.

Nushagak
Nuyakuk · 1532
Lake Ualik
M? Waskey
L. Kulit
716
L. Aleknagik
Nushagak Pen.
Dillingham

Finn Mtn · 756
M? Ketok · 516

Lime Hills · 700
1153
Halfway Mtn · 985
Cairn Mtn
Whitefish L.

Unga I. · 619
Unga · Sand Point
Shumagin Islands
Popof I.
Nagai I. · 562
Kupreanof P?
Bird I.
Chernabura I. · 490
413 · Little Koniuji I.
Simeonof I?
Karovin I.
Big Koniuji I.
Paul I.
Chiachi I.
Perryville
Chignik

M?
Veniaminof · 2507
Strogonof P?
Port Heiden
Aniakchak Crater · 1303

C. Greig
Egegik
Ugashik L.
Becharof Lake
C. Constantine
Nushagak
Kvichak B.
Naknek
King Salmon
Igiugik
Kvichak

Mesa Mtn · 975
Bonanza Hills · 1067
Old Village
Lake Telaquana

Mitrofania I.
Seal C.
Chankliut I.
Nakchamik I.
Sutwik I.
Chiginagak · 2134
1500
Katmai
Kanatak
Knife P? · 2312
Nat. Monument
M? Denison · 2304
M? Douglas · 2153
1197
Augustine I.

Newhalen
Port Alsworth
Pile Bay
Chenik
Iliamna Vol. · 3053
Oil P?
3108 · Redoubt Vol.
M? Sp
Kalgin I.
Chigmit Mtns

Semidi Islands
C. Iguak
Puale B.
Shelikof Str.

Chirikof I.
Tugidak I.
Trinity Islands
C. Ikolik
Low C.
Larsen Bay
Karluk · 1011
Kaguyak
Old Harbor · 1353
1064
Kodiak
Black P?
Sitkalidak I.
Kiliuda B.
Ugak B.
C. Chiniak
Uganik I.
Kodiak Island
Afogniak I.
678
Shuyak I.
Marmot I.
Spruce I.
C. Douglas

Anchor Point
Ninilchik
Homer · 712
Soldatna
Ster
Kenai
KENAI · 2016
Kenai Pe
Kenai Mtns

100 Kilomètres
50
0
50 Statute Miles
0

J 115

68°                    72°

CHUKCHI SEA

USSR
USA
Bering
C. Dejnev
Uelen
In'čoun
Nun'amo
O. Ratmanova
Diomede Is.
Little Diomede
Strait
Arctic Circle

Point Hope
C. Lisburne
620

ARCTIC OCEAN

C. Prince of Wales
Wales
King I.
885
Brooks Mtn
Shishmaref
Teller
1437
Imuruk Basin
Taylor
SEWARD
Point Lay
Kasegaluk Lag.
Icy Cape
Naokok
Kukpowruk
Tingmerkpuk Mtn
1097
Delong Mountains
Mulgrave Hills
Wainwright
Pt Franklin
Ivisaruk
Kokolik
Kukpuk
Nome
Dahl
Bunker Hill
C. Espenberg
Kotzebue Sound
Noatak
694
Igichuk Hills
Misheguk Mtn
1489
864
Lookout Ridge
Avatik
Ketik
Peard B.
Meade
Barrow
Pt Barrow
Port Safety
Dickson
1137
Iron Creek
Council
PEN.
Baldwin Pen.
Kotzebue
Deviation Pt
815
Baird Mountains
BROOKS
Nuka
Kurupa
Tapkaluk Is
Plover Is
Tangent Pt
Dease Inlet
C. Simpson
Rocky Pt
White Mountain
Monument
Mount 742
Candle
Deering
Buckland
Eschscholtz Bay
Selawik Lake
Noorvik
Kiana
Salmon
1311
1676
Ipnavik
Teshekput Lake
C. Halkeet
Golovin
Darby Mtn
C. Darby
Elim
Dime Landing
Haycock
Koyuk
884
Selawik
Inland L.
1008
Waring Mtns
549
Schwatka Mtns
Colville
Ikpikpuk
Price
560
Harrison Bay
Michael
C. Denbigh
Ungalik
Egavik
Unalakleet
1036
Traverse Peak
Huslia
Tagagawik
Kobuk
1280
2682
2328
Okokmilaga
Killik
Umiat
Colville
Pingok I.
Jones Is
Stuart I.
Tolstoi Pt
Golsovia
1402
Debauch Mtn
1209
Kateel
Purcell Mtn
1219
Angutikada Pk
1372
Castle Mtn
1135
2319
Midway Is
Beechey Pt
Mc Clure I.
391
White Hills
Stockton I.
Maguire Is
UKON
Kaiyuh
820
Galena
Zane Hills
Lookwood Hills
Koyukuk
Hogatza
John
Anaktuvuk
Nanushuk
Kupatuk
Kawik
Flaxman I.
Brownlow Pt
Camden Bay
Dishkakat
Davenport
Ruby
Melozitna
Hughes
1290
Allakaket
Lookout Mtn
645
Bettles
2499
Philip Smith Mountains
Mt Salisbury
2286
2152
Shublik Mtn
Kaktovik
Martin Pt
Ganes Creek
1250
Cloudy Mtn
Kokrines
Placerville
Sulatna
1518
Kokrines Hills
Kanuti
Caro
Coldfoot
North F.
2761
Mt Chamberlain
Mt Michelson
Aichilik
1341
Mc Grath
Susulatna
Nowitna
Ray Mountains
1804
2749
Franklin Mtns
Romanzof Mtns
2699
Isto
Gordon
1374
Von Frank Mtn
N.F. Kuskokwim
Tanana
Tozitna
1682
Hodzana
Stevens Village
East Fork Chandalar
Arctic Village
1981
MOUNTAINS
YUKON
971
Tofty
Eureka
Rampart
1472
Hess
Christian
Beaver
Shoulder Mtn
1295
Davidson Mtns
Kongakut
Firth
British Mountains
2045
Farewell
ALASKA
Kantishna
Sawtooth Mtn
Livengood
Sheenjek
Porcupine
1676
Mt Dall
2668
Mt Mc Kinley
Kantishna
Bearpaw
Chatanika
Beaver
Fort Yukon
1981
Mt Foraker
5304
6193
(U.S.A.)
White Mtns
1536
Coleen
Mt Gerdine
Mt McKINLEY
Na'Park
Nenana
Chatanika
Crazy Mtns
1124
Central
Rapid
Old Rampart
Babbage
Petersville
Mc Kinley Park
Fairbanks North Star
Chena
Birch
Circle
856
Blow
Chulitna
2053
Cantwell
Wood
West Point
Little Black R.
Porcupine
RANGE
Talkeetna
1691
Deadman Mtn
Little Delta
Chatanika
1804
Woodchopper
1372
1585
1981
ANCHORAGE
Willow
Susitna
Talkeetna Mtns
4176
Mt Hayes
Delta Junction
Saldha
Yukon
Charley
Nation
CANADA
Hope
Palmer
Sutton
2334
Chickaloon
Donnelly
Goodpaster
Kandik
Porcupine
Beluga L.
Portage
Mount Marcus Baker
4016
Nelchina
Paxson
Mt Kimball
3154
Mt Harper
1985
Mt Veta
1646
Glacier Mtn
Eagle
Mt Klotz
1799
Plateau
1990
Eureka Lodge
1743
Mt Harper
Sourdough

HACHETTE-IGN

H          J 160          K          L          M          N          P

64°

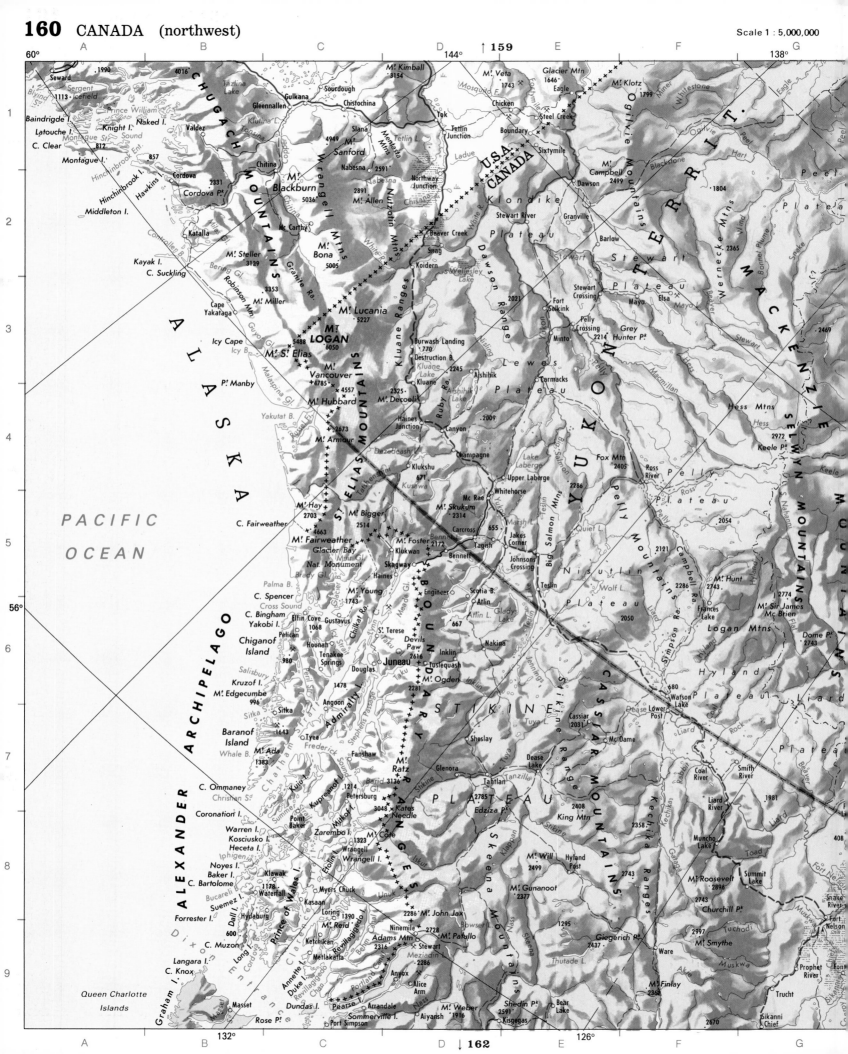

PACIFIC

OCEAN

ALASKA

CHUGACH MOUNTAINS

St. ELIAS MOUNTAINS

ALEXANDER ARCHIPELAGO

YUKON TERRITORY

MACKENZIE MOUNTAINS

SELWYN MOUNTAINS

BOUNDARY RANGES

STIKINE PLATEAU

CASSIAR MOUNTAINS

Queen Charlotte Islands

## Scale

0 — 50 — 100 Kilomètres
0 — 50 Statute Miles

↑ **155**

→ **15**
→ **15**
→ **15**

↓ **163**

© HACHETTE-IGN

**NORTH WEST TERRITORIES**

**DISTRICT OF MACKENZIE**

**MACKENZIE MOUNTAINS PRESERVE**

**YELLOWKNIFE PRESERVE**

**VICTORIA ISLAND**

AMUNDSEN GULF

GREAT BEAR LAKE

GREAT SLAVE LAKE

Coronation Gulf

Prince Albert Sound

Dolphin and Union Str.

Shaler Mtns

Prince Albert Peninsula

Wollaston Peninsula

Reindeer Grazing Preserve

Inuvik
Sitidgi Lake
Stanton
Fort Pherson
Arctic Red River
Bernard House
Fort Good Hope
Norman Wells
Fort Norman
Fort Franklin
Canol
Wrigley
Nahanni Butte
Fort Simpson
Trout L.
Mills Lake
Fort Providence
Hay River
Enterprise
Alexandra Falls
Buffalo Lake
Kahntah
Habay
Meander River
M. Watt
Pine Point
Dawson Landing
Fort Resolution
Fort Smith
Rocher River
Rat River
Snowdrift
Reliance
Yellowknife
Rae
Thompson Landing

Paulatuk
Letty Harbour
Cape Parry
Booth I.
C. Lyon
Keats P.
C. Lambton
De Salis B.
Berkeley P.
C. Peter Richards
C. Wollaston
Holman Island
C. Baring
C. Ernest Kendall
Clifton P.
C. Young
C. Hope
Read Island
Lady Franklin P.
Duke of York Arch.
Coppermine
Jameson I.
C. Barrow
Banks Pen.
Bathurst Inlet
Peacock Hills
Melville Hills
Bluenose Lake

Mackenzie
Mackenzie River
Franklin Mountains
Horn Mtns
Cameron Hills
Grizzly Bear Mtns
Scented Grass Hills

Keith Arm
Smith Arm
Dease Arm
Mc Tavish Arm
Richardson I.
Port Radium
Sawmill Bay
Mc Vicar Arm
North Arm
Keith Arm

M. Clark 1443
M. Davy 610
M. Bumpus 518
M. Watt
1036
1039
2164
472
244
686
262
157 +20
265
143
156 403
503
817
553
620
472
297
375
762
353
560
914
900
656
280
352
701
651

Arctic Circle

Nahanni
Redstone
Canyon Ranges
Backbone Ranges

Wallaston
Kagloryuak
Tahiryuak Lake
Minto Inlet
Simpson B.
Walker B.

ALASKA (U.S.A.)

BRITISH COLUMBIA

VANCOUVER ISLAND

PACIFIC OCEAN

HECATE STRAIT

Queen Charlotte Islands

Nechako Plateau

FRASER PLATEAU

ROCKY MOUNTAINS

WASHINGTON

Columbia Basin

Prince George

Quesnel

Williams Lake

Kamloops

VANCOUVER

North Vancouver

New Westminster

Victoria

Bellingham

SEATTLE

TACOMA

Olympia

PORTLAND

Vancouver

Salem

Corvallis

SPOKANE

CALGARY

Lethbridge

Red Deer

Banff

Prince Rupert

Port Edward

Kitimat

Terrace

Smithers

Hazelton

Fort St. John

Dawson Creek

Grande Prairie

Peace River

Fort Fraser

Vanderhoot

Bella Coola

Anahim Lake

Tatla Lake

Alexis Creek

Hanceville

Lillooet

Merritt

Princeton

Penticton

Kelowna

Vernon

Revelstoke

Golden

Nelson

Trail

Cranbrook

Fernie

Kimberley

Everett

Bremerton

Aberdeen

Yakima

Wenatchee

Ellensburg

Moses Lake

Astoria

Longview

Mt. Waddington 3994

Mt. Robson 3954

Mt. Columbia

Mt. Rainier 4392

Mt. St. Helens 2948

Mt. Hood 3430

Mt. Baker 3285

Mt. Olympus 2428

132° 126° 120° 114°

52° 48°

160 166

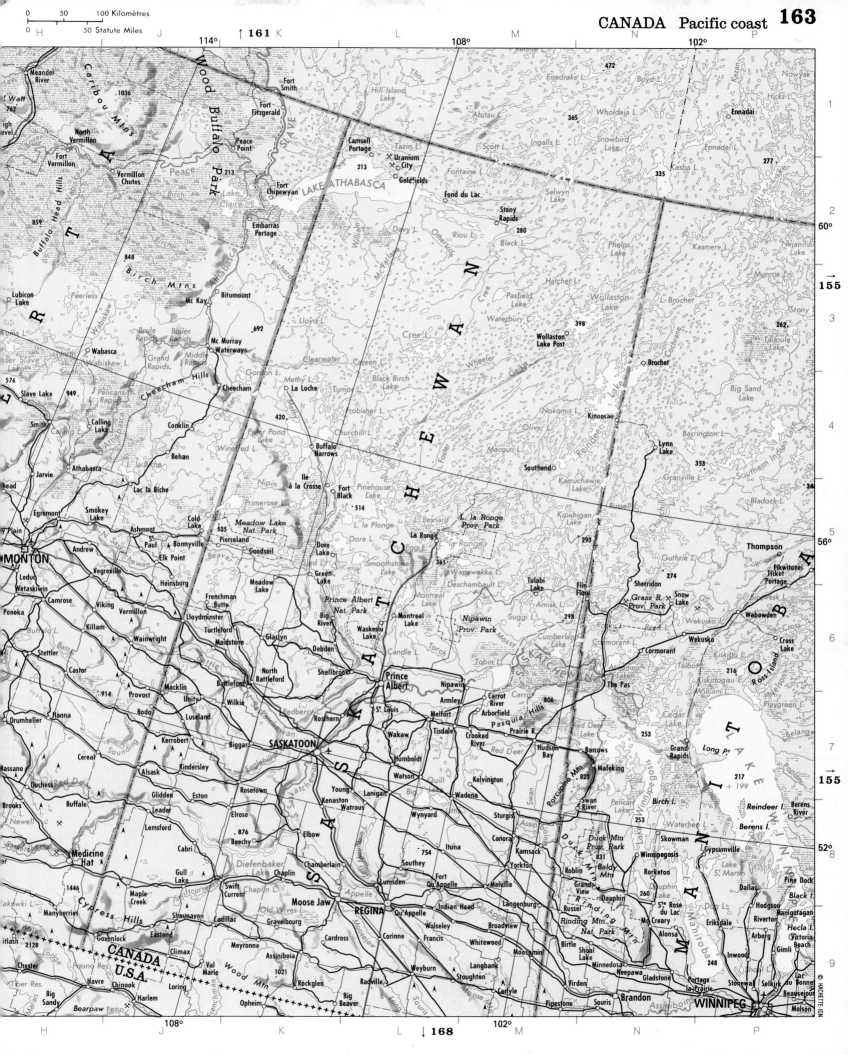

Belcher Islands

Flaherty I.
Tukarak I.

78°
L. d'Iberville
Petite R. de la Baleine
L. Bienville
L. Dolu
L. Sandy
Scheffervile
Menihek
Petitsikapau L.
Wade L.
66°

56°

Poste de la Baleine
(Great Whale River)
La Grande Rivière
Burton
L. Delorme
L. Caniapiscau
Lac Clairambault
Shabogamo
Livingstone
Emeril

Pte Louis XIV
Long Island
Long Island St.
823
Labrador City
L. Opiscoteo
Wabush Lake
Ashuan
975
940

Bear I.

Chisasibi
Radisson
L. Sakami
L. la Salle
L. Frigate
L. Naococane
Petit Lac Manicouagan
Mitchequon
Pi

JAMES

N. Twin I.
Houston Pt
160
L. Rossignol
Iles Otish
1128
Gagnon
1056

Ekwan Pt
S. Twin I.
Nouveau-Comptoir
(Paint Hills)
L. Opinaca
1056

Akimiski I.
BAY
C. Duncan
Eastmain
Neoskweskau
L. Woollett
QUÉBEC
819

Kapiskau

Fort Albany
Charlton I.
Eastmain
Réserve de Mistassini
L. Manicouagan

Nomansland Pt
Charlton Depot
165
Fort-Rupert
(Rupert House)
Nemiscau
Marten
Q
Réserve de
Mistassini
Post
L. Albanel
Godbout

Halfway Pt
B. de Rupert
Broadback
Réserve de
Assinica
Baie-Comeau

52°

Moosonee
Hannah B.
Broadback
231
L. Evans
Lac aux Goëlands
L. Chibougamau
L. Manouane
U
Mistassini
Raguenau

Moose Factory
Moose
Abitibi
Réserve de
Assinica
556
Chibougamau
Réserve de
Chibougamau
L. Périboncan
L. Berté

Moose River
Kesagami Lake
Mattagami
Waswanipi
Chapais
Dolbeau
Réserve de
Chicoutimi
Forestville
St-Paul-du-Nord
Mont-Joli

Ranoke
L. Waswanipi
L. Surprise
St-Félicien
Kénogami
Chicoutimi
Tadoussac
Rimouski

Coral Rapids
Smoky Falls
Fraserdale
Island Falls
Mattagami
Lac aux Goëlands
Mistassini
Roberval
Jonquière
Arvida
Rivière-du-Loup
Rés. de Horton Kedg. Game Res

Kapuskasing
St-Jean
98
Trois-Pistoles
Cabano
N.-D.-du-L.

Smooth Rock Falls
Cochrane
264
Tascherau
Amos
Beattyville
L. Parent
R° de Gouin
Lac-Edouard
Parc des Laurentides
la Malbaie
Ste-Anne-de-
St-Siméon
Edmu

Porquis Junction
L. Abitibi
la Sarre
Barraute
Senneterre
Oskelaneo
Parent
Sanmaur
Baie St-Paul
St-Jean
1190
Rivière Bleue

S. Porcupine
Matheson
575
Rouyn
Paradis
La Mo
La Tuque
Grand'Mère
Québec
Ste-Anne-de-Beaupré
Montmagny

Timmins
Kirkland Lake
Malartic
Val-d'Or
Rivière-à-Pierre
Ste-Foy
Lévis
Lac Frontière
884

Foleyet
Swastika
L. Simard
Lac Victoria
Parc de la Vérendrye
L. Kempt
L. Taureau
Hervey
Ste-Tite
Grand'Mère
Vallée Jonction
Chamberlain

48°

Gogama
Earlton
N.-D.-du-Nord
Laforce
Rés° de Cabonga
220
Ste-Anne-du-Lac
Shawihigan
Cap de la Madeleine
Plessisville
St-Georges
Baxter State Park 1606

Elk L.
519
Angliers
Réserve de Kipawa
St-Michel-des-Saints
Trois-Rivières
Thetford Mines
Mt Katah

Matachewan
Ville Marie
L. Baskatong
St-Alexis-des-Monts
Parc de la Mtre Tremblante
Nicolet
Victoriaville
Rockwood

Newliskeard
Haileybury
Réserve Kipawa
Dumoine
St-Donat
Mont-Laurier
P. Johannsen
960
Berthierville
Drummondville
Mégantic
Jackman

Biscotasing
Timagami
Témiscamingue
Maniwaki
Labelle
Ste Agathe des M.
Joliette
Richmond
Mtne Mégantic
1150

Mississagi Prov. For.
Marten River
Coulonge
N.-D. du-Laus
St-Jérôme
Sorel
St-Pierre
Sherbrooke
Stratton
Sugarloaf Mtn 1291

Benny
Capreol
Wanapitei
Fort-Coulonge
Buckingham
St-Eustache
Laval
Cartier
Granby
Magog
Skowhegan

Levack
Sturgeon Falls
197
Mattawa
Pembroke
Hull
Hawkesbury
Lachine
Verdun
MONTRÉAL
CANADA
U.S.A.
Newport
Farmington

Elliot Lake
Sudbury
North Bay
Algonquin Prov. Park
Barrys Bay
Eganville
Renfrew
Arnprior
OTTAWA
Cornwall
Valleyfield
St-Jean
Champlain
Colebrook
Errol
1273

Blind River
Espanola
Ludgate
Sundridge
Algonquin Park
Whitney
Wallace
Carleton Place
Perth
Smiths Falls
Massena
Malone
Morrisville
Burlington
St-Albans
Plattsburgh
Berlin
1916
Mt Washington

Little Current
Manitoulin I.
Georgian B. Prov. Forest
Parry Sound
Hunstville
Bancroft
Sharbot Lake
Brockville
Ogdensburg
Canton
Potsdam
Saranac
Montpelier
Barre
1260
Littleton
Auburn

S. Baymouth
Tobermory
C. Hurd
Bruce Pen.
L. HURON
176
Wiarton
Midland
Orillia
Minden
Fenelon Falls
Kaladar
Napanee
Kingston
Gouverneur
Topper L.
628
Adirondack
1485
Woodsville
Portland

Southampton
Owen Sound
Collingwood
Barrie
Lindsay
Peterborough
Madoc
Belleville
Trenton
Watertown
Lowville
Indian L.
Ticonderoga
Rutland
1292
White River Jc.
Concord
Manchester
Biddeford

Kincardine
Durham
Shelburne
Newmarket
Oshawa
Cobourg
L. ONTARIO
Thousand Is.
637
Glenfalls
Georges
Claremont
Rochester
Dover
Portsmouth

TORONTO
78°
170
72°

PACIFIC OCEAN

CANADA
U.S.A.
MONTANA
IDAHO
OREGON
WASHINGTON

CALGARY
VANCOUVER
North Vancouver
New Westminster
Victoria
SEATTLE
TACOMA
Everett
Bremerton
Olympia
Bellingham
PORTLAND
Salem
EUGENE
Springfield
Corvallis
Albany
SPOKANE
Yakima
Ellensburg
Wenatchee
Pasco
Richland
Kennewick
Walla Walla
Pendleton
La Grande
Baker
Bend
Medford
Klamath Falls
Eureka
Arcata
Fortuna
Red Bluff
Redding
BOISE
Nampa
Caldwell
Ontario
Vale
Twin Falls
Pocatello
Blackfoot
Idaho Falls
American Falls
Missoula
Helena
Butte
Anaconda
Deer Lodge
Dillon
Burley

BITTERROOT RANGE
SALMON RIVER MOUNTAINS
BLUE MOUNTAINS
Lost River Range
Lemhi Range
Sawtooth Ra.
COLUMBIA PLATEAU
GREAT BASIN
Columbia Basin
Cabinet Mountains
Clearwater Mountains
Wallowa Mtns
Steens Mtns
Warner Mtns
Fremont Mountains
Klamath Mountains
Siskiyou Mtns
Salish Mountains
Owyhee Mtns
High Desert
Harney Basin

Strait of Juan de Fuca
VANCOUVER I.
Grays Harbor
Willapa Bay
C. Disappointment
C. Blanco
Pt St George
C. Mendocino
Pt Gorda

Mt Rainier 4392
Mt Adams 3751
Mt St Helens 2948
Mt Hood 3430
Mt Shasta 4317
Mt McLoughlin 2894
Mt Olympus 2428
Mt Baker 3285
Three Sisters
Crater Lake Nat. Park
Lassen Volcanic Nat. Park

Glacier Nat. Park
Mt Cleveland 3185
Flathead Lake
Pend Oreille Lake
Coeur d'Alene
Snake River
Columbia R.
Clark Fork
Salmon
Clearwater
He Devil 2868
Hells Canyon
Borah Peak 3857
Matterhorn 3304

120° 126° 44° 48° 40°

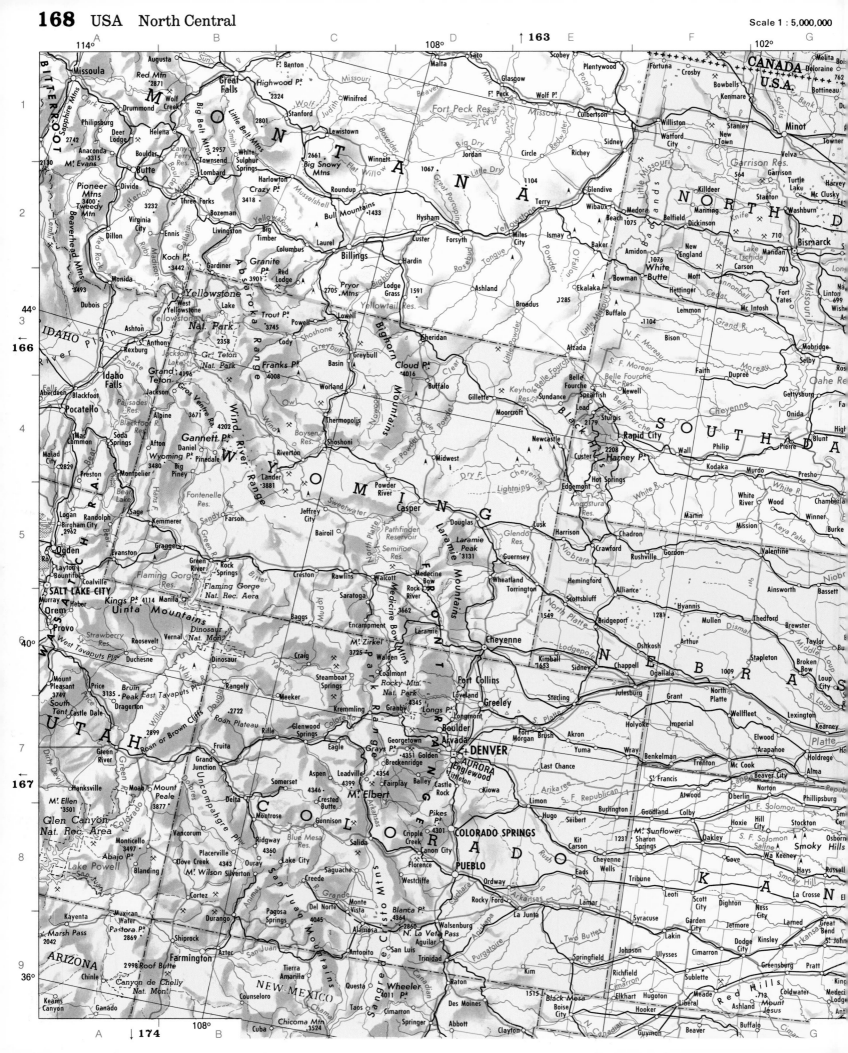

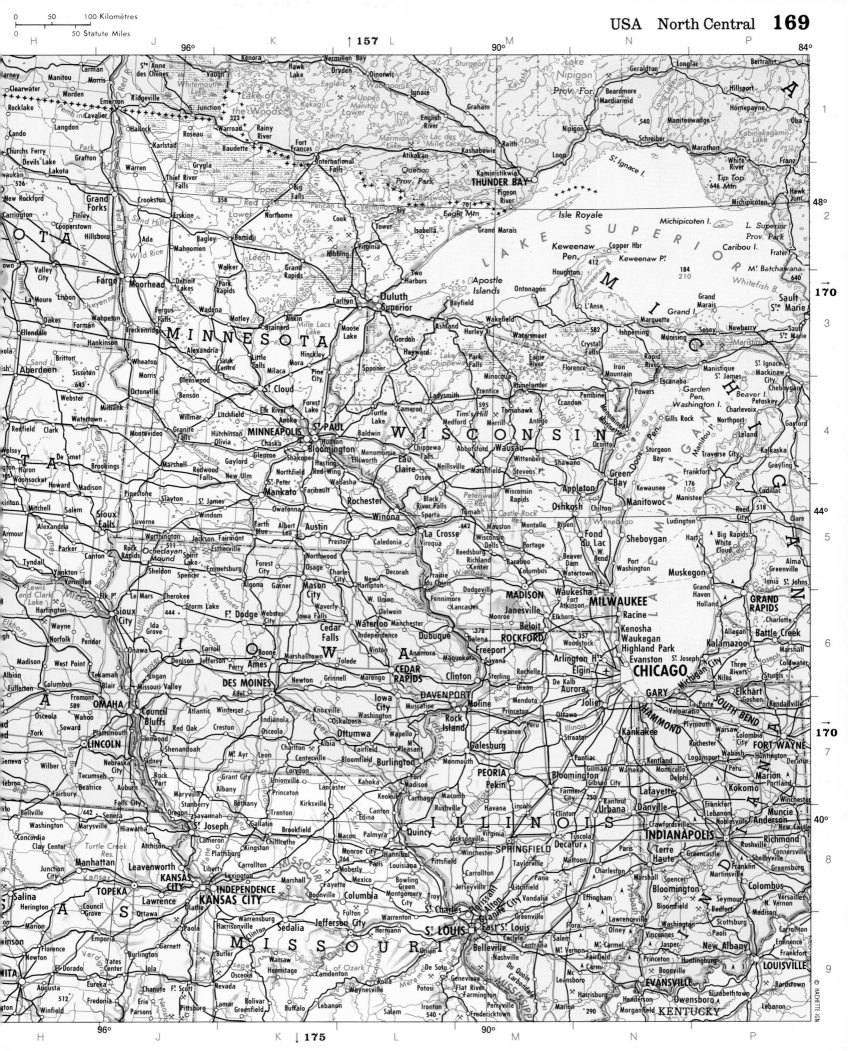

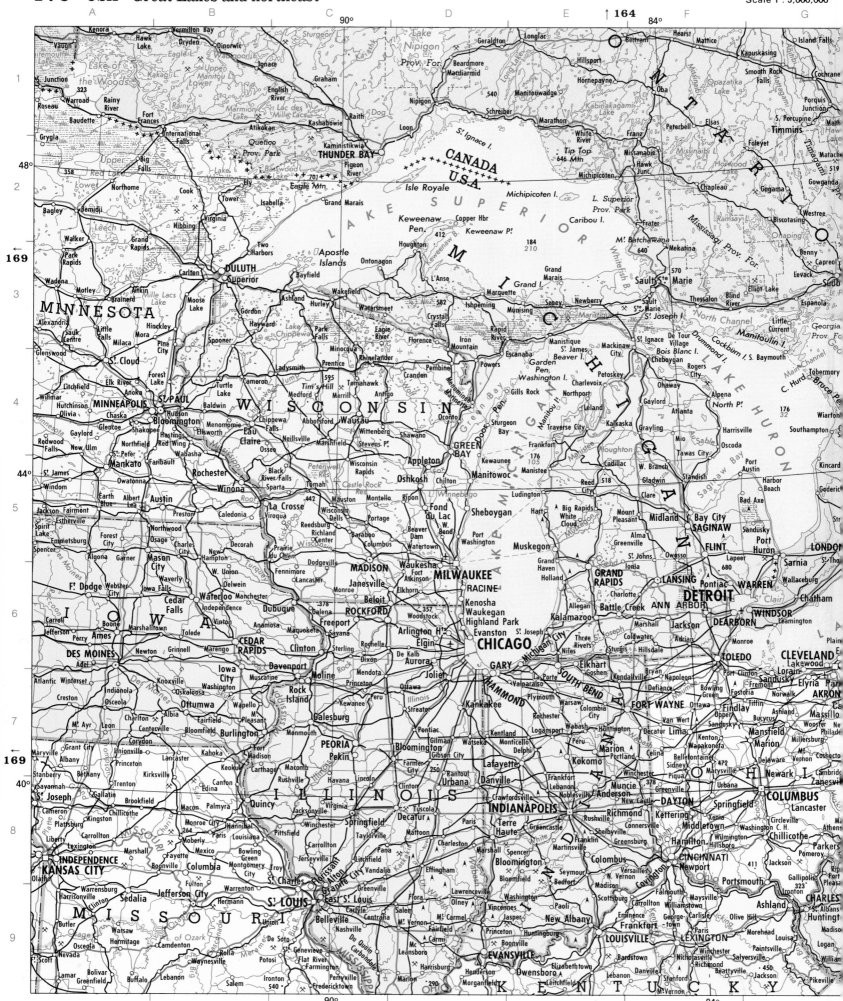

50   100 Kilomètres
50 Statute Miles

↑ 165

78°   72°   66°

**CANADA** / **USA**

**NEW BRUNSWICK**

Chicoutimi · Jonquière · Arvida · Roberval · Alma · Kénogami · Tadoussac · Rivière-du-Loup · Cabano · N.-D.-du-Lac · Edmundston · St-Léonard · Grand Falls · Plaster Rock · Renous · Newcastle · Mc Carleton · Lower Neguac · Chatham · Blackville

Normétal · la Sarre · Taschereau · Amos · Barraute · Rouyn · Malartic · Val-d'Or · Senneterre · Oskélaneo · Parent · Sanmaur · St-Félicien · St-Jean · Kedgwick Game Refuge · St-Quentin · Plaster Rock · St-George · Eastport

**QUÉBEC** · Ste-Foy · Lévis · **MONTRÉAL** · Laval · Lachine · Verdun · St-Jean · Granby · Sherbrooke · Drummondville · Trois-Rivières · Shawinigan · Grand'Mère · Cap-de-la-Madeleine · Nicolet · Sorel · Richmond · Victoriaville · Thetford Mines

**OTTAWA** · Hull · Cornwall · Valleyfield · Plattsburgh · Burlington · Montpelier · Barre · Middlebury · Rutland

**MAINE** · Bangor · Old Town · Augusta · Waterville · Skowhegan · Farmington · Rumford · Bethel · Lewiston · Auburn · Mt Washington · Berlin · Lancaster · Littleton

**TORONTO** · Oshawa · Hamilton · Niagara Falls · St Catharines · Welland · **BUFFALO** · Lockport · Batavia · **ROCHESTER** · **SYRACUSE** · Auburn · Geneva · Canandaigua · Oswego · Pulaski · Watertown · Rome · Utica · Amsterdam · Schenectady · **ALBANY** · Troy · Saratoga Springs · Glens Falls · Ticonderoga

**NEW YORK** · Ithaca · Binghamton · Elmira · Corning · Hornell · Olean · Jamestown · Dunkirk · **ERIE** · Ashtabula · Warren · Bradford

**NEW HAMPSHIRE** · Concord · Manchester · Nashua · Keene · Claremont · Laconia

**VERMONT** · Rochester · Dover · Portsmouth · Haverhill · Lawrence · Lowell · Lynn · Gloucester · **BOSTON** · Cambridge · Quincy · Brockton · Provincetown · **Cape Cod**

**MASSACHUSETTS** · Worcester · Springfield · Holyoke · Chicopee · Pittsfield · Fitchburg · Greenfield · New Bedford · Nantucket · Martha's Vineyard

**CONNECTICUT** · **HARTFORD** · New Britain · Meriden · Waterbury · Danbury · Bridgeport · Stamford · Norwalk · **NEW HAVEN** · New London · Middletown · Torrington

**RHODE ISLAND** · **PROVIDENCE** · Pawtucket · Cranston · Warwick · Fall River · Newport

Kingston · Poughkeepsie · Newburgh · Middletown · Port Jervis · White Plains · Yonkers · **NEW YORK** · Jersey City · Newark · Elizabeth · New Brunswick · Trenton · Long Island

**PENNSYLVANIA** · **PITTSBURGH** · Johnstown · Altoona · Williamsport · Scranton · Wilkes-Barre · Hazleton · Harrisburg · Lancaster · York · Reading · **ALLENTOWN** · Bethlehem · Easton · Pottstown · Norristown · Chester · **PHILADELPHIA** · Camden

**NEW JERSEY** · Atlantic City · Vineland · Bridgeton · Cape May · Wildwood · Toms River · Lakewood · Red Bank

**MARYLAND** · **BALTIMORE** · Towson · Dundalk · Annapolis · Rockville · Silver Spr. · Hagerstown · Frederick · Cumberland · Salisbury · Ocean City · Cambridge

**DELAWARE** · Dover · Wilmington · Georgetown · Rehoboth Beach

**WASHINGTON** · Arlington · Alexandria · Warrenton

**WEST VIRGINIA** · Morgantown · Fairmont · Clarksburg · Elkins · Weston · Sutton

**VIRGINIA** · **RICHMOND** · Charlottesville · Lynchburg · **ROANOKE** · Fredericksburg · Culpeper · Harrisonburg · Staunton · **NEWPORT NEWS** · **HAMPTON** · **NORFOLK** · **PORTSMOUTH** · **VIRGINIA BEACH** · Cape Charles · Williamsburg · Petersburg

**ATLANTIC OCEAN**

LAKE ONTARIO · LAKE ERIE · Chesapeake Bay · Delaware Bay · Massachusetts Bay

ADIRONDACK MTNS · Mt Marcy 1628 · GREEN MTNS · WHITE MTNS · Mt Washington 1916 · APPALACHIAN MOUNTAINS · ALLEGHENY MOUNTAINS · Catskill Mts

© HACHETTE-IGN

↓ 177

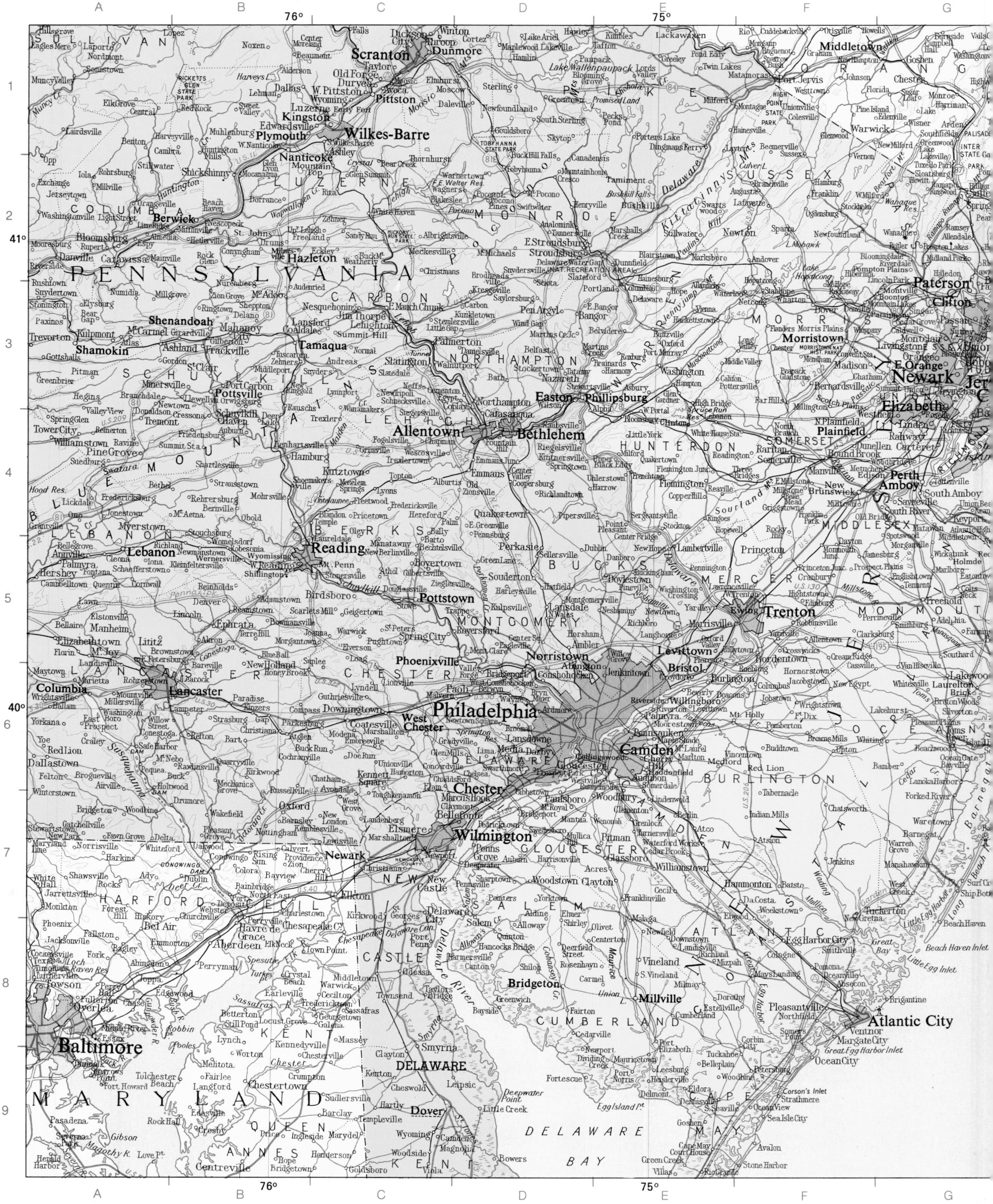

A
B
C
D
E
F
G
76°
75°
41°
40°
1
2
3
4
5
6
7
8
9
PENNSYLVANIA
MARYLAND
DELAWARE
NEW JERSEY
SULLIVAN
LUZERNE
COLUMBIA
CARBON
MONROE
PIKE
SCHUYLKILL
NORTHAMPTON
LEHIGH
BERKS
LEBANON
LANCASTER
CHESTER
MONTGOMERY
BUCKS
DELAWARE
HARFORD
CECIL
KENT
QUEEN ANNES
NEW CASTLE
SALEM
GLOUCESTER
CAMDEN
BURLINGTON
ATLANTIC
CUMBERLAND
CAPE MAY
OCEAN
MONMOUTH
MERCER
MIDDLESEX
SOMERSET
HUNTERDON
WARREN
MORRIS
SUSSEX
ORANGE
UNION
BLUE MOUNTAIN
DELAWARE BAY
Scranton
Dunmore
Pittston
Kingston
Wilkes-Barre
Plymouth
Nanticoke
Berwick
Bloomsburg
Hazleton
Shenandoah
Shamokin
Tamaqua
Pottsville
Allentown
Bethlehem
Easton
Phillipsburg
Lebanon
Reading
Pottstown
Lancaster
Columbia
Norristown
Phoenixville
West Chester
Philadelphia
Chester
Wilmington
Camden
Levittown
Bristol
Trenton
Newark
Paterson
Clifton
Elizabeth
Plainfield
Perth Amboy
Morristown
Middletown
Atlantic City
Bridgeton
Millville
Vineland
Dover
Baltimore
Towson
Aberdeen
Elkton
Stroudsburg
Lancaster
Hershey
Ephrata
Manheim
Lititz
Flemington
Princeton
Somerville
New Brunswick
Freehold
Lakewood
Toms River
Ocean City
Cape May
Salem
Glassboro
Woodbury
Doylestown
Quakertown
Lansdale
Media
Paoli
Bel Air
Havre de Grace
Chestertown
Smyrna

H J K 73° L M 72° N P

CONNECTICUT

Cold Spring
Kent Cliffs
Towners
Putnam Lake
New Fairfield
Southbury
Southford
Brooksvale
Wallingford
E. Haddam
Montville
Uncasville
Wood River Junc.
Wakefield
Narragansett Pier
Newport Bay

Carmel
Putnam
Southford
Oxford
Beacon Falls
NEW HAVEN
Chesterfield
Ledyard
N. Stonington
Ashaway
Charlestown

**Danbury**
Bethel
Newtown
Seymour
McCarmel
Northford
Rockland
Chester
Hamburg E. Lyme
Old Mystic
Pawcatuck
Mystic
**Westerly**
Ninigret Pond
Pt. Judith

Redding
Botsford
**Hamden**
N. Guilford
Madison
Deep River
Essex
Laysville
**New London**
Groton
Noank
Stonington
RHODE ISLAND

Monroe
Woodbridge
**Ansonia**
Orange
N. Branford
Guilford
Ivoryton
Old Saybrook
Old Lyme
Waterford
Quonochontaug
Galilee

Shelton
Derby
**New Haven**
E. Haven
Stony Creek
Westbrook
Clinton
Watch Hill

FAIRFIELD
**Stratford**
**West Haven**
Sachem Hd.
Falkner I.
Cornfield Pt.
Fort Terry
Plum I.
Fishers I.
Block Island Sound
Sandy Pt.

**Bridgeport**
Fairfield
Stratford Pt.
Orient
Orient Pt.
Great Salt Pond
Block I.
Southeast Pt.

**Norwalk**
**Stamford**
LONG ISLAND SOUND
Greenport
Gardiners Bay
Gardiners I.
Montauk Pt.

**Greenwich**
Port Chester
Southold
Shelter Island
Napeague
Montauk
HITHER HILLS ST. PK.
Napeague Beach

**White Plains**
WESTCHESTER
Eatons Neck Pt.
Old Field Pt.
Peconic Bay
Little Peconic Bay
North Haven
Sag Harbor
Springs
Amagansett

**Yonkers**
**New Rochelle**
Smithtown
Setauket
Port Jefferson
Shoreham
Wading Riv.
Aquebogue
**Riverhead**
Great Peconic Bay
Bridgehampton
Water Mill
E. Hampton

M' Vernon
Glen Cove
Oyster Bay
Huntington
Stony Brook
Rocky Point
Calverton
Flanders
Southampton
Sagaponack

BRONX
NASSAU
Northport
Kings Park
Middle Island
Manorville
Riverhead
Westhampton
Shinnecock B.

QUEENS
Hicksville
Central Islip
Ronkonkoma
Brookhaven
Moriches
Eastport
Quogue

**NEW YORK**
Westbury
Brentwood
Patchogue
Bellport
Mastic Beach

Jamaica
**Hempstead**
Farmingdale
Deer Park
Sayville
W. Sayville
SUFFOLK

Brooklyn
Wantagh
Lindenhurst
**Babylon**
**Bay Shore**
Islip
South Beach
GREAT SOUTH BEACH
NATIONAL SEASHORE

Rockville Centre
Amityville
Great South Bay
Ocean Beach
Cherry Grove
Fire Island

Rockaway Beach
**Long Beach**
Saltaire
Oak Beach
JONES BEACH STATE PARK

GATEWAY NATIONAL RECREATION AREA

Ambrose Channel
L. Ambrose Channel

Highlands

Silver
**Long Branch**

**bury Park**
Ocean Grove
by the Sea

Lake

squan
Pleasant

oking

Barnegat

41°

40°

**ATLANTIC OCEAN**

0  5  10        20        30 Statute Miles
0  5 10     20    30    40    50 Kilometres

© HACHETTE-BARTHOLOMEW

H J K 73° L M 72° N P

100 Kilometres
50 Statute Miles
Scale 1 : 5,000,000

114° ↑ **167**

108°

**ARIZONA**

**NEW**

Gulf of Sto Catalina
Oceanside
Vista
Escondido
Indio
Vidal
Parker
Prescott
Cottonwood
Sanders
Petrified Forest Nat. Park
Mt Ta
599
S. Clemente I.
El Cajon
Julian
Salton Sea
Blythe
Quartzsite
Wickenburg
2430
Mount Union
Clints Well
Pine
Holbrook
Zuni
Grants
Fence Lake
San Diego
Chula Vista
Anza-Borrego Desert State Park
Calipatria
Brawley
El Centro
Calexico
1373
73
Signal Pk
1471
Avondale
Glendale
Scottsdale
Roosevelt
Mc Nary
Baldy Peak 3533
Springerville
Alpine
Quemando
Datil
I: Coronados
Tijuana
Tecate
Mexicali
Descanso
Yuma
Gila
Phoenix
Mesa
Tempe
Miami
Superior
Globe
Fort Apache
Concho
St. Johns
Magdalen
S. Baldy
32°
Ensenada
1830
Lag. Salada
Batagues
1060
S. Luis R. Colorado
960
Wellton
Gila Bend
Casa Grande
Coolidge
Florence
Hayden
Salt
San Carlos L.
Apache Creek
Reserve
Whitewater Baldy 3320
Black Springs
I: de Todos Santos
Pta Banda
Pta Sto Tomás
Mayor
Rito
Desierto de Altar
Ajo
Eloy
549
Picacho Pass
Mt Lemmon 2800
Mt Graham 3265
Clifton
Safford
Thruth or Consequences (Hot Springs)
El Alamo
S. Vicente
Cerro del Pinacate 1390
Sonoita
Organ Pipe Cactus Nat. Mon.
1476
Quijotoa
Tucson
Duncan
Silver City
Santa Rita
S. Lorenzo
Arrey
Hatch
R.
C. Colnett
So San Pedro Martir
Cº de la Encantada 3078
S. Felipe
Pta S. Felipe
Pta Estrella
Pto Peñasco
B. de Adair
Sells
2356
Palo Alto
Baboquivari Pk
Continental
Mt Wrightson 2879
Sonoita
Miller Pk 2885
Tombstone
Chiricahua Pk 2985
Rodeo
Hachita
Deming
Las Cruces
Columbus
I. S. Martín
S. Quintín
C. S. Quintín
B. de S. Jorge
1213
Desemboque
Heroica Caborca
Sasabe
Sarío
Heroica Nogales
Nogales
Sta Cruz
2039
Cº Cibuta
Imuris
Benson
Animas
U.S.A. MEXICO
Ciudad Juarez
Rosario
Pta Baja
Pta S. Antonio
Sta Catarina
Pta Canoas
S. Fernando
I. S. Luis
B. S. Luis Gonzaga
Puerto Libertad
C. Lobos
Pitiquito
Altar
Trincheras
Benjamin Hill
Magdalena
Santa Anna
Cananea
Agua Prieta
Douglas
Colonia Morelos
Guzmán
Ascension
Nueva Casas Grandes
Jarios
28°
Rosario
Pta Rosarito
Sierra de S. Borjas
I. Angel de la Guarda
C. Tepoca
P. de Johnson
1023
Sa de S. Antonio
Arizpe
Nacozari
2452
Bavispe
2769
Juárez
Galeana
El Sueco
Buenaventura
1555 Cº dos Picachos
1315
I. Tiburón
1218
Bahía Kino
1019
Ures
Moctezuma
Villa Ahumada
Carmen
Puerta Prieta
I. S. Benito
I. Cedros
1204
Bahía Sebastián Vizcaíno
Sto Domingo
1907
I. S. Esteban
I. S. Lorenzo
Pta Baja
Cabo S. Miguel
Sonora
2192
Hermosillo
Mazatán
Presa El Novillo
Sahuaripa
Madera
Sierra
Chihua
I. Natividad
Pta Eugenia
4335
La Colorada
Cº Otatal
1364
Tetoripa
Tonichi
Temosachic
El Sauz
B. de S. Cristobal
Pta S. Pablo
935
Desierto de Vizcaíno
Sierra Vizcaíno
Vol. las Tres Virgenes 1996
S. Ignacio
C. Virgenes
I. Tortuga
2668
Ciudad Guerrero 3102
La Junta
Chihuahua
Cuauhtémoc
Pta S. Hipólito
B. S. Hipólito
935
Santa Rosalía
I. S. Marcos
Pta Chivato
I. Lobos
Presa Obregón
Gl. Trias
Sta Rosalia de las Cuevas
Creel
Pta Abreojos
B. Ballenas
1776
Mulegé
B. Sta Inés
Pta Concepción
742
Pta Sta Teresa
Guaymas
C. Haro
Ciudad Obregón
Yaqui
Presa Macuzari
Oteros
2793
Valle del Sauz
Pta Sto Domingo
Pta Pequeña
Pta S. Juanico
La Purísima
Comomdu
1766
Rosario
Pta Púlpito
I. Coronados
Loreto
479
Huatabampo
Pta Rosa
Navojoa
Alamos
1790
El Fuerte
Choix
Creel
2437
2713
Rosa
Rocas Alijos
PACIFIC
OCEAN
Sto Domingo
I. Carmen
I. Monserrate
I. Sta Catalina
Pta S. Marcial
3295
Los Mochis
Higueras de Zaragoza
S. Blas
Sinaloa de Leyva
Guadaloupe y Calvo
3150
Cerro Chorreras
Isla
C. S. Lázaro
Magdalena
Bahía Magdalena
688
I. S. José
1524
I. Sta Cruz
Pta Sta Maria
I. de S. Ignacio
Guasave
Verdura
2192
Guamúchil
S. Francis del Oro
Sta Barbara
24°
I. Sto Margarita
I. Cresciente
Llano de la Magdalena
9 Hilario
762
I. Espíritu Santo
I. Cerralvo
Boca del Rio
Badiraguato
Presa Sanalona
Pericos
Altata
2622
Culiacán
Tepeh
Papasq
Tropic of Cancer
2164
Todos Santos
Santiago
Pta Arena
La Paz
S. Pedro
El Triunfo
Ensenada
Pta de la Ventana
Sierra de S. Lázaro
Eldorado
Cosalá
2474
La Cruz
S. Ignacio
Du
El Sal
S. Lucas
C. Falso
C. S. Lucas
S. José del Cabo
Pta Piaxtla

114°
108°

↑ **168**

→ **176**

↓ **178**

USA states/regions: **MEXICO**, **OKLAHOMA**, **TEXAS**, **COAHUILA**, **NUEVO LEON**, **DURANGO**

**GULF OF MEXICO**

Coordinates: 96°, 102°, 36°, 32°, 28°

Grid columns: I, J, K, L, M, N, P
Grid rows: 1, 2, 3, 4, 5, 6, 7, 8, 9

© HACHETTE-IGN

Cities and place names (selection):

Los Alamos, Santa Fe, San Ysidro, Las Vegas, Wagon Mound, Roy, Mosquero, Conchas Dam, Stratford, Perryton, Woodward, Ponca City, Pawhuska, Bartlesville, Vinita, ALBUQUERQUE, Sandia Pk, Tucumcari, Logan, Nara Visa, Dumas, Stinnett, Borger, Canadian, Enid, Perry, Pawnee, Cleveland, Claremore, TULSA, Pryor, Los Lunas, Belen, Estancia, Sta Rosa, San Jon, Vega, Pampa, Panhandle, Cheyenne, Elk City, Kingfisher, Guthrie, Cushing, Wagoner, Tahlequah, Muskogee, Sallisaw, AMARILLO, Claude, Canyon, Wheeler, Shamrock, Sayre, Clinton, El Reno, OKLAHOMA CITY, Midwest City, Shawnee, Seminole, Wewoka, Okmulgee, Eufaula, Stigler, Poteau, Willard, Mountainair, Corona, Clovis, Farwell, Hereford, Dimmit, Tulia, Memphis, Wellington, Mangum, Hollis, Anadarko, Chickasha, Norman, Purcell, Holdenville, Wilburton, Carrizozo, Sierra Blanca Pk, Portales, Elida, Muleshoe, Silverton, Turkey, Childress, Altus, Snyder, Frederick, Duncan, Pauls Valley, Ada, Mac Alester, Coalgate, Salinas Peak, Roswell, Bledsoe, Morton, Littlefield, Plainview, Floydada, Matador, Quanah, Paducah, Vernon, Lawton, Walters, Davis, Sulphur, Atoka, Antlers, Clayton, Tularosa, Hondo, Two Rivers Reservoir, Tatum, Lovington, Plains, Brownfield, LUBBOCK, Slaton, Dickens, Crosbyton, Benjamin, Seymour, WICHITA FALLS, Henrietta, Bowie, Gainesville, Bonham, Denison, Madill, Durant, Hugo, Idabel, Clarksville, De Kalb, Carlsbad, Hobbs, Seminole, Lamesa, Gail, Snyder, Roby, Aspermont, Haskell, Throckmorton, Graham, Jacksboro, Decatur, Denton, Mac Kinney, Greenville, Commerce, Cooper, Paris, Mount Pleasant, Guadalupe Pk, Salt Flat, Jal, Eunice, Andrews, Colorado City, Sweetwater, ABILENE, Baird, Cisco, Breckenridge, Mineral Wells, Ft WORTH, IRVING, GARLAND, DALLAS, Terrell, Longview, Sierra Blanca, Kermit, Mentone, Odessa, MIDLAND, Garden City, Sterling City, Robert Lee, Winters, Coleman, Comanche, Hico, Hamilton, Meridian, Hillsboro, Waxahachie, Ennis, Corsicana, Tyler, Kilgore, Van Horn, Kent, Toyahvale, Pecos, Monahans, Crane, Rankin, Big Lake, San Angelo, Ballinger, Brownwood, Goldthwaite, Gatesville, WACO, Marlin, Groesbeck, Buffalo, Rusk, Nacogdoches, Felix U. Gomez, Valentine, Mt Livermore, Ft Davis, Fort Stockton, Mc Camey, Iraan, Ozona, Eldorado, Menard, San Saba, Brady, Mason, Lampasas, Belton, Temple, Cameron, Hearne, Madisonville, Groveton, Crockett, Lufkin, Marfa, Chinati Pk, Alpine, Marathon, Sheffield, Sonora, Junction, Llano, Burnet, Georgetown, Taylor, Rockdale, Bryan, Navasota, Huntsville, Livingston, Woodville, Presidio, Ojinaga, Coyame, Sanderson, Dryden, Comstock, Rocksprings, Fredericksburg, Johnson City, Kerrville, Comfort, AUSTIN, Bastrop, Elgin, Giddings, Brenham, Hempstead, Conroe, Cleveland, Liberty, Ciudad Delicias, Caballos Mesteños, Study Butte, Big Bend Nat Park, Emory Pk, Del Rio, Brackettville, Leakey, Bandera, Boerne, New Braunfels, SAN ANTONIO, San Marcos, Seguin, Luling, Schulenburg, La Grange, Columbus, Sealy, HOUSTON, PASADENA, Baytown, Anahuac, M. Venavides, Acuña, S. Carlos, Jimenez, Uvalde, Hondo, Devine, Floresville, Stockdale, Gonzales, Hallettsville, Yoakum, Wharton, Rosenberg, West Columbia, Alvin, Texas City, Galveston, Piedras Negras, Zaragoza, Eagle Pass, La Pryor, Crystal City, Pearsall, Pleasanton, Karnes City, Kenedy, Cuero, El Campo, Bay City, Lake Jackson, Freeport, Allende, Nava, Carrizo Springs, Cotulla, Tilden, Three Rivers, Goliad, Victoria, Edna, Palacios, Port Lavaca, Matagorda, Matagorda B., Nueva Rosita, Sabinas, V. Unión, Encinal, George West, Beeville, Refugio, Aransas Pass, Rockport, Melchor Múzquiz, San Diego, Alice, Robstown, CORPUS CHRISTI, Freer, Sinton, Juárez, No LAREDO, Laredo, Hebbronville, Kingsville, Baffin B., Padre Island, Ocampo, Cuatrociénegas de Carranza, S. Blas, S. Buenaventura, Anahuac, Zapata, Falfurrias, Sarita, Villa Frontera, MONCLOVA, Lampazos, Villaldama, Sabinas Hidalgo, Rio Grande City, Raymondville, Port Isabel, Gómez Palacio, TORREON, Matamoros, Cd Lerdo, Paredón, Azul, Cerralvo, Los Aldamas, Camargo, Mc ALLEN, Edinburg, Pharr, Mercedes, Harlingen, Brownsville, Jimulco, Viesca, Parras de la Fuente, Paila, SALTILLO, MONTERREY, China, Valle Hermoso, MATAMOROS, REYNOSA, Rodeo, Pedriceña, Cuencamé, S. Juan de Guadalupe, Concepción del Oro, Montemorelos, S. Lorenzo, VICTORIA DE DURANGO, Miguel Auza, Estación Camacho, Canelo, Linares, Rastro, S. Carlos, S. Fernando, B. Sto Maria, Rio Grande, Santander Jimenez

**DURANGO**, **NUEVO LEON**, **COAHUILA**

Rivers/features: Pecos, Canadian, Rio Grande, Rio Bravo del Norte, Red R., Brazos, Colorado, Concho, Nueces, Rio Salado, Conchos, Nazas, Aguanaval, Laguna Madre, LLANO ESTACADO, EDWARDS PLATEAU, Davis Mtns, Sacramento Mtns, Bolson de Mapimi

GULF OF MEXICO

MEXICO

MATAMOROS

States and major cities: OKLAHOMA, OKLAHOMA CITY, TULSA, MISSOURI, SPRINGFIELD, ARKANSAS, LITTLE ROCK, MEMPHIS, TENNESSEE, NASHVILLE, MISSISSIPPI, JACKSON, ALABAMA, BIRMINGHAM, TEXAS, DALLAS, FT. WORTH, HOUSTON, AUSTIN, WACO, CORPUS CHRISTI, BROWNSVILLE, LOUISIANA, SHREVEPORT, BATON ROUGE, NEW ORLEANS, MOBILE, PENSACOLA

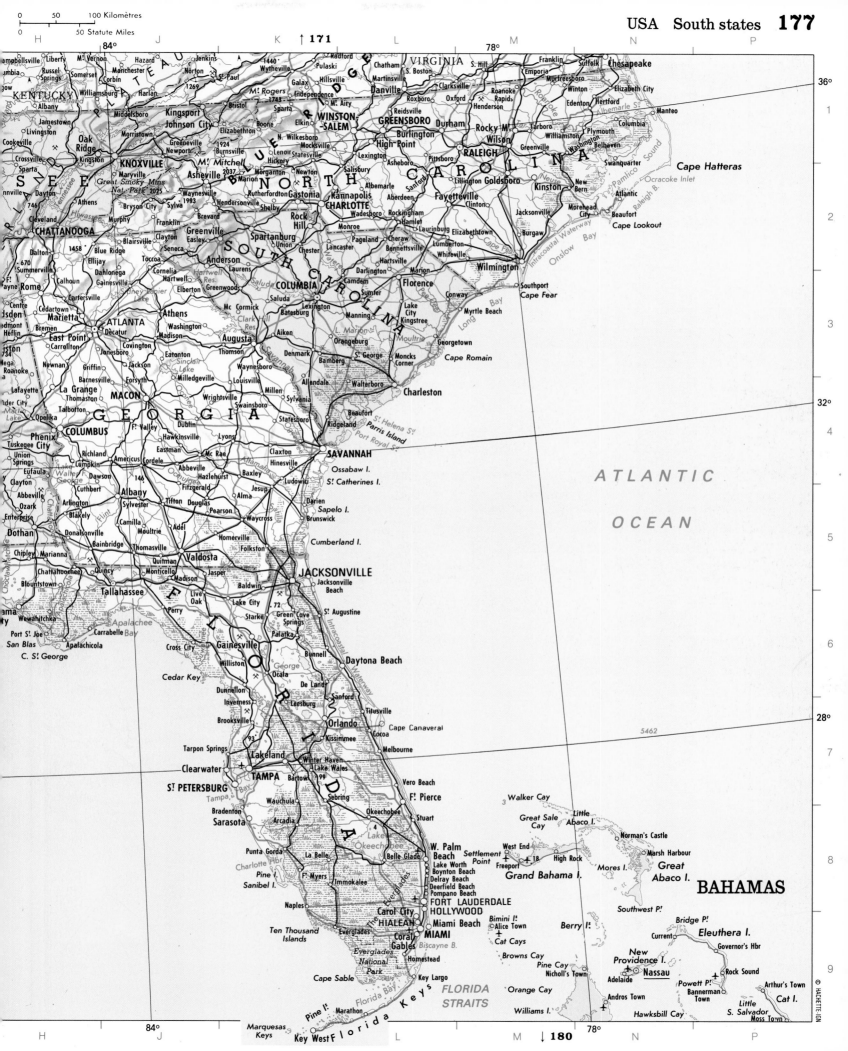

Scale 1 : 5,000,000

↑ **175** 102°

108°

**PACIFIC OCEAN**

**COLIACÁN** · Pericos · Altata · Eldorado · Cosalá · La Cruz · S. Ignacio · Pta Piaxtla · **MAZATLÁN** · Concordia · V. Unión · Rosario · Escuinapa de Hidalgo · Teacapan · Tecuala · Acaponeta · Rosa Morada · Rosamorada · Tuxpán · Santiago Ixcuintla · S. Blas · Sta Cruz · Pta Gorda · Pta Raza · Compostela · Valle de Banderas · Pta de Mita · B. de Banderas · Puerto Vallarta · C. Corrientes · Tulto · Chamela · Barra de Navidad · Playa Blanca · Manzanillo

I. S. Juanito · I. M. Madre · I. M. Magdalena · I. M. Cleofas · I.s Las Tres Marias

**DURANGO** · Tepehuanes · Santiago Papasquiaro · Rodeo · Canatlán · Francisco I. Madero · **VICTORIA DE DURANGO** · El Salto · Bayas · Vicente Guerrero · Mezquital · Concordia

**ZACATECAS** · Río Grande · Sombrerete · Sain Alto · Cañitas de F. Pescador · Fresnillo de G. Echeverría · Valparaiso · Jerez de G. Salinas · **Zacatecas** · Jesús Maria · Colotlán · Villanueva · Rincón de Romos

Gómez Palacio · Cº Lerdo · **TORREÓN** · Matamoros · Jimulco · Cuencamé · Pedriceña · Nazas · S. Juan de Guadalupe · Guadalupe Victoria · Juan Aldama · Miguel Auza · Estación Camacho · Viesca · Paila · Parras de la Fuente · **SALTILLO** · Concepción del Oro · Sto Domingo · Matehuala · Dr. Arroyo · Salinas de Hidalgo · Ojo Caliente · Pinos · Loreto · Vº Hidalgo

**NUEVO LEÓN** · **MONTERREY** · China · Montemorels · Linares · Potosí · Canelo · Rastro · Entronque Huizache · Cerro Peña Nevada 4054 · Tula

**TAMAULIPAS** · **REYNOSA** · **MATAMOROS** · S. Fernando · S. Carlos · Santander Jiménez · Soto la Marina · **CIUDAD VICTORIA** · Palmillas · Ciudad Mante · Gonzales · Manuel · Antiguo Morelos · Cárdenas · Elbano · **CIUDAD MADERO** · **TAMPICO** · Pánuco

**SAN LUIS POTOSÍ** · Charcas · Cerritos · **S. LUIS POTOSÍ** · Río Verde · Ciudad del Maiz · Ciudad Valles · Jalpan · Tamazunchale · Tamuín

**NAYARIT** · **TEPIC** · Ahuacatlán · Tequila

**JALISCO** · **GUADALAJARA** · Tlaquepaque · Ameca · Tala · Tequila · Mascota · Autlán de Navarro · Unión de Tula · Cocula · Sayula · L. de Chapala · Chapala · Ocotlán · La Barca · Ciudad Guzmán · Tuxpan · Tapalpa · Juchipila · Yahualica de G. Gallo · Teocaltiche · Jalostotitlán · Tepatitlán de Morelos · Arandas · Atotonilco el Alto · S. Juan de los Lagos · Lagos de Moreno · León · **LEÓN** · S. Francisco del Rincón · Silao · **GUANAJUATO** · **IRAPUATO** · **SALAMANCA** · **CELAYA** · Salvatierra · Acámbaro

**AGUASCALIENTES** · Calvillo · Jalpa · Tlaltenango de S. Román · Encarnación de Díaz · Ojuelos de Jalisco · S. Felipe · Cuna de la Ind. Nal. · S. Miguel de Allende · S. Luis de la Paz

Nevado de Colima · Colima · **COLIMA** · Tecomán · Coahuayana · Coalcomán de Matamoros · Cabeza Negra · Pta S. Telmo · Arteaga · Aguililla · Apatzingán de la Constitución · Tepalcatepec · Playa Azul · Pta Mangrove · La Unión · B. de Petacalco · Ixtapa Zihuatanejo · Pta Maldonado

**MICHOACÁN** · **URUAPAN** · Los Reyes Zacapu de Salgado · Pátzcuaro · Ario de Rosales · Vol. de S. Andres · Tacámbaro de Codallos · Huetamo de Núñez · Infiernillo · Presa del Infiernillo · Presa de la Villita · Altamirano · Arcelia · Heroica Zitacuaro · **MORELIA** · Ciudad Hidalgo · Moroleón · Valle de Santiago · La Piedad Cavadas · Sahuayo de Díaz · Zamora de Hidalgo · Jiquilpan de Juárez

**QUERETARO** · **QUERETARO** · Tequisquiapan · S. Juan del Río · Zimapán · Ixmiquilpan

**HIDALGO** · Actopan · **Pachuca de Soto** · Tula de Allende · Atlacomulco de Fabela · Ciudad Hidalgo · Tulancingo · Huauchinango · Apan · Zacatlán

**MÉXICO** · **NAUCALPAN DE MÉXICO** · Teotihuacan · **TOLUCA DE LERDO** · Metepec · Nevado de Toluca 4373 · Tenango del Aire · **CUERNAVACA** · **MORELOS** · Cuautla · Morelos · Amecameca de J. · Popocatepetl 5452 · Martín Texmelucan · **PUEBLA** · Tlaxcala de X. · Apizaco · Oriental

**GUERRERO** · **Chilpancingo de los Bravo** · Tixtla · Chilapa de Alvarez · Tecpan de Galeana · Cruz Grande · **ACAPULCO DE JUAREZ** · Ometepec · S. Marcos · Tlapa de Comonfort · Cuajinicuilapa · Santiago Pinotepa Nacional · Putla de Guerrero · Iguala de la Ind. · Huitzuco de Figueroa · Chiautla de Tapia · Balsas · Mezcala · Jojutla de Juárez · Izúcar de Matamoros · Acatlán de Osorio · Tehua · Atlixco · Tepeaca · Justlahuaca · Sta Maria Asunción Tla · Huajuapan de León

**SIERRA MADRE DEL SUR** · **SIERRA MADRE OCCIDENTAL** · **SIERRA MADRE ORIENTAL**

Río Grande de Santiago · L. de Chapala · R. Balsas · R. Verde · R. Pánuco · R. Montezuma · Lag. del Caimanero · Presa del Infiernillo

Elevations: 3209 · 2622 · 2888 · 3137 · 3440 · 3751 · 2499 · 3195 · 3592 · 4054 · 3035 · 1311 · 3226 · 2474 · 2696 · 3109 · 2895 · 2590 · 2301 · 2956 · 640 · 2120 · 2926 · 3190 · 1338 · 1067 · 2740 · 2960 · 1502 · 3183 · 3627 · 4265 · 3933 · 5452 · 4373 · 2754 · 5121 · 2652 · 4703 · 3414 · 3375 · 4380 · 5291 · 5291

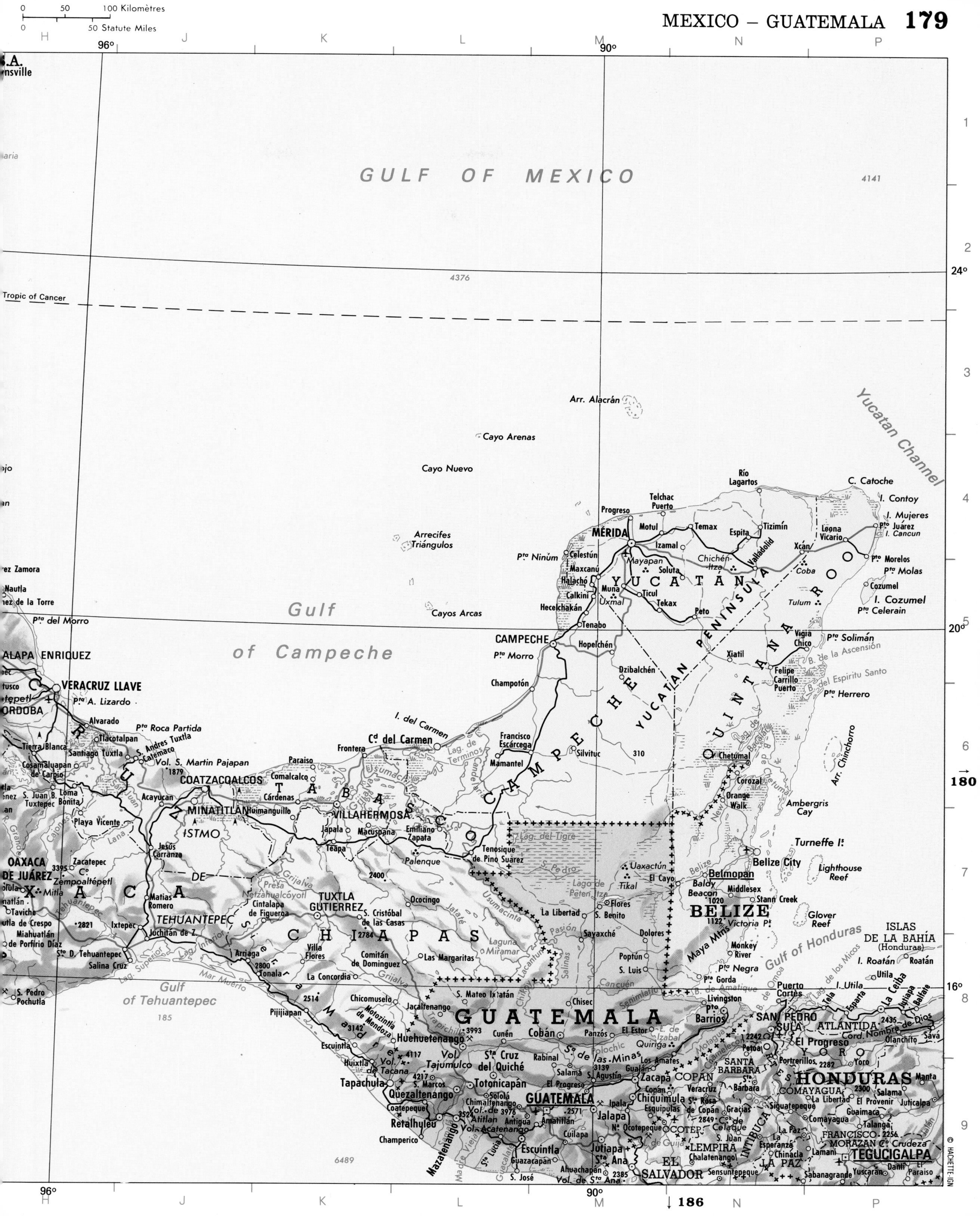

0 50 100 Kilomètres
0 50 Statute Miles

H 96° J K L M 90° N P

U.S.A.
nsville

1

GULF OF MEXICO
4141

2
24°

Tropic of Cancer

3

Arr. Alacrán

Cayo Arenas

Cayo Nuevo
Río Lagartos
C. Catoche
I. Contoy
4
Progreso Telchac Puerto
I. Mujeres
Pta Juárez
I. Cancun
MÉRIDA Motul Temax Espita Tizimín Leona Vicario
Arrecifes Triángulos
Pta Ninúm Celestún Izamal Soluta Chichén-Itzá Valladolid Xcan
Pto Morelos
Mayapan YUCATÁN Coba Pto Molas
Maxcanú Muna Cozumel
Halachó Ticul I. Cozumel
Calkini Uxmal Tekax Pto Celerain
Hecelchakán Peto
Cayos Arcas Tenabo
5
Gulf
of Campeche
20°
ALAPA ENRIQUEZ CAMPECHE Hopelchén Vigia Chico Pta Solimán
Pta del Morro Pta Morro Xiatil B. de la Ascensión
VERACRUZ LLAVE Dzibalchén Felipe Carrillo Puerto
Pta A. Lizardo Champotón Hopelchén Pta Herrero
CORDOBA
Alvarado I. del Carmen
Tierra Blanca Tlacotalpan Pta Roca Partida Cd del Carmen Francisco Escárcega
Santiago Tuxtla Frontera Silvituc
Cosamaluapan Andres Tuxtla Catemaco Lag. de Términos Mamantel 310 Chetumal Arr. Chinchorro
de Carpio Vol. S. Martin Pajapan Paraiso
1879 COATZACOALCOS Comalcalco Corozal 6
S. Juan B. Loma Bonita Cárdenas Orange Walk Ambergris Cay
Tuxtepec Acayucan MINATITLAN Huimanguillo
Playa Vicente VILLAHERMOSA
ISTMO Japala Lag. del Tigre Turneffe Is.
Zacatepec Jesús Carranza Macuspana Uaxactún Belize 7
OAXACA Matias Romero Teapa Tenosique Belize City
DE JUÁREZ 3395 Zempoaltépetl 2400 de Pino Suárez El Cayo Belmopan Lighthouse Reef
Mitla Palenque Lago de Petén Itzá Baldy Beacon
Tavicha Cintalapa Ocosingo Tikal 1020 Middlesex Stann Creek
Miahuatlán de Porfirio Díaz 2821 Ixtepec TUXTLA de Figueroa Flores S. Benito BELIZE Glover
Ixtepec GUTIERREZ S. Cristóbal 1122 Victoria Pk Reef
Juchitán de Z de las Casas La Libertad
S D Tehuantepec 2784 Dolores ISLAS
Salina Cruz CHIAPAS Sayaxché Maya Mins DE LA BAHÍA
TEHUANTEPEC Villa Flores Laguna Poptún Monkey (Honduras)
2800 Comitán Miramar River I. Roatán Roatán
Arriaga Tonala de Dominguez S. Luis Pta Negra Utila
Gulf of Tehuantepec Las Margaritas Pta Gorda I. Utila
185 La Concordia S. Mateo Ixtatán Cancuén Puerto Cortés La Ceiba 16°
2514 Chicomuselo Chisec Livingston Tela
Pijijiapan Jacaltenango Los Amates Barrios SAN PEDRO ATLÁNTIDA 2435
3142 Motozintla L. de Izabal SULA Savá
Huehuetenango 3993 Cunén Cobán Panzós El Estor Quiriga El Progreso YORO Olanchito Savá 8
Escuintla Rabinal Santa 2242 Portrerillos Yoro
4117 Sta Cruz Salamá S. Agustín Zacapa Bárbara 2282 GUATEMALA
Huixtla Vol. del Quiché 3139 COPAN Sta Rosa HONDURAS Manta
Tapachula de Tacana Totonicapán El Progreso Gualán Chiquimula de Copán COMAYAGUA 2300 Salama 9
4217 S. Marcos Sololá GUATEMALA Ipala Esquipulas Gracias La Libertad El Provenir Juticalpa
Quezaltenango Chimaltenango 2571 Jalapa 2849 Siguatepeque Comayagua Guaimaca
3524 Antigua Amatitlán N° Ocotepeque Guía La Paz Talanga
Retalhuleu Vol. de Fuego Cuilapa FRANCISCO
Champerico Escuintla Jutiapa LEMPIRA MORAZAN 2256
6489 Sta Ana EL Chinacla TEGUCIGALPA
Guazacapán S. Ana SALVADOR Yuscarán
2385 S. José Ahuachapán Paraiso

H 96° J K L M 90° N P

HACHETTE-IGN

180

186

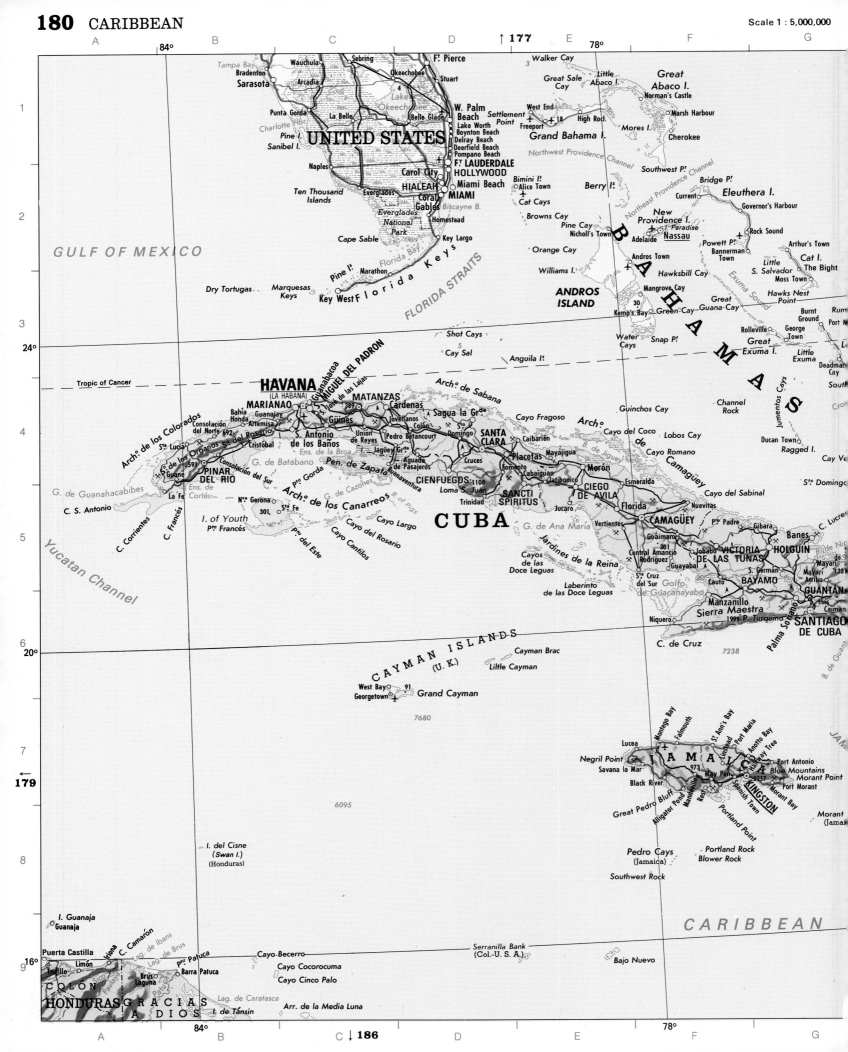

Scale 1 : 5,000,000

**GULF OF MEXICO**

**UNITED STATES**

Tampa Bay
Bradenton
Sarasota
Wauchula
Sebring
F.t Pierce
Okeechobee
Stuart
Punta Gorda
Arcadia
La Belle
Belle Glade
W. Palm Beach
Lake Worth
Boynton Beach
Delray Beach
Deerfield Beach
Pompano Beach
Pine I.t
Sanibel I.
Naples
Ten Thousand Islands
Carol City
HIALEAH
Everglades
Coral Gables
HOLLYWOOD
Miami Beach
MIAMI
F.t LAUDERDALE
Everglades National Park
Homestead
Cape Sable
Key Largo
Pine I.t
Marathon
Dry Tortugas
Marquesas Keys
Key West
Florida Keys
Florida Straits
Biscayne B.
Lake Okeechobee

Walker Cay
Great Sale Cay
West End
Freeport
Settlement Point
High Rock.
Grand Bahama I.
Little Abaco I.
Great Abaco I.
Norman's Castle
Marsh Harbour
Mores I.
Cherokee
Southwest P.t
Bridge P.t
Current
Eleuthera I.
Governor's Harbour
Rock Sound
Bimini I.t
Alice Town
Cat Cays
Browns Cay
Pine Cay
Nicholl's Town
Berry I.t
New Providence I.
Adelaide
Paradise
Nassau
Powett P.t
Bannerman Town
Arthur's Town
Cat I.
The Bight
Moss Town
Orange Cay
Andros Town
Hawksbill Cay
Little S. Salvador
Williams I.
Mangrove Cay
Hawks Nest Point
Kemp's Bay
Water Cays
Snap P.t
Green Cay
Great Guana Cay
Burnt Ground
Port N
Rolleville
George Town
Great Exuma I.
Little Exuma
Deadman Cay
Sou
Le

**ANDROS ISLAND**

**B A H A M A S**

Northwest Providence Channel
Northeast Providence Channel
Exuma Sound
Jumentos Cays

Shot Cays
Cay Sal
Anguila I.t
Tropic of Cancer

24°

**CUBA**

Guanahatoa
MIGUEL DEL PADRON
HAVANA (LA HABANA)
MARIANAO
Ios de las Lajas
MATANZAS
Cárdenas
Bahía Honda
Guanajay
Güines
Jovellanos
Sagua la Gr.de
Arch.o de Sabana
Consolación del Norte
Artemisa
S. Antonio de los Baños
Unión de Reyes
Colón
Domingo
SANTA CLARA
Caibarién
Cayo Fragoso
Arch.o
Cayo del Coco
Guinchos Cay
Channel Rock
Ducan Town
S.ta Lucía
Sa del Rosario
Pedro Betancourt
Caba
Placetas
Mayajigua
B. de Jiguey
Cayo Romano
Ragged I.
S.to Domingo
Cay
S.ta Fe
Cristóbal
Jaguey Gr.de
Aguada de Pasajeros
Cruces
Fomento
Cabaiguán
Morón
Esmeralda
Pinar del Rio
Consolación del Sur
Pen. de Zapata
Buenaventura
CIENFUEGOS
Loma S. Juan
Trinidad
SANCTI SPIRITUS
Jatibonico
CIEGO DE AVILA
Florida
Cayo del Sabinal
Nuevitas
Guane
Arch.o de los Colorados
Arch.o de los Organos
La Fe
Ens. de Cortés
N.va Gerona
I. of Youth
P.to Francés
Arch.o de los Canarreos
Cayo Largo
Cayo del Rosario
Cayo Cantilos
Jucaro
Vertientes
CAMAGÜEY
P.to Padre
Gibara
Banes
C. Lucre
C. S. Antonio
C. Corrientes
C. Frances
P.to Gorda
G. de Cazones
B.t of Pigs
G. de Ana María
Guáimaro
Central Amancio Rodríguez
VICTORIA DE LAS TUNAS
HOLGUIN
de Ni
G. de Batabano
Cayos de las Doce Leguas
Guayabal
S.ta Cruz del Sur
Mayari
S. German
Mayari Arriba
G. de Guanahacabibes
Jardines de la Reina
Golfo de Guacanayabo
Cauto
BAYAMO
GUANTAN
Laberinto de las Doce Leguas
C. de Cruz
Manzanillo
Sierra Maestra
1999 P. Turquino
SANTIAGO DE CUBA
B. de Guan
Niquero
Palma Soriano
Luis Caiman
7238

20°

**Yucatan Channel**

**CAYMAN ISLANDS (U.K.)**
Cayman Brac
Little Cayman
West Bay
Georgetown
Grand Cayman
7680

6095

**J A M A I C A**
Montego Bay
Falmouth
S.t Ann's Bay
Port Maria
Anotto Bay
Lucea
Linstead
Halfway Tree
Port Antonio
Negril Point
Savana la Mar
May Pen
Blue Mountains
Morant Point
Black River
Mandeville
KINGSTON
Port Morant
Morant Bay
Great Pedro Bluff
Alligator Pond
Spanish Town
Portland Point
Rest
Morant (Jamai
Portland Bight
I. del Cisne (Swan I.) (Honduras)

Pedro Cays (Jamaica)
Portland Rock
Blower Rock
Southwest Rock

**CARIBBEAN**

I. Guanaja
Guanaja
Puerta Castilla
C. Camarón
Serranilla Bank (Col.-U.S.A.)
Bajo Nuevo
Trujillo
Limón
Bruso Laguna
Barra Patuca
Cayo Becerro
Cayo Cocorocuma
Cayo Cinco Palo
**C O L O N**
**HONDURAS**
**G R A C I A S   A   D I O S**
Lag. de Caratasca
Arr. de la Media Luna
I. de Tánsin
16°

84°

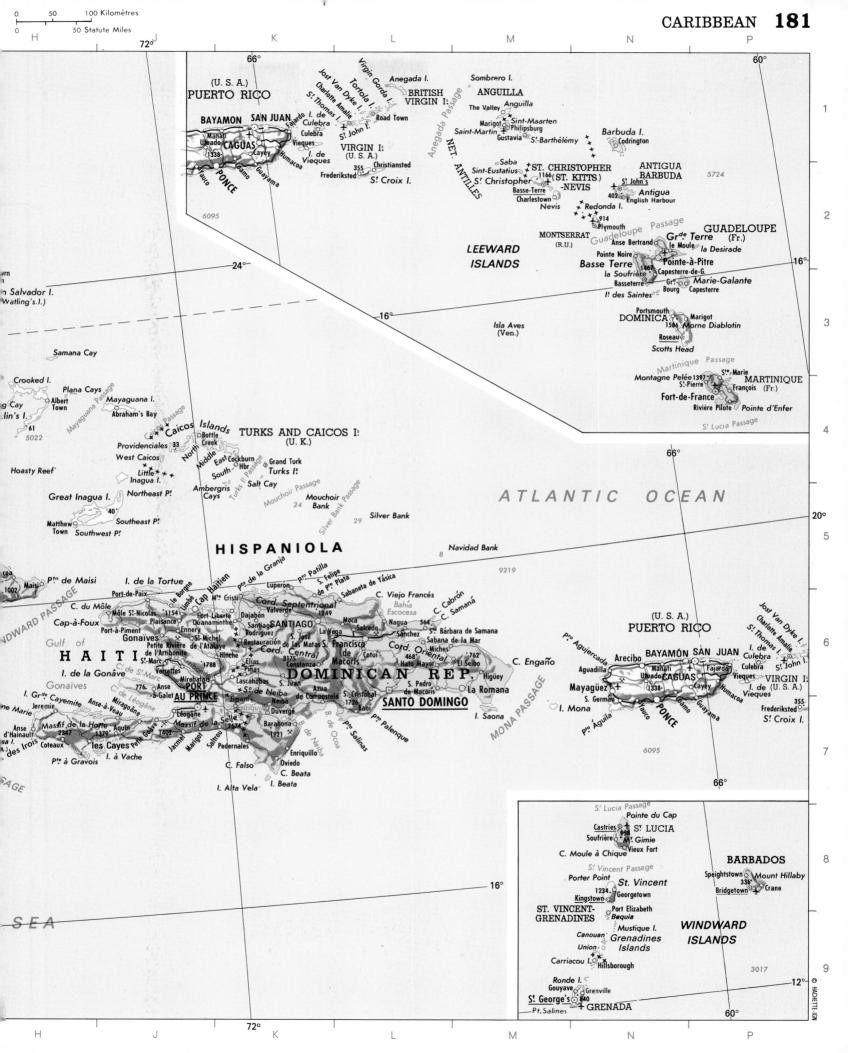

50   100 Kilomètres
50 Statute Miles

PUERTO RICO (U.S.A.)
BAYAMON   SAN JUAN
Manati   Fajardo I. de
Utuado   Culebra
CAGUAS   Culebra
(1338)   Cayey   I. de
Humacao   Vieques
Ponce   Guayama
Yauco   Salinas   355
Christiansted
Frederiksted   St Croix I.

Virgin Gorda I.
Jost Van Dyke I.   Anegada I.
Charlotte Amalie   BRITISH
St Thomas I.   VIRGIN Is
Tortola I.
Road Town
St John I.
VIRGIN Is
(U.S.A.)

Sombrero I.
ANGUILLA
The Valley   Anguilla
Marigot   Sint-Maarten
Saint-Martin   Philipsburg
Gustavia   St-Barthélémy
NET. ANTILLES

Saba   ST. CHRISTOPHER
Sint-Eustatius   1166 (ST. KITTS)
St Christopher   -NEVIS   St John's
Basse-Terre   402
Charlestown   English Harbour
Nevis   Antigua
914   Redonda I.
Plymouth
MONTSERRAT   (R.U.)

ANTIGUA
BARBUDA
Barbuda I.
Codrington

5724

LEEWARD
ISLANDS

Isla Aves
(Ven.)

Anse Bertrand   Grde Terre   (Fr.)
Pointe Noire   le Moule   la Desirade
Basse Terre   Pointe-à-Pitre
la Soufrière 1467   Capesterre-de-G.
Basseterre   Grde   Marie-Galante
Grd   Bourg   Capesterre
Is des Saintes

GUADELOUPE

Portsmouth   Marigot
DOMINICA   1586   Morne Diablotin
Roseau
Scotts Head

Montagne Pelée 1397   Ste-Marie
St-Pierre   MARTINIQUE
Fort-de-France   François   (Fr.)
Rivière Pilote   Pointe d'Enfer
St Lucia Passage

HISPANIOLA

Samana Cay

Crooked I.
Plana Cays
Albert   Mayaguana I.
Town   Abraham's Bay
61   5022

Hoasty Reef

Caicos Islands
Providenciales   33   Bottle
West Caicos   Creek
East Cockburn
Little   Middle   Hbr
Inagua I.   South
Great Inagua I.   Ambergris   Salt Cay
Matthew   40   Cays
Town   Southeast Pt
Southwest Pt   Northeast Pt

TURKS AND CAICOS Is
(U.K.)

Grand Turk
Turks Is

24
Mouchoir Passage
29   Mouchoir
Bank
Silver Bank

ATLANTIC   OCEAN

Navidad Bank
8
9219

Pta de Maisi
Maisi   I. de la Tortue
1002   Port-de-Paix   le Borgne
C. du Môle   Limbé
Cap-à-Foux   Môle St-Nicolas   1154   Fort Liberté
Port-à-Piment   Plaisance   Ouanaminthe
Gonaïves   Ennery   Dajabón
Petite Rivière   St-Michel   Santiago
St-Marc   de l'Artibonite   Rodriguez
I. de la Gonâve   Hinche   Restauración
HAITI   1788   Elias   de las Matas
Golfe de St-Marc   Piñas
Gonaïves   776   Verrettes   Lascahobas   3175
Anse   Mirebalais   San Juan
I. Grde Cayemite   à-Galet   Jimani   de Neiba
Miragoâne   PORT   Duvergé
Jeremie   Anse-à-Veau   AU PRINCE   2674
Léogâne   Sde la Selle
ne Marie   Massif de la Hotte   Marigot   Barahona
Anse   2347   1379   1402   Saltrou   1921
d'Hainault   Aquin   Petit Goâve   Pedernales
les Cayes   Jacmel   C. Falso
Coteaux   I. à Vache   Oviedo
Pte à Gravois   I. Alta Vela   C. Beata
I. Beata

Pta de la Granja
Pto Patilla
S. Felipe   Luperon   Pto de Pta Plata
Cap Mte Cristi   Valverde   1249
Cord. Septentrional   Moca
Santiago   La Vega   Salcedo
SANTIAGO   564
S. José   Cotui   Sánchez
Cord.   S. Francisco   Sabana de la Mar
Central   de   Miches
Constanza   Macoris   Cord.
DOMINICAN REP.   Oriental   468
Azua   S. Cristóbal   Hato Mayor   762
de Compostela   1726   S. Pedro   El Seibo
Baní   de Macoris   Higüey
SANTO DOMINGO   La Romana
Pta Salinas   I. Saona
C. Engaño

Sabaneta de Yásica
C. Viejo Francés   C. Cabrón
Bahía   C. Samaná
Escocesa
Nagua   Bárbara de Samana

PUERTO RICO (U.S.A.)
Pto Aguijercada
Arecibo   BAYAMÓN   SAN JUAN
Aguadilla   Manati   Fajardo
Utuado   CAGUAS   I. de
Mayagüez   (1338)   Culebra
S. Germán   Cayey   Culebra
Ponce   Humacao
Yauco   Guayama   I. de (U.S.A.)
I. Mona   Vieques   355
Pto Águila   Frederiksted
St Croix I.
MONA PASSAGE

Jost Van Dyke I.
Charlotte Amalie
St Thomas I.
VIRGIN Is
I. de
Culebra
Vieques

6095

S.t Lucia Passage
Pointe du Cap
Castries   958   ST. LUCIA
Soufrière   Mt. Gimie
C. Moule à Chique   Vieux Fort

St Vincent Passage
Porter Point
St. Vincent
1234   Georgetown
Kingstown
ST. VINCENT-
GRENADINES   Port Elizabeth
Bequia
Mustique I.
Canouan   Grenadines
Union   Islands
Carriacou I.   Hillsborough

Ronde I.
Gouyave   Grenville
St George's   840
Pt. Salines   GRENADA

BARBADOS
Speightstown   Mount Hillaby
336
Bridgetown   Crane

WINDWARD
ISLANDS

3017

© HACHETTE-IGN

Scale 1 : 5,000,000

↑ **179**

# MEXICO

**GUATEMALA**

**BELIZE**

Tuxtla Gutiérrez
S. Cristóbal de las Casas
Ococingo
Arriaga
Tonalá
Lag. Inferior
Mar Muerto
Vol. Flores
2784
2800
la Concordia
Comitán de Domínguez
las Margaritas
Lag. Miramar
Usumacinta
Belize
Turneffe I.
Lighthouse Reef
Pijijiapán
2514
Chicomuselo
S. Mateo Ixtatán
3142
Chisec
Sayaxché
Dolores
Maya 990
Wilson Peak
El Cayo
Baldy Beacon
Victoria Peak 1122
Middlesex
Belmopan
S. Andrés
Flores
la Libertad
Poptún
S. Luis
Stann Creek
Glover Reef
Escuintla
Motozintla de Mendoza
Vol. de Tacaná
3990
Jacaltenango
Alto Cuchumatanes
Ixcán
Chixoy
Cobán
Panzós
El Estor
Lago de Petén Itzá
Tikal
S. Benito
Golfo de Honduras
ISLAS DE LA BAHÍA
I. Roatán
Roatán
I. Guanaja
I. Guanaja
I. Barbareta
Huixtla
4117
Vol. Tajumulco
4217
S. Marcos
Huehuetenango
Sta. Cruz del Quiché
Cunén
Rabinal
Salamá
3139
Sa. de las Minas
Polochic
L. de Izabal
Livingston
Pto. Barrios
Quiriga
Motagua
Quiriguá
S. PEDRO SULA
2242
I. Utila
Utila
Tapachula
Quezaltenango
Totonicapán
Coatepeque
Sololá
Chichicastenango
El Progreso
S. Agustín
Los Amates
Gualán
COPÁN
Copán
Veracruz
SANTA BÁRBARA
Sta. Bárbara
El Progreso
2300
Salamá
Manta
Tela
la Ceiba
Esparta
Trujillo
ATLÁNTIDA
Puerta Castilla
Lag. Guaimo
Retalhuleu
Atitlán
3975
Vol. Acatenango
3524
Antigua
GUATEMALA
2571
Escuintla
Cuilapa
Chiquimula
Jalapa
Ipala
Esquipulas
Sta. Rosa de Copán
Nº Ocotepeque
OCOTEP
2849
COMAYAGUA
2407
YORO
Yoro
P. Pijol 2282
Nombre
Olanchito
Savá
S. Esteban
HONDURAS
OLANCHO
Catacamas
Champerico
Sta. Lucía
Mazatenango
Guazacapán
Jutiapa
Metapán
Celaque 2849
Cº de S. Juan
Siguatepeque
Guaimaca
Talanga
COMAYAGUA
Juticalpa
Mazatenango
Madre Vieja
Chalatenango
2256
la Esperanza
LEMPIRA
INTIBUCÁ
Tutule
Lamani
FRANCISCO MORAZÁN
Cº Crudeza
Ahuachapán
Vol. de Sta. Ana
2385
Chinacla
Chinacla
La Paz
S. Francisco Gotera
LA PAZ
Sabanagrande
Yuscarán
TEGUCIGALPA
Jalapa
SEGOVIA
Garrobo
San José
Sonsonate
Acajutla
2134
S. Vicente
Usulután
Conchagua
Pta. S. Juan
La Unión
San Miguel
VALLE
Nacaome
Goascorán
Choluteca
Sómoto
Ocotal
1963
MADRIZ
Cordillera Isa
Nº S. Salvador
SAN SALVADOR
L. de Ilopango
Zacatecoluca
Vol. 1250
CHOLUTECA
G. de Fonseca
Vol. Cosigüina
CHINANDEGA
El Viejo
Vol. El Viejo
El Sauce
Estelí
Sébaco
ESTELÍ
Jinotega
MATAGAL
Cord. del Da
Chinandega
1780
León Viejo
Dario
Sta. Rosa
Momotombo
1258
León
L. de Managua
Teustepe
Boaco
BOACO
Juigalpa
Pto. Corinto
Pto. Sandino
MANAGUA
MANAGUA
Masaya
Granada
Acoyapa
NICARAGUA
CHON
Diriamba
Vol. Mombacho
Pto. Masachapa
Jinotepe 1363
GRANADA
I. Zapatera
CARAZO
RIVAS
S. Jorge
Vol. Concepción
1556
I. de Ometepe
S. Juan del Sur
Rivas
Nicaragua
I. de Solentin
B. de Salinas
la Cruz
C. Sta. Elena
Golfo de Papagayo
Vol. Cord.
Miravalles
2020
Liberia
GUANACASTE
C. Velas
Nicoya
la Mansión
Sta. Cruz
Puntare
Pto. Jesús
Lepanto
4353 Pta. Guiones
Pen. de Nicoya
C. Blanco
9
3553
6489
6350

## PACIFIC OCEAN

---

### ARCHIPIÉLAGO DE COLÓN
(Ecuador)

I. Culpepper
I. Wenman
320
PACIFIC OCEAN
I. Pinta
I. Marchena
I. Genovesa
Roca Redonda
Pta. Albemarle
Vol. Wolf
**ISLAS GALAPAGOS**
Equator
C. Berkeley
B. de Bancos
1707
I. S. Salvador
884
I. Fernandina
C. Douglas
Vol. la Cumbre
1494
ISLA
I. Baltra
I. Sta. Cruz
Pta. Pitt
B. Isabel
C. de Isabela
864
Pto. Ayora
I. Sta. Fé
I. S. Cristóbal
**ISABELA**
Vol. Sto. Tomas 1500
Pto. Cristóbal
Cº Azul 1689
I. Pinzón
C. de Sta. Cruz
I. Sta. Fé
Pto. Baquerizo
896
Pto. Villamil
C. Rosa
Floreana
I. Sta. María
I. Española
Pto. Wreck
90°
Equator
0°
-8°
90°
16°
12°

100 Kilomètres
50 Statute Miles

JAMAICA

Lucea
Montego Bay
Falmouth
Saint Ann's Bay
Port Maria
Anotto Bay
Negril Point
Savana la Mar
973
Linstead
Port Antonio
Halfway Tree
Blue Mountains
Black River
May Pen
Port Morant
2257
Morant Point
Great Pedro Bluff
Rest
Spanish Town
KINGSTON
Morant Bay
Alligator Pond
Mandeville
Portland Point

Morant Cays
(Jamaica)

I. del Cisne (Swan I.)
(Honduras)

6095

Pedro Cays
(Jamaica)
Portland
Rock
Blower Rock

Southwest Rock

Camarón
Lag. de Ibans
de Brus
Cayo Becerro
Brus Laguna
Pto Patuca
Barra Patuca

Cayo Cocorocuma
Cayo Cinco Palo

GRACIAS
AS DIOS
Lag. de Caratasca
Serranilla Bank
Bajo Nuevo
16°

Wampusirpi
Mosquitia
I. de Tánsin
Puerto Lempira
Arr. de la Media Luna

Auasbila
Leimus
C. Gracias a Dios
Arr. Edinburgh
BO GRACIAS A DIOS
Waspan
Cabo Gracias a Dios
Quita Sueno
Bank

Cayos
Morrison
Cayo Muerto

onanza
Yacaltara
Lag. Uskira
Dacura
Cayos Miskito
Serrana Bank
U A
a Luz
Tunki
Pto Cabezas
Cayo Ned Thomas

epi
Macantaca
Carata
Lag. Carata
Huahue
Prinzapolca
Lag. Huaunta
Huaunta
Roncador Cay
4532

Grande
553
Lag. de
las Perlas
I. de Providencia
(Colombia)

Huapi
La Barra
Curinhuas
Pta de Perlas
C A R I B B E A N       S E A

Squil
Rama
I. del Maiz
(Corn I.)
(Nicaragua)
I. de S. Andrès
(Colombia)
103   S. Andrés
Cayos de Courtown

Bluefields
El Bluff
I. Venado
Cayos de Albuquerque

d. Yolaina
Punta Gorda
Pta del Mono

SAN JUAN
B. de S. Juan
del Norte

St. Juan
del Norte
12°

HEREDIA
Pto Viejo
Tortuguero

BARRANQUILLA
Pta Faro
Pto Colombia
Soledad
Baranoa
ATLANTICO
Sabanalarga
S. Estanislao

Limón
CARTAGENA

Guápiles
Siquires
Pta Canoas
Pto Baru
B. Barba

JOSE
Cartagos
Pandora
Pto Cahuita
Cahuita
Is del Rosario

Turrialba
Suretka
Is de S. Bernardo
S. Onofre
841
Plato
Zambrano
JOSE
Chirripó Gde
Pico Blanco
I. de Colón
Bocas del Toro
Archipiélago
Portobelo
Pta Manzanilla
Pen. de S. Blas
El Porvenir
Playón Grande
Golfo
de Darien
I. Fuerte
S. Bernardo
Coveñas
Sincelejo
Corozal
186

Buenos
Aires
3565
I. Bastimentos
de Bocas del Toro
COLON
Mandinga
Blas
Pta Portogandí
Pto Escondido
Lorica
Chinu
Magangué

Dominical
El General
I. Popa
Pen. Valiente
Cristobal
Madden
823
Pta Arboletes
Arboletes
Cereté
Since
Benito

Palmar
Pando
Robalo
Escudo de Veraguas
PANAMÁ
Chepo
Perme
MONTERIA
Colomboy
SUCRE
Marcos

Pen. de Osa
Disquis
G. de los Mosquitos
Cristobal
Balboa
Sasardi
Pto Arboletes
Mulatos
Planeta
Rica
Majagual

Golfito
Vol. Chiriqui
Chitré
La Chorrera
Pta Chame
San
Pta Caribana
Acandí
Nicocli
CORDOBA

C. Matapalo
David
Boquete
3478
COCLÉ
Penonomé
Puno
Darien
1410
Tierra
Alta
Ayapel

la Cuesta
2826
Aguadulce
S. Carlos
I. Pedro
Gonzáles
221
I. del
Rey
la Palma
Cº Tacarcuna
1910

Golfo
Pta Armuelles
Pedregal
Boca
del Monte
Remedios
Santiago
Río Hato
I. S. José
DARIÉN
El Real
Garachiné
2000
Caucasia

Pto Burica
I. Sevilla
Sona
HERRERA
Ocú
DE LAS PIEDRAS
Parc
Naturel Sautatá
3960

I. Ladrones
Is Secas
Macaracas
las Tablas
Golfo de Panamá
Darien
1565
Chigorodó

I. Contreras
PEN. DE AZUERO
LOS SANTOS
Pedasi
Jaqué
Cº Puno
COLOMBIA

I. Montuosa
I. Coiba
416
I. Cebaco
Cº Cambutal   1829
Tonosi
Pta Mala
Cocalito
Pavarandocito
Zaragoza

I. Jicarón
Pto Mariato
Morro de Puercos
Juradó
Ituango

© HACHETTE-IGN

A 78° B C D E 72° F G

12°
1

**CARIBBEAN SEA**

PENINSULA DE GUAJIRA

(Ven.)
I.ˢ los Monjes

Nazareth

Manaure  Uribia  ·801  Pᵗᵒ López
Pᵗᵒ Estrella  853.

Riohacha

Maicao  Paraguaipoa  Golfo de Venezuela

C. de la Aguja  Dibulla  Sinamaica  Capatárida

Pᵗᵒ Faro  SANTA MARTA  Cᵒ Quemado 2946  Carrasquero  San Rafael  Dabajuro

BARRANQUILLA  Ciénaga  SIERRA NEVADA  P. Cristóbal  Campo Mara  Mene

Pᵗᵒ Colombia  Soledad  Ciénaga Grᵈᵉ  Sᵗᵃ Marta 5775  Colón  MARACAIBO  Sᵗᵃ Rita  de Mauroa

Baranoa  ATLÁNTICO  DE Sᵗᵃ MARTA  San  la Paz  Sᵗᵃ Rita

Pᵗᵃ Canoas  Sitio Nuevo  la Concepción  Concepción  CABIMAS  Cᵃ Cerro

CARTAGENA  Sabanalarga  VALLEDUPAR  los Negrones  Ciudad Ojeda  1900

536  Estanislao  Pivijay  Rosario  Lagunillas

I.ˢ del Rosario  Arjona  Calamar  CÉSAR  Machiques  Barranquitas  Bachaquero

Pᵗᵒ Barú  Mahates  Juan  Becerri  Cᵒˢ Irapa  ZULIA  Sᵗᵃ Timoteo

B. Barbacoas  Nepomuceno  Plato  3750  Mene Grᵈᵉ

Ciénaga de Sapayan  El Difícil  Arjona  Lago de

PANAMA  S. Onofre  Zambrano  Rincón Hondo  Maracaibo

Pᵗᵃ Manzanilla  I. Fuerte  El Carmen  Chiriguana  Sierra de  la Ceiba  TRUJI

Portobelo  Pen. de S. Blas  Morrosquillo  Tolú  El Banco  Cᵒˢ de Bobali  Encontrados  Bodures  Betijoque

COLON  El Porvenir  Coveñas  Sincelejo  Momíl  (2521)  Palmarito  S. Antonio

Mandinga  S. Bernardo  Lorica  Mompós  la Gloria  Palmira  la Solita  VALERA

920  Cᵒˢ de S. Blas  Chepo  Sᵉʳ  Pᵗᵒ Escondido  Cereté  Chinú  SUCRE  Ayacucho  Encontrados

827ᵗ  Pᵗᵒ Cariban  Arboletes  San  Sincé  S. Marcos  Castigua

PANAMÁ  Sasardí  Pᵗᵒ  Arboletes  Benito  Majagual  NORTE  El Vigía  MÉRIDA  Merida

la  Balboa  Permé  C. Tiburón  Acandí  Mulatos  Colomboy  Aguachica  3750  la Fría  Tovar  5008  PICO

Chorrera  B.ᵃ de  Chiman  Nicocli  Planeta  DE  Ejido  BOLÍVAR

Pᵗᵒ Chame  Panamá  Turbo  MONTERIA  Rica  Ayapel  Ocaña  3200  Cúcuta  S. Cristóbal

S. Carlos  ARCHIPIÉLAGO  la Palma  Cᵒ Puno  2000  Ayapel  Caucasia  Abrego  Gramalote  TÁCHIRA  CORD.

Río Hato  I. Pedro  221°  Cᵒ Tacarcuna  Tierra  CÓRDOBA  la Raya 2400  Negro  Cachira  Rubio  S.ᵗᵃ Bárbara

Gonzáles  I. del  1910+  Alta  Alto de  SANTANDER  S. Carlos

I. S. José  Rey  El Real  Quimari  Zaragoza  Pamplona  152

DE LAS PIEDRAS  Garachiné  DARIÉN  de Urabá  Pavarandocito  Río Negro  BUCARAMANGA  Arauca

Pedasi  C. Escarpado  Jaqué  1565  Chigorodó  Ituango  Remedios  Piedecuesta  4400  132

Pᵗᵒ Mala  Sautatá  Paramillo  Yarumal  Barrancabermeja  Mesa Colorada  Arauca

Golfo de Panamá  3960  Amalfi  1239  S. Andrés  Guas

C. Marzo  Cupica  Frontino  ANTIOQUIA  3110  Sᵗᵃ Rosa  Cisneros  S. Gil  Cerrito

Golfo de  Paramo  Antioquia  Girardota  Pᵗᵒ Berrío  los Cobardes 3500  Socorro  Onzaga 5493  Tame  Pᵗᵒ Rondón

Cupica  Frontino  Bello  Capitanejo  ARAUC

Pte San Francisco  4080  4350  Chita  Hato de Corozal

Solano  Urrao  MEDELLIN  SANTANDER  Alto Ritacuva

4468  Alto del Buey  Itagüí  Rionegro  Vélez  Socha

1810  Fredonia  Envigado  Sᵗᵃ Bárbara  Niño  Barbosa  Duitama  Támara

Golfo de  Quibdó  Bolívar  Sonsón  Peña de Saboyá  Chiquinquira  Sogamoso  Pore  Ariporo

Tibuga  CHOCÓ  Andes  4003  TUNJA  Sevilla  Guachiria  S. Pablo

Nuquí  Salamina  Aguadas  la Dorada  Pᵗᵃ Boyacá  Lag. de Tota  Miraflores  Trinidad

C. Corrientes  CALDAS  Neira  Boyacá  3795  Sᵗᵃ Sᵗᵃ

Cértegui  Supía  Mariquita  Ubaté  Orocué  Pauto

Cᵒ Tamaná  Anserma  Honda  Chocontá  BOYACÁ  CASANARE  Meta

Pizarro  4200  Armero  Zipaquirá  Maní

Baudó  MANIZALES  Fresno  Madrid  Gacheta  S. Pedro

Cᵒ Torra  RISARALDA  Nevᵈᵒ  del Libano  Facatativá  Gachalá  de Arimena

PEREIRA  3670  del Ruiz 5400  CUNDINAMARCA  Cuisiana

Sipí  Cartago  Sᵗᵃ Rosa de Cabal  Beltrán  la Mesa  BOGOTA  Muco

Roldanillo  la Unión  Calarcá  Tocaima  Girardot  4033  Chaviva

El Porvenir  4250  QUINDIO  Ibagué  Soacha  Meta

I. Cacahua  Togoromá  Zarzal  Caicedonia  Fusagasugá  Guatiquía  Vichada

Tuluá  Sevilla  El Corazón  Espinal  Cᵒ Nevado  Guayuriba  Pᵗᵒ López

Pᵗᵃ Magdalena  VALLE DEL CAUCA  San  Ortega  Guamo  Villavicencio  Guarrojo

Buga  Antonio  Purificación  Acacías  S.

BUENAVENTURA  Cerrito  Chaparral  3830  S. Martín  Uvá

Dagua  Coyaima  Alto de  4650  COLOMB

PACIFIC OCEAN  Pradera  las Oseras  Pᵗᵒ Limón  la Serranía  Uvá  Manaveni

CALI  PALMIRA  Natagaima  Colombia  Iteviare

I. Ají  Cᵒ Naya  Timba  Uribe  Chafurray  Lag. Uvá

I. Gorgona  San José  2650  Pᵗᵒ Tejada  Tello  Ariari  METÁ  Mapiripán

Pᵗᵒ Coco  Naya  Nev. del Huila  NEIVA  Salto de  Guaviare

I. Cacahua  Santander  5750  Palermo  Cᵒ Leiva  Angostura II.  Puerto la  Salto de

Timbiquí  Morales  3520  Concordia  Angostura III

Mosquera  El Tambo  Campoalegre  Ser. de la Macarena  S. José  Inírida

POPAYAN  Gigante  NEIVA  del Guaviare

Guapí  Piendamó  Silvia  Paez  Salto de  VAUP

I. Sᵗᵃ Rosa  Iscuandé  El Bordo  la Plata  Guacamaya  Angostura  Cᵒ Otare  Calamar

Tumaco  Barbacoas  Timbío  Altamira  Losada  910

C. Manglares  .150  CAUCA  Bolívar  Garzón  Casa Agapito  Mesa de

B. de Ancon de Sardinas  4700  Pitalito  Florencia  Llanos de  Lindosa  Papunaua

Lag. de Chimbuso  Vol. Puracé  San  Yarí  Mesa de

Ens. de Tumaco  Iscuandé  4250  Augustín  Belén  Yambi

Rioverde  NARIÑO  Vol. Cutanga  CAQUETÁ  El Dorado  Cuquiarí

la Tola  Samaniego  4300  Montañita  Sᵒ de Chiribiquete  Isana

Muisne  Sandoná  Vol. Doña  869

Mocoa  Juana  Lag. Chaira  Uaurá Ipana  Yaupés  Pedro Chico

Tambo  PASTO  Mecay  Ortegaza  Pirá  Raudal Yupurari

Túquerres  4266  Pᵗᵒ Limón  Mesas de  Guanapiana

Vol. de Pasto  PUTUMAYO  Tres Esquinas  Tunaima  Iguaje

Esmeraldas  Ipiales  la Cocha  Cunaré  Macujer

Vol. de Chiles  Putumayo  Guamués  Cᵒ Cumare  UAUPÉS

4748  Caguán  720

ECUADOR  Tulcán  Puerto Asís

IMBABURA  CARCHI

78°  188  72°

50 100 Kilomètres
50 Statute Miles

↑ 181
66° 60°

NEDERLANDSE ANTILLEN
(NETHERLANDS ANTILLES)
Aruba 188
Sint Nicolaas
Curaçao ·372
de Bonaire
S!ª Catharina
Willemstad Kralendijk

ST-VINCENT-
GRENADINES
Cannouan I.
Union I.
Carriacou I.
Hillsborough
Ronde I.
Gouyave ·840 Greenville
St-George's GRENADA
Point Saline

Pueblo Nuevo
Adicora
·815

Cardón
Ismo de
Médanos P!ª Manzanillo
P!ª Gavilán
Coro Cumarebo
Churuguara
S? de S. Luís ·1502
Mirimire
S. Juan de los Cayos
Tucacas
Tucuyo de la Costa
G. Triste
P!º Cabello
Maiquetía
La Guaira
los Caracas
Chirimera
C. Codera
Higuerote
Río Chico
Caucagua
S!ª Teresa
El Guapo

I. Orchila
(Venezuela)
I! los Hermanos
I! los Testigos
NUEVA ESPARTA
P!ª de Piedras
I. de Margarita
Juangriego ·1160 ·957
la Asunción
Porlamar
I. Cubagua
I. Coche
Río Caribe
Morro de Chacopata

I! la Sola
I! los Frailes
Carúpano
Pen. de Paria
Irapa
P!ª de Hierro
P!ª de Peñas
Yaguaraparo
Güiria
I. Antica
Tunapuna ·939
Galera P!
Arima
Sangre Gr!º
Port
of Spain

Charlotteville ·576
Tobago
Crown P! Scarborough
TRINIDAD
and
TOBAGO

FALCÓN
DISTRITO FEDERAL
CARACAS
los Teques
Petare
Guatire

DISTRITO FEDERAL
MARACAY
VALENCIA
MIRANDA
Villa de Cura
Guatopo
S. Casimiro
S. Sebastián
Camatagua

CUMANÁ
Pen. de Araya
Cariaco
El Rincón
Casanay
S. Fernando

TRINIDAD
Chaguanas
Río Claro
Siparia Galeota P!
Icacos Town
Boca de la Sierpe
Bonasse

BRAZIL

R O R A I M A

GUYANA

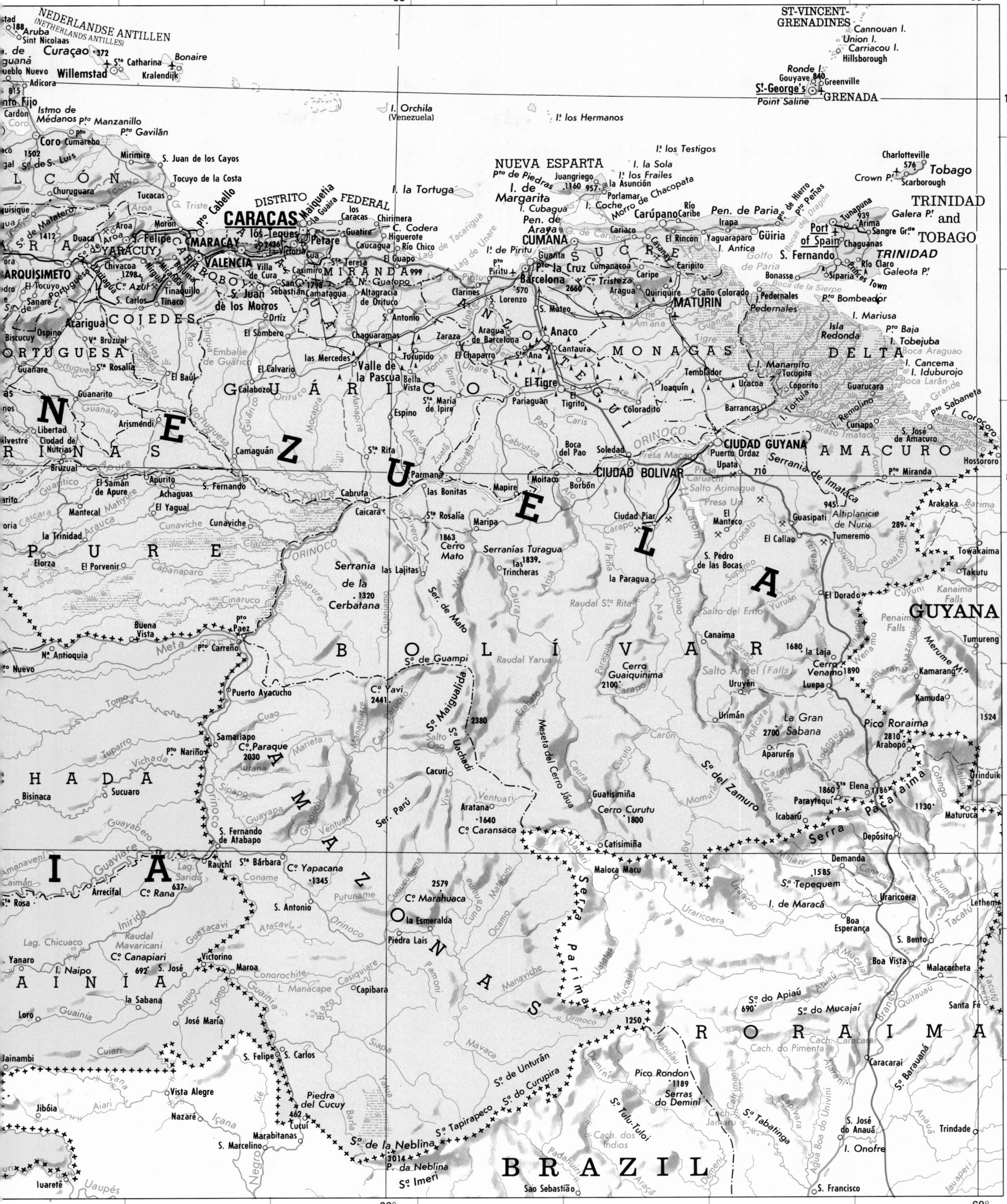

→ 192

↓ 183

© HACHETTE-IGN

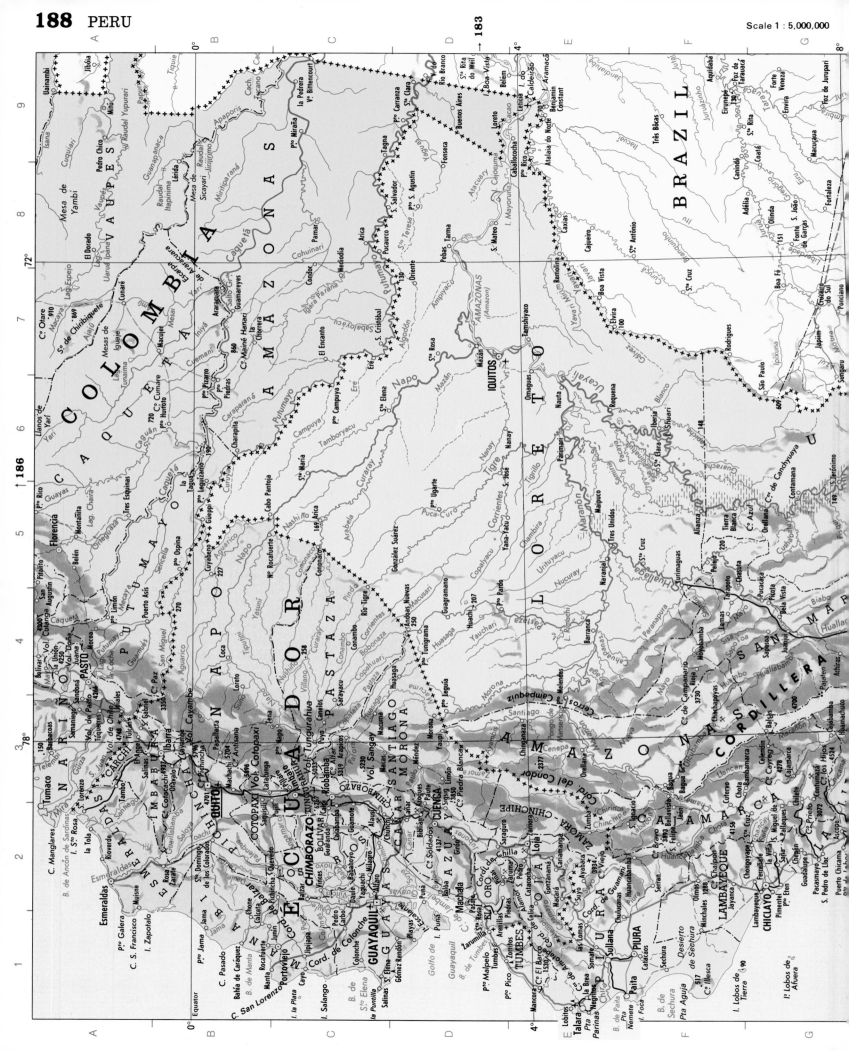

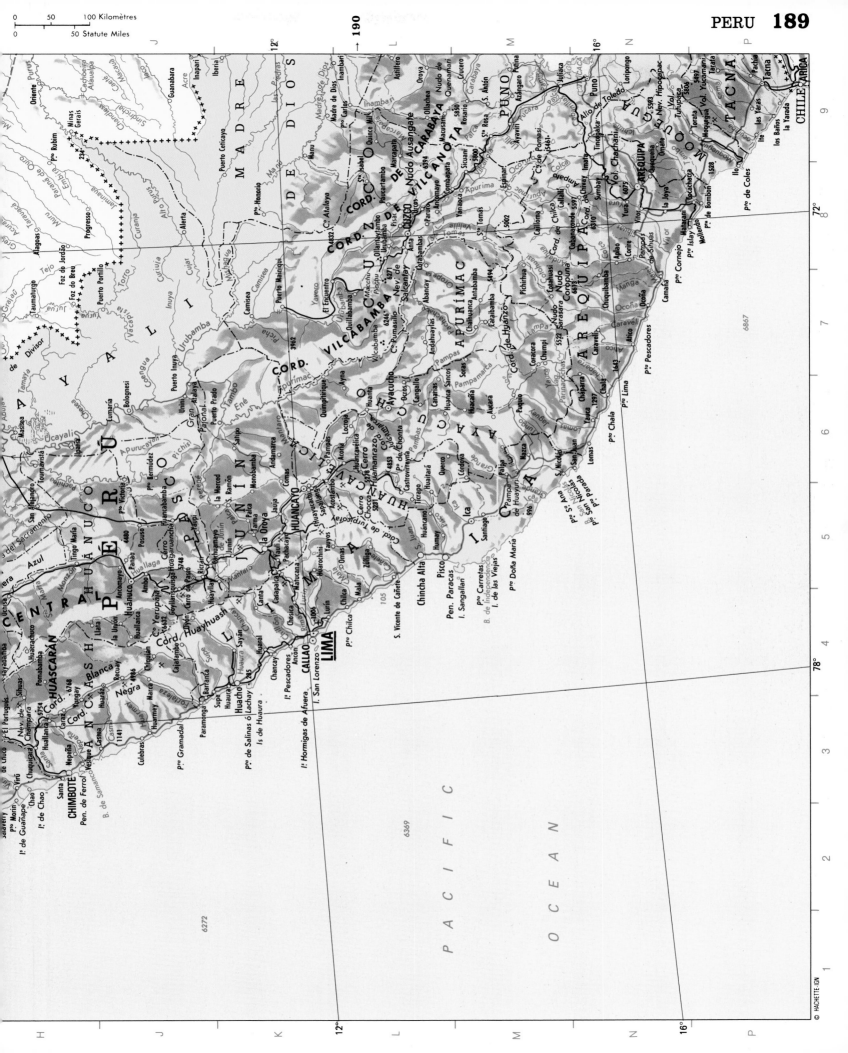

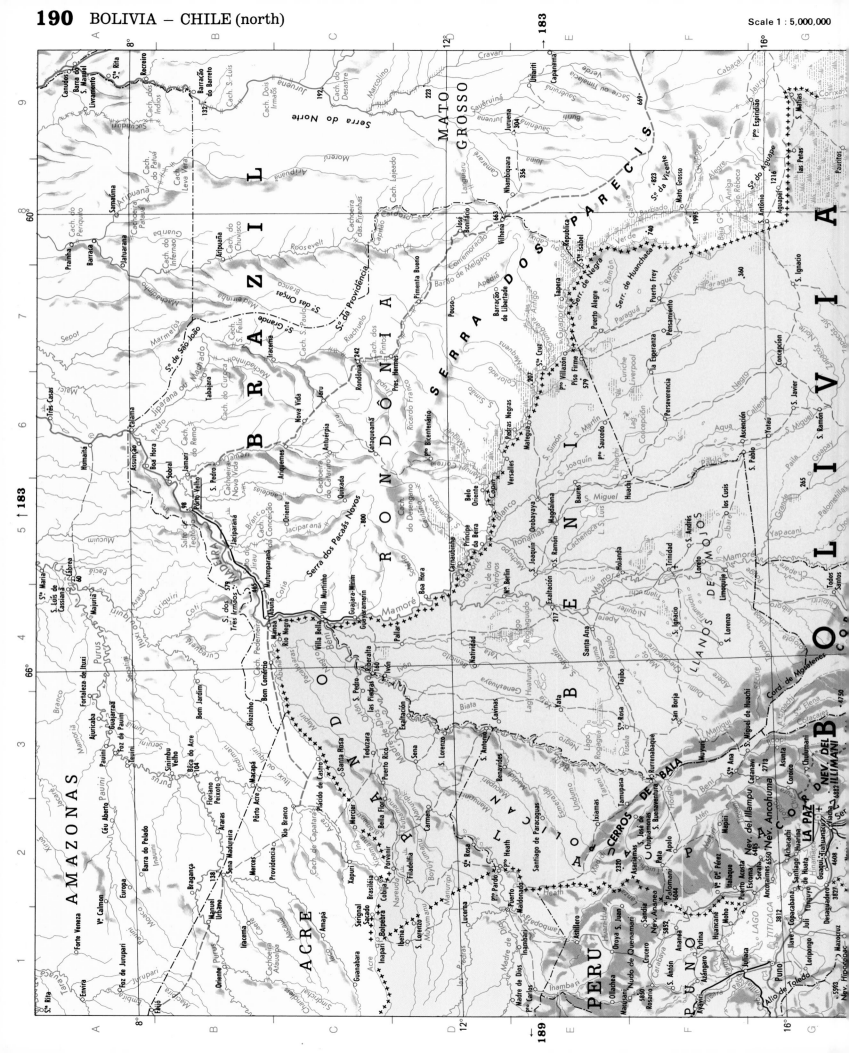

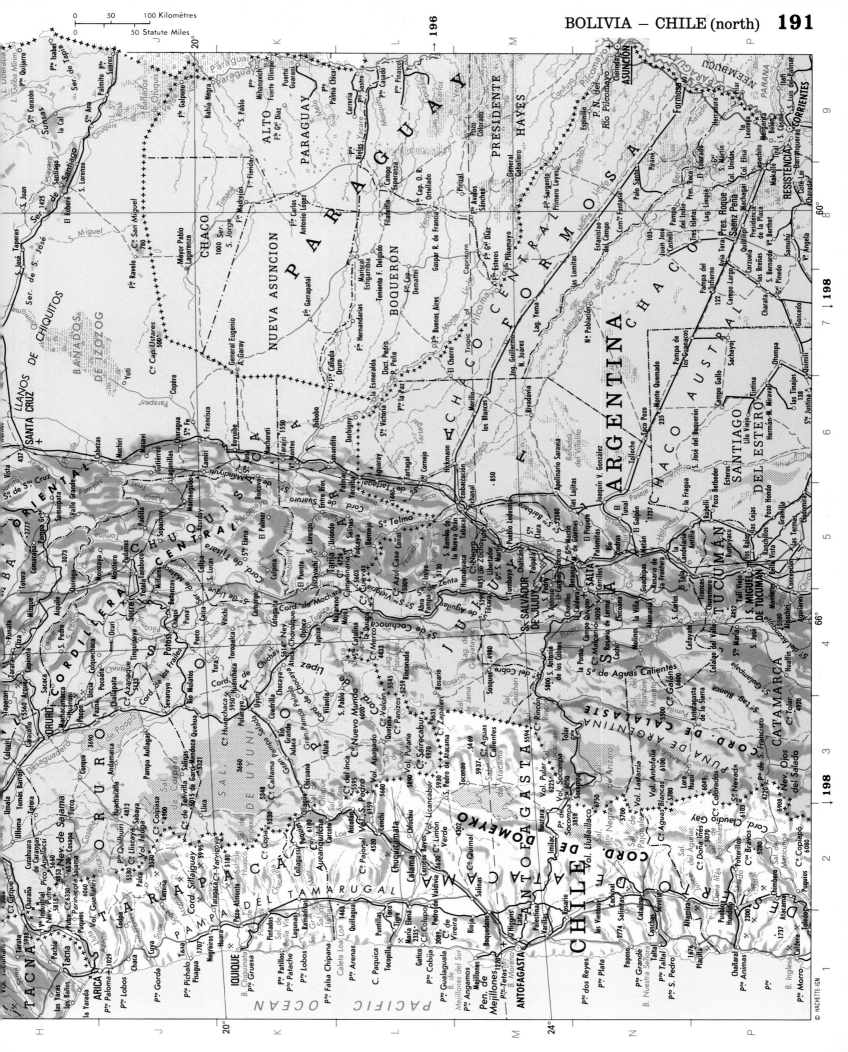

VENEZUELA

GUYANA

SURINAM

FRENCH GUIANA

RORAIMA

AMAZONAS

AMAPÁ

PARÁ

BRASIL

Curiapo · S. José de Amacuro · I. Corocoro · Pto Miranda · Hossororo · Baramanni · Marlborough · Charity · Danielstown · Suddie · Spring Garden · Wakenaam I. · Enterprise · Parika · Hog I. · GEORGETOWN · Vreed en Hoop · Buxton · Hyde Park · Enmore · Mahaicony · Fort Wellington · New Amsterdam · Rosignol · Mackenzie · Mara · Skeldon · Nieuw Nickerie · Totness · PARAMARIBO · Nieuw Amsterdam · Braams Punt · Wageningen · Groningen · Potribo · Tamarin · Mana · Organabo · Iracoube · De Goede Hoop · Paranam · Moengo · Albina · Ste-Laurent · Sinnamary · Zanderij · Kwakoegron · Java · Herminadorp · Apatou · Gare Tigre · Kourou · Tonate · Cayenne · Heidoti · Brokopondo · Affobakka · Massif Décou-Décou · Délices · Ste-Elie · Mgne de la Trinité · Rémire · Brownsweg · Roura · Cacao · Kaw · Guisanbourg · Régina · Ste-Louis · Ste-Georges

Altiplanicie de Nuria · Tumeremo · Arakaka · Towakaima · Takutu · Penaima Falls · Peter's Mine · Tumureng · Kartabu · Bartica · Kamarang · Merume Mts · Kamuda · Pico Roraima · Arabopó · Sta Elena · Orinduik · Depósito · Maturuca · Demanda · Uraricoera · Boa Esperança · S. Bento · Boa Vista · Malacacheta · Dadanawa · Shea · Santa Fé · Isherton · Caracarai · Biloku · Trindade · S. José do Anauá · I. Onofre · Anamá · Airão · Sto Antônio · Tauapeçaçu · Conceição · Caapiranga · Manacapuru · Caldeirão · MANAUS · I. do Careiro · Careiro · Itacoatiara · Murutinga · Autazes · Nova Olinda do Norte · Repartimento · Maués · Ariaú · Pedras · Barreirinha · Parintins · Silves · Itapiranga · Urucará · Albano · Nhamundá · Faro · Juruti · Óbidos · Oriximiná · Alenquer · Monte Alegre · Santarém · Belterra · Boim · Aveiro · Pacoval · Sousel · Independência · Belo Mont · Altamira · Paquicama · Carvalho · Veiros · Pôrto de Moz · Almeirim · Arere · Pôrto San Mazagá · Terezinha · Serra do Navio · Cupixi · Acampamento Grande · Mapireme · Iaripo · Maloca · Dansia · Akótipa · Curicha · Tacalé · Pôrto Poet · Kapiting · Sikima · S. Acari · S. Makoa · S. Iricoumé · Cofuini · Aldea dos Indios Sucane · Amuku Mountains · Kuyuwini · Oronoque · New River · Biloku

Equator

↑ **193**

54° A B C D 48° E F G

14°

Cach. Grande do Iriri · Cach. Pariaxa · Joana-Peres · Tucurui · S.ra da Desordem · Penalva · Monção · Vitória do Mearim

Cach. Soledade · Cach. Camaleão · Cachoeira Coruaga · Lontra · Cach. Tocunduba · Remansão · Jacundá · Jatobal · 396 · Pio XII · Bacabal

Cach. Sêca · P.to Alegre · Cach. do Ipixuna · Serra do Tocantins · Pedreira

Paga Conta · Sem Tripa · Jatobá · P.to de Lontra · Itupiranga · Marabá · S. Felix · S.ra do Gurupi · MARANH

2

Cach. da Boca · Entre Rios · Belo Horizonte · Araparí · S. João do Araguaia · S. Bento · Araguatins · Imperatriz · Amarante do Maranhão · Barra do Corda · Presidente

Cach. S. Francisco · PARA · S. Sébastião · S.ta Isabel do Araguaia · Cach. de S.ta Isabel · Itaguatins · Montes Altos · 430 · Grajaú · S.ra Branca

Cach. do Limão · Cach. Manuel Jorge · Nazaré · Cach. Xafeturu · Tocantinópolis · Porto Franco · S.ra da Cinta · S.ra Negra · S.ra Canelas · 549 · S.ra do Itapicuru

3

Araras · Cach. da Saudade · Pombal · Triunfo · S. Félix do Xingu · Xambioá · Araguanã · Gameleira · 640 · S.ra da Croeira · S. Raimundo das Mangabeiras · S. Félix do Balsas

Cach. P.to Seguro · Nova Olinda · Branco · Fresco · S.ta Maria · Muricizal · Muricizal · Araguaína · Cach. Mortandade · Farinha · Fortaleza dos Nogueiras · Loreto

183 · Cach. Sabia · Cach. Araras · S.ra da Seringa · Neves · Pau d'Arco · Filadélfia · Carolina · Riachão · 235 · Sambaiba

Baú · Cach. Ananás · Gradaus · Cach. Capivara · Jenipapo Cunhãs · Balsas · Sereno · S.ra do Gado Bravo · Ribeiro Gonçalves

8°

Curuá · Riozinho · Itapora · Vamos Ver · Piacá · S.ra do Penitente · Balsalsinhos

4

Cach. do Uba · Cach. da Pedra Sêca · Arraias do Araguaia · Conceição do Araguaia · Couto Magalhães · Tupiratins · Itacajá · Ouro · 540 · Brejo da Porta · Cach. S.ra do Caititu · S.ra Grande

Ipiranga · Serra dos Gradaús · S.ra do Inajá · Goianorte · Agua Fria · S.ra da Cangalha · Cach. d'Areia · S.ta Filomena

Fresco · Inajá · S.ta Maria das Barreiras · Araguacema · S.ra do Gomes · Tupirama · Pedro Afonso · Perdida · Alto Parnaiba · 240 · S.ra do Uruçui

5

Irirí Novo · Cachoeira Pedras · Cach. Von Martius · Beleza · Santana · Miracema do Norte · Tocantínia · Três Pedras · Lizarda · Curupá · Monte Alegre do Piauí · Gilbués

Cach. da Pedra · S.ra do Matão · Côco · Piedade · Lajeado · Cach. do Piloes · Novo Acôrdo · Espingarda · Caracol · 750 · Chapada das Mangabeiras

Crisôstomo · Sancho · Luzia · Cach. do Jaú · Claro · Corrente

6

Huaiá-Missu · S.ta Terezinha · S.ra do Tapirapé · Tapirapé · Cristalândia · Pium · Mangues · Ponte Alta do Norte · Sono · Formosa do R. Prêto · S.ta Rita de Cass.

Campo de Diauarum · Xingu · Vertentes · Ilha do Bananal · Porto Nacional · Cach. Cerreira Comprida · Balsal · S.ra Geral ou Grande · 870 · S.ra Geral · Tabati

Manissauá Missu · Gameleira · Liberdade · Urubu · Brejinho de Nazaré · Cach. do Canoeiro · Preto · Ouro · Caiparé

Suiá-Missu · Dueré · S. de S.to Antônio · Surubim · Bagagem · Almas · Dianópolis

12°

Arraias · S. João · S. Felix · Gurupi · Travessão Jacaré · Peixe · Manuel Alves · Natividade · Jupag

7

Steinen · Pôrto dos Meinacos · Tanguro · Canoană · Peixe · Cach. de Tropêço · Valerio · Conceição do Norte · P.ta Alta do Bom Jesus · Palmeira · Barreiras · Angica · Cristópolis

263 · Culuene · S. João · Alvorada · Paraná · Taguatinga · Pedras · Ondas · Tabocas · Brejo Ve

183 · 265 · Sote de Setiembro · Baracaiu · 186 · Araguaçu · 670 · Paraná · Manhã · Almas · S. Domingos

8

MATO GROSSO · Cach. Cururi · Culuene · 670 · S. Miguel do Araguaia · S. Domingos · 1188 · Porangatu · Douro da Almas · Arraias · Campos Belos · Galheirão · Meio · Correntina · Corrente

Cach. Formosa · Bandeirante · Mutunópolis · Monte Alegre de Goiás · Cavalcante · S. Domingos · Gatos

Cach. da Saudade · Crixás-Açu · Estrêla do Norte · Amaro Leite · Cana Brava · Cach. Anta · 1555 · Posse · Arroiado · Correntina

Cach. das Garças · PLANALTO · Crixás · Campinorte · Colinas · Alto Paraiso de Goiás · 861 · Iaciara · Côcos Serr.

792 · GOIÁS · Chavantina · Mozarlândia · Hidrolina · Uruaçu · 664 · Niquelândia · S. João da Aliança · Damianopolis · Mambai · S.ra da Capivara · Jibão · Coxá

9

DE · Itapaci · Aruanã · 210 · Pindaiba · Rubiataba · Barro Alto · Maranhão · Alto Paraitinzinho · Formoso · Sitio da Abadia · Tabocas · Bonito

MATO GROSSO · Britânia · Ceres · Rialma · Goianésia · Padre Bernardo · Serra Bonita · 929 · Itacatar

Pres. Murtinho · G.al Carneiro · Araguaiana · Registro do Araguaia · Itapuranga · Uruana · Itaguaru · Verde · DISTRITO FEDERAL · Serra das Araras

Poxoréu · Britânia · **BRASILIA**

54° A ↓ **196** C D E F G

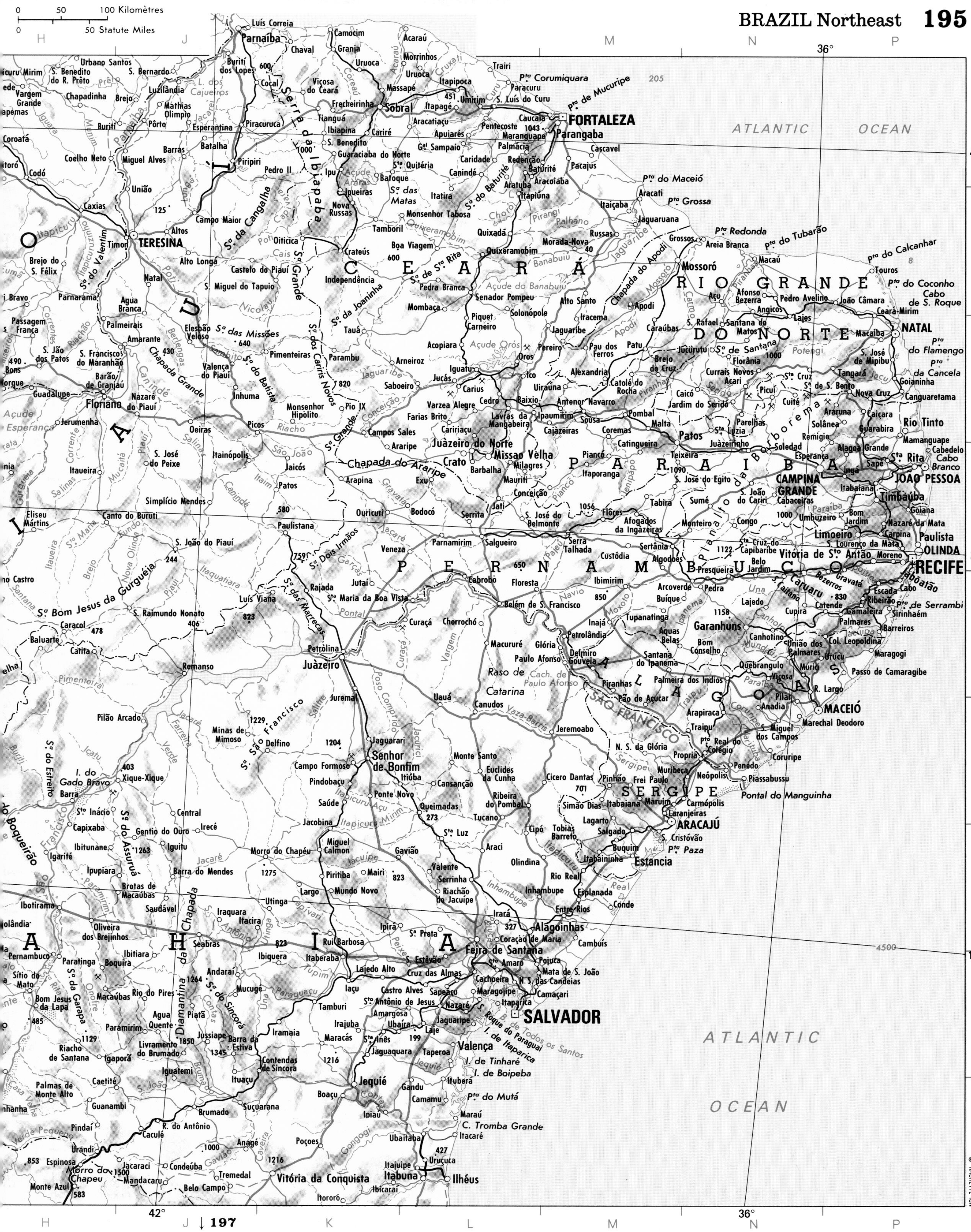
0 50 100 Kilomètres
0 50 Statute Miles
ATLANTIC OCEAN
CEARÁ
PIAUÍ
RIO GRANDE DO NORTE
PARAÍBA
PERNAMBUCO
ALAGOAS
SERGIPE
BAHIA
FORTALEZA
NATAL
JOÃO PESSOA
RECIFE
OLINDA
MACEIÓ
ARACAJÚ
SALVADOR
TERESINA
Parnaíba
Sobral
Mossoró
Campina Grande
Caruaru
Garanhuns
Juàzeiro do Norte
Crato
Petrolina
Juàzeiro
Feira de Santana
Vitória da Conquista
Jequié
Ilhéus
Itabuna
Floriano
Caxias
Picos
Patos
Senhor de Bonfim
Alagoinhas
Estancia
Chapada do Araripe
Chapada Diamantina
Sa da Ibiapaba
Raso de Catarina
Baía de Todos os Santos
São Francisco
Pontal do Manguinha
Cabo Branco
Pta do Calcanhar
4°
8°
12°
36°
42°
© HACHETTE-IGN

↓197

MATO GROSSO

BOLIVIA

MATO GROSSO DO SUL

SERTÃO DE CAIAPÓ

GOIÂNIA

ALTO PARAGUAY

SÃO PAULO

PARAGUAY

PRESIDENTE HAYES

CONCEPCIÓN

SERRA DE MARACAJU

SERRA DO BODOQUENA

AMAMBAÍ

PARANÁ

SERRA PARANAPIAC

MISIONES

CAAZAPÁ

ITAPUA

ÑEEMBUCÚ

GUAIRÁ

ASUNCIÓN

CURITIBA

SERRA DO MAR

SANTA CATARINA

ARGENTINA

CORRIENTES

POSADAS

Pto Espiridião
S. Matias
Cáceres
Cuiabá
Coxipó da Ponte
Sto Antônio do Leverger
Pres. Murtinho
Gel Carneiro
Araguaiana
Itaipuranga
Itaguaru
Itáguaru
Jaraguá
Pirenópolis
Padre Rapa
Uruana

Corumbá
Ladário
Porto Novo
Pto Quijarro
Pto Isabel
la Cal
Sta Ana
Palmito
Suárez
Amolar
Nhecolândia
Albuquerque
Vista Alegre
Pto Esperança
Coimbra
Bahía Negra
Miranda
Aquidauana
Campo Grande
Água Clara
Três Lagoas

Anápolis
GOIÂNIA
Uberlândia
Prata
Campina Verde
Frutal

Bonito
Jardim
Guia Lopes da Laguna
Maracaju
Nioaque
Sidrolândia
Bela Vista
Rio Brilhante
Itaporã
Dourados
Ponta Porã
Amambaí
Carapó
Juti
Iguatemi

Bauru
Jaú
Marília
Pres. Prudente
Araçatuba
S. José do R. Prêto
Catanduva
Lins
Assis
Londrina
Maringá
Apucarana
Ponta Grossa
Paranaguá
Joinville
Blumenau
Itajaí
Florianópolis

Asunción
Villarrica
Caazapá
Encarnación
Posadas
Formosa
Pilar
Humaitá

Foz do Iguaçu
Cascavel
Guaíra
Toledo
Campo Mourão
Guarapuava
União da Vitória
Mafra
Canoinhas
Chapecó
Concórdia
Erechim
Lajes

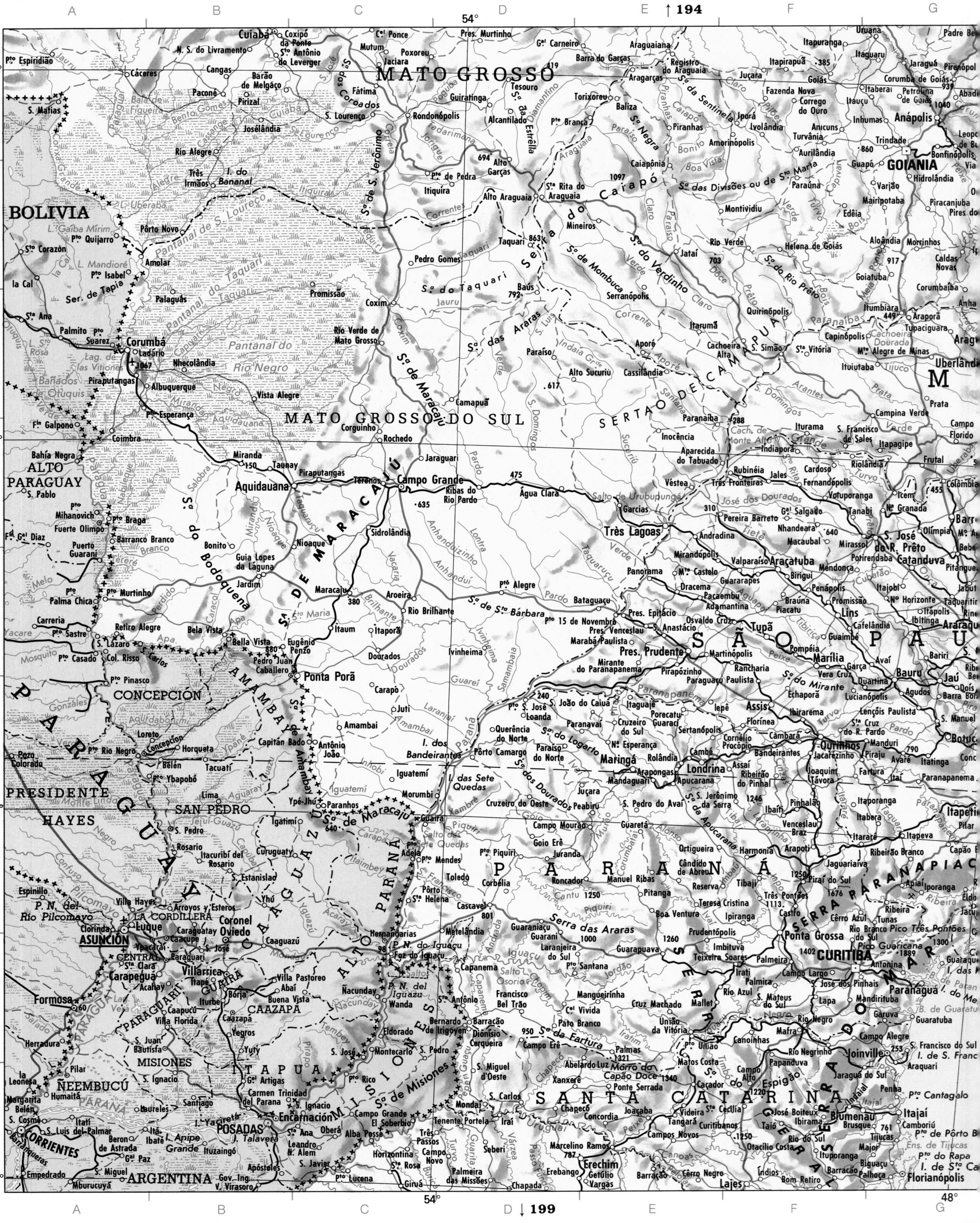

0  50  100 Kilomètres
0  50 Statute Miles

↑ 195

42°

**BRASILIA**

TO FEDERAL

Formosa  929  Serra das Araras  Bonito  Chapeu  Mandacaru  Tremedal  Vitória da Conquista  Itabuna  Ilhéus
Cabeceiras  Buritis  Januária  Varzelândia  Monte Azul  583  S. Joao do Paraíso  Belo Campo  Itambé  Itororó  Ibicaraí  Una
Arinos  S. Francisco  Porteirinha  Itapetinga  Aratacá  Camacã
Garapuava  Janaúba  Taiobeiras  Vereda do Paraíso  Encruzilhada  1000  Macarani  Potiraguá  Mascote  Canavieiras
Unaí  S. Romão  Riacho-dos-Machados  1216  André Fernandes  Bandeira  Jordânia  333  Itapebi  Belmonte
1233  Cristalina  Capão Redondo  Brasília  Salinas  953  Medina  Pedra Azul  Almenara  Salto da Divisa  Rubim  Jacinto  Gabiarra  Serrinha  Stª Cruz Cabrália
Morro de Padre  Paracatu  Caatinga  1000  Coração de Jesus  Barrocão  1311  Grão Mogol  Cel Murta  Almenara  Jequitinhonha  Pôrto Seguro
962  Guarda-Mor  Ibiaí  Montes Claros  Francisco Sá  950  Virgem da Lapa  Itinga  Itaobim  Buranhém  Pta de Corumbaú
Pirapora  425  Juramento  Araçuaí  Carai  Machacalis  Mt Pascoal  536  Recifes Itacolomis
Campo Alegre de Goiás  Terra Branca  Minas Novas  752  Sª do Chifre  Itanhém  Medeiros Neto  Prado
774  Várzea da Palma  Carbonita  1047  Novo Cruzeiro  Crispim Jaques  Alcobaça  Recifes das Timbebas
Três Ranchos  Coromandel  João Pinheiro  Lassance  Capelinha  Malacacheta  Poté  Pavão  Carlos Chagas  Nanuque  Ibirapuã  Pta da Baleia
Mt Carmelo  Pres Olegário  Canoeiros  1192  Senador Mourão  1004  Teófilo Otoni  Caravelas  Recifes da Pedra Grande
7005  Patos de Minas  1025  S. Gonçalo do Abaeté  Buenópolis  Mendanha  Diamantina  2033 Pico do Itambé  Rio Vermelho  Atalaia  Mucuri  Morro d'Anta  Mucuri  42  Arquipélago dos Abrolhos
Patrocínio  1147  Corinto  Felixlândia  Sêrro  Sª Negra  Stª Maria do Suaçuí  Cibrão  Ecoporanga  Itaúnas  Caçumba
Paranaíba  Tiros  Sª do Salitre  Pompeu  Curvelo  Pto de Parauna  Senhora do Pôrto  Virgolândia  Peçanha  Gdor Valadares  Mendes Pimentel  Conceição da Barra
Araxá  Ibiá  Abaeté  Martinho Campos  Conc. do Mato Dentro  Guanhães  Coroaci  635  S. Gabriel  Nova Venécia  S. Mateus
Sacramento  S. Gotardo  Carmo do Paranaíba  Dores do Indaiá  Caetanópolis  Morro do Pilar  Joanésia  Turiritinga  Itanhomi  Cons. Pena  Pancas  Barra Sêca
Rifaina  1250  Tapiraí  Bom Despacho  Papagaios  Sete Lagoas  Ferros  Naque  Tarumirim  Resplendor  Colatina  Linhares
Franca  1200  Guia Lopes  Bambuí  Pedro Leopoldo  Itabira  Inhapim  Aimorés  Itapina  Colatina
Delfinópolis  Formiga  Araújos  Pará de Minas  1400  Sabará  Cel Fabriciano  Antônio Dias  Pocrane  Mutum  825  Pta da Regência  Regência
Cássia  Alpinópolis  Divinópolis  Itaúna  Nova Lima  2107  Barão de Cocais  1195  Bom Jesus do Galho  Conc. de Ipanema  João Neiva  Riacho
Batatais  Passos  1349  **BELO HORIZONTE**  Itabirito  Dionísio  Raul Soares  Carangola  Manhuaçu  Stª Leopoldina  1098  VITÓRIA
Guaranésia  Guaxupé  Oliveira  Itaguara  Ouro Prêto  Rio Casca  Manhumirim  Iúna  Domingos Martins  Espírito Santo (Vila Velha)
Mococa  Múzambinho  Alfenas  Boa Esperança  Conselheiro Lafaiete  Ponte Nova  Abre Campo  2890 Pico da Bandeira  Espera Feliz  Matilde  Guarapari
S. José do R. Pardo  Machado  Campo Belo  S. Tiago  Viçosa  1859  Carangola  Alegre  Castelo  Iconha  Anchieta
Poços de Caldas  Campanha  1270  Entre Rios de Minas  Ponte Nova  Visconde do R. Branco  Miradouro  Porciúncula  Mimoso do Sul  Mugui  Cachoeiro de Itapemirim
S. João da Boa Vista  1834  Três Pontas  Lavras  Itutinga  S. João del Rei  1554  Ubá  Muriaé  Cataguases  Itaperuna  Itapemirim
Pirassununga  Aguaí  Varginha  Três Corações  Barbacena  Santos Dumont  1455  Guarani  Leopoldina  Miracema  Itabapoana  Bom Jesus do Itabapoana  Morro do Côco
Pinhal  1692 JUIZ DE FORA  S. João Nepomuceno  Recreio  S. Fidélis  Ituporanga  S. João da Barra
Mogi Guaçu  Campinho  Andrelândia  Bom Jardim de Minas  Bicas  Leopoldina  Itaocara  1879  CAMPOS  S. Amaro de Campos
Itapira  Ouro Fino  Pouso Alegre  Stª Rita do Sapucaí  Liberdade  Além Paraíba  Carmo  Itaperuna  Elesbão  C. de S. Tomé
Limeira  Itabira  Lambari  Caxambu  Passa Vinte  R. Preto  Valença  Três Rios  Sumidouro  Pico S. Mateus  Cordeiro  Carapebus
Americana  Itajubá  Pico das Agulhas Negras 2787  Resende  Rio Prêto  Sumidouro  Nova Friburgo  Macaé  Lag. Feia
CAMPINAS  Paraisópolis  Barra Mansa  Volta Redonda  Barra do Pirai  2264  Teresópolis  Casimiro de Abreu  I. de Santana
Bragança Paulista  Lorena  Cruzeiro  PETRÓPOLIS  Magé  Barra de S. João  Cabo Frio
Jundiaí  Paulista  Pindamonhangaba  Guaratinguetá  Nª IGUAÇU  DUQUE DE CAXIAS  R. Bonito  C. dos Búzios  C. Frio
CABA da Rocha  Franco da Rocha  Taubaté  Caçapava  Paraú  1425  NITERÓI  **RIO DE JANEIRO**  S. GONÇALO  Araruama
S. ROQUE  Guarulhos  Jacareí  Mogi das Cruzes  I. Grande  I. Grossa da Marambaia  Lag. de Araruama
**SÃO PAULO**  S. CAETANO DO SUL  Caraguatatuba  Ubatuba  Angra dos Reis
nardo do Campo  ANDRÉ  Ilhabela  S. Sebastião  I. dos Porcos
SANTOS  1379  I. dos Búzios
S. Vicente  Guarujá  Pta do Boi
Pedro Toledo  Itanhaém  de S. Sebastião  Laje de Santos
450  Peruíbe  de Deus  I. Queimadas
prida

Tropic of Capricorn

1945

**ATLANTIC  OCEAN**

MINAS GERAIS

SERRA DO ESPINHAÇO

SERRA DA MANTIQUEIRA

SERRA DO CHAPARÃO

ESPÍRITO SANTO

RIO DE JANEIRO (GUANABARA)

Serra dos Aimorés

Represa das Tres Marias (Dam)

Represa de Furnas (Dam)

16°

20°

24°

42°

H  J  K  L  M  N  P

© HACHETTE-IGN

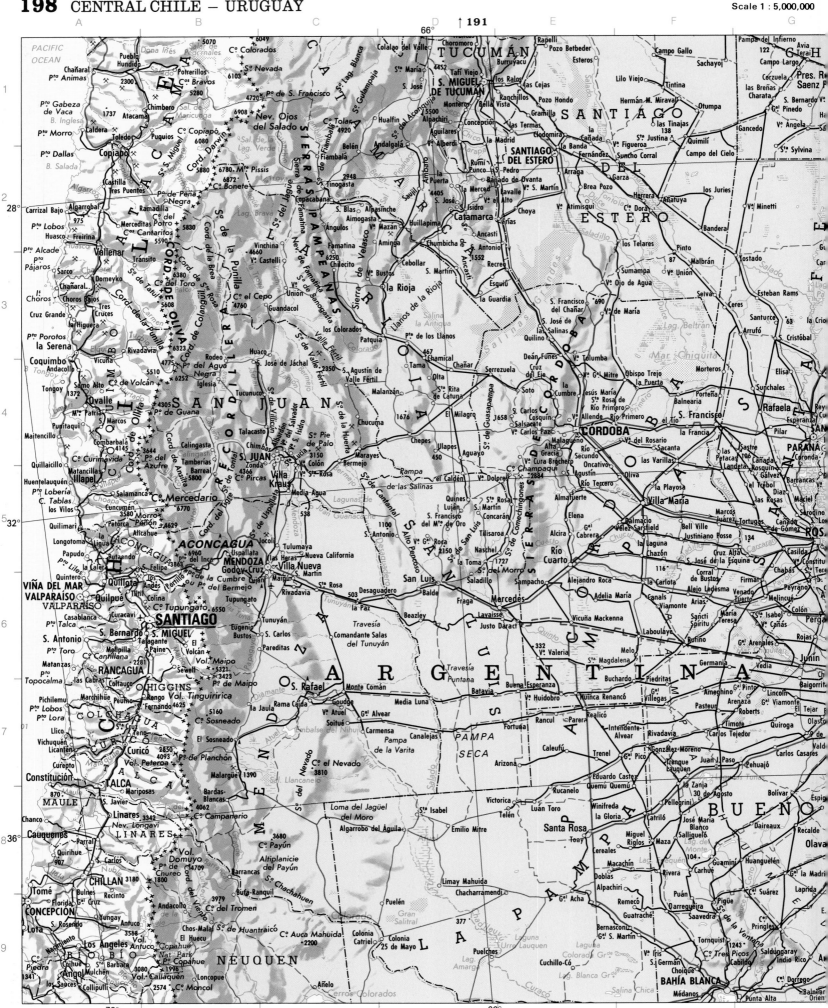

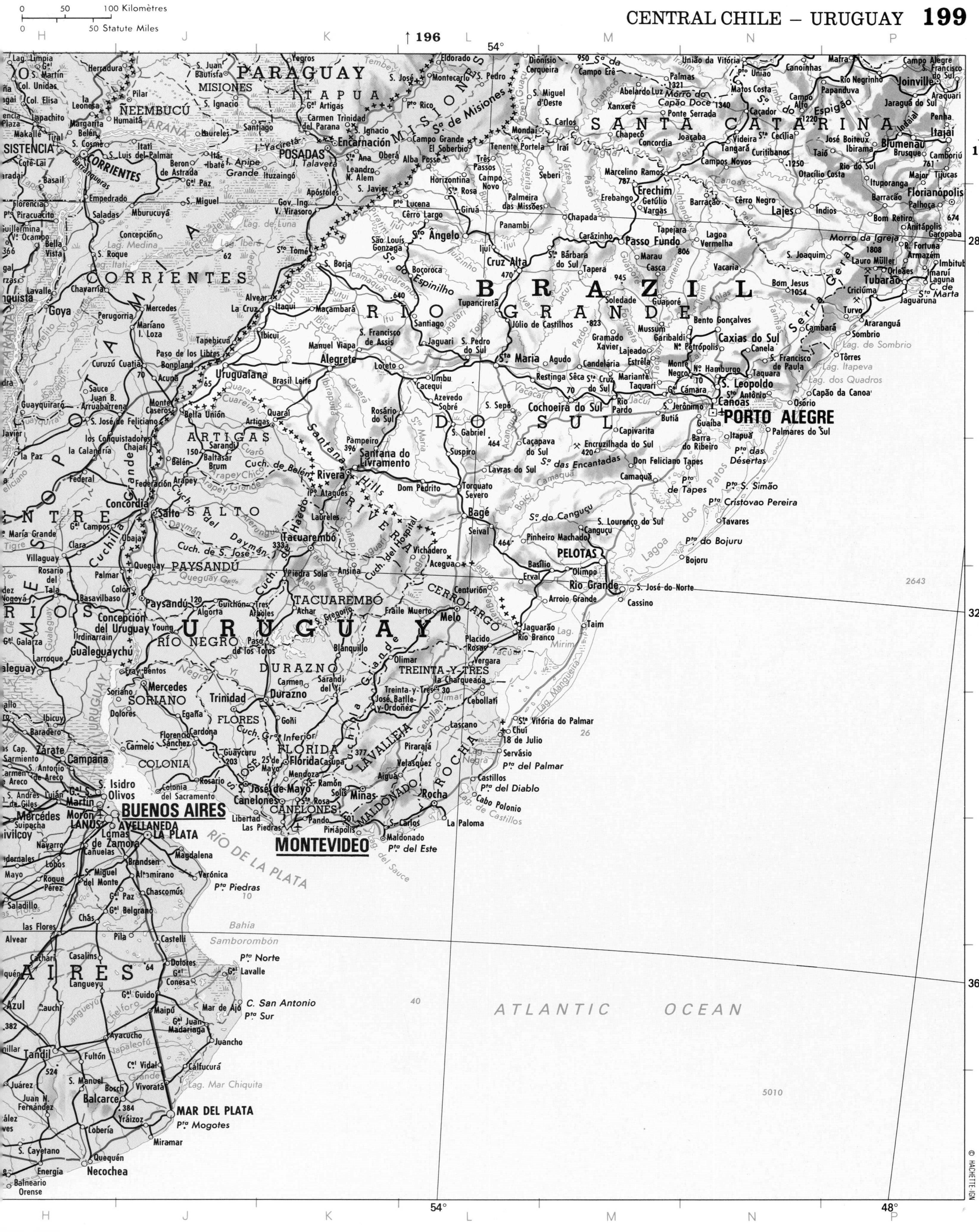

0 50 100 Kilomètres
0 50 Statute Miles

↑ 196
→ 196

**PARAGUAY**
MISIONES
ITAPUA
ÑEEMBUCÚ

**CORRIENTES**

**BRAZIL**
SANTA CATARINA
RIO GRANDE DO SUL

**URUGUAY**
ARTIGAS
SALTO
RIVERA
TACUAREMBÓ
CERRO LARGO
RÍO NEGRO
DURAZNO
TREINTA-Y-TRES
SORIANO
FLORES
FLORIDA
LAVALLEJA
COLONIA
CANELONES
ROCHA
MALDONADO

**MONTEVIDEO**

**BUENOS AIRES**
LA PLATA
AVELLANEDA
LANÚS

AIRES

**Porto Alegre**
Pelotas
Rio Grande

Posadas
Encarnación
Concordia
Salto
Paysandú
Mercedes
Gualeguaychú
Trinidad
Durazno
Minas
Rocha
Maldonado
Mar del Plata
Necochea
Tandil
Balcarce

Passo Fundo
Cruz Alta
Caxias do Sul
Sta Maria
Bagé
Melo
Tacuarembó

Florianópolis
Blumenau
Joinville
Tubarão
Criciúma
Lajes
Itajaí

**ATLANTIC OCEAN**

RÍO DE LA PLATA

© HACHETTE-IGN

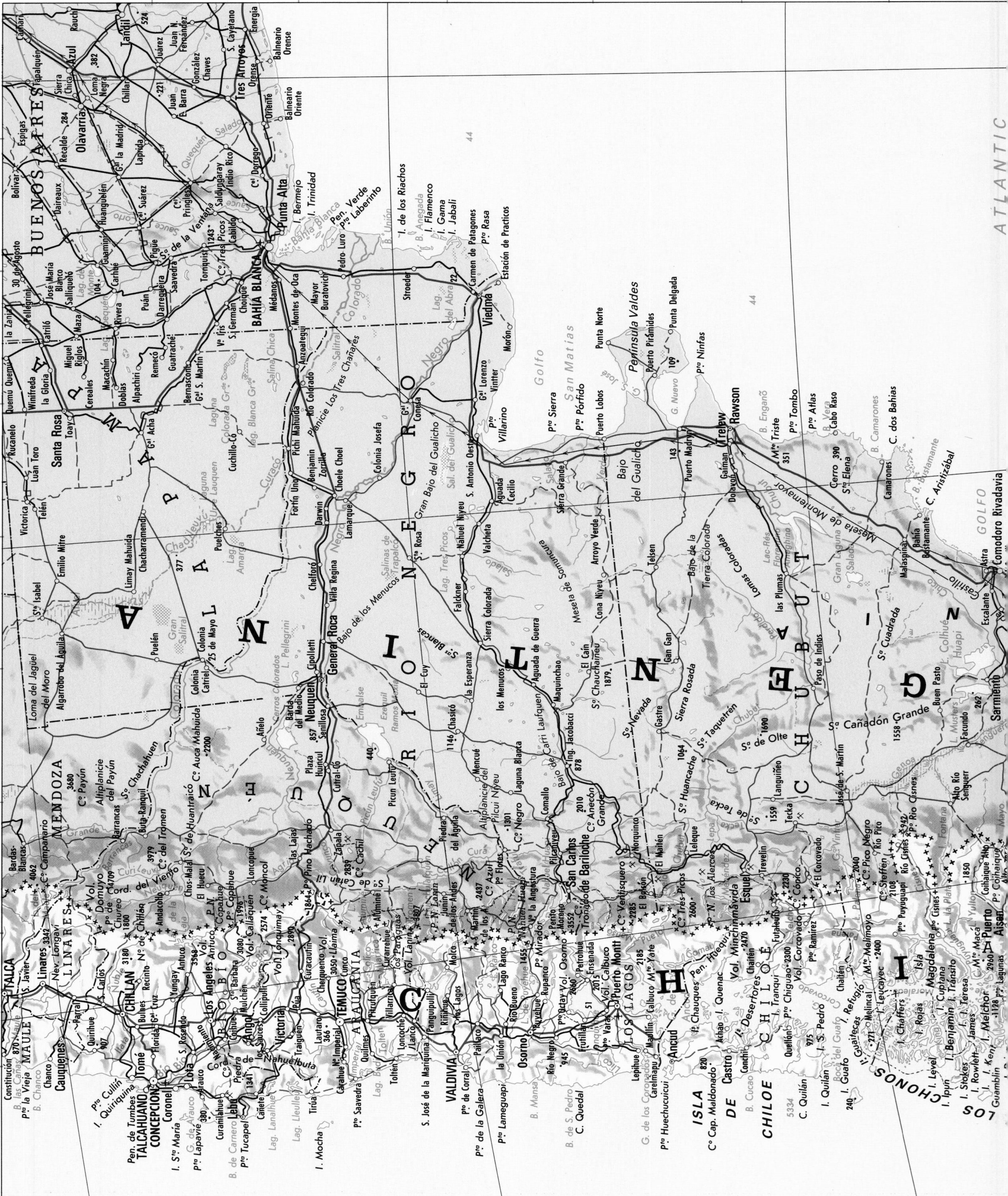

Scale 1 : 5,000,000

BUENOS AIRES

LA PAMPA

MENDOZA

NEUQUEN

RIO NEGRO

CHUBUT

LOS LAGOS

CHILOE

LOS CHONOS

ATLANTIC

GOLFO San Matias

Península Valdés

Santa Rosa

Bahía Blanca

General Roca

Neuquén

San Carlos de Bariloche

Rawson

Trelew

Concepción

Temuco

Valdivia

Osorno

Puerto Montt

Castro

Ancud

Esquel

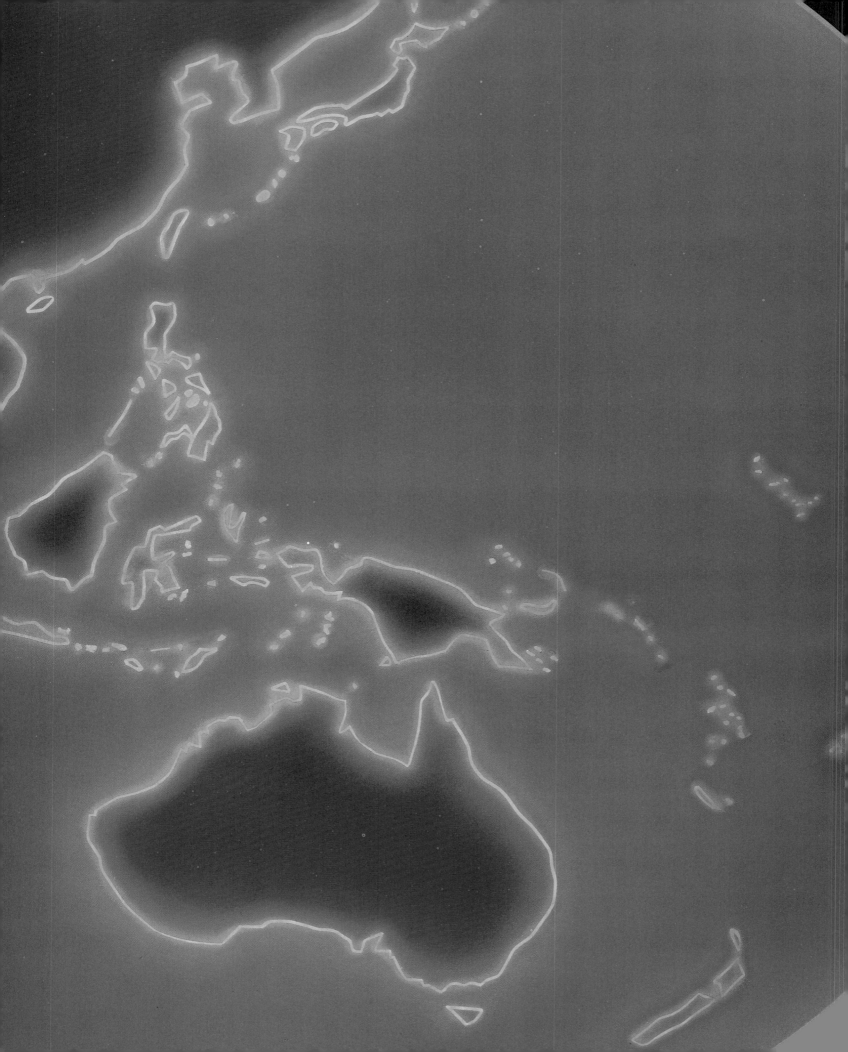

# AUSTRALIA – OCEANIA

| COUNTRY | OFFICIAL LANGUAGE(S) | AREA in sq mi | POPULATION | POPULATION DENSITY pop/sq mi | GNP in billions of $ (1982) | WORLD RANK | PER CAPITA Income (1982 dollars) | WORLD RANK | CAPITOL | POPULATION | PER CAPITA ELEC. CONSUMPTION in millions of kwh | No. of VEHICLES per 1,000 inhabitants | No. of DOCTORS per 1,000 inhabitants | % POPULATION less than 15 years of age |
|---|---|---|---|---|---|---|---|---|---|---|---|---|---|---|
| AUSTRALIA | english | 2,966,428 | 15,500,000 | 5 | 150.50 | 14 | 9,760 | 21 | CANBERRA | 251,000 | 6,936 | 469 | 1.8 | 27.2 |
| COOK IS. | english | 93 | 18,000 | 194 | 0.021 | 193 | 1,050 | 116 | AVARUA | 2,355 | 526 | — | 1 | 42.7 |
| FIJI IS. | english | 7,056 | 684,000 | 97 | 1.14 | 133 | 1,675 | 93 | SUVA | 71,000 | 498 | 38 | 0.46 | 38 |
| KIRIBATI | english | 281 | 62,000 | 221 | 0.030 | 190 | 500 | 152 | TARAWA | 20,148 | 98 | — | 0.27 | 41.1 |
| NAURU | english | 8 | 8,400 | 1,032 | 0.042 | 187 | 6,000 | 44 | NAURU | — | 3,375 | — | 1.5 | — |
| NEW ZEALAND | english | 103,746 | 3,270,000 | 32 | 22.20 | 54 | 7,025 | 37 | WELLINGTON | 342,500 | 7,886 | 496 | 1.57 | 27 |
| NIUE | english | 100 | 3,400 | 34 | 0.004 | 200 | 1,000 | 120 | ALOFI | — | 750 | — | 0.8 | 42.7 |
| PAPUA NEW GUINEA | pidgin english | 178,276 | 3,257,000 | 18 | 2.31 | 109 | 725 | 135 | PORT MORESBY | 144,000 | 406 | 5.7 | 0.06 | 43.8 |
| SOLOMON IS. | english | 10,984 | 269,000 | 25 | 0.160 | 168 | 615 | 145 | HONIARA | 20,842 | 97 | — | 0.16 | 48.4 |
| TONGA | tongan | 270 | 106,000 | 401 | 0.080 | 182 | 800 | 129 | NUKU'ALOFA | 20,564 | 115 | 5.6 | 0.38 | 44.4 |
| TUVALU | tuvaluan, english, french | 61 | 8,800 | 137 | 0.005 | 198 | 570 | 148 | FUNAFUTI | 1,000 | — | — | 0.43 | — |
| WESTERN SAMOA | english, samoan | 1,097 | 163,000 | 148 | 0.148 | 171 | 990 | 123 | APIA | 33,170 | 248 | 8.6 | 0.40 | 48.2 |
| VANUATU | english, bichlamer | 5,701 | 126,000 | 22 | 0.080 | 183 | 666 | 140 | VILA | 14,797 | 176 | 18.3 | 0.18 | 57 |

Scale 1 : 5,000,000

↑ **146**

A   B   C   D   102°   E   F   G

Equator

P. Tanahmasa

Bukittinggi   Pajakumbuh   PEMATANG   R I A U   G. Daix 1163   P. Lingga

P. Tanahbala   D. Mahindju   2891   Airmolek   Tel. Kuala   Tjenaku   P. Selajar
Luahasibuka   Padangpandjang   G. Marapi   Rengat   Tembilahan   P. Singkep   P. Saja
P. Bodjo   Pariaman   Sawahlunto   Taluk   Sungaisalak   Tg. Basu   475
Selat Siberut   Solok   Muara   Sel. Barhala
1795   PADANG   G. Talang   Sungaidareh   Tg. Djabung   Kep. Tudjuh
Telukbajur   2597   Alahanpandjang   Muarakumpe   Belinju

P. 406   SUMATERA   Muarabungo   Muaratebo   Muaratembesi   TELANAIPURA   Tel. Sekanak   G. Maras 669
Muarasiberut   BARAT   G. Kerintji   Tg.   Temping   Tel. Kampa   Pangkalpina
Simansih   Kambang   3805   Bangko   Betung   Bajunglintjir   Mentok   Tg.
SELAT   Airhadji   DJAMBI   Koba
Siberimanua   P. Sipora   Sungaipenuh   Sarolanguno   SUMATERA   654
Tg.   Tapan   G. Masurai   Surulangun   Rawas   Sekaju   Talangbetutu   SE   Batubetumbah
Inderapura   2934   Muarabeliti   PALEMBANG   Sungaigerung   Toboali
Mukomuko   Lubuklinggau   Perabumulih   Tandjungradja   Djerembarengas   Tg. Kait
P. Pagai   Muaraaman   Tjurup   Tebingtinggi   Kajuagung
Utara   2467   Kepahiang   Lahat   Muaraenim   S
Matobe   372   Sikakap   Lais   Bengkulu   Muarabeliti   Tg. Lumut
368   Bake   P. Pagai   U. Telukpunggur   Pagaralam   R
Selatan   P. Sanding   Tais   G. Dempo 3159   Baturadja   A
P. Mega   Manna   2817   Martapura   Menggala   Tulangbawang

Bintuhan   D. Ranau   G. Pesagi 2232   Kotabumi   Gunungsugih   Sukadana
Krui   Seputih   Metro
P. Enggano   LAMPUNG   Tegineneng   TANJUNGKARANG
281   Kajaapu   TELUKBETUNG   Kep. Se
6036   Kotaagung   Pandjang   Djabung
Belimbing   Kalianda   Ketapang   Tg. Pudjut
Tg. Rata   1281   Merak   Tg. Tua   Tang
Anak Krakatau 813   Selat Sunda   Serang
P. Rakata   Anjer Lor   Rangkasbit
P. Panaitan   Labuhan   Pandeglang   1778   DI
5225   Sem. Djungkulon   Malingping
P. Tindjil   Pelabuanra
P. Deli   Djamp
Kulo
Genteng
Tg. Genteng

I N D I A N   O C E A N

Christmas Island
(Austr.)

0  50  100 Kilomètres

0  50 Statute Miles

↑ 147

CHINA

SEA

INDONESIA

**PONTIANAK**  KALIMANTAN BARAT

B O R N E O
(K A L I M A N T A N)

KALIMANTAN
TIMUR

T E N G A H

KALIMANTAN
SELATAN

Sungaikakap
Tajan
Kertamulta
Nangapinoh
G. Saran 1758
Nangamuntatal
Nangatajap
Bukit Baja 2778
Peg. Schwaner
Muaradjuloi
Longiram
Intu
D. Semajang
D. Melintang
Puruktjahu
Sungaipinang
Muarateweh
Muarabenangin
Pajang
Muarapajang
·1233
G. Sarempaka 1380
Tanahgrogot

P. Padangtikar
P. Panebangan
P. Maja
Telukbatang
Sukadana
Sandai
Kualakurun
Daju
Tandjung

P. Karimata
P. Serutu
·1030
·996
Ketapang
Serengka
Panopah
·879
Rawi
Palangkaraya
Negara ·1893
G. Besar
Amuntai
Kandangan

Kualapesaguan
Kendawangan
Sukaradja
Sukamara
Kotawaringin
Pangkalanbuun
Kumai
Telegapulang
Semuda
Bangkal
Sampit
Pulangpisau
Bapuju
Marabahan
Negara
Rantau
Peg. Meratus
SELATAN
Kotabaru
Sebuku

Tandjungpandan
Belitung
Manggar
P. Selandu
Dendang
P. Selui
P. Kebatu
Tg. Sambar
Tg. Kluang
Tg. Puting
Kualapembuang
Tel. Kumai
Tel. Sampit
Tel. Sebangan
Tel. Malatajur
BANJARMASIN
Martapura
Kintap
Pleihari
Laut
Pagatan
Karambu
Batakan
Djorong
Tg. Selatan
Tg. Lajar
P. Marabatua

SELAT KARIMATA

Kep. Nangka
P. Gaspar
Nadur

L A U T   J A W A
(JAVA SEA)

Kep. Laut Ketjil
P. Keramian
P. Masalembo-Besar

Kep. Karimundjawa
P. Parang
P. Karimundjawa
P. Bawean

**BANDUNG**
**SEMARANG**
**SURABAJA**
**KUDUS**
**MAGELANG**
**SURAKARTA**
**MADIUN**
**KEDIRI**
**MALANG**
**BANJUWANGI**
**JOGJAKARTA**
**TJIREBON**
**PEKALONGAN**
**TASIKMALAJA**
**MATARAM**

Tg. Klawang
Bekasi
Krawang
Indramaju
Pamanukan
Kandanghaur
Tjikampek
Subang
Sumedang
Pemalang
Batang
Kendal
Demak
Pati
Lasem
Tuban
Lamongan
Gresik
Madura
Ambunten
Sumenep
Pabean
P. Kangean

Purwakarta
Tjimahi
G. Bukittunggul 2209
Kuningan
Brebes
Tegal
Slawi
Tjiledug
Wonosobo
Ambarawa
Salatiga
Bodjonegoro
Babat
Bangkalan
Sampang
Pamekasan
P. Sapudi
P. Raas
P. Paliat
P. Sepandjang

Tjiandjur
G. Patuha 2434
G. Tjikurai 2821
Garut
Tjiamis
Bandjar
Purwokerto
G. Slamet 3428
G. Merbabu
G. Lawu 3265
Solo
Ngawi
Modjokerto
Sidoardjo
Bangil
Pasuruan
Paiton
Situbondo
Bondowoso
Banjuwedang
Tedjakula
Kubu
Singaradja

Pameungpeuk
Garut
Tjikadjang
Kebumen
Tjilatjap
Prambanan
Borobudur
Klaten
Baturetno
Slaung
Ponorogo
Tulungagung
Blitar
Wlingi
G. Semeru 3676
G. Kelakah
Djember
3332 Raung
Gilimanuk
Negara
Denpasar
Klungkung
Karangasem
Mataram
Praja
Awang

Kroja
Bantu
Wonosari
Peg. Sewu
Patjitan
Popoh
P. Sempu
Nusa Barung
Puger
Gradjagan
Djimbaran
Nusa Penida
Tg. Mebulu
Tg. Batugendang
Lombok

D J A W A   T E N G A H
B A R A T
J A W A
(JAVA)

LAUT BALI
(BALI SEA)
BALI

7450

© HACHETTE-IGN

↑ **149**

← **207**

**SULAWESI TENGAH**

TELUK TOMINI

LAUT MALUKU (MOLUCCA SEA)

SULAWESI (CELEBES)

SULAWESI SELATAN

TELUK BONE

TELUK TOLO

SULAWESI TENGGARA

Kep. Sula

Kep. Banggai

LAUT JAWA (JAVA SEA)

LAUT BALI

LAUT FLORES

LAUT BAND

INDON

NUSA TENGGARA BARAT

NUSA TENGGARA TIMUR

LAUT SAVU

INDIAN OCEAN

Semajang
Mahakam
Santan
Equator
2530
Mapaga
Toribulu
P. Unauna
Kep. Togian
P. Waleabahi
Tenggarong
Bangsalsembera
SAMARINDA
2019
Donggala
Parigi
P. Batudaka
P. Puah
P. Togian
P. Waleakodi
P. Talatakoh
Tg. Pangkalsiang
Sambodja
Palu
Sausu
Uebonti
Teluk Uebonti
Pangimanan
Teku
Muaratunan
BALIKPAPAN
G. Nokilalaki
3311
Tel. Poso
2400
Luwuk
Sabal
Tg. Pemali
Pasangkaju
3127
Poso
3505
Toili
Basiano
P. Peleng
Tanahgrogot
Lariang
C.D. Lingu
Lemoro
Peg. Batui
Kembani
Banggai
P. Banggai
Todeli
1157
P. Mang
Tg. Aru
Karosa
Watukama
Pendolo
Kolonodale
Bangkulu
P. Labobo
P. Salue
P. Taliabu
Kep. Balabalangan
Peg. Takolekaju
Tel. Tomori
Timpaus
Lekitobi
Auponhia
Sanana
Tel. Pamukan
Sampaga
2950
3016
Malili
Saroako
P. Salue Timpaus
Kep. Sula
P. Sanana
Tel. Klumpeng
Tg. Rangasa
G. Gandadiwata
3074
Kambuno
Masamba
G. Balease
Bungku
Tg. Palp
P. Takatalu
Mamuqju
Peg. Quarles
Rantepao
Larona
D. Towuti
Labota
Kep. Salabangka
Tg. Kai
SELAT
Palopo
2799
Peg. Mekongga
Labota
Kotabaru
Onan
Peg.
Madjene
Peg. Matana
P. Labengke
P. Padea
P. Sebuku
SULAWESI
Makale
Konaweha
Lasolo
P. Manui
P. Lari Larian
G. Rantekombola
Wawotobi
Laut Karambu
3455
Enrekang
Malamala
Tel. Lasolo
Pinrang
Rappang
Tomboli
Kolaka
Kendari
Langara
MAKASSAR
Parepare
D. Tempe
Sengkang
P. Padamarang
Monse
P. Wowoni
Tg. Lajar
Watansoppeng
Pampanua
TENGGARA
Benua
Kolono
Sumpangbinangae
Watampone
Torobuku
1190
Buapinang
Poleang
Tampo
Bonelipu
Kep. Masalima
Kep. Sangkarang
Samak
Raha
Tel. Kolowana Watobo
P. Butongbutongan
Sindjai
Dualo
Muna
P. Wangiwangi
P. Kalukalukuang
P. Marasende
UJUNG-PANDANG (MAKASSAR)
Kadjang
Sikelio
1570
Mawasangka
P. Langkesi
P. Doangdoangan-Besar
2900
G. Lompobattang
Butung
P. Kaledupa
Bonthain
Bulukumba
P. Kabaena
Baubau
Lawele
P. Tanakeke
P. Kadatuang
Pasarwadjo
P. Tomea
Djeneponto
Bonelohe
P. Siumpu
P. Binongko
P. Taka Rewataje
P. Kabia
P. Moromaho
Barangbarang
Kep. Tukangbesi
P. Tambolongang
Kep. Taka Bonerate
P. Batuata
Sabalana
P. Kajuadi
P. Kabia
INDON
P. Tanahdjampea
Labuhanmarege
P. Karompa
P. Kalao
P. Kalagtoá
P. Bonerate
P. Setengar
Kep. Tenga
5121
P. Sukun
P. Komba
Liop
LAUT BALI
P. Sangeang
Tg. Kopondei
P. Lomblen
P. Pantar
Taramana
830
I. Ata
Bajan
Katupa
G. Api
1949
P. Banta
Komodo
Reo
Pota
P. Paloe
Larantuka
P. Adonara
Balaurin
Kabir
Kalabahi
G. Rindjani
P. Mojo
2850
Labuhanbadjo
Besar
1659
Waiwerang
Kajan
P. Alor
1839
Mataru
Dili
MATARAM
3726
Lombok
G. Tambora
Dompu
Naga
2382
Kuteng
Maumere
1704
Kep. Solor
Kep. Alor
Maubara
Ermera
2980
Praja
Selong
Sumbawa
1790
Rabe
Sape
Aimere
G. Inerie
Ende
P. Solor
Liquiça
Tata Ma
Awang
Taliwang
Parado
2245
Pante Macassar
Bobonaro
Bet
LOMBOK
Lunjuk
Plampang
FLORES
Atambua
Kefamenanu
Suai
NUSA TENGGARA BARAT
SUMBAWA
Tg. Sasar
Memboro
Tg. Karósso
Karuni
G. Mutis
2427
Besikama
Soe
Tossi
Waikabubak
Waingapu
P. Semau
Kupang
SUMBA
G. Wanggameti
1225
Melolo
Baun
P. Mangkudu
Baing
P. Raidjua
Seba
P. Sawu
Baa
430
P. Roti
P. Dana
Nembrala
P. Ndao
Tg. Ngundju
P. Dana
5066
Hibernia Reef
Ashmore Reef (Australia)

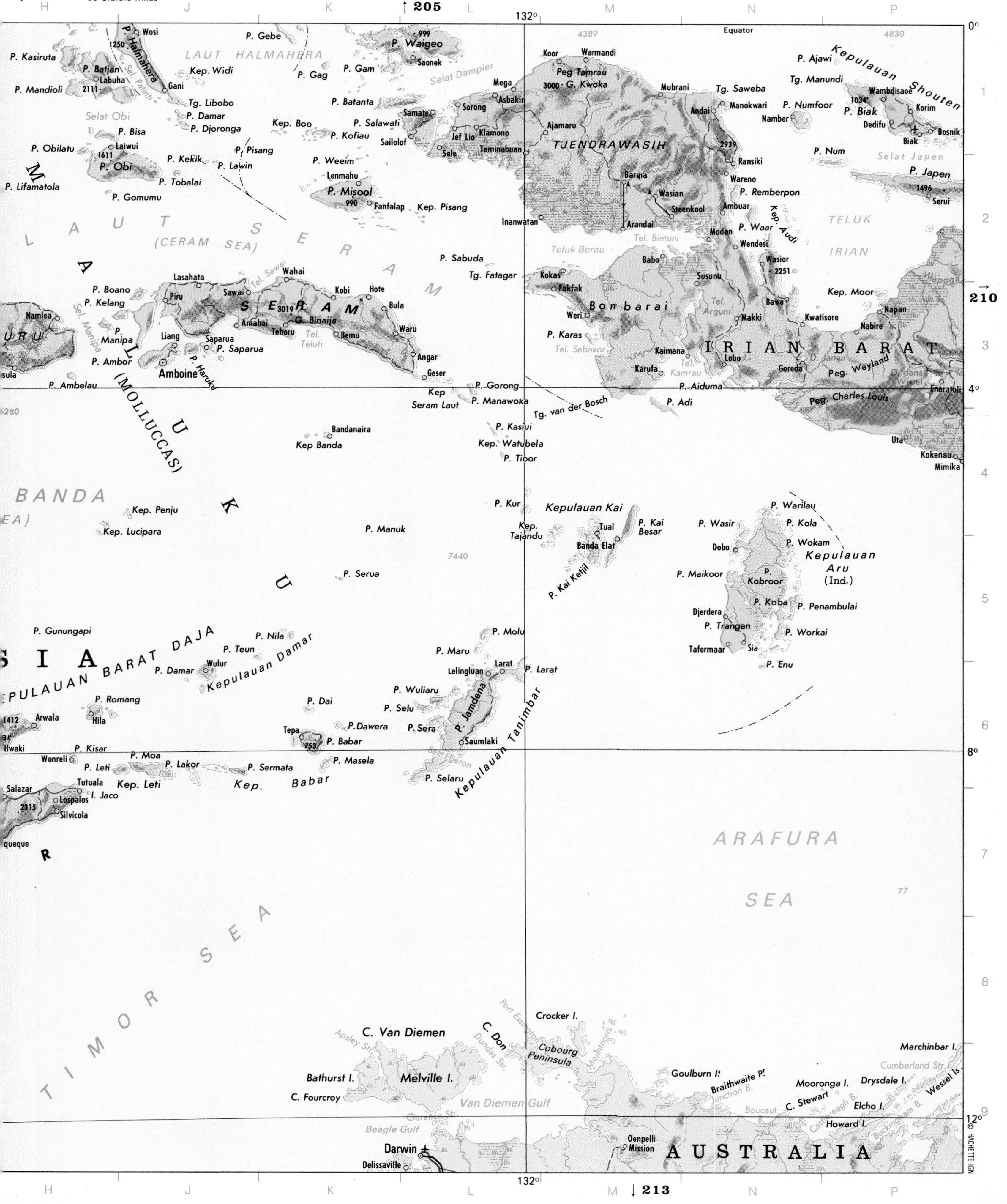

0 50 100 Kilomètres
0 50 Statute Miles

↑ 205

132°

H J K L M N O P

Equator 0°

4389 4830

P. Wosi
P. Halmahera 1250
P. Kasiruta
P. Batjan
P. Mandioli 2111
Labuha
Gani
LAUT HALMAHERA
Kep. Widi
P. Gebe
P. Waigeo · 999
P. Gam
Saonek
Selat Dampier
Koor Warmandi
Peg. Tamrau
3000 · G. Kwoka
Mubrani
Tg. Saweba
Tg. Manundi
P. Ajawi
Kepulauan Shouten
Mega
Asbakin
Sorong
Andai
Manokwari
P. Numfoor
Number
1034·
P. Biak
Wambdisaoe
Korim
Bosnik

P. Mandioli
P. Bisa
Laiwui
1611
P. Obilatu
P. Obi
P. Kekik
P. Djoronga
Kep. Boo
P. Kofiau
P. Pisang
P. Lawin
Samate
Klamono
Jef Lio
Sailolof
Sele
Teminabuan
Ajamaru
TJENDRAWASIH
2939
Ransiki
Barma
Wasian
Wareno
P. Remberpon
Steenkool
Ambuar
Dedifu
Biak
P. Num
Selat Japen
P. Japen
1496
Serui

P. Lifamatola
P. Tobalai
P. Gomumu
P. Weeim
Lenmahu
P. Misool
990
Fanfalap
Kep. Pisang
Inanwatan
Arandai
Tel. Bintuni
Modan
P. Waar
Wendesi
Kep. Audi
Wasior · 2251
TELUK
IRIAN

LAUT SERAM
(CERAM SEA)
SERAM
P. Sabuda
Tg. Fatagar
Teluk Berau
Babo
Susunu
Kep. Moor
Napan

P. Boano
Lasahata
Wahai
Tel. Sawai
Kobi
Hote
Kokas
Fakfak
Bonbarai
Makki
Bawe
Kwatisore
Nabire

P. Kelang
Piru
Sawai
SERAM 3019
G. Binaija
Bula
Weri
P. Karas
Tel. Arguni
Goreda
Peg. Weyland
D. danau Wissel

Namlea
P. Manipa
Liang
Amahai
Tehoru
Bemu
Waru
Angar
Geser
Kaimana
Karufa
Tel. Kamrau
Lobo
D. Jamur
Enaratoli

P. Ambor
Amboine
P. Haruku
Saparua
P. Saparua
Tel. Teluti
P. Gorong
Kep Seram Laut
P. Manawoka
Tg. van der Bosch
P. Aiduma
P. Adi
Peg. Charles Louis
Uta
Kokenau
Mimika

P. Ambelau
(MOLUCCAS)
P. Kasiui
Kep. Watubela
P. Tioor
P. Kur
Kepulauan Kai
P. Warilau
P. Kola

BANDA
Kep. Penju
Kep. Lucipara
P. Manuk
7440
Kep. Tajandu
Tual
P. Kai Besar
Banda Elat
P. Wasir
Dobo
P. Wokam
Kepulauan Aru (Ind.)
P. Maikoor
Kobroor
P. Koba
P. Penambulai

Bandanaira
Kep Banda
P. Serua
P. Kai Kejil
Djerdera
P. Trangan
P. Koba
P. Workai

P. Gunungapi
P. Nila
P. Molu
Tafermaar
Sia
P. Enu

KEPULAUAN BARAT DAJA
P. Teun
Kepulauan Damar
P. Maru
Larat
P. Larat

SIA
P. Damar
Wulur
Lelingluan
P. Wuliaru
P. Romang
P. Dai
P. Selu
Hila
Tepa
P. Dawera
P. Sera
P. Jamdena

1412
Arwala
P. Dawera
P. Babar
P. Sera
Saumlaki
Kepulauan Tanimbar

Ilwaki
P. Kisar
P. Moa
P. Lakor
P. Sermata
P. Masela
Wonreli
P. Leti
Kep. Leti
Kep. Babar
P. Selaru

Salazar
Tutuala
I. Jaco
2315
Lospalos
Silvicola
queque
R

ARAFURA
SEA
77

TIMOR SEA

Crocker I.
C. Van Diemen
C. Don
Port Essington
Cobourg Peninsula
Marchinbar I.

Apsley Str.
Dundas Str.
Goulburn I.
Braithwaite P!
Mooronga I.
Drysdale I.
Cumberland Str.

Bathurst I.
Melville I.
Junction B.
C. Stewart
Elcho I.
Wessel Is.

C. Fourcroy
Van Diemen Gulf
Howard I.
12°

Beagle Gulf
Clarence Str.
Oenpelli Mission
© HACHETTE-IGN

Darwin
Delissaville
AUSTRALIA

PACIFIC

0° Equator

↑ **205**

138°

1

Mubrani
Andai
Manokwari
P. Ajawi
Tg. Saweba
Tg. Manundi
P. Numfoor
Namber
1034
P. Biak
Wambdisaoe
Dedifu
Korim
Bosnik
Biak
Bosnik
Kep. Padeaido

2939
Barma
Wasian
Ransiki
Wareno
P. Num
Selat Japen
4830
Tg. d'Urville
Kep. Kunamba
Sarmi

Wasian
Steenkool
Ambuar
P. Remberpon
P. Japen
1496
Serui
Bono
D. Rombebai
Pionierbivak
Bufareh
Armopa
Demta

2
Arandal
Tel. Bintuni
Modan
Wendesi
P. Waar Audi
TELUK
IRIAN
Waren
Wonti
Mamberamo
Pegunungan van Rees
2164
Jayapura
(Sukarnapura)
Vanimo
Leitre

209 ←

Babo
Susunu
Wasior
2251
Bawe
Makki
Tel. Arguni
Kep. Moor
Napan
Nabire
G. Dom
1340
Wapoga
Tariku
Tarifatu
D. Sentani
Gerjem
Pagi
Moari
Aitape
Val

Kaimana
Karufa
Lobo
Goreda
Tel. Kamrau
D. Jamur
Peg. Weyland
D. danau
Wi sel
Derewa
Enaratoli
Mbambawa
3741
G. Angemuk
Warula
Sobger
Sepik
Wagu
Dreikikir
Om
Wagad

3

P. Aiduma
P. Adi

IRIAN BARAT

PEGUNUNGAN MAOKE

4° 
Peg. Charles Louis
Peg. Sudirman
5030
Puncak Jaya
(Sukarno)
Uta
Kokenau
Mimika
Tjemara
4730
Trikora
Peg. Jalawidjaja
4702 G. Mandala
3860
Turnwald Ra.
Victor Emmanuel Ra.
CENTR
Lagu
Bivi

4
Tel. Flamingo
Agats
Lorentz
Baliem
Pulau
Digul
Muller Ra.
Karius Ra.
Ta

P. Kai
Besar
P. Wasir
P. Warilau
P. Kola
Dobo
P. Wokam
Kepulauan
Aru
(Ind.)

5
P. Maikoor
P.
Kobroor
P. Koba
P. Penambulai
Djerdera
P. Trangan
Sia
P. Workai
Tafermaar
P. Enu

INDONESIA
Birufu
Mindiptana
Tanahmerah
Kiunga
Mt. Bosavi
2895

Birab
Kepi
Asike
Mava
Murray
Wawoi

6
Tg. de Jongs
Mapi
Kai
P. Kolepom
Bulaka
Kumbe
Aramia
Gair

8° 
Tg. Vals
Wan
P. Komoran
Okaba
Merauke
Sehajo
Rouku
Buk
Koabu
Tonda
Buji
Sebidiro
Dar

77

Boigu I.
Deliverance I.
Turnagain I.
Sabai I.
Dungene

7
Turu Cay
Gabba I.
Mulgrave I.
Long I.
Banks I.

TORRES STRAIT

8

A R A F U R A   S E A

Horn I.
C. York
Prince of Wales I.
Somerset
Newcastle B.
Endeavor Strait

C. Wessel

9
Marchinbar I.
Cumberland Str.
Goulburn I.
Braithwaite Pt.
Mooronga I.
Drysdale I.
Wessel Islands
The English Company's I.
Truant I.
C. Stewart
Elcho I.
C. Wilber Force
Boucaut
Caslereagh B.
Junction B.
Howard I.
Buckingham B.
Melville
Bremer I.
CAPE YORK
PENINSULA
Port Musgrave
Cullen Pt.
Mapoon

12°
Oenpelli
Mission
Yirrkala
Mission
C. Arnhem
Wenlock
Shelbur

**AUSTRALIA**

138°

↓ **214**

A    B    C    D    E    F    G

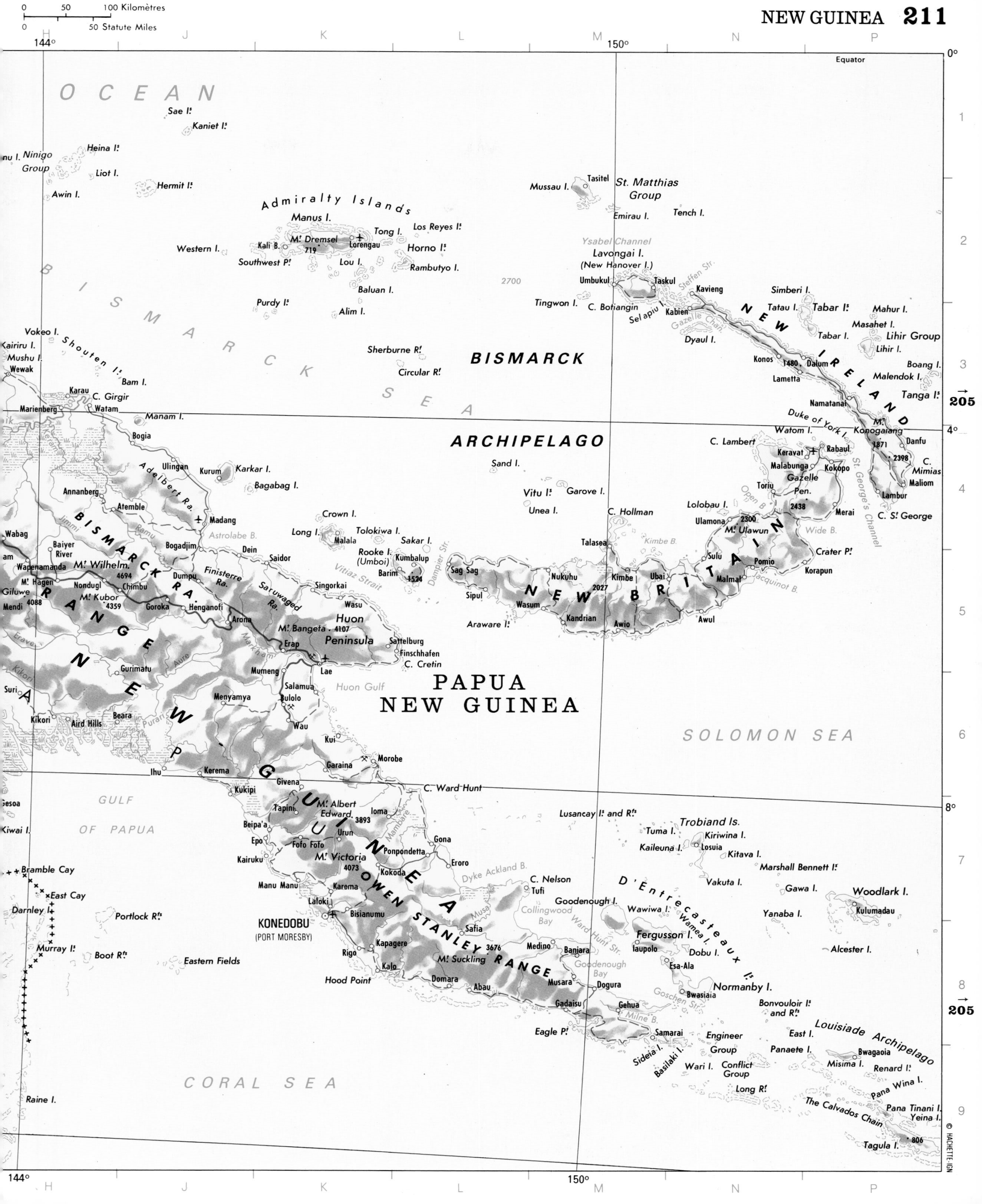

50 100 Kilomètres
50 Statute Miles

144° 150° 0°
Equator

O C E A N

Ninigo Group
nu I.
Heina I.
Liot I.
Awin I.
Hermit I!
Sae I!
Kaniet I!

Admiralty Islands
Manus I.
M! Dremsel 719
Kali B.
Lorengau
Tong I.
Los Reyes I!
Horno I!
Western I.
Southwest P!
Lou I.
Rambutyo I.
Purdy I!
Baluan I.
Alim I.

Mussau I.
Tasitel
St. Matthias Group
Emirau I.
Tench I.

Ysabel Channel
Lavongai I. (New Hanover I.)
Umbukul
Taskul
Steffen Str.
Kavieng
Tingwon I.
C. Botiangin
Selapiu I.
Kabien
Dyaul I.
Simberi I.
Tatau I.
Tabar I!
Mahur I.
Masahet I.
Lihir Group
Tabar I.
Lihir I.
Boang I.
Malendok I.
Tanga I!

Sherburne R!
Circular R!

BISMARCK

NEW IRELAND

2700

BISMARCK SEA

Vokeo I.
Kairiru I.
Mushu I.
Wewak
Shouten Is.
Bam I.
Karau
C. Girgir
Watam
Marienberg
Manam I.

ARCHIPELAGO

Sand I.
Vitu I!
Unea I.
Garove I.

Konos 1480 Dalum
Lametta
Namatanai
Watom I.
Duke of York I.
M! Konogaiang 1871
Danfu
2398
C. Mimias
Maliom
Lambur
C. S! George

Keravat
Malabunga
Kokopo
Gazelle Pen.
Toriu
Rabaul
St. George's Channel

C. Lambert
C. Hollman
Lolobau I.
Ulamona 2300
M! Ulawun
Sulu
Ubai
Merai
Korapun

4°

Bogia
Ulingan
Kurum
Karkar I.
Bagabag I.
Annanberg
Atemble
Madang
Astrolabe B.
Bogadjim
Crown I.
Long I.
Malala
Tolokiwa I.
Sakar I.
Rooke I. (Umboi)
Barim 1524
Kumbalup
Dein
Saidor
Singorkai
Vitiaz Strait
Dampier Str.

Talasea
Kimbe B.
2438
Nukuhu 2027
Kimbe
Pomio
Malmal
Crater P!
Jacquinot B.

Sag Sag
Sipul
Wasum
NEW BRITAIN
Kandrian
Awio
Awul

Araware I!
Wide B.
SOLOMON SEA

Wabag
Baiyer River
M! Wilhelm 4694
Nondugl
Chimbu
M! Kubor 4359
Goroka
Henganofi
Arona
Wapenamanda
M! Hagen
Giluwe
Mendi 4088
Suri
Gurimatu
BISMARCK RANGE
Finisterre Ra.
Saruwaged Ra.
Dumpu
Wasu
Huon Peninsula
M! Bangeta 4107
Erap
Sattelburg
Finschhafen
C. Cretin
Lae
Markham
NEW GUINEA RANGE

PAPUA NEW GUINEA

Kikori
Aird Hills
Beara
Menyamya
Mumeng
Salamua
Bulolo
Wau
Kui
Garaina
Morobe

Eraves
Kikori
Purari
Aire

Ihu
Kerema
Givena
Kukipi
Beipa'a
Tapini
Epo
Fofo Fofo
Kairuku
M! Victoria 4073
M! Albert Edward 3893
Urun
Ioma
Ponpondetta
Gona
Eroro
Kokoda
C. Ward Hunt
C. Nelson
Tufi

OWEN STANLEY RANGE

GULF OF PAPUA

Gesoa
Kiwai I.
Bramble Cay
East Cay
Darnley I.
Portlock R!!
Murray I!
Boot R!!
Eastern Fields
Manu Manu
Laloki
Bisianumu
KONEDOBU (PORT MORESBY)
Rigo
Kapagere
Kalo
Hood Point
Domara
Abau
Musara
Gadaisu
Gehua
Dogura
Eagle P!
M! Suckling 3676

Dyke Ackland B.
Safia
Collingwood Bay
Goodenough I.
Wawiwa I.
Wamea I.
D'Entrecasteaux Is.
Fergusson I.
Dobu I.
Esa-Ala
Normanby I.
Goodenough Bay
Banjara
Medino
Iaupolo
Bwasiaia
Milne B.
Samarai
Sideia I.
Basilaki I.
Wari I.
Engineer Group
Conflict Group
Long R!

Lusancay I! and R!!
Trobiand Is.
Tuma I.
Kiriwina I.
Kaileuna I.
Losuia
Kitava I.
Vakuta I.
Gawa I.
Marshall Bennett I!
Woodlark I.
Kulumadau
Yanaba I.
Alcester I.

Bonvouloir I! and R!!
Louisiade Archipelago
East I.
Panaete I.
Misima I.
Renard I!
Pana Wina I.
Bwagaoia
The Calvados Chain
Pana Tinani I.
Yeina I.
Tagula I. 806

CORAL SEA

Raine I.
Raine I.

144° 150°

→ 205
→ 205
© HACHETTE-IGN

Scale 1 : 5,000,000

A       B       C       D       E       F       G

114°                                    120°

1

12°

6840

2                                                               Seringapatam Reef

Scott Reef

Sandy I.

3                                                               Lynher Reef

3373

*I N D I A N   O C E A N*

4

16°                                                             Lacepede

C. Baske

Mermaid Reef

Rowley Shoals    Clerke Reef

5                                                               Gantheaun

Imperieuse Reef

C. Latouche Treville

C. Bossut

6                                                               Anna

Eighty    Mile    Beach

Bedout I.                              Mandora

Turtle I!                              Wallal

De Grey    Pardoo

7       Port Hedland    M! Goldsworthy              GR

Dampier      Legendre I.                  Warrawagine

Arch.                        Talgatalga

Monte Bello I!          Nickol B.

20°                    Enderby I.    Port Samson          Marble Bar

Dampier                               M! Sy

Preston    Roebourne        Abydos

Barrow I.                            Mungaroona Range    Nullagine

Yarraloola    Millstream                Chichester Ra.

8       Thevenard I.            831.                    Fortescue

Muron I!    Onslow        M! Pyrton

North West Cape                            Wittenoom    Roy Hill

Minderoo    Hamersley

HAMERSLEY    RANGE

Learmonth              M! Brockman              1226

1113        1075  M! Bruce    WESTERN

Exmouth Gulf    Boolaloo    Wyloo    M! Wall    M! Tom/Price    Ophtalmia Ra.

9                    M! Alexander    948              M! Newman    Ethel Creek

Giralia                        Paraburdoo        1128

P! Cloates

P! Maud    Winning    M! Palgrave

Pool                704        Mundiwindi

A       B       C    **216**    E       F       G

114°        120°

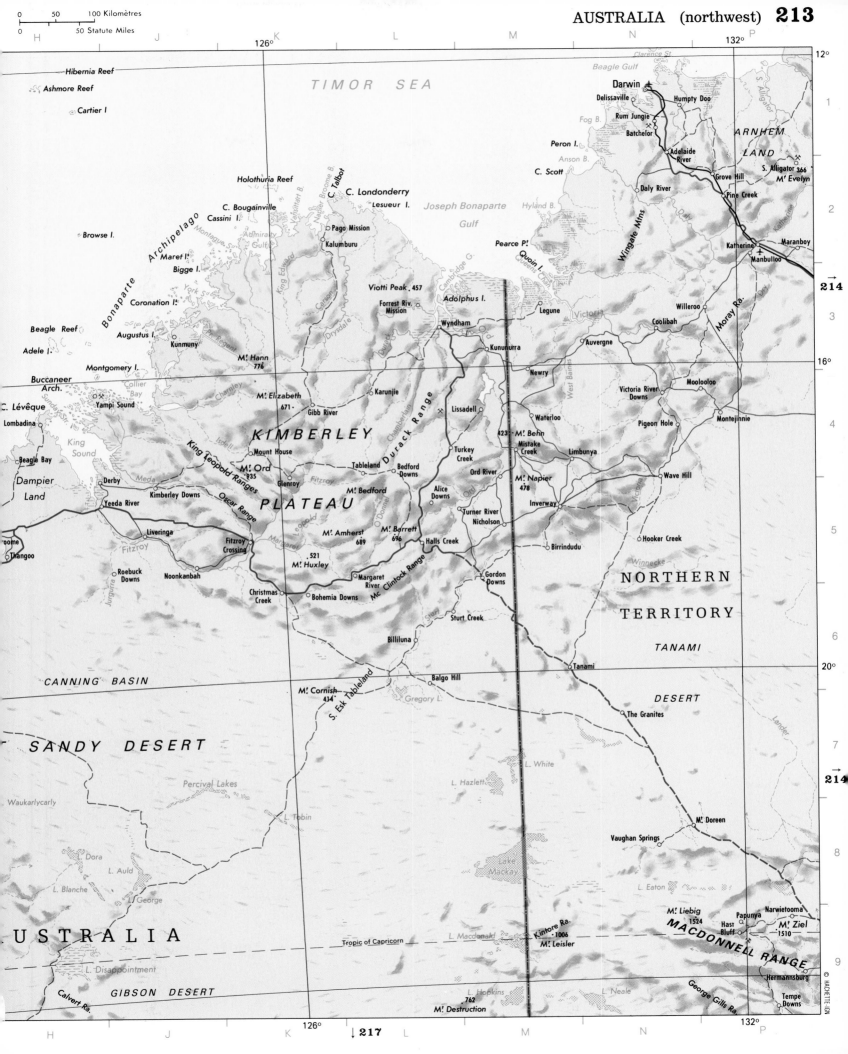

↓ 217

TIMOR SEA

Hibernia Reef
Ashmore Reef
Cartier I.
Browse I.

Holothuria Reef
C. Bougainville
Cassini I.
Maret I.
Bigge I.
Coronation I.
Augustus I.
Montgomery I.
Beagle Reef
Adele I.
Buccaneer Arch.

Bonaparte Archipelago

C. Talbot
C. Londonderry
Lesueur I.
Pago Mission
Kalumburu

Joseph Bonaparte Gulf

C. Scott
Pearce P.
Quoin I.
Adolphus I.

Clarence St.
Beagle Gulf
Darwin
Delissaville
Rum Jungle
Batchelor
Adelaide River
Daly River
Grove Hill
Pine Creek

Humpty Doo
S. Alligator 366
M. Evelyn
Katherine
Manbulloo
Maranboy

ARNHEM LAND

Fog B.
Anson B.
Peron I.
Wingate Mtns

Viotti Peak 457
Forrest Riv. Mission
Wyndham
Kununurra

Legune
Auvergne
Newry
Victoria

Willeroo
Coolibah

Moray Ra.

C. Lévêque
Yampi Sound
Lombadina
Beagle Bay
Dampier Land

King Sound
Collier Bay

M. Hann 776
M. Elizabeth 671
Gibb River
Mount House
M. Ord 935
Glenroy
Tableland
Bedford Downs
M. Bedford

KIMBERLEY

PLATEAU

Durack Range
Chamberlain
Karunjie
Lissadell
Turkey Creek
Ord River
423 M. Behn
Mistake Creek
M. Napier 478

Waterloo
Limbunya

Victoria River Downs
Pigeon Hole

Moolooloo

Montejinnie

Derby
Kimberley Downs
Yeeda River
Liveringa
Roebuck Downs
Noonkanbah
Fitzroy Crossing

King Leopold Ranges
Oscar Range
Meda
Fitzroy
Margaret

M. Amherst 689
M. Barrett 696
521
M. Huxley
Margaret River
Bohemia Downs
Christmas Creek

Alice Downs
Halls Creek
Turner River
Nicholson
Inverway

Mc Clintock Range
Gordon Downs

Wave Hill
Hooker Creek
Birrindudu

NORTHERN

TERRITORY

Broome
Thangoo

Jurguira
Fitzroy

Sturt
Sturt Creek
Biliiluna
Balgo Hill

Tanami

TANAMI

DESERT

M. Cornish 414
S. Esk Tableland
Gregory L.

Winnecke

The Granites

CANNING BASIN

SANDY DESERT

Percival Lakes
Waukarlycarly
L. Tobin

L. White
L. Hazlett

M. Doreen

L. Dora
L. Auld
L. Blanche
L. George

Lake Mackay
L. Eaton

Vaughan Springs

M. Liebig 1524
Hast Bluff
Papunya
Narwietooma
M. Ziel 1510

USTRALIA

Tropic of Capricorn
L. Macdonald
L. Disappointment
Calvert Ra.

GIBSON DESERT

L. Hopkins
M. Destruction 762

Kintore Ra. 1006
M. Leisler

MACDONNELL RANGE

George Gills Ra.
Hermannsburg
Tempe Downs

L. Neale

© HACHETTE-IGN

A B C 138° D E ↑ **210** F G

**ARAFURA SEA**

77

PAPUA NEW GUINEA

Buji
Deliverance I. Boigu I. Sabai I. Dungeness
Turnagain I.
Turu Cay Gabba I.
Mulgrave I. Long I. Banks I. Half
**TORRES STRAIT**

C. Wessel
Marchinbar I.
Cumberland Str.
Goulburn I. Wessel Islands Horn I.
Braithwaite P. Mooronga I. Drysdale I. The English Company's I. Prince of Wales I. C. York
Junction B. Truant I. Somerset
Boucaut C. Stewart Castlereagh B. Elcho I. C. Wilber Force Newcastle B.
Howard I. Endeavour Strait
Melville
12° Buckingham B. Bremer I. Cullen P. Port Musgrave Shelburn
Oenpelli Nhulunbuy C. Arnhem Mapoon **CAPE YORK** Gre
Mission
**ARNHEM** Frederick Hills Duifken P. Moreton S.W. Thompson Ra.
Parsons Ra. Caledon B. Albatross B. Weipa 555 Lock River M
213 C. Grey Pera Head Wenlock **PENINSULA**
C. Shield Archer B. Wenlock
**LAND** Blue Woodah I. C. Keer-Weer Aurukun Archer
Mainoru Mud North East I. Rokeby
B. Groote Holroyd
4 Rose River Bickerton I. **Eylandt** Coen
Mission 213 Warwick Chan. Yarraden Musgra
Roper River C. Beatrice Coleman
Mission Edward I. **GULF OF** Strathmay
Mataranka Roper Valley Maria I. Limmen Bight Wallaby I. Pottalah C.
Elsey Rose **CARPENTARIA** Mitchell River Alice
Hodgson C. Pellew Rutland Plains Crosbi
Larrimah Downs West I. Sir Edward Pellew Nassau
Birdum Arnold Cox Group Mitchell
Nutwood Vanderlin I. Palmer
Downs Limmen Bight
16° Tanumbirini Borroloola Manangoora Dunbar
Daly Waters Bauhinia Sandy Head Inkerman Galbraith
Downs Wellesley I. Staaten
Leila McArthur Mornington I. Macaroni Gambo
Dunmarra O.T. Downs Foelsche Pungalina C. Van Diemen Delta Downs
6 Robinson Calvert Forsyth I. Vanrook Gilbert
Beetaloo Robinson River Bentinck I. Karumba Miranda
**NORTHERN** Foelsche Wollogorang S. Wellesley I. Downs Abingdon Einasleigh
Newcastle Calvert Hills Westmoreland Normanton Carron Etheridge
Waters Elliot Cliffdale Burketown Inverleigh Haydon Blackbull
L. Woods **BARKLY** Seigals Corinda Floraville Milgarra Croydon Gilbert River
Anthony Lagoon Creek Nicholson Albert Vena Park Georgetown
**TERRITORY** Fish River Augustus Downs Norman Forsayth
Banka Banka Brunette **TABLELAND** Lawn Hill Gregory Downs Donors Hills Iffley Clara Esmeralda
Brunette Downs Leichhardt Alexandra Gregory
Rockampton Riversleigh Canobie Gilberton
Downs Playford Fiery Taldora Range
M. Woodcock 373 Alexandria Morstone Kamileroi Millungera Woolgar
Flynn Memorial Frewena Alroy Downs Georgina M. Margaret Dobbyn Corella
436 Ranken Store M. Oxide Kajabbi Koolamarra Dalgonally Saxby
M. Samuel Tennant Creek Avon Camooweal Yelvertoft Cambridge
20° Soudan Downs Buckley Mary Cloncurry Gilliat Maxwellton Downs
Greenwood Murchinson Epenarra Mingera Kathleen **QUEENS** Dutton
Wauchope Davenport Ra. Templeton Mount Isa Oorindi Julia Creek Richmond
636 Hatches Creek Lake Nash **Selwyn** Malbon Mc Kinlay Marathon
Murray Downs Elkedra Annitowa **Range** Duchess Cassilis
Barrow Creek Trekelano Selwyn Stamford

A 138° D ↓ **218** E F G

← 213
← 213

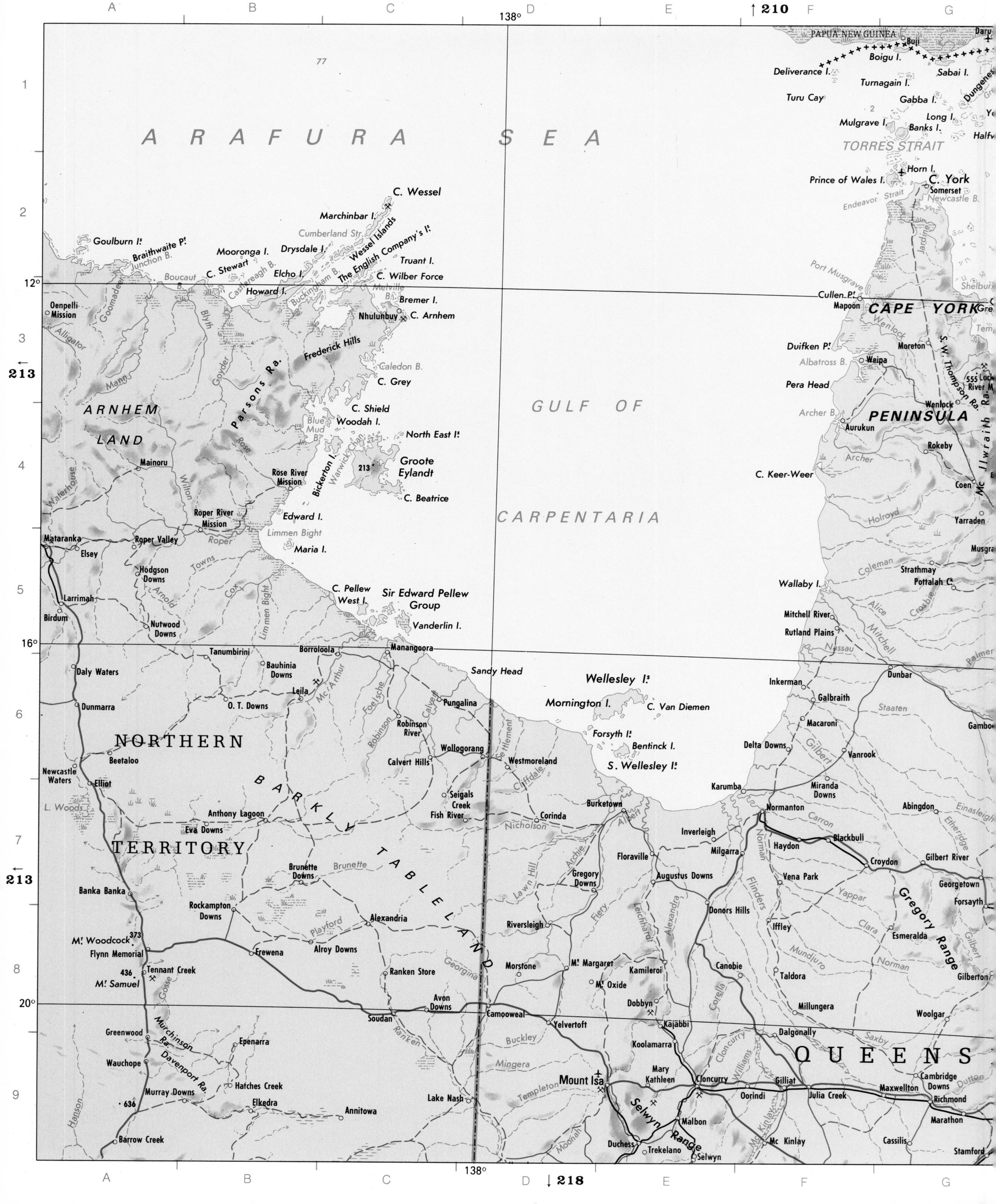

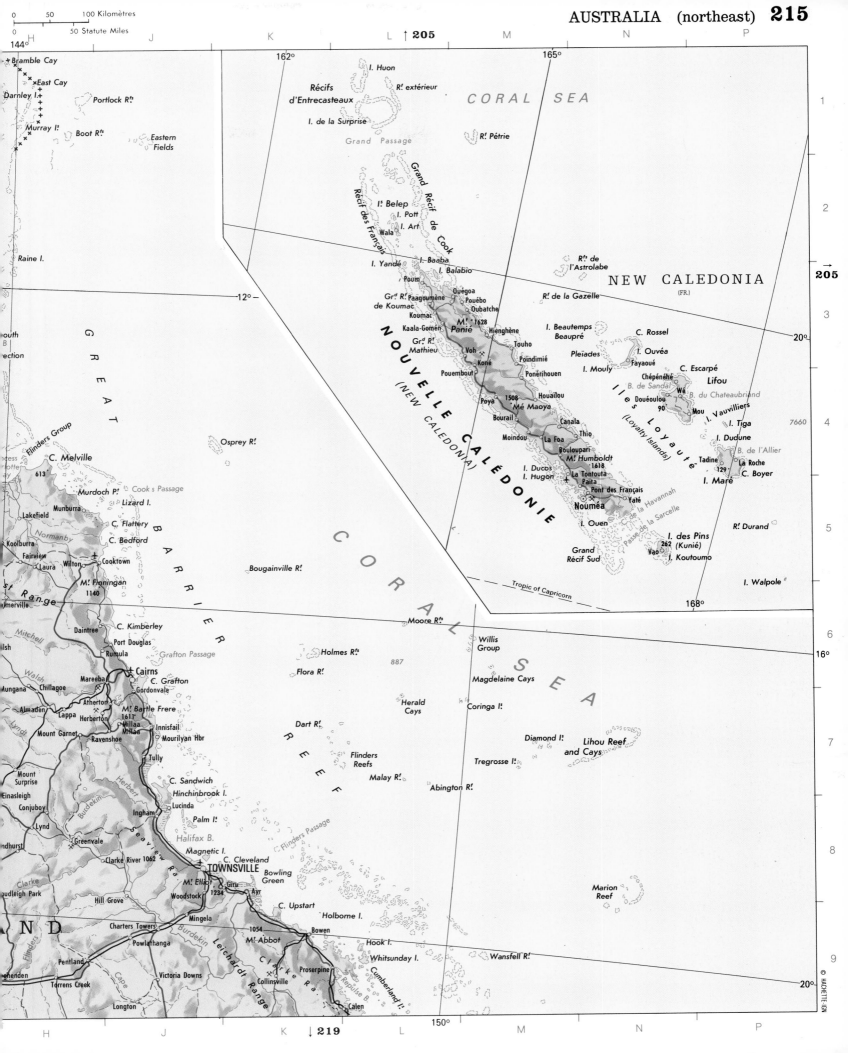

Scale 1 : 5,000,000

↑ 212

A 114° B C D E 120° F G

Tropic of Capricorn

INDIAN OCEAN

WESTERN AUSTRALIA

P! Maud
Winning Pool
Lyndon
Williambury
Minilya
M! Palgrave 704
Barlee Ra.
698 Boggola
Mundiwindi
M! Thomson 392
Minnie Creek
M! Augustus
584 M! Vernon
M! Vernon
Ashburton
C. Cuvier
M! Augustus 1105
M! Egerton 994
M! Wonyulgunna 776
M! Essendon 910
Bernier I. Carnarvon
M! Gascoyne 789
Landor
M! Labouchere
Milgun 722
Horse Shoe
Dorre I.
Grey's Plains
Gascoyne Junction
M! Fraser 801
Robinson Ranges
Peak Hill
C. Inscription Peron Pen.
Shark Bay
Naturaliste Channel
Wooramel
Coor de Wandy 553
M! Hale 732
Meekatharra
Patoo
Dirk Hartogs I.
Denham
Milly Milly
Berringarra
Mileura
Wiluna
Byro
L. Way
Steep P!
Hamelin Pool
Meeberrie
M! Murchison 520
M! Lulworth 701
Nannine
Tamala
Murgoo
Nicholson Ra. 530 M! Luke
Big Bell
Cue
Barrambie
Billybillong
L. Austin
Sandstone
Lawlers
Pinegrove
651 M! Dalgaranger
M! Magnet
M! Wyemandoo 543
Salt Lakes
Bluff P!
Galena
Ajana
453 Tallering P!
Yalgoo
Youanmi
Lynton
Northampton
Wurarga
L. Barlee
L. Giles
Mullewa
Geraldton
Mingenew
248 Morawa
M! Singleton 698
Johnston Ra.
M! Budd
Paynes Find
Dongara
Arrino
Perenjori
447
M! Jackson 686
Three Springs
Carnamah
Lake Moore
L. Deborah
Beagle I.
Green Head
Wubin
Bonnie Rock
Bullab
Island Point
M! Lesueur 313
Gunyidi
Kalannie
Beacon
L. Seabrook
Pithara
Burakin
Mukinbudin
Bullfinch
Moora
Milling
Koorda
Bencubbin
Dandaragan
Piawaning
L. Brown
Southern Cross
Wedge I.
Wongan Hills
Dowerin
Wyalkatchem
Nungarin
463
Marvel Loch
Calingiri
Goomalling
Kellerberrin
Merredin
Muntgadin
Toodyay
Cunderdin
C. Leschenault
Gingin
Bruce Rock
Parker Ra.
Yanchep
Michea
Northam
376
The Johnston Lakes
PERTH
York
Midland Jn
Quairading
Rottnest I.
Fremantle
Armadale
Beverley
Brookton
Corrigin
Kondinin
Hyden
L. Camnody
Garden I.
Medina
Pingelly
L. Hope
Mandurah
M! Cooke 582
C. Bouvard
Pinjarra
Dwellingup
Wickepin
Jitarning
Pingaring
Harvey
Narrogin
L. Grace
Newdegate
L. Kings
Lake King
Bunbury
Collie
Darkan
Williams
Arthur Riv.
Wagin
Dumbleyung
Pingrup
L. Grace
L. Magenta
Ravensthy
Bowelling
Katanning
Nyabing
Hope
Donnybrook
Kojonup
Gnowangerup
Ongerup
529
Cape Naturaliste
Busselton
Boyup Brook
Tambellup
Hood Point
Margaret River
Bridgetown
Cranbrook
Nat. Park 1096
Bremer Bay
C. Knob
Nannup
Manjimup
Rocky Gully
Stirling Ra. Bluff Knoll
Cheyne B.
Augusta
Pemberton
M! Barker
562
Bald I.
Cape Leeuwing
Northcliffe
Nornalup
Denmark
Albany
Flinders Bay
P! d'Entrecasteaux
P! Nuyts
West Cape Howe
Bald Head
King George Sound

Houtman Abrolhos
Geelvink Channel
Wallabi Gr.
Faure I.
Hamelin Pool
Denham Sound
Geographe Channel
Lake Mc.Leod
Kennedy Ra.
Minilya
Gascoyne
Murchison
Murchison
Lake McLeod
5395

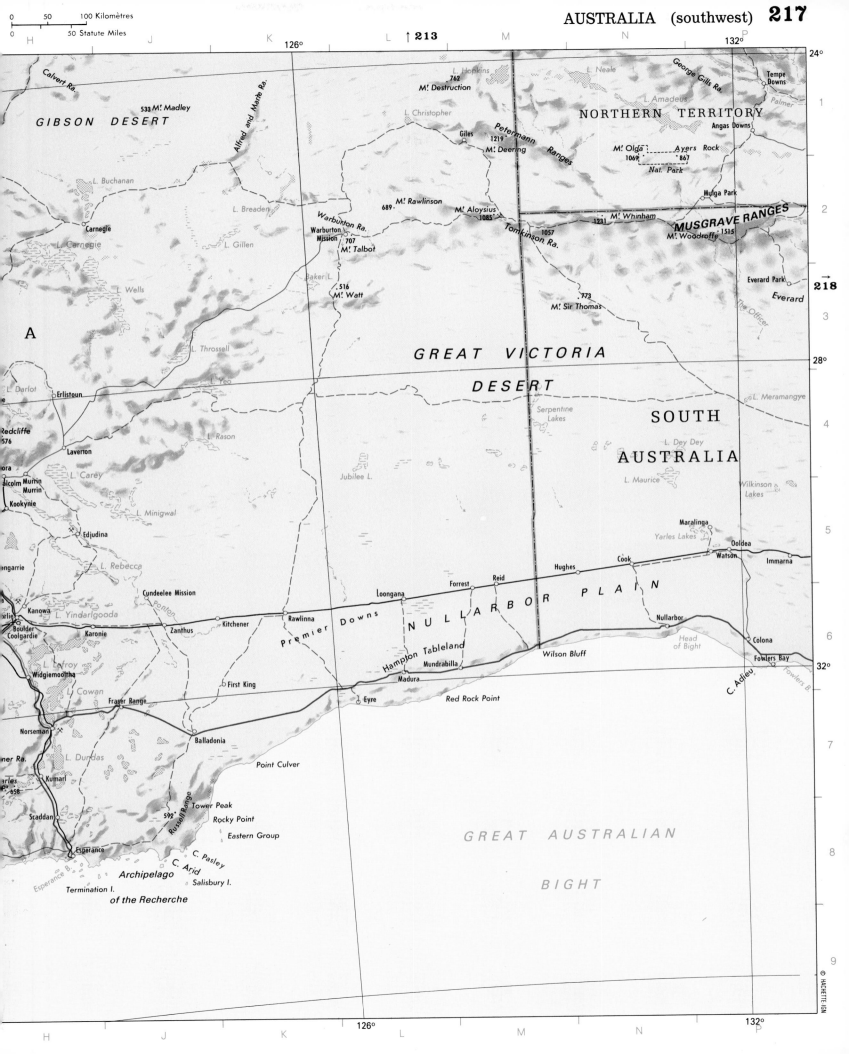

0  50  100 Kilomètres

0   50 Statute Miles

126°   ↑ **213**   132°

24°

Calvert Ra.

L. Hopkins   L. Neale   George Gills Ra.   Tempe Downs

.762   Mt Destruction

Palmer

533 Mt Madley   **NORTHERN   TERRITORY**

**GIBSON   DESERT**   L. Christopher   L. Amadeus

1

L. Buchanan   Giles   1219   Petermann   Angas Downs

Mt Deering   Ranges

L. Breaden   Mt Olga   Ayers Rock

Carnegie   Warburton Ra.   Mt Rawlinson   1069   . 867

Warburton   689.   Mt Aloysius   Nat. Park   Mulga Park

L. Carey... no

L. Gillen   Mission   1085   **MUSGRAVE RANGES**

707   1231   Mt Whinham

Mt Talbot   Tomkinson Ra.   1057   Mt Woodroffe   .1515

2

L. Wells   Baker L.   .516   Mt Watt

Everard Park

.773   Everard

L. Throssell   Mt Sir Thomas   → **218**

The Officer

**A**

L. Yeo   **GREAT   VICTORIA**   28°

L. Darlot   Erlistoun   **DESERT**   L. Meramangye

**SOUTH**

Redcliffe   L. Rason   Serpentine   Lakes

576   Laverton   **AUSTRALIA**

3

Jubilee L.   L. Dey Dey

alcolm Murrin   L. Carey   L. Maurice   Wilkinson

Murrin   Lakes

Kookynie   L. Minigwal   Maralinga

4

Edjudina   Yarles Lakes   Ooldea

L. Rebecca   Cook   Watson   Immarna

ongarrie   Cundeelee Mission   Hughes

Kanowa   Ponton   Forrest   Reid

5

L. Yindarlgooda   Loongana   Nullarbor

orlie   Zanthus   Kitchener   Rawlinna   **NULLARBOR   PLAIN**   Colona

Boulder   Premier Downs   Head   Fowlers Bay

Coolgardie   Karonie   Wilson Bluff   of Bight

6

Widgiemooltha   Hampton Tableland   32°

L. Lefroy   First King   Mundrabilla

L. Cowan   Madura

Norseman   Fraser Range   Eyre

Red Rock Point   C. Adieu   Fowlers B.

7

er Ra.   Balladonia

L. Dundas   Point Culver

Kumari

arles   .658   Tower Peak

Pt   592.   Rocky Point

Tay   Russell Range   Eastern Group   **GREAT   AUSTRALIAN**

8

Scaddan   C. Pasley

Esperance   C. Arid   Salisbury I.

Esperance B.   Archipelago   **BIGHT**

Termination I.   of the Recherche

9

126°   132°

© HACHETTE-IGN

H   J   K   L   M   N   P

Scale 1 : 5,000,000

138°  ↑ 214

**QUEEN**

MACDONNELL RA.

NORTHERN
TERRITORY

SIMPSON
DESERT

Tropic of Capricorn

GREAT

ARTES

BASIN

LAKE EYRE BASIN

Lake Eyre

SOUTH
AUSTRALIA

Stuart Range

STURT
DESERT

GREY RANGE

Flinders Ranges

Lake Torrens

Lake Gairdner

Gawler Ranges

Eyre Peninsula

138°  ↓ 220

144°

← 217

← 217

24°

28°

32°

Barrow Creek
Stirling
Ammaroo
Tea Tree
Harper Springs
Woodgreen
Utopia
Aileron
M. Swan
Mc Donald Downs
Indiana
Lucy Creek
M. Hay 1249
M. Laughlen 1169
Bond Springs
Arltunga
Ringwood
Alice Springs
James Ra.
Henbury
Deep Well
Rodinga
Indracowra
Erldunda
Horseshoe Bend
Finke
Kulgera
Umbeara
M. Cavenagh
Abminga
Tieyon
De Rose Hill
Lambina
Alberga
Welbourn Hill
Wintinna
M. Willoughby
Oodnadatta
M. Dutton
Algebuckina
Warrina
Edwards Creek
Boorthanna
Anna Creek
William Creek
Coober Pedy
Ingomar
Coward Springs
Bopechee
Marree
Mulgathing
The Twins 227
Millers Creek
Bon Bon
M. Eba
Tarcoola
Malbooma
Kingoonya
Andamooka
Coondambo
Pimba
Woomera
Woocalla
Penong
Koonibba
Ceduna
Wirrulla
Poochera
Nukey Bluff 472
Minnipa
Buckleboo
Iron Knob
Kyancutta
Port Kenny
Iron Baron
Kimba
Port Pirie
Whyalla
Port Augusta
Quorn
Wilmington
Carrieton
Orroroo
Nackara
Peterborough
Terowie
Jamestown
Gladstone
Spalding
Burra
Clare
Snowtown
Wallaroo
Port Broughton
Cowell
Cleve
Arno Bay
Lock
Elliston
M. Wedge
C. Finniss
Flinders I.
Investigator Group
Anxious Bay
C. Radstock
C. Blanche
P. Westall
C. Wondoma
Nuyts P. Arch.
Streaky Bay
Denial B.
Smoky B.
Brown

Urandangi
Duchess
Trekelano
Selwyn
Mc Kinlay
Kynuna
Cassilis
Dajarra
Carandotta
Noranside
Middleton
Ayrshire Downs
Collingwood
Winton
Dillcar
Corfield
Roxborough Downs
Warenda
Boulia
Hamilton
Glenormiston
Herbert Downs
Marion Downs
Springvale
Vergemont
Evesham
Coorabulka
Diamantina Lakes
Sandringham
Bedourie
Davenport Downs
Connemara
Warbreccan
Stonehenge
Cooyeana
L. Philippi
Cluny
Glengyle
L. Machattie
Monkira
Palparara
Jundah
Annandale
Mooraberree
Currawilla
Momey
Windorah
Hammond Downs
Roseberth
Betoota
Tanbar
Gilleppe
Thylungra
Birdsville
Alton Downs
L. Etamunbanie
Kyabra
M. Howitt
L. Yamma Yamma
Clifton Hills
Arrabury
Eromanga
Quilpie
Durham Downs
Mc Gregor Ra.
Cowarie
Nappamerry
Tobermory
Toompi
Innamincka
Noccundra
Norley
Thargomindah
Mungerannie
Bransby
Bulloo Downs
Urimbin
Etadunna
L. Gregory
Hungerford
L. Wyara
Muloorina
L. Blanche
Caryapundy Swamp
Callabonna
Tibooburra
Farina
Lyndhurst
Milparinka
Whyjonta
Leigh Creek
Wooltana
Mount Arrowsmith
Tongo
M. Hack 1128
Lake Frome
Blinman
Parachilna
White Cliffs
Momba
Wilpena
M. Robe 1486
Torrowangee
Mount Murchison
Wilcannia
Cultowa
Hawker
St. Mary P. 1189
Curnamona
Silverton
Cockburn
Mingary
Broken Hill
Hesso
Macfarlane
Olary
Radium Hill
L. Menindee
Menindee
Yunta
Mannahill 710
Cawndilla
Victoria L.
Canopus
Oakbank
L. Popilta
Travellers L.
Darnick
Ivanhoe
Pooncarie
Mussgiel
Willandra Billabong
Conobl

Georgina (Herbert)
Pituri
Burke
Wokingham
Diamantina
Mulligan
Eyre
Hay
Finke
Hamilton
Emery Ra.
The Macumba
Peera Peera Poolanna L.
Poolowanna L.
L. Thomas
Moonda L.
Beal Ra.
Mirranponga Pongunna L.
The Neales
Peake
Strzelecki
Barcoo or Cooper
Thomson
Barcoo
Eurinilla
Willochra
Main Barrier Ra.
Paroo
Darling
Mt. Remarkable 969
M. Bryan 934
Lake Younghusband
L. Harris
Everard
Hart
L. Labyrinthe
Pernatty Lagoon
Island Lagoon
Hambridge Nat. Park
Murlong Land Nicholls Nat. Park
Franklin Harbour
L. Gilles
Cadibarrawirracanna L.

1128 M. Brassey
12

D ↑ **218**

138° 144°

## SOUTH AUSTRALIA

Denial B. Smoky B.

Nuyts P.¹ Brown
Arch.

C. Wondoma
P.¹ Westall
C. Blanche
C. Radstock

Streaky
Bay
Port Kenny

Anxious
Bay

C. Finnis
Elliston
M.¹ Wedge
Flinders I.
Investigator Group
Mount Hope
Drummond P.¹
Kapinnie
Coffin Bay Pen.
P.¹ Whidbey
Whidbey I.¹

Wirrulla
Poochera
Nukey Bluff
·472
Minnipa
Kyancutta
Buckleboo

Lock
Murlong
and Nicholls
Nat. Park
Arno
Bay
Cummins
Tumby Bay
Wangary
Bank's
Group

Hambridge
Nat. Park
Cleve
Cowell

Hesso

Port Augusta
Wilmington
Snowtown

Iron Knob
Iron Baron
Whyalla
Port Pirie

Quorn
Carrieton
Orroroo

Mingary

Cockburn
Broken Hill

Olary
Radium Hill
Yunta
Mannahill
710

L. Menindee
Cawndilla
Lake
Tandou

Menindee

Darnick
Ivanohe

Victoria L.

Mossgiel

Nackara
Peterborough
969 M.¹
Remarkable

Oakbank

L. Popilta

Travellers

Pooncarie

Port Broughton
Gladstone
Terowie
Jamestown
M.¹ Bryan
934
Burra
Canopus

Darling

Eyre Peninsula

Spalding

Spencer Gulf

Port Kenny

Bostan I.

Maitland
Moonta
Kadina
Wallaroo

Port
Wakefield

Wardang I.
Ardrossan
Minlaton

Hardwicke
Bay

C. Donington
Corny P.¹
Thistle I.

Port
Lincoln

C. Carnot

Sleaford B.
Gambier I.¹
C. Catastrophe
C. Spencer

Stenhouse
Bay

Parndana
229·
Kingscote

C. Borda

Kangaroo I.

Maupertuis B.
Vivonne B.
D'Estree B.
C. du Couedic
C. Gantheaume
C. Willoughby
C. Hart

Clare
Robertstown
Morgan

Riverton
Eudunda
Waikerie
Kapunda
Truro

Angaston
Blanche
Town
Sedan
Yinkanie
Swan Reach

Barmera
Renmark
Loxton

Berri
Meringur

Wentworth
Merbein
Mildura

Booli
Oxley

L. Pitarpunga

Euston

L. Victoria

Red Cliffs

Robinvale

Kulwin

Maude
Hay

Balranald

Moulamein

Pcnneshaw

Investigator
Strait

36°

Parndana

Lacepede B.

C. Jaffa

C. Dombey
Robe

Kingston

Naracoorte

Penola

Millicent

·244

M.¹ Gambier

C. Banks
C. Northumberland

Discovery B.

Bordertown

Kaniva

Dimbola
Goroke
Carpolac

Aspley
Edenhope

Coleraine

Casterton

Dartmoor
Branxholme

Hamilton
Duqkeld

Portland
Port
Mc. Donnell

Heywood

Bridgewater
C. Nelson
P.¹ Danger
Portland B.
Port Fairy
Warrnambool
Port
Campbell

C. Bridgewater

C. Otway

Nhill

Natimuk
Horsham

Mortlake
Koroit

Camperdown
Colac
Timboon

Apollo Bay
Lavers Hill

Yanac

Yapeet

Hopetoun
Beulah

Birchip

Warracknabeal

Charlton

Stawell
Avoca

Ararat

Skipton
Willaura

Cressy

Queenscliff

Lismore

Jeparit

Sea Lake
Ultima

Kerang

Wycheproof
Boor

Korong
Vale
Donald

Bolangum

Maryborough

Beaufort

Skipton

Werribee

Mornington

P. Nebean
Portsea
Rosebud

Mornington Pen.

Western Port

French I.
Crib
Point

Philip I.
P. Paterson

Mt. William
1167

Rocklands
Res.

L. Bolac

L. Hindmarsh

L. Albacutya

L. Tyrrell

Swan Hill

Piangil

Ouyen

Murrayville

Wyperfield
Nat. Park

Halton Lakes
Nat. Park

Pinnaroo

Peebinga

Mindarie

Karoonda Nat. Park

Meribah

Wanganella

Conargo
Deniliquin

Kondrook

Cohuna

Mathoura

Finle
Tocumwa

Echuca

Durham Ox

Elmore
Girgarr

Bendigo

Numur

Warang
Res.

Heathcote
Mangalore

Castlemaine

Daylesford

Kyneton
Kilmore

Seymour

Broadford

800·

Alexan

Ballarat
Bacchus
Marsh

GEELONG

MELBOURNE

Healesvi

Warburton

Emeral
Dandenong
Mordialloc
Warragul

Wonthaggi

Warragu
Korumb

W. Promo
Nat.

C. Liptrap

L. Corangamite

Murray

Murray Bridge
Mannum
Tailem Bend

Meningie

Tintinara
Keith

Messent
Nat. Park

Messent
Nat. Park

A. Makin
Nat. Park

L. Alexandrina
L. Albert

Younghusband Pen.

Encounter
Bay

Willunga
Rapid
Bay
Victor Hbr

ADELAIDE

Edithburg

Elizabeth

Gawler

Mount
Baker
M.¹ Pleasant

M.¹ McDonnell

Milang

Backstairs Pass.

Port
Victoria

St Vincent
Gulf

Y O R K E

P E N.

Gambier I.¹

Mt. Lofty

S O U T H

R A N G E S

GREAT AUSTRALIAN

BIGHT

5605

INDIAN OCEAN

4960

40°
40°

944°

KING I.

Phoques B.
Yambacoona
Currie
M.¹ Stanley 213
Naracoopa

C. Wickham

Stokes P.¹

Three Hummock

Hunter I.
C. Grim

Hunter I.¹
Robbins I.

Smithton
Marrawah
Temma

Stanley
Rocky C.
Table C.
Wynyard
Burnie

Trowutta

Sawyer B.

Sandy C.

M.¹ Cleveland
914·

Hampshire

Ulverstone
Devonport

Delora

Corinna

1539·
Zeehan
Barn Bluff
Rosebery

Mole
Creek

C. Sorell

Strahan

Cradle Nat. Park

Queenstown

Derwent Bridge

1617 M.¹ Ossa

Miena
Bro
Pa

Macquarie Hbr.

P.¹ Hibbs

Pieman

Nat. Park 1450

Great Lake

Frenchman
Cap

Gordon

Hamilton

Maydena

Low Rocky P.¹

Elliot B.

Port Davey

Cox Bight

Nat.
Park

Huonvi
New Norfo

1323
M.¹ Picton
Hastings
Catamaran

Geeves

South E
Cape

BAS

VICTORIA

0   50   100 Kilomètres
0   50 Statute Miles

↑ **219**

H        J        K        150°        L        M        N        P   156°

Hermidale
Nyngan                Warrumbungle Nat. Park        Bellbrook
EW SOUTH              Gulargambone                           Smoky C.
Nymagee   Nevertire   Collie   Caraghnan Mtn   Coonabarabran   Mullaley   Walcha   Kempsey
WALES     Warren   Gilgandra   Binnaway   Tamworth   1494   Wauchope   Pt Plomer
Gilgunnia  Bobadah  Albert  573  Trangie  Mendooran  Coolah  Werris Creek  Black Sugarloaf  Port Macquarie
Mt Hope   Melrose   Narromine   Dunedoo   Cassilis   Scone   Hastings Ra.   Camden Haven
Tullamore   Dubbo   Gulgong   Merriwa   Wingham   Crowdy Head
Condobolin   Trundle   Peak Hill   Wellington   Mudgee   Muswellbrook   Gloucester   Taree
Lake      Euabalong   Bogan   Mt Barrington   Dungog   Nabiac   C. Hawke
Cargelligo  Burcher  Gate  Parkes  Molong  Rylstone  1585  Singleton  Sugarloaf Pt
Naradhan           Forbes   Orange   Hunter  1274   Maitland
Ungarie   Eugowra   1395   Bathurst   Ra.  Coricudgy   Cessnock   NEWCASTLE
Rankins           Canowindra   Blayney   Lithgow   Port Stephens
Springs   W. Wyalong   Grenfell   1204   Taralga   Blue Mtns   Broken B.   5941
Leeton   Ardlethan   Temora   Cowra   Oberon   Penrith   Gosford
Narrandera   Young   Boorowa   Blue Mountains   Parramatta   Port Jackson
Kywong          Cootamundra   Morrumburrah   (Katoomba)   SYDNEY
Wagga Wagga   Junee   Crookwell   Warragamba   Liverpool   Botany B.
Urana                Gundagai   Yass   Goulburn   Campbelltown   Sutherland
Rand   Culcairn   Tarcutta   Burrinjuck   Picton   Bulli   WOLLONGONG
Albury   Holbrook   Tumut   Res.  George   Moss Vale   Port Kembla
Wodonga          Batlow   Nowra   Shellharbour
Wangaratta   Tumbarumba   CANBERRA   Queanbeyan   Kiama
Beechworth   Yackandandah   1912   A.C.T.   Braidwood   Pt Perpendicular
Myrtleford   Corryong   Mt Bimberi   Captains   1131   Jervis Bay   A.C.T.
Bright   1721   Kosciusko   Flat   Ulladulla   St George Hd
Mt Buffalo   1986   Nat. Park   Batemans B.
Nat. Park   Mt Bogong   2230   Mt Kosciusko   Moruya   Batemans Bay
1806      Omeo   Nimmitabel   Cooma   Batehaven
1742   Dargo   Mt Cobberas   Bodalla
Mt Bowen   1837   Narooma   C. Dromedary
1372   Bonang   Cobargo   5250
Buchan   Bega
Maffra   Bairnsdale   Orbost   Cann Riv.   Bombala   Eden
Sale   Nat. Park   1295   Delegate   Green C.
Wellington   L. King   Mallacoota   Twofold B.
90 Miles Beach   C. Conran   C. Howe
02   Yarram   C. Everard   Gabo I.
Alberton   Ram Head
Snake I.
son's Promontory
East Point

TASMAN   SEA

148

Kent Group

TRAIT        Palana   North Pt
C. Frankland   316   Flinders I.
Hummock I.   Emita
Whitemark
Chappell I.   Lady Barron   FURNEAUX GROUP
686   C. Barren I.
C. Portland   Clarke I.
Bridport   Gladstone
Eddystone Pt
Herrick   B. of Fires
field   Scottsdale
Launceston   St Helens Pt
Nat. Park   1573   St Helens
Legges Tor   St Marys
Campbell   Bicheno   TASMANIA
Town
Swansea   Freycinet Pen.
Oatlands   Nat. Park
Schouten I.
Maria I.
Sorell   Marion B.
Dunalley
Forestier Pen.
BART   Port Arthur
C. Pillar
Tasman Pen.

1°   32°   2
    36°
    40°

© HACHETTE-IGN

H   150°   J   K   156°   L   M   156°   N   P

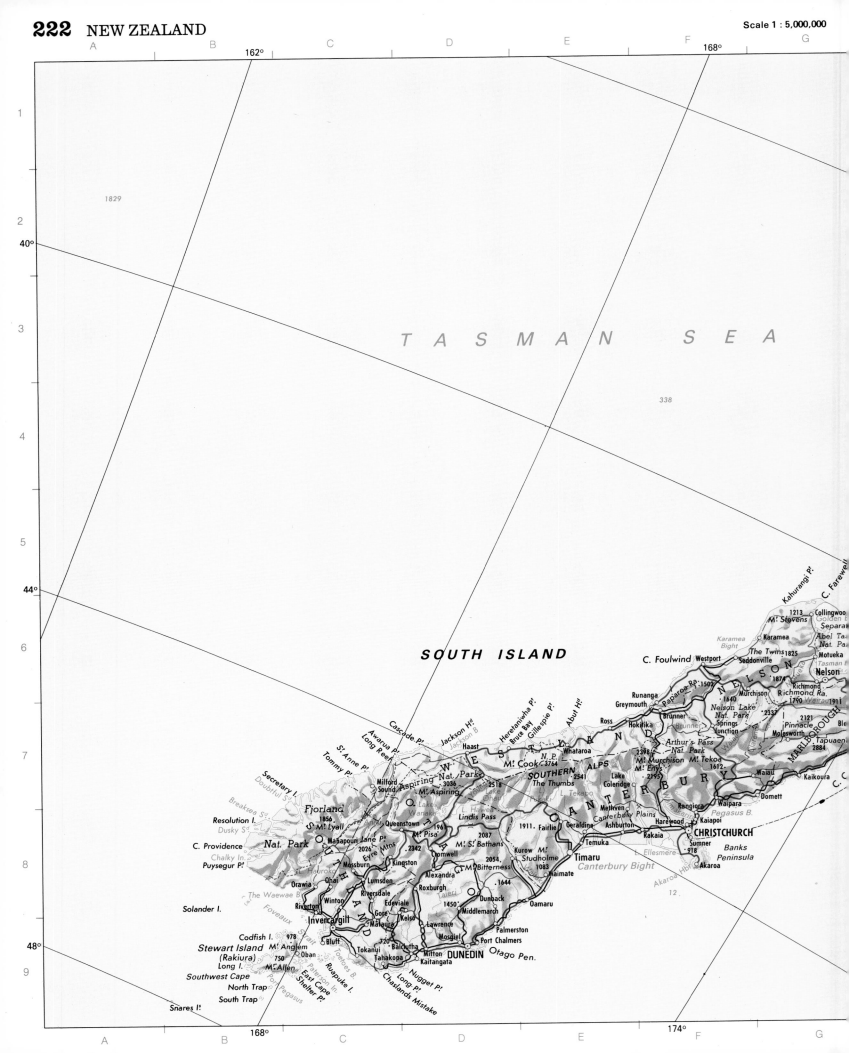

162°

168°

40°

T A S M A N   S E A

*1829*

*338*

44°

SOUTH ISLAND

1213
M! Stevens     Collingwoo
Karamea Bight        Karamea        Separa
Abel Ta
Nat. Pa
C. Foulwind   Westport   Seddonville   The Twins 1825   Motueka
187
Runanga   Paparoa Ra. 1502   Murchison   Richmond   Nelson
Greymouth   Brunner   1640   Richmond Ra.
Ross   Hokitika   Brunner   1790   Wairau 1911
Nelson Lake   2333
Nat. Park   Springs   Pinnacle   2121   Tapuaen
Junction   Molesworth   2884
Cascade P!   Jackson Hd   Heretaniwha P!   Arthur's Pass   2398
Bruce Bay   Gillespie P!   Nat. Park   Ble
Awarua P!   Haast   Abut Hd   Whataroa   M! Murchison M! Tekoa
Long Reef   Jackson B   M! Cook · 3764   M! Murchison   1612
St. Anne P!   Whataroa   M! Enys · 2195   Waiau
Tommy P!   SOUTHERN ALPS   2541   Kaikoura
Secretary I.   WEST   N. P.   The Thumbs   Lake   Domett
Doubtful S!   Milford   · 3036   Coleridge
Breaksea S!   Sound   Aspiring Nat. Park   2518   L. Tekapo
Resolution I.   Fjorland   · 2026   M! Aspiring   L. Hawea   Canterbury Plains   Rangiora   Waipara
Dusky S!   1856   Lake   Methven   Pegasus B.
M! Lyell   Wanaka   Lindis Pass   1911 · Fairlie   Geraldine   Harewood   Kaiapoi
C. Providence   Nat. Park   Queenstown   1961   2087   Ashburton   CHRISTCHURCH
Chalky In.   Manapouri Jane P!   M! Pisa   M! St Bathans   Rakaia   Sumner
Puysegur P!   2026   · 2342   2054   Kurow M!   Temuka   · 918
Eyre Mtns   Cromwell   M! Bitterness   Studholme   Timaru   Banks
Orawia   Mossburn   Alexandra   1083   Canterbury Bight   Peninsula
Ohai   Kingston   Naimate   Akaroa
Lumsden   Roxburgh   1450!   · 1644   Oamaru   Akaroa Hbr
Riverdale   Taieri   Dunback   12
Winton   Edeviale   Middlemarch
Riverton   Gore   Kelso   1450!   Palmerston
Solander I.   Invercargill   Mataura   Lawrence   Mosgiel   Port Chalmers
Codfish I.   978   Bluff   Kaitangata   Mitton   DUNEDIN   Otago Pen.
Stewart Island   M! Anglem   Oban   Tokanyi   Balclutha
(Rakiura)   750   Tahakopa   Nugget P!
Long I.   M! Allen   Ruapuke I.   Long P!
Southwest Cape   East Cape   Chaslands Mistake
North Trap   Shelter P!
Snares I!   South Trap

48°

168°         174°

A   B   C   D   E   F   G

Three Kings Is.

C. Reinga
C. Maria van Diemen
North Cape
Te Apua
Parengarenga Hbr
Te Kao
Great Exhibition B.
Rangaunu B.
Ahipara B.
Awanui
C. Karikari
Doubtless B.
Berghan P.
Tauroa P.
Kaitaia
Manganui

Cavalli I.

Okaihau
Russell
B. of Islands
C. Brett
Kaikohe
Kawakawa
Home P.
Hokianga Hbr
776

NORTHLAND

Hikurangi
Whangaruru Hbr
Dargaville
Whangarei
Poor Knights I.

Ngunguru B.
Bream Hd

Hen and Chickens I.
N. Head
Wellsford
Bream Tail
Mokohinau I.
Kaipara Harbour
Warkworth
357
C. Rodney
Helensville
722
Little
Barrier I.
Tokatu P.
Needles P.
Kawau I.
Great Barrier I.
621
C. Barrier

CENTRAL AUCKLAND
Haraki
Chan.
C. Colville
**AUCKLAND**
892
Moehau
Titirangi
Takapuna
Waiheke I.
Mercury I. (Iles d'Haussez)
Manukau Hbr
Papatoetoe
Manurewa
Papakura
Mercury B.
Waiuku
Pukekohe
Camels Back
Coromandel Peninsula
818
Thames
The Aldermen I.
Raglan Hbr
Firth of Thames

Gannet I.
Huntly
Paeroa
Kawhia Harbour
Ngaruawahia
Waihi
Albatross P.
**HAMILTON**
Morrinsville
357
Raglan
Te Aroha
Mayor I.
Tirua P.
Cambridge
Matakana I.
Te Awamutu
Matamata
M. Maunganui
Otorohanga
**Tauranga**
805
**SOUTH AUCKLAND**
Motiti I.
Awakino
Te Kuiti
Paturaru
**BAY OF PLENTY**
White I.
New Plymouth
Mangakino
321
C. Egmont
Mokau
166
Kinleith
Rotorua
Kawerau
M. Egmont
M. Pureora
Mount 1110
Whakatane
Opunake
2517
Taumarunui
Tarawera
Taneatua
Kutarere
**TARANAKI**
Murupara
Opotiki
C. Runaway
Strafford
Taupo
Urewera
Matakoa P.
Manaia
Nat. Park
Hawera
359
Huiarau Ra.
East Cape
S. Taranaki
Ngaeruhce
1403
Hikurangi
Bight
Raetihi
2291
Tongariro
Lake
1753
Patea
Ohakune
2797
Nat. Park
Waikaremoana
Ruatoria
Ruapehu
Tokomaru
Wanganui
Waiouru
Kaweka
**EAST COAST**
Taihape
724
Kaweka
Raukumara Ra.
Putorino
Tolaga Bay
Marton
1733
Gisborne
Ohakea
Napier
Poverty B.
Feilding
Hawke B.
402
**Palmerston N.**
**HAWKE'S BAY**
Table C. (Kahutara P.)
Foxton
Dannevirke
Hastings
Pen. Mahia
Levin
Woodville
Waipukurau
Otaki
1571
C. Kidnappers
802
C. Stephens
D'Urville I.
Kapiti I.
Tawa
**WELLINGTON**
Hupper Hutt
Masterton
Lower Hutt
Caterton
Featherston
Martinborough
Castelpoint
983
M. Ross
C. Turnagain
C. Palliser

NORTH
ISLAND

COOK STRAIT

**PACIFIC**

**OCEAN**

8010

0    50    100 Kilomètres
0    50 Statute Miles
H    J    174°    K    L    M    N    P
32°
2
3
4
5
36°
6
7
8
9
40°
44°
H    J    180°    K    L    M    N    P
© HACHETTE-IGN

Somes P.
177°
C. Pattison
Chatham I.
158
Te Whanga
Lagoon
Durham P.
Waitangi
C. l'Evêque
286
Hanson B.
Manukau P.
Pitt Strait
**CHATHAM ISLANDS**
295
Pitt I.
**(N. Z.)**

Scale 1 : 33,000,000

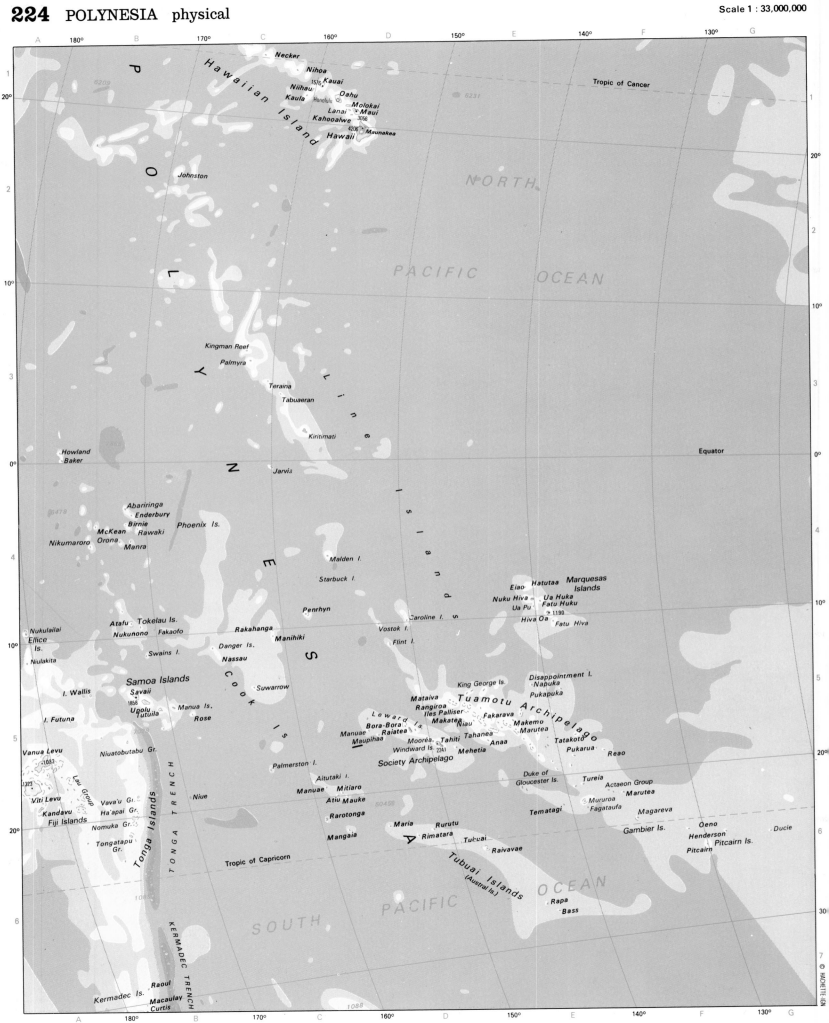

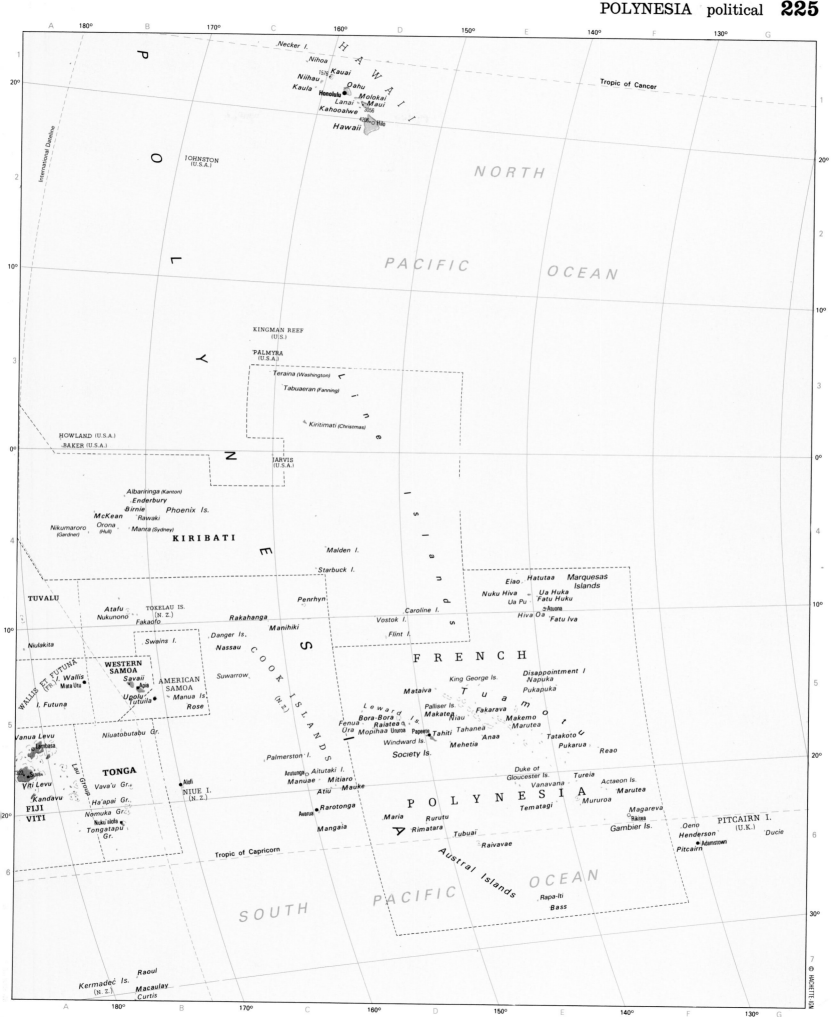

A 180° B 170° C 160° D 150° E 140° F 130° G

1

Necker I.
Nihoa
Niihau 1576 Kauai
Kaula Oahu
Honolulu Molokai
Lanai Maui
Kahooalwe 3056
Hawaii 4206 Hilo

HAWAII

Tropic of Cancer

20°

JOHNSTON
(U.S.A.)

NORTH

2

PACIFIC OCEAN

10°

KINGMAN REEF
(U.S.)

PALMYRA
(U.S.A.)

3

Teraina (Washington)
Tabuaeran (Fanning)

Kiritimati (Christmas)

Line

HOWLAND (U.S.A.)
BAKER (U.S.A.)

JARVIS
(U.S.A.)

0°

Albariringa (Kanton)
Enderbury
Birnie Phoenix Is.
McKean Rawaki
Nikumaroro Orona
(Gardner) (Hull) Manra (Sydney)

KIRIBATI

Malden I.

Starbuck I.

4

Eiao Hatutaa Marquesas
Nuku Hiva Ua Huka Islands
Ua Pu Fatu Huku
Hiva Oa Atuona
Fatu Iva

TUVALU

Atafu TOKELAU IS.
Nukunono (N.Z.)
Fakaofo

Penrhyn

Rakahanga

Caroline I.

Vostok I.

Flint I.

10°

Niulakita

Manihiki

Danger Is.
Nassau

Swains I.

WESTERN
SAMOA
Savaii
Apia
Upolu
Tutuila

Suwarrow

AMERICAN
SAMOA
Manua Is.
Rose

FRENCH

King George Is.
Disappointment I.
Napuka
Mataiva Pukapuka

5

WALLIS ET FUTUNA
(FR.) I. Wallis
Mata Utu
I. Futuna

Lewards Is.
Fenua Bora-Bora
Ura Mopihaa Ururoa
Raiatea
Papeete Tahiti
Windward Is.
Society Is.

Palliser Is.
Makatea
Niau Fakarava
Makemo
Marutea
Tahanea
Anaa
Mehetia Tatakoto
Pukarua
Reao

Tuamotu

Vanua Levu
Lambasa

Niuatobutabu Gr.

COOK ISLANDS (N.Z.)

Palmerston I.

Duke of
Gloucester Is. Tureia
Vanavana Actaeon Is.
Marutea

20°

TONGA

Vava'u Gr.

Alofi
NIUE I.
(N.Z.)

Arutunga Aitutaki I.
Manuae Mitiaro
Atiu
Mauke

Tematagi Mururoa
Magareva
Rikitea
Gambier Is.

PITCAIRN I.
(U.K.)
Oeno
Henderson Ducie
Adamstown
Pitcairn

323 Suva
Viti Levu
Kandavu
FIJI
VITI

Lau Group

Ha'apai Gr.
Nomuka Gr.
Nuku'alofa
Tongatapu Gr.

Avarua Rarotonga

Mangaia

Maria Rurutu
Rimatara
Tubuai
Raivavae

POLYNESIA

6

30°

Tropic of Capricorn

Austral Islands

Rapa-Iti
Bass

SOUTH PACIFIC OCEAN

7

Raoul
Kermadec Is. Macaulay
(N.Z.) Curtis

A 180° B 170° C 160° D 150° E 140° F 130° G

International Dateline

POLYNESIA

© HACHETTE-IGN

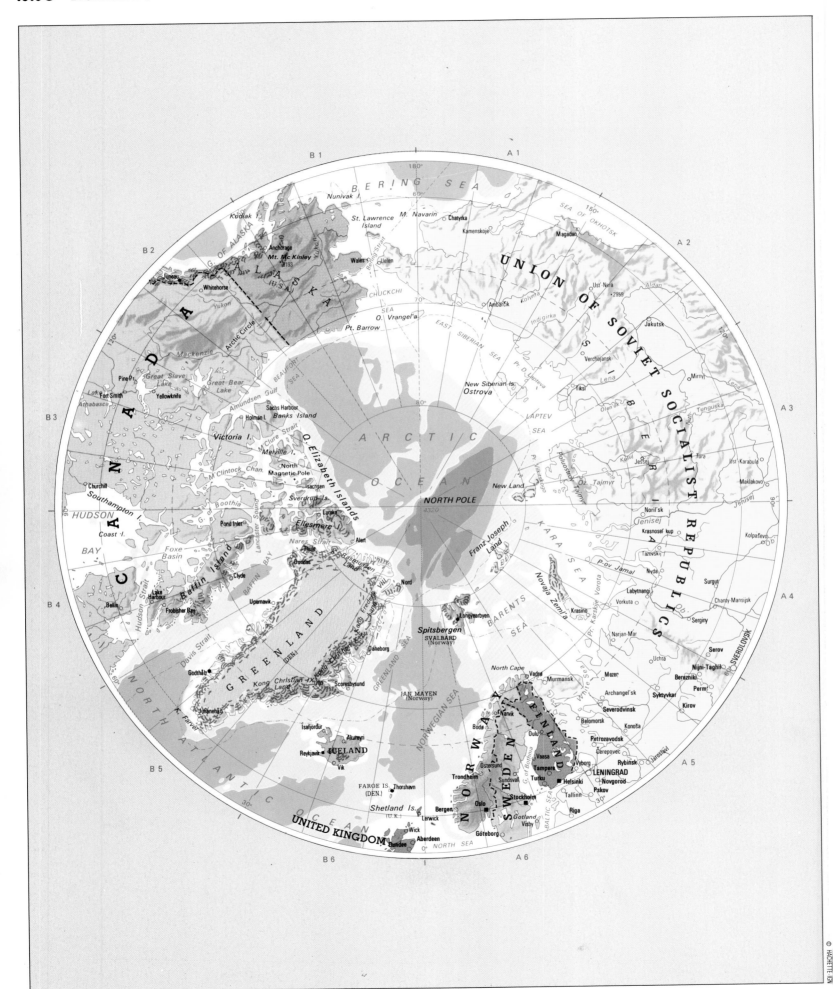

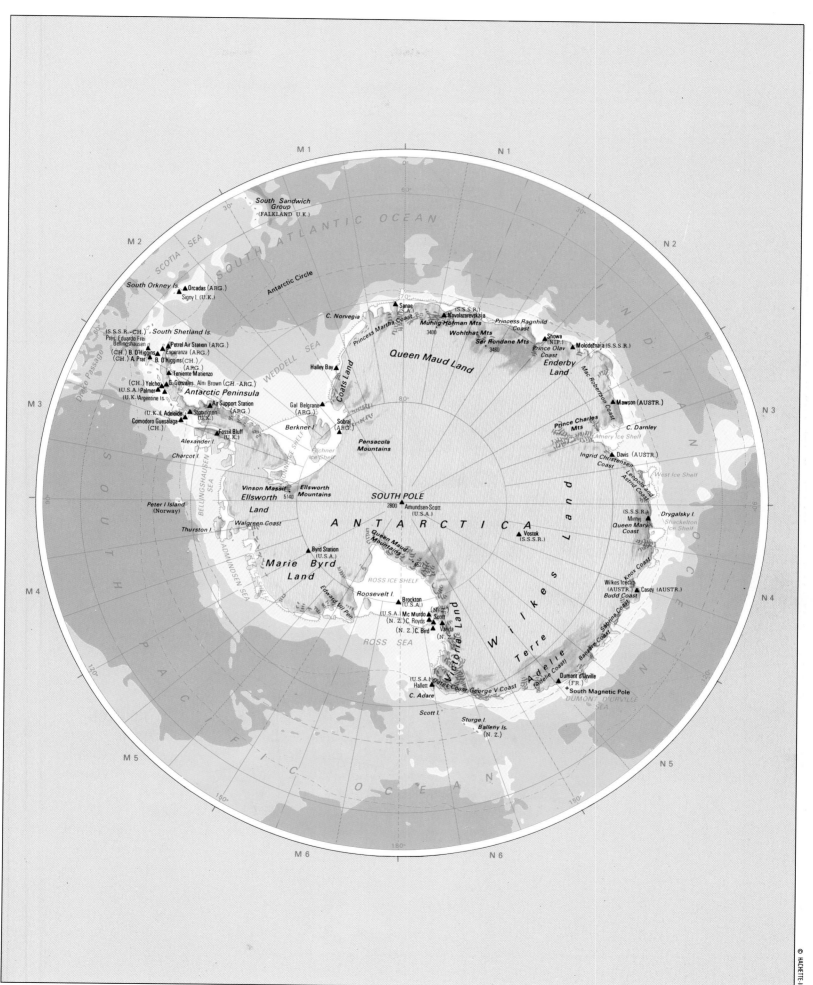

SOUTH ATLANTIC OCEAN

South Sandwich
Group
(FALKLAND U.K.)

SCOTIA SEA

Antarctic Circle

South Orkney Is.  ▲ Orcadas (ARG.)
Signy I. (U.K.)

C. Norvegia        ▲ Sanae (S.A.)
                              ▲ Novolazarevskaja (S.S.S.R.)
                              Mühlig Hofman Mts
Princess Martha Coast        Princess Ragnhild
                              Coast
(S.S.R.-CH.) South Shetland Is.   3400   Wohlthat Mts
Prés. Eduardo Frei                     Sör Rondane Mts        Showa
Bellingshausen                              3460              (N.IP.)
(CH.) B. O'Higgins  ▲ Petrel Air Station (ARG.)        Prince Olav   ▲ Molodeznaja (S.S.S.R.)
(CH.) A. Prat ▲ Esperanza (ARG.)      Queen Maud Land    Coast
         ▲ B. O'Higgins (CH.)                          Enderby
              (ARG.)              Coats Land                Land
         ▲ Teniente Matienzo   Halley Bay                           Mac Robertson Coast
(CH.) Yelcho ▲  G. Gonzales  Alm Brown (CH.-ARG.)
(U.S.A.) Palmer ▲                                                    ▲ Mawson (AUSTR.)
(U.K.) Argentine Is.   Antarctic Peninsula
(U.K.) Adelaide ▲ Stonington   Air Support Station   Gal Belgrano   Prince Charles   C. Darnley
              (U.K.)            (ARG.)    (ARG.)       Mts
Comodoro Guesalaga ▲           Sobral                        Amery Ice Shelf
(CH.)      ▲ Fossil Bluff      Berkner I.  ▲ (ARG.)
              (U.K.)                                   Ingrid Christensen  ▲ Davis (AUSTR.)
Alexander I.                   Pensacola              Coast
Charcot I.                     Mountains                    Leopold and
                                                            Astrid Coast   West Ice Shelf
           Vinson Massif   Ellsworth
           Ellsworth  5140  Mountains   SOUTH POLE
Peter I Island    Land                  ● 2800  Amundsen-Scott
(Norway)                                        (U.S.A.)              (S.S.S.R.)
                  Walgreen Coast    ANTARCTICA                        Mirnyj    Drygalsky I.
Thurston I.                                                           Queen Mary   Shackelton
                                                 ▲ Vostok             Coast         Ice Shelf
              ▲ Byrd Station   Queen Maud         (S.S.S.R.)
                 (U.S.A.)      Mountains                      Wilkes
     Marie Byrd                    4521                              Wilkes Icecap   Knox Coast
        Land                                                         (AUSTR.) ▲   ▲ Casey (AUSTR.)
              Edward VII Pen.  ROSS ICE SHELF                        Budd Coast
                       Roosevelt I.                                  Sabrina Coast
                       ▲ Brockton
                          (U.S.A.)                                            Banzare Coast
                   (U.S.A.) Mc Murdo ▲  Scott
                   (N. Z.)  C. Royds ▲ (N. Z.)         Adélie
                       (N. Z.) C. Bird ▲ Vanda         Terre        ▲ Dumont d'Urville
                                        (N. Z.)        Adélie         (FR.)
                                              Victoria  (Adélie Coast)  + South Magnetic Pole
ROSS SEA                          (U.S.A.)  Land                      DUMONT D'URVILLE
                                  ▲ Hallett  Oates Coast George V Coast   SEA
                                  C. Adare

                       Scott I.
                            Sturge I.
                            Balleny Is.
                            (N. Z.)

WEDDELL SEA
FILCHNER ICE SHELF
Filchner Ice Shelf
BELLINGSHAUSEN SEA
AMUNDSEN SEA
SOUTH PACIFIC OCEAN
Drake Passage
INDIAN OCEAN

© HACHETTE-IGN

## Scale of 1: 33,000,000 at the equator
Aitoff-Wagner projection, modified by the French National
Geographical Institute

### Heights and Depths

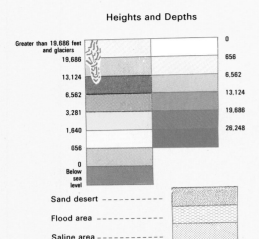

| | |
|---|---|
| Greater than 19,686 feet and glaciers | 0 |
| 19,686 | 656 |
| 13,124 | 6,562 |
| 6,562 | 13,124 |
| 3,281 | 19,686 |
| 1,640 | 26,248 |
| 656 | |
| 0 Below sea level | |

Sand desert - - - - - - - - - -

Flood area - - - - - - - - - -

Saline area - - - - - - - - - -

City, population greater than 1,000,000 - - - - - - - - - - - ○   PARIS

City, population 100,000 to 1,000,000 - - - - - - - - - - - ○   Geneva

City, population less than 100,000 - - - - - - - - - - - ○   Dover

National capital - - - - - - - - - - - ■  ■  ▪

State or provincial capital - - - - - - - - - - - ●  ●  ·

Antarctic base - - - - - - - - - - - ▲

Railway (1)   Railway under construction (2) - - - - - - (1)  (2)

Road (1)   Track (2) - - - - - - - - - - - (1)  (2)

International boundary - - - - - - - - - - - - - - - -

Spot height (1)   Sounding (2) - - - - - - - - - - - 4807 (1)  7451 (2)

Limit of ice shelf - - - - - - - - - - -

Limit of ice field - - - - - - - - - - -

---

## Scale of 1: 5,000,000
Transverse double Mercator projection

**Kilometers**
0  25  50  100  150  200  250

**Nautical miles**
0  25  50  100  150

**Statute miles**
0  50  100  150

Railway - - - - - - - - - - - - - - - - - - - - - -

Main road, year-round usability - - - - - - - - - - -

Main road, seasonal usability; or major track - - - - - -

Secondary road, year-round usability - - - - - - - - -

Secondary road, seasonal usability; or track - - - - - -

1. Main road under construction; 2. Pass - - - - - - - 1  2

Watercourse: (a) perennial; (b) seasonal - - - - - - - a  b

1. Navigable canal; 2. Non-navigable canal - - - - - - 1  2

1. Dam; 2. Waterfall or rapids; 3. Water source - - - - 1  2  3

1. Ferry; 2. Car ferry - - - - - - - - - - - 1  1  2

1. Aqueduct; 2. Oil or gas pipeline - - - - - - - - -

1. Flood area or seasonal lake; 2. Marsh or mangrove swamp - - - 1  2

1. Saline area or salt lake; 2. Sandy wetland - - - - - 1  2

1. Paddy field; 2. Coral reef; reef or shelf - - - - - 1  2  +

Boundary of park or natural reserve - - - - - - - - -

1. International airport; 2. Oil or gas field; 3. Mine - - - 1 +  2 ▴  3 ⤬

City, population greater than 1,000,000 - - - - - - - ⌂ ▢ **HOUSTON**

City, population 500,000 to 1,000,000 - - - - - - - ▢ **GLASGOW**  ▢ **QUITO**

City, population 100,000 to 500,000 - - - - - - - ◯ **PASADENA**  ◯ **MONTERIA**

City, population 25,000 to 100,000 - - - - - - - ○ Lorient  ○ Sarmiento

City, population less than 25,000; or major landmark - - - ○ Cavaillon

National capital - - - - - - - - - - - **PARIS**   **ANKARA**

Administrative center - - - - - - - - - - - ⬠  ⊡  ⊙  ⊙  ◎

International boundary - - - - - - - - - - - +++++++++++++++

++  +++  +++  +++

Other administrative boundary - - - - - - - - - -

1. Spot height; 2. Sounding - - - - - - - - - 1. 1275   2 3574

**Boundary lines:** On these topographical maps, the French National Geographical Institute has merely indicated the boundaries between states described in materials at its disposal

# INDEX

● To the left of each name the reader will find the page number followed by alpha-numerical coordinates enabling him to find the name on the map:
**61 N-8 Palermo** means that the city of **Palermo** is found on page **61** near the intersection of line N and line 8.
Abbreviations in italics specify the geographical nature of names other than those of cities:
**61 P-8 Messina** *strt.* refers to the Strait of Messina, found on page **61** near the intersection of line P and line 8.

● The names in this index are listed alphabetically.

For names of two or more words, alphabetical order holds for each word beginning with a capital letter:
**Aborlan**
**Abou Dabi**
**Abou Deia**
**Abou Simbel**
**Abounamy**

Names beginning with an article (*La; Le, Los,* etc.) are alphabetized under that article, except for France and its overseas departments and territories:
**La Habana** is listed under **La Habana**
**La Rochelle** is listed under **Rochelle (La)**

● When the name of a city, country, river, etc., has changed, the former name will most often be found in parentheses:
**109 H-7 Toamasina (Tamatave)**
For ease of reference, the following listing also will be found:
**109 H-7 Tamatave (Toamasina)**

● To clarify their location, some names — mainly countries and their capitals, large geographical regions, and principal relief lines — bear references to two different pages:
The **Appalachians** *mt* are found at G-3 on the physical map of North America (scale: 1: 33,000,000) on page **156** and at K-6 on the map of the United States (Great Lakes and North-East) (scale 1: 5,000,000) on page **171**.

## ABBREVIATIONS

| | | | | | |
|---|---|---|---|---|---|
| *bas* | basin | *lag* | lagoon, pond | *sea* | sea |
| *bay* | bay, cove | *lake* | lake, reservoir, marsh, swamp | *site* | site |
| *cal* | canal | | | *stat* | state |
| *cap* | cape, promontory | *mt* | mount, mountain, massif, summit, peak, jebel | *strt* | strait, passage |
| *col* | hill | | | *val* | valley |
| *dam* | dam | *na.p.* | natural parkland | *vol* | volcano |
| *des* | desert | *pass* | pass | *well* | well, shaft |
| *fj* | fjord | *pen* | peninsula | | |
| *ft* | forest | *pl* | plain | | |
| *glac* | glacier | *plat* | plateau | | |
| *gulf* | gulf | *pte* | point | | |
| *holl* | low-lying area | *reg* | region | | |
| *isl* | island | *rf* | reef | | |
| *isls* | islands, archipelago | *rge* | mountain range | | |
| *isth* | isthmus | *riv* | river | | |

## A

| | | |
|---|---|---|
| 50 | G-7 | Aachen |
| 57 | N-8 | Aalbeek |
| 56 | E-6 | Aalburg *reg.* |
| 56 | F-5 | Aalburg |
| 50 | F-7 | Aalet |
| 56 | D-1 | Aalsmeer |
| 56 | F-5 | Aalst (Netherlands) |
| 56 | G-4 | Aalst (Netherlands) |
| 56 | G-8 | Aalst (Netherlands) |
| 57 | M-4 | Aalten |
| 57 | N-7 | Aan den Berg |
| 49 | H-8 | Aänekoski |
| 104 | F-4 | Aansluit |
| 56 | B-8 | Aanwas |
| 56 | D-2 | Aar *riv.* |
| 59 | H-2 | Aar Wanger |
| 61 | K-1 | Aarau |
| 58 | F-3 | Aarberg |
| 59 | H-1 | Aarburg |
| 59 | J-5 | Aare *riv.* |
| 58 | F-3 | Aare *cal.* |
| 59 | H-2 | Aargau (Ober) *reg.* |
| 57 | H-7 | Aarle-Rixtel |
| 59 | H-2 | Aarwangen |
| 127 | H-7 | Ab-e Istādeh-ye Moqor *lake* |
| 127 | L-4 | Ab-e Panj *riv.* |
| 90 | B-7 | Aba (Nigeria) |
| 94 | D-7 | Aba (Zaïre) |
| 83 | J-4 | Abā ad Dūd |
| 93 | K-3 | Abadab *mt* |
| 83 | L-1 | Abādān |
| 73 | M-8 | Abādeh |
| 196 | G-1 | Abadiâna |
| 78 | F-5 | Abadla |
| 197 | J-3 | Abaete |
| 193 | J-8 | Abaetetuba |
| 132 | E-2 | Abagaqi |
| 196 | B-8 | Abai |
| 168 | A-8 | Abajo *mt* |
| 90 | C-6 | Abakaliki |
| 122 | E-4 | Abakan |
| 122 | D-4 | Abakan *riv.* |
| 122 | D-4 | Abakanskij *mt* |
| 100 | B-3 | Abakwasimbo |
| 88 | G-8 | Abala |
| 122 | F-1 | Abalakova |
| 122 | G-2 | Aban *riv.* |
| 122 | G-2 | Aban |
| 189 | L-7 | Abancay |
| 98 | C-2 | Abanga *riv.* |
| 63 | L-3 | Abano Terme |
| 73 | M-8 | Abarqū |
| 136 | A-7 | Abasiri |
| 211 | L-8 | Abau |
| 121 | H-4 | Abay |
| 95 | J-5 | Abaya *lake* |
| 122 | D-4 | Abaza |
| 58 | A-6 | Abbaye (L') |
| 56 | B-5 | Abbenbroek |
| 56 | C-2 | Abbenes |
| 53 | N-3 | Abberton |
| 50 | E-7 | Abbeville |
| 176 | D-6 | Abbeville (USA) |
| 177 | H-5 | Abbeville (USA) |
| 62 | D-3 | Abbiategrasso |

| | | |
|---|---|---|
| 215 | K-9 | Abbot *mt* |
| 52 | C-9 | Abbotsbury |
| 170 | C-4 | Abbotsford |
| 168 | D-9 | Abbott |
| 127 | L-7 | Abbottābād |
| 56 | E-1 | Abcoude |
| 96 | F-9 | Abd al Kūri *isl.* |
| 97 | H-2 | Abdal Qadr |
| 73 | H-8 | Abdānān |
| 70 | A-1 | Abdulino |
| 97 | H-1 | Abe *lake* |
| 91 | L-1 | Abéché |
| 222 | G-6 | Abel Tasman *na.p.* |
| 196 | E-8 | Abelardo Luz |
| 95 | J-3 | Abelti |
| 89 | N-3 | Abengourou |
| 51 | J-4 | Abenra |
| 89 | N-8 | Abeokuta |
| 166 | F-4 | Aber *lake* |
| 52 | A-4 | Aber Gwynft |
| 52 | A-4 | Aberavon |
| 50 | C-5 | Aberayron |
| 52 | B-4 | Abercarn |
| 101 | G-3 | Aberdare *na.p.* |
| 52 | A-4 | Aberdare |
| 152 | H-3 | Aberdeen *lake* |
| 104 | G-8 | Aberdeen (South Africa) |
| 50 | E-2 | Aberdeen (UK) |
| 176 | F-3 | Aberdeen (USA) |
| 177 | L-2 | Aberdeen (USA) |
| 169 | H-3 | Aberdeen (USA) |
| 168 | A-4 | Aberdeen (USA) |
| 162 | B-8 | Aberdeen (USA) |
| 52 | B-2 | Aberedw |
| 52 | B-4 | Aberfart |
| 52 | C-4 | Abergavenny |
| 52 | A-2 | Abergwesyn |

| | | |
|---|---|---|
| 52 | B-4 | Abersychan |
| 52 | B-5 | Aberthaw |
| 52 | B-4 | Abertillery |
| 50 | C-5 | Aberystwyth |
| 63 | J-8 | Abetone |
| 96 | B-1 | Abhā |
| 73 | J-5 | Abhar |
| 185 | N-9 | Abibe *mt* |
| 89 | P-3 | Abidjan |
| 175 | L-3 | Abilene |
| 214 | G-7 | Abingdon (Australia) |
| 52 | G-4 | Abingdon (UK) |
| 172 | A-8 | Abingdon (USA) |
| 215 | L-7 | Abington *rf* |
| 53 | L-2 | Abington |
| 72 | A-1 | Abinsk |
| 79 | H-7 | Abiod *riv.* |
| 79 | N-2 | Abiod |
| 163 | M-1 | Abitau *lake* |
| 164 | B-6 | Abitibi *lake* |
| 170 | G-1 | Abitibi *riv.* |
| 93 | N-7 | Abiy Adi |
| 72 | B-2 | Abkhaz ASSR *reg.* |
| 54 | E-2 | Ableiges |
| 218 | B-4 | Abminga |
| 81 | P-4 | Abnūb |
| 80 | E-9 | Abo *mt* |
| 94 | G-4 | Abodo |
| 139 | L-2 | Abohar |
| 89 | P-3 | Aboisso |
| 89 | N-7 | Abomey |
| 58 | C-8 | Abondance |
| 90 | F-8 | Abong Mbang |
| 149 | H-7 | Aborlan |
| 91 | K-3 | Abou Déïa |
| 192 | E-4 | Abounamy *riv.* |
| 83 | N-4 | Abqaiq |
| 200 | C-7 | Abra (del) *lag.* |

| | | |
|---|---|---|
| 191 | L-4 | Abra Pampa |
| 96 | D-4 | Abrad *riv.* |
| 181 | J-4 | Abraham's Bay |
| 60 | A-5 | Abrantes |
| 80 | F-5 | Abraq *riv.* |
| 197 | L-4 | Abre Campo |
| 186 | E-4 | Abrego |
| 174 | B-6 | Abreojos *pte* |
| 53 | L-4 | Abridge |
| 133 | K-4 | Abrog *riv.* |
| 197 | P-3 | Abrolhos *islds* |
| 172 | F-8 | Absecon |
| 92 | F-1 | Abū al Huşayn *well* |
| 82 | E-1 | Abū al Huşayn *lake* |
| 83 | L-1 | Abū al Khaşib |
| 83 | N-3 | Abū Ali *isl.* |
| 96 | C-1 | Abū'Arīsh |
| 81 | M-7 | Abū Ballāş *mt* |
| 82 | E-9 | Abū Dārah *cap.* |
| 82 | B-5 | Abū Darbah |
| 93 | H-6 | Abū Dawn |
| 118 | A-4 | Abu Dhabi |
| 84 | E-4 | Abu Dhabi *reg.* |
| 84 | D-4 | Abu Dhabi |
| 84 | D-5 | Abu Dhabi |
| 93 | J-6 | Abū Dulayq |
| 83 | M-3 | Abū Hadrīyah |
| 93 | H-3 | Abū Hamad |
| 93 | J-7 | Abū Harāz |
| 94 | B-1 | Abū Jābirah |
| 82 | E-7 | Abū Madd *cap.* |
| 94 | A-2 | Abū Maţariq |
| 81 | L-5 | Abū Minqār |
| 81 | M-3 | Abū Muḥarrik *dés* |
| 81 | N-2 | Abū Qīr |
| 82 | B-3 | Abū Qurūn *cap.* |

| | | |
|---|---|---|
| 93 | H-7 | Abū Qūţah |
| 139 | J-7 | Abu Road |
| 93 | L-2 | Abū Shajarah *pte* |
| 92 | E-7 | Abū Shanab |
| 81 | P-8 | Abu Simbel *site* |
| 83 | H-1 | Abū Sukhayr |
| 72 | G-9 | Abū Sukhayr |
| 81 | P-5 | Abu Tig |
| 92 | G-6 | Abū'Urug |
| 92 | F-2 | Abū Wulayd *mt* |
| 92 | F-9 | Abū Zabad |
| 82 | B-4 | Abū Zanīmah |
| 82 | B-4 | Abuja |
| 189 | H-6 | Abujao *riv.* |
| 136 | G-8 | Abukuma Kōti *mt* |
| 91 | M-8 | Abumonbazi |
| 190 | B-4 | Abunā |
| 190 | C-4 | Abunā *riv.* |
| 93 | N-8 | Abuna Josef *mt* |
| 222 | E-7 | Abut *pen.* |
| 148 | G-3 | Abuyog |
| 94 | E-3 | Abwong |
| 89 | P-3 | Aby *lag.* |
| 92 | D-8 | Abyad |
| 92 | E-4 | Abyad *mt* |
| 95 | K-4 | Abyata *lake* |
| 212 | F-8 | Abydos |
| 81 | P-5 | Abydos *site* |
| 94 | C-2 | Abyei |
| 186 | E-7 | Acaciás |
| 196 | B-8 | Acahay |
| 196 | G-8 | Acajutla |
| 184 | D-3 | Acajutla |
| 98 | B-1 | Acalayong |
| 178 | E-5 | Acámbaro |
| 192 | F-6 | Acampamento Grande |
| 185 | N-8 | Acandí |
| 178 | B-2 | Acaponeta *riv.* |
| 178 | F-7 | Acapulco de Juarez |

Al B-Alp □ 231


65 L-8 Al Basīt *cap.*
83 N-3 Al Bāṭinah *isl.*
93 J-4 Al Bauga
81 M-4 Al Bawīti
83 M-7 Al Bayād *mt*
96 E-4 Al Baydā
81 H-1 Al Baydā *reg.*
93 P-3 Al Birk
80 D-2 Al Bū'ayrāt
81 P-2 Al Buḥayrah al Murra *lake*
84 D-6 Al Buraymī
96 F-3 Al Burayqah
93 K-6 Al Buṭanah *mt*
72 F-8 Al Fallūja
82 F-8 Al Far'ah
96 D-6 Al Fardah
83 N-3 Al Fārisīyah *isl.*
96 B-9 Al Fatk
83 L-1 Al Faw
83 H-5 Al Fawwārah
96 B-9 Al Faydamī
96 E-2 Al Fāzih
91 L-4 Al Fifī
80 E-5 Al Fuqahā
81 J-2 Al Ghabi *well*
96 C-8 Al Ghal
73 H-9 Al Gharraf *riv.*
83 K-5 Al Ghāṭ
96 D-7 Al Ghaydah
84 D-4 Al Ghubbah *isl.*
72 E-9 Al Ghudāf *riv.*
82 B-6 Al Ghudaqah (Hurgada)
81 L-4 Al Ghurd al Kabir *hill*
80 B-3 Al Ghuzayliyah *well*
72 F-8 Al Habbānīyah
84 D-9 Al Hadd
80 F-6 Al Hadh *riv.*
72 E-8 Al Hadīthah (Iran)
82 D-2 Al Hadīthah (Iraq)
72 E-7 Al Hadr
96 C-5 Al Hajr
85 J-8 Al Hallānīyah *isl.*
82 F-2 Al Hamād *mt*
80 A-3 al Hamrā *dés*
82 F-8 Al Hamra (Saudi Arabia)
84 E-7 Al Hamra (Oman)
82 G-7 Al Hanākīyah
81 H-6 Al Harash *well*
83 L-7 Al Harīq
65 P-7 Al Hasakah
85 J-7 Al Hāsikiyah *isl.*
81 N-2 Al Hawāmidīyah
93 K-8 Al Hawātah
82 G-9 Al Hawīyah
73 J-9 Al Hawizah *lake*
96 E-5 Al Hawrā
96 D-6 Al Hawṭah
73 H-9 Al Hayy
83 L-7 Al Hillah (Saudi Arabia)
72 G-9 Al Hillah (Iraq)
92 E-8 Al Hillal
72 F-9 Al Hindīyah
83 M-4 Al Hinnah
78 F-2 Al-Hoceima
96 E-2 Al Hudaydah
83 M-5 Al Hunayy
93 J-7 Al Husayḥisah
96 C-2 Al Huṣaynīyah *well*
80 G-3 Al Husayyāt *well*
96 F-3 Al Huwaymi
82 E-3 Al Isawīyāh
81 P-2 Al Ismā'īlīyah
93 H-8 Al Jabalayn
83 P-6 Al Jāfūrah *mt*
81 J-3 Al Jaghbūb
83 L-2 Al Jahral
82 F-3 Al Jawf (Saudi Arabia)
81 J-7 Al Jawf (Libya)
93 H-6 Al Jaylī
93 H-7 Al Jazirah *mt*
84 E-4 Al Jiwā
85 J-8 Al Jubaylah *isl.*
80 D-4 Al Jufrah *riv.*
80 E-3 Al Jufrah
82 B-4 Al Junaynah *mt*
83 N-3 Al Jurayd *isl.*
83 H-6 Al Jurdhāwīyah
93 J-6 Al Kāmilīn
93 H-3 Al Kanīsah
82 C-3 Al Karak
93 H-7 Al Kawah
72 F-8 Al Kāzimīyah
64 P-7 Al Khābūr *riv.*
84 D-7 Al Khābūrah
72 F-8 Al Khālis
84 F-8 Al Khaluf
96 A-2 Al Khamasin
81 K-2 Al Khamsah *well*
92 G-4 Al Khandaq
96 D-3 Al Kharāb
81 N-6 Al Khārijah
81 N-6 Al Khārijah (Al Wāhat)
83 M-6 Al Kharj *mt*
84 B-5 Al Khaṣab
83 J-7 Al Khāṣirah
83 P-4 Al Khawr
96 D-1 Al Khawtamah *isl.*
93 N-4 Al Khubar
80 C-1 Al Khums
80 C-2 Al Khums *reg.*
83 N-6 Al Khunn
83 J-9 Al Khurmah *mt*
83 P-4 Al Khuwayr
84 F-5 Al Kidn *dés*
92 D-8 Al Kū *riv.*
72 G-9 Al Kūfah
92 G-4 Al Kuru *site*
72 G-9 Al Kūt
83 L-2 Al Kuwayt *state*
82 G-3 Al Labbah *plat.*
65 L-8 Al Ladhiqiyah (Latakia)
93 N-2 Al Līth
96 D-1 Al Luḥayyah
96 G-6 Al Madōw *mt*
82 C-2 Al Mafraq
96 D-5 Al Maghārīm
96 E-5 Al Maḥfaz
72 F-8 Al Mahmūdiyah
94 C-2 Al Malamm
93 H-7 Al Manāqil
83 L-2 Al Manāqish
96 E-3 Al Manṣūrī
80 G-1 Al Marj
84 E-4 Al Marta
96 F-4 Al Maṣāni'
84 F-9 Al Masīrah *isl.*
96 G-7 Al Maskad *mt*
93 J-5 Al Matammah
81 P-1 Al Matarīyah
72 E-6 Al Mausil
65 P-8 Al Mayādin
72 G-8 Al Miqdādīyah
83 N-5 Al Mubarraz
82 F-6 Al Mudarraj
94 B-1 Al Muglad
96 D-6 Al Mukalla
96 F-2 Al Mukhā
93 J-7 Al Musallamīyah
82 F-7 Al Musayīd
72 F-9 Al Musayyib
82 G-5 Al Mustajiddah
83 H-8 Al Muwayh
78 C-4 Al Ourir
96 B-5 Al Qa'āmīyāt *dés*
93 K-7 Al Qadārif
80 D-2 Al Qaddāḥiyah
93 P-3 Al Qaḥmah
65 P-6 Al Qāmishlī
81 P-2 Al Qanṭarah
82 F-3 Al Qārah
96 E-5 Al Qarn
84 D-3 Al Qarnayn *isl.*
80 C-3 Al Qaryah ash Sharqiyah
65 M-9 Al Qaryatayn
83 K-5 Al Qaṣab
80 C-1 Al Qaṣabāt
81 M-6 Al Qaṣr
83 N-4 Al Qatīf
80 D-7 Al Qatrūn
83 K-3 Al Qayṣūmah
83 N-3 Al Qiran *isl.*
93 P-3 Al Qunfudhah
92 D-4 Al Qurayyah *site*
82 D-2 Al Qurayyāt *reg.*
83 K-1 Al Qurnah
82 B-3 Al Quṣaymah
82 C-6 Al Quṣayr (Egypt)
65 M-9 Al Quṣayr (Libya)
65 M-9 Al Quṭayfah (Libya)
82 C-1 Al Quṭayfah (Syria)
93 H-7 Al Qutaynah
83 K-7 Al Quway'īyah
96 D-6 Al Quzah
84 G-2 Al Ubaylah
83 G-8 Al Ubayyid
72 G-9 Al Ubayyid *riv.*
82 E-6 Al Ula'
82 E-4 Al Uqayb *riv.*
80 F-3 Al'Uqaylah
83 H-5 Al'Uqaylāt
96 D-1 Al'Uqbān *isl.*
82 F-4 Al Urayq *mt*
84 G-5 Al Urūq al Mutaridah *reg.*
83 N-5 Al Uthmānīyah
80 F-2 Al'Uwayjah
81 K-9 Al Uwaynāt *mt*
72 F-8 Al Uzaym *riv.*
81 M-4 Al Wāḥat al Baḥriyah
83 M-4 Al Wannān
83 N-3 Al Wāsiṭah
92 G-7 Al Wazz
93 H-8 Al Wusā'
83 M-6 Al Yamāmah
63 J-2 Ala
72 E-4 Ala *mt*
69 M-4 Al'a (L') *riv.*
176 G-4 Alabama *state*
176 G-5 Alabama *riv.*
157 E-3 Alabama *state*
148 E-5 Alabat *isl.*
120 F-9 Alabel *pass*
65 K-5 Alaca
65 K-5 Alacahüyük *site*
65 K-4 Alacam
179 M-3 Alacrán *rf*
73 N-2 Alādagh *mt*
65 L-6 Aladağlar *mt*
130 D-4 Alag *lake*
130 A-6 Alag-Erdene
128 G-8 Alagan
130 D-3 Alaghayrhan *mt*
72 D-1 Alagir
62 B-1 Alagna Valsesia
195 P-4 Alagoa Grande
195 M-5 Alagoas *reg.*
189 H-8 Alagoas
195 L-7 Alagoinhas
206 C-1 Alahanpandjang
127 M-2 Alajskiy *mt*
185 H-7 Alajuela
158 G-3 Alakanuk
139 P-3 Alaknanda *riv.*
128 B-6 Alakol' *lake*
48 E-9 Alakurtti
192 A-7 Alalaū *riv.*
84 B-3 Alāmarvdasht *riv.*
97 M-2 Alamashindo
93 N-8 Alamata
148 C-7 Alaminos
175 H-3 Alamogordo
188 E-1 Alamor *mt*
188 E-1 Alamor *riv.*
174 E-7 Alamos
168 C-9 Alamosa
131 P-2 Alanduc
146 D-8 Alang Besar *isl.*
89 M-2 Alangouassou
63 L-1 Alano di Piave
131 L-4 Alanquan *lake*
90 F-4 Alantika *mt*
65 J-8 Alanya
108 G-6 Alaotra *lake*
89 M-9 Alapa
69 N-5 Alapayevsk
208 A-7 Alas *strt.*
122 C-5 Alaš *riv.*
64 G-7 Alaşehir
131 H-6 Alashan *reg.*
131 H-9 Alashanzuochi
152 C-3 Alaska *rge*
157 A-1 Alaska *state*
158 C-7 Alaska *pen.*
152 C-4 Alaska *pen.*
160 B-4 Alaska *state*
62 B-8 Alassio
71 L-7 Alat
159 L-5 Alatna *riv.*
67 L-1 Alatyr'
67 K-2 Alatyr' *riv.*
188 C-2 Alausi
72 E-3 Alaverdi
62 B-6 Alba
64 D-1 Alba Lulia
196 C-9 Alba Posse
60 E-6 Albacete
220 E-3 Albacutya *lake*
164 E-4 Albanel *lake*
47 E-5 Albania *state*
63 J-9 Albano *mt*
192 C-8 Albano
62 C-3 Albano Vercellese
216 F-9 Albany (Australia)
177 H-5 Albany (USA)
171 L-5 Albany (USA)
175 M-3 Albany (USA)
170 A-7 Albany (USA)
166 D-3 Albany (USA)
198 C-4 Albardón
63 K-3 Albaredo d'Adige
62 F-7 Albareto
223 J-4 Albatross *pte*
214 F-3 Albatross *bay*
124 D-3 Albazino
184 A-8 Albemarle *pte*
177 L-2 Albemarle
177 N-1 Albemarle *strt.*
62 F-1 Alben *mt*
62 B-8 Albenga
218 B-4 Alberga *riv.*
220 D-3 Albert *lake*
221 J-1 Albert
214 E-7 Albert *riv.*
211 K-7 Albert Edward *mt*
170 A-5 Albert Lea
181 H-4 Albert Town
162 G-5 Alberta *state*
198 G-7 Alberti
221 H-6 Alberton
61 J-2 Albertville
63 L-3 Albettone
58 E-6 Albeuve
60 G-3 Albi
170 B-7 Albia
63 L-3 Albignásego
102 A-4 Albina *pte*
192 E-3 Albina
63 H-6 Albinea
58 G-8 Albinen
62 F-2 Albino
169 H-6 Albion
59 K-9 Albiona *mt*
62 C-7 Albisola Marina
62 C-7 Albisola Superiore
56 C-5 Alblasserdam
56 D-4 Alblasserwaard *reg.*
78 F-2 Alborán *isl.*
78 F-2 Alboran *sea*
60 D-8 Alborán (Esp.) *isl.*
51 J-3 Alborg
162 E-5 Albreda
172 C-2 Albrightsville
58 G-7 Albristhorn *mt*
59 K-8 Albrun *pass*
185 K-5 Albuquerque *islds*
196 A-3 Albuquerque (Brazil)
175 H-1 Albuquerque (USA)
172 C-4 Alburns
221 H-4 Albury (Australia)
53 J-6 Albury (UK)
60 A-6 Alcácer do Sal
198 A-2 Alcade *pte*
148 B-5 Alcala
60 F-5 Alcalá de Chivert
60 B-7 Alcalá de Guadaira
60 D-5 Alcalá de Henares
61 M-8 Alcamo
60 C-4 Alcañices
60 F-5 Alcañiz
193 M-8 Alcântara
196 D-1 Alcantilado
60 C-6 Alcaracejos
60 D-6 Alcaraz
60 D-6 Alcaraz *mt*
60 D-6 Alcázar de S. Juan
211 P-8 Alcester *isl.*
52 E-2 Alcester
123 H-4 Alchadyr *mt*
198 E-5 Alcira
60 E-6 Alcira
197 N-3 Alcobaca
53 J-1 Alconbury
53 J-1 Alconbury Hill
60 E-6 Alcoy
60 G-6 Alcudia
108 A-5 Aldabra *islds*
178 G-3 Aldama (Mexico)
175 H-6 Aldama (Mexico)
124 C-1 Aldan *riv.*
130 B-5 Aldarhaan
52 F-5 Aldbourne
192 B-6 Aldea dos Indios Sucane
53 P-2 Aldeburgh
197 H-2 Aldeia *mt*
63 J-1 Aldeno
52 G-6 Aldermaston
223 K-4 Aldermen (The) *islds*
52 F-2 Alderminster
50 C-7 Alderney *isl.*
53 H-6 Aldershot
172 B-1 Alderson
53 P-3 Alderton
172 D-7 Aldine
52 F-4 Aldsworth
86 E-4 Aleg
78 D-8 Alegranza *isl.*
196 B-2 Alegre *riv.*
193 J-8 Alegre (Brazil)
197 M-5 Alegre (Brazil)
199 K-3 Alegrete
121 M-5 Alej *riv.*
199 H-3 Alejandra
198 E-6 Alejandro Roca
198 F-6 Alejo Ledesma
121 N-4 Alejsk
158 E-6 Aleknagik *lake*
66 G-8 Aleksandrija
67 H-2 Aleksandrov
67 N-4 Aleksandrov
70 A-1 Aleksandrovka
69 L-5 Aleksandrovsk
125 M-2 Aleksandrovsk-Sachalinskij
124 B-5 Aleksandrovskij Zavod
122 C-1 Aleksandrovskoje
128 A-8 Aleksejevka (SSSR)
121 H-2 Aleksejevka (SSSR)
121 N-2 Aleksejevka (SSSR)
121 H-1 Aleksejevka (SSSR)
123 L-1 Aleksejevsk
66 G-3 Aleksin
97 J-1 Alem Maya
197 L-6 Alem Paraiba
191 N-4 Alemaniá
50 D-8 Alençon
192 E-8 Alenquer
89 P-3 Alépé
65 M-7 Aleppo (Halab)
128 G-7 Alerji
189 J-8 Alerta
61 H-3 Alès
61 K-3 Alessandria *reg.*
62 C-5 Alessandria *reg.*
49 H-1 Alesund
128 B-9 Aletai
59 J-7 Aletschhorn *mt*
124 G-4 Aleun *riv.*
158 C-8 Aleutian *rge*
227 M-3 Alexander *isl.*
212 D-9 Alexander *mt*
156 A-1 Alexander *islds*
160 B-7 Alexander *islds*
104 B-5 Alexander *bay*
177 H-4 Alexander City
214 E-8 Alexandra *riv.*
112 C-1 Alexandra *isl.*
220 G-5 Alexandra (Australia)
161 K-9 Alexandra
222 D-8 Alexandra (New Zealand)
81 N-2 Alexandria
105 H-9 Alexandria (South Africa)
214 C-8 Alexandria (Australia)
195 M-3 Alexandria (Brazil)
64 E-3 Alexandria (Romania)
171 K-8 Alexandria (USA)
176 D-5 Alexandria (USA)
170 A-3 Alexandria (USA)
169 H-5 Alexandria (USA)
220 D-3 Alexandrina *lake*
64 F-5 Alexandroúpolis
162 D-4 Alexis Creek
188 C-2 Alfaro
197 J-5 Alfenas
64 D-8 Alfios *riv.*
53 J-7 Alfold
63 M-6 Alfonsine
195 N-2 Alfonso Bezerra
55 J-6 Alfortville
49 J-1 Alfotbreen *isl.*
162 C-5 Alfred *mt*
217 K-1 Alfred and Marie *mt*
53 L-8 Alfriston
70 D-2 Alga
70 A-3 Algabas
198 A-2 Algarrobal *riv.*
198 A-2 Algarrobal
200 A-4 Algarrobo del Aguilla
125 H-1 Algazeja
218 B-5 Algebuckina
60 B-8 Algeciras
77 C-1 Algeria *state*
61 K-6 Alghero
77 C-1 Algiers
79 K-2 Algiers
105 H-9 Algoa *bay*
195 M-4 Algodoes
188 D-7 Algodón *riv.*
170 A-5 Algona
164 C-8 Algonquin *na.p.*
199 J-5 Algorta
78 F-2 Alhucemas *islds*
82 B-8 Ali *dam.*
73 H-9 Ali al Gharbi
72 G-2 Ali Bajramly
139 J-9 Ali Rājpur
73 K-6 Aliābad *mt*
64 C-6 Aliakmon *riv.*
188 F-5 Alianza
140 C-2 Alībāg
95 J-2 Alibo
89 J-8 Alibori *riv.*
198 B-5 Alicahue
60 E-7 Alicante
219 H-3 Alice *riv.*
175 M-7 Alice
162 C-1 Alice Arm
62 C-6 Alice bel Colle
62 B-3 Alice Castello
213 L-5 Alice Downs
218 A-2 Alice Springs
180 E-2 Alice Town
105 H-9 Alicedale
176 F-4 Aliceville
61 N-7 Alicudi *isl.*
139 N-5 Alīgarh (Koil)
73 J-7 Alīgūdarz
124 D-5 Alihe
174 A-7 Alijos *rf*
73 L-8 Alījūd *mt*
211 K-3 Alim *isl.*
98 F-3 Alima *riv.*
91 M-7 Alindao
131 P-2 Alingongba
51 K-2 Alingsas
129 M-4 Alingshan *mt*
142 F-5 Alipore
139 J-2 Alīpur
142 G-2 Alīpur Duār
129 K-8 Aliushan
64 E-7 Aliverion
105 H-7 Aliwal North
96 F-2 Alkabir *isl.*
56 C-2 Alkemade *reg.*
53 P-6 Alkham
50 G-5 Alkmaar
89 N-7 Allada
142 B-2 Allāhābād (India)
139 J-3 Allāhābād (Pakistan)
159 L-6 Allakaket
58 B-7 Allaman
172 E-3 Allanmichy
80 B-2 Allāq *well*
82 C-9 Allāquī *riv.*
60 B-3 Allariz
170 E-6 Allegan
171 H-8 Allegheny *mt*
171 H-6 Allegheny *riv.*
156 F-3 Allegheny *rge*
160 C-2 Allen *mt*
148 F-3 Allen
177 K-3 Allendale
175 K-6 Allende
172 F-5 Allentown (USA)
172 C-4 Allentown (USA)
141 K-4 Alleppey
52 F-1 Allesley
53 M-5 Allhallow
171 H-7 Alliance (USA)
168 E-6 Alliance (USA)
215 P-4 Allier *bay*
61 H-2 Allier *riv.*
213 P-1 Alligator *riv.*
180 F-7 Alligator Pond
51 L-4 Allinge-Sandvig
58 B-8 Allinges
52 E-6 Allington
162 B-4 Allison Harbour
50 D-2 Alloa
172 D-8 Alloway
172 D-8 Alloway's *riv.*
54 E-5 Alluets *ft*
54 E-5 Alluets-le-Roi (Les)
227 M-2 Alm Brown
164 E-5 Alma (Canada)
165 J-7 Alma (Canada)
177 K-5 Alma (USA)
168 G-7 Alma (USA)
170 F-5 Alma (USA)
128 C-2 Alma Ata
60 A-5 Almada
215 H-7 Almaden
198 E-5 Almafuerte
71 P-4 Almalyk
60 E-6 Almansa
194 E-7 Almas
194 D-9 Almas *riv.*
194 G-7 Almas
60 E-4 Almazán
120 D-9 Almazar
172 A-2 Almedia
192 F-8 Almeirim
192 F-7 Almeirim *mt*
57 N-1 Almelo
57 L-2 Almen
197 M-1 Almenara
60 B-6 Almendralejo
62 F-2 Almenno san Salvatore
52 E-8 Almer
56 F-1 Almere
56 F-1 Almere Haven
60 D-8 Almería *gulf*
60 D-8 Almeria
69 L-9 Al'met'yevsk
51 L-3 Almhult
78 E-1 Almina *pte*
201 N-5 Almirantazgo (Seno del) *strt.*
185 J-8 Almirante
201 M-3 Almirante Montt *gulf*
64 D-6 Almirós
56 E-5 Almkerk
60 A-6 Almodôvar
52 D-5 Almonsbury
129 N-1 Almora
88 E-6 Almoustarat
69 L-8 Alnaši
78 D-5 Alnif
50 E-3 Alnwick
196 G-2 Aloândia
145 L-2 Along *bay*
143 K-1 Along
98 C-3 Alonha
64 E-6 Alonnisos *isl.*
163 N-9 Alonsa
196 E-7 Alonso *riv.*
208 G-6 Alor *isl.*
208 F-7 Alor *islds*
146 D-5 Alor Setar
191 K-3 Alota
217 M-2 Aloysius *mt*
198 D-1 Alpachiri (Argentina)
200 A-7 Alpachiri (Argentina)
60 B-5 Alpalhão
198 C-2 Alpasinche
62 G-7 Alpe di Succiso *mt*

50 C-4 Anglesey *pen.*
175 P-6 Angleton
164 B-7 Angliers
94 A-7 Ango
106 G-8 Angoche
107 H-8 Angoche *isl.*
77 D-6 Angola *state*
160 C-7 Angoon
71 P-7 Angor
200 D-3 Angostura
168 E-5 Angostura *lake*
60 G-2 Angoulême
197 K-6 Angra dos Reis
71 P-3 Angren
91 P-8 Angu
124 E-9 Anguang
180 E-3 Anguila *islds*
181 M-1 Anguilla *isl.*
63 L-4 Anguillara Veneta
165 L-4 Anguille *cap.*
142 D-6 Angul
198 C-2 Angulos
100 A-2 Angumu
132 E-6 Anguo
172 F-2 Angusta
159 K-5 Angutikada *mt*
103 N-5 Angwa *riv.*
135 M-7 Anhai
196 D-5 Anhandui *riv.*
196 D-4 Anhanduizinho *riv.*
196 G-3 Anhangüera
134 D-1 Anhe *riv.*
133 L-6 Anheung
51 K-3 Anholt
134 G-5 Anhua
135 L-2 Anhui *reg.*
158 F-5 Aniak *riv.*
158 F-5 Aniak
158 C-7 Aniakchak Crater *vol.*
201 M-4 Anibal Pinto *lake*
196 F-1 Anicuns
89 M-6 Anie *riv.*
194 A-7 Aniia *riv.*
193 M-9 Anil
198 A-1 Animas *pte*
191 P-1 Animas *pte*
174 F-3 Animas
168 B-8 Animas *riv.*
64 C-2 Anina
199 P-2 Anitápolis
125 P-5 Aniva *bay*
125 P-4 Aniva
125 P-5 Aniva *cap.*
108 D-8 Anivorano Nord
131 P-9 Aniyue
82 C-1 Anjar *site*
138 G-7 Anjar
99 P-2 Anjenje
206 G-5 Anjer Lor
134 G-6 Anjiang
140 F-3 Anjidiv *islds*
138 E-2 Anjira
108 F-6 Anjobony *riv.*
109 H-6 Anjozorobe
134 F-2 Ankang
108 F-5 Ankara *plat.*
65 J-5 Ankara
47 G-6 Ankara
108 F-5 Ankarafantsika *na.p.*
109 K-4 Ankaramena
109 J-5 Ankaratra *reg.*
109 H-4 Ankavandra
109 K-3 Ankazoabo
109 H-5 Ankazobe
97 H-4 Ankhor
51 K-5 Anklam
140 A-3 Anklesvar
95 L-2 Ankober
89 N-4 Ankobra *riv.*
100 C-3 Ankole *reg.*
99 P-7 Ankoro
90 C-5 Ankwé *riv.*
134 D-7 Anlong
145 J-7 Anlong Vêng
135 H-3 Anlu
133 M-7 Anmyeon *isl.*
170 F-6 Ann Arbor
67 J-5 Anna
218 B-6 Anna Creek
212 G-6 Anna Plains
79 M-2 Annaba (Bône)
192 B-4 Annai
145 L-5 Annam Cordillera *rge*
211 H-4 Annanberg
218 D-3 Annandale
171 K-8 Annapolis
165 J-7 Annapolis Royal
129 P-4 Annapürna *mt*
61 J-2 Annecy
61 J-2 Annemasse
57 P-7 Annendaal
68 D-8 Annenskij Most
55 M-5 Annet-sur-Marne
160 C-9 Annette *isl.*
165 M-3 Annieopsquotch *mt*
134 B-7 Anning

134 B-5 Anninghe *riv.*
177 H-3 Anniston
214 C-9 Annitowa
58 G-9 Anniviers *val.*
61 J-2 Annonay
62 E-1 Annone *lake*
63 N-1 Annone Veneto
172 A-5 Annville
201 P-6 Año Nuevo (Seno) *gulf*
158 E-4 Anogok
170 A-4 Anoka
109 J-6 Anosibe
109 J-4 Anosimbazaha
192 G-5 Anotaie *riv.*
180 F-7 Anotto Bay
145 N-2 Anpu
135 K-3 Anqing
133 H-7 Anqiu
83 J-3 Anşâb
51 J-8 Ansbach
170 D-3 Anse
181 J-6 Anse à Galet
181 J-7 Anse à Veau
181 N-2 Anse Bertrand
181 H-7 Anse d'Hainault
93 M-5 Anseba *riv.*
133 M-6 Anseong
186 D-6 Anserma
133 J-4 Anshan
134 D-7 Anshun
198 B-5 Ansilta *mt*
199 K-4 Ansina
213 N-2 Anson *bay*
175 L-3 Anson
88 G-6 Ansongo
173 K-1 Ansonia
189 L-7 Anta
194 E-8 Anta *riv.*
189 M-7 Antabamba
65 M-7 Antakya (Hatay)
108 E-8 Antalaha
80 G-2 Antalát *well*
108 F-4 Antalihy *bay*
65 H-8 Antalya
65 J-8 Antalya *gulf*
108 F-7 Antanambalana *riv.*
109 H-6 Antananarivo
77 G-6 Antananarivo
109 J-5 Antanifotsy
109 M-3 Antanimora
227 M-3 Antarctic *pen.*
49 J-9 Antarctique (Océan glacial)
62 F-3 Antegnate
103 L-9 Antelope
195 M-3 Antenor Navarro
60 C-7 Antequera
58 C-1 Anteuil
62 A-1 Antey St André
168 G-9 Anthony
176 A-1 Anthony (USA)
214 B-7 Anthony Lagoon
58 B-8 Anthy
78 B-5 Anti Atlas *mt*
61 K-4 Antibes
187 N-2 Antica *isl.*
165 J-4 Anticosti *isl.*
190 E-7 Antigo *riv.*
170 C-4 Antigo
165 K-6 Antigonish
59 K-8 Antigorio *val.*
181 N-2 Antigua *isl.*
179 L-9 Antigua
190 F-8 Antigua *lake*
157 H-5 Antigua and Barbuda *state*
178 F-3 Antiguo Morelos
191 N-5 Antilla
186 B-5 Antioquia *reg.*
186 D-5 Antioquia
188 B-3 Antisana *mt*
175 P-2 Antlers
191 M-2 Antofagasta *reg.*
191 M-1 Antofagasta
191 P-3 Antofagasta de la Sierra
191 N-3 Antofalla *vol.*
191 N-3 Antofalla *lake*
62 E-6 Antola *mt*
179 H-6 Antón Lizardo *pte*
108 F-8 Antongil *bay*
196 G-8 Antonina
201 H-6 Antonio de Biedma
197 L-4 Antonio Díaz
196 C-6 Antonio João
193 H-8 Antonio Lemos
168 C-9 Antonito
121 H-1 Antonovka (SSSR)
128 B-5 Antonovka (SSSR)
55 H-7 Antony
67 K-7 Antracit
108 E-7 Antsakabary
109 H-4 Antsalova
108 C-8 Antseranana
109 J-5 Antsirabe
108 E-6 Antsohihy

133 M-1 Antu
200 B-2 Antuco
200 B-2 Antuco *vol.*
190 C-6 Antuérpia
96 D-1 Antufush *isl.*
56 B-9 Antwerp
50 F-6 Antwerp
56 D-9 Antwerpen *reg.*
121 P-5 Anuj *riv.*
125 L-4 An'uj *riv.*
89 N-5 Anum *riv.*
139 K-3 Anüpgarh
139 N-5 Anüpshahr
141 M-7 Anuradhapura
159 G-4 Anvik *riv.*
159 G-4 Anvik
220 A-1 Anxious *bay*
132 E-8 Anyang
162 B-1 Anyox
122 F-3 Anža *riv.*
62 B-1 Anza *riv.*
174 B-1 Anza-Borrego *na.p.*
122 C-2 Anzhero Sudzhensk
61 M-5 Anzio
187 L-3 Anzoategui *reg.*
200 B-7 Anzoategui
127 K-2 Anzob *mt*
71 P-5 Anzob *strt.*
63 K-6 Anzola dell'Emilia
132 G-3 Aohanqi
136 D-7 Aomori
62 A-3 Aosta *reg.*
61 K-2 Aosta
61 K-2 Aosta *val.*
91 L-4 Aouk *riv.*
91 M-3 Aoukalé *riv.*
86 D-7 Aoukâr *reg.*
88 A-5 Aouker *reg.*
79 H-9 Aoulef el Ared
78 B-5 Aoulime *mt*
86 F-6 Aourou
133 N-2 Aozi
80 E-9 Aozou
145 K-9 Ap Tuyên
196 B-5 Apa *riv.*
187 N-6 Apácara *riv.*
174 G-2 Apache Creek
188 E-4 Apaga *riv.*
191 L-3 Apagado *vol.*
177 J-6 Apalachee *bay*
177 H-6 Apalachicola *riv.*
177 H-6 Apalachicola
178 G-3 Apan
188 B-9 Apaporis *riv.*
196 E-4 Aparecida do Tabuado
148 B-5 Aparri
187 N-6 Aparurén
64 B-2 Apatin
48 D-9 Apatity
192 E-3 Apatou
178 D-5 Apatzingán de la Constitución
123 N-4 Apcharok
190 D-7 Apediá *riv.*
57 K-2 Apeldoorn
57 J-1 Apeldoorns *cal.*
62 C-7 Apennin Ligure *mt*
46 E-5 Apennines *rge*
190 E-4 Apere *riv.*
64 G-3 Aphrodisias *site*
208 C-6 Api (Indonesia) *mt*
129 N-2 Api (Nepal) *mt*
225 B-5 Apia
196 G-7 Apiaí
187 N-8 Apiaú *riv.*
187 N-8 Apiaú *mt*
69 K-2 Apin (L') *riv.*
196 B-9 Apipe Grande *isl.*
168 D-9 Apishapa *riv.*
178 G-5 Apizaco
189 N-8 Aplao
149 J-2 Apo *vol.*
148 F-6 Apo *rf*
195 M-5 Apodi *riv.*
195 M-2 Apodi
191 M-5 Apolinario Savaria
82 B-7 Apollinopolis Magna (Idfu)
220 F-6 Apollo Bay
81 H-1 Apollonia *site*
190 F-2 Apolo
64 B-5 Apolonia *site*
187 N-6 Apónguao *riv.*
196 B-9 Apóstoles
66 G-9 Apostolovo
171 K-6 Appalachian *rge*
156 N-5 Appalachian *mt*
50 G-6 Appeldoorn
57 H-5 Appeltern

61 L-1 Appenzell
62 D-2 Appiano Gentile
53 M-7 Appledore
58 B-6 Apples
170 D-5 Appleton
192 G-3 Approuague *riv.*
123 P-1 Aprel'sk
54 B-4 Apremont
72 B-1 Apsheronsk
209 K-9 Apsley *strt.*
61 J-3 Apt
196 E-6 Apucarana *mt*
196 E-6 Apucarana
61 L-1 Apuiarés
64 D-1 Apulum *site*
187 H-5 Apure *reg.*
187 H-4 Apure *riv.*
189 M-8 Apurima *riv.*
189 K-6 Apurímac *riv.*
189 M-7 Apurímac
187 J-4 Apurito
189 J-6 Apurucayali *riv.*
71 P-8 Aq Chäh
127 H-4 Aq Koprük
82 C-4 Aqaba *gulf*
127 H-3 Aqcheh
73 M-7 Aqdâ
72 E-6 Aqrah
60 E-4 Aqreda
190 F-6 Aqua *riv.*
193 H-5 Aqua Doce
174 F-3 Aqua Prieta
195 M-5 Aquas Belas
173 L-2 Aquebogue
167 M-5 Aqueduct *riv.*
188 F-9 Aquidabá
196 B-6 Aquidabonmi *riv.*
196 B-4 Aquidauana *riv.*
196 B-4 Aquidauana
61 N-5 Aquila (L')
181 J-7 Aquin
187 J-8 Aquio *riv.*
130 C-3 Ar *mt*
92 G-8 Ar Rahad
93 J-7 Ar Rahad *riv.*
72 F-8 Ar Ramādi
80 G-5 Ar Ramlah
82 C-1 Ar Ramtha
65 N-7 Ar Raqqah
81 M-6 Ar Rāshidah
83 J-5 Ar Rass
65 M-8 Ar rastān
64 P-9 Ar Ratqah *riv.*
83 J-9 Ar Rawdah (Saudi Arabia)
96 E-5 Ar Rawdah (Yémen Sud)
73 H-9 Ar Rifa'i
83 L-5 Ar Rimāh
84 G-3 Ar Rimal *reg.*
82 G-8 Ar Rubad
83 L-1 Ar Rumaylah
83 N-4 Ar Rumaytha
65 P-9 Ar Rutbah
82 F-1 Ar Ruţbah
83 K-7 Ar Ruwaydah (Saudi Arabia)
83 J-5 Ar Ruwaydah (Saudi Arabia)
97 L-1 Ara Fana
93 K-4 Arab *riv.*
82 C-3 Arabah *riv.*
188 C-5 Arabela *riv.*
116 B-5 Arabian *sea*
85 M-7 Arabian *sea*
76 G-2 Arabian *pen.*
140 D-1 Arabian *sea*
76 F-2 Arabian Desert *dés*
82 B-6 Arabian Desert *dés*
187 P-6 Arabopó
187 M-9 Araçá *riv.*
195 M-6 Aracaju
194 E-1 Aracandéua *riv.*
186 E-2 Aracataca
195 M-2 Aracati
195 L-1 Aracatiaçu
196 F-5 Aracatuba
187 K-4 Aracay *riv.*
148 G-6 Araceli
195 L-7 Araci
195 L-1 Aracoiaba
187 L-2 Aracruz
197 L-2 Aracuaí
64 C-1 Arad
84 E-4 Arādah
122 E-5 Aradan
192 E-8 Aradions *riv.*
93 N-6 Arafali
93 N-1 Arafat *mt*
204 D-1 Arafura *sea*
72 E-3 Aragac *mt*
196 E-1 Aragarcas
60 E-5 Aragon *reg.*
60 E-4 Aragon *riv.*

187 M-3 Aragua
187 K-3 Aragua *reg.*
187 L-3 Aragua de Barcelona
194 D-5 Araguacema
194 D-7 Araguaçu
196 D-1 Araguaia *riv.*
196 E-1 Araguaiana
194 E-3 Araguaína
194 E-3 Araguaña
196 G-3 Araguari *riv.*
196 G-3 Araguari
194 E-2 Araguatins
88 D-1 Arãguîb *reg.*
86 B-4 Arãguîb ej Jahfa *val.*
194 D-4 Araias do Araguaia *riv.*
193 P-9 Araioses
73 J-7 Arãk
187 P-4 Arakaka
116 E-4 Arakan *rge*
143 J-7 Arakan *reg.*
143 K-7 Arakan Yoma *mt*
72 G-3 Araks *riv.*
112 D-5 Aral *sea*
70 G-3 Aral'sk
120 B-3 Aral'sk
70 B-4 Aralsor (SSSR) *lake*
67 N-5 Aralsor (SSSR) *lake*
193 H-7 Aramá *riv.*
219 H-2 Aramac
188 E-9 Aramacá *isl.*
190 F-6 Aramia *riv.*
140 C-7 Arãn *riv.*
50 B-2 Aran *isl.*
60 D-4 Aranda de Duero
209 M-2 Arandai
178 D-4 Arandas
127 L-6 Arandu
60 D-5 Aranjuez
104 D-2 Aransas
175 N-7 Aransas Pass
141 K-6 Arantãngi
196 F-3 Arantes *riv.*
145 H-7 Aranyaprathet
137 M-2 Arao
88 D-4 Araouane
168 G-7 Arapahoe
194 D-2 Arapari
199 J-4 Arapey
199 J-4 Arapey Chico *riv.*
199 J-4 Arapey Grande *riv.*
188 C-3 Arapicos
195 K-4 Arapiná
195 N-6 Arapiraca
192 E-8 Arapiri *isl.*
65 M-5 Arapkir
197 M-3 Araponga *dam.*
196 E-6 Arapongas
196 G-3 Araporã
196 F-7 Arapoti
196 G-5 Araquari
82 F-2 Ar'ar *riv.*
188 B-7 Araracuara
199 P-3 Araranguá
196 G-5 Araraquara
196 D-7 Araras *mt*
197 H-6 Araras
220 F-4 Ararat
72 E-3 Ararat (SSSR)
193 M-9 Arari
193 J-7 Arari *lake*
193 J-8 Arari *riv.*
142 F-2 Arãria
197 L-6 Araruama *lag.*
197 L-6 Araruama
195 P-3 Araruna
64 P-4 Aras *riv.*
197 N-1 Arataca
187 L-7 Aratana
86 D-8 Aratâne *well*
193 H-9 Arataú *riv.*
192 F-4 Arataye *riv.*
193 H-4 Araticu
195 L-1 Aratuba
190 A-4 Arauá *riv.*
186 G-5 Arauca
187 H-4 Arauca *riv.*
186 G-5 Arauca *riv.*
200 C-2 Araucania *reg.*
200 B-1 Arauco *gulf*
200 B-1 Arauco
197 J-4 Araujos
116 C-4 Aravalli *rge*
139 L-5 Arãvalli *mt*
211 L-5 Araware *islds*
197 H-4 Araxá
187 L-2 Araya *pen.*
95 L-3 Arba Gugu *mt*
95 J-5 Arba Minch
124 A-5 Arbagar
78 D-2 Arbaoua
51 K-8 Arbe *mt*
59 N-9 Arbedo
124 E-2 Arbi *riv.*
51 L-1 Arboga
185 N-8 Arboletes
185 N-8 Arboletes *pte*

163 M-7 Arborfield
163 P-9 Arborg
62 C-3 Arborio
91 J-2 Arboutchatak
50 D-2 Arbroath
58 A-9 Arbusigny
80 F-3 Arc des Philènes *site*
167 J-4 Arc Dome *mt*
58 B-3 Arc-sous-Cicon
60 F-2 Arcachon
177 K-8 Arcadia
179 L-5 Arcas *rf*
166 F-1 Arcata
178 E-6 Arcelia
57 K-8 Arcen
58 F-2 Arch
58 A-9 Archamps
68 F-4 Archangel'skaya Oblast *reg.*
124 G-5 Archara
125 H-5 Archara *riv.*
54 C-1 Archemont
92 C-1 Archenu *mt*
214 F-4 Archer *bay*
214 F-4 Archer *riv.*
101 H-2 Archer's Post
214 D-7 Archie *riv.*
201 J-1 Archipel Guayaneco *islds*
62 D-1 Arcisate
64 G-1 Arciz
63 J-1 Arco (Italy)
166 F-8 Arco (USA)
63 K-3 Arcole
58 B-4 Arçon
62 E-2 Arcore
195 N-5 Arcorverde
46 E-1 Arctic Ocean
55 J-6 Arcueil
63 L-3 Arcugnano
64 E-5 Arda (Bulgaria) *riv.*
62 F-5 Arda (Italy) *riv.*
72 G-4 Ardabil
72 D-3 Ardahan
73 M-9 Ardakãn
73 M-7 Ardakãn
49 J-2 Ardalstangen
67 L-1 Ardatov
67 J-2 Ardatov
97 H-4 Arde *mt*
50 B-3 Ardee
52 F-1 Arden *ft*
172 G-1 Arden
60 D-4 Ardenne *mt*
72 C-3 Ardeşen
73 L-6 Ardestãn
53 N-3 Ardleigh
221 H-3 Ardlethan
175 N-2 Ardmore
218 G-5 Ardoch
72 D-1 Ardon
220 C-2 Ardrossan
173 H-4 Ardsley
49 H-4 Are
94 D-7 Arebi
181 N-6 Arecibo
197 J-1 Areia
195 N-2 Areia Branca
192 F-7 Areião *mt*
149 H-6 Arena *isl.*
201 J-2 Arenales *mt*
179 L-4 Arenas *rf*
191 L-1 Arenas *pte*
198 G-7 Arenaza
51 J-1 Arendal
56 E-9 Arendonk
188 D-1 Arenillas
62 C-7 Arenzano
189 N-7 Arequipa *reg.*
189 N-8 Arequipa
62 F-1 Arera *mt*
126 D-6 Arere (Afghanistan)
192 F-7 Arere (Brazil)
95 K-6 Arero
199 J-4 Arerunguá *riv.*
93 M-6 Aresa
58 C-4 Areuse
61 M-4 Arezzo
130 D-8 Argaiin *riv.*
130 E-9 Argalinta
69 P-7 Argazi *lake*
62 E-1 Argegno
63 L-6 Argenta
50 D-8 Argentan
55 H-4 Argenteuil
165 P-3 Argentia
55 P-9 Argentières
62 A-8 Argentina *riv.*
183 D-6 Argentina (La) *state*
227 M-3 Argentine *isl.*
201 L-3 Argentino *lake*
60 G-1 Argenton-sur-Creuse
64 E-2 Argeşul *riv.*
126 F-7 Arghandāb *riv.*
97 M-1 Argheile

124 F-2 Argi *riv.*
95 H-3 Argio
92 F-3 Argo
64 D-8 Argolis *gulf*
64 D-8 Argos
64 C-7 Argostolion
124 C-4 Argoun *riv.*
167 L-1 Arguelle *pte*
72 E-1 Argun
89 J-9 Argungu
209 N-3 Arguni *bay*
130 B-7 Arhangay *reg.*
51 J-3 Arhus
141 P-1 Ari *isl.*
104 D-5 Ariamsvlei
63 M-5 Ariano *isl.*
63 M-5 Ariano nel Polésine
186 E-7 Ariari *riv.*
198 F-6 Arias
192 C-9 Ariaú
89 H-5 Aribinda
189 P-9 Arica (Chile)
188 C-8 Arica (Colombia)
188 C-5 Arica (Peru)
165 L-6 Arichat
217 J-8 Arid *cap.*
137 K-5 Arida
139 K-2 Arifwāla
186 E-2 Ariguani *riv.*
65 M-8 Ariḥa
168 E-7 Arikaree *riv.*
137 M-2 Arikawa
187 P-2 Arima
96 B-1 Arīn *riv.*
197 J-1 Arinos
178 D-5 Ario de Rosales
186 G-5 Ariporo *riv.*
190 B-8 Aripuaña
190 A-8 Aripuanã *riv.*
192 D-8 Ariranha *riv.*
187 L-5 Arisa *riv.*
187 J-4 Arismendi
162 A-2 Aristazabal *isl.*
200 G-6 Aristizábal *cap.*
109 H-5 Arivonimamo
191 N-3 Arizaro *lake*
198 E-7 Arizona
174 E-4 Arizona *state*
157 C-3 Arizona *state*
174 E-4 Arizpe
51 K-1 Arjäng
48 F-5 Arjeplog
186 E-3 Arjona
67 K-4 Arkadak
176 D-3 Arkadelphia
141 H-4 Arkalgud
120 F-2 Arkalyk
176 D-3 Arkansas *state*
168 G-9 Arkansas *riv.*
157 E-3 Arkansas *state*
176 B-1 Arkansas City
56 E-5 Arkel
68 E-5 Arkhangel'sk
80 D-9 Arkiafera *mt*
50 B-4 Arklow
51 K-4 Arkona *cap.*
141 H-7 Arkonam
61 H-3 Arles
52 D-1 Arley
52 D-4 Arlingham
177 H-5 Arlington (USA)
171 K-8 Arlington (USA)
175 N-3 Arlington (USA)
162 C-7 Arlington (USA)
170 D-6 Arlington Heigths
50 G-8 Arlon
218 B-2 Arltunga
89 J-7 Arly *na.p.*
216 E-7 Armadale
50 B-3 Armagh
83 L-5 Armah *mt*
96 B-7 Armah *riv.*
55 M-7 Armainvilliers *ft*
210 D-4 Armandville *riv.*
82 B-7 Armant
67 L-9 Armavir
199 P-2 Armazém
72 E-3 Armenia *rép*
114 C-5 Armenia *rép*
186 D-6 Armero *site*
219 L-8 Armidale
163 M-7 Armley
210 E-2 Armopa
169 H-5 Armour
160 C-4 Armour *mt*
52 C-1 Arms
125 L-6 Armu *riv.*
140 D-7 Armür
62 A-2 Arnad
48 A-1 Arnarfjördur *bay*
72 E-5 Arnas *mt*
65 J-9 Arnaútis *cap.*
175 M-1 Arnett
58 B-5 Arnex
214 C-3 Arnhem *cap.*
50 G-6 Arnhem

214 A-4 Arnhem Land *reg.*
213 P-1 Arnhem Land *reg.*
141 H-7 Arni
173 H-4 Arnionk
104 D-9 Arniston
119 N-6 Arno *isl.*
63 H-1 Arno *lake*
61 L-4 Arno *riv.*
220 B-2 Arno Bay
214 A-5 Arnold *riv.*
55 J-4 Arnouville-lès-Gonesse
54 C-5 Arnouvilles-lès-Mantes
48 C-6 Arnøy *isl.*
164 D-8 Arnprior
187 M-4 Aro *riv.*
187 H-2 Aroa *mt*
187 J-2 Aroa *riv.*
187 H-2 Aroa
104 D-4 Aroab
196 C-5 Aroeira
62 A-1 Arolla
191 J-1 Aroma *riv.*
191 K-1 Aroma *riv.*
211 J-5 Arona (Papua New Guinea)
62 C-2 Arona (Italie)
158 F-4 Aropuk *lake*
148 F-4 Aroroy
100 G-2 Arorr *riv.*
174 F-5 Aros *riv.*
60 A-3 Arosa *mt*
191 F-5 Aroua *mt*
88 B-2 Arouâkim *reg.*
63 L-3 Arquà Petrarca
63 L-4 Arquà Polesine
62 D-6 Arquata Scrivia
191 H-4 Arque
218 E-4 Arrabury
198 E-2 Arraga
142 D-3 Arrah (Bangladesh)
89 N-3 Arrah (Ivory Coast)
194 A-6 Arraias
194 E-7 Arraias *riv.*
194 F-8 Arraias
50 C-2 Arran *strt.*
162 B-1 Arrandale
50 F-7 Arras
187 H-7 Arrecifal
78 D-8 Arrecife
199 H-6 Arrecifes *riv.*
50 C-8 Arrée *mt*
174 G-2 Arrey
179 J-8 Arriaga
180 G-5 Arriba
53 K-2 Arrington
216 D-5 Arrino Three Springs
79 L-3 Arris
199 M-5 Arroio Grande
194 F-8 Arrojado *riv.*
50 D-7 Arromanches-les-Bains
54 G-1 Arronville
162 E-6 Arrowhead
200 E-6 Arroyo Verde
196 B-7 Arroyos y Esteros
198 G-3 Arrufó
121 H-2 Aršaly *riv.*
73 N-9 Arsenjän
125 K-8 Arsenjev
63 L-1 Arsiè
63 K-1 Arsiero
141 H-4 Arsikere
69 K-9 Arsk
215 L-2 Art *isl.*
96 G-2 Arta (Afars et Issas)
64 C-7 Arta (Greece)
178 D-6 Arteaga
180 B-4 Artemisa
63 L-1 Arten
175 J-3 Artesia
105 H-2 Artésia
59 L-3 Arth
54 D-2 Arthies
54 D-1 Arthieul
220 G-7 Arthur *riv.*
168 F-6 Arthur
216 E-8 Arthur River
222 F-7 Arthur's Pass *na.p.*
180 G-2 Arthur's Town
69 N-7 Arti
181 J-6 Artibonite *riv.*
226 A-1 Artic Ocean
161 H-2 Artic Red *riv.*
161 H-1 Artic Red River
159 N-7 Artic Village
199 J-3 Artigas *reg.*
199 K-3 Artigas
72 E-3 Artik
161 N-8 Artillery *lake*
54 E-2 Artimont
93 J-4 Artoli
133 N-1 Art'om
73 H-2 Art'om-Ostrov
122 F-3 Art'omovsk
67 J-7 Art'omovsk
123 N-1 Art'omovskij (SSSR)
69 N-5 Artomovskiy (SSSR)

65 L-5 Artova
227 M-2 Arturo Prat
72 C-3 Artvin
73 P-1 Artyk
208 A-2 Aru *cap.*
204 D-2 Aru *islds*
94 D-7 Aru
146 C-6 Aru *bay*
94 E-7 Arua
194 C-9 Aruaña
187 H-1 Aruba *isl.*
142 F-2 Arun (Nepal) *riv.*
143 K-1 Arunachal Pradesh *reg.*
53 J-8 Arundel
218 C-3 Arunta *dés*
141 L-5 Aruppukkottai
96 F-3 Arūs
101 H-5 Arusha
100 G-5 Arusha *reg.*
101 H-5 Arusha Chini
95 K-3 Arusi *mt*
141 L-7 Aruvi *riv.*
99 N-1 Aruwimi *riv.*
168 D-7 Arvada
130 D-8 Arvayheer
58 A-9 Arve *riv.*
164 F-6 Arvida
48 F-6 Arvidsjaur
51 K-1 Arvika
209 H-6 Arwala
71 N-3 Arys' *riv.*
120 D-5 Arys *lake*
120 D-5 Arys'
67 K-1 Arzamas
79 H-2 Arzew *gulf*
79 H-2 Arzew
67 N-8 Arzgir
63 K-3 Arzignano
58 F-9 Arzinol *mt*
72 E-3 Arzni
60 B-2 Arzua
60 L-8 As
57 L-8 As
   H-1 As Ela
84 D-5 Aş Sadr
81 P-3 Aş Saff
82 C-3 Aş Şāfiyah
81 J-4 Aş Şaḩrā al Libiyah *dés*
65 M-8 As Salamīyah
96 E-1 As Salif
84 E-4 As Salīmah
81 K-2 As Sallūm
83 J-2 As Salmān
82 C-2 As Salt
83 P-5 As Salwa
83 J-1 As Samāwah
84 F-3 As Sanām *hill*
84 L-7 As Sawāda *mt*
85 J-8 As Sawdā *isl.*
82 G-9 As Sayl al Kabīr
93 N-1 As Sayl al Kabīr
93 H-3 As Shallāl
93 H-1 As Sibū *site*
80 F-3 As Sidar
94 D-4 As Sudd *reg.*
96 E-6 As Sufāl
93 K-6 As Sufayyah
65 N-8 As Sukhnah
72 G-6 As Sulaymāniyah
83 M-6 As Sulaymīyah
83 L-9 As Sulayyil
83 M-5 As Sulb *mt*
94 B-2 As Sumayḩ
83 K-4 Aş Summān *mt*
83 H-9 As Sūq
96 E-4 Aş Surrah
96 E-4 Aş Suwār
82 D-1 As Suwaydā
73 H-8 As Suwayqiyah *lake*
72 G-9 As Suwayrah
187 M-5 Asa *riv.*
90 B-6 Asaba
73 H-6 Asadābād
146 D-8 Asahan *riv.*
136 B-7 Asahi *mt*
136 B-6 Asahikawa
93 P-7 Asale *lake*
89 N-5 Asamankese
122 G-2 Asansk
142 E-4 Asansol
190 F-2 Asariamas
49 H-4 Asarna
96 G-1 Asayta
209 L-1 Asbakin
95 L-2 Asbe Teferi
104 F-5 Asbesberge *mt*
69 N-6 Asbest
172 E-3 Asbury Park
173 H-5 Asbury Park
82 B-2 Ascalon *site*
190 F-6 Ascención
174 G-4 Ascension
179 P-5 Ascensión *bay*
56 F-4 Asch
51 H-8 Aschaffenburg

120 D-6 Aščikol' *lake*
121 K-4 Aščisu *riv.*
120 F-2 Aščitasty
61 N-4 Ascoli Piceno
59 M-9 Ascona
188 G-2 Ascope
53 H-5 Ascot
191 K-3 Ascotan *lake*
191 L-2 Ascotán
96 F-2 Aseb
95 K-3 Asela
48 G-5 Asele
100 F-2 Asembo
95 J-4 Asendabo (Ethiopia)
95 J-2 Asendabo (Ethiopia)
64 A-2 Asenovgrad
53 P-6 Ash
92 F-1 Ash Shabb (Egypt) *well*
81 N-8 Ash Shabb (Libya)
84 E-7 Ash Sham *mt*
72 G-9 Ash Shāmīyah
72 E-7 Ash Shaqāt
83 K-6 Ash Shaqrā
84 E-8 Ash Sharqīyah *reg.*
80 C-5 Ash Shāṭi *riv.*
83 J-1 Ash Shaṭrah
83 J-8 Ash Shifā *mt*
96 D-7 Ash Shiḩr
83 J-5 Ash Shiṣar *well*
83 H-4 Ash Shu'aybah
83 L-4 Ash Shumlūl
93 P-4 Ash Shuqayq
93 J-4 Ash Shurayk
93 M-1 Ash Shuyūkh
69 N-8 Asha
89 N-4 Ashanti *reg.*
173 J-2 Asharoken
173 N-1 Ashaway
222 E-8 Ashburton
216 E-1 Ashburton *riv.*
52 F-5 Ashbury
82 C-2 Ashdod
176 C-3 Ashdown
177 L-1 Asheboro
177 J-2 Asheville
53 N-6 Ashford
52 C-7 Ashill
53 J-8 Ashington
73 N-1 Ashkhabad
166 E-3 Ashland (USA)
168 G-9 Ashland (USA)
170 C-3 Ashland (USA)
168 D-3 Ashland (USA)
170 G-7 Ashland (USA)
170 G-3 Ashland (USA)
164 G-6 Ashland (USA)
168 G-3 Ashley
163 J-5 Ashmont
213 H-1 Ashmore *rf*
81 N-2 Ashmūn
139 M-7 Ashoknagar
52 D-2 Ashperton
82 B-7 Ashqelon
139 L-8 Ashta
171 H-6 Ashtabula
53 K-6 Ashtead
168 A-3 Ashton
164 G-2 Ashuanipi *lake*
72 E-7 Ashur *site*
53 L-7 Ashurst
53 K-3 Ashwell
63 K-1 Asiago
136 B-6 Asibetu
63 K-3 Asigliano Veneta
62 D-4 Asigliano Vercellese
137 H-7 Asikaga
210 E-5 Asike
78 E-2 Asilah
61 K-5 Asinara *gulf*
61 K-5 Asinara *isl.*
122 C-1 Asino
96 B-1 Asīr *reg.*
137 L-4 Asizuri *pte*
72 C-4 Askale
93 N-2 Askar *pte*
68 B-8 Askel'a
51 J-1 Asker
104 E-4 Askham
51 K-1 Askim
122 D-4 Askiz
48 C-3 Askja *vol.*
49 J-1 Askøy *isl.*
93 M-6 Asmera
51 L-3 Asnen *lake*
78 C-4 Asni
55 H-5 Asnières
55 J-1 Asnières-sur-Oise
63 H-4 Asola
63 L-2 Asolo
94 G-2 Asosa
93 K-3 Asoteriba *mt*
73 M-9 Aspās
168 C-7 Aspen
56 E-4 Asperen
175 L-3 Aspermont
222 D-7 Aspiring *na.p.*

222 D-7 Aspiring *mt*
220 E-4 Aspley
120 E-8 Assa *riv.*
78 A-6 Assa
93 P-7 Assa Ela
86 E-6 Assâba *reg.*
196 F-6 Assaí
143 J-2 Assam *reg.*
109 K-2 Assassins *bay*
171 L-9 Assateague *isl.*
105 L-4 Assegaai *riv.*
88 F-8 Assekkârai *riv.*
51 H-5 Assen
51 J-4 Assens
190 F-2 Assigny *lake*
163 K-5 Assiniboia
162 F-7 Assiniboine *mt*
163 M-8 Assiniboine *riv.*
164 D-4 Assinica *lake*
164 D-4 Assinica *rés*
196 F-6 Assis
62 E-1 Asso
87 P-2 Assomada
64 E-7 Assoro
88 E-3 Assouairt *mt*
108 A-6 Assumption *isl.*
190 A-6 Assunção
195 J-7 Assuruá *mt*
72 E-3 Aštarak
57 H-8 Asten
61 K-3 Asti
62 B-5 Asti *reg.*
189 L-9 Astillero
64 F-8 Astipalaia *isl.*
138 C-4 Astola *isl.*
52 E-3 Aston Cross
162 A-8 Astoria
108 A-7 Astove *isl.*
200 G-5 Astra
72 G-3 Astrachan bazar (Džalilabad)
121 H-2 Astrachanka (SSSR)
125 J-8 Astrachanka (SSSR)
70 B-7 Astrachanskij *islds*
70 A-7 Astrakan
211 J-4 Astrolabe *bay*
215 N-3 Astrolabe *rf*
60 C-3 Asturias *mt*
53 J-2 Astwood
174 B-6 Asunción *bay*
183 E-5 Asuncion
119 K-5 Asuncion *isl.*
196 A-7 Asunción (Assomption)
178 G-7 Asuncion Nochistlán
190 G-3 Asunta
84 E-6 Aswad (Al) *mt*
76 D-2 Aswan *dam.*
82 B-8 Aswān
82 B-8 Aswan
136 B-7 Asyoro
81 P-4 Asyūt
81 N-4 Asyut
128 D-1 At Baši
145 J-6 At Samat
82 C-3 Aṭ Tafilah
93 N-1 Aṭ Ṭā'if
81 J-7 At Taj
81 J-7 Aṭ Ṭallab *well*
81 H-8 Aṭ Ṭarhūni *mt*
84 E-4 Aṭ Ṭarīf
82 F-3 Aṭ Ṭawīl *mt*
92 G-8 Aṭ Ṭayyārah
72 E-9 Aṭ Ṭubal *riv.*
82 D-4 Aṭ Ṭubayq *mt*
82 B-5 Aṭ Ṭūr
82 C-2 Aṭ Ṭurayf
96 F-2 At Turbah
198 B-1 Atacama *reg.*
191 M-3 Atacama *lake*
191 M-2 Atacama *dés*
198 B-1 Atacama
182 D-5 Atacama *dés*
187 J-7 Atacavi *riv.*
188 D-8 Atacuary *riv.*
224 B-4 Atafu *isl.*
123 H-3 Atagaj
89 L-7 Atakora *reg.*
89 K-7 Atakora *mt*
89 M-6 Atakpamé
188 E-9 Atalaia do Norte
123 J-4 Atalanka
189 J-6 Atalaya
189 J-4 Atalaya *mt*
197 M-3 Ataléia
190 G-3 Atamachi *riv.*
123 P-6 Atamanovka
122 F-2 Atamanovo
208 G-7 Atambua
91 K-4 Ataouay
96 E-5 Atāq
199 K-4 Ataques
86 B-5 Atar
144 E-6 Ataran *riv.*
167 K-2 Atascadero
120 G-4 Atasu

189 H-9 Ataualpa *dam.*
208 G-6 Atauro *isl.*
208 G-6 Atauro
93 J-4 Atbara
93 K-5 Aṭbarah *riv.*
120 G-1 Atbasar
176 D-6 Atchafalaya *bay*
169 J-8 Atchison
158 G-4 Atchueelin *riv.*
159 G-4 Atcheelinguk *riv.*
172 E-7 Atco
89 M-5 Atebubu
211 H-4 Atemble
190 F-2 Atén *riv.*
192 D-4 Atereboto
172 B-6 Atglen
72 E-7 Ath Tharthār *riv.*
163 K-2 Athabasca *lake*
163 H-3 Athabasca
163 J-4 Athabasca *riv.*
127 K-9 Athārān Hazāri
50 A-3 Athenry
47 F-6 Athens
170 G-8 Athens (USA)
175 P-4 Athens (USA)
176 G-2 Athens (USA)
177 J-3 Athens (USA)
177 H-2 Athens (USA)
215 J-7 Atherton
93 P-2 Athfālah
142 D-6 Athgarh
101 J-4 Athi *riv.*
89 N-7 Athième
55 J-8 Athis-Mons
142 C-6 Athmalik
140 E-4 Athni
172 C-5 Athol
162 A-3 Athone *isl.*
64 E-6 Athos *isl.*
91 K-1 Ati
80 C-8 Ati *mt*
94 E-7 Atiak
189 N-7 Atico *riv.*
189 N-7 Atico
163 N-6 Atikameg *lake*
170 B-1 Atikokan
165 H-2 Atikonak *lake*
141 K-7 Atirāmpattinam
158 D-9 Atitak *bay*
184 C-2 Atitlán *lake*
184 C-3 Atitlán *vol.*
224 D-6 Atiu *isl.*
146 A-7 Atjeh *reg.*
146 A-6 Atjeh *riv.*
67 L-4 Atkarsk
178 F-5 Atlacomulco de Fabela
170 F-4 Atlanta (USA)
176 C-4 Atlanta (USA)
177 H-3 Atlanta (USA)
172 F-8 Atlantic *reg.*
170 A-7 Atlantic (USA)
177 N-2 Atlantic (USA)
173 H-4 Atlantic Beach
171 L-7 Atlantic City
172 G-4 Atlantic Highlands
182 F-7 Atlantic Ocean
76 B-7 Atlantic Ocean
156 H-3 Atlantic Ocean
184 F-2 Atlántida *reg.*
172 A-3 Atlas
200 F-6 Atlas *pte*
76 B-1 Atlas *rge*
130 E-5 Atlas Bogd *mt*
79 H-4 Atlas Saharien *mt*
76 C-1 Atlas Saharien *rge*
79 K-2 Atlas Tellien *rge*
160 D-6 Atlin
160 D-6 Atlin *lake*
82 C-1 Atlit *site*
171 J-7 Atloona
140 F-6 Atmakür
176 G-5 Atmore
92 F-1 Aṭmur al Kubaysh
162 C-2 Atna *mt*
191 K-4 Atocha
175 P-2 Atoka
91 M-7 Atongo-Bakari
178 D-4 Atotonilco el Alto
86 B-3 Atoui *riv.*
88 C-3 Atouila *dés*
142 G-3 Atrai *riv.*
73 M-2 Atrak *riv.*
186 C-6 Atrato *riv.*
73 L-3 Atrek *riv.*
172 F-7 Atsion
172 F-7 Attachie
55 J-3 Attainville
58 D-7 Attalens
176 G-3 Attalla
145 L-6 Attapu
79 K-4 Attar *riv.*
155 K-4 Attawapiskatt
59 M-4 Attinghausen
127 L-7 Attock

195 L-3 Baixio
102 E-5 Baixo Longa
87 H-1 Baixos do Sul *lag.*
132 F-6 Baiyangdian *lake*
132 A-6 Baiyantaohai
211 H-5 Baiyer River
93 H-4 Baiyuda *dés*
143 N-1 Baiyunding
132 B-4 Baiyunebo
135 K-4 Baizha
122 F-6 Baj-Chak
122 D-5 Baj-Tajga *mt*
64 B-2 Baja
174 B-3 Baja (Mexico) *pte*
187 P-3 Baja (Vénézuela) *pte*
156 C-4 Baja California *reg.*
174 B-3 Baja California *reg.*
208 A-7 Bajan
121 K-4 Bajanaul
123 K-5 Bajandaj
129 N-2 Bājang
130 A-8 Bajangol
123 H-3 Bajer
121 N-3 Bajevo
131 J-3 Bajiachaïdamuhu *lake*
96 E-2 Bajil
134 A-9 Bajinghe *riv.*
120 E-7 Bajkadam
123 K-6 Bajkal
69 P-5 Bajkalovo
123 K-6 Bajkal'sk
123 M-3 Bajkal'skoje
69 M-8 Bajkibaševo
71 H-1 Bajkonir
70 C-1 Bajmak
201 J-4 Bajo de los Caracoles
185 M-3 Bajo Nuevo *isl.*
131 L-5 Bajongshankou *mt*
219 L-3 Bajool
120 D-8 Bajrkum
71 M-4 Bajrkum
123 N-4 Bajsa
71 P-6 Bajsuntau *mt*
128 A-2 Bajtajlak
206 E-2 Bajunglintjir
129 N-2 Bājura
71 M-2 Bajžansaj
93 P-6 Baka *isl.*
94 D-6 Baka
69 P-8 Bakal
91 L-6 Bakala
121 K-7 Bakanas *riv.*
128 B-2 Bakanas
91 J-6 Bakassa *riv.*
121 P-1 Bakčar
206 B-3 Bake
86 F-5 Bakel
154 J-3 Baker *lake*
162 C-7 Baker *mt*
160 B-8 Baker *isl.*
201 J-3 Baker *riv.*
201 J-2 Baker *strt.*
162 C-7 Baker (USA) *lake*
167 L-5 Baker (USA)
168 E-2 Baker (USA)
166 E-6 Baker (USA)
167 L-3 Bakersfield
162 E-4 Bakerville
73 N-9 Bakhtegan *lake*
73 K-8 Bakhtiari *reg.*
192 D-3 Bakhuis *mt*
73 K-1 Bakinskich Komissarov
73 H-3 Bakinskich Komissarov
73 H-2 Bakinskij *islds*
48 B-4 Bakkafjördur
90 A-4 Bako *riv.*
95 H-5 Bako
64 A-1 Bakony *mt*
64 A-1 Bakony *reg.*
91 N-7 Bakouma
86 G-6 Bakoy *riv.*
69 P-9 Bakruz'ak
121 P-1 Baksa *riv.*
72 D-1 Baksan
94 D-8 Baku
73 H-2 Baku
146 G-9 Bakung *isl.*
146 B-7 Bakungan
72 D-2 Bakuriani
65 J-5 Balâ
126 F-3 Bālā Morghāb
116 G-6 Balabac *strt.*
149 J-8 Balabac
149 J-9 Balabac *strt.*
149 J-8 Balabac *isl.*
91 L-9 Balabala
208 A-2 Balabalangan *islds*
215 L-3 Balabio *isl.*
122 D-3 Balachčin
67 J-1 Balachna
122 E-3 Balachta
97 P-4 Bal'ad
72 F-8 Balad
83 K-6 Balādin as Sakrān
123 M-6 Bal'aga
123 J-4 Balagansk
140 C-4 Bālāghāt *mt*
140 B-8 Bālāghāt
133 H-1 Balahushi
147 L-9 Balaikarangan
91 L-6 Balakété
67 H-7 Balakleya
67 M-3 Balakovo
129 P-6 Balaling *mt*
149 K-9 Balambangan *isl.*
185 H-3 Balana
148 D-6 Balanga
99 J-2 Balangala
67 K-4 Balashov
142 E-6 Balasore
66 A-9 Balassagyarmat
64 A-1 Balaton *lake*
208 F-6 Balaurin
148 E-6 Balayan
185 L-8 Balboa
50 C-4 Balbriggan
199 J-9 Balcarce
64 F-3 Balčik
222 D-9 Balclutha
53 K-7 Balcombe
167 K-5 Bald *mt*
216 G-9 Bald *isl.*
216 F-9 Bald Head *cap.*
176 D-2 Bald Knob
198 D-6 Balde
59 K-2 Baldegg
59 K-2 Baldegger *lake*
62 B-5 Baldichieri d'Asti
63 J-2 Baldo *mt*
53 K-3 Baldock
159 K-3 Baldwin *pen.*
170 B-4 Baldwin (USA)
177 K-5 Baldwin (USA)
173 H-1 Baldwin Place
162 D-7 Baldy (Canada) *mt*
163 N-8 Baldy (Canada) *mt*
184 E-1 Baldy Beacon *mt*
174 F-1 Baldy Peak *mt*
100 E-1 Bale
97 M-2 Bale *reg.*
60 G-6 Balearic *islds*
46 D-6 Balearic *isl.*
208 D-2 Balease *mt*
147 N-8 Baleh *riv.*
197 P-3 Baleia *pte*
124 A-5 Balej
148 D-5 Baler
69 K-7 Balezino
179 P-8 Balfate
105 K-4 Balfour (South Africa)
162 E-7 Balfour (Canada)
59 H-9 Balfrin *mt*
122 F-6 Balgazyn
57 H-5 Balgoij
213 L-6 Balgoo Hill
96 E-6 Balḥāf
96 G-1 Balho
207 N-7 Bali *strt.*
204 B-2 Bali *sea*
207 P-7 Bali *isl.*
91 L-6 Bali (Rép. Centrafricaine) *riv.*
149 H-4 Baliangao
210 E-4 Baliem *riv.*
146 C-8 Balige
142 C-6 Bāliguda
64 G-6 Balikesir
208 A-1 Balikpapan
130 E-3 Balikun
130 E-3 Balikunhu *lake*
149 L-6 Balimbing
147 M-7 Balingian
148 A-5 Balintang *strt.*
148 A-5 Balintang *islds*
132 G-2 Balinzuoqi
65 N-7 Balis *site*
196 E-1 Baliza
93 P-2 Baljarshī *reg.*
91 H-5 Balkabra
64 E-4 Balkan *rge*
121 H-1 Balkašino
71 P-8 Balkh
127 H-3 Balkh
127 H-4 Balkh *riv.*
127 H-4 Balkh *reg.*
112 F-5 Balkhash *lake*
121 H-6 Balkhash
121 H-7 Balkhash *lake*
128 A-2 Balkhash *lake*
62 E-1 Ballábio
217 J-7 Balladonia
58 B-5 Ballaigues
55 H-8 Ballainvilliers
48 D-5 Ballangen
220 F-5 Ballarat
216 G-5 Ballard *lake*
50 D-2 Ballater
86 F-8 Ballé
174 C-4 Ballenas *strt.*
174 C-6 Ballenas *bay*
201 N-4 Ballenero *strt.*
227 N-6 Balleny *islds*
168 D-7 Balley
142 D-2 Ballia
219 N-7 Ballina (Australia)
50 A-3 Ballina (UK)
175 L-4 Ballinger
142 C-7 Ballipadar
172 C-4 Bally
50 C-3 Ballycastle
50 C-3 Ballymena
58 F-4 Balm
201 L-3 Balmaceda *mt*
201 M-4 Balmaceda *lake*
201 H-3 Balmaceda
58 G-7 Balmhorn *mt*
62 B-1 Balmuccia
198 F-4 Balnearia
200 B-9 Balneario Orense
200 B-9 Balneario Oriente
188 D-2 Balóa
188 D-2 Baloa *riv.*
140 C-9 Balod
102 C-2 Balombo
102 B-2 Balombo *riv.*
131 K-4 Balong
219 K-5 Balonne *riv.*
139 J-5 Bālotra
142 C-1 Balrāmpur
220 F-4 Balranald
188 G-3 Balsas
178 F-6 Balsas
194 F-4 Balsas (Brazil) *riv.*
178 E-6 Balsas (Mexico) *riv.*
195 H-3 Balseiros *riv.*
53 L-2 Balsham
194 F-4 Balsinhas *riv.*
59 H-1 Balsthal
66 E-9 Balta
199 J-4 Baltasar Brum
112 A-4 Baltic *sea*
226 A-6 Baltic *sea*
46 E-4 Baltic *sea*
66 A-4 Baltijsk
68 C-6 Baltijskij Kan *lake*
81 N-1 Balṭim
50 A-1 Baltimore (UK)
171 K-8 Baltimore (USA)
172 A-8 Baltimore (USA)
127 N-6 Baltit
184 B-8 Baltra *isl.*
59 H-8 Baltschieder
123 H-1 Balturino
211 K-2 Baluan *isl.*
195 H-5 Baluarte
116 B-4 Baluchistan *reg.*
138 D-8 Baluchistan *reg.*
147 P-8 Balui *riv.*
142 G-3 Bālurghāt
108 F-4 Baly *bay*
122 C-5 Balykča
122 D-4 Balyksa
70 B-6 Balyksi
122 G-7 Balyktyg-Chem *riv.*
188 C-2 Balzar
188 B-1 Balzar *mt*
73 N-2 Bām
91 H-5 Bam
211 J-3 Bam *isl.*
134 E-8 Bama (China)
90 F-3 Bama (Nigeria)
77 B-3 Bamako
87 H-8 Bamako
87 H-8 Bamako *reg.*
191 H-4 Bamba *reg.*
88 F-5 Bamba
91 L-7 Bamba *riv.*
188 F-3 Bambamarca
185 H-4 Bambana *riv.*
91 L-7 Bambari
172 G-6 Bamber
177 K-3 Bamberg
94 A-7 Bambesa
86 F-2 Bambey
94 A-7 Bambili
91 J-8 Bambio
89 M-4 Bamboï
90 D-7 Bamboutos *mt*
99 P-2 Bambudjo
197 J-4 Bambui
123 P-3 Bambujka *riv.*
123 P-3 Bambujka
90 D-7 Bamenda
73 M-1 Bami
127 H-5 Bāmiān
133 J-2 Bamiancheng
91 K-5 Bamingui *riv.*
91 L-5 Bamingui
91 K-5 Bamingui Bangoran *na.p.*
129 N-8 Bamohu *lake*
52 A-7 Bampton (UK)
52 F-4 Bampton (UK)
146 C-7 Bampu *riv.*
126 A-9 Bampūr *riv.*
126 A-9 Bampūr
210 G-6 Bamu *riv.*
89 H-4 Ban
145 J-3 Ban Ban
145 H-2 Ban Boun Tai
145 L-6 Ban Buang Nam
146 D-3 Ban Don *bay*
145 L-8 Ban Dôn
94 F-2 Ban Donige
145 L-7 Ban Hans Phya Bac
144 F-4 Ban Hong
144 G-2 Ban Houayxay
146 C-3 Ban Kapong
145 H-4 Ban Keun
145 L-8 Ban Mê Thuôt
146 D-3 Ban Na San
145 K-4 Ban Napè
144 G-3 Ban Pakkhop
145 H-5 Ban Phai
145 H-4 Ban Phu
144 F-6 Ban Rai
146 D-4 Ban Ron Phibun
96 E-3 Banā *riv.*
195 M-2 Banabuiu *riv.*
198 D-2 Bañado de Ovanta
196 A-3 Bañados de Otuquis *lake*
191 H-7 Bañados de Izozog *lake*
191 M-6 Bañados del Viñalito
100 F-4 Banagi
48 C-7 Banak
99 N-1 Banalia
87 H-9 Banamba
87 L-4 Banana *islds*
219 L-3 Banana
194 D-4 Bananal *riv.*
196 B-2 Bananal (Brazil) *isl.*
194 C-7 Bananal (Brazil) *isl.*
89 L-1 Banandjé
146 A-4 Bananga
94 A-5 Banangi
82 D-8 Banās *cap.*
139 K-6 Banās *riv.*
64 H-6 Banaz *riv.*
52 G-2 Banbury
218 F-7 Bancannia *lake*
184 J-7 Bancoran *isl.*
184 A-8 Bancos *bay*
164 C-9 Bancroft
126 G-5 Band-e Bāyān
126 G-4 Band-e Torkestan *mt*
71 P-9 Band-i-Turkistan *mt*
117 H-7 Banda *sea*
94 B-6 Banda
139 P-7 Bānda
174 A-2 Banda *pte*
209 K-4 Banda *islds*
204 C-2 Banda *sea*
146 A-5 Banda Atjeh
127 K-7 Bānda Dāūd Shāh
209 M-5 Banda Elat
87 M-5 Bandajuma
89 P-2 Bandama *riv.*
89 L-2 Bandama Blanc *riv.*
126 C-6 Bandān
209 K-4 Bandanaira
140 F-8 Bandar
84 A-5 Bandar Abbās
73 H-4 Bandar-Anzali
84 B-4 Bandar-e Chārak
83 M-1 Bandar-e Deylam
84 B-4 Bandar-e Lengeh
73 K-9 Bandar-e Ma Shur
83 M-1 Bandar-e Ma'shūr
126 G-4 Bandar-e Mollāhā
84 B-3 Bandar-e Nakhīlū
83 N-1 Bandar-e Rīg
73 L-3 Bandar-e Shah
83 M-1 Bandar-e Shāhpūr
118 G-6 Bandar Seri Begawan
141 N-8 Bandarawela
139 P-3 Bandarpunch *mt*
197 N-1 Bandeira
197 M-5 Bandeira *mt*
194 C-8 Bandeirante
196 C-6 Bandeirantes *isl.*
196 F-6 Bandeirantes
105 L-2 Bandelierkop
198 F-2 Bandera (Argentina)
175 M-5 Bandera (USA)
178 B-4 Banderas *bay*
140 C-8 Bandia *riv.*
88 G-3 Bandiagara
88 G-4 Bandiagara *mt*
139 M-5 Bāndikūi
130 G-8 Bandingtuoluogai
64 G-5 Bandirma
207 J-6 Bandjar
50 A-5 Bandon
140 C-2 Bāndra
129 N-2 Bandu
99 H-5 Bandundu
99 J-4 Bandundu *reg.*
207 H-6 Bandung
72 G-6 Baneh
180 G-5 Banes
162 F-6 Banff *na.p.*
162 F-6 Banff (Canada)
50 E-1 Banff (UK)
89 K-2 Banfora *mt*
89 K-2 Banfora
145 K-5 Bang-Hiang *riv.*
146 D-1 Bang Saphan
99 K-6 Banga
94 B-6 Bangadi
141 H-5 Bangalore
140 F-6 Banganapalle
90 D-7 Bangangté
142 F-5 Bangaon
91 N-7 Bangassou
135 K-1 Bangbu
131 P-4 Bangda
211 K-5 Bangeta *mt*
208 F-2 Banggai *isl.*
208 F-2 Banggai
208 E-2 Banggai *islds*
149 J-8 Banggi *isl.*
80 G-4 Banghāzi *reg.*
127 K-4 Bangī *riv.*
207 M-6 Bangil
132 F-5 Bangjun
149 N-2 Bangka (Indonesia) *isl.*
206 G-3 Bangka (Selat) *strt.*
207 M-2 Bangkai
207 M-6 Bangkalan
146 B-8 Bangkaru *isl.*
146 E-9 Bangkinang
206 D-2 Bangko
118 F-5 Bangkok
144 G-7 Bangkok
208 E-2 Bangkulu
118 E-4 Bangladesh *state*
91 J-4 Bangneu
129 K-1 Bangonghu *lake*
129 K-2 Bangongshan *mt*
50 C-3 Bangor (UK)
164 G-8 Bangor (USA)
91 L-5 Bangoran *riv.*
142 E-5 Bāngriposi
208 A-1 Bangsalsembera
148 B-6 Bangued
91 K-8 Bangui
77 E-4 Bangui
146 C-7 Bangunpurba
106 C-1 Bangweulu *lake*
132 C-5 Banhangedu
57 N-9 Banholt
181 L-7 Baní
78 C-6 Bani *mt*
89 H-2 Bani *riv.*
89 H-6 Bani
88 G-8 Bani Bangou
96 A-3 Banī Ma'ārid *dés*
81 N-3 Banī Mazār
93 P-2 Banī Sharfā
80 C-2 Banī Walīd
83 P-9 Banī Zaynān Hādh *reg.*
211 M-8 Baniara
89 J-1 Banifing *riv.*
91 N-7 Banima
82 C-1 Bāniyās
146 B-8 Banjak *islds*
140 A-9 Banjār *riv.*
207 N-3 Banjarmasin
206 F-3 Banjuasin *riv.*
86 G-2 Banjul
77 A-3 Banjul
207 N-7 Banjuwangi
207 N-7 Banjuwedang
185 K-4 Bank *isl.*
142 E-3 Bānka
214 A-7 Banka Banka
98 G-5 Bankana
89 H-3 Bankass
88 G-6 Bankilaré
162 D-8 Banks *lake*
161 P-5 Banks *pen.*
204 G-3 Banks *islds*
204 E-6 Banks *strt.*
220 D-5 Banks *cap.*
220 B-2 Bank's *islds*
222 F-8 Banks *pen.*
221 H-7 Banks *strt.*
210 G-8 Banks (Australia) *isl.*
162 B-2 Banks (Canada) *isl.*
142 E-5 Bānkura
132 B-5 Banlaqidu
143 L-4 Banmauk
146 E-5 Bannang Sata
180 F-2 Bannerman Town
62 B-1 Bannio Anzino
127 J-7 Bannu
139 N-8 Bans *mt*
140 B-3 Bānsda
142 C-1 Bānsi
66 A-9 Banska-Bystrica
90 E-6 Banso
53 K-6 Banstead
138 K-8 Bānswāra
101 M-1 Banta
208 C-7 Banta *isl.*
148 G-4 Bantayan *isl.*
148 G-4 Bantayan
207 N-7 Bantenan *cap.*
58 G-3 Bantiger *hill*
146 E-7 Banting
148 E-5 Banton *isl.*
50 A-4 Bantry
207 K-7 Bantul
138 F-8 Bāntva
52 C-6 Banwell
90 E-6 Banyo
149 J-9 Banyueansha (Half Moon) *rf*
227 N-5 Banzare Coast
92 B-6 Bao *riv.*
145 J-1 Bao Ha
145 K-1 Bao Lac
145 L-9 Bao Lôc
135 J-9 Baoan
132 F-5 Baodi
132 F-6 Baoding
125 J-7 Baodong
135 H-1 Baofeng
133 H-3 Baoguotu
134 E-1 Baoji
134 F-5 Baojing
134 E-1 Baojixian
134 G-2 Baokang
131 N-9 Baolunyuan
125 H-6 Baonanzhen
125 J-7 Baoqing
143 N-4 Baoshan
132 C-5 Baotou
86 G-7 Baoulé *riv.*
86 G-8 Baoulé *na.p.*
131 P-7 Baoxing
135 M-1 Baoying
139 J-4 Bāp
140 F-8 Bāpatla
207 N-3 Bapuju
131 L-3 Baqiakkusaier
191 M-1 Baquedano
66 D-8 Bar (SSSR)
64 B-4 Bar (Yugoslavia)
165 H-8 Bar Harbour
50 G-8 Bar-le-Duc
50 F-9 Bar-sur-Aube
209 H-3 Bara
127 N-9 Barā Lācha Lā *pass*
133 N-1 Barabaš
121 M-1 Barabinsk
121 M-1 Barabinskaya *pl.*
170 C-5 Baraboo
88 G-5 Baraboulé
195 L-2 Barabuiu *lake*
60 E-3 Baracaldo
181 H-5 Baracoa
194 C-7 Baracuju *riv.*
199 H-6 Baradero
219 K-8 Baradine *riv.*
101 H-1 Baragoi
187 H-2 Baragua *mt*
92 G-8 Bārah
181 K-7 Barahona
143 J-3 Barāil *mt*
143 J-4 Barāk *riv.*
96 D-6 Barākah *mt*
93 L-4 Barakah *riv.*
142 E-4 Barākar *riv.*
127 J-6 Barakī Barak
142 D-6 Bārākot
219 L-5 Barakula
219 L-3 Baralaba
147 P-6 Baram *riv.*
147 N-6 Baram *cap.*
192 B-1 Barama *riv.*
192 B-1 Baramanni
140 D-4 Bārāmati
219 M-5 Barambah *riv.*
127 M-7 Bārāmūla
126 C-5 Bārān *mt*
139 L-7 Bārān
66 E-4 Baran
142 F-5 Baranagar
126 D-5 Barang *reg.*
208 D-5 Barangbarang
89 H-3 Barani
185 P-7 Baranoa
160 B-7 Baranof *isl.*
66 C-5 Baranovichi
197 K-4 Barão de Cocais
195 H-3 Barão de Granjau
190 D-7 Barão de Melgaço *riv.*
196 B-1 Barão de Melgáco
207 M-6 Barat *bay*
209 H-6 Barat Daja *islds*
144 A-8 Baratang *isl.*
59 H-4 Bārau
187 P-9 Barauaná *mt*
139 N-4 Baraut
145 K-8 Barayn
185 H-7 Barba *vol.*
197 K-5 Barbacena
188 A-3 Barbacoas
185 P-7 Barbacoas *bay*
190 F-8 Barbado *riv.*
181 P-8 Barbados *isl.*
157 H-5 Barbados *state*
195 L-4 Barbalha

93 J-4 Barbar
63 L-3 Barbarano Vicentino
184 G-2 Barbareta isl.
62 G-3 Barbariga
60 F-4 Barbastro
63 K-8 Barberino di Mugello
105 L-4 Barberton
60 F-2 Barbezieux
63 H-9 Barbona mt
186 E-5 Barbosa
181 N-1 Barbuda isl.
219 H-2 Barcaldine
193 J-8 Barcarena
61 P-8 Barcellona
60 G-5 Barcelona
187 L-3 Barcelona (Vénézuela)
61 J-3 Barcelonnette
57 M-2 Barchem
172 C-9 Barclay
218 D-6 Barcoo riv.
218 G-3 Barcoo riv.
55 P-3 Barcy
62 A-2 Bard
72 F-2 Barda
200 B-4 Barda del Medio
80 E-9 Bardagué riv.
80 E-9 Bardaï
48 C-3 Bardarbunga mt
200 A-3 Bardas-Blancas
66 A-8 Bardejov
54 D-6 Bardelle
97 P-2 Bärdere
62 F-6 Bardi
81 K-1 Bardīyah
48 C-4 Bardneshorn isl.
170 E-9 Bardstown
48 D-5 Bardufoss
96 F-8 Bareda
139 P-5 Bareilly
59 P-6 Bären mt
56 C-5 Barendrecht
112 C-2 Barents sea
226 A-5 Barents sea
46 H-2 Barents sea
48 B-8 Barents sea
93 M-6 Barentu
59 N-1 Bäretswil
172 B-6 Bareville
52 E-7 Barford (UK)
52 F-2 Barford (UK)
63 H-8 Barga
96 G-8 Bärgāl
83 M-1 Barganshar
142 C-6 Bargarh
63 H-2 Barghe
55 P-1 Bargny
52 B-4 Bargoed
123 M-4 Barguzin riv.
123 M-4 Barguzin
123 M-4 Barguzinskij mt
123 M-5 Barguzinskij Zaliv bay
123 M-4 Barguzinskij Zapovednik rés
142 E-3 Bārh
206 F-1 Barhala strt.
142 D-4 Barhi
139 M-6 Bāri
61 P-8 Bari
138 K-7 Bari Sādri
61 L-6 Bari Sardo
187 K-9 Baría riv.
100 F-4 Bariadi
63 L-6 Baricella
160 C-7 Barid glac.
82 E-7 Baridi cap.
62 F-6 Barigazzo mt
96 F-2 Bāriḥ
79 L-3 Barika
127 L-6 Barīkowt
211 L-5 Barim
192 B-1 Barima riv.
187 H-4 Barinas reg.
187 H-3 Barinas
161 M-2 Baring cap.
99 K-2 Baringa
100 G-2 Baringo
100 G-2 Baringo lake
186 G-3 Barinitas
142 E-5 Baripāda
196 G-5 Bariri
81 N-6 Bāris
142 G-5 Barisal
206 D-3 Barisan mt
58 G-3 Bäriswil
207 N-2 Barito riv.
80 B-6 Barjuj riv.
84 D-7 Barkā
83 M-1 Barkan cap.
127 H-9 Bärkhān
53 L-5 Barking
162 B-6 Barkley strt.
214 C-7 Barkly plat.
105 J-7 Barkly East
53 K-3 Barkway
87 N-2 Barlavento reg.
216 D-1 Barlee mt

216 G-5 Barlee lake
61 P-5 Barletta
53 K-3 Barley
87 L-4 Barlo pte
161 P-9 Barlow lake
160 E-2 Barlow
123 J-4 Barluk
122 D-6 Barlyk riv.
209 M-2 Barma
139 H-5 Barmer
220 E-2 Barmera
220 G-8 Barn Bluff
59 P-7 Barna pass
122 B-3 Barnaul
121 P-3 Barnaul
121 N-4 Barnaulka riv.
55 M-9 Barneau
172 G-6 Barnegat bay
172 G-7 Barnegat
172 G-7 Barnegat Light
177 J-4 Barnesville
53 K-4 Barnet
53 K-4 Barnet Wood Green na.p.
57 H-2 Barneveld
53 M-1 Barnham
50 D-4 Barnsley (UK)
172 B-7 Barnsley (USA)
50 C-6 Barnstaple
52 A-8 Barnstapple Cross
90 B-5 Baro
94 G-3 Baro riv.
104 G-8 Baroe
158 G-6 Barometer mt
55 M-1 Baron
56 D-6 Baronie van Breda reg.
127 M-5 Barowghīl mt
143 H-3 Barpeta
187 H-2 Barquisimeto
84 F-9 Barr al Hikmān riv.
107 M-4 Barra pte
195 H-6 Barra
50 C-1 Barra isl.
196 G-6 Barra Bonita
195 J-8 Barra da Estiva
178 B-5 Barra de Navidad
197 L-6 Barra de São João
194 G-2 Barra do Corda
197 J-4 Barra do Funchal
196 E-1 Barra do Garcas
195 J-7 Barra do Mendes
190 A-2 Barra do Pelado
197 K-6 Barra do Pirai
199 N-3 Barra do Ribeiro
190 A-9 Barra do San Manuel
107 M-4 Barra Falsa pte
197 K-6 Barra Mensa
185 H-2 Barra Patuca
197 N-4 Barra Seca
219 L-8 Barraba
192 G-7 Barraca da Boca
196 F-9 Barracão
190 D-7 Barração de Libertade
190 B-9 Barração do Barreto
216 F-3 Barrambie
188 E-4 Barranca (Peru)
189 J-3 Barranca (Peru)
186 E-5 Barrancabermeja
200 A-3 Barrancas riv.
200 A-3 Barrancas (Argentina)
198 G-5 Barrancas (Argentina)
196 A-4 Barranca Branco
196 A-9 Barranqueras
185 P-7 Barranquilla
186 F-2 Barranquitas
195 J-1 Barras
164 C-6 Barraute
164 F-9 Barre
198 B-5 Barreal
194 G-7 Barreiras
192 C-9 Barreirinha
193 N-9 Barreirinhas
60 A-5 Barreiro
195 P-5 Barreiros
144 B-8 Barren isl.
108 G-2 Barren (Madagascar) islds
158 F-9 Barren (USA) islds
196 G-4 Barretos
213 L-5 Barrett mt
163 H-5 Barrhead
164 B-9 Barrie
223 K-3 Barrier cap.
204 E-3 Barrier Reef (Great) rf
162 E-6 Barriere
221 L-2 Barrington mt
163 N-4 Barrington lake
194 D-9 Barro Alto
193 N-9 Barro Duro riv.
197 L-2 Barrocão
212 C-7 Barron isl.
159 N-3 Barrow
153 J-2 Barrow strt.
161 P-4 Barrow (Canada) cap.

109 M-2 Barrow (Madagascar) pte
159 P-3 Barrow (USA) pte
214 A-9 Barrow Creek
50 D-4 Barrow in Furness
163 N-7 Barrows
52 B-5 Barry
164 C-8 Barrys Bay
70 G-4 Barsakel'mes isl.
70 G-6 Barsakel'mes lake
89 H-5 Barsalogo
101 H-1 Barsaloi
121 K-6 Baršatas
58 F-1 Bärschwil
140 D-4 Bärsi
120 G-3 Baršin
167 M-4 Barstow
172 B-6 Bart
145 J-3 Barthélemy pass
192 B-2 Bartica
65 J-4 Bartin
215 J-7 Bartle Frère mt
175 P-1 Bartlesville
161 K-6 Bartlett lake
168 G-6 Bartlett
172 C-4 Barto
160 B-8 Bartolome cap.
53 J-3 Barton
53 M-1 Barton Mills
66 A-5 Bartoszyce
177 K-7 Bartow
185 P-7 Baru riv.
146 D-8 Barumun riv.
123 M-7 Barun Sibertuj mt
124 A-6 Barun Torej lake
207 M-7 Barung riv.
146 C-8 Barus
130 C-2 Baruun Huuray mt
123 P-9 Baruun-Urt
89 H-1 Barwéli
219 J-7 Barwon riv.
67 L-2 Baryš
122 C-2 Barzas
62 E-1 Barzio
122 G-5 Baš Chem riv.
58 F-9 Bas-Hérémence
87 N-6 Basa hill
84 B-5 Bāsa'idū
199 H-2 Basail
127 L-7 Basāl
62 C-5 Basaluzzo
99 J-1 Basankusu
67 L-8 Bašanta
128 A-2 Basaral mt
199 H-5 Basavilbaso
121 N-5 Baščelakskij mt
61 K-1 Basel
148 G-3 Basey
105 J-8 Bashee riv.
129 H-6 Bashikejike
129 H-9 Bashikuergan
129 H-7 Bashimaergong
130 G-2 Bashituogelake
69 N-9 Bashkirskaya reg.
73 L-9 Bāsht
208 E-1 Basiano
211 M-9 Basilaki isl.
149 K-4 Basilan isl.
149 K-5 Basilan
53 L-5 Basildon
90 C-8 Basile (Santa Isabel) mt
63 P-1 Basiliano
61 P-6 Basilicata reg.
199 M-5 Basílio
140 C-6 Bāsim
168 C-3 Basin
50 D-6 Basingstoke
142 F-5 Basīrhāt
72 E-5 Başkale
171 J-2 Baskatong lake
122 C-6 Baškaus riv.
193 N-9 Baskerville cap.
67 N-6 Baskunčak lake
67 K-3 Bašmakovo
59 L-7 Basodino mt
99 M-1 Basoko
83 L-1 Basra
220 G-7 Bass strt.
224 E-6 Bass isl.
204 E-5 Bass strt.
163 H-7 Bassano (Canada)
61 M-2 Bassano (Italy)
63 L-2 Bassano del Grappa
89 L-6 Bassari
91 M-7 Basse-Kotto reg.
86 G-3 Basse Santa Su
181 M-2 Basse-Terre
181 N-2 Basse-Terre isl.
58 F-1 Bassecourt
143 K-9 Bassein riv.
144 C-5 Bassein (Birman)
140 B-3 Bassein (India)
54 A-6 Basses-Lisières
52 G-7 Basset
181 N-3 Basseterre

157 H-5 Basseterre
168 G-5 Bassett
139 M-2 Bassī
88 F-2 Bassikounou reg.
92 A-5 Basso mt
101 L-2 Basso Giuba reg.
170 C-2 Basswood lake
84 B-4 Bastak
73 M-3 Bastam
66 G-9 Baštanka
142 C-1 Basti
61 L-4 Bastia
62 A-7 Bastia Mondovi
63 J-6 Bastiglia
185 J-8 Bastimentos isl.
50 G-7 Bastogne
176 D-4 Bastrop (USA)
175 N-5 Bastrop (USA)
206 E-1 Basu cap.
103 K-8 Basuto
186 E-6 Batá riv.
98 C-1 Bata
180 B-4 Batabano gulf
56 G-8 Batadorp
148 F-3 Batag isl.
196 E-5 Bataguacu
208 B-6 Batahai strt.
127 J-7 Batai Kandao pass
207 N-4 Batakan
195 J-1 Batalha
146 G-9 Batam isl.
70 D-1 Batamšinskij
148 E-3 Batan isl.
207 K-6 Batang
131 P-5 Batang
146 E-7 Batang Berjuntai
98 B-2 Batanga
91 K-6 Batangafo
149 L-7 Batangas
209 E-6 Batangas
209 K-1 Batanta isl.
174 C-2 Bataques
197 H-5 Batatais
198 D-7 Batavia (Argentina)
171 J-5 Batavia (USA)
67 K-8 Bataysk
170 F-2 Batchawana mt
213 N-1 Batchelor
98 F-5 Batéké plat.
199 H-3 Batelito riv.
221 K-4 Batemans bay
221 K-4 Batemans Bay Batehaven
57 H-5 Batenburg
177 K-3 Batesburg
176 D-2 Batesville
56 A-8 Bath (Netherlands)
50 D-4 Bath (UK)
164 G-9 Bath (USA)
171 J-6 Bath (USA)
91 L-1 Batha riv.
91 K-1 Batha reg.
52 D-5 Bathford
57 L-1 Bathmen
209 K-9 Bathurst isl.
153 J-2 Bathurst isl.
161 P-5 Bathurst bay
221 K-2 Bathurst (Australia)
165 H-5 Bathurst (Canada)
161 P-5 Bathurst Inlet
58 E-9 Bâtiax (La)
83 K-2 Bāţin riv.
84 D-6 Bāţinah reg.
195 J-3 Batista mt
209 H-1 Batjan isl.
73 M-7 Bātlaq-e Gāvkhuni lake
221 J-4 Batlow
65 P-5 Batman
79 L-3 Batna
176 E-5 Baton Rouge
146 C-5 Batong isl.
195 K-1 Batoque
90 G-8 Batouri
65 M-9 Batroun
48 B-8 Båtsfjord
172 F-7 Batsto
100 A-1 Batsumoni
63 L-3 Battáglia Terme
145 H-8 Battambang
58 F-2 Bätterkinden
58 G-2 Bätterkinden
146 A-3 Batti Malv isl.
141 M-8 Batticaloa
163 H-6 Battle riv.
53 M-8 Battle
170 E-6 Battle Creek
167 H-5 Battle Mountain
163 K-6 Battleford
95 L-4 Batu mt
206 A-1 Batu (Indonesia) islds
146 C-9 Batu (Indonesia) islds
146 F-8 Batu Pahat
146 E-6 Batu Puteh mt
208 E-5 Batuata isl.

206 G-3 Batubetumbang
208 D-1 Batudaka isl.
207 P-7 Batugendang cap.
208 E-1 Batui mt
147 P-9 Batukelau
72 C-3 Batumi
149 P-7 Batuputih
206 E-4 Baturadja
207 L-7 Baturetno
195 L-1 Baturité
195 L-2 Baturité mt
67 L-1 Batyrevo
147 L-8 Bau
194 B-3 Baú riv.
208 E-4 Baubau
90 D-3 Bauchi reg.
90 D-3 Bauchi
170 A-1 Baudette
142 C-6 Baudh
186 C-5 Baudó mt
186 C-5 Baudó
186 C-6 Baudó riv.
165 M-1 Bauld cap.
50 C-9 Baule-Escoublac (La)
58 B-5 Baulmes
58 B-5 Baulmes mt
59 N-1 Bauma
55 M-2 Baumarchais
58 C-8 Baume (La)
58 B-1 Baume-les-Dames
208 F-8 Baun
146 G-9 Baun isl.
123 N-3 Baunt
123 N-3 Baunt lake
190 E-5 Baures
196 D-3 Baus
57 N-9 Bautsch
51 L-7 Bautzen
59 L-8 Bavona val.
59 L-7 Bavona
91 K-8 Bavula
207 K-3 Bawal isl.
89 P-4 Bawdia
53 P-3 Bawdsey
143 M-5 Bawdwin
209 N-3 Bawe
207 M-5 Bawean isl.
89 K-6 Bawku
143 M-8 Bawlake
97 H-2 Bawn
132 F-6 Baxian
177 K-4 Baxley
164 G-7 Baxter na.p.
165 P-3 Bay Bulls
170 F-5 Bay City (USA)
175 N-6 Bay City (USA)
165 P-2 Bay de Verde
176 G-5 Bay Minette
223 K-5 Bay of Plenty riv.
176 F-6 Bay Saint Louis
173 J-3 Bay Shore
176 F-4 Bay Springs
180 F-6 Bayamo
181 K-1 Bayamon
132 D-1 Bayan riv.
124 G-8 Bayan (China)
123 L-9 Bayan (Mongolia)
130 C-4 Bayan (Mongolia)
123 N-8 Bayan-Adraga
130 B-4 Bayan Ayrag mt
132 A-2 Bayan Dobo Suma
130 C-9 Bayan Hushuu well
132 C-1 Bayan Mönhö Suma
130 A-2 Bayan-Olgiy reg.
130 C-9 Bayan-Ondör (Mongolia)
130 D-6 Bayan-Ondör (Mongolia)
123 N-9 Bayan-Ovoo (Mongolia)
132 A-3 Bayan-Ovoo (Mongolia)
130 D-6 Bayan Tsagaan mt
123 H-6 Bayan Uul mt
130 A-5 Bayan-Uul (Mongolia)
130 C-4 Bayan-Uul (Mongolia)
139 M-5 Bayāna
130 C-6 Bayanbulag
130 A-6 Bayandzürch
91 H-9 Bayanga
123 L-8 Bayangol
130 A-5 Bayanhayrhan
131 K-5 Bayanhe riv.
130 C-7 Bayanhongor
123 M-9 Bayanjargalan
131 L-4 Bayankalashan mt
123 M-9 Bayanmön
123 N-9 Bayanterem
130 D-6 Bayantsagaan

58 B-4 Bayards (Les)
178 C-2 Bayas
149 H-4 Bayawan
148 G-3 Baybay
72 C-4 Bayburt
80 F-4 Bayda
112 E-3 Baydarackaya bay
130 C-6 Baydrag riv.
51 J-8 Bayern reg.
50 D-7 Bayeux
170 C-2 Bayfield
96 E-4 Bayhān al Qisāb
64 G-7 Bayindir
82 D-3 Bāyir
113 J-4 Baykal rge
113 J-4 Baykal lake
123 L-5 Baykal lake
123 L-4 Baykal'skiy rge
120 E-4 Baykonir
91 N-8 Baykumbala
81 K-2 Bayli well
52 G-3 Baynards Green
84 E-3 Baynūnah reg.
148 G-5 Bayo pte
148 C-6 Bayombong
60 E-3 Bayonne (France)
172 G-4 Bayonne (USA)
176 D-3 Bayou Bartholomew riv.
176 C-4 Bayou Bodeau lake
51 J-8 Bayreuth
132 D-1 Bayshinta Süme
172 D-8 Bayside
173 J-3 Bayville
69 M-8 Baza riv.
60 D-7 Baza
54 B-6 Bazainville
71 P-8 Bazār-i-Sharīf
72 F-2 Bazard'uzu mt
107 L-4 Bazaruto isl.
60 F-2 Bazas
54 D-5 Bazemont
134 D-3 Bazhong
126 A-8 Bazmān
126 A-8 Bazmān mt
54 D-7 Bazoches-sur-Guyonne
63 J-6 Bazzano
65 M-9 Bcharré
145 L-9 Be riv.
168 E-2 Beach
172 B-2 Beach Haven (USA)
172 B-2 Beach Haven (USA)
172 G-8 Beach Haven Inlet cap.
52 C-4 Beachley
172 G-6 Beachwood
53 L-8 Beachy Head cap.
216 F-6 Beacon
173 K-1 Beacon Falls
221 H-8 Beaconsfield (Australia)
53 J-4 Beaconsfield (UK)
216 D-6 Beagle
201 N-6 Beagle cal.
213 H-3 Beagle rf
213 N-1 Beagle gulf
213 H-4 Beagle Bay
218 F-4 Beal mt
108 E-7 Bealanana
162 A-6 Beale cap.
52 C-8 Beaminster
109 M-4 Beampingaratra mt
46 F-2 Bear isl.
164 A-2 Bear isl.
168 A-4 Bear riv.
172 G-1 Bear mt
172 C-2 Bear Creek
172 A-3 Bear Gap
162 D-1 Bear Lake
168 A-5 Bear Lake lake
211 H-6 Beara
170 D-1 Beardmore
52 A-8 Beare
172 G-2 Bearfort mt
139 N-8 Beärma riv.
159 J-7 Bearpaw
163 H-9 Bearpaw mt
139 N-2 Beäs riv.
181 K-7 Beata cap.
181 K-7 Beata isl.
59 H-5 Beatenberg
214 C-4 Beatrice cap.
169 H-7 Beatrice (USA)
103 N-7 Beatrice (Zimbabwe)
162 F-1 Beatton riv.
162 F-1 Beatton River
166 F-3 Beatty (USA)
167 K-5 Beatty (USA)
164 C-6 Beattyville (Canada)
170 F-9 Beattyville (USA)
54 G-3 Beauchamp
201 M-9 Beauchene isl.

54 A-8 Beauchêne
219 N-6 Beaudesert
220 F-5 Beaufort
226 B-2 Beaufort *sea*
149 L-9 Beaufort
177 N-2 Beaufort (USA)
177 L-4 Beaufort (USA)
104 F-8 Beaufort West
161 L-8 Beaulieu *riv.*
52 F-8 Beaulieu
50 C-4 Beaumaris
167 M-4 Beaumont (USA)
176 C-6 Beaumont (USA)
219 H-8 Beaumont Hill
55 H-1 Beaumont-sur-Oise
50 F-9 Beaune
163 P-9 Beausejour
215 M-3 Beautemps Beaupré *isl.*
54 B-8 Beauterne
50 E-8 Beauvais
55 P-9 Beauvoir
50 C-9 Beauvoir-sur-Mer
159 H-6 Beaver *mt*
168 D-1 Beaver *riv.*
170 E-4 Beaver *isl.*
176 C-1 Beaver *lake*
160 F-3 Beaver (Canada) *riv.*
162 F-6 Beaver (Canada)
159 L-7 Beaver (USA)
159 L-7 Beaver (USA) *riv.*
168 F-9 Beaver (USA)
167 K-7 Beaver (USA)
171 H-7 Beaver (USA)
168 G-7 Beaver City
160 D-2 Beaver Creek
170 D-5 Beaver Dam
201 L-7 Beaver Island *isl.*
172 B-2 Beaver Meadows
168 A-2 Beaverhead *mt*
161 P-8 Beaverhill *lake*
162 F-3 Beaverlodge
139 K-6 Beäwar
198 D-6 Beazley
91 H-5 Bébédja
196 G-5 Bebedouro
91 H-6 Béboura III
53 P-1 Beccles
64 B-2 Bečej
60 B-3 Becerrea
186 E-3 Becerri
185 J-2 Becerro *islds*
78 F-5 Béchar
158 D-8 Becharof *lake*
89 M-4 Bechem
158 A-6 Bechevin *bay*
172 C-5 Bechtelsville
59 L-3 Beckenried
154 J-3 Becker Lake
52 E-3 Beckford
52 E-5 Beckhampton
52 D-6 Beckington
171 H-9 Beckley
57 N-2 Beckum
58 G-9 Becs de Bosson *mt*
165 J-4 Becscie
127 H-6 Bed Mashk
78 B-3 Beddouza (Cantin) *cap.*
95 H-3 Bedele
122 E-5 Bedelig *mt*
95 L-3 Bedessa
97 J-3 Bedewanak
213 L-5 Bedford *mt*
215 J-5 Bedford *cap.*
171 J-7 Bedford
53 J-2 Bedford *reg.*
53 J-2 Bedford (UK)
213 L-4 Bedford Downs
173 H-1 Bedford Hills
53 L-1 Bedford Level *reg.*
170 E-9 Bedfort
91 K-3 Bédi
138 F-8 Bedi Bandar
72 D-2 Bediani
122 G-5 Bedij *riv.*
59 P-7 Bedoletta *pass*
62 F-6 Bedonia
218 D-3 Bedourie
212 F-6 Bedout *isl.*
59 L-7 Bedretto *val.*
59 L-7 Bedretto
52 F-1 Bedworth
159 P-5 Beechey
221 H-4 Beechworth
163 K-8 Beechy
57 N-6 Beegden
57 J-5 Beek (Netherlands)
57 H-7 Beek en Donk
57 J-2 Beekbergen
56 E-7 Beekse Bergen *hill*
172 F-1 Beemerville
219 N-6 Beenleigh
52 B-9 Beer
82 C-3 Be'er Sheva
46 C-2 Beerenberg
57 J-6 Beers
56 D-9 Beerse
56 F-8 Beerze *riv.*
56 F-4 Beesd
57 K-9 Beesel
105 J-3 Beestekraal
214 A-6 Beetaloo
175 M-6 Beeville
99 K-2 Befale
108 E-7 Befandriana Nord
109 K-2 Befandriana Sud
99 L-2 Befori
221 K-5 Bega
93 L-8 Begemdir-Simen *reg.*
130 D-5 Beger
130 D-5 Beger *riv.*
94 G-2 Begi
70 G-9 Begiarslan *mt*
113 K-2 Begičev *isl.*
58 A-7 Begnins
66 D-4 Begoml'
71 P-4 Begovat
192 G-3 Béhague *pte*
163 J-4 Behan
73 L-9 Behbehān
160 C-9 Behm *cal.*
213 M-4 Behn *mt*
54 C-6 Béhoust
73 L-4 Behshahr
124 F-6 Beian
131 J-5 Beidahe *riv.*
62 C-7 Béigua *mt*
145 M-2 Beihai
135 J-8 Beijiang *riv.*
145 P-5 Beijiao *isl.*
129 L-2 Beijie
134 G-9 Beiliu
91 H-5 Béinamar
62 A-4 Beinasco
62 A-7 Beinette
59 K-1 Beinwil
211 K-7 Beipa'a
134 C-7 Beipanjiang *riv.*
134 D-4 Beipei
133 H-3 Beipiao
107 K-4 Beira
47 G-6 Beirut
82 C-1 Beirut
130 F-3 Beishanmo *mt*
103 M-9 Beit Bridge
57 N-9 Beitel
64 C-1 Beiuş
124 F-6 Beixing
133 H-3 Beizhen
122 D-4 Beja
60 A-6 Beja (Spain)
79 N-2 Béja (Tunisia)
79 L-2 Bejaïa *gulf*
79 L-2 Bejaïa
60 C-5 Béjar
126 B-2 Bejestān
73 P-4 Bejestān
126 G-9 Beji *riv.*
70 E-6 Bejneu
124 D-3 Bejtonovo
187 J-2 Bejuma
90 G-9 Bek *riv.*
207 H-5 Bekasi
70 E-9 Bekdaš
64 C-1 Bekescsaba
109 M-3 Bekily
70 F-9 Bekmurat *mt*
95 K-4 Bekoji
121 H-6 Bektauata *mt*
54 G-9 Bel-Air
172 A-8 Bel Air
142 B-2 Bela (India)
138 E-4 Bela (Pakistan)
100 B-2 Bela (Zaïre)
64 C-2 Bela Crkva
196 B-5 Bela Vista (Brazil)
107 P-1 Bela Vista (Mozambique)
188 G-4 Bela Vista (Peru)
90 F-7 Belabo
147 N-8 Belaga
121 M-5 Belagaš
69 M-8 Belaja *riv.*
123 H-5 Belaja (bol.) *riv.*
69 J-7 Belaja Chelunica
67 L-9 Belaja Glina
67 K-7 Belaja Kalitva
70 C-1 Bel'ajevka
64 G-1 Bel'ajevka
140 D-7 Belampalli
149 P-2 Belang
163 P-7 Belanger *riv.*
146 B-7 Belangpidie
59 J-8 Belap
119 J-6 Belau *isl.*
146 C-7 Belawan
66 E-7 Belaya Tserkov
62 B-6 Belbo *riv.*
66 D-9 Belcesti
155 K-4 Belcher *isl.*
153 J-2 Belcher *strt.*
156 F-2 Belcher *islds*
164 A-1 Belcher *islds*
126 G-4 Belcherāgh
71 P-9 Belchiragh
66 E-9 Bel'cy
69 M-9 Belebey
97 M-4 Beled Weyne
193 J-8 Belem
188 D-9 Belém (Colombia)
195 L-5 Belém de Sao Francisco
199 K-4 Belén *mt*
198 C-2 Belén *riv.*
175 H-1 Belen
198 C-2 Belén (Argentina)
196 A-9 Belén (Argentina)
188 A-5 Belén (Colombia)
196 B-6 Belen (Paraguay)
199 J-4 Belén (Uruguay)
64 E-3 Belene
134 D-2 Belen'kaja
215 L-2 Belep *islds*
70 F-6 Beleuli *site*
194 C-5 Beleza *riv.*
105 L-3 Belfast (South Africa)
50 C-3 Belfast (UK)
164 G-8 Belfast (USA)
172 D-3 Belfast (USA)
58 E-4 Belfaux
57 K-9 Belfeld
168 F-2 Belfield
94 G-2 Belfodio
50 G-9 Belfort
140 E-3 Belgaum
62 E-4 Belgioioso
47 D-4 Belgium *state*
67 H-6 Belgorod
64 G-1 Belgorod-Dnestrovskiy
47 F-5 Belgrade
64 C-3 Belgrade
227 M-2 Belgrano
177 N-1 Belhaven
79 L-6 Belhirane
66 G-7 Beliki
206 F-5 Belimbing
122 G-5 Belin *riv.*
98 E-1 Belinga *mt*
206 G-2 Belinju
67 K-3 Belinskij
125 N-4 Belinskoje
207 J-3 Belitung *isl.*
157 F-5 Belize *state*
184 E-1 Belize *state*
184 E-1 Belize *riv.*
184 F-1 Belize
179 N-7 Belize City
158 A-6 Belkofski
113 M-2 Bel'kovskij *isl.*
219 M-5 Bell
165 M-1 Bell *isl.*
164 C-5 Bell *riv.*
159 P-9 Bell (Canada) *riv.*
198 F-5 Bell Ville
62 C-1 Bella *isl.*
162 B-3 Bella Coola
190 C-2 Bella Flor
58 G-8 Bella Tola *mt*
199 J-3 Bella Unión
191 K-1 Bella Vista *lake*
199 H-2 Bella Vista (Argentina)
198 D-1 Bella Vista (Argentina)
196 B-5 Bella Vista (Brazil)
60 G-1 Bellac
62 E-1 Bellagio
172 A-5 Bellaire
62 E-1 Bellano
63 N-8 Bellaria
140 F-5 Bellary
219 K-7 Bellata
188 F-2 Bellavista
54 D-1 Bellay-en-Vexin (Le)
221 M-1 Bellbrook
54 B-4 Belle Côte (La)
55 H-1 Belle-Eglise
168 E-3 Belle Fourche *lake*
168 E-4 Belle Fourche
168 E-3 Belle Fourche *riv.*
177 L-8 Belle Glade
50 B-8 Belle-île *isl.*
165 L-1 Belle-Isle *strt.*
172 F-4 Belle Mead
55 K-2 Bellefontaine (France)
170 F-7 Bellefontaine (USA)
171 J-7 Bellefonte
61 J-2 Bellegarde
172 A-5 Bellegrove
58 C-1 Belleherbe
58 E-1 Bellelay
165 N-3 Belleoram
172 E-9 Belleplain
58 B-8 Bellevaux
164 C-9 Belleville
170 C-9 Belleville (USA)
219 M-8 Bellingen
162 C-7 Bellingham
227 M-3 Bellingshausen *sea*
62 C-2 Bellinzago Novara
61 L-2 Bellinzona
186 D-5 Bello
55 J-2 Belloy-en-France
173 K-3 Bellport
61 M-2 Belluno
104 C-9 Bellville (South Africa)
169 H-8 Bellville (USA)
172 G-5 Belmar
58 C-7 Belmont
104 G-6 Belmont (South Africa)
171 J-6 Belmont (USA)
197 P-1 Belmonte
157 F-5 Belmopan
184 E-1 Belmopan
197 M-1 Belo Campo
197 K-4 Belo Horizonte (Brazil)
194 B-2 Belo Horizonte (Brazil)
195 N-5 Belo Jardim
192 G-9 Belo Monte
190 D-5 Belo Oriente
109 H-3 Belo sur Tsiribihina
109 H-4 Belobaka
124 F-4 Belogorsk (SSSR)
122 D-2 Belogorsk (SSSR)
109 M-2 Beloha
170 C-6 Beloit (USA)
169 H-8 Beloit (USA)
69 P-6 Belojarskij
121 P-5 Belokuricha
68 C-5 Belomorsk
68 C-6 Belomorsk *riv.*
68 E-4 Belomorsko-Kulojskoje *plat.*
143 H-5 Belonia
66 G-6 Belopolje
72 A-1 Belorečensk
69 P-8 Beloretsk
114 A-4 Belorussia *rép*
112 A-4 Belorusskaja Gra'da *mt*
161 J-3 Belot *lake*
121 N-6 Belousovka
66 G-4 Bel'ov
122 C-3 Belovo
67 J-6 Belovodsk
68 E-8 Belozersk
58 G-4 Belp
58 G-4 Belp *hill*
122 E-1 Bel'skoje
192 E-9 Belterra
175 N-5 Belton
198 F-3 Beltrán *lag.*
186 D-6 Beltrán
57 M-3 Beltrum
122 D-4 Bel'tyrskij
122 B-6 Belucha *mt*
159 H-8 Beluga *lake*
121 P-6 Belukha *mt*
141 H-4 Belūr
149 K-8 Beluran
219 J-2 Belyando *riv.*
122 D-3 Belyi Ljus *riv.*
66 F-3 Belyj
112 F-2 Belyj *isl.*
176 E-4 Belzoni
86 G-7 Béma
108 G-3 Bemaraha *plat.*
108 F-6 Bemarivo *riv.*
98 F-7 Bembe
89 K-8 Bembéréké
103 M-8 Bembesi
52 G-9 Bembridge Foreland
57 M-9 Bemelen
170 A-2 Bemidji
57 J-4 Bemmel
209 K-3 Bemu
50 D-1 Ben Dearg *mt*
79 P-5 Ben Gardane
50 D-1 Ben Nevis *mt*
78 D-3 Ben-Slimane
99 L-5 Bena Dibele
72 F-5 Benāb
97 P-4 Benadir *reg.*
78 C-3 Benahmed
221 H-4 Benalla
142 C-2 Benares (Vārānasi)
60 C-3 Benavente
190 D-3 Benavides
50 C-1 Benbecula *isl.*
216 F-6 Bencubbin
166 D-4 Bend
207 L-6 Benda *cap.*
90 A-6 Bendel *reg.*
99 H-5 Bendela
159 J-3 Bendeleben *mt*
219 L-8 Bendemeer
97 H-8 Bender Bäyla
96 G-7 Bendersiyada
64 G-1 Bendery (SSSR)
66 E-9 Bendery (SSSR)
220 G-4 Bendigo
62 A-6 Bene Vagienna
194 G-3 Benedito Leite
53 J-1 Benefield
109 L-3 Benenitra
61 N-6 Benevento
192 E-8 Benfica *dam.*
144 G-2 Bèng *riv.*
116 D-6 Bengal *gulf*
142 F-8 Bengal *gulf*
99 N-2 Bengamisa
80 G-1 Benghazi
147 K-9 Bengkajang
146 F-8 Bengkalis *isl.*
146 E-8 Bengkalis *strt.*
146 E-8 Bengkalis
206 D-4 Bengkulu
98 F-9 Bengo *riv.*
102 B-2 Benguela *reg.*
102 B-2 Benguela
78 C-4 Benguerir
107 L-4 Benguérua *isl.*
129 L-6 Bengwaluoteshan *mt*
81 N-2 Benha
100 B-2 Beni
190 E-4 Beni *reg.*
190 F-3 Beni *riv.*
78 F-6 Beni Abbès
78 D-4 Beni-Mellal
78 G-5 Beni-Ounif
78 G-2 Beni Saf
81 N-3 Beni Suef
161 M-7 Beniah *lake*
60 F-5 Benicarló
190 D-4 Benicito *riv.*
77 C-3 Benin *state*
76 C-4 Benin *gulf*
90 A-6 Benin City
140 D-5 Benithora *riv.*
186 E-5 Benito
175 M-3 Benjamin
200 G-2 Benjamin *isl.*
188 E-9 Benjamin Constant
174 D-4 Benjamin Hill
200 C-6 Benjamin Zorrilla
168 F-7 Benkelman
56 C-1 Bennebroek
54 A-3 Bennecourt
57 H-4 Bennekom
160 D-5 Bennett *lake*
160 D-5 Bennett
177 L-2 Bennettsville
171 L-5 Bennington
164 A-8 Benny
146 E-7 Benom *mt*
105 K-4 Benoni
79 H-5 Benoud *well*
90 G-5 Bénoué *riv.*
91 H-4 Bénoye
210 F-7 Bensbach *riv.*
56 E-3 Benschop
174 E-5 Benson (USA)
169 J-4 Benson (USA)
84 A-8 Bent
146 E-7 Benta
56 C-3 Benthuizen
102 A-4 Bentiaba *riv.*
146 C-1 Bentinck (Birman) *isl.*
94 D-3 Bentiu
194 G-2 Bento *riv.*
196 B-1 Bento Gomes *riv.*
199 N-3 Bento Gonçalves
172 A-1 Benton
146 E-7 Bentong
147 J-9 Benua *isl.*
208 E-4 Benua
90 C-6 Benué *reg.*
90 B-5 Benue *riv.*
53 K-1 Benwick
133 K-3 Benxi
192 E-4 Benzdorp
149 L-1 Beo
133 M-7 Beobseongpo
139 P-8 Beohāri
89 M-1 Béoumi
137 L-3 Beppu
181 N-9 Bequia *isl.*
193 M-8 Bequimão
97 J-4 Ber
88 E-4 Bérabich *mt*
138 K-7 Berach *riv.*
109 M-3 Beraketa
146 G-9 Berakit *cap.*
100 C-3 Berarara *riv.*
64 C-5 Berat
209 M-2 Berau (Teluk) *gulf*
97 H-4 Berbera
91 H-8 Berbérati
192 C-3 Berbice *riv.*
62 G-6 Berceto
58 C-5 Bercher
54 A-6 Berchères-sur-Vesgre
70 E-3 Berčogur
121 P-3 Berd' *riv.*
67 J-9 Berd'ansk
69 P-7 Berd'aus
66 E-7 Berdičev
121 P-2 Berdsk
89 M-1 Béré *riv.*
52 D-8 Bere Regis
86 F-6 Bérédji Kourou *mt*
122 D-1 Beregajevo
66 B-9 Beregovo
62 D-4 Bereguardo
89 M-4 Berekum
56 B-9 Berendrecht
163 P-8 Berens *isl.*
163 P-8 Berens River
79 M-5 Beressof *well*
64 C-1 Berettyoujfalu
66 F-7 Berezan'
66 C-8 Berezany
66 E-5 Berezina *riv.*
66 D-5 Berezino
68 F-6 Bereznik
69 L-5 Berezniki
66 D-7 Berezno
57 M-9 Berg
57 J-5 Berg en Dal
64 F-6 Bergama
56 D-4 Bergambacht
61 L-2 Bergamo
62 F-2 Bergamo *reg.*
62 F-2 Bergamo (Bergame)
63 K-4 Bergantino
51 H-1 Berganuten
172 G-2 Bergen *reg.*
49 J-1 Bergen (Norway)
57 K-7 Bergen (Netherlands)
56 B-8 Bergen op Zoom
173 H-2 Bergenfield
56 G-9 Bergeyk
57 L-4 Bergh *reg.*
223 K-2 Berghan *pte*
57 H-5 Bergharen
57 H-5 Berghem
56 C-4 Bergschenhoek
56 E-6 Bergse Maas *riv.*
105 K-5 Bergville
123 N-9 Berh
146 D-7 Berhala *isl.*
142 F-4 Berhampore
142 C-7 Berhampur
63 L-3 Berici *mt*
206 G-2 Berikat *cap.*
160 B-2 Bering *glac.*
226 A-1 Bering *sea*
113 S-3 Bering *strt.*
113 Q-4 Bering *sea*
57 J-9 Beringen
91 P-2 Beringil
59 J-8 Berisal
66 G-9 Berislav
65 M-6 Berit *mt*
49 H-3 Berkåk
124 D-1 Berkakit
78 F-2 Berkane
56 C-4 Berkel
57 L-2 Berkel *riv.*
56 B-4 Berkel en Rodenrijs *reg.*
161 M-1 Berkeley *pte*
184 A-8 Berkeley *cap.*
52 D-4 Berkeley (UK)
167 H-2 Berkeley (USA)
201 L-9 Berkeley Sound *bay*
56 D-4 Berkenwoude
53 H-4 Berkhamsted
78 E-3 Berkine
227 M-2 Berkner *isl.*
64 D-4 Berkovica
172 C-4 Berks *reg.*
53 H-5 Berkshire *reg.*
162 F-4 Berland *riv.*
195 J-3 Berlengas *riv.*
48 B-8 Berlevåg
56 G-6 Berlicum
47 E-4 Berlin (GDR)
51 K-6 Berlin (GDR)
51 K-6 Berlin (FRG)
172 E-7 Berlin (USA)
164 F-8 Berlin (USA)
175 J-8 Bermejillo
200 C-8 Bermejo *isl.*
198 C-5 Bermejo *riv.*
198 C-4 Bermejo *riv.*
198 B-6 Bermejo *riv.*
164 F-2 Bermen *lake*
60 C-4 Bermillo de Sayago
142 E-4 Bermo
156 H-3 Bermuda *islds*
159 N-9 Bern *riv.*
47 D-5 Bern
61 K-1 Bern
175 H-1 Bernalillo
146 E-7 Bernam *riv.*
161 H-2 Bernard House
175 H-1 Bernardo
196 D-8 Bernardo de Irigoyen
172 F-3 Bernardsville
200 B-7 Bernasconi
55 P-8 Bernay-Vilbert
51 K-6 Bernburg
58 F-4 Berne
55 H-1 Bernes-sur-Oise
58 C-8 Bernex

216 B-2 Bernier isl.
56 A-5 Bernisse reg.
172 B-4 Bernville
102 A-4 Bero riv.
58 A-6 Berolle
59 K-2 Beromünster
196 A-9 Beron de Astrada
109 K-3 Beroroha
49 J-9 Ber'osovyj isl.
89 K-8 Bérouhouay
66 C-6 Ber'oza
125 K-8 Ber'ozovaja mt
66 F-9 Ber'ozovka
124 F-5 Ber'ozovka (SSSR)
69 L-1 Ber'ozovo
69 N-6 Ber'ozovskij
124 F-2 Ber'ozovyj
63 M-5 Berra
58 E-5 Berra (La) mt
78 C-3 Berrechid
220 E-2 Berri
79 J-4 Berrian
79 K-5 Berriane
221 H-3 Berrigan
216 E-3 Berringarra
79 J-2 Berrouaghia
180 E-2 Berry islds
167 H-2 Berryessa lake
66 E-8 Beršad'
164 G-3 Berté lake
54 B-1 Berthenonville
164 E-7 Berthierville
93 N-9 Berthor
193 H-9 Bertinho
63 M-8 Bertinoro
195 H-4 Bertólinia
90 F-8 Bertoua
170 E-1 Bertram
141 N-7 Beruwala
54 F-1 Berville
172 B-2 Berwick
50 E-3 Berwick upon Tweed
172 D-6 Berwyn
108 F-3 Besalampy
61 J-1 Besançon
146 F-8 Besar mt
208 E-7 Besar isl.
207 P-3 Besar (Indonesia) mt
128 B-5 Besbaskan mt
66 D-4 Bešenkivici
208 G-7 Besikama
66 A-8 Beskidy mt
72 D-1 Beslan
163 L-5 Besnard lake
65 M-6 Besni
54 G-3 Bessancourt
64 G-1 Bessarabka
176 G-3 Bessemer
56 G-7 Best
121 J-2 Bestobe
68 F-6 Bestuževo
109 J-5 Betafo
99 K-4 Betamba
108 G-6 Betampona na.p.
191 M-5 Betania
208 G-7 Betano
191 J-4 Betanzos (Bolivia)
60 B-2 Betanzos (Spain)
90 G-7 Bétaré Oya
89 L-7 Bétérou
105 K-4 Bethal
104 C-3 Bethanie
170 A-7 Bethany
158 F-5 Bethel (USA)
164 G-8 Bethel (USA)
55 H-3 Béthemont-la-Forêt
104 G-8 Bethesda
105 J-5 Bethlehem (South Africa)
82 C-2 Bethlehem (Israel)
171 L-7 Bethlehem (USA)
173 J-3 Bethpage
50 F-7 Béthune
60 C-7 Betica rge
186 G-3 Betijoque
109 L-2 Betioky
147 M-8 Betong (Malaysia)
146 E-5 Betong (Thailand)
218 E-4 Betoota
120 E-6 Betpak-Dala dés
109 L-4 Betroka
59 N-4 Betschwanden
164 F-5 Betsiamites riv.
108 G-5 Betsiboka riv.
80 F-9 Bette mt
59 J-8 Betten
172 B-8 Betterton
142 D-2 Bettiah
159 L-6 Bettles
59 J-8 Bettlihorn mt
62 F-5 Bettola
140 A-7 Betül
206 E-2 Betung
139 M-8 Betwa riv.
55 P-1 Betz
57 J-6 Beugen

220 F-3 Beulah (Australia)
52 A-2 Beulah (UK)
57 J-5 Beuningen
56 F-4 Beusichem
55 M-4 Beuvronne riv.
58 D-4 Bevaix
158 E-6 Beveley lake
216 E-7 Beverley (Australia)
50 E-4 Beverley (UK)
172 E-6 Beverly
63 K-4 Bevilacqua Boschi
52 D-1 Bewdley
58 D-8 Bex
53 M-8 Bexhill on Sea
53 L-5 Bexley
65 L-6 Bey mt
87 L-7 Beyla
96 F-1 Beylul
54 D-6 Beynes
65 J-5 Beypazari
141 J-4 Beypore
64 J-7 Beyşehir gulf
65 J-7 Beyşehir
53 M-2 Beyton
142 C-3 Bhabua
138 F-8 Bhādar riv.
127 M-8 Bhadarwāh
142 E-1 Bhādgaon
142 C-2 Bhadohi
140 G-4 Bhadra lake
140 G-4 Bhadra riv.
142 E-6 Bhadrakh
139 H-8 Bhādran
140 G-4 Bhadrāvati
142 E-3 Bhāgalpur
139 P-3 Bhāgirathi riv.
142 C-1 Bhairawa
127 J-8 Bhakkar
139 N-2 Bhākra lake
140 D-6 Bhālki
143 M-4 Bhamo
140 B-8 Bhandāra
139 N-7 Bhānder
139 L-7 Bhānpura
139 N-8 Bhanrer mt
139 M-5 Bharatpur
142 G-5 Bhātiāpāra Ghāt
139 L-3 Bhatinda
140 G-3 Bhatkal
142 F-5 Bhātpāra
127 L-8 Bhaun
140 A-2 Bhavnagar
142 B-7 Bhawānipatna
127 L-8 Bhera
129 P-2 Bheri riv.
140 B-9 Bhilai
139 K-6 Bhilwāra
140 D-4 Bhīma riv.
140 F-9 Bhīmavaram
142 D-1 Bhīmphedi
139 N-6 Bhind
140 C-3 Bhiwandi
139 M-4 Bhiwāni
142 F-2 Bhojpur
140 E-7 Bhongīr
139 M-8 Bhopāl
140 D-8 Bhopālpatnam
140 D-3 Bhor
142 D-7 Bhubaneswar
138 F-7 Bhuj
140 B-5 Bhusāwal
118 E-4 Bhutan state
143 H-2 Bhutan (Druk-Yul) reg.
145 M-8 Bi Doup mt
89 N-3 Bia riv.
73 N-6 Biābanak
188 G-4 Biabo riv.
98 A-1 Biafra gulf
93 L-7 Biagundi
91 M-8 Biakété
66 B-6 Biala Podlaska
66 B-5 Bialystok
210 E-6 Bian riv.
62 G-8 Bianca pte
63 M-5 Bianco cal.
62 C-2 Biandrate
91 L-7 Bianga
87 M-8 Biankouma
58 A-3 Bians-lès-Usiers
62 B-3 Bianzè
139 L-8 Biaora
129 L-1 Biar
73 M-3 Bīārjmand
99 N-2 Biaro
149 N-2 Biaro isl.
60 E-3 Biarritz
59 N-8 Biasca

190 D-3 Biata riv.
89 H-4 Biba
81 N-3 Bibã
136 B-6 Bibai
102 A-4 Bibala
79 K-2 Bibans mt
63 H-6 Bibbiano Traversetolo
63 L-9 Bibbiena
59 M-2 Biberbrugg
58 G-2 Biberist
89 N-4 Bibiania
141 M-8 Bibile
188 D-2 Biblián
52 F-4 Bibury
192 F-4 Bicade
197 L-5 Bicas
64 C-1 Bîcaul riv.
46 C-5 Bicay gulf
64 E-1 Bicaz
72 B-3 Bičenekskij strt.
52 G-3 Bicester
125 K-5 Bičevaja
163 J-5 Biche lake
95 J-1 Bichena
221 H-8 Bicheno
125 K-2 Biči riv.
162 G-5 Bickerdike
214 C-4 Bickertorn isl.
52 A-8 Bickleigh
90 A-4 Bida
140 D-6 Bīdar
164 G-9 Biddeford
53 M-7 Biddenden
52 E-2 Bidford
91 K-9 Biduni
125 J-6 Bidžan
125 H-6 Bidžan riv.
102 D-2 Bié reg.
51 P-5 Biebrza riv.
66 B-5 Biebrza lake
61 K-1 Biel
58 E-3 Biel lake
59 K-7 Biel
58 F-2 Biel
51 M-7 Bielawa
51 H-6 Bielefeld
62 B-2 Biella
61 K-2 Bielle
66 B-6 Bielsk Podalski
145 L-9 Biên Hoa
63 H-9 Bientina
155 L-4 Bienville lake
164 D-1 Bienville lake
58 A-9 Bière
56 D-5 Biesbos lag.
59 H-7 Bietschhorn
55 H-6 Bièvre riv.
54 G-7 Bièvres
59 N-5 Bifertenstock mt
98 E-3 Bifoum
161 K-8 Big isl.
170 C-9 Big riv.
159 H-5 Big (USA) riv.
163 K-9 Big Beaver
216 E-4 Big Bell
168 B-1 Big Belt mt
175 J-5 Big Bend na.p.
176 E-4 Big Black riv.
169 H-7 Big Blue riv.
168 D-1 Big Dry riv.
170 A-2 Big Falls
158 B-7 Big Koniuji isl.
175 K-4 Big Lake
168 E-5 Big Piney
170 E-5 Big Rapids
163 K-6 Big River
160 E-5 Big Salmon riv.
160 E-5 Big Salmon mt
163 P-4 Big Sand lake
163 H-9 Big Sandy
169 H-4 Big Sioux riv.
168 C-2 Big Snowy mt
175 K-3 Big Springs
168 B-2 Big Timber
64 F-5 Biga
64 G-6 Bigadic
163 K-7 Biggar
213 J-3 Bigge isl.
219 M-4 Biggenden
160 C-5 Bigger mt
53 J-2 Biggleswade
168 C-3 Bighorn riv.
168 C-3 Bighorn mt
58 G-4 Biglen
59 M-4 Bignasco
87 H-2 Bignona
62 A-9 Bignone mt
167 K-4 Bigpine
52 C-4 Bigsweir
196 G-9 Biguacu
61 P-3 Bihac
142 D-3 Bihār reg.
142 D-3 Bihār
100 D-4 Biharamulo
97 H-6 Bihen well
136 A-7 Bihoro

136 A-6 Bihuka
122 B-4 Bija riv.
87 J-1 Bijagos islds
140 E-4 Bījāpur
140 D-8 Bījāpur
73 H-6 Bījārd
129 P-2 Bijauri
64 B-3 Bijeljina
143 N-3 Bijiang
134 D-6 Bijie
56 E-1 Bijlmermeer
139 N-4 Bijnor
139 L-2 Bikaner cal.
139 K-4 Bīkaner
119 N-5 Bikar isl.
132 C-5 Bikeqi
125 K-6 Bikin riv.
125 K-6 Bikin
119 M-5 Bikini isl.
99 H-3 Bikoro
146 D-8 Bila riv.
93 P-2 Bilād Ghamid mt
93 P-2 Bilād Zahrān mt
124 D-6 Bilahe riv.
139 K-5 Bilāra
139 P-4 Bilāspur (India)
142 B-5 Bilāspur (India)
139 N-2 Bilāspur (India)
149 P-4 Bilato
144 F-7 Bilauktaung mt
129 P-1 Bilauri
60 E-3 Bilbao
81 P-2 Bilbays
123 M-6 Bil'čir
53 N-3 Bildeston
51 M-8 Bilé Karpaty mt
65 H-5 Bilecik
139 P-6 Bilhaur
91 N-8 Bili riv.
91 H-2 Bili
144 E-5 Bilin
90 E-4 Biliri
148 F-9 Bilitan isl.
53 L-4 Billericay
220 E-3 Billiat na.p.
213 L-6 Billiluna
168 C-2 Billings
53 J-7 Billingshurts
52 D-1 Billingsley
216 D-4 Billybillong
95 J-3 Bilo
219 L-3 Biloela
192 B-5 Biloku
176 F-6 Biloxi
218 E-3 Bilpamorea Claypan riv
81 N-1 Bil'qas
59 N-2 Bilten
56 F-2 Bilthoven
92 A-7 Biltine reg.
48 D-6 Bilto
144 E-5 Bilugyun isl.
94 A-7 Bima riv.
102 C-2 Bimbe
221 J-4 Bimberi mt
89 L-6 Bimbila
91 K-8 Bimbo
180 E-2 Bimini islds
139 M-8 Bīna
209 K-3 Binaija mt
148 G-4 Binalbagan
126 D-1 Bīnālūd mt
73 P-2 Bīnālūd mt
62 D-3 Binasco
147 M-8 Binatang
219 K-5 Bindago
146 C-7 Bindjai
219 K-6 Bindle
103 N-6 Bindura
78 D-4 Bine el Ouidane
89 L-3 Bineda riv.
103 L-6 Binga
219 L-7 Binga
141 J-1 Bingaram isl.
57 N-8 Bingelrade
160 B-6 Bingham cap.
171 K-6 Binghamton
65 N-5 Bingöl
145 K-9 Binh Khiêm-Cuong
133 H-9 Binhai
143 L-8 Binhon Taung hill
52 G-1 Binley
59 K-8 Binn
221 K-1 Binnaway
59 K-8 Binnen val.
208 F-5 Binongko isl.
146 G-9 Bintan isl.
146 D-6 Bintang mt
149 P-3 Bintauna
206 E-4 Bintuhan
147 N-7 Bintulu
209 M-2 Bintuni bay
124 G-3 Binxian
132 B-9 Binxian
132 G-7 Binxian
134 F-9 Binyang

79 N-2 Binzert (Bizerte)
97 J-8 Bio Addo
200 B-2 Bio Bio reg.
200 B-1 Bio Bio riv.
62 B-2 Bioglio
61 P-4 Biograd
90 C-8 Bioko (Fernando Poo)
58 C-8 Biot
140 C-5 Bīr
96 E-6 Bi'r Alī
84 B-8 Bīr Bālā
95 H-3 Bir-Bir riv.
79 M-3 Bir-el-Ater
81 J-2 Bir Hakeîm well
82 D-4 Bi'r Ibn Hirmās
90 G-1 Bir Louri plat.
82 F-7 Bi'r Nașīf
88 B-4 Bir Ounâne well
79 K-2 Bir-rabalou
81 P-3 Bi'r Za Fāranah
125 J-5 Bira
210 D-5 Birab
126 B-9 Bīrag mt
125 H-5 Birakan
91 N-3 Birao
163 N-7 Birch isl.
163 J-3 Birch riv.
161 K-7 Birch lake
163 J-2 Birch riv.
159 L-8 Birch (USA) riv.
107 K-2 Birchenough Bridge
53 P-5 Birchington
220 F-3 Birchip
158 A-7 Bird isl.
227 N-6 Bird
52 E-3 Birdlip
172 C-5 Birdsboro
218 D-4 Birdsville
214 A-5 Birdum
65 M-7 Birecik
146 B-6 Bireuen
142 D-1 Birganj
168 A-5 Birgham City
94 A-4 Biri riv.
196 F-5 Birigui
122 D-4 Birikčul'
122 E-1 Biril'ussy
126 B-4 Bīrjand
83 H-9 Birkah
82 C-2 Birkat al Qațrānah
81 N-3 Birkat Qārīm lake
86 G-2 Birkelane
50 D-4 Birkenhead
64 F-1 Bîrlad
128 B-1 Birlik
124 G-4 Birma riv.
59 L-1 Birmensdorf
50 D-5 Birmingham reg.
50 D-5 Birmingham
176 G-3 Birmingham (USA)
142 D-3 Birmitrapur
90 B-3 Birna-Gwari
89 H-8 Birni-Ngaouré
90 A-1 Birni-Nkonni
89 J-9 Birnin-Kebbi
90 D-3 Birnin-Kudu
125 J-5 Birobidžan
125 J-5 Birofel'd
59 N-9 Bironico
50 B-4 Birr
213 M-5 Birrindudu
139 J-4 Birsilpur
69 M-8 Birsk
163 M-9 Birtle
131 N-2 Biru
67 H-9 Bir'učij isl.
210 D-5 Birufu
123 L-4 Bir'ul'ka
71 J-7 Biruni
122 G-2 Bir'usa (Ona) riv.
122 G-4 Birva (bol.) riv.
122 G-4 Birva (mal.) riv.
66 B-3 Biržai
209 J-1 Bisa isl.
129 P-1 Bisalpur
174 E-3 Bisbee
60 D-7 Biscay gulf
177 L-9 Biscayne bay
164 A-7 Biscotasing
187 H-3 Biscucuy
63 K-9 Bisenzio riv.
69 N-6 Bisert'
93 M-6 Bisha
96 B-1 Bīshah riv.
96 A-1 Bīshah reg.
92 A-1 Bishārah well
92 G-3 Bisharin dés
142 E-5 Bishnupur
167 K-4 Bishop
52 G-7 Bishops
52 C-1 Bishops Castle
52 D-8 Bishop's Caundle
52 E-3 Bishop's Cleeve
165 M-2 Bishop's Falls
52 B-7 Bishops Lydeard

53 L-3 Bishops Stortford
65 N-8 Bishri mt
211 K-7 Bisianumu
129 K-8 Bisikan
187 H-7 Bisinaca
59 M-4 Bisisthal
122 D-4 Biskamža
52 L-3 Biskra
79 L-3 Biskra
53 J-6 Bisley
149 J-2 Bislig
168 G-2 Bismarck
117 K-7 Bismarck islds
117 K-7 Bismarck sea
211 L-4 Bismarck islds
211 H-5 Bismarck mt
65 P-6 Bismil
168 F-3 Bison
108 C-5 Bison rf
73 H-7 Bisotūn
77 A-3 Bissau
87 H-2 Bissau
87 H-2 Bissora
62 C-6 Bistagno
161 J-8 Bistcho lake
64 D-1 Bistrita
142 B-1 Biswān
94 A-5 Bita riv.
98 D-1 Bitam
66 B-7 Bitgoraj
91 K-2 Bitkine
91 K-2 Bitlis
64 C-5 Bitola
61 P-6 Bitonto
141 H-1 Bitra isl.
188 C-7 Bittencourt
168 B-5 Bitter riv.
104 C-7 Bitterfontein
52 G-8 Bitterne
222 D-8 Bitterness mt
168 A-1 Bitterroot reg.
89 K-6 Bittou
67 J-7 Bit'ug riv.
163 J-3 Bitumount
149 N-2 Bitung
90 F-3 Biu
210 G-4 Biviraka
137 J-5 Biwa lake
96 E-1 Biyād
81 N-1 Biyalā
121 P-4 Biysk
105 K-7 Bizana
79 N-2 Bizerte (Binzert)
64 D-3 Bjala Slatina
48 A-1 Bjargtangar cap.
61 P-2 Bjelovar
51 K-1 Bjørkelangen
89 H-2 Bla
56 C-5 Blaak
163 P-8 Black isl.
112 B-5 Black sea
176 D-5 Black riv.
158 D-9 Black pte
46 D-5 Black ft
163 M-2 Black (Canada) lake
158 C-7 Black (USA) lake
159 M-8 Black (USA) riv.
175 N-1 Black Bear riv.
163 L-4 Black Birch lake
168 E-4 Black Hills mt
168 E-9 Black Mesa plat.
167 L-6 Black Mountains mt
52 B-3 Black Mountains hill
180 F-7 Black River
145 J-2 Black River (Sông Da) riv.
170 C-5 Black River Falls
166 G-4 Black Rock dés
174 G-2 Black Springs
221 L-1 Black Sugarloaf mt
219 H-3 Blackall
53 L-7 Blackboys
214 F-7 Blackbull
160 C-2 Blackburn mt
50 D-4 Blackburn
52 B-7 Blackdown hill
168 A-4 Blackfoot
168 A-4 Blackfoot River lake
50 D-4 Blackpool
160 F-1 Blackstone riv.
165 H-6 Blackville
53 M-3 Blackwater riv.
161 J-5 Blackwater lake
219 K-3 Blackwater (Australia)
53 H-6 Blackwater (UK)
52 G-9 Blackwater (UK)
52 B-4 Blackwood
216 E-9 Blackwood riv.
56 F-9 Bladel
163 P-5 Bladock lake
52 A-8 Blaenavon
52 A-4 Blaengarw
52 A-4 Blaenrhondda
52 B-7 Blagdon
67 M-9 Blagodarnoje
64 D-4 Blagoevgrad
121 M-3 Blagoreščenka

124 F-5 Blagovechtchensk
69 N-8 Blagoveshchensk
162 C-7 Blaine
169 J-6 Blair
144 B-7 Blair *bay*
219 K-2 Blair Athol
50 D-2 Blairgowrie
172 E-2 Blairstown
177 J-2 Blairsville
80 B-9 Blaka *riv.*
177 H-5 Blakely
52 C-2 Blakemere
52 D-4 Blakeney
172 C-2 Blakeslee
207 N-7 Blambangan *pen.*
54 D-1 Blamecourt
58 D-1 Blamont
79 N-2 Blanc *cap.*
165 L-1 Blanc- Sablon
60 G-1 Blanc (Le)
50 D-9 Blanc (Le)
55 K-4 Blanc-Mesnil (Le)
168 D-9 Blanca *riv.*
201 M-4 Blanca *lake*
200 B-6 Blanca Grande *lag.*
218 D-6 Blanche
220 A-1 Blanche *cap.*
213 H-8 Blanche *lake*
220 D-2 Blanche Town
191 K-4 Blanco *riv.*
184 G-7 Blanco (Costa Rica) *cap.*
166 E-2 Blanco (USA) *cap.*
48 B-2 Blanda *riv.*
52 E-8 Blandford
168 A-8 Blanding
172 C-4 Blandon
146 B-7 Blangkedjeren
58 F-6 Blankenburg
187 L-1 Blanquilla *isl.*
199 K-5 Blanquillo
106 G-4 Blantyre
56 F-1 Blaricum
54 A-3 Blaru
59 M-6 Blas *mt*
59 H-7 Blatten
58 G-6 Blau *lake*
56 D-6 Blauwe Sluis
60 F-2 Blaye
221 K-2 Blayney
76 D-6 Ble *plat.*
201 L-9 Bleaker Island *isl.*
53 N-6 Blean
175 K-2 Bledsoe
63 J-1 Bleggio
56 C-3 Bleiswijk
51 L-3 Blekinge *reg.*
222 G-7 Blenheim
59 N-7 Blenio Riviera *val.*
57 K-8 Blerick
56 D-5 Bleskengraaf en Hofwegen *reg.*
53 H-3 Bletchley
53 J-2 Bletsoe
52 G-5 Blewbury
79 K-2 Blida
51 M-1 Blidö *isl.*
54 G-9 Bligny
164 A-8 Blind River
59 K-7 Blindenhorn *mt*
53 K-6 Blindley Heath
218 D-7 Blinman
166 F-7 Bliss
162 B-5 Bliss Landing
53 H-7 Blisworth
207 M-7 Blitar
89 M-6 Blitta
57 K-7 Blitterswijk
171 M-6 Block *isl.*
173 P-1 Block Island
173 N-1 Block Island *strt.*
52 F-3 Blockley
105 H-6 Bloemfontein
105 H-4 Bloemhof
50 E-9 Blois
58 D-7 Blonay
48 B-2 Blönduos
170 B-7 Bloomfield (USA)
170 E-8 Bloomfield (USA)
172 E-1 Blooming Grove
172 G-2 Bloomingdale
170 A-4 Bloomington (USA)
170 E-8 Bloomington (USA)
171 K-6 Bloomsburg
172 K-4 Bloomsbury
207 L-6 Blora
177 H-5 Blountstown
159 P-8 Blow *riv.*
180 F-8 Blower Rock *isl.*
52 G-3 Bloxham
221 K-2 Blue
172 B-5 Blue Ball
165 M-4 Blue Hills of Couteau *mt*
168 C-8 Blue Mesa *lake*

180 G-7 Blue Mountains (Jamaica) *mt*
221 K-2 Blue Mountains (Katoomba)
166 D-6 Blue Mountains (USA) *mt*
214 B-4 Blue Mud *bay*
76 F-3 Blue Nile *riv.*
173 K-3 Blue Point
162 F-1 Blueberry
171 H-9 Bluefield
185 H-5 Bluefields
161 L-3 Bluenose *lake*
216 C-4 Bluff *pte*
222 C-9 Bluff
216 F-9 Bluff Knoll *mt*
196 F-9 Blumenau
58 G-5 Blumenstein
59 H-7 Blümlisalp
146 F-8 Blumut *mt*
168 G-4 Blunt
160 A-1 Blyind *strt.*
214 B-3 Blyth *riv.*
174 C-1 Blythe
176 E-2 Blytheville
87 M-5 Bo
133 M-8 Bo-gtl *isl.*
144 F-7 Bo Phloi
94 B-4 Bo River
87 L-8 Boa *riv.*
197 J-5 Boa Esperanca
195 H-3 Boa Esperança *lake*
188 G-7 Boa Fé
190 D-4 Boa Hora (Bolivia)
190 A-6 Boa Hora (Brazil)
196 E-7 Boa Ventura
195 L-2 Boa Viagem
196 E-2 Boa Vista *riv.*
193 H-8 Boa Vista (Brazil)
187 P-8 Boa Vista (Brazil)
188 E-7 Boa Vista (Brazil)
87 N-3 Boa Vista (Cape Verde) *isl.*
188 D-9 Boa Vista (Colombia) *isl.*
149 K-7 Boaan
148 K-5 Boac
184 G-5 Boaco *reg.*
184 G-5 Boaco
195 K-8 Boaçu
132 D-9 Boaj
91 J-7 Boali
87 M-5 Boama
108 F-5 Boanamary
211 P-3 Boang *isl.*
209 H-3 Boano *isl.*
63 L-4 Boara Polesine
62 G-1 Boario Terme
219 J-5 Boatman
221 H-1 Bobadah
134 G-9 Bobai
186 E-3 Bobali *mt*
62 E-5 Bobbio
89 K-3 Bobo-Dioulasso
208 G-7 Bobonaro
188 C-4 Bobonaza *riv.*
103 L-9 Bobonong
66 F-8 Bobrinec
121 K-1 Bobrinka
67 J-5 Bobrov
66 F-6 Bobrovica
66 D-5 Bobruysk
109 K-4 Boby *mt*
194 A-2 Boca *riv.*
187 P-3 Boca Araguao *riv.*
200 F-2 Boca del Guafo *gulf*
185 J-8 Boca del Monte
187 M-4 Boca del Pao
174 F-8 Boca del Rio
190 B-3 Boca do Acre
187 P-4 Boca Grande *riv.*
187 P-3 Boca Larán *riv.*
197 K-2 Bocaiúva
91 H-6 Bocaranga
185 J-7 Bocas del Toro
185 K-8 Bocas del Toro *islds*
184 G-3 Bocay
62 F-6 Boccolo dei Tassi
123 K-5 Bochan
133 M-3 Bocheonbo
66 A-8 Bochnia
57 L-6 Bocholt
57 N-9 Bocholtz
51 H-6 Bochum
102 B-2 Bocoio
186 G-3 Bocono
199 L-2 Boçoroca
91 J-8 Boda
123 N-1 Bodajbo
91 M-9 Bodalangi
221 K-4 Bodalla
90 A-4 Bode-Sadu
91 K-8 Bodebe
56 D-3 Bodegraven

48 F-6 Boden
52 C-2 Bodenham
140 D-6 Bodhan
141 K-5 Bodináyakkanür
59 N-7 Bodio
91 M-9 Bodjaki
206 A-1 Bodjo *isl.*
91 L-8 Bodjokole
207 L-6 Bodjonegoro
172 A-9 Bodkin *pte*
163 J-7 Bodo
48 E-4 Bodø
195 L-4 Bodocó
130 C-3 Bodonchiin Hüryee
196 B-4 Bodoquena *mt*
91 J-7 Bodoupa
64 G-8 Bodrum
186 G-3 Bodures
58 B-9 Boege
57 H-7 Boekel
57 N-2 Boekelo
99 K-2 Boende
99 K-1 Boendu
57 H-7 Boerdonk
175 M-5 Boerne
129 H-1 Boertashi
128 E-8 Boertushan *pass*
176 D-4 Boeuf *riv.*
54 C-7 Bœuf-Couronné (Le)
87 K-3 Boffa
211 J-5 Bogadjim
176 E-5 Bogalusa
221 J-1 Bogan *riv.*
221 J-2 Bogan Gate
89 H-6 Bogandé
91 K-7 Bogangolo
219 J-3 Bogantungan
65 K-5 Bogazköy *site*
65 L-5 Boğazliyan
97 N-1 Bogbol Manyo
99 J-1 Bogbonga
130 D-7 Bogd
69 P-6 Bogdanovič
128 D-8 Bogeduoshan *rge*
121 J-2 Bogembaj
48 D-5 Bogen
104 B-4 Bogenfels
70 D-1 Bogetsaj
58 B-9 Bogève
129 M-6 Bogezhanghe *riv.*
219 L-6 Boggabilla
219 K-8 Boggabri
216 E-1 Boggola *mt*
211 J-4 Bogia
59 K-9 Bognanco *val.*
48 D-5 Bognes
59 P-9 Bogno
53 J-8 Bognor Regis
90 G-3 Bogo (Cameroon)
148 G-3 Bogo (Philippines)
67 J-1 Bogodorsk
125 L-6 Bogoladza *mt*
221 H-4 Bogong *mt*
186 E-6 Bogota *riv.*
186 E-6 Bogota *pass*
183 C-2 Bogota
122 D-2 Bogotol
142 G-4 Bogra
122 D-3 Bograd
122 G-1 Bogučany
67 K-6 Bogučar
86 E-4 Bogué
66 E-4 Boguševsk
66 F-7 Boguslav
147 P-9 Boh *riv.*
133 J-6 Bohai *strt.*
132 G-6 Bohai *gulf*
132 G-6 Bohaiwan *bay*
213 K-6 Bohemia Downs
51 K-8 Bohemian *ft*
46 K-3 Bohemian *rge*
89 N-7 Bohicon
130 A-2 Böhmörön
126 C-3 Bohnābād
149 H-3 Bohol *pass*
97 M-3 Bohol Washago *riv.*
91 M-5 Bohou *riv.*
135 K-3 Bohu *lake*
199 L-4 Boici *riv.*
210 F-7 Boigu *isl.*
163 J-3 Boiler Rapids *riv.*
192 E-9 Boim
143 J-5 Boinu *riv.*
54 C-5 Boinville-en-Mantois
54 B-5 Boinvilliers
195 L-8 Boipeda *isl.*
196 F-2 Bois *riv.*
161 K-3 Bois (Canada) *lake*
58 D-2 Bois (Les)
170 F-3 Bois Blanc *isl.*
54 F-6 Bois-d'Arcy
55 K-3 Bois-du-Coudray

54 A-2 Bois-Jérôme-Saint- Ouen
50 G-6 Bois-le-Duc (St-Hertogenbosch)
54 B-2 Bois-Roger (Le)
55 K-1 Bois-Saint-Denis (Le)
166 F-7 Boise *riv.*
166 F-6 Boise
168 E-9 Boise City
54 F-3 Boisemont
54 B-8 Boissière-Ecole (La)
54 A-8 Boissy
55 P-1 Boissy-Fresnoy
54 F-2 Boissy-l'Aillerie
54 B-4 Boissy-Mauvoisin
54 D-6 Boissy-sans-Avoir
55 K-7 Boissy-St-Léger
66 E-7 Bojarka
148 B-6 Bojeador *cap.*
73 N-2 Bojnürd
199 M-3 Bojoru
199 N-4 Bojoru *pte*
145 J-9 Bok Kou
98 E-1 Boka Boka *mt*
91 K-8 Bokada
129 J-9 Bokalike
89 M-2 Bokanda
99 J-3 Bokatola
87 J-3 Boké
128 D-8 Bokedafeng *mt*
124 D-7 Boketu
104 E-5 Bokhara
219 J-7 Bokhara *riv.*
90 E-8 Bokito
51 H-1 Boknafjorden *fj.*
49 K-1 Boknafjorden *bay*
98 F-6 Boko
99 K-2 Bokolongo
122 D-2 Bokonbajevskoje
99 L-2 Bokondo
91 J-2 Bokoro
146 C-1 Bokpyin
125 K-3 Boktor
99 L-3 Bokungu
90 G-1 Bol
73 K-1 Bol. Balchan *mt*
120 A-2 Bol Barsuki *dés*
67 N-1 Bol. Kinel' *riv.*
69 M-3 Bol. Ous *riv.*
121 N-6 Bol'Senarymskoje
69 M-1 Bol Son *lake*
69 L-7 Bol. Sosnova
69 M-2 Bol Tap *riv.*
91 K-3 Bola *riv.*
91 N-9 Bolama
87 J-2 Bolama (Guinée-Bissau)
91 L-9 Bolama (Zaïre)
138 F-2 Bolān *riv.*
94 A-4 Bolanda *mt*
142 C-6 Bolángir
220 F-4 Bolangum
178 C-3 Bolanos *riv.*
50 E-7 Bolbec
59 H-1 Bölchent'luh *mt*
113 J-2 Bolchevik *isl.*
66 G-4 Bolchov
52 F-8 Boldre
128 C-5 Bole
95 J-4 Bole (Ethiopia)
89 L-4 Bole (Ghana)
66 C-8 Bolechov
99 H-1 Bolekhid
99 J-2 Bolenge
51 L-7 Bolestawiec
89 K-5 Bolgatanga
64 F-1 Bolgrad
125 H-8 Boli
91 J-6 Bolia (Centrafrique)
99 H-3 Bolia (Zaïre)
48 G-6 Boliden
129 M-1 Bolin
67 M-3 Bol.Irgiz *riv.*
186 E-3 Bolívar *reg.*
186 C-8 Bolívar *pass*
200 A-8 Bolívar (Brazil)
188 A-4 Bolívar (Colombia)
170 A-9 Bolívar (USA)
176 F-2 Bolívar (USA)
183 D-4 Bolívar *state*
62 E-2 Bollate
58 G-3 Bolligen
49 J-5 Bollnäs
219 J-6 Bollon
51 K-3 Bolmen *lake*
53 K-7 Bolney
72 E-2 Bolnisi
98 G-4 Bolobo
61 M-3 Bologna
63 K-6 Bologna (Bologne)
189 J-6 Bolognesi
66 F-1 Bologoye

99 J-2 Bolomba
99 L-1 Bolombo *riv.*
125 K-4 Bolon *lake*
125 K-4 Bolon'
99 J-2 Bolondo
121 P-2 Bolotnoje
145 K-6 Bolovens *plat.*
190 C-1 Bolpebra
122 F-2 Bol'saja Murta
121 L-4 Bol'šaja Vladimirovka
123 J-3 Bol'šeokinskoje
69 N-7 Bol'šeust'ikinskoje
89 H-7 Bolsi
125 L-2 Bol'sije Kiri *lake*
133 P-1 Bolsoj Kamen'
123 L-4 Bol'šoj Onguren
123 H-6 Bol'šoj Sajan *mt*
122 E-2 Bol'šoj Uluj
123 K-6 Bol'šoje Goloustnoje
58 F-5 Boltigen
50 D-4 Bolton
65 H-5 Bolu
128 E-7 Boluoha *mt*
67 N-4 Bol.Uzen *riv.*
65 H-5 Bolvadin
190 B-4 Bom Comércio
197 J-4 Bom Despacho
195 P-4 Bom Jardim (Brazil)
190 B-4 Bom Jardim (Brazil)
197 K-6 Bom Jardim de Minas
194 G-5 Bom Jesus (Brazil)
199 N-2 Bom Jesus (Brazil)
195 H-5 Bom Jesus da Gurguéia *mt*
195 H-8 Bom Jesus da Lapa
197 L-4 Bom Jesus do Galho
197 M-5 Bom Jésus do Itabapoanna
196 F-9 Bom Retiro
197 J-5 Bom Successo
98 E-6 Boma
98 F-2 Bomandjokou
99 H-1 Bomango
87 P-2 Bomba *pte*
221 J-5 Bombala
94 G-2 Bombashi
140 C-2 Bombay
187 P-3 Bombeador *pte*
108 E-5 Bombetoka *bay*
98 G-6 Bombo *riv.*
100 E-2 Bombo
99 G-2 Bömbögör
99 J-1 Bomboma
143 J-2 Bomdila
131 P-3 Bomi
87 M-6 Bomi Hills Vaitown
100 A-1 Bomili
56 F-5 Bommelerwaard
124 F-2 Bomnak
94 B-7 Bomokandi *riv.*
91 K-8 Bomotu
146 A-3 Bompoka *isl.*
79 P-2 Bon *cap.*
146 C-3 Bon *isl.*
218 B-7 Bon Bon
160 C-2 Bona *mt*
142 D-5 Bonaigarh
187 J-1 Bonaire *isl.*
221 J-5 Bonang
185 H-4 Bonanza
158 E-2 Bonanza Hills *mt*
213 J-2 Bonaparte *islds*
159 G-5 Bonasila *riv.*
158 G-5 Bonasila Dome *mt*
187 N-3 Bonasse
62 F-5 Bonassola
63 K-4 Bonavigo
165 P-2 Bonavista
165 N-2 Bonavista *bay*
165 P-2 Bonavista *cap.*
209 M-3 Bonbarai *riv.*
218 A-2 Bond Springs
63 K-5 Bondeno
91 N-8 Bondo
148 E-5 Bondoc *pen.*
55 J-3 Bondoufle
89 M-4 Bondoukou
207 N-6 Bondowoso
69 L-9 Bond'užskij
55 K-5 Bondy
79 M-2 Bone (Annaba)
208 D-4 Bone (Teluk) *gulf*
208 E-4 Bonelipu
208 D-5 Bonelohe
208 D-6 Bonerate *isl.*
198 B-2 Bonete *mt*
196 G-1 Bonfinópolis
55 P-9 Bonfruit
87 N-7 Bong *reg.*
87 N-6 Bong (Liberia)
57 K-9 Bong (Netherlands)
95 H-4 Bonga
148 F-5 Bongabong
91 L-9 Bongado

99 K-1 Bongandanga
208 D-1 Bongka *riv.*
91 N-4 Bongo *mt*
98 C-4 Bongo
149 J-3 Bongo *isl.*
89 K-6 Bongo-Da
109 H-4 Bongolava *reg.*
91 M-9 Bongolu
91 H-3 Bongor
89 N-2 Bongouanou
175 P-3 Bonham
204 C-2 Boni *gulf*
61 K-5 Bonifacio *strt.*
61 L-5 Bonifacio
59 H-5 Bönigen
59 K-1 Boniswil
197 L-6 Bonito
196 E-1 Bonito *riv.*
197 K-1 Bonito (Brazil)
196 B-4 Bonito (Brazil)
192 E-4 Boniville
47 D-4 Bonn
51 H-7 Bonn
48 E-5 Bonnå
165 L-3 Bonne *bay*
58 A-9 Bonne
54 F-9 Bonnelles
162 E-5 Bonners Ferry
163 P-9 Bonnet *lake*
160 G-2 Bonnet Plume *riv.*
55 K-4 Bonneuil-en-France
58 C-8 Bonnevaux
61 J-2 Bonneville
220 E-5 Bonney *lake*
216 F-6 Bonnie Rock
54 B-3 Bonnières-sur-Seine
90 B-8 Bonny
89 J-5 Bonnyville
163 J-5 Bonnyville
210 D-2 Bono
137 N-3 Bônotu
199 J-3 Bonpland
219 L-7 Bonshaw
208 C-5 Bonthain
87 M-4 Bonthe
148 C-6 Bontoc
52 B-5 Bonvilston
211 N-8 Bonvouloir *islds*
209 K-1 Boo *islds*
87 L-7 Boola
212 D-9 Boolaloo
220 G-2 Booligal
170 A-6 Boone (USA)
177 K-1 Boone (USA)
176 F-2 Booneville
219 J-2 Boongoondoo
170 D-9 Boonsville
172 G-3 Boonton
130 D-6 Bööntsagaan *lake*
170 B-8 Boonville
221 J-3 Boorowa
57 M-8 Boorsem
220 F-4 Boort
218 B-6 Boorthanna
211 H-8 Boori *rf*
161 L-1 Booth *islds*
153 J-2 Boothia *pen.*
98 D-2 Booué
218 C-6 Bopechee
105 J-3 Bophuthatswana *reg.*
104 G-4 Bophuthatswana *reg.*
132 F-7 Boping
135 L-7 Bopingling *mt*
87 M-6 Bopulu
191 L-7 Boqueron *reg.*
185 J-8 Boquete
195 H-8 Boquira
94 E-5 Bor (Sudan)
64 C-3 Bor (Yugoslavia)
130 B-4 Bor Har *mt*
224 D-5 Bora-Bora *isl.*
166 F-8 Borah *mt*
97 H-2 Bôramo
55 J-1 Boran-sur-Oise
51 K-2 Boras
83 N-1 Borāzjān
148 G-3 Bordo
187 M-4 Borbón
195 N-4 Borborema *plat.*
182 G-3 Borborema *plat.*
171 N-5 Borckton
57 M-3 Borculo
54 E-2 Bord-Haut-de-Vigny (Le)
220 B-3 Borda *cap.*
60 F-2 Bordeaux
165 K-6 Borden
153 K-2 Borden *pen.*
172 F-5 Bordentown
220 E-4 Bordertown
58 E-9 Bordes (Les)
48 B-2 Bordeyri
62 A-9 Bordighera
79 L-2 Bordj Bou-Arréridj
78 E-8 Bordj Fly Sainte Marie (Bou Bernous)
79 K-2 Bordj Ménaïel

79 N-7 Bordj Messouda
62 F-6 Bore
55 M-1 Borest
48 B-1 Borgarnes
62 A-4 Bórgaro Torinese
175 L-1 Borger
57 M-9 Borgharen
63 J-2 Borghetto
62 F-8 Borghetto di Vara
62 F-4 Borghetto Lodi
51 M-3 Borgholm
63 H-8 Borgo a Mozzano
62 B-3 Borgo d'Ale
63 K-6 Borgo Panigale
63 K-8 Borgo San Lorenzo
62 C-2 Borgo Ticino
62 F-7 Borgo Val di Taro
62 C-3 Borgo Vercelli
63 J-4 Borgoforte
62 A-3 Borgofranco d'Ivrea
62 C-3 Borgolavezzaro
62 C-2 Borgomanero
62 B-8 Borgomaro
62 E-4 Borgonovo
62 B-2 Borgosesia
89 K-8 Borgou reg.
130 A-4 Borig Del Els mt
145 J-4 Borikhan reg.
66 B-8 Borislav
67 K-5 Borisoglebsk
66 D-4 Borisov
67 H-4 Borisovka
66 F-7 Borispol'
60 E-4 Borja (Spain)
196 B-8 Borja (Paraguay)
56 G-9 Borkel
57 N-5 Borken
92 A-4 Borkou-Ennedi-Tibesti reg.
51 H-5 Borkum
49 K-4 Borlänge
61 K-3 Bormida riv.
62 B-7 Bormida
62 B-6 Bormida di Millesimo riv.
62 B-7 Bormida di Spigno riv.
57 M-7 Born
57 N-1 Borne
54 G-1 Bornel
207 M-1 Bornéo
108 C-5 Bornéo rf
149 N-7 Borneo reg.
57 N-1 Bornerbroek
60 B-4 Bornes mt
51 L-4 Bornholm isl.
51 L-4 Bornholm strt.
90 F-2 Borno reg.
62 G-1 Borno
64 F-7 Bornova
86 G-9 Boro
94 A-3 Boro riv.
207 K-6 Borobudur site
95 J-5 Borodda
121 M-5 Borodulicha
91 M-4 Boromara
89 J-4 Boromo
148 F-2 Borongan
87 L-8 Borotou
53 L-6 Borough
66 E-1 Bŏroviči
121 P-4 Borovl'anka
121 H-1 Borovoje
66 G-3 Borovsk
97 H-7 Borrän
214 C-5 Borroloola
66 C-9 Borsa
139 H-8 Borsad
66 D-8 Borščev
124 B-4 Borshchovochnyy mt
95 K-3 Borshoto
57 N-1 Borskoje
59 H-1 Boru hill
99 H-4 Boruempe riv.
73 L-8 Borüjen
73 J-7 Borüjerd
124 A-6 Borza riv.
124 A-6 Borz'a
66 F-6 Borzna
72 D-2 Boržomi
62 E-7 Borzonasca
121 H-5 Bosaga
96 G-7 Bösáso
210 G-5 Bosavi mt
199 J-9 Bosch
57 M-7 Bosch Beek riv.
56 F-9 Boscheind
63 K-4 Boschi Santa Anna
59 L-8 Bosco
63 J-2 Bosco Chiesanuova
62 C-5 Bosco Marengo
52 E-8 Boscombe
62 A-3 Bosconero
99 L-1 Bosenge
133 M-8 Boseong
132 G-7 Boshan
105 H-5 Boshof

126 B-2 Boshrüyeh (Iran)
62 E-2 Bosisio Parini
128 E-8 Bositenghu lake
56 C-3 Boskoop
64 A-3 Bosna riv.
125 M-3 Bošn'akovo
64 A-3 Bosnia Herce-govina reg.
137 H-8 Bōsō pen.
99 J-1 Boso Djafo
91 L-8 Bosobolo
91 J-6 Bossangoa
91 J-7 Bossembélé
91 H-7 Bossentelé
176 C-4 Bossier City
90 F-1 Bosso
89 H-8 Bosso riv.
62 B-6 Bossolasco
212 G-6 Bossut cap.
126 F-8 Bostān
72 G-4 Bostānābād-e Bala
177 L-1 Boston
176 C-2 Boston mt
220 B-2 Boston bay
50 E-5 Boston (UK)
171 M-5 Boston (USA)
89 N-5 Bosumtwi lake
139 H-8 Botād
221 L-3 Botany bay
53 N-1 Botesdale
64 D-4 Botevgrad
105 H-4 Bothaville
112 A-3 Bothnia gulf
49 J-7 Bothnia gulf
46 F-3 Bothnia gulf
221 H-8 Bothwell
211 M-3 Botiangin cap.
103 J-8 Botletle riv.
52 G-8 Botley (UK)
52 G-4 Botley (UK)
99 H-3 Botola
99 J-2 Botoro
66 D-9 Botoşani
89 M-2 Botro
173 J-1 Botsford
168 G-1 Bottineau
53 L-2 Bottisham
181 J-4 Bottle Creek
63 M-4 Bottrighe
196 G-6 Botucatu
165 M-2 Botwood
124 B-4 Boty
89 L-1 Bou riv.
78 C-5 Bou-Azzer
78 E-8 Bou Bernous (Bordj Fly Sainte Marie)
88 D-4 Boû Djébéha well
79 J-3 Bou Ismaïl
78 A-6 Bou-Izakarn
79 H-3 Bou Ktoub
78 E-3 Bou Naceur mt
86 C-5 Boû Nâga
78 D-3 Bou Regreg riv.
86 C-4 Boû Rjeîmât well
79 K-3 Bou Saâda
86 F-8 Bou Staîla
89 M-1 Bouaflé
54 E-4 Bouafle
89 M-2 Bouaké
78 F-4 Bouânane
89 M-1 Bouandougou
91 H-7 Bouar
78 F-4 Bouârfa
90 G-5 Bouba-Njidda na.p.
89 N-1 Boubérédou
91 K-6 Bouca
214 A-3 Boucaut bay
54 B-7 Bouchemont
165 K-2 Boucher lake
58 A-2 Bouclans
54 E-1 Bouconvillers
78 E-4 Boudenib
58 D-4 Boudry
98 E-5 Bouenza riv.
98 E-5 Bouenza reg.
79 K-2 Boufarik
55 H-3 Bouffémont
79 L-2 Bougaa
215 K-6 Bougainville rf
213 K-2 Bougainville cap.
79 M-2 Bougaroun cap.
52 B-2 Boughrood
79 L-2 Bougie (Bejaïa)
54 G-6 Bougival
89 J-1 Bougoukouroula
87 J-8 Bougouni
89 K-3 Bougouriba riv.
58 B-7 Bougy
55 P-2 Bouillancy
79 K-2 Bouira
78 D-4 Boujâd
98 C-4 Boukolo
78 C-3 Boulaouane
54 B-7 Boulay (Le)
168 B-2 Boulder riv.

217 H-6 Boulder (Australia)
168 D-7 Boulder (USA)
167 L-5 Boulder City
78 E-3 Boulemane
55 P-5 Bouleurs
218 E-2 Boulia
54 F-8 Boullay-les-Troux
55 H-6 Boulogne ft
55 H-6 Boulogne-Billancourt
50 E-7 Boulogne-sur-Mer
91 M-6 Boulouba
215 M-4 Bouloupari
89 J-5 Boulsa
78 D-5 Boumalne
91 H-9 Boumba riv.
90 G-7 Boumbé II riv.
90 G-7 Boumbé 1 riv.
86 E-6 Boumdeïd
89 L-3 Bouna
172 F-4 Bound Brook
160 E-1 Boundary
160 D-6 Boundary (Canada) mt
167 J-4 Boundary (USA) mt
89 L-1 Boundiali
98 F-3 Boundji
88 G-1 Boundjiguiré
145 L-6 Boung riv.
91 M-5 Boungou riv.
168 A-5 Bountiful
55 J-3 Bouquenal
215 M-4 Bourail
79 N-9 Bourarhet dés
54 B-7 Bourdonné
88 F-6 Bourem
61 J-2 Bourg-en-Bresse
60 B-3 Bourg-Madame
61 H-1 Bourges
55 K-4 Bourget (Le)
61 J-2 Bourgoin
219 H-7 Bourke
50 D-6 Bournemouth
90 F-3 Bourrah
78 C-3 Bouskoura
91 H-3 Bousso
55 L-8 Boussy-Saint-Antoine
54 D-3 Bout-d'en-Haut (Le)
55 P-5 Boutigny
54 B-7 Boutigny-Prouais
86 D-2 Boutilimit
98 D-3 Boutipabo
89 L-3 Boutourou mt
214 A-2 Braithwaite pte
216 D-8 Bouvard cap.
58 D-7 Bouveret
94 A-5 Bouyé riv.
78 D-3 Bouznika
62 G-2 Boyengo
172 C-5 Bovertown
62 A-7 Boves
52 A-9 Bovey Tracey
52 D-9 Bovington
63 M-3 Bovolenta
63 K-4 Bovolone
162 G-7 Bow riv.
168 F-1 Bowbells
216 E-8 Bowelling
215 K-9 Bowen
221 J-5 Bowen mt
219 H-2 Bowen Downs
172 D-9 Bowers
219 J-1 Bowie (Australia)
175 N-3 Bowie (USA)
174 F-3 Bowie (USA)
162 F-8 Bowlder mt
215 K-8 Bowling Green cap.
170 F-7 Bowling Green (USA)
170 B-8 Bowling Green (USA)
176 G-1 Bowling Green (USA)
168 F-3 Bowman
162 D-5 Bowman mt
172 B-5 Bowmansville
162 E-3 Bowron riv.
162 E-4 Bowron Lake na.p.
160 D-9 Bowser lake
52 D-9 Box
168 C-1 Boxelder riv.
53 M-3 Boxford
132 F-9 Boxian (China)
135 K-1 Boxian (China)
53 M-6 Boxley
57 J-6 Boxmeer
56 G-7 Boxtel
65 K-4 Boyabat
186 F-6 Boyaca reg.
186 C-5 Boyajá riv.
163 N-1 Boyd lake
161 P-9 Boyd (Canada) lake
99 J-2 Boyenge
169 J-6 Boyer riv.
215 P-4 Boyer cap.
73 L-9 Boyer Ahmadiye reg.
50 B-3 Boyle
177 L-8 Boynton Beach
168 C-4 Boysen lake
191 K-6 Boyuibe
216 E-8 Boyup Brook
190 D-2 Boyuyumanu riv.

143 M-1 Bozangbujiang riv.
64 G-7 Bozdoğan
168 B-2 Bozeman
132 F-6 Bozhen
58 F-2 Bözingen
131 P-3 Bozong
91 H-6 Bozoum
65 H-5 Bozüyük
63 H-4 Bozzolo
62 A-6 Bra
61 P-4 Bracki cap.
192 E-2 Braams pte
56 C-9 Braaschaat
61 D-7 Brác isl.
80 C-5 Brach
57 N-7 Brachterbeek
49 H-4 Bräcke
175 L-6 Brackettville
52 G-3 Brackley
53 H-5 Bracknell
194 D-6 Braço Menor do Araguaia ou Javes riv.
64 D-1 Brad
177 K-8 Bradenton
52 G-5 Bradfield
53 M-2 Bradfield Combust
50 D-4 Bradford (UK)
171 J-6 Bradford (USA)
173 H-5 Bradley Beach
53 N-4 Bradwell
175 M-4 Brady
160 C-5 Brady glac.
50 D-2 Braemar
60 B-3 Braga
198 G-7 Bragado
194 E-9 Bragagem riv.
60 B-3 Bragança (Spain)
190 B-2 Bragança (Peru)
197 H-6 Bragança Paulista
138 F-5 Brahmanābād site
143 H-4 Brāhmanbāria
142 D-6 Brāhmani riv.
129 N-3 Brahmapoutre riv.
116 E-4 Brahmaputra riv.
143 H-3 Brahmaputra riv.
129 P-7 Brahmaputra riv.
221 K-4 Braidwood
64 F-2 Braila
170 A-3 Brainerd
53 M-3 Braintree
53 M-6 Braithwaite
105 K-1 Brak riv.
56 E-5 Brakel
86 D-5 Brakna reg.
105 K-4 Brakpan
102 D-9 Brakwater
162 C-5 Bralorne
172 E-3 Bramards
215 H-1 Bramble Cay rf
211 H-7 Bramble Cay
57 L-2 Bramel
53 P-1 Bramfield
53 N-2 Bramford
53 J-6 Bramley
58 F-8 Bramois
171 H-5 Brampton (Canada)
53 K-1 Brampton (UK)
53 P-1 Brampton (UK)
194 G-2 Branca mt
165 P-4 Branch
172 A-3 Branchdale
172 F-2 Branchville
87 N-1 Branco isl.
194 C-3 Branco riv.
190 E-8 Branco (Cabixi) riv.
102 C-3 Brandberg mt
51 K-6 Brandenburg
51 K-6 Brandenburg reg.
105 H-5 Brandfort
163 N-9 Brandon (Canada)
53 M-1 Brandon (UK)
51 L-7 Brandý-na-Labem
173 L-1 Branford
66 A-5 Braniewo
192 B-6 Branquinho riv.
218 F-6 Bransby
176 D-1 Branson
124 E-1 Br'antsk riv.
171 H-5 Brantford
220 E-5 Branxholme
62 F-1 Branzi
192 C-8 Brás
165 N-5 Bras d'Or lake
199 K-3 Brasil Leite
190 C-2 Brasiléia
87 F-4 Brasilia
197 H-1 Brasilia
64 E-2 Braşov
218 B-2 Brassey (Australia) mt
149 M-2 Brassey (Malaysia) mt
58 A-6 Brassus (Le)
53 L-6 Brasted
51 M-9 Bratislava
123 J-2 Bratsk

66 F-8 Bratskoje
123 J-3 Bratskoje lake
171 M-5 Brattleboro
53 K-3 Braughing
196 F-5 Braúna
51 J-6 Braunschweig
59 N-4 Braunwald
87 P-1 Brava
101 N-1 Brava
188 F-2 Brava mt
191 P-2 Bravos mt
174 B-1 Brawley
54 B-1 Bray-et-Lû
162 F-5 Brazeau mt
162 G-5 Brazeau riv.
183 F-4 Brazil state
182 E-4 Brazilian Highland plat.
186 E-3 Brazo de Loba riv.
186 E-3 Brazo de Mompos riv.
187 N-4 Brazo Imataca riv.
201 L-4 Brazo sur del Coig riv.
175 P-6 Brazos riv.
77 D-5 Brazzaville
98 F-5 Brazzaville
198 E-2 Brea Pozo
217 K-2 Breaden lake
222 B-8 Breaksea strt.
52 D-9 Bream
223 K-3 Bream cap.
223 K-3 Bream Tail
54 F-1 Bréançon
64 E-2 Breaza
60 B-3 Brebes
54 A-8 Bréchamps
56 C-9 Brecht
168 C-7 Breckenridge (USA)
169 J-3 Breckenridge (USA)
175 M-3 Breckenridge (USA)
53 M-1 Breckland reg.
201 N-4 Brecknock pen.
52 B-3 Brecon
52 A-3 Brecon Beacons hill
50 G-6 Breda
63 M-2 Breda di Piave
104 D-9 Bredasdorp
221 J-4 Bredbo
53 M-7 Brede
57 M-4 Bredevoort
53 M-6 Bredhurst
52 E-3 Bredon
57 M-7 Bree
104 D-9 Brée riv.
57 J-5 Breedeweg
63 L-2 Breganze
61 L-1 Bregenz
63 H-1 Breguzzo
55 P-2 Brégy
48 A-1 Breidafjördur bay
48 A-1 Breidavik
48 C-4 Breiddalsvik
59 P-5 Breil (Brigels)
59 H-7 Breithorn
194 E-6 Brejinho de Nazaré
195 H-4 Brejo riv.
193 N-9 Brejo
194 F-4 Brejo da Porta
195 M-3 Brejo do Cruz
195 H-2 Brejo do São Félix
195 H-7 Brejolândia
49 H-3 Brekken
48 G-3 Brekstad
58 E-8 Brelaye
49 H-1 Bremangerlandet isl.
62 F-1 Brembana val.
62 F-1 Brembo riv.
177 H-3 Bremen
51 H-5 Bremen
214 C-3 Bremer isl.
216 G-9 Bremer bay
217 H-7 Bremer mt
51 H-5 Bremerhaven
162 B-8 Bremerton
59 K-1 Bremgarten
219 J-6 Brenda
63 K-3 Brendola
52 A-7 Brendon hill
58 A-5 Brenet lake
58 C-3 Brenets (Les)
175 N-5 Brenham
61 M-1 Brenner strt.
63 H-1 Breno
52 C-6 Brent (UK)
58 D-7 Brent (Switzerland)
61 M-2 Brenta riv.
53 J-5 Brentford
63 L-4 Brentónico
53 L-4 Brentwood (UK)
173 K-3 Brentwood (USA)
53 N-7 Brenzett
63 H-5 Brescello
62 G-2 Brescia reg.
61 L-2 Brescia
62 E-4 Bressana Bottarone
60 F-1 Bressuire

50 D-9 Bressuire
50 B-7 Brest
66 B-6 Brest Litovsk
59 K-1 Brestenberg
50 C-8 Bretagne reg.
54 F-6 Bretèche (La)
54 E-4 Breteuil
52 E-2 Bretfortor
55 J-9 Brétigny-sur-Orge
176 F-6 Breton Sound strt.
172 G-6 Breton Woods
58 C-2 Bretonvillers
223 K-2 Brett cap.
146 A-5 Breueh isl.
54 C-4 Breuil-Bois-Robert
62 A-1 Breuil Cervinia
56 E-2 Breukelen
57 M-9 Breust
54 A-4 Bréval
177 J-2 Brevard
193 H-8 Breves
54 D-8 Bréviaires (Les)
58 C-3 Brévine (La)
58 B-9 Brevon riv.
219 J-7 Brewarrina
168 G-6 Brewster
221 H-2 Brewster lake
176 G-5 Brewton
105 L-4 Breyten
69 L-9 Brezhnev
79 H-4 Brézina
54 E-2 Brézolles
91 M-6 Bria
167 K-7 Brian Head
61 K-3 Briançon
62 E-2 Brianza reg.
173 H-2 Briarcliff Manor
172 G-6 Brick
109 H-6 Brickaville
180 F-2 Bridge pte
162 D-5 Bridge Lake
173 M-2 Bridgehampton
52 A-5 Bridgend
168 E-6 Bridgeport (USA)
167 J-3 Bridgeport (USA)
171 M-6 Bridgeport (USA)
171 L-7 Bridgeport
181 P-8 Bridgetown
157 H-5 Bridgetown
216 E-9 Bridgetown
165 K-8 Bridgewater
220 E-8 Bridgewater cap.
164 G-9 Bridgton
50 C-6 Bridgwater
52 B-6 Bridgwater Bay bay
50 E-4 Bridlington
221 H-7 Bridport
52 C-8 Bridport (UK)
55 L-8 Brie-Comte-Robert
56 A-4 Brielle
59 J-5 Brienz
59 J-5 Brienzer lake
52 E-1 Brierley Hill
59 J-8 Brig
165 L-1 Brig Bay
172 G-8 Brigantine
52 G-9 Brighstone
221 H-4 Bright
53 L-7 Brightling
53 N-3 Brightlingsea
53 D-6 Brighton
53 P-2 Brightwell
54 E-1 Brignancourt
62 A-8 Brigue (La)
54 G-9 Briis-sous-Forges
86 G-1 Brikama
66 G-9 Brilevka
196 C-5 Brilhante riv.
53 L-2 Brinkley
52 G-1 Brinklow
52 E-5 Brinkworth
165 K-5 Brion isl.
59 M-8 Brione
61 H-2 Brioude
219 N-6 Brisbane
59 L-4 Brisen mt
63 L-7 Brisighella
59 M-9 Brissago
59 M-5 Bristen
59 M-5 Bristenstock mt
52 B-6 Bristol bay
152 C-4 Bristol bay
158 C-6 Bristol bay
50 D-6 Bristol (UK)
177 K-1 Bristol (USA)
175 P-5 Bristow
194 C-9 Britânia
162 C-6 Britannia Beach
159 P-7 British mt
104 F-7 Britstown
59 H-7 Brittnau
59 H-3 Britton
60 G-2 Brive
60 D-3 Briviesca
53 H-1 Brixworth

128 B-1 Brlik
51 M-8 Brno
180 C-4 Broa *bay*
140 A-3 Broach
219 L-2 Broad *strt.*
52 A-8 Broad Clyst
164 B-4 Broadback *riv.*
220 G-5 Broadford (Australia)
50 C-1 Broadford (UK)
53 P-5 Broadstairs
168 E-3 Broadus
163 M-9 Broadview
52 D-2 Broadwas
52 E-3 Broadway (UK)
52 D-9 Broadway (UK)
52 C-8 Broadwinsor
58 E-6 Broc
163 N-3 Brochet *lake*
163 N-3 Brochet
52 F-8 Brockenhurst
212 E-9 Brockman *mt*
227 M-6 Brockton
164 D-9 Brockville
100 F-2 Broderick Falls
153 K-2 Brodeur *pen.*
172 D-2 Brodheadsville
50 C-2 Brodick
66 A-5 Brodnica
66 C-7 Brody
57 K-8 Broekhuizen
57 K-7 Broekhuizenvorst
57 K-1 Broekland
59 M-8 Broglio
172 A-6 Brogueville
220 G-4 Broken *riv.*
221 L-3 Broken *bay*
168 G-6 Broken Bow
220 E-1 Broken Hill
176 E-5 Brokhaven
192 E-3 Brokopondo
59 M-9 Brolla *pass*
52 C-1 Bromfield
52 E-5 Bromham
53 K-5 Bromley
52 E-1 Bromsgrove
52 D-2 Bromyard
51 J-2 Brønderslev
89 M-4 Brong-Ahafo *reg.*
62 E-4 Broni
57 K-3 Bronkhorst
105 K-3 Bronkhorstspruit
52 B-3 Bronllys
48 F-1 Brønnøysund
57 K-2 Bronsbergen
175 L-4 Bronte
220 G-8 Bronte Park
173 H-3 Bronx
105 K-4 Broodsnyersplaas
53 J-2 Brook End
53 L-4 Brook Street
149 H-8 Brooke's Point
170 A-8 Brookfield
173 K-3 Brookhaven
169 J-4 Brookings (USA)
166 E-2 Brookings (USA)
53 N-7 Brookland
173 H-3 Brooklyn
162 A-4 Brooks *bay*
158 E-8 Brooks *lake*
162 A-5 Brooks *pen.*
163 H-7 Brooks
152 C-3 Brooks *rge*
159 J-2 Brooks (USA) *mt*
173 K-1 Brooksvale
177 K-7 Brooksville
216 E-7 Brookton
171 J-7 Brookville
172 D-6 Broomall
213 H-5 Broome
53 L-4 Broomfield
54 E-8 Brosse (La)
195 J-7 Brotas de Macaúba
55 L-5 Brou-sur-Chantereine
54 A-7 Broué
53 H-3 Broughton
57 H-8 Brouwhuis
66 E-7 Brovary
220 A-1 Brown *pte*
216 F-6 Brown *lake*
180 E-2 Brown Cay *rf*
175 K-3 Brownfield
162 G-9 Browning
159 P-6 Brownlow *pte*
172 F-6 Browns Mills
172 B-5 Brownstown
176 F-2 Brownsville
178 G-1 Brownsville (USA)
192 E-3 Brownsweg
175 M-4 Brownwood
213 H-2 Browse *isl.*
58 D-5 Broye *riv.*
58 D-4 Broye
63 K-9 Brozzi
62 G-2 Brozzo
59 J-5 Brtenzer Rothorn *mt*
212 E-9 Bruce *mt*

164 A-9 Bruce *pen.*
222 D-7 Bruce Bay
216 F-7 Bruce Rock
56 F-5 Bruchem
67 K-9 Br'uchoveckaja
61 P-1 Bruck an der Mur
52 C-6 Brue *riv.*
54 D-3 Brueil-en-Vexin
63 H-1 Bruffione *mt*
50 F-6 Brugge
57 K-9 Brüggen
63 M-3 Brügine
63 N-1 Brugnera
62 E-6 Brugneto *lake*
168 A-6 Bruin *riv.*
56 A-6 Bruinisse
147 L-8 Bruit *isl.*
165 H-2 Brûlé *lake*
163 J-3 Brule Rapids *riv.*
195 J-9 Brumado *riv.*
195 J-9 Brumado
57 K-3 Brummen
166 G-6 Bruneau *riv.*
147 P-6 Brunei *reg.*
118 G-6 Brunei *state*
214 C-7 Brunette *riv.*
165 N-4 Brunette *isl.*
214 B-7 Brunette Downs
49 H-4 Brunflo
59 K-5 Brünig *pass*
59 J-5 Brünigen
59 P-1 Brunnadern
59 H-9 Brunnegghorn *mt*
59 M-3 Brunnen
222 F-7 Brunner
222 F-7 Brunner *lake*
59 M-3 Brunni
55 K-8 Brunoy
51 J-5 Brunshüttelkoog
57 N-8 Brunssum
164 G-9 Brunswick
201 N-4 Brunswick *pen.*
177 K-5 Brunswick
221 H-9 Bruny *isl.*
185 J-8 Brus *riv.*
185 H-2 Brus *lag.*
185 H-2 Brus Laguna
62 B-4 Brusasco
68 G-7 Brusenec
168 E-7 Brush
196 G-9 Brusque
47 D-4 Brussels
50 F-7 Brussels
62 A-2 Brusson
52 D-7 Bruton
55 L-7 Bruyères (Les)
187 H-4 Bruzual
55 K-6 Bry-sur-Marne
220 D-1 Bryan *mt*
170 F-7 Bryan (USA)
175 N-5 Bryan (USA)
66 F-4 Bryansk
167 L-7 Bryce Canyon *na.p.*
52 B-4 Bryhmdwr
52 A-5 Bryn Cethin
172 D-6 Bryn Mawr
51 H-1 Bryne
177 J-2 Bryson City
51 M-7 Brzeg
64 H-7 Bü *riv.*
72 E-4 Bü Ağri *mt*
80 E-3 Bü Ash Shawk *riv.*
84 C-4 Bü Müsa *isl.*
80 D-3 Bü Nujaym
92 A-1 Bü Sunbul *mt*
72 E-5 Bü-zap *riv.*
106 E-3 Bua *riv.*
133 M-7 Buan (South Korea)
90 B-7 Buan (Nigeria)
128 A-8 Buarjin
208 D-4 Buapinang
146 E-9 Buatan
87 J-3 Buba
100 B-4 Bubanza
87 J-2 Bubaque
62 B-6 Bubbio
103 L-7 Bubi *riv.*
83 L-2 Bübiyän *isl.*
100 G-6 Bubu *riv.*
129 N-4 Bubuduo
99 H-1 Buburu
103 M-9 Bubye *riv.*
54 G-7 Buc
64 F-7 Buca
66 C-8 Bučač
65 H-7 Bucak
186 E-5 Bucaramanga
160 B-8 Bucareli *bay*
149 H-1 Bucas Grande *isl.*
213 H-4 Buccaneer *islds*
221 J-5 Buchan
217 H-2 Buchanan *lake*
173 H-1 Buchanan
87 N-6 Buchanan (Liberia)
165 M-3 Buchans
64 E-2 Bucharest
47 F-5 Bucharest

58 F-2 Buchegg *mt*
54 B-4 Buchelay
54 C-1 Buchet
121 P-7 Buchtarma *riv.*
57 M-7 Buchten
53 J-7 Buck Barn
172 D-1 Buck Hill Falls
172 C-2 Buck Mont
172 C-6 Buck Run
53 K-1 Buckden
214 B-3 Buckingham *bay*
164 D-8 Buckingham (Canada)
53 H-3 Buckingham (UK)
172 E-5 Buckingham (USA)
219 K-3 Buckland *plat.*
159 J-4 Buckland *riv.*
159 J-3 Buckland
52 D-6 Buckland Denham
214 D-9 Buckley *riv.*
220 B-1 Buckleyboo
166 G-3 Bucks *mt*
172 E-5 Bucks *reg.*
53 J-7 Bucks Green
98 D-6 Buco Zau
170 G-7 Bucyrus
49 H-2 Bud
143 K-6 Budalin
64 B-1 Budapest
47 E-5 Budapest
48 B-1 Budardalur
70 A-3 Budarino
139 P-5 Budaun
97 N-5 Budbud
216 D-5 Budd *mt*
227 N-4 Budd Coast
172 F-6 Buddtown
50 C-6 Bude (UK)
176 E-5 Bude (USA)
57 H-9 Budel
200 C-1 Budi *lag.*
48 B-1 Búdir (Iceland)
48 C-4 Búdir (Norway)
91 L-9 Budjala
52 B-9 Budleigh Salterton
63 N-1 Budoia
63 L-6 Budrio
100 F-1 Budula
124 G-5 Budunda *riv.*
90 C-8 Buéa
200 G-4 Buen Pasto
201 L-5 Buen Tempo *cap.*
198 E-7 Buena Esperanza
167 L-3 Buena Vista *lake*
191 H-5 Buena Vista (Bolivia)
196 B-8 Buena Vista (Paraguay)
171 J-9 Buena Vista (USA)
187 J-5 Buena Vista (Vénézuela)
186 C-7 Buenaventura (Colombia)
180 C-4 Buenaventura (Cuba)
174 G-5 Buenaventura (Mexico)
148 E-5 Buenavista
52 A-5 Buenga *riv.*
197 K-3 Buenópolis
201 H-4 Buenos Aires *lake*
183 D-6 Buenos Aires (Argentina)
200 A-8 Buenos Aires (Argentina)
199 H-7 Buenos Aires (Argentina)
188 D-9 Buenos Aires (Colombia)
185 H-8 Buenos Aires (Costa Rica)
131 N-3 Buerhanbutashan *mt*
129 N-9 Buerhu *lake*
128 A-8 Buerjin
130 A-1 Buerjinhe *riv.*
210 D-2 Bufareh
221 H-4 Buffalo *na.p.*
163 J-1 Buffalo *riv.*
163 H-6 Buffalo *lake*
161 K-9 Buffalo (Canada) *riv.*
163 H-7 Buffalo (Canada)
161 K-9 Buffalo (Canada) *lake*
168 G-9 Buffalo (USA)
168 E-3 Buffalo (USA)
170 A-9 Buffalo (USA)
168 D-4 Buffalo (USA)
171 J-5 Buffalo (USA)
175 P-4 Buffalo (USA)
163 H-2 Buffalo Head *mt*
163 K-4 Buffalo Narrows
104 C-5 Buffels *riv.*
51 P-6 Bug *riv.*
66 D-8 Bug *riv.*
186 C-7 Buga
133 M-4 Bugcheong
97 N-6 Bugda Kösär *well*
207 L-5 Bugel *cap.*
57 N-6 Buggenum
78 B-1 Bugio *isl.*
100 E-2 Bugiri

100 F-1 Bugisu *reg.*
133 L-4 Bugjin
100 E-1 Bugondo
68 E-1 Bugrino
149 J-8 Bugsuk *isl.*
69 M-9 Bugul'ma
71 M-3 Bugun' *riv.*
120 D-8 Bugun *riv.*
123 P-4 Bugunda
67 N-1 Buguruslan
166 G-7 Buhl
97 K-5 Bühödle
64 E-1 Buhuşi
54 C-1 Buhy
89 M-4 Bui *dam.*
67 L-1 Buinsk
195 M-5 Buique
52 A-2 Buith Wells
210 G-7 Buji
77 K-5 Bujumbura
100 B-5 Bujumbura
210 G-7 Buk
124 A-4 Bukačača
100 D-2 Bukakata
71 K-5 Bukantau *mt*
100 B-8 Bukavu
129 N-8 Bukechi *lake*
100 F-1 Bukedea
100 F-2 Bukedi *reg.*
131 K-6 Bukehe *riv.*
84 B-5 Bukha
71 L-7 Bukhara
120 A-9 Bukhara
149 M-2 Bukide *isl.*
207 M-1 Bukit Baja *mt*
146 F-6 Bukit Besi
206 B-1 Bukittinggi
207 H-6 Bukittunggul *mt*
100 D-3 Bukoba
100 D-5 Bukombe
121 M-6 Bukon *riv.*
124 A-5 Bukuka
73 M-8 Bül *mt*
209 K-3 Bula
210 E-6 Bulaka *riv.*
72 B-4 Bulancak
139 N-4 Bulandshahr
121 P-4 Bulanicha
72 D-4 Bulanik
103 L-8 Bulawayo
64 G-7 Buldan
140 B-5 Buldāna
189 H-4 Buldibuyo
52 F-6 Bulford
130 C-2 Bulgan *riv.*
130 C-2 Bulgan (Mongolia)
130 B-8 Bulgan (Mongolia)
130 E-8 Bulgan (Mongolia)
130 B-2 Bulgan (Mongolia)
47 F-5 Bulgaria *state*
149 J-8 Buliluyan *cap.*
95 H-5 Bulki
168 C-2 Bull *mt*
201 M-8 Bull Point *pte*
176 D-1 Bull Shoals *lake*
216 G-6 Bullabulling
97 H-3 Bullahār
58 E-6 Bulle
221 H-5 Buller *mt*
216 F-6 Bullfinch
221 L-3 Bulli
54 F-9 Bullion
218 F-6 Bulloo *lake*
219 H-4 Bulloo *riv.*
218 F-6 Bulloo Downs
130 B-6 Bulnayn *mt*
200 A-2 Bulnes
97 N-4 Bulo Burti
220 F-4 Buloke *lake*
211 K-6 Bulolo
131 K-4 Bulunjierhe *riv.*
131 K-2 Buluntai
148 E-3 Bulusan *vol.*
149 P-3 Buluwa *riv.*
129 N-8 Bum Tsho *lake*
98 G-5 Buma *riv.*
99 L-1 Bumba
100 D-4 Bumbiri *isl.*
87 L-5 Bumbuna
143 M-3 Bumhpa Bum *mt*
161 N-2 Bumpus *mt*
143 H-2 Bumtang *riv.*
99 J-5 Buna
133 M-8 Bunam *isl.*
81 J-1 Bunbah *gulf*
216 E-8 Bunbury
219 M-4 Bundaberg
219 L-8 Bundarra

57 M-9 Bunde
139 L-6 Bündi
100 C-2 Bundibugyo
145 J-4 Bung Kan
148 F-2 Bunga *pte*
90 D-3 Bunga
206 B-2 Bungalaut *strt.*
53 P-1 Bungay
219 K-5 Bungil *riv.*
208 E-2 Bungku
113 M-6 Bungo *strt.*
137 L-4 Bungo *strt.*
98 F-8 Bungo
100 F-2 Bungoma
100 C-1 Bunia
127 M-6 Bunji
149 M-8 Bunju *isl.*
219 N-3 Bunker Group *islds*
159 J-3 Bunker Hill
167 J-5 Bunker Hill *hill*
177 K-6 Bunnell
56 F-3 Bunnik
56 G-2 Bunschoten
89 N-5 Bunsu
90 B-2 Bunsuru *riv.*
53 K-3 Buntingford
57 N-2 Buntok
65 L-6 Bünyan
100 D-1 Bunyoro *reg.*
59 K-1 Bünzen
93 J-8 Bunzuqah
59 L-3 Buochs
145 M-8 Buôn Blech
113 M-2 Buor Khaya *cap.*
96 G-8 Buq'Atöti
83 N-4 Buqayq
195 M-7 Buquim
123 L-1 Bur
123 L-1 Bür Gabo
97 P-3 Bür Hakkaba
82 C-6 Bür Safajah
81 P-2 Bür Tawfiq
101 J-5 Bura (Kenya)
101 K-3 Bura (Kenya)
69 M-8 Burajevo
216 E-6 Burakin
91 P-3 Buram
72 A-8 Buran
197 N-2 Buranhem *riv.*
197 N-2 Buranhem
70 D-6 Burankol'
63 N-3 Burano
97 J-4 Burao
97 J-4 Burao Kibir
83 J-5 Buraydah
52 F-6 Burbage
167 M-3 Burbank
130 D-5 Burchanbuudaj *mt*
59 H-8 Bürchen
221 J-2 Burcher
130 C-8 Bürd
97 J-5 Bürdab *mt*
215 H-8 Burdekin *riv.*
68 F-3 Burduj
65 H-7 Burdur
142 F-5 Burdwān
125 J-3 Bureinskyy *rge*
124 G-5 Bureja *riv.*
124 G-5 Bureja
58 F-2 Büren
56 F-4 Buren
122 F-6 Buren *riv.*
130 B-8 Bürengiyn *mt*
54 E-4 Bures (France)
53 M-3 Bures (UK)
54 G-8 Bures-sur-Yvette
52 F-4 Burford
51 K-6 Burg
122 E-4 Burgan
64 F-4 Burgas
177 M-2 Burgaw
58 G-3 Burgdorf
59 L-3 Bürgenstock *hill*
165 M-4 Burgeo
105 H-7 Burgersdorp
53 K-7 Burgess Hill
53 H-5 Burgfield
59 M-4 Bürglen
60 D-3 Burgos
49 M-6 Burgsvik
64 F-6 Burhaniye
140 B-5 Burhānpur
142 D-2 Burhi *riv.*
93 N-6 Buri *pen.*
142 D-1 Buri Gandaki *riv.*
148 F-4 Burias *isl.*
185 H-9 Burica *pte*
199 L-2 Buricá *riv.*
124 A-8 Büridelin Hudag *well*
165 N-4 Burin *mt*
165 N-4 Burin

124 D-3 Burinda *riv.*
145 H-6 Buriram
142 G-6 Burishwar *lag.*
195 H-1 Buriti
195 H-6 Buriti *riv.*
193 P-9 Buriti dos Lopes
194 F-2 Buriticupu *riv.*
197 J-1 Buritis
218 E-1 Burke *riv.*
162 B-3 Burke *strt.*
168 G-5 Burke
171 J-9 Burkesville
214 E-7 Burketown
77 B-3 Burkina Faso *state*
121 H-5 Burkit *mt*
121 N-7 Burkitaul *mt*
121 M-3 Burla *riv.*
121 M-3 Burla
166 G-7 Burley
52 C-2 Burley Gate
70 A-2 Burli
172 F-6 Burlington *reg.*
169 J-9 Burlington (USA)
170 B-7 Burlington (USA)
168 E-8 Burlington (USA)
177 L-1 Burlington (USA)
125 K-6 Burlit
118 E-4 Burma *state*
69 L-3 Burmantovo
162 A-2 Burnaby *isl.*
175 M-5 Burnet
219 M-4 Burnett *riv.*
166 G-3 Burney
52 D-6 Burnham
53 M-4 Burnham on Crouch
220 G-7 Burnie
50 D-4 Burnley
71 N-2 Burnoje
166 E-5 Burns
162 C-2 Burns Lake
161 N-5 Burnside *riv.*
172 G-1 Burnside
177 K-1 Burnsville
180 G-3 Burnt Ground
122 G-1 Burnyj
94 G-3 Buro
59 J-2 Büron
62 B-3 Buronzo
100 C-5 Burundi *riv.*
77 E-5 Burundi *state*
100 G-5 Burungi *lake*
100 C-5 Bururi
195 H-2 Buruti Bravo
90 A-7 Burutu
52 D-1 Burwarton
53 L-7 Burwash
160 D-3 Burwash Landing
53 L-1 Burwell (UK)
168 G-6 Burwell (USA)
50 E-1 Burwick
50 E-5 Bury St.Edmunds
123 L-6 Buryatskaya *rép*
66 G-6 Buryn'
70 C-7 Burynšik
54 B-1 Bus-Saint-Rémy
149 K-3 Busa *mt*
62 D-6 Busalla
133 N-7 Busan
63 H-7 Busana
103 K-4 Busanga
123 N-3 Busani *riv.*
65 P-8 Buşayrah
100 E-2 Busembatia
83 N-2 Büshehr
100 C-3 Bushenyi
53 J-4 Bushey
99 M-8 Bushimaie *riv.*
172 E-2 Bushkill
100 F-2 Busia
91 L-8 Businga
99 J-2 Busira *riv.*
100 F-2 Busiu
49 J-2 Buskerud
66 A-7 Busko Zdrój
100 E-2 Busoga *reg.*
124 F-4 Busse
216 E-8 Busselton
58 G-1 Büsserach
94 B-5 Busseri *riv.*
62 G-5 Busseto

58 B-6 Bussigny
63 J-3 Bussolengo
56 F-1 Bussum
58 F-3 Busswil
55 M-6 Bussy-Saint-Georges
55 M-6 Bussy-Saint-Martin
200 G-7 Bustamante *bay*
62 D-2 Busto Arsizio
99 K-1 Busu Djanoa
99 K-1 Busu Melo
99 J-1 Busu Mokiri
148 F-6 Busuanga
148 F-7 Busuanga *isl.*
89 L-5 Busunu
91 P-9 Buta
200 A-3 Buta-Ranquil
95 K-3 Butajira
100 C-4 Butaré
162 B-5 Bute Inlet *gulf*
130 A-9 Büteeliyn *mt*
124 D-7 Butehaqi
100 B-2 Butembo
100 F-2 Butere
105 J-5 Butha-Buthe
199 M-3 Butiá
100 D-1 Butiaba
161 M-9 Butledge *lake*
170 A-9 Butler (USA)
171 H-7 Butler (USA)
208 B-4 Butongbutongan *isl.*
54 G-2 Butry-sur-Oise
59 N-1 Bütschwil
53 H-7 Butser *hill*
63 J-3 Buttapietra
168 A-2 Butte
162 B-5 Butte *lake*
166 D-5 Butter *riv.*
105 J-8 Butterworth (South Africa)
146 D-6 Butterworth (Malaysia)
58 B-4 Buttes
59 J-2 Buttisholz
172 E-3 Buttzville
149 H-2 Butuan
199 K-2 Butui *riv.*
208 E-4 Butung *strt.*
208 E-4 Butung *isl.*
67 K-5 Buturlinovka
56 F-4 Buurmalsen
57 N-2 Buurse
57 M-2 Buurser beek *riv.*
57 N-2 Buurser Zand *reg.*
130 C-6 Buutsagaan
142 D-2 Buxar
162 A-3 Buxton *mt*
104 G-4 Buxton (South Africa)
192 C-2 Buxton (Guyana)
68 F-9 Buy
132 C-1 Buyant
72 F-1 Buynaksk
87 N-9 Buyo
124 B-8 Buyr Nuur *lake*
70 C-7 Buzači *pl.*
64 F-2 Buzau
64 E-2 Buzaul *riv.*
81 H-7 Buzaymah
69 M-9 Buzd'ak
129 K-2 Buzhun
107 K-3 Buzi *riv.*
107 K-3 Buzi
127 L-3 Buzīn
197 L-6 Buzios *cap.*
124 F-4 Buzuli
70 A-2 Buzuluk
67 K-5 Buzuluk *riv.*
123 H-2 Buzykanovo
211 P-9 Bwagaoia
211 N-8 Bwasiaia
86 G-2 Bwian
52 B-3 Bwlch
153 H-2 Byam Martin *strt.*
65 M-9 Byblos *site*
66 E-5 Bychov
125 M-3 Byčij *cap.*
51 M-5 Bydgoszcz
66 E-4 Byelorussia *reg.*
52 G-2 Byfield
53 J-6 Byfleet
51 H-1 Bykle
125 N-4 Bykov
67 M-5 Bykovo
153 L-2 Bylot *isl.*
141 H-1 Byramgore *isl.*
227 M-5 Byrd Station
124 B-6 Byrka
216 D-3 Byro
219 H-8 Byrock
219 N-7 Byron *cap.*
219 N-7 Byron Bay
201 L-8 Byron Sound *bay*
113 J-2 Byrranga *rge*
124 G-3 Byssa *riv.*
124 G-3 Byssa
128 C-2 Bystrovka
121 P-6 Bystruchinskij Spil' *mt*
53 J-1 Bythorn
51 M-7 Bytom
100 C-3 Byumba
51 M-2 Byxelkrok


# C


145 K-4 Ca *riv.*
126 E-1 Caača
196 B-8 Caacupe
196 C-7 Caaguazu *reg.*
196 B-8 Caaguazu
162 B-2 Caamaño *strt.*
192 A-9 Caapiranga
196 B-8 Caapucu
197 J-2 Caatinga
196 B-8 Caazapa *reg.*
195 N-4 Cabaceiras
149 H-2 Cabadbaran
180 E-4 Cabaiguan
188 E-9 Caballococha
175 H-6 Caballos Mesteños *pl.*
189 N-8 Cabanaconde
148 D-6 Cabanatuan
189 L-9 Cabanillas
164 G-6 Cabano
148 C-7 Cabarruyan *isl.*
56 E-4 Cabauw
197 H-1 Cabeceiras
195 P-4 Cabedelo
178 C-6 Cabeza Negra *pte*
191 H-6 Cabezas
200 B-8 Cabildo
186 G-2 Cabimas
98 D-6 Cabinda
98 D-6 Cabinda *reg.*
162 F-9 Cabinet *mt*
190 E-8 Cabixi (Branco) *riv.*
195 P-5 Cabo
201 H-6 Cabo Blanco
195 P-4 Cabo Branco
106 E-7 Cabo Delgado *reg.*
197 L-6 Cabo Frio
185 J-3 Cabo Gracias a Dios
185 H-3 Cabo Gracias a Dios *reg.*
193 H-5 Cabo Norte *cap.*
188 B-5 Cabo Pantoja
199 L-6 Cabo Polonio
200 F-6 Cabo Raso
176 D-1 Cabool
219 N-6 Caboolture
106 G-2 Cabora Bassa *dam.*
165 L-5 Cabot *strt.*
153 N-5 Cabot *strt.*
197 K-2 Cabral *mt*
60 B-3 Cabreira *mt*
60 G-6 Cabrera *bay*
163 J-8 Cabri
195 L-5 Cabrobo
181 L-6 Cabrón *cap.*
187 K-4 Cabruta
187 L-4 Cabrutica *riv.*
148 B-6 Cabugao
67 M-6 Caca
196 E-9 Caçador
186 B-6 Cacahua *isl.*
64 C-3 Čačak
188 D-9 Cacao *isl.*
192 G-3 Cacao
197 J-6 Caçapava
199 L-4 Caçapava do Sul
61 K-6 Cáccia *cap.*
199 L-3 Cacequi
196 B-1 Cáceres (Brazil)
60 B-5 Caceres (Spain)
200 A-9 Cachari
162 D-6 Cache Creek
166 G-7 Cache Peak *mt*
190 E-5 Cachenoca *riv.*
87 H-2 Cacheu *riv.*
87 H-2 Cacheu
191 N-4 Cachi
200 C-3 Cachil *mt*
99 K-8 Cachimo
191 N-2 Cachinal
186 F-4 Cachira
195 L-8 Cachoeira
196 F-3 Cachoeira Alta
193 J-7 Cachoeira de Arari
197 M-5 Cachoeiro de Itapemirim
130 D-4 Cachryn Tore
87 J-2 Cacine *lag.*
99 J-9 Cacolo
102 C-3 Caconda
197 H-5 Caconde
102 D-3 Cacuchi *riv.*
195 J-9 Caculé
102 B-5 Caculuvar *riv.*
87 J-3 Cacumba
197 P-3 Caçumba *isl.*
187 L-6 Cacuri
98 G-9 Cacuso
122 D-5 Cadan
219 L-5 Cadarga
52 A-8 Cadbury
63 H-5 Cadelbosco di Sopra
62 E-1 Cadenabbia
59 N-9 Cadenazzo
62 F-5 Cadéo
218 B-6 Cadibarrawirracanna *lake*
57 M-9 Cadier en Keer
148 E-5 Cadig *mt*
163 J-9 Cadillac (Canada)
170 E-5 Cadillac (USA)
60 A-7 Cádiz *gulf*
60 B-7 Cádiz
148 G-4 Cadiz (Philippines)
176 F-1 Cadiz (USA)
167 M-5 Cadiz (USA)
52 F-8 Cadnam
63 J-1 Cadria *mt*
64 F-1 Cadyr-Lunga
50 D-7 Caen
52 C-4 Caerleon
52 C-4 Caernarvon
50 C-4 Caernarvon Bay *bay*
52 B-5 Caerphilly
52 C-4 Caerwent
82 C-2 Caesarea *site*
197 K-4 Caetanópolis
190 B-1 Caete *riv.*
193 L-8 Caeté *bay*
197 K-4 Caeté
195 H-9 Caetité
191 N-4 Cafayate
196 F-5 Cafelândia
130 A-6 Cagaan *mt*
123 M-6 Cagan-Churtej *mt*
122 D-6 Cagan-Sibetu *mt*
149 H-6 Cagayan *islds*
149 J-3 Cagayan de Oro
149 K-7 Cagayan Sulu *isl.*
61 K-7 Cágliari *gulf*
61 K-7 Cagliari
68 D-9 Cagoda
148 E-3 Cagrary *isl.*
188 B-5 Cagua *vol.*
188 A-6 Caguán *riv.*
181 K-1 Caguas
70 F-9 Cagyl
60 G-3 Cahors
188 E-4 Cahuapanas *riv.*
185 J-7 Cahuita
185 J-7 Cahuita *pte*
89 J-8 Cahungula
199 N-3 Caí *riv.*
107 H-4 Caia
196 E-1 Caiapo *riv.*
196 D-2 Caiapo *mt*
196 E-2 Caiaponia
194 D-5 Caiapós *riv.*
193 J-9 Caiari
180 E-4 Caibarien
148 F-3 Caibiran
187 H-4 Caicara *riv.*
187 K-4 Caicara
195 P-3 Caiçara
186 D-7 Caicedonia
195 N-3 Caicó
181 J-4 Caicos *strt.*
181 J-4 Caicos *islds*
189 M-8 Cailloma
187 H-7 Caimán *lake*
170 G-6 Caimanera
178 B-2 Caimanero *lag.*
158 G-7 Cairn *mt*
215 J-6 Cairns
176 F-1 Caïro
81 N-2 Cairo
77 F-2 Cairo
62 B-7 Cairo Montenotte
195 K-2 Cais *riv.*
194 G-4 Caititu *riv.*
102 D-4 Caiundo
219 H-6 Caiwaro
191 J-4 Caiza
135 K-3 Caizuhu *lake*
123 M-2 Caja *riv.*
188 C-2 Cajabamba
188 G-3 Cajabamba
188 F-2 Cajamarca *reg.*
188 G-3 Cajamarca
71 M-2 Cajan
193 M-9 Cajapió
189 J-4 Cajatambo
125 K-2 Cajatyn *mt*
195 M-3 Cajázeiras
128 C-1 Cajek
148 F-4 Cajidiocan
69 L-8 Cajkovski
188 D-8 Cajocuma *isl.*
179 H-7 Cajones *riv.*
193 P-9 Caju *isl.*
194 E-1 Cajuapara *riv.*
188 E-8 Cajueiro
193 P-9 Cajueros *lake*
130 A-8 Cakir
90 C-7 Calabar
187 J-3 Calabozo
61 P-7 Calabria *reg.*
46 E-6 Calabria *reg.*
63 N-8 Calabrine
191 H-2 Calacoto
64 D-3 Calafat
201 L-3 Calafate
148 D-4 Calagua *islds*
102 C-3 Calai *riv.*
165 H-7 Calais (Canada)
50 E-6 Calais (France)
191 N-3 Calalaste *mt*
190 A-6 Calama (Brazil)
191 L-2 Calama (Chile)
185 P-7 Calamar (Bolivia)
186 F-8 Calamar (Colombia)
190 G-2 Calamarca
148 F-7 Calamian *islds*
59 P-8 Calanca
59 P-8 Calancascia *riv.*
98 G-9 Calandula
148 E-6 Calapan
64 F-3 Calarași
186 D-6 Calarcá
148 E-6 Calatanga
60 E-4 Cãlatayud
148 E-5 Calauag
148 E-6 Calavite *cap.*
149 K-3 Calawag
148 A-6 Calayan *isl.*
148 F-3 Calbayog
200 E-2 Calbuco *vol.*
200 E-2 Calbuco
195 P-2 Calcanhar *pte*
192 G-5 Calçaoene *riv.*
176 D-5 Calcasieu *riv.*
176 C-6 Calcasieu *lake*
188 B-1 Calceta
191 N-4 Calchaqui *riv.*
63 H-9 Calci
63 H-3 Calcinato
62 F-3 Calcio
193 H-5 Calçoene
142 F-5 Calcutta
186 D-6 Caldas *reg.*
60 A-5 Caldas de Rainha
196 G-2 Caldas Novas
107 H-8 Caldeira *isl.*
192 D-8 Caldeirão *isl.*
192 A-9 Caldeirão
191 P-1 Caldera (Chile)
198 A-1 Caldera (Chile)
63 K-6 Calderara di Reno
219 J-4 Caldervale
52 C-5 Caldicot
63 K-2 Caldogno
63 K-1 Caldonazzo
63 K-1 Caldonazzo *lake*
175 N-5 Caldwell (USA)
166 F-6 Caldwell (USA)
105 H-7 Caledon *riv.*
104 D-9 Caledon
214 C-3 Caledon *bay*
170 B-5 Caledonia (USA)
50 D-1 Caledonian Canal *cal.*
62 G-6 Calestano
201 H-5 Caleta Olivia
198 E-7 Caleufú
174 B-1 Calexico
199 J-8 Calfucurá
162 G-7 Calgary
177 H-3 Calhoun
186 C-7 Cali
62 F-7 Calice al Cornoviglio
62 B-8 Calice Ligure
148 G-2 Calicoan *isl.*
141 J-4 Calicut
167 K-6 Caliente
190 G-6 Caliente *riv.*
172 E-3 Califon
167 H-2 California *state*
157 C-3 California *state*
156 C-4 California *gulf*
174 D-6 California *gulf*
198 B-4 Calingasta *riv.*
216 E-6 Calingiri
174 B-1 Calipatria
167 H-2 Calistoga
104 E-9 Calitzdorp
62 B-7 Calizzano
179 M-5 Calkini
218 E-6 Callabonna *lake*
189 M-8 Callali
191 K-4 Callama *riv.*
50 D-2 Callander
189 K-4 Callao (Peru)
167 J-7 Callao (USA)
200 B-3 Callaquén *vol.*
63 J-1 Calliano
62 B-4 Calliano
163 H-4 Calling *riv.*
163 H-4 Calling Lake
198 B-4 Callingasta
219 M-3 Calliope
190 A-2 Calmon
52 E-5 Calne
148 E-3 Calolbon
62 E-2 Calolziocorte
148 D-6 Caloocan
188 C-2 Calpi
61 N-8 Caltagirone
191 K-3 Caltama *mt*
63 K-2 Caltrano
99 J-8 Caluango *riv.*
102 D-1 Calucinga
98 F-9 Calulo
102 C-3 Caluquembo
62 A-3 Caluso
211 P-9 Calvados *mt*
63 K-8 Calvana *mt*
172 B-7 Calvert
162 A-4 Calvert *isl.*
213 H-9 Calvert *mt*
214 C-6 Calvert *riv.*
214 C-6 Calvert Hills
173 L-3 Calverton
61 K-4 Calvi
178 D-3 Calvillo
104 D-7 Calvinia
63 H-3 Calvisano
53 L-1 Cam *riv.*
145 M-8 Cam Lâm
145 M-9 Cam Ranh *bay*
123 J-3 Cama *riv.*
59 P-8 Cama
98 F-8 Camabatela
197 N-1 Camacá
195 M-8 Camaçari
102 D-2 Camacupa
187 J-4 Camaguán
180 F-4 Camagüey *islds*
180 F-5 Camagüey
63 H-9 Camaiore
194 B-1 Cameleâo *riv.*
192 C-8 Camaleão *dam.*
193 J-7 Camaleão *isl.*
195 L-9 Camamu
189 N-7 Camana
192 A-8 Camanaū *riv.*
196 C-3 Camapuã
199 M-3 Camaquã
199 M-4 Camaquã *riv.*
199 M-3 Cámara
193 H-8 Camaraipi *riv.*
61 J-4 Camarat *cap.*
190 D-8 Camaraté *riv.*
191 K-4 Camargo
185 H-2 Camarón *cap.*
191 K-1 Camarones *riv.*
200 F-6 Camarones *bay*
200 F-6 Camarones
187 K-3 Camatagua
116 C-4 Camba *gulf*
98 F-9 Cambambe *dam.*
196 F-6 Cambara
139 H-9 Cambay *gulf*
139 H-8 Cambay
196 E-6 Cambé
53 H-6 Camberley
191 K-5 Camblaya *riv.*
98 G-8 Cambo *riv.*
118 F-5 Cambodia *state*
219 L-4 Camboon
196 G-9 Camboriú
172 B-1 Cambra
50 F-7 Cambrai
167 K-2 Cambria
213 L-3 Cambridge *gulf*
223 K-5 Cambridge (New Zealand)
53 K-2 Cambridge (UK)
52 D-4 Cambridge (UK)
171 K-8 Cambridge (USA)
170 G-7 Cambridge (USA)
171 M-5 Cambridge (USA)
214 G-9 Cambridge Downs
195 M-7 Cambuís
185 K-9 Cambutal *mt*
177 L-3 Camdem
172 E-7 Camden *reg.*
159 P-6 Camden *bay*
176 G-4 Camden (USA)
176 D-3 Camden (USA)
171 L-7 Camden (USA)
170 B-9 Camdenton
59 M-9 Camedo
102 G-2 Caméia *na.p.*
223 K-4 Camels Back *mt*
62 C-3 Cameri
161 J-9 Cameron *hill*
175 N-5 Cameron (USA)
176 C-6 Cameron (USA)
170 A-8 Cameron (USA)
167 M-7 Cameron (USA)
170 B-4 Cameron (USA)
77 D-4 Cameroon *state*
76 C-4 Cameroon *mt*
193 J-8 Cameta
148 A-5 Camiguin *isl.*
177 J-5 Camilla
191 J-2 Camiña
62 G-1 Camino *mt*
193 L-8 Camiranga
191 J-6 Camiri
63 L-3 Camisano Vicentino
189 K-7 Camisea
189 K-7 Camisea *riv.*
195 K-1 Camocim
59 P-9 Camoghe *mt*
62 E-7 Camogli
219 H-2 Camoola
214 D-8 Camooweal
192 F-5 Camopi *riv.*
192 G-4 Camopi
146 A-4 Camorta *isl.*
186 G-5 Camoruco
148 G-3 Camotes *sea*
148 G-3 Camotes *islds*
63 M-3 Campagna Lupia
201 J-1 Campana *isl.*
199 H-6 Campana
191 L-5 Campanaria *mt*
188 F-3 Campanario
197 J-5 Campanha
200 A-3 Campaniaro *mt*
61 N-6 Campanie *reg.*
188 E-3 Campaquiz *mt*
222 G-7 Campbell *cap.*
161 N-8 Campbell *lake*
162 A-3 Campbell *isl.*
160 E-2 Campbell (Canada) *mt*
160 F-5 Campbell (Canada) *mt*
172 G-1 Campbell Hall
162 B-5 Campbell River
221 H-8 Campbell Town
127 L-7 Campbellpore
177 H-1 Campbellsville
165 H-5 Campbellton
221 K-3 Campbelltown (Australia)
172 A-5 Campbelltown (USA)
50 C-2 Campbeltown
179 K-5 Campeche *gulf*
179 M-5 Campeche
179 M-6 Campeche *reg.*
156 E-5 Campeche *gulf*
220 F-5 Camperdown
63 K-9 Campi Bisenzio
62 A-2 Campiglia
195 N-4 Campina Grande
196 G-3 Campina Verde
197 H-6 Campinas
56 F-7 Campinase Heide *reg.*
194 D-8 Campinorte
62 D-1 Campione d'Italia
90 D-9 Campo *rés*
59 L-8 Campo *val.*
90 D-9 Campo (Cameroon)
59 N-6 Campo (Switzerland)
196 G-8 Campo Alegre (Brazil)
186 D-8 Campo Alegre (Colombia)
197 H-2 Campo Alegre de Goias
196 F-9 Campo Alfo
193 H-6 Campo Belo (Brazil)
197 J-5 Campo Belo (Brazil)
194 A-6 Campo de Dianarum
198 G-2 Campo del Cielo
196 D-8 Campo Ere
191 L-8 Campo Esperanza
196 G-4 Campo Florido
195 K-6 Campo Formoso
198 F-1 Campo Gallo (Argentina)
191 P-6 Campo Gallo (Brazil)
196 C-9 Campo Grande (Argentina)
196 C-4 Campo Grande (Brazil)
191 P-7 Campo Largo (Argentina)
196 F-8 Campo Largo (Brazil)
62 C-6 Campo Ligure
195 J-2 Campo Maior
186 G-2 Campo Mara
196 E-7 Campo Mourão
196 D-9 Campo Novo
191 N-4 Campo Quijano
59 M-7 Campo Tencia *mt*
61 N-5 Campobasso
63 L-3 Campodarsego
63 J-6 Campogalliano
63 M-3 Campolongo Maggiore
62 D-6 Campomorone
63 M-3 Camponogara
63 H-8 Camporgiano

197 M-6 Campos
197 J-4 Campos Altos
194 F-8 Campos Belos
197 J-6 Campos de Jordão
196 E-9 Campos Novos
195 K-3 Campos Sales
63 L-2 Camposampiero
63 K-5 Camposanto
188 C-6 Campuya *riv.*
163 H-6 Camrose
161 M-7 Camsell *lake*
163 L-1 Camsell Portage
63 K-8 Camugnano
128 D-1 Camyndy
67 L-2 Camzinka
64 F-6 Can
147 H-2 Can Tho
194 D-7 Cana Brava *riv.*
155 L-5 Canada *state*
198 G-5 Cañada de Gómez
198 G-5 Cañada-Rosquín
175 K-1 Canadian *riv.*
175 L-1 Canadian
200 F-4 Cañadón Grande *mt*
187 M-5 Canaima
64 F-6 Canakkale
162 F-7 Canal Flats
215 M-4 Canala
62 B-5 Canale
198 D-7 Canalejas
198 F-6 Canals
171 J-5 Canandaigua
174 E-4 Cananea
196 G-8 Cananéia
187 J-8 Canapiari *mt*
188 D-2 Canar *riv.*
188 D-2 Cañar *reg.*
188 D-2 Cañar
193 P-9 Canarias *isl.*
189 L-6 Canarias
180 C-5 Canarreos *islds*
187 P-7 Canaruana *riv.*
78 B-8 Canary *islds*
191 L-5 Cañas
197 H-4 Canastra *mt*
194 D-7 Canastra *riv.*
178 C-1 Canatlán
197 P-1 Canavieiras
221 J-4 Canberra
205 C-5 Canberra
166 F-3 Canby
192 B-9 Cançari *lake*
195 P-3 Cancela *pte*
187 P-3 Cancema *isl.*
191 N-1 Canchas
188 G-6 Canchyuaya *mt*
184 D-2 Cancuén *riv.*
179 P-4 Cancun *isl.*
63 K-8 Canda *mt*
64 F-6 Candarli
190 B-5 Candeias *riv.*
63 P-9 Candelara
179 L-6 Candelaria *riv.*
199 M-3 Candelária
62 B-2 Candelo
62 A-3 Candia Canavese
62 C-4 Candia Lomellina
63 M-4 Candiana
196 E-7 Cândido de Abreu
193 L-8 Cândido Mendes
159 J-3 Candle
163 L-6 Candle *lake*
169 H-1 Cando
148 C-6 Candon
199 N-3 Canela
194 F-3 Canelas *mt*
62 B-6 Canelli
178 F-2 Canelo
199 K-6 Canelones
199 K-6 Canelones *reg.*
188 C-3 Canelos
189 L-5 Cañete *riv.*
200 B-1 Cañete
195 J-2 Cangalha (Brazil) *mt*
194 F-4 Cangalha (Brazil) *mt*
189 L-6 Cangallo
102 F-3 Cangamba
196 B-1 Cangas
60 C-2 Cangas de Narcea
133 H-7 Cangkou
98 G-8 Cangola
102 F-4 Cangombe
187 H-4 Canguá *riv.*
199 M-3 Canguçu
199 M-3 Canguçu *mt*
143 N-5 Cangyuan
132 F-6 Cangzhou
195 N-5 Canhotino
195 N-5 Canhoto *riv.*
164 E-1 Caniapiscau *lake*
61 N-8 Canicatti
162 E-5 Canim *lake*
195 L-1 Canindé
195 J-3 Canindé *riv.*
149 J-8 Canipaan
178 D-2 Cañitas de Felipe Pescador
87 M-1 Canjana *pte*
192 C-3 Canje *riv.*
65 K-5 Cankiri
148 G-4 Canlaon
148 G-4 Canlaon *vol.*
216 G-7 Canmody *lake*
221 J-5 Cann River
64 F-4 Cannakkala Bag *strt.*
141 J-3 Cannanore
62 C-1 Cannero Riviera
61 K-4 Cannes
63 H-4 Canneto sull'Oglio
159 N-6 Canning *riv.*
213 J-6 Canning *pool*
168 F-3 Cannonball *riv.*
187 N-1 Canouan *isl.*
187 N-3 Caño Araguao *riv.*
187 M-3 Caño Colorado
187 N-3 Caño Macare *riv.*
187 N-3 Caño Manamo *riv.*
187 N-3 Caño Mariúsa *riv.*
187 K-6 Caño Parucito *riv.*
196 E-9 Canoa *riv.*
194 D-7 Canoaná
199 N-2 Canoas *riv.*
199 N-3 Canoas
185 P-7 Canoas (Colombia) *pte*
174 B-4 Canoas (Mexico) *pte*
214 F-8 Canobie
162 F-5 Canoe *riv.*
194 E-6 Canoeiro *riv.*
197 J-3 Canoeiros
196 F-8 Canoinhas
161 H-4 Canol
168 D-8 Canon City
220 E-2 Canopus
163 M-8 Canora
61 P-6 Canosa di Puglia
221 J-2 Canowindra
195 P-3 Canquaretama
86 A-2 Cansado
195 L-6 Cansanção
165 L-6 Canso
189 K-4 Canta
46 C-5 Cantabrian *rge*
60 C-3 Cantabrica *rge*
107 H-3 Cantadica
63 K-8 Cantagallo
196 G-9 Cantagalo *pte*
198 D-5 Cantantal *mt*
198 B-2 Cantaritos *mt*
187 L-3 Cantaura
64 B-2 Cantavir
222 E-8 Canterbury *bay*
222 E-8 Canterbury *bay*
50 E-6 Canterbury
149 H-2 Cantilan
198 A-6 Cantillana *mt*
180 C-5 Cantilos *isl.*
78 B-3 Cantin (Beddouza) *cap.*
195 H-4 Canto do Buruti
135 J-9 Canton
164 D-9 Canton (Canada)
175 P-4 Canton (USA)
176 E-4 Canton (USA)
170 G-7 Canton (USA)
170 B-8 Canton (USA)
169 J-5 Canton (USA)
196 D-7 Cantu *riv.*
62 E-2 Cantù
159 J-8 Cantwell
190 A-9 Canudos (Argentina)
195 L-6 Canudos (Brazil)
199 H-7 Cañuelas
53 M-5 Canvey
121 M-1 Cany *lake*
121 M-1 Cany
161 H-4 Canyon *mt*
160 D-4 Canyon (Canada)
175 K-1 Canyon (USA)
166 E-5 Canyon City
168 A-9 Canyon de Chelly
168 B-1 Canyon Ferry *lake*
166 E-3 Canyonville
99 L-8 Canzar
145 K-1 Cao Bâng
145 K-9 Cao Lanh
134 C-6 Caohai *lake*
98 G-8 Caombo
63 P-2 Caorle *lag.*
63 P-2 Caorle
62 F-4 Caorso
149 K-6 Cap *isl.*
78 C-3 Cap Blanc (El Jorf-Lasfar) *cap.*
171 L-9 Cap Charles *cap.*
165 H-4 Cap-Chat
164 E-7 Cap-de-la-Madeleine
181 J-6 Cap Haïtien
70 A-4 Capajevo
187 J-5 Capanaparo *riv.*
196 D-8 Capanema *riv.*
193 K-8 Capanema (Brazil)
196 D-8 Capanema (Brazil)
190 E-9 Capanema (Brazil)
63 H-9 Capannori
196 G-7 Capão Bonito
199 N-3 Capão da Canoa
197 J-2 Capão Redondo
186 G-4 Caparo *riv.*
190 C-2 Capatara *riv.*
186 G-2 Capatárida
60 G-6 Capdepera
53 N-3 Capdock
221 J-7 Cape Barren *isl.*
165 L-6 Cape Breton *isl.*
153 N-5 Cape Breton *isl.*
165 L-5 Cape Breton Highlands *reg.*
177 L-7 Cape Canaveral
171 L-9 Cape Charles
89 P-5 Cape Coast
171 N-5 Cape Cod *bay*
177 M-2 Cape Fear *riv.*
176 F-1 Cape Girardeau
171 L-8 Cape May
87 M-5 Cape Mount *reg.*
87 N-5 Cape Mount *cap.*
161 L-1 Cape Parry
162 A-4 Cape Scott
161 L-4 Cape St George
77 E-8 Cape Town
87 N-2 Cape Verde *islds*
86 F-1 Cape Verde *cap.*
157 G-4 Cape Verde *state*
160 B-3 Cape Yakataga
214 G-3 Cape York *pen.*
210 G-8 Cape York *pen.*
53 K-6 Capel
197 L-3 Capelinha
219 K-2 Capella
56 C-4 Capelle aan den Ijssel
102 D-4 Capelongo
104 E-7 Cape's Province *reg.*
181 N-3 Capesterre
181 N-3 Capesterre de Grande Terre
104 C-9 Capetown
62 B-1 Capezzone *mt*
187 K-8 Capibara
193 K-8 Capim
196 F-3 Capinópolis
191 H-4 Capinota
62 B-1 Capio *mt*
201 N-4 Capitan Aracena *isl.*
196 C-6 Capitán Bado
186 F-5 Capitanejo
190 C-8 Capitão *riv.*
167 K-8 Capitol Reef *na.p.*
194 G-9 Capivara *mt*
194 E-4 Capivara *riv.*
196 B-3 Capivari *riv.*
197 H-6 Capivari
199 M-3 Capivarita
195 H-7 Capixaba
67 J-4 Caplygin
63 H-1 Capo di Ponte
106 F-2 Capoche *riv.*
219 M-7 Capoompeta *mt*
65 L-6 Cappadocia *reg.*
61 L-4 Capraia *isl.*
164 A-8 Capreol
61 L-5 Caprera *isl.*
62 C-6 Capriata d'Orba
219 M-2 Capricorn *strt.*
219 N-3 Capricorn Group *islds*
62 E-2 Caprino Bergamasco
63 J-2 Caprino Veronese
103 H-6 Caprivi *val.*
165 L-5 Capstick
221 K-4 Captains Flat
196 B-7 Capubary *riv.*
192 B-8 Capucapu *riv.*
188 A-6 Caquetá *reg.*
188 A-4 Caquetá *riv.*
121 M-6 Car *riv.*
146 A-3 Car Nicobar *isl.*
124 A-1 Cara
148 F-5 Carabao *isl.*
189 L-9 Carabaya *riv.*
189 L-8 Carabaya *mt*
187 J-3 Carabobo *reg.*
64 E-3 Caracal
187 N-8 Caracarai *riv.*
187 P-8 Caracarai
183 D-2 Caracas
187 K-2 Caracas
187 H-3 Carache
87 J-2 Carache *isl.*
195 H-5 Caracol
196 B-5 Caracol *riv.*
191 H-3 Caracollo
221 K-1 Caraghnan *mt*
197 J-7 Caraguatatuba
198 G-3 Caraguatay (Argentina)
196 B-7 Caraguatay (Paraguay)
200 C-2 Carahue
197 M-2 Caraí
189 M-7 Caraibamba
194 A-2 Carajari *riv.*
194 C-2 Carajás *mt*
148 E-4 Caramoan *pen.*
190 G-3 Caranavi
218 D-1 Carandotta
197 L-5 Carangola
193 M-9 Caranguejos *isl.*
187 L-7 Caransaca *mt*
64 C-2 Caransebes
196 C-7 Carapa *riv.*
193 H-5 Carapaporis *cap.*
188 B-6 Caraparaná *riv.*
197 L-6 Carapebus
196 B-8 Carapeguá
187 M-4 Carapo *riv.*
196 C-6 Carapó
165 J-5 Caraquet
186 E-5 Carare *riv.*
59 N-9 Carasso
185 J-4 Carata *lag.*
185 J-4 Carata
185 H-3 Caratasca *lag.*
62 E-2 Carate Brianza
197 L-4 Caratinga
195 M-3 Caraúbas
62 F-3 Caravaggio
87 J-2 Caravela *isl.*
197 N-3 Caravelas
189 N-7 Caraveli
189 N-7 Caravelli *riv.*
189 H-3 Caraz
199 M-2 Carázinho
184 F-5 Carazo *reg.*
60 B-3 Carballino
60 B-2 Carballo
172 C-3 Carbon *reg.*
172 D-3 Carbon
79 L-2 Carbon *cap.*
61 L-7 Carbonara *cap.*
63 K-4 Carbonara di Po
170 C-9 Carbondale
165 P-3 Carbonear
61 K-7 Carbonia
197 L-2 Carbonita
161 H-3 Carcajou *riv.*
148 G-4 Carcar
198 G-5 Carcaraña *riv.*
62 B-7 Carcare
201 L-8 Carcass *isl.*
60 G-4 Carcassonne
188 A-3 Carchi *reg.*
191 K-2 Carcote
160 D-5 Carcross
116 C-6 Cardamom *rge*
141 K-4 Cardamom *hill*
141 J-1 Cardamum *isl.*
180 C-4 Cardenas (Cuba)
178 F-3 Cárdenas (Mexico)
179 K-6 Cárdenas (Mexico)
201 J-4 Cardiel *lake*
50 C-5 Cardiff
50 C-5 Cardigan
50 C-5 Cardigan *bay*
199 J-6 Cardóna
190 C-8 Cardoso *riv.*
196 G-8 Cardoso *isl.*
196 F-4 Cardoso
163 K-9 Cardross
162 G-8 Cardston
163 L-3 Careen *lake*
63 K-2 Carega *mt*
66 B-9 Carei
192 B-9 Careiro *isl.*
59 P-9 Carena
217 H-4 Carey *lake*
50 C-8 Carhaix-Plouguer
52 A-6 Carhampton
189 J-5 Carhuamayo
200 A-7 Carhué
187 M-2 Cariaco
187 M-2 Cariaco *gulf*
188 E-2 Cariamanga
185 N-8 Caribana *pte*
185 L-5 Caribbean *sea*
156 G-5 Caribbean *sea*
162 E-4 Cariboo *mt*
164 G-6 Caribou
170 E-2 Caribou *isl.*
163 H-1 Caribou *mt*
184 F-4 Caridad
195 L-1 Caridade
62 A-5 Carignano
219 J-8 Carinda
194 F-9 Carinhanha *riv.*
195 H-9 Carinhanha
194 G-7 Cariparé
187 M-3 Caripe
187 M-3 Caripito
195 K-1 Cariré
195 L-3 Caririaçu
195 K-3 Cariris Novos *mt*
187 M-4 Caris *riv.*
52 G-9 Carisbrooke
195 L-3 Carius
165 H-6 Carleton *mt*
164 D-8 Carleton Place
105 J-4 Carletonville
167 H-6 Carlin
50 D-3 Carlisle
170 F-9 Carlisle (USA)
201 N-3 Carlos *isl.*
198 G-7 Carlos Casares
197 M-3 Carlos Chaguas
50 B-4 Carlow
175 J-3 Carlsbad
170 B-3 Carlton
163 M-9 Carlyle (Canada)
170 C-9 Carlyle (USA)
160 E-3 Carmacks
62 A-5 Carmagnola
169 H-1 Carman
165 N-2 Carmanville
50 C-5 Carmarthen
173 H-1 Carmel (USA)
172 E-8 Carmel (USA)
197 H-3 Carmelo (Brazil)
199 J-6 Carmelo (Uruguay)
174 D-7 Carmen *isl.*
174 G-4 Carmen *riv.*
190 D-2 Carmen (Bolivia)
149 H-3 Carmen (Philippines)
199 K-5 Carmen (Uruguay)
199 H-6 Carmen de Areco
200 D-7 Carmen de Patagones
196 B-9 Carmen del Parana
198 C-7 Carmensa
170 D-9 Carmi
219 L-1 Carmila
62 B-8 Carmo *mt*
197 H-4 Carmo *riv.*
197 L-6 Carmo
197 J-3 Carmo do Paranaíba
98 F-8 Carmona (Angola)
60 B-7 Carmona (Spain)
195 N-6 Carmópolis
216 D-5 Carnamah
104 F-7 Carnarvon
190 D-5 Carnaubinha
219 K-4 Carnavaron *mt*
216 C-2 Carnavon
219 J-4 Carnavon Gorge *na.p.*
217 H-2 Carnegie *lake*
217 H-2 Carnegie
199 M-2 Carneiro *riv.*
55 H-2 Carnelle *ft*
200 B-1 Carnero *bay*
55 M-5 Carnetin
61 M-2 Carnic *mt*
91 H-7 Carnot
220 B-3 Carnot *cap.*
50 B-5 Carnsore *pte*
161 J-2 Carnwath *riv.*
159 M-7 Caro
192 B-6 Caroaebe *riv.*
177 L-9 Carol City
194 E-3 Carolina (Brazil)
105 L-4 Carolina (South Africa)
177 K-2 Carolina (North) *state*
177 K-2 Carolina (South) *state*
117 K-6 Caroline *islds*
224 E-4 Caroline *isl.*
119 K-6 Carolines *islds*
170 A-8 Carollton
62 F-1 Carona
187 M-4 Caroni *riv.*
62 D-2 Caronno Pertus
187 H-2 Carora
58 A-9 Carouge
162 E-3 Carp *lake*
62 F-5 Carpaneto Piacentino
66 A-8 Carpathian *mt*
112 A-5 Carpathians *rge*
63 H-3 Carpenedolo
62 C-6 Carpeneto
214 D-4 Carpentaria *gulf*
204 D-3 Carpentaria *gulf*
61 J-3 Carpentras
63 J-5 Carpi
62 C-3 Carpignano Sesia
195 P-4 Carpina
63 H-7 Carpineti
220 E-4 Carpolac Goroke
217 H-6 Carrabelle
187 N-5 Carrao *riv.*
193 N-8 Carrapatal *isl.*
62 G-8 Carrara *reg.*
62 G-8 Carrara
186 F-2 Carrasquero
192 G-8 Carrazedo
196 A-5 Carreira
201 H-3 Carrera *lake*
189 M-4 Carretas *pte*
200 D-4 Carri Laufquen *bay*
187 N-1 Carriacou *isl.*
50 B-3 Carrick on Shannon
54 G-5 Carrières
54 A-4 Carrières (Les)
54 F-5 Carrières-sous-Bois
54 F-4 Carrières-sous-Poissy
220 D-1 Carrieton
169 H-2 Carrington
198 A-2 Carrizal Bajo
175 L-6 Carrizo Springs
175 H-2 Carrizozo
163 M-6 Carro *riv.*
62 F-7 Carrodano
170 A-6 Carroll
177 H-3 Carrollton (USA)
170 F-9 Carrollton (USA)
170 C-8 Carrollton (USA)
214 F-7 Carron *riv.*
62 D-6 Carrósio
163 M-7 Carrot River
62 A-7 Carrú
72 A-4 Carşamba
127 H-3 Caršanga
162 G-7 Carseland
121 M-6 Carsk
213 K-3 Carson *riv.*
167 H-4 Carson *lake*
167 H-3 Carson City
185 P-7 Cartagena
60 E-7 Cartagena
186 C-6 Cartago (Colombia)
185 H-7 Cartago (Costa Rica)
172 G-4 Carteret
177 H-3 Cartersville
79 P-2 Carthage *site*
176 C-4 Carthage (USA)
176 C-1 Carthage (USA)
170 B-7 Carthage (USA)
213 H-1 Cartier *isl.*
63 P-9 Cartoceto
193 L-9 Caru *riv.*
187 M-4 Caruachi *dam.*
195 N-5 Caruaru
187 M-6 Carún *riv.*
187 M-2 Carúpano
193 L-8 Carutapera
176 F-1 Caruthersville
71 N-3 Carvak
192 G-8 Carvalho
60 A-5 Carvoeiro *cap.*
87 M-1 Carvoeiros
218 F-6 Caryapundy Swamp *lake*
221 L-2 Carycudgy *mt*
128 C-4 Caryn *riv.*
128 C-4 Caryn
121 N-4 Caryš *riv.*
201 L-9 Carysfort *cap.*
121 N-5 Caryšskoje
63 L-8 Carzolano *mt*
186 E-8 Casa Agapito
197 H-5 Casa Branca
174 E-2 Casa Grande
195 H-9 Casa Velha *riv.*
78 C-3 Casablanca
198 A-6 Casablanca (Chile)
63 L-8 Casaglia *pass*
62 B-4 Casalborgone
62 G-4 Casalbuttano
61 K-3 Casale Monferrato
63 K-7 Casalecchio di Reno
62 F-3 Casaletto Ceredano
62 F-3 Casaletto Vaprio
63 J-6 Casalgrande
199 H-8 Casalins
63 H-5 Casalmaggiore
62 G-3 Casalmorano
63 H-4 Casaloldo
62 F-4 Casalpusterlengo
62 C-3 Casalvolone
87 H-2 Casamance *riv.*
87 H-3 Casamance *reg.*
186 G-5 Casanare *riv.*
187 M-2 Casanay
71 N-8 Casanga
189 K-5 Casapalca
63 P-1 Casarsa della Delizia
174 F-4 Casas Grandes *riv.*
62 G-2 Casazza
199 M-2 Casca
197 K-5 Casca *riv.*
156 B-2 Cascade *rge*
166 E-7 Cascade
222 D-7 Cascade *pte*
195 M-1 Cascavel (Brazil)
196 D-7 Cascavel (Brazil)
62 D-4 Casei Gerola
62 D-6 Casella
62 A-4 Caselle Torinese
63 M-7 Casemurate
63 L-9 Casentino *val.*
61 N-6 Caserta
227 N-4 Casey
219 K-6 Cashmere
52 E-8 Cashmoore Corner
186 F-3 Casigua
148 C-5 Casiguran
198 G-5 Casilda
197 L-6 Casimoro de Abreu
63 H-6 Casina
219 N-7 Casino
187 K-8 Casiquiare *riv.*

189 J-3 Casma *riv.*
189 J-3 Casma
62 G-8 Casola in Lunigiana
63 L-7 Casola Val Senio
62 D-3 Casorate Primo
63 K-1 Casotto
168 D-5 Casper
112 C-5 Caspian *holl.*
112 C-5 Caspian *sea*
70 A-5 Caspian *holl.*
102 G-1 Cassai *riv.*
102 F-3 Cassamba
196 B-1 Cassange *riv.*
62 F-3 Cassano d'Adda
62 D-5 Cassano Spinola
197 H-4 Cássia
160 E-7 Cassiar
160 E-7 Cassiar *mt*
196 E-3 Cassilândia
221 K-1 Cassilis
62 C-5 Cassine
102 D-4 Cassinga
213 J-2 Cassini *isl.*
199 M-5 Cassino
192 G-5 Cassiporé *riv.*
193 H-4 Cassiporé *cap.*
63 L-2 Cassola
62 D-3 Cassolnovo
172 F-5 Cassville
63 K-4 Castagnaro
62 B-5 Castagnole Lanze
193 K-8 Castanhal
198 B-4 Castaño *riv.*
62 D-2 Castano Primo
62 E-5 Casteggio
63 L-7 Castel Bolognese
63 J-4 Castel d'Ario
63 L-8 Castel del Rio
63 H-3 Castel Goffredo
63 K-6 Castel Maggiore
62 E-4 Castel san Giovanni
63 L-9 Castel San Niccoló
63 L-7 Castel San Pietro Terme
63 J-4 Castelbelforte
63 J-6 Castelfranco Emilia
63 L-2 Castelfranco Veneto
63 K-2 Castelgomberto
60 F-2 Casteljaloux
62 B-5 Castell'Alfero
62 F-5 Castell'Arquato
61 N-6 Castellammare di Salerno
62 A-3 Castellamonte
61 J-3 Castellane
62 D-2 Castellanza
63 J-6 Castellarano
62 C-5 Castellazo Bórmida
62 F-4 Castelleone
62 C-2 Castelletto
63 J-2 Castelletto di Brenzone
199 J-7 Castelli
62 C-5 Castello d'Annone
63 J-7 Castello di Serravalle
60 F-6 Castellon de la Plana
63 H-4 Castellúcchio
220 G-4 Castelmaine
63 K-4 Castelmassa
60 G-3 Castelnaudary
63 H-5 Castelnovo di Sotto
63 H-7 Castelnovo ne'Monti
63 H-8 Castelnuovo di Garfagnana
62 G-8 Castelnuovo di Magra
63 J-3 Castelnuovo di Verona
62 B-4 Castelnuovo Don Bosco
62 D-5 Castelnuovo Scrivia
197 M-5 Castelo
60 B-5 Castelo Branco
195 J-2 Castelo do Piauí
223 J-7 Castelpoint
56 D-8 Castelre
210 B-9 Castelreagh *bay*
60 G-3 Castelsarrasin
61 M-8 Castelvetrano
63 K-6 Castenaso
62 G-3 Castenedolo
57 K-8 Castenraij
56 F-8 Casteren
220 E-5 Casterton
62 F-7 Castiglione Chiavari
62 F-4 Castiglione d'Adda
62 D-1 Castiglione d'Intelvi
63 K-8 Castiglione dei Pepoli
63 H-3 Castiglione del Stiviere
63 H-8 Castiglione di Garfagnana
46 C-5 Castilla *reg.*
198 A-2 Castilla
60 D-5 Castilla la Nueva *reg.*
60 D-4 Castilla la Vieja *reg.*
199 L-6 Castillos *lag.*
199 L-6 Castillos
62 B-6 Castino
59 N-8 Castione
62 G-1 Castione della Presolana
166 F-7 Castle *mt*
159 M-5 Castle (USA) *mt*
52 F-1 Castle Bromwich
52 D-7 Castle Cary
168 A-7 Castle Dale
53 M-3 Castle Hedingham
168 D-7 Castle Rock
170 C-5 Castle Rock *rés*
50 A-3 Castlebar
50 C-1 Castlebay
162 E-7 Castlegar
214 B-3 Castlereagh *bay*
219 J-8 Castlereagh *riv.*
52 B-5 Castleton
52 D-9 Castletown
163 H-6 Castor
108 C-6 Castor *rf*
60 G-3 Castres
157 H-5 Castries
181 N-8 Castries
196 F-7 Castro (Brazil)
200 E-2 Castro (Chile)
195 L-8 Castro Alves
63 M-8 Castrocaro
60 C-2 Castropol
61 P-7 Castrovillari
189 L-6 Castrovirreyna
60 C-6 Castuera
69 L-7 Castyje
107 H-7 Casuarina *isl.*
199 K-6 Casupa
180 G-2 Cat *isl.*
180 E-2 Cat Cays *rf*
184 G-3 Catacamas
188 F-1 Catacáos
188 E-2 Catacocha
196 G-5 Cataduva
197 L-5 Cataguases
148 F-3 Cataiñgan
197 H-3 Cataláo
64 G-5 Catalca
65 K-7 Catalhöyük *site*
165 P-2 Catalina (Canada)
191 N-2 Catalina (Chile)
60 G-4 Catalonia *reg.*
220 G-9 Catamaran
198 D-2 Catamarca
198 D-2 Catamarca *reg.*
191 P-3 Catamarca *reg.*
188 E-1 Catamayo *riv.*
200 C-3 Catán Lil *mt*
148 E-3 Catanduanes *islds*
193 M-9 Catanhede
61 N-8 Catania
61 N-8 Catanissetta
61 P-7 Catanzaro
190 C-6 Cataqueamã
190 C-6 Catarino *riv.*
148 F-3 Catarman
172 D-3 Catasauqua
220 B-3 Catastrophe *cap.*
186 F-3 Catatumbo *riv.*
172 A-2 Catawissa
148 F-3 Catbalogan
179 J-6 Catemaco
223 H-7 Caterton
194 A-3 Catete *riv.*
98 E-9 Catete
105 H-8 Cathcart
195 M-4 Catingueira
87 J-2 Catió
187 M-7 Catisimiña
195 H-5 Catita
71 P-2 Catkal *riv.*
71 P-3 Catkal'skij *mt*
179 P-4 Catoche *cap.*
195 M-3 Catolé do Rocha
158 A-6 Caton *isl.*
200 A-7 Catriló
187 N-9 Catrimani *riv.*
171 L-6 Catskill *na.p.*
57 M-8 Catsop
63 P-8 Cattolica
107 P-1 Catuane
148 F-3 Catubig
102 B-2 Catumbela *riv.*
147 K-2 Catwick *islds*
128 D-1 Catyrk'ol' *lake*
128 D-1 Catyrtaš
145 K-1 Cau *riv.*
145 K-3 Câu Giat
98 G-8 Cauale *riv.*
194 E-1 Cauaxi *riv.*
148 C-5 Cauayan
186 C-8 Cauca *reg.*
185 P-9 Cauca *riv.*
187 K-2 Caucagua
185 P-9 Caucasia
112 C-5 Caucasus (Greater) *rge*
72 C-1 Caucasus (Greater) *rge*
112 C-5 Caucasus (Lesser) *rge*
72 D-2 Caucasus (Lesser) *rge*
191 M-3 Cauchari *lake*
59 P-8 Cauco
107 H-2 Cauerési *riv.*
190 E-2 Caupolican *reg.*
200 A-2 Cauquenes
187 L-5 Caura *riv.*
164 G-5 Causapscal
190 D-5 Cautário *riv.*
60 F-3 Cauterets
200 C-2 Cautin *riv.*
180 F-5 Cauto
180 G-5 Cauto *riv.*
141 H-4 Cauvery *riv.*
58 D-7 Caux
62 E-4 Cava Manara
62 B-3 Cavaglià
61 J-3 Cavaillon
194 E-8 Cavalcante
169 H-1 Cavalier
87 P-8 Cavalla *riv.*
62 A-6 Cavallermaggiore
223 K-2 Cavalli *islds*
79 L-2 Cavallo *cap.*
50 B-3 Cavan
63 M-4 Cavárzere
122 F-5 Cavaš *riv.*
63 J-1 Cavédine
195 K-9 Caveiro *riv.*
53 M-2 Cavendish
199 K-3 Caverã *riv.*
59 M-8 Cavergno
53 H-5 Caversham
193 H-7 Caviana *isl.*
59 M-9 Caviano
149 H-6 Cavili *isl.*
190 D-3 Cavinas
148 D-6 Cavite
72 C-3 Cavka *mt*
63 H-6 Cavriago
149 H-1 Cawit *pte*
220 F-1 Cawndilla *lake*
197 J-6 Caxambu
195 H-2 Caxias (Brazil)
188 E-8 Caxias (Brazil)
199 N-3 Caxias do Sul
98 E-8 Caxito
192 G-8 Caxiuana *riv.*
53 K-2 Caxton
53 K-2 Caxton Gibbet
65 H-6 Cay
180 G-4 Cay Verde *rf*
189 H-6 Cayali *reg.*
188 B-3 Cayambe *vol.*
188 B-3 Cayambe
72 C-3 Cayeli
192 G-3 Cayenne
181 K-1 Cayey
65 L-5 Cayiralan
180 D-6 Cayman *islds*
180 E-6 Cayman Brac *isl.*
52 C-1 Caynham
188 C-1 Cayo
180 E-4 Cayo del Coco *isl.*
180 F-5 Cayo del Sabinal *isl.*
180 E-4 Cayo Fragosco *isl.*
185 J-3 Cayo Muerto *islds*
180 F-4 Cayo Romano *rf*
180 E-5 Cayos de las Doce Leguas *rf*
188 G-3 Cayreg *mt*
171 K-5 Cazenovia
103 H-2 Cazombo
180 C-5 Cazones *gulf*
72 C-2 Cchakaja
72 C-2 Cchaltubo
195 K-2 Ceará *reg.*
195 P-2 Ceara-Mirim
185 K-9 Cebaco *isl.*
69 P-7 Cebarkul
69 J-9 Ceboksary
198 D-3 Cebollar
199 L-6 Cebollatí *riv.*
199 L-6 Cebollatí
148 G-3 Cebu
148 G-4 Cebu *isl.*
70 B-9 Čečen' *isl.*
66 E-5 Cečersk
125 N-4 Cechov
66 G-3 Cechov Stupino
172 E-7 Cecil
219 L-6 Cecil Plains
172 C-8 Cecilton
123 M-2 Cečuj *riv.*
123 L-1 Cečujsk
163 N-7 Cedar *lake*
168 F-3 Cedar *riv.*
172 E-7 Cedar Brook
167 K-7 Cedar City
175 N-4 Cedar Creek *lake*
170 B-6 Cedar Falls
172 G-3 Cedar Grove
177 J-6 Cedar Key *isl.*
170 B-6 Cedar Rapids
177 H-3 Cedartown
172 D-8 Cedarville
53 J-1 Ceddington
195 L-3 Cedro
174 B-5 Cedros *isl.*
218 A-8 Ceduna
61 N-8 Cefalu
125 H-3 Cegdomyn
63 N-2 Ceggia
64 B-1 Cegled
57 K-7 Ceijsteren
123 J-3 Cekanovskij
130 F-7 Ceke
69 M-8 Cekmaguš
125 H-4 Cekunda
184 E-3 Celaque *mt*
178 E-4 Celaya
67 K-9 Celbas *riv.*
124 C-1 Cel'baus *mt*
129 H-3 Cele
117 H-6 Celebes *sea*
149 N-4 Célèbes (Sulawesi)
73 K-2 Celeken
73 K-2 Celeken *pen.*
188 G-3 Celendin
179 P-5 Celerain *pte*
179 M-4 Celestún
188 E-2 Celica
58 A-8 Céligny
170 F-7 Celina
121 P-4 Celinnoje
121 H-3 Celinograd
61 P-2 Celje
70 F-3 Celkar
51 J-6 Celle
54 E-9 Celle-des-Bordes (La)
54 G-6 Celle-St-Cloud
121 P-5 Cemal
172 D-3 Cementon
188 E-3 Cenepa *riv.*
62 F-6 Ceno *riv.*
134 G-9 Cenqi
62 A-6 Centallo
176 C-4 Center
172 E-4 Center Bridge
172 B-1 Center Moreland
173 L-3 Center Moriches
172 D-5 Center Square
172 D-4 Center Valley
172 D-8 Centerton
170 B-7 Centerville
63 K-6 Cento
62 F-7 Cento Croci *mt*
210 G-4 Central *rge*
181 K-6 Central *mt*
73 K-5 Central *reg.*
195 J-6 Central (Brazil)
148 B-6 Central (Philippines) *mt*
159 L-8 Central (USA)
172 A-1 Central (USA)
77 E-4 Central African Republic *state*
180 F-5 Central Amancio Rodriguez
223 J-3 Central Auckland *reg.*
176 G-1 Central City
169 H-7 Central City
173 K-3 Central Islip
105 J-6 Central Range (South Africa) *rge*
112 B-4 Central Russian Uplands *mt*
172 G-1 Central Valley
59 M-6 Centrale *mt*
162 B-8 Centralia (USA)
170 C-9 Centralia (USA)
66 E-2 Central'nolesnoj Zapov *rés*
122 C-2 Central'nyj
177 H-3 Centre
176 G-4 Centreville
200 G-3 Centro Rio Mayo
199 L-5 Centurión
69 L-7 Cepca *riv.*
64 C-7 Cephalonia *isl.*
62 A-9 Ceppo *mt*
95 K-5 Ceralatto
204 C-2 Ceram *sea*
62 D-3 Cerano
187 K-5 Cerbatana *mt*
61 H-4 Cerbère
61 H-4 Cerbère *cap.*
62 A-5 Cercenasco
68 F-2 Cercle polaire arctique
67 M-1 Cerdakly
69 K-5 Cerdyn'
63 K-4 Cerea
163 H-7 Cereal
63 L-4 Ceregnano
122 F-4 Ceremšanka
121 P-3 Cerepanovo
104 D-8 Ceres (South Africa)
198 F-3 Ceres (Argentina)
194 D-9 Ceres (Brazil)
63 H-4 Ceresara
62 A-5 Ceresole Alba
60 G-4 Céret
185 P-8 Ceretè
108 A-9 Cerf *isl.*
62 D-4 Cergnago
54 F-3 Cergy
62 B-8 Ceriale
62 A-9 Ceriana
61 P-5 Cerignola
64 D-9 Cerigo *isl.*
65 J-4 Cerkeş
64 G-5 Cerkezköy
121 K-1 Cerlak
121 K-2 Cerlakskij
69 M-8 Cermasan *riv.*
65 N-6 Cermik
66 E-7 Cern'achov
66 A-4 Cern'achovsky
124 E-3 Cern'ajevo
54 E-8 Cernay-la-Ville
68 G-7 Cerncovo
52 D-8 Cerne Abbas
58 D-3 Cernier
125 K-8 Cernigovka (SSSR)
67 H-9 Cernigovka (SSSR)
62 D-1 Cernóbbio
66 E-6 Cernobyl'
122 E-4 Cernogorsk
65 H-1 Cernomorskoje
121 L-3 Cernoreck
121 M-2 Cernovka
69 H-8 Cernovskoje
69 M-7 Cernuška
124 D-2 Cernyseva *mt*
125 K-8 Cernyševka
124 A-4 Cernyševsk
67 L-7 Cernyškovskij
124 A-3 Cernyšova *mt*
174 E-9 Cerralvo *isl.*
175 L-8 Cerralvo
194 E-6 Cerreira Comprida *riv.*
62 G-7 Cerreto *pass*
63 J-9 Cerreto Guidi
191 N-5 Cerrilos
186 F-5 Cerrito (Colombia)
186 C-7 Cerrito (Colombia)
178 F-3 Cerritos
191 L-2 Cerritos Bayos
200 F-6 Cerro *mt*
196 F-7 Cerro Azul
189 J-4 Cerro de Pasco
187 L-6 Cerro Jáua *plat.*
196 E-9 Cerro Negro
199 L-5 Cerrolargo *reg.*
186 G-2 Cerrón *mt*
200 B-4 Cerros Colorados *lake*
190 F-3 Cerros de Bala *mt*
124 A-4 Cerskogo *mt*
186 C-6 Cértegui
67 K-6 Certkovo
62 E-4 Certosa di Pavia
62 A-7 Certosa di Pesio
123 H-1 Cerv'anka
148 C-6 Cervantes
62 G-6 Cervellino *mt*
66 D-5 Cerven
64 D-3 Cerven Brjag
62 A-6 Cervere
63 N-7 Cérvia
62 A-1 Cervino (Matterhorn) *mt*
62 B-9 Cervo
62 B-3 Cervo *riv.*
186 E-2 César *riv.*
186 E-2 César *reg.*
63 M-1 Cesen *mt*
61 M-3 Cesena
63 N-7 Cesenatico
59 P-9 Cesero *mt*
62 B-8 Cesio
66 C-2 Cesis
51 L-7 Ceská Lipa
51 L-8 Ceské Budejovice
51 L-8 Ceskomoravska *mt*
64 F-7 Ceşme
221 L-2 Cessnock
87 N-7 Cestos *riv.*
122 D-1 Cet' *riv.*
68 G-3 Cetlasskij Kamen *mt*
63 H-1 Ceto
190 A-2 Ceu Aberto
124 G-4 Ceugda
78 E-1 Ceuta
62 B-7 Ceva
61 H-3 Cévennes *mt*
59 M-8 Cevio
65 L-7 Ceyhan
72 A-7 Ceyhan *riv.*
65 P-6 Ceylanpinar
145 J-1 Cha Pa
122 G-1 Cha'a
56 D-7 Chaam
56 E-7 Chaamsee Bos *ft*
68 G-2 Chabaricha
198 G-5 Chabás
58 B-8 Chablais *reg.*
191 J-1 Chaca
201 H-3 Chacabuco *riv.*
198 G-6 Chacabuco
191 K-2 Chacarilla *riv.*
200 A-4 Chachahuen *mt*
189 N-8 Chachani *vol.*
188 F-3 Chachapoyas
139 H-3 Chācharān
200 A-6 Chacharramendi
144 G-7 Chachoengsao
72 G-1 Chačmas
191 J-8 Chaco *reg.*
191 N-6 Chaco Austral *reg.*
191 M-7 Chaco Central *reg.*
187 M-2 Chacopata
77 D-3 Chad *state*
90 G-1 Chad *lake*
52 E-1 Chaddesley Corbett
172 C-6 Chaddsford
200 B-5 Chadileuvú *riv.*
159 M-5 Chadler *riv.*
168 E-5 Chadron
72 B-1 Chadysensk
78 F-2 Chafarinas *islds*
200 G-2 Chaffers *isl.*
58 A-4 Chaffois
186 E-7 Chafurray
126 E-9 Chāgai
126 D-8 Chāgai *reg.*
130 F-8 Chagandianlisu
124 F-9 Chaganhu *lake*
127 K-6 Chaghasarāy
61 J-1 Chagny
188 G-3 Chagual
187 N-2 Chaguanas
187 K-3 Chaguaramas
84 B-9 Chāh Bahār
127 K-4 Chah-e Ab
126 A-8 Chah Gheyoi *lake*
126 D-8 Chāh Sandan *well*
132 D-4 Chahaeryouhouqi
132 D-5 Chahaeryouqianqi
132 D-4 Chahaeryouzhongqi
131 H-2 Chahanchilatu
131 L-7 Chahanjin
132 G-2 Chahanmulunhe *riv.*
126 C-7 Chahār Borjak
142 D-5 Chaibāsa
131 J-2 Chaidam *holl.*
131 J-3 Chaidamushan *mt*
98 D-4 Chaillu *mt*
123 L-5 Chaim
144 F-6 Chainat
54 E-6 Chaîne (La)
188 A-5 Chaira *lake*
54 C-9 Chaises (Les)
200 F-2 Chaitén
146 C-3 Chaiya
145 H-6 Chaiyaphum Bua Yai
199 J-4 Chajari
127 M-2 Chajdarken
135 L-1 Chajian
129 M-6 Chajing Tsho *lake*
127 M-9 Chak Amru
94 B-3 Chak Chak
131 K-6 Chaka
159 G-8 Chakachamna *lake*
126 G-9 Chākar *riv.*
103 M-6 Chakari
131 K-6 Chakayanchi *lake*
101 K-6 Chake Chake
129 L-5 Chakechumushankou *pass*
126 C-6 Chakhānsūr
131 K-8 Chakouyi
142 D-5 Chakradharpur
127 L-8 Chakwāl
189 N-6 Chala
189 N-6 Chala *pte*
127 H-2 Chalač
58 G-8 Chalais
184 E-3 Chalatenango
106 G-7 Chalaua
95 J-7 Chalbi *dés*
123 N-5 Chal'di *mt*
52 G-9 Chale
101 K-6 Chale Point *pte*
165 H-5 Chaleur *bay*
53 J-4 Chalfont Saint Giles
52 E-4 Chalford
189 M-7 Chalhuanca
201 K-4 Chalia *riv.*
191 M-5 Chalicán
55 N-5 Chalifert
70 C-1 Chalilovo
135 J-6 Chaling
140 B-4 Chālisgaon
222 B-8 Chalky *bay*
62 A-2 Challand St Anselme
191 J-3 Challapata
61 J-1 Chalon-sur-Saône
50 F-8 Châlons-sur-Marne
188 F-2 Chalpon *mt*
127 M-6 Chalt
69 J-7 Chalturin
129 K-3 Chaluolehu *lake*
73 K-4 Chālus
191 L-3 Chalviri *lake*
51 K-8 Cham (FRG)
59 L-2 Cham (Switzerland)
168 B-9 Chama *riv.*

132 E-4 Chicheng
212 F-8 Chichester mt
50 D-6 Chichester
159 H-9 Chickaloon
176 F-5 Chickasawhay riv.
175 N-2 Chickasha
160 E-1 Chicken
52 E-7 Chicklade
188 G-2 Chiclayo
188 G-2 Chiclín
166 G-2 Chico
201 J-4 Chico riv.
191 N-4 Chicoana
179 K-8 Chicomuselo
171 M-5 Chicopee
164 F-5 Chicoutimi rés
164 F-6 Chicoutimi
187 H-8 Chicuaco lake
107 L-1 Chicualacuala
191 K-3 Chicuana
141 J-7 Chidambaram
53 J-7 Chiddingfold
52 C-8 Chideack
160 G-9 Chief riv.
144 F-3 Chieng Mai
100 B-9 Chiengi
62 A-4 Chieri
63 H-3 Chiese riv.
61 N-5 Chieti
132 G-3 Chifeng
197 M-2 Chifre riv.
103 H-2 Chifumage riv.
160 B-6 Chiganof isl.
158 D-8 Chiginagak mt
158 F-8 Chigmit mt
165 J-7 Chignecto cap.
165 J-7 Chignecto bay
158 C-8 Chignik bay
158 C-7 Chignik
107 M-2 Chigombe riv.
185 N-9 Chigorodó
200 F-2 Chiguao pte
107 M-2 Chigubo
53 L-4 Chigwell
135 L-2 Chihe riv.
174 G-6 Chihuahua
174 G-5 Chihuahua reg.
128 G-3 Chijilika
131 H-5 Chijinbao
141 H-5 Chik Ballāpur
135 H-9 Chikan
140 B-5 Chikhli
140 G-4 Chikmagalūr
145 J-8 Chikrêng
145 J-7 Chikrêng riv.
158 F-6 Chikuminuk lake
106 G-4 Chikwawa
162 D-3 Chilako riv.
178 F-7 Chilapa de Alvarez
127 M-6 Chilās
141 M-7 Chilaw
189 L-4 Chilca
189 L-4 Chilca pte
189 M-8 Chilca mt
219 M-4 Childers
175 L-2 Childress
188 A-3 Chile vol.
183 C-6 Chile state
201 H-3 Chile Chico
198 C-3 Chilecito
188 G-2 Chilete
123 M-4 Chilgana
53 N-6 Chilham
92 A-6 Chili (Chad) riv.
103 L-2 Chililabombwe
142 D-7 Chilka lake
160 C-6 Chilkat mt
162 C-5 Chilko lake
162 C-4 Chilko riv.
162 D-5 Chilkotin riv.
188 D-2 Chilla mt
215 H-6 Chillagoe
200 A-2 Chillán mt
200 A-2 Chillan
200 A-2 Chillar
200 A-9 Chillar
170 G-8 Chillicothe (USA)
170 A-8 Chillicothe (USA)
162 C-7 Chilliwack
189 K-4 Chillón riv.
58 D-7 Chillon
55 J-8 Chilly-Mazarin
98 D-9 Chiloango riv.
200 F-2 Chiloe reg.
123 N-6 Chilok riv.
123 M-6 Chilok
178 F-7 Chilpancingo de los Bravo
53 H-4 Chiltern hill
170 D-5 Chilton
52 F-5 Chilton Foliat
106 C-4 Chilumba
135 P-7 Chilung
106 F-4 Chilwa lake
52 G-7 Chilworth
184 C-3 Chimaltenango
185 M-8 Chiman

107 K-2 Chimanimani na.p.
129 J-9 Chimanshan mt
107 K-3 Chimbabava
198 C-4 Chimbas
71 H-6 Chimbay
191 P-2 Chimbero
188 C-2 Chimbo riv.
188 C-3 Chimbobazo
188 C-2 Chimborazo reg.
189 H-3 Chimbote
211 J-5 Chimbu
186 B-8 Chimbuso lag.
103 L-6 Chimene riv.
107 J-3 Chimio
71 N-3 Chimkent
120 D-8 Chimkent
66 G-2 Chimki
143 J-6 Chin reg.
118 F-3 China state
178 F-1 China
204 A-1 China sea
117 H-4 China (East) sea
113 L-6 China (East) sea
116 G-6 China (South) sea
184 E-3 Chinacla
184 F-4 Chinandega reg.
184 F-5 Chinandega
175 J-5 Chinati mt
189 L-5 Chincha Alta
162 G-1 Chinchaga riv.
219 L-5 Chinchilla
188 E-2 Chinchipe riv.
179 P-6 Chinchorro rf
107 J-5 Chinde
143 K-5 Chindwin riv.
188 E-3 Chinganaza
141 H-7 Chingleput
103 L-2 Chingola
135 N-7 Ch'ingshui
102 D-2 Chinguar
86 B-6 Chinguetti
86 B-6 Chinguetti hill
103 N-6 Chinhoyi
139 P-2 Chīni
158 E-9 Chiniak isl.
127 L-9 Chiniot
145 K-8 Chinit riv.
91 P-5 Chinko riv.
168 A-9 Chinle
53 H-4 Chinnor
50 D-9 Chinon
166 D-4 Chinook lake
163 J-9 Chinook
106 C-2 Chinsali
142 F-5 Chinsura
106 D-4 Chinteche
106 G-2 Chioco
61 M-3 Chioggia
64 F-7 Chios isl.
64 F-7 Chios
162 G-5 Chip lake
103 P-3 Chipata
106 E-2 Chipata (Fort-Jameson)
106 G-4 Chiperone mt
107 K-2 Chipinga
190 G-4 Chipitiri riv.
177 H-5 Chipley
140 D-3 Chiplūn
165 J-6 Chipman
106 C-4 Chipoka
52 E-5 Chippenham
170 C-3 Chippewa lake
170 B-4 Chippewa riv.
170 B-4 Chippewa Falls
52 F-3 Chipping Campden
52 F-3 Chipping Norton
53 L-4 Chipping Ongar
52 D-5 Chipping Sodbury
58 G-8 Chippis
189 J-4 Chiquian
184 D-3 Chiquímula
191 K-1 Chiquinata bay
186 E-6 Chiquinquira
188 E-1 Chira riv.
140 F-8 Chīrāla
71 P-9 Chirās
139 L-4 Chirāwa
73 M-9 Chiraz
120 D-9 Chirchik
71 N-3 Chirchik
107 K-1 Chiredzi
187 J-3 Chirgua riv.
188 A-7 Chiribiquete mt
174 F-3 Chiricahua mt
186 E-3 Chiriguana
152 C-4 Chirikof isl.
158 C-9 Chirikof isl.
187 K-2 Chirimera
188 E-2 Chirinos riv.
185 J-8 Chiriqui lag.
185 J-9 Chiriqui gulf
185 J-8 Chiriqui vol.
142 B-4 Chirmiri
106 G-4 Chiromo
59 N-7 Chironico

185 H-6 Chirripo riv.
185 H-7 Chirripó Grande mt
103 M-5 Chirundu
103 M-4 Chisamba
106 D-4 Chisamulo isl.
160 D-2 Chisana riv.
164 B-2 Chisasibi
184 D-2 Chisec
135 N-8 Chishan
135 M-5 Chishizhen
139 K-2 Chishtiān Mandi
134 D-5 Chishui
66 E-4 Chislaviči
52 F-5 Chisledon
53 L-5 Chislehurst
160 C-1 Chistochina
69 L-9 Chistopol
123 P-5 Chita
186 F-5 Chita
102 D-3 Chitembo
106 C-4 Chitimba
160 C-2 Chitina riv.
160 C-2 Chitina
100 E-9 Chitipa
139 P-2 Chitkul
138 K-7 Chitorgarh
127 L-5 Chitrā
140 G-5 Chitradurga
140 G-6 Chitravati riv.
185 K-9 Chitré
143 H-6 Chittagong
142 E-4 Chittaranjan
141 H-7 Chittoor
187 M-5 Chiuao riv.
191 L-2 Chíuchiu
106 D-6 Chiulezi riv.
102 G-1 Chiumbe riv.
102 G-4 Chiume
106 E-8 Chiure Novo
62 A-7 Chiusa di Pesio
63 M-9 Chiusi di Verna
106 F-4 Chiuta lake
191 K-4 Chiva riv.
71 J-7 Chiva
187 H-2 Chivacoa
62 A-4 Chivasso
187 L-4 Chivata riv.
174 D-6 Chivato pte
189 N-8 Chivay
199 H-7 Chivilcoy
103 M-3 Chiwefwe
184 C-2 Chixoy riv.
66 D-8 Chmel'nik
133 K-5 Cho isl.
160 E-1 Cho Oyu mt
145 J-7 Choâm Khsant
198 A-5 Choapa riv.
103 J-7 Chobe na.p.
103 H-6 Chobe riv.
103 J-7 Chobe reg.
53 J-6 Chobham
191 K-3 Chocaya mt
191 K-4 Chocaya
189 L-5 Chocca mt
186 C-5 Chocó reg.
174 C-1 Chocolate mt
186 E-6 Chocontá
188 G-2 Chocope
177 H-6 Choctawhatchee riv.
140 E-9 Chodavaram
66 C-8 Chodorov
71 N-8 Chodžambas
51 M-6 Chodziez
125 M-1 Choe
200 C-6 Choele Choel
145 H-5 Choen riv.
123 K-5 Chogot
139 H-5 Chohtan
200 B-7 Choique
54 F-8 Choisel
201 L-9 Choiseul Sound bay
55 J-7 Choisy-le-Roi
174 F-7 Choix
69 J-1 Chojma strt.
51 M-5 Chojnice
66 E-6 Chojniki
107 N-2 Chokwe
124 A-5 Cholbon
52 F-6 Cholderton
50 D-9 Cholet
66 E-2 Cholm
68 E-5 Cholmogorskaja
68 E-5 Cholmogory
125 N-4 Cholmsk
72 A-1 Cholmskij
106 G-4 Cholo
130 A-8 Choltoson
184 F-4 Choluteca riv.
184 F-4 Choluteca
184 F-4 Choluteca reg.
121 N-6 Cholzun riv.
144 E-4 Chom Thong
103 L-5 Choma
125 L-2 Chomi mt
142 G-1 Chomo Lhāri mt
139 L-5 Chōmu

51 K-7 Chomutov
123 K-5 Chomutovo
144 G-7 Chon Buri
123 L-6 Choncholoj
188 B-1 Chone
145 J-7 Chong Kal
135 L-5 Chongan
135 N-2 Chongmingdao isl.
102 B-3 Chongoroi
188 G-2 Chongoyape
135 K-5 Chongren
103 M-5 Chongwe riv.
135 M-7 Chongwu
134 E-9 Chongzuo
201 H-1 Chonos islds
189 L-6 Chonta mt
184 G-5 Chontales reg.
140 A-5 Chopda
196 D-8 Chopim riv.
67 L-3 Chop'or riv.
125 K-5 Chor riv.
125 K-5 Chor
191 M-4 Chorillos
135 M-5 Chorinsk
190 G-5 Choro riv.
195 L-2 Choró riv.
127 L-4 Chorog
125 J-8 Chorol'
66 G-7 Chorol
191 K-4 Chorolque mt
198 D-1 Choromoro
198 A-3 Choros islds
198 A-3 Choros Bajos
174 G-8 Chorreras mt
195 L-5 Chorrochó
67 H-8 Chortica
122 F-6 Chorumnug mt
200 B-3 Chos-Malal
133 L-3 Chosan
189 K-4 Chosica
188 F-3 Chota
188 F-2 Chota riv.
162 G-9 Choteau
138 G-8 Chotila
66 D-8 Chotin
86 B-5 Choûm
122 E-6 Chovu Aksy
141 K-4 Chowghat
198 E-2 Choya
123 P-8 Choybalsan
132 B-1 Choyr
222 F-8 Christchurch (Australia)
52 F-8 Christchurch (UK)
160 B-7 Christian strt.
163 K-4 Christian riv.
172 C-7 Christiana
104 G-5 Christiana (South Africa)
181 L-2 Christiansted
161 M-8 Christie bay
172 C-2 Christmans
224 D-3 Christmas isl.
213 K-6 Christmas Creek
217 L-1 Christopher lake
70 D-2 Chromtau
145 M-6 Chrouy Samit
145 H-9 Chrouy Yéay Sên
125 L-8 Chrustal'nyj
145 M-8 Chu Yang Sin mt
184 C-2 Chuacús mt
142 F-4 Chuādānga
135 N-2 Chuansha
200 E-3 Chubut riv.
200 F-4 Chubut reg.
162 D-2 Chuchi lake
198 E-5 Chucul riv.
198 A-4 Chucuma
190 G-2 Chucura riv.
72 G-1 Chudat
52 A-9 Chudleigh
215 H-8 Chudleigh Park
123 N-5 Chudunskij mt
158 F-9 Chugach islds
160 B-1 Chugach mt
129 L-2 Chugang
128 B-6 Chuguchak (Tacheng)
199 L-6 Chui
133 M-8 Chuja isl.
101 H-2 Chuka
146 F-6 Chukai
113 S-3 Chukchi sea
113 S-3 Chukchi pen.
226 B-1 Chukchi sea
129 M-6 Chukehu lake
174 A-1 Chula Vista
69 K-1 Chulga riv.
159 J-8 Chulitna
72 C-2 Chulo
188 E-1 Chulucanas
190 G-3 Chulumani
130 B-7 Chuluut riv.
144 F-6 Chum Saeng
131 K-2 Chumaerhe riv.
129 L-1 Chumar
129 K-1 Chumātang

198 D-2 Chumbicha
135 N-4 Chumen
145 J-9 Chumnoab
146 D-2 Chumphon
189 M-7 Chumpi
144 F-3 Chun
142 C-3 Chunār
188 C-2 Chunchi
133 M-5 Chunchon
185 M-8 Chuncunaque riv.
125 K-3 Chungari riv.
125 K-3 Chungari
135 N-8 Chunghsing
133 M-6 Chungju
134 D-4 Chungking
135 N-7 Chungli
133 N-7 Chungmu
135 N-8 Chungyangshanmo mt
133 N-1 Chunhua
139 L-2 Chūnīān
129 N-4 Chunitehu lake
100 E-9 Chunya
124 D-8 Chuoerhe riv.
145 H-8 Chuor Phnum Krâvanh
189 N-7 Chuquibamba
191 L-2 Chuquicamata
189 H-3 Chuquicara
191 J-5 Chuquisaca reg.
61 L-1 Chur
172 B-9 Church Hill
163 N-5 Churchill riv.
154 J-4 Churchill mt
154 J-4 Churchill
163 L-4 Churchill lake
164 A-1 Churchill strt.
52 C-6 Churchill (UK)
165 H-1 Churchill Falls
169 H-1 Churchs Ferry
172 B-7 Churchville
200 A-3 Chureo mt
125 K-3 Churmuli
139 L-4 Churu
187 H-2 Churuguara
129 K-1 Chushul
69 M-6 Chusovoy
66 B-9 Chust
71 P-3 Chust
130 C-9 Chusuur mt
122 F-5 Chut riv.
125 L-3 Chuvi riv.
190 B-8 Chuvisco riv.
72 G-6 Chuwārtah
135 L-2 Chuxian
134 A-7 Chuxiong
67 M-3 Chvalynsk
101 J-7 Chwaka
101 H-4 Chyulu mt
63 H-6 Ciano d'Enza
122 F-3 Cibižek
197 M-3 Cibrão riv.
174 E-3 Cibuta mt
62 E-7 Cicagna
124 C-3 Cičatka
123 K-4 Cičkova
62 G-4 Cicognolo
65 J-4 Cide
66 A-6 Ciechanow
180 E-5 Ciego de Avila
186 E-2 Ciénaga
185 P-8 Ciénaga de Caimito lake
185 P-8 Ciénaga Grande lake
180 D-4 Cienfuegos
60 E-7 Cieza
65 H-6 Cifteler
128 A-1 Ciganak
66 F-7 Cigirin
62 B-3 Cigliano
65 J-6 Cihanbeyli
178 C-5 Cihuatlán
71 K-3 Ciili
127 N-2 Cijirčik pass
123 K-4 Cikan
123 L-7 Cikoj
123 L-7 Cikoj riv.
69 J-2 Cikšino
62 D-3 Cilavegna
64 P-3 Cildir gulf
134 G-4 Cili
128 C-3 Cilik
70 B-2 Cilik
56 C-5 Cillaarshoek
68 G-3 Cil'ma riv.
67 L-1 Cil'na
72 E-5 Cilo mt
67 L-7 Cimalmotto
59 L-8 Cim'anskoje Vochr. riv.
168 F-9 Cimarron
168 E-9 Cimarron riv.
186 E-4 Cimitarra riv.
67 L-7 Ciml'ansk

63 J-8 Cimone mt
64 D-1 Cîmpia-Turzii
64 E-2 Cîmpina
64 E-2 Cîmpulung
66 C-9 Cîmpulung-Mold
71 P-6 Cintarga mt
123 N-4 Cina riv.
187 J-5 Cinaruco riv.
191 L-4 Cincel riv.
170 F-8 Cincinnati
180 C-9 Cinco Palo isl.
185 J-3 Cinco Palo islds
52 D-4 Cinderford
64 G-7 Cine
69 P-1 Cingaly
123 P-5 Cingikan mt
121 L-6 Cingiz-Tau mt
166 F-6 Cinnabar mt
144 A-9 Cinque islds
194 F-3 Cinta mt
179 K-7 Cintalapa de Figueroa
61 K-5 Cinto mt
63 P-1 Cinto Caomaggiore
196 F-6 Cinzas riv.
61 J-4 Ciotat (La)
124 A-3 Cipa riv.
123 N-3 Cipikan
123 N-3 Cipikan riv.
195 L-7 Cipó
192 E-8 Cipoal
200 C-4 Cipolletti
67 L-6 Cir riv.
71 N-6 Cirakči
71 N-4 Circik riv.
168 E-1 Circle (USA)
159 M-8 Circle (USA)
170 G-8 Circleville
211 L-3 Circular rf
207 J-6 Cirebon
52 E-4 Cirencester
62 A-4 Cirié
190 B-4 Ciriquiri riv.
• 68 B-6 Cirka Kem' riv.
64 E-2 Cirpan
191 H-2 Cirque mt
62 G-7 Cisa pass
175 M-4 Cisco
132 E-8 Cishan
105 H-8 Ciskei reg.
63 L-1 Cismon del Grappa
69 N-9 Cišmy
185 J-1 Cisne isl.
180 B-8 Cisne (Swan) isl.
186 D-5 Cisneros
200 C-3 Cisnes riv.
63 M-1 Cison di Valmarino
59 K-8 Cistella mt
121 L-1 Cistooz'ornoje
120 G-1 Cistopolje
192 E-6 Citaré riv.
72 E-2 Citeli-Ckaro
178 G-6 Citlatepetl mt
104 D-8 Citrusdal
61 M-4 Citta di Castello
63 L-2 Cittadella
178 E-6 Ciudad Altamirano
187 M-4 Ciudad Bolivar
186 G-4 Ciudad Bolivia
175 M-3 Ciudad Camargo
187 H-4 Ciudad de Nutrias
179 L-6 Ciudad del Carmen
178 F-3 Ciudad del Maiz
175 H-6 Ciudad Delicias
174 F-6 Ciudad Guerrero
187 N-4 Ciudad Guyana
178 C-5 Ciudad Guzmán
178 E-5 Ciudad Hidalgo
174 G-3 Ciudad Juarez
178 D-1 Ciudad Lerdo
178 G-3 Ciudad Madero
178 F-3 Ciudad Mante
174 E-6 Ciudad Obregón
186 G-2 Ciudad Ojeda
187 M-4 Ciudad Piar
60 C-6 Ciudad Real
60 B-4 Ciudad Rodrigo
178 F-3 Ciudad Valles
178 F-2 Ciudad Victoria
61 H-6 Ciudadela
72 A-4 Civa pte
62 E-1 Civenna
54 B-1 Civières
67 L-1 Civil'sk
61 M-5 Civitavecchia
63 M-8 Civitella di Romagna
60 G-1 Civray
65 H-7 Civril
54 B-5 Civry-la-Forêt
123 M-4 Civyrkujskij Zaliv bay
68 E-3 Ciža (SSSR)
71 N-3 Ciža (SSSR)
121 J-1 Ckalovo
125 K-8 Ckalovskoje
52 B-3 Ckrickhowell
54 B-3 Clachalôze
53 N-4 Clacton on Sea

166 F-2 Clair Engle *lake*
164 F-1 Clairambault *lake*
163 K-2 Claire *lake*
54 E-9 Clairefontaine-en-Yvelines
55 H-6 Clamart
50 F-9 Clamecy
53 J-6 Clandon
52 F-4 Clanfield (UK)
53 H-7 Clanfield (UK)
176 G-4 Clanton
104 D-8 Clanwilliam
146 C-2 Clara *isl.*
214 F-8 Clara *riv.*
199 H-4 Clara
50 A-3 Clare *isl.*
220 D-2 Clare (Australia)
53 M-2 Clare (UK)
170 F-5 Clare (USA)
164 F-9 Claremont
175 P-1 Claremore
50 A-3 Claremorris
204 C-3 Clarence *strt.*
201 N-4 Clarence *isl.*
222 F-7 Clarence *riv.*
213 N-1 Clarence (Australia) *strt.*
160 C-8 Clarence (USA) *strt.*
175 L-2 Clarendon
58 D-7 Clarens
165 N-3 Clarenville
59 N-4 Claridenstock *mt*
187 L-3 Clarines
171 H-7 Clarion
169 H-4 Clark
159 G-8 Clark *lake*
161 J-5 Clark (Canada) *mt*
167 L-5 Clark (USA) *mt*
168 A-1 Clark Fork *riv.*
177 K-3 Clark Hill *lake*
215 K-9 Clarke *mt*
215 H-8 Clarke *riv.*
221 J-7 Clarke *isl.*
164 G-4 Clarke City
215 J-8 Clarke River
165 J-8 Clark's Harbour
171 H-8 Clarksburg
176 E-3 Clarksdale
177 L-1 Clarksville (USA)
176 G-1 Clarksville (USA)
176 C-2 Clarksville (USA)
175 P-3 Clarksville (USA)
59 P-8 Claro *mt*
59 N-8 Claro
194 F-5 Claro *riv.*
175 L-1 Claude
198 B-1 Claudio *mt*
191 P-2 Claudio Gay *mt*
148 B-6 Claveria
46 B-2 Clavering *isl.*
177 K-4 Claxton
169 H-8 Clay Center
53 N-2 Claydon
55 M-4 Claye-Souilly
54 E-6 Clayes-sous-Bois (Les)
172 D-7 Claymont
53 K-8 Clayton (UK)
168 E-9 Clayton (USA)
177 J-2 Clayton (USA)
175 P-2 Clayton (USA)
177 H-4 Clayton (USA)
199 H-5 Clé *riv.*
168 D-3 Clear *riv.*
166 F-3 Clear *lake*
160 A-1 Clear *cap.*
162 F-2 Clear *mt*
159 K-8 Clear (USA) *riv.*
162 F-2 Clear Prairie
171 J-7 Clearfield
166 D-8 Clearwater *riv.*
166 D-7 Clearwater *mt*
163 K-3 Clearwater *riv.*
162 E-5 Clearwater (Canada)
169 H-1 Clearwater (USA)
177 K-7 Clearwater (USA)
175 N-4 Cleburne
52 D-1 Cleehill
192 G-4 Clément
201 H-1 Clemente *isl.*
172 E-7 Clementon
52 E-1 Clent
52 E-1 Clent *hill*
52 D-1 Cleobury Mortimer
52 D-1 Cleobury North
172 A-5 Cleona
149 H-7 Cleopatra Needle *mt*
212 F-5 Clerke *rf*
219 K-2 Clermont (Australia)
50 E-8 Clermont (France)
61 H-2 Clermont-Ferrand
58 B-1 Clerval
54 D-2 Cléry-en-Vexin
144 B-7 Cleugh *strt.*
220 B-2 Cleve
52 C-5 Clevedon
215 K-8 Cleveland *cap.*
162 G-8 Cleveland *mt*
220 G-8 Cleveland (Australia) *mt*
170 G-6 Cleveland (USA)
175 P-1 Cleveland (USA)
177 H-2 Cleveland (USA)
175 P-5 Cleveland (USA)
176 E-3 Cleveland (USA)
55 H-5 Clichy
55 K-5 Clichy-sous-Bois
50 A-3 Clifden
214 D-6 Cliffdale *riv.*
53 M-5 Cliffe
52 B-2 Clifford
161 M-2 Clifton *pte*
219 J-6 Clifton (Australia)
52 C-5 Clifton (UK)
174 F-2 Clifton (USA)
171 H-9 Clifton Forge
218 D-5 Clifton Hills
163 J-9 Climax
56 A-9 Clinge
162 D-5 Clinton (Canada)
170 D-8 Clinton (USA)
170 A-9 Clinton (USA)
170 C-6 Clinton (USA)
176 E-5 Clinton (USA)
177 M-2 Clinton (USA)
176 D-2 Clinton (USA)
175 M-1 Clinton (USA)
174 E-1 Clints Well
191 H-4 Cliza
105 J-6 Clocolan
191 P-5 Clodomira
198 E-1 Clodomira
214 E-9 Cloncurry *riv.*
214 E-9 Cloncurry
50 B-4 Clonmel
53 J-3 Clophill
51 H-5 Cloppenburg
196 A-7 Clorinda
173 H-2 Closter
168 D-3 Cloud *mt*
159 H-6 Cloudy *mt*
167 H-1 Cloverdale
175 K-2 Clovis
52 D-1 Clow's Top
64 D-1 Cluj
52 C-1 Clun *riv.*
52 C-1 Clun
52 B-1 Clun *ft*
218 E-3 Cluny
58 B-4 Cluse (La)
62 G-1 Clusone
50 D-2 Clydebank
52 B-2 Clyro
52 A-8 Clyst Honiton
52 A-8 Clyst Saint Mary
67 J-3 Cna *riv.*
172 D-2 Cnadensis
72 E-2 Cnorr
147 H-3 Cô Chiên *strt.*
178 C-6 Coahuayana
175 K-7 Coahuila *reg.*
160 F-7 Coal *riv.*
162 A-4 Coal Harbour
160 F-7 Coal River
178 D-6 Coalcomán *mt*
178 C-6 Coalcomán de Matamoros
167 J-4 Coaldale
175 P-2 Coalgate
167 K-2 Coalinga
168 C-6 Coalmont
168 A-5 Coalville
181 K-1 Coamo
215 H-5 Coast (Australia) *mt*
219 M-5 Coast (Australia) *mt*
188 G-8 Coatá
155 K-3 Coata *isl.*
153 K-3 Coata *isl.*
156 F-1 Coata *isl.*
179 H-5 Coatepec
179 L-9 Coatepeque
172 C-6 Coatesville
227 M-1 Coats Land *reg.*
179 J-6 Coatzacoalcos
179 N-5 Coba *site*
184 D-2 Cobán
219 H-8 Cobar
221 K-4 Cobargo
221 J-5 Cobberas *mt*
53 J-6 Cobham
191 L-1 Cobija *pte*
190 C-2 Cobija
164 C-9 Cobourg
209 M-8 Cobourg *pen.*
220 G-4 Cobram
191 M-4 Cobre *mt*
106 D-4 Cobuè
51 J-7 Coburg
188 B-4 Coca
188 B-3 Coca *riv.*
189 P-8 Cocachacra
193 P-9 Cocal
185 M-9 Cocalito
63 M-7 Coccolia
62 B-4 Cocconato
191 H-4 Cochabamba
187 M-2 Coche *isl.*
141 K-4 Cochin
191 L-4 Cochinoca *mt*
180 C-5 Cochinos (Bay of Pigs) *bay*
199 M-3 Cochoeira do Sul
201 H-3 Cochrane *lake*
163 N-3 Cochrane *riv.*
164 A-6 Cochrane (Canada)
201 J-3 Cochrane (Chile)
172 B-6 Cochranville
170 F-3 Cockburn *isl.*
201 N-4 Cockburn *strt.*
220 E-1 Cockburn
181 K-4 Cockburn Harbour
181 H-3 Cockburn Town
172 A-8 Cockeysville
185 K-8 Coclé *reg.*
186 B-8 Coco *pte*
184 G-4 Coco *riv.*
144 B-7 Coco *strt.*
144 B-7 Coco *islds*
177 L-7 Cocoa
98 C-2 Cocobeach
195 P-2 Coconho *pte*
180 C-9 Cocorocuma *isl.*
185 J-3 Cocorocuma *islds*
194 G-9 Cocos
178 C-4 Cocula
171 N-5 Cod *cap.*
187 K-2 Codera *cap.*
222 B-9 Codfish *isl.*
53 K-3 Codicote
63 M-5 Codigoro
97 H-7 Codmo *riv.*
195 H-1 Codó
62 F-4 Codogno
195 H-2 Codozinho *riv.*
191 J-1 Codpa
181 N-1 Codrington
63 P-1 Codroipo
168 C-3 Cody
195 H-1 Coelho Neto
214 G-4 Coen
189 J-6 Coengua *riv.*
192 C-4 Coeroeni *riv.*
162 E-9 Coeur d'Alene
176 B-1 Coffeyville
220 B-2 Coffin *bay*
220 B-2 Coffin Bay *pen.*
219 M-8 Coff's Harbour
192 C-6 Cofuini *riv.*
124 G-1 Cogar *riv.*
53 M-3 Coggeshall
62 B-2 Coggiola
59 M-8 Coglio
60 F-1 Cognac
98 C-1 Cogo
62 C-7 Cogoleto
63 K-2 Cogollo del Cengio
172 D-8 Cohansey *riv.*
188 C-8 Cohuinari *riv.*
220 G-3 Cohuna
185 J-9 Coiba *isl.*
201 L-5 Coig *riv.*
54 E-7 Coignières
200 G-3 Coihaique
200 G-3 Coihaique Alto *pte*
200 G-3 Coihaique Alto
200 B-2 Coihue
141 J-5 Coimbatore
196 A-3 Coimbra (Brazil)
60 A-4 Coimbra (Portugal)
191 J-2 Coipasa *mt*
191 K-3 Coipasa *lake*
122 B-4 Coja
187 J-3 Cojedes *riv.*
187 J-3 Cojedes *reg.*
201 H-4 Cojudo Blanco *mt*
184 E-4 Cojutepeque
52 C-8 Coker
62 A-9 Col di Rodi
220 F-5 Colac
198 D-1 Colalao del Valle
198 B-3 Colangüil *mt*
197 M-4 Colatina
220 G-4 Colbinabbin
168 F-8 Colby
189 M-8 Colca *riv.*
198 A-7 Colchagua *reg.*
50 E-6 Colchester
163 J-5 Cold *lake*
52 D-5 Cold Ashton
163 J-5 Cold Lake
53 M-4 Cold Norton
173 H-1 Cold Spring
173 J-3 Cold Spring Harbor
159 M-6 Coldfoot
168 G-9 Coldwater (USA)
170 F-6 Coldwater (USA)
164 F-8 Colebrook
159 N-8 Coleen *riv.*
52 D-4 Coleford
214 F-5 Coleman *riv.*
162 F-8 Coleman (Canada)
175 M-4 Coleman (USA)
72 E-5 Cölemerik (Hakkâri)
220 E-5 Coleraine (Australia)
50 C-2 Coleraine (UK)
141 K-6 Coleroon *riv.*
189 P-8 Coles *pte*
104 G-7 Colesberg
52 E-4 Colesborne
52 F-1 Coleshill
172 F-1 Colesville
176 D-5 Colfax (USA)
162 E-9 Colfax (USA)
200 G-5 Colhué Huapi *lake*
62 E-6 Coli
200 C-2 Colico *lake*
178 C-5 Colima
188 C-1 Colimes *riv.*
198 B-6 Colina
195 H-3 Colinas (Brazil)
194 E-8 Colinas (Brazil)
50 C-1 Coll *isl.*
59 P-9 Colla
62 G-7 Collagna
191 K-2 Collagussi
219 K-7 Collarenebri
62 G-6 Collecchio
55 M-6 Collégien
62 A-4 Collegno
216 E-8 Collie
213 J-4 Collier *bay*
63 J-8 Collina *pass*
52 F-6 Collingbourne Kingston
172 E-6 Collingswood
211 M-7 Collingwood *bay*
164 B-9 Collingwood (Canada)
222 G-6 Collingwood (Nouvelle Zélande)
176 F-5 Collins
215 K-9 Collinsville
63 H-2 Collio
200 B-2 Collipulli
79 M-2 Collo
58 D-8 Collombey
200 D-3 Collon Curá *riv.*
58 A-8 Collonge
58 A-9 Collonges (France)
58 E-9 Collonges (Switzerland)
50 B-3 Collooney
191 J-5 Collpa
50 G-9 Colmar
53 J-5 Colnbrook
53 M-3 Colne *riv.*
174 A-3 Colnett *cap.*
172 F-6 Colnnibus
63 K-3 Cologna Veneta
172 F-8 Cologne (USA)
62 F-2 Cologno al Serio
55 H-5 Colombes
183 C-2 Colombia *state*
196 G-4 Colombia (Brazil)
186 D-7 Colombia (Colombia)
170 E-7 Colombia City
154 F-4 Colombie britannique
58 B-6 Colombier (Switzerland)
58 D-3 Colombier (Switzerland)
63 H-1 Colombine *mt*
118 D-6 Colombo
141 N-7 Colombo (Sri Lanka)
185 P-8 Colomboy
170 E-8 Colombus (USA)
176 F-3 Colombus (USA)
184 C-7 Colón *islds*
185 J-7 Colón *isl.*
184 G-3 Colón *mt*
198 G-6 Colón (Argentina)
180 D-4 Colón (Cuba)
184 G-2 Colón (Honduras) *reg.*
184 C-7 Colón (Galapagos) *islds*
185 L-8 Colón (Panama) *reg.*
185 L-8 Colon (Panama)
199 J-5 Colón (Uruguay)
217 P-6 Colona
188 C-1 Colonche *mt*
188 C-1 Colonche
197 N-1 Colonia *riv.*
199 J-6 Colonia *reg.*
200 B-4 Colonia Catriel
199 J-6 Colonia del Sacramento
199 H-1 Colonia Elisa
200 C-6 Colonia Josefa
195 P-5 Colonia Leopoldina
174 F-4 Colonia Morelos
196 A-5 Colonia Risso
199 H-1 Colonia Unidas
200 B-5 Colonia 25 de Mayo
171 K-9 Colonial Heights
50 C-2 Colonsay *isl.*
172 B-7 Colora
186 F-5 Colorada *plat.*
200 B-6 Colorada Grande *lag.*
187 M-4 Coloradito
167 L-8 Colorado *state*
156 C-3 Colorado *riv.*
156 C-3 Colorado *plat.*
157 D-3 Colorado *state*
200 B-4 Colorado (Argentina) *riv.*
168 A-8 Colorado (USA) *riv.*
175 L-3 Colorado City
168 D-8 Colorado Springs
191 P-3 Colorados *mt*
180 A-4 Colorados *islds*
63 H-5 Colorno
178 D-3 Colotlán
128 C-2 Colpon-Ata
191 H-4 Colquechaca
191 H-3 Colquiri
198 A-7 Coltauco
172 G-5 Colts Neck
102 C-4 Colui *riv.*
156 B-2 Columbia *riv.*
162 D-9 Columbia *pool*
162 E-5 Columbia *mt*
162 F-7 Columbia *lake*
162 C-9 Columbia *riv.*
166 D-5 Columbia *plat.*
172 A-2 Columbia (District)
170 B-8 Columbia (USA)
177 K-3 Columbia (USA)
176 D-4 Columbia (USA)
177 H-1 Columbia (USA)
177 N-1 Columbia (USA)
176 G-2 Columbia (USA)
176 E-5 Columbia (USA)
60 F-6 Columbretes *islds*
169 H-6 Columbus (USA)
168 C-2 Columbus (USA)
170 C-5 Columbus (USA)
170 G-8 Columbus (USA)
176 C-1 Columbus (USA)
175 N-6 Columbus (USA)
177 H-4 Columbus (USA)
174 G-3 Columbus (USA)
191 L-2 Colupo *mt*
167 H-2 Colusa
159 M-4 Colville *riv.*
162 E-8 Colville
161 J-3 Colville *lake*
223 K-3 Colville *cap.*
223 K-3 Colville *strt.*
50 C-4 Colwyn Bay
52 B-8 Colyford
63 M-6 Comacchio
63 M-6 Comacchio *lag.*
179 K-6 Comalcalco
200 D-3 Comallo
175 M-4 Comanche
192 G-8 Comandai *isl.*
191 N-8 Comandante Fontana
201 K-5 Comandante Luis Piedrabuena
198 C-6 Comandante Salas
64 E-1 Comaneşti
63 J-1 Cománo
191 H-5 Comarapa
189 K-5 Comas
200 E-2 Comau *riv.*
184 F-3 Comayagua *reg.*
184 F-3 Comayagua
179 P-9 Comayagua
58 E-7 Comballaz
189 L-8 Combapata
198 A-4 Combarbalá
143 J-8 Combermere *bay*
58 D-5 Combremont-le-Grand
55 L-9 Combs-la-Ville
164 G-5 Comeau *bay*
198 E-5 Comechingones *mt*
190 D-8 Comemoracao *riv.*
219 K-3 Comet
219 K-3 Comet *riv.*
175 M-5 Comfort
143 H-5 Comilla
61 L-6 Comino *cap.*
179 K-8 Comitán de Dominguez
55 K-1 Commelles *lake*
54 E-2 Commeny
175 P-3 Commerce
50 G-8 Commercy
63 H-4 Commessaggio
192 E-3 Commewijne *riv.*
149 J-9 Commodore (Silingjiao) *rf*
61 L-2 Como *lake*
61 L-2 Como
62 E-1 Como *lake*
62 D-2 Como (Côme)
227 M-3 Comodoro Guesalaga
200 G-5 Comodoro Rivadavia
89 L-3 Comoé *na.p.*
89 N-3 Comoé *riv.*
59 L-9 Comologno
174 C-7 Comomdú
108 C-3 Comores *reg.*
141 M-5 Comorin *cap.*
108 B-4 Comoros *islds*
77 G-6 Comoros *state*
76 G-6 Comoros *islds*
55 M-4 Compans
172 B-6 Compass
50 F-8 Compiègne
87 J-3 Compony *lag.*
178 C-4 Compostela
197 H-7 Comprida *isl.*
175 K-5 Comstock
145 K-3 Con *riv.*
63 M-4 Cona
200 E-5 Cona Niyeu
77 A-3 Conakry
87 K-3 Conakry
188 C-4 Conambo *riv.*
188 C-4 Conambo
187 J-7 Coname *riv.*
220 G-3 Conargo
63 N-9 Conca *riv.*
198 E-5 Concarán
50 B-8 Concarneau
197 J-1 Conceião *riv.*
195 K-3 Conceição *riv.*
195 M-4 Conceicão (Brazil)
192 A-9 Conceição (Brazil)
197 N-3 Conceicão da Barra
197 M-4 Conceição de Ipanema
194 D-4 Conceição do Araguaia
197 K-3 Conceição do Matro Dentro
194 E-7 Conceição do Norte
184 G-6 Concepción *vol.*
201 L-2 Concepcion *strt.*
174 D-6 Concepcion *pte*
198 D-1 Concepción (Argentina)
199 J-2 Concepción (Argentina)
191 P-4 Concepción (Argentina)
190 F-6 Concepción (Bolivia) *lake*
190 G-7 Concepcion (Bolivia)
200 B-1 Concepcion (Chile)
196 A-6 Concepción (Uruguay)
191 H-7 Concepción (Uruguay) *lake*
186 G-2 Concepción (Vénézuela)
178 E-1 Concepción del Oro
199 J-5 Concepción del Uruguay
165 P-3 Conception *bay*
104 A-2 Conceptionbaai *bay*
62 G-2 Concésio Nave
184 E-4 Conchagua *vol.*
196 G-6 Conchas
175 J-1 Conchas Dam
55 M-6 Conches
191 L-2 Conchi (Chile)
200 F-2 Conchi (Chile)
175 L-4 Concho *riv.*
174 F-1 Concho
175 H-5 Conchos *riv.*
58 C-4 Concise
167 H-2 Concord
196 E-9 Concordia (Brazil)
178 B-2 Concordia (Mexico)
199 J-4 Concordiá (Uruguay)
169 H-8 Concordia (USA)
63 P-2 Concordia Sagittaria
63 J-5 Concordia sulla Secchia
172 C-6 Concordville
62 E-2 Concorezzo
162 C-7 Concrete
219 L-5 Condamine
195 M-7 Conde
55 N-5 Condé-Sainte-Libiaire
54 B-7 Condé-sur-Vesgre
54 E-3 Condécourt
195 J-9 Condeúba
63 H-1 Condino
221 J-2 Condobolin
60 F-3 Condom
166 D-5 Condon
188 E-3 Condor *mt*
188 C-7 Condor
176 G-5 Conecuh *riv.*
63 M-1 Conegliano
172 A-6 Conestoga
172 B-5 Conestoga *riv.*
173 H-4 Coney Island
54 F-4 Conflans-Sainte-Honorine
211 N-9 Conflict Group *islds*
60 G-1 Confolens
196 A-7 Confuso *riv.*
173 H-2 Congers
135 J-8 Conghua
134 F-7 Congjiang
128 D-5 Congliu
195 N-4 Congo

76 E-4 Congo *pool*
77 D-5 Congo *state*
98 G-3 Congo *riv.*
195 K-9 Congogi *riv.*
52 C-6 Congresbury
197 M-5 Conha
200 F-3 Cónico *mt*
215 H-8 Conjuboy
163 J-4 Conklin
171 H-6 Conneaut
157 G-3 Connecticut *state*
171 M-5 Connecticut *riv.*
171 M-5 Connecticut *state*
171 J-7 Connellsville
218 F-3 Connemara
170 F-8 Connersville
52 B-6 Connington
219 L-1 Connors *mt*
188 C-5 Cononaco *riv.*
188 C-5 Cononaco
187 K-8 Conorochite *riv.*
172 B-7 Conowingo *dam.*
172 B-7 Conowingo
197 H-4 Conquista
162 G-9 Conrad
221 J-6 Conran *cap.*
175 P-5 Conroe
160 G-9 Conroy *riv.*
63 L-6 Consandolo
197 K-5 Conselheiro Lafaiete
197 M-4 Conselheiro Péna
63 L-6 Conselice
63 L-4 Conselve
172 D-6 Conshohocken
180 B-4 Consolación del Norte
180 B-4 Consolación del Sur
64 G-2 Constanta
158 D-7 Constantine *cap.*
79 M-2 Constantine
181 K-6 Constanza
198 A-7 Constitución
219 K-3 Consuelo
166 G-7 Contact
142 F-6 Contai
188 G-5 Contamara
63 M-4 Contarina
195 J-8 Contas *riv.*
195 K-8 Contendas de Sincora
58 F-9 Conthey
174 E-3 Continental
194 D-4 Conto Magalhães
179 P-4 Contoy *isl.*
185 J-9 Contreras *islds*
201 M-2 Contreras *isl.*
160 B-2 Controlle *bay*
87 H-3 Contuboé
188 G-3 Contumazá
161 N-6 Contwoyto *lake*
186 E-4 Convención
177 L-3 Conway (USA)
176 D-2 Conway (USA)
172 B-2 Conyngham
218 B-6 Coober Pedy
142 G-2 Cooch Behār
53 M-8 Cooden Beach
222 E-7 Cook *mt*
223 H-7 Cook *strt.*
159 G-8 Cook *gulf*
224 C-5 Cook *islds*
201 P-5 Cook *bay*
217 N-5 Cook (Australia)
170 B-2 Cook (USA)
52 E-2 Cook Hill
216 E-7 Cooke *mt*
177 H-1 Cookeville
53 H-5 Cookham
105 H-8 Cookhouse
215 J-5 Cooks *strt.*
165 L-1 Cooks Harbour
215 H-5 Cooktown
219 H-8 Coolabah
221 K-1 Coolah
219 N-6 Coolangatta
217 H-6 Coolgardie
53 J-7 Coolham
213 N-3 Coolibah
174 E-2 Coolidge
102 C-2 Coolo
221 J-4 Cooma
52 E-7 Coombe Bisset
52 E-3 Coombe Hill
221 K-1 Coonabarabran
219 J-8 Coonamble
218 B-7 Coondambo
140 G-3 Coondapoor
212 F-8 Coongan *riv.*
216 G-5 Coongarrie *lake*
219 H-5 Coongoola
141 J-5 Coonoor
175 P-3 Cooper
218 D-6 Coopers *riv.*
172 D-4 Coopersburg
169 H-2 Cooperstown
216 D-2 Coor de Wandy *mt*
218 E-2 Coorabulka
219 N-5 Cooroy
166 D-2 Coos Bay
176 G-4 Coosa *riv.*
221 J-3 Cootamundra
219 M-5 Cooyar
218 D-3 Cooyeana
66 B-9 Cop
191 K-2 Copa *mt*
198 C-2 Copacabana (Argentina)
190 G-2 Copacabana (Bolivia)
188 C-4 Copahuari *riv.*
200 B-3 Copahue *mt*
200 B-3 Copahue *na.p.*
188 D-5 Copalyacu *riv.*
184 E-3 Copán
184 E-2 Copán *site*
188 C-3 Copataza *riv.*
47 D-4 Copenhagen
51 K-3 Copenhagen
191 J-6 Copère
62 E-4 Copiano
198 A-2 Copiapó *riv.*
198 A-2 Copiapó
54 C-1 Copierres
172 D-3 Coplay
187 N-3 Coporito
102 B-3 Coporolo *riv.*
63 L-5 Copparo
192 D-3 Coppename *riv.*
160 C-1 Copper *riv.*
162 E-8 Copper Butte *mt*
170 D-2 Copper Harbour
172 E-4 Copper Hill
103 M-6 Copper Queen
103 L-3 Copperbelt *reg.*
161 M-4 Coppermine
161 M-4 Coppermine *riv.*
58 A-8 Coppet
86 C-3 Coppolani
108 C-8 Coq *hill*
99 H-2 Coquilhatville (Mbandaka)
166 D-2 Coquille
198 A-4 Coquimbo *reg.*
198 A-3 Coquimbo
123 K-3 Cora *riv.*
64 E-3 Corabia
197 K-2 Coracão de Jesus
195 L-7 Coração de Maria
189 M-7 Coracora
204 F-3 Coral *sea*
177 L-9 Coral Gables
155 K-3 Coral Harbour
164 A-5 Coral Rapids
173 K-3 Coram
220 F-5 Corangamite *lake*
50 E-8 Corbeil-Essonnes
196 D-7 Corbélia
54 C-5 Corbeville
58 D-8 Corbeyrier
54 A-1 Corbie
58 E-6 Corbières
177 H-1 Corbin
172 F-8 Corbin City
64 M-4 Córbola
53 J-1 Corby
58 D-4 Corcelles
200 F-2 Corcovado *vol.*
200 F-2 Corcovado *gulf*
60 A-2 Corcubion
194 E-3 Corda *riv.*
197 L-6 Cordeiro
177 J-4 Cordele
175 M-1 Cordell
63 N-1 Cordenons
194 E-4 Cordilheiras *mt*
188 F-3 Cordillera Central *mt*
156 G-6 Cordillera centrale
60 E-4 Cordillera iberica *rge*
182 C-2 Cordillera Occidental *rge*
156 G-6 Cordillera occidentale
182 C-2 Cordillera Oriental *rge*
191 H-5 Cordillera Oriental *mt*
156 G-6 Cordillera orientale
198 E-5 Cordoba *reg.*
198 E-4 Córdoba
198 E-4 Cordoba *mt*
198 P-9 Córdoba *reg.*
60 C-7 Cordoba
201 J-5 Cordón Alto *mt*
55 P-9 Cordoux
160 B-9 Cordova *bay*
160 B-2 Cordova
160 B-2 Cordova *mt*
189 M-6 Córdova
201 N-4 Cordova *pen.*
63 P-1 Cordovado
195 K-1 Coreaú *riv.*
137 L-1 Corée *strt.*
63 H-8 Coreglia Antelminelli
214 E-8 Corella *riv.*
195 M-3 Coremas
52 E-9 Corfe Castle
218 G-1 Corfield
64 B-6 Corfu *strt.*
58 E-2 Corgémont
196 C-3 Corguinho
63 N-8 Coriano
194 B-1 Coriarí *riv.*
214 D-7 Corinda
215 M-7 Coringa *islds*
220 G-8 Corinna
163 L-9 Corinne
64 D-7 Corinth *gulf*
176 F-2 Corinth (USA)
197 K-3 Corinto
62 A-3 Corio
59 N-9 Corippo
189 N-8 Corire
98 B-2 Corisco *bay*
98 B-2 Corisco *isl.*
196 A-1 Corixa Grande *riv.*
218 F-2 Cork (Australia)
50 A-4 Cork (UK)
52 F-1 Corley
63 L-1 Corlo *lake*
64 G-5 Corlu
55 H-4 Cormeilles-en-Parisis
54 F-2 Cormeilles-en-Vexin
163 N-6 Cormorant *lake*
163 N-6 Cormorant
69 L-6 Cormoz
194 B-1 Cornaga (Brazil) *riv.*
69 N-4 Cornaja *riv.*
68 E-8 Cornaja Sloboda
63 K-2 Cornedo Vicentino
189 N-7 Cornejo *pte*
177 J-2 Cornelia
196 F-6 Cornelio Procopio
221 H-6 Corner *bay*
165 L-3 Corner Brook
58 C-8 Cornettes (Les) *mt*
63 J-1 Cornetto *mt*
173 M-1 Cornfield *pte*
58 A-9 Cornier
62 G-7 Corniglio
176 E-1 Corning (USA)
171 K-6 Corning (USA)
166 G-2 Corning (USA)
219 H-2 Cornish *riv.*
213 K-6 Cornish *mt*
63 J-8 Corno alle Scale
62 F-1 Corno Stella *mt*
63 M-1 Cornuda la Valle
164 E-8 Cornwall
153 J-2 Cornwallis *isl.*
220 C-2 Corny *pte*
67 M-6 Cornyj Jar
187 H-1 Coro *gulf*
187 H-1 Coro
197 L-3 Coroaci
196 C-1 Coroados *mt*
195 H-1 Coroatá
187 P-4 Corocoro *isl.*
191 H-2 Corocoro
190 G-3 Coroico
223 K-4 Coromandel *pen.*
197 H-3 Coromandel
116 D-5 Coromandel Coast
148 F-6 Coron
148 F-6 Coron *isl.*
175 H-2 Corona
185 H-8 Coronado *bay*
174 A-1 Coronados *islds*
174 D-7 Coronados *isl.*
213 J-3 Coronation *islds*
160 B-8 Coronation *isl.*
161 N-4 Coronation *gulf*
198 G-4 Coronda
200 B-1 Coronel
191 L-6 Coronel Cornejo
200 B-8 Coronel Dorrego
197 L-4 Coronel Fabriciano
197 L-2 Coronel Murta
196 B-7 Coronel Oviedo
196 C-1 Coronel Ponce
200 B-8 Coronel Pringles
200 A-8 Coronel Suarez
199 J-8 Coronel Vidal
196 D-8 Coronel Vivida
64 C-6 Corovode
221 H-4 Corowa
185 P-8 Corozal (Colombia)
179 N-6 Corozal (Honduras)
201 K-5 Corpen
175 N-7 Corpus Christi
191 H-3 Corque
198 F-5 Corral de Bustos
63 J-5 Corréggio
148 E-6 Corregidor *isl.*
197 J-4 Corrego Danta
196 F-1 Corrego do Ouro
196 C-1 Correia *riv.*
196 E-3 Corrente *riv.*
194 G-6 Corrente
196 D-2 Correntes *riv.*
194 G-8 Correntina *riv.*
194 G-8 Correntina
174 G-1 Correo
63 K-4 Correzzo
63 M-4 Corrèzzola
50 A-3 Corrib *lake*
196 A-9 Corrientes
199 J-2 Corrientes *reg.*
188 C-4 Corrientes *riv.*
186 B-6 Corrientes (Colombia) *cap.*
180 A-5 Corrientes (Cuba) *cap.*
178 B-4 Corrientes (Mexico) *cap.*
216 F-7 Corringin
60 A-3 Corrubedo *cap.*
171 H-6 Corry
221 J-4 Corryong
61 K-4 Corse *cap.*
52 E-5 Corsham
61 L-5 Corsica *isl.*
46 D-5 Corsica *isl.*
175 N-4 Corsicana
62 E-3 Corsico
58 A-8 Corsier
172 F-9 Corson's inlet *isl.*
72 D-6 Corston
58 D-4 Cortaillod
61 L-5 Corte
58 E-2 Cortébert
63 N-2 Cortellazzo
62 G-5 Cortemaggiore
62 B-6 Cortemilia
62 E-4 Corteolona
180 B-5 Cortés *bay*
179 N-9 Cortes *reg.*
184 E-2 Cortes *mt*
168 B-8 Cortez
61 M-2 Cortina d'Ampezzo
66 C-8 Cortkov
171 K-5 Cortland
200 A-8 Corto *riv.*
87 J-3 Corubal *riv.*
60 A-5 Coruche
64 N-4 Coruh *riv.*
65 K-4 Corum
196 G-1 Corumba *riv.*
196 A-3 Corumbá
196 G-1 Corumba de Goiás
196 G-3 Corumbaíba
196 E-7 Corumbatai *riv.*
197 P-2 Corumbaú
190 E-7 Corumbiara *riv.*
195 L-1 Corumiquara *pte*
195 N-5 Coruripe *riv.*
197 L-1 Corutuba *riv.*
162 A-9 Corvallis
170 A-7 Corydon
53 M-5 Coryton
198 G-1 Corzuela
64 G-8 Cos
178 B-1 Cosalá
179 H-6 Cosamaluapan de Carpio
191 H-2 Cosapa
191 H-2 Cosapa *riv.*
61 P-7 Cosenza
52 G-8 Cosham
170 G-7 Coshocton
184 E-4 Cosigüina *vol.*
108 A-7 Cosmoledo *islds*
61 H-1 Cosne
50 E-9 Cosne-Cours-sur-Loire
198 E-4 Cosquín
62 B-2 Cossato
55 M-8 Cossigny
58 B-6 Cossonay
185 H-4 Costa de los Mosquitos
63 L-4 Costa di Rovigo
157 F-6 Costa Rica *state*
62 B-5 Costigliole d'Asti
189 L-7 Cotabambas
149 J-3 Cotabato
188 B-2 Cotacachi *mt*
190 G-3 Cotacajes *riv.*
191 K-4 Cotagaita
189 M-7 Cotahuasi
180 D-8 Cote *mt*
58 A-7 Côte (La) *reg.*
199 H-1 Coté-Lai
181 H-7 Coteaux
194 G-7 Cotegipe
50 D-7 Cotentin *pen.*
53 K-6 Coterham
56 F-3 Cothen
219 K-2 Cotherstone
190 B-4 Coti *riv.*
190 C-4 Cotia *riv.*
63 M-7 Cotignola
187 P-6 Cotingo *riv.*
189 M-7 Cotohuasi *riv.*
89 N-7 Cotonou
188 B-2 Cotopaxi *reg.*
188 B-3 Cotopaxi *vol.*
166 D-3 Cottage Grove
51 L-6 Cottbus
53 L-1 Cottenham
58 E-5 Cottens
53 K-3 Cottered
192 E-3 Cotticá *riv.*
53 H-1 Cottingham
174 E-1 Cottonwood
181 L-6 Cotuí
175 M-6 Cotulla
54 A-5 Couarde (La)
55 M-8 Coubert
55 M-8 Coubert *ft*
60 E-1 Coubre *pte*
55 L-5 Coubron
54 A-6 Coudray (Le)
220 B-4 Couedic *cap.*
55 P-5 Couilly-Pont-aux-Dames
162 D-8 Coulee City
54 A-9 Coulombs
55 P-5 Coulommes
171 J-3 Coulonge *riv.*
166 E-7 Council
159 H-3 Council (USA)
169 J-7 Council Bluffs
169 H-9 Council Grove
168 B-9 Counselor
54 D-6 Couperie (La)
162 C-7 Coupeville
55 N-5 Coupvray
161 M-7 Courageous Lake *lake*
192 C-3 Courantyne (Corantijn) *riv.*
55 H-5 Courbevoie
55 P-7 Courbon
54 F-8 Courcelle
54 G-1 Courcelles
54 F-2 Courcelles-sur-Vexin
55 J-9 Courcouronnes
54 F-3 Courdimanche
54 B-5 Courgent
55 J-5 Courneuve (La)
55 N-8 Courquetaine
58 F-1 Courrendlin
58 F-1 Courroux
58 F-2 Court
172 E-9 Court House
58 E-2 Courtelary
162 B-6 Courtenay (Canada)
58 F-1 Courtetelle
55 P-9 Courtomer
55 L-5 Courtry
176 C-4 Coushatta
50 D-7 Coutances
55 N-5 Coutevroult
185 K-5 Coutown *islds*
58 C-4 Couvet
58 D-9 Coux *pass*
201 K-1 Covadonga *isl.*
107 L-3 Covane
173 H-1 Cove
185 P-8 Coveñas
172 F-3 Covent Station
50 D-5 Coventry
60 B-4 Covilhã
158 E-8 Coville *lake*
176 E-2 Covington (USA)
176 E-5 Covington (USA)
177 J-3 Covington (USA)
171 H-9 Covington (USA)
170 F-8 Covington (USA)
200 C-3 Covunca *riv.*
217 H-6 Cowan *lake*
218 C-6 Coward Springs
218 D-5 Cowarie
52 A-5 Cowbridge
53 L-7 Cowden
220 C-2 Cowell
52 G-8 Cowes
53 K-7 Cowfold
162 B-8 Cowlitz *riv.*
221 J-2 Cowra
214 B-5 Cox *riv.*
220 G-9 Cox *bay*
194 G-9 Coxá *riv.*
196 C-3 Coxim
196 C-3 Coxim *riv.*
196 B-1 Coxipó da Ponte
143 H-6 Cox's Bāzār
87 K-4 Coyah
186 D-7 Coyaima
175 H-5 Coyame
55 K-1 Coye *ft*
55 K-1 Coye-la-Forêt
179 P-5 Cozumel *isl.*
179 P-5 Cozumel
219 L-4 Cracow
220 G-8 Cradle *na.p.*
105 H-8 Cradock
52 A-3 Crai
168 C-6 Craig
219 L-5 Craigs *mt*
64 D-3 Craiova
172 A-6 Craley
59 M-8 Cramalina *mt*
91 K-6 Crampel
164 E-3 Cran Cassé *riv.*
52 E-8 Cranborne
216 F-9 Cranbrook (Australia)
162 F-8 Cranbrook (Canada)
53 M-7 Cranbrook (UK)
172 F-5 Cranbury
170 D-4 Crandon
181 P-8 Crane (Antilles)
175 K-4 Crane (USA)
166 E-5 Crane (USA)
53 J-1 Cranford Saint John
53 J-7 Cranleigh
58 A-8 Crans (Switzerland)
58 F-8 Crans (Switzerland)
171 M-5 Cranston
58 A-7 Crassier
211 P-5 Crater *mt*
166 E-3 Crater Lake *na.p.*
195 L-4 Crato
190 D-9 Cravari *riv.*
59 L-9 Craveggia
102 B-2 Craveiro Lopes *dam.*
52 C-1 Craven
54 A-4 Cravent
197 H-5 Cravinhos
186 G-5 Cravo
186 G-5 Cravo Norte *riv.*
186 F-6 Cravo Sur *riv.*
168 E-5 Crawford
170 E-8 Crawfordsville
50 D-6 Crawley
159 L-8 Crazy (USA) *mt*
168 B-2 Crazy (USA) *mt*
172 F-5 Cream Ridge
55 P-7 Crécy *ft*
55 P-6 Crécy-la-Chapelle
52 C-2 Credenhill
52 A-8 Crediton
163 L-3 Cree *lake*
163 M-3 Cree *riv.*
168 C-8 Creede
174 F-6 Creel
55 P-4 Crégy-lès-Meaux
50 E-8 Creil
62 F-3 Crema
61 L-3 Cremona
62 G-4 Cremona
61 N-3 Cres *isl.*
145 P-5 Crescent *isl.*
166 E-2 Crescent City
62 B-4 Crescentino
62 E-3 Crescenzago
174 C-8 Cresciente *isl.*
54 F-1 Cresnes
63 K-2 Crespadoro
63 L-1 Crespano
54 E-5 Crespières
63 L-5 Crespino
198 G-5 Crespo
54 D-6 Cressay
54 F-8 Cressely
58 E-4 Cressier
172 B-4 Cressona
220 F-5 Cressy
168 C-8 Crested Butte
162 E-8 Creston (Canada)
168 C-5 Creston (USA)
170 A-7 Creston (USA)
176 G-5 Crestview
64 E-9 Crete *isl.*
55 K-7 Créteil
211 L-5 Cretin *cap.*
61 H-4 Creus *cap.*
60 G-1 Creuse *riv.*
58 C-4 Creux du Van
62 B-2 Crevacuore
63 K-6 Crevalcore
55 P-7 Crèvecoeur-en-Brie
52 A-4 Crevnant
59 K-9 Crevola
50 D-4 Crewe
52 C-8 Crewkerne
220 G-5 Crib Point
199 P-2 Criciúma
52 G-1 Crick
52 E-4 Cricklade
50 D-2 Crieff
66 E-9 Crigoriopol'
220 F-7 Crim *cap.*
112 B-5 Crimea *rép*
65 J-1 Crimea *reg.*
192 A-7 Criminosa *riv.*
168 D-8 Cripple Creek
53 M-7 Cripps Corner
194 C-5 Crisostomo *riv.*
197 M-3 Crispim Jaques
98 E-6 Cristal *mt*
194 D-6 Cristalândia
197 H-2 Cristalina
194 C-8 Cristalino *riv.*
159 M-7 Cristian *riv.*
195 H-5 Cristino Castro
184 A-9 Cristóbal *pte*
185 L-8 Cristobal
186 E-2 Cristóbal Colon *mt*
194 G-7 Cristópolis
199 N-4 Cristovao Pereira *pte*
64 C-1 Crisul-Alb *riv.*
194 D-9 Crixás
194 C-8 Crixás-açu *riv.*
194 C-8 Crixás-Mirim *riv.*
64 B-4 Crna Gora *reg.*

207 P-7 Denpasar
53 M-2 Denston
58 C-8 Dent d'Oche *mt*
58 E-6 Dent de Brenleire *mt*
58 D-7 Dent de Lys *mt*
58 E-9 Dent de Mordes *mt*
58 E-6 Dent de Ruth *mt*
58 D-9 Dent du Midi *mt*
53 H-2 Denton (UK)
53 L-8 Denton (UK)
175 N-3 Denton (USA)
168 D-7 Denver
172 F-3 Denville
139 N-3 Deoband
142 D-6 Deogarh (India)
139 K-6 Deogarh (India)
139 N-8 Deogarh (India)
142 E-4 Deoghar
133 L-6 Deogjeog *isl.*
129 P-1 Deoha *riv.*
140 B-3 Deolāli
139 L-6 Deoli
139 N-8 Deori
142 D-2 Deoria
127 N-7 Deosai *mt*
90 C-4 Dep (Nigeria) *riv.*
124 F-2 Dep (SSSR) *riv.*
172 B-7 Deposit Webster
187 P-7 Depósito
52 E-7 Deptford
143 N-1 Deqin
139 J-2 Dera Ghāzi Khān
127 J-8 Dera Ismāil Khān
122 F-6 Deraik *riv.*
139 J-3 Derāwar Fort
66 D-8 Derazn'a
71 P-7 Derbent
122 E-3 Derbina *riv.*
91 P-7 Derbisaka
213 H-5 Derby (Australia)
50 D-5 Derby (UK)
173 K-1 Derby (USA)
58 G-2 Derendingen
68 C-7 Derev'anka
69 J-5 Derev'ansk
210 C-3 Derewa *riv.*
67 N-3 Dergači (SSSR)
67 H-6 Dergači (SSSR)
65 P-6 Derik
65 K-6 Derinkuyu
97 M-2 Derka Dur
104 B-4 Dernburg *cap.*
176 E-6 Dernières *islds*
143 N-1 Derong
93 K-4 Derudeb
220 G-8 Derwent *riv.*
220 G-8 Derwent Bridge
120 F-1 Deržavinskij
170 A-5 Des Moines *riv.*
170 A-6 Des Moines
198 D-6 Desaguadero
198 D-5 Desaguadero *riv.*
62 C-4 Desana
224 F-5 Désappointement *islds*
190 C-9 Desastre *riv.*
53 H-1 Desborough
174 A-2 Descanso
163 M-5 Deschambault *lake*
166 D-4 Deschutes *riv.*
63 M-3 Dese *riv.*
201 M-4 Deseado *cap.*
201 H-4 Deseado *riv.*
174 C-3 Desemboque
190 D-5 Desengano *riv.*
201 K-6 Desengano *pte*
63 H-3 Desenzano del Garda
167 H-8 Deseret *mt*
78 B-1 Deserta Grande *isl.*
199 N-4 Désertas *pte*
78 B-1 Desertas *islds*
200 F-2 Desertores *islds*
93 M-8 Deshen *mt*
139 K-4 Deshnoke
62 E-2 Desio
66 F-5 Desna *riv.*
201 N-3 Desolacion *isl.*
148 G-2 Desolation *pte*
193 L-4 Desordem *mt*
51 K-6 Dessau
58 C-2 Dessoubre *riv.*
213 M-9 Destruction *mt*
160 D-3 Destruction *bay*
145 K-6 Det Udom
53 M-6 Detling
170 F-6 Detroit
169 J-3 Detroit Lakes
103 K-7 Dett
55 H-4 Deuil-la-Barre
57 J-8 Deurne
57 N-1 Deurningen
147 H-3 Deux Frères (Les) *isl.*
64 D-2 Deva
141 K-6 Devakottai
65 L-6 Develi
51 H-6 Deventer
59 K-8 Devero *val.*

159 K-3 Deviation *mt*
141 K-5 Devikolam
139 H-4 Devīkot
175 L-5 Devils *riv.*
141 L-7 Devil's *pte*
169 H-2 Devils Lake
160 D-6 Devils Paw *mt*
175 M-6 Devine
52 E-6 Devizes
142 B-8 Devodi Munda *mt*
153 K-2 Devon *isl.*
220 G-8 Devonport
65 J-4 Devrek
103 N-8 Devure *riv.*
146 A-7 Dewa *pte*
139 L-8 Dewās
105 H-6 Dewetsdorp
217 N-4 Dey Dey *lake*
131 P-9 Deyang
73 P-5 Deyhūk
73 J-7 Dez *riv.*
160 D-4 Dezadeash *lake*
72 G-6 Dezh Shāhpūr
132 F-7 Dezhou
82 C-5 Dhahad
83 N-4 Dhahran
118 E-4 Dhaka
143 J-5 Dhaleswari *riv.*
140 B-7 Dhāmangaon
96 E-3 Dhamār
140 C-9 Dhamtar
80 C-7 Dhan Murzuk *dés*
142 E-4 Dhānbād
129 P-1 Dhangarhi
142 F-2 Dhankuta
141 L-6 Dhanushkodi
139 K-9 Dhār
142 B-7 Dharamgarh
141 K-5 Dhārāpuram
85 K-6 Dharbat Ali *cap.*
140 A-1 Dhāri
141 J-6 Dharmapuri
140 G-5 Dharmavaram
142 C-5 Dharmjaygarh
127 N-9 Dharmsāla
140 F-4 Dhārwār
139 N-7 Dhasān *riv.*
129 P-3 Dhaulāgiri *mt*
127 M-9 Dhavlādhar *mt*
138 K-7 Dhebar *lake*
65 K-9 Dhekelia
64 D-7 Dhelfoi *site*
142 D-4 Dhenkānal
64 F-9 Dhia *isl.*
64 F-5 Dhidhimótikhon
116 D-4 Dhivehi Rajjge *islds*
64 C-6 Dhodhoni
85 J-6 Dhofar *reg.*
139 H-3 Dholka
139 N-6 Dholphur
64 D-6 Dhomokós
140 C-4 Dhond
140 F-6 Dhone
138 G-8 Dhorāji
139 H-8 Dhrāngadhra
96 F-2 Dhubāb
142 G-3 Dhubri
140 B-4 Dhūlia
142 F-4 Dhulīan
61 N-6 Di Capri *isl.*
145 M-9 Di Linh
88 G-2 Dia
87 H-8 Dia *riv.*
58 E-8 Diablerets *mt*
58 E-8 Diablerets (Les)
58 G-9 Diablons *mt*
88 G-3 Diaka *isl.*
86 G-4 Dialakoto
89 H-3 Diallassagou
181 P-4 Diamant *pte*
198 G-5 Diamante
198 B-7 Diamante *riv.*
197 K-3 Diamantina
218 F-1 Diamantina *riv.*
195 J-8 Diamantina da Chapada *mt*
218 F-2 Diamantina Lakes
196 D-1 Diamantino *riv.*
167 H-4 Diamond *mt*
215 M-7 Diamond *islds*
142 F-5 Diamond Harbour
145 N-2 Diamnai
134 B-8 Dianchi *lake*
86 H-7 Diandoumé
86 G-7 Diangounté-Camara
62 B-6 Diano d'Alba
62 B-9 Diano Marina
194 F-7 Dianópolis
89 L-1 Dianra
89 J-7 Diapaga
87 H-2 Diattacounda
144 B-8 Diavolo *hill*
198 G-5 Diaz
143 L-2 Dibāng *riv.*
99 L-7 Dibaya

99 J-5 Dibaya-Lubue
143 K-2 Dibrugarh
91 P-2 Dibs
65 N-7 Dibsi 'Afnān
186 E-1 Dibulla
53 K-8 Dichting
175 L-3 Dickens
53 L-8 Dick.
168 F-2 Dickinson
53 N-1 Dickleburgh
159 H-3 Dickson (USA)
176 G-1 Dickson (USA)
172 C-1 Dickson City
65 N-5 Dicle *riv.*
63 L-9 Dicomano
57 K-4 Didam
125 K-2 Didbiran
52 G-5 Didcot
95 H-2 Diddessa *riv.*
93 P-8 Didhav
148 A-5 Didicas *vol.*
86 G-8 Didiéni
87 H-1 Diembéring
56 E-1 Diemen
58 G-6 Diemtig *val.*
145 H-2 Dien Biên Phu
57 M-2 Diepenheim
57 K-1 Diepenveen
51 H-6 Diepholz
165 J-6 Dieppe (Canada)
50 E-7 Dieppe (France)
57 K-3 Dieren
56 F-8 Diessen
59 L-2 Dietwil
101 L-1 Dif
90 F-1 Diffa
141 N-2 Difuri *isl.*
139 M-5 Dig
94 A-6 Digba
143 L-2 Digboi
165 J-8 Digby
165 J-8 Digby Neck *cap.*
168 F-8 Dighton
140 D-6 Diglūr
61 J-3 Digne
61 H-1 Digoin
149 K-2 Digos
138 F-5 Digri
210 E-5 Digul *riv.*
165 J-8 Dijlah *riv.*
71 H-3 Diirmentobe
61 J-1 Dijon
91 J-4 Dik
97 H-1 Dikhil
143 K-3 Dikhu *riv.*
72 E-1 Diklosmta *mt*
89 L-1 Dikodougou
103 K-1 Dikuluwe *riv.*
90 G-2 Dikwa
95 A-5 Dila
208 G-7 Dili (Célèbes)
94 B-7 Dili (Zaïre)
144 B-8 Diligent *strt.*
72 K-3 Diližan
218 G-1 Dillcar
158 E-6 Dillingham
168 A-2 Dillon
86 G-9 Dilly
103 H-1 Dilolo
52 C-2 Dilwyn
131 M-2 Dimaersang
99 M-6 Dimbelenge
89 N-2 Dimbokro
220 E-4 Dimbola
159 J-4 Dime Landing
64 H-4 Dimitrovgrad
67 M-1 Dimitrovgrad
175 K-2 Dimmit
82 C-3 Dimona
148 G-2 Dinagat *isl.*
148 G-2 Dinagat
142 G-3 Dinājpur
50 C-8 Dinan
88 G-4 Dinangourou
50 G-7 Dinant
73 M-9 Dīnar *mt*
65 H-7 Dīnar
61 P-4 Dinara Planina *mt*
46 E-5 Dinaric Alps *rge*
94 H-4 Dincha *riv.*
93 K-8 Dindar *na.p.*
140 E-6 Dindi *riv.*
141 K-5 Dindigul
98 G-6 Dinga
132 A-7 Dingbian
143 N-1 Dinggu *riv.*
142 F-1 Dingjie
132 A-5 Dingkouzhen

172 E-1 Dingmans Ferry
219 L-3 Dingo
131 N-3 Dingqing
142 F-1 Dingri
142 F-1 Dingrihe *riv.*
135 M-2 Dingshan
87 J-6 Dinguiraye
50 D-1 Dingwall
131 L-9 Dingxi
132 E-6 Dingxing
132 F-6 Dingxiang
145 L-2 Dinh Lâp
142 G-3 Dīnhāta
57 P-2 Dinkel *riv.*
89 H-8 Dinnik *plat.*
170 B-1 Dinorwic
168 B-6 Dinosaur *na.p.*
168 B-6 Dinosaur
97 P-2 Dinsōr
56 B-6 Dintel Mark *riv.*
56 B-6 Dinteloord
56 B-6 Dinteloord en Prinsenland
56 G-6 Dinther
139 H-7 Diodâr
89 H-1 Dioila
159 J-1 Diomede *islds*
87 K-7 Dion *riv.*
197 L-4 Dionísio
196 D-8 Dionisio Cerqueira
89 H-1 Dioro
89 K-1 Diou
86 G-2 Diouloulou
86 G-8 Dioumara
88 G-2 Dioura
86 F-2 Diourbel
86 F-2 Diourbel *reg.*
143 J-3 Diphu
138 G-6 Diplo
149 H-4 Dipolog
127 L-6 Dīr
88 F-4 Diré
97 J-1 Dire Dawa
215 H-3 Direction *cap.*
184 F-5 Diriamba
102 F-6 Dirico
216 B-3 Dirk Hartogs *isl.*
56 A-5 Dirksland
219 K-6 Dirranbandi
97 N-5 Dirri
168 A-7 Dirty Devil *riv.*
162 A-8 Disappointement *cap.*
213 H-9 Disappointment *lake*
220 E-5 Discovery *bay*
59 N-5 Disentis (Muster)
159 H-5 Dishkakat
161 L-4 Dismal *lake*
168 F-6 Dismal *riv.*
66 D-3 Disna *riv.*
185 H-8 Disquis *riv.*
53 N-1 Diss
96 C-1 Dissān *isl.*
81 N-2 Disūq
87 J-6 Dité
52 D-1 Ditton Priors
140 A-1 Diu
140 F-3 Diu *reg.*
149 H-2 Diuata *mt*
59 K-9 Divedro *val.*
98 D-4 Divénié *rés*
98 D-4 Divénié
140 F-8 Divi *pte*
72 G-2 Diviči
168 A-2 Divide
172 E-9 Dividing Creek
204 E-4 Dividing Range (Great) *rge*
197 J-4 Divinópolis
196 F-2 Divisoes *mt*
189 H-7 Divisor *mt*
122 E-2 Divnogorsk
67 M-8 Divnoje
89 N-2 Divo
58 A-8 Divonne
65 M-5 Divriği
130 D-2 Diwopo
156 A-1 Dixon *strt.*
160 B-9 Dixon *strt.*
170 C-6 Dixon
162 G-2 Dixonville
72 G-7 Diyāla *mt*
72 G-7 Diyālā *riv.*
65 N-6 Diyarbakir
73 J-8 Dizful
90 F-9 Dja *rés*
90 F-8 Dja *riv.*
206 F-1 Djabung *cap.*
206 G-5 Djabung
98 E-2 Djadié *riv.*
80 B-9 Djado
80 B-9 Djado *plat.*
79 J-8 Djafou
81 H-4 Djado
79 L-4 Djamâa
98 F-4 Djambala
206 D-2 Djambi *reg.*

146 B-6 Djambuair *cap.*
206 G-6 Djampang Kulon
80 A-7 Djanet
99 J-2 Djanori
79 H-9 Djaret *riv.*
207 H-5 Djatinegara
207 H-6 Djawa Barat *reg.*
207 K-6 Djawa Tengah *reg.*
147 M-9 Djawe
91 K-3 Djébren
91 K-1 Djedaa
79 K-4 Djedi *riv.*
79 K-3 Djelfa
94 A-5 Djéma
147 H-8 Djemadja *isl.*
207 M-7 Djember
79 L-2 Djemila *site*
207 P-1 Djempang *lake*
79 N-6 Djenein
208 C-5 Djeneponto
89 H-3 Djenné
209 N-5 Djerdera
90 G-6 Djerem *riv.*
206 F-3 Djerembarengas
79 M-4 Djerid *holl.*
90 G-2 Djermaya
91 M-6 Dji *riv.*
89 H-5 Djibo
77 G-3 Djibouti
77 G-3 Djibouti *state*
96 G-2 Djibouti
207 P-7 Djimbaran
99 J-3 Djobe
99 L-2 Djobu
207 M-6 Djombang
90 N-4 Djorong
209 J-1 Djoronga *isl.*
98 F-5 Djoué *riv.*
89 L-7 Djougou
90 F-9 Djoum
91 L-3 Djouna
100 C-1 Djugu
206 F-6 Djungkulon *pen.*
51 H-2 Djupedalsknuten
48 C-3 Djúpivogur
79 K-2 Djurdjura *reg.*
66 G-5 Dmitriev-L'govskij
66 F-6 Dmitrijevka
66 G-2 Dmitrov
66 G-5 Dmitrovsk-Orlovskij
66 G-8 Dneprodzerzhinsk
67 H-8 Dnepropetrovsk
66 H-9 Dneproskaja
66 F-3 Dniepr *riv.*
64 G-1 Dniestr *riv.*
66 D-2 Dno
88 F-4 Do *lake*
127 J-5 Do Ab-e Mīkh-e Zarrīn
197 J-7 Do Boi *pte*
196 B-1 Do Livramento
196 G-8 Do Mel *isl.*
127 K-5 Do Rāh *mt*
126 D-4 Do Shākh *mt*
208 A-4 Doangdoangan-Besar *isl.*
91 J-5 Doba
173 H-2 Dobbs Ferry
214 E-8 Dobbyn
95 L-7 Dobel
66 B-3 Dobele
200 A-7 Doblas
209 N-5 Dobo
64 A-3 Doboj
69 L-6 Dobr'anka
67 H-7 Dobropolje
66 F-8 Dobrovelíčkovka
66 E-5 Dobrus
211 N-8 Dobu *isl.*
197 N-4 Doce *riv.*
52 D-2 Docklow
178 F-2 Doctor Arroyo
191 L-7 Doctor Pedro Peña
141 H-5 Dod Ballāpur
127 M-8 Doda
53 K-1 Doddington
53 M-6 Doddirgton
64 F-8 Dodecanese *islds*
57 H-4 Dodewaard
168 F-9 Dodge City
170 C-6 Dodgeville
63 K-1 Dodici *mt*
95 K-4 Dodola
77 F-5 Dodoma
100 G-7 Dodoma
100 G-7 Dodoma *reg.*
172 C-6 Doe Run
56 B-9 Doel
144 F-6 Doem Bang Nang Buat
57 K-3 Doesburg
57 L-4 Doetinchem
163 P-8 Dog (Canada) *lake*
170 C-1 Dog (Canada) *lake*
65 J-7 Doğanhisar
52 D-5 Dogdington Ash
62 B-6 Dogliani

137 J-3 Dōgo *isl.*
89 H-9 Dogondoutchi
89 H-9 Dogonkiria
72 E-4 Doğubayazit
90 A-1 Dogueraoua
211 M-8 Dogura
83 P-4 Doha
118 A-4 Doha
139 J-8 Dohad
143 H-6 Dohāzāri
80 F-9 Dohou *riv.*
144 E-4 Doi Inthanon *mt*
196 G-6 Dois Corregos
195 K-4 Dois Irmãos *mi*
93 K-7 Doka
72 D-1 Dokšukino
210 D-6 Dolak *riv.*
211 D-6 Dolak
200 E-6 Dolavon
164 E-5 Dolbeau
63 J-2 Dolce
62 A-9 Dolceacqua
62 B-9 Dolcedo
59 H-7 Doldenhorn *mt*
61 J-1 Dole
98 D-4 Dolé *riv.*
94 E-3 Doleib Hill
50 C-5 Dolgelley
122 G-2 Dolgij Most
125 P-4 Dolinsk
63 M-3 Dolo
61 M-2 Dolomiti *mt*
128 D-1 Dolon *pass*
121 L-5 Dolon'
168 B-7 Dolores *riv.*
199 J-8 Dolores (Argentina)
184 E-1 Dolores (Honduras)
179 M-8 Dolores (Mexico)
148 F-2 Dolores (Philippines)
199 J-6 Dolores (Uruguay)
97 N-2 Dōlow
201 L-9 Dolphin *cap.*
161 M-3 Dolphin and Union *strt.*
133 N-8 Dolsan *isl.*
159 K-9 Dolta *riv.*
164 F-1 Dolu *lake*
67 J-9 Dolžanskaja
210 C-2 Dom (Australia) *mt*
59 H-9 Dom (Switzerland) *mt*
145 K-6 Dom Noi *riv.*
199 L-4 Dom Pedrito
194 G-2 Dom Pedro
145 K-7 Dom Yai *riv.*
69 N-9 D'oma *riv.*
101 L-1 Domadare
211 L-8 Domara
72 C-1 Dombaj
70 D-1 Dombarovskij
49 H-2 Dombås
107 K-3 Dombe
220 D-4 Dombey *cap.*
87 H-6 Dombia
64 A-1 Dombovar
58 D-3 Dombresson
58 D-4 Domdidier
160 G-6 Dome *mt*
57 J-1 Domein Bossen *ft*
222 G-7 Domett
198 A-3 Domeyko
191 M-2 Domeyko *mt*
50 D-8 Domfront
197 M-5 Domingos Martins
157 H-5 Dominica *state*
181 N-3 Dominica *isl.*
185 H-7 Dominical
157 H-5 Dominican Republic *state*
165 J-1 Dominion *lake*
56 G-7 Dommel *riv.*
56 G-9 Dommelen
97 K-5 Domo
59 K-9 Domodossola
108 C-4 Domoni
55 H-3 Domont
58 D-4 Dompierre
208 B-7 Dompu
200 A-3 Domuyo *vol.*
162 B-3 Don *pen.*
112 C-4 Don *pl.*
145 K-6 Dôn *riv.*
140 E-5 Don (India) *riv.*
67 K-8 Don (SSSR) *riv.*
60 B-6 Don Benito
199 M-3 Don Feliciano
191 P-2 Doña Iñes *mt*
188 A-4 Doña Juana *vol.*
189 M-4 Doña Maria *pte*
63 M-4 Donada
162 D-2 Donald Landing
172 A-4 Donaldson
176 E-6 Donaldsonville
177 H-5 Donalsonville
133 N-8 Donaro *isl.*

51 J-8 Donaüwörth
50 E-4 Doncaster
91 M-8 Dondo
141 N-7 Dondra *cap.*
67 K-7 Donec *riv.*
67 J-8 Doneck
67 K-7 Doneck
67 J-7 Doneckij Kraž *mt*
50 B-3 Donegal
50 B-3 Donegal *bay*
145 L-1 Dông Dâng
145 L-4 Dông Hoi
145 K-1 Dông Khê
145 L-9 Dông Nai *riv.*
134 D-9 Dong Van
90 D-5 Donga *riv.*
135 L-8 Dongahan
134 G-6 Dongan
216 D-5 Dongara
131 L-1 Dongbulijin
131 L-2 Dongbulizhadamo
134 B-7 Dongchuan
131 P-7 Dongeluo
56 E-6 Dongen
145 M-3 Dongfang
133 K-2 Dongfeng
208 C-1 Donggala
143 J-1 Donggazong
135 M-5 Donggongshan *mt*
135 J-9 Dongguan
133 H-9 Donghai
145 N-2 Donghaidao *isl.*
133 M-4 Donghan *bay*
132 F-2 Donghaojitewangfu
134 D-3 Donghe *riv.*
145 K-5 Dôngphên
129 M-5 Donghu *lake*
59 N-7 Dongio
135 H-7 Dongjiang
131 P-2 Dongjiu
149 P-6 Dongkalang
134 E-8 Donglan
133 K-2 Dongliaohe *riv.*
128 G-8 Donglike
133 L-3 Dongmungeori
125 J-9 Dongning
91 K-9 Dongo
99 H-1 Dongou
132 F-8 Dongpihghu *riv.*
132 F-8 Dongping (China)
124 E-8 Dongping (China)
133 N-7 Dongrae
132 C-5 Dongsheng
135 H-4 Dongtinhu *lake*
93 L-9 Dongur
103 J-3 Dongwe *riv.*
132 F-1 Dongwuzhumuqinqi
134 D-5 Dongxi
135 K-5 Dongxiang
124 G-8 Dongxing
89 K-5 Doninga
220 B-2 Donington *cap.*
64 A-3 Donji Vakuf
143 H-6 Donmânick *islds*
48 F-3 Dønna *isl.*
62 A-2 Donnas
159 K-9 Donnelly
167 H-3 Donner *mt*
162 G-3 Donnley
216 E-8 Donnybrook
91 J-4 Dono-Manga
214 E-7 Donors Hills
67 H-3 Donskoi
70 E-5 Donyztau *hill*
123 H-6 Dood *lake*
170 D-4 Door *pen.*
56 G-3 Doorn
57 J-4 Doorwerth
59 J-3 Doppleschwand
213 H-8 Dora *lake*
175 K-2 Dora
198 F-2 Dora
62 A-2 Dora Baltea *riv.*
161 N-9 Doran *lake*
191 L-6 Dorbigny
52 D-8 Dorchester (UK)
52 G-4 Dorchester (UK)
104 C-1 Dordabis
60 G-2 Dordogne *riv.*
105 H-7 Dordrecht (South Africa)
56 D-5 Dordrecht (Netherlands)
56 C-5 Dordtse Kil *riv.*
163 L-5 Dore *lake*
163 K-5 Dore Lake
197 J-4 Dores de Indaiá
130 B-3 Dörgön *lake*
89 H-6 Dori
104 D-7 Doring *riv.*
53 J-6 Dorking
125 K-5 Dormidontovka
52 D-2 Dormington
61 L-1 Dornbirn
62 D-4 Dorno
50 D-1 Dornoch
50 D-1 Dornoch Firth *gulf*
123 P-8 Dornod *reg.*
132 B-2 Dornogovi *reg.*
94 F-2 Doro *riv.*
88 F-5 Doro
66 D-9 Dorohoi
94 A-8 Doromo
172 E-8 Dorothy
57 L-6 Dorplein
96 G-1 Dorra
172 B-2 Dorrance
216 B-2 Dorre *isl.*
219 M-8 Dorrigo
166 F-3 Dorris
52 D-8 Dorset *reg.*
56 D-7 Dorst
52 C-2 Dorstone
51 H-6 Dortmund
65 L-7 Dörtyol
94 B-6 Doruma
126 B-1 Dorūneh
73 N-4 Dorūneh
197 J-7 Dos Buzios *isl.*
107 M-1 Dos Elefantes *riv.*
199 M-4 Dos Patos *lake*
197 J-7 Dos Porcos *islds*
199 P-3 Dos Quadros *lag.*
123 H-2 D'ošima
89 H-8 Dosso *reg.*
89 J-8 Dosso
63 J-3 Dossobuono
70 C-5 Dossor
177 H-5 Dothan
165 N-2 Doting Cove
58 F-2 Dotzigen
50 F-7 Douai
90 D-8 Douala
90 D-8 Douala-Edéa *rés*
50 B-8 Douarnenez
219 N-5 Double Island *pte*
175 L-3 Double Mountain Fork Brazos *riv.*
58 B-4 Doubs
61 J-1 Doubs *riv.*
222 C-7 Doubtful *strt.*
223 K-2 Doubtless *bay*
88 G-4 Douentza
215 N-4 Douéoulou
79 N-2 Dougga *site*
158 F-9 Douglas *cap.*
158 F-8 Douglas *mt*
168 B-7 Douglas *riv.*
104 G-5 Douglas (South Africa)
184 A-8 Douglas (Ecuador) *cap.*
50 C-3 Douglas (UK)
160 C-6 Douglas (USA)
174 F-3 Douglas (USA)
177 J-5 Douglas (USA)
168 D-5 Douglas (USA)
172 C-5 Douglassville
92 A-5 Dougouro *riv.*
78 B-3 Doukkala *reg.*
90 F-8 Doumé
90 G-8 Doumé *riv.*
88 G-5 Douna
87 N-8 Douobe *riv.*
194 D-8 Dourada *mt*
196 G-3 Dourada *dam.*
196 C-5 Dourados *riv.*
196 D-6 Dourados *mt*
196 C-5 Dourados
60 B-4 Douro *riv.*
58 A-8 Douvaine
55 P-2 Douy-la-Ramée
63 M-8 Dovadola
168 B-8 Dove Creek
50 E-6 Dover
176 F-1 Dover (USA)
171 L-8 Dover (USA)
164 G-9 Dover (USA)
164 G-8 Dover Foxcroft
53 P-3 Dovercourt
172 E-5 Dovlestown
49 H-2 Dovrefjell *plat.*
49 H-2 Dovrefjell *mt*
66 E-5 Dovsk
103 J-9 Dow *lake*
83 N-1 Dow Gonbadān
73 J-7 Dow rūd
106 E-3 Dowa
127 H-8 Dowah Chīnī Qal'eh
172 C-9 Dower
216 E-6 Dowerin
52 B-4 Dowlais
126 G-5 Dowlat Yār
126 G-3 Dowlatābād
167 M-3 Downey
167 H-3 Downieville
172 C-6 Downingtown
50 C-3 Downpatrick
172 E-8 Downstown
52 F-7 Downton
162 C-3 Downton *mt*
127 J-5 Dowshī
52 F-8 Dowton
124 E-2 Doždlivyj
63 L-7 Dozza
78 A-6 Dra'a *riv.*
78 C-6 Draâ *dés*
79 K-2 Draa-el-Zan
196 E-5 Dracema
64 D-2 Dragaşani
168 A-7 Dragerton
63 K-5 Dragoncello
187 N-2 Dragon's Mouth *strt.*
61 J-4 Draguignan
227 M-3 Drake *strt.*
105 K-6 Drakensberg *rge*
76 E-8 Drakensberg *rge*
64 E-5 Dráma
51 J-1 Drammen
55 K-5 Drancy
48 A-2 Drangajökull *glac.*
58 C-8 Dranse *riv.*
127 N-7 Drās
127 L-5 Drasar
61 N-1 Drau *riv.*
64 A-2 Drava *riv.*
55 J-8 Draveil
219 M-6 Drayton
162 G-5 Drayton Valley
56 D-2 Drecht *riv.*
210 G-3 Dreikikir
57 K-3 Drempt
211 K-2 Dremsel *mt*
51 K-7 Dresden
56 G-5 Dreumel
50 E-8 Dreux
49 J-3 Drevsjø
57 H-1 Drie
56 F-3 Driebergen
56 F-3 Driebergen Rijsenburg *reg.*
56 D-3 Driebruggen
56 G-2 Driedorp
57 J-4 Driel
56 D-6 Drimmelen
64 C-4 Drin *riv.*
64 B-3 Drina *riv.*
200 G-1 Dring *isl.*
176 C-4 Driskill *mt*
63 J-1 Dro
54 C-3 Drocourt
50 C-3 Drogheda
66 C-6 Drogičin
66 B-8 Drogobych
58 E-2 Droit *mt*
52 E-2 Droitwich
55 N-1 Drojzelles
221 K-4 Dromedary *cap.*
56 E-6 Drongelen
60 G-2 Dronne *riv.*
127 L-6 Drosh
123 N-6 Drov'anaja
66 C-3 Druja
52 A-9 Drumbridge
163 H-7 Drumheller
168 A-1 Drummond
170 F-3 Drummond *isl.*
220 B-2 Drummond *pte*
219 J-3 Drummond *mt*
164 F-8 Drummondville
172 B-7 Drumore
53 L-2 Drumpington
56 G-4 Drumpt
172 B-2 Drums
56 F-6 Drunen
59 M-3 Drusberg *mt*
66 B-5 Druskininkai
57 H-4 Druten
69 N-6 Družinino
213 P-3 Dry *riv.*
180 B-3 Dry Tortugas *isl.*
170 B-1 Dryden (Canada)
175 K-5 Dryden (USA)
227 N-4 Drygalsky *isl.*
214 B-2 Drysdale *isl.*
213 K-3 Drysdale *riv.*
90 D-7 Dschang
171 J-7 Du Bois
170 C-9 Du Quoin
187 H-2 Duaca
208 E-4 Dualo
134 E-8 Duan
219 L-3 Duaringa
196 F-6 Duartina
84 C-5 Dubai *reg.*
84 C-5 Dubai
73 H-2 Dubannyj
161 P-9 Dubawnt *riv.*
56 D-5 Dubbeldam
221 J-1 Dubbo
59 M-1 Dübendorf
70 C-1 Dubenskij
159 J-5 Dubli *riv.*
47 C-4 Dublin
50 B-4 Dublin (Bayle Atha Cliath)
172 D-5 Dublin (USA)
175 M-4 Dublin (USA)
177 J-4 Dublin (USA)
172 B-7 Dublin (USA)
66 G-2 Dubna
66 C-7 Dubno
168 A-3 Dubois
66 E-9 Dubóssary
67 M-6 Dubovka
87 K-4 Dubreka
69 L-7 Dubrova
66 D-6 Dubrovica
66 F-4 Dubrovka
64 B-4 Dubrovnik
123 M-1 Dubrovskoje
170 C-6 Dubuque
154 J-3 Dubwant *lake*
87 P-7 Dubwe *riv.*
145 L-8 Duc Lâp
145 M-9 Duc Trong
180 G-4 Ducan Town
168 A-6 Duchesne
214 E-9 Duchess
163 H-7 Duchess (Canada)
224 G-6 Ducie *isl.*
163 M-8 Duck *mt*
163 N-8 Duck Mtn *na.p.*
167 J-6 Duckwater *mt*
215 M-4 Ducos *isl.*
142 E-1 Dudh Kosi *riv.*
142 C-3 Dūdhi
58 E-4 Düdingen
50 D-5 Dudley
140 C-5 Dudna *riv.*
97 H-8 Dūdo *riv.*
97 H-8 Dūdo
66 G-4 Dudorovskij
97 L-5 Dudub *well*
215 P-4 Dudune *isl.*
125 M-2 Due
87 N-8 Duékoué
201 H-1 Duende *pen.*
124 E-8 Duerbote (Taikang)
194 D-6 Dueré
60 D-4 Duero *riv.*
63 L-2 Dueville
166 G-4 Duffer *mt*
62 A-1 Dufour *mt*
124 G-2 Dugda *riv.*
61 N-3 Dugi Otok *isl.*
55 J-4 Dugny
93 L-2 Dugunab
134 G-2 Duhe *riv.*
214 F-3 Duifken *pte*
129 P-8 Duilongdeqing
50 G-6 Duisburg
186 E-5 Duitama
57 K-4 Duiven
56 E-1 Duivendrecht
105 L-2 Duiwelskloof
56 F-9 Duizel
91 M-2 Duju
101 M-1 Dujūma
94 E-4 Duk Fadiat
94 E-4 Duk Faiwil
95 J-6 Dukana
211 P-4 Duke of York *isl.*
161 N-4 Duke of York *islds*
131 N-7 Dukehe *riv.*
83 P-4 Dukhān
126 G-9 Duki
73 J-8 Dūl Gap
148 G-3 Dulag
131 K-5 Dulan
198 F-3 Dulce *riv.*
184 G-3 Dulce Nombre de Culmi
123 P-6 Dul'durga
95 J-6 Dulei *riv.*
91 P-9 Dulia
53 L-1 Dullingham
143 M-1 Dulonghe *riv.*
64 F-3 Dulovo
72 F-1 D'ul'tydag
129 J-3 Duluo
170 B-3 Duluth
52 A-7 Dulvertono
94 B-6 Duma *riv.*
82 C-1 Dūmā
149 H-4 Dumaguete
146 E-8 Dumai
148 G-4 Dumanjug
148 G-6 Dumaran *isl.*
201 P-5 Dumas *pen.*
175 K-1 Dumas
216 F-8 Dumbleyung
50 D-3 Dumfries
190 F-4 Dumi *riv.*
142 F-4 Dumka
171 J-2 Dumoine *lake*
227 N-5 Dumont d'Urville
227 N-5 Dumont d'Urville *sea*
211 J-5 Dumpu
81 P-1 Dumyāt
50 B-4 Dun Laoghaire
133 P-1 Dunaj
124 A-5 Dunajeno
66 D-8 Dunajevcy
221 H-9 Dunalley
64 B-1 Dunaújváros
113 L-2 Dunay *isl.*
222 D-8 Dunback
214 G-6 Dunbar
52 F-7 Dunbridge
144 A-9 Duncan *strt.*
164 A-3 Duncan *cap.*
162 F-7 Duncan *lake*
162 B-6 Duncan (Canada)
175 N-2 Duncan (USA)
174 F-2 Duncan (USA)
50 E-1 Duncansby *cap.*
52 G-1 Dunchurh
53 J-8 Duncton
66 A-2 Dundaga
50 C-3 Dundalk *bay*
50 B-3 Dundalk (Ireland)
171 K-8 Dundalk (USA)
217 H-7 Dundas *lake*
209 L-9 Dundas *strt.*
162 B-1 Dundas *isl.*
105 L-5 Dundee (South Africa)
50 D-2 Dundee (UK)
130 D-9 Dundgovi *reg.*
99 K-8 Dundo
218 G-5 Dundoo
222 D-9 Dunedin
221 K-1 Dunedoo
172 F-4 Dunellen
50 D-2 Dunfermline
50 B-3 Dungannon
139 J-7 Dūngarpur
50 B-4 Dungarvan
210 G-7 Dungeness *isl.*
130 G-3 Dunghuang
50 C-3 Dungiven
221 L-2 Dungog
94 C-7 Dungu
94 C-7 Dungu *riv.*
133 L-1 Dunhua
95 L-3 Dunkata *riv.*
220 F-5 Dunkeld
50 F-6 Dunkerque
52 A-6 Dunkery Beacon *hill*
171 H-6 Dunkirk
93 L-2 Dunkunāb *gulf*
89 N-4 Dunkwa
214 A-6 Dunmarra
172 C-1 Dunmore
177 K-6 Dunnellon
172 E-2 Dunnfield
92 G-4 Dunqulah
92 G-4 Dunqulah al Qadīmah
50 D-3 Duns
168 G-1 Dunseith
53 J-7 Dunsfold
53 J-3 Dunstable
52 A-6 Dunster
50 C-1 Dunvegan
53 P-1 Dunwich
139 J-2 Dunyāpur
124 E-5 Duobukuerhe *riv.*
124 E-5 Duobukuershan *mt*
128 C-5 Duoheyan
129 M-2 Duokocheng
132 F-3 Duolun
131 N-4 Duomula
134 G-7 Dupangling *mt*
129 L-7 Dupeilikesishan *mt*
168 F-4 Dupree
197 K-6 Duque de Caxias
201 L-2 Duque of York *isl.*
97 H-8 Dur
80 F-5 Dūr al Abraq *mt*
95 H-1 Dura *riv.*
65 P-8 Dura-Europos *site*
213 L-3 Durack *riv.*
213 L-4 Durack *mt*
61 J-3 Durance *riv.*
215 P-5 Durand *rf*
178 C-1 Durango *reg.*
60 E-3 Durango (Spain)
168 B-9 Durango (USA)
176 E-4 Durant (USA)
175 N-2 Durant (USA)
199 K-6 Durazno
199 K-5 Durazno *reg.*
105 L-7 Durban
66 A-3 Durbe
128 D-1 D'urbel'džin
122 C-6 Durbet Daba *mt*
96 G-8 Durbo
97 H-3 Durdur *riv.*
97 J-8 Durdura *cap.*
138 E-4 Dureji
50 G-7 Duren
140 B-9 Durg
142 E-4 Durgāpur
223 N-9 Durham *pte*
164 B-9 Durham (Canada)
50 E-3 Durham (UK)
177 L-1 Durham (USA)
218 F-5 Durham Downs
220 G-4 Durham Ox
146 F-9 Durian *strt.*
83 L-6 Durma
64 B-4 Durmitor *mt*
50 D-1 Durness
70 C-6 Durneva *islds*
59 H-3 Dürrenroth
64 B-5 Durrës
50 A-4 Dursey *cap.*
52 D-4 Dursley
52 B-7 Durston
64 G-6 Dursunbey
69 M-8 D'urt'uli
126 C-5 Dūruḥ
97 J-4 Duruksi
82 D-1 Duruz *mt*
172 C-1 Durvea
52 D-8 Durweston
71 P-9 Durzāb
97 M-5 Dusa Marel
73 P-1 Dušak
134 E-7 Dushan
127 K-3 Dushanbe
71 P-6 Dushanbe
128 D-7 Dushanzi
222 B-8 Dusky *strt.*
50 G-7 Dusseldorf
56 E-6 Dussen
59 N-5 Düssistock *mt*
129 L-6 Dutaliutexingsishan *mt*
141 L-7 Dutch *bay*
104 G-2 Dutlhe
69 J-3 Dutovo
214 G-2 Dutton *riv.*
127 P-9 Dutung
69 N-7 Duvan
181 K-7 Duvergé
84 F-9 Duwwah
134 E-6 Duyun
65 H-5 Düzce
66 C-3 Dvinsk (Daugavpils)
68 D-4 Dvinskaya *gulf*
106 E-3 Dwangwa *riv.*
138 F-8 Dwārka
102 E-6 Dwase
216 E-8 Dwellingup
66 A-6 Dwor Maz
104 E-8 Dwyka *riv.*
89 J-7 Dyamongou *riv.*
66 F-4 Dyat'kovo
211 N-3 Dyaul *isl.*
72 D-1 Dychtau *mt*
176 F-1 Dyersburg
211 L-7 Dyke Ackland *bay*
53 N-7 Dymchurch
52 D-3 Dymock
88 G-4 Dyoundé *mt*
124 B-2 Dyryndinskij *mt*
130 C-6 Dzag
130 E-4 Dzagtich Sajr *riv.*
125 J-4 Džaki-Unachta-Jakbyjana *mt*
71 P-7 Džakurgan
71 J-3 Džalagaš
127 N-2 Džalal Abad
72 G-3 Džalilabad (Astrachan Bazar)
124 D-3 Džalinda
70 B-7 Džambajskij *isl.*
70 B-3 Džambejty
128 A-1 Džambul *hill*
120 G-5 Džambul
130 C-6 Dzamiin *well*
132 C-2 Dzamïn Üüd
130 D-4 Dzamyn Sand *well*
70 G-9 Dzanak *mt*
128 B-4 Džansugurov
108 C-4 Dzaoudzi
127 J-3 Džarkurgan
125 L-3 Džaur *riv.*
72 D-2 Džava
130 B-4 Dzavhan *reg.*
130 B-4 Dzavhan *rf*
130 B-4 Dzavhanmandal
131 N-4 Dze *riv.*
73 K-1 Džebel
124 D-2 Dželtulak
130 B-3 Dzereg
128 D-3 Džergalan
72 F-3 Džermuk
67 J-1 Dzerzhinsk (SSSR)
66 D-5 Dzeržinsk (SSSR)
66 D-7 Dzeržinsk (SSSR)
122 D-3 Dzeržinskij
71 N-4 Džetysaj
120 E-4 Džezdy
124 G-2 Dzhagdy *mt*
120 E-8 Dzhambul
71 N-1 Dzhambul
65 J-1 Dzhankoy
120 E-4 Dzhezkazgan
130 A-8 Dzhidinskiy *mt*
113 M-4 Dzhugdzhur *rge*
121 L-9 Dzhungarskiy Altau *rge*
131 N-4 Dzi *riv.*
179 M-5 Dzibalchén
130 A-9 Dzidā
123 J-6 Džida *riv.*

51 M-7 Dzierzoniów
71 K-6 Džingil'dy
127 M-3 Džirgatal'
71 N-5 Džizak
124 F-1 Džugdyr mt
72 F-4 Džul'fa
71 N-6 Džuma
112 G-5 Dzungaria reg.
112 F-5 Dzungaria rge
128 C-8 Dzungarian pool
122 B-9 Dzungarian Basin pool
128 B-5 Dzungarskiy rge
120 C-5 Džusaly
71 J-3 Džusaly
130 F-7 Dzüün Ada well
132 B-2 Dzüünbayan
130 C-8 Dzüünbayan-Uaan
130 A-4 Dzüüngovi
123 L-8 Dzüünharaa
123 L-9 Dzuunmod

# E

145 L-8 Ea riv.
168 E-8 Eads
160 G-1 Eagle (Canada) riv.
170 B-1 Eagle (Canada) lake
211 M-8 Eagle (Papua-niugini) mt
170 C-2 Eagle (USA) mt
164 G-7 Eagle (USA) lake
166 B-3 Eagle (USA) lake
168 C-7 Eagle (USA)
166 G-4 Eagle (USA) mt
164 G-6 Eagle Lake
175 L-6 Eagle Pass
201 L-9 Eagle Passage strt.
170 C-3 Eagle River
163 K-7 Eaglehill riv.
172 A-1 Eagles Mere
172 D-5 Eagleville
97 H-2 Eali-Sabih
53 J-5 Ealing
52 C-2 Eardisland
162 B-6 Earl Cove
172 B-8 Earleville
53 M-3 Earls Colne
164 B-7 Earlton
170 A-5 Earth Blue
96 G-1 Easal lake
53 H-7 Easebourne
177 J-2 Easley
211 N-8 East isl.
173 H-3 East riv.
223 L-5 East cap.
172 D-3 East Bangor
172 A-6 East Boro
181 K-4 East Caicos isl.
222 C-9 East Cape cap.
215 H-1 East Cay rf
211 H-7 East Cay
223 K-6 East Coast reg.
52 G-8 East Cowes
159 G-4 East Fork Andreafsky riv.
51 H-5 East Frisian islds
172 D-4 East Greenville
53 K-7 East Grinstead
173 M-1 East Haddam
173 M-2 East Hampton
53 N-1 East Harling
173 L-1 East Haven
53 L-8 East Hoathly
53 L-5 East Horndon
173 K-3 East Islip
52 E-7 East Knoyle
171 H-7 East Liverpool
52 E-9 East Lulworth
173 M-1 East Lyme
172 C-3 East Mauch Chunk
172 F-4 East Millstone
173 J-2 East Norwalk
172 G-3 East Orange
162 F-2 East Pine
165 K-6 East Point pte
177 H-3 East Point
170 C-9 East Saint Louis
172 D-2 East Stroudsburg
168 A-7 East Tavaputs plat.
50 E-6 Eastbourne
53 N-5 Eastchurch
105 K-6 Eastcourt
53 L-8 Eastdean
163 J-9 Eastend
53 J-8 Eastgate

211 J-8 Eastern Fields islds
215 J-1 Eastern Fields rf
217 J-8 Eastern Group islds
62 E-7 Eastern Riviera
139 K-3 Eastern Sādiqia cal.
122 G-4 Eastern Sajan rge
53 H-5 Easthampsted
175 M-4 Eastland
52 G-7 Eastleigh
164 B-3 Eastmain
164 C-3 Eastmain riv.
177 J-4 Eastman
52 D-3 Eastnor
52 D-9 Easton (UK)
172 D-3 Easton (USA)
171 L-7 Easton (USA)
173 J-1 Easton (USA)
165 H-8 Eastport (USA)
173 L-3 Eastport (USA)
53 P-6 Eastry
171 L-9 Eastville
213 N-8 Eaton lake
53 J-2 Eaton Socon
177 J-3 Eatonton
172 G-5 Eatontown
170 B-4 Eau Claire
55 H-4 Eaubonne
52 B-4 Ebbw Vale
98 D-1 Ebébiyin
57 M-9 Eben Emaal
171 J-7 Ebensburg
51 L-6 Eberswalde
136 C-6 Ebetu
134 B-4 Ebian
59 K-3 Ebikon
59 P-1 Ebnat
91 M-8 Ebola riv.
90 E-9 Ebolowa
99 P-6 Ebombo
119 M-6 Ebon isl.
89 P-2 Ebrié lag.
60 E-4 Ebro riv.
62 E-6 Ebro mt
73 H-6 Ecbatane site
64 F-6 Eceabat
79 J-2 Ech Cheliff
79 H-3 Ech Chergui holl.
58 C-6 Echallens
196 F-6 Echaporã
90 B-5 Echau
55 M-8 Echelle (L') ft
135 J-3 Echeng
72 E-3 Echmiadzin
57 N-7 Echt
56 G-4 Echteld
57 N-7 Echterbosch
220 G-4 Echuca
60 C-7 Ecija
56 G-4 Eck
51 J-4 Eckernförde
52 E-2 Eckington
172 C-2 Eckley
58 B-6 Eclépens
197 M-3 Ecoporanga
54 B-1 Ecos
55 J-3 Ecouen
54 E-4 Ecquevilly
61 J-3 Ecrins (Barre des) mt
183 C-3 Ecuador state
58 D-6 Ecublens (Switzerland)
58 B-6 Ecublens (Switzerland)
96 F-1 Ed
78 E-7 Ed Daoura riv.
140 B-5 Edalābād
100 G-2 Edama-Ravine
221 J-8 Eddystone pte
176 F-1 Eddyville
89 M-9 Ede
57 H-3 Ede (Netherlands)
90 D-8 Edéa
196 F-2 Edeia
221 K-5 Eden (Australia)
175 L-4 Eden (USA)
53 K-6 Edenbridge
105 H-6 Edenburg
220 E-4 Edenhope
177 N-1 Edenton
172 F-1 Edenville
57 H-3 Ederveen
172 B-9 Edesville
222 D-8 Edeviale
171 N-6 Edgartown
46 F-2 Edge isl.
52 G-2 Edge hill
160 B-6 Edgecumbe mt
169 H-3 Edgeley
168 E-5 Edgemont
172 A-8 Edgewood
53 K-4 Edgware
64 D-5 Edhessa
88 B-8 Edina
175 M-8 Edinburg
50 D-2 Edinburgh
185 J-3 Edinburgh rf
52 E-6 Edington
64 F-4 Edirne

172 F-4 Edison
227 M-2 Edith Ronne reg.
220 C-3 Edithburg
79 N-9 Edjeleh
88 E-7 Edjerir riv.
88 E-7 Edjerir oua-n-Tabarint riv.
217 H-5 Edjudina
163 H-5 Edmonton (Canada)
53 K-4 Edmonton (UK)
164 G-6 Edmundston
175 N-6 Edna
61 L-2 Edolo
192 F-5 Edouard
227 M-6 Edouard VII pen.
64 F-6 Edremit
130 E-5 Edrengiyn mt
49 J-5 Edsbyn
162 G-5 Edson
52 F-2 Edstone
141 N-2 Edu Faro isl.
198 E-7 Eduardo Castex
227 M-2 Eduardo frei Bellingshausen
214 B-4 Edward isl.
100 C-2 Edward lake
175 L-5 Edwards plat.
218 B-5 Edwards Creek
172 B-1 Edwardsville
160 D-7 Edziza mt
57 L-2 Eefde
158 E-5 Eek
158 E-5 Eek riv.
166 G-2 Eel riv.
56 F-1 Eem
56 F-1 Eemmeer lake
56 F-2 Eemmes
56 A-4 Eendracht strt.
57 K-3 Eerbeek
56 F-9 Eersel
56 E-6 Eethen
109 L-5 Efatsy
170 D-8 Effingham
90 A-5 Efon
61 M-8 Egadi islds
167 J-6 Egan mt
199 J-6 Egaña
164 C-8 Eganville
159 H-4 Egavik
90 A-5 Egbe
93 P-7 Egcoji lake
158 D-7 Egegik
158 D-7 Egegik bay
66 A-9 Eger
209 L-6 Egeron strt.
51 H-1 Egersund
53 M-6 Egerton
216 E-2 Egerton mt
163 L-5 Egg lake
172 F-8 Egg Harbour City
59 J-7 Eggishorn mt
59 H-4 Eggiwil
172 E-9 Eggsland pte
53 J-5 Egham
57 J-9 Eghel
48 C-4 Egilsstadir
130 A-7 Egiyn riv.
130 C-7 Egiyn Davaa
165 L-5 Egmont cap.
223 H-5 Egmont cap.
223 H-5 Egmont na.p.
223 H-5 Egmont mt
163 H-5 Egremont (Canada)
54 D-7 Egremont (France)
65 H-7 Egridir
65 J-7 Egridir lake
96 G-2 Eguereleïta mt
77 F-2 Egypt state
172 D-3 Egypt
128 D-6 Ehabuteshan mt
224 E-4 Eiao isl.
57 M-3 Eibergen
51 H-1 Eide
219 M-4 Eidsvold
93 J-1 Eiger mt
59 J-6 Eiger mt
50 C-1 Eigg isl.
141 M-1 Eight Degree Channel
212 G-6 Eighty Mile Beach
93 K-3 Eigrim mt
57 P-8 Eijgelshoven
57 N-9 Eijs
161 N-8 Eileen lake
192 D-4 Eilerts de Haan mt
48 B-3 Einarsstadir
214 G-7 Einasleigh riv.
215 H-7 Einasleigh
57 J-9 Eind lake
50 G-6 Eindhoven
58 G-5 Einigen
59 M-2 Einsiedeln
188 G-8 Eiru riv.

188 F-9 Eirunepé
57 M-8 Eisden
51 J-7 Eisenach
61 P-1 Eisenstadt
109 M-2 Ejeda
186 G-4 Ejido
89 M-5 Ejura
179 H-7 Ejutla de Crespo
168 E-3 Ekalaka
56 B-9 Ekeren
90 C-7 Eket
113 R-2 Ekiatapsky rge
121 K-3 Ekibastuz
125 H-2 Ekimčan
90 D-7 Ekom
99 L-1 Ekombe
90 C-7 Ekoundou-Titi
51 L-2 Eksjö
102 C-6 Ekumo riv.
98 G-2 Ekwamou
164 A-3 Ekwan pte
79 J-2 El Abadia
79 H-4 El Abiodh Sidi Cheikh
198 D-1 El Aconquija
79 M-9 El Adeb Larache
79 L-6 El-Agreb
198 B-4 El Agua Negra mt
86 C-6 El Aguer reg.
81 M-2 El Alamein
174 B-2 El Alamo
188 A-3 El Angel
79 M-3 El Aouinet
79 K-2 El Arba Nait Irathen
78 B-3 El-Aricha
82 B-3 El Arish
86 E-6 El Assâba plat.
198 B-4 El Azufre mt
81 P-5 El Badari
186 E-3 El Banco
188 E-1 El Barco mt
187 J-3 El Baúl
79 H-4 El Bayadh
90 G-2 El Beid riv.
79 H-4 El Biod
185 H-8 El Blanco pte
185 H-5 El Bluff
200 E-3 El Bolsón
186 C-8 El Bordo
79 N-6 El Borma
78 C-4 El Borouj
60 D-4 El Burgo de Osma
200 D-5 El Caín
174 A-1 El Cajon
198 D-5 El Caldén
187 N-5 El Callao
187 K-3 El Calvario
175 N-6 El Campo
191 M-5 El Carmen (Argentina)
185 P-8 El Carmen (Colombia)
184 E-1 El Cayo
174 B-1 El Centro
198 B-3 El Cepo mt
191 H-7 El Cerro
187 L-3 El Chaparro
191 L-7 El Chorro
191 P-8 El Colorado
186 D-7 El Corazón
200 F-3 El Coreovado
200 C-4 El Covi
185 M-8 El Darién mt
97 M-2 El Dere
97 M-2 El Dere well
199 L-6 El Diablo pte
186 E-2 El Difícil
79 P-3 El Djem
188 A-8 El Dorado (Colombia)
169 H-9 El Dorado (USA)
176 D-3 El Dorado (USA)
187 N-5 El Dorado (Vénézuela)
189 K-7 El Encuentro
78 B-8 El Escobonal
184 D-2 El Estor
79 L-2 El Eulma
79 N-2 El Fahs
81 N-3 El Faiyum
92 C-8 El Fasher
81 N-3 El Fashn
60 B-2 El Ferrol del Caudillo
174 F-7 El Fuerte
96 G-8 El Gâl
185 H-4 El Gallo
191 N-5 El Galpón
78 C-3 El Gara
79 L-3 El-Gassi
185 H-7 El General
86 E-7 El Gharbi plat.
81 N-2 El Giza site
97 M-3 El Goran
187 K-2 El Guapo
79 N-4 El Guéttar
79 L-5 El Hadjira
78 E-3 El-Hajeb
78 D-3 El Hammam
97 K-7 El Hamurre

79 K-2 El Harrach
86 E-6 El Hasseïra plat.
79 H-7 El Homr
200 B-3 El Huecu
189 M-6 El Ingenio riv.
78 C-3 El-Jadida (Mazagan)
198 C-2 El Jagüe mt
78 C-3 El Jorf-Lasfar (cap Blanc) cap.
79 N-2 El Kala
79 L-3 El Kantara
79 N-2 El Kef
78 C-4 El-Kelaa-des-Srarhna
97 M-1 El Kere
86 A-7 El Khatt val.
91 L-3 El Kouk
78 F-8 El Krebs dés
78 D-4 El Ksiba
86 A-5 El Maersa reg.
81 N-2 El Mahallah el Kubra
200 E-3 El Maitén
81 P-5 El Manshah
81 N-2 El Mansura
187 N-4 El Manteco
79 H-2 El Marsa
79 L-4 El Meghaïer
97 M-1 El Mendo
79 J-6 El Menia
88 C-1 El Mereie reg.
198 D-4 El Milagro
79 L-2 El Milia
81 N-4 El Minya
185 H-6 El Mono pte
86 B-9 El Mrâyer well
86 A-9 El Mreïti well
88 B-7 El Mreyer well
198 B-4 El Msilé mt
198 C-7 El Nevado mt
95 L-6 El Niabo
148 G-7 El Nido
174 L-6 El Novillo dam.
188 D-2 El Oro reg.
79 M-4 El Oued
199 L-6 El Palmar pte
191 K-5 El Palmar
175 H-8 El Palmito
200 E-3 El Paraiso reg.
184 F-4 El Paraíso
175 H-3 El Paso
191 N-5 El Piquete
201 H-4 El Pluma
189 H-3 El Portugués
186 C-7 El Porvénir
185 M-8 El Porvenir (Panama)
187 H-5 El Porvenir (Vénézuela)
198 B-2 El Potro mt
184 D-2 El Progreso (Guatémala)
184 F-2 El Progreso (Honduras)
184 F-3 El Provenir
191 K-4 El Puente
60 B-7 El Puerto de Santa María
82 C-1 El Qunatirah
81 N-4 El Qusiya
185 M-9 El Real
175 N-1 El Reno
187 M-2 El Rincon
191 H-8 El Roboré
185 N-7 El Rosario isl.
201 J-5 El Salado
178 B-2 El Salto
201 J-3 El Saltón
149 H-3 El Salvador
187 H-4 El Samán de Apure
185 M-9 El Sapo mt
199 K-7 El Sauce lag.
184 F-4 El Sauce
174 G-5 El Sauz
181 M-6 El Seibo
97 P-1 El Shama
196 C-9 El Soberbio
187 K-3 El Sombero
198 B-7 El Sosneado
174 G-5 El Sueco
191 N-5 El Tala
186 C-8 El Tambo
198 G-7 El Tejar
199 H-4 El Tigre riv.
198 B-3 El Tigre
187 L-3 El Tigre
187 M-3 El Tigrito
82 B-4 El Tih mt
187 H-3 El Tío
187 H-4 El Tocuyo
198 B-3 El Toro mt
198 G-5 El Trébol
174 D-9 El Triunfo
191 N-5 El Tunal
201 L-4 El Turbio
184 F-4 El Viejo vol.
184 F-5 El Viejo
186 G-3 El Vigia
198 B-6 El Volcán

95 M-7 El Wak
187 J-4 El Yagual
201 M-4 El Zurdo
52 A-1 Elan val.
54 E-7 Elancourt
105 J-3 Elands riv.
64 D-6 Elassón
82 C-4 Elat
65 N-5 Elazig
61 L-4 Elba isl.
177 H-5 Elba
178 G-3 Elbano
64 C-5 Elbasan
51 K-6 Elbe riv.
168 C-7 Elbert mt
177 J-3 Elberton
50 E-8 Elbeuf
65 M-6 Elbistan
49 P-6 Elblag
64 C-5 Elbonas
163 K-8 Elbow
112 C-5 Elbrus mt
97 M-5 Elbür
112 D-6 Elburz rge
73 K-4 Elburz (Reshteh-ye kūhhā-ye) rge
60 E-7 Elche
214 B-2 Elcho isl.
60 E-7 Elda (Spain)
48 G-3 Elda (Norway)
97 J-5 Eldab
57 J-4 Elden
172 E-9 Eldora
196 C-5 Eldorado (Argentina)
196 G-7 Eldorado (Brazil)
178 A-1 Eldorado (Mexico)
175 L-5 Eldorado (USA)
100 G-2 Eldoret
201 H-2 Elefantes gulf
122 E-6 Elegest
93 J-2 Elei riv.
67 H-2 Elektrostal
90 B-7 Elele
57 M-7 Elen
198 E-5 Elena
143 H-6 Elephant (Bangladesh) pte
141 M-8 Elephant (Sri Lanka) pte
197 L-6 Elesbão
195 J-3 Elesbáo Veloso
72 D-4 Eleşkirt
156 G-4 Eleuthera isl.
180 F-2 Eleuthera isl.
176 E-1 Eleven Point riv.
64 E-7 Elevsís
64 E-5 Elevtheroúpolis
160 C-6 Elfin Cove
124 C-2 El'gakan
93 M-4 Elgena
50 D-1 Elgin (UK)
170 D-6 Elgin (USA)
175 N-5 Elgin (USA)
100 F-1 Elgon mt
53 N-6 Elham
64 F-4 Elhovo
181 K-6 Elias Piñas
175 J-3 Elida
100 A-4 Elila riv.
159 H-3 Elim
99 M-4 Elingampangu
131 L-4 Elinghu lake
99 M-3 Elipa
198 G-4 Elisa
104 B-4 Elisabethbaai
54 D-4 Elisabethville
103 L-2 Elisabethville (Lubumbashi)
49 J-9 Elisenvaara
195 H-4 Eliseu Mártins
67 M-8 Elista
220 D-4 Eliza lake
213 K-4 Elizabeth mt
220 D-2 Elizabeth (Australia)
171 L-6 Elizabeth (USA)
177 N-1 Elizabeth City
170 E-9 Elizabeth Town
177 K-1 Elizabethton
172 A-5 Elizabethtown
177 M-2 Elizabethtown
66 B-5 Elk
162 F-8 Elk mt
176 G-2 Elk riv.
175 M-1 Elk City
166 G-2 Elk Creek
172 A-1 Elk Grove
164 B-7 Elk Lake
172 B-8 Elk Neck
163 J-5 Elk Point
170 A-4 Elk River
214 B-9 Elkedra
170 E-6 Elkhart (USA)
168 E-9 Elkhart (USA)
169 H-6 Elkhorn riv.
170 D-6 Elkhorn
177 K-1 Elkin

171 H-8 Elkins
162 F-8 Elko (Canada)
167 H-6 Elko (USA)
171 J-9 Elkton (USA)
166 D-3 Elkton (USA)
57 M-6 Ell
168 A-8 Ellen *mt*
169 H-3 Ellendale
162 C-8 Ellensburg
222 F-8 Ellesmere *lake*
153 L-2 Ellesmere *isl.*
54 C-5 Elleville
224 B-4 Ellice *islds*
177 H-2 Ellijay
53 J-1 Ellington
220 G-9 Elliot *bay*
215 J-8 Elliot *mt*
105 J-7 Elliot (South Africa)
214 A-7 Elliot (Australia)
164 A-8 Elliot Lake
220 B-2 Elliston
50 E-1 Ellon
227 M-3 Ellsworth *mt*
168 G-8 Ellsworth (USA)
170 B-4 Ellsworth (USA)
165 H-8 Ellsworth (USA)
227 M-4 Ellsworth Land *reg.*
59 P-4 Elm
65 J-5 Elmadağ
65 H-8 Elmali
65 H-8 Elmali *mt*
172 D-7 Elmer
172 D-1 Elmhurst
171 K-6 Elmira
220 G-4 Elmore
51 J-5 Elmshorn
99 H-4 Elombe
187 H-5 Elorza
174 E-2 Eloy
198 A-3 Elqui *riv.*
163 K-8 Elrose
160 F-3 Elsa
170 F-1 Elsas
57 J-7 Elsendorp
214 A-5 Elsey
167 M-3 Elsinore
57 M-8 Elsloo
172 C-7 Elsmere
57 J-1 Elspeet
56 G-4 Elst (Netherlands)
57 J-4 Elst (Netherlands)
53 H-6 Elstead
172 A-5 Elstonville
53 J-2 Elstow
53 K-4 Elstree
57 K-4 Elten
53 L-5 Eltham
53 K-2 Eltisley
67 N-5 El'ton *lake*
67 N-5 El'ton
140 E-8 Elūru
66 C-1 Elva
60 B-5 Elvas
48 C-6 Elvebakken
53 M-1 Elveden
172 C-5 Elverson
188 E-7 Elvira
62 B-3 Elvo *riv.*
168 G-7 Elwood
52 B-7 Elworthy
52 B-5 Ely *riv.*
53 L-1 Ely
170 B-2 Ely (USA)
167 J-6 Ely (USA)
170 G-7 Elyria
172 A-3 Elysburg
57 M-1 Elzen
97 M-5 Emadle
101 G-4 Emali
127 K-4 Emām Sāḥeb
51 L-2 Emån *riv.*
70 E-3 Emba
70 C-5 Emba *riv.*
198 C-7 Embalse del Nihuil *rés*
191 M-5 Embarcación
163 K-2 Embarras Portage
189 H-8 Embira *riv.*
99 J-2 Embondo
193 L-8 Emborai *bay*
172 C-6 Embreeville
101 G-3 Embu
51 H-5 Emden
134 C-4 Emei
128 B-6 Emel *riv.*
55 L-6 Emerainville
220 G-5 Emerald
164 G-2 Emeril
169 J-1 Emerson
218 B-4 Emery *mt*
64 G-6 Emet
80 C-9 Emi Fezzane *mt*
61 L-3 Emilia-Romagna *reg.*
179 L-7 Emiliano Zapata
200 A-5 Emilio Mitre
128 B-7 Emin
170 F-9 Eminence
211 M-2 Emirau *isl.*
65 H-6 Emirdağ
221 H-7 Emita
51 L-3 Emmaboda
172 D-4 Emmaus
172 D-4 Emmaus Junction
59 H-4 Emme *riv.*
51 H-5 Emmen
58 G-3 Emmental *reg.*
57 L-5 Emmerich (Emmerik)
219 H-3 Emmet
166 E-6 Emmet (USA)
170 A-5 Emmetsburg
59 L-4 Emmetten
172 A-8 Emmorton
175 J-5 Emory *mt*
174 D-6 Empalme
105 L-6 Empangeni
196 A-9 Empedrado
56 F-6 Empel
191 K-2 Empexa *lake*
63 J-9 Empoli
169 J-9 Emporia
171 J-6 Emporium
57 J-1 Emst
53 H-8 Emsworth
219 M-3 Emu Park
124 D-3 Emuerhe *riv.*
124 C-4 Emuershan *mt*
99 N-5 Emungu
133 L-1 Emusuo
136 A-6 Enbetu
168 C-6 Encampment
174 B-3 Encantada *mt*
199 M-3 Encantadas *mt*
196 B-9 Encarnación
178 D-4 Encarnación de Díaz
148 D-5 Encato *cap.*
89 N-3 Enchi
175 L-7 Encinal
186 F-3 Encontrados
220 D-3 Encounter *bay*
197 M-1 Encruzilhada
199 M-3 Encruzilhada do Sul
131 P-4 Enda
146 F-8 Endau *riv.*
146 F-8 Endau
208 D-7 Ende
214 F-2 Endeavour *strt.*
95 J-3 Endeber
224 B-4 Enderbury *isl.*
212 D-7 Enderby *isl.*
227 N-2 Enderby Land *reg.*
159 M-5 Endicott *mt*
129 J-6 Endiluopuhu *lake*
190 B-3 Endimari *riv.*
62 G-2 Endine *lake*
189 K-6 Ené *riv.*
63 L-1 Enego
200 B-9 Energia
69 P-2 Eretor *lake*
64 F-5 Enez
54 D-2 Enfer
181 P-4 Enfer *pte*
79 P-2 Enfida
53 K-4 Enfield
146 A-4 Enfok
200 F-6 Enganó *bay*
148 B-5 Engaño *cap.*
181 M-6 Engáno *cap.*
136 A-7 Engaru
105 J-8 Engcobo
59 L-4 Engelberg
59 K-4 Engelbergeraa *riv.*
56 F-6 Engelen
67 M-4 Engels
206 D-5 Enggano *isl.*
55 H-4 Enghien-les-Bains
59 J-6 Engi (Switzerland)
59 P-3 Engi (Switzerland)
160 D-5 Engineer
211 N-8 Engineer Group *islds*
147 M-9 Engkili
206 D-3 Engkulu *reg.*
50 D-5 England *reg.*
165 M-1 Englee
168 D-7 Englewood
58 F-4 Englisberg
50 E-6 English *strt.*
142 F-3 English Bāzār
210 C-9 English
Company's *islds*
181 N-2 English Harbour
170 C-1 English River
172 G-5 Englishtown
59 K-5 Engstlen *lake*
58 G-6 Engstligen *mt*
58 G-7 Engstligen Alpe *mt*
58 E-7 Enhaut *reg.*
175 N-1 Enid
119 M-5 Eniwetok *isl.*
103 N-7 Enkeldoorn
51 M-1 Enköping
192 C-2 Enmore
61 N-8 Enna
163 P-1 Ennadai *lake*
163 P-1 Ennadai
92 A-5 Ennedi *mt*
59 P-3 Ennenda
80 B-8 Enneri Achelouma *riv.*
54 F-2 Ennery (France)
181 J-6 Ennery (Haiti)
58 E-6 Enney
219 H-7 Enngonia
50 A-4 Ennis (Ireland)
175 N-4 Ennis (USA)
168 B-2 Ennis (USA)
50 B-4 Enniscorthy
50 B-3 Enniskillen
48 D-7 Enontekiö
208 C-3 Enrekang
181 K-7 Enriquillo *lake*
181 K-7 Enriquillo
51 H-6 Enschede
200 D-2 Ensenada (Chile)
174 E-9 Ensenada (Mexico)
174 B-2 Ensenada (Mexico)
134 F-4 Enshi
56 F-4 Enspijk
52 F-3 Enstone
100 E-2 Entebbe
57 M-1 Enter
161 K-8 Enterprise (Canada)
192 C-2 Enterprise (Guyana)
177 H-5 Enterprise (USA)
166 D-6 Enterprise (USA)
167 K-6 Enterprise (USA)
59 J-1 Entfldn
59 J-3 Entlebu *rge*
59 J-3 Entlebuch
199 H-5 Entre Ríos *reg.*
191 K-5 Entre Rios (Bolivia)
194 A-2 Entre Rios (Brazil)
195 M-7 Entre Rios (Brazil)
197 K-5 Entre Rios de Minas
211 M-7 Entrecasteaux *islds*
216 E-9 Entrecasteaux *pte*
204 F-2 Entrecasteaux *islds*
215 K-1 Entrecasteaux *rf*
178 F-3 Entronque Huízache
90 B-6 Enugu
186 D-5 Envigado
52 D-1 Enville
188 G-9 Envira
91 J-9 Enyélé
222 F-7 Enys *mt*
63 H-5 Enza *riv.*
133 N-2 Eorang *cap.*
89 N-9 Epe (Nigeria)
57 J-1 Epe (Netherlands)
57 N-9 Epen
99 H-1 Epéna
214 B-9 Epenarra
58 C-5 Ependes
200 A-7 Epequen *lag.*
50 F-8 Epernay
58 B-9 Epernon
64 G-7 Ephesus *site*
172 B-5 Ephrata (USA)
162 D-8 Ephrata (USA)
55 L-3 Epiais-lès-Louvres
54 F-2 Epiais-Rhus
64 D-8 Epidhavros
50 G-9 Epinal
55 J-2 Epinay-Champlâtreux
55 H-8 Epinay-sur-Oise
55 K-8 Epinay-sur-Seine
54 B-8 Epinette (L')
100 B-1 Epini
192 C-5 Epira
54 G-3 Epluches
211 K-7 Epo
98 B-1 Epole *pte*
54 D-4 Epône
53 L-4 Epping
53 K-4 Epping *ft*
57 K-2 Epse
50 D-6 Epsom
53 K-6 Epsom (UK)
54 B-2 Epte *riv.*
102 F-9 Epukiro *riv.*
100 B-1 Epulu *riv.*
73 M-8 Eqlid
77 C-4 Equatorial
Guinea *state*
62 G-8 Equi Terme
97 H-5 Er Dur Elan *well*
94 D-6 Era (Na'am) *riv.*
63 N-2 Eraclea
61 M-8 Eraclea *site*
54 F-3 Eragny
162 B-9 Erange *reg.*
211 K-5 Erap
211 H-5 Erave *riv.*
62 E-1 Erba (Italy)
93 L-3 Erba (Sudan)
72 A-4 Erbaa
63 J-2 Erbezzo
72 E-5 Ercek *lake*
72 E-4 Erciş
65 L-6 Erciyas *mt*
49 H-1 Erd
133 L-2 Erdaojiang *riv.*
64 G-5 Erdek
65 K-7 Erdemli
123 L-9 Erdene
130 A-6 Erdenebulgan
130 A-3 Erdenebüren
130 D-9 Erdenedalay
130 B-7 Erdenemandal
130 C-9 Erdenesant
132 E-1 Erdenetsagaan
130 C-7 Erdenetsogt
92 A-4 Erdi *mt*
78 B-5 Erdouz *mt*
188 C-7 Eré
188 C-6 Eré *riv.*
196 D-9 Erebango
187 L-6 Erebato *riv.*
196 D-9 Erechim
124 A-6 Ereen Cav
123 N-8 Ereen Davaani *mt*
65 H-4 Ereğli (Turkey)
65 K-7 Ereğli (Turkey)
192 D-8 Erepucu *lake*
97 K-1 Erer *riv.*
78 E-5 Erfoud
51 J-7 Erfurt
76 B-2 Erg Chech *mt*
76 B-1 Erg occidental *reg.*
76 C-1 Erg oriental
(Great) *rge*
54 E-7 Ergal
65 N-5 Ergani
69 N-1 Erginskij *lake*
66 C-2 Ergli
134 A-7 Erhai *lake*
135 N-8 Erhlin
165 H-2 Eric *lake*
164 G-2 Eric
60 A-5 Ericeira
83 K-1 Eridu *site*
171 H-6 Erie *lake*
156 F-2 Erie *lake*
169 J-9 Erie (USA)
171 H-6 Erie (USA)
97 H-5 Erigābo
88 C-3 Erigât *reg.*
163 P-9 Eriksdale
136 C-7 Erimo *cap.*
59 H-3 Eriswil
93 N-6 Eritrea *reg.*
93 L-3 Erkowit
58 E-3 Erlach *pass*
51 J-8 Erlangen
218 A-3 Erldunda
58 G-6 Erlenbach
58 B-8 Erli
132 C-3 Erlian
217 H-4 Erlistoun
133 K-2 Erlongshan *lake*
123 P-7 Ermana *mt*
105 K-4 Ermelo (South Africa)
57 H-1 Ermelo (Netherlands)
65 K-8 Ermenek
55 L-1 Ermenonville *ft*
55 M-2 Ermenonville
208 G-7 Ermera
92 E-8 Ermil Post
165 N-4 Ermitage *bay*
55 H-4 Ermont-Franconville
64 E-8 Ermoúpolis
141 K-4 Ernākulam
50 B-3 Erne *lake*
161 M-2 Ernest Kendall *cap.*
141 J-5 Erode
218 G-4 Eromanga
102 C-9 Erongoberg *mt*
211 L-7 Eroro
57 H-7 Erp
141 F-6 Erramala *mt*
50 B-2 Errigal *mt*
50 A-3 Erris *cap.*
164 F-8 Errol
58 G-1 Erschwil
169 J-2 Erskine
59 M-4 Erstfeld
67 J-4 Ertil'
199 L-5 Erval
52 B-2 Erwood Chapel
143 N-3 Eryuan
132 A-6 Erzidi
122 F-6 Erzin *riv.*
122 F-7 Erzin
72 B-4 Erzincan
72 C-4 Erzurum
211 M-8 Esa-Ala
136 C-6 Esan *cap.*
136 E-7 Esasi (Japan)
136 A-6 Esasi (Japan)
136 D-6 Esasi (Japan)
56 F-8 Esbeek
51 H-4 Esbjerg
55 N-5 Esbly
195 P-5 Escada
188 D-1 Escalante *islds*
200 G-5 Escalante (Argentina)
167 K-8 Escalante (USA)
175 H-7 Escalón
170 D-4 Escanaba
188 B-7 Escarpa de
Araracuara *mt*
148 B-5 Escarpada *pte*
185 M-9 Escarpado *cap.*
215 N-3 Escarpé *cap.*
56 B-9 Escaut *riv.*
56 F-7 Esch
57 H-5 Escharen
59 K-2 Eschenbach
59 J-4 Escholzmatt
159 K-3 Eschscholtz *bay*
181 L-6 Escocesa *bay*
190 G-2 Escoma
185 H-5 Escondido *riv.*
174 B-1 Escondido
90 A-7 Escravos *strt.*
89 P-9 Escravos *riv.*
185 K-8 Escudo de Veraguas
178 B-2 Escuinapa
de Hidalgo
49 J-1 Ese
90 E-8 Eséka
73 M-8 Esfandārān
195 H-4 Esfolado *riv.*
53 J-6 Esher
127 L-5 Eshkāshem
105 L-6 Eshowe
62 G-1 Esipe
219 M-5 Esk
48 C-4 Eskifjörður
51 M-1 Eskilstuna
154 J-3 Eskimo Point
65 H-5 Eskişehir
60 C-4 Esla *riv.*
190 E-2 Esmeralda *riv.*
201 K-1 Esméralda *isl.*
214 G-8 Esmeralda (Australia)
180 E-5 Esmeralda (Cuba)
188 A-2 Esmeraldas *riv.*
188 A-2 Esmeraldas *reg.*
184 C-9 Española *isl.*
164 A-8 Espanola
184 F-2 Esparta
188 A-7 Espejo *lake*
159 K-3 Espenberg *cap.*
197 L-5 Espera Feliz
196 E-6 Esperanca
195 N-4 Esperança (Brazil)
106 E-5 Esperança
(Mozambique)
217 H-8 Esperance
217 H-8 Esperance *bay*
54 D-6 Espérance (L')
201 L-3 Esperanza *isl.*
201 L-4 Esperanza (Argentina)
198 G-4 Esperanza (Argentina)
162 A-5 Esperanza
Inlet *gulf*
60 A-6 Espichel *cap.*
60 C-6 Espiel
196 F-9 Espigão *mt*
194 F-7 Espigão Mestre *mt*
200 A-9 Espigas
186 D-7 Espinal
189 M-8 Espinar
194 E-5 Espingarda *riv.*
197 L-1 Espinhaco *reg.*
199 L-2 Espinilho *mt*
196 A-7 Espinillo
187 K-4 Espino
195 H-9 Espinosa
197 N-3 Espirito Santo *reg.*
197 M-5 Espirito Santo (Vila
Velha)
179 P-6 Espiritu Santo *bay*
174 D-8 Espiritu Santo *isl.*
201 M-6 Espiritu Santo *cap.*
179 N-4 Espita
195 M-7 Esplanada
107 K-2 Espungabera
172 A-2 Espy
200 F-3 Esquel
179 M-9 Esquipulas
198 D-3 Esquiú
78 B-4 Essaouira (Mogador)
54 E-8 Essarts-le-Roi (Les)
86 G-2 Essau
90 E-8 Essé
56 B-8 Essen (Belgium)
57 H-2 Essen (Netherlands)
51 H-6 Essen (FRG)
216 G-2 Essendon *mt*
192 C-5 Essequibo *riv.*
58 C-6 Essertes
58 C-5 Essertines
53 M-3 Essex (UK)
173 M-1 Essex (USA)
172 A-8 Essex (USA)
171 K-8 Essex (USA)
103 M-8 Essexvale
59 M-1 Esslingen
98 F-2 Essoukou
56 F-5 Est
175 K-3 Estacado *pl.*
178 D-1 Estación Camacho
200 D-7 Estación de Practisos
182 D-8 Estados *isl.*
201 N-8 Estados *isl.*
84 A-3 Estahbānāt
195 M-7 Estancia (Brazil)
175 H-1 Estancia (USA)
126 B-5 Estand *mt*
191 N-8 Estanislao
del Campo
191 L-4 Estarca *riv.*
58 D-4 Estavayer-le-Lac
180 C-5 Este *pte*
63 L-4 Este
198 G-3 Esteban Rams
184 F-4 Esteli *reg.*
184 F-4 Esteli
60 E-3 Estella
172 E-8 Estelville
98 B-2 Esterias *cap.*
198 E-1 Esteros (Argentina)
191 P-6 Esteros (Brazil)
199 J-2 Esteros
del Iberá
163 L-9 Estevan
162 A-2 Estevan Group *islds*
170 A-5 Estherville
194 G-4 Estiva *riv.*
163 J-7 Eston
66 B-1 Estonia *reg.*
114 A-4 Estonia *rép*
112 A-4 Estonia *rep*
66 C-1 Estonie *rép*
60 A-5 Estoril
220 C-3 Estrees *bay*
195 H-6 Estreito
60 B-4 Estrela *mt*
199 M-3 Estrêla
194 D-8 Estrela do Norte
197 H-3 Estrela do Sul
196 D-1 Estrella *mt*
174 C-3 Estrella *pte*
60 B-5 Estremoz
194 D-5 Estrondo *mt*
218 D-6 Etadunna
139 N-5 Etah
58 A-2 Etalans
165 K-2 Etamamu *riv.*
50 E-8 Etampes
218 E-4 Etamunbanie *lake*
54 F-5 Etang-la-
Ville (L')
139 N-6 Etāwah
212 G-9 Ethel Creek
214 G-7 Etheridge *riv.*
77 F-4 Ethiopia *state*
76 F-4 Ethiopian *plat.*
136 G-7 Etigo *mt*
55 K-9 Etiolles
58 E-7 Etivaz (L')
61 N-8 Etna *mt*
99 M-2 Etoka
158 E-3 Etolin *strt.*
160 C-8 Etolin *isl.*
158 E-3 Etolin *cap.*
219 L-1 Eton (Australia)
53 J-5 Eton (UK)
102 B-6 Etosha *rés*
102 D-7 Etoshapan *lake*
98 F-2 Etoumbi
58 B-7 Etoy
55 P-3 Etrépilly
57 L-4 Etten
56 C-7 Etten Leur
52 F-2 Ettington
132 B-6 Etuokeqi
59 M-2 Etzel *mt*
221 H-2 Euabalong
64 E-7 Euboea *isl.*
170 G-6 Euclid
195 L-6 Euclides
da Cunha
221 J-4 Eucumbene *lake*
220 D-2 Eudunda
175 P-2 Eufaula *lake*
177 H-4 Eufaula (USA)
175 P-2 Eufaula (USA)
63 L-3 Euganean *hill*
166 D-3 Eugene
174 B-5 Eugenia *pte*
198 B-6 Eugenio Bustos
196 B-5 Eugenio Penzo
221 J-2 Eugowra
133 M-6 Euijeongbu
133 K-4 Euiju
133 N-6 Euiseong
219 H-6 Eulo
219 K-1 Eungela *na.p.*
175 J-3 Eunice (USA)
176 D-5 Eunice (USA)
83 H-1 Euphrates *riv.*
72 D-8 Euphrates
153 K-2 Eureka *strt.*
166 F-1 Eureka (USA)
169 H-9 Eureka (USA)
167 J-6 Eureka (USA)

167 J-8 Eureka (USA)
159 K-7 Eureka (USA)
162 F-8 Eureka (USA)
159 J-9 Eureka Lodge
176 C-1 Eureka Springs
218 E-8 Eurinilla riv.
220 G-4 Euroa
190 A-2 Europa
60 D-3 Europa mt
56 A-4 Europoort
220 F-2 Euston (Australia)
53 M-1 Euston (UK)
176 F-4 Eutaw
162 C-3 Eutsuk lake
214 B-7 Eva Downs
102 C-5 Evale
219 N-7 Evans cap.
168 A-2 Evans mt
164 C-5 Evans lake
168 A-5 Evanston (USA)
170 D-6 Evanston (USA)
170 D-9 Evansville
175 M-4 Evant
55 M-2 Eve
54 E-3 Evecquemcnt
213 P-2 Evelyn mt
52 F-3 Evenlode riv.
223 N-9 Eveque (L') cap.
221 J-6 Everard cap.
217 P-3 Everard mt
218 B-8 Everard lake
217 P-3 Everard Park
52 D-7 Evercreech
56 F-4 Everdingen
142 F-1 Everest (Zhumu-langmafeng) mt
162 C-7 Everett
177 L-9 Everglades na.p.
177 L-8 Everglades islds
177 K-9 Everglades
176 G-5 Evergreen
53 H-6 Eversley
52 F-2 Evesham val.
218 G-2 Evesham (Australia)
52 E-2 Evesham (UK)
58 C-7 Evian-les-Bains
58 E-2 Evilard
58 A-3 Evillers
98 C-1 Evinayong
58 E-9 Evionnaz
51 H-1 Evje
58 G-9 Evolène
60 A-6 Evora
125 K-3 Evoron lake
50 E-8 Evreux
55 J-9 Evry
55 L-9 Evry-Grégy-sur-Yerre
64 E-6 Evstratios isl.
125 K-2 Evur riv.
172 B-1 Ewans Falls
100 G-3 Ewaso Ngiro riv.
53 K-6 Ewell
52 A-5 Ewenni
53 J-6 Ewhurst
57 H-4 Ewijk
172 F-5 Ewing
98 F-3 Ewo
190 D-3 Exaltación
172 A-2 Exchange
52 A-6 Exe riv.
50 C-6 Exeter
52 A-7 Exford
52 A-9 Exminster
52 A-9 Exmouth
212 C-9 Exmouth gulf
215 L-1 Extérieur rf
52 A-7 Exton
60 B-5 Extremadura reg.
195 L-4 Exu
180 F-3 Exuma gulf
180 G-3 Exuma isl.
100 F-5 Eyasi lake
53 N-1 Eye
143 M-1 Eyihe riv.
48 B-3 Eyjafjördur bay
97 K-8 Eyl
72 B-3 Eynesil
53 L-6 Eynsford
52 G-4 Eynsham
222 C-8 Eyre mt
220 B-1 Eyre pen.
217 L-7 Eyre
218 C-5 Eyre lake
218 D-5 Eyre holl.
218 D-3 Eyre riv.
73 K-5 Eyvānakī
86 B-5 Ez Zerga reg.
55 J-3 Ezanville
200 C-4 Ezequil Ramos Mexia lake
88 G-8 Ezgueret riv.
64 F-6 Ezine
69 H-5 Ežva
78 D-3 Ezzhiliga

# F

89 H-6 Fa riv.
87 K-7 Fabala
62 E-5 Fabbrica Curone
63 J-5 Fabbrico
175 H-4 Fabens
161 K-6 Faber lake
51 J-4 Faborg
61 M-4 Fabriano
186 E-6 Facatativá
200 G-4 Facundo
92 A-5 Fada
89 J-6 Fada-Ngourma
113 N-2 Faddejevskij isl.
94 E-3 Faddoi
83 M-4 Fadhili
141 N-2 Fadiffolu isl.
63 M-7 Faenza
46 C-3 Faeroes islds
91 J-6 Fafa riv.
86 G-3 Fafakourou
97 L-3 Fafen riv.
64 E-2 Fagaras
224 F-6 Fagataufa isl.
49 K-4 Fagersta
63 L-8 Faggiola mt
88 F-3 Faguibine lake
48 C-3 Fagurhólsmýri
94 D-2 Fagwir
108 F-7 Fahambahy riv.
79 K-5 Fahl riv.
126 A-7 Fahraj
59 K-1 Fahrwangen
145 L-2 Fai Tsi Long bay
81 P-2 Fā'id
59 M-7 Faido
159 K-8 Fairbanks-North Star
169 H-7 Fairbury
173 J-1 Fairfield reg.
175 N-4 Fairfield (USA)
170 D-9 Fairfield (USA)
166 F-7 Fairfield (USA)
170 B-7 Fairfield (USA)
167 H-2 Fairfield (USA)
52 F-4 Fairford
176 G-5 Fairhope
172 G-3 Fairlawn
172 B-9 Fairlee
222 E-8 Fairlie
170 A-5 Fairmont (USA)
171 H-8 Fairmont (USA)
168 C-7 Fairplay
172 D-8 Fairton
215 H-5 Fairview (Australia)
162 G-3 Fairview (Canada)
160 B-5 Fairweather cap.
160 C-5 Fairweather mt
168 F-4 Faith
142 C-1 Faizābād
181 K-1 Fajardo
82 A-7 Fajr riv.
144 G-4 Fak Tha
224 B-4 Fakaefo isl.
224 E-5 Fakarava isl.
209 M-3 Fakfak
143 H-2 Fakiragram
126 C-4 Fakrūd riv.
133 J-3 Faku
87 K-5 Falaba
161 K-8 Falaise lake
54 D-4 Falaise (La)
119 K-6 Falaurep isl.
200 D-5 Falckner
187 H-2 Falcón reg.
175 L-8 Falcón dam.
78 G-2 Falcon cap.
87 H-6 Faléa
87 H-6 Falemé riv.
175 M-7 Falfurrias
51 K-3 Falkenberg
50 D-7 Falkirk
182 E-8 Falkland islds
201 M-8 Falkland islds
201 M-9 Falkland (East) reg.
201 K-7 Falkland (West) reg.
173 L-1 Falkner isl.
51 K-2 Falköping
171 N-5 Fall River
59 M-1 Fällanden
167 H-4 Fallon
201 K-2 Fallos strt.

172 C-1 Falls
168 A-4 Falls riv.
169 J-8 Falls City
172 A-8 Fallston
53 K-8 Falmer
50 B-6 Falmouth (UK)
180 F-7 Falmouth (USA)
170 F-9 Falmouth (USA)
86 G-8 Falou
191 K-1 Falsa Chipana pte
158 A-6 False Pass
192 G-6 Falsino riv.
174 E-9 Falso (Mexico) cap.
181 K-7 Falso (Saint Domingue) cap.
51 K-4 Falster isl.
142 F-5 Falta
63 L-9 Falterona mt
66 D-9 Falticeni
49 K-4 Falun
198 C-2 Famatina
198 C-2 Famatina mt
90 E-5 Fan riv.
145 J-1 Fan Si Pan mt
89 H-1 Fana
108 D-8 Fanambana riv.
63 J-8 Fanano
109 J-5 Fandriana
59 P-6 Fanella mt
209 K-2 Fanfalap
144 F-3 Fang
94 D-3 Fangak
145 M-1 Fangcheng (China)
135 H-1 Fangcheng (China)
134 G-2 Fangxian
224 D-3 Fanning isl.
84 A-8 Fannúj
51 H-4 Fanø
61 N-4 Fano
160 C-7 Fanshaw
58 E-4 Faoug
81 P-2 Fāqus
82 G-8 Far riv.
172 F-3 Far Hills
62 C-2 Fara Novara
71 L-7 Farab
94 D-7 Faradje
109 L-5 Farafangana
81 M-5 Farâfirah (Wāhat)
126 D-5 Farah
63 F-5 Farāh riv.
119 K-5 Farallon de Medinilla isl.
119 K-5 Farallon de Pajaros isl.
87 K-6 Faranah
96 D-1 Farasan islds
109 H-5 Faratsiho
52 G-8 Fareham
222 G-5 Farewell cap.
159 H-7 Farewell
49 J-2 Fargernes
169 J-3 Fargo
108 A-9 Farguhar islds
195 L-3 Farias Brito
170 A-5 Faribault
139 M-4 Farīdābād
139 L-2 Farīdkot
142 G-4 Farīdpur
81 H-5 Fārigh riv.
62 B-6 Farigliano
87 H-3 Farim
126 D-2 Farīmān
218 D-7 Farina
52 F-4 Faringdon
62 F-6 Farini d'Olmo
120 B-9 Fariš
51 M-3 Färjestaden
52 D-6 Farmboro
170 D-7 Farmer City
173 J-3 Farmingdale (USA)
172 G-5 Farmingdale (USA)
164 G-8 Farmington (USA)
170 C-9 Farmington (USA)
168 B-9 Farmington (USA)
171 J-9 Farmville
53 H-6 Farnborough
162 F-7 Farnham mt
53 H-6 Farnham (UK)
53 P-2 Farnham (UK)
52 E-8 Farnham cap.
53 J-5 Farnham Royal
53 L-5 Farningham
53 L-6 Farnoorough
192 D-8 Faro
185 P-6 Faro pte
90 F-6 Faro riv.
90 F-5 Faro rés
49 L-6 Fårö isl.
60 A-7 Faro
48 D-1 Faroe islds
49 L-6 Fårösund
63 M-1 Farra di Soligo
218 F-3 Farrars riv.
83 P-1 Farrāshband
195 J-6 Farreira riv.

52 D-6 Farrington Gurney
126 C-3 Farrokhī
139 P-5 Farrukhābād
64 D-9 Fársala
126 E-4 Fārsī
168 B-5 Farson
96 C-9 Fartak cap.
52 G-3 Fartinghoe
196 D-8 Fartura mt
196 F-6 Fartura
58 E-5 Farvagny
175 M-1 Farview
175 K-2 Farwell
71 N-9 Faryab reg.
126 G-3 Fāryāb reg.
84 A-3 Fasā
66 E-7 Fastov
209 L-2 Fatagar cap.
87 J-4 Fatala riv.
86 G-7 Fatao
139 M-3 Fatehābād
139 L-4 Fatehpur (India)
139 P-7 Fatehpur (India)
66 G-5 Fatež
94 E-4 Fathai
88 F-3 Fati lake
86 F-2 Fatick
96 F-2 Fatmab isl.
72 A-4 Fatsa
59 N-4 Fätschbach
224 F-5 Fatu Hiva isl.
224 F-4 Fatu Huku isl.
185 H-2 Fatuca riv.
59 P-3 Faulegg mt
58 G-6 Faulensee
59 J-5 Faulhorn mt
168 G-4 Faulkton
162 E-7 Fauquier
48 E-4 Fauske
162 G-4 Faust
109 N-3 Faux-Cap
54 B-8 Faverolles
53 N-6 Faversham
54 B-6 Favières
54 B-4 Favrieux
119 K-6 Favu isl.
52 G-8 Fawley
172 A-7 Fawn Grove
48 B-1 Faxaflói bay
215 N-3 Fayaoué
176 G-3 Fayette (USA)
176 E-5 Fayette (USA)
170 B-8 Fayette (USA)
176 G-2 Fayetteville (USA)
176 C-1 Fayetteville (USA)
177 L-2 Fayetteville (USA)
83 L-2 Faylakah isl.
89 L-6 Fazao na.p.
196 F-1 Fazenda Nova
139 L-2 Fāzilka
83 N-4 Fazran
86 A-6 Fdérik
177 M-3 Fear cap.
223 H-7 Featherston
50 E-7 Fécamp
52 E-2 Feckenham
127 M-2 Fedčenko
199 J-4 Federación
199 H-4 Federal
67 M-2 Federovska
51 K-4 Fehmarn isl.
51 J-4 Fehmarn Belt strt.
59 M-1 Fehraltdorf
197 M-6 Feia lag.
135 L-2 Feidong
188 G-9 Feijó
223 J-6 Feilding
103 N-5 Feira
195 L-7 Feira de Santana
132 G-8 Feixian
79 N-4 Fejaj holl.
65 L-6 Feke
53 K-7 Felbridge
51 H-9 Feldberg mt
61 L-1 Feldkirch
62 A-3 Feletto
60 B-4 Felgueiras
199 H-4 Feliciano riv.
62 G-6 Felino
179 N-5 Felipe Carrillo Puerto
175 H-4 Felix U. Gomez
197 K-3 Felixlândia
53 P-3 Felixstove
62 C-5 Felizzano
63 K-5 Felonica
86 G-6 Félou (chutes)
53 J-8 Felpham
172 A-6 Felton
63 L-1 Feltre
167 H-4 Femley
49 H-3 Femund lake
174 C-9 Fenelon Falls
108 G-7 Fénérivo

93 N-8 Feneroa
135 K-5 Fengcheng (China)
133 K-4 Fengcheng (China)
135 N-9 Fengchiang
132 E-8 Fengfeng
134 E-5 Fenggang
135 N-3 Fenghua
134 F-3 Fengjie
133 J-1 Fengku
135 N-4 Fenglin
132 E-9 Fengqiu
132 G-5 Fengrun
134 E-8 Fengshan (China)
135 N-9 Fengshan (Formose)
134 D-1 Fengxian
134 E-1 Fengxiang
135 N-7 Fengyuan
132 D-5 Fengzhen
132 D-8 Fenhe riv.
143 H-5 Feni
170 C-6 Fennimore
109 H-5 Fenoarino Centre
125 H-7 Fenshuigang mt
66 C-6 Fenstanton
132 D-7 Fenyang
65 K-1 Feodosiya
79 M-2 Fer cap.
54 C-6 Féranville
52 E-8 Ferdown
73 P-4 Ferdows
87 L-8 Ferédougouba riv.
97 M-4 Ferfer
127 M-2 Fergana
127 N-2 Ferganskij mt
169 J-3 Fergus Falls
211 M-8 Fergusson isl.
79 N-3 Feriana
89 L-2 Ferké
89 L-2 Ferkessédougou
86 F-4 Ferlo reg.
86 F-4 Ferlo riv.
55 P-9 Fermeté (La)
63 P-9 Fermignano
60 C-4 Fermoselle
50 A-4 Fermoy
198 E-2 Fernández
184 A-8 Fernandina isl.
90 C-8 Fernando Poo (Bioko)
196 F-4 Fernandópolis
197 K-1 Fernao Dias
106 F-8 Fernào Veloso bay
53 H-7 Fernhurst
162 F-8 Fernie
165 L-1 Ferolle pte
55 P-5 Férolles
55 L-7 Férolles-Attilly
63 L-5 Ferrara riv.
61 M-3 Ferrara
63 L-6 Ferrara (Ferrare) na.p.
63 J-2 Ferrara di Monte Baldo
79 H-2 Ferrat cap.
193 H-6 Ferreira Gomes
188 G-2 Ferreñate
162 A-5 Ferrer pte
62 E-6 Ferriere
55 M-6 Ferrières ft
55 M-6 Ferrières
199 J-4 Ferro
189 H-2 Ferrol pen.
197 L-4 Ferros
165 P-3 Ferryland
78 E-3 Fès
99 H-7 Feshi
59 P-5 Fess pass
168 G-2 Fessenden
135 L-2 Fetesti
55 H-8 Fethiye
70 D-8 Fetisovo
54 E-4 Feucherolles
59 J-4 Feurestein mt
61 H-2 Feurs
55 C-5 Fey
127 L-4 Feyzābād (Afghanistan)
126 B-4 Feyzābād (Iran)
76 D-2 Fezzan dés
62 C-6 Fezzan riv.
80 C-4 Fezzan mt
198 C-1 Fiambalá riv.
198 C-2 Fiambalá mt
198 C-2 Fiambalá
89 K-4 Fian
109 K-5 Fianarantsoa
90 G-4 Flanga
62 A-4 Fiano
63 K-5 Ficarolo
95 K-2 Fiche
51 K-8 Fichtel Geb mt
105 J-5 Ficksburg
62 G-5 Fidenza
166 F-5 Fields
64 B-5 Fieri
214 E-8 Fiery riv.

147 N-3 Fiery Cross (Yongshujiao) rf
59 J-7 Fiesch
59 J-6 Fiescherhorn mt
59 M-7 Fiesso
87 J-7 Fifa
78 G-2 Figalo cap.
60 G-2 Figeac
103 L-8 Figtree
60 A-4 Figueira da Foz
60 G-4 Figueras
78 G-5 Figuig
109 L-2 Fiherenana riv.
225 A-5 Fiji state
224 B-5 Fiji islds
56 C-6 Fijnaart
56 B-6 Fijnaart en Heijningen
97 K-2 Fik
103 M-8 Filabusi
190 D-2 Filadelfia (Bolivia)
194 E-3 Filadélfia (Brazil)
191 L-8 Filadelfia (Paraguay)
227 M-3 Filchner Ice Shelf glac.
64 C-6 Filiátes
64 D-8 Filiatrá
122 G-2 Filimonovo
89 H-8 Filingué
51 L-1 Filipstad
167 L-8 Fillmore
52 D-5 Filton
95 L-5 Filtu
95 L-5 Filtu mt
99 H-4 Fimi riv.
87 H-8 Fina rés
62 B-8 Finalborgo
63 K-5 Finale Emilia
62 C-8 Finale Ligure
62 C-8 Finale Pia
53 L-3 Finchingfield
72 C-3 Findikli
170 F-7 Findlay
53 J-8 Findon
53 H-1 Finedon
59 L-9 Finero
106 F-2 Fingoè
65 H-8 Finike
211 J-5 Finisterre mt
60 A-2 Finisterre cap.
159 J-3 Fink Creek
218 A-3 Finke riv.
218 A-3 Finke
46 F-3 Finland plat.
47 F-3 Finland state
112 A-4 Finland gulf
162 E-1 Finlay riv.
162 E-1 Finlay mt
220 G-3 Finley (Australia)
169 H-2 Finley (USA)
162 E-1 Finley Ranges
52 G-3 Finmere
158 F-6 Finn
215 H-5 Finningan mt
220 A-2 Finnis cap.
48 C-7 Finnmark reg.
48 D-5 Finnsness
62 D-2 Fino Mornasco
58 C-3 Fins (Les)
211 L-5 Finschhafen
51 L-1 Finspang
51 K-2 Finsteraarhorn mt
51 K-6 Finsterwalde
50 C-2 Fionnphort
63 L-1 Fior mt
63 J-6 Fiorano Modenese
62 G-5 Fiorenzuola d'Arda
63 P-8 Fiorenzuola di Focara
159 H-9 Fire isl.
173 K-4 Fire Island pte
173 K-4 Fire Island National Seashore isth.
163 M-1 Firedrake lake
63 K-9 Firenze reg.
63 K-9 Firenze (Florence)
63 K-8 Firenzuola
221 H-8 Fires bay
198 G-6 Firmat
61 H-2 Firminy
66 F-1 Firovo
139 N-5 Firozābād
139 L-2 Firozpur
217 K-6 First King
159 P-8 Firth riv.
50 D-2 Firth of Forth gulf
50 C-2 Firth of Lorn gulf
223 K-4 Firth of Thames bay
73 N-1 Fīr'uza
83 P-1 Fīrūzābād
73 L-5 Fīrūzkuh
59 N-1 Fischenthal
87 M-7 Fisébu
161 J-6 Fish lake
159 H-5 Fish riv.
214 D-7 Fish River
52 G-8 Fishbourne
162 F-8 Fisher mt
173 N-1 Fishers isl.

48 G-3 Frohavet *gulf*
59 M-3 Frohnalpstock *mt*
67 L-5 Frolovo
218 D-7 Frome *lake*
52 D-6 Frome
52 D-2 Fromes Hills
168 D-6 Front Range *mt*
171 J-8 Front Royal
179 K-6 Frontera
186 C-5 Frontino
61 N-5 Frosinone
54 G-1 Frouville
48 G-2 Frøya *isl.*
168 B-7 Fruita
120 G-9 Frunze
128 A-3 Frunze
128 C-1 Frunze
66 E-9 Frunzovka
196 G-4 Frutal
58 G-6 Frutigen
200 D-2 Frutillan
81 L-2 Fu'ād *well*
135 M-5 Fuan
58 C-2 Fuans
55 P-4 Fublaines
63 J-9 Fucecchio
135 M-4 Fuchunliang *riv.*
135 N-5 Fuding
125 L-8 Fudzin *riv.*
60 B-6 Fuente de Cantos
185 N-8 Fuerte *isl.*
174 E-7 Fuerte *riv.*
196 A-4 Fuerte Olimpio
78 C-9 Fuerteventura *isl.*
148 B-6 Fuga *isl.*
48 D-1 Fuglefjord.
143 N-3 Fugong
128 B-8 Fuhai
84 E-7 Fuhud *well*
84 C-6 Fujairah
135 L-6 Fujian *reg.*
125 J-6 Fujin
135 P-7 Fukueichiao *cap.*
87 H-3 Fulacunda
73 L-4 Fūlād Maḥalleh
127 H-5 Fūlādī *mt*
124 E-8 Fulaerji
51 J-7 Fulda
134 E-4 Fuling
125 H-7 Fulitun
169 H-6 Fullerton
58 E-9 Fully
133 J-1 Fulongquan
199 H-8 Fultōn
170 B-9 Fulton (USA)
176 F-1 Fulton (USA)
176 F-3 Fulton (USA)
204 H-5 Fumante *isl.*
223 L-4 Fumante *isl.*
134 B-7 Fumin
134 E-9 Funan
78 B-1 Funchal
186 E-2 Fundación
197 M-4 Fundão
197 K-2 Fundo *riv.*
165 J-7 Fundy *bay*
165 J-7 Fundy *na.p.*
107 M-3 Funhalouro
134 D-8 Funing (China)
133 H-9 Funing (China)
132 G-5 Funing (China)
165 N-1 Funk *isl.*
219 K-2 Funnel *riv.*
90 B-2 Funtua
59 N-6 Fuorns
132 B-9 Fuping
135 M-6 Fuqing
186 E-6 Fúquene *lake*
106 F-3 Furancungo
84 A-4 Furg
84 A-5 Fürgun *mt*
59 L-8 Furka *pass*
67 H-1 Furmanov
128 A-1 Furmanovka
70 A-4 Furmanovo
197 J-5 Furnas *dam.*
221 J-7 Furneaux *islds*
61 P-1 Fürstendeld
51 L-6 Fürstenwalde
51 J-8 Fürth
186 E-7 Fusagasugá
134 C-4 Fushun (China)
133 J-3 Fushun Shenyang (Mukden)
63 M-7 Fusignano
63 H-3 Fusina
59 M-7 Fusio
133 L-2 Fusong
175 J-7 Fuste *mt*
63 K-8 Futa *pass*
200 F-3 Futaleufú
224 B-5 Futuna *isl.*
135 L-6 Futunqi *riv.*
81 N-2 Fuwah
133 J-5 Fuxian
134 B-8 Fuxianhu *lake*

133 H-3 Fuxin
134 A-9 Fuxinzhen
135 K-2 Fuyang
132 F-7 Fuyanghe *riv.*
135 N-6 Fuyaoshan *isl.*
134 G-6 Fuyishui *riv.*
124 F-9 Fuyu (China)
124 E-7 Fuyu (China)
125 J-6 Fuyuan (China)
134 C-7 Fuyuan (China)
124 F-7 Fuyuerhe *riv.*
130 B-2 Fuyun
135 M-6 Fuzhou (China)
135 K-5 Fuzhou (China)
133 J-5 Fuzhou (China)
53 L-4 Fyfield
51 J-4 Fyn *isl.*

# G

133 K-5 Ga *isl.*
96 G-6 Ga'ān
57 L-4 Gaanderen
91 M-2 Gabassour
214 G-1 Gabba *isl.*
97 J-8 Gabba'
102 B-1 Gabela
166 G-1 Gaberville
79 P-4 Gabès *gulf*
79 N-4 Gabès
198 A-1 Gabeza de Vaca *pte*
62 B-4 Gabiano
197 N-2 Gabiarra
100 C-3 Gabiro
221 K-5 Gabo *isl.*
77 C-4 Gabon *state*
98 B-2 Gabon *gulf*
171 J-2 Gabonga *lake*
77 E-7 Gaborone
105 H-2 Gaborone
69 J-5 Gabovo
94 A-2 Gabras
109 N-9 Gabriel *isl.*
84 B-7 Gābrīk
64 E-4 Gabrovo
133 M-3 Gabsan
94 B-7 Gabu
62 B-2 Gaby
83 N-1 Gach Sārān
186 E-6 Gachala
186 E-6 Gacheta
94 C-7 Gada *riv.*
66 G-6 Gad'ač
140 F-4 Gadag
211 M-8 Gadaisu
54 D-2 Gadancourt
140 A-7 Gādarwāra
48 G-4 Gäddede
146 D-9 Gadis *riv.*
59 K-5 Gadmen *riv.*
59 K-5 Gadmen
195 H-6 Gado Bravo *isl.*
194 F-4 Gado Bravo *mt*
177 H-3 Gadsden
91 H-7 Gadzi
133 L-4 Gaecheon
133 L-5 Gaeseong
61 N-5 Gaeta
79 N-4 Gafsa
209 K-1 Gag *isl.*
90 G-4 Gagal
66 F-3 Gagarin
90 B-2 Gagere *riv.*
62 D-3 Gaggiano
89 N-1 Gagnoa
164 F-3 Gagnon
161 M-8 Gagnon *lake*
55 K-5 Gagny
72 B-2 Gagra
142 C-2 Gahmar
196 A-2 Gaiba Mirim *lake*
142 G-3 Gaibānda
175 L-3 Gail
60 G-3 Gaillac
173 L-4 Gaillard *lake*
54 D-3 Gaillon-sur-Montcient
54 D-3 Gaillonnet
210 G-7 Gaima
200 E-6 Gaiman
175 N-3 Gainesville (USA)
177 K-6 Gainesville (USA)
177 J-3 Gainesville (USA)
133 J-4 Gaiping
218 B-8 Gairdner *lake*
129 L-6 Gaishasihu *lake*

70 D-1 Gaj
69 K-5 Gajny
66 E-8 Gajsin
68 E-9 Gajutino
66 E-8 Gajvoron
149 K-2 Gal Santos
97 N-5 Gal Tardo
125 H-1 Galam *riv.*
191 N-4 Galán *mt*
101 K-5 Galana *riv.*
101 K-5 Galana
64 F-2 Galaţi
129 J-9 Galawutelake
177 K-1 Galax
132 A-3 Galbin Govi *mt*
214 F-6 Galbraith
97 L-6 Galcaio
174 G-4 Galeana
63 M-8 Galeata
216 D-4 Galena (Australia)
170 C-6 Galena (USA)
159 J-5 Galena (USA)
59 L-6 Galenstock *mt*
187 P-3 Galeota *pte*
190 E-8 Galera *riv.*
200 D-1 Galera (Chile) *pte*
187 P-2 Galera (Vénézuela) *pte*
170 C-7 Galesburg
93 J-8 Galgani
57 J-3 Galgenberg *hill*
59 N-2 Galgenen
194 G-7 Galheirão *riv.*
72 C-2 Gali
68 G-9 Galič
60 B-3 Galicia *reg.*
173 P-1 Galilee
82 C-1 Galilee *sea*
219 J-1 Galilee *lake*
90 F-6 Galim
79 N-1 Galite *islds*
82 C-1 Galliate
63 H-8 Gallicano
55 N-4 Galliéni *site*
62 B-8 Gallinara *isl.*
63 L-1 Gallio
64 B-6 Gallipoli
170 G-8 Gallipolis
48 E-6 Gallivare
53 L-5 Gallows Corner
54 D-7 Galluis
167 M-9 Gallup
63 K-9 Galluzzo
58 E-4 Galmiz
196 A-3 Galpono
123 N-9 Galshir
171 H-5 Galt
175 P-6 Galveston *bay*
175 P-6 Galveston
198 G-5 Gálvez
188 F-7 Gálvez *riv.*
50 A-3 Galway *bay*
50 A-3 Galway
209 K-1 Gam *isl.*
145 K-1 Gam *riv.*
200 C-8 Gama *isl.*
195 P-5 Gamaleira
98 C-4 Gamba
89 K-5 Gambaga
54 B-7 Gambais
54 C-7 Gambaiseuil
62 G-4 Gàmbara
94 G-3 Gambela
158 G-1 Gambell
63 N-8 Gambettola
77 A-3 Gambia *state*
86 G-2 Gambie *riv.*
224 F-6 Gambier *islds*
165 N-2 Gambo (Canada)
91 M-7 Gambo (Centrafrique)
62 D-4 Gamboló
98 G-4 Gamboma
214 G-6 Gamboola
90 G-8 Gamboula
54 F-5 Gameren
104 C-5 Gamka *riv.*
51 M-2 Gamleby
95 J-5 Gamo Gofa *reg.*
86 G-4 Gamon
59 H-8 Gampel
133 N-7 Gampo
141 M-7 Gampola
95 K-6 Gamud *mt*
48 B-7 Gamvik
72 F-3 G'amyš

200 E-5 Gan Gan
168 A-9 Ganado
101 M-1 Ganäne *riv.*
66 C-5 Gancevići
102 C-3 Ganda
208 C-2 Gandadiwata *mt*
99 M-7 Gandajika
142 D-2 Gandak *riv.*
138 F-2 Gandāva
165 N-2 Gander *riv.*
165 N-2 Gander *lake*
165 N-2 Gander
139 L-7 Gāndhi Sagar *dam.*
60 E-6 Gandia
62 G-1 Gandino
195 L-9 Gandu
131 K-7 Gandutang
159 H-6 Ganes Creek
162 D-5 Gang Ranch
139 L-3 Gangānagar
139 M-6 Gangāpur
143 K-6 Gangaw
143 K-6 Gangaw Yoma *mt*
131 K-6 Gangcha
139 L-8 Gangdhar
129 M-2 Gangdisihan *mt*
116 D-3 Gangdisishanmo *mt*
57 N-8 Gangelt
133 M-3 Ganggu
133 L-3 Ganggye
133 L-6 Ganghwa
133 M-8 Gangjin
133 L-4 Gangnam-Sanmack *mt*
102 C-1 Gango *riv.*
129 M-1 Gangotrī *mt*
133 N-5 Gangreung
142 G-2 Gangtok
131 N-5 Gangtuo
131 L-9 Gangu
124 D-5 Ganhe *riv.*
209 J-1 Gani
90 G-7 Ganjiang *riv.*
124 E-7 Gannan
59 M-6 Ganneretsch *mt*
223 J-4 Gannet *isl.*
168 B-4 Gannett *mt*
104 D-9 Gansbaai
58 F-1 Gänsbrunnen
131 J-2 Gansen
133 M-5 Ganseong
131 H-7 Gansu *mt*
87 M-7 Ganta
56 E-5 Gantelwijk
212 G-3 Gantheaume *pte*
58 F-5 Gantrisch *mt*
70 B-6 Gan'uškino
133 H-8 Ganyu
135 J-7 Ganzhou
131 H-6 Ganzhouhe *riv.*
124 B-7 Ganzhuermiao
131 N-6 Ganzi
88 D-5 Gao *reg.*
88 F-6 Gao (Mali)
94 C-7 Gao (Zaïre)
135 K-5 Gaoan
135 K-5 Gaohefou
135 J-5 Gaokeng
143 N-3 Gaoligongshan *mt*
133 H-7 Gaomi
132 D-8 Gaoping
135 M-7 Gaoshan
131 H-6 Gaotai
132 F-7 Gaotang
89 K-3 Gaoua
87 J-4 Gaoual
132 F-9 Gaoyou
135 M-1 Gaoyou
135 L-1 Gaoyouhu *lake*
145 N-1 Gaozhou
61 J-3 Gap (France)
172 B-6 Gap (USA)
125 H-6 Gar' *mt*
124 F-3 Gar' *riv.*
97 J-1 Gara Muleta *mt*
95 H-4 Gara Nasi *mt*
97 K-7 Gara'ad
185 M-9 Garachiné
219 K-7 Garah
211 K-6 Garaina
78 A-7 Garajonay *mt*
87 K-9 Garalo
94 D-6 Garamba *na.p.*
54 C-6 Garancières
197 K-5 Garandai
195 N-5 Garanhuns
119 K-5 Garapan
197 J-1 Garapuava
91 L-4 Garba
62 C-3 Garbagna Novara
97 N-2 Garbahārrey
91 N-1 Garboldisham
196 F-5 Garça
195 K-4 Garças *riv.*
54 G-6 Garches
196 E-4 Garcias

61 H-3 Gard *riv.*
63 J-2 Garda *lake*
61 L-2 Garda (Italy) *lake*
101 J-2 Garda Tula
72 E-2 Gardabani
73 J-5 Gardaneh *mt*
73 J-6 Gardaneh-ye Aveh *mt*
73 L-4 Gardaneh-ye Gadūk *mt*
161 P-8 Garde (Canada) *lake*
170 E-4 Garden *pen.*
216 D-7 Garden *isl.*
192 B-2 Garden
175 K-4 Garden City
168 F-9 Garden City
167 M-3 Garden Grove
162 B-2 Garder *strt.*
57 H-2 Garderen
127 J-6 Gardez
168 B-3 Gardiner
173 N-2 Gardiners *isl.*
173 M-2 Gardiners *bay*
224 B-4 Gardner *isl.*
63 H-2 Gardone Riviera
62 G-2 Gardone Valtrompia
192 F-3 Gare Tigre
62 B-8 Garessio
172 G-3 Garfield
138 F-3 Garhi Khairo
139 N-4 Garhmuktesar
69 N-4 Gari
162 C-6 Garibaldi *na.p.*
199 N-3 Garibaldi
104 C-5 Garies
101 K-3 Garissa
175 N-3 Garland
62 D-4 Garlasco
62 E-1 Garlate *lake*
127 L-3 Garm
61 M-1 Garmisch Partenkirchen
73 L-5 Garmsār
54 E-8 Garne
170 A-5 Garner
172 G-1 Garnerville
169 J-9 Garnett
165 N-4 Garnish
143 H-3 Gāro-Khāsī-Jaintiyā *reg.*
97 J-7 Garoe
60 G-3 Garonne *riv.*
199 P-2 Garopaba
88 F-4 Garou *lake*
90 F-4 Garoua
90 G-7 Garoua Boulai
211 M-4 Garove *isl.*
168 G-2 Garrison
168 F-2 Garrison *lake*
184 G-4 Garrobo
101 K-4 Garsen
91 N-2 Garsila
52 A-2 Garth (UK)
52 A-4 Garth (UK)
207 H-6 Garut
196 G-8 Garuva
142 C-3 Garwa
170 D-7 Gary
198 E-2 Garza
186 D-8 Garzón
170 B-9 Gasconade *riv.*
216 C-2 Gascoyne *mt*
216 C-2 Gascoyne *riv.*
216 C-2 Gascoyne junction
93 L-6 Gash *riv.*
135 L-2 Gashunhu *lake*
130 F-7 Gashunnuoer *lake*
130 F-2 Gashunshamo *mt*
54 B-2 Gasny
207 H-3 Gaspar *strt.*
191 L-8 Gaspar R. de Francia
165 J-4 Gaspé
165 J-4 Gaspé *bay*
165 J-4 Gaspé *cap.*
165 H-5 Gaspésie *na.p.*
165 H-5 Gaspésie *reg.*
89 H-3 Gassan
57 J-6 Gassel
54 C-3 Gassicourt
62 A-4 Gássino Torinese
125 N-3 Gastello
58 G-7 Gastern *val.*
177 K-2 Gastonia
200 E-4 Gastre
65 K-9 Gáta *cap.*
160 F-8 Gataga *riv.*
172 A-7 Gatchellville
68 B-9 Gatchina
50 E-3 Gateshead
175 N-4 Gatesville
191 L-1 Gatico
88 F-3 Gatié-Loumo

171 K-2 Gatineau *riv.*
54 E-6 Gâtines (Les)
194 G-8 Gatos
62 C-2 Gattinara
219 M-6 Gatton
185 L-8 Gatun *lake*
143 H-3 Gauhāti
66 C-2 Gauja *riv.*
127 H-2 Gaurdak
129 P-1 Gauri Phānta
227 N-3 Gauss *mt*
220 C-4 Gautheaume *cap.*
73 M-7 Gäv Khūni
63 H-2 Gavardo
60 F-3 Gave de Pau *riv.*
62 D-6 Gavi
195 K-7 Gavião
195 J-9 Gavião *riv.*
86 F-7 Gavinané
62 D-1 Gavirate
49 K-5 Gävle
49 J-5 Gavleborg *reg.*
67 H-1 Gavrilov Jam
68 G-5 Gavrilovo
211 N-7 Gawa *isl.*
56 A-8 Gawege
140 B-6 Gāwīlgarh *na.p.*
220 D-2 Gawler
57 N-3 Gaxel
142 D-3 Gaya (India)
89 J-8 Gaya (Niger)
91 J-4 Gayam
52 G-2 Gaydon
89 J-6 Gayéri
53 H-2 Gayhurst
170 F-4 Gaylord (USA)
170 A-4 Gaylord (USA)
219 M-4 Gayndah
126 A-7 Gaz *riv.*
82 B-2 Gaza
107 M-2 Gaza *reg.*
73 L-3 Gazan-Kuli
90 C-1 Gazaoua
211 P-4 Gazelle *pen.*
215 M-3 Gazelle *rf*
211 N-3 Gazelle *cal.*
54 C-9 Gazeran *ft*
65 M-7 Gaziantep
124 B-5 Gazimur *riv.*
124 B-4 Gazimurskij *mt*
124 B-5 Gazimurskij Zavod
65 J-8 Gazipaza
71 L-7 Gazli
63 H-4 Gazoldo degli Ippoliti
63 J-4 Gazzo Veronese
63 H-4 Gazzuolo
87 K-8 Gbanhala *riv.*
87 M-7 Gbarnga
87 M-6 Gbeya *riv.*
90 C-5 Gboko
51 M-5 Gdansk
49 P-5 Gdansk *bay*
51 M-5 Gdanski
201 J-4 Gdor. Gregores
66 C-1 Gdov
51 M-4 Gdynia
166 F-3 Gearhart
87 H-2 Geba *cal.*
87 H-3 Geba *riv.*
129 M-5 Gebailang
209 K-1 Gebe *isl.*
97 J-3 Gebile *well*
64 G-5 Gebze
95 H-4 Gecha
65 H-6 Gediz
64 G-6 Gediz *riv.*
95 J-3 Gedo
51 K-4 Gedser
220 G-5 Geelong
216 C-5 Geelvink *strt.*
129 L-2 Geerhe *riv.*
131 K-3 Geermu
56 D-6 Geertruidenberg
56 B-5 Geervliet
57 M-2 Geesteren
51 J-5 Geesthacht
220 G-9 Geeveston
79 P-5 Gefara *reg.*
56 G-6 Geffen
211 M-8 Gehua
90 E-2 Geidam
172 C-5 Geigertown
163 M-3 Geikie *riv.*
57 P-8 Geilenkirchen
49 J-2 Geilo
49 H-2 Geiranger
100 D-4 Geita
134 B-9 Gejiu
94 D-5 Gel *riv.*
61 N-8 Gela
97 L-5 Geladi
97 L-5 Gelam *isl.*
146 F-7 Gelang *cap.*
57 J-3 Gelderland *reg.*
56 F-4 Geldermalsen
57 H-8 Geldrop

95 L-3 Gelemso
72 A-1 Gelendžik
64 F-5 Gelibolu
65 J-8 Gelidonya cap.
129 P-8 Gelinshankou pass
208 E-7 Geliting strt.
57 M-9 Gellik
58 A-5 Gellin
97 L-5 Gellinsör well
59 K-6 Gelmer lake
95 L-3 Gelolcha
57 M-2 Gelselaar
51 H-6 Gelsenkir
51 J-4 Gelting
146 F-8 Gemas
91 L-8 Gemena
129 N-7 Gemenghu lake
65 L-5 Gemerek
57 H-7 Gemert
64 G-5 Gemlik
59 H-5 Gemmenalp mt
58 G-7 Gemmi pass
129 L-5 Gemu
129 L-5 Gemuzhakechi lake
54 C-2 Genainville
56 E-6 Genderen
57 L-4 Gendringen
57 J-4 Gendt
91 M-1 Geneina
200 A-6 General Acha
198 C-7 General Alvear
198 G-6 General Arenales
196 B-9 General Artigas
199 H-6 General Belgrano
191 M-8 General Caballero
198 E-5 General Cabrera
199 H-4 General Campos
196 D-1 General Carneiro
200 C-7 General Conesa
199 J-8 General Conesa
200 B-2 General Cruz
191 K-7 General Eugenio A. Garay
199 H-5 General Galarza
199 J-8 General Guido
199 J-8 General Juan Madariaga
200 A-8 General la Madrid
199 J-7 General la Paz
200 D-7 General Lorenzo Vintter
191 M-5 General Martin M. de Güemes
196 A-9 General Paz
198 G-1 General Pinedo
200 C-5 General Roca
196 F-4 General Salgado
195 L-1 General Sampaio
200 B-7 General San Martín
199 H-6 General San Martín (Argentina)
174 G-6 General Trías
200 F-3 General Vintter lake
190 D-4 Geneshuaya riv.
95 K-3 Genet Alem
61 J-1 Geneva lake
61 J-2 Geneva (Switzerland)
171 K-5 Geneva (USA)
169 H-7 Geneva (USA)
132 C-4 Genghis Khan Wall site
143 N-5 Gengma
124 C-6 Genhe riv.
94 F-4 Geni'Khawr riv.
67 H-9 Geničesk
54 F-2 Génicourt
97 N-1 Gennale riv.
61 K-6 Gennargentu mt
57 J-6 Gennep
55 H-5 Gennevilliers
61 L-3 Genoa
62 D-7 Genoa reg.
62 D-7 Genoa
62 D-8 Genoa gulf
62 A-6 Genola
184 C-8 Genovesa isl.
59 K-5 Gental riv.
206 G-6 Genteng cap.
206 G-6 Genteng
51 K-6 Genthin
58 A-8 Genthod
55 J-6 Gentilly
195 J-7 Gentio do Ouro
94 C-6 Genze riv.
129 N-7 Genzhou
133 N-7 Geochang
216 D-8 Géographe bay
216 B-2 Géographe Channel strt.
133 M-8 Geogum isl.
133 N-7 Geoje isl.
73 N-1 Geok-Tepe
72 F-2 Geokčaj
133 N-8 Geomun isl.
104 F-9 George
177 K-6 George lake

165 L-6 George bay
212 E-8 George riv.
220 D-4 George (Australia) lake
221 K-3 George (Australia) lake
159 H-9 George (USA) lake
217 N-1 George Gills mt
201 M-8 George Island isl.
221 H-7 George Town (Australia)
180 G-3 George Town (Bahamas)
170 F-9 George Town (USA)
227 N-6 George V Coast
175 M-6 George West
112 C-2 Georges isl.
214 G-7 Georgetown
180 C-6 Georgetown (Antilles)
165 K-6 Georgetown (Canada)
86 G-3 Georgetown (Gambia)
181 N-8 Georgetown (Grenada)
183 E-2 Georgetown (Guyana)
192 C-2 Georgetown (Guyana)
175 M-5 Georgetown (USA)
177 L-3 Georgetown (USA)
171 L-8 Georgetown (USA)
168 D-7 Georgetown (USA)
67 J-5 Georghiu-Dej
177 J-4 Georgia state
112 C-5 Georgia rép
114 C-5 Georgia rép
157 E-3 Georgia state
162 B-6 Georgia strt.
182 G-8 Georgia (South) isl.
170 G-4 Georgian bay
164 B-9 Georgian bay
72 C-3 Georgian state
164 B-8 Georgian Bay na.p.
128 C-1 Georgijevka
214 C-8 Georgina riv.
218 D-1 Georgina (Herbert) riv.
67 M-9 Georgiyevsk
51 K-7 Gera
199 P-2 Geral mt
194 F-7 Geral de Goiás mt
194 E-9 Geral do Paraná mt
194 F-6 Geral ou Grande mt
222 E-8 Geraldine
216 D-5 Geraldton
170 D-1 Geraldton (USA)
159 H-8 Gerdine mt
65 J-5 Gerede
126 E-6 Geresh
210 E-3 Gerjem
166 G-4 Gerlach
58 G-2 Gerlafingen
97 L-4 Gerlogubi
54 A-7 Germainville
47 M-8 German Democratic Republic state
198 F-6 Germania
153 S-1 Germania Land
162 D-2 Germansen Landing
47 D-4 Germany (Federal Republic of) state
72 G-3 Germi
55 P-4 Germigny-l'Evêque
105 J-4 Germiston
54 F-2 Gérocourt
60 G-4 Gerona
59 M-8 Gerra
53 J-5 Gerrards Cross
59 L-3 Gersau
61 P-6 Gervati mt
57 H-8 Gerwen
65 K-4 Gerze
209 L-3 Geser
129 J-9 Geshun
211 H-7 Gesoa
56 G-8 Gestel
55 N-3 Gesvres-le-Chapitre
124 D-2 Getkan riv.
58 C-9 Gets (Les)
59 J-2 Gettnau
168 G-4 Gettysburg
196 E-9 Getúlio Vargas
100 C-1 Gety
227 M-4 Getz glac.
57 M-8 Geulle
133 M-7 Geum riv.
133 N-8 Geum isl.
146 A-6 Geumpang
146 B-6 Geureudong mt
72 E-5 Gevaş
64 D-5 Gevgelija
95 L-2 Gewani
108 C-5 Geyser rf
131 H-1 Gezikulihu lake
142 F-2 Gezing
79 N-7 Ghadamès (Ghudāmis)
85 J-5 Ghadūn riv.
84 G-6 Ghāfah (dunes)
139 M-3 Ghaggar riv.
142 D-2 Ghāghara riv.
138 F-3 Ghaibidero

96 D-7 Ghal Bā Wazir
77 B-4 Ghana state
138 G-7 Ghāntila
102 G-9 Ghanzi reg.
102 G-9 Ghanzi
84 D-6 Ghārb reg.
79 K-5 Ghardaïa
82 B-5 Ghārib mt
138 E-5 Gharo
83 K-1 Gharraf riv.
79 M-4 Gharsa holl.
80 C-1 Gharyān
80 B-2 Gharyān reg.
80 A-6 Ghāt
142 F-5 Ghātāl
140 C-3 Ghātghar lake
172 F-3 Ghatham
140 E-4 Ghātprabha riv.
116 D-5 Ghats (Eastern) rge
116 C-5 Ghats (Western) rge
78 G-2 Ghazaouet
139 J-2 Ghāzi Ghāt
139 N-4 Ghāziābād
142 C-2 Ghāzīpur
127 H-7 Ghaznī riv.
127 H-6 Ghaznī
62 G-3 Ghedi
94 G-3 Ghemi mt
62 C-2 Ghemme
50 F-6 Ghent
64 G-2 Gheorghe riv.
64 E-1 Gheorghe
64 E-1 Gheorghieni
64 E-1 Gheorghiu-Dej mt
62 C-1 Ghiffa
123 L-7 Ghilok riv.
95 H-3 Ghimbi
201 H-3 Ghio lake
78 A-5 Ghir cap.
140 C-3 Ghod riv.
126 G-5 Ghowr reg.
79 N-7 Ghudāmis (Ghadamès)
123 N-6 Ghudun riv.
127 H-7 Ghulam Haidar Kili
126 D-3 Ghūriān
145 L-9 Gia Dinh
145 L-8 Gia Nghia
97 H-8 Giahel riv.
63 K-2 Giazza
180 G-5 Gibara
213 K-4 Gibb River
172 D-7 Gibbstown
104 C-2 Gibeon
58 E-5 Gibloux mt
48 D-5 Gibostad
60 B-8 Gibraltar
60 B-8 Gibraltar strt.
76 B-1 Gibraltar strt.
78 L-1 Gibraltar strt.
172 A-9 Gibson isl.
213 J-9 Gibson dés
204 C-4 Gibson dés
217 J-1 Gibson dés
170 D-7 Gibson City
162 C-6 Gibsons
130 D-5 Gichgeniyn mt
94 G-3 Gidami
138 E-3 Gidar Dhor riv.
175 N-5 Giddings
95 J-5 Gidole
160 E-9 Giegerich mt
50 E-9 Gien
56 D-9 Gierle
57 K-3 Giesbeek
59 J-5 Giessbach
51 H-7 Giessen
56 E-5 Giessenburg
57 K-2 Gietelo
54 G-8 Gif-sur-Yvette
73 N-2 Gifān
58 F-7 Gifferhorn mt
58 E-5 Giffers
124 G-1 Giga riv.
67 L-8 Gigant
174 D-8 Giganta mt
186 D-8 Gigante
90 B-4 Giggan mt
61 L-5 Giglio isl.
137 J-6 Gihu
60 C-2 Gijon
100 C-4 Gikongoro
162 B-2 Gil isl.
174 C-2 Gila riv.
174 D-2 Gila Bend
73 H-5 Gilan reg.
117 N-7 Gilbert islds
201 P-4 Gilbert isl.
214 F-6 Gilbert riv.
214 G-7 Gilbert River
214 G-8 Gilberton (Australia)
172 B-3 Gilbertown (USA)
172 C-5 Gilbertsville
129 L-6 Gilbués
106 G-6 Gilé
218 F-4 Gileppee
217 M-1 Giles

216 G-5 Giles lake
92 C-1 Gilf Kabir plat.
162 B-4 Gilford isl.
221 K-1 Gilgandra
100 G-3 Gilgil
127 M-6 Gilgit riv.
127 M-6 Gilgit
221 H-1 Gilgunnia
207 N-7 Gilimanuk
133 M-3 Gilju
217 K-2 Gillen lake
54 A-5 Gilles
220 C-1 Gilles lake
222 E-7 Gillespie pte
168 D-4 Gillette
58 B-3 Gilley
214 F-9 Gilliat
53 M-5 Gillingham
52 D-7 Gillingham
170 E-4 Gills Rock
58 A-7 Gilly
170 D-7 Gilman
175 P-3 Gilmer
94 G-4 Gilo riv.
127 M-6 Giloit Kashmir reg.
167 J-2 Gilroy
124 D-2 Gil'uj riv.
211 H-5 Giluwe mt
52 B-3 Gilwern
56 E-7 Gilze
56 E-7 Gilze en Rijen reg.
133 N-7 Gimcheon
58 A-7 Gimel
133 M-5 Gimhwa
181 N-8 Gimie pte
163 P-9 Gimli
141 N-7 Gin riv.
219 M-4 Gin an Gin
93 N-6 Ginda
216 E-7 Gingin
149 H-2 Gingoog
99 H-6 Gingungi
95 L-4 Ginir
57 H-3 Ginkel
56 D-7 Ginneken
60 B-3 Ginzo de Limia
63 K-8 Gioge di Scarperia hill
61 P-6 Gioia di Colle
64 D-7 Giona mt
59 N-7 Giornico
59 L-8 Giove mt
63 K-9 Giovi hill
63 H-8 Giovo mt
221 H-5 Gippsland reg.
58 F-5 Gipsera
140 A-1 Gīr na.p.
212 C-9 Giralia
186 D-7 Girardot
186 D-5 Girardota
172 B-3 Girardville
102 A-4 Giraul riv.
72 B-4 Giresun
81 P-5 Girga
220 G-4 Girgarr
211 H-3 Girgir cap.
99 J-1 Giri riv.
142 E-4 Giridih
140 B-4 Girnā riv.
188 D-2 Girón
60 F-2 Gironde riv.
53 J-2 Girtford
53 K-2 Girton
215 K-8 Giru
196 C-9 Giruá
50 C-3 Girvan
129 P-2 Girwa riv.
159 J-5 Gisasa riv.
223 L-6 Gisborne
100 B-3 Gisenyi
71 P-6 Gissar
127 K-2 Gissarskij mt
71 P-6 Gissarskij mt
59 K-4 Giswil
100 C-4 Gitarama
100 C-5 Gitega
59 N-9 Giubiasco
64 E-3 Giurgiu
62 E-2 Giussano
62 C-7 Giusvalla
211 K-6 Giverny
54 A-2 Giverny
50 G-7 Givet
61 J-2 Givors
81 N-2 Giza
125 G-8 Gīzāb
120 A-9 Gīžduvan
66 A-5 Gizycko
64 C-6 Gjirokastër
49 J-3 Gjovik
160 C-5 Glacier bay
162 F-6 Glacier (Canada) na.p.
159 M-9 Glacier (USA) mt
162 C-8 Glacier (USA) mt

160 C-5 Glacier Bay (National monument)
175 P-4 Gladewater
48 F-3 Gladstad
220 D-1 Gladstone (Australia)
221 H-8 Gladstone (Australia)
163 N-9 Gladstone (Canada)
170 F-5 Gladwin
160 E-6 Gladys lake
49 J-3 Glåma riv.
52 A-5 Glamorgan reg.
58 A-7 Gland
58 D-6 Glåne riv.
57 P-2 Glanerbrug
59 N-3 Glärnisch mt
59 N-3 Glarus reg.
59 N-3 Glarus
61 L-1 Glarus
59 N-4 Glarus Alps rge
168 D-1 Glasgow
50 D-5 Glasgow (UK)
177 H-1 Glasgow (USA)
163 K-6 Glaslyn
171 L-7 Glassboro
52 C-7 Glastonbury
53 J-1 Glatton
59 J-6 Gleckstein Hôtel
160 C-1 Gleennallen
166 F-7 Gleens Ferry
173 J-2 Glen Brook
172 A-9 Glen Burnie
168 A-8 Glen Canyon na.p.
167 L-7 Glen Canyon
173 J-3 Glen Cove
172 E-3 Glen Gardner
219 M-7 Glen Innes
172 B-2 Glen Lyon
172 D-6 Glen Mils
175 N-4 Glen Rose
50 B-8 Glénan islds
221 L-1 Glenbawn lake
171 K-8 Glenburnie
105 K-5 Glencoe (South Africa)
170 A-4 Glencoe (USA)
103 N-6 Glendale (South Africa)
167 M-3 Glendale (USA)
174 D-1 Glendale (USA)
168 E-2 Glendive
168 D-5 Glendo lake
220 E-4 Glenelg riv.
218 E-3 Glengyle
219 L-5 Glenmorgan
59 P-5 Glenner riv.
62 G-1 Gleno mt
160 D-7 Glenora
218 D-2 Glenormiston
213 K-4 Glenroy
171 L-5 Glensfalls
105 L-6 Glenside
170 A-4 Glenswood
169 J-7 Glenwood
168 C-7 Glenwood Springs
58 D-1 Glère
163 J-7 Glidden
58 D-7 Glion
59 J-8 Glis
51 M-7 Gliwice
174 E-2 Globe
66 G-7 Globino
51 L-7 Glogow
48 F-6 Glommersträsk
72 A-1 Glor'ačij-Kluč
195 M-5 Glória
200 A-7 Gloria (la)
108 C-5 Glorieuses islds
172 E-6 Gloucester
221 L-1 Gloucester (Australia)
224 E-6 Gloucester (Duke of) islds
52 E-4 Gloucester (UK) reg.
50 D-5 Gloucester (UK)
171 N-5 Gloucester (USA)
58 L-7 Glovelier
165 M-3 Glover isl.
184 F-1 Glover rf
165 N-2 Glovertown
124 F-3 Glubokij (SSSR)
121 M-5 Glubokoje
66 G-6 Glukhov
66 D-5 Glusk
52 A-4 Glyncorrwg
52 A-4 Glynneath
52 A-3 Glyntawe
51 L-9 Gmünd
61 N-1 Gmunden
94 C-5 Gnap
51 M-6 Gniezno
64 C-4 Gnjilane
59 N-3 Gnosca
216 F-8 Gnowangerup
147 H-2 Go Công
127 H-6 Go-i-Ahan
140 F-3 Goa reg.
143 H-3 Goālpāra

93 L-8 Goang riv.
94 A-5 Goangoa riv.
184 E-4 Goascorán
89 N-4 Goaso
95 L-4 Goba (Ethiopia)
107 P-1 Goba (Mozambique)
102 E-9 Gobabis
113 J-5 Gobi dés
130 G-8 Gobi dés
137 K-5 Gobo
64 D-5 Goce Delčev
57 K-6 Goch
104 D-2 Gochas
53 J-6 Godalming
140 E-9 Godavari riv.
164 G-4 Godbout
63 N-1 Godego di Sant'Urbano
170 G-5 Goderich
51 H-7 Godesberg
139 J-8 Godhra
90 G-4 Godi riv.
62 D-5 Godiasco
97 L-5 Godinlabe
53 K-1 Godmanchester
52 D-8 Godmanstone
64 B-1 Gödöllö
198 C-5 Godoy-Cruz
52 G-9 Godshill
53 K-6 Godstone
164 C-5 Goëlands lake
108 B-9 Goelette isl.
133 N-7 Goesong
164 A-7 Gogama
124 F-3 Gogolevka
94 B-3 Gogrial
86 F-7 Gogui
133 M-8 Goheung
97 M-6 Gohō
195 P-4 Goiana
195 P-3 Goianésia
194 D-9 Goianinha
194 D-4 Goianorte
194 E-8 Goiás reg.
196 F-1 Goiás
196 G-2 Goiatuba
141 P-1 Goidu isl.
196 D-7 Goio riv.
196 D-7 Goio Ere
56 E-7 Goirle
63 H-4 Goito
95 J-4 Gojeb riv.
140 E-4 Gokāk
70 G-9 Goklenkui (Karašor) lake
72 A-6 Göksu riv.
65 L-6 Göksun
103 M-7 Gokwe
49 J-2 Gol
143 K-3 Golāghāt
125 L-4 Golaja mt
65 H-5 Gölcük
162 E-2 Gold Bar
166 E-2 Gold Beach
89 P-5 Gold Coast
219 N-6 Gold Coast
167 H-7 Gold Hi
59 L-3 Goldau
58 G-5 Goldiwil
58 H-5 Goldiwil
177 M-2 Goldsboro
212 F-7 Goldsworthy mt
175 M-4 Goldthwaite
51 L-5 Goleniow
200 G-7 Golfe San Jorge gulf
185 H-8 Golfito
185 H-8 Golfo Dulce gulf
65 H-7 Gölhisar
175 N-6 Goliad
72 A-4 Gölköy
105 M-5 Gollel
58 B-6 Gollion
91 K-4 Golongosso
159 H-3 Golovin
159 H-3 Golovnin bay
136 A-8 Golovnino
73 K-7 Golpāyegān
126 E-3 Golrān
159 H-4 Golsovia
123 H-1 Gol't'avino
123 J-5 Golumet'
100 B-3 Goma
129 P-1 Gomati riv.
94 C-8 Gombari
90 E-3 Gombe
90 F-4 Gombi

62 G-9 Gombo
66 E-5 Gomel'
194 E-4 Gomes *mt*
54 G-8 Gometz-la-Ville
54 G-8 Gometz-le-Châtel
178 D-1 Gómez Palacio
188 D-1 Gomez Rendón
54 B-2 Gommecourt
209 J-2 Gomumu *isl.*
133 M-2 Gomusan
211 L-7 Gona
126 C-2 Gonābād
181 J-6 Gonaïves
124 E-1 Gonam *riv.*
181 H-6 Gonâve *isl.*
181 H-6 Gonâve *gulf*
73 M-3 Gonbad-e Kāvus
126 E-6 Gonbadeh
195 H-8 Gonçalo *riv.*
142 B-1 Gonda
138 G-8 Gondal
93 M-8 Gonder *site*
91 K-4 Gondey
140 B-8 Gondia
59 H-2 Gondiswill
59 J-9 Gondo
64 G-6 Gönen
55 K-4 Gonesse
131 J-8 Gongdahe *riv.*
134 B-4 Gonggashan *mt*
129 P-8 Gongge
127 P-4 Gonggeershan (Kungur) *mt*
131 K-6 Gonghe
133 M-6 Gongju
129 M-2 Gonglong
90 D-3 Gongola *riv.*
90 E-5 Gongola *reg.*
219 J-7 Gongolgon
143 N-2 Gongshan
129 M-4 Gongshiya
133 H-2 Gongyefu
199 K-6 Goñi
137 L-2 Gonoura
58 A-2 Gonsans
63 J-5 Gonzaga (Italy)
148 B-5 Gonzaga (Philippines)
196 A-6 Gonzales *riv.*
178 G-3 Gonzáles (Mexico)
227 M-3 Gonzales (Pôle Sud)
175 N-6 Gonzales (USA)
200 B-9 González Chaves
188 D-5 González Suárez
188 E-2 Gonzanamá
165 N-3 Goobies
104 C-9 Good Hope *cap.*
192 B-4 Good Hope
211 M-8 Goodenough *bay*
211 M-7 Goodenough *isl.*
104 C-5 Goodhouse
166 F-7 Gooding
168 F-8 Goodland
158 D-5 Goodnews *bay*
158 D-5 Goodnews
158 E-5 Goodnews *riv.*
219 J-7 Goodooga
159 L-9 Goodpaster *riv.*
52 C-3 Goodrich
163 K-5 Goodsoil
162 G-3 Goodwin
56 F-1 Gooi ('t) *reg.*
56 F-1 Gooimeer *lake*
221 H-2 Goolgowi
214 A-3 Goomadeer *riv.*
216 E-7 Goomalling
219 H-7 Goombalie
219 M-6 Goombungee
219 M-5 Goomeri
219 L-6 Goondiwindi
217 H-5 Goongarrie
219 K-1 Goonyella
57 M-2 Goor
162 A-3 Goose *isl.*
166 F-4 Goose *lake*
165 J-1 Goose *riv.*
140 F-6 Gooty
142 D-2 Gopālganj
142 B-3 Gopat *riv.*
141 J-5 Gopichettipālaiyam
51 H-9 Göppingen
122 D-2 Gor'ačegorsk
72 G-3 Goradiz
149 P-1 Goraitji *islds*
138 G-9 Gorakhnath *mt*
142 C-1 Gorakhpur
124 B-4 Gorbica
124 G-4 Gorbyl' *riv.*
191 J-1 Gorda (Chile) *pte*
180 C-4 Gorda (Cuba) *pte*
178 B-4 Gorda (Mexico) *pte*
166 F-1 Gorda (USA) *pte*
171 J-9 Gordensville
64 G-6 Gördes
59 M-9 Gordevio
91 M-4 Gordil
59 N-9 Gordola
220 G-9 Gordon *riv.*
201 N-5 Gordon *isl.*
161 L-7 Gordon (Canada) *lake*
163 K-3 Gordon (Canada) *lake*
159 P-7 Gordon (USA)
168 F-5 Gordon (USA)
170 B-3 Gordon (USA)
213 M-5 Gordon Downs
215 J-6 Gordonvale
59 N-9 Gorduno
158 F-9 Gore *pte*
91 H-5 Goré
95 H-3 Gore
209 N-3 Goreda
65 K-6 Göreme *site*
122 F-2 Gorevoje
126 A-7 Gorg
73 L-3 Gorgān
73 M-2 Gorgān *riv.*
63 N-1 Gorgo al Monticano
86 F-5 Gorgol *reg.*
86 E-5 Gorgol *riv.*
86 E-5 Gorgol el Abiod *riv.*
86 E-5 Gorgol el Akhdar *riv.*
186 B-7 Gorgona (Colombia) *isl.*
61 L-4 Gorgona (Italy) *isl.*
62 E-3 Gorgonzola
93 M-8 Gorgora
72 D-2 Gori
56 E-5 Gorinchem
72 F-3 Goris
61 N-2 Gorizia
66 E-4 Gorki (SSSR)
67 K-1 Gorky
66 A-8 Gorlice
51 L-7 Görlitz
67 J-7 Gorlovka
64 E-3 Gorna Orjahovica
121 M-5 Gorn'ak
62 A-1 Gornergrat *mt*
62 F-1 Gorno
121 P-5 Gorno-Altajsk
122 B-5 Gorno Altayskaya *reg.*
127 M-4 Gorno Badachsanskaja
123 M-1 Gorno-Cujskij
66 G-9 Gornostajevka
125 N-5 Gornozavodsk
67 N-3 Gornyj
63 M-5 Goro
91 M-4 Goro *riv.*
66 C-7 Gorochov
67 J-1 Gorochovec
125 H-2 Gorod-Makit *mt*
67 J-1 Gorodec
67 F-7 Gorodišče (SSSR)
67 L-3 Gorodišče (SSSR)
66 D-7 Gorodnica
68 G-7 Gorodok (SSSR)
66 D-8 Gorodok (SSSR)
66 B-8 Gorodok (SSSR)
66 D-3 Gorodok (SSSR)
211 J-5 Goroka
88 G-6 Gorom-Gorom
209 L-3 Gorong *isl.*
107 J-3 Gorongosa *na.p.*
107 J-3 Gorongosa *mt*
149 P-4 Gorontalo
89 J-7 Goroubi *riv.*
88 G-6 Gorouol *riv.*
62 E-6 Gorreto
62 B-6 Gorrino
57 K-2 Gorssel
57 J-1 Gortel
125 J-3 Gor'un *riv.*
66 D-6 Goryn *riv.*
62 B-6 Gorzegno
51 L-6 Gorzów Wielkopolski
142 E-1 Gosainthan *mt*
133 M-5 Gosan
66 D-7 Gošča
211 N-8 Goschen *strt.*
59 L-6 Göschenen
59 L-6 Göschenental *val.*
59 L-6 Göscheneralpsee *lake*
133 M-5 Goseong
221 L-2 Gosford
59 J-1 Gösgen
170 E-7 Goshen
51 J-6 Goslar
52 G-8 Gosport
86 F-2 Gossas
59 M-1 Gossau
214 A-8 Gosse *riv.*
88 F-5 Gossi
94 A-3 Gossinga
64 C-5 Gostivar
66 A-6 Gostynin
136 D-6 Gosyogawara
97 J-1 Gota
51 K-2 Götaälv *riv.*
51 K-2 Göteborg
51 K-2 Göteborg och bohus *reg.*
90 E-6 Gotel *mt*
51 J-7 Gotha
89 H-7 Gothèye
51 M-3 Gotland *reg.*
137 M-1 Gotō *islds*
49 L-6 Gotska Sandön *isl.*
162 C-6 Gott *mt*
62 F-7 Gottero *mt*
51 J-6 Göttingen
62 G-3 Gottolengo
172 A-3 Gottshalls
51 M-8 Gottwaldow
137 K-3 Gōtu
97 H-3 Gouban *reg.*
133 J-3 Goubangzi
56 D-3 Gouda
56 D-4 Gouderak
198 C-7 Goudge
53 M-7 Goudhurst
86 G-5 Goudiri
90 E-1 Goudoumaria
56 E-4 Goudriaan
56 B-5 Goudswaard
164 D-6 Gouin *lake*
86 G-6 Gouina
90 B-1 Goulbin Kaba *val.*
214 A-2 Goulburn *islds*
221 K-3 Goulburn
220 G-4 Goulburn *riv.*
172 D-1 Gouldsboro
78 A-6 Goulimime
78 E-4 Goulmima
86 G-9 Goumbou
64 D-5 Goumenitsa
58 C-6 Goumoëns la Ville
58 D-1 Goumois
91 M-5 Gounda *riv.*
88 F-3 Goundam
91 J-4 Goundi
91 H-4 Gounou-Gaya
54 C-5 Goupillières
79 J-2 Gouraya
89 H-4 Gourcy
60 G-2 Gourdon
90 D-1 Gouré
104 E-9 Gourits *riv.*
88 F-5 Gourma *reg.*
88 F-5 Gourma-Rharous
50 E-7 Gournay-en-Bray
55 L-6 Gournay-sur-Marne
54 A-7 Goussainville
55 C-5 Goussonville
55 M-6 Gouvernes
164 D-9 Gouverneur
55 J-1 Gouvieux
187 N-1 Gouyave
54 E-2 Gouzangrez
168 F-8 Gove
163 H-9 Govenlock
180 F-2 Governor's Harbour
66 C-9 Goverta *mt*
130 C-4 Govi Altay *reg.*
130 E-7 Govi Altayn *mt*
132 A-1 Govi-Ugtaal
62 B-5 Govone
219 H-3 Gowan *mt*
126 C-7 Gowd-e Zereh *lake*
133 M-4 Goweon
164 A-7 Gowganda
127 H-7 Gowmal Rowd *riv.*
199 H-2 Goya
214 B-3 Goyder *riv.*
165 K-2 Goyette *lake*
189 J-4 Goyllarisquisga
65 H-5 Göynük
91 M-2 Goz Beïda
91 M-3 Goz Sassoulko *mt*
61 N-9 Gozo
137 K-5 Gozyō
62 C-2 Gozzano
104 G-8 Graaff Reinet
57 M-3 Graafschap *reg.*
56 A-9 Graauw
87 P-8 Grabo
59 H-9 Grächen
184 E-3 Gracias
185 H-3 Gracias a Dios *reg.*
185 J-3 Gracias a Dios *cap.*
78 D-8 Graciosa *isl.*
70 A-1 Gračovka
194 C-4 Gradaús *mt*
194 C-4 Gradaús
207 N-7 Gradjagan *bay*
207 N-7 Gradjagan
175 K-1 Grady
172 D-6 Gradyville
48 B-1 Grafarnes
215 J-6 Grafton *cap.*
201 N-3 Grafton *islds*
215 J-6 Grafton *strt.*
219 M-7 Grafton (Australia)
171 H-8 Grafton (USA)
169 J-1 Grafton (USA)
160 B-9 Graham *isl.*
162 E-1 Graham *riv.*
153 K-2 Graham *strt.*
174 F-2 Graham *mt*
170 C-1 Graham (Canada)
175 M-3 Graham (USA)
112 E-1 Graham Bell *isl.*
105 H-9 Grahamstown
79 N-4 Graïba
53 M-5 Grain
87 N-6 Grain Coast *reg.*
189 H-7 Grajaú
189 H-7 Grajaú *riv.*
66 B-5 Grajewo
189 J-3 Gramadal *pte*
199 M-3 Gramado Xavier
186 F-4 Gramalote
198 E-1 Gramilla
58 D-8 Grammont
122 C-3 Gramoteino
50 D-2 Grampian *mt*
201 J-4 Gran Altiplanicie Central *plat.*
200 C-6 Gran Bajo del Gualicho *bay*
78 B-9 Gran Canaria *isl.*
182 D-5 Gran Chaco *reg.*
192 E-4 Gran Dahomeij
189 J-6 Gran Pajonal *mt*
191 K-3 Gran Pampa Pelada *reg.*
191 K-3 Gran Pampa Salada *reg.*
192 D-4 Gran Rio *riv.*
200 B-5 Gran Salitral
61 N-4 Gran Sasso d'Italia *mt*
78 C-9 Gran Tarajal
62 A-1 Gran Tournalin *mt*
184 G-5 Granada
60 C-7 Granada
78 B-9 Granadilla de Abona
63 K-6 Granarolo dell'Emilia
192 E-4 Granbori
175 M-3 Granbury
162 E-7 Granby *riv.*
164 E-8 Granby (Canada)
168 D-7 Granby (USA)
171 P-3 Grand *lake*
170 E-5 Grand *riv.*
165 N-4 Grand Bank
87 N-7 Grand Bassa *reg.*
89 P-3 Grand Bassam
87 P-9 Grand Bérébi
181 N-3 Grand-Bourg
55 P-9 Grand-Bréau
50 B-4 Grand Canal *cal.*
167 L-7 Grand Canyon *na.p.*
167 L-6 Grand Canyon *val.*
165 H-5 Grand Cascapedia
180 D-6 Grand Cayman *rf*
87 P-8 Grand Cess
87 P-8 Grand Cess *riv.*
214 G-1 Grand Chenal du N.E. *strt.*
79 H-6 Grand Erg Occidental *dés*
79 M-6 Grand Erg Oriental *dés*
165 H-6 Grand Falls
165 M-3 Grand Falls
162 E-7 Grand Forks
169 J-2 Grand Forks
87 N-8 Grand Gedeh *reg.*
164 G-3 Grand-Germain *lake*
170 E-5 Grand Haven
169 H-7 Grand Island
170 E-3 Grand Island (USA) *isl.*
176 E-6 Grand Isle *isl.*
176 E-6 Grand Isle
201 L-8 Grand Jason *isl.*
168 B-7 Grand Junction
165 H-8 Grand Lac *lake*
167 H-7 Grand Lac Salé *dés*
89 P-2 Grand Lahou
165 H-7 Grand Lake *lake*
171 P-2 Grand Lake *lake*
176 D-6 Grand Lake *lake*
165 H-8 Grand Manan *isl.*
170 E-3 Grand Marais
170 C-2 Grand Marais
165 L-2 Grand Mecatina *isl.*
164 E-7 Grand'Mère
58 E-8 Grand Muyeran *mt*
192 F-4 Grand Pont
89 N-7 Grand-Popo
175 N-3 Grand Prairie
163 J-3 Grand Rapids *riv.*
163 N-7 Grand Rapids
170 E-6 Grand Rapids
170 A-2 Grand Rapids
215 L-2 Grand récif de Cook
168 B-3 Grand Teton *na.p.*
181 K-4 Grand Turk
163 N-8 Grand View
192 D-4 Grandam
54 B-8 Grandchamp
58 D-4 Grandcour
201 J-5 Grande *lake*
197 J-6 Grande *bay*
63 M-8 Grande *hill*
87 J-2 Grande *lag.*
190 G-5 Grande *riv.*
191 N-1 Grande *pte*
190 C-7 Grande *mt*
197 K-6 Grande (Brazil) *isl.*
109 N-9 Grande-Baie
220 B-5 Grande Baie Australienne
181 H-7 Grande Cayemite *isl.*
58 C-3 Grande Combe (La)
192 G-8 Grande de Gurupá *isl.*
192 A-9 Grande de Manacapuru *lake*
193 P-9 Grande de Santa Isabel *isl.*
186 E-2 Grande de Santa Marta *lake*
192 D-8 Grande do Curuai *lake*
193 P-9 Grande do Paulino *isl.*
192 E-8 Grande do Tapará *isl.*
165 K-5 Grande-Entrée
162 F-3 Grande Prairie
164 B-2 Grande Rivière *riv.*
165 J-5 Grande-Rivière
164 B-1 Grande rivière de la Baleine *riv.*
166 D-6 Grande Ronde *riv.*
181 N-2 Grande-Terre *isl.*
55 K-1 Grandes Ecuries
175 K-4 Grandfalls
161 K-6 Grandin *lake*
122 F-4 Grandioznyj *mt*
58 C-5 Grandson
58 F-1 Grandval
58 E-6 Grandvillard
55 P-9 Grandvillé
58 C-8 Grange *mt*
54 D-7 Grange-du-Bois (La)
168 B-5 Granger
58 F-8 Granges
58 D-5 Granges
58 A-5 Granges Sainte-Marie
49 K-4 Grängesberg
166 D-7 Grangeville
59 J-1 Gränichen
160 C-2 Granite *mt*
168 B-2 Granite (USA) *mt*
166 G-4 Granite (USA) *mt*
170 C-9 Granite City
169 J-4 Granite Falls
213 N-7 Granites (The)
71 P-1 Granitogorsk
120 F-9 Granitogorsk
195 K-1 Granja
181 K-6 Granja *pte*
168 F-7 Grant
170 A-7 Grant City
50 E-5 Grantham
174 G-1 Grants
166 E-2 Grants Pass
167 H-8 Grantsville
163 N-4 Granville *riv.*
160 E-2 Granville
50 D-8 Granville
197 L-2 Grão Mogol
63 L-1 Grappa *mt*
58 B-3 Gras (Les)
57 J-9 Grashoek
105 L-3 Graskop
49 K-6 Gräsö *isl.*
159 M-8 Grass *riv.*
163 N-6 Grass River *na.p.*
167 H-3 Grass Valley
61 K-3 Grasse
48 E-4 Gråtånes
165 P-2 Grates *pte*
57 N-6 Grathem
195 P-5 Gravatá
57 H-5 Grave
60 F-1 Grave *pte*
60 E-1 Grave *pte*
163 K-9 Gravelbourg
62 C-1 Gravellona Toce
56 C-5 Gravendeel ('s)
164 B-9 Gravenhurst
56 E-6 Gravenmoer ('s)
56 C-9 Gravenwezel ('s)
56 A-3 Gravenzande
53 L-5 Gravesend
50 E-6 Gravesend
181 H-7 Gravois *pte*
170 F-4 Grayling
53 L-5 Grays
168 C-7 Grays *mt*
162 A-8 Grays Harbor *gulf*
50 E-6 Grays Thurrock
61 P-1 Graz
220 G-8 Great *lake*
180 F-1 Great Abaco
156 G-4 Great Bahama *isl.*
180 E-1 Great Bahama *isl.*
53 L-3 Great Bardfield
223 K-3 Great Barrier *isl.*
215 J-6 Great Barrier Reef *rf*
53 M-4 Great Barrow
156 C-2 Great Basin *pool*
172 G-8 Great Bay *bay*
161 J-4 Great Bear *riv.*
161 K-4 Great Bear lake *lake*
168 G-9 Great Bend
53 N-2 Great Blakenham
50 E-3 Great Britain *reg.*
162 B-6 Great Central
53 M-7 Great Chart
53 L-2 Great Chesterford
53 N-3 Great Clacton
147 N-2 Great Discovery (Daxianjiao) *rf*
53 L-3 Great Dunmow
53 L-3 Great Easton
172 F-8 Great Egg *riv.* Harbour
223 J-1 Great Exhibition *bay*
168 B-1 Great Falls
53 N-2 Great Finborough
180 F-3 Great Guana Cay *rf*
165 N-3 Great Gull *lake*
156 G-4 Great Inagua *isl.*
181 H-5 Great Inagua *isl.*
139 H-4 Great Indian *dés*
165 M-3 Great Lake *lake*
52 E-2 Great Malvern
173 H-3 Great Neck
53 J-3 Great Offley
173 L-2 Great Peconic Bay *bay*
180 F-7 Great Pedro Bluff *cap.*
168 D-2 Great Porcupine *riv.*
100 F-8 Great Ruaha *riv.*
180 E-1 Great Sale Cay *isl.*
156 C-2 Great Salt Lake *lake*
167 H-8 Great Salt Lake *lake*
173 P-1 Great Salt Pond *cap.*
213 H-7 Great Sandy Desert *dés*
52 F-5 Great Shefford
161 K-8 Great Slave Lake *lake*
177 H-2 Great Smoky Mounts *na.p.*
173 K-3 Great South Bay *bay*
173 K-3 Great South Beach *isth.*
53 M-5 Great Wakering
131 H-6 Great Wall *site*
53 L-4 Great Waltham
53 J-1 Great Weldon
52 D-1 Great Witley
50 E-5 Great Yarmouth
89 N-6 Greater Accra *bay*
156 G-5 Greater Antilles *islds*
53 H-7 Greatham
53 N-7 Greatstone on Sea
66 F-7 Grebenka
60 C-5 Gredos
47 F-6 Greece *state*
168 D-7 Greeley
153 K-1 Greely *fj.*
170 D-4 Green *bay*
171 L-5 Green *mt*
221 K-5 Green *cap.*
170 D-4 Green Bay
180 F-3 Green Cay *rf*
177 K-6 Green Cove Springs
172 E-9 Green Creek
216 D-6 Green Head *pte*
163 K-5 Green Lake
172 D-5 Green Lane
164 F-9 Green Montains *mt*
168 A-7 Green R. *riv.*
168 A-7 Green River
172 A-3 Greenbrier
170 E-8 Greencastle
177 J-1 Greeneville
171 M-5 Greenfield (USA)
170 A-9 Greenfield (USA)
173 J-2 Greenfield Hill
153 S-2 Greenland *reg.*
153 S-2 Greenland *sea*
46 C-2 Greenland *sea*
226 B-6 Greenland *sea*
50 D-2 Greenock
171 M-6 Greenport
176 G-4 Greensboro (USA)
177 L-1 Greensboro (USA)
171 H-7 Greensburg (USA)
168 G-9 Greensburg (USA)
170 E-8 Greensburg (USA)
172 D-1 Greentown
215 H-8 Greenvale
187 N-1 Greenville (Grenada)
87 P-7 Greenville (Liberia)
164 G-7 Greenville (USA)
171 H-6 Greenville (USA)
170 F-8 Greenville (USA)
170 E-5 Greenville (USA)
170 C-9 Greenville (USA)
177 M-1 Greenville (USA)
177 J-2 Greenville (USA)
176 G-4 Greenville (USA)
175 N-3 Greenville (USA)
176 E-3 Greenville (USA)
173 J-2 Greenwich
53 K-5 Greenwich (UK)

172 D-8 Greenwich (USA)
214 A-9 Greenwood
176 E-3 Greenwood (USA)
176 C-2 Greenwood (USA)
177 K-3 Greenwood (USA)
172 G-1 Greenwood Lake
54 D-9 Greffiers
188 G-8 Gregorio *riv.*
213 L-7 Gregory *lake*
218 D-6 Gregory *lake*
214 G-8 Gregory *mt*
216 G-2 Gregory *lake*
214 D-7 Gregory Downs
55 L-8 Gregy-sur-Yerre
59 M-1 Greifensee
59 M-1 Greifensee *lake*
51 K-5 Greifswald
158 D-7 Greig *cap.*
59 N-6 Greina *pass*
52 C-7 Greinton
65 L-9 Greko *cap.*
68 C-3 Gremicha
69 M-6 Gremyachinsk
51 J-3 Grená
157 H-5 Grenada *state*
156 H-5 Grenada *isl.*
176 E-3 Grenada
187 N-1 Grenade *isl.*
187 N-1 Grenadines *islds*
58 F-2 Grenchen
221 J-2 Grenfell
59 J-8 Grengiols
172 E-7 Grenloch
61 J-2 Grenoble
214 G-3 Grenville *cap.*
181 N-9 Grenville
59 L-3 Greppen
207 M-6 Gresik
54 F-4 Grésillons (Les)
54 B-6 Gressey
62 A-1 Gressoney la Trinité
62 A-2 Gressoney St Jean
55 M-4 Gressy
55 N-7 Gretz-Armainvilliers
64 C-6 Grevená
57 M-7 Grevenbicht
201 P-6 Grevy *isl.*
214 C-3 Grey *cap.*
218 F-6 Grey *mt*
165 M-3 Grey *lake*
160 F-3 Grey Hunter *mt*
168 C-3 Greybull *riv.*
168 C-3 Greybull
222 F-7 Greymouth
216 C-2 Grey's plains *pl.*
105 L-6 Greytown
63 J-3 Grezzana
67 K-5 Gribanovskij
162 B-2 Gribbell *isl.*
91 K-5 Gribingui *riv.*
91 K-6 Gribingui *reg.*
57 J-8 Griendtsveen
59 K-7 Gries *pass*
177 H-3 Griffin
221 H-3 Griffith
172 F-4 Griggstown
62 E-1 Grigna *mt*
62 C-2 Grignasco
63 L-1 Grigno
54 E-6 Grignon
179 K-7 Grijalva *riv.*
146 E-6 Grik
91 L-7 Grimari
58 G-9 Grimentz
58 G-6 Grimmialp
54 B-1 Grimonval
50 E-4 Grimsby
59 K-6 Grimsel *pass*
59 K-6 Grimsel *lake*
48 A-3 Grimsey *isl.*
162 G-3 Grimshaw
48 B-3 Grimsstadir
51 J-2 Grimstad
172 C-4 Grimville
48 B-1 Grindavik
59 J-6 Grindelwald
170 B-6 Grinnell
105 K-7 Griqualand East *reg.*
104 F-5 Griqualand West *reg.*
104 F-5 Griquatown
63 L-3 Grisignano di Zocco
60 G-3 Grisolles
54 F-2 Grisy-les-Plâtres
55 M-8 Grisy-Suisnes
161 K-5 Grizzly Bear *mt*
48 B-4 Grjótnes
165 M-1 Groais *isl.*
105 K-3 Groblersdal
104 F-5 Groblershoop
58 F-7 Grodei
66 B-5 Grodno
76 D-8 Groeie Hoop *cap.*
56 F-2 Groenekan
56 C-3 Groenendijk
57 K-6 Groeningen
57 M-3 Groenlo

104 F-5 Groenwater *riv.*
175 N-4 Groesbeck (USA)
57 J-5 Groesbeek (Netherlands)
57 K-4 Groessen
50 B-8 Groix *isl.*
58 E-4 Grolley
62 G-1 Gromo
57 P-2 Gronau
48 G-3 Grong
51 M-3 Grönhögen
51 H-5 Groningen (Netherlands)
192 D-3 Groningen (Suriname)
59 P-8 Grono
57 M-9 Gronsveld
53 L-7 Groombridge
104 G-8 Groot *riv.*
56 D-4 Groot Ammers
104 D-8 Groot-Berg *riv.*
57 N-8 Groot Genhout
104 D-4 Groot Karasberge *mt*
105 J-8 Groot-Kei *riv.*
57 J-5 Groot Linden
104 G-8 Groot-Vis *riv.*
104 E-6 Groot Vjoer *lake*
214 C-4 Groote Eylandt *isl.*
57 K-6 Groote Horst
102 E-7 Grootfontein
102 E-8 Grootlaagte *riv.*
62 D-4 Gropello Cairoli
195 L-3 Gros *lake*
161 L-8 Gros *cap.*
161 N-6 Gros *lake*
165 L-3 Gros Morne *mt*
168 B-4 Gros Ventre *mt*
214 G-5 Grosbie *riv.*
55 J-4 Groslay
52 C-3 Grosmont
54 C-7 Grosrouvre
195 M-2 Grossa *pte*
197 K-6 Grossa de Marambaia *pte*
59 H-2 Grossdietwil
61 M-4 Grosseto
125 M-4 Grossevici
61 M-1 Grossglockner *mt*
59 J-4 Grossteil
58 G-7 Grosstrubel *mt*
59 J-2 Grosswangen
219 K-1 Grosvenor Downs
173 N-1 Groton
49 H-2 Grotti
78 D-3 Grou *riv.*
89 M-3 Groumania
213 P-2 Grove Hill
175 P-5 Groveton
72 E-1 Groznyj
57 K-8 Grubbenvorst
58 F-6 Grubenwald
51 M-5 Grudziadz
191 K-1 Gruesa *pte*
173 H-1 Grugers
62 A-4 Grugliasco
57 L-7 Gruitrode
104 C-4 Grünau
53 N-2 Grundisburgh
59 M-1 Grüningen
59 H-5 Grütschalp
58 E-6 Gruyère *lake*
58 E-6 Gruyères
72 C-3 Gruzinskaja *rép*
67 J-4 Gryazi
51 L-5 Gryfice
170 A-2 Grygla
58 E-8 Gryon
59 H-7 Gspaltenhorn *mt*
58 F-7 Gstaadt
58 F-7 Gsteig
146 E-6 Gua Musang
185 J-7 Guabito
184 C-3 Guacalate *riv.*
186 D-8 Guacamaya
180 F-5 Guacanayabo *gulf*
191 N-4 Guachipas
191 N-5 Guachipas *riv.*
186 G-6 Guachiria *riv.*
196 E-8 Guacu *riv.*
60 D-5 Guadalajara (Spain)
178 D-4 Guadalajara (Mexico)
60 C-7 Guadalquivir *riv.*
175 N-6 Guadalupe *riv.*
195 H-3 Guadalupe (Brazil)
60 C-5 Guadalupe (Spain) *mt*
188 G-2 Guadalupe (Peru)
175 H-3 Guadalupe (USA) *mt*
175 H-4 Guadalupe Bravos
178 C-1 Guadalupe Victoria
174 G-7 Guadalupe y Calvo
60 D-5 Guadarrama *mt*
181 P-2 Guadeloupe *isl.*
60 A-6 Guadiana *riv.*
200 F-1 Guafo *isl.*
188 D-4 Guagramano
148 D-6 Guagua
199 N-3 Guaíba

188 B-2 Guaillabamba *riv.*
184 F-3 Guaimaca
180 F-5 Guáimaro
196 F-5 Guaimbé
184 G-2 Guaimoreto *lag.*
187 H-8 Guainia *riv.*
187 H-8 Guainía *reg.*
54 A-5 Guainville
187 M-6 Guaiquinaima *mt*
196 B-8 Guaira *reg.*
196 C-7 Guaira
200 F-2 Guaitecas *islds*
192 F-8 Guajará *riv.*
190 C-4 Guajara-Mirim
190 A-3 Guajarraã
156 G-5 Guajira *pen.*
186 F-1 Guajira *pen.*
191 L-1 Gualaguala *pte*
129 N-2 Gualamandatashan *mt*
184 D-2 Gualán
199 H-5 Gualeguay
199 H-5 Gualeguay *riv.*
199 H-5 Gualeguaychú
200 E-6 Gualicho *bay*
191 H-2 Guallatiri *vol.*
63 H-5 Gualtieri
119 K-5 Guam *isl.*
193 K-8 Guama
193 J-8 Guama *riv.*
188 E-2 Guamani *mt*
188 B-7 Guamareyes
200 G-1 Guamblin *isl.*
194 E-3 Guameleira
194 B-6 Guameleira *riv.*
200 A-8 Guamimi
186 D-7 Guamo
188 C-2 Guamote
187 L-5 Guampi *mt*
184 G-3 Guampú *riv.*
174 F-8 Guamúchil
188 A-4 Guamués *riv.*
198 B-4 Guana *mt*
180 C-4 Guanabacoa
189 J-9 Guanabara
198 C-5 Guanacache *lag.*
184 G-6 Guanacaste *reg.*
201 H-5 Guanaco *bay*
180 A-5 Guanahacabibes *gulf*
180 A-9 Guanaja
180 B-4 Guanajay
178 E-4 Guanajuato
195 H-9 Guanambi
186 G-6 Guanapalo *riv.*
188 B-4 Guanapanaca *riv.*
189 H-2 Guañape *islds*
187 H-3 Guanare
187 H-4 Guanare *riv.*
187 H-3 Guanarito
131 L-8 Guanbao
198 C-2 Guanchin *riv.*
198 C-3 Guandacol
133 L-1 Guanditun
197 M-4 Guandu *riv.*
180 B-4 Guane
135 L-5 Guanfeng
134 D-3 Guangan
135 J-8 Guangdong *reg.*
135 H-9 Guanghai
131 P-8 Guanghan
131 L-8 Guanghe
134 G-2 Guanghua
135 K-4 Guangji
132 E-5 Guangling
133 J-5 Guangludao *isl.*
134 C-8 Guangnan
134 F-8 Guangxi Zhuangzu Zizhiqu *reg.*
131 N-9 Guangyuan
197 L-3 Guanhães
187 K-5 Guaniamo *riv.*
187 N-3 Guanipa *riv.*
131 N-8 Guankou
134 E-3 Guanmianshan *mt*
133 K-4 Guanshui
187 L-2 Guanta
180 G-6 Guantánamo
180 G-6 Guantanamo *bay*
132 F-7 Guantao
131 P-8 Guanxian
134 G-7 Guanyang
135 N-5 Guaotou
197 J-5 Guapé
186 B-8 Guapi *riv.*
185 H-7 Guápiles
196 G-2 Guapó
190 D-5 Guaporé *riv.*
199 M-2 Guaporé
187 K-7 Guapuchi *riv.*
190 G-2 Guaqui
195 P-3 Guarabira
188 F-6 Guaracha *riv.*
195 K-1 Guaraciaba do Norte
188 C-2 Guaranda
197 H-5 Guaranésia
196 D-7 Guarani (Brazil)

197 L-5 Guarani (Brazil)
196 D-7 Guaraniacu
187 P-5 Guaranpin *riv.*
197 M-5 Guarapari
187 M-3 Guarapiche *riv.*
196 E-8 Guarapuava
196 F-5 Guararapes
197 J-6 Guaratinguetá
196 G-8 Guaratuba
196 G-8 Guaratuba *bay*
60 B-4 Guarda
197 H-2 Guarda-Mor
196 D-6 Guarei *riv.*
196 E-7 Guaretá
190 B-8 Guariba *riv.*
187 K-3 Guárico *reg.*
187 J-3 Guárico *lake*
186 F-7 Guarrojo *riv.*
187 P-3 Guarucara
197 H-7 Guarujá
197 H-6 Guarulhos
187 J-7 Guasacavi *riv.*
198 D-4 Guasapampa *mt*
186 F-2 Guasare *riv.*
174 F-8 Guasave
186 G-5 Guasdualito
187 N-4 Guasipati
63 H-5 Guastalla
157 E-5 Guatemala *state*
184 D-3 Guatemala
157 E-5 Guatemala City
186 E-7 Guatiquía *riv.*
187 K-2 Guatire
187 M-7 Guatisimiña
200 B-7 Guatraché
187 H-7 Guaviare *riv.*
197 H-5 Guaxupé
180 F-5 Guayabal
186 D-8 Guayabero *riv.*
187 J-7 Guayapa *riv.*
199 H-3 Guayquiraró (Argentina)
199 J-6 Guaycurú (Uruguay)
174 D-6 Guaymas
199 H-3 Guayquiraró *riv.*
192 G-4 Guisanbourg
187 N-2 Güiria
186 E-7 Guayuriba *riv.*
184 D-3 Guazacapán
130 G-4 Guazhoukou
103 K-1 Guba
69 K-1 Gubakha
148 E-3 Gubat
95 H-3 Gubba *riv.*
51 L-6 Guben
125 K-7 Guberovo
90 F-2 Gubio
67 H-5 Gubkin
127 M-4 Gudara
72 B-2 Gudaut
95 J-2 Guder *riv.*
72 E-1 Gudermes
140 F-8 Gudivāda
141 H-6 Gudiyāttam
65 J-5 Güdül
49 J-1 Gudvangen
134 G-8 Gueijiang *riv.*
186 E-8 Güejar *riv.*
87 L-6 Guékédou
91 H-3 Guélengdeng
86 E-4 Guéllouâr *riv.*
79 M-2 Guelma
171 H-5 Guelph
188 B-5 Güeppi
86 A-2 Guera *mt*
55 P-6 Guérard
78 F-3 Guercif
187 L-3 Guere *riv.*
92 A-7 Guéréda
60 G-1 Guéret
55 M-6 Guermantes
54 B-3 Guernes
60 E-3 Guernica y Luno
168 D-5 Guernsey
50 C-7 Guernsey *isl.*
79 K-5 Guerrara
178 E-6 Guerrero *reg.*
131 J-3 Guertuangeer
54 C-4 Guerville
88 B-4 Guettâra *well*
87 N-9 Guétuzon
89 N-1 Guéyo
59 P-3 Gufelstock *mt*
59 N-6 Güferhorn *mt*
73 L-5 Gügerd
58 F-5 Guggisberg
95 J-5 Gughe *mt*

84 B-7 Güh Küh *mt*
78 B-9 Guía de Gran Canaria
197 H-4 Guia Lopes
196 B-5 Guia Lopes da Láguna
182 D-2 Guiana Highlands *plat.*
156 H-6 Guiana Highlands *plat.*
135 L-3 Guichi
199 J-5 Guichón
91 H-4 Guidari
131 K-7 Guide
90 G-4 Guider
90 D-1 Guidiguir
86 F-5 Guidimaka *reg.*
90 D-1 Guidimouni
134 E-6 Guiding
63 H-3 Guidizzolo
86 E-3 Guier *lake*
63 J-7 Guiglia
87 N-8 Guiglo
55 N-9 Guignes
135 K-1 Guile *riv.*
184 D-3 Guija *lake*
107 N-2 Guija
148 G-5 Guimaras *islds*
193 M-8 Guimarães (Brazil)
60 B-3 Guimaraes (Spain)
148 G-5 Guimaras *islds*
180 F-4 Guinchos Cay *rf*
149 H-3 Guindulman
76 C-4 Guinea *gulf*
77 A-3 Guinea *state*
90 A-8 Guinea *gulf*
77 A-3 Guinea Bissau *state*
180 C-4 Güines
50 C-8 Guingamp
86 F-2 Guinguinéo
184 F-7 Guiones *pte*
54 C-9 Guiperreux
134 G-9 Guiping
78 F-5 Guir *riv.*
78 F-5 Guir *dés*
196 D-1 Guiratinga
187 N-2 Güiria
54 D-2 Guiry-en-Vexin
192 G-4 Guisanbourg
61 K-7 Guispini
87 H-8 Guissoumalé
54 C-3 Guitrancourt
89 P-2 Guitri
148 G-2 Guiuan
134 F-9 Guixian
135 H-7 Guiyang (China)
134 D-6 Guiyang (China)
188 A-3 Güiza *riv.*
134 D-6 Guizhou *reg.*
133 L-4 Gujang
127 L-8 Gūjar Khān
138 G-8 Gujarat *reg.*
127 L-9 Gujrānwāla
127 L-8 Gujrat
67 K-7 Gukovo
121 H-7 Gul'Sad
124 C-3 Gul'a
67 H-8 Gul'ajpole
191 P-4 Gulampaja *mt*
131 J-8 Gulang
221 J-1 Gulargambone
140 E-5 Gulbarga
66 C-2 Gulbene
176 F-6 Gulfport
221 K-1 Gulgong
134 D-5 Gulin
126 F-8 Gulistān (Pakistan)
127 L-1 Gulistan (SSSR)
160 C-1 Gulkana
67 L-9 Gul'keviči
162 G-6 Gull *lake*
163 J-8 Gull Lake
93 H-8 Gulli
59 P-3 Gulmen
65 K-8 Gülnar
57 N-9 Gulpen
94 E-7 Gulu
129 K-2 Guluo
100 G-7 Gulwe
127 J-8 Gumal *riv.*
91 M-9 Gumba
69 P-8 Gumbejka *riv.*
94 D-6 Gumbiri *mt*
90 D-2 Gumel
142 D-4 Gumla
58 E-4 Gummeni
58 E-7 Gummfluh *mt*
90 A-2 Gummi
72 B-4 Gümüşhane
93 M-9 Guna *mt*

95 L-3 Gunä (Ethiopia)
139 M-7 Guna (India)
160 E-8 Gunanoot *mt*
221 J-3 Gundagai
91 M-9 Gundji
140 F-7 Gundlakamma *riv.*
64 G-7 Güney
99 J-6 Gungu
130 D-8 Günnariyn
168 C-8 Gunnison (USA)
167 J-8 Gunnison (USA)
172 A-8 Gunpowder *riv.*
133 M-7 Gunsan
127 M-4 Gunt *riv.*
140 F-5 Guntakal
140 F-8 Guntür
209 H-5 Gunungapi *isl.*
146 B-9 Gunungsitoli
206 F-5 Gunungsugih Metro
146 D-8 Gunungtua
142 C-7 Gunupur
216 E-6 Gunyidi
135 K-1 Guohe *riv.*
131 M-6 Guoluoshan *mt*
135 K-1 Guoyang
132 G-9 Gupeizhou
127 M-5 Gupis
129 N-4 Guqigu
129 N-7 Gura Gyalong *mt*
95 K-3 Gurage *mt*
123 H-4 Guran
90 B-4 Gurara *riv.*
94 B-6 Gurba *riv.*
123 J-6 Gurban-Daban *mt*
130 D-6 Gurban Subita Hudag
127 M-9 Gurdāspur
72 E-2 Gurdžaani
139 M-4 Gurgaon
91 P-1 Gurgei *mt*
194 G-5 Gurgueía *riv.*
139 H-6 Gürha
95 L-4 Guri
95 L-4 Gurie
211 J-6 Gurimatu
122 C-3 Gurjevsk
142 D-1 Gurkha
71 H-7 Gurlen
58 F-5 Gurnigelbad
94 G-4 Gurrafarda
49 H-1 Gurskøy *isl.*
58 F-4 Gurten *mt*
59 M-5 Gurtnellen
139 J-6 Guru Sikhar *mt*
106 G-5 Gurue
100 F-4 Gurumeti *riv.*
65 M-5 Gürün
193 L-8 Gurupi *riv.*
193 L-7 Gurupi *cap.*
194 E-2 Gurupi *mt*
194 D-7 Gurupi
130 E-8 Gurvan Sayhan *mt*
130 C-6 Gurvanbulag
123 P-8 Gurvandzagal
70 B-6 Gur'yev
66 D-8 Gus'atin
90 B-2 Gusau
122 B-3 Gusek *hill*
133 K-4 Guseong
66 B-4 Gusev
133 K-4 Gushan
135 K-2 Gushi
89 L-6 Gushiago
123 L-6 Gusinoje *lake*
123 L-6 Gusinoje-Ozero
123 L-6 Gusinoozersk
67 H-2 Gus'khrustal'nyy
62 G-2 Gussago
63 H-5 Gussola
181 M-1 Gustavia
160 C-6 Gustavus
51 K-5 Güstrow
122 G-4 Gutarskij *mt*
173 L-2 Gutchogue
51 H-6 Gütersloh
163 N-5 Guthrie *lake*
175 L-2 Guthrie (USA)
175 N-1 Guthrie (USA)
172 C-6 Guthriesville
135 M-6 Gutian
191 J-6 Gutiérrez
179 H-5 Gutiérrez Zamora
59 K-6 Guttanen
107 J-1 Gutu
187 J-7 Guyabero *riv.*
181 K-2 Guyama
183 E-2 Guyana *state*
54 F-7 Guyancourt

200 H-1 Guyaneco *islds*
132 C-4 Guyang
168 F-9 Guymon
160 B-3 Guyot *glac.*
219 L-8 Guyra
132 E-4 Guyuan

71 N-7 Guzar
135 K-1 Guzhen
174 G-4 Guzmán
66 A-4 Gvardejsk
65 J-1 Gvardejskoje
125 K-5 Gvas'ugi
143 K-9 Gwa (Birman)
94 E-2 Gwa (Sudan)
219 K-8 Gwabegar
138 A-3 Gwadar
138 A-3 Gwādar West *bay*
103 L-7 Gwai *riv.*
103 L-7 Gwai
91 K-9 Gwalangu
139 N-6 Gwalior
219 L-4 Gwambagwine
103 M-9 Gwanda
94 A-6 Gwane
133 M-7 Gwangju
138 A-3 Gwātar *bay*
58 G-5 Gwatt
103 M-7 Gwelo *riv.*
52 C-4 Gwent *reg.*
103 M-7 Gweru
219 L-7 Gwydir *riv.*
144 E-5 Gyaing *riv.*
112 F-2 Gydanskaya *bay*
112 F-2 Gydanskiy *pen.*
126 C-7 Gydar-i-Shah *site*
133 N-5 Gyebang-san *mt*
133 L-6 Gyeonggi *bay*
133 N-7 Gyeongju
133 M-2 Gyeongseong
133 N-2 Gyeongseong *bay*
133 M-2 Gyerim
219 N-5 Gympie
66 A-9 Gyöngyos
64 A-1 Gyor
163 P-8 Gypsumville


# H


145 K-2 Ha Dông
145 K-1 Ha Giang
146 G-2 Ha Tiên
145 K-4 Ha Tinh
56 F-5 Haaften
57 N-2 Haaksbergen
66 C-2 Haanja. Kõrgustik *mt*
224 B-5 Ha'apai *islds*
48 G-8 Haapajärvi
49 H-8 Haapamäki
66 B-1 Haapsalu
56 F-7 Haaren
57 L-1 Haarle
50 G-6 Haarlem
56 D-1 Haarlemmermeer *reg.*
57 M-3 Haarlo
56 F-6 Haarsteeg
56 E-3 Haarzuilens
57 N-9 Haasdal
222 D-7 Haast
56 D-3 Haastrecht
138 E-3 Hab *riv.*
138 E-5 Hab Nadi Chowki
132 E-3 Habaga
128 A-8 Habahe
129 K-3 Habahu *lake*
96 B-9 Habarūt
101 K-1 Habaswein
96 C-2 Habawnā *riv.*
162 G-1 Habay (Canada)
101 N-1 Habay (Somalia)
96 E-5 Habbān
72 G-9 Habbāniyah *riv.*
143 H-4 Habiganj
59 H-5 Habkern
136 A-6 Haboro
88 C-2 Habr oû Gdoûr *reg.*
174 F-3 Hachita
65 K-6 Hacibektas
218 D-7 Hack *mt*
173 H-2 Hackensack *riv.*
172 G-3 Hackensack
172 E-3 Hackettstown
83 H-9 Hadan *mt*
93 P-1 Hadan *vol.*
54 D-1 Hadancourt-le-Haut-Clocher
82 E-9 Hadāribah *cap.*
93 L-1 Hadāribah *pte*
130 B-8 Hadasan
84 D-9 Hadd *cap.*
93 M-1 Haddā'
97 H-5 Hadded *reg.*
53 K-1 Haddenham
172 E-6 Haddondfield
90 D-2 Hadejia
128 D-6 Hadekehe *riv.*
82 C-2 Hadera
51 J-4 Haderslev
83 P-8 Hadīdah *mt*
65 J-7 Hadim
82 F-6 Hadīyah
90 G-2 Hadjer el Hamis
79 J-2 Hadjout
53 M-5 Hadleigh (UK)
53 N-3 Hadleigh (UK)
53 L-6 Hadlow
133 N-7 Hadong
96 D-6 Hadramawi *mt*
96 C-7 Hadramawt *riv.*
48 D-4 Hadseløya *isl.*
199 K-4 Haedo *mt*
133 L-5 Haeju
57 N-6 Haelen
133 M-8 Haenam
124 G-8 Haerbin
133 J-3 Haertao
131 H-3 Haertenghe *riv.*
83 K-3 Hafar al Bāṭin
84 D-5 Hafit *mt*
127 L-9 Hāfizābād
143 J-4 Hāflong
48 B-1 Hafnarfjördur
73 K-9 Haft Gel
96 G-9 Hāfun *cap.*
96 G-9 Hāfun *bay*
96 G-9 Hāfun
140 G-5 Hagari *riv.*
158 D-6 Hagemeister *isl.*
158 D-5 Hagemeister *strt.*
211 H-5 Hagen *mt*
173 K-3 Hagerman
171 J-8 Hagerstown
56 F-4 Hagestein
49 K-4 Hagfors
59 K-1 Hägglingen
48 A-1 Hagi (Iceland)
137 K-3 Hagi (Japan)
52 E-1 Hagley
97 K-4 Hagoga
50 F-6 Hague
50 D-7 Hague (La) *cap.*
132 G-2 Hahéilihe *riv.*
145 K-2 Hai Duong
135 M-1 Haian
104 C-5 Haib *riv.*
124 F-7 Haibei
133 J-4 Haicheng
54 A-3 Haie-de-Béranville (La)
82 C-1 Haifa
135 K-9 Haifeng (China)
124 F-7 Haifeng (China)
132 F-5 Haihe *riv.*
145 N-2 Haikang (Leizhou)
145 N-3 Haikou
82 G-4 Hā'il
82 G-4 Hā'il *reg.*
124 C-7 Hailaer
124 C-7 Hailaerhe *riv.*
143 J-4 Hailākāndi
125 H-9 Hailanghe *riv.*
166 F-7 Hailey
164 B-7 Haileybury
125 H-9 Hailin
145 P-1 Hailingdao *isl.*
133 K-2 Hailong
53 L-8 Hailsham
124 F-7 Hailun
48 F-7 Hailuoto *isl.*
135 N-4 Haimen (China)
135 L-8 Haimen (China)
137 P-5 Haimi
145 N-3 Hainan Dao *isl.*
160 D-5 Haines
160 D-4 Haines Junction
172 E-2 Hainesburg
172 E-1 Hainesville
135 N-3 Haining
145 L-2 Haiphong
86 F-6 Haïré Koro *mt*
135 N-6 Haitandao *isl.*
157 G-5 Haiti *state*
131 H-4 Haitun
131 K-7 Haiyan
134 G-7 Haiyanqxu
131 K-9 Haiyuan
91 N-3 Hajar Banga
84 C-6 Hajarayn *mt*
66 B-9 Hajdúböszörmény
64 C-1 Hajdúzoboszló
129 J-2 Hāji Langar
131 J-2 Hajier
142 D-2 Hājīpur
93 J-7 Hājj Abd Allah
96 D-2 Hajjah
84 A-3 Hājjiābād
66 B-6 Hajnowka
123 N-9 Hajuu Hudag
143 J-5 Haka
99 N-8 Hakansson *mt*
84 F-9 Hakkān
72 E-5 Hakkâri *mt*
72 E-5 Hakkâri (Cölemerik)
95 K-4 Hakō
136 D-6 Hakodate
137 H-6 Haku *mt*
138 F-5 Hāla
65 M-7 Halab (Aleppo)
83 K-7 Halaban
72 G-7 Halabjah
179 M-5 Halachó
131 J-5 Halahu *lake*
93 K-1 Halā'ib
82 E-9 Halā'ib al Kabīrah *isl.*
129 H-5 Halamulanhe *riv.*
65 M-9 Halba
51 J-6 Halberstadt
52 A-4 Halberton
148 E-6 Halcon *mt*
52 B-7 Halcon Corner
51 K-1 Halden
129 N-1 Haldwāni
132 D-1 Haldzan
130 D-3 Haldzan *mt*
216 E-3 Hale *mt*
53 L-6 Hale Street Yalding
96 F-2 Haleb *isl.*
172 G-2 Haledon
52 E-1 Halesowen
53 P-1 Halesworth
89 P-3 Half Assini
149 J-9 Half Moon (Banyueansha) *rf*
84 F-8 Halfīn *riv.*
52 F-2 Halford
214 G-1 Halfway *isl.*
162 F-2 Halfway *riv.*
158 G-7 Halfway *mt*
164 A-4 Halfway *pte*
180 F-7 Halfway Tree
124 C-8 Halhing *riv.*
93 P-3 Hali *reg.*
165 K-7 Halifax
215 J-8 Halifax *bay*
97 J-7 Halin
159 P-4 Halkeet *cap.*
119 L-6 Hall *isl.*
172 A-6 Hallam
162 E-5 Hallam *mt*
53 L-8 Halland
51 K-3 Halland *reg.*
82 D-4 Hallat Ammār
51 K-7 Halle
167 H-6 Halleck
51 L-1 Hällefors
227 N-6 Hallett
175 N-6 Hallettsville
227 M-1 Halley Bay
48 G-6 Hällnäs
158 E-8 Hallo *bay*
169 J-1 Hallock
213 L-5 Halls Creek
49 K-6 Hallstavik
59 K-1 Hallwiler *lake*
209 J-1 Halmahera *isl.*
117 H-6 Halmahera *sea*
149 P-1 Halmahera (Indonesia) *isl.*
223 J-4 Halmiton
51 K-3 Halmstad
140 A-9 Hālon *riv.*
79 P-2 Halq el Oued
53 M-3 Halstead
56 B-7 Halsteren
48 D-6 Haltia
220 E-2 Halton Lakes *na.p.*
132 F-1 Haluhe *riv.*
84 D-3 Hālūl *isl.*
82 C-3 Haluza *site*
138 G-7 Halvad
57 H-2 Halvinkhuizen
48 C-7 Halvøya *isl.*
104 D-5 Ham (South Africa) *riv.*
79 K-2 Ham (Algeria) *riv.*
147 H-2 Ham Luong *strt.*
145 L-9 Ham Tân
136 A-6 Hama-Tombetu
137 K-3 Hamada
73 H-6 Hamadan
73 H-6 Hamadān *reg.*
78 F-5 Hamaguir
65 M-8 Hamāh
137 J-7 Hamamatsu
49 J-3 Hamar
97 K-2 Hamaro Hadad
82 D-8 Hamāṭah *mt*
141 N-8 Hambantota
53 H-8 Hambledon
52 C-7 Hambridge
220 B-1 Hambridge *na.p.*
52 D-5 Hambroock
51 J-5 Hamburg
172 B-4 Hamburg (USA)
172 F-2 Hamburg (USA)
173 M-1 Hamburg (USA)
176 D-4 Hamburg (USA)
199 N-3 Hamburgo
82 F-7 Hamd *riv.*
96 B-1 Hamdah
126 E-3 Hamdam Ab *reg.*
93 N-2 Hamdānah
173 K-1 Hamden
49 J-8 Häme *reg.*
49 J-8 Hämeenlinna
54 A-4 Hamel (Le)
216 C-3 Hamelin Pool
216 C-3 Hamelin Pool *lake*
95 J-6 Hamer Koke
212 E-8 Hamersley
212 E-9 Hamersley *rge*
133 M-3 Hamgyeong-sanmaek *rge*
133 M-4 Hamheung
130 E-3 Hami
130 E-2 Hami *holl.*
92 F-2 Hamid *mt*
218 B-4 Hamilton *riv.*
158 F-5 Hamilton *mt*
220 E-5 Hamilton (Australia)
171 H-5 Hamilton (Canada)
50 D-2 Hamilton (UK)
170 F-8 Hamilton (USA)
176 F-3 Hamilton (USA)
175 M-4 Hamilton (USA)
165 H-1 Hamilton (USA) *riv.*
81 J-3 Hamin *riv.*
49 J-9 Hamina
139 P-7 Hamīrpur
177 L-2 Hamlet
172 D-1 Hamlin
72 E-6 Hammām al Alil
79 P-2 Hammam Lif
79 P-2 Hammamet
79 P-2 Hammamet *gulf*
83 K-1 Hammār *lake*
49 H-4 Hammerdal
48 C-6 Hammerfest
170 D-7 Hammond (USA)
176 E-5 Hammond (USA)
218 G-4 Hammond Downs
172 E-7 Hammonton
181 M-6 Hamona *cal.*
56 G-9 Hamont
172 C-6 Hamorton
93 M-4 Hamoyet *mt*
165 M-2 Hampden
52 G-7 Hampshire *reg.*
220 G-8 Hampshire
217 L-6 Hampton *plat.*
53 J-5 Hampton (UK)
171 K-9 Hampton (USA)
176 D-3 Hampton (USA)
173 L-3 Hampton Bays
133 M-8 Hampyeong
92 E-7 Hamrat ash Shaykh
72 F-7 Hamrin *mt*
53 N-7 Hamstreet
84 A-7 Hāmūn-e Jāz Mūrīan *lake*
89 K-4 Han
87 N-9 Hana *riv.*
82 E-7 Hanak
82 G-6 Hanākīyah *riv.*
136 E-7 Hanamaki
100 G-6 Hanang *mt*
162 D-4 Hanceville
132 C-8 Hancheng
171 J-8 Hancock (USA)
171 K-6 Hancock (USA)
172 D-8 Hancocks Bridge
96 G-9 Handa
132 E-7 Handan
53 K-7 Handcross
59 K-6 Handegg
57 H-7 Handel
101 H-6 Handeni
52 E-7 Handley
82 C-3 Hanegev *reg.*
59 H-2 Hanenstein
167 K-3 Hanford
133 M-6 Hang *riv.*
144 F-4 Hang Dong
130 B-6 Hangay
130 C-6 Hangayn nuruu *rge*
97 H-7 Hanghei
132 A-5 Hangjinhouqi
104 D-9 Hangklip *cap.*
97 H-7 Hangorta Hodan
132 G-5 Hangu (China)
127 K-7 Hangu (Pakistan)
135 M-3 Hangzhou
135 N-3 Hangzhouwan *bay*
123 H-6 Hanh
130 A-4 Hanhöhiy *mt*
65 N-5 Hani
141 M-1 Hanimadu *isl.*
96 F-1 Hanish *islds*
96 F-2 Hanish al Kabir *islds*
135 K-8 Hanjiang *riv.*
135 M-7 Hanjiang
56 D-6 Hank
144 F-6 Hankha
169 J-3 Hankinson
49 K-7 Hanko
168 A-7 Hanksville
129 L-1 Hanle
52 E-2 Hanley Cas
132 G-1 Hanmiao
213 K-3 Hann *mt*
163 H-7 Hanna
164 B-4 Hannah *bay*
54 D-4 Hanneucourt
170 B-8 Hannibal
51 L-3 Hanöbukten *bay*
145 K-2 Hanoi
118 F-5 Hanoi
51 J-6 Hanover
201 L-2 Hanover *isl.*
104 G-7 Hanover
133 M-9 Hanra-san *mt*
133 M-9 Hanrim
168 A-5 Hans F. *riv.*
162 E-3 Hansard
135 H-3 Hanshui *riv.*
139 M-4 Hānsi
214 A-9 Hanson *riv.*
223 N-9 Hanson *bay*
136 A-8 Hantō
139 L-3 Hanumāngarh
142 E-2 Hanumānnagar
130 B-7 Hanuy *riv.*
134 B-4 Hanyuan
134 E-2 Hanzhong
132 G-9 Hanzhuang
125 H-7 Haoli
125 H-7 Haoliaohé
143 P-3 Haoqing
131 H-8 Haotaolaohai *well*
92 A-6 Haouach *riv.*
79 L-5 Haoud el Hamra
48 F-7 Haparanda
56 F-8 Hapert
56 F-9 Hapertse Heide *reg.*
143 K-2 Hāpoli
166 F-2 Happy Camp
165 J-1 Happy Valley
57 J-6 Haps
139 N-4 Hāpur
82 C-4 Haql
127 L-7 Har-ipur
130 A-3 Har Us *lake*
97 L-1 Hara Bonel
97 L-1 Hara Buri
123 L-8 Haraa *riv.*
83 N-6 Harad
96 C-1 Harajā
139 K-2 Harappa *site*
97 M-6 Harardere
77 F-6 Harare
103 N-6 Harare (Salisbury)
54 F-1 Haravilliers
91 K-1 Haraz
92 G-6 Harāzah *mt*
91 L-4 Harazé Mangueigne
65 M-8 Harbiye
170 G-5 Harbor Beach
165 N-4 Harbour Breton
165 M-2 Harbour Deep
165 P-3 Harbour Grace
201 L-9 Harbours *bay*
140 A-6 Harda
49 J-1 Hardanger *fj.*
57 H-1 Harderwijk
54 D-1 Hardeville
212 E-9 Hardey *riv.*
59 K-6 Hardidegg
168 D-2 Hardin
105 K-7 Harding
159 G-9 Harding *glac.*
56 D-5 Hardinxveld Giessendam
161 K-6 Hardisty *lake*
139 P-6 Hardoi
54 D-3 Hardricourt
139 N-3 Hardwār
53 H-3 Hardwick
52 D-4 Hardwicke
220 C-2 Hardwicke *bay*
176 E-1 Hardy
201 P-6 Hardy *pen.*
165 M-1 Hare *bay*
161 J-3 Hare Indian *riv.*
49 H-1 Hareidlandet *isl.*
57 H-5 Haren
97 J-1 Harer
97 K-2 Harer *reg.*
222 F-8 Harewood
52 C-3 Harewood End
172 D-5 Harfield
172 B-7 Harford Cecil *reg.*
54 C-5 Hargeville
97 J-3 Hargeysa
122 D-7 Harhiraa Uul *mt*
206 C-1 Hari *riv.*
78 D-8 Haria
96 E-3 Harīb
96 E-3 Harīb *riv.*
88 F-4 Haribongo *lake*
88 A-4 Haricha *dés*
54 A-2 Haricourt
139 H-7 Hārij
84 B-5 Harim *mt*
142 G-6 Hāringhāta *lag.*
56 A-5 Haringvliet *strt.*
126 F-4 Harirud *riv.*
172 A-7 Harkins
177 J-1 Harlan
50 C-4 Harlech
163 J-9 Harlem
53 P-1 Harleston
172 D-5 Harleysville
50 G-5 Harlingen (Netherlands)
175 M-8 Harlingen (USA)
50 E-6 Harlow
64 E-4 Harmanli
56 E-3 Harmelen
172 D-8 Harmersville
196 F-7 Harmonia
172 E-3 Harmony
140 D-2 Harnai (India)
126 G-9 Harnai (Pakistan)
53 H-8 Harndean
166 E-5 Harney *pool*
168 E-4 Harney *mt*
166 E-5 Harney *lake*
49 H-5 Härnösand
60 E-3 Haro
174 D-6 Haro *cap.*
124 B-7 Harori Hudag *well*
140 F-4 Harpanahalli
53 J-4 Harpenden
159 L-9 Harper *mt*
166 E-6 Harper (USA)
218 A-1 Harper Springs
96 D-7 Harrah
82 D-5 Harrat al Uwayrid *mt*
97 J-1 Harrawa
57 M-4 Harreveld
164 B-6 Harricana *riv.*
164 B-5 Harricanaw *riv.*
53 M-6 Harrietsham
172 G-1 Harriman
165 K-2 Harrington Harbour
218 B-7 Harris *lake*
170 D-9 Harrisburg
105 K-5 Harrismith
168 E-5 Harrison
159 N-4 Harrison *bay*
171 J-8 Harrisonburg (USA)
176 D-5 Harrisonburg (USA)
170 A-9 Harrisonville
162 C-6 Harrisson *lake*
176 D-1 Harrisson (USA)
170 F-4 Harrisville
50 D-4 Harrogate
53 J-5 Harrow (UK)
172 D-4 Harrow (USA)
96 G-5 Harshō
57 H-2 Harskamp
48 D-5 Harstad
53 K-2 Harston
140 A-6 Harsūd
166 F-4 Hart *mt*
170 E-5 Hart
218 C-7 Hart *lake*
160 G-1 Hart *riv.*
220 C-3 Hart *cap.*
104 E-5 Hartbees *riv.*
53 H-6 Hartely Wintney
53 L-7 Hartfield
171 M-8 Hartford
169 H-6 Hartington
52 E-1 Hartlebury
162 B-2 Hartley Bay
172 C-9 Hartly
104 G-5 Harts *riv.*
177 L-2 Hartsville
177 J-3 Hartwell
177 J-3 Hartwell *lake*
209 J-3 Haruku *isl.*
139 K-3 Hārunābād
126 C-5 Hārūt *riv.*
216 E-8 Harvey (Australia)
168 G-2 Harvey (USA)
172 B-1 Harveys *lake*
172 B-1 Harveyville
52 G-5 Harwell
53 P-3 Harwich
139 M-3 Haryana *reg.*
51 J-6 Harz *mt*
130 C-4 Hasagt
130 C-4 Hasagt Hayrhan *mt*
65 K-6 Hasan *mt*
139 N-4 Hasanpur
83 H-1 Hasb *riv.*
53 J-7 Hascombe
142 B-4 Hasdo *riv.*
130 C-8 Hashaat
84 F-9 Hashīsh *bay*

73 H-4 Hashtpar
85 J-7 Hasik
139 K-2 Hāsilpur
175 M-3 Haskell
59 J-3 Hasle (Switzerland)
58 G-3 Hasle (Switzerland)
53 H-7 Haslemere
59 N-3 Haslen
59 K-5 Haslital *val.*
93 H-1 Hasmat'Umar *riv.*
141 H-4 Hassan
82 E-7 Hassānī *isl.*
80 C-4 Hassauna *mt*
153 J-2 Hassel *strt.*
50 G-7 Hasselt
79 J-9 Hassi Abadra
79 L-5 Hassi-Messaoud
79 J-4 Hassi R'Mel
86 A-6 Hassiâne *mt*
213 P-9 Hast Bluff
221 L-1 Hastings *mt*
220 G-9 Hastings (Australia)
223 K-6 Hastings (New Zealand)
50 E-6 Hastings (UK)
168 G-7 Hastings (USA)
170 B-4 Hastings (USA)
173 H-2 Hastings on Hudson
48 C-6 Hasvik
81 L-3 Hasy al Qaṭṭar *well*
146 D-4 Hat Yai
93 H-2 Haṭab *riv.*
65 M-7 Hatay (Antakya)
174 G-3 Hatch
214 B-9 Hatches Creek
163 M-3 Hatchet *lake*
57 J-5 Hatert
137 P-6 Hateruma *isl.*
53 K-4 Hatfield
53 L-4 Hatfield Heath
53 M-4 Hatfield Peverel
139 N-5 Hāthras
143 H-5 Hātia *lag.*
137 J-6 Hatiman
136 D-7 Hatinohe
137 H-7 Hatiôzi
137 K-8 Hatizyō
137 K-8 Hatizyō *isl.*
186 F-5 Hato de Corozal
181 L-6 Hato Mayor
72 E-7 Hatra *site*
201 J-3 Hatscher *mt*
139 N-8 Hatta
177 N-2 Hatteras *cap.*
48 F-4 Hattfjelldal
142 B-7 Hatti *riv.*
176 F-5 Hattiesburg
52 F-1 Hatton
144 E-8 Hattras *strt.*
224 F-4 Hatutaa *isl.*
145 M-7 Hâu Bôn
147 H-3 Hâu Giang *strt.*
97 K-4 Haud Harerge *reg.*
51 H-1 Haugesund
48 E-4 Haugvik
49 K-2 Haukelingren
48 F-7 Haukipudas
49 H-9 Haukivesi *lake*
163 L-4 Haultain *riv.*
198 G-1 Haumonía
144 E-5 Haungtharaw *riv.*
223 K-3 Hauraki *gulf*
222 C-8 Hauroko *lake*
223 K-4 Haussey (Mercury) *islds*
59 N-4 Hausstock *mt*
54 A-5 Haut-Arbre (Le)
78 D-4 Haut Atlas *mt*
91 P-6 Haut Mbomou *reg.*
58 F-9 Haute
54 B-2 Haute-Isle
91 M-5 Haute-Kotto *reg.*
91 H-8 Haute-Sangha *reg.*
54 C-2 Haute-Souris
54 B-8 Hauteville (La)
54 E-1 Hautiers (Les)
54 F-3 Hautil (L')
58 C-9 Hauts Forts (Les) *mt*
170 C-7 Havana
180 C-4 Havana
157 F-4 Havana
215 N-5 Havannah *cap.*
53 H-8 Havant
139 L-2 Haveli
127 L-7 Haveliān
105 L-4 Havelock
144 B-8 Havelock *isl.*
54 A-7 Havelu
50 C-5 Haverfordwest
53 L-2 Haverhill (UK)
171 M-5 Haverhill (USA)
173 H-2 Haverstraw
57 N-7 Havert
51 M-8 Havirov
64 F-6 Havran
163 H-9 Havre
50 D-7 Havre (Le)
165 K-5 Havre-Aubert
172 B-8 Havre de Grace
165 J-3 Havre-St-Pierre
64 F-5 Havsa
130 D-3 Havtag Uul Tahiyn Shar *mt*
66 A-5 Hawa
225 D-1 Hawaii *state*
224 C-1 Hawaii *islds*
224 D-2 Hawaii *isl.*
224 D-2 Hawaii
93 P-6 Hawakil *isl.*
90 F-3 Hawal *riv.*
83 L-2 Hawali
222 D-8 Hawea *lake*
223 H-5 Hawera
50 D-3 Hawick
65 N-8 Hawiṭ ar Ra's *mt*
170 F-2 Hawk Junction
170 A-1 Hawk Lake
223 K-6 Hawke *bay*
221 M-2 Hawke *cap.*
53 M-2 Hawkedon
218 D-8 Hawker
223 J-6 Hawke's bay *reg.*
162 B-2 Hawkesbury *isl.*
164 E-8 Hawkesbury
53 M-7 Hawkhurst
160 A-2 Hawkins *isl.*
177 J-4 Hawkinsville
180 G-3 Hawks Nest Point *pte*
180 F-3 Hawksbill Cay *rf*
219 L-4 Hawkwood
171 L-6 Hawley
72 E-9 Hawrān *riv.*
167 J-4 Hawthorne
124 C-6 Hawuluohe *riv.*
93 N-7 Hawzien
52 B-2 Hay
220 G-3 Hay (Australia)
218 A-2 Hay (Australia) *mt*
218 C-2 Hay (Australia) *riv.*
161 H-9 Hay (Canada) *lake*
161 K-9 Hay (Canada) *riv.*
163 H-1 Hay (Canada) *riv.*
160 C-5 Hay (USA) *mt*
55 H-7 Hay-les-Roses (L')
219 L-1 Hay Point
161 K-8 Hay River
159 J-4 Haycock
174 E-2 Hayden
214 F-7 Haydon
54 A-6 Haye (La)
159 K-9 Hayes *mt*
96 C-2 Hayjān
53 H-8 Hayling *isl.*
65 J-6 Haymana
64 F-5 Hayrabolu
96 D-1 Hayrān
168 G-8 Hays (USA)
96 F-2 Hays (Yémen)
167 J-7 Haystack *mt*
167 J-2 Hayward (USA)
170 B-3 Hayward (USA)
53 K-7 Haywards Heath
93 L-4 Hayyā
96 B-6 Hazar *riv.*
73 P-2 Hazār Masjed *mt*
126 G-6 Hazār Qadam
177 J-1 Hazard
127 J-3 Hazāreh Toghāy
172 D-4 Hazārībāgh
176 E-4 Hazelhurst
162 C-1 Hazelton *mt*
162 C-1 Hazelton
167 H-4 Hazen
158 E-3 Hazen *bay*
153 H-2 Hazen *strt.*
56 C-3 Hazerswoude *reg.*
56 C-2 Hazerswoude
136 F-6 Haziki *pte*
177 K-4 Hazlehurst
172 B-6 Hazleton
171 K-6 Hazleton
213 M-7 Hazlett *lake*
96 C-7 Hbshīyah *mt*
166 E-7 He Devil *mt*
217 N-5 Head of Bight *bay*
53 M-6 Headcorn
220 G-5 Healesville
159 L-9 Healy *riv.*
175 N-5 Hearne
170 F-1 Hearst
168 F-2 Heart *riv.*
220 G-4 Heathcote
54 F-1 Heaulme (Le)
175 M-7 Hebbronville
219 J-6 Hebel
168 A-6 Heber
176 D-2 Heber Springs
132 E-8 Hebi
50 C-1 Hebrides *sea*
50 C-1 Hebrides *islds*
82 C-2 Hebron (Israel)
169 H-7 Hebron (USA)
131 K-4 Hebuxunhu *lake*
162 A-2 Hecate *strt.*
156 A-1 Hecate *strt.*
179 M-5 Hecelchakán
160 B-8 Heceta *isl.*
134 E-8 Hechi
134 D-4 Hechuan
53 H-6 Heckfield
163 P-9 Hecla *isl.*
49 H-4 Hede
56 F-6 Hedel
56 F-6 Hedikhuizen
79 M-4 Hedjila *well*
49 J-3 Hedmark *reg.*
54 G-1 Hédouville
57 N-9 Heek
57 N-6 Heel
57 H-4 Heelsum
57 M-4 Heelweg
56 C-1 Heemstede
56 A-5 Heenvliet
57 M-9 Heer
56 G-5 Heere-Waarden
57 L-4 Heerenberg
56 C-5 Heerjansdam
57 N-9 Heerlen
57 N-8 Heerlerheide
129 M-6 Heermo
57 M-9 Hees (Netherlands)
57 J-5 Hees (Netherlands)
56 F-6 Heesbeen
56 G-6 Heesch
56 G-6 Heeswijk
57 L-1 Heeten
57 H-8 Heeze
135 L-2 Hefei
177 H-3 Heflin
125 H-7 Hegang
88 E-7 Hegbane *mt*
172 A-3 Hegins
136 G-5 Hegura *isl.*
56 E-4 Hei en Boeicop
145 K-2 Hêi Xuân
57 J-9 Heibloem
130 F-7 Heicheng (Khara Khoto) *site*
132 A-8 Heichengzhen
51 J-5 Heide
105 J-4 Heidelberg
158 C-7 Heiden *bay*
51 J-9 Heidenheim
192 D-3 Heidoti
173 H-6 Heights
57 K-6 Heijen
56 B-6 Heijningen
57 J-9 Heijthuizen
56 E-7 Heikant
105 J-4 Heilbron
51 H-8 Heilbronn
51 H-8 Heildeberg
124 D-6 Heilongjiang *reg.*
58 G-5 Heimberg
58 G-3 Heimiswil
211 H-1 Heina *islds*
56 C-5 Heinenoord
49 J-8 Heinola
57 P-7 Heinsberg
163 J-5 Heinsburg
144 E-6 Heinze *bay*
97 H-5 Heis
133 J-3 Heishan
132 G-3 Heishui
172 E-9 Heislerville
58 F-4 Heitenried
57 J-8 Heitrak
132 F-6 Hejian
134 D-5 Hejiang
132 C-8 Hejin
128 E-7 Hejing
65 M-5 Hekimhan
48 C-5 Hekla *mt*
135 J-3 Hekou (China)
131 K-8 Hekou (China)
145 J-1 Hekou (China)
51 M-4 Hel
49 H-4 Helagsfjället
132 A-6 Helan
131 J-9 Helanshan *mt*
57 K-9 Helden
168 B-1 Helena (USA)
176 E-3 Helena (USA)
196 F-2 Helena de Goias
57 J-8 Helenaveen
223 J-3 Helensville
51 H-4 Helgoland *reg.*
132 C-5 Helingeer
65 M-9 Heliopolis *site*
108 D-7 Hell-Ville
83 N-1 Helleh *riv.*
49 H-1 Hellesylt
56 A-5 Hellevoetsluis
60 E-6 Hellin
56 F-5 Hellouw
166 D-7 Hells Canyon *val.*
126 E-7 Helmand *reg.*
126 D-7 Helmand *riv.*
104 B-3 Helmeringhausen
57 H-8 Helmond
50 D-1 Helmsdale
51 J-6 Helmstedt
133 M-2 Helong
51 K-5 Helpter *mt*
56 E-4 Helsdingen
59 K-8 Helsenhorn *mt*
51 K-3 Helsingborg
51 K-3 Helsingør
47 F-3 Helsinki
49 K-8 Helsinki
198 G-4 Helvecia
56 F-6 Helvoirt
81 P-2 Helwan
126 A-4 Hemar *riv.*
141 H-4 Hemāvati *riv.*
59 P-1 Hemberg
57 M-4 Hemden
53 J-4 Hemel Hempstead
167 M-4 Hemet
168 E-5 Hemingford
173 J-1 Hemlock *rés*
175 N-5 Hempstead
49 M-6 Hemse
49 H-6 Hemsö *isl.*
223 K-3 Hen and Chickens *islds*
135 H-1 Henan *reg.*
60 D-5 Henarès *riv.*
136 E-6 Henasi *pte*
218 A-3 Henbury
65 H-5 Hendek
224 G-6 Henderson *isl.*
170 D-9 Henderson (USA)
167 L-5 Henderson (USA)
177 M-1 Henderson (USA)
175 P-4 Henderson (USA)
177 J-2 Hendersonville
84 C-3 Hendorābi *isl.*
52 A-5 Hendre Forgan
56 C-5 Hendrick Ido Ambacht
105 H-7 Hendrik Verwoerd *dam.*
192 D-4 Hendriktop *mt*
53 K-8 Henfield
84 B-5 Hengam *isl.*
211 J-5 Henganofi
135 N-9 Hengch'un
57 N-1 Hengelo
57 L-3 Hengelo
129 L-6 Henglitaoliangshan *mt*
132 D-6 Hengshan *mt*
135 H-6 Hengshan
132 F-7 Hengshui
134 F-9 Hengxian
135 H-6 Hengyang
146 A-5 Henhoaha
165 L-1 Henley Harbour
52 F-1 Henley in Arden
53 H-5 Henley on Thames
171 L-8 Henlopen *cap.*
53 K-3 Henlow
105 J-5 Hennenman
54 A-1 Hennezis
58 D-5 Henniez
175 M-2 Henrietta
54 E-7 Henriville
144 B-8 Henry Lawrence *isl.*
175 P-1 Henryetta
172 D-2 Henryville
52 D-7 Henstridge
102 B-9 Hentiesbaai
123 M-8 Hentiy *reg.*
123 L-8 Hentiyn Nuruu *mt*
57 N-4 Henxel
143 K-9 Henzada
166 D-5 Heppner
145 M-1 Hepu
132 C-6 Hequ
215 L-7 Herald Cays *rf*
172 A-9 Herald Harbor
126 E-4 Herat
215 J-7 Herbert *riv.*
218 D-2 Herbert Downs
144 A-8 Herbertābād
215 J-7 Herberton
54 D-5 Herbeville
59 H-9 Herbriggen
57 L-9 Herderen
185 H-6 Heredia *reg.*
175 K-2 Hereford
50 D-5 Hereford (UK)
52 D-2 Hereford and Worcester *reg.*
58 F-9 Hérens *val.*
222 E-7 Heretaniwha *pte*
51 H-6 Herford
59 K-3 Hergiswil (Switzerland)
59 J-3 Hergiswil (Switzerland)
169 H-8 Herington
59 P-1 Herisau
57 P-6 Herkenbosch
56 A-6 Herkingen
123 N-9 Herlen *riv.*
191 P-6 Hermán Miraval
148 D-7 Hermana Mayor *isl.*
58 A-8 Hermance
170 B-9 Hermann
213 P-9 Hermannsburg
104 D-9 Hermanus
65 M-9 Hermel
54 B-9 Hermeray
221 H-1 Hermidale
78 A-8 Hermigua
192 E-3 Herminadorp
162 C-9 Hermiston
211 J-2 Hermit *islds*
170 A-9 Hermitage
201 P-6 Hermite *islds*
174 E-5 Hermosillo
196 C-7 Hernandarias
199 H-5 Hernández
53 N-6 Herne
53 N-5 Herne Bay
57 H-5 Hernen
51 J-3 Herning
174 D-3 Heroica Caborca
174 E-3 Heroica Nogales
178 E-5 Heroica Zitacuaro
57 L-8 Herongen
54 G-2 Hérouville
73 H-4 Herowābād
57 H-5 Herpen
56 F-6 Herpt
196 A-8 Herradura
185 K-9 Herrera *reg.*
198 F-2 Herrera
179 P-6 Herrero *pte*
53 H-6 Herriard
221 H-8 Herrick
172 A-5 Hershey
53 L-8 Herstmonceux
59 L-3 Hertenstein
53 K-3 Hertford *reg.*
53 K-4 Hertford
177 N-1 Hertford (USA)
50 G-6 Hertogenbosch
164 E-7 Hervey
219 N-4 Hervey *bay*
57 K-4 Herwen
57 K-4 Herwen en Aerdt *reg.*
56 F-5 Herwijnen
59 H-2 Herzogenbuchsee
57 P-9 Herzogenrath
127 H-5 Heṣar *mt*
132 F-1 Heshimiao
128 B-8 Heshituoluogai
132 E-7 Heshun
160 G-4 Hess *mt*
160 G-4 Hess (Canada) *riv.*
159 L-7 Hess (USA) *riv.*
51 H-7 Hessen *reg.*
220 C-1 Hesso
145 J-2 Hèt *riv.*
56 G-9 Het Loo
57 K-8 Het Vorst
57 H-4 Heteren
128 F-4 Hetianhe *riv.*
172 B-2 Hetlerville
132 C-4 Hetongmiao
57 L-4 Hettenheuvel *hill*
168 F-3 Hettinger
54 A-1 Heubécourt-Haricourt
57 M-9 Heugem
133 L-8 Heugsan *isl.*
133 L-4 Heuicheon
57 J-5 Heumen *reg.*
133 M-4 Heungnam
54 B-5 Heurteloup
57 J-8 Heusden (Netherlands)
56 F-6 Heusden (Netherlands)
58 G-6 Heustrich
53 L-6 Hever
172 G-2 Hewitt
135 H-8 Hexian
131 J-7 Hexibao
131 L-5 Heyakutuer
72 F-5 Heydarābād
57 J-8 Heydse *lake*
52 E-6 Heytesbury
135 J-8 Heyuan
220 E-5 Heywood
132 F-8 Heze
131 J-2 Hezhaerzake
134 C-6 Hezhang
131 L-8 Hezheng
135 J-6 Hezhiao
131 L-8 Hezuo
177 L-9 Hialeah
169 J-8 Hiawatha
170 B-2 Hibbing
220 F-8 Hibbs *pte*
213 H-1 Hibernia *rf*
172 F-2 Hibernra
191 L-6 Hickmann
177 K-2 Hickory
172 C-2 Hickory Run State *na.p.*
163 P-1 Hicks *lake*
173 J-3 Hicksville
175 M-4 Hico
137 H-6 Hida *mt*
136 B-7 Hidaka *mt*
178 F-5 Hidalgo *reg.*
175 H-7 Hidalgo del Parral
80 F-5 Hidān *riv.*
196 G-2 Hidrolândia
194 D-9 Hidrolina
215 M-3 Hienghène
82 B-7 Hieraconpolis *site*
65 H-7 Hierapolis *site*
57 H-1 Hierden
78 A-9 Hierro *isl.*
145 K-9 Hiêu Thiên
48 G-2 Hifra *isl.*
137 M-2 Higasi-Sonogi
137 K-5 Higasiôsaka
172 E-3 High Bridge
166 E-4 High Desert *dés*
163 H-1 High Level
177 L-1 High-Point
172 F-1 High Point State *na.p.*
162 G-3 High Prairie
162 G-7 High River
180 E-1 High Rock
53 H-4 High Wycombe
53 J-1 Higham Ferrers
52 B-6 Highbridge
52 G-6 Highclere
167 K-6 Highland *mt*
170 D-6 Highland Park
173 H-4 Highlands
172 G-1 Highlands Mills
168 G-4 Highmore
172 F-5 Hightstown
168 B-1 Highwood *mt*
52 F-4 Highworth
174 E-7 Higueras de Zaragoza
187 K-2 Higuerote
181 M-6 Higüey
89 M-6 Hihéatro
97 N-4 Hiiraan *reg.*
66 A-1 Hiiumaa *isl.*
83 H-2 Hijārah *dés*
82 F-7 Hijaz *mt*
76 F-2 Hijaz *reg.*
223 L-5 Hikurangi *mt*
223 K-2 Hikurangi
209 H-6 Hila
81 H-1 Hilal *pte*
51 J-6 Hildesheim
84 F-9 Hilf *cap.*
53 K-1 Hill
168 G-8 Hill City (USA)
166 F-7 Hill City (USA)
215 J-8 Hill Grove
163 L-1 Hill Island *lake*
172 G-2 Hillburn
56 B-4 Hillegersberg
56 C-1 Hillegom
92 A-8 Hilléket
51 K-3 Hillerød
46 C-5 Hills of Brittany *mt*
162 B-9 Hillsboro (USA)
170 F-8 Hillsboro (USA)
169 J-2 Hillsboro (USA)
175 N-4 Hillsboro (USA)
187 N-1 Hillsborough
170 F-6 Hillsdale
52 D-4 Hillsley
170 E-1 Hillsport
221 H-2 Hillston
177 K-1 Hillsville
148 G-3 Hilongos
58 G-5 Hilterfingen
56 F-8 Hilvarenbeek
50 G-6 Hilversum
139 N-2 Himāchal Pradesh *reg.*
116 C-3 Himalaya *rge*
85 K-6 Himār *cap.*
139 J-7 Himatnagar
137 L-3 Hime *isl.*
137 K-5 Himezi
137 H-6 Himi
101 H-5 Himo
65 M-8 Himṣ (Homs)
146 B-9 Hinako *islds*
190 G-2 Hinamarca *lake*
149 J-2 Hinatuan
181 K-6 Hinche
160 A-1 Hinchinbrook *strt.*
215 J-7 Hinchinbrook (Australia) *isl.*
160 A-2 Hinchinbrook (USA) *isl.*
170 B-3 Hinckley
39 M-6 Hindaun
58 G-3 Hindelbank
53 H-7 Hindhead
220 E-3 Hindmarsh *lake*
52 E-7 Hindon
127 K-5 Hindu Kush *reg.*
112 F-6 Hindu Kush *rge*
126 G-8 Hindubāgh
140 G-5 Hindupur
116 D-4 Hindustan *rge*

162 G-2 Hines Creek
177 K-4 Hinesville
140 B-7 Hinganghāt
138 D-4 Hinglāj
138 D-4 Hingol riv.
140 C-6 Hingoli
72 D-4 Hinis
52 B-6 Hinkley Point
137 K-4 Hino
137 M-3 Hinokage
59 P-4 Hinter-Steinibach
59 P-6 Hinterrhein mt
59 P-6 Hinterrhein
53 N-2 Hintlesham
162 F-5 Hinton
52 F-8 Hinton (UK)
148 G-2 Hinundayan
59 M-1 Hinwil
189 N-9 Hipocapac mt
137 L-2 Hirado
137 L-2 Hirado isl.
142 C-5 Hīrākūd dam.
101 K-3 Hiraman riv.
137 P-6 Hirara
137 K-3 Hirata
136 C-7 Hiratori
140 G-3 Hirebhāskara lake
149 P-1 Hiri isl.
140 G-5 Hiriyūr
136 C-7 Hiroo
136 D-6 Hirosaki
137 K-3 Hirosima
50 F-7 Hirson
51 J-2 Hirtshals
52 A-4 Hirwain
96 F-3 Hisha mt
130 B-8 Hishig-Ondör
96 B-8 Hisī al Athbār well
96 C-5 Hişn al-'Abr
96 E-5 Hişn Bal'id
96 D-6 Hisn Layjūn
139 M-3 Hissār
53 L-2 Histon
72 E-8 Hīt
137 L-3 Hita
136 G-8 Hitati
53 N-2 Hitcham
53 J-3 Hitchin
137 M-3 Hitoyosi
59 K-2 Hitzkirch
224 E-5 Hiva Oa isl.
82 B-7 Hiw
177 H-2 Hiwassee riv.
219 N-2 Hixon cap.
95 J-3 Hiywet
51 L-1 Hjälmaren lake
49 H-2 Hjerkinn
51 J-2 Hjørring
143 M-2 Hkakabo Razi mt
144 E-5 Hlaingbwe
105 L-4 Hlatikulu
105 M-5 Hluhluwe
89 N-6 Ho
143 N-5 Ho-pang
145 K-2 Hoa Binh
145 M-7 Hoai Nhon
145 J-1 Hoang Lien Son mt
102 B-7 Hoanib riv.
102 A-7 Hoarusib riv.
181 H-4 Hoasty rf
133 M-3 Hoban
221 H-9 Hobart (Australia)
175 M-2 Hobart (USA)
175 J-3 Hobbs
172 G-3 Hoboken
51 J-3 Hobro
97 M-7 Hobyā
59 P-7 Hochberg mt
59 K-2 Hochdorf
59 L-3 Hochftuh
61 N-1 Hochgolling mt
58 G-4 Höchstetten
52 F-1 Hockley Heath
53 J-3 Hockliffe
53 K-4 Hoddesdon
54 C-1 Hodent
163 P-8 Hodgson
214 A-5 Hodgson Downs
86 E-8 Hodh reg.
64 C-1 Hódmezóvásárhely
79 L-2 Hodna mt
79 K-3 Hodna holl.
51 M-9 Hodonin
159 L-7 Hodzana riv.
56 A-4 Hoek van Holland
56 B-5 Hoeksa Waard isl.
57 J-5 Hoenderberg hill
57 J-2 Hoenderloo
133 M-6 Hoengseong
56 D-3 Hoenkoop
57 N-8 Hoensbroek
133 M-4 Hoeryong
56 G-2 Hoevelaken
56 C-7 Hoeven
56 B-9 Hoevenen
51 K-7 Hof

105 H-7 Hofmeyr
48 C-3 Höfn
49 K-5 Hofors
48 B-2 Hofsjökull glac.
83 N-5 Hofuf
149 L-7 Hog pte
192 B-2 Hog isl.
51 K-3 Höganäs
159 K-5 Hogatza riv.
56 G-1 Hoge Vaart cal.
57 J-3 Hoge-Veluwe na.p.
124 A-7 Hoh Nuur lake
59 M-2 Hohe Rone mt
58 G-1 Hohe Winde mt
59 K-5 Hohenstollen mt
59 H-5 Hohgant
59 H-8 Hohgleifen mt
123 P-7 Höhö Uula mt
172 G-2 Hohokus
158 G-5 Hoholitna riv.
137 L-3 Hōhu
145 M-6 Hôi An
100 D-1 Hoima
223 J-2 Hokianga
222 E-7 Hokitika
136 B-8 Hokkaido isl.
73 N-2 Hokmābād
190 E-5 Holanda
51 K-4 Holbœk
215 K-9 Holborne isl.
221 H-4 Holbrook (Australia)
174 F-1 Holbrook (USA)
175 P-2 Holdenville
200 G-5 Holdich
168 G-7 Holdrege
141 H-4 Hole Narsipur
180 G-5 Holguin
96 G-2 Holhol
158 F-6 Holitna riv.
56 G-2 Holk
51 L-9 Hollabrunn
104 A-2 Hollams Voëleiland isl.
170 E-6 Holland (USA)
54 D-7 Hollande lake
56 C-6 Hollands Diep est.
56 D-3 Hollandse Ijssel riv.
53 M-6 Hollingbourne
175 M-2 Hollis
167 J-2 Hollister
211 M-4 Hollman cap.
176 F-2 Holly Springs
177 L-8 Hollywood
161 M-1 Holman Island
48 A-2 Hólmavik
172 G-5 Holmde
53 K-1 Holme
164 E-1 Holmer lake
215 K-6 Holmes rf
48 G-6 Holmsund
52 D-8 Holnest
82 C-2 Holon
104 C-4 Holoog
213 K-2 Holothuria rf
214 F-4 Holroyd riv.
49 J-1 Holsnøy isl.
51 J-3 Holstebro
51 J-5 Holstein reg.
52 D-7 Holt Heath
57 L-1 Holten
57 N-7 Holtum
172 A-6 Holtwood
158 G-5 Holy Cross (USA)
53 H-6 Holybourne
50 C-4 Holyhead
171 M-5 Holyoke (USA)
168 E-7 Holyoke (USA)
165 P-3 Holyrood
52 D-8 Holywell
59 K-1 Hom hill
100 F-3 Homa Bay
143 K-4 Homalin
88 G-5 Hombori
88 G-5 Hombori Tondo mt
191 N-4 Hombre Muento lake
223 K-2 Home pte
158 G-9 Homer (USA)
176 D-4 Homer (USA)
53 P-1 Homersfield
177 J-5 Homerville
177 L-9 Homestead
57 K-6 Hommersum
140 D-6 Homnabad
107 M-3 Homoine
148 G-2 Homonhon isl.
65 M-8 Homs (Hims)
146 G-3 Hon Buông isl.
146 G-2 Hon Chông
146 G-3 Hon Chuôi isl.
145 L-2 Hon Gai
145 M-8 Hon Tre isl.
65 H-7 Honaz mt
136 B-7 Honbetu
186 D-6 Honda
187 L-3 Honda riv.
104 C-6 Hondeklipbaai
175 D-2 Hondo

190 F-3 Hondo riv.
137 M-2 Hondo (Japan)
175 M-6 Hondo (USA)
175 H-2 Hondo (USA)
157 F-5 Honduras state
179 N-8 Honduras gulf
184 F-2 Honduras gulf
180 A-9 Honduras reg.
49 K-2 Hønefoss
59 H-5 Honegg mt
171 K-6 Honesdale
166 G-3 Honey lake
172 B-6 Honey Brook
59 L-1 Höng
133 L-8 Hong isl.
145 J-1 Hong Ha (Red River)
135 J-9 Hong Kong
145 K-9 Hông Ngu
133 M-3 Hongcheon
132 D-8 Hongdong
57 N-7 Hongen
130 A-1 Hongerzake
133 M-3 Honggun
135 K-9 Honghaiwan bay
134 B-9 Honghe
135 J-1 Honghe riv.
135 H-4 Honghu
134 F-6 Hongjiang
132 A-6 Hongliushu
130 G-4 Hongliuyuan
132 D-1 Hongor
130 E-8 Hongor Oboo
133 K-1 Hongqi
133 M-6 Hongseong
134 E-8 Hongshuihe riv.
165 J-4 Honguedo strt.
133 M-4 Hongweon
135 L-1 Hongzehu lake
205 G-2 Honiara
53 M-1 Honington
52 B-8 Honiton
48 B-7 Honningsvåg
224 D-1 Honolulu
56 A-3 Honselersdijk
136 G-9 Honshu isl.
113 M-6 Honshu reg.
56 F-4 Honswijk
136 E-7 Honzyō
53 M-5 Hoo
161 N-5 Hood riv.
172 A-4 Hood rés
216 G-9 Hood pte
211 K-8 Hood (Papua-niugini) mt
162 B-9 Hood (USA) mt
162 B-9 Hood River
56 D-1 Hoofddorp
56 D-1 Hoofdvaart cal.
57 J-2 Hoog Soeren
56 E-4 Hoogblokland
57 N-9 Hoogcruts
56 D-6 Hooge en Lage Zwaluwe reg.
56 F-7 Hooge Haghorst
56 F-8 Hooge Mierde
56 D-6 Hooge Zwaluwe
56 F-8 Hoogeind
56 F-8 Hoogelooon
56 B-8 Hoogerheide
142 F-6 Hooghly lag.
56 C-2 Hoogmade
56 D-8 Hoogstraten
56 B-4 Hoogvliet
53 J-6 Hook
215 L-9 Hook isl.
168 F-9 Hooker
213 N-5 Hooker Creek
160 C-6 Hoonah
57 M-2 Hoonte
158 F-3 Hooper Bay
56 E-4 Hoornaar
72 C-3 Hopa
172 F-2 Hopatcong
172 F-2 Hopatcong lake
161 M-3 Hope cap.
176 C-3 Hope
216 G-7 Hope lake
162 C-7 Hope (Canada)
159 H-9 Hope riv.
165 H-1 Hope Montains mt
52 C-2 Hope Under Dinmore
104 C-8 Hopefield
179 M-5 Hopelchén
49 H-2 Hopen
220 F-3 Hopetoun (Australia)
216 G-8 Hopetoun (Australia)
104 G-8 Hopetown
171 K-9 Hopewell
143 L-4 Hopin
58 A-2 Hôpital du Grosbois (L')
220 F-5 Hopkins lake
176 G-1 Hopkinsville
162 B-8 Hoquiam
72 D-4 Horasan

191 N-5 Horcones riv.
49 K-1 Hordaland reg.
210 F-3 Horden riv.
123 H-6 Hordil-Saridag mt
59 L-1 Horgen
130 A-1 Horgon lake
196 G-5 Horizonte
196 C-9 Horizontina
53 K-6 Horley
126 B-7 Hormak
189 K-3 Hormigas de Afuera islds
122 E-6 Hormoson-Gol riv.
84 B-4 Hormoz
84 B-4 Hormoz mt
116 A-4 Hormuz strt.
84 B-5 Hormuz strt.
161 K-7 Horn riv.
48 A-2 Horn cap.
51 L-9 Horn
182 D-8 Horn cap.
201 P-6 Horn cap.
214 G-2 Horn isl.
161 J-7 Horn (Canada) mt
158 G-5 Horn (USA) mt
48 A-2 Horn Horn
51 N-9 Hornád riv.
161 L-2 Hornaday riv.
48 F-5 Hornavan lake
53 L-5 Horndon
49 H-6 Hörnefors
171 J-6 Hornell
170 E-1 Hornepayne
172 F-6 Hornerstown
59 N-1 Hörnli mt
211 L-2 Horno islds
201 P-6 Hornos isl.
109 L-3 Horombe reg.
136 B-7 Horosiri Dake mt
196 B-6 Horqueta
141 P-1 Horsburgh isl.
165 M-2 Horse islds
216 E-4 Horse Shoe
166 F-7 Horse Shoe Bend
53 L-8 Horsebridge
162 E-5 Horsefly lake
53 J-6 Horsell
51 J-3 Horsens
218 A-3 Horseshoe Bend
220 E-4 Horsham (Australia)
53 J-7 Horsham (UK)
172 E-5 Horsham (USA)
53 J-6 Horsley
57 H-5 Horssen
57 H-1 Horst (Netherlands)
57 K-8 Horst (Netherlands)
51 J-1 Horten
161 K-1 Horton riv.
164 G-5 Horton rés
161 K-3 Horton lake
52 E-8 Horton (UK)
52 C-7 Horton (UK)
59 K-3 Horw
170 F-2 Horwood lake
95 J-4 Hosaina
140 G-4 Hosdurga
147 N-8 Hose mt
81 H-8 Hosenofu well
140 A-7 Hoshangābād
139 M-2 Hoshiārpur
59 L-6 Hospenthal
140 F-5 Hospet
199 K-4 Hospital mt
60 G-5 Hospitalet
59 K-6 Hospiz mt
59 J-8 Hospiz pass
187 P-4 Hossororo
201 P-5 Hoste isl.
144 E-4 Hot
168 E-5 Hot Springs (USA)
176 D-3 Hot Springs (USA)
129 H-3 Hotan
162 G-2 Hotchkiss
209 K-3 Hote
159 K-3 Hotham Inlet gulf
48 G-5 Hoting
130 A-1 Hoton lake
130 C-8 Hotont
161 K-5 Hottah lake
104 A-3 Hottentotsbaai bay
215 M-4 Houaïlou
144 G-2 Houakhong reg.
145 J-3 Houaphan reg.
54 B-7 Houdan
170 D-3 Houghton
170 E-4 Houghton lake
132 B-5 Hougouzi
54 G-4 Houilles
165 H-7 Houlton
132 C-8 Houma (China)
176 E-6 Houma (USA)
79 P-4 Houmt Souk (Jerba)
89 J-3 Houndé
53 J-5 Hounslow
173 K-1 Housatonic riv.
55 P-7 Houssaye-en-Brie (La)

162 C-2 Houston
164 A-3 Houston pte
176 D-1 Houston (USA)
175 P-5 Houston (USA)
57 H-8 Hout
56 F-3 Houten
57 M-9 Houthem
57 K-8 Houthuizen
53 K-6 Hove
57 K-8 Hovd
130 B-3 Hovd
130 A-1 Hovd riv.
123 H-6 Hövsgöl lake
132 B-3 Hövsgöl
130 A-6 Hövsgöl reg.
92 B-6 Hovsha
92 D-5 Howai riv.
214 B-3 Howard isl.
219 N-4 Howard (Australia)
169 H-5 Howard (USA)
221 K-5 Howe cap.
105 K-6 Howick
164 G-8 Howland
224 B-3 Howland isl.
142 F-5 Howrah
176 E-1 Hoxie (USA)
168 F-8 Hoxie (USA)
53 N-1 Hoxne
50 E-1 Hoy strt.
49 J-1 Høyanger
137 L-6 Hôyo pen.
64 H-7 Hoyran gulf
100 C-2 Hoysha
130 B-6 Hoyt Terhiin riv.
122 G-6 Hoyto Aguy Uula mt
65 N-5 Hozat
51 L-8 Hradec Krlové
51 M-8 Hranice
51 N-9 Hron riv.
48 C-2 Hruni
143 M-5 Hsenwi
143 N-7 Hsim riv.
135 N-7 Hsinchu
135 N-8 Hsinying
143 M-6 Hsipaw
135 N-7 Hsuehshan mt
143 N-3 Htawgaw
144 F-8 Hua Hin
146 D-4 Hua Sai
189 M-6 Huacaña
191 J-2 Huachacalla
190 E-6 Huachi lake
190 E-5 Huachi (Bolivia)
188 D-4 Huachi (Peru)
189 M-6 Huacho
125 H-7 Huachuan
198 C-3 Huaco
189 H-4 Huacrachuco
132 E-4 Huade
133 L-2 Huadian
135 L-1 Huafa
189 J-5 Huagaruancha mt
185 H-4 Huahua riv.
146 D-4 Huai Yot
194 A-6 Huaiá-Missu riv.
132 C-6 Huaian (China)
133 H-9 Huaian (China)
133 K-2 Huaide
135 K-1 Huaihe riv.
134 F-6 Huaihua
135 H-8 Huaiji
132 E-5 Huailai
135 K-2 Huainan
135 K-3 Huaining
132 F-5 Huairou
189 L-5 Huaitará
135 J-1 Huaiyang
133 H-9 Huaiyin (China)
135 K-1 Huaiyuan
178 G-7 Huajuapan de León
191 P-4 Hualfin (Argentina)
198 C-1 Hualfin (Argentina)
135 P-8 Hualien
188 G-4 Huallabamba riv.
188 G-4 Huallaga riv.
189 J-4 Huallanca (Peru)
189 H-3 Huallanca (Peru)
189 H-3 Huamachuco
189 L-6 Huamanrazo mt
102 C-2 Huambo reg.
102 C-2 Huambo
189 L-6 Huanca Sancos
188 F-2 Huancabamba riv.
188 F-2 Huancabamba (Peru)
189 J-3 Huancabamba (Peru)
200 E-4 Huancache rf
190 F-1 Huancané
189 L-5 Huancane
189 L-6 Huancavélica
189 L-5 Huancavélica reg.
189 K-5 Huancayo
191 K-3 Huanchaca mt

191 K-4 Huanchaca
135 J-2 Huangchuan
135 J-3 Huanggang
132 C-5 Huanghe riv.
131 K-8 Huanghe (Yellow river) riv.
135 L-5 Huangjinbu
132 B-8 Huangling
145 M-4 Huangliu
132 C-8 Huanglong
134 G-2 Huanglongzhen
135 K-4 Huangmei
133 L-1 Huangnihe
135 J-3 Huangpi
135 J-3 Huangshan mt
135 J-3 Huangshi
200 A-8 Huanguelén
133 H-6 Huangxian
131 K-7 Huangyuan
185 J-3 Huani lag.
135 P-2 Huaniaoshan isl.
133 K-3 Huanren
135 N-5 Huanshan
189 L-6 Huanta
200 B-3 Huantraicó mt
189 H-6 Huánuco reg.
189 J-5 Huánuco
191 H-3 Huanumi
189 M-7 Huanzo mt
185 H-5 Huapi mt
191 K-1 Huara
189 K-4 Huaral
189 J-4 Huaráz
190 E-1 Huari-Huari riv.
190 G-2 Huarina
189 J-3 Huarmey
189 J-3 Huarmey riv.
189 K-5 Huarochiri
135 H-4 Huarong
188 D-4 Huasaga
188 C-3 Huasaga riv.
189 H-4 Huascarán reg.
191 K-2 Huasco lake
198 A-2 Huasco
198 A-2 Huasco riv.
174 E-7 Huatabampo
190 E-4 Huatunas lake
179 H-6 Huatusco
178 G-5 Huauchinango
185 H-4 Huaunta
185 J-4 Huaunta lake
189 K-4 Huaura
189 K-4 Huaura riv.
189 K-3 Huaura islds
179 H-6 Huautla de Jiménez
132 E-8 Huaxian (China)
135 J-8 Huaxian (China)
189 J-4 Huayhuash mt
189 J-5 Huayllay
134 F-5 Huayuan
189 K-5 Huayucachi
189 M-5 Huayuri pl.
145 N-1 Huazhou
160 C-4 Hubbard mt
135 H-3 Hubei reg.
140 F-4 Hubli
133 L-3 Huchang
82 D-8 Hudayn riv.
50 D-4 Huddersfield
97 J-6 Huddun
97 N-3 Huddur Hadama
49 J-5 Hudiksvall
130 G-8 Hudo well
155 K-4 Hudson bay
156 F-1 Hudson bay
153 L-3 Hudson strt.
156 G-1 Hudson strt.
155 L-3 Hudson strt.
201 H-2 Hudson riv.
171 L-5 Hudson (USA)
170 B-4 Hudson (USA)
163 M-7 Hudson Bay
171 L-5 Hudson Falls (USA)
164 E-9 Hudson Falls (USA)
162 E-2 Hudson Hope
172 G-3 Hudson Queens reg.
145 L-5 Huê
200 E-1 Huechucuicui pte
200 C-3 Huechulafquen lake
184 C-2 Huehuetenango
60 B-7 Huelva
201 H-3 Huemules riv.
198 A-5 Huentelauquén
200 E-2 Huequi pen.
60 F-4 Huesca
178 E-6 Huetamo de Núñez
80 F-3 Hufrah
82 E-4 Hufrah mt
91 P-4 Hufrat an Naḥas
58 F-7 Hugeligrat mt
215 H-9 Hughenden
172 F-1 Hughenot
159 K-6 Hughes
168 E-8 Hugo (USA)
175 P-2 Hugo (USA)

215 M-4 Hugon isl.
168 F-9 Hugoton
132 C-5 Huhehaote
135 M-7 Huian
223 K-6 Huiarau mt
104 B-4 Huib plat.
134 B-6 Huidong
133 L-2 Huifahe riv.
125 H-8 Huifaheng
56 B-8 Huijbergen
102 C-4 Huila reg.
186 D-8 Huila riv.
186 C-8 Huila vol.
134 B-6 Huili
198 D-2 Huillapima
179 K-7 Huimanguillo
132 G-7 Huimin
133 K-2 Huinan
198 E-7 Huinca Renancó
57 H-2 Huinen
131 L-9 Huining
134 D-7 Huishui
50 D-8 Huisne riv.
57 H-5 Huisseling
57 J-4 Huissen
134 F-6 Huitong
49 J-7 Huittinen
178 F-6 Huitzuco de Figueroa
134 D-1 Huixian
179 K-9 Huixtla
135 J-9 Huiyang
134 B-6 Huize
57 H-3 Huize Kernhem site
56 F-1 Huizen
82 E-4 Hüj mt
130 C-8 Hujirt (Mongolia)
130 B-2 Hujirt (Mongolia)
136 B-6 Hukagawa
136 E-6 Hukaura
137 M-1 Hukue isl.
137 M-1 Hukue
137 H-5 Hukui
104 F-2 Hukuntsi
137 L-2 Hukuoka
136 D-7 Hukuoka
136 F-7 Hukusima
137 K-4 Hukuyama
124 G-8 Hulan
124 F-8 Hulanhe riv.
82 G-6 Hulayfah
130 D-9 Huld
224 B-4 Hull isl.
164 D-8 Hull
57 N-9 Hulsberg
56 F-8 Hulsel
57 H-1 Hulshorst
57 H-1 Hulshorster Zand reg.
56 A-9 Hulst
56 E-7 Hulten
51 L-2 Hultsfred
124 B-7 Hulunchi lake
124 E-4 Huma
181 K-1 Humacoa
124 D-4 Humaerhe riv.
124 D-4 Humaerwojishan mt
191 M-5 Humahuaca
190 A-6 Humaita
196 A-9 Humaitá
104 G-9 Humansdorp
93 J-4 Humar riv.
189 L-5 Humay
193 N-9 Humberto de Campos
215 M-4 Humboldt
163 L-7 Humboldt (Canada)
176 F-2 Humboldt (USA)
166 G-5 Humbolt riv.
221 H-4 Hume lake
66 B-8 Humenné
129 N-2 Hūmla Karnāli riv.
57 L-3 Hummelo
48 G-2 Hummelvik
221 H-7 Hummock isl.
201 H-2 Humos riv.
167 M-7 Humphreys mt
213 N-1 Humpty Doo
80 D-4 Hun
48 A-2 Hunafloi bay
134 G-6 Hunan reg.
96 F-2 Hunayshīyah
133 N-1 Hunchun
51 K-3 Hundested
52 B-2 Hundred
64 D-2 Hunedoara
145 K-2 Hung Yên
47 E-5 Hungary state
218 G-6 Hungerford (Australia)
52 F-5 Hungerford (UK)
162 G-9 Hungry Horse lake
133 J-3 Hunhe riv.
133 K-3 Hunjiang riv.
57 M-6 Hunsel
50 E-5 Hunstanton
164 B-8 Hunstville
141 H-4 Hunsür
160 F-5 Hunt mt
220 G-7 Hunter islds

221 L-2 Hunter riv.
221 K-2 Hunter mt
220 F-7 Hunter (Australia) isl.
162 A-3 Hunter (Canada) isl.
172 E-4 Hunterdon
143 J-8 Hunters bay
162 D-8 Hunters
219 K-4 Hunterton
170 E-9 Huntingburg
50 E-5 Huntingdon (UK)
171 J-7 Huntingdon (USA)
172 A-2 Huntington riv.
173 J-3 Huntington
173 J-2 Huntington bay
170 G-9 Huntington (USA)
170 E-7 Huntington (USA)
166 E-6 Huntington (USA)
172 B-1 Huntington Mills
52 D-3 Huntley
223 K-4 Huntly
175 P-5 Huntsville (USA)
176 G-2 Huntsville (USA)
130 B-7 Hünüg riv.
106 G-1 Hunyani riv.
132 D-5 Hunyuan
127 N-6 Hunza riv.
128 C-4 Huocheng
132 G-1 Huolehe riv.
124 E-5 Huolongmon
132 E-6 Huolu
215 L-1 Huon isl.
211 K-6 Huon gulf
211 K-5 Huon pen.
220 G-9 Huon riv.
145 L-5 Huong Hoa
145 K-4 Huong Khê
220 G-9 Huonville
135 K-3 Huoshan
132 D-7 Huoshan mt
125 H-6 Huoshaoying
57 N-3 Huppel
223 H-7 Hupper Hutt
136 B-7 Hurano
164 A-9 Hurd cap.
96 G-9 Hurdiyo
82 B-6 Hurgada (Al Ghudaqah)
123 M-8 Hurhïn riv.
95 J-7 Huri hill
52 A-6 Hurlestone pte
53 H-5 Hurley (UK)
174 F-7 Hurley (USA)
170 C-3 Hurley (USA)
169 H-4 Huron
170 G-4 Huron lake
156 F-2 Huron lake
167 L-7 Hurricane
52 G-7 Hursley
52 G-6 Hurstbourne
52 F-6 Hurstbourne Tarrant
53 K-8 Hurstpierpoint
198 A-4 Hurtado riv.
136 F-7 Hurukawa
48 B-3 Husávik
53 H-1 Husband's Bosworth
97 K-1 Husen
130 D-9 Hushuu Hiid
64 F-1 Husi
137 H-7 Husi San vol.
51 L-2 Huskvarna
144 A-9 Hut bay
130 A-8 Hutag
146 D-9 Hutanopan
170 A-4 Hutchinson
57 L-5 Huthum
131 H-2 Hutonghu lake
124 E-4 Hutongzhen
125 K-7 Hutou
219 K-4 Hutton mt
52 C-6 Hutton
59 H-2 Huttwill
128 D-8 Hutubi
128 D-8 Hutubihe riv.
132 E-6 Hutuhohe riv.
135 N-8 Huwei
134 F-1 Huxian (China)
132 B-9 Huxian (China)
213 K-5 Huxley (USA)
178 C-3 Huynamota riv.
135 M-3 Huzhou
131 K-7 Huzhu
137 J-7 Huzi
137 H-7 Huzi-Yosida
137 H-7 Huzisawa
61 P-4 Hvar isl.
61 P-4 Hvarski cap.
48 B-2 Hvita riv.
48 C-1 Hvolsvöllur
133 L-5 Hwangju
168 F-6 Hyannis
130 A-4 Hyargas lake
130 A-4 Hyargas
160 C-8 Hydaburg
153 Q-1 Hyde fj.
192 C-2 Hyde Park
216 F-7 Hyden

140 E-6 Hyderābād
138 F-5 Hyderabad
49 J-1 Hyen
61 J-4 Hyères
61 J-4 Hyères islds
133 M-3 Hyesan
58 B-1 Hyèvre
213 L-2 Hyland bay
160 F-6 Hyland riv.
160 F-6 Hyland plat.
160 G-5 Hyland riv.
160 E-8 Hyland Post
51 J-1 Hynnekleiv
48 F-8 Hyrynsalmi
168 D-2 Hysham
52 G-8 Hythe (UK)
53 N-7 Hythe (UK)
137 M-3 Hyuga
49 J-8 Hyvinkaa

# I

224 C-5 I Sisifo islds
64 A-3 I Zenica
78 F-8 Iabes dés
113 K-4 Iablonovy rge
189 J-9 Iaco riv.
109 L-4 Iakora
64 E-2 Ialomita riv.
109 J-4 Iandratsay riv.
196 F-7 Iapo riv.
197 L-4 Iapu
192 E-6 Iaripo
66 D-9 Iaşi
142 C-5 Ib riv.
59 M-3 Ibach
89 M-8 Ibadan
186 D-6 Ibagué
196 F-7 Ibaiti
100 C-2 Ibanda
201 H-3 Ibáñez riv.
185 H-2 Ibans lag.
190 F-5 Ibare riv.
188 B-3 Ibarra
96 E-3 Ibb
94 C-6 Ibba
94 C-5 Ibba riv.
91 N-9 Ibembo
91 J-9 Ibenga riv.
199 J-2 Iberá lag.
59 M-3 Iberg
188 F-6 Iberia (Peru)
190 D-1 Iberia (Peru)
46 C-5 Iberic rge
164 C-1 Iberville lake
197 H-4 Ibiaí
197 K-2 Ibiaí
195 K-1 Ibiapaba mt
195 K-1 Ibiapina
93 K-1 Ibib riv.
191 K-6 Ibibobo
197 N-1 Ibicaraí
199 K-3 Ibicuí riv.
199 K-3 Ibicui
199 H-6 Ibicuy
195 M-5 Ibimirim
100 B-2 Ibina riv.
195 K-8 Ibiquera
196 F-9 Ibirama
197 N-3 Ibirapuã
199 K-3 Ibirapuita riv.
196 F-6 Ibirarema
199 K-3 Ibiroca riv.
195 J-8 Ibitiara
196 G-5 Ibitinga
195 H-7 Ibitunane
60 F-6 Ibiza
60 F-6 Ibiza isl.
65 L-8 Ibn Hanï cap.
96 C-7 Ibn Qawrah
106 E-8 Ibo
195 H-7 Ibotirama
98 D-3 Iboundji mt
84 D-8 Ibrā
91 P-3 Ibrah riv.
93 N-2 Ibrāhïm riv.
67 L-1 Ibresi
84 E-7 Ibri
81 N-3 Ibshawāy
52 F-8 Ibsley
137 N-3 Ibusuki
189 M-5 Ica riv.
189 M-5 Ica reg.
189 M-5 Ica

121 M-1 Iča
187 N-7 Icabarú
187 N-6 Icabarú riv.
199 K-2 Icamaquã riv.
187 J-9 Içana riv.
193 M-9 Icatu
195 H-6 Icatu riv.
47 B-3 Iceland state
196 G-4 Icem
123 M-1 Ičera
140 E-3 Ichalkaranji
142 C-7 Ichchāpuram
191 H-5 Ichilo riv.
190 G-4 Ichoa riv.
189 N-9 Ichuña riv.
53 M-1 Icklingham
66 F-6 Ičn'a
195 L-3 Ico
159 M-2 Icy cap.
160 C-6 Icy strt.
160 B-3 Icy bay
160 B-3 Icy Cape cap.
84 D-3 Id al Sharqi well
91 M-1 Id el Gara
169 J-6 Ida Grove
175 P-3 Idabel
90 B-6 Idah
168 A-3 Idaho state
157 C-2 Idaho state
168 A-3 Idaho Falls
97 L-7 Idān
91 P-3 Idd al Ghanam
68 C-6 Idel'
130 B-7 Ider riv.
130 B-5 Ider
123 N-9 Idermeg
82 B-7 Idfu (Apollinopolis Magna)
64 E-9 Idhi mt
64 E-8 Idhra isl.
63 K-7 Idice riv.
97 M-3 Ididole
99 J-6 Idiofa
88 E-9 Idiotya mt
159 H-5 Iditarod riv.
100 B-4 Idjwi isl.
65 M-8 Idlib
49 J-4 Idre
122 E-3 Idrinskoje
63 H-2 Idro lake
63 H-2 Idro
187 P-3 Iduburojo isl.
105 J-8 Idutywa
122 E-5 Idžim
51 L-7 Ielenia-Gora
100 G-8 Ifakara
90 A-5 Ifaki
109 K-5 Ifanadiana
89 M-9 Ife
91 K-1 Ifénat
58 F-7 Iffigen
214 F-8 Iffley
90 A-6 Ifon
88 E-7 Iforas mt
78 E-3 Ifrane
124 G-3 Iga riv.
100 E-2 Iganga
195 H-8 Igaporã
188 C-7 Igara Paraná riv.
197 H-4 Igarapava
193 K-8 Igarapé-Açu
193 J-8 Igarapé-Miri
195 H-7 Igarité
196 C-7 Igatimi
140 B-3 Igatpuri
89 L-9 Igbetti
72 E-3 Iğdir
90 D-2 Iggy riv.
79 H-2 Ighil Izane
78 D-4 Ighil Mgoun mt
159 K-3 Igichuk mt
123 K-2 Igirma
123 K-2 Igirma riv.
158 F-7 Igiugik
198 B-4 Iglesia riv.
198 B-4 Iglesia
61 K-7 Iglesias
78 F-6 Igli
170 B-1 Ignace
66 C-4 Ignalina
124 C-7 Ignašino
144 A-9 Ignoitijala
55 H-7 Igny
100 D-6 Igombe riv.
64 C-6 Igoumenitsa
69 L-7 Igra
199 P-2 Igreja mt
69 L-1 Igrim
197 K-6 Iguacu
196 D-3 Iguacu riv.
158 D-8 Iguak cap.
178 F-6 Iguala de la Ind.
60 G-5 Igualada
197 H-7 Iguape
197 J-4 Iguatama
196 C-6 Iguatemi riv.

195 J-8 Iguatemi (Brazil)
196 C-6 Iguatemi (Brazil)
196 C-8 Iguazu na.p.
98 B-4 Iguela
86 D-3 Iguîdi reg.
88 A-8 Iguidi in Afarag reg.
195 J-7 Iguitu
103 L-8 Igusi
130 D-7 Ih Bogd mt
130 B-6 Ih-Uul
141 M-1 Ihavandiffulu isl.
137 M-8 Iheya isl.
91 P-8 Ihgasu
132 B-1 Ihhet
90 B-7 Ihiala
109 K-4 Ihosy
109 K-4 Ihosy riv.
109 K-2 Ihotry lake
130 C-7 Ihtamir
64 D-4 Ihtiman
69 M-8 Ik riv.
211 J-6 Ihu
48 F-8 Iijoki riv.
101 K-3 Ijara
89 N-8 Ijebu-Ode
88 B-2 Ijoubbâne reg.
56 B-5 IJsselmonde isl.
56 C-4 IJsselmonde
56 E-3 Ijsselstein
57 J-8 Ijsselstein (Netherlands)
199 K-2 Ijui riv.
199 L-2 Ijui
199 L-2 Ijuizinho riv.
57 L-4 IJzevoorde
69 M-9 Ikire
72 C-3 Ikizdere
158 D-9 Ikolik cap.
90 C-7 Ikom
108 G-5 Ikopa riv.
109 H-5 Ikopa
89 N-8 Ikorodu
100 A-4 Ikosi
90 B-7 Ikot-Ekpene
98 C-3 Ikoy riv.
159 N-4 Ikpikpuk riv.
69 P-3 Iksa riv.
63 M-1 Il Montello hill
130 A-6 Il-Uul
90 A-5 Ila
88 B-7 Ilaferh riv.
141 K-6 Ilaiyānkudi
73 H-8 Ilām reg.
73 H-8 Ilām (Iran)
142 F-2 Ilām (Nepal)
135 P-7 Ilan
122 G-2 Ilanskij
59 P-5 Ilanz
190 G-1 Ilave
52 C-7 Ilchester
201 P-5 Ildefonso islds
163 K-5 Ile à la Crosse
200 F-1 Ile de Chiloé isl.
99 K-5 Ilebo
70 B-7 Ileck riv.
100 E-4 Ilemera
89 N-8 Iléro
90 A-5 Ilesha
59 H-4 Ilfis riv.
50 C-6 Ilfracombe
52 G-2 Ilfton
123 K-4 Ilga riv.
65 J-4 Ilgaz mt
65 J-4 Ilgaz
65 J-6 Ilgin
197 J-7 Ilhabela
197 P-1 Ilhéus
128 C-3 Ili
128 A-7 Ili riv.
158 F-8 Iliamna vol.
149 J-3 Iligan
149 J-3 Iligan bay
123 J-2 Ilim riv.
123 K-2 Ilimsk
148 F-5 Ilin isl.
123 H-4 Ilir riv.
123 H-3 Ilir
158 G-5 Ilivit mt
71 H-7 Iljaly
120 C-9 Iljič
122 F-2 Iljinka
125 N-4 Iljinskij

190 G-2 Illampu mt
149 J-3 Illana bay
198 A-5 Illapel
198 A-5 Illapel riv.
63 K-3 Illasi
95 H-6 Illeret
188 F-1 Illesca mt
59 M-3 Illgau
192 D-7 Ilhinha dam.
58 D-9 Illiez val.
57 M-7 Illikhoven
190 G-3 Illimani mt
170 C-7 Illinois riv.
170 C-8 Illinois state
157 F-2 Illinois state
192 B-4 Illiwa riv.
79 M-9 Illizi
66 E-1 Il'men' riv.
52 C-8 Ilminster
189 P-8 Ilo
89 M-9 Ilobu
148 G-4 Iloilo
89 M-9 Ilorin
72 A-1 Il'skij
94 G-4 Ilubabor reg.
49 P-6 Ilwa
209 H-6 Ilwaki
137 L-4 Ilwazima
137 K-4 Imabari
192 C-7 Imanis mt
136 C-6 Imagane
109 L-3 Imaloto riv.
125 K-7 Iman riv.
125 K-7 Iman
68 B-3 Imandra lake
124 B-1 Imangra riv.
199 P-2 Imaruí
189 N-9 Imata
187 N-4 Imataca mt
49 J-9 Imatra
81 N-2 Imbabah
188 B-2 Imbabura reg.
196 F-7 Imbaú riv.
199 P-2 Imbitub
196 F-8 Imbituva
57 K-3 Imbosch na.p.
64 E-6 Imbros isl.
121 J-1 Imeni Molodogvardejcev
125 J-2 Imeny Poliny Osipenko
187 K-9 Imeri mt
109 H-5 Imerina reg.
99 H-1 Imese
78 C-3 Imfout
133 M-5 Imgin riv.
97 L-2 Imi
78 B-5 Imi-n'Tanoute
191 M-2 Imilac
78 D-4 Imilchil
72 G-3 Imišlij
217 P-5 Immarna
59 L-3 Immensee
177 K-8 Immokalee
159 J-3 Immuruk Lake lake
90 B-7 Imo reg.
61 M-3 Imola
78 B-5 Imouzzer-des-Ida-Outanane
78 E-3 Imouzzer-du-Kandar
194 E-2 Imperatriz
62 A-9 Imperia reg.
61 B-9 Imperia
62 B-9 Imperia Porto Maurizio
200 C-2 Imperial
200 C-1 Imperial riv.
168 F-7 Imperial
212 F-5 Imperieuse rf
99 H-1 Impfondo
143 K-4 Imphal
63 K-9 Impruneta
174 E-4 Imuris
159 J-2 Imuruk Basin lake
79 N-8 In Amenas
88 C-6 In Arhata mt
88 B-8 In Dagouber
80 B-8 In Ezzane well
88 A-8 In Hihaou riv.
88 C-6 In Naj dés
88 C-8 In Ouzzal riv.
88 C-6 In Sâkâne dés
79 J-9 In Salah
79 K-7 In Sokki riv.
88 D-9 In Tabarakkat mt
88 F-8 In-Tallak
122 B-2 In'a riv.
121 N-5 Ina riv.
121 P-6 In'a
137 H-6 Ina (Japan)
123 M-4 Ina (SSSR)
195 M-5 Inajá
194 D-4 Inajá riv.
194 C-4 Inajá mt
189 K-9 Inambari
137 K-8 Inanba isl.
209 L-2 Inanwatan

189 J-9 Inapari
123 M-2 In'aptuk *mt*
48 D-8 Inari *lake*
48 D-7 Inari
48 D-7 Inarijoki *riv.*
124 E-2 Inarogda
159 N-3 Inaru *riv.*
190 B-2 Inauni *riv.*
136 G-7 Inawasiro *lake*
60 G-6 Inca
191 L-3 Inca (del) *mt*
191 M-3 Incahuasi *lake*
65 K-3 Ince *cap.*
65 K-8 Incekum *cap.*
65 L-6 Incesu
86 B-4 Inchîri *reg.*
133 M-6 Inch'on
62 C-5 Incisa Scapaccino
107 N-1 Incomati *riv.*
159 J-1 Inčoun
61 L-5 Incudine *mt*
93 M-7 Inda Silase
197 J-3 Indaia *riv.*
196 E-3 Indaia Crde *riv.*
196 F-9 Indaial
197 H-6 Indaiatuba
143 L-4 Indaw
143 L-4 Indawgyi *lake*
59 N-9 Indémini
58 G-8 Inden
189 M-5 Indepencia *bay*
166 G-6 Independence *mt*
153 Q-1 Independence *fj.*
176 B-1 Independence (USA)
177 K-1 Independence (USA)
170 B-6 Independence (USA)
170 A-8 Independence (USA)
167 K-4 Independence (USA)
190 G-3 Independencia (Bolivia)
195 K-2 Independência (Brazil)
70 B-5 Inder *lake*
206 E-1 Inderagiri *riv.*
206 C-2 Inderapura *cap.*
70 B-5 Inderborskij
58 D-1 Indevillers
140 E-5 Indi
118 C-4 India *state*
163 L-8 Indian Head
164 E-9 Indian Lake
172 F-7 Indian Mills
204 B-3 Indian Ocean
76 G-7 Indian Ocean
116 C-7 Indian Ocean
167 M-8 Indian Wells
170 E-8 Indiana *state*
157 F-2 Indiana *state*
218 B-2 Indiana (Australia)
171 J-7 Indiana (USA)
170 E-8 Indianapolis
176 E-3 Indianola (USA)
170 A-7 Indianola (USA)
197 H-3 Indianópolis
196 F-4 Indiaporã
68 F-2 Indiga
113 N-2 Indigirskaya Nizmennost *pl.*
64 B-2 Indija
161 L-6 Indin *lake*
185 H-6 Indio *riv.*
174 B-1 Indio
200 B-8 Indio Rico
196 F-9 Indios
190 A-9 Indios *riv.*
118 F-7 Indonesia *state*
139 L-9 Indore
142 B-6 Indra *riv.*
218 A-3 Indracowra
207 J-5 Indramaju
140 D-8 Indrāvati *riv.*
50 D-9 Indre *riv.*
62 D-1 Induno Olona
138 E-6 Indus *est.*
138 E-6 Indus *riv.*
116 B-4 Indus *riv.*
191 H-1 Industrial
105 J-7 Indwe
65 J-4 Inebolu
64 G-5 Inegöl
208 D-7 Inerie *mt*
201 J-4 Iñes *mt*
78 B-5 Inezgane
148 D-5 Infanta
184 A-1 Inferior *lag.*
190 B-8 Infernao *riv.*
178 D-6 Infiernillo
178 D-6 Infiernillo *dam.*
60 C-2 Infiesto
144 G-3 Ing *riv.*
195 P-4 Ingá
98 E-6 Inga *dam.*
143 K-9 Ingabu
163 M-1 Ingalls *lake*
53 L-4 Ingatestone
56 G-4 Ingen
99 J-2 Ingende
215 J-8 Ingham (Australia)
53 M-1 Ingham (UK)
120 B-9 Ingička
153 M-2 Inglefield Land
198 A-1 Inglesa *bay*
172 B-9 Ingleside
219 L-6 Inglewood (Australia)
167 M-3 Inglewood (USA)
159 J-4 Inglutalik *riv.*
123 N-6 Ingoda (SSSR) *riv.*
124 A-5 Ingoda (SSSR) *riv.*
51 J-9 Ingoldstadt
153 S-1 Ingolfs *fj.*
218 B-6 Ingomar
165 L-5 Ingonish
227 N-3 Ingrid Christensen Coast
66 G-9 Ingul *riv.*
66 G-8 Ingulec *riv.*
66 G-8 Ingulec
123 P-4 Ingur
72 D-1 Ingušskaja *reg.*
107 P-2 Inhaca *isl.*
107 M-4 Inhambane *bay*
107 M-4 Inhambane
107 M-3 Inhambane *reg.*
195 L-7 Inhambupe *riv.*
195 L-7 Inhambupe
107 J-4 Inhaminga
199 M-2 Inhanduva *riv.*
193 K-8 Inhangapi
197 L-4 Inhapim
107 L-4 Inhassoro
194 G-2 Inhaúma *mt*
196 C-6 Inhobi *riv.*
195 J-3 Inhuma
196 G-1 Inhumas
90 E-4 Ini *riv.*
192 E-4 Inini
192 F-4 Inini *riv.*
186 G-8 Iniriba *riv.*
188 B-7 Iniyá *riv.*
219 K-4 Injune
52 E-2 Inkberrow
214 F-6 Inkerman
98 F-6 Inkisi *riv.*
160 D-6 Inklin
160 D-6 Inklin *riv.*
159 K-4 Inland *lake*
143 L-7 Inle *lake*
61 L-2 Inn *riv.*
218 E-5 Innamincka
48 E-4 Inndyr
132 D-3 Inner Mongolia *reg.*
59 K-5 Innertkirchen
215 J-7 Innisfail
125 K-4 Innokentjevka
125 M-4 Innokentjevskij
159 G-5 Innoko *riv.*
137 K-4 Innosima
61 M-1 Innsbrück
196 E-4 Inocencia
99 H-4 Inongo
98 F-4 Inoni
155 L-4 Inoucdjouac
51 M-6 Inowrocław
190 G-3 Inquisivi
58 E-3 Ins
67 K-2 Insar
216 B-3 Inscription *cap.*
144 D-5 Insein
49 J-1 Instelfjord
69 J-1 Inta
93 N-7 Inteho
61 K-1 Interlaken
170 B-1 International Falls
144 A-8 Interview *isl.*
184 E-3 Intibuca *reg.*
176 C-6 Intracoastal Waterway *lake*
59 M-9 Intragna
62 E-1 Intróbio
207 P-1 Intu
137 H-8 Inubo *cap.*
137 L-3 Inukai
201 N-5 Inutil *bay*
161 H-1 Inuvik
189 J-7 Inuya *riv.*
50 C-2 Inveraray
222 C-9 Invercargill
219 L-7 Inverell
214 E-7 Inverleigh
165 L-6 Inverness (Canada)
50 D-1 Inverness (UK)
177 K-7 Inverness (USA)
213 M-5 Inverway
220 A-2 Investigator *islds*
220 C-3 Investigator *strt.*
149 J-9 Investigator (Yuyaansha) *rf*
163 P-9 Inwood
107 H-2 Inyanga
107 H-2 Inyanga *mt*
167 L-4 Inyokern
100 D-7 Inyonga
67 L-2 Inza
67 K-4 Inžavino
69 N-8 Inzer
69 N-8 Inzer *riv.*
99 H-6 Inzia *riv.*
137 N-3 Iō *isl.*
172 C-5 Ioanna
64 C-6 Ioánnina
169 J-9 Iola
63 M-5 Iolanda di Savoia
121 P-5 Iolgo *mt*
71 M-9 Iolotan'
126 F-2 Iolotan
211 K-7 Ioma
172 A-5 Iona
102 A-5 Iona *na.p.*
109 L-4 Ionaivo *riv.*
66 B-4 Ionava
170 E-5 Ionia
64 C-7 Ionian *islds*
64 B-8 Ionian *sea*
46 E-6 Ionian *sea*
66 B-3 Ioniškis
64 E-8 Ios
170 A-6 Iowa *state*
157 E-2 Iowa *state*
170 B-6 Iowa City
170 A-6 Iowa Falls
184 D-3 Ipala
196 G-2 Ipameri
195 N-5 Ipanema *riv.*
189 H-6 Iparía
67 M-8 Ipatovo
195 L-3 Ipaumirim
91 J-9 Ipendja *riv.*
160 B-8 Iphigenia *bay*
188 A-3 Ipiales
195 K-9 Ipiaú
196 F-7 Ipiranga
194 A-5 Ipiranga *riv.*
187 L-3 Ipire *riv.*
64 C-6 Ipiros *reg.*
194 B-2 Ipixuna *riv.*
159 M-4 Ipnavik *riv.*
146 E-6 Ipoh
195 P-5 Ipojuca *riv.*
196 F-1 Iporá
196 G-7 Iporanga
91 M-6 Ippy
64 F-5 Ipsala
219 M-6 Ipswich (Australia)
50 E-6 Ipswich (UK)
169 H-3 Ipswish
195 K-1 Ipu
193 H-9 Ipuana *dam.*
195 K-8 Ipueiras
200 G-1 Ipun *isl.*
66 F-5 Iput *riv.*
195 H-1 Iquara *riv.*
191 K-1 Iquique
190 C-3 Iquiri (Ituxi) *riv.*
188 D-7 Iquitos
91 M-7 Ira Banda
175 K-4 Iraan
137 P-6 Irabu *isl.*
195 M-3 Iracema (Brazil)
190 B-7 Iracema (Brazil)
192 F-3 Iracoube
192 F-3 Iracoubo *riv.*
97 H-7 Irādame
59 N-8 Iragna
196 D-9 Iraí
69 H-3 Irajol'
195 K-8 Irajuba
64 F-9 Iraklion (Candia)
114 D-6 Iran *state*
204 B-1 Iran (Peg) *rge*
141 L-7 Iranamadu *lake*
141 L-7 Iranativu *isl.*
72 G-6 Irānshah
126 A-9 Iranshār
187 N-2 Irapa
186 F-2 Irapa *mt*
178 E-4 Irapuato
193 H-8 Irapuru
77 G-1 Iraq *state*
195 J-7 Iraquara
195 L-7 Irará
194 B-1 Irata *riv.*
192 G-7 Iratapuru *riv.*
196 F-8 Irati
199 M-1 Iratim *riv.*
123 H-1 Irba
122 F-3 Irbejskoje
51 P-2 Irbes Saurums *strt.*
66 A-2 Irbes Sauruns *strt.*
82 C-1 Irbid
72 F-6 Irbil
69 P-5 Irbit
99 H-3 Irebu
195 J-7 Irecé
47 C-4 Ireland *state*
50 B-3 Ireland (Northern) *reg.*
69 P-8 Iremel' *mt*
192 B-4 Ireng *riv.*
70 F-2 Irgiz
70 E-1 Irgiz *riv.*
79 K-9 Irharhar *riv.*
78 B-5 Irherm
133 M-7 Iri
194 A-5 Iri Novo *riv.*
117 J-7 Irian *bay*
210 B-2 Irian (Teluk) *bay*
92 A-7 Iriba
192 C-6 Iricoumé *mt*
148 E-4 Iriga
70 D-1 Iriklinskij
100 F-9 Iringa *reg.*
100 G-8 Iringa
89 L-3 Iringo *riv.*
123 K-1 Irinja *mt*
137 P-5 Iriomote *isl.*
185 H-2 Iriona
194 A-1 Iriri *riv.*
200 B-7 Iris
46 C-4 Irish *sea*
50 C-4 Irish *sea*
193 K-8 Irituia
123 J-6 Irkut *riv.*
123 K-5 Irkutsk
120 A-6 Irlir *mt*
193 L-7 Irmaos *isl.*
91 K-4 Iro *lake*
137 J-7 Irō *pte*
181 H-7 Irois *cap.*
220 C-1 Iron Baron
159 H-3 Iron Creek
220 C-1 Iron Knob
170 D-3 Iron Mountain
170 G-9 Ironton (USA)
170 C-9 Ironton (USA)
161 J-2 Iroquois *riv.*
66 E-7 Irpen'
83 J-8 Irq as Subayb *mt*
96 E-5 Irqah
143 K-8 Irrawaddy *riv.*
144 C-5 Irrawaddy *reg.*
88 E-2 Irrigi *reg.*
53 J-1 Irthlingborough
69 P-1 Irthyš *riv.*
121 K-1 Irtyš
121 L-2 Irtyš *riv.*
121 K-2 Irtyšsk
100 C-1 Irumu
60 E-3 Irun
191 L-5 Iruya *riv.*
191 L-5 Iruya
175 N-3 Irving
173 H-2 Irvington
133 N-6 Irweeol-San *mt*
216 D-5 Irwir *riv.*
172 G-3 Irymgton
93 K-1 Is *mt*
69 M-5 Is
127 K-8 Isa Khel
219 L-2 Isaac *riv.*
184 A-8 Isabel *bay*
201 M-4 Isabel *isl.*
184 A-9 Isabela *isl.*
184 B-8 Isabela *cal.*
184 G-4 Isabelia *mt*
170 B-2 Isabella
48 A-2 Isafjardardjúp *fj.*
137 M-2 Isahaya
99 J-4 Isaka
137 M-8 Isakawa
109 K-3 Isalo *mt*
186 G-8 Isana *riv.*
99 L-4 Isandja
108 G-5 Isandrano *riv.*
99 L-3 Isanga
106 C-1 Isangano *rés*
99 M-2 Isangi
79 M-8 Isaouane-N-Irarraren *reg.*
79 L-9 Isaouane-N-Tifernine *reg.*
51 J-9 Isar *riv.*
191 K-5 Iscayachi
61 N-6 Ischia *isl.*
186 B-8 Iscuandé *riv.*
186 B-8 Iscuandé
213 J-4 Isdell *riv.*
137 J-6 Ise *gulf*
137 J-6 Ise
59 K-9 Iselle
59 J-5 Iseltwald
137 L-8 Isen
57 N-7 Isenbruch
59 L-4 Isenthal
62 G-2 Iseo
62 G-2 Iseo *lake*
58 E-9 Isérables
61 J-2 Isère *riv.*
89 M-8 Iseyin
73 L-7 Isfahan *reg.*
73 L-7 Isfahan
127 M-2 Isfara
97 P-3 Isha Baydabo
53 H-1 Isham
192 B-5 Isherton
101 G-3 Ishiara
69 N-9 Ishimbay
127 M-5 Ishkumān
170 D-3 Ishpeming
190 G-4 Isiboro *riv.*
137 P-6 Isigaki
137 P-6 Isigaki *isl.*
136 B-7 Isikari *mt*
136 B-6 Isikari *gulf*
136 B-6 Isikari
120 F-2 Išim *riv.*
120 G-1 Išimka
149 P-4 Isimu
123 N-5 Isinga
94 B-7 Isiro
219 H-3 Isisford
137 L-4 Isizuti *mt*
120 D-9 Iskandar
64 D-3 Iskar *riv.*
127 L-5 Iškašim
65 L-7 Iskenderun
64 L-7 Iskenderun Körfezi *bay*
65 K-4 Iskilip
122 D-5 Iškin
70 C-5 Iskininskij
121 P-2 Iskitim
125 K-4 Iskra
97 H-8 Iskushuban
160 D-8 Iskut *riv.*
181 M-3 Isla Aves *isl.*
200 G-2 Isla Magdalena
65 M-7 Islâhiye
118 C-3 Islamabad
127 L-8 Islamabad
138 G-6 Islāmkot
218 C-8 Island *lag.*
155 S-3 Island *state*
172 G-7 Island Beach *bay*
164 A-6 Island Falls
172 G-6 Island Heights
216 D-6 Island Point *pte*
165 L-3 Islands *bay*
223 K-2 Islands *bay*
50 C-2 Islay *isl.*
189 N-8 Islay *pte*
60 G-2 Isle *riv.*
58 B-6 Isle (L')
55 H-2 Isle-Adam (L')
55 H-2 Isle-Adam (L') *ft*
170 D-2 Isle Royale *isl.*
53 L-1 Isleham
55 N-5 Isles-lès-Villenoy
52 G-4 Islip (UK)
173 K-3 Islip (USA)
191 J-2 Isluga *vol.*
168 E-2 Ismay
82 B-7 Isnā
109 M-3 Isoanala
106 C-3 Isoka
62 B-5 Isola d'Asti
62 D-6 Isola del Cantone
63 J-4 Isola della Scala
63 K-3 Isola Rizza
63 K-2 Isola Vicentina
62 A-9 Isolabona
101 H-2 Isolio
59 N-9 Isone
136 F-8 Isonomaki
63 H-3 Isorella
65 H-7 Isparta
72 C-4 Ispir
62 C-1 Ispra
200 G-1 Isquiliac *isl.*
47 G-6 Israël *state*
93 N-5 Isratu *isl.*
192 B-3 Issano
100 F-7 Issaua *riv.*
57 M-5 Isselburg
79 K-2 Isser *riv.*
89 N-1 Issia
194 F-8 Issiara
62 A-2 Issime
61 H-2 Issoire
54 D-4 Issou
61 H-1 Issoudun
97 H-3 Issutugan *riv.*
55 H-6 Issy-les-Moulineaux
128 D-2 Issyk-Kul' *lake*
64 G-5 Istanbul
64 G-5 Istanbul Boğazi *strt.*
71 P-4 Istara
64 D-7 Istiaía
186 C-6 Istmina
187 H-1 Istmo de Médanos
159 P-7 Isto *mt*
63 M-2 Istrana
120 B-9 Ištychan
196 A-9 Itá-Ibaté
195 P-4 Itabaiana
195 M-7 Itabaininha
197 M-5 Itabapoana
196 G-7 Itabera
195 K-8 Itaberaba
196 F-1 Itaberai
197 L-4 Itabira
197 K-4 Itabirito
197 P-1 Itabuna
194 D-2 Itacaiúna *riv.*
194 E-4 Itacajá
197 L-2 Itacambirucu *riv.*
194 G-9 Itacarambi
195 L-9 Itacaré
195 J-7 Itacira
192 C-9 Itacoatiara
197 P-2 Itacolomis *rf*
188 E-9 Itacua'i *riv.*
196 B-7 Itacuribí del Rosario
197 M-4 Itaguacu
197 K-6 Itaguai
196 E-6 Itaguaje
197 K-4 Itaguara
194 G-9 Itaguari *riv.*
196 G-1 Itaguaru
194 E-2 Itaguatins
186 D-5 Itagüi
196 G-6 Itai
195 M-2 Itaiçaba
195 K-4 Itaim *riv.*
196 C-7 Itaimbey *riv.*
195 J-4 Itainópolis
196 C-7 Itaipu
196 G-9 Itajai
196 G-9 Itajai *riv.*
196 G-5 Itajobi
197 J-6 Itajuba
124 B-3 Itaka
190 F-2 Italaque
47 E-5 Italy *state*
197 L-3 Itamarandiba
193 L-8 Itamataré
197 N-1 Itambé
197 L-3 Itambé *mt*
197 J-6 Itamonte
109 M-2 Itampolo
143 K-2 Itanagar
192 E-8 Itandeua *lake*
94 G-3 Itang
197 H-7 Itanhaém
197 N-3 Itanhem *riv.*
197 N-2 Itanhém
197 M-4 Itanhomi
197 M-2 Itaobim
197 L-6 Itaocara
194 D-9 Itapaci
195 L-1 Itapagé
196 G-4 Itapagipe
195 L-8 Itaparica *isl.*
195 L-8 Itaparica
196 B-8 Itapé
197 N-1 Itapebi
197 J-4 Itapeceria
197 M-5 Itapemirim
197 N-4 Itaperina *pte*
197 L-5 Itaperuna
197 N-1 Itapetinga
196 G-6 Itapetininga
199 P-3 Itapeva *lag.*
196 G-7 Itapeva
194 G-3 Itapicuru *riv.*
195 M-7 Itapicuru *riv.*
195 K-6 Itapicuru-Açu *riv.*
195 K-6 Itapicuru-Mirim *riv*
193 M-9 Itapicuru Mirim
195 H-2 Itapicuruzinho *riv.*
197 M-4 Itapina
188 B-8 Itapinima *dam.*
195 L-1 Itapipoca
197 H-6 Itapira
192 C-9 Itapiranga
196 F-1 Itapirapuã
195 L-2 Itapiúna
196 G-9 Itapocu *riv.*
196 G-5 Itápolis
196 C-5 Itaporã (Brazil)
194 E-4 Itapora (Brazil)
195 M-4 Itaporanga (Brazil)
196 F-6 Itaporanga (Brazil)
199 N-3 Itapuã
196 B-9 Itapua *reg.*
196 F-1 Itapuranga
195 J-5 Itaquatiara *riv.*
199 K-2 Itaqui
196 F-6 Itararé *riv.*
196 F-7 Itararé
140 A-7 Itārsi
196 E-3 Itarumã
200 A-2 Itata *riv.*
196 A-9 Itati
199 J-2 Itati *lag.*
197 H-6 Itatiba
196 G-6 Itatinga
195 L-2 Itatira
122 C-1 Itatka
122 D-2 Itatskij
192 G-7 Itatupã
191 L-5 Itau *riv.*
193 H-5 Itaúbal
196 F-1 Itaucu
195 H-4 Itaueira *riv.*
195 H-4 Itaueira
196 C-5 Itaum
197 K-4 Itaúna
197 N-3 Itaúnas
185 H-7 Itazu *vol.*
52 G-8 Itchen

161 M-5 Itchen lake
189 P-9 Ite
121 H-2 Itemgen lake
186 G-7 Iteviare riv.
171 K-5 Ithaca
64 C-7 Itháki
82 F-5 Ithnayn mt
52 B-2 Ithon riv.
137 H-8 Itikawa
99 M-1 Itimbiri riv.
197 M-2 Itinga
197 M-1 Itinga riv.
194 E-1 Itinga riv.
137 J-6 Itinomiya
136 E-7 Itinoseki
196 C-2 Itiquira
196 C-2 Itiquira riv.
195 L-6 Itiúba
191 L-6 Itiyuro riv.
159 N-5 Itkillik riv.
137 J-7 Itō
136 G-6 Itoigawa
99 L-3 Itoko
109 M-4 Itomampy riv.
137 M-8 Itoman
190 E-5 Itonamas riv.
197 N-1 Itorocó
79 L-4 Ittel riv.
57 M-8 Itteren
57 M-6 Ittervoort
188 F-8 Itu riv.
197 H-6 Itu (Brazil)
90 C-7 Itu (Nigeria)
195 J-9 Ituaçu
185 P-9 Ituango
195 L-9 Itubera
199 N-2 Ituim riv.
196 G-3 Ituiutaba
100 A-5 Itula
196 G-3 Itumbiara
163 L-8 Ituna
192 C-3 Ituni
194 D-2 Itupiranga
196 F-9 Ituporanga
192 E-9 Ituqui isl.
196 F-4 Iturama
196 B-8 Iturbe
100 A-1 Ituri riv.
197 K-5 Itutinga
197 H-4 Ituverava
190 C-3 Ituxi (Iquiri) riv.
51 J-5 Itzehoe
78 E-4 Itzèr
187 H-9 Iuaretê
199 L-2 Ivai riv.
109 M-4 Ivakoany mt
48 D-8 Ivalo
66 C-1 Ivangorod
66 E-6 Ivankov
125 J-5 Ivankovcy
66 C-8 Ivano-Frankovsk
220 G-1 Ivanohe
124 K-5 Ivanovka (SSSR)
125 K-9 Ivanovka (SSSR)
67 H-1 Ivanovo
121 N-6 Ivanovskij mt
123 P-2 Ivanovskij
69 L-4 Ivdel'
53 J-5 Iver heath
55 N-3 Iverny
98 D-2 Ivindo riv.
53 J-3 Ivinghe
196 D-5 Ivinheima
196 D-5 Ivinheima riv.
159 M-3 Ivisaruk riv.
159 N-6 Ivishak riv.
109 L-4 Ivohibe
196 F-1 Ivolândia
190 D-4 Ivón riv.
190 C-4 Ivón
109 H-6 Ivondro riv.
89 P-1 Ivory Coast
77 B-4 Ivory Coast state
173 M-1 Ivoryton
62 A-3 Ivrea
55 J-6 Ivry
53 N-7 Ivrychurch
136 G-8 Iwaki
137 K-3 Iwakuni
136 B-6 Iwamizawa
136 C-6 Iwanai
136 E-7 Iwate mt
136 E-7 Iwate
133 M-3 Iweon
89 M-9 Iwo
184 C-2 Ixcán riv.
190 E-2 Iximas
178 F-4 Ixmiquilpan
105 K-7 Ixopo
178 D-6 Ixtapa pte
179 J-7 Ixtepec
53 M-1 Ixworth
92 F-8 Iyal Bakhit
137 L-4 Iyo
137 L-3 Iyo Nada sea
69 L-8 Iž riv.

184 E-2 Izabal lake
179 N-4 Izamal
66 D-7 Izáslav
73 K-8 Izeh
137 M-8 Izena isl.
70 F-4 Izendy
72 F-1 Izerbaš
69 L-8 Izhevsk
84 D-8 Izkī
69 H-3 Izma riv.
69 H-2 Iźma
64 G-2 Izmail
64 F-7 Izmir (Smyrna) site
65 H-5 Izmit
122 C-2 Ižmorskij
65 H-5 Iznik
64 H-5 Iznik gulf
67 L-9 Izobil'nyj
137 J-7 Izu pen.
137 J-8 Izu islds
113 N-6 Izu Bonins foss
178 G-6 Izúcar de Matamoros
137 L-1 Izuhara
67 H-7 Iz'um
137 K-3 Izumo
112 G-2 Izvestij cik isl.
125 H-5 Izvestkovyj
137 N-3 Izyuin

# J

195 P-5 Jaboatão
93 H-6 Jabal al Awliyā
80 D-6 Jabal Bin Ghanimah mt
83 N-7 Jabal Dab'
127 J-5 Jabal os Sarāj
200 D-8 Jabali isl.
140 A-8 Jabalpur
57 N-8 Jabeek
93 H-2 Jabjabah riv.
65 M-8 Jablah
64 A-3 Jablanica
55 N-5 Jablines
123 N-6 Jablonovo
72 A-1 Jablonovskij
83 P-2 Jabrīn isl.
196 G-5 Jabuticabal
197 K-4 Jabuticatubas
60 F-4 Jaca
184 C-2 Jacaltenango
195 J-9 Jacaraci
197 J-5 Jacaré riv.
197 J-6 Jacarei
196 F-6 Jacarezinho
198 B-4 Jáchal riv.
69 P-2 Jachtur lake
196 C-1 Jaciara
197 N-2 Jacinto
190 B-5 Jaciparaná
190 C-6 Jaciparaná riv.
162 E-5 Jackman (Canada)
164 G-7 Jackman (USA)
175 M-3 Jacksboro
219 L-5 Jackson
216 G-6 Jackson mt
168 B-3 Jackson lake
222 D-7 Jackson bay
222 D-7 Jackson cáp.
177 J-3 Jackson (USA)
176 F-2 Jackson (USA)
176 E-4 Jackson (USA)
176 F-5 Jackson (USA)
170 F-6 Jackson (USA)
170 A-5 Jackson (USA)
167 H-3 Jackson (USA)
170 G-8 Jackson (USA)
168 B-4 Jackson (USA)
170 G-9 Jackson (USA)
165 M-2 Jackson's Arm
175 P-4 Jacksonville (USA)
177 M-2 Jacksonville (USA)
177 J-5 Jacksonville (USA)
170 C-8 Jacksonville (USA)
177 K-5 Jacksonville Beach
181 J-7 Jacmel
209 H-4 Jaco isl.
167 L-7 Jacob Lake
138 G-3 Jacobābād
200 D-4 Jacobacci
195 K-7 Jacobina
172 F-6 Jacobstown
161 J-3 Jacques lake
165 J-3 Jacques Cartier strt.

164 E-8 Jacques Cartier
211 N-5 Jacquinot bay
195 P-3 Jacu riv.
199 M-3 Jacui riv.
195 P-5 Jacuipa riv.
195 K-7 Jacuipe riv.
194 D-1 Jacundá
193 H-8 Jacunda riv.
196 G-7 Jacupiranda
193 L-9 Jacureconga dam.
195 L-6 Jacurici riv.
138 B-4 Jaddi pte
204 G-6 Jade islds
222 D-6 Jade isl.
92 D-8 Jadīd Ra's al Fil
67 K-1 Jadrin
80 B-2 Jādū
60 C-7 Jaén
188 F-2 Jaen
88 C-1 Jafene reg.
220 D-4 Jaffa cap.
141 L-7 Jaffna lag.
141 L-7 Jaffna
139 N-3 Jagādhrī
142 G-4 Jagannāthganj Ghāt
140 D-9 Jagdalpur
105 H-6 Jagersfontein
140 E-6 Jaggayyapeta
122 G-3 Jagi mt
55 K-2 Jagny-sous-Bois
159 P-7 Jago riv.
69 N-3 Jagodnyj
66 F-7 Jagotin
139 M-2 Jagraon
140 D-7 Jagtiāl
195 K-8 Jaguaquara
199 L-5 Jaguarão
199 L-5 Jaguarão riv.
195 K-6 Jaguarari
199 L-3 Jaguari riv.
199 L-3 Jaguari
196 F-7 Jaguariaíva
195 M-2 Jaguaribe riv.
195 M-3 Jaguaribe
195 L-8 Jaguaripe
195 M-2 Jaguaruana
199 P-2 Jaguaruna
198 B-2 Jaguē riv.
189 M-6 Jaguey riv.
180 C-4 Jagüey Grande
142 D-3 Jahānābād
84 A-3 Jahrom
197 L-1 Jaiba mt
195 K-4 Jaicós
143 J-4 Jaintiāpur
139 L-5 Jaipur
82 J-3 Jair riv.
139 H-4 Jaisalmer
125 L-2 Jaj riv.
122 C-1 Jaja
129 P-2 Jājarkot
73 M-3 Jājarm
71 P-3 Jājpur
142 E-6 Jājpur
69 L-5 Jajva
118 F-7 Jakarta
207 H-5 Jakarta
160 E-5 Jakes Corner
138 F-7 Jakhāu
67 H-6 Jakoulevo
125 K-8 Jakovlevka
69 L-8 Jakšur-Bodja
175 J-3 Jal
83 K-5 Jalājil
127 K-6 Jalālābād (Afghanistan)
129 P-1 Jalālābād (India)
127 L-8 Jalālpur
82 F-2 Jalāmīd
84 E-9 Ja'lān reg.
179 P-9 Jalán riv.
184 G-3 Jalán riv.
184 D-3 Jalapa
184 G-4 Jalapa
179 H-5 Jalapa Enriquez
139 N-6 Jālaun
126 G-7 Jaldak
196 F-4 Jales
142 E-2 Jaleswar
140 B-5 Jālgaon
90 B-4 Jalingo
178 C-4 Jalisco reg.
127 M-6 Jalkot
140 C-5 Jālna
60 L-8 Jalón riv.
139 J-6 Jālor
178 D-3 Jalpa
142 G-2 Jalpaiguri
178 F-4 Jalpan
81 H-4 Jālū
81 H-4 Jālū (Wāhat)
119 N-6 Jaluit isl.
126 D-2 Jam riv.
125 H-2 Jam-Altin mt

138 F-8 Jām Jodhpur
188 B-1 Jama pte
188 B-1 Jama riv.
188 B-1 Jama
191 M-3 Jama lake
90 D-2 Jamaare riv.
157 G-5 Jamaica state
173 H-3 Jamaica
180 G-7 Jamaïque cal.
142 G-3 Jamālpur (Bangladesh)
142 E-3 Jamālpur (India)
101 M-2 Jamāme
58 D-7 Jaman pass
69 N-8 Jamantau mt
190 B-6 Jamari riv.
190 B-6 Jamari
123 M-7 Jamarovka
187 N-9 Jamaru riv.
58 B-9 Jambaz pass
188 D-1 Jambeli cap.
149 K-8 Jambongan isl.
54 D-3 Jambville
209 L-6 Jamdena
200 G-2 James isl.
164 A-3 James bay
218 A-2 James mt
169 H-5 James riv.
155 K-4 James (Canada) bay
172 F-5 Jamesburg
161 P-4 Jameson islds
173 L-2 Jamesport
220 D-1 Jamestown
105 H-7 Jamestown (South Africa)
177 H-1 Jamestown (USA)
171 H-6 Jamestown (USA)
169 H-2 Jamestown (USA)
189 H-8 Jaminaua riv.
142 F-6 Jāmira lag.
140 E-4 Jamkhandi
127 M-8 Jammu
127 M-8 Jammu reg.
129 J-1 Jammu-Kashmir reg.
138 F-3 Jāmnagar
140 B-5 Jāmner
66 D-7 Jampol (SSSR)
66 G-5 Jampol' (SSSR)
139 J-2 Jāmpur
49 J-8 Jamsa
82 B-5 Jamsah
142 E-5 Jamshedpur
142 E-4 Jāmtāra
142 E-3 Jamūi
142 G-3 Jamuna lake
210 B-3 Jamur lake
69 J-4 Jamžačnaja Parma mt
46 C-2 Jan Mayen isl.
83 N-3 Janah isl.
142 E-4 Janakpur
192 B-9 Janauacá lake
197 L-1 Janaúba
193 H-6 Janaucu isl.
69 M-8 Janaul
127 K-7 Jand
73 M-5 Jandaq
188 E-9 Jandiatuba riv.
219 M-5 Jandowae
222 C-8 Jane mt
170 C-6 Janesville
126 B-4 Jangal riv.
140 E-7 Jangaon
133 M-7 Janghang
133 M-6 Janghoweon
71 P-3 Jangiabad
71 N-4 Jangijer
71 N-4 Jangijul'
71 N-5 Jangikišlak
71 P-3 Jangikurgan
142 F-4 Jangipur
133 L-4 Jangjin
133 L-3 Jangjin-gang riv.
133 K-6 Jangsan-Got cap.
133 L-4 Jangsang
71 P-3 Jangybazar
133 L-5 Jangyeon
82 C-2 Janin
68 B-7 Janisjarvi lake
124 A-2 Jankan mt
174 F-4 Janos
104 G-3 Jansenville
64 E-3 Jantra riv.
197 K-1 Januária
54 G-9 Janvry
71 L-3 Jany-Kurgan
138 K-3 Jaora
179 K-7 Japala
117 K-3 Japan foss
113 N-6 Japan foss
119 J-3 Japan state
113 M-5 Japan sea
117 J-2 Japan sea
210 B-2 Japan strt.
188 G-7 Japiim
185 M-9 Jaqué
69 K-7 Jar
70 A-7 Jar

65 M-7 Jarābulus
196 G-1 Jaraguá
196 F-9 Jaraguá do Sul
196 C-4 Jaraguari
93 P-1 Jārah riv.
146 D-7 Jarak isl.
60 D-5 Jarama riv.
201 H-5 Jaramillo
69 J-8 Jaransk
127 L-9 Jarānwāla
82 C-8 Jarārah riv.
82 C-2 Jarash site
192 F-8 Jarauçu riv.
66 F-3 Jarcevo
196 B-5 Jardim
195 N-3 Jardim do Seridó
214 G-2 Jardine riv.
180 E-5 Jardines de la Reina islds
72 G-3 Jardymli
69 H-3 Jarega
49 K-3 Jaren
69 H-5 Jarenga
69 H-5 Jarensk
123 M-9 Jargalthaan
143 H-4 Jāria
194 A-6 Jarina riv.
121 M-2 Jarki
72 F-7 Jarmo site
51 M-6 Jarocin
66 B-8 Jaroslaw
49 H-4 Järpen
130 C-5 Jarqalan
73 K-9 Jarrāchi riv.
83 L-1 Jarrāḥī riv.
95 J-5 Jarso
190 C-6 Jaru
190 C-6 Jaru riv.
127 M-8 Jammu reg.
49 G-8 Järvenpää
163 H-4 Jarvie
224 D-4 Jarvis isl.
142 C-1 Jarwa
64 B-1 Jásbereny
138 G-3 Jasdan
133 L-3 Jaseong
142 C-4 Jashpurnagar
67 J-8 Jasinovataja
84 B-7 Jāsk
122 C-2 Jaškino
67 N-8 Jaškul'
66 B-8 Jaslo
67 H-3 Jasnogorsk
70 D-1 Jasnyj
201 L-7 Jason Islands islds
162 F-5 Jasper
162 F-5 Jasper (Canada) na.p.
176 C-5 Jasper (USA)
176 G-3 Jasper (USA)
177 J-5 Jasper (USA)
170 E-9 Jasper (USA)
196 E-2 Jataí
192 B-7 Jatapu riv.
184 C-1 Jataté riv.
140 E-4 Jath
138 F-6 Jāti
195 L-8 Jati
180 E-4 Jatibonico
60 E-6 Játiva
194 B-2 Jatobá
194 A-7 Jatoba riv.
194 D-1 Jatobal
190 A-8 Jatuarana
196 G-6 Jaú
194 E-5 Jaú riv.
187 P-9 Jauaperi riv.
192 F-8 Jauari mt
189 K-5 Jauja
58 F-6 Jaun
58 F-6 Jaun mt
142 C-2 Jaunpur
196 A-1 Jauru riv.
116 G-7 Java sea
192 E-3 Java
204 B-3 Java foss
141 H-4 Javādi na.p.
127 K-3 Javan
192 B-9 Javari dam.
201 J-2 Javier riv.
66 B-3 Javorov
207 K-7 Jawa isl.
139 J-6 Jawai riv.
138 K-8 Jawf
140 B-3 Jawhār
141 J-7 Jayamkondacho-lapuram
188 F-2 Jayanca
210 F-2 Jayapura (Sukarnapura)
210 E-4 Jayawidjaya mt
142 E-4 Jaynagār
142 E-2 Jaynagar
65 M-9 Jayrūd
175 L-3 Jayton

96 E-1 Jazā'ir az Zubayr isl.
65 M-9 Jbail
78 C-4 Jbilet reg.
138 E-3 Jebri
133 N-6 Jecheon
50 D-3 Jedburgh
66 D-9 Jedincy
66 A-7 Jedrzejów
162 A-2 Jedway
209 L-1 Jef Lio
168 A-2 Jefferson riv.
167 J-5 Jefferson mt
170 A-6 Jefferson (USA)
176 C-4 Jefferson (YSA)
170 B-9 Jefferson City
168 C-5 Jeffrey City
165 L-4 Jeffrey's
89 J-9 Jega
58 G-3 Jegenstorf
121 K-5 Jegindydbulak
71 H-2 Jegizkara mt
67 H-2 Jegorjevsk
67 L-8 Jegorlyk riv.
126 C-6 Jehīl-e Pūzak lake
201 H-3 Jeinemeni mt
67 K-8 Jeja
133 M-9 Jeju
196 B-7 Jejui-Guazú riv.
66 C-3 Jekabpils
69 M-4 Jekaterininka
124 G-5 Jekaterinoslavka
67 L-4 Jekaterinovka
94 F-3 Jekaw
120 E-2 Jekidin
146 E-6 Jelai riv.
67 L-5 Jelan'
123 L-5 Jelancy
128 B-5 Jel'atj
67 M-1 Jelchovska
122 C-4 Jel'covka
123 N-4 Jeleninskij
66 G-8 Jelizarovo
66 D-5 Jelizovo
66 F-4 Jel'n'a
73 J-8 Jelow Gir
69 H-4 Jelva riv.
66 B-3 Jelvaga (Mitau)
78 B-3 Jemâa-Shaîm
146 G-8 Jemaluang
68 E-6 Jemca
68 E-6 Jemca riv.
68 E-5 Jemeck
66 D-7 Jemil'čino
119 M-5 Jemo isl.
51 J-7 Jena (GDR)
176 D-5 Jena (USA)
67 J-7 Jenakijevo
79 N-2 Jendouba
69 N-1 Jendra lake
194 D-4 Jenipapo riv.
192 G-4 Jenipapo
122 E-3 Jenisej lake
122 F-5 Jenisej (bol.) riv.
122 F-5 Jenisej (mal.) riv.
177 J-1 Jenkins
172 E-6 Jenkintown
160 E-6 Jennings riv.
176 D-6 Jennings
172 E-3 Jennyjump riv.
67 N-7 Jenotajevka
68 C-3 Jenozero lake
133 M-7 Jeongeub
133 K-4 Jeongju
133 M-7 Jeonju
220 E-4 Jeparit
195 L-8 Jequié riv.
195 K-9 Jequié
197 K-2 Jequitaí riv.
197 K-2 Jequitaí
197 M-2 Jequitinhonha
197 N-1 Jequitinhonha riv.
78 F-3 Jerada
70 D-8 Jeralijev
146 F-7 Jerantut
64 F-9 Jerápetra
123 N-5 Jeravnoje (bol.) lake
79 P-4 Jerba isl.
71 J-9 Jerbent
68 E-7 Jercevo
181 H-7 Jeremie
195 M-6 Jeremoabo
178 D-3 Jerez de G. Salinas
60 B-7 Jerez de la Frontera
82 C-2 Jericho
221 H-3 Jerilderie
121 L-3 Jermak
123 L-2 Jermaki
122 E-3 Jermakovskoje
121 J-3 Jermentau
67 J-2 Jermiš
70 B-1 Jermolajevo
124 C-3 Jerofej Pavlovič
166 G-7 Jerome
199 M-3 Jerônimo
68 G-2 Jersa riv.
50 C-7 Jersey isl.

171 L-6 Jersey City
172 A-2 Jerseytown
170 C-8 Jerseyville
67 N-3 Jeršov
195 H-3 Jerumenha
47 G-6 Jérusalem
67 M-4 Jeruslan *riv.*
221 K-3 Jervis *bay*
221 K-4 Jervis Bay
120 G-1 Jesil'
63 N-2 Jésolo
72 C-1 Jessentuki
49 K-3 Jessheim
142 G-5 Jessore
97 M-1 Jestro *riv.*
177 K-5 Jesup
168 G-9 Jesus *mt*
179 J-7 Jesús Carranza
198 E-4 Jesús María (Argentina)
178 C-3 Jesus María (Mexico)
87 H-2 Jeta *isl.*
138 G-8 Jetpur
54 A-3 Jeufosse
125 H-5 Jevrejskaja *reg.*
142 B-7 Jeypore
100 D-2 Jeza
48 C-7 Jfjord
138 K-8 Jhābua
139 M-4 Jhajjar
138 F-2 Jhal
138 D-3 Jhal Jaho
139 L-7 Jhālawār
140 B-8 Jhanda Dongar *mt*
127 K-9 Jhang
143 H-4 Jhānjail
139 N-7 Jhānsi
142 F-2 Jhāpa
142 E-5 Jhārgrām
142 E-4 Jharia
142 D-1 Jhawani
127 K-9 Jhelum *riv.*
127 L-8 Jhelum
142 G-4 Jhenida
139 L-4 Jhūnjhunu
129 L-2 Jiachulafu
135 N-2 Jiading
129 M-3 Jiaigong
134 C-4 Jiajiang
145 M-3 Jialai
131 P-2 Jiali
134 D-3 Jialingjiang *riv.*
129 N-4 Jialonghu *lake*
132 B-4 Jiamenhudugu
125 H-7 Jiamusi
135 J-6 Jian (China)
135 L-3 Jian (China)
133 K-3 Jianchang (China)
133 H-4 Jianchang (China)
132 G-5 Jianchangying
143 N-3 Jianchuan
135 M-4 Jiande
134 C-5 Jiang'an
134 A-9 Jiangcheng
134 B-8 Jiangchuan
129 L-2 Jiangchum
135 M-2 Jiangdu
131 N-9 Jiange
133 H-3 Jiangjidian
134 D-4 Jiangjin
124 C-8 Jiangjunmiao
135 M-2 Jiangjyin
134 F-5 Jiangkou (China)
134 E-4 Jiangkou (China)
135 L-6 Jiangle
135 H-3 Jiangling
135 H-9 Jiangmen
133 L-1 Jiangmifeng
145 M-2 Jiangping
135 L-4 Jiangshan
135 M-1 Jiangsu *reg.*
135 K-6 Jiangxi *reg.*
132 D-8 Jiangxian
135 M-1 Jiangyan
142 G-1 Jiangzi
135 L-6 Jianning
135 L-6 Jianou
132 G-4 Jianping
134 F-3 Jianshi
134 B-8 Jianshui
134 C-4 Jianwei
131 P-9 Jianyang
133 L-1 Jiaohe
133 H-2 Jiaolianhe *riv.*
128 E-9 Jiaoluoshan *mt*
133 H-7 Jiaoxian
132 D-9 Jiaozuo
135 L-1 Jiashan
132 G-9 Jiawang
135 H-1 Jiaxian
135 N-3 Jiaxing
129 K-6 Jiayunhu *lake*
135 K-9 Jiazi
97 H-8 Jibalei
194 G-9 Jibão *mt*
90 B-1 Jibiya
188 A-9 Jibóia
185 J-9 Jicarón *isl.*
89 L-5 Jidanyile
93 M-1 Jiddah
84 G-7 Jiddat al Harāsis *pl.*
129 M-9 Jidingxilin
132 C-6 Jiehekou
135 K-9 Jieshi
135 K-9 Jieshiwan *bay*
135 J-1 Jieshou
48 C-7 Jiešjavrre *lake*
132 D-7 Jiexiu
135 K-8 Jieyang
180 E-4 Jiguey *bay*
51 L-8 Jihlava
126 D-5 Jijah
79 L-2 Jijel
97 J-2 Jijiga
131 M-6 Jikehe *riv.*
124 C-5 Jilalin
131 H-9 Jilantai
131 H-9 Jilantaiyanchi *lake*
101 M-2 Jilib
131 M-2 Jilibulake
133 K-1 Jilin
133 K-1 Jilin *reg.*
129 P-4 Jilong
172 C-3 Jim Thorpe
95 J-4 Jima
181 K-7 Jimaní
64 C-2 Jimbolia
175 H-7 Jiménez (Mexico)
175 L-6 Jiménez (Mexico)
89 L-5 Jimle
211 H-4 Jimmi *riv.*
178 D-1 Jimulco *mt*
128 A-8 Jimunai
128 D-9 Jimusaer
133 M-8 Jin *isl.*
132 D-8 Jincheng
139 M-3 Jind
133 M-8 Jindo
51 L-8 Jindrichuv Hradec
132 B-7 Jingbian
133 M-1 Jingbohu *lake*
132 A-9 Jingchuan
135 L-3 Jingde
135 L-4 Jingdezhen
134 A-8 Jingdong
134 A-8 Jinggu
132 B-9 Jinghe *riv.*
128 C-6 Jinghe
135 M-2 Jingjiang
132 D-6 Jingle
135 H-3 Jingmen
131 L-9 Jingning
135 H-3 Jingshan
131 K-8 Jingtai
134 D-9 Jingxi
134 F-6 Jingxian
124 E-8 Jingxing
133 L-2 Jingyu
131 K-9 Jingyuan
133 N-7 Jinhae
124 C-5 Jinhe
135 M-4 Jinhua
132 D-4 Jining (China)
132 F-8 Jining (China)
100 E-2 Jinja
132 A-7 Jinji
133 N-7 Jinju
134 B-8 Jinning
184 G-4 Jinotega
184 G-4 Jinotega *reg.*
184 F-5 Jinotepe
134 F-6 Jinping
134 D-6 Jinsha
134 A-6 Jinshajiang *riv.*
135 H-4 Jinshi
130 E-6 Jinst *mt*
130 D-7 Jinst
148 F-4 Jintolo *strt.*
140 C-5 Jintūr
133 H-4 Jinxi
133 J-5 Jinxian
132 F-8 Jinxiang
134 B-5 Jinyang
133 N-7 Jinyeong
133 H-4 Jinzhou
133 J-5 Jinzhouwan *bay*
188 C-1 Jipijapa
193 H-5 Jipioca *isl.*
178 D-5 Jiquilpan de Juárez
188 B-9 Jirijirimo *dam.*
129 H-8 Jishibuyang
131 L-6 Jishishan *mt*
134 F-5 Jishou
65 M-8 Jisr ash Shughūr
128 D-9 Jitai
216 F-8 Jitarning
133 M-2 Jiuantu
128 E-8 Jiuheshi
132 E-5 Jiuhuaian
135 K-4 Jiujiang
130 F-5 Jiujinkeng
64 D-2 Jiul *riv.*
135 J-5 Jiulingshan *mt*
134 A-5 Jiulong
135 L-7 Jiulongjiang *riv.*
135 L-6 Jiulongqi *riv.*
135 K-7 Jiupingyuan
131 H-5 Jiuquann
133 K-1 Jiutai
131 L-8 Jiutaosha
135 H-1 Jiuxian
132 D-9 Jiuyuanqu
133 K-1 Jiuzhan
138 A-3 Jīwani
135 L-3 Jixi
132 E-8 Jixian (China)
132 F-5 Jixian (China)
96 C-8 Jiz *riv.*
82 E-6 Jizl *riv.*
196 E-9 Joacaba
86 F-1 Joal Fadiout
193 H-9 Joana-Peres
193 J-7 Joanes
197 L-4 Joanésia
195 K-3 Joaninha
193 H-9 João
195 P-2 João Câmara
193 J-8 João Coelho
102 B-4 Joao de Almeida
197 M-4 João Neiva
195 P-4 João Pessoa
197 J-2 Joao Pinheiro
87 J-2 Joao Vieira *isl.*
196 F-6 Joaquim Távora
187 M-3 Joaquín
180 F-5 Jobabo
172 F-6 Jobstown
59 L-5 Joch *pass*
198 C-5 Jocoli
123 J-1 Jodarma *riv.*
123 J-1 Jodarma
139 J-5 Jodhpur
138 G-8 Jodiya
49 H-9 Joensuu
133 L-5 Joeryeong
96 D-3 Jof *riv.*
162 F-7 Joffre *mt*
108 C-8 Joffreville
207 K-7 Jog Jakarta
73 N-3 Jogbatāy
127 N-9 Jogindarnagar
126 F-9 Johān
165 J-3 Johan-Beetz *bay*
167 L-4 Johannesburg
105 J-4 Johannesburg (South Africa)
164 E-7 Johannsen *mt*
142 B-4 Johilla *riv.*
159 L-6 John *riv.*
166 E-5 John Day
166 D-5 John Day *riv.*
160 D-8 John Jax *mt*
174 D-5 Johnson *mt*
168 E-9 Johnson
175 M-5 Johnson City (USA)
177 J-1 Johnson City (USA)
160 E-5 Johnsons Crossing
216 F-5 Johnston *mt*
224 C-2 Johnston *isl.*
216 G-7 Johnston (The) *lake*
103 M-1 Johnston Falls
162 B-5 Johnstone *strt.*
171 H-7 Johnstown
146 F-8 Johor *reg.*
146 G-8 Johor Baharu
50 G-8 Joinville
196 G-8 Joinville (Brazil)
55 K-6 Joinville-le-Pont
178 F-6 Jojutla de Juarez
48 E-8 Joki *riv.*
48 F-6 Jokkmokk
48 C-3 Jökulsá à Fjöllum *riv.*
72 F-4 Jolfa
170 D-7 Joliet
164 E-8 Joliette
149 K-5 Jolo
149 K-5 Jolo Grande *isl.*
148 D-5 Jomalig *isl.*
102 E-1 Jombo *riv.*
100 E-5 Jomu
54 B-8 Joncs (Les)
59 L-1 Jonen
153 K-2 Jones *strt.*
159 P-5 Jones *islds*
177 H-3 Jonesboro (USA)
176 D-4 Jonesboro (USA)
176 E-2 Jonesboro (USA)
172 A-4 Jonestown
87 M-5 Jong *riv.*
94 E-4 Jonglei
210 D-5 Jongs *cap.*
142 B-6 Jonk *riv.*
51 L-2 Jönkoping
164 F-6 Jonquière
60 F-2 Jonzac
176 C-1 Joplin
172 A-8 Joppa
139 M-6 Jora
58 C-6 Jorat *mt*
148 G-4 Jordan
77 F-1 Jordan *state*
82 C-2 Jordan (Israel) *riv.*
166 F-6 Jordan (USA) *riv.*
168 D-1 Jordan (USA)
166 F-6 Jordan Valley
197 N-1 Jordânia
196 E-8 Jordão *riv.*
201 L-2 Jorge Montt *isl.*
143 K-2 Jorhāt
196 C-1 Jorigue *riv.*
127 L-4 Jorm
48 G-6 Jörn
198 B-2 Jorquera *riv.*
68 G-4 Jortom
87 M-6 Joru
90 C-4 Jos *plat.*
199 K-6 José Batle-y-Ordonez
196 F-9 José Boiteux
190 D-8 José Bonifacio
200 F-4 José de S. Martin
196 F-4 José dos Dourados *riv.*
187 J-8 José María
200 A-7 José Maria Blanco
196 B-1 Josélândia
164 G-2 Joseph *lake*
46 A-2 Joseph *fj.*
213 L-2 Joseph Bonaparte *gulf*
129 M-1 Joshnnath
167 M-4 Joshua tree *na.p.*
55 N-6 Jossigny
181 L-1 Jost Van Dike *isl.*
49 J-2 Jostedalsbreen *glac.*
49 J-2 Jotunheimen *mt*
54 D-7 Jouars-Ponchartrain
58 B-5 Jougne
175 M-6 Jourdanton
48 E-8 Joutsijärvi
58 A-6 Joux *lake*
58 A-6 Joux *val.*
54 G-7 Jouy-en-Josas
54 F-3 Jouy-la-Fontaine
54 G-2 Jouy-le-Comte
54 F-3 Jouy-le-Moutier
54 B-4 Jouy-Mauvoisin
66 C-1 Jõvega
180 C-4 Jovellanos
97 P-4 Jowhar
127 H-3 Jowzjān *reg.*
71 P-8 Jowzjan *reg.*
178 D-2 Juan Aldama
199 J-3 Juan B. Arruabarrena
182 B-7 Juan de Fuca *strt.*
108 F-2 Juan de Nova (St-Cristophe) *isl.*
200 B-9 Juan E. Barra
191 N-8 Juan José Castelli
200 B-9 Juan N.Fernandez
162 A-2 Juan Perez Sound *strt.*
201 J-1 Juan Stuven *isl.*
199 J-8 Juancho
187 M-2 Juangriego
188 G-4 Juanjui
174 B-2 Juárez *mt*
200 B-9 Juárez (Argentina)
175 L-7 Juárez (Mexico)
174 F-4 Juárez (Mexico)
197 K-7 Juatinga *pte*
195 N-4 Juazeirinho
195 K-5 Juázeiro
195 L-4 Juázeiro do Norte
94 E-6 Juba
83 N-3 Jubail
93 K-2 Jubayt
82 G-4 Jubbah
217 L-4 Jubilee *lake*
124 E-3 Jubilejnyj
188 D-2 Jubones *riv.*
78 D-9 Juby *cap.*
60 E-6 Jucar *riv.*
196 F-1 Jucara
196 E-6 Jucara (Brazil)
193 N-9 Juçaral *riv.*
180 E-5 Jucaro
178 D-4 Juchipila
179 J-8 Juchitán
66 G-3 Juchnov
197 N-2 Jucurucu *riv.*
197 N-2 Jucurucu
195 N-3 Jucurutu
82 F-2 Judayyidat Ar'ar
61 N-1 Judenburg
173 P-1 Judith *pte*
168 C-1 Judith *riv.*
68 G-7 Jug *riv.*
69 L-7 Jugo-Kamskij
135 P-7 Juifang
184 G-5 Juigalpa
55 M-3 Juilly
197 K-5 Juiz de Fora
191 M-4 Jujuy *reg.*
113 P-3 Jukagirskoje Ploskogorje *plat.*
69 N-1 Jukonda *riv.*
68 F-5 Jula *riv.*
191 K-3 Julaca
189 L-6 Julcamarca *mt*
190 G-1 Juli
214 F-9 Julia Creek
189 M-9 Juliaca
174 B-1 Julian
61 N-2 Julian Alps *mt*
57 N-7 Juliana *cal.*
192 D-4 Julianatop *mt*
199 L-3 Júlio de Castilhos
139 M-2 Jullundur
191 H-5 Julpa *riv.*
140 A-5 Julwānia
68 B-5 Juma
83 H-3 Jumaymah
101 L-4 Jumbo *cap.*
101 L-3 Jumbo
54 D-5 Jumeauville
180 G-4 Jumentos Cays *rf*
129 N-2 Jumla
94 E-5 Jummayzah
170 C-4 Jump *riv.*
130 E-5 Jumt *mt*
138 G-9 Junāgadh
133 H-8 Junan
191 N-2 Juncal *riv.*
175 L-5 Junction
214 A-2 Junction *bay*
170 A-1 Junction (Canada)
167 K-7 Junction (USA)
176 D-4 Junction City (USA)
169 H-8 Junction City (USA)
218 G-3 Jundah
197 H-6 Jundiai
160 C-6 Juneau
221 J-3 Junee
59 J-6 Jungfrau
59 J-6 Jungfrau *mt*
59 J-6 Jungfraujoch
138 E-5 Jungshāhi
189 K-5 Junin *lake*
189 K-5 Junín *reg.*
198 G-6 Junín (Argentina)
188 B-1 Junin (Ecuador)
189 K-5 Junín (Peru)
200 C-3 Junín de los Andes
140 C-3 Junnar
166 E-5 Juntura
194 G-7 Jupaguá
197 H-7 Juquiá
50 C-2 Jura *isl.*
58 E-1 Jura *reg.*
46 D-5 Jura Souabe *reg.*
185 M-9 Juradó
191 N-5 Juramento *riv.*
197 L-2 Juramento
196 D-7 Juranda
197 M-4 Juraparanã *lake*
106 D-7 Jurege *riv.*
195 K-5 Juremal
121 L-1 Jur'evo
122 B-2 Jurga
213 J-6 Jurgurra *riv.*
87 M-5 Juring
69 J-9 Jurino
69 J-7 Jurja
67 H-1 Jurjev-Pol'skij
68 G-9 Jurjevec
67 H-7 Jurjevka
69 K-6 Jurla
66 B-3 Jurmala
122 G-3 Jurty
188 G-8 Juruá *riv.*
188 G-7 Juruá Mirim *riv.*
188 F-9 Juruazinho *riv.*
190 C-9 Juruena *riv.*
190 D-9 Juruena *riv.*
188 G-9 Jurupari *riv.*
193 H-6 Jurupari *isl.*
192 D-8 Juruti
69 N-8 Jur'uzan' *riv.*
68 B-5 Juškozero
195 J-8 Jussiape
58 A-8 Jussy
198 F-5 Justiniano Posse
178 G-7 Justlahuaca
198 E-6 Justo Daract
188 F-9 Jutai *riv.*
192 F-8 Jutai *mt*
195 K-5 Jutai
196 C-6 Juti
184 D-3 Jutiapa (Guatemala)
184 G-2 Jutiapa (Honduras)
184 G-3 Juticalpa
179 P-9 Juticalpa
55 J-8 Juvisy
133 H-8 Juxian
132 F-8 Juye
73 P-4 Jūyma
126 C-2 Jūymand
84 A-3 Jūyom
67 J-1 Juža
54 D-4 Juziers
127 M-4 Južno-Aličurskij *mt*
122 C-6 Južno Cujskij *mt*
125 N-4 Južno-Kamyšovyj *mt*
136 A-8 Južno-Kuril'sk
123 N-3 Južno-Mujskij *mt*
125 P-4 Juzno-Sachalinsk
67 N-9 Južno-Suchokumsk
122 B-7 Juznyi Altaj *mt*
51 J-3 Jylland *reg.*
46 D-4 Jylland *pen.*


# K


90 A-2 Ka *riv.*
73 P-1 Kaachka
215 L-3 Kaala-Gomén
48 D-8 Kaamanen
102 B-9 Kaapkruis
105 L-3 Kaapmuiden
76 E-7 Kaapplato *rge*
86 G-7 Kaarta *reg.*
56 G-6 Kaathoven
149 J-2 Kaatoan *mt*
56 E-6 Kaatsheuvel
87 K-5 Kaba *riv.*
208 E-4 Kabaena *strt.*
208 D-4 Kabaena *isl.*
71 L-7 Kabakly
124 C-1 Kabaktan
87 K-5 Kabala
100 C-3 Kabale
100 A-6 Kabambare
146 C-7 Kabandjahe
149 H-4 Kabankalan
123 L-6 Kabansk
100 B-4 Kabare
100 G-2 Kabarnet
149 J-4 Kabasalan
90 A-5 Kabba
141 J-4 Kabbani *riv.*
100 C-4 Kabgaye
91 H-4 Kabia *riv.*
208 E-5 Kabia *isl.*
211 N-3 Kabien
144 G-7 Kabin Buri
170 E-1 Kabinakagami *lake*
99 M-7 Kabinda
73 H-8 Kabir *mt*
208 F-6 Kabir
82 C-6 Kabīr *isl.*
120 E-1 Kabirga *riv.*
92 C-8 Kabkabiyah
93 H-3 Kabna
91 K-5 Kabo
103 J-3 Kabompo
103 J-3 Kabompo *riv.*
99 N-8 Kabongo
79 P-3 Kaboudia *pte*
84 E-9 Kabsh *cap.*
73 P-1 Kabud Gonbad
127 J-6 Kabul *riv.*
127 J-6 Kabul
118 B-3 Kabul
100 D-2 Kabula
100 D-2 Kabulasoke
100 A-8 Kabumba *lake*
100 A-8 Kabumbulu
103 M-2 Kabunda
100 B-3 Kabunga
149 M-1 Kaburuang *isl.*
92 G-8 Kabūshah
93 J-5 Kabūshiya
103 M-4 Kabwe
76 C-1 Kabylie *reg.*
64 C-4 Kačanik
126 B-7 Kāchā *mt*
138 F-7 Kachchh (Kutch) *reg.*
139 H-3 Kāchelo
158 F-9 Kachemak *bay*
72 F-2 Kachi
90 C-4 Kachia
103 J-6 Kachikau
143 M-3 Kachin *reg.*
66 G-9 Kachovka
123 L-7 K'achta (SSSR)
123 J-4 K'achta (SSSR)
121 L-2 Kačiry
69 M-5 Kackanar
72 C-3 Kackar *mt*
123 K-4 Kačug
123 J-3 Kada *riv.*
143 M-9 Kadaingti
141 L-5 Kadaiyanallūr
124 B-5 Kadaja
144 E-8 Kadan *isl.*
126 F-8 Kadaney *riv.*
208 E-5 Kadatuang *isl.*

89 N-5 Kade
90 G-7 Kadei *riv.*
82 B-8 kadhdhāb *mt*
67 J-7 Kadijévka
220 C-2 Kadina
145 J-4 Kading (Theun) *riv.*
65 J-6 Kadinhani
207 J-4 Kadipaten
140 G-6 Kadiri
65 L-7 Kadirli
91 M-1 Kadja *riv.*
208 D-4 Kadjang
67 J-2 Kadom
103 M-7 Kadoma
144 C-5 Kadônkani
90 B-2 Kaduna *reg.*
90 A-4 Kaduna *riv.*
90 B-3 Kaduna
94 D-1 Käduqlī
122 G-5 Kadyr-Os *riv.*
72 F-4 Kadžaran
69 J-2 Kadžerom
128 D-2 Kadži-Saj
86 E-4 Kaédi
90 G-4 Kaélé
99 M-9 Kafakumba
72 F-3 Kafan
90 C-4 Kafanchan
126 G-6 Kafar Jar Ghar *mt*
73 P-2 Kafar qal eh
126 D-1 Kāfar Qal'eh
86 G-2 Kaffrine
127 H-5 Kāfir Qal'a *site*
127 J-3 Kafirnigan *riv.*
86 G-1 Kafountine
81 N-2 Kafr ad Dawwār
81 N-2 Kafr ash Shaykh
81 N-2 Kafr az Zayyat
81 N-2 Kafr Shukr
93 L-7 Kafta
103 K-4 Kafue *riv.*
103 L-5 Kafue
103 K-4 Kafue *na.p.*
100 D-8 Kafufu *riv.*
137 H-5 Kaga
71 M-7 Kagan
66 F-7 Kagarlyk
129 J-7 Kagelike
100 D-3 Kagera *riv.*
100 C-3 Kagera *na.p.*
72 D-3 Kaġiman
59 K-4 Kägiswil
161 P-2 Kagloryuak *riv.*
92 G-7 Kagmar
137 N-3 Kagosima
64 F-1 Kagul
158 D-9 Kaguyak
207 M-1 Kahajan *riv.*
100 E-5 Kahama
99 J-7 Kahemba
72 G-5 Kâhju
162 G-1 Kahntah
170 B-7 Kahoka
224 D-1 Kahooalwe *isl.*
65 M-6 Kahramanmaras (Maras)
139 J-2 Kahror Pakka
100 C-2 Kahunge
222 G-5 Kahurangi *pte*
223 L-6 Kahutara *pte*
208 B-3 Kai *isl.*
209 M-4 Kai *islds*
210 E-6 Kai
209 M-4 Kai Besar *isl.*
209 M-5 Kai Ketjil *isl.*
89 L-9 Kaiama
222 F-8 Kaiapoi
170 C-1 Kaiashk *riv.*
128 E-7 Kaiduhe *riv.*
131 N-3 Kaierluotang
192 B-3 Kaieteur Fall
132 E-9 Kaifeng
223 K-2 Kaikohe
222 G-7 Kaikoura
124 D-3 Kaikukang
143 H-4 Kailâshahar
211 M-7 Kaileuna *isl.*
134 K-6 Kaili
133 H-2 Kailu
192 B-1 Kailuma *riv.*
139 P-5 Kaimganj
104 D-6 Kaimoepslaagte
142 B-3 Kaimur *reg.*
137 K-5 Kainan
120 F-2 Kaindy *riv.*
89 L-9 Kainji *dam.*
223 J-3 Kaipara
139 N-4 Kairâna
211 H-3 Kairiru *isl.*
79 N-3 Kairouan
211 K-7 Kairuku
58 F-6 Kaiseregg *mt*
133 M-2 Kaishantun
66 B-4 Kaišjadoris
206 G-3 Kait *cap.*
223 J-2 Kaitaia

222 D-9 Kaitangata
139 M-3 Kaithal
131 K-1 Kaitonghu *lake*
134 E-3 Kaixian
134 E-6 Kaiyang
133 J-2 Kaiyuan (China)
134 B-8 Kaiyuan (China)
159 H-5 Kaiyuh *mt*
92 B-7 Kaja *riv.*
48 G-8 Kajaani
206 D-5 Kajaapu
214 E-8 Kajabbi
126 F-6 Kajakī
208 F-7 Kajan
147 P-8 Kajan *riv.*
70 D-7 Kajdak *lake*
101 G-4 Kajiado
123 K-2 Kajmonovo
121 K-5 Kajnar
94 E-7 Kajo Kaji
71 P-4 Kajrakkum
208 D-5 Kajuadi *isl.*
206 F-3 Kajuagung
170 A-1 Kakagi *lake*
94 G-7 Kakamari
104 E-5 Kakamas
100 F-2 Kakamega
146 A-3 Kakana
87 N-6 Kakata
137 L-8 Kakeroma *isl.*
104 G-2 Kakia
140 E-9 Kākinada
161 J-8 Kakisa *riv.*
161 J-8 Kakisa *lake*
100 C-3 Kakogawa
89 L-3 Kakpin
87 J-4 Kakrima *riv.*
159 P-6 Kaktovik
136 E-7 Kakunodate
162 F-4 Kakwa *riv.*
127 K-7 Kālābagh
208 F-6 Kalabahi
64 C-6 Kalabáka
103 H-4 Kalabo
82 B-8 Kalabsha *site*
67 K-5 Kalač
67 L-6 Kalač-na-Donu
121 L-1 Kalačinsk
143 J-5 Kaladan *riv.*
164 C-9 Kaladar
132 G-3 Kalaginqi
131 L-5 Kalahai *lake*
104 E-3 Kalahari *na.p.*
76 E-7 Kalahari *dés*
140 G-7 Kālahasti
142 G-1 Kalahu *lake*
127 L-3 Kalai-Chumb
126 E-3 Kalai-Mor
123 N-1 Kalajka
48 G-7 Kalajoki
48 G-7 Kalajoki *riv.*
124 A-3 Kalakan
128 G-3 Kalakashihe *riv.*
129 L-1 Kalake
127 L-6 Kalâm
149 M-2 Kalama *isl.*
64 D-8 Kalámai
162 E-7 Kalamalka *lake*
170 E-6 Kalamazoo
143 J-3 Kalang *riv.*
124 A-5 Kalanguj
216 E-6 Kalannie
81 H-5 Kalansho *dés*
208 D-6 Kalao *isl.*
208 E-6 Kalaotoa *isl.*
124 B-2 Kalar
124 A-2 Kalarskij *mt*
129 K-9 Kalashankou
147 P-9 Kalasin (Indonesia)
145 J-5 Kalasin (Thailand)
126 B-3 Kalāt *mt*
126 F-9 Kalāt
64 D-7 Kalávrita
143 L-7 Kalaw
84 C-6 Kalbā
121 M-6 Kalbinskij *mt*
57 K-9 Kaldenkirchen
65 K-5 Kalecik
208 F-4 Kaledupa
144 E-6 Kalegauk *isl.*
100 B-4 Kalehe
100 B-7 Kalemie
143 K-6 Kalemyo
48 F-9 Kalevala
143 K-5 Kalewa
48 C-2 Kalfarell
68 D-6 Kalgačicha
158 G-8 Kalgin *isl.*
217 H-6 Kalgoorlie
128 A-7 Kalguty
129 N-1 Kāli (India) *riv.*
89 L-9 Kali (Nigeria) *riv.*
211 K-2 Kali B.
139 L-7 Kāli Sindh *riv.*
64 G-3 Kaliakra *cap.*

206 G-5 Kalianda
148 F-5 Kalibo
99 P-4 Kalima
207 M-1 Kalimantan
147 N-8 Kalimantan *reg.*
147 L-9 Kalimantan Barat *reg.*
147 N-9 Kalimantan Tengah *reg.*
149 N-9 Kalimantan Timur *rge*
64 F-8 Kalimnos
142 G-2 Kālimpong
71 H-7 Kalinin (SSSR)
66 F-7 Kalinin (SSSR)
66 A-4 Kaliningrad
67 L-4 Kalininsk
66 E-6 Kalinkovici
66 E-8 Kalinovka
100 E-2 Kaliro
97 J-7 Kalis
207 N-7 Kalisat
162 F-9 Kalispell
51 M-6 Kalisz
67 K-7 Kalitva *riv.*
141 J-7 Kaliveli *lake*
48 F-7 Kalix
48 E-6 Kalixalven *riv.*
121 K-3 Kalkaman
57 L-5 Kalkar
170 E-4 Kalkaska
102 D-8 Kalkfeld
102 G-9 Kalkfontein
104 G-6 Kalkfontein *dam.*
104 C-2 Kalkrand
141 M-8 Kalkudah
192 C-3 Kalkuni
66 C-1 Kallaste
49 H-9 Kallavesi *lake*
58 E-3 Kallnach
56 B-9 Kallo
48 G-4 Kallsjön *lake*
71 J-1 Kalmakkyrgan *riv.*
121 P-4 Kalmanka
51 L-3 Kalmar
51 L-3 Kalmarsund *strt.*
56 C-8 Kalmthout
141 M-8 Kalmunai
70 B-4 Kalmykovo
67 M-7 Kalmytskaya *reg.*
142 F-5 Kālna
143 H-4 Kālni *riv.*
211 K-8 Kalo
64 B-1 Kalocsa
139 H-8 Kālol
100 D-9 Kalombo
103 K-6 Kalomo *riv.*
103 K-6 Kalomo
162 B-3 Kalone *mt*
129 N-8 Kalong
100 G-1 Kalossia
141 K-2 Kalpeni *isl.*
139 P-7 Kālpi
141 M-7 Kalpitiya
73 N-3 Kālshūr *riv.*
140 B-3 Kalsūbai *mt*
122 C-3 Kaltan
59 L-3 Kaltbad
59 N-2 Kaltbrunn
58 F-5 Kalte Sense *reg.*
141 N-7 Kalu *riv.*
138 E-5 Kālu
66 G-3 Kaluga
208 A-4 Kalukalukuang *isl.*
103 L-3 Kalulushi
100 C-8 Kalumbi
213 K-2 Kalumburu
100 A-8 Kalumendongo *riv.*
100 D-2 Kalumiro
128 D-1 Kalunak
51 J-4 Kalundborg
103 P-1 Kalungu *riv.*
103 N-1 Kalungwishi *riv.*
89 L-5 Kalurakun *riv.*
66 C-8 Kalush
141 N-7 Kalutara
100 C-7 Kalya
140 C-3 Kalyān
140 G-5 Kalyāndrug
140 D-5 Kalyāni
128 A-8 Kal'žir *riv.*
90 E-5 Kam (Nigeria) *riv.*
145 J-5 Kam (Thailand) *riv.*
69 L-7 Kama *lake*
69 K-5 Kama *riv.*
99 P-5 Kama (Zaïre) *riv.*
137 L-3 Kamae
80 E-9 Kamai
143 L-3 Kamaing
136 E-8 Kamaisi
87 K-5 Kamakwie
127 K-9 Kamālia
145 L-6 Kaman *riv.*
139 M-5 Kāman
65 K-5 Kamaran
88 F-3 Kamango *lake*
103 L-1 Kamangombe *riv.*
192 D-5 Kamani *riv.*

102 C-7 Kamanjab
100 B-4 Kamanyola
96 E-1 Kamarān *isl.*
96 E-1 Kamarān
187 P-6 Kamarang
187 P-6 Kamarang *riv.*
71 N-7 Kamaši
91 J-6 Kambakota
71 L-1 Kambaly
206 C-2 Kambang
207 J-6 Kambangan *isl.*
138 F-3 Kambar
69 L-8 Kambarka
87 L-4 Kambia
103 K-1 Kambove
208 C-2 Kambuno *mt*
145 K-9 Kâmchay Méa
64 F-3 Kamčija *riv.*
127 L-6 Kamdesh
91 H-2 Kamé
208 D-5 Kameda *pen.*
67 N-3 Kamenka (SSSR)
67 K-3 Kamenka (SSSR)
67 H-8 Kamenka (SSSR)
67 F-8 Kamenka (SSSR)
49 J-9 Kamennogorsk
72 B-1 Kamennomostskij
68 B-6 Kamenoje *lake*
123 L-6 Kamensk
67 K-7 Kamensk-Shakhtinskiy
69 P-6 Kamensk-Ural'skiy
67 M-4 Kamenskij
115 Q-3 Kamenskoye
56 D-3 Kamerik
67 H-1 Kameškovo
129 M-1 Kāmet *mt*
137 M-3 Kami *isl.*
133 P-7 Kami-Tusima
137 N-3 Kami-Yaku
166 D-7 Kamiah
104 C-6 Kamieskroon
136 B-7 Kamikawa
214 E-8 Kamileroi
158 F-8 Kamishak *bay*
100 B-4 Kamituga
120 E-7 Kamkaly
162 D-6 Kamloops
162 D-6 Kamloops *plat.*
123 N-2 Kamniokan
136 G-7 Kamo *riv.*
72 E-3 Kamo (SSSR)
137 K-5 Kamoda *cap.*
127 L-9 Kāmoke
100 E-2 Kampala
77 F-4 Kampé
146 F-9 Kampar *riv.*
146 E-9 Kampar Kanan *riv.*
146 E-9 Kampar Kiri *riv.*
206 F-2 Kampe *bay*
100 A-5 Kapeme
144 F-5 Kamphaeng Phet
140 F-5 Kampli
103 N-2 Kapolombo *lake*
145 K-8 Kâmpong Cham
145 J-8 Kâmpong Chhnang
146 F-5 Kâmpong Raja
145 H-9 Kâmpóng Saôm *bay*
145 J-9 Kâmpong Spoe
145 J-8 Kâmpong Thum
140 B-8 Kamptee
89 K-3 Kampti
209 M-3 Kamrau *bay*
163 M-8 Kamsack
87 J-3 Kamsar
67 M-1 Kamskoje-Ustje
99 J-6 Kamtsha *riv.*
163 M-5 Kamuchawie *lake*
187 P-6 Kamuda
136 C-5 Kamui *cap.*
100 E-2 Kamuli
67 M-5 Kamyshin
69 P-5 Kamyshlov
120 B-3 Kamyslybas *lake*
122 F-2 Kan *riv.*
94 E-3 Kan
103 L-7 Kana *riv.*
164 C-2 Kanaaupscow *riv.*
167 L-1 Kanab
167 L-7 Kanab *riv.*
187 P-5 Kanaima Falls
81 M-2 Kanā'is *cap.*
146 C-6 Kanana *riv.*
99 L-6 Kananga (Luluabourg)
67 L-1 Kanash

158 D-8 Kanatak
171 H-9 Kanawha *riv.*
137 H-5 Kanazawa
143 L-5 Kanbalu
144 F-7 Kanchanaburi
142 F-1 Kanchenjunga *mt*
141 H-7 Kānchipuram
68 D-5 K'anda
70 D-2 Kandagač
126 F-7 Kandahar
145 J-9 Kândal *reg.*
48 E-9 Kandalaksha
68 B-4 Kandalakshskiy Zaliv *gulf*
207 P-3 Kandangan
207 J-5 Kandanghaur
122 D-1 Kandat *riv.*
122 D-1 Kandat
224 B-5 Kandavu *isl.*
89 L-6 Kandé
58 G-6 Kanderbrück
58 G-6 Kandergrund
58 G-7 Kandersteg
138 G-3 Kandhkot
89 K-8 Kandi (Dahomey)
142 F-4 Kāndi (India)
138 F-3 Kandiāro
159 M-9 Kandik *riv.*
87 H-4 Kandika
91 L-7 Kandjia
138 G-7 Kandla
108 G-4 Kandreho
211 M-5 Kandrian
141 M-1 Kandufuri *isl.*
140 F-7 Kandukūr
141 N-1 Kandute *isl.*
141 M-7 Kandy
158 E-5 Kanektok *riv.*
86 F-4 Kanel
90 G-1 Kanem *mt*
91 H-1 Kanem *reg.*
68 D-3 Kanevka
67 K-9 Kanevskaja
104 F-2 Kang
87 J-8 Kangaba
65 M-5 Kangal
83 P-2 Kangân
146 D-5 Kangar
87 J-8 Kangaré
220 B-3 Kangaroo *isl.*
73 H-7 Kangâvar
132 E-4 Kangbao
129 P-9 Kangbupashankou *pass*
131 P-7 Kangding
207 P-6 Kangean *isl.*
94 F-5 Kangen *riv.*
142 G-1 Kangma
129 N-5 Kangmaer
129 L-2 Kangnichumike
98 C-2 Kango
94 G-8 Kangole
133 J-2 Kangping
135 N-9 Kangshan
143 J-1 Kangto *mt*
132 F-5 Kangzhuang
140 A-7 Kanhan *riv.*
142 C-4 Kanhar *riv.*
143 K-6 Kani (Birman)
89 L-1 Kani (Ivory Coast)
99 M-8 Kaniama
71 P-4 Kanibadam
211 J-1 Kaniet *islds*
140 F-7 Kanigiri
71 M-6 Kanimech
68 D-2 Kanin *pen.*
112 C-3 Kanin Kamen *pen.*
68 D-2 Kanin Nos
88 F-4 Kanioumé
136 D-6 Kanita
122 F-3 Kanitonovka
220 E-4 Kaniva
170 D-7 Kankakee
87 K-7 Kankan
140 C-9 Kānker
141 K-7 Kankesanturai
86 F-6 Kankossa
139 K-6 Kānkroli
122 D-5 Kanlegir *riv.*
146 C-1 Kanmaw *isl.*
177 K-2 Kannapolis
139 P-6 Kannauj
57 M-9 Kanne
140 A-6 Kannod
90 C-2 Kano
90 C-2 Kano *reg.*
90 C-3 Kano *riv.*
65 N-6 Kanona
106 E-1 Kanona
137 K-4 Kan'onzi
217 H-6 Kanowit
147 M-8 Kanowit
137 N-3 Kanoya
143 K-6 Kanpetlet
139 P-6 Kanpur
89 J-2 Kanrangana
71 P-4 Kansaj

157 D-3 Kansas *state*
169 H-8 Kansas *riv.*
169 H-8 Kansas *state*
169 J-8 Kansas City
122 G-2 Kansk
128 C-1 Kant
146 D-4 Kantang
89 J-7 Kantchari
145 J-7 Kantharalak
159 K-7 Kantishna *riv.*
159 J-7 Kantishna
224 B-4 Kanton *isl.*
70 G-5 Kantubek
126 D-8 Kanuk
192 B-4 Kanuku *mt*
136 G-7 Kanuma
159 L-6 Kanuti *riv.*
105 H-3 Kanye
147 K-8 Kanyi *mt*
122 D-3 Kanym (bol.) *mt*
103 J-8 Kanyu
103 K-1 Kanzenze
146 F-2 Kaôh Chrâluk *isl.*
145 H-9 Kaôh Kong *reg.*
146 F-2 Kaôh Tang *isl.*
135 N-9 Kaohsiung
89 K-9 Kaoje
102 B-7 Kaokoveld *plat.*
86 F-2 Kaolack
103 J-4 Kaoma
129 H-5 Kapa
139 J-8 Kapadvanj
211 K-8 Kapagere
99 L-8 Kapanga
100 F-1 Kapchorwa
61 N-3 Kapel
56 B-9 Kapellen
100 F-1 Kapenguria
61 P-1 Kapfenberg
119 L-6 Kapingamarangi *isl.*
220 B-2 Kapinnie
103 M-3 Kapiri Mposhi
127 J-6 Kāpīsā
164 A-3 Kapiskau
147 N-8 Kapit
223 H-6 Kapiti *isl.*
192 E-5 Kapiting
92 A-7 Kapka *mt*
64 A-1 Kaposvar
59 L-2 Kappel (Switzerland)
59 P-1 Kappel (Switzerland)
102 D-9 Kapps
100 F-2 Kapsabet
66 B-4 Kapsukas
143 J-5 Kaptai
147 N-9 Kapuas *lake*
207 K-1 Kapuas *riv.*
147 L-9 Kapuas (Indonesia) *riv.*
147 N-8 Kapuas Hulu *mt*
220 D-2 Kapunda
139 M-2 Kapûrthala
164 A-6 Kapuskasing (Canada)
67 M-6 Kapustin Jar
72 F-4 Kapydzik *mt*
112 F-2 Kara *sea*
89 L-6 Kara *riv.*
226 A-4 Kara *sea*
128 C-1 Kara-Balty
73 J-1 Kara-Bogaz *gulf*
122 D-5 Kara-Chol'
73 M-4 Kara-Kala
120 F-3 Kara-Kengir *riv.*
71 P-2 Kara-Kul'
112 D-5 Kara Kum *rge*
71 J-8 Kara-Kum *dés*
127 N-2 Kara-Su
71 N-2 Kara-Tau
120 E-2 Kara Turgaj *riv.*
70 E-9 Kara–Bogaz–Gol *bay*
127 H-4 Karaalma
127 N-3 Karaart
121 L-6 Karaaul
65 L-5 Karabas *mt*
128 B-8 Karabas *riv.*
121 H-4 Karabas
70 B-4 Karabau
71 M-8 Karabekaul
71 N-9 Karabil' *mt*
128 A-6 Karabuga *riv.*
65 J-4 Karabük
128 B-4 Karabulak
64 F-7 Karaburun
70 E-1 Karabutak
65 N-6 Karaca *mt*
64 F-7 Karacabey
72 C-1 Karačajevsk
66 G-4 Karačev
138 E-5 Karachi
140 D-3 Karâd
123 N-4 Karaftit
69 L-6 Karagaj
121 J-5 Karagajly
124 C-3 Karagan

121 H-4 Karaganda
73 K-2 Karagel'
72 A-4 Karagöl mt
122 D-5 Karagoš mt
65 H-7 Karahalli
69 N-7 Karaidel'skij
141 K-6 Kāraikkudi
141 K-7 Kāraitivu isl.
73 K-5 Karaj
121 K-4 Karakabak
70 F-6 Karakalpakskaya reg.
149 L-1 Karakelong isl.
149 M-2 Karakitang isl.
71 K-1 Karakoin lake
128 D-2 Karakolka
127 P-6 Karakoram reg.
129 H-1 Karakoram pass
127 N-3 Karakul' lake
71 L-7 Karakul'
69 L-8 Karakulino
128 A-5 Karakum
71 M-9 Karakumskij cal.
121 L-5 Karakus mt
102 F-7 Karakuwisa
123 L-3 Karam
208 C-2 Karama riv.
65 K-7 Karaman
190 C-2 Karamanu riv.
208 A-3 Karambu
222 F-6 Karamea bay
222 G-6 Karamea
71 M-8 Karamet-Nijaz
94 G-7 Karamoja reg.
64 G-5 Karamürsel
123 J-1 Karamyševo
144 E-5 Karan reg.
192 B-4 Karanambo
72 G-7 Karand
207 P-7 Karangasem
140 B-6 Kāranja
142 D-6 Karanjia
139 K-3 Karanpur
128 A-2 Karaoj
121 M-7 Karaotkel
65 K-7 Karapinar
209 M-3 Karas isl.
104 D-5 Karasburg
70 E-8 Karašek lake
121 J-6 Karašengel'
48 C-7 Karasjok
48 D-7 Karašjokka riv.
121 J-4 Karasor riv.
70 G-9 Karašor (Goklenkui) lake
121 K-3 Karasu riv.
65 H-5 Karasu
72 C-4 Karasu-Aras mt
121 M-2 Karasuk riv.
121 M-2 Karasuk
128 A-3 Karatal riv.
65 L-7 Karataş
120 E-8 Karatau mt
71 H-7 Karatau
70 B-3 Karatobe
71 L-2 Karatou rge
142 G-3 Karatoya riv.
70 G-4 Karatup pen.
128 C-3 Karaturuk
122 K-4 Karatuzskoje
211 H-3 Karau
128 F-7 Karaul
71 M-7 Karaulbazar
139 M-6 Karauli
70 C-3 Karaulkel'dy
71 P-2 Karavan
91 L-8 Karawa
61 N-2 Karawanken mt
81 M-5 Karawayn well
120 G-5 Karažal
68 G-6 Kar'ažma
72 F-9 Karbalā
64 C-1 Karcag
72 C-3 Karcal
64 D-6 Kardhítsa
141 P-1 Kardiva cal.
141 P-2 Kardiva isl.
141 P-1 Kardiva strt.
66 A-1 Kärdla
64 E-5 Kârdžali
68 C-6 Karelskaya reg.
211 K-7 Karema
100 C-7 Karema (Tanzania)
144 B-8 Karen
124 A-4 Karenga riv.
139 N-7 Karera
48 D-6 Karesuando
126 A-8 Kārevāndar
121 N-2 Kargat riv.
121 N-2 Kargat
65 K-9 Kargi
127 N-7 Kargil
68 E-7 Kargopol'
122 D-6 Kargy riv.
49 J-8 Karhula
90 D-3 Kari
78 E-2 Karia-ba-Mohammed

103 L-6 Kariba lake
103 M-5 Kariba
102 C-9 Karibib
104 F-8 Kariega riv.
64 E-6 Karies
48 C-7 Karigasniemi
141 K-7 Karikal
223 K-2 Karikari cap.
92 G-4 Karima
207 J-2 Karimata isl.
207 J-3 Karimata (Selat) strt.
143 J-4 Karīmganj
140 D-7 Karīmnagar
123 P-6 Karimskoje
146 F-9 Karimun isl.
207 K-5 Karimundjawa islds
207 K-5 Karimundjawa isl.
97 H-4 Karin (Ethiopia)
96 G-7 Karin (Somalia)
100 B-3 Karisimbi mt
64 E-7 Káristos
210 G-5 Karius mt
126 D-4 Kārīz-e Dasht
49 K-7 Karjaa
68 E-4 Karjepolje
211 J-4 Karkar isl.
97 H-7 Karkar mt
121 J-5 Karkaralinsk
73 L-7 Karkas
93 J-8 Karkawj
138 F-3 Karkh
73 J-9 Karkheh riv.
64 J-1 Karkinitskij bay
49 J-8 Karkkila
82 D-6 Karkūmā cap.
51 K-7 Karl-Marx-Stadt
61 P-2 Karlovak
67 H-7 Karlovka
64 E-4 Karlovo
51 K-8 Karlovy Vary
51 L-3 Karlshamn
51 L-1 Karlskoga
51 L-3 Karlskrona
51 H-8 Karlsruhe
51 K-1 Karlstad (Sweden)
169 J-1 Karlstad (USA)
158 D-9 Karluk lake
92 F-3 Karmah
140 D-4 Karmāla
82 B-7 Karnak site
139 N-3 Karnāl
129 N-2 Karnāli riv.
143 H-5 Karnaphuli lake
140 F-4 Karnataka reg.
175 M-6 Karnes City
64 F-4 Karnobat
91 K-3 Karo
103 M-6 Karoi
126 E-6 Karokh
208 E-6 Karompa isl.
106 C-3 Karonga
217 H-6 Karonie
104 F-8 Karoo (Great)
104 E-6 Karoo (Hoë) reg.
104 E-9 Karoo (little) reg.
220 D-3 Karoonda
127 J-9 Karor
93 M-4 Karora
208 C-2 Karosa
208 B-7 Karosso cap.
64 F-9 Karpathos isl.
64 D-7 Karpenísion
59 P-4 Kärpf mt
69 M-4 Karpinsk
68 F-5 Karpogory
72 D-3 Kars
120 E-4 Karsakpaj
127 H-1 Karshi
71 N-7 Karshi
112 D-2 Karskiye strt.
69 K-7 Karsovaj
192 B-2 Kartabu
69 H-7 Kartajol'
64 G-5 Kartal
108 B-3 Kartala mt
69 H-5 Kartkeros
125 K-7 Kartun
209 M-3 Karufa
214 F-7 Karumba
83 L-1 Kārūn riv.
73 K-8 Kārūn riv.
208 C-7 Karuni
213 L-4 Karunjie
141 J-6 Karūr
51 M-8 Karvina
140 F-3 Kārwār
139 P-7 Karwi
123 J-4 Karymskoje
70 E-8 Karynžaryk mt
65 H-8 Kaş
160 C-8 Kasaan
142 E-5 Kāsai (India) riv.
99 J-5 Kasai (Zaïre) riv.
99 K-5 Kasai Occidental reg.
99 M-5 Kasai Oriental reg.
103 H-1 Kasaji

100 C-6 Kasalu
106 C-1 Kasama
71 M-7 Kasan
103 J-6 Kasane
106 D-1 Kasanka rés
71 P-2 Kasansaj
137 K-4 Kasaoka
141 H-3 Kāsaragod
137 L-9 Kasari
139 N-2 Kasauli
163 N-2 Kasba lake
78 D-4 Kasba-Tadla
137 N-3 Kaseda
159 M-2 Kasegaluk lag.
103 K-3 Kasempa
103 M-1 Kasenga
100 C-1 Kasenyi
100 A-3 Kasese
145 J-6 Kaset Wisai
139 N-5 Kāsganj
170 C-1 Kashabowie
126 E-2 Kashaf riv.
73 K-6 Kāshān
128 E-1 Kashi
128 F-2 Kashigaerhe riv.
128 C-5 Kashihe riv.
139 P-4 Kashīpur
71 N-6 Kashkadar' inskaya reg.
93 K-6 Kashm el Girba
73 N-3 Kāshmar
139 H-3 Kashmor
72 G-2 Kasi-Magomed
142 D-2 Kasia
99 M-8 Kasidishi riv.
67 J-2 Kasimov
66 G-1 Kašin
100 C-2 Kasindi
209 H-1 Kasiruta isl.
209 L-4 Kasiui isl.
137 H-8 Kasiwa
136 G-6 Kasiwazaki
121 L-5 Kaskabulak
71 M-7 Kaškadarja riv.
170 D-8 Kaskakia riv.
128 C-2 Kaskelen
49 H-6 Kaskinen
69 P-6 Kasli
162 F-7 Kaslo
121 N-3 Kasmala riv.
163 P-2 Kasmere lake
100 A-6 Kasongo
98 G-7 Kasongo Lunda
64 G-9 Kasos isl.
72 D-2 Kaspi
70 A-8 Kaspijskij
72 F-1 Kaspiysk
93 M-4 Kasr pte
93 L-6 Kassala
93 K-4 Kassalā reg.
87 H-6 Kassama
64 D-6 Kassandra pen.
51 J-7 Kassel
79 N-3 Kasserine
65 J-4 Kastamonu
64 E-9 Kastellion
64 G-9 Kastellou cap.
65 H-8 Kastelorizon isl.
64 C-5 Kastoría
67 H-5 Kastornoje
64 E-6 Kastron
137 J-6 Kasugai
99 N-4 Kasuku riv.
72 F-1 Kasumkent
106 E-3 Kasungu rés
106 E-3 Kasungu
139 L-2 Kasūr
123 J-1 Kata riv.
103 J-5 Kataba
164 G-7 Katahdin mt
160 B-2 Katalla
123 K-1 Katanga riv.
125 M-1 Katangli
216 F-8 Katanning
141 N-8 Kataragama
129 P-2 Katarniān Ghāt
146 A-4 Katchall isl.
159 J-5 Kateel riv.
125 L-6 Katen riv.
99 L-7 Katende
64 D-6 Katerini
160 D-7 Kates Needle mt
143 L-4 Katha
94 G-5 Kathangor mt
213 P-2 Katherine riv.
213 P-2 Katherine
138 G-8 Kathiawar reg.
118 D-4 Kathmandu
142 E-1 Kathmandu
127 M-9 Kathua
87 H-8 Kati

142 F-3 Katihār
103 J-6 Katima Mulilo
89 M-2 Katiola
158 E-8 Katmai site
158 E-8 Katmai bay
140 B-7 Kātol
99 P-7 Katompe
121 P-7 Katon-Karagaj
173 H-1 Katonah
221 K-2 Katoomba (Blue Mountains)
99 N-4 Katopa
82 B-5 Katrīnah mt
51 L-1 Katrineholm
108 F-5 Katsépy
90 C-1 Katsina
90 C-5 Katsina Ala riv.
171 L-5 Katskill mt
71 M-6 Kattakurgan
164 B-5 Kattawagami riv.
137 L-2 Katumoto
122 B-4 Katun riv.
67 J-1 Katúnki
121 P-6 Katunskij mt
208 B-7 Katupa
142 F-4 Katwa
100 C-2 Katwe
56 B-2 Katwijk reg.
56 B-2 Katwijk aan de Rijn
56 B-2 Katwijk aan Zee
146 C-2 Kau-Ye isl.
224 C-1 Kauai
224 D-1 Kauai isl.
61 M-1 Kaufbeuren
175 N-3 Kaufman
102 G-7 Kaukau Veld plat.
224 C-1 Kaula
48 E-7 Kauliranta
66 B-4 Kaunas (Kovno)
49 K-8 Kauniainen
90 B-2 Kaura Namoda
129 P-2 Kauriāla Ghāt
48 D-7 Kautokeino
64 C-5 Kavadarci
64 B-5 Kavajë
125 L-8 Kavalerovo
140 G-7 Kāvali
64 E-5 Kavālla
141 J-1 Kavaratti
141 J-1 Kavaratti isl.
119 M-6 Kaven isl.
87 K-5 Kavendou mt
139 H-8 Kāvi
211 N-2 Kavieng
159 N-6 Kavik riv.
126 A-1 Kavīr dés
73 M-5 Kavīr (Dasht-e)
73 P-4 Kavīr-e Namak mt
192 G-3 Kaw
92 G-3 Kawa site
137 H-7 Kawagoe
137 H-7 Kawaguti
223 K-2 Kawakawa
149 L-2 Kawalusu isl.
100 B-9 Kawambwa
137 K-4 Kawanoe
140 B-9 Kawardha
137 H-8 Kawasaki
223 K-3 Kawau isl.
223 K-6 Kaweka mt
223 K-5 Kawerau
223 J-4 Kawhia Harbour
149 L-2 Kawio isl.
144 E-5 Kawkareik
143 L-5 Kawlin
146 C-2 Kawthaung
89 H-5 Kaya
143 M-8 Kayah reg.
160 A-2 Kayak isl.
119 J-6 Kayangel isl.
141 L-4 Kāyankulam
86 F-1 Kayar
168 A-9 Kayenta
86 G-6 Kayes (Congo)
98 D-5 Kayes (Congo)
86 G-6 Kayes (Mali)
93 M-5 Kelamet
192 D-4 Käyser mt
65 L-2 Kayseri
100 E-2 Kayunga
64 F-6 Kaz mt
72 E-2 Kazach
120 F-5 Kazachskaja rép
70 F-3 Kazachskaja rép
70 D-9 Kazachskij bay
72 D-2 Kazachstan
123 L-3 Kazačinskoje
67 H-6 Kazačja Lopan
71 H-6 Kazakdarja
125 K-5 Kazakevičevo
120 G-4 Kazakh pl.
112 E-5 Kazakh Steppes pl.

71 H-3 Kazalinsk
69 K-9 Kazan
163 P-1 Kazan riv.
72 F-2 Kazanbulak
73 L-1 Kazandžik
125 J-5 Kazanka
64 E-4 Kazanlâk
65 K-1 Kazantip cap.
127 P-2 Kazarman
66 E-7 Kazatin
72 D-1 Kazbek mt
83 N-1 Kāzerūn
69 J-6 Kazim
101 J-7 Kazim Kazi cap.
66 A-9 Kazincbarcika
67 N-4 Kaztalovka
99 L-7 Kazumba
103 J-6 Kazungula
122 F-4 Kazyr riv.
125 L-6 Kchucin riv.
86 F-2 Kébémer
100 E-1 Keberamaido
79 N-4 Kebili
48 E-5 Kebnekaise mt
97 L-3 Kebri Dehar
207 K-6 Kebumen
64 D-4 Kecani
160 F-8 Kechika mt
160 F-8 Kechika riv.
65 H-7 Kecirborlu
64 B-1 Kecskmet
146 D-5 Kedah reg.
66 B-4 Kédainiai
164 G-5 Kedgwick Game Refuge na.p.
56 E-5 Kedichem
86 A-6 Kediet ej Jill mt
207 L-6 Kediri
124 F-7 Kedong
87 H-5 Kédougou
160 G-4 Keele mt
161 H-4 Keele riv.
171 M-5 Keene
219 L-8 Keepit lake
214 F-4 Keer–Weer cap.
124 G-6 Keerfenhe riv.
130 E-3 Keerleikeshan mt
133 J-1 Keerqinzuozhongqi
129 L-2 Keerzong
104 C-4 Keetmanshoop
95 H-4 Kefa reg.
65 H-4 Kefken cap.
48 B-1 Keflavik
162 G-2 Keg River
141 M-7 Kegalla
128 D-3 Kegen
128 D-6 Kegen riv.
129 M-7 Kegongzhake
59 K-3 Kehrsitens
57 L-3 Keienburg
104 E-5 Keimoes
91 K-4 Keita riv.
161 K-4 Keith strt.
220 D-3 Keith (Australia)
50 D-1 Keith (UK)
162 E-4 Keithley Creek
68 C-3 Kejvy mt
57 K-5 Kekerdom
131 L-2 Kekeshili
209 J-2 Kekik isl.
141 M-7 Kekirawa
122 F-2 Kekur
78 D-5 Kelâa-des-Mgouna
97 M-3 Kelafo
141 M-1 Kelai isl.
129 K-7 Kelalihu lake
95 H-6 Kelam
128 C-7 Kelamayi
93 M-5 Kelamet
129 J-7 Kelamulun-shankou pass
132 C-6 Kelan
209 H-3 Kelang isl.
146 E-7 Kelang
128 B-9 Kelanhe riv.
146 E-5 Kelantan reg.
207 M-6 Kelapang
128 E-6 Kelashaerhe riv.
128 D-7 Kelawuchengshan mt
68 E-4 Kel'da riv.
57 H-7 Keldonk
71 N-3 Keles riv.
71 N-3 Keles
108 G-4 Kelifely plat.

126 G-2 Kelifskij Uzbol lake
147 L-9 Kelingkang mt
71 M-8 Kelistkij Uzboj lake
129 J-3 Keliyahe riv.
129 J-3 Keliyashankou hill
64 L-4 Kelkif riv.
72 B-4 Kelkit
98 F-2 Kéllé
161 J-5 Keller lake
216 F-7 Kellerberrin
50 B-3 Kells
161 J-3 Kelly lake
53 H-1 Kelmarsh
91 H-4 Kélo
162 D-7 Kelowna
162 B-5 Kelsey Bay
162 B-9 Kelso
222 D-5 Kelso (Australia)
167 M-5 Kelso (USA)
71 N-2 Kel'temašat
86 A-7 Kelulunhe riv.
124 F-6 Keluohe riv.
53 M-3 Kelvedon
163 M-7 Kelvington
97 J-7 Kelyched
68 C-5 Kem'
68 C-5 Kem riv.
149 L-9 Kemabong
65 N-5 Kemah
208 E-2 Kembani
91 M-8 Kembé
172 C-7 Kemblesville
122 E-1 Kemčug riv.
147 N-7 Kemena riv.
122 C-2 Kemerovo
48 E-8 Kemi riv.
48 F-7 Kemi
48 E-8 Kemijarvi lake
48 E-8 Kemijärvi
67 K-2 Keml'a
168 A-5 Kemmerer
91 K-7 Kemo-Gribingui reg.
175 M-2 Kemp lake
69 K-1 Kempaz riv.
56 F-8 Kempenland reg.
180 F-3 Kemp's Bay
221 M-1 Kempsey
53 J-2 Kempston
171 K-2 Kempt lake
61 L-1 Kempten
139 P-7 Ken riv.
78 F-5 Kenadsa
158 G-9 Kenai pen.
158 G-8 Kenai
158 G-9 Kenai mt
165 J-1 Kenamu riv.
163 K-8 Kenaston
207 K-6 Kendal (Indonesia)
50 D-4 Kendal (UK)
170 E-7 Kendallville
208 E-3 Kendari
208 E-3 Kendari bay
207 K-2 Kendawangan
141 N-2 Kendikolu isl.
142 E-6 Kendrāpāra
100 F-3 Kendu
175 M-6 Kenedy
87 M-5 Kenema
143 M-7 Keng Tawng
143 N-7 Keng Tung
98 G-6 Kenge
104 E-6 Kenhardt
87 H-6 Keniéba
87 H-6 Kéniékéniéko
87 H-9 Kénikou
219 J-5 Kenilworth (Australia)
52 F-1 Kenilworth (UK)
149 L-9 Keningau
78 D-2 Kenitra
168 F-1 Kenmare
52 C-5 Kenn
175 J-2 Kenna
171 N-3 Kennebec riv.
103 L-7 Kennedy
216 C-2 Kennedy mt
158 F-9 Kennedy strt.
162 B-6 Kennedy lake
177 L-7 Kennedy cap.
172 B-8 Kennedyville
52 A-8 Kennerleigh
52 F-5 Kennet riv.
176 E-1 Kennet
172 C-6 Kennet Spare
162 D-9 Kennewick
53 N-1 Kenninghall
164 F-6 Kénogami
170 A-1 Kenora
170 D-6 Kenosha
173 H-2 Kensico rés
200 G-1 Kent isl.
221 H-6 Kent islds
53 L-6 Kent (UK) reg.
172 B-8 Kent (USA) reg.
166 D-5 Kent (USA)
175 J-4 Kent (USA)

173 H-1 Kent Cliffs
71 M-2 Kentau
53 M-1 Kentford
170 D-7 Kentland
170 F-7 Kenton
170 F-8 Kentucky *riv.*
170 E-9 Kentucky *state*
157 E-3 Kentucky *state*
176 G-1 Kentucky *lake*
165 J-7 Kentville
101 H-2 Kenya *mt*
77 F-5 Kenya *state*
142 D-6 Keonjhargarh
206 D-3 Kepahiang
210 E-5 Kepi
128 E-3 Keping
128 E-2 Kepingshan *mt*
219 M-3 Keppel *bay*
201 L-8 Keppel *isl.*
141 J-4 Kerala *reg.*
141 H-3 Kerala *mt*
211 H-4 Keram *riv.*
137 M-8 Kerama *islds*
207 N-4 Keramian *isl.*
89 K-6 Kéran *na.p.*
220 F-3 Kerang
211 P-4 Keravat
125 J-2 Kerbi *riv.*
65 K-1 Kerč
64 K-1 Kerčenskij *strt.*
69 J-5 Kerčomja
79 K-5 Kerdiz *riv.*
95 H-5 Kere
120 G-3 Kerej *lake*
211 J-6 Kerema
162 D-7 Keremeos
93 M-6 Keren
86 G-2 Kerewan
68 G-5 Kerga
93 H-8 Keri Kera
100 G-3 Kericho
206 C-2 Kerintji *mt*
206 C-2 Kerintji *lake*
100 G-1 Kerio *riv.*
56 G-4 Kerk Avezaath
56 G-5 Kerkdriel
79 P-4 Kerkenna *islds*
71 N-8 Kerki
64 B-6 Kérkira *isl.*
64 C-6 Kerkira
57 P-9 Kerkrade
224 B-6 Kermadec *islds*
224 B-6 Kermadec *foss*
73 P-8 Kermān *reg.*
73 H-7 Kermansha
73 N-7 Kermānshāhan
72 G-7 Kermānshāhan *reg.*
175 J-4 Kermit
126 G-5 Kermu *mt*
52 D-3 Kerne
92 B-8 Kernoya
59 K-4 Kerns
87 L-7 Kérouané
163 J-7 Kerrobert
175 M-5 Kerrville
52 B-1 Kerry *hill*
46 C-4 Kerry *mt*
207 J-1 Kertamulta
146 F-6 Kertch (Malaysia)
78 F-7 Kerzaz
58 E-3 Kerzers
164 A-5 Kesagami *lake*
64 F-5 Keşan
136 E-8 Kesennuma
124 F-7 Keshan
129 N-6 Keshangdamu
128 F-1 Keshier
128 E-4 Keshierbulake
132 F-2 Keshikelengqi
140 A-1 Keshod
72 C-4 Kesis *mt*
49 H-8 Keski Suomi *reg.*
65 K-5 Keskin
170 B-7 Keskuk
57 K-9 Kessel (Netherlands)
56 G-5 Kessel (Netherlands)
57 K-9 Kesseleijk
57 M-6 Kessenich
105 K-5 Kestell
48 E-9 Kesten'ga
57 H-4 Kesteren
53 K-6 Keston
129 J-7 Kesuke
122 E-1 Ket *riv.*
89 N-6 Keta
95 K-2 Ketama
206 G-5 Ketapang (Indonesia)
207 K-2 Ketapang (Indonesia)
160 C-9 Ketchikan
56 C-4 Keten
159 M-3 Ketik *riv.*
128 D-4 Ketmen *mt*
158 F-7 Ketok *mt*
129 H-7 Ketonghuan
89 M-8 Kétou
66 A-5 Ketrzyn
50 E-5 Kettering (UK)
170 F-8 Kettering (USA)
162 E-7 Kettle *riv.*
162 E-8 Kettle Falls
162 D-8 Kettle River *mt*
123 J-1 Keul'
57 K-9 Keup
86 E-2 Keur Massène
57 L-7 Kevelaer
170 C-7 Kewanee
170 D-5 Kewaunee
170 D-3 Keweenaw *bay*
170 D-2 Keweenaw *pen.*
170 D-2 Keweenaw *pte*
128 G-9 Kexilangcha
177 L-9 Key Largo
177 K-9 Key West
168 G-5 Keya Paha *riv.*
129 P-4 Keyanggeyapu
168 E-4 Keyhole *lake*
52 D-5 Keynsham
172 G-4 Keyport
69 L-7 Kez
129 K-2 Kezihu *lake*
123 J-1 Kežma
64 A-1 Kezsthely
104 E-2 Kgalagadi *reg.*
105 H-2 Kgatleng *reg.*
158 F-4 Kgun *lake*
125 K-5 Khabarovsk
143 K-8 Khadaungnge *mt*
144 F-6 Khaeng *riv.*
83 M-2 Khafji
142 B-2 Khāga
140 B-9 Khairāgarh
138 G-3 Khairpur
73 L-9 Khāīz *mt*
122 D-4 Khakasskaya *reg.*
127 N-8 Khalatse
128 D-4 Khalik Tau *mt*
64 G-8 Khalki *isl.*
64 E-7 Khalkís
140 A-9 Khamaria
138 F-8 Khambhāliya
140 B-6 Khāmgaon
96 D-2 Khamir
96 B-1 Khamīs-Mushayţ
140 E-8 Khammam
145 J-5 Khammouan
145 H-3 Khan *riv.*
65 M-8 Khān Shaykhūn
82 B-3 Khān Yūnis
127 K-4 Khanābād *riv.*
127 K-4 Khānābād
140 D-4 Khānāpur
72 G-7 Khānaqin
140 A-6 Khandwa
72 F-6 Khāneh
139 K-2 Khānewāl
147 H-3 Khanh Hung
64 E-9 Khaniá
139 H-3 Khānpur
69 N-1 Khanty-Mansiysk
97 H-4 Khānzūr *cap.*
144 G-7 Khao Laem *mt*
144 F-6 Khao Mokochu *mt*
145 H-8 Khao Soi Dao Tai *mt*
127 N-7 Khapalu
73 M-7 Khār *mt*
73 H-5 Khar Rūd *riv.*
130 F-7 Khara Khoto (Heicheng) *site*
142 E-5 Kharagpur (India)
142 E-3 Kharagpur (India)
126 E-9 Khārān
140 A-5 Khargon
139 L-6 Khāri *riv.*
82 C-8 Kharīt *riv.*
83 N-1 Khārk
67 H-6 Khar'kov
93 H-6 Khartoum
77 F-3 Khartoum
93 H-6 Khartoum (North) *reg.*
126 E-6 Khāsh *riv.*
126 D-6 Khāsh (Afghanistan)
126 B-8 Khāsh (Iran)
116 E-4 Khasi *rge*
83 J-7 Khāşirah *reg.*
64 E-4 Khaskovo
96 G-5 Khatib *cap.*
73 N-8 Khātūn *mt*
102 G-7 Khaudun *riv.*
138 G-6 Khāvda
85 H-3 Khawr Mahyūbah *well*
93 P-3 Khay'
82 G-6 Khaybar *mt*
82 F-6 Khaybar
145 J-3 Khé Bô
140 C-3 Khed
139 J-7 Khed Brahma
139 N-8 Khēda *mt*
143 L-2 Khela
79 J-2 Khemis
78 B-3 Khemis des Zemamra
78 D-3 Khemisset
145 K-6 Khemmarat
79 M-3 Khenchela
78 D-3 Khénifra
127 J-5 Khenjān
79 L-2 Kherrata
73 L-8 Khersan *riv.*
139 J-7 Kherwāra
127 L-8 Khewra
127 J-4 Kheyrābād
124 D-6 Khingan (Greater) *rge*
113 K-5 Khingan (Greater) *rge*
124 F-6 Khingan (Lesser) *rge*
113 L-5 Khingan (Lesser) *rge*
146 C-3 Khiri Rat Nikhom
83 H-1 Khirr *riv.*
129 J-2 Khitai Dawan *pass*
72 G-4 Khiyav
144 F-5 Khlong Khlung
146 C-4 Khlong Thom
145 H-9 Khlong Yai
66 D-8 Khmel'nitsky
88 B-4 Khnâchêch *reg.*
146 G-4 Khoai *isl.*
71 H-7 Khodzheyli
126 F-8 Khojak *hill*
144 G-6 Khok Samrong
127 J-4 Kholm
127 J-4 Kholm *riv.*
104 B-1 Khomas Highland *mt*
86 F-2 Khombol
103 J-8 Khomo
145 H-7 Khon Buri
145 H-5 Khon-Kaen
144 G-5 Khon San
145 K-7 Không
145 K-6 Khôngxédôn
84 B-3 Khonj
96 G-2 Khor Angar
84 C-6 Khor Fakkan
138 C-4 Khor Kalmat *bay*
64 E-9 Khora Sfakon
116 A-3 Khorassan
126 D-5 Khormāleq
83 P-2 Khormuj *mt*
73 J-7 Khorramābād
83 L-1 Khorramshahr
72 E-6 Khorsabad *site*
126 G-9 Khost
78 D-3 Khouribga
143 H-4 Khowai
83 M-1 Khowr-e Mūsa *bay*
73 N-7 Khowrnag *mt*
127 J-7 Khowst
64 E-5 Khrisoúpolis
145 J-4 Khuang *riv.*
83 J-4 Khubb al Mazhūr *mt*
83 K-6 Khuff
126 F-7 Khūgīānī
82 G-9 Khulayş
142 G-5 Khulna
127 H-7 Khumbur Khūle Ghar *mt*
144 E-3 Khun Yuam
142 D-4 Khunti
126 B-3 Khūr
139 M-8 Khurai
73 N-4 Khurasan *reg.*
83 M-5 Khurayş
92 D-8 Khurayt
142 D-7 Khurda
139 N-5 Khurja
83 J-8 Khurmah Wādī *riv.*
82 G-2 Khurr *riv.*
83 M-3 Khursaniyah
126 B-4 Khūsf
126 D-5 Khush
126 B-3 Khushāb
127 K-8 Khushāb
92 F-8 Khuwayy
138 E-2 Khuzdār
73 J-9 Khuzistan *reg.*
126 D-3 Khvāf
127 K-4 Khvājeh Ghār
127 K-5 Khvājeh Moham-mad *mt*
73 K-7 Khvonsar
73 N-5 Khvor
83 N-2 Khvormuj
72 F-4 Khvoy
144 E-7 Khwae (Kwaī) *riv.*
127 K-6 Khyber Pass *pass*
221 K-3 Kiama
149 K-3 Kiamba
100 A-8 Kiambi
175 P-2 Kiamichi *riv.*
159 K-3 Kiana
99 P-6 Kiangwe *riv.*
94 C-7 Kibali *riv.*
98 D-5 Kibangou
149 J-2 Kibawe
95 H-6 Kibish *riv.*
100 D-2 Kiboga
99 N-5 Kibombo
100 C-5 Kibondo
100 C-4 Kibungo
100 B-4 Kibuye
101 J-4 Kibwesi
64 C-5 Kičevo
170 C-5 Kickapo *riv.*
88 E-7 Kidal
52 D-1 Kidderminster
94 G-7 Kidepo *na.p.*
100 E-1 Kidera
86 G-5 Kidira
52 G-4 Kidlington
223 K-6 Kidnappers *cap.*
96 B-8 Kidyūt *riv.*
51 J-4 Kiel
66 A-7 Kielce
56 A-9 Kieldrecht
51 J-4 Kieler *bay*
147 H-3 Kiên Long
103 L-1 Kienge
90 D-9 Kienke *riv.*
59 H-5 Kiental *reg.*
59 H-5 Kiental
58 G-4 Kiesen
66 E-7 Kiev
87 H-4 Kifaya
86 E-6 Kiffa
64 E-7 Kifisiá
72 F-7 Kifrt
100 C-4 Kigali
77 E-5 Kigali
159 M-4 Kigalik *riv.*
100 C-3 Kigezi *reg.*
159 H-2 Kigluaik *mt*
100 C-5 Kigoma *reg.*
100 C-6 Kigoma
99 P-4 Kigombe
100 D-5 Kigosi *riv.*
66 B-8 Kihnu *isl.*
101 J-6 Kihurio
137 K-5 Kii *strt.*
137 K-6 Kii *pen.*
121 H-6 Kiik
66 A-1 Kiipsaarenukk *cap.*
122 C-1 Kija *riv.*
121 H-3 Kijevka
120 G-1 Kijma
137 L-9 Kikai *isl.*
64 C-2 Kikinda
136 D-6 Kikonai
211 H-6 Kikori *riv.*
211 H-6 Kikori
137 M-3 Kikuchi
67 L-5 Kikvidze
99 J-6 Kikwit
51 K-1 Kil
141 L-6 Kilakkarai
158 F-5 Kilbuck *mt*
219 M-5 Kilcay
50 B-4 Kildare
57 L-4 Kilder
48 C-9 Kil'din *isl.*
48 C-9 Kil'din *isl.*
103 N-6 Kildonan
175 P-4 Kilgore
100 F-3 Kilgoris
101 K-5 Kilifi
101 H-5 Kilimanjaro *reg.*
101 H-5 Kilimanjaro *rge*
65 J-4 Kilimli
101 K-5 Kilindini
101 K-8 Kilindoni
173 L-1 Kilingworth
65 M-7 Kilis
158 E-9 Kiliuda *bay*
64 G-2 Kiliya
50 B-4 Kilkenny
64 D-5 Kilkís
163 H-6 Killam
219 M-6 Killarney (Australia)
50 A-4 Killarney (Ireland)
169 H-1 Killarney (USA)
168 F-2 Killdeer
56 E-5 Kille
175 N-4 Killeen
159 M-5 Killik *riv.*
64 D-7 Killini *mt*
64 C-7 Killini
50 A-4 Killorglin
50 B-3 Killybegs
50 D-2 Kilmarnoch
69 K-8 Kil'mez' *riv.*
69 K-8 Kil'mez'
100 G-9 Kilombero *riv.*
101 H-7 Kilosa
50 A-4 Kilrush
52 G-1 Kilsby
141 J-2 Kiltān *isl.*
99 N-8 Kilubi *riv.*
100 B-9 Kilwa
101 K-9 Kilwa Kisiwani *isl.*
101 J-9 Kilwa Kivinje
101 J-9 Kilwa Masoko
168 E-9 Kim
90 E-7 Kim *riv.*
220 B-1 Kimba
168 E-6 Kimball
159 K-9 Kimball *mt*
211 M-4 Kimbe *bay*
211 M-5 Kimbe
204 C-3 Kimberley *plat.*
213 K-5 Kimberley *plat.*
104 G-5 Kimberley (South Africa)
215 J-6 Kimberley (Australia)
162 F-7 Kimberley (USA)
213 J-5 Kimberley Downs
172 E-1 Kimbles
53 J-1 Kimbolton
87 L-8 Kimbrila-Sud
101 H-8 Kimhandu *mt*
64 E-7 Kimi
64 E-8 Kimolos *isl.*
67 H-3 Kimovsk
89 H-2 Kimparana
49 H-7 Kimpeli
66 G-1 Kimry
143 L-5 Kin-u
149 K-8 Kinabalu *mt*
162 F-5 Kinbasket *lake*
170 G-5 Kincardine
99 N-9 Kinda
101 H-3 Kindaruma *dam.*
176 D-5 Kinder
56 C-4 Kinderdijk
163 J-7 Kindersley
89 J-4 Kindi
87 K-4 Kindia
99 N-4 Kindu
67 N-2 Kinel
67 N-1 Kinel'čerkasy
68 G-9 Kineshma
100 F-3 Kinesi
52 F-2 Kineton
162 B-3 King *isl.*
160 E-8 King *mt*
204 C-3 King *strt.*
213 H-4 King *strt.*
216 G-8 King *lake*
200 G-2 King *cap.*
220 F-6 King (Australia) *isl.*
159 H-2 King (USA) *isl.*
127 N-3 King Ata Tagh *mt*
167 K-2 King City
158 A-6 King Cove
213 K-3 King Edward *riv.*
216 F-9 King George *strt.*
201 L-8 King George Bay *bay*
224 E-5 King Georges *islds*
112 B-2 King Karl's Land *isl.*
213 J-4 King Leopold *mt*
158 E-7 King Salmon *riv.*
158 E-7 King Salmon
105 J-8 King William's Town
219 M-5 Kingaroy
52 E-1 Kinge Norton
175 N-1 Kingfisher
52 B-1 Kinghton
66 A-2 Kingisepp (SSSR)
66 C-1 Kingisepp (SSSR)
224 C-3 Kingman *rf*
167 M-6 Kingman (USA)
168 G-9 Kingman (USA)
218 B-7 Kingoonya
127 H-9 Kingri
168 A-6 Kings *mt*
167 K-3 Kings Canyon *na.p.*
53 J-4 King's Langley
50 E-5 King's Lynn
173 J-3 Kings Park
52 F-7 Kings Somborne
52 G-6 Kingsclere
220 C-3 Kingscote
53 L-6 Kingsdown
53 J-7 Kingsfold
53 P-5 Kingsgate
53 H-7 Kingsley
177 J-1 Kingsport
52 A-9 Kingsteignton
180 F-7 Kingston
157 G-5 Kingston
164 D-9 Kingston (Canada)
222 C-8 Kingston (New Zealand)
52 E-9 Kingston (UK)
53 K-5 Kingston (UK)
177 H-2 Kingston (USA)
170 A-8 Kingston (USA)
171 L-6 Kingston (USA)
52 G-4 Kingston Bagpuize
50 E-4 Kingston-Upon-Hull
220 D-4 Kingstone
157 H-5 Kingstown
177 L-3 Kingstree
175 M-7 Kingsville
52 C-2 Kington
98 C-2 Kinguélé *dam.*
64 F-6 Kinik
138 F-5 Kinjhar Dhand *lake*
98 F-5 Kinkala
87 J-5 Kinkon
108 F-4 Kinkony *lake*
223 K-5 Kinleith
50 E-1 Kinnairds *cap.*
163 N-4 Kinoosao
57 M-6 Kinrooi
49 K-1 Kinsarvik
77 D-5 Kinshasa
98 F-5 Kinshasa (Léopoldville)
168 G-9 Kinsley
52 E-8 Kinson
177 M-2 Kinston
89 M-4 Kintampo
207 P-3 Kintap
213 M-9 Kintore *mt*
100 G-7 Kinyasungwe *riv.*
94 F-7 Kinyeti *mt*
172 B-6 Kinzers
59 M-4 Kinzig *pass*
166 D-5 Kinzua
158 F-6 Kiokluk *mt*
176 A-1 Kiowa
163 M-5 Kipahigan *lake*
64 D-8 Kiparíssia
164 B-7 Kipawa *lake*
171 H-2 Kipawa *lake*
71 H-7 Kipčak
100 E-8 Kipembawe
106 C-4 Kipengere *mt*
100 C-8 Kipili
101 K-4 Kipini
158 E-4 Kipnuk
59 H-7 Kippel
103 L-2 Kipushi
67 L-1 Kir'a
86 F-7 Kirané
141 J-7 Kīranūr
68 C-4 Kirbej *cap.*
176 C-5 Kirbyville
58 G-3 Kirchberg
59 K-2 Kirchbühl
58 G-5 Kirchdorf
123 H-4 Kirej *riv.*
123 L-2 Kirenga *riv.*
123 L-1 Kirensk
90 A-3 Kirfo
114 F-5 Kirghiz *rép*
129 H-1 Kirghiz Jangal
122 F-7 Kirghizistan *rép*
127 P-1 Kirgizskaya *reg.*
120 F-9 Kirgizskij *mt*
99 J-3 Kiri
225 C-4 Kiribati *state*
65 L-7 Kirikhan
65 K-5 Kirikkale
141 N-8 Kirinda
109 J-2 Kirindy *riv.*
68 C-9 Kiriši
211 N-7 Kiriwina *isl.*
64 G-6 Kirkağac
50 D-2 Kirkcaldy
50 D-3 Kirkcudbright
140 C-3 Kirkee
48 C-8 Kirkenes
164 B-6 Kirkland Lake
64 F-4 Kirklareli
170 B-8 Kirksville
72 F-7 Kirkūk
50 E-1 Kirkwall
104 G-9 Kirkwood (South Africa)
172 C-7 Kirkwood (USA)
172 B-6 Kirkwood (USA)
101 K-8 Kirongwe
66 F-4 Kirov (SSSR)
69 J-7 Kirov (SSSR)
72 F-2 Kirovabad
72 E-3 Kirovakan
71 P-4 Kirovo
69 J-7 Kirovo-Chepetsk
66 F-8 Kirovograd
66 E-5 Kirovsk
73 P-1 Kirovsk
48 D-9 Kirovsk (SSSR)
124 E-2 Kirovskij (SSSR)
124 D-2 Kirovskij (SSSR)
128 B-3 Kirovskij (SSSR)
125 K-8 Kirovskij (SSSR)
70 A-7 Kirovskij (SSSR)
71 N-2 Kirovskoje
69 K-6 Kirs
67 K-4 Kirsanov
65 K-6 Kirşehir
138 F-3 Kirthar *mt*
48 E-6 Kiruna
99 N-3 Kirundu
137 H-7 Kiryū
101 H-8 Kisaki
99 P-8 Kisale *lake*
100 G-8 Kisanga
99 N-2 Kisangani (Stanleyville)
209 H-6 Kisar *isl.*
158 F-5 Kisaralik *riv.*
146 D-7 Kisaran
101 J-8 Kisarawe
83 H-8 Kisbh *mt*
122 C-3 Kiselevsk
125 L-2 Kisel'ovka
162 C-1 Kisgegas
72 G-9 Kish *site*
142 F-2 Kishangani

139 L-5 Kishangarh
139 H-3 Kishangarh
89 L-8 Kishi
66 E-9 Kishinov
143 H-4 Kishorganj
127 N-8 Kishtwär
100 F-7 Kisigo riv.
100 F-3 Kisii
101 J-8 Kisiju
72 D-3 Kisir mt
137 K-5 Kisiwada
162 F-3 Kiskatinaw riv.
163 P-6 Kiskitto lake
163 P-6 Kiskittogisu lake
64 B-1 Kiskunfelegyháza
64 B-1 Kiskunhalas
72 C-1 Kislovodsk
101 M-2 Kismaayo
100 C-3 Kisoro
87 L-5 Kissidougou
177 K-7 Kissimmee
92 C-2 Kissü mt
59 N-4 Kisten pass
100 F-2 Kisumu
137 M-1 Kisyuku
168 E-8 Kit Carson
87 H-7 Kita
136 G-8 Kita-Ibaraki
137 L-2 Kita-Kyüsyü
71 N-6 Kitab
136 E-7 Kitakami
136 E-7 Kitakami Köti mt
136 G-7 Kitakata
100 F-1 Kitale
136 A-6 Kitami mt
136 A-7 Kitami
100 F-5 Kitangiri lake
211 N-7 Kitava isl.
217 K-6 Kitchener (Australia)
171 H-5 Kitchener (Canada)
91 P-7 Kitesa
94 F-7 Kitgum
94 F-7 Kitgum Matidi
64 E-8 Kithnos isl.
162 B-2 Kitimat
123 K-5 Kitoj
123 J-5 Kitoj riv.
53 M-6 Kits Coty Ho
109 H-5 Kitsamby riv.
48 F-6 Kittajaur
171 H-7 Kittanning
172 E-2 Kittatinny's monts rge
48 E-7 Kittilä
101 J-3 Kitui
137 L-3 Kituki
162 C-1 Kitwanga
103 M-3 Kitwe
61 M-1 Kitzbühel
99 P-9 Kiubo
210 F-5 Kiunga
48 G-8 Kiuruvesi
101 K-6 Kiuyu cap.
159 K-2 Kivalina
122 C-4 Kivda hill
124 G-5 Kivdinskij
66 C-7 Kivercy
66 C-1 Kiviöli
100 A-4 Kivu reg.
100 B-4 Kivu lake
125 J-1 Kivun mt
211 H-7 Kiwai isl.
158 E-4 Kiwigillingok
72 F-4 Kiyämaki mt
69 L-5 Kizel
122 G-5 Kiži-Chem riv.
65 M-5 Kizil mt
65 J-5 Kizilcahamam
72 A-5 Kizilirmak riv.
72 E-1 Kiziljurt
65 P-6 Kiziltepe
123 M-6 Kižinga
122 F-4 Kizir riv.
70 A-8 Kizl'arskij bay
70 A-9 Kizlyar
69 L-8 Kizner
73 M-1 Kizyl-Arvat
73 L-3 Kizyl-Atrek
71 N-8 Kizylajak
48 B-7 Kjøllefjord
64 D-4 Kjustendil
116 H-1 Kkingan (Greater) rge
56 B-5 Klaaswaal
149 N-2 Klabat mt
206 G-2 Klabat bay
51 K-8 Kladno
144 G-8 Klaeng
61 N-2 Klagenfurt
66 A-3 Klaipéda (Memel)
207 M-7 Klakah
48 D-2 Klaksvig
166 F-2 Klamath
166 F-2 Klamath mt
166 F-2 Klamath riv.
166 F-3 Klamath Falls
209 L-1 Klamono
160 E-8 Klappan riv.

49 J-4 Klarälven riv.
57 K-2 Klarenbeek
207 K-6 Klaten
51 K-8 Klatovy
61 N-1 Klaus
59 M-4 Klausen pass
160 C-8 Klawak
104 D-7 Klawer
67 J-1 Kl'az'ma riv.
66 D-5 Kleck
48 B-2 Kleifar
152 C-4 Kleinfeltersville
104 C-6 Kleinsee
57 H-6 Kleinwijk
105 H-4 Klerksdorp
66 F-4 Kletn'a
67 L-6 Kletskaja
57 K-5 Kleve (Kleef)
124 B-6 Klička
162 B-9 Klickitat riv.
68 C-7 Klimeckij isl.
57 N-9 Klimmen
66 F-4 Klimoviči
66 G-2 Klin
51 K-7 Klinovec mt
51 M-2 Klintehamn
66 K-7 Klintsy
105 K-5 Klip riv.
104 G-8 Klipplaat
51 M-7 Kłodzko
59 N-3 Klön val.
160 E-2 Klondike plat.
144 F-7 Klong riv.
59 N-3 Klöntaler lake
51 L-9 Klosterneuburg
67 L-5 Klotovo
159 M-9 Klotz mt
160 D-3 Kluane mt
160 D-3 Kluane lake
160 D-3 Kluane
146 F-8 Kluang
207 K-3 Kluang cap.
124 B-4 Kl'učevskij
72 C-1 Kluchorskij strt.
121 M-3 Kl'uči
51 M-7 Kluczbork
160 D-4 Klukshu
160 D-5 Klukwan
208 A-3 Klumpeng bay
56 C-6 Klundert
207 P-7 Klungkung
160 B-1 Klutina lake
56 B-7 Klutsdorp
125 K-1 Kn'azevo
56 G-8 Knegsel
64 D-3 Kneža
158 E-8 Knife mt
168 F-2 Knife riv.
160 A-1 Knight isl.
162 B-5 Knight Inlet gulf
52 D-9 Knighton
61 P-3 Knin
61 N-1 Knittelfeld
216 G-9 Knob cap.
50 F-6 Knokke
59 L-2 Knonau
64 F-9 Knossós site
52 F-1 Knowle
160 B-9 Knox cap.
119 N-6 Knox isl.
227 N-4 Knox Coast
177 J-1 Knoxville (USA)
170 B-7 Knoxville (USA)
153 M-2 Knud-Rasmussen Land
59 J-2 Knutwil
104 F-9 Knysna
136 D-6 Ko isl.
135 L-6 Ko mt
144 G-8 Ko Kram Yai isl.
146 D-3 Ko Samui
210 G-7 Koabu
101 J-7 Koani
123 J-3 Kob'
89 H-1 Koba riv.
206 G-2 Koba
209 N-5 Koba isl.
137 M-3 Kobayasi
137 K-5 Kobe
66 G-7 Kobel'aki
209 K-3 Kobi
137 N-5 Kobi Syo isl.
51 H-7 Koblenz
93 N-8 Kobo
94 E-7 Koboko
125 H-2 Koboldo
68 D-9 Koboža
69 J-6 Kobra
209 N-6 Kobroor isl.
159 K-4 Kobuk
159 K-4 Kobuk riv.
72 C-2 Kobuleti
123 K-3 Kočenga riv.
67 J-4 Kočetovka
168 B-2 Koch mt
137 L-4 Kochi

67 H-1 Kochma
56 E-2 Kockengen
121 N-2 Kočki
68 C-6 Kočkoma
127 N-2 Kočkor-Ata
128 C-1 Kočkorka
123 H-1 Koda riv.
168 F-4 Kodaka
140 E-8 Kodär
141 L-8 Koddivar bay
152 C-4 Kodiak isl.
158 E-9 Kodiak
158 D-9 Kodiak isl.
68 F-6 Kodima
140 A-1 Kodinär
68 E-5 Kodino
94 E-2 Kodok (Fashoda)
66 E-9 Kodyma
104 G-9 Koega riv.
104 D-5 Koel riv.
104 D-3 Koes
64 F-4 Kofcaz
104 G-6 Koffiefontein
209 K-1 Kofiau isl.
89 N-5 Koforidua
137 H-7 Koga
51 K-4 Køge
94 G-3 Kogille
87 J-3 Kogon riv.
69 J-6 Kojgorodok
68 F-4 Kojnas
216 F-8 Kojonup
143 N-7 Kok riv.
127 N-2 Kok-Jangak
91 M-4 Kokab
128 D-1 K'okajgyr
71 J-7 Kokand
70 G-4 Kokaral riv.
209 M-2 Kokas
121 H-1 Kokčetavskaja vozvyšennost' plat.
121 H-1 Kokchetav
49 J-7 Kokemaki
141 L-8 Kokkilai lag.
48 G-5 Kokkola
95 H-2 Koko
211 K-7 Kokoda
159 M-2 Kokolik riv.
170 E-7 Kokomo
211 P-4 Kokopo
146 A-7 Kokpekty riv.
121 M-6 Kokpekty
159 J-6 Kokrines
159 K-6 Kokrines mt
71 M-3 Koksaraj
120 B-4 Kokšekol' lake
128 E-2 Kokšhaal Tau mt
105 K-7 Kokstad
128 B-3 Koksu
120 F-5 Koktas riv.
137 M-3 Kokubu
70 E-2 Kokžar
68 B-3 Kola riv.
209 N-4 Kola isl.
48 C-9 Kola
48 D-9 Kola riv.
142 B-7 Kolab riv.
138 C-3 Kolâchi riv.
87 L-6 Kolahun
208 D-3 Kolaka
141 H-6 Kolär
141 H-6 Kolär Gold Fields
48 E-7 Kolari
139 K-4 Kolâyat
48 A-3 Kolbeinsey isl.
101 L-3 Kolbio
127 K-3 Kolchozabad
67 H-2 Kol'čugino
87 H-3 Kolda
51 J-4 Kolding
99 N-1 Kole (Zaïre)
99 L-5 Kole (Zaïre)
79 K-2 Koléa
123 K-4 Kolenga riv.
87 K-4 Kolente riv.
210 D-6 Kolepom isl.
48 C-4 Kolfreyjustaður
46 H-3 Kolgujev isl.
68 E-1 Kolguyev isl.

140 E-3 Kolhäpur
105 H-4 Koligny
86 F-6 Kolimbiné riv.
51 L-8 Kolin
95 J-4 Kolito
66 B-2 Kolkasrags cap.
48 A-2 Kollabudir
141 H-5 Kollegäl
140 E-9 Kolleru lake
59 J-1 Kölliken
89 L-4 Kolmasa
66 B-4 Kolmè
51 H-7 Köln
51 M-6 Koło
51 L-5 Kołobrzeg
66 E-3 Kolodn'a
68 G-8 Kologriv
87 H-8 Kolokani
97 K-1 Kololo
67 H-2 Kolomna
66 C-4 Kolomya
89 J-1 Kolondiéba
119 L-6 Kolonia
208 E-4 Kolono
208 D-2 Kolonodale
208 E-4 Kolowana Watobo strt.
71 H-1 Kolšekol' lake
68 C-3 Kol'skiy Poluostrov pen.
122 G-3 Koltoši
67 N-1 Koltubanovskij
201 H-5 Koluel Kayke
125 L-7 Kolumbe riv.
121 H-2 Koluton riv.
121 H-2 Koluton
69 H-1 Kolva riv.
103 K-1 Kolwezi
113 P-2 Kolymskaya Nizmennost' pl.
113 P-3 Kolymskiy rge
122 C-1 Kolyon
67 J-3 Kolyšlej
121 P-2 Kolyvan'
98 C-1 Kom riv.
101 J-8 Kom isl.
95 J-3 Koma
90 E-2 Komadugu Gana riv.
90 F-1 Komadugu Yobé riv.
137 H-6 Komagane
100 C-1 Komanda
125 J-1 Komandnaja mt
113 Q-4 Komandorskije islds
121 N-4 Komaricha
69 M-6 Komarichinsk
66 G-5 Komariči
105 L-4 Komati riv.
105 M-3 Komatipoort
94 C-4 Komaton
137 H-5 Komatsu
137 K-5 Komatusima
208 F-6 Komba isl.
98 D-2 Kombo
100 E-2 Kome isl.
206 F-4 Komering riv.
68 G-3 Komi reg.
69 K-5 Komi-Permyak Nat'L. Okrug reg.
57 J-5 Kommerdijk
122 D-3 Kommunar
67 J-7 Kommunarsk
127 M-3 Kommunizma mt
49 J-2 Komsomol'sk
125 K-3 Komsomol'sk-na-Amur
69 K-4 Komsomol'sk-na Pečore
69 M-3 Komsomol'skij
120 G-3 Kon riv.
88 G-3 Kona
66 G-2 Konakovo
127 K-6 Konar riv.
142 J-9 Konâr lake
127 K-6 Konar-e Khäs
142 D-7 Konârak
142 J-8 Konârhä reg.
208 D-3 Konaweha riv.
69 P-2 Konda riv.
69 M-2 Konda
140 C-9 Kondagaon

216 F-7 Kondinin
69 P-2 Kondinskoje
100 G-6 Kondoa
99 P-1 Kondolole
125 K-3 Kondon
126 C-2 Kondor (Iran)
73 P-3 Kondor (Iran)
123 H-2 Kondratjevo
220 G-3 Kondrook
66 G-3 Kondrovo
67 N-1 Kondurča riv.
215 M-3 Koné
68 E-7 Konevo
145 H-9 Kong isl.
145 K-7 Kông riv.
89 L-2 Kong
91 M-7 Kongbo
128 D-5 Kongjisihe riv.
130 G-2 Kongkuduke
143 J-1 Kongmo La mt
103 H-6 Kongola
99 P-6 Kongolo
94 E-4 Kongor
89 H-5 Kongoussi
128 F-7 Kongqiaohe riv.
51 J-1 Kongsberg
49 K-3 Kongsvinger
100 G-7 Kongwa
89 H-2 Koni riv.
51 M-6 Konin
125 J-1 Konin riv.
57 L-1 Koningsbelt hill
57 N-7 Koningsbosch
64 C-6 Kónitsa
61 K-1 Köniz
140 D-3 Konkan pl.
104 C-4 Konkiep riv.
87 A-4 Konkouré riv.
123 N-2 Konkudera
125 K-3 Konošanovo
68 E-7 Konosha
66 F-6 Konotop
67 J-7 Konstantinovka
67 L-7 Konstantinovskij
61 L-1 Konstanz
140 E-9 Konta
90 A-3 Kontagora
123 P-4 Kontalakskij Golec mt
90 F-5 Kontcha
145 L-7 Kontum
65 J-7 Konya
65 K-7 Konya Ovasi pl.
128 C-4 Konyrolen
70 B-4 Konystanu
101 G-4 Konza
69 M-5 Konžakovskij Kamen' mt
158 G-1 Kookooligit mt
217 H-5 Kookynie
214 E-9 Koolamarra
215 H-5 Koolburra
218 A-8 Koonibba
104 G-5 Koopmansfontein
209 M-1 Koor
221 J-3 Koorawatha
216 E-6 Koorda
166 D-7 Kooskia
162 F-7 Kootenay lake
162 F-8 Kootenay riv.
162 F-6 Kootenay na.p.
104 E-7 Kootjieskolk
57 J-2 Kootwijk
57 H-2 Kootwijkerbroek
128 C-2 Kopa
140 B-4 Kopargaon
48 B-2 Kópasker
51 H-1 Kopervik
73 P-2 Kopet mt
69 P-7 Kopeysk
51 L-1 Köping
122 D-3 Kopjevo
208 E-6 Kopondei cap.
140 F-4 Koppal
49 J-3 Koppang
49 J-3 Kopparberg
125 L-4 Koppi riv.
58 G-2 Koppigen
61 P-2 Koprivnica
73 M-9 Kor riv.
61 P-2 Korčulski cap.
67 J-3 Korablino
97 L-3 Korahe
140 E-6 Korangal
138 E-5 Korangi
211 P-5 Korapun
142 B-7 Koraput
88 G-3 Korarou lake
116 F-5 Korat plat.
142 B-5 Korba (India)
79 P-2 Korba (Tunisia)

91 J-4 Korbol
146 E-6 Korbu mt
64 C-5 Korcë
121 N-3 Korčino
72 G-6 Kord Estan rép
73 L-3 Kord Kuy
92 A-5 Kordi riv.
92 F-8 Kordofan reg.
69 M-6 Kordon
133 K-5 Korea bay
113 L-6 Korea strt.
113 L-6 Korea bay
119 H-3 Korea (North) state
119 H-3 Korea (South) state
66 D-7 Korec
140 D-3 Koregaon
68 G-1 Koregavka
66 G-6 Korenovo
67 K-9 Korenovsk
69 K-4 Korepino
86 F-8 Koréra-Koré
125 K-5 Korfovskij
72 A-4 Korgan
121 N-5 Korgonskij mt
89 L-1 Korhogo
138 E-6 Kori bay
87 M-5 Koribundu
88 G-3 Korientzé
78 G-4 Korima riv.
64 D-7 Korinthos
101 N-1 Korioley
136 G-7 Köriyama
69 P-7 Korking
65 H-7 Korkuteli
65 K-8 Kormakitis cap.
121 K-1 Kormilovka
121 J-4 Kornejevka
66 E-9 Kornešty
89 H-4 Koro
121 N-4 Korobejnikovo
65 J-5 Köröğlu mt
101 J-6 Korogwe
220 E-5 Koroit
91 K-3 Korom riv.
149 K-3 Koronadal
86 F-9 Koronga
220 F-4 Korongvale
119 J-6 Koror
64 C-1 Körös riv.
66 E-6 Korosten'
66 E-7 Korostyšev
100 E-1 Koroto
158 B-7 Korovin isl.
91 J-7 Korpélé
49 J-7 Korpo
125 P-4 Korsakov
89 H-5 Korsimoro
51 K-4 Korsør
123 M-1 Koršunova
56 E-2 Kortenhoef
92 G-4 Korti
50 F-7 Kortrijk
50 F-7 Kortrijk
66 F-6 Kor'ukovka
220 G-5 Korumburra
122 C-6 Koš Agač
69 K-5 Kosa
69 K-6 Kosa riv.
70 A-6 Košalak
70 C-5 Koščagyl
51 M-6 Koscian
176 E-4 Kosciusko
160 B-8 Kosciusko isl.
221 J-4 Kosciusko na.p.
221 J-4 Kosciusko mt
126 E-3 Koshk-e Kohneh
139 M-5 Kosi
129 N-1 Kosi (India)
139 P-4 Kosi (India) riv.
142 E-2 Kosi (Nepal) riv.
66 A-9 Kosice
137 N-2 Kosikizima islds
69 M-5 Kosja
69 J-1 Kosju
70 C-5 Koškar
68 G-4 Koslan
121 L-6 Kosoba mt
64 C-4 Kosova I Metohiyan reg.
64 C-4 Kosovska Mitrovica
95 J-3 Kossa
105 J-3 Koster
123 J-1 Kostino
127 P-2 Košt'ob'o
66 D-7 Kostopol'
68 F-9 Kostroma
68 F-9 Kostroma riv.
51 L-6 Kostrzyn
51 L-5 Koszalin
127 J-9 Kot Addu
138 G-3 Kot Diji
139 L-2 Kot Kapüra
139 L-7 Kota
149 K-9 Kota Belud
146 F-5 Kota Bharu
149 K-9 Kota Kinabalu

206 F-5 Kotaagung
208 A-3 Kotabaru
206 F-4 Kotabumi
137 P-2 Kotakara *isl.*
149 P-3 Kotamabagu
121 K-6 Kotanemel' *mt*
146 D-8 Kotapinang
146 D-9 Kotatengah
207 L-2 Kotawaringin
161 H-9 Kotcho *lake*
139 P-4 Kotdwāra
69 J-8 Kotel'nich
67 L-7 Kotel'nivoko
113 M-2 Kotel'nyi *isl.*
66 G-7 Kotel'va
123 N-3 Kotera *riv.*
140 C-8 Koti *riv.*
94 G-7 Kotido
138 E-4 Kotīro
49 J-8 Kotka
68 G-6 Kotlas
70 G-8 Kotlovina *lake*
89 N-2 Kotobi
64 B-4 Kotor *strt.*
64 F-1 Kotovsk (SSSR)
66 E-9 Kotovsk (SSSR)
67 K-4 Kotovsk (SSSR)
139 M-5 Kotputli
139 J-7 Kotra
138 F-5 Kotri
138 E-6 Kotri Allāhrakhio
140 E-8 Kottagūdem
141 L-5 Kottai Malai *mt*
141 L-4 Kottārakara
141 K-4 Kottayam
57 N-4 Kotten
91 N-5 Kotto *riv.*
97 H-8 Kotton
140 F-4 Kottūru
73 K-2 Koturdepe
159 K-3 Kotzebue
159 J-3 Kotzebue *bay*
86 G-7 Kouaga *riv.*
89 K-7 Kouandé
91 L-7 Kouango
91 L-3 Koubo Abou Gara
56 C-2 Koudekerk aan de Rijn
89 J-4 Koudougou
129 J-3 Kouen louen *rge*
104 F-9 Kougaberge *mt*
98 C-2 Kougouleu
98 D-5 Kouilou *reg.*
98 D-5 Kouilou *riv.*
79 L-4 Kouinine
91 J-6 Kouki
91 L-6 Koukourou *riv.*
90 B-1 Koukouta
98 D-3 Koulamoutou
87 H-9 Koulikoro
87 H-4 Koulountou *riv.*
87 J-3 Kouloye Magesan
91 K-7 Kouma *riv.*
215 L-3 Koumac *rf*
215 L-3 Koumac
219 L-1 Koumala
87 J-4 Koumba *riv.*
87 H-3 Koumbakara
91 L-4 Koumbala *riv.*
91 N-5 Koumou *riv.*
86 G-3 Koumpenntoum
91 J-4 Koumra
87 H-4 Koundara
87 H-6 Koundian
89 J-2 Koundougou
86 G-3 Koungheul
91 K-3 Koungouri
87 H-4 Kounkandé
121 H-6 Kounradskij
88 E-5 Kounta *reg.*
175 P-5 Kountze
89 J-6 Koupéla
87 H-7 Kouragué
87 K-8 Kouraï *riv.*
89 J-2 Kouri
192 F-3 Kourou *riv.*
192 F-3 Kourou
87 H-6 Kouroukoto
86 G-7 Kourouninkoto
87 K-7 Kouroussa
86 G-4 Koussanar
86 G-5 Koussane
90 G-2 Kousseri
89 J-2 Koutiala
89 L-3 Koutouba
215 N-5 Koutoumo
49 J-8 Kouvola
98 G-3 Kouyou *riv.*
123 J-2 Kova *riv.*
123 H-1 Kova
121 L-3 Kovalevka
48 D-9 Kovdor
68 B-4 Kovdozero *lake*
66 C-7 Kovel'
69 N-1 Kovenskaja *riv.*
141 L-5 Kovilpatti
123 J-1 Kovinskaja Cr'da *mt*
66 B-4 Kovno (Kaunas)
123 K-1 Kovrižka *mt*
67 H-1 Kovrov
67 K-2 Kovylkino
127 K-4 Kowkcheh *riv.*
135 J-9 Kowloon (Jiulong)
127 J-6 Kowt-e 'Ashrow
159 J-4 Koyuk
159 J-5 Koyukuk
159 K-5 Koyukuk *riv.*
129 K-1 Koyul
72 A-4 Koyulhisar
137 M-8 Koza
120 E-1 Kožachmet
65 L-7 Kozan
64 C-6 Kozáni
61 P-3 Kozara Planina *mt*
122 B-1 Koževnikovo
69 J-1 Kožim
69 K-3 Kožimiz *mt*
65 H-4 Kozlu
69 J-9 Koz'modem'yansk
68 F-4 Koz'mogorodskoje
137 J-8 Kōzu *isl.*
122 C-2 Kožuch *riv.*
122 E-2 Kozul'ka
69 J-2 Kožva
69 H-2 Kožva *riv.*
89 N-6 Kpalimé
89 M-6 Kpandae
89 N-6 Kpandu
89 N-7 Kpémé
87 M-6 Kpo *mt*
116 F-6 Kra *isth.*
146 C-2 Kra *isth.*
146 C-2 Kra Buri
105 H-7 Kraai *riv.*
56 A-7 Krabbe *est.*
56 A-8 Krabbendijke
146 C-4 Krabi
145 K-8 Krâchéh
51 J-1 Kragerø
64 C-3 Kragugevac
69 J-9 Krai-Russkije
65 M-8 Krak des Chevaliers *site*
206 G-5 Krakatau *vol.*
91 M-5 Krakoma
66 A-8 Krakow
187 J-1 Kralendijk
64 C-3 Kraljevo
67 J-7 Kramatorsk
49 H-5 Kramfors
56 A-6 Krammer Volkerak *est.*
57 K-5 Kranenburg
64 D-8 Kranídhion
61 N-2 Kranj
105 L-6 Kranskop
122 C-2 Krapivinskij
68 G-6 Krasavino
66 D-8 Krasilov
120 G-1 Krasivoje
133 N-1 Kraskino
66 C-3 Krāslava
66 B-7 Kraśnik
67 J-8 Krasnoarmejsk
67 M-4 Krasnoarmejsk (SSSR)
67 K-9 Krasnoarmejskaja (SSSR)
68 G-6 Krasnoborsk
122 C-3 Krasnobrodskij
72 A-1 Krasnodar
67 K-9 Krasnodar *reg.*
67 K-7 Krasnodon
66 G-2 Krasnogorsk
69 K-7 Krasnogorskoje
67 H-7 Krasnograd
71 N-5 Krasnogvardejsk
69 P-5 Krasnogvardejskij
65 J-1 Krasnogvardejskoje (SSSR)
67 L-9 Krasnogvardejskoje (SSSR)
124 F-4 Krasnojarovo
122 B-2 Krasnoje
126 F-2 Krasnoje Znam'a
69 L-6 Krasnokamsk
121 K-2 Krasnokutskij
121 L-2 Krasnokutskoje
67 J-5 Krasnolesnyj
65 J-1 Krasnoperekopsk
66 G-6 Krasnopolje
125 L-8 Krasnorečenskij
121 N-4 Krasnošč'okovo
67 M-6 Krasnoslobodsk (SSSR)
67 K-2 Krasnoslobodsk (SSSR)
69 M-4 Krasnotur'insk
69 M-7 Krasnoufimsk
69 N-5 Krasnoural'sk
69 N-9 Krasnousol'skij
125 M-3 Krasnova *mt*
69 L-5 Krasnovišersk
73 J-1 Krasnovodsk
73 K-1 Krasnovodsk *plat.*
122 E-2 Krasnoyarsk
69 H-5 Krasnozatonskij
121 M-2 Krasnozerskoje
120 G-2 Krasnoznamenskij
67 K-7 Krasnyi Sulin
70 A-7 Krasnyj Barrikady
66 G-1 Krasnyj Cholm
123 M-7 Krasnyj-Cikoj
122 C-1 Krasnyj Jar (SSSR)
123 P-4 Krasnyj-Jar (SSSR)
125 K-1 Krasnyj Jar (SSSR)
70 A-7 Krasnyj Jar (SSSR)
67 M-4 Krasnyj Kut
67 J-7 Krasnyj Liman
67 J-7 Krasnyj Luch
69 H-9 Krasnyje Baki
66 B-7 Krasnystaw
121 J-7 Krasnyy Okt'abr'
207 H-5 Krawang
207 H-5 Krawang *cap.*
68 D-6 Kr'az Vetrenyi Pojas
68 E-7 Krečetovo
50 G-6 Krefeld
66 G-7 Kremenchug
66 C-7 Kremenec
66 G-7 Kremges
55 J-6 Kremlin-Bicêtre (Le)
168 C-7 Kremmling
172 D-3 Kresgeville
66 E-1 Krestcy
72 E-1 Krestovyj *strt.*
66 A-3 Kretinga
59 N-1 Kreuzegg *mt*
90 D-9 Kribi
66 E-4 Krichev
64 E-4 Kričim
59 K-3 Kriens
86 G-6 Krigou *riv.*
125 P-5 Kriljon *cap.*
125 P-5 Kriljonskij *pen.*
56 C-4 Krimpen aan den Ijssel
56 C-4 Krimpen aan den Lek
56 D-4 Krimpenerwaard *reg.*
59 N-1 Krinau
140 E-8 Krishna *riv.*
141 H-6 Krishnagiri
142 F-5 Krishnanagar
141 H-4 Krishnarājāsāgara *lake*
51 H-2 Kristiansand
51 L-3 Kristianstad
49 H-2 Kristiansund
49 H-6 Kristiinankaupunki
69 H-8 Kriv'ačka
66 G-8 Krivoy Rog
61 N-3 Krk *isl.*
66 C-6 Krobin
146 E-5 Kroh
207 J-6 Kroja
48 F-4 Kroken
105 L-3 Krokodil *riv.*
66 F-6 Krolevec
104 D-7 Krom *riv.*
66 G-5 Kromy
145 L-8 Krong *riv.*
145 H-9 Krong Kaôh Kong
145 J-9 Krong Kêb
51 L-3 Kronoberg *reg.*
68 B-9 Kronštadt
105 J-5 Kroonstad
67 L-9 Kropotkin (SSSR)
123 P-1 Kropotkin (SSSR)
123 P-1 Kropotkina (SSSR) *mt*
124 A-3 Kropotkina (SSSR) *mt*
66 B-8 Krosno
48 E-8 Krtinen *riv.*
57 P-6 Krüchten
105 M-2 Kruger *na.p.*
69 P-7 Kruglica *mt*
206 E-5 Krui
104 E-8 Kruidfontein
56 G-6 Kruigstraat
56 A-8 Kruiningen
56 B-7 Kruisland
64 B-5 Krujë
59 P-1 Krummenau
66 D-4 Krupki
159 K-2 Krusenstern
64 C-3 Kruševac
121 N-3 Kruticha
160 B-6 Kruzof *isl.*
67 K-8 Krylovskaja
72 A-1 Krymsk
65 J-2 Krymskije *mt*
122 F-4 Kryžina *mt*
66 E-8 Kryžopol
51 L-6 Krzyz
88 B-2 Ksaib (puits)
79 J-2 Ksar el Boukhari
78 D-2 Ksar el Kebir
78 E-4 Ksar-es-Souk
79 H-4 Ksel *mt*
124 B-4 Ksenjevka
67 H-5 Kšenskij
78 G-4 Ksour *mt*
79 P-3 Ksour-Essaf
67 K-1 Kstovo
65 K-9 Ktema
121 K-5 Ku *mt*
91 P-1 Kū *riv.*
146 C-7 Kuala
146 F-6 Kuala Dungun
146 D-6 Kuala Kangsar
146 E-7 Kuala Klawang
146 E-6 Kuala Krai
146 E-7 Kuala Kubu Baharu
146 E-7 Kuala Lipis
118 F-6 Kuala Lumpur
146 E-7 Kuala Lumpur
146 D-5 Kuala Nerang
149 L-9 Kuala Penyu
147 P-5 Kuala Penyu
146 F-8 Kuala Pilah
146 E-7 Kuala Selangor
206 E-1 Kuala Tjenaku *bay*
146 F-6 Kuala Trengganu
207 N-1 Kualakurun
146 C-6 Kualalangsa
207 M-3 Kualapembuang
207 K-2 Kualapesaguan
149 L-8 Kuamut
124 A-2 Kuanda *riv.*
149 P-4 Kuandang
133 K-4 Kuandian
206 D-1 Kuantan *riv.*
146 F-7 Kuantan
72 G-1 Kuba
72 A-1 Kuban *riv.*
72 F-3 Kubatly
91 N-2 Kubbum
68 F-8 Kubena *riv.*
68 E-8 Kubenskoje *lake*
211 H-5 Kubor *mt*
207 P-7 Kubu
137 P-8 Kubumesaai
147 P-5 Kubura
142 E-5 Kuchaiburi
128 E-5 Kuche
145 J-5 Kuchinarai
142 C-5 Kuchinda
149 L-8 Kuching
126 E-7 Kūchnay Darvīshān
124 F-3 Kuchterin Lug
121 M-3 Kučukskoje *lake*
138 E-3 Kūd *riv.*
123 L-5 Kudara
149 K-8 Kudat
56 D-2 Kudelstaart
92 B-1 Kūdī *hill*
81 J-7 Kūdī
141 L-7 Kudremalai *pte*
207 L-6 Kudus
69 K-6 Kudymkar
130 B-2 Kueerjisihe *riv.*
128 C-6 Kueidunhe *riv.*
124 G-5 Kuerbin
132 E-2 Kuerchahanbo *lake*
128 E-7 Kuerchu
128 E-7 Kuerle
131 J-4 Kuerleikehu *lake*
131 J-4 Kuerleikeshan *mt*
81 J-7 Kufrah (Wāhat)
61 M-1 Kufstein
161 J-1 Kugaluk *riv.*
71 P-7 Kugilantau *mt*
127 J-3 Kugitangtau *mt*
97 L-2 Kugno
84 B-6 Kūh *cap.*
73 H-6 Kūh-e Alvand
72 G-4 Kūh-e Bozqūsh
73 P-3 Kūh-e Sorkh *mt*
84 B-9 Kūh Lab *cap.*
93 H-3 Kuḥali
73 P-7 Kūhbonān
73 H-8 Kuhdasht
84 B-6 Kuhestak
126 D-3 Kūhestān
72 G-4 Kūhhā-ye Sabalan *mt*
48 G-9 Kuhmo
73 L-7 Kūhpāyeh
84 A-7 Kūhrān *mt*
211 K-6 Kui
120 E-1 Kuikkol' *lake*
126 E-6 Kuiluohe *riv.*
104 B-1 Kuiseb *riv.*
135 K-9 Kuitan
102 D-2 Kuito
160 C-7 Kuiu *isl.*
48 F-7 Kuivaniemi
89 M-5 Kujani (Game Réserve) *na.p.*
121 M-1 Kujbyšev
127 M-2 Kujbyševo
127 K-3 Kujbyševskij
69 M-7 Kujeda
128 A-2 Kujgan
71 N-4 Kujl'uk
68 B-5 Kujto *lake*
48 F-9 Kujto *lake*
123 J-4 Kujtun
158 C-8 Kujulik *bay*
159 M-3 Kuk *riv.*
125 J-5 Kukan
125 J-4 Kukanskij *mt*
104 G-1 Kuke
64 C-4 Kukës
128 D-5 Kukeshui *riv.*
128 G-1 Kukeya
211 J-6 Kukipi
158 F-8 Kuklalek *lake*
69 K-9 Kukmor
104 F-2 Kukong
159 L-2 Kukpowruk *riv.*
159 L-2 Kukpuk *riv.*
123 L-2 Kukujskij-Mys
124 B-5 Kukul'bej *mt*
146 F-9 Kukup
129 K-8 Kukushilishanmo *mt*
84 A-5 Kūl *riv.*
64 D-3 Kula (Romania)
64 G-7 Kula (Turkey)
64 B-4 Kula (Yugoslavia)
64 B-2 Kula (Yugoslavia)
143 H-1 Kula Gangri *mt*
127 K-3 Kul'ab
70 B-5 Kulagino
146 F-8 Kulai
122 F-1 Kulakovo
70 D-5 Kulakši
70 B-7 Kulaly *isl.*
120 A-3 Kulandy *pen.*
120 A-3 Kulandy
70 F-4 Kulandy *pen.*
131 M-2 Kulanheer
121 H-4 Kulanutpes *riv.*
72 C-2 Kulaši
125 K-1 Kul'či
66 A-3 Kuldīga
125 H-5 Kul'dur
67 J-2 Kulebaki
145 J-7 Kulén
218 A-4 Kulgera
158 E-6 Kulik *lake*
71 K-5 Kulkuduk
169 H-3 Kulm
59 J-1 Kulm
59 L-3 Kulm (Switzerland)
68 E-4 Kuloj *riv.*
68 F-7 Kuloj
158 G-2 Kulowiyi
89 K-5 Kulpawn *riv.*
172 A-3 Kulpmont
172 D-5 Kulpsville
70 D-5 Kul'sary
70 C-7 Kultaj
48 G-4 Kultsjöluspen
123 J-6 Kultur
65 J-3 Kulu
128 F-8 Kulukeshanmo *mt*
93 P-6 Kululli
211 P-7 Kulumadau
143 J-1 Kulunamuji
121 M-3 Kulunda
121 M-3 Kulunda *riv.*
121 M-3 Kulundinskaya *pl.*
121 M-3 Kulundinskoje *lake*
133 H-3 Kulunqi
158 E-4 Kulvagavik
220 F-3 Kulwin
73 L-1 Kum-Dag
67 P-8 Kuma *riv.*
70 A-8 Kuma
137 H-7 Kumagaya
207 L-3 Kumai *bay*
207 L-3 Kumai
70 D-1 Kumak
192 C-4 Kumaka
137 M-3 Kumamoto
137 K-6 Kumano
64 C-4 Kūmanovo
124 F-4 Kumara
217 H-7 Kumarl
89 N-4 Kumasi
90 D-7 Kumba
211 L-5 Kumbalup
219 L-6 Kumbarilla
210 E-6 Kumbe *riv.*
210 E-6 Kumbe
129 P-2 Kumbher
141 N-8 Kumbukkan *riv.*
96 A-3 Kumdah
137 M-7 Kume *isl.*
70 B-1 Kumertau
100 F-1 Kumi
69 P-3 Kuminskyj
65 H-8 Kumluca
143 M-3 Kumon Taungdan *mt*
145 H-5 Kumphawapi
140 F-3 Kumta
94 A-7 Kumu
72 F-1 Kumuch
129 K-9 Kumuhuan *lake*
129 J-8 Kumukeer
128 E-8 Kumushi
130 G-2 Kumutakeshamo *mt*
71 H-7 Kun'a-urgenč
210 E-2 Kunamba *islds*
69 P-6 Kunašak
136 A-8 Kunašir *isl.*
139 N-7 Künch
127 N-9 Kund Barā
127 H-8 Kundar *riv.*
100 A-9 Kundelungu *mt*
140 F-6 Kunderu *riv.*
127 K-8 Kundiān
140 A-2 Kundla
146 F-9 Kundur *isl.*
122 F-4 Kundusuk
102 A-5 Kunene (Cunene) *riv.*
142 G-6 Kunga *lag.*
128 C-2 Kungej Alatau *mt*
162 A-2 Kunghit *isl.*
70 G-6 Kungrad
91 K-9 Kungu
69 M-6 Kungur
122 G-6 Kungur-Tuk
219 K-1 Kungurri
122 G-3 Kungus *riv.*
144 D-5 Kungyangon
215 N-5 Kunié *isl.*
137 M-8 Kunigami
207 J-6 Kuningan
172 D-3 Kunkletown
143 N-5 Kunlong
112 G-6 Kunlun *rge*
129 J-5 Kunlun shan *rge*
134 B-7 Kunming
213 J-3 Kunmuny
57 N-9 Kunrade
135 N-2 Kunshan
86 G-3 Kuntaur
139 M-6 Kunu *riv.*
213 M-3 Kununurra
219 L-2 Kunwarara
139 M-6 Kunwāri *riv.*
100 F-1 Kunyao
48 E-8 Kuolajarvi
49 H-8 Kuopio *reg.*
49 H-8 Kuopio
61 P-2 Kupa *riv.*
123 K-3 Kupa *riv.*
208 F-8 Kupang
67 J-6 Kup'ansk
159 N-5 Kupatuk *riv.*
121 L-2 Kupino
66 B-3 Kupiškis
158 B-7 Kupreanof *pte*
158 E-9 Kupreanof *strt.*
160 C-7 Kupreanof *isl.*
124 F-1 Kupuri *riv.*
124 F-1 Kupuri
209 L-4 Kur *isl.*
125 J-4 Kur *riv.*
72 E-2 Kura *riv.*
72 D-3 Kura Cildir *riv.*
128 B-1 Kuragaty *riv.*
120 G-9 Kuragaty *riv.*
122 E-4 Kuragino
122 C-6 Kuraj
127 K-7 Kuram *riv.*
127 M-1 Kuraminskij *mt*
71 P-3 Kuraminskij *mt*
137 K-4 Kurasiki
137 J-4 Kurayosi
123 M-5 Kurba *riv.*
123 M-5 Kurbinskij *mt*
128 A-7 Kürčum
128 A-8 Kurčumskij *mt*
128 C-1 Kurdaj
72 G-2 K'urdamir
140 D-4 Kurduvadi
137 K-5 Kure
120 G-3 Kurgal'džino
127 K-3 Kurgan-T'ube
72 B-1 Kurganinsk
116 A-5 Kuria Muria *islds*
85 J-7 Kuria Muria *islds*
79 P-3 Kuriate *islds*
49 H-7 Kurikka
102 E-6 Kuring Kuru
137 M-3 Kurino
137 N-3 Kurio
121 N-4 Kurja
124 B-4 Kurleja
94 G-2 Kurmuk
140 F-6 Kurnool
137 N-2 Kuro *isl.*
136 D-6 Kuroisi
123 P-6 Kurort-Darasun
222 E-8 Kurow *mt*
66 B-3 Kuršėnai
142 F-2 Kurseong
67 H-5 Kursk
66 A-4 Kurskaja Kosa *pen.*
65 P-5 Kurtalan
122 E-5 Kurtušibinskij *mt*
128 B-2 Kurty *riv.*
94 A-4 Kuru *riv.*
143 H-2 Kuru (Bhutan) *riv.*
65 J-4 Kurucaşile
211 J-4 Kurum
104 F-4 Kuruman
104 E-4 Kuruman *riv.*
104 F-4 Kuruman-Heuwells *hill*
137 L-2 Kurume

123 M-4 Kurumkan
141 M-7 Kurunegala
142 B-5 Kurung lake
159 M-4 Kurupa riv.
192 B-3 Kurupukari
92 G-2 Kurur mt
92 G-2 Kurūsh mt
117 L-2 Kuryl foss
113 P-5 Kuryl islds
113 P-5 Kuryl foss
113 P-4 Kuryl strr.
64 F-4 Kus gulf
69 P-7 Kusa
64 G-7 Kuşadasi
137 N-2 Kusagaki isl.
119 M-6 Kusaie isl.
131 K-2 Kusaihu lake
121 J-6 Kusak riv.
160 D-4 Kusawa lake
67 K-8 Kuščevskaja
140 F-5 Kushtagi
142 G-4 Kushtia
130 F-3 Kushui
69 M-5 Kushva
137 N-3 Kusima
137 K-6 Kusimoto
136 B-8 Kusiro
126 E-3 Kuška
126 F-3 Kuška riv.
158 G-6 Kuskokwim mt
158 E-5 Kuskokwim bay
159 H-7 Kuskokwin riv.
68 D-4 Kuškušara
129 P-3 Kusma
59 L-1 Küsnacht
123 M-6 Kusotuj mt
59 L-3 Küssnacht
136 A-7 Kussyaro lake
93 H-8 Küsti
70 A-4 Kušum riv.
145 H-9 Kut isl.
73 J-8 Küt-e Gapu site
122 G-5 Kut-Tajga mt
123 K-2 Kuta riv.
65 H-6 Kütahya
72 C-2 Kutaisi
146 A-7 Kutanibong
223 K-5 Kutarere
116 B-4 Kutch gulf
138 F-6 Kutch lake
138 F-7 Kutch gulf
138 F-7 Kutch (Kachchh) reg.
137 N-3 Kutierabu isl.
123 L-2 Kutima
123 M-2 Kutima riv.
137 P-3 Kutino isl.
72 F-2 Kutkašen
66 A-6 Kutno
48 D-8 Kuttusvaara
136 C-6 Kuttyan
99 H-4 Kutu
143 H-6 Kutubdia isl.
123 J-5 Kutulik
92 C-7 Kutum
158 C-7 Kutuzof cap.
172 C-4 Kutztown
161 P-2 Kuuk riv.
73 J-1 Kuuli Majak
48 F-8 Kuusamo
49 J-8 Kuusankoski
70 C-1 Kuvandyk
127 M-2 Kuvasaj
66 F-2 Kuvšinovo
83 L-2 Kuwait
77 G-2 Kuwait
77 G-2 Kuwait state
67 N-2 Kuybyshev
72 F-6 Kūysanjaq
64 G-7 Kuyucak
192 B-5 Kuyuwini riv.
122 C-4 Kuzedejevo
136 D-7 Kuzi
124 E-3 Kuznecovo
67 L-3 Kuznetsk
122 D-3 Kuznetskiy Alatau mt
68 C-4 Kuzomen
67 M-2 Kuzovatovo
137 L-3 Kuzyū mt
48 C-5 Kvaløy isl.
48 C-7 Kvaløya isl.
48 C-7 Kvalsund
49 J-1 Kvanndal
72 E-2 Kvareli
61 N-3 Kvarner gulf
61 N-3 Kvarneric gulf
158 E-7 Kvichak riv.
158 E-7 Kvichak
158 E-7 Kvichak bay
48 E-5 Kvikkjokk
51 H-1 Kvina riv.
112 B-1 Kvit isl.
46 G-1 Kvit isl.
48 C-6 Kvoenangen bay
98 G-4 Kwa riv.
56 E-8 Kwaalburg
89 M-5 Kwadjokrom

144 E-7 Kwaï (Khwae) riv.
101 L-4 Kwaihu isl.
119 M-6 Kwajalein isl.
192 E-3 Kwakoegron
192 C-3 Kwakwani
101 J-8 Kwale isl.
101 K-6 Kwale (Kenya)
90 B-7 Kwale (Nigeria)
98 G-5 Kwamouth
102 G-4 Kwando (Cuando) riv.
99 H-5 Kwango riv.
102 E-2 Kwanza riv.
90 A-5 Kwara reg.
209 N-3 Kwatisore
103 M-7 Kwekwe
104 G-2 Kweneng reg.
99 H-7 Kwenge riv.
158 E-5 Kwethluk riv.
158 F-5 Kwethluk
198 F-6 Kwiguk
158 D-3 Kwigamiut
158 G-3 Kwigut
93 N-7 Kwiha
98 F-6 Kwilu riv.
192 B-4 Kwitara riv.
209 M-1 Kwoka mt
82 G-5 Kwrayzīyah
145 K-4 Ky Anh
144 E-5 Kya-in Seikkyi
91 K-4 Kyabé
218 G-4 Kyabra
143 L-9 Kyaikto
100 D-3 Kyaka
220 B-1 Kyancutta
94 B-4 Kyango
143 L-9 Kyaukkyi
143 K-7 Kyaukpadaung
143 J-8 Kyaukpyu
143 L-6 Kyaukse
144 D-5 Kyauktan
143 J-7 Kyauktaw
144 C-5 Kyaunggon
143 L-6 Kyawkku
100 D-2 Kyegegwa
127 N-9 Kyelang
100 C-2 Kyenjojo
100 E-1 Kyere
70 G-9 Kyjamatdag mt
103 N-8 Kyle dam.
50 D-1 Kyle
49 J-8 Kymi reg.
69 M-6 Kyn
220 G-5 Kyneton
218 F-1 Kynuna
100 E-1 Kyoga lake
137 J-5 Kyōga cap.
219 M-7 Kyogle
143 L-7 Kyong
137 J-5 Kyōto
120 F-3 Kypšak lake
65 K-8 Kyréneia
69 P-7 Kystym
143 K-5 Kyunhla
113 M-6 Kyushu reg.
137 M-4 Kyushu isl.
221 H-3 Kywong
49 H-7 Kyyjärvi
122 D-5 Kyzas
122 F-5 Kyzyl
122 G-6 Kyzyl-Chem riv.
127 N-4 Kyzyl-Dzhiik
127 M-2 Kyzyl-Kija
120 F-3 Kyzyl-Kommuna
71 K-4 Kyzyl-Kum dés
122 D-6 Kyzyl-Mažalyk
128 B-5 Kyzylagaš
127 N-3 Kyzylart
121 H-6 Kyzylespe
121 K-2 Kyzylkak lake
112 E-5 Kyzylkum reg.
120 B-7 Kyzylkum dés
127 L-3 Kyzylsu riv.
121 J-5 Kyzyltas mt
120 F-4 Kyzylžar
71 J-3 Kzyl-Orda
121 J-1 Kzyltu
127 N-7 K2 (Godwin Austen) mt

# L

198 D-3 La Antiqua lake
187 M-2 La Asunción
175 K-6 La Babia

198 E-2 La Banda
60 C-3 La Bañeza
178 D-5 La Barca
185 H-5 La Barra
177 K-8 La Belle
90 F-4 La Bénoué na.p.
163 J-4 La Biche lake
175 H-6 La Boquilla
188 E-1 La Brea
198 B-3 La Brea mt
175 H-8 La Cadena
191 N-4 La Cadera
196 A-2 La Cal
196 A-2 La Cal riv.
199 H-4 La Calandría
198 A-5 La Cale
198 E-1 La Cañada
191 N-5 La Candelaria
60 B-3 La Cañiza
198 F-6 La Carlota (Argentina)
148 G-4 La Carlota (Philippines)
184 F-2 La Ceiba
186 G-3 La Ceiba
199 L-5 La Charqueaoa
188 B-7 La Chorrera
188 A-4 La Cocha lake
201 J-3 La Colonia
174 E-5 La Colorada
186 G-2 La Concepción
179 K-3 La Concordia
196 A-7 La Cordillera Central reg.
60 B-2 La Coruña reg.
198 G-3 La Criolla
170 B-5 La Crosse
184 G-6 La Cruz
185 J-8 La Cuesta
184 A-8 La Cumbra vol.
198 E-4 La Cumbre
181 P-2 La Desirade isl.
186 D-6 La Dorada
191 L-6 La Esmeralda (Paraguay)
187 L-7 La Esmeralda (Venezuela)
200 D-4 La Esperanza (Argentina)
190 F-7 La Esperanza (Bolivia)
184 E-3 La Esperanza (Honduras)
60 B-3 La Estrada
180 B-5 La Fe
215 M-4 La Foa
191 N-5 La Fragua
198 F-4 La Francia
186 F-4 La Fría
186 E-6 La Gloria
78 A-8 La Gomera isl.
187 N-6 La Gran Sabana reg.
166 D-6 La Grande
175 N-5 La Grange (USA)
177 H-4 La Grange (USA)
186 F-4 La Grita
181 N-2 La Guadeloupe cal.
187 K-2 La Guaira
186 F-1 La Guajira reg.
198 D-3 La Guardia
198 A-3 La Higuera
198 C-4 La Huerta mt
198 B-7 La Jaula
189 N-8 La Joya
168 E-8 La Junta
198 F-5 La Laguna
187 N-5 La Laja
196 A-9 La Leonesa
188 G-2 La Libertad reg.
184 D-4 La Libertad (El Salvador)
184 D-1 La Libertad (Guatémala)
179 P-9 La Libertad (Honduras)
198 A-5 La Ligua
60 B-8 La Línea
163 K-4 La Loche
185 H-4 La Luz
198 D-1 La Madrid
164 F-6 La Malbaie
60 D-6 La Mancha reg.
184 G-7 La Mansión
181 P-3 La Martinique cal.
161 K-6 La Martre lake
185 J-3 La Media Luna rf
189 J-5 La Merced
186 D-6 La Mesa
62 B-6 La Morra
185 H-3 La Mosquitia reg.
164 C-6 La Motte lake
169 H-3 La Moure
78 D-9 La Oliva
78 B-8 La Orotava
189 K-5 La Oroya
78 A-8 La Palma isl.
185 M-8 La Palma
199 L-6 La Paloma

187 M-5 La Paragua
198 C-6 La Paz
199 H-4 La Paz
184 F-3 La Paz
184 E-3 La Paz reg.
186 F-2 La Paz
190 F-2 La Paz reg.
174 D-9 La Paz (Mexico)
188 C-9 La Pedrera
178 G-2 La Pesca
198 G-4 La Picada
178 D-4 La Piedad Cavadas
187 M-5 La Piña riv.
166 E-4 La Pine
175 L-6 La Pryor
200 G-3 La Plata lake
188 C-1 La Plata isl.
199 J-7 La Plata (Argentina)
186 D-8 La Plata (Colombia)
198 F-5 La Playosa
163 L-5 La Plonge lake
191 N-4 La Poma
170 E-6 La Porte
175 L-6 La Porte
198 D-2 La Puerta (Argentina)
198 F-4 La Puerta (Argentina)
188 C-1 La Puntilla pte
174 C-7 La Purísima
191 L-4 La Quiaca
198 D-3 La Rioja
198 D-3 La Rioja pl.
198 D-3 La Rioja reg.
60 D-6 La Roda
181 M-5 La Romana
163 L-5 La Ronge
163 L-5 La Ronge lake
187 J-8 La Sabana
60 D-7 La Sagra mt
164 D-2 La Salle lake
164 B-6 La Sarre
165 M-2 La Scie
198 A-3 La Serena
62 B-3 La Serra mt
186 F-7 La Serrania mt
187 M-2 La Sola isl.
186 F-3 La Solita
181 N-3 La Soufrière vol.
61 L-3 La Spezia
62 F-7 La Spezia reg.
165 K-2 La Tabatière
188 B-6 La Tagua
188 A-2 La Tola
198 D-5 La Toma
215 M-4 La Tontouta
148 C-6 La Trinidad
187 H-5 La Trinidad
198 B-3 La Troya riv.
198 D-7 La Varita pl.
181 K-6 La Vega
187 H-4 La Victoria (Vénézuela)
187 K-2 La Victoria (Vénézuela)
191 N-4 La Viña (Argentina)
188 G-2 La Viña (Peru)
189 P-9 La Yarada
175 H-8 La Zarca
57 L-3 Laag Keppel
57 K-3 Laag-Soeren
59 N-7 Laak
59 P-4 Laax
59 P-4 Laaxer val.
67 L-9 Laba riv.
138 D-3 Labach
147 N-7 Labang
54 G-2 Labbeville
88 G-6 Labbezanga
87 J-5 Labé
51 L-7 Labe riv.
164 D-7 Labelle
208 E-3 Labengke isl.
160 E-4 Laberge lake
200 C-8 Laberinto pte
180 E-5 Laberinto de las Doce Leguas islds
72 B-1 Labinsk
146 F-8 Labis
208 F-2 Labobo isl.
89 L-4 Laboni riv.
208 E-3 Labota
216 C-2 Labouchere mt
60 F-2 Labouheyre
198 F-6 Laboulaye
153 N-3 Labrador sea
164 G-2 Labrador City
190 A-3 Lábrea
52 F-7 Labscombe Corner
147 P-6 Labuan isl.
209 H-1 Labuha
206 G-6 Labuhan

208 C-7 Labuhanbadjo
146 D-3 Labuhanbilik
208 D-6 Labuhanmarege
144 C-5 Labutta
129 P-5 Labuzhonghu lake
218 B-7 Labyrinthe lake
58 C-3 Lac (Villers)
165 J-3 Lac-Allard
164 E-6 Lac-Edouard
164 G-2 Lac-Frontière
68 E-7 Lača lake
179 L-8 Lacantun riv.
116 C-6 Laccadive sea
116 C-6 Laccadive islds
62 E-3 Lacchiarella
220 D-4 Lacepede bay
212 G-4 Lacepede islds
220 G-2 Lachan riv.
68 B-8 Lachdenpochja
142 G-1 Lachen (India)
59 N-2 Lachen (Switzerland)
164 E-8 Lachine
164 E-8 Lachute
172 E-1 Lackawaxen
53 M-1 Lackford
52 E-5 Lacock
162 G-6 Lacombe
164 F-9 Laconia
195 K-8 Laçu
127 P-8 Ladakh mt
196 A-3 Ladário
52 G-2 Ladbroke
68 C-8 Ladejnoje Pole
65 L-4 Lâdik
104 E-3 Ladismith
126 B-8 Lâdiz
94 E-6 Lado mt
68 C-8 Ladoga lake
164 D-2 Ladrillero gulf
201 M-4 Ladrillero mt
165 M-2 Ladrones islds
160 D-1 Ladue riv.
221 H-7 Lady Barron
219 N-3 Lady Elliot isl.
187 M-2 Lady Evelyne
161 N-3 Lady Franklin pte
105 J-7 Lady Grey
105 J-6 Ladybrand
170 C-4 Ladysmith
105 K-5 Ladysmith (South Africa)
162 B-6 Ladysmith (Canada)
120 G-2 Ladyženka
119 M-6 Lae isl.
211 K-5 Lae
145 H-8 Laem Ngop
146 E-5 Laem Pho isl.
146 D-2 Laem Pracham Hiang isl.
146 D-3 Laem Sui isl.
146 D-3 Laem Talumphuk isl.
177 H-4 Lafayette (USA)
176 D-6 Lafayette (USA)
170 E-7 Lafayette (USA)
83 P-4 Laffán cap.
90 C-5 Lafia
90 A-4 Lafiagi
164 B-7 Laforce
84 B-5 Läft
210 G-4 Lagaip riv.
197 H-3 Lagamar
143 H-1 Lagangzong
48 C-3 Lagarflót riv.
63 J-2 Lagarina val.
195 M-6 Lagarto
83 J-1 Lagash site
73 H-9 Lagawe
148 C-6 Lagawe
129 P-5 Lage
56 F-8 Lage Mierde
56 F-2 Lage-Vuursche
56 D-6 Lage Zwaluwe
56 C-7 Lagedonk
49 J-3 Lågen riv.
56 D-2 Lagenbroek
57 H-6 Lagepeel
129 M-2 Lageshi lake
50 C-2 Lagg
127 K-6 Laghmân reg.
79 J-4 Laghouat
55 M-2 Lagny-le-Sec
55 M-2 Lagny-sur-Marne
201 N-5 Lago Blanco lake
201 K-4 Lago Cardiel
201 N-6 Lago Fagnano lake
201 J-3 Lago Posadas
200 D-2 Lago Ranco
201 K-3 Lago St. Martin
201 K-3 Lago Viedma
197 J-4 Lagoa da Prata
197 K-4 Lagoa Santa
199 N-2 Lagoa Vermelha
89 N-8 Lagos
77 C-4 Lagos
178 D-4 Lagos de Moreno
63 M-5 Lagosanto

129 M-5 Lagu
199 P-2 Laguna
193 H-8 Laguna isl.
200 D-4 Laguna Blanca
198 C-1 Laguna Blanca mt
201 K-4 Laguna Grande
179 J-8 Laguna Inferior lag.
191 P-8 Laguna Limpia
179 J-8 Laguna Superior lag.
198 B-2 Laguna Verde lake
191 M-7 Laguna Yema
191 K-1 Lagunas
198 F-7 Lagunas Tunas lag.
191 J-6 Lagunillas (Bolivia)
186 G-2 Lagunillas (Vénézuela)
124 E-7 Laha
149 L-7 Lahad Datu
149 P-9 Laham
139 N-6 Lahär
206 E-4 Lahat
146 B-9 Lahewa
96 F-3 Lahij
73 J-4 Lāhījān
127 L-9 Lahore
49 J-8 Lahti
145 H-1 Lai Châu
143 M-7 Lai-hka
211 H-5 Laiagam
91 H-4 Laï
134 F-8 Laibin
134 F-4 Laifeng
62 B-8 Laigueglia
104 E-3 Laingsburg
54 D-3 Lainville
172 A-1 Lairdsville
50 D-1 Lairg
91 J-3 Laïri
206 D-3 Lais (Indonesia)
149 P-6 Lais (Indonesia)
149 K-2 Lais (Philippines)
101 H-1 Laisamis
58 A-1 Laissey
132 G-8 Laiwu
209 H-1 Laiwui
133 H-7 Laiyang
132 E-6 Laiyuan
133 H-7 Laizhouwan bay
200 B-3 Laja lag.
69 H-1 Laja riv.
208 A-4 Lajar cap.
68 E-1 Lajdennyj cap.
195 L-8 Laje
192 D-7 Laje dam.
197 J-7 Laje de Santos bay
194 E-5 Lajeado
194 F-3 Lajeado riv.
195 N-5 Lajedo
195 K-8 Lajedo Alto
196 F-9 Lajes (Brazil)
195 N-3 Lajes (Brazil)
58 E-1 Lajoux
69 P-3 Lajtamak
101 L-1 Lak Bissigh riv.
101 K-1 Lak Boggal riv.
101 K-1 Lak Bor riv.
101 K-2 Lak Dera riv.
95 L-7 Lak Katueo
86 G-7 Lakamané
168 B-3 Lake
169 H-5 Lake Andes
172 D-1 Lake Ariel
221 H-2 Lake Cargelligo
176 C-6 Lake Charles
177 L-3 Lake City (USA)
177 K-6 Lake City (USA)
168 C-8 Lake City (USA)
222 E-7 Lake Coleridge
162 B-6 Lake Cowichan
164 E-9 Lake Georges
175 P-6 Lake Jackson
216 G-8 Lake King
162 F-6 Lake Louise
214 D-9 Lake Nash
176 D-9 Lake Providence
176 E-3 Lake Village
177 K-7 Lake Wales
171 L-7 Lake Wood
177 L-8 Lake Worth
215 H-5 Lakefield
172 G-6 Lakehurst
177 K-7 Lakeland
162 C-2 Lakelse
166 G-1 Lakeport
221 H-5 Lakes na.p.
167 J-3 Lakeshore
167 H-8 Lakeside
166 F-4 Lakeview
172 D-1 Lakeville (USA)
172 G-1 Lakeville (USA)
167 M-3 Lakewood (USA)
170 G-6 Lakewood (USA)
64 G-8 Lakhania
79 K-2 Lakhdaria
139 L-6 Lakheri

129 P-1 Lakhīmpur
82 C-2 Lakhish site
140 A-8 Lakhnãdon
142 B-1 Lakhnau
138 F-6 Lakhpat
143 H-4 Lakhya riv.
168 F-9 Lakin
127 J-8 Lakki
64 D-8 Lakonia gulf
209 J-6 Lakor isl.
89 N-1 Lakota (Ivory Coast)
169 H-2 Lakota (USA)
143 H-5 Lãkshãm
127 L-8 Lãla Mũsa
206 F-2 Lalana riv.
109 L-3 Lalanna riv.
98 D-2 Lalara
106 F-6 Lalava riv.
52 A-5 Laleston
142 F-4 Lãlgola Ghãt
73 J-8 Lãli
93 N-8 Lalibela
60 B-3 Lalín
208 E-3 Lalindu riv.
124 G-9 Lalinhe riv.
129 L-3 Lalishan mt
139 N-7 Lalitpur
129 N-1 Lalkuwan
127 J-3 L'al'mikar
71 P-7 L'al'mikar
211 K-7 Laloki
69 H-6 Lal'sk
139 M-6 Lãlsot
145 L-2 Lam
89 L-7 Lama-Kara
63 J-7 Lama Mocogno
149 L-8 Lamag
207 L-2 Lamandau riv.
184 F-3 Lamaní
168 E-8 Lamar
200 C-6 Lamarque
188 F-4 Lamas
131 L-4 Lamatuoluogai
98 C-3 Lambaréné
197 J-5 Lambari
188 F-2 Lambayeque
53 L-7 Lamberhurst
211 N-4 Lambert cap.
227 N-3 Lambert glac.
104 C-7 Lambertsbaai
172 E-5 Lambertville
218 A-4 Lambina
52 F-5 Lambourg
62 E-4 Lambro riv.
161 L-1 Lambton cap.
211 P-4 Lambur
68 D-5 L'amca
200 D-1 Lameguapi pte
175 K-3 Lamesa
211 N-3 Lametta
64 D-7 Lamiá
146 A-6 Lammeulo
142 G-1 Lamohu lake
63 L-1 Lamon
63 L-7 Lamone riv.
207 M-6 Lamongan
55 J-1 Lamorlaye
119 K-6 Lamotrek isl.
189 M-7 Lampa riv.
144 F-4 Lampang
175 M-5 Lampasas
175 L-7 Lampazos
172 B-6 Lampeter
144 F-4 Lamphun
63 J-9 Lamporecchio
53 H-1 Lamport
206 F-5 Lampung reg.
206 F-5 Lampung bay
56 A-9 Lamswaarde
101 L-4 Lamu
101 L-4 Lamu isl.
179 J-7 Lana riv.
224 D-1 Lanai isl.
129 N-8 Lanake mt
57 M-9 Lanaken
129 K-2 Lanakeshankou mt
200 B-1 Lanalhue lag.
50 D-2 Lanark
146 C-2 Lanbi isl.
149 J-4 Lanboyan pte
143 N-6 Lancang
131 M-3 Lancangjiang (Mekong) riv.
153 K-2 Lancaster strt.
165 J-7 Lancaster (Canada)
50 D-4 Lancaster (UK)
164 F-8 Lancaster (USA)
177 K-2 Lancaster (USA)
170 B-7 Lancaster (USA)
170 C-6 Lancaster (USA)
170 G-8 Lancaster (USA)
167 L-3 Lancaster (USA)
200 C-2 Lanco
133 H-7 Lancun
66 B-8 Lancut
56 E-5 Land van Altena reg.

98 D-6 Lândana
51 H-8 Landau
126 D-7 Landay
61 M-1 Landeck
172 C-7 Landenberg
213 P-7 Lander riv.
168 C-4 Lander
60 F-2 Landes reg.
198 F-5 Landeta
144 B-7 Landfall isl.
52 F-7 Landford
127 K-7 Landi Kotal
172 E-8 Landisville (USA)
172 A-5 Landisville (USA)
59 M-2 Lãndli
216 E-2 Landor
58 B-2 Landresse
62 E-3 Landriano
50 B-6 Land's end pte
61 M-1 Landsberg
51 K-9 Landshut
51 K-3 Landskrona
53 H-4 Lane End
143 M-6 Lang riv.
145 L-1 Lang Son
146 C-2 Lang Suan
64 D-5 Langadhás
95 K-4 Langana lake
127 M-5 L'angar
127 M-5 Langar
71 M-6 L'angar
160 B-9 Langara isl.
126 E-6 Langara
73 J-4 Langarũd
163 M-9 Langbank
56 F-3 Langbroek reg.
129 M-2 Langchuhe riv.
169 H-1 Langdon
59 K-1 Langdorf
93 L-4 Langeb riv.
104 C-8 Langebaan
104 D-9 Langeberg rge
104 F-5 Langeberge mt
51 J-4 Langeland isl.
59 H-1 Langenbruck
163 M-8 Langenburg
51 J-6 Langenhagen
59 H-2 Langenthal
56 D-2 Langeraar
56 D-4 Langerak
56 C-8 Langeschouw
59 H-2 Langeten riv.
56 C-6 Langeweg
124 D-7 Langfeng
172 B-9 Langford
201 N-3 Langford (Seno) bay
62 B-6 Langhe reg.
62 G-6 Langhirano
172 E-5 Langhorne
48 B-2 Langjökull glac.
146 D-5 Langkawi isl.
143 H-1 Langkazi
208 F-4 Langkesi isl.
149 K-9 Langkon
165 N-4 Langlade isl.
162 C-7 Langley
219 H-4 Langlo riv.
219 H-4 Langlo Crossing
59 L-1 Langnau (Switzerland)
59 H-4 Langnau (Switzerland)
100 E-1 Lango reg.
60 F-2 Langon
48 D-4 Langøya isl.
52 C-7 Langport
50 G-9 Langres
129 H-2 Langru
146 C-6 Langsa bay
146 C-6 Langsa
49 H-5 Långsele
132 A-4 Langshan
131 H-7 Langshoushan mt
56 E-6 Langstraat reg.
146 D-5 Langsa
199 H-8 Langueyu
199 H-8 Langueyú riv.
190 D-8 Languiaru riv.
200 F-4 Languiñeo
52 A-1 Langurig
131 N-9 Langzhong
135 P-9 Lanhsu isl.
52 A-1 Lanidloes
163 L-7 Lanigan
200 C-3 Lanin na.p.
200 C-2 Lanin vol.
132 E-9 Lankao
57 M-8 Lanklaar
50 C-7 Lannion
172 G-6 Lanoka Harbor
149 K-6 Lanparan isl.
131 N-3 Lanping
172 D-5 Lansdale
172 D-6 Lansdowne
172 C-3 Lansford
135 H-7 Lanshan
170 F-6 Lansing
146 C-4 Lanta isl.

199 H-7 Lanus
149 H-2 Lanuza
124 F-8 Lanxi (China)
135 M-4 Lanxi (China)
190 F-2 Lanza (Bolivia) riv.
59 H-8 Lanza (Switzerland) riv.
78 D-8 Lanzarote isl.
131 K-8 Lanzhou
144 F-3 Lao riv.
145 J-1 Lao Kay
148 B-6 Laoag
148 F-3 Laoang isl.
148 F-3 Laoang
143 N-5 Laobieshan mt
134 E-1 Laocheng (China)
133 J-2 Laocheng (China)
132 G-3 Laohahe riv.
133 N-1 Laoheishan
50 F-8 Laon
145 K-6 Laongam
118 F-5 Laos state
116 F-4 Laos reg.
133 J-7 Laoshanwan bay
125 H-8 Laoyeling mt
196 F-8 Lapa
199 H-1 Lapachito
90 B-4 Lapai
200 B-3 Lapavié pte
170 F-5 Lapeer
172 A-1 Laporte
215 H-7 Lappa
49 H-7 Lappajarvi lake
49 J-9 Lappeenranta
112 A-3 Lappland reg.
124 D-1 Lapri
200 A-8 Laprida
113 K-2 Laptev sea
226 A-2 Laptev sea
148 G-3 Lapu Lapu
49 H-7 Lapua
129 N-5 Lapujun mt
92 E-3 Laqīyat al Arba'īn
59 J-9 Laquinhorn
98 D-2 Lara riv.
187 H-2 Lara reg.
89 L-4 Larabanga
78 D-2 Larache
84 B-5 Lãrak isl.
168 D-5 Laramie mt
168 D-6 Laramie
196 C-6 Laranjai riv.
196 D-8 Laranjeira do Sul
195 M-6 Laranjeiras
196 F-7 Laranjinha riv.
208 E-6 Larantuka strt.
208 E-7 Larantuka
209 L-6 Larat
124 C-1 Larba riv.
173 H-2 Larchmont
107 H-7 Larde
101 H-2 Lare
60 D-3 Laredo (Spain)
175 L-7 Laredo (Mexico)
56 F-1 Laren (Netherlands)
57 L-2 Laren (Netherlands)
195 K-7 Largo
180 C-5 Largo isl.
208 A-3 Lari Larian isl.
208 C-2 Lariang
208 C-1 Lariang riv.
64 D-6 Larisa
53 L-1 Lark riv.
138 F-3 Lãrkãna
58 B-4 Larmont mt
65 K-9 Lárnax
50 C-3 Larne
168 G-9 Larned
89 J-4 Laro
208 D-3 Larona
94 E-7 Laropi
108 G-7 Larrée pte
214 A-5 Larrimah
199 H-5 Larroque
83 J-1 Larsa site
158 E-9 Larsen Bay
60 F-3 Laruns
51 J-1 Larvik
187 J-1 Las Aves isl.
187 L-4 Las Bonitas
198 G-1 Las Breñas
198 A-7 Las Cabras
200 A-2 Las Cañas bay
184 G-6 Las Cejas
198 E-1 Las Cejas
174 G-3 Las Cruces
97 H-7 Lãs Dawa'o
199 H-8 Las Flores
199 H-5 Las Flores riv.
199 H-2 Las Garzas
201 H-5 Las Heras
198 C-5 Las Heras (Argentina)
201 J-4 Las Horquetas
200 C-3 Las Lajas
191 M-5 Las Lajitas

188 E-1 Las Lomas
191 M-8 Las Lomitas
179 L-8 Las Margaritas
187 K-3 Las Mercedes
184 D-2 Las Minas mt
186 E-7 Las Oseras mt
174 B-2 Las Palmas riv.
78 C-9 Las Palmas de Gran Canaria
185 H-5 Las Perlas lag.
198 F-4 Las Petacas
189 K-9 Las Piedras riv.
190 C-3 Las Piedras (Bolivia)
199 K-7 Las Piedras (Uruguay)
200 F-5 Las Plumas
198 G-5 Las Rosas
198 D-5 Las Salinas pl.
185 K-9 Las Tablas
191 P-5 Las Termas
191 P-6 Las Tinajas
178 A-5 Las Tres Marias islds
187 L-5 Las Trincheras
198 B-6 Las Tunas riv.
198 F-4 Las Varillas
175 J-1 Las Vegas (USA)
167 L-5 Las Vegas (USA)
189 M-4 Las Viejas isl.
189 P-9 Las Yaras
209 J-3 Lasahata
129 P-8 Lasahe riv.
181 K-6 Lascahobas
199 L-6 Lascano
97 H-4 Lãsdãred
207 L-6 Lasem
126 C-6 Lash-e joven
143 M-5 Lashio
129 K-5 Lashunhu lake
146 B-8 Lasia isl.
73 L-5 Lãsjerd
208 E-3 Lasolo bay
208 E-3 Lasolo
162 B-6 Lasqueti isl.
197 K-3 Lassance
166 G-3 Lassen mt
166 G-3 Lassen Volcanic na.p.
149 K-5 Lassitan
55 K-2 Lassy
168 E-7 Last Chance
163 L-8 Last Mountain lake
191 N-3 Lastarria vol.
63 K-1 Latebasse
98 E-3 Lastoursville
61 P-4 Lastovski cap.
63 K-9 Lastra a Signa
191 M-1 Lata
188 B-3 Latacunga
72 A-8 Latakia
65 L-8 Latakia (Al Ladhiqiyah)
142 E-8 Latehãr
167 K-5 Lathrop Wells
61 M-5 Latina
63 P-2 Latisana
160 A-1 Latouche isl.
212 G-5 Latouche Treville cap.
48 A-2 Látrar
221 H-6 Latrobe mt
140 D-5 Lãtũr
114 A-4 Latvia rép
66 B-3 Latvia rép
224 B-5 Lau islds
94 D-5 Lau riv.
191 H-2 Lauca riv.
161 P-3 Lauchlan riv.
58 F-7 Lauenen
59 L-3 Lauerz
59 L-3 Lauerzer lake
218 A-2 Laughlen mt
53 L-8 Laughton
221 H-6 Launceston (Australia)
50 C-6 Launceston (UK)
144 E-7 Langlon
58 E-4 Laupen
59 H-3 Lauperswil
211 M-8 Laupolo
215 H-5 Laura
176 F-5 Laurel (USA)
168 C-4 Laurel (USA)
172 C-4 Laureldale
196 A-9 Laureles (Argentina)
199 K-4 Laureles (Brazil)
172 G-6 Laurel Hill
177 K-2 Laurens
156 E-1 Laurentian plat.
164 F-6 Laurentides na.p.
177 L-2 Laurinburg
49 J-9 Lauritsala
199 P-2 Lauro Müller
58 C-6 Lausanne
61 K-1 Lausanne
69 P-3 Laut
147 K-6 Laut isl.
207 P-3 Laut strt.

207 P-4 Laut Ketjil islds
201 K-3 Lautaro vol.
200 C-2 Lautaro
59 H-5 Lauterbrunnen
59 H-1 Lautetfingen
54 C-3 Lavacourt
62 E-7 Lavagna riv.
62 E-7 Lavagna
198 E-6 Lavaisse
164 E-8 Laval (Canada)
50 D-8 Laval (France)
172 G-6 Lavalette
199 H-2 Lavalle (Argentina)
198 D-2 Lavalle (Argentina)
199 K-6 Lavalleja reg.
63 L-8 Lavane mt
109 N-2 Lavanono bay
73 P-8 Lavar Meydãn lake
63 K-1 Lavarone
191 N-5 Lavayén riv.
68 C-8 Lavda-Vetka
53 J-2 Lavendon
53 M-2 Lavenham
63 H-2 Lavenone
52 A-4 Laveron
58 D-9 Lavey
63 L-6 Lavezzola
54 E-1 Lavilletertre
58 B-2 Laviron
59 M-7 Lavizzara val.
211 M-2 Lavongai (New Hanover) isl.
59 N-7 Lavorgo
197 J-5 Lavras
195 L-3 Lavras da Mangabeira
199 L-4 Lavras do Sul
64 E-7 Lavrion
103 N-2 Lavushi Manda rés
207 M-6 Lawang
147 P-6 Lawas
96 E-4 Lawdar
208 E-3 Lawele
209 J-2 Lawin isl.
146 F-6 Lawit mt
143 L-7 Lawksawk
172 A-5 Lawn
214 D-7 Lawn Hill riv.
83 H-3 Lawqah
89 K-4 Lawra
222 D-9 Lawrence
144 B-8 Lawrence (J.) isl.
169 J-8 Lawrence (USA)
171 M-5 Lawrence (USA)
176 G-2 Lawrenceburg
170 D-9 Lawrenceville
175 M-2 Lawton
207 L-6 Lawu mt
82 C-5 Lawz mt
59 J-7 Lax
51 L-1 Laxa
53 P-1 Laxfield
131 M-4 Laxiu
54 E-8 Layes (Les)
83 M-8 Laylã
173 M-1 Laysville
168 A-5 Layton
158 A-6 Lazaref cap.
125 L-1 Lazarev
123 L-2 Lazareva
125 J-6 Lazarevo
129 P-6 Lazi
61 M-5 Lazio Campania reg.
63 J-3 Lazise
125 L-9 Lazo (SSSR)
125 K-2 Lazo (SSSR)
137 M-8 Le isl.
172 B-6 Leacock
165 H-8 Lead mt
168 E-4 Lead
53 L-2 Leaden Roding
163 J-8 Leader
168 C-7 Leadville
176 F-5 Leaf riv.
175 L-5 Leakey
52 G-1 Leam
170 G-6 Leamington
196 C-9 Leandro N. Alem
50 A-5 Lear riv.
212 C-9 Learmonth
53 J-6 Leatherhead
162 C-8 Leavenworth
169 J-8 Leavenworth (USA)
51 M-4 Leba
149 K-3 Lebak

47 G-6 Lebanon state
172 A-4 Lebanon reg.
166 D-3 Lebanon (USA)
176 G-1 Lebanon (USA)
170 E-8 Lebanon (USA)
170 B-9 Lebanon (USA)
170 F-9 Lebanon (USA)
71 K-7 Lebanga
121 L-4 Leb'ažje
69 J-8 Leb'ažje
122 C-4 Lebed' riv.
67 H-4 Lebed'an'
66 G-6 Lebedin
58 G-1 Lebern mt
48 C-7 Lebesby
98 G-4 leboma riv.
105 M-4 Lebombo mt
51 M-4 Lebork
186 E-4 Lebrija riv.
200 B-1 Lebu
64 B-6 Lecce
61 L-2 Lecco
62 E-1 Lecco lake
135 J-7 Lechang
52 F-4 Lechlade
66 A-6 Leczyca
68 F-6 Led riv.
52 D-3 Ledbury
98 G-4 Lediba
125 L-5 Ledinka riv.
68 F-2 Ledkovo
147 K-9 Ledo
98 E-9 Lêdo cap.
145 M-4 Ledong
63 H-1 Ledro lake
131 K-7 Ledu
163 H-5 Leduc
173 N-1 Ledyard
52 G-8 Lee on the Solent
167 J-3 Lee Vining
170 A-2 Leech lake
50 D-4 Leeds (UK)
176 G-3 Leeds (USA)
57 H-9 Leende
51 H-5 Leer
56 E-4 Leerbroek
56 E-4 Leerdam
57 N-6 Leerop
56 G-3 Leersum
177 K-7 Leesburg
176 C-5 Leesville
221 H-3 Leeton
50 G-5 Leeuwarden
56 C-4 Leeuwen (Netherlands)
57 N-6 Leeuwen (Netherlands)
216 D-9 Leeuwing cap.
98 A-4 Léfini riv.
98 F-4 Léfini na.p.
64 E-9 Lefka mt
65 K-8 Lefkónikos
217 H-6 Lefroy lake
98 F-7 Lefunde riv.
148 E-4 Legazpi
212 D-7 Legendre isl.
221 H-8 Legges Tor na.p.
166 G-1 Leggett
63 K-4 Legnago
62 D-2 Legnano
63 M-3 Legnaro
51 L-7 Legnica
213 M-3 Legune
127 P-8 Leh
167 J-8 Lehi
172 C-4 Lehigh reg.
172 C-2 Lehigh riv.
172 C-3 Lehighton
98 E-2 Lehiri riv.
172 B-1 Lehman
127 J-9 Leiah
61 P-2 Leibnitz
134 C-5 Leibo
50 D-5 Leicester
215 K-9 Leichardt mt
214 E-8 Leichhardt riv.
50 G-6 Leiden
56 C-2 Leiderdorp
56 B-3 Leidschendam
53 L-6 Leigh
218 D-7 Leigh Creek
53 M-5 Leigh on Sea
57 N-8 Leijenbroek
49 J-1 Leikanger
214 B-6 Leila
56 D-2 Leimuiden
185 H-3 Leimus
62 A-4 Leini
172 C-9 Leipsic
51 K-7 Leipzig
48 E-2 Leiranger
60 A-5 Leiria
48 C-8 Leirpollen
213 M-9 Leisler mt
59 H-5 Leissigen
53 P-2 Leiston

132 C-7 Lishi
135 M-4 Lishui
134 G-7 Lishui *riv.*
125 J-8 Lishuzhen
67 J-7 Lisichansk
50 D-8 Lisieux
219 N-7 Lismore
53 H-7 Liss
213 M-4 Lissadell
56 C-1 Lisse
55 M-9 Lissy
51 H-2 Lista *fj.*
50 A-4 Listowel (Ireland)
170 G-5 Listowel (USA)
219 H-4 Listowel Downs
123 K-6 Listv'anka
131 P-6 Litang (China)
149 L-7 Litang (Philippines)
134 A-5 Litanghe *riv.*
52 G-6 Litchfield (UK)
170 A-4 Litchfield (USA)
170 C-8 Litchfield (USA)
56 G-5 Lith
221 K-2 Lithgow
56 G-5 Lithoijen
114 A-4 Lithuania *rép*
112 A-4 Lithuania *rép*
66 B-4 Lithuania *rép*
172 A-5 Lititz
125 K-4 Litovko
59 K-3 Littau
175 P-2 Little *riv.*
164 A-5 Little Abitibi *riv.*
223 K-3 Little Barrier *isl.*
168 B-1 Little Belt *mt*
159 M-8 Little Black *riv.*
169 H-7 Little Blue *riv.*
162 G-8 Little Bow *riv.*
161 L-9 Little Buffalo *riv.*
174 F-1 Little Colorado *riv.*
172 D-9 Little Creek
164 A-8 Little Current
159 K-8 Little Delta *riv.*
159 J-1 Little Diomede *isl.*
168 D-2 Little Dry *riv.*
172 G-7 Little Egg Harbour *bay*
172 G-8 Little Egg Inlet *cap.*
180 G-3 Little Exuma *isl.*
170 A-3 Little Falls
170 B-2 Little Fork *riv.*
172 C-3 Little Gap
52 C-1 Little Hereford
158 B-7 Little Koniuji *isl.*
168 F-2 Little Missouri *riv.*
173 M-2 Little Peconic *bay*
162 E-2 Little Prairie
176 D-2 Little Rock
100 G-8 Little Ruaha *riv.*
180 G-3 Little San Salvador *isl.*
87 K-5 Little Scarcies *riv.*
172 G-5 Little Silver
162 F-4 Little Smoky *riv.*
53 K-1 Little Stukeley
53 L-2 Little Thurlow
170 D-8 Little Wabash *riv.*
53 M-4 Little Witham
172 E-4 Little York
53 N-6 Littlebourne
53 L-3 Littlebury
175 K-2 Littlefield
53 J-8 Littlehampton
53 L-1 Littleport
53 N-7 Littlestone on Sea
168 D-7 Littleton (USA)
164 F-9 Littleton (USA)
135 K-2 Liuan
134 E-1 Liuba
135 N-9 Liuchiuhsu *isl.*
134 D-6 Liuchonghe *riv.*
135 L-2 Liuhe
135 P-3 Liuhengdao *isl.*
124 D-9 Liuhucun
134 F-8 Liujiang *riv.*
132 A-9 Liupanshan *mt*
106 G-8 Liupo
129 J-3 Liushishan *mt*
103 H-4 Liuwa Plain *na.p.*
135 J-5 Liuyang
134 F-8 Liuzhou
64 D-7 Livanatai
66 C-3 Livāni
177 J-6 Live Oak
201 L-9 Lively Island *isl.*
159 L-7 Livengood
63 P-2 Livenza *riv.*
55 N-8 Liverdy-en-Brie
213 J-5 Liveringa
175 J-4 Livermore *mt*
221 K-1 Liverpool *mt*
165 K-8 Liverpool (Canada)
50 D-4 Liverpool (UK)
54 F-2 Livilliers
179 N-8 Livingston (Guatémala)
177 H-1 Livingston (USA)
175 P-5 Livingston (USA)
176 F-4 Livingston (USA)
168 B-2 Livingston (USA)
106 C-4 Livingstone *mt*
164 G-1 Livingstone (Canada)
76 D-5 Livingstone (Falls)
103 K-6 Livingstone (Maramba)
172 G-3 Livingstone (USA)
106 C-4 Livingstonia
67 H-4 Livny
61 L-4 Livorno
62 B-3 Livorno Ferraris
193 H-6 Livramento
195 J-8 Livramento do Brumado
55 K-5 Livry-Gargan
84 C-6 Liwa
106 C-7 Liwale
131 M-9 Lixian
134 B-9 Lixianjiang *riv.*
64 C-7 Lixoúrion
136 G-6 Liyama
135 M-2 Liyang
215 J-5 Lizard *isl.*
50 B-6 Lizard *cap.*
194 F-5 Lizarda
137 L-2 Lizuka
63 J-8 Lizzano in Belvedere
123 H-3 Lja *riv.*
61 N-2 Ljubljana
49 H-4 Ljungam *riv.*
51 L-3 Ljungby
49 H-4 Ljungdalen
49 J-5 Ljusdal
49 J-5 Ljusne
148 C-5 Llagan
200 C-2 Llaima *vol.*
189 L-9 Llalli *riv.*
191 K-1 Llamara *lake*
52 B-1 Llanbistero
188 F-3 Llancan *riv.*
198 C-7 Llancanelo (Argentina) *lake*
52 B-5 Llandaf
52 B-1 Llandinam Dolforo
50 C-5 Llandovery
52 B-2 Llandrindod Wells
50 C-5 Llanelly
52 A-3 Llanfrynacho
52 A-2 Llangammarch Wells
52 B-3 Llangorse
175 L-5 Llano *riv.*
175 M-5 Llano
182 D-4 Llanos *reg.*
191 H-6 Llanos de Chiquitos
190 F-4 Llanos de Mojos *reg.*
200 E-2 Llanquihue *lake*
52 C-4 Llansay
52 B-3 Llanthony *hill*
52 A-5 Llantrisant
52 A-5 Llantwit Majoro *na.p.*
52 C-3 Llanvetherin
52 C-3 Llanvihangel Crucorney
52 A-2 Llanwrtyd Wells
52 B-2 Llanyre
189 J-4 Llata
68 D-6 Lleksa *riv.*
60 B-6 Llerena
69 K-9 Llet' *riv.*
200 B-1 Lleulleu *lag.*
172 B-3 Llewellyn
53 L-5 Llford
158 F-8 Lliamna *lake*
191 J-2 Llica
200 E-2 Llico *riv.*
198 A-7 Llico
191 J-2 Lliscaya *mt*
69 L-6 Lljinskij
68 B-7 Llomantsi
184 D-4 Llopango *lake*
67 J-8 Llovajsk
67 L-6 Llovl'a
67 K-5 Llovl'a *riv.*
215 H-3 Lloyd *bay*
163 K-3 Lloyd *lake*
173 J-3 Lloyd Harbor
163 J-6 Lloydminster
52 G-5 Llsley
191 N-2 Llullaillaco *vol.*
126 A-5 Llüt *dés*
69 K-3 Llyč *riv.*
165 M-3 Llyods *riv.*
52 B-3 Llyswen
145 K-1 Lo *riv.*
99 L-4 Lo
61 N-3 Losinj *isl.*
191 L-2 Loa *riv.*
167 K-8 Loa
172 C-5 Loag
147 N-2 Loaita (Daomingqunjiao) *rf*
196 D-6 Loanda
99 J-6 Loandji *riv.*
99 J-7 Loange *riv.*
62 B-8 Loano
149 H-3 Loay
69 K-8 Loban *riv.*
105 H-3 Lobatse *reg.*
105 H-3 Lobatse
91 J-8 Lobaye *riv.*
91 J-8 Lobaye *reg.*
198 A-5 Lobería *pte*
199 H-9 Lobería
57 K-4 Lobith
102 B-2 Lobito
188 E-1 Lobitos
209 N-3 Lobo
87 N-9 Lobo *riv.*
78 D-9 Lobo *isl.*
174 D-6 Lobos *isl.*
174 C-4 Lobos *cap.*
198 A-7 Lobos *pte*
199 H-7 Lobós
198 A-2 Lobos *pte*
180 F-4 Lobos Cay *rf*
188 G-1 Lobos de Afuera *islds*
188 F-1 Lobos de Tierra *isl.*
89 K-1 Lobougoula
69 M-4 Lobva
145 L-8 Lôc Ninh
59 M-9 Locarno
62 E-3 Locate Triuizi
50 C-2 Lochaline
57 M-2 Lochem
57 M-2 Lochemerberg *hill*
60 G-1 Loches
50 C-2 Lochgilphead
50 D-1 Lochinver
50 C-1 Lochmaddy
166 D-8 Lochsa *riv.*
57 P-9 Locht
66 G-7 Lochvica
220 B-2 Lock
171 J-6 Lock Haven
172 A-8 Lock Raven *rés*
159 K-5 Lock Wood *mt*
165 J-8 Lockeport
175 N-5 Lockhart
161 M-7 Lockhart *lake*
214 G-3 Lockhart River Mission
52 C-6 Locking
171 J-5 Lockport
58 C-3 Locle (Le)
59 M-9 Loco
61 P-8 Locri
189 L-6 Locroja
189 P-9 Locumba *riv.*
172 B-8 Locust Grove
220 F-4 Loddon *riv.*
61 H-3 Lodève
163 H-9 Lodge *riv.*
168 D-3 Lodge Grass
168 E-6 Lodgepole *riv.*
139 J-2 Lodhrān
62 E-3 Lodi (Italy)
167 H-2 Lodi (USA)
99 K-5 Lodi (Zaïre)
62 E-3 Lodi Vecchio
48 D-5 Lødingen
99 M-5 Lodja
59 N-8 Lodrino
63 H-1 Lodrone
58 A-3 Lods
95 H-7 Lodwar
66 A-6 Lodz
144 G-4 Loei
98 D-6 Loémé *riv.*
57 K-3 Loenen
56 C-8 Loenhout
104 D-7 Loeriesfontein
56 F-3 Loerik
87 M-6 Loffa *reg.*
87 M-6 Loffa *riv.*
103 L-1 Lofoi
48 D-3 Lofoten *islds*
220 D-2 Lofty *mt*
89 H-8 Loga
170 G-9 Logan
160 C-3 Logan *mt*
175 K-1 Logan (USA)
169 J-6 Logan (USA)
168 A-5 Logan (USA)
170 E-7 Logansport
196 D-6 Logarto *mt*
98 E-8 Loge *riv.*
54 F-5 Loges (Les)
54 G-7 Loges-en-Josas (Les)
90 G-2 Logone *riv.*
91 H-5 Logone *riv.*
91 H-5 Logone Oriental *reg.*
62 G-3 Lograto
60 E-4 Logrono
142 D-4 Lohārdaga
139 M-4 Lohāru
49 K-7 Lohjo
58 G-7 Lohner
143 M-8 Loi-kaw
143 M-7 Loi-lem
143 M-5 Loi Lun Taungdan *mt*
143 N-7 Loi Mwe
63 K-7 Loiano
99 K-4 Loile *riv.*
49 J-7 Loimaa
50 D-9 Loir *riv.*
61 H-1 Loire *riv.*
55 L-2 Loisy
60 C-7 Loja
188 E-2 Loja
188 E-2 Loja *reg.*
66 E-6 Lojev
68 C-7 Lojmola
190 G-4 Lojojota *riv.*
94 E-6 Loka
99 N-4 Lokandu
68 C-3 Lokanga *riv.*
73 H-2 Lokbatan
99 L-4 Lokedi *riv.*
95 H-8 Lokicharr
94 G-6 Lokichoggio
95 H-6 Lokitaung
48 D-8 Lokka *lake*
66 D-2 Lokn'a
108 E-8 Lokoho *riv.*
90 B-5 Lokoja
99 J-4 Lokolama
99 L-1 Lokolenge
99 J-3 Lokolo *riv.*
91 H-9 Lokomo
99 J-4 Lokoro *riv.*
89 N-7 Lokossa
121 N-5 Loktevka *riv.*
94 B-3 Lol *riv.*
87 M-8 Lola
167 H-3 Lola *mt*
99 L-2 Lolingo
100 G-4 Loliondo
51 K-4 Lolland *isl.*
98 D-3 Lolo *riv.*
100 A-4 Lolo
211 N-4 Lolobau *isl.*
90 D-8 Lolodorf
100 E-2 Lolui *isl.*
90 G-7 Lom *riv.*
49 J-2 Lom
144 G-5 Lom Sak
87 L-5 Loma *mt*
179 H-6 Loma Bonita
200 A-4 Loma del Jagüel del Moro
200 A-9 Loma Negra
180 D-4 Loma San Juan *mt*
127 K-1 Lomakino
99 M-2 Lomami *riv.*
189 M-6 Lomas
200 E-5 Lomas Coloradas *mt*
199 H-7 Lomas de Zamora
102 F-4 Lomba *riv.*
213 H-4 Lombadina
149 P-3 Lombagin
168 B-2 Lombard
192 G-5 Lombarda *mt*
61 L-2 Lombardy *reg.*
208 F-6 Lomblen *isl.*
207 P-7 Lombok *strt.*
208 A-7 Lombok
208 A-7 Lombok *isl.*
89 N-6 Lomé
77 C-4 Lomé
94 M-4 Lomela
99 L-3 Lomela *riv.*
62 D-4 Lomello
90 F-9 Lomié
57 K-8 Lomm
54 A-4 Lommoye
68 B-9 Lomonosov
58 C-1 Lomont *rge*
67 K-3 Lomov
208 C-4 Lompobottang *mt*
167 L-2 Lompoc
62 D-2 Lonate Pozzolo
63 H-3 Lonato
140 C-3 Lonauli
200 C-2 Loncoché
200 B-3 Loncopue
125 H-5 Londoko
201 N-4 London *isl.*
50 E-6 London
47 C-4 London
170 G-5 London (USA)
53 K-4 London Colney
147 M-3 London Reefs (Yinqingqunjiao) *rf*
201 P-4 Londonderry *isl.*
213 L-2 Londonderry *cap.*
50 B-2 Londonderry
196 E-6 Londrina
167 K-4 Lonefine
103 M-7 Lonely Mine
177 L-3 Long *bay*
163 P-7 Long *pte*
163 L-9 Long *riv.*
113 R-2 Long *strt.*
143 H-1 Long
210 G-8 Long (Australia) *isl.*
214 G-1 Long (Australia) *isl.*
219 L-2 Long (Australia) *isl.*
180 G-3 Long (Bahamas) *isl.*
160 B-9 Long (Canada) *isl.*
222 C-7 Long (Nouvelle Zélande) *rf*
222 D-9 Long (Nouvelle Zélande) *pte*
149 H-7 Long (Philippines) *pte*
168 G-3 Long (USA) *lake*
147 P-7 Long Akah
167 M-3 Long Beach
172 G-7 Long Beach *isth.*
173 H-5 Long Branch
52 D-8 Long Burton
181 H-4 Long Cay *isl.*
52 F-3 Long Compton
53 H-4 Long Credon
173 K-1 Long Hill
171 M-6 Long Island *isl.*
164 B-1 Long Island *strt.*
164 A-2 Long Island (Canada) *isl.*
173 K-2 Long Island Sound *gulf*
170 E-1 Long lake *lake*
53 M-2 Long Melford
171 H-6 Long Point *bay*
165 L-2 Long Range Mountains *mt*
53 N-1 Long Stratton
52 C-7 Long Sutton
147 H-3 Long Toan
172 F-3 Long Valley
147 H-2 Long Xuyên
102 E-5 Longa *riv.*
102 C-1 Longa *riv.*
195 J-2 Longá *riv.*
134 E-9 Longan
63 L-3 Longara
63 L-3 Longare
99 K-7 Longatshimo *riv.*
200 A-2 Longavi *mt*
147 P-9 Longbangun
149 P-9 Longbeleh
52 E-6 Longbridge Deverhill
129 N-4 Longbushan *mt*
134 D-4 Longchang
54 F-9 Longchêne
135 K-8 Longchuan
143 M-4 Longchuanjiang *riv.*
132 A-8 Longde
52 D-3 Longdon
123 P-1 Longdor *mt*
221 H-8 Longford
50 B-3 Longford (Ireland)
52 E-8 Longham
135 K-4 Longhu *lake*
132 F-4 Longhua
101 G-4 Longido
207 P-1 Longiram
135 K-8 Longjiang *riv.*
124 E-8 Longjiang
133 M-2 Longjing
55 H-8 Longjumeau
129 N-4 Longkaergongba
170 E-1 Longlac
143 P-6 Longlangshan *mt*
134 E-6 Longli
134 D-8 Longlin
143 N-4 Longling
129 K-3 Longmatuoke
135 J-8 Longmen
168 D-7 Longmont
129 K-3 Longnakeshankou *pass*
135 J-7 Longnan
147 P-8 Longnawan
54 B-5 Longnes
198 A-5 Longotoma
55 M-3 Longperrier
129 P-5 Longpoganleishan *mt*
55 H-9 Longpoint-sur-Orge
135 M-5 Longquan
218 G-2 Longreach
131 N-7 Longriba
168 D-7 Longs *mt*
134 E-8 Longshan
134 F-7 Longsheng
131 J-5 Longshijin
215 J-9 Longton
54 E-3 Longuesse
50 G-8 Longuyon
175 P-4 Longview (USA)
162 B-8 Longview (USA)
149 P-9 Longwai
50 G-8 Longwy
131 L-9 Longxi
132 A-9 Longxian
135 L-7 Longyan
135 M-4 Longyou
124 F-6 Longzhen
134 E-9 Longzhou
143 J-1 Longzi
63 K-3 Lonigo
99 L-4 Lonkonia *riv.*
57 P-1 Lonneker
200 B-2 Lonquimay *vol.*
61 J-1 Lons-le-Saunier
196 D-4 Lontra *riv.*
194 B-1 Lontra
149 P-5 Lonu
57 K-4 Loo
148 F-5 Looc
50 A-4 Lood *cap.*
177 N-2 Lookout *cap.*
162 E-9 Lookout *pass*
159 L-6 Lookout *mt*
100 G-5 Loolmalasin *mt*
170 D-1 Loon
56 E-6 Loon op Zand
217 L-6 Loongana
162 E-4 Loos
57 H-6 Loosbroek
56 E-2 Loosdrecht *reg.*
56 A-3 Loosduinen
144 G-6 Lop Buri
70 B-9 Lopatin
125 N-2 Lopatina *mt*
94 F-5 Lopaye
124 C-2 Lopča
124 C-2 Lopča *riv.*
98 B-3 Lopez *cap.*
56 E-4 Lopik
56 E-4 Lopikerkapel
56 E-3 Lopikerwaard *reg.*
99 L-2 Lopori
99 L-2 Lopori *riv.*
48 C-6 Lopphavet *gulf*
68 D-5 Lopšen'ga
69 J-5 Lopydino
198 A-7 Lora *pte*
186 F-3 Lora *riv.*
126 E-9 Lora (hamun-i) *riv.*
126 E-9 Lora (Pishin) *riv.*
60 B-7 Lora del Rio
170 G-6 Lorain
126 G-9 Loralai
126 G-9 Loralai *riv.*
60 D-7 Lorca
174 F-3 Lordsburg
63 M-2 Loreggia
197 J-6 Lorena
211 K-2 Lorengau
210 D-4 Lorentz *riv.*
63 M-4 Loreo
188 E-5 Loreto *reg.*
190 F-5 Loreto (Bolivia)
199 K-3 Loreto (Brazil)
194 G-3 Loreto (Brazil)
188 D-9 Loreto (Colombia)
188 B-4 Loreto (Ecuador)
178 E-3 Loreto (Mexico)
174 D-7 Loreto (Mexico)
196 B-6 Loreto (Paraguay)
63 L-2 Loria
185 P-8 Lorica
50 C-8 Lorient
163 J-9 Loring (Canada)
160 C-8 Loring (USA)
189 N-9 Loripongo
54 A-9 Lormaye
187 H-8 Loro
191 N-3 Loro Huasi
89 K-3 Loropéni
95 H-7 Lorukumu
87 K-3 Los *islds*
175 L-8 Los Aldamas
200 E-3 Los Alerces *na.p.*
184 E-2 Los Amates
198 B-6 Los Andés
200 B-2 Los Angeles (Chile)
167 M-2 Los Angeles (USA)
201 H-3 Los Antiguos
190 D-5 Los Arroyos *lake*
189 P-9 Los Baños
167 J-2 Los Banos
191 M-6 Los Blancos
187 K-2 Los Caracas
185 H-7 Los Cartagos
186 E-5 Los Cobardes *mt*
198 C-3 Los Colorados
199 H-3 Los Conquistadores
200 E-1 Los Coronados *gulf*
190 F-5 Los Cusis
191 J-4 Los Frailes *mt*
187 M-2 Los Frailes *islds*
187 L-1 Los Hermanos *islds*
188 G-3 Los Hijos *mt*
198 F-2 Los Juries
200 E-2 Los Lagos *reg.*
200 D-2 Los Lagos
78 A-8 Los Llanos de Aridane
175 H-1 Los Lunas
200 D-4 Los Menucos
200 C-5 Los Menucos *bay*
179 P-8 Los Micos *lag.*
174 E-7 Los Mochis
186 G-1 Los Monjes *islds*
201 J-6 Los Nodales *bay*
200 C-2 Los Paraguas *mt*
198 B-5 Los Platos *riv.*
198 E-1 Los Ralos
191 P-5 Los Ralos
211 L-2 Los Reyes *islds*

69 H-2 Lyža
69 H-2 Lyža riv.

# M

108 B-3 M'Beni
98 E-7 M'Bridge riv.
145 M-8 M'Drak
79 K-3 M'Sila
79 K-5 M'Zab reg.
79 K-5 M'Zab riv.
145 H-2 Ma riv.
148 G-4 Ma-ao
141 N-2 Ma Faro isl.
81 H-9 Ma' tan as Sarra well
81 J-8 Ma tan Bishârah well
93 H-7 Ma'Tûq
144 C-5 Ma-ubin
79 K-2 Maâdid mt
57 P-6 Maalbroek
82 C-3 Ma'an
83 H-2 Ma'ânîyah
135 L-2 Maanshan
57 H-9 Maarheeze
56 G-3 Maarn
65 M-8 Ma'arrat an Nu'mân
56 G-3 Maarsbergen
56 E-2 Maarssen
56 F-2 Maartensdijk
56 F-5 Maas riv.
57 J-5 Maas-Waal cal.
57 N-6 Maasbracht
57 K-9 Maasbree
56 C-5 Maasdam
56 A-4 Maasdijk
56 F-5 Maasdriel reg.
57 M-7 Maaseik
57 K-7 Maashees
148 G-3 Maasin
56 B-4 Maasland
57 N-6 Maasniel
56 A-4 Maassluis
50 G-7 Maastricht
81 P-4 Maaza plat.
135 L-1 Maba
103 M-8 Mabalabala
107 M-2 Mabalane
96 E-3 Ma'bar
97 H-8 Mabber cap.
143 L-5 Mabein
162 K-6 Mabel lake
99 H-5 Mabenga
134 C-5 Mabian riv.
95 H-2 Mabil
107 H-3 Mabote
82 C-3 Mabrak mt
98 E-8 Mabubas dam.
100 E-4 Mabuki
81 H-6 Ma'būs Yūsuf
175 P-2 Mac Alester
168 A-4 Mac Cammon
175 N-3 Mac Kinney
169 H-9 Mac Pherson
200 G-2 Macá
200 A-7 Macachín
193 H-8 Macacos isl.
197 L-6 Macaé
187 M-4 Macagua dam.
195 P-3 Macáiba
199 K-2 Maçambará
185 H-4 Macantaca
135 J-9 Macao (Aomen)
190 B-3 Macapa (Brazil)
193 H-7 Macapa (Brazil)
192 F-6 Macaquara dam.
188 E-2 Macará
188 E-2 Macara riv.
185 K-9 Macaracas
197 N-1 Macarani
186 E-8 Macarena mt
214 F-6 Macaroni
188 C-3 Macas
208 C-4 Macassar (Ujung-Pandang)
195 N-2 Macaú
189 J-9 Macaua riv.
196 F-4 Macaubal
224 B-6 Macauley isl.
188 A-7 Macaya riv.
62 D-1 Maccagno
189 L-7 Macchu Picchu site
170 D-1 Macdiarmid
213 M-9 Macdonald lake
218 A-2 Macdonnell mt

60 B-4 Macedo de Cavaleiros
64 D-6 Macedonia reg.
195 M-1 Maceió pte
195 N-6 Maceió
87 L-7 Macenta
61 N-4 Macerata
63 N-9 Macerata Feltria
126 F-9 Mach
197 M-2 Machacalis
191 H-3 Machacamarca
188 B-3 Machachi
190 B-7 Machadinho riv.
197 J-5 Machado
190 B-7 Machado riv.
105 L-3 Machadodorp
101 H-3 Machakos
188 D-2 Machala
70 B-5 Machambet
105 J-1 Machaneng
72 C-2 Macharadze
56 G-5 Macharen
191 K-6 Machareti
218 E-3 Machattie lake
107 K-2 Machaze
107 H-2 Macheke
52 B-5 Machen
135 J-3 Macholamarca
140 E-7 Macherla
165 H-8 Machias
103 J-5 Machili riv.
58 A-8 Machilly
186 F-2 Machiques
190 E-5 Machupo riv.
107 N-2 Macia
198 G-5 Maciel
219 L-6 Macintyre riv.
189 H-9 Macipira riv.
213 M-8 Mackay lake
219 L-1 Mackay (Australia)
166 F-8 Mackay (USA)
192 C-2 Mackenzie
161 J-5 Mackenzie reg.
160 G-3 Mackenzie mt
219 K-2 Mackenzie (Australia) riv.
161 H-1 Mackenzie (Canada) riv.
170 E-3 Mackinaw
101 J-5 Mackinnon Road
163 J-6 Macklin
219 N-7 Maclean
105 J-7 Maclear
217 H-4 Maclolm
160 F-3 Macmillan riv.
58 E-2 Macolin
170 C-7 Macomb
61 K-6 Macomer
106 E-8 Macomia
61 J-1 Macon
177 J-4 Macon (USA)
176 F-4 Macon (USA)
170 B-8 Macon (USA)
103 J-2 Macondo
107 H-3 Macossa
163 M-4 Macoun lake
107 L-4 Macovane pte
221 H-8 Macquarie riv.
220 G-8 Macquarie Harbour bay
219 J-8 Macquarie Marshes lake
55 P-1 Macquelines
188 G-9 Macucaua
62 B-1 Macugnaga
188 B-7 Macujer
188 D-3 Macuma riv.
188 C-3 Macuma
218 B-5 Macumba riv.
190 D-3 Macupari riv.
188 D-4 Macurasi riv.
195 L-5 Macururé
189 L-9 Macusani
179 K-7 Macuspana
174 E-6 Macuzari dam.
90 C-5 Madá Ramat
82 E-5 Madá in Sâlih
101 H-9 Madaba
77 G-6 Madagascar state
140 G-5 Madakasira
80 C-9 Madama
97 P-4 Madamarodi
73 N-3 Ma'dan
141 H-6 Madanapalle
165 L-6 Madane isl.
211 J-4 Madang
90 A-1 Madaoua
142 G-5 Mâdârïpur
143 L-6 Madaya
61 L-5 Maddalena isl.
185 L-8 Madden lake
97 L-2 Maddiso riv.
56 D-6 Made
56 D-6 Made en Drimmelen reg.
94 C-4 Madeir
78 A-1 Madeira isl.

78 A-1 Madeira islds
76 A-1 Madeira isl.
190 B-5 Madeira riv.
190 B-7 Madeirinha riv.
66 C-4 M'adel
165 K-5 Madeleine islds
65 N-5 Maden
103 K-7 Madenassa pl.
174 F-5 Madera (Mexico)
167 K-3 Madera (USA)
59 M-5 Maderaner val.
63 H-4 Maderno
96 D-2 Madhab riv.
142 E-2 Madhipura
142 E-2 Madhubani
142 G-5 Madhumati riv.
140 A-7 Madhya Pradesh reg.
94 E-7 Madi reg.
94 F-7 Madi Opei
190 E-2 Madidi riv.
175 N-2 Madill
98 F-6 Madimba
87 H-8 Madina
87 L-9 Madinani
96 F-3 Madinat Ash Sha'b
98 E-5 Madingou
82 C-5 Madiq Jûbâl isl.
108 F-5 Madirovalo
172 F-3 Madison
168 A-2 Madison riv.
177 J-5 Madison (USA)
170 C-5 Madison (USA)
170 G-9 Madison (USA)
169 H-5 Madison (USA)
170 E-9 Madison (USA)
176 G-1 Madisonville (USA)
175 P-5 Madisonville (USA)
59 H-2 Madiswill
207 L-6 Madiun
208 C-3 Madjene
217 J-1 Madley mt
52 C-3 Madley
164 C-9 Madoc
94 B-3 Madol
66 C-2 Madona
59 N-8 Madone Grosso mt
91 L-6 Madonguéré
85 H-9 Madrakah cap.
141 H-7 Madras
141 J-5 Madras (Amil Nadu) reg.
166 D-4 Madras (USA)
148 B-5 Madre mt
175 N-8 Madre lag.
179 K-8 Madre (Sierra) mt
201 L-2 Madre de Dios isl.
189 K-8 Madre de Dios reg.
189 K-9 Madre de Dios
190 D-3 Madre de Dios riv.
178 F-7 Madre del Sur (Sierra) mt
174 G-8 Madre Occidental (Sierra) mt
178 F-3 Madre Oriental (Sierra) mt
179 L-9 Madre Vieja riv.
186 E-6 Madrid pass
47 C-5 Madrid
60 C-5 Madrid
60 D-6 Madridejos
184 F-4 Madriz reg.
99 N-2 Madula
131 L-5 Maduo
217 L-6 Madura
207 M-6 Madura isl.
207 M-6 Madura strt.
141 K-5 Madurai
141 M-8 Maduru riv.
73 N-8 Madvâr mt
82 D-5 Madyan mt
144 E-4 Mae Chaem
144 E-3 Mae Hong Son
145 J-4 Mae Nam Khong (Mékong) riv.
144 E-5 Mae Ramat
144 F-2 Mae Sai
144 E-4 Mae Sariang
144 E-5 Mae Sot
144 F-3 Mae Suai
144 F-3 Mae Taeng
137 H-7 Maebasi
52 A-4 Maerdy
57 M-9 Maerland
148 F-5 Maest. de Campo isl.
52 A-4 Maesteg
63 N-5 Maestra pte
180 F-6 Maestra mt
108 E-7 Maevarano riv.
108 G-5 Maevatanana
105 H-3 Mahaleshwar (South Africa)
163 N-7 Mafeking (Canada)
105 J-6 Mafeteng
55 H-2 Mafflers
221 H-5 Maffra
101 K-8 Mafia isl.

101 J-8 Mafia strt.
196 F-8 Mafra
100 G-4 Magadi
59 N-9 Magadino
148 E-4 Magallanes
201 M-3 Magellan strt.
201 M-3 Magallanes reg.
182 C-8 Magellan strt.
185 P-8 Magangué
224 F-6 Magareva isl.
90 C-1 Magaria
176 C-2 Magazine mt
87 L-5 Magburaka
124 E-3 Magdagači
186 B-7 Magdalena pte
186 E-2 Magdalena reg.
174 C-8 Magdalena dés
174 C-8 Magdalena pen.
199 J-7 Magdalena (Argentina)
190 E-5 Magdalena (Bolivia)
186 E-4 Magdalena (Colombia) riv.
174 D-4 Magdalena (Mexico) riv.
174 E-4 Magdalena (Mexico)
174 G-2 Magdalena (USA)
215 M-6 Magdelaine Cays rf
197 L-6 Magé
207 K-6 Magelang
62 D-3 Magenta
216 G-8 Magenta lake
48 B-7 Magerøya isl.
59 P-3 Magerram mt
207 L-6 Magetan
59 M-8 Maggia
59 M-8 Maggia val.
62 E-6 Maggiorasca mt
62 C-1 Maggiore (Lago) lake
81 N-3 Maghâghah
86 F-5 Maghama
127 K-9 Maghiâna Gojra
54 C-1 Magny-en-Vexin
55 N-5 Magny-le-Hongre
54 F-7 Magny-les-Hameaux
55 P-5 Magny-Saint-Loup
125 K-1 Mago
106 G-2 Mâgoé
164 F-8 Magog
52 C-5 Magor
172 A-9 Magothy riv.
165 H-3 Magpie
165 H-3 Magpie riv.
62 G-7 Magra riv.
83 M-8 Magran riv.
162 G-8 Magrath
125 J-1 Magu mt
193 P-9 Magu riv.
134 C-9 Maguan
193 J-7 Maguarinho cap.
107 N-2 Magude
159 P-6 Maguire islds
142 G-5 Magura
143 K-7 Magwe
143 K-7 Magwe reg.
100 E-2 Magyo
141 M-7 Maha riv.
145 H-5 Maha Sarakham
72 F-6 Mahâbâd
140 E-3 Mahâbaleshwar
141 H-7 Mahâbalipuram
109 J-3 Mahabo
97 P-4 Mahadday Weyne
140 A-7 Mahâded na.p.
109 L-2 Mahafaly plat.
100 D-1 Mahagi
100 D-1 Mahagi-Port
142 F-3 Mahahanda riv.
192 C-2 Mahaica riv.
192 C-2 Mahaicony
108 F-5 Mahajamba riv.
108 E-5 Mahajamba bay
139 K-3 Mahâjan
108 F-5 Mahajanga
109 H-4 Mahajilo riv.
147 P-9 Mahakam riv.
105 J-1 Mahalapye
108 F-8 Mahalevona
73 K-7 Mahallat
140 C-9 Mahânadi riv.
106 C-5 Mahanje
109 J-6 Mahanoro
172 A-3 Mahanoy riv.
172 B-3 Mahanoy City

140 C-5 Mahârâshtra reg.
79 P-4 Maharès
109 J-3 Maharivo riv.
83 P-1 Mahârlu lake
97 N-5 Mahâs
185 P-7 Mahates
108 G-4 Mahavavy riv.
141 M-8 Mahaweli riv.
140 E-6 Mahbûbnagar
82 G-8 Mahd adh Dhahab
79 P-3 Mahdia
141 M-7 Maho
139 P-7 Mahoba
61 H-6 Mahón
161 J-2 Mahony lake
173 H-1 Mahopac
173 H-1 Mahopac Falls
142 B-4 Mahora mt
60 E-6 Mahora
96 B-8 Mahrât mt
96 B-8 Mahrât riv.
139 N-8 Mahroni
211 P-3 Mahur isl.
140 A-2 Mahuva
99 H-1 Mai-Ndombe lake
106 F-8 Maiaia
193 K-7 Maiaú pte
186 F-1 Maicao
58 D-2 Maiche
93 H-4 Maichew
190 A-6 Maici riv.
192 E-1 Maicuru riv.
141 K-4 Maïdân mt
172 C-4 Maiden mt
52 D-7 Maiden Bradley
52 D-8 Maiden Newton
53 H-5 Maidenhead
163 J-6 Maidstone (Canada)
50 E-6 Maidstone (UK)
90 F-2 Maiduguri
128 F-2 Maigaiti
187 L-6 Maigualida mt
95 J-4 Maigudo mt
142 A-5 Maikala mt
100 A-2 Maiko riv.
100 A-3 Maiko na.p.
209 N-5 Maikoor isl.
142 C-4 Mailan mt
129 P-1 Mailâni
198 F-2 Mailin riv.
220 F-2 Mailin riv.
139 K-2 Mailsi
71 N-9 Maimâna
164 A-9 Main cal.
165 L-2 Main riv.
218 E-8 Main Barrier mt
165 M-1 Main Brook
170 G-4 Main Channel strt.
54 E-8 Maincourt-sur-Yvette
157 G-2 Maine state
164 G-8 Maine state
188 B-7 Mainé Hanari mt
90 E-1 Maïné-Soroa
50 E-1 Mainland pen.
214 A-4 Mainoru
139 N-6 Mainpuri
108 G-3 Maintirano
55 K-8 Mainville (France)
172 A-2 Mainville (USA)
51 H-8 Mainz
87 P-2 Maio
87 P-3 Maio isl.
198 B-7 Maipo mt
198 B-6 Maipo riv.
198 B-6 Maipo vol.
198 C-5 Maipú (Argentina)
199 J-8 Maipú (Argentina)
188 E-5 Maipuco
187 K-2 Maiquetia
62 F-4 Mairago
201 N-7 Maire (Le) strt.
195 K-7 Mairi
196 G-2 Mairipotaba
181 H-5 Maisi pte
181 H-5 Maisi
143 H-6 Maiskhâl isl.
54 E-7 Maison-Blanche (La)
54 G-9 Maisons-Laffitte
198 A-4 Maitencillo
142 E-4 Maithon dam.
216 G-3 Maitland lake
221 L-2 Maitland (Australia)
220 C-2 Maitland (Australia)
185 J-5 Maiz isl.
137 J-5 Maizuru

124 G-1 Maja riv.
207 J-1 Maja isl.
185 P-8 Majagual
127 L-4 Majakovskogo
187 N-7 Majari riv.
96 E-6 Majdarah
133 M-5 Majeon
189 N-7 Majes riv.
61 K-2 Majeur lake
95 H-5 Maji
121 K-3 Majkain
128 A-4 Majkamys
69 L-6 Majkor
67 L-2 Majna
192 D-5 Majoli
67 G-9 Major
92 D-7 Majrur riv.
125 M-4 Majskij
124 G-1 Majskij rge
121 L-4 Majskoje
128 A-2 Majtan
149 P-1 Maju isl.
190 A-4 Majuriã
119 N-6 Majuro isl.
145 H-9 Mak isl.
70 C-5 Makai
103 H-8 Makalamabedi
208 C-3 Makale
199 H-1 Makallé
142 F-1 Makâlu mt
128 A-6 Makanči
100 C-7 Makari mt
103 K-8 Makarikari lake
68 G-9 Makarjev
125 N-3 Makarov
123 L-2 Makarovo
127 K-7 Makarwâl Khejli
116 G-7 Makassar strt.
172 C-4 Makassar strt.
149 P-7 Makassar strt.
204 B-2 Makassar strt.
208 B-2 Makassar (Selat) strt.
224 E-5 Makatea isl.
109 J-3 Makay mt
224 E-5 Makemo isl.
87 L-5 Makeni
67 J-7 Makeyevka
72 F-1 Makhachkala
83 K-2 Makhfar al Buşayyah
65 N-7 Makhfar al Hammâm
72 E-7 Makhmûr
149 P-1 Makian isl.
220 E-3 Makian na.p.
121 H-1 Makinsk
100 F-6 Makiwo riv.
82 G-9 Makkah reg.
209 N-3 Makki
122 F-1 Maklakovo
64 C-1 Makó
87 H-5 Mako (Senegal)
192 C-6 Makoa mt
98 B-2 Makok
98 E-2 Makokou (Gabon)
91 L-2 Makokou (Chad)
87 L-6 Makona riv.
94 A-7 Makongo
98 G-2 Makoua
122 K-1 Makovskoje
138 B-3 Makrân Coast mt
139 L-5 Makrâna
66 F-1 Maksaticha
123 M-5 Maksimicha
79 N-3 Maktar
72 E-4 Makû
136 B-7 Makubetu
100 F-9 Makumbako
99 K-6 Makumbi
135 M-8 Makung
141 N-1 Makunudu isl.
90 C-5 Makurdi
84 B-3 Makûyeh
100 G-5 Makuyuni
105 H-4 Makwassie
61 K-6 Mal di Ventre isl.
69 M-2 Mal. So'va riv.
185 L-9 Mala pte
189 L-4 Mala
189 L-5 Mala riv.
149 J-3 Malabang
141 J-3 Malabâr
116 C-5 Malabar (Coast)
77 C-4 Malabo
90 C-8 Malabo
211 P-4 Malabunga
187 P-8 Malacacheta
197 L-3 Malacachete
116 E-6 Malacca isl.
116 E-6 Malacca
146 D-7 Malacca strt.
146 E-8 Malacca
168 A-4 Malad City
54 F-5 Maladrerie (La)
54 E-5 Maladrerie (La)

60 C-7 Malaga (Spain)
172 E-7 Malaga (USA)
100 C-6 Malagarasi riv.
198 E-4 Malagueño
146 A-5 Malaka strt.
94 E-2 Malakāl
140 D-9 Malakanagiri
127 L-6 Malākand
55 J-6 Malakoff
211 K-4 Malala
63 L-6 Malalbergo
208 D-3 Malamala
149 H-8 Malambunga
63 N-3 Malamocco
100 E-5 Malampaka
138 D-4 Malān pte
207 M-7 Malang
98 G-9 Malange
142 E-2 Malangwa
102 E-1 Malanje reg.
98 G-9 Malanje reg.
198 D-4 Malanzán
51 M-1 Malaren lake
198 B-7 Malargüe
129 M-1 Mālari
164 C-6 Malartic
160 C-3 Malaspina glac.
200 G-5 Malaspina
54 F-9 Malassis
207 M-3 Malatajur cap.
65 M-6 Malatya
139 L-2 Malaut
141 H-5 Malavalli
73 H-8 Malavi
149 K-8 Malawali isl.
77 F-6 Malawi state
93 L-6 Malawiya
116 F-6 Malay pen.
146 F-5 Malay pen.
215 L-7 Malay rf
136 A-9 Malaya Kuril'skaja Gr'ada islds
149 J-2 Maybalay
73 J-7 Malāyer
118 F-6 Malaysia state
72 D-4 Malazgirt
67 H-9 Mal.Beloz'orka
214 E-9 Malbon
218 A-7 Malbooma
49 F-6 Malbork
192 B-1 Malborough
198 F-3 Malbrán
57 J-4 Malburgen
191 N-4 Malcanió mt
63 J-2 Malcesine
123 M-7 Malchanskij mt
224 D-4 Malden (l.)
57 J-5 Malden (R.F.A.)
176 E-1 Malden (USA)
118 C-6 Maldives state
141 P-2 Maldives islds
53 M-4 Maldon
199 K-7 Maldonado
200 E-1 Maldonado mt
199 K-6 Maldonado reg.
178 F-8 Maldonado pte
118 C-6 Malé
141 P-1 Malé isl.
141 P-1 Male isl.
141 P-2 Male isl.
51 M-9 Malé Karpaty mt
64 E-8 Maleas cap.
64 D-9 Maleas cap.
140 B-4 Mālegaon
126 B-7 Malek Siāh mt
98 D-5 Maléké
106 F-6 Malema
211 P-3 Malendok isl.
68 D-6 Malen'ga
139 M-2 Māler Kotlā
59 L-9 Malesco
123 M-6 Maletā
63 H-1 Malga Boazzo lake
72 D-1 Malgobek
92 D-7 Malha
60 A-6 Malhão mt
166 F-5 Malheur lake
166 E-6 Malheur riv.
77 B-3 Mali state
144 E-8 Mali isl.
143 M-3 Mali riv.
87 H-5 Mali
132 B-8 Malianhe riv.
92 G-5 Malik riv.
126 D-8 Malik Nāro mt
208 D-2 Malili
100 B-8 Malimba mt
66 H-7 Malin
149 M-9 Malinau
149 J-3 Malindang mt
101 K-5 Malindi
206 G-6 Malingping
149 P-8 Malino mt
109 K-3 Malio riv.
211 P-4 Maliom
134 C-9 Malizhen

95 K-6 Malka Guba
140 B-5 Malkāpur
64 F-5 Malkara
221 K-5 Mallacoota lake
221 J-5 Mallacoota
50 C-1 Mallaig
81 N-4 Mallawi
58 F-2 Malleray
196 E-8 Mallet
60 G-6 Mallorca isl.
46 D-6 Mallorca isl.
50 A-4 Mallow
211 N-5 Malmal
104 D-8 Malmesbury (South Africa)
52 E-5 Malmesbury (UK)
51 K-4 Malmö
51 K-4 Malmohüs reg.
69 K-8 Malmyž
62 D-2 Malnate
63 K-2 Malo
199 K-5 Malo (Uruguay) riv.
192 E-4 Malobbi
192 D-6 Maloca
187 M-7 Maloca Macu
119 N-6 Maloelap isl.
66 G-3 Malojaroslavec
69 N-8 Malojaz
123 K-5 Maloje Goloustnoje
123 L-5 Maloje-More bay
69 J-2 Malokožvinskaja Vozv.
136 A-9 Malokuril'skoje
148 D-5 Malolos
106 F-4 Malombe lake
164 E-8 Malone
103 H-1 Malonga
66 B-6 Malorita
141 N-1 Malosmadulu isl.
68 D-6 Malošyjka
227 M-1 Malouines (Sandwich du Sud) islds
49 H-1 Måløy
68 F-1 Malozeml'skaja Tundra pl.
188 D-1 Malpelo pte
140 F-4 Malprabha riv.
139 L-6 Mālpura
76 D-1 Malta isl.
61 N-9 Malta
61 N-9 Malta
47 E-6 Malta state
195 M-3 Malta (Brazil)
168 D-1 Malta (USA)
104 C-2 Maltahöhe
59 K-3 Malters
54 B-9 Maltorne riv.
204 C-2 Maluceas islds
90 C-2 Malumfashi
49 J-4 Malung
126 B-6 Malüsän mt
149 K-5 Maluso
94 E-2 Malüt
105 J-6 Maluti mt
67 N-4 Mal.Uzen riv.
59 N-7 Malvaglia
140 E-2 Mālvan
52 D-2 Malvern hill
176 D-3 Malvern
172 C-6 Malvern
219 H-3 Malvern Hills
52 D-2 Malvern Link
52 D-2 Malvern Wells
201 M-8 Malvinas islds
182 M-8 Malvinas islds
66 E-1 Mal.Višera
139 L-7 Malwā Pathār reg.
125 K-7 Malyj Chingan mt
121 M-2 Malyje Cany lake
123 N-1 Mama
123 N-2 Mama riv.
69 L-9 Mamadyš
149 L-1 Mamahan
123 N-2 Mamakan riv.
123 N-1 Mamakan
195 P-3 Mamanguape
179 L-6 Mamantel
173 H-2 Mamaroneck
194 F-9 Mambaí
211 K-7 Mambare riv.
100 B-1 Mambasa
210 D-2 Mamberamo riv.
91 H-7 Mambéré riv.
106 C-8 Mambi riv.
90 E-6 Mambila mt
98 F-2 Mambili riv.
87 H-7 Mambiri
52 D-1 Mamble
101 K-5 Mambrui
148 E-6 Mamburao
57 N-9 Mamelis
50 D-8 Mamers
90 D-7 Mamfé
192 E-8 Mamiá riv.
58 A-2 Mamirolle
66 A-4 Mamonovo
121 N-4 Mamontovo

190 F-5 Mamoré riv.
192 B-9 Mamori riv.
190 A-3 Mamoriá riv.
87 K-5 Mamou
108 C-4 Mamoudzou
108 F-6 Mampikony
99 J-2 Mampoko
66 A-5 Mamry lake
82 C-3 Mamshit site
208 B-2 Mamuaju
102 F-9 Mamuno
192 D-9 Mamuru riv.
124 F-3 Mamyn riv.
140 D-4 Mān riv.
87 M-8 Man
50 C-3 Man isl.
143 J-8 Man-aung strt.
143 M-5 Mān Panglao
192 F-3 Mana riv.
97 K-1 Mana (Ethiopia) riv.
192 F-3 Mana (Guyane)
122 F-3 Mana (SSSR) riv.
129 M-1 Māna-Barāhoti
188 B-1 Manabi reg.
187 K-8 Manacape lake
192 A-9 Manacapuru
60 A-9 Manacor
149 N-2 Manado
157 F-5 Managua
184 F-5 Managua lake
184 F-5 Managua reg.
184 F-5 Managua
172 G-7 Manahawkin
223 H-5 Manaia
108 F-7 Manakalampona mt
109 L-5 Manakara
96 E-2 Manākhah
211 J-3 Manam isl.
118 A-4 Manama
83 N-4 Manama
108 G-3 Manambaho riv.
109 H-3 Manambolo riv.
109 M-4 Manambondro
109 M-3 Manambovo riv.
187 N-3 Manamito isl.
108 F-7 Manana riv.
132 E-2 Manan Gegeen Süme
109 K-4 Mananantanana riv.
108 F-7 Mananara
108 F-7 Mananara riv.
214 C-5 Manangoora
109 K-5 Mananjary
87 K-9 Manankoro
109 M-4 Manantenina
141 J-4 Manantoddy
148 C-6 Manaoag
187 K-6 Manapiarre riv.
187 K-4 Manapire riv.
222 C-8 Manapouri
141 L-5 Manappād pte
192 A-9 Manaquiri lake
108 F-5 Manaratsandry
71 P-2 Manas strt.
120 E-9 Manas mt
143 H-2 Manās riv.
129 M-2 Manasarowar lake
129 M-1 Manashankou mt
128 D-7 Manasi
128 C-7 Manasihe riv.
128 C-8 Manasihu lake
129 P-4 Manāslu mt
172 G-5 Manasquan riv.
172 G-5 Manasquan
172 C-5 Manatawny
181 K-1 Manati
208 G-7 Manatuto
186 F-1 Manaure
192 B-9 Manaus
186 G-7 Manaveni riv.
65 J-8 Manavgat
187 L-8 Manaviche riv.
209 L-3 Manawoka riv.
149 H-3 Manbajao
91 H-7 Manbéré reg.
65 M-7 Manbij
132 A-3 Manbogd
213 P-2 Manbulloo
160 B-3 Manby pte
50 B-7 Manchela
132 E-6 Mancheng
140 D-7 Mancherāl
50 D-4 Manchester (UK)
171 M-5 Manchester (USA)
170 B-6 Manchester (USA)
164 F-9 Manchester (USA)
176 G-2 Manchester (USA)
177 J-1 Manchester (USA)
138 E-4 Manchhar lake
113 L-5 Manchuria pl.
124 E-9 Manchurian pl.
133 H-1 Manchurian pl.
188 E-1 Mancora
142 C-5 Mānd riv.
83 P-2 Mand riv.
106 C-4 Manda
91 P-5 Manda mt

109 J-3 Mandabe
197 M-1 Mandacaru
196 E-6 Mandaguari
132 B-2 Mandah
51 H-2 Mandal
130 E-9 Mandal-Ovoo
210 F-4 Mandala mt
143 L-6 Mandalay
139 K-6 Mandalgarh
132 A-1 Mandalgovi
72 G-8 Mandali
51 H-1 Mandalselva
168 G-1 Mandan
148 F-4 Mandaon
208 C-3 Mandar bay
90 F-3 Mandara mt
61 K-6 Mandas
138 K-7 Mandasor
131 H-3 Mandata
126 D-4 Mandel
62 E-1 Mandello di Lario
180 F-7 Mandelville
139 N-2 Mandi
146 F-6 Mandi Angin mt
127 L-8 Mandi Bahāuddīn
139 K-2 Mandi Burewāla
87 K-8 Mandiana
106 G-3 Mandié
106 F-5 Mandimba
185 L-8 Mandinga
209 H-1 Mandioli isl.
196 A-2 Mandioré riv.
196 F-8 Mandirituba
191 K-6 Mandiyuti mt
140 A-9 Mandla
212 G-6 Mandora
109 H-4 Mandoto
91 J-8 Mandoukou
89 K-6 Mandouri
109 M-3 Mandrare riv.
55 L-8 Mandres-les-Roses
63 M-9 Mandrioli pass
108 F-7 Mandritsara
140 A-5 Māndu
143 N-6 Mandun
216 E-8 Mandurah
196 F-6 Manduri
64 A-6 Manduria
138 F-7 Māndvi
141 H-5 Mandya
142 B-4 Manendragarh
90 D-7 Manengouba mt
140 D-7 Māner riv.
63 H-2 Manerba della Garda
62 G-3 Manerbio
66 C-7 Manevići
81 N-4 Manfalūt
61 P-5 Manfredonia
189 N-7 Manga riv.
99 J-5 Manga
224 D-6 Mangaia isl.
223 K-5 Mangakino
99 M-2 Mangakia
143 J-3 Mangaldai
64 G-3 Mangkacha
91 K-2 Mangalmé
220 G-4 Mangalore (Australia)
141 H-3 Mangalore (India)
223 K-2 Manganui
197 K-6 Mangaratiba
142 B-3 Mangawān
129 L-4 Mange
142 G-1 Mangen
207 J-3 Manggar
143 L-4 Mangin Yoma mt
70 C-8 Mangistau mt
71 H-7 Mangit
149 P-7 Mangkalihat pte
208 C-8 Mangkudu isl.
208 A-7 Mangkun cap.
127 L-8 Mangla
188 A-2 Manglares cap.
109 K-3 Mangoky riv.
208 G-2 Mangole isl.
109 H-6 Mangoro riv.
140 A-1 Māngrol
178 D-6 Mangrove pte
180 F-3 Mangrove Cay rf
91 M-3 Mangueigne
199 M-5 Mangueira (Uruguay) lag.
196 E-8 Mangueirinha
80 B-8 Mangueni plat.
194 D-6 Mangues riv.
103 N-6 Mangula Mine
175 M-2 Mangum
193 M-8 Mangunça isl.
100 B-2 Manguredjipa
107 H-1 Mangwendi
70 D-8 Mangyšlak plat.
70 C-7 Mangyšlakskij bay
129 N-9 Mangzha
194 F-7 Manhā
197 L-4 Manhacu riv.
130 B-3 Manhan
129 K-4 Manhanmuchi lake

173 H-3 Manhattan isl.
169 H-8 Manhattan
172 A-5 Manheim
107 N-2 Manhica
197 L-4 Manhuacu
197 L-4 Manhumirim
186 F-6 Maní
191 K-2 Mani (Chile) riv.
87 M-7 Mani (Liberia) riv.
109 J-4 Mania riv.
109 H-6 Maniakandriana
106 E-4 Maniamba
140 A-9 Maniari lake
142 B-5 Maniāri lake
90 D-5 Manica reg.
107 J-2 Manica
103 P-7 Manicaland reg.
107 J-2 Manicaland plat.
164 G-4 Manicouagan riv.
164 F-3 Manicouagan lake
164 F-4 Manicouagan
219 M-2 Manifold cap.
131 N-5 Manigange
163 P-9 Manigotagan
224 C-5 Manihiki isl.
99 P-9 Manika plat.
127 H-8 Manikhawa
168 B-6 Manila
119 H-5 Manila
148 D-6 Manila
219 L-8 Manilla
109 K-3 Manja
107 N-2 Manjacaze
73 J-5 Manjil
216 E-9 Manjimup
140 C-5 Manjlegaon
140 D-5 Mānjra riv.
142 G-3 Mankacha
120 C-1 Mankanaj
170 A-5 Mankato (USA)
169 H-8 Mankato (USA)
127 J-9 Mankera
89 M-1 Mankono
141 L-7 Mankulam
140 B-4 Manmād
214 A-3 Mann riv.
206 E-4 Manna
87 M-4 Manna pte
220 D-1 Mannahill
129 M-1 Mannan
141 L-7 Mannar
141 L-6 Mannar gulf
141 K-7 Mannārgudi
59 M-2 Mannedorf
140 G-7 Manneru riv.
51 H-8 Mannheim
59 J-3 Männlichen
58 G-6 Männlifluh mt
220 D-3 Mannum
87 M-5 Mano riv.
87 M-5 Mano
190 B-4 Manoa
55 P-2 Manoeuvre
209 N-1 Manokwari
125 K-4 Manoma riv.
109 L-2 Manombo
108 F-4 Manombo riv.
100 E-5 Manonga riv.
100 A-8 Manono
173 L-3 Manorville
164 F-4 Manouane isl.
164 E-4 Manouane lake
91 L-5 Manovo riv.

133 L-3 Manpo
128 A-7 Manrak mt
60 G-4 Manresa
172 E-9 Manricetown
50 D-8 Mans (Le)
103 M-1 Mansa
139 M-3 Mānsa
200 D-1 Mansa bay
86 G-2 Mansa Konko
127 L-7 Mānsehra
153 L-3 Mansel isl.
155 K-3 Mansel isl.
156 G-1 Mansel isl.
188 E-3 Manseriche dam.
50 D-5 Mansfield (UK)
170 G-7 Mansfield (USA)
176 C-4 Mansfield (USA)
143 L-4 Mansi
194 A-9 Manso ou das Mortes riv.
87 H-2 Mansoa
52 D-7 Manston
63 N-1 Mansuè
188 B-1 Manta bay
188 C-1 Manta (Ecuador)
184 G-3 Manta (Honduras)
149 H-8 Mantalingajan
100 E-4 Mantare
189 K-5 Mantaro riv.
187 H-4 Mantecal
129 L-8 Mantekamuhu lake
197 M-3 Mantena
197 M-3 Mantenopolis
177 N-1 Manteo
149 N-3 Manterawu isl.
54 B-4 Mantes-la-Jolie
54 C-4 Mantes-la-Ville
197 K-5 Mantiqueira mt
172 G-6 Mantoloking
49 H-7 Mänttä
172 D-7 Mantua
63 J-4 Mantua reg.
63 J-4 Mantua
219 J-3 Mantuan Downs
69 H-8 Manturovo
211 H-1 Manu isl.
189 K-8 Manú riv.
189 K-9 Manu
211 K-7 Manu Manu
224 C-5 Manua islds
224 D-5 Manuae isl.
164 F-4 Manuanis riv.
161 J-2 Manuel lake
178 G-3 Manuel
194 E-4 Manuel Alves riv.
190 D-6 Manuel Correia riv.
194 A-2 Manuel Jorge riv.
196 E-7 Manuel Ribas
190 B-1 Manuel Urbano
175 J-6 Manuel Venavides
199 K-3 Manuel Viapa
208 F-3 Manui riv.
84 A-6 Manüjän
209 K-4 Manuk isl.
223 J-4 Manukan
209 N-1 Manundi cap.
223 K-4 Manurewa
190 D-2 Manuripi riv.
172 F-4 Manville
176 C-5 Many
219 M-3 Many Peaks
100 G-5 Manyara lake
100 G-5 Manyara na.p.
163 H-8 Manyberries
67 L-8 Manyč-Gudilo lake
100 F-7 Manyoni
122 G-1 Man'z'a
127 J-8 Manzai
185 L-7 Manzanilla pte
187 H-1 Manzanillo pte
180 F-6 Manzanillo (Cuba)
178 C-5 Manzanillo (Mexico)
73 K-6 Manzariyeh
124 B-6 Manzhouli
126 C-8 Manzil
105 L-4 Manzini
125 K-8 Manzovka
123 K-5 Manzurka
91 H-1 Mao
125 K-3 M'ao Can mt
124 C-6 Maoershan
210 E-4 Maoke mt
204 D-2 Maoke isl.
138 K-7 Maoli
131 K-8 Maomaoshan mt
145 N-1 Maoming
130 G-6 Maoxian
88 G-9 Maouri val.
131 N-8 Maowen
124 F-9 Maoxing
208 C-1 Mapaga
107 L-1 Mapai
192 F-6 Mapari riv.
94 D-4 Maper

210 E-6 Mapi
210 E-5 Mapi riv.
175 J-8 Mapimí
175 J-8 Mapimí holl.
107 L-3 Mapinhane
187 L-4 Mapire
192 E-6 Mapireme
190 F-2 Mapiri
190 C-3 Mapiri riv.
186 G-8 Mapiripán riv.
186 F-8 Mapiripán lake
169 H-2 Maple riv.
163 J-8 Maple Creek
172 E-6 Maple Shade
172 D-1 Maplewood
214 F-3 Mapoon
210 G-3 Maprik
192 C-7 Mapuera riv.
187 M-8 Mapuiau riv.
107 N-1 Mapulanguene
105 M-5 Maputo riv.
77 F-7 Maputo
107 P-1 Maputo (Lourenço Marques)
86 A-7 Maqteïr mt
129 N-3 Maquanhe riv.
98 F-7 Maquela do Zombo
200 D-4 Maquinchao
170 C-6 Maquoketa
198 F-3 Mar Chiquita lake
199 J-9 Mar Chiquita lag.
199 J-8 Mar de Ajó
199 J-9 Mar del Plata
60 E-7 Mar Menor
179 J-8 Mar Muerto lag.
100 F-4 Mara reg.
100 F-3 Mara riv.
161 N-5 Mara riv.
192 C-2 Mara (Guyana)
143 K-1 Mara (India)
194 D-2 Marabá
196 E-5 Maraba Paulista
207 N-3 Marabahan
207 P-4 Marabatua isl.
187 K-9 Marabitanas
193 H-5 Maracá
192 G-7 Maracá riv.
193 H-5 Maracá isl.
193 L-8 Maracaçumé riv.
156 G-5 Maracaibo lake
186 G-3 Maracaibo lake
186 G-2 Maracaibo
196 C-5 Maracaju
196 C-4 Maracajú mt
193 K-7 Maracanã
192 F-7 Maracanaquará plat.
195 K-8 Maracás
187 J-2 Maracay
58 D-6 Maracon
192 F-8 Maracu lake
80 F-4 Marādah
90 B-1 Maradi reg.
90 B-1 Maradi
72 G-5 Maragheh
195 P-5 Maragogi
195 L-1 Maragojipe
83 K-6 Marāh
89 N-1 Marahoué na.p.
89 N-1 Marahoué riv.
187 L-7 Marahuaca mt
163 H-9 Marais riv.
193 H-7 Marajo isl.
193 K-7 Marajo bay
72 F-4 Marākand
124 D-8 Marakaton
101 H-1 Maralal
217 P-5 Maralinga
149 J-2 Maramag
103 K-6 Maramba (Livingstone)
108 F-4 Marambitsy bay
142 B-6 Maramsilli lake
146 F-7 Maran
126 F-9 Mārān mt
213 P-2 Maranboy
72 F-4 Marand
63 J-6 Maranello
127 P-9 Marang mt
195 L-1 Maranguape
194 F-2 Maranhão reg.
194 D-9 Maranhão riv.
63 K-2 Marano Vicentino
219 J-4 Maranoa riv.
188 E-3 Marañon riv.
92 A-7 Maraoné mt
198 D-2 Marapa riv.
193 K-7 Marapanim
206 C-1 Marapi mt
192 D-6 Marapi riv.
206 G-2 Maras mt
65 M-6 Maras (Kahramanmaras)
208 B-4 Marasende isl.
192 D-3 Maratakka riv.
214 G-9 Marathon (Australia)
170 E-1 Marathon (Canada)

175 J-5 Marathon (USA)
149 N-7 Maratua isl.
199 M-2 Marau
195 L-9 Maraú
73 M-2 Marâveh Tappeh
187 J-8 Maravicani riv.
149 J-3 Marawi (Philippines)
92 G-4 Marawī (Sudan)
198 C-4 Marayes
59 H-4 Marbach
212 F-7 Marble Bar
105 K-3 Marble Hall
51 H-7 Marburg
189 J-4 Marca
189 L-9 Marcapata
63 H-4 Marcaria
196 E-9 Marcelino Ramos
58 A-6 Marchairuz pass
58 A-1 Marchaux
61 M-4 Marche reg.
54 A-6 Marchefroy
55 N-3 Marchémoret
60 B-7 Marchena
184 B-8 Marchena isl.
54 A-7 Marchezais
198 A-7 Marchihüe
214 C-2 Marchinbar isl.
55 P-3 Marcilly
63 J-1 Marco
190 C-9 Marcolino riv.
63 M-2 Marcon
197 H-1 Marcos riv.
198 F-5 Marcos Juárez
55 H-9 Marcoussis
54 D-6 Marcq
159 H-9 Marcus Baker mt
172 D-7 Marcus Hook
164 E-9 Marcy mt
127 L-7 Mardan
53 M-6 Marden
65 P-6 Mardin
215 P-5 Maré rf.
195 N-6 Marechal Deodoro
215 J-6 Mareeba
97 N-6 Mãreg
55 J-2 Mareil-en-France
54 D-7 Mareil-le-Guyon
54 F-5 Mareil-Marly
54 D-5 Mareil-sur-Mauldre
56 G-5 Maren
86 G-6 Maréna
62 A-6 Marene
170 B-6 Marengo (USA)
60 F-1 Marennes
53 L-7 Maresfield
213 J-2 Maret islds
79 N-4 Mareth
55 P-5 Mareuil-lès-Meaux
175 J-5 Marfa
52 A-5 Margam
67 H-8 Marganec
74 F-3 Margao
213 K-5 Margaret riv.
213 L-5 Margaret River
187 L-2 Margarita isl.
196 A-9 Margarita
105 K-7 Margate (South Africa)
50 E-6 Margate (UK)
172 F-8 Margate City
55 H-3 Margency
143 L-2 Mārgherita
126 A-3 Marghūb mt
54 F-1 Margicourt
127 M-2 Margitan
149 J-4 Margosatubig
126 D-7 Mārgow dés
57 N-9 Margraten
57 H-6 Mariaheide
161 K-7 Marian lake
119 K-5 Mariana foss
117 K-5 Mariana islds
117 K-5 Mariana foss
180 C-4 Marianao
177 H-5 Marianna (USA)
176 E-2 Marianna (USA)
62 E-2 Mariano Comense
199 J-3 Mariano I. Loza
199 M-3 Mariante
185 K-9 Mariato pte
96 D-3 Ma'rib
51 K-4 Maribo
61 P-2 Maribor
64 E-4 Marica riv.
105 J-2 Marico riv.

191 P-2 Maricunga lake
94 C-6 Marīdī
94 C-5 Marīdī riv.
227 M-5 Marie Byrd Land reg.
181 N-3 Marie-Galante
49 K-6 Mariehamn
211 H-3 Marienberg
104 C-2 Mariental
51 L-1 Mariestad
187 K-6 Marieta riv.
170 G-3 Marietta (USA)
177 H-3 Marietta (USA)
90 B-3 Mariga rīv.
58 B-9 Marignier
181 J-7 Marigot (Haiti)
181 N-3 Marigot (Martinique)
181 M-1 Marigot (Saint-Martin)
122 D-2 Mariinsk
125 L-2 Mariinskoje
196 F-5 Marilia
98 G-8 Marimba
108 G-7 Marimbona riv.
62 G-8 Marina di Carrara
62 G-8 Marina di Massa
63 M-6 Marina di Ravenna
148 E-5 Marinduque isl.
54 E-1 Marines
170 D-4 Marinette
99 K-2 Maringa riv.
196 E-6 Maringá
107 H-3 Maringue
177 L-3 Marion lake
215 N-8 Marion rf
221 H-9 Marion bay
176 F-1 Marion (USA)
176 G-4 Marion (USA)
177 K-2 Marion (USA)
177 L-3 Marion (USA)
170 G-7 Marion (USA)
170 E-7 Marion (USA)
218 E-2 Marion Downs
187 L-4 Maripa
192 E-4 Maripasoula
167 J-3 Mariposa
186 D-6 Mariquita
149 P-5 Marisa
191 L-8 Mariscal Estigarribia
170 E-3 Maristique lake
195 N-5 Marituba riv.
123 K-6 Marituj
187 P-3 Mariusa isl.
148 E-6 Mariveles
69 J-9 Mariyskaya ASSR reg.
66 B-1 Märjamaa
82 C-1 Marjayoun
59 J-7 Marjelen S.
66 D-5 Marjina Gorka
52 C-6 Mark
101 P-1 Marka
88 G-1 Markabougou
121 P-7 Markakol' lake
89 H-1 Markala
127 H-5 Mārkandeh site
51 K-3 Markaryd
57 M-2 Markelo
121 P-1 Markelovo
176 D-5 Markesville
53 H-1 Market Harborough
52 E-6 Market Lavington
211 J-5 Markham riv.
167 H-3 Markleeville
91 J-5 Markounda
123 L-2 Markovo
88 G-6 Markoye
53 M-3 Mark's Tey
127 M-5 Marksa mt
172 E-2 Marksboro
52 D-6 Marksbury
53 J-3 Markvate Street
172 G-5 Marlboro
214 B-5 Maria isl.
222 G-7 Marlborough reg.
219 L-2 Marlborough (Australia)
52 F-5 Marlborough (UK)
175 N-4 Marlin
171 H-9 Marlinton
53 H-5 Marlow
172 E-6 Marlton
58 E-5 Marly
55 K-2 Marly-la-Ville
54 F-6 Marly-le-Roi
140 F-3 Marmagao
60 F-2 Marmande
64 G-5 Marmara islds
64 G-5 Marmara sea
64 G-5 Marmaris
170 B-1 Marmion lake
63 J-4 Marmirolo
158 E-9 Marmot bay
158 F-9 Marmot isl.
85 J-7 Marmul
55 M-5 Marne riv.
55 L-6 Marne riv.
54 G-6 Marnes-la-Coquette

72 E-2 Marneuli
90 A-1 Marnona
59 P-9 Marnotto mt
91 K-5 Maro
187 J-8 Maroa
108 F-8 Maroantsetra
108 E-8 Marojezy riv.
127 N-7 Marol
109 J-6 Marolambo
54 A-7 Marolles
55 L-7 Marolles-sur-Brie
108 E-6 Maromandia
108 E-7 Maromokotro mt
108 E-6 Maromony pte
103 N-7 Marondera
62 G-2 Marone
63 L-2 Marostica
90 G-3 Maroua
192 F-5 Marouini riv.
108 F-5 Marovoay
192 E-3 Marowijne (Maroni) riv.
65 P-7 Marqādah
105 J-5 Marquard
224 F-4 Marquesas islds
177 K-9 Marquesas Keys islds
170 D-3 Marquette
92 C-8 Marra mt
218 G-8 Marra
63 L-8 Marradi
96 D-1 Marrāk isl.
78 C-4 Marrakech
220 F-7 Marrawah
195 K-5 Marrecas mt
107 J-4 Marromeu
106 E-6 Marrupa
165 H-7 Mars Hill
82 C-7 Marsá al Alam
81 H-1 Marsá Süsah
95 K-8 Marsabit
95 K-8 Marsabit na.p.
61 M-8 Marsala
55 N-6 Marsange riv.
61 J-4 Marseille
48 F-4 Marsfjället mt
176 D-6 Marsh isl.
52 B-8 Marsh
160 E-5 Marsh lake
180 F-1 Marsh Harbour
168 A-9 Marsh Pass
218 C-2 Marshall riv.
170 F-6 Marshall
119 M-5 Marshall islds
117 M-6 Marshall islds
87 N-6 Marshall (Liberia)
176 D-2 Marshall (USA)
176 C-4 Marshall (USA)
169 J-4 Marshall (USA)
158 F-4 Marshall (USA)
211 P-7 Marshall Bennett islds
172 E-2 Marshalls Creek
172 C-6 Marshallton
170 A-6 Marshalltown
52 C-1 Marshbrook
52 D-5 Marshfield (UK)
176 B-9 Marshfield (USA)
170 C-4 Marshfield (USA)
73 L-7 Mārshinān mt
52 C-3 Marstow
142 D-1 Marsyandi riv.
144 D-5 Martaban gulf
144 E-5 Martaban
90 F-6 Martap
207 N-3 Martapura (Indonesia)
206 F-4 Martapura (Indonesia)
90 G-2 Marte
63 M-2 Martellago
121 N-1 Martemjanovskij
164 C-4 Marten riv.
164 B-7 Marten River
171 N-6 Martha's Vineyard isl.
61 K-2 Martigny
61 J-4 Martigues
177 H-4 Martin lake
153 H-4 Martin isl.
168 F-5 Martin
159 P-6 Martin pte
52 E-2 Martin Hussingtree
223 H-7 Martinborough
62 F-2 Martinengo
179 H-5 Martinez de la Torre
197 J-4 Martinho Campos
181 P-4 Martinique isl.
196 E-5 Martinópolis
172 D-3 Martins
172 D-3 Martins Creek
52 D-9 Martinstown
177 L-1 Martinsville
52 D-2 Martley
52 C-7 Martock
223 J-6 Marton (Nouvelle Zélande)
52 G-1 Marton (UK)
60 C-7 Martos

48 E-8 Martti
70 C-2 Martuk
72 E-3 Martuni
209 L-5 Maru isl.
187 J-8 Maruā
108 F-8 Marūb bay
82 E-9 Mar'ūb bay
147 P-6 Marudi
126 G-7 Ma'ruf
126 F-7 Ma'ruf riv.
137 K-6 Marugame
210 G-3 Marui
195 M-6 Maruim
102 F-6 Marunga
100 B-8 Marungu mt
224 F-6 Marutea isl.
224 E-5 Marutea isl.
73 M-9 Marv Dasht
73 N-8 Marvast
216 G-6 Marvel Loch
139 K-6 Mārwār
67 M-3 Marx
161 P-9 Mary lake
126 F-1 Mary
161 P-8 Mary Frances lake
214 E-9 Mary Kathleen
219 N-4 Maryborough
104 F-6 Marydale
172 C-9 Marydel
171 K-6 Maryland state
157 G-3 Maryland state
87 P-8 Maryland (Liberia) reg.
172 A-7 Maryland Line
166 G-5 Marys riv.
165 N-4 Marystown
167 K-7 Marysvale
165 H-7 Marysville (Canada)
170 F-7 Marysville (USA)
169 H-8 Marysville (USA)
167 H-2 Marysville (USA)
177 J-2 Maryville
63 K-7 Marzabotto
186 B-5 Marzo cap.
62 A-2 Marzo mt
80 C-6 Marzūq
211 P-3 Masahet isl.
100 G-6 Masai pl.
101 G-4 Masai Amboseli rés
100 F-3 Masai Mara rés
100 D-2 Masaka
100 D-3 Masaka reg.
207 N-5 Masalembo-Besar isl.
208 A-4 Masalima islds
72 G-3 Masally
133 N-7 Masan
100 B-7 Masanga
106 C-7 Masasi
191 J-6 Masavi
184 G-5 Masaya
148 F-4 Masbate
148 F-4 Masbate isl.
79 H-2 Mascara
109 N-8 Mascarene islds
76 G-8 Mascarene islds
59 J-1 Maschwanden
178 C-4 Mascota
197 N-1 Mascote
209 K-6 Masela isl.
63 M-1 Maser
59 N-9 Masera
63 L-3 Masera di Padova
63 M-2 Maserada sul Piave
164 D-6 Masères lake
105 J-6 Maseru
77 E-7 Maseru
103 J-6 Masese
103 N-8 Mashaba
82 D-7 Mashābih isl.
126 D-1 Mashal
99 L-6 Mashala
127 K-4 Mashhad riv.
138 D-3 Mashkai riv.
126 C-9 Māshke lake
138 C-2 Māshkel riv.
126 C-8 Mashki Chāh
138 B-2 Māshkīd riv.
103 N-6 Mashonaland reg.
94 C-3 Mashra'ar Raqq
127 H-7 Mashūray
48 C-3 Masi
99 H-6 Masi-Manimba
109 M-5 Masianaka lake
133 L-5 Masigryeong-sanmaeg mt
136 B-6 Masike
69 P-9 Masim mt
100 D-1 Masindi
100 D-1 Masindi-Port
84 G-9 Masirah gulf
189 H-6 Masisea
100 B-3 Masisi
137 J-6 Masita riv.
73 K-8 Masjed Soleymān
65 N-7 Maskanah
121 P-3 Masl'anino

61 P-3 Maslenica
96 E-6 Maşna'ah
108 F-8 Masoala cap.
108 F-8 Masoala isl.
108 F-7 Masokamena mt
109 J-6 Masomeloka
175 M-5 Mason
170 A-5 Mason City
62 D-6 Masone
187 H-4 Masparro riv.
84 D-7 Masqaţ reg.
62 G-7 Massa reg.
62 G-8 Massa
78 B-5 Massa riv.
63 M-5 Massa Fiscaglia
63 L-7 Massa Lombarda
171 M-5 Massachusetts state
171 L-5 Massachusetts bay
157 G-3 Massachusetts state
63 H-9 Massaciuccoli lake
91 H-2 Massaguet
91 J-2 Massalassef
107 L-2 Massangena
195 K-1 Massapê
59 M-7 Massari mt
97 N-4 Massarole well
63 H-9 Massarosa
93 N-5 Massawa strt.
164 D-8 Massena
91 H-3 Massénya
62 B-2 Masserano
104 F-1 Massering
162 A-1 Masset
162 A-1 Masset Sound strt.
172 C-8 Massey
201 J-2 Massier strt.
46 D-5 Massif central mt
61 H-2 Massif Central mt
181 H-7 Massif de la Hotte mt
181 K-7 Massif de la Selle mt
89 J-1 Massigui
170 G-7 Massillon
88 G-3 Massina reg.
107 M-4 Massinga
107 M-1 Massingir
58 D-8 Massongex
55 H-8 Massy
93 M-2 Mastābah
73 H-2 Maštaga
223 H-7 Masterton
56 A-6 Mastgat strt.
173 L-3 Mastic Beach
127 L-5 Mastūj riv.
126 F-9 Mastung
82 F-8 Mastūrah
137 K-3 Masuda
206 D-3 Masurai mt
107 K-1 Masvingo
65 M-8 Masyaf
145 J-3 Mat riv.
195 M-8 Mata de S. João
103 L-8 Matabeleland reg.
191 J-5 Mátaca mt
164 B-7 Matachewan
187 L-7 Matacuni riv.
124 A-8 Matad
98 E-6 Matadi
175 L-2 Matador
184 G-4 Matagalpa
184 G-4 Matagalpa reg.
175 N-6 Matagorda
175 N-6 Matagorda bay
224 E-5 Mataiva isl.
128 B-4 Mataj
125 K-6 Mataj riv.
147 H-7 Matak isl.
223 K-4 Matakana isl.
223 L-5 Matakana pte
102 C-4 Matala
141 M-7 Matale
86 F-4 Matam
223 K-5 Matamata
90 C-1 Matamèye
172 F-1 Matamoras
178 D-1 Matamoros
208 D-2 Matana lake
149 K-4 Matanal pte
198 A-5 Matancillas
101 J-9 Matandu riv.
164 G-5 Matane
159 H-9 Matanuska riv.
159 H-9 Matanuska Susitna
198 A-6 Matanzas (Chile)
180 C-4 Matanzas (Cuba)
194 C-5 Matão mt
185 H-8 Matapalo cap.
64 D-9 Matapan cap.
198 A-7 Mataquito riv.
93 N-6 Matara site
141 N-7 Matara
207 P-7 Mataram
208 A-7 Matarani
189 N-8 Matarani
214 A-5 Mataranka
208 E-3 Matarape bay
60 G-5 Mataro

195 L-2 Matas *mt*
187 H-2 Matatero *mt*
105 J-7 Matatiele
222 C-9 Mataura
172 G-4 Matawan
103 H-5 Matebale *pl.*
190 E-6 Mategua
178 E-2 Matehuala
106 K-9 Matemo *isl.*
61 P-6 Matera
66 B-9 Mátészalka
103 K-6 Matetsi
103 K-6 Matetsi *riv.*
79 N-2 Mateur
164 B-6 Matheson
62 A-3 Mathi
193 N-9 Mathias Olimpio
215 L-3 Mathieu *rf*
175 M-7 Mathis
220 G-3 Mathoura
139 N-5 Mathura
149 K-2 Mati
179 J-7 Matias Romero
91 N-7 Matibika
197 M-5 Matilde
193 M-9 Matinha
197 L-4 Matipo *riv.*
109 L-5 Matitanana *riv.*
187 H-4 Matiyure *riv.*
142 F-6 Mātlā *lag.*
138 F-5 Matli
79 N-4 Matmata
187 L-5 Mato *riv.*
187 L-5 Mato *mt*
182 E-4 Mato Grosso *plat.*
190 F-8 Mato Grosso
194 A-8 Mato Grosso *reg.*
194 A-9 Mato Grosso *plat.*
206 B-3 Matobe
143 K-8 Maton *riv.*
103 L-8 Matopo *hill*
103 L-8 Matopos *na.p.*
103 L-8 Matopos
190 F-4 Matos *riv.*
196 E-8 Matos Costa
60 A-4 Matosinhos
66 A-9 Matra *mt*
84 D-8 Maţraḥ
58 E-5 Matran
104 D-8 Matroosberg *mt*
125 N-3 Matrosovo
87 M-5 Matru
81 L-2 Maţrūḥ
109 K-4 Matsiatra *riv.*
135 N-6 Matsu Shan *isl.*
137 L-4 Matsuyama
59 P-3 Matt
164 C-5 Mattagami *lake*
164 A-5 Mattagami *riv.*
164 C-5 Mattagami
63 J-1 Mattarello
164 C-8 Mattawa
165 H-7 Mattawamkeag
62 A-1 Matterhorn (Cervino) *mt*
61 K-2 Matterhorn (Switzerland) *mt*
166 G-7 Matterhorn (USA) *mt*
181 H-5 Matthew Town
170 F-1 Mattice
173 L-2 Mattituck
170 D-8 Mattoon
59 P-2 Mattstock *mt*
207 K-3 Matua
189 K-5 Matucana
137 J-3 Matue
82 B-7 Matūlī *riv.*
136 D-6 Matumae
136 D-6 Matumae *pen.*
137 H-6 Matumoto
91 N-8 Matundu
137 L-4 Matuno
173 P-1 Matunuck
187 M-3 Maturin
208 F-7 Maturu
187 P-7 Maturuca
149 K-2 Matutum *vol.*
137 L-2 Matuura
137 J-6 Matuzaka
67 K-8 Matvejev-Kurgan
100 G-3 Mau *mt*
142 B-2 Mau
139 N-7 Mau Rānipur
148 E-5 Mauban
208 G-7 Maubara
50 F-7 Maubeuge
54 G-3 Maubuisson *site*
216 B-1 Maud *pte*
220 G-2 Maude
54 C-2 Maudétour-en-Vexin
59 J-2 Mauensee
192 C-9 Maues
119 K-5 Maug *isl.*
142 B-3 Mauganj
224 D-1 Maui *isl.*
224 D-6 Mauke *isl.*

54 D-6 Mauldre *riv.*
200 A-2 Maule
200 A-2 Maule *reg.*
54 D-5 Maule
200 A-3 Maule (del) *lake*
54 B-7 Maulette
200 E-2 Maullín
54 A-3 Maulu
143 H-4 Maulvi Bāzār
170 F-7 Maumee *riv.*
208 E-7 Maumere
103 H-8 Maun
224 D-2 Maunakea *mt*
143 J-7 Maungdaw
161 K-3 Maunoir *lake*
220 B-3 Maupertuis *bay*
224 D-5 Maupihaa *isl.*
59 M-1 Maur
64 C-7 Maura *isl.*
54 F-4 Maurecourt
55 L-3 Mauregard
54 E-7 Maurepas
191 H-2 Mauri *riv.*
60 G-2 Mauriac
217 N-5 Maurice *lake*
172 E-8 Maurice *riv.*
56 G-4 Maurik
77 A-3 Mauritania *state*
195 L-4 Mauriti
109 P-9 Mauritius *isl.*
76 G-8 Mauritius *isl.*
77 G-8 Mauritius *state*
170 C-5 Mauston
149 P-5 Mautong
210 F-5 Mava (Nouvelle Guinée)
94 B-7 Mava (Zaïre)
187 L-8 Mavaca *riv.*
102 F-5 Mavinga
107 J-2 Mavita
101 J-9 Mavuji *riv.*
106 G-3 Mavuzi *riv.*
146 C-1 Maw Daung
208 E-4 Mawasangka
143 M-8 Mawchi
143 M-7 Mawkmai
143 K-5 Mawlaik
82 G-5 Mawqaq
96 D-2 Mawr *riv.*
96 F-2 Mawshij
227 N-3 Mawson
91 K-9 Mawuya
107 L-2 Maxaila
179 M-5 Maxcanú
107 M-3 Maxixe
214 G-9 Maxwellton
180 F-7 May Pen
184 E-1 Maya *mt*
181 J-4 Mayaguana *isl.*
181 H-4 Mayaguana *strt.*
181 N-6 Mayagüez
180 E-4 Mayajigua
98 F-5 Mayama
73 M-3 Mayámey
179 M-5 Mayapan *site*
180 G-5 Mayari *mt*
180 G-5 Mayari
220 F-4 Mayborough
96 G-5 Mayd
96 G-5 Mayd *isl.*
220 G-9 Maydena
96 D-1 Maydī
50 D-8 Mayenne
50 D-8 Mayenne *riv.*
96 E-5 Mayfa'ah
53 L-7 Mayfield (UK)
176 F-1 Mayfield (USA)
53 J-6 Mayford
131 L-9 Mayingzhen
72 B-1 Maykop
143 L-6 Maymyo
218 F-2 Mayne *riv.*
201 L-3 Mayo *mt*
160 F-3 Mayo
160 F-3 Mayo *lake*
200 G-3 Mayo (Argentina) *riv.*
188 A-4 Mayo (Ecuador) *riv.*
90 E-6 Mayo Darlé
90 F-5 Mayo Déo *riv.*
90 G-5 Mayo-Djarendi
90 G-4 Mayo Kebbi *reg.*
90 G-4 Mayo Kebbi *riv.*
98 E-4 Mayoko
98 E-5 Mayombe *reg.*
148 E-4 Mayon *vol.*
174 B-2 Mayor
223 K-4 Mayor *isl.*
200 C-7 Mayor Buratovich
191 J-8 Mayor Pablo Lagerenza
188 D-8 Mayoruna *riv.*
108 C-4 Mayotte *isl.*
148 B-6 Mayraira *pte*
172 F-8 Mays Landing
170 F-9 Maysville
172 A-6 Maytown

143 J-6 Mayu *riv.*
98 C-5 Mayumba
129 N-3 Mayumushankou
141 J-7 Māyūram
93 J-8 Mayyah
82 C-5 Mayyah *bay*
200 A-7 Maza
103 L-5 Mazabuka
78 C-3 Mazagan (El-Jadida)
192 G-7 Mazagão
162 D-7 Mazama
60 G-2 Mazamet
188 D-7 Mazán
188 D-6 Mazán *riv.*
73 L-3 Mazanderan *reg.*
127 H-3 Mazar-i-Charif
61 M-8 Mazara
201 H-6 Mazarredo *bay*
201 H-6 Mazarredo
60 E-7 Mazarron *gulf*
187 P-5 Mazaruni *riv.*
174 E-5 Mazatán
179 L-9 Mazatenango
178 B-2 Mazatlán
66 B-3 Mažeinai
82 C-4 Mazḩafah *mt*
73 N-3 Mazīnān
66 A-2 Mazirbe
190 G-1 Mazocruz
106 G-2 Mazoe *riv.*
130 F-4 Mazongshan *mt*
130 G-5 Mazongshan *riv.*
122 E-2 Mazul'skij
103 M-9 Mazunga
105 L-4 Mbabane
77 F-7 Mbabane
86 F-2 Mbacké
91 L-8 Mbada
91 H-8 Mbaéré ou Ghali *riv.*
89 M-2 Mbahiakro
91 J-8 Mbaiki
90 F-6 Mbakaou *dam.*
100 D-9 Mbala
100 F-1 Mbale
90 E-8 Mbalmayo
90 E-6 Mbam *riv.*
106 D-4 Mbamba Bay
210 D-3 Mbambawa
99 H-2 Mbandaka (Coquilhatville)
90 D-8 Mbanga
98 C-5 Mbanio *lake*
98 F-7 Mbanza-Congo
98 F-6 Mbanza-Ngungu
99 H-6 Mbao
86 F-2 Mbar
106 C-6 Mbarangandu *riv.*
100 C-3 Mbarara
106 C-1 Mbawala *isl.*
90 F-5 Mbé
89 K-1 Mbengué
90 G-6 Mbéré *riv.*
100 E-8 Mbeya *reg.*
100 E-9 Mbeya
91 J-7 Mbi *riv.*
98 D-4 Mbigou
98 E-4 Mbinda
98 B-1 Mbini
98 C-1 Mbini *riv.*
107 K-1 Mbizi
91 K-5 Mbo
94 A-6 Mboki
91 N-7 Mbomou *riv.*
91 N-7 Mbomou *reg.*
86 F-2 Mboro
90 D-7 Mbouda
86 F-1 Mbour
86 E-5 Mbout
91 L-6 Mbrès
99 M-7 Mbuji-Mayi
100 E-2 Mbulamuti
91 P-8 Mbuma
196 A-9 Mburucuyá
106 C-7 Mbwemburu *riv.*
165 H-7 Mc Adam
172 B-3 Mc Adoo
175 M-8 Mc Allen
214 C-6 Mc Arthur *riv.*
166 E-7 Mc Call
175 K-4 Mc Camey
160 C-2 Mc Carthy
162 B-1 Mc Cauley *isl.*
153 H-2 Mc Clintock *strt.*
213 L-5 Mc Clintock *mt*
159 P-5 Mc Clure *isl.*
168 G-2 Mc Clusky
176 E-5 Mc Comb
171 J-7 Mc Connellsburg
168 F-7 Mc Cook
177 K-3 Mc Cormick
163 N-9 Mc Creary
160 E-7 Mc Dame
166 G-5 Mc Dermitt
162 F-9 Mc Donald *mt*
218 B-1 Mc Donald Downs
161 K-4 Mc Donnel *cap.*

220 E-5 Mc Donnell
220 C-3 Mc Donnell *mt*
163 L-2 Mc Farlane *riv.*
176 D-3 Mc Gehee
165 H-6 Mc Givney
159 H-6 Mc Grath
218 F-5 Mc Gregor *mt*
166 E-7 Mc Guire *mt*
214 G-4 Mc Ilwraith *mt*
168 F-3 Mc Intosh
163 J-3 Mc Kay
161 N-7 Mc Kay *lake*
224 B-4 Mc Kean *isl.*
214 F-9 Mc Kinlay
214 F-9 Mc Kinlay *riv.*
153 R-1 Mc Kinley *sea*
159 J-8 Mc Kinley *mt*
159 J-7 Mc Kinley *na.p.*
159 K-8 Mc Kinley Park
167 L-2 Mc Kittrick
170 D-9 Mc Leansboro
153 H-6 Mc Lear *strt.*
216 C-1 Mc Leod *lake*
161 M-8 Mc Leod *bay*
166 E-3 Mc Loughlin *mt*
175 J-3 Mc Millan *lake*
177 H-2 Mc Minnville (USA)
162 A-9 Mc Minnville (USA)
227 N-6 Mc Murdo
163 J-3 Mc Murray
174 F-1 Mc Nary
219 N-6 Mc Pherson *mt*
160 D-5 Mc Rae (Canada)
177 A-4 Mc Rae (USA)
227 N-2 Mc Robertson Coast
161 L-4 Mc Tavish *strt.*
161 K-5 Mc Vicar *strt.*
66 G-4 Mcensk
106 E-3 Mchinji
124 E-7 Mdidawaqi
215 M-4 Mé Maoya *mt*
167 L-6 Mead *lake*
167 L-6 Mead *na.p.*
168 F-9 Meade
160 D-6 Meade *glac.*
159 M-3 Meade *riv.*
163 K-5 Meadow Lake *na.p.*
167 K-6 Meadow Valley Wash *riv.*
171 H-6 Meadville
219 L-5 Meandarra
163 H-1 Meander River
194 G-2 Mearim *riv.*
50 F-8 Meaux
207 P-7 Mebulu *cap.*
106 F-5 Mecanhelas
188 A-4 Mecaya *riv.*
93 M-1 Mecca
82 G-9 Mecca
106 F-6 Mecequesse *riv.*
172 B-6 Mechanics Grove
95 L-3 Mechara
50 G-7 Mechelen
57 N-9 Mechelen
57 M-8 Mechelen aan de Maas
78 G-4 Mecheria
79 N-6 Mechiquig
65 K-4 Mecitözü
172 C-2 Meckersville
51 K-5 Mecklenburger *bay*
106 G-8 Meconta
64 B-2 Mecsek
106 F-8 Mecuburi *riv.*
106 F-7 Mecuburi
106 E-8 Mecufi
106 D-6 Mecula
106 G-2 Mecumbura
213 J-4 Meda *riv.*
140 D-6 Medak
54 E-4 Medan (France)
146 C-7 Medan (Sumatra)
200 B-7 Médanos
201 J-6 Medanosa *pte*
141 L-7 Medawachchiya
57 N-3 Medde
62 D-4 Mede
79 J-2 Medea
168 D-5 Medecine Bow
168 G-9 Medecine Lodge
197 N-2 Medeiros Neto
59 M-6 Medel *val.*
59 N-6 Medel *mt*
186 D-5 Medellín
79 P-5 Médenine
86 D-3 Méderdra
62 G-5 Medesano
65 K-7 Medetsiz *mt*
176 A-1 Medford (USA)
170 C-4 Medford (USA)
166 E-3 Medford (USA)
64 F-2 Medgidia
94 D-6 Medi
172 D-6 Media
198 C-5 Media Agua
198 D-7 Media Luna
180 C-9 Média Luna *rf*

64 D-1 Mediaş
63 L-6 Medicina
168 C-6 Medicine Bow *mt*
163 H-8 Medicine Hat
197 M-1 Medina
199 J-2 Medina *lag.*
82 F-7 Medina
216 E-7 Medina (Australia)
60 C-4 Medina de Ríoseco
60 C-4 Medina del Campo
87 H-4 Médina Gonasse
86 G-2 Médina Saback
60 E-4 Medinaceli
211 M-8 Medino
188 C-7 Mediodiá
78 C-3 Mediouna
46 D-6 Mediterranean *sea*
94 B-8 Medje
96 G-7 Medjourtine *mt*
70 C-1 Mednogorsk
63 H-3 Médole
168 F-2 Medora
98 C-2 Médouneu
79 H-3 Medrissa
63 N-1 Meduna *riv.*
66 G-1 Medvedica *riv.*
69 K-8 Medvedok
68 C-7 Medvezh'yegorsk
113 Q-2 Medvežje *isl.*
69 J-2 Medvežskaja
53 L-6 Medway *riv.*
55 P-8 Mée (Le)
216 D-3 Meeberrie
216 F-3 Meekatharra
168 C-7 Meeker
56 D-8 Meer
56 A-9 Meerdonk
56 E-4 Meerkerk
56 D-8 Meerle
57 K-7 Meerlo
57 M-9 Meerssen
139 N-4 Meerut
57 M-8 Meeswijk
56 F-6 Meeuwen
206 C-4 Mega *isl.*
209 L-1 Mega (Célèbes)
95 K-6 Mega (Ethiopia)
95 L-4 Megalo
64 D-8 Megalópolis
65 K-1 Meganom *cap.*
164 F-8 Mégantic
164 F-8 Mégantic *mt*
64 D-7 Megara
106 C-8 Megaruma *riv.*
142 E-6 Megasini *mt*
57 L-5 Megchelen
57 H-5 Megen
123 K-5 Meget
58 B-9 Mégevette
95 K-2 Megezez *mt*
59 L-3 Meggen
143 H-3 Meghalaya *reg.*
143 H-5 Meghna *riv.*
68 C-8 Megrega
72 F-4 Megri
138 F-3 Mehar
78 D-2 Mehdiya
142 C-1 Mehndāwal
84 B-4 Mehran *riv.*
73 H-8 Mehrān
139 H-7 Mehsāna
100 G-7 Meia Meia
196 G-2 Meia Ponte *riv.*
135 K-3 Meichuan
128 E-2 Meidanshan *mt*
59 H-9 Meiden
59 L-5 Meien *val.*
57 J-9 Meijel
143 L-7 Meiktila
59 M-1 Meilen
58 C-7 Meillerie
62 C-2 Meina
51 J-7 Meiningen
58 F-2 Meinisberg
194 G-8 Meio *riv.*
131 P-8 Meishan
51 K-7 Meissen
59 K-1 Meisterschwanden
134 E-5 Meitan
135 K-8 Meixian
112 C-3 Mejducharskij *isl.*
191 M-1 Mejillones del Sur *bay*
191 M-1 Mejillones *pen.*
191 M-1 Mejillones

127 H-9 Mekhtar
90 F-6 Mekié *riv.*
78 D-3 Meknès
131 M-3 Mekong (Lancangjiang)
145 J-4 Mékong (Mae Nam Khong) *riv.*
208 D-3 Mekongga *mt*
158 E-3 Mekoryok
89 K-7 Mekrou *riv.*
67 K-3 Mekša *riv.*
97 H-8 Meladen
149 L-9 Melalap
106 F-8 Melamo *cap.*
204 F-2 Melanesia *reg.*
207 M-1 Melawi *riv.*
62 C-6 Melazzo
53 K-2 Melbourn
220 G-5 Melbourne
70 C-1 Melbourne (USA)
177 L-7 Melbourne (USA)
48 D-4 Melbu
52 E-7 Melbury Abbas
59 K-4 Melch *val.*
59 H-2 Melchnau
200 G-2 Melchior *isl.*
175 K-7 Melchor Múzquiz
59 K-4 Melchthal
63 M-8 Meldola
91 M-4 Mélé
62 B-8 Mele *cap.*
62 E-3 Melegnano
106 G-6 Melela *riv.*
67 J-2 Melenki
70 B-1 Meleuz
59 M-9 Melezzo *riv.*
91 J-3 Melfi
163 L-7 Melfort
193 H-8 Melgaco
79 L-4 Melghir *holl.*
87 L-6 Meli *riv.*
57 N-6 Melick
62 D-1 Melide
78 F-2 Melilla
200 F-2 Melimoyo *mt*
200 F-2 Melincal
198 G-6 Melincué
207 P-1 Melintang *lake*
198 A-6 Melipilla
56 A-5 Melissant
168 G-1 Melita
67 H-9 Melitopol'
172 B-9 Melitota
52 E-6 Melksham
62 G-3 Mella *riv.*
49 H-5 Mellansel
79 L-2 Mellegue *riv.*
51 K-1 Mellerud
92 D-7 Mellit
201 J-3 Mellizo Sur *mt*
105 L-6 Melmoth
122 B-1 Mel'nikovo
196 A-5 Melo *riv.*
198 F-6 Melo (Argentina)
199 L-5 Melo (Uruguay)
208 D-8 Melolo
59 L-7 Melora *mt*
159 K-6 Melozitna *riv.*
217 H-4 Melrose (Australia)
221 H-1 Melrose (Australia)
175 J-2 Melrose (USA)
107 J-2 Melsetter
48 E-7 Meltaus
48 E-7 Meltosjärvi
147 M-8 Meluan
106 G-7 Meluli *riv.*
50 E-8 Melun
55 L-9 Melun-Sénart
141 K-6 Melūr
153 M-2 Melville *bay*
153 H-2 Melville *strt.*
153 M-8 Melville *isl.*
155 K-3 Melville *pen.*
214 C-3 Melville *bay*
215 H-4 Melville *cap.*
161 L-2 Melville *hill*
161 P-4 Melville *strt.*
163 M-8 Melville (Canada)
173 J-3 Melville (USA)
62 E-3 Melzo
106 F-8 Memba
106 F-8 Memba *bay*
208 C-7 Memboro
66 A-3 Memel (Klaipéda)
61 L-1 Memmingen
145 K-9 Mémot
147 K-9 Mempawah
176 E-2 Memphis
81 N-3 Memphis *site*
136 B-7 Memuro
95 L-5 Mena *riv.*
66 F-6 Mena (SSSR)
176 C-2 Mena (USA)
62 E-1 Menaggio
88 G-8 Ménaka
109 K-3 Menamaty *riv.*
54 F-3 Menandon

109 L-4 Menarahaka *riv.*
109 M-2 Menarandra *riv.*
175 L-5 Menard
63 M-6 Menate
108 G-5 Menavava *riv.*
92 C-8 Menawashei
200 D-4 Mencué
207 H-3 Mendanau *isl.*
197 K-3 Mendanha
147 J-9 Mendarik *isl.*
62 A-8 Mendatica
207 M-2 Mendawai *riv.*
61 H-3 Mende
95 K-4 Mendebo *mt*
122 E-1 Mendel *riv.*
176 E-4 Mendenhall
158 D-3 Mendenhall *cap.*
64 H-7 Menderes *riv.*
197 M-3 Mendes Pimentel
188 D-3 Mendez
172 F-3 Mendham
94 G-2 Mendi (Ethiopia)
211 H-5 Mendi (Nouvelle Guinée)
52 C-6 Mendip *hill*
166 F-1 Mendocino *cap.*
146 F-9 Mendol *isl.*
196 F-5 Mendonça
129 N-5 Mendongsi
221 K-1 Mendooran
170 C-7 Mendota (USA)
167 K-2 Mendota (USA)
198 C-5 Mendoza
200 A-3 Mendoza *reg.*
198 C-5 Mendoza (Argentina) *riv.*
199 K-6 Mendoza (Uruguay)
62 D-1 Mendrisio
186 G-2 Mene de Mauroa
186 G-3 Mene Grande
62 F-6 Menegosa *mt*
64 F-7 Menemen
200 E-3 Menéndez *lake*
124 B-8 Menengiyn Tal *mt*
54 B-4 Ménerville
90 F-6 Meng *riv.*
149 K-9 Mengalum *isl.*
143 P-6 Mengban
135 K-1 Mengcheng
72 E-5 Mengene *mt*
206 F-4 Menggala
143 P-6 Menghai
143 N-5 Menglang
143 N-6 Menglian
100 E-2 Mengo (East) *reg.*
100 D-2 Mengo (West) *reg.*
90 E-9 Mengong
132 G-8 Mengshan *mt*
132 G-8 Mengyin
134 B-9 Mengzi
164 F-1 Menihek
164 G-1 Menihek Lakes *lake*
55 H-9 Ménil (Le)
54 A-4 Ménil-Guyon
220 F-1 Menindee
220 F-1 Menindee *lake*
220 D-3 Meningie
149 P-9 Menjapa *mt*
124 E-6 Menluhe *riv.*
87 N-8 Méno *riv.*
58 B-9 Ménoge *riv.*
170 D-4 Menominee
170 B-4 Menomomie
102 E-4 Menongue
46 D-6 Menorca *isl.*
61 H-6 Menorca *isl.*
54 G-1 Ménouville
129 M-2 Menshi
149 K-9 Mentanani *isl.*
160 D-1 Mentasta *mt*
206 A-2 Mentawai (Kepulauan) *islds*
206 B-2 Mentawai (Selat) *strt.*
206 F-2 Mentok
61 K-3 Menton
175 J-4 Mentone
54 E-3 Menucourt
211 J-6 Menyamya
131 J-7 Menyuan
123 M-7 Menza *riv.*
59 J-3 Menzberg
79 N-2 Menzel-Bourguiba
79 P-2 Menzel Temime
69 L-8 Menzelinsk
216 G-5 Menzies
59 K-2 Menziken
59 L-2 Menzingen
59 J-3 Menznau
59 M-8 Menzonio
63 N-2 Méolo
52 G-8 Meon *riv.*
53 L-6 Meopham
175 H-6 Meoqui
98 E-7 Mepozo *riv.*
50 G-5 Meppel
107 H-4 Mepuse *riv*
190 D-7 Mequens *riv.*
142 C-5 Mer Dongar *hill*
211 P-4 Merai
206 G-5 Merak
49 H-3 Meraker
217 P-4 Meramangye *lake*
170 B-9 Meramec *riv.*
206 D-2 Merangin *riv.*
54 A-8 Mérangle
61 M-2 Merano
149 L-9 Merapak
165 N-4 Merasheen *isl.*
62 E-2 Merate
207 P-3 Meratus *rge*
210 F-6 Merauke *riv.*
210 E-7 Merauke
207 K-6 Merbabu *mt*
220 F-2 Merbein
141 H-4 Mercāra
63 M-8 Mercato Saraceno
167 J-2 Merced
198 B-5 Mercedario *mt*
198 E-6 Mercedes (Argentina)
199 H-6 Mercedes (Argentina)
199 J-5 Mercedes (Uruguay)
175 M-8 Mercedes (USA)
198 A-2 Merceditas
171 H-7 Mercer
172 F-5 Mercer *reg.*
190 B-2 Merces
190 C-2 Mercier
191 L-4 Merco *mt*
162 F-5 Mercoal
223 K-4 Mercury *bay*
223 K-4 Mercury (îles d'Haussey) *islds*
54 D-7 Méré
52 D-7 Mere
93 M-6 Mèreb *riv.*
201 L-7 Meredith *cap.*
175 L-1 Meredith *lake*
67 H-7 Merefa
146 C-7 Merek
53 L-6 Mereworth
70 A-4 Mergenevo
59 N-9 Mergoscia
62 C-1 Mergozzo
116 E-5 Mergui *islds*
146 C-1 Mergui
90 G-3 Méri
220 E-2 Meribah
54 B-3 Méricourt
186 G-3 Merida *reg.*
186 G-3 Merida *rge*
60 B-6 Mérida (Spain)
179 M-4 Mérida (Mexico)
186 G-3 Merida (Vénézuela)
52 F-1 Meriden (UK)
171 M-6 Meriden (USA)
176 F-4 Meridian
54 G-2 Mériel
60 F-2 Mérignac
220 E-2 Meringur
201 J-2 Merino Jarpa *isl.*
192 F-6 Meripatari *dam.*
120 F-9 Merke
57 N-8 Merkelbeek
56 B-9 Merksem
56 D-9 Merksplas
63 K-4 Merlara
59 H-5 Merligen
212 F-5 Mermaid *rf*
93 J-5 Méroé *site*
93 H-6 Meroe *reg.*
79 L-3 Merouana
79 L-4 Merouane *holl.*
216 F-7 Merredin
170 C-4 Merrill
104 F-7 Merriman
162 D-6 Merritt
221 K-1 Merriwa
53 J-6 Merrow
78 G-2 Mers-el-Kebir
93 N-6 Mersa Fatma
53 N-4 Mersea *isl.*
57 J-7 Merselo
65 L-7 Mersin
166 G-8 Mersing
66 B-2 Mersrags
139 K-5 Merta
139 K-5 Merta-Road
50 C-5 Merthyr
52 B-4 Merthyr Tydfil
101 J-1 Merti
60 A-6 Mértola
70 D-6 Mertvyy Kultuk *lake*
175 L-4 Mertzon
101 H-5 Meru *mt*
101 J-2 Meru *rés*
101 H-2 Meru
187 P-5 Merume *mt*
126 F-1 Merv *site*
58 G-1 Mervelier
162 B-9 Mervin *lake*
56 E-4 Merwede *cal.*
54 G-2 Méry-sur-Oise
65 K-4 Merzifon
174 E-1 Mesa
158 F-7 Mesa *mt*
188 A-8 Mesa de Yambi *plat.*
188 B-7 Mesai *riv.*
188 A-7 Mesas de Iguaje *plat.*
72 C-4 Mescit *mt*
67 H-2 Meščora
93 M-7 Mesfinto
73 P-2 Meshed
139 J-8 Meshva *riv.*
79 M-3 Meskiana
54 C-8 Mesle (Le)
95 L-5 Meslo
54 C-3 Mesnil (Château)
55 L-3 Mesnil-Amelot (Le)
55 J-3 Mesnil-Aubry (Le)
55 H-1 Mesnil-en-Thelle (Le)
55 G-4 Mesnil-le-Roi (Le)
54 B-2 Mesnil-Milon (Le)
54 E-7 Mesnil-Saint-Denis (Le)
55 H-1 Mesnil-Saint-Martin (Le)
54 E-8 Mesnil-Sevin
54 A-5 Mesnil-Simon (Le)
54 D-7 Mesnuls (Les)
59 P-7 Mesocco
63 M-5 Mésola
59 P-8 Mesolcina *val.*
64 C-7 Mesolongion
79 K-4 Messaad
80 B-7 Messak Mellet *mt*
106 D-8 Messalo *riv.*
90 F-8 Méssaména
54 G-1 Messelan
220 D-3 Messent *na.p.*
73 L-2 Messerian *site*
58 A-8 Messery
105 L-1 Messina
61 P-8 Messina
61 N-8 Messina *strt.*
64 D-8 Messini *site*
64 D-8 Messini *gulf*
55 M-4 Messy
64 D-5 Mesta *riv.*
63 M-3 Mestre
63 L-3 Mestrino
206 F-4 Mesudji *riv.*
87 N-6 Mesurado *cap.*
144 G-3 Met *riv.*
186 F-7 Meta *reg.*
187 J-5 Meta *riv.*
176 E-6 Metairie
51 K-7 Métallifères *mt*
103 N-4 Métamboa *riv.*
191 N-5 Metán
106 E-4 Metangula
184 D-3 Metapán
63 P-9 Metauro *riv.*
95 L-3 Metehara
196 D-7 Metelândia
93 L-8 Metema
178 F-5 Metepec
56 F-5 Meteren
56 F-6 Meterij *reg.*
57 K-8 Meterik
222 E-8 Methven
163 K-4 Methy *lake*
163 K-4 Methy *riv.*
186 E-7 Metica *riv.*
160 C-9 Metlakatla
79 K-5 Metlili Chaamba
129 K-3 Metmahu *lake*
64 C-6 Metsovan
53 P-1 Metthingham
59 J-3 Mettlen
59 L-2 Mettmenstetten
141 J-5 Mettuppālaiyam
141 J-5 Mettūr
95 H-3 Metu
172 G-4 Metuchen
50 G-8 Metz
54 G-6 Meudon
146 A-6 Meulaboh
54 E-3 Meulan
146 A-6 Meureudu
50 G-6 Meuse *riv.*
175 N-4 Mexia
193 H-7 Mexiana *isl.*
174 B-2 Mexicali
156 D-4 Mexican *plat.*
168 A-9 Mexican Water
178 F-5 Mexico *reg.*
157 E-5 Mexico *state*
157 D-4 Mexico *state*
178 F-5 Mexico (Mexico)
170 B-8 Mexico (USA)
157 D-4 Mexico City
157 E-5 Mexico City
176 E-8 Mexique *gulf*
179 L-1 Mexique *gulf*
73 M-7 Meybod
73 P-9 Meydan-e Gel
126 G-7 Meydān Kalay
105 J-4 Meyerton
126 G-3 Meymaneh
126 G-3 Meymaneh *riv.*
73 K-7 Meymeh
57 P-6 Meynweg *na.p.*
163 K-9 Meyronne
143 L-5 Meza *riv.*
82 C-2 Mezad *site*
178 F-6 Mezcala
122 C-3 Meždurečenskij
68 E-3 Mezen'
68 E-3 Mezenskaya *gulf*
160 D-9 Meziadin *lake*
54 A-6 Méziard (Le)
58 C-6 Mézières
54 A-1 Mézières-en-Vexin
54 D-4 Mézières-sur-Seine
66 A-9 Mezokövesd
64 C-1 Mezotur
122 F-2 Mežovo
178 C-2 Mezquital
54 D-3 Mézy-sur-Seine
62 E-7 Mezzanego
63 M-7 Mezzano
63 M-5 Mezzogoro
100 F-3 Mfwanganu *isl.*
125 M-2 Mgači
66 F-5 Mglin
78 D-6 Mhamid
140 D-4 Mhāsvād
57 M-9 Mheer
140 A-5 Mhow
137 K-2 Mi *isl.*
79 J-7 Mia *riv.*
179 H-8 Miahuatlán de Porfirio Díaz
139 H-5 Miājlar
91 L-4 Miaméré
170 F-8 Miami *riv.*
177 L-9 Miami (USA)
175 L-1 Miami (USA)
176 C-1 Miami (USA)
174 E-2 Miami (USA)
177 L-9 Miami Beach
139 K-2 Miān Channūn
73 N-2 Miānābād
72 G-5 Miāndow Ab
109 H-4 Miandrivazo
124 D-7 Mianduhe
72 G-5 Miāneh
149 L-1 Miangas *isl.*
138 F-8 Miāni
134 A-6 Mianmianshan *mt*
134 B-5 Mianning
138 G-4 Miāno
127 K-8 Miānwāli
134 D-2 Mianxian
135 H-3 Mianyang
131 P-8 Mianzhu
133 H-6 Miaodaoqundao *isl.*
135 N-7 Miaoli
134 E-6 Miaoling *mt*
109 H-5 Miarinarivo
69 P-7 Miass
51 M-5 Miastko
134 E-2 Micangshan *mt*
67 H-3 Michajlov
121 M-4 Michajlovskij
216 E-7 Michea
123 K-2 Michejevo
162 C-3 Michel *mt*
52 G-7 Micheldever
159 P-7 Michelson *mt*
181 L-6 Miches
157 F-2 Michigan *state*
156 F-2 Michigan *lake*
170 E-4 Michigan *lake*
170 D-3 Michigan *state*
170 E-6 Michigan City
170 E-2 Michipicoten *isl.*
170 E-2 Michipicoten
178 D-6 Michoacán *reg.*
67 J-4 Michurinsk
53 K-6 Mickelham
52 F-2 Mickelton
185 H-5 Mico *riv.*
98 C-1 Micomeseng
119 K-5 Micronésia *islds*
117 L-6 Micronesia *reg.*
64 F-4 Mičurin
105 L-7 Mid Illovo
53 H-8 Mid Lavant
147 J-7 Midai *isl.*
78 F-2 Midar
57 K-1 Middel
57 J-6 Middelaar
56 F-8 Middelbeers
105 K-3 Middelburg (South Africa)
104 G-7 Middelburg (South Africa)
56 A-5 Middelharnis
56 E-4 Middelkoop
177 J-1 Middelsboro
56 B-6 Middelsluis
105 J-3 Middelwit
201 P-6 Middle *isl.*
166 F-4 Middle Alkali *lake*
181 J-4 Middle Caicos *isl.*
173 K-3 Middle Island
168 G-6 Middle Loup *riv.*
163 J-3 Middle Rapids *riv.*
165 N-3 Middle Ridge *lake*
172 A-8 Middle River
162 D-2 Middle River Village
172 E-3 Middle Valley
164 E-9 Middlebury
222 D-8 Middlemarch
52 D-8 Middlemarsh (UK)
172 B-3 Middleport
50 E-3 Middlesbrough
184 E-1 Middlesex (Honduras)
172 F-4 Middlesex (USA)
160 A-2 Middleton *isl.*
218 F-1 Middleton
165 J-7 Middleton (Canada)
52 G-3 Middleton Stoney
171 M-6 Middletown (USA)
170 F-8 Middletown (USA)
171 L-6 Middletown (USA)
78 E-4 Midelt
53 H-7 Midhurst
164 B-9 Midland (Canada)
175 K-4 Midland (USA)
170 F-5 Midland (USA)
216 E-7 Midland JN
172 G-2 Midland Park
103 M-7 Midlands (Zimbabwe) *reg.*
142 E-5 Midnapore
109 M-4 Midongy du Sud
149 J-3 Midsayap
159 P-5 Midway *islds*
168 D-4 Midwest
175 N-1 Midwest City
65 P-6 Midyat
64 D-3 Midžur *mt*
98 F-1 Miélé (Congo)
91 K-2 Miélé (Chad)
66 B-7 Mielec
220 G-8 Miena
175 L-8 Mier
64 E-1 Miercurea-Ciuc
60 C-3 Mieres
57 H-8 Mierlo
131 K-2 Miesaituo
95 L-2 Miesso
58 B-9 Mieussy
172 B-2 Mifflinville
101 J-7 Migasi *riv.*
63 M-5 Migliarino
62 F-5 Mignano *lake*
58 A-5 Mignovillard-Petit-Villard
179 H-6 Miguel Alemán *dam.*
195 J-1 Miguel Alves
178 D-2 Miguel Auza
195 K-7 Miguel Calmon
174 F-7 Miguel Hidalgo *dam.*
200 A-7 Miguel Riglos
137 K-4 Mihara
70 C-4 Mijaly
56 D-2 Mijdrecht
97 H-8 Mijirten *reg.*
56 C-5 Mijnsheerenland
136 B-6 Mikasa
64 D-3 Mikhaylovgrad
106 C-8 Mikindani
143 J-3 Mikir *mt*
49 J-8 Mikkeli
49 H-9 Mikkeli *reg.*
163 J-2 Mikkwa *riv.*
109 K-2 Mikoboka *mt*
98 C-2 Mikongo *mt*
64 F-8 Míkonos *site*
68 E-2 Mikulkin *cap.*
51 M-9 Mikulov
101 H-8 Mikumi *rés*
101 H-8 Mikumi
69 H-5 Mikun'
137 J-8 Mikura *isl.*
126 D-5 Mīl Kūh *mt*
79 L-2 Mila
170 A-3 Milaca
141 N-2 Miladummadulu *isl.*
195 L-4 Milagres
188 C-2 Milagro
129 M-1 Milam
62 E-3 Milan
61 L-2 Milan
128 G-8 Milan
176 F-2 Milan (USA)
220 D-3 Milang
62 E-3 Milano *reg.*
64 G-7 Milâs
169 J-4 Milbank
52 D-8 Milborne Saint Andrew
53 M-1 Mildenhall
220 F-2 Mildura
134 B-8 Mile
219 L-5 Miles
160 B-2 Miles *glac.*
168 D-2 Miles City
64 G-7 Miletus *site*
216 E-3 Mileura
53 J-6 Milford (UK)
167 K-7 Milford (USA)
171 L-6 Milford (USA)
171 L-8 Milford (USA)
50 C-5 Milford Haven
222 C-7 Milford Sound
214 F-7 Milgarra
216 E-2 Milgun
81 K-1 Milh *pte*
72 E-7 Milhat Ashqar *riv.*
72 F-8 Milhath Tharthār *lake*
57 J-7 Milheeze
119 N-6 Mili *isl.*
79 J-2 Miliana
163 H-9 Milk *riv.*
162 G-9 Milk *riv.*
57 J-6 Mill
166 D-4 Mill City
215 J-7 Millaa Millaa
191 J-4 Millares
61 H-3 Millau
170 C-1 Mille lacs *lake*
177 J-4 Milledgeville
54 C-6 Millemont
57 N-7 Millen
177 K-4 Millen (USA)
169 H-4 Miller
160 C-3 Miller (Canada) *mt*
174 E-3 Miller (USA) *mt*
67 K-7 Millerovo
218 B-7 Millers Creek
170 G-7 Millersburg
172 A-6 Millersville
165 M-3 Millerton Junction
165 M-3 Millertown
54 A-5 Millerus (Les)
62 B-7 Millesimo
172 A-3 Millgrove
220 D-5 Millicent
216 E-6 Milling
57 K-4 Millingen an de Rijn
176 E-2 Millington
164 G-7 Millinocket
219 L-6 Millmerran
161 J-7 Mills *lake*
161 J-8 Mills Lake
57 J-6 Millsbeek
172 F-5 Millstone *riv.*
172 F-4 Millstone
212 D-8 Millstream
172 F-4 Milltown
214 F-8 Millungera
172 E-8 Millville
171 L-7 Millville
216 E-3 Milly Milly
172 E-8 Milmay
211 M-8 Milne *bay*
172 B-2 Milnesville
164 G-8 Milo
87 K-7 Milo *riv.*
54 F-8 Milon-la-Chapelle
64 E-8 Milos *site*
67 H-3 Miloslayskoje
218 F-7 Milparinka
176 G-5 Milton
53 J-2 Milton Ernest
53 H-3 Milton Keynes
52 B-7 Milverton
172 A-2 Milville
170 D-5 Milwaukee
133 N-7 Milyang
211 P-4 Mimias *cap.*
60 F-2 Mimizan
53 K-4 Mimms
98 D-3 Mimongo
197 M-5 Mimoso do Sul
128 D-1 Min Kuš
123 L-2 Min'a *riv.*
82 G-9 Mina
79 H-2 Mina *riv.*
93 N-1 Miná
82 D-8 Mīnā'Baranīs
83 L-2 Mīnā' Su ūd
84 A-6 Mīnāb
137 M-3 Minamata
137 N-3 Minamitane
165 K-7 Minas *pool*
146 E-9 Minas (Sumatra)
199 K-6 Minas (Uruguay)
195 J-6 Minas de Mimoso
197 H-3 Minas Gerais *reg.*
189 H-9 Minas Gerais
197 L-2 Minas Novas
179 J-7 Minatitlán
143 K-7 Minbu
143 J-7 Minbya
50 C-1 Minch (Little) *strt.*
188 F-1 Minchales
200 E-2 Minchinmāvida *vol.*
63 J-4 Mincio *riv.*
175 P-3 Mincola
149 H-3 Mindanao *sea*
149 J-3 Mindanao *reg.*
220 E-3 Mindarie

87 M-1 Mindelo
164 C-9 Minden (Canada)
51 H-6 Minden (FRG)
167 H-3 Minden (USA)
176 C-4 Minden (USA)
56 D-8 Minderhout
122 F-2 Minderla
212 C-8 Minderoo
90 G-3 Mindif
210 E-5 Mindiptana
143 K-8 Mindon
148 F-6 Mindoro strt.
148 F-7 Mindoro isl.
98 F-5 Mindouli
72 F-4 Mindživan
137 L-3 Mine
50 C-6 Minehead
196 E-2 Mineiros
173 H-3 Mineola
160 F-1 Miner riv.
175 M-3 Mineral Wells
72 C-1 Mineral'nyje Vody
63 L-6 Minerbio
172 B-3 Minersville
129 H-4 Minfeng
103 L-1 Minga
91 M-7 Mingala
165 H-3 Mingan
165 J-2 Mingan rés
165 J-3 Mingan islds
220 E-1 Mingary
72 E-2 Mingečaurskoje riv.
72 F-2 Mingechaur
215 J-9 Mingela
216 D-5 Mingenew
214 D-9 Mingera riv.
143 K-5 Mingin
106 C-8 Mingoyo
130 F-4 Mingshui
127 N-5 Mingtiegaidafan
135 N-2 Minhang
131 K-8 Minhe
143 K-7 Minhla
141 L-2 Minicoy isl.
166 G-8 Minidoka
217 J-5 Minigwal lake
216 C-1 Minilya
216 C-1 Minilya riv.
165 K-1 Minipi lake
89 H-4 Minissia
69 N-8 Minjar
135 M-6 Minjiang riv.
123 L-6 Minjiyn riv.
220 C-2 Minlaton
131 J-7 Minle
90 B-4 Minna
170 A-4 Minneapolis
163 N-9 Minnedosa
170 A-4 Minnesota riv.
170 A-3 Minnesota state
157 E-2 Minnesota state
49 K-3 Minnesund
169 H-2 Minnewaukan
216 D-1 Minnie Creek
220 B-1 Minnipa
60 B-3 Miño riv.
137 J-6 Mino-Kamo
170 C-3 Minocqua
168 G-1 Minot
131 J-8 Minqin
135 M-6 Minqing
124 F-7 Minsgshui
131 M-8 Minshan mt
66 D-5 Minsk
53 M-5 Minster (UK)
53 P-6 Minster (UK)
90 F-8 Minta
160 E-3 Minto
161 N-1 Minto bay
81 M-2 Minûf
122 E-4 Minusinsk
98 D-1 Minvoul
96 C-5 Minwach
131 L-8 Minxian
148 D-7 Minzhujiao
   (Scaborough
   Shoal) isl.
170 F-4 Mio
128 D-8 Miquan
165 N-4 Miquelon isl.
72 F-3 Mir-Basir mt
63 M-3 Mira
188 A-2 Mira riv.
197 K-1 Mirabela
62 C-4 Mirabello Monferrato
197 L-5 Miracema
194 E-5 Miracema do Norte
200 D-2 Mirador
197 L-5 Miradouro
186 E-6 Miraflores
181 J-7 Miragoâne
140 E-3 Miraj
219 L-1 Miram
127 J-7 Mīram Shāh
199 J-9 Miramar
184 C-1 Miramar lag.

165 J-6 Miramichi bay
196 B-3 Miranda riv.
187 K-3 Miranda riv.
196 B-4 Miranda (Brazil)
187 J-2 Miranda (Vénézuela)
60 E-3 Miranda de Ebro
60 C-4 Miranda do Douro
214 F-6 Miranda Downs
60 F-3 Mirande
60 B-4 Mirandela
63 J-5 Mirandola
196 E-5 Mirandópolis
63 M-3 Mirano
196 F-6 Mirante mt
196 E-5 Mirante do
   Paranapanema
196 F-4 Mirassol
184 G-6 Miravalles vol.
85 K-7 Mirbāt
54 A-5 Mirbel
220 G-5 Mirboo North
181 J-6 Mirebalais
72 F-6 Mirgah Sūr
66 G-7 Mirgorod
147 N-6 Miri
143 K-1 Miri mt
140 E-7 Miriālgūda
219 M-3 Miriam Vale
199 M-5 Mirim lag.
187 J-2 Mirimire
199 J-3 Miriñay riv.
188 B-8 Miritiparaná riv.
126 B-8 Mīrjāveh
124 A-6 Mirnaja
227 N-4 Mirnyj
58 D-1 Miroir hill
66 F-7 Mironovka
123 M-1 Mironovo
127 L-8 Mīrpur
138 F-5 Mīrpur Khās
138 G-3 Mīrpur Māthelo
138 E-5 Mīrpur Sakro
218 C-4 Mirranponga
   Pongunna lake
90 D-1 Mirria
219 J-1 Mirtna
64 E-8 Mirtoan sea
103 N-5 Miruro
142 C-3 Mirzāpur
92 E-1 Misālah well
63 P-8 Misano Monte
136 D-7 Misawa
165 J-5 Miscou pte
165 J-5 Miscou isl.
123 J-5 Mišelevka
81 P-1 Misfaq
127 N-5 Misgār
189 K-7 Mishagua riv.
125 J-8 Mishan
159 L-3 Misheguk mt
143 L-1 Mishmī mt
211 P-9 Misima isl.
196 C-9 Misiones mt
196 C-8 Misiones reg.
83 J-6 Miskah
69 M-8 Miškino
185 J-4 Miskito islds
66 A-9 Miskolc
93 K-4 Mismār
209 K-2 Misool isl.
81 N-2 Mișr al Jadīdah
93 K-3 Misrar riv.
80 D-1 Misratah
80 E-3 Misrātah reg.
195 J-3 Missoes mt
62 E-2 Missaglia
170 F-2 Missanabie
195 L-4 Missao Velha
53 H-4 Missenden
170 F-2 Missinaibi lake
170 F-1 Missinaibi riv.
168 G-5 Mission
162 C-7 Mission City
201 N-6 Mission Fagnano
86 G-4 Missira
170 F-2 Mississagi reg.
164 A-8 Mississagi na.p.
156 E-3 Mississippi riv.
157 E-3 Mississippi state
176 D-5 Mississippi riv.
176 E-3 Mississippi state
168 A-1 Missoula
78 E-4 Missour
168 C-1 Missouri riv.
176 D-1 Missouri state
157 E-3 Missouri state
156 E-3 Missouri riv.
169 J-6 Missouri Valley
219 J-2 Mistake riv.
213 M-4 Mistake Creek
221 H-9 Mistaken cap.
164 E-5 Mistassini riv.
164 D-4 Mistassini lake
164 D-4 Mistassini rés

164 D-4 Mistassini Post
57 N-4 Miste
52 C-8 Misterton
80 D-1 Mistrātah pte
137 M-3 Misumi
81 N-2 Mīt Gharm
178 B-4 Mita pte
66 B-3 Mitau (Jelvaga)
52 D-3 Mitcheldean
214 F-5 Mitchell riv.
177 J-2 Mitchell mt
219 K-5 Mitchell (Australia)
169 H-5 Mitchell (USA)
214 F-5 Mitchell River
52 C-4 Mitchell Troy
164 E-2 Mitchequon
127 K-8 Mitha Tiwāna
138 G-6 Mithi
64 F-6 Mithimna
224 D-5 Mitiaro isl.
64 F-6 Mitilíni
179 H-7 Mitla site
136 G-8 Mito
201 N-6 Mitre pen.
158 B-8 Mitrofania isl.
55 L-4 Mitry-le-Neuf
55 L-4 Mitry-Mory
108 B-3 Mitsamiouli
108 F-3 Mitsinjo
93 N-6 Mitsiwa
221 H-4 Mitta Mitta riv.
54 B-8 Mittainville
51 J-8 Mittelfranken mt
58 F-4 Mittelland reg.
222 D-9 Mitton
188 A-9 Mitú
136 C-7 Mituisi
100 B-5 Mitumba mt
99 P-9 Mitwaba
136 D-6 Miumaya
132 E-9 Mixian
83 H-7 Miyah riv.
137 J-8 Miyake isl.
137 J-8 Miyake
137 P-7 Miyako isl.
136 E-8 Miyako
137 M-3 Miyakonozyō
137 M-3 Miyazaki
137 J-5 Miyazu
134 B-6 Miyi
137 K-4 Miyosi
95 H-4 Mizan Teferi
80 C-2 Mizdah
64 E-2 Mizil
143 J-5 Mizoram reg.
172 E-8 Mizpah
191 H-4 Mizque riv.
191 H-4 Mizque
137 J-6 Mizunami
72 D-1 Mizurskij
136 E-7 Mizusawa
100 F-2 Mjanji
51 L-2 Mjölby
49 J-3 Mjøsa riv.
101 K-6 Mkoani
101 J-7 Mkokotoni
101 J-6 Mkomazi
101 J-6 Mkomazi rés
101 K-8 Mkumbi cap.
105 M-5 Mkuze riv.
105 M-5 Mkuze
107 K-1 Mkwasini riv.
51 L-7 Mladá Boleslav
64 C-3 Mladenovac
106 G-4 Mlange mt
106 G-4 Mlange
103 L-6 Mlibizi riv.
64 A-4 Mljet
48 F-4 Mo
209 J-6 Moa isl.
87 L-7 Moa riv.
168 A-7 Moab
190 A-1 Moaco riv.
107 N-1 Moamba
98 E-3 Moanda
167 L-6 Moapa
210 F-3 Moari
100 C-7 Moba
137 H-8 Mobara
91 M-8 Mobaye
91 M-8 Mobayi-Mbongo
99 H-2 Mobenzélé
170 B-8 Moberly
176 F-5 Mobile
176 F-5 Mobile bay
168 G-3 Mobridge
100 C-1 Mobutu Sese
   Seko lake
145 J-5 Môc Châu
145 K-9 Môc Hoa
181 L-6 Moca
193 J-9 Mocajuba
172 B-2 Mocanaqua
187 K-4 Mocapra riv.
200 C-1 Mocha isl.

191 K-4 Mochara mt
189 H-3 Moche riv.
105 H-2 Mochudi
106 D-8 Mocimboa da Praia
177 K-1 Mocksville
102 C-2 Môco mt
188 A-4 Mocoa
197 H-5 Mococa
193 J-7 Mocoes riv.
174 E-4 Moctezuma riv.
174 E-4 Moctezuma
107 H-5 Mocuba
209 N-2 Modan
61 K-2 Modane
139 J-7 Modāsa
104 G-5 Modder riv.
172 C-6 Modena
63 J-7 Modena reg.
61 L-3 Modena
63 J-6 Modena (Modène)
167 J-2 Modesto
61 N-9 Modica
63 J-6 Modigliana
91 M-9 Modjamboli
207 M-6 Modjokerto
221 H-5 Moe
223 K-4 Moehau mt
99 J-1 Moeko riv.
49 J-3 Moelv
192 E-3 Moengo
167 M-8 Moenkopi
56 E-6 Moer
56 C-6 Moerdijk
56 F-7 Moergestel
50 D-3 Moffat
158 B-6 Moffet bay
139 M-2 Moga (India)
99 P-4 Moga (Zaïre)
77 G-4 Mogadiscio
97 P-4 Mogadishu
78 B-4 Mogador (Essaouira)
60 B-4 Mogadouro
105 K-1 Mogalakwena riv.
99 M-1 Mogandjo
143 M-3 Mogaung riv.
143 M-4 Mogaung
125 J-4 Mogdy
59 P-1 Mogeisberg
62 F-1 Moggio
197 H-7 Mogi das Cruzes
196 G-5 Mogi-Guacu riv.
197 H-5 Mogi-Guacu riv.
197 H-6 Mogi-Guacu
197 H-6 Mogi Mirim
219 K-7 Mogil Mogil
66 E-4 Mogil'ov
66 E-8 Mogil'ov-Podol'skij
106 G-8 Mogincual
106 G-7 Mogincual riv.
93 J-3 Moglal riv.
63 J-5 Móglia
63 M-2 Mogliano Veneto
124 B-3 Mogoča
94 E-3 Mogode
123 P-6 Mogojtuj
143 L-5 Mogok
105 J-2 Mogol riv.
174 E-1 Mogollon Rim mt
124 D-2 Mogot riv.
199 J-9 Mogotes pte
123 P-6 Mogotujskij mt
95 J-4 Mogu
124 D-8 Moguqi
91 L-8 Mogwaka
123 N-6 Mogzon
105 J-6 Mohales Hoek
105 G-6 Mohalés Hoek
79 H-2 Mohammadia
78 C-3 Mohammedia
139 M-6 Mohana
143 H-4 Mohanganj
142 D-3 Mohani riv.
142 C-3 Mohania
172 F-2 Mohawk lake
124 C-3 Mohe
146 A-4 Mohean
138 F-3 Mohenjodero site
158 E-3 Mohican cap.
143 L-4 Mohnyin
190 F-1 Moho
101 J-9 Mohoro
172 B-4 Mohrsville
95 K-7 Moiale
215 M-4 Moindou
64 E-1 Moinești
121 H-6 Mointy
66 B-2 Mõisaküla
123 J-4 Moisejevka
165 H-4 Moisie
164 G-3 Moisie riv.
91 J-5 Moïssala
55 L-3 Moisselles
54 B-2 Moisson
54 B-3 Moisson ft
55 L-9 Moissy-Cramayel
187 L-4 Moitaco
175 J-7 Mojada mt

167 L-3 Mojave
167 L-4 Mojave dés
156 C-3 Mojave dés
134 A-9 Mojiang
97 K-1 Mojo riv.
208 A-7 Mojo isl.
191 L-4 Mojo (Bolivia)
95 K-3 Mojo (Ethiopia)
191 H-5 Mojocaya
191 J-5 Mojotoro
193 J-8 Moju
193 J-8 Moju riv.
91 J-9 Mokala riv.
103 M-2 Mokambo
142 E-3 Mokameh
223 J-5 Mokav riv.
105 K-6 Mokhotlong
119 L-6 Mokil isl.
124 B-2 Mokla riv.
79 P-3 Moknine
223 K-3 Mokohinau islds
143 K-3 Mokokchūng
90 G-3 Mokolo (Cameroon)
99 H-1 Mokolo (Zaïre)
99 M-6 Mokombe riv.
133 M-8 Mokpo
84 A-9 Mokrān reg.
67 J-2 Moksa riv.
67 K-3 Mokšan
50 G-6 Mol
99 K-1 Molanda
64 D-8 Moláoi
62 C-6 Molare
59 N-7 Molare mt
179 P-5 Molas pte
95 K-2 Molate
200 D-2 Molco
114 A-5 Moldavia rép
66 E-9 Moldavia rép
66 E-9 Moldavia reg.
49 H-2 Molde
48 E-4 Moldjorda
64 C-2 Moldova Noua
64 E-2 Moldoveanu
89 L-5 Molé riv.
53 J-6 Mole riv.
181 J-6 Mole cap.
58 B-9 Môle (Le) mt
220 G-8 Mole Creek
89 L-4 Mole Game na.p.
181 J-6 Môle St-Nicolas
91 L-8 Molegbe
57 K-8 Molen beek riv.
56 D-4 Molenaarsgraaf
57 M-6 Molenbeersel
59 N-8 Moleno
105 H-2 Molepolole
58 D-6 Moléson mt
222 G-7 Molesworth (Nouvelle
   Zélande)
53 J-1 Molesworth (UK)
61 P-5 Molfetta
121 L-4 Molgary
54 F-8 Molières (Les)
54 B-1 Molincourt
170 C-7 Moline
63 L-6 Molinella
191 N-4 Molinos
100 C-8 Moliro
61 N-5 Molise reg.
100 E-1 Molitar
189 N-8 Mollendo
59 P-3 Mollis
67 H-9 Moločansk
68 F-8 Moločnoje
106 G-6 Molocué riv.
66 C-4 Molodechno
227 N-2 Molodežnaja
66 G-8 Molod'ožnoje
66 F-1 Mologa riv.
224 D-1 Molokai isl.
221 K-2 Molong
192 C-7 Molongo dam.
104 E-4 Molopo riv.
98 F-1 Moloundou
59 P-2 Mols
163 P-9 Molson
105 H-7 Molteno
209 L-5 Molu isl.
117 H-6 Molucca sea
117 H-7 Moluccas islds
106 G-5 Molumbo
209 J-4 Moluques reg.
107 H-7 Moma
107 H-7 Moma
   (Mozambique) isl.
99 M-3 Moma (Zaïre)
100 D-9 Momba riv.
218 G-8 Momba
195 L-2 Mombaça
184 L-2 Mombacho vol.
63 P-9 Mombaroccio
62 C-5 Mombaruzzo
101 K-5 Mombasa
62 B-4 Mombello Monferrato
62 B-5 Mombercelli

101 J-6 Mombo
99 M-1 Mombongo
99 J-3 Momboyo riv.
196 E-2 Mombuca mt
126 C-4 Mo'menābād mt
185 P-8 Momil
140 C-5 Mominābād
62 C-2 Momo
184 F-5 Momotombo vol.
99 L-2 Mompono
186 E-3 Mompós
187 M-7 Momurán riv.
51 K-4 Møn isl.
143 K-7 Mon riv.
144 E-6 Mon reg.
143 J-2 Mon Yul mt
181 N-7 Mona isl.
47 D-5 Monaco
61 K-3 Monaco
47 D-5 Monaco state
187 M-3 Monagas reg.
50 B-3 Monaghan
175 K-4 Monahans
106 G-7 Monapo riv.
106 G-8 Monapo
141 N-8 Monaragala
162 C-4 Monarch mt
162 E-6 Monashee mt
62 C-6 Monastero Bormida
79 P-3 Monastir
66 C-8 Monastyriska
90 E-8 Monatélé
136 C-7 Monbetu
136 A-7 Monbetu
62 A-5 Moncalieri
62 B-4 Moncalvo
193 M-9 Monção
58 A-1 Moncey
59 J-6 Monch mt
59 M-1 Mönchaltorf
48 D-9 Monchegorsk
50 G-6 Mönchengladbach
62 G-7 Monchio
60 A-6 Monchique mt
177 L-3 Moncks Corner
175 K-7 Monclova
200 B-3 Moncol mt
165 J-6 Moncton
62 B-4 Moncucco Torinese
125 N-5 Moneron isl.
62 B-7 Monesiglio
69 N-6 Monetnyj
176 C-1 Monett
61 N-2 Monfalcone
62 B-5 Monferrato reg.
62 B-6 Monforte d'Alba
143 N-7 Möng Hpäyak
143 M-6 Möng Hsu
143 M-6 Möng Küng
143 L-5 Möng Mit
143 M-7 Möng Nai
143 N-7 Möng Nawng
143 M-7 Möng Sit
143 N-7 Möng Ton
143 M-6 Möng Yai
143 N-6 Möng Yang
143 P-7 Möng Yawng
91 N-8 Monga
94 E-6 Mongalla
172 F-1 Monganp
100 C-1 Mongbwalu
145 L-2 Mongcai
216 E-5 Monger lake
63 K-7 Monghidoro
142 E-3 Monghyr
62 D-6 Mongiardino Ligure
62 A-8 Mongioie mt
145 H-8 Môngkól Borei riv.
87 K-5 Mongo riv.
91 K-2 Mongo
106 F-4 Mongoche
130 B-4 Mongol mt
130 B-2 Mongol Altay rge
99 J-1 Mongola riv.
115 J-5 Mongolia state
130 C-6 Mongolie rég.
124 B-8 Mongolie reg.
98 D-1 Mongomo
90 F-2 Mongonu
91 M-2 Mongororo
91 K-8 Mongoumba
62 B-3 Mongrando
55 K-1 Mongrésin
103 H-4 Mongu

130 B-2 Mönh Hayrhan *mt*
130 D-4 Mönh Tsast *mt*
123 N-9 Mönhhaan
99 H-1 Moniangi
168 A-3 Monida
167 J-5 Monitor *mt*
197 K-3 Monjolos
106 F-4 Monkey Bay
179 N-8 Monkey River
218 E-3 Monkira
99 K-3 Monkoto
53 M-2 Monks Eleigh
172 A-7 Monkton
172 G-5 Monmouth *reg.*
162 C-5 Monmouth *mt*
52 C-4 Monmouth (UK)
170 C-7 Monmouth (USA)
172 F-5 Monmouth Junction
58 A-9 Monnetier
52 C-3 Monnow *riv.*
89 N-7 Mono *riv.*
89 N-7 Mono *reg.*
167 J-3 Mono *lake*
189 K-5 Monobamba
64 A-5 Monopoli
92 A-6 Monou
60 E-5 Monreal del Campo
162 C-8 Monroe
176 D-4 Monroe (USA)
170 C-6 Monroe (USA)
170 F-6 Monroe (USA)
170 B-8 Monroe City
176 G-5 Monroeville
77 A-4 Monrovia
50 F-7 Mons
208 E-3 Monse
195 L-2 Monsehor Tabosa
63 L-4 Monselice
174 D-7 Monserrate *isl.*
56 A-3 Monster
51 L-3 Mönsteras
63 J-9 Monsummano Terme
58 C-6 Mont (Le)
172 A-4 Mont Aetna
105 K-6 Mont aux Sources *mt*
61 K-2 Mont Blanc
172 A-3 Mont Carmel (USA)
173 K-1 Mont Carmel (USA)
172 D-5 Mont Clare
58 A-5 Mont d'Or *mt*
165 H-4 Mont-de-Jacques-Cartier *mt*
165 H-8 Mont Desert *isl.*
172 E-6 Mont Holly
172 F-3 Mont Hope
221 H-1 Mont Hope
164 G-5 Mont-Joli
172 A-5 Mont Joy
173 H-1 Mont Kisco
58 B-6 Mont-la-Ville
172 E-6 Mont Laurel
164 D-7 Mont-Laurier
165 H-4 Mont-Louis
172 D-2 Mont Michaels
172 A-6 Mont Nebo
172 C-5 Mont Penn
55 P-5 Mont-Pichet
172 D-7 Mont Royal
58 D-2 Mont-Soleil
50 D-8 Mont-St.-Michel
173 H-3 Mont Vernon
62 B-5 Monta
62 B-5 Montafia
63 K-4 Montagnana
172 E-1 Montagne
108 D-8 Montagne d'Ambre *na.p.*
181 P-4 Montagne Pelée *mt*
164 D-7 Montagne Tremblante *na.p.*
54 D-1 Montagny-en-Vexin
55 M-2 Montagny-Sainte-Félicité
160 A-1 Montague *strt.*
160 A-1 Montague *isl.*
213 K-2 Montague (Australia) *strt.*
174 C-3 Montague (Mexico) *isl.*
54 D-5 Montainville
60 E-5 Montalbán
63 J-9 Montale
54 D-3 Montalet-le-Bois
54 E-5 Montamets
157 C-2 Montana *state*
168 D-2 Montana *state*
168 C-1 Montana *state*
78 D-8 Montaña Clara *isl.*
62 A-4 Montanaro
62 A-7 Montanera
188 A-5 Montañita
50 E-9 Montargis
60 G-3 Montauban
173 N-2 Montauk *pte*
173 N-2 Montauk
55 P-5 Montbarbin
50 F-9 Montbard
58 E-6 Montbarry
50 G-9 Montbéliard
58 B-3 Montbenoit
55 P-6 Montbrieux
61 J-1 Montceau-les-Mines
54 B-5 Montchauvet
58 D-1 Montcheroux
172 G-3 Montclair
50 F-7 Montdidier
191 N-8 Monte *riv.*
200 A-7 Monte (del) *lag.*
179 H-7 Monte Alban *site*
192 E-8 Monte Alegre
194 E-8 Monte Alegre de Goias
196 G-3 Monte Alegre de Minas
194 G-5 Monte Alegre do Piauí
196 F-4 Monte Alto *dam.*
197 L-1 Monte Azul
212 C-7 Monte Bello *islds*
199 J-3 Monte Caseros
196 E-5 Monte Castelo
59 N-9 Monte Céneri
198 C-7 Monte Comán
181 K-6 Monte Cristi
63 N-9 Monte Grimano
196 A-6 Monte Linda *riv.*
199 N-3 Monte Negro
198 A-4 Monte Patria
191 N-6 Monte Quemado
195 L-6 Monte Santo
168 C-9 Monte Vista
191 J-5 Monteagudo
63 K-3 Montebello Vicentino
63 M-2 Montebelluna
62 E-6 Montebruno
63 N-9 Montecalvo in Foglia
196 C-8 Montecarlo
63 J-9 Montecatini Terme
63 H-6 Montécchio Emilia
63 K-3 Montecchio Maggiore
62 B-4 Montechiaro d'Asti
61 L-5 Montechristo *isl.*
59 K-9 Montecrestese
63 J-7 Montecreto
63 M-9 Montefeltro *mt*
63 H-7 Montefiorino
180 F-7 Montego Bay
195 N-4 Monteiro
213 P-4 Montejinnie
61 J-3 Montélimar
170 C-5 Montello
62 B-6 Montelupo Albese
63 J-9 Montelupo Fiorentino
62 C-5 Montemagno
200 F-6 Montemayor *mt*
63 L-9 Montemignaio
178 F-1 Montemorelos
63 J-9 Montemurlo
106 E-7 Montepuez *riv.*
106 E-7 Montepuez
147 K-9 Monterado
63 K-7 Monterenzio
167 J-1 Monterey *bay*
171 J-9 Monterey (USA)
167 J-1 Monterey (USA)
185 P-8 Montería
191 H-6 Montero
198 D-1 Monteros
62 F-8 Monterosso al Mare
178 F-1 Monterrey
194 F-2 Montes Altos
197 K-2 Montes Claros
200 B-7 Montes de Oca
63 J-7 Montese
54 G-5 Montesson
63 J-7 Monteveglio
183 E-6 Montevideo
199 K-7 Montevideo
169 J-4 Montevideo (USA)
55 M-5 Montevrain
58 E-1 Montfaucon
57 L-4 Montferland *reg.*
55 L-5 Montfermeil
56 E-3 Montfoort
57 N-7 Montfort
54 D-7 Montfort-l'Amaury
55 N-3 Montgé-en-Goelle
55 K-8 Montgeron
54 F-2 Montgeroult
139 K-2 Montgomery
172 D-5 Montgomery *reg.*
213 J-3 Montgomery *isl.*
176 G-4 Montgomery (USA)
170 B-8 Montgomery City
172 D-5 Montgomeryville
55 P-6 Monthérand
58 C-6 Montheron
58 D-8 Monthey
55 N-3 Monthyon
63 N-1 Monticano *riv.*
62 G-4 Monticelli d'Ongina
177 J-5 Monticello (USA)
176 E-5 Monticello (USA)
170 E-7 Monticello (USA)
168 A-8 Monticello (USA)
62 B-6 Monticello Alba
63 H-3 Montichiari
62 B-4 Montiglio
54 F-7 Montigny-le-Bretonneux
185 K-9 Montijo *gulf*
60 A-5 Montijo
60 C-7 Montilla
196 E-2 Montividiu
55 M-5 Montjay-la-Tour
62 A-2 Montjovet
58 C-3 Montlebon
55 H-9 Montlhéry
55 H-3 Montlignon
55 M-1 Montlognon
61 H-1 Montluçon
164 F-7 Montmagny
55 L-2 Montmélian
55 H-4 Montmorency
55 H-3 Montmorency *ft*
60 G-1 Montmorillon
219 M-4 Monto
63 M-7 Montone *riv.*
60 B-3 Montorte
58 F-2 Montoz *mt*
164 F-9 Montpelier (USA)
168 A-4 Montpelier (USA)
61 H-3 Montpellier
164 E-8 Montréal
163 L-6 Montreal *lake*
55 K-6 Montreuil
50 E-7 Montreuil
54 C-1 Montreuil-s-Epte
58 D-7 Montreux
58 B-6 Montricher
58 C-9 Montriond
50 E-2 Montrose (UK)
168 B-8 Montrose (USA)
55 J-6 Montrouge
55 N-5 Montry
165 H-5 Monts de Notre Dame *mt*
58 E-6 Montsalvens *lake*
87 N-6 Montserrado *reg.*
181 M-2 Montserrat (UK)
192 F-3 Montsinery
55 H-2 Montsoult
185 J-9 Montuosa *isl.*
173 M-1 Montville (USA)
172 G-3 Montville (USA)
159 J-3 Monument *site*
143 K-6 Monywa
61 L-2 Monza
103 L-5 Monze
189 H-5 Monzón *riv.*
63 K-7 Monzuno
105 K-6 Mooirivier
57 J-5 Mook
213 P-4 Mooloolоo
214 D-9 Moonah *riv.*
218 E-4 Moonda *lake*
219 L-6 Moonie *riv.*
220 C-2 Moonta
216 E-6 Moora
218 E-3 Mooraberree
168 E-4 Moorcroft
56 C-4 Moordrecht
216 E-5 Moore *lake*
215 L-6 Moore *rf*
224 D-5 Mooréa *isl.*
171 J-8 Moorefield
172 E-6 Moorestown
169 J-3 Moorhead
214 B-2 Mooronga *isl.*
164 A-4 Moose *bay*
163 N-6 Moose *lake*
164 A-4 Moose Factory
163 K-8 Moose Jaw
170 B-3 Moose Lake
163 M-9 Moose Mtn *riv.*
164 A-5 Moose River
164 G-7 Moosehead *lake*
163 L-9 Moosejaw *riv.*
172 C-1 Moosic *riv.*
59 J-1 Moosleerau
163 M-9 Moosomin
164 A-4 Moosonee
107 H-4 Mopeia
57 L-9 Mopertingen
103 J-8 Mopipi
88 G-3 Mopti
88 G-3 Mopti *reg.*
97 N-5 Moqokorei
127 H-7 Moqor
189 P-9 Moquegua
189 P-9 Moquegua *riv.*
189 N-9 Moquegua *reg.*
90 G-3 Mora (Cameroon)
49 J-4 Mora (Sweden)
175 J-1 Mora (USA) *riv.*
170 A-3 Mora (USA)
195 M-2 Morada-Nova
197 J-3 Morada Nova de Minas
139 N-4 Morādābād
108 G-3 Morafenobe
54 E-5 Morainvilliers
200 G-2 Moraleda *cap.*
186 C-8 Morales
109 H-6 Moramanga
142 F-2 Morang
55 J-8 Morangis
55 H-1 Morangles
143 K-2 Moranhāt
62 C-4 Morano Po
180 G-7 Morant Bay
180 G-8 Morant Cays *isl.*
180 G-7 Morant Point *pte*
129 K-1 Morari *lake*
141 N-7 Moratuwa
64 C-3 Morava *riv.*
51 M-9 Morava (Czechoslovakia) *riv.*
64 C-3 Morava (Yugoslavia)
46 E-5 Moravia *reg.*
216 D-5 Morawa
213 P-3 Moray *mt*
50 D-1 Moray Firth *gulf*
63 N-9 Morciano di Romagna
52 E-8 Morden (UK)
169 H-1 Morden (USA)
220 G-5 Mordialloc
52 D-3 Mordiford
67 K-2 Mordvinian *reg.*
158 A-5 Mordvinof *cap.*
125 P-4 Mordvinova *bay*
49 H-2 Møre Og Romsdal *reg.*
168 F-3 Moreau *riv.*
219 K-7 Moree
170 G-9 Morehead
177 N-2 Morehead City
59 J-8 Mörel
178 E-5 Morelia
218 G-2 Morella
60 F-5 Morella (Spain)
178 F-6 Morelos *reg.*
103 H-7 Moremi *rés*
139 N-6 Morena
60 C-6 Morena *mt*
64 E-2 Moreni
191 M-1 Moreno *bay*
195 P-4 Moreno
190 C-8 Morerú *riv.*
180 F-1 Mores *isl.*
52 G-7 Morestead
219 N-6 Moreton *cap.*
219 N-6 Moreton *bay*
219 N-6 Moreton *isl.*
214 G-3 Moreton (Australia)
52 C-2 Moreton (UK)
52 F-3 Moreton in Marsh
62 A-5 Moretta
62 F-6 Morfasso
220 D-2 Morgan
176 E-6 Morgan City
170 D-9 Morganfield
177 K-2 Morganton
171 H-8 Morgantown
172 G-5 Morganville
59 M-3 Morgarten
58 B-7 Morges
73 N-9 Morghāb
58 D-8 Morgins
58 D-9 Morgins *val.*
142 D-3 Morhar *riv.*
136 C-6 Mori
63 J-1 Mori (Italy)
219 H-6 Moriarty *mt*
162 C-2 Morice *lake*
162 C-1 Moricetown
173 L-3 Moriches *bay*
191 M-6 Morillo
136 E-7 Morioka
50 C-8 Morlaix
55 P-9 Mormant
181 N-3 Morne Diablotin *mt*
218 F-3 Morney
220 G-6 Mornington *pen.*
220 G-5 Mornington
214 D-6 Mornington *isl.*
201 K-1 Mornington *isl.*
149 K-3 Moro *gulf*
162 C-9 Moro
198 A-1 Moro *pte*
167 K-2 Moro Bay
59 P-9 Morobbia *val.*
211 K-6 Morobe
77 B-1 Morocco *state*
101 H-7 Morogoro
101 H-7 Morogoro *reg.*
108 E-6 Morolahy *pte*
178 E-5 Moroleón
208 G-5 Moromaho *isl.*
109 K-2 Morombe
130 A-6 Mörön
130 B-7 Mörön
123 M-9 Mörön
58 F-1 Moron *mt*
200 D-7 Morón
180 E-4 Morón (Cuba)
187 J-2 Morón (Vénézuela)
60 B-7 Morón de la Frontera
188 D-4 Morona *riv.*
188 D-3 Morona
109 J-3 Morondava
109 J-3 Morondava *riv.*
108 B-3 Moroni
77 G-6 Moroni
94 G-8 Moroto *mt*
94 G-8 Moroto
67 L-7 Morozovsk
62 A-7 Morozzo
50 E-3 Morpeth
176 D-2 Morrilton
196 G-2 Morrinhos
169 J-4 Morris
172 F-3 Morris *reg.*
172 F-3 Morris Plains
185 J-3 Morrison *islds*
177 J-1 Morristown
172 F-3 Morristown *na.p.*
164 F-8 Morrisville (Canada)
172 E-5 Morrisville (USA)
191 P-1 Morro (Chile) *pte*
179 H-5 Morro (Mexico) *pte*
197 N-3 Morro d'Anta
197 H-2 Morro de Padre *mt*
196 E-9 Morro do Capão Doce *mt*
195 H-9 Morro do Chapeu *mt*
195 K-7 Morro do Chapéu
197 M-5 Morro do Coco
197 L-4 Morro do Pilar
192 E-8 Morro Grande *mt*
198 B-5 Morro Peñón *mt*
185 P-8 Morrosquillo *gulf*
107 H-4 Morrumbala
107 M-4 Morrumbene
67 N-2 Morša
55 J-9 Morsang-sur-Orge
63 P-1 Morsano al Tagliamente
59 M-3 Morschach
67 J-3 Morshansk
70 C-7 Morskoj *isl.*
79 M-3 Morsott
214 D-8 Morstone
50 E-8 Mortagne-au-Perche
194 F-3 Mortandade *riv.*
62 D-4 Mortara
55 P-7 Mortcerf
58 C-3 Morteau
55 L-2 Mortefontaine
198 F-4 Morteros
94 G-2 Mortesoro
52 C-4 Mortimers Cross
220 F-5 Mortlake
175 K-2 Morton
196 C-6 Morumbi
221 K-4 Moruya
61 H-1 Morvan *mt*
219 J-4 Morven
138 G-8 Morvi
221 H-5 Morwell
55 L-4 Mory
112 C-3 Morzhovets *isl.*
58 C-9 Morzine
68 E-3 Moržovec *isl.*
69 K-9 M'oša *riv.*
144 E-7 Moscos Kyunzu *islds*
66 G-2 Moscow
114 B-4 Moscow
162 E-9 Moscow (USA)
172 C-4 Moselem Springs
50 G-9 Moselle *riv.*
195 K-3 Mosenhor Hipolito
162 D-9 Moses Lake
190 G-4 Mosetenes *mt*
222 D-9 Mosgiel
104 F-4 Moshaveng *riv.*
101 H-5 Moshi
172 C-1 Mosic
99 M-2 Mosite
48 F-4 Mosjøen
48 E-4 Moskenesøya *isl.*
121 P-2 Moškovo
71 L-7 Moskovsk
127 K-3 Moskovskij
59 N-1 Mosnang
186 B-8 Mosquera
175 J-1 Mosquero
196 A-5 Mosquito (Brazil) *riv.*
159 L-9 Mosquito (USA) *riv.*
185 K-8 Mosquitos *gulf*
51 K-1 Moss
180 G-3 Moss Town
221 K-3 Moss Vale
98 G-3 Mossaka
222 C-8 Mossburn
104 E-9 Mosselbaai
98 E-4 Mossendjo
58 E-7 Mosses *pass*
220 G-2 Mossgiel
195 M-2 Mossoró *riv.*
195 M-2 Mossoró
106 G-8 Mossuril
163 M-6 Mossy *riv.*
51 K-7 Most
64 A-4 Mostar
52 C-8 Mosterton
72 B-1 Mostovskoj
66 C-5 Mosty
149 L-7 Mostyn
60 C-4 Mota del Marquès
99 H-1 Motaba *riv.*
179 N-8 Motagua *riv.*
51 L-2 Motala
139 N-7 Moth
149 P-1 Moti *isl.*
58 C-4 Môtiers
142 D-2 Motihāri
60 E-6 Motilla del Palancar
223 K-5 Motiti *isl.*
170 A-3 Motley
94 C-7 Moto
122 E-4 Motorskoje
68 B-2 Motovskij *bay*
48 C-9 Motovskij Zal. *gulf*
179 K-8 Motozintla de Mendoza
60 C-8 Motril
223 K-4 Motrinsville
168 F-3 Mott
136 C-5 Motta *cap.*
62 G-4 Motta Baluffi
63 N-2 Motta di Livenza
62 D-3 Motta Visconti
63 J-4 Motteggiana
224 D-5 Motu One *isl.*
222 G-6 Motueka *riv.*
222 G-6 Motueka
179 M-4 Motul
143 L-1 Motuo
122 F-1 Motygino
67 J-4 Motyra *riv.*
145 J-1 Mou *riv.*
215 N-4 Mou
164 F-3 Mouchalagane *riv.*
181 K-5 Mouchoir *strt.*
181 K-5 Mouchoir Bank *isl.*
134 A-7 Mouding
86 D-5 Moudjéria
98 C-4 Mouila
71 M-1 Mouioum-Koum *dés*
91 M-6 Mouka
98 C-4 Moukalaba *riv.*
220 G-3 Moulamein *riv.*
220 G-3 Moulamein
181 N-8 Moule à Chique *cap.*
61 H-1 Moulins
144 E-5 Moulmein
144 C-5 Moulmeingyun
78 E-4 Moulouya *riv.*
177 J-5 Moultrie
177 L-3 Moultrie *lake*
215 N-3 Mouly *isl.*
98 E-3 Mounana
91 H-5 Moundou
171 H-8 Moundsville
145 H-8 Moung Roessei
90 F-5 Moungel
90 D-1 Mounio *reg.*
177 K-1 Mount Airy
218 E-7 Mount Arrowsmith
216 E-1 Mount Augustus
170 A-7 Mount Ayr
220 D-3 Mount Baker
170 D-9 Mount Carmel
218 A-4 Mount Cavenagh
106 G-1 Mount Darwin
213 N-8 Mount Doreen
219 J-1 Mount Douglas
219 H-8 Mount Drysdale
218 B-5 Mount Dutton
218 B-7 Mount Eba
175 P-4 Mount Enterprise
105 K-7 Mount Frere
215 H-7 Mount Garnet
181 P-8 Mount Hillaby *mt*
220 B-2 Mount Hope
213 K-4 Mount House
218 F-4 Mount Howitt
214 D-9 Mount Isa *mt*
216 E-4 Mount Magnet
214 D-8 Mount Margaret
223 K-5 Mount Maunganui
219 L-3 Mount Morgan
218 G-8 Mount Murchinson
214 D-8 Mount Oxide
219 M-4 Mount Perry
220 D-2 Mount Pleasant (Australia)
175 P-3 Mount Pleasant (USA)
170 B-7 Mount Pleasant (USA)
170 F-5 Mount Pleasant (USA)
168 A-6 Mount Pleasant (USA)
162 C-8 Mount Rainier *na.p.*
166 F-3 Mount Shasta
165 K-6 Mount Steward
215 H-7 Mount Surprise
218 B-1 Mount Swan
171 J-7 Mount Union
162 C-7 Mount Vernon

143 J-7 Myengun *cap.*
160 C-8 Myers Chuck
172 A-4 Myerstown
48 D-1 Myggenaes *islds*
143 K-6 Myingyan
144 E-7 Myinmoletkat *mt*
143 L-6 Myinmu
143 M-4 Myitkyinä
143 K-9 Myitmaka *riv.*
143 L-6 Myitnge *riv.*
144 E-7 Myitta
143 K-5 Myittha *riv.*
143 L-6 Myittha
143 H-4 Mymensingh
128 A-1 Mynaral
120 A-6 Mynbulak
104 G-7 Mynfontein
52 A-2 Mynydd Eppynt
143 J-7 Myohaung
143 K-7 Myothit
48 C-2 Myrdalsjökull *glac.*
48 D-4 Myre
177 M-3 Myrtle Beach
221 H-4 Myrtleford
122 C-3 Myski
66 G-1 Myškino
66 A-8 Myslenice
51 L-6 Mysliborz
141 H-5 Mysore
173 N-1 Mystic
66 A-7 Myszków
59 M-3 Mythen *mt*
66 G-2 Mytishchi
48 L-8 Myvatn *lake*
106 D-3 Mzimba
106 D-3 Mzuzu

# N

88 A-8 N'Ataram *dés*
66 C-8 N'Atyn
100 A-1 N'Gayu *riv.*
145 L-1 Na Säm
146 D-5 Na Thawi
56 A-4 Naaldwijk
78 G-4 Naama
49 K-7 Naantali
56 F-1 Naarden
56 E-1 Naardermeer *lake*
50 B-4 Naas
97 J-2 Nabadid
142 F-5 Nabadwip
148 F-5 Nabas
216 G-2 Nabberru *lake*
160 D-2 Nabesna *riv.*
160 C-2 Nabesna
79 P-2 Nabeul
139 M-3 Näbha
93 H-2 Nabi *riv.*
96 D-2 Nabi Sha'ib *mt*
221 M-2 Nabiac
125 M-1 Nabil' *riv.*
100 F-1 Nabilatuk
196 A-4 Nabileque *riv.*
165 J-3 Nabisipi *riv.*
82 C-2 Nablus
100 F-1 Naboa
89 L-5 Nabogo
105 K-2 Naboomspruit
82 C-5 Nabq
107 H-7 Naburi
106 F-8 Naçala
184 F-4 Nacaome
106 F-8 Nacaroa
106 C-7 Nachingwea
200 B-2 Nacimiento
220 D-1 Nackara
175 P-4 Nacogdoches
174 E-4 Nacozari
196 C-8 Nacunday *riv.*
196 C-8 Nacunday
125 J-5 Nadeždinskoje
139 J-8 Nadiäd
162 C-2 Nadina River
64 C-1 Nadlac
78 F-2 Nador
207 H-3 Naduk *isl.*
124 E-5 Nadulihe *riv.*
68 C-6 Nadvoicy
66 C-8 Nadvornaja
133 M-5 Naegeumgang
59 N-2 Näfels
73 K-8 Naft-e Safid
72 G-8 Naft-e Shäh

83 H-6 Nafud al Urayq *mt*
80 B-2 Nafüsah *mt*
138 D-2 Näg
93 J-5 Naga *site*
137 L-3 Naga *isl.*
208 C-7 Naga (Australia)
148 E-4 Naga (Philippines)
137 J-5 Nagahama
158 B-7 Nagai *isl.*
143 K-3 NagaLand *reg.*
137 H-6 Nagano
136 G-6 Nagaoka
141 K-7 Nägappattinam
138 G-6 Nagar Pärkar
140 E-7 Nägärjuna *lake*
184 F-5 Nagarote
137 M-2 Nagasaki
137 L-3 Nagato
139 K-5 Nägaur
142 C-8 Nägävali *riv.*
133 N-7 Nagdong *riv.*
141 L-5 Nägercoil
94 F-6 Nagichot
139 N-4 Nagina
126 B-2 Nagineh
63 J-1 Nago (Italy)
137 M-8 Nago (Japan)
139 P-8 Nägod
124 D-1 Nagornyj
69 J-7 Nagorsk
94 B-8 Nagosira
137 J-6 Nagoya
140 B-7 Nagpur
129 N-9 Nagqu
181 L-6 Nagua
141 M-1 Naguri *isl.*
64 B-1 Nagykörös
137 M-8 Naha
147 P-9 Nahabuan
139 N-3 Nähan
138 B-2 Nahang *riv.*
161 H-7 Nahanni Butte
82 C-1 Nahariyya
73 J-7 Nahävand
124 E-7 Nahe
93 N-5 Nahelej *isl.*
81 M-2 Nähid *well*
93 J-7 Nahr ad Dindar *riv.*
93 L-5 Nahr al Qäsh *riv.*
81 P-8 Nahr an Nil *riv.*
127 J-5 Nahrin
200 D-3 Nahuel Huapi *lake*
200 D-3 Nahuel Huapi *na.p.*
200 D-5 Nahuel Niyeu
200 B-2 Nahuelbuta *mt*
131 K-3 Naichitai
143 J-1 Naidong
52 C-5 Nailsea
52 E-4 Nailsworth
93 H-7 Na'ima
133 H-3 Naimanqi
73 M-7 Nä'in
129 N-1 Naini-Täl
140 A-8 Naipur
187 H-8 Naipo
131 K-3 Naiqiguoluehe *riv.*
50 D-1 Nairn
101 G-3 Nairobi
77 F-5 Nairobi
106 E-7 Nairoto
58 A-2 Naisey
100 G-3 Naivasha
73 L-7 Najafäbäd
125 K-4 Najchin
139 N-4 Najibäbäd
133 N-2 Najin
133 N-2 Najman
128 A-9 Najramdal *mt*
96 B-3 Najrän *reg.*
96 C-2 Najrän *riv.*
96 C-2 Najrän
48 G-3 Namsos
133 M-8 Naju *isl.*
133 M-8 Naju
120 G-4 Najza *mt*
136 A-8 Naka-Sibetu
137 M-1 Nakadöri *isl.*
136 G-8 Nakaminato
137 L-4 Nakamura
137 H-6 Nakano
137 J-3 Nakano (Japan) *isl.*
137 P-3 Nakano (Japan) *isl.*
137 P-3 Nakanosima *strt.*
137 H-7 Nakanozyö
136 D-6 Nakasato
100 E-1 Nakasongola
137 L-3 Nakatu
158 C-8 Nakchamik *isl.*
129 N-3 Nakechabe
129 K-2 Nakecuo *lake*
160 A-1 Naked *isl.*
93 M-5 Nakfa
72 F-4 Nakhichevan
126 B-5 Nakhl *riv.*
133 P-1 Nakhodka
145 H-6 Nakhon

144 F-7 Nakhon Chai Si *riv.*
144 G-7 Nakhon Nayok
144 F-7 Nakhon Pathom
145 J-5 Nakhon Phanom
144 F-6 Nakhon Sawan
146 D-3 Nakhon Si Thammarat
144 G-5 Nakhon Thai
160 D-6 Nakina
51 M-5 Naklo n.
158 E-7 Naknek
158 E-7 Naknek *lake*
100 E-9 Nakonde
89 K-5 Nakong
69 L-3 N'aksinvol'
51 J-4 Nakskov
100 G-2 Nakuru
162 E-7 Nakusp
138 E-2 Näl
138 D-3 Näl *riv.*
128 D-5 Nalateshan *mt*
123 L-9 Nalayh
201 H-2 Nalcayec *isl.*
72 C-1 Nal'chik
49 H-4 Nälden
126 G-4 Naleng
140 E-7 Nalgonda
124 B-4 Nalimsk
130 E-7 Nalinhe *riv.*
140 F-7 Nallamalla *mt*
129 P-7 Nalong
80 B-2 Nälüt
146 G-3 Näm Cän
145 K-2 Nam Dinh
146 G-3 Nam Du *isl.*
143 N-6 Nam Hka *riv.*
144 G-4 Nam Pat
119 L-6 Nama *isl.*
107 P-1 Namaacha
107 H-5 Namacurra
126 B-2 Namak *dés*
73 P-8 Namaki *riv.*
108 F-4 Namakia
104 B-3 Namaland (Groot) *reg.*
76 D-7 Namaland (Groot) *reg.*
127 M-1 Namangan
106 F-8 Namapa
104 C-5 Namaqualand *reg.*
86 F-4 Namari
106 G-5 Namarroi
100 E-1 Namasagali
100 E-1 Namasale
211 P-3 Namatanai
209 N-1 Namber
219 N-5 Nambour
142 F-2 Namchi
144 G-3 Namèo
106 G-7 Nametil
133 N-8 Namhae
133 N-8 Namhae *isl.*
143 M-5 Namhkam
143 M-5 Namhsan
102 B-8 Namib *dés*
76 D-7 Namib *dés*
102 A-4 Namibe *reg.*
102 A-4 Namibe
104 B-2 Namibia *reg.*
77 D-7 Namibia *state*
73 H-4 Namin
106 G-6 Namiroe *riv.*
209 H-3 Namlea
106 E-7 Namoto
124 F-6 Namoer
124 E-6 Namoerhe *riv.*
219 K-7 Namoi *riv.*
78 G-5 Namous *riv.*
166 F-6 Nampa
88 F-2 Nampala
133 L-5 Nampo
133 M-2 Nampotae-san *mt*
143 L-3 Nampuk *riv.*
106 G-7 Nampula
50 G-7 Namur
95 H-6 Namuruputh
102 D-7 Namutoni
129 N-3 Namuzhashankou
106 G-7 Namva *riv.*
103 K-5 Namwala
133 M-7 Namweon
144 G-3 Nan
144 G-4 Nan *riv.*
91 H-7 Nana *riv.*
91 J-5 Nana Barya *riv.*
90 G-7 Nana Manbéré *reg.*
162 B-6 Nanaimo
133 M-2 Nanam
219 M-5 Nanango
137 H-5 Nanao

135 L-8 Nanaodao *isl.*
136 G-5 Nanatu *isl.*
188 D-6 Nanay
188 D-6 Nanay *riv.*
134 D-3 Nanbu
125 H-7 Nancha
135 K-5 Nanchang
135 K-5 Nancheng
134 D-3 Nanchong
134 E-4 Nanchuan
146 A-4 Nancowry *isl.*
58 A-2 Nancray
50 G-8 Nancy
129 M-1 Nandä Devi *mt*
134 E-7 Nandan
140 C-6 Nänder
219 L-8 Nandewar *mt*
143 N-5 Nandinghe *riv.*
145 N-3 Nanduhe *riv.*
140 A-4 Nandurbär
140 F-6 Nandyäl
135 K-6 Nanfeng
145 H-7 Nang Rong
90 F-7 Nanga-Eboko
127 N-6 Nangä Parvat *mt*
207 L-1 Nangamuntatai
207 L-1 Nangapinoh
147 N-9 Nangaraun
127 K-6 Nangarhar *reg.*
106 F-8 Nangata *pte*
207 K-2 Nangatajap
207 J-2 Nangka *islds*
132 F-7 Nangong
131 N-4 Nangqian
133 L-3 Nangrim-Sanmack *mt*
130 D-7 Nangua
130 E-1 Nanhu
134 A-7 Nanhua
141 H-5 Nanjangüd
134 A-7 Nanjian
134 E-2 Nanjiang *riv.*
134 D-2 Nanjiang
135 N-5 Nanjishan *isl.*
127 L-9 Nankäna Sähib
135 L-2 Nanking
134 F-5 Nankou
132 F-5 Nankou
135 H-7 Nanling *mt*
135 L-3 Nanling
129 P-7 Nanmulin
216 F-3 Nannine
134 E-9 Nanning
216 E-9 Nannup
134 C-7 Nanpanjiang *riv.*
129 P-2 Nänpära
135 H-4 Nanping (China)
135 L-6 Nanping (China)
135 M-5 Nanpuqi *riv.*
135 M-7 Nanridao *isl.*
153 J-1 Nansen *strt.*
131 H-5 Nanshan *mt*
148 G-9 Nanshandao *isl.*
147 N-3 Nanshaqundao (Spratly) *islds*
100 E-4 Nansio
131 M-7 Nansongling *mt*
52 B-5 Nant Garw
52 A-4 Nant y Moel
52 A-2 Nant-y-mwyn
143 K-3 Nantaleik *riv.*
54 G-5 Nanterre
50 C-9 Nantes
55 N-1 Nanteuil-le-Haudouin
55 P-4 Nanteuil-lès-Meaux
143 J-9 Nantha *cap.*
172 B-1 Nanticoke
54 A-5 Nantilly
135 N-2 Nantong
135 N-8 Nant'ou
55 M-3 Nantouillet
61 J-2 Nantua
171 N-6 Nantucket *strt.*
171 N-6 Nantucket *isl.*
171 N-6 Nantucket
172 G-2 Nanuet
197 N-3 Nanuque
159 M-5 Nanushuk *riv.*
124 C-5 Nanuteshan *mt*
147 M-3 Nanweidao (Spratly) *isl.*
134 C-5 Nanxi
135 H-4 Nanxian
135 N-2 Nanxiang
135 J-7 Nanxiong
135 H-2 Nanyang
101 H-2 Nanyuki
132 F-7 Nanyunhe *cal.*
125 L-5 Nanza *mt*
134 G-2 Nanzhang
103 K-5 Nanzhila *riv.*
60 F-7 Nao *cap.*
164 E-2 Naococane *lake*
136 G-6 Naoetu
133 M-2 Nanam
159 M-4 Naokok
138 G-6 Naokot
125 J-6 Naolihe *riv.*

126 C-5 Näomid *reg.*
123 L-7 Naoški
64 D-5 Náousa
145 N-2 Naozhoudao *isl.*
167 H-2 Napa
158 F-5 Napaiskak
149 N-9 Napakule
199 J-8 Napaleofú *riv.*
158 G-6 Napamute
164 D-9 Napanee
94 G-7 Napass
92 G-4 Napata *site*
173 N-2 Napeague *bay*
173 N-2 Napeague Beach *isth.*
165 K-1 Napetipi *riv.*
59 J-3 Napf *mt*
213 M-5 Napier *mt*
223 K-6 Napier
213 K-2 Napier Broome *bay*
61 N-6 Naples
177 K-8 Naples (USA)
131 P-2 Napo
188 B-3 Napo *riv.*
188 B-3 Napo *reg.*
64 D-1 Napoca *site*
168 G-3 Napoleon
218 E-5 Nappamerry
224 E-5 Napuka *isl.*
82 B-7 Naqadäh
72 F-5 Naqadeh
82 C-3 Naqb *cap.*
197 L-4 Naque
131 N-1 Naquhe (Salween) *riv.*
138 G-4 Nära *cal.*
137 J-5 Nara (Japan)
88 F-1 Nara (Mali)
175 K-1 Nara Visa
220 F-6 Naracoopa
220 E-4 Naracoorte
221 H-2 Naradhan
130 C-5 Naran
188 E-5 Naranjal
185 H-7 Naranjo
178 G-4 Naranjos
137 H-8 Narasino
123 N-7 Narasun
146 E-5 Narathiwat
143 H-4 Näräyanganj
61 H-4 Narbonne
98 D-7 Narca *pte*
144 B-7 Narcondam *isl.*
73 M-3 Nardin
186 D-5 Nare *riv.*
138 F-2 Näri *riv.*
108 B-6 Narinda *bay*
188 A-3 Nariño
122 E-6 Nariyn-Gol *riv.*
130 D-7 Nariynteel
68 G-1 Narjan-Mar
140 A-4 Narmada *riv.*
139 M-4 Närnaul
66 G-4 Naro-Fominsk
112 D-3 Narodnaja *pl.*
69 J-1 Narodnaja *mt*
100 G-3 Narok
221 K-4 Narooma
66 E-6 Narovl'a
127 M-9 Närowäl
219 K-8 Narrabri
173 P-1 Narragansett Pier
219 J-7 Narran *riv.*
219 J-7 Narran or Terewah *lake*
221 H-3 Narrandera
216 E-8 Narrogin
221 J-1 Narromine
140 A-8 Narsimhapur
139 M-8 Narsinghgarh
142 D-6 Narsinghpur
142 B-8 Narsïpatnam
104 D-4 Narubis
122 F-3 Narva
66 C-1 Narva *riv.*
48 D-5 Narvik
139 M-3 Narwäna
213 P-9 Narwietooma
121 N-7 Narymskij *mt*
128 D-1 Naryn *riv.*
122 F-7 Naryn *riv.*
122 F-7 Naryn (SSSR)
130 A-5 Naryn (SSSR)
128 D-1 Naryn (SSSR)
128 D-4 Narynkol
62 A-6 Narzole
90 C-5 Nasarawa
64 D-1 Nasaud
198 E-5 Naschel
52 A-5 Nash
158 E-3 Nash Harbor
188 C-5 Nashiño *riv.*
171 M-5 Nashua

170 C-9 Nashville (USA)
176 C-1 Nashville (USA)
89 K-5 Nasia *riv.*
140 B-3 Näsik
94 F-3 Näşir
139 K-6 Nasïräbäd
81 N-2 Naşr
73 H-8 Naşrïan-e Pa'in
162 C-1 Nass *riv.*
173 J-3 Nassau *reg.*
157 G-4 Nassau
201 P-6 Nassau *bay*
224 C-5 Nassau *isl.*
214 F-5 Nassau *riv.*
180 F-2 Nassau
81 P-8 Nasser (Birkat) *lake*
89 L-2 Nassian
51 L-2 Nassjö
155 L-4 Nastapoka *isl.*
148 E-6 Nasugbu
103 K-8 Nata *riv.*
103 K-8 Nata
186 D-7 Natagaima
105 L-6 Natal *reg.*
195 P-3 Natal (Brazil)
195 J-2 Natal (Brazil)
146 C-9 Natal (Indonesia)
73 L-6 Natanz
102 A-6 Natas *riv.*
165 J-2 Natashquan *riv.*
165 J-3 Natashquan
176 E-5 Natchez
176 C-5 Natchitoches
59 J-8 Naters
84 E-7 Näţih *well*
220 E-4 Natimuk
162 E-2 Nation *riv.*
89 K-7 Natitingou
82 C-9 Natityäy *mt*
174 B-5 Natividad *isl.*
190 D-4 Natividad
194 E-7 Nátividade
136 F-7 Natori
100 G-4 Natron *lake*
143 L-8 Nattaung *mt*
142 G-2 Natu La *mt*
216 D-3 Naturaliste *cap.*
216 B-3 Naturaliste Channel *strt.*
51 K-7 Naumburg
119 M-7 Nauru *state*
188 E-6 Nauta
142 C-1 Nautanwa
48 A-2 Nauteyri
179 H-5 Nautla
56 A-8 Nauw van Bath *est.*
62 A-8 Nava *pass*
175 L-6 Nava
140 A-4 Naväpur
127 H-6 Nävar *dés*
201 N-6 Navarino *isl.*
60 E-3 Navarra *reg.*
199 H-7 Navarro
67 J-2 Naväšina
175 N-5 Navasota
181 H-7 Navassa *isl.*
172 G-4 Navesink
181 M-5 Navidad Bank *isl.*
195 M-5 Navio *riv.*
66 G-5 Navl'a
138 G-7 Navlakhi
120 A-9 Navoi
174 E-6 Navojoa
64 D-7 Návpaktos
64 D-8 Návplion
89 K-5 Navrongo
140 A-3 Navsäri
139 J-3 Nawa Kot
142 B-1 Nawäbganj
142 D-3 Nawäda
127 H-7 Näwah
142 E-1 Nawäkot
139 L-4 Nawalgarh
142 B-6 Nawäpära
139 M-2 Nawäshahr
83 J-9 Nawäşif *mt*
93 P-1 Nawäşif *vol.*
143 K-8 Nawin *riv.*
85 K-7 Naws *cap.*
129 N-3 Nawukehe *riv.*
178 C-3 Nayarit *reg.*
53 M-3 Nayland
136 A-6 Nayoro
190 G-2 Nazacara
188 G-8 Nazaré (Bolivia)
194 B-3 Nazaré (Brazil)
187 J-9 Nazaré (Peru)

195 P-4 Nazaré da Mata
195 J-3 Nazaré da Piaui
191 K-4 Nazareno
186 G-1 Nazareth *pass*
82 C-1 Nazareth (Israël)
172 D-3 Nazareth (USA)
123 L-2 Nazarovo (SSSR)
122 E-2 Nazarovo (SSSR)
178 C-1 Nazas
178 C-1 Nazas *riv.*
189 M-6 Nazca
86 F-1 Naze *cap.*
54 G-2 Naze (La)
69 N-7 N'azepetrovsk
68 C-9 Nazija
126 B-8 Nāzil
64 G-7 Nazilli
143 H-5 Nāzir Hāt
162 D-4 Nazko
162 D-4 Nazko *riv.*
95 K-3 Nazret
84 D-7 Nazwa
69 N-1 Nazym *riv.*
103 L-2 Nchanga
106 F-4 Ncheu
103 N-3 Ndabala
98 F-9 Ndalatando
89 L-8 Ndali
208 E-8 Ndao *isl.*
91 L-5 Ndélé
98 D-4 Ndendé *rés*
98 D-4 Ndendé
90 E-7 Ndieké *riv.*
90 G-3 Ndiguina
90 E-7 Ndikiniméki
86 E-3 Ndioum
77 D-3 Ndjamena
90 G-2 Ndjamena
90 E-7 Ndjim *riv.*
98 C-2 Ndjolé
90 F-7 Ndo *riv.*
98 C-4 Ndogo *riv.*
103 M-3 Ndola
90 E-8 Ndom
90 D-5 Ndoro *hill*
89 N-2 Ndoussi
91 N-7 Ndu
105 M-4 Ndumu *mt*
100 B-1 Nduye
100 B-1 Nduye *riv.*
219 J-5 Neabul *riv.*
50 C-3 Neagh *lake*
217 N-1 Neale *lake*
218 B-5 Neales *riv.*
64 F-9 Neápolis (Greece)
64 D-8 Neápolis (Greece)
129 L-3 Near
50 C-5 Neath
52 A-4 Neath *riv.*
54 E-6 Neauphle-le-Château
54 D-6 Neauphle-le-Vieux
54 A-5 Neauphlette
89 K-4 Nebbou
220 G-5 Nebean *strt.*
51 H-4 Nebel
59 J-2 Nebikon
219 J-5 Nebine *riv.*
73 K-1 Nebit-Dag
187 K-9 Neblina *mt*
219 K-1 Nebo
68 D-9 Nebolči
168 F-6 Nebraska *state*
157 D-2 Nebraska *state*
169 J-7 Nebraska City
123 P-1 Nečera *riv.*
123 P-1 Nečera
162 B-7 Nech Bay
162 D-3 Nechako *riv.*
162 C-2 Nechako *plat.*
224 C-1 Necker *isl.*
199 H-9 Necochéa
185 J-4 Ned Thomas *islds*
148 G-3 Nedellin
56 F-4 Neder Betuwe *reg.*
57 H-5 Nederasselt
56 F-5 Nederhemert
56 E-1 Nederhorst den Berg
56 F-3 Nederlangbroek
57 H-9 Nederweert
66 G-6 Nedrigajlov
57 M-2 Neede
53 N-2 Needham Market
167 M-5 Needles
223 K-3 Needles *pte*
196 A-9 Neembucú *reg.*
139 L-5 Neemka Thāna
163 N-9 Neepawa
172 B-7 Neer *riv.*
57 K-9 Neer
56 E-5 Neer Andel
57 M-7 Neerglabbeek
57 M-8 Neerharen
57 M-6 Neeritter
57 J-9 Neerkant
57 M-7 Neeroeteren
93 N-6 Nefasit
172 C-3 Neffs
79 M-4 Nefta
73 H-2 Neft'anye Kamni *isl.*
67 N-9 Neftekumsk
76 G-2 Nefud *dés*
98 F-8 Negage
87 H-8 Négala
207 N-3 Negara
207 P-2 Negara *riv.*
95 L-5 Negele
146 E-8 Negeri Sembilan *reg.*
196 B-5 Negla *riv.*
106 D-7 Negomano
141 M-7 Negombo
199 L-6 Negra *lag.*
184 E-2 Negra *pte*
190 E-7 Negra (Bolivia) *mt*
197 L-3 Negra (Brazil) *mt*
194 F-3 Negra (Brazil) *mt*
63 J-3 Negrar
60 B-2 Negreira
191 J-1 Negreiros
66 B-9 Negresti
180 E-7 Negril Point *pte*
79 M-4 Negrine
188 E-1 Negritos
186 E-4 Negro *mt*
192 A-8 Negro (Brazil) *riv.*
196 A-7 Negro (Chile) *riv.*
186 F-3 Negro (Vénézuela) *riv.*
191 M-5 Negro de Zucho *mt*
149 H-5 Negros *isl.*
162 A-8 Nehalem *riv.*
126 B-5 Nehbandān
181 K-7 Neiba *bay*
181 K-6 Neiba
109 P-7 Neiges *mt*
134 D-4 Neijiang
144 B-8 Neill *isl.*
170 C-4 Neillsville
186 D-6 Neira
62 E-7 Neirone
51 L-7 Neisse *riv.*
186 D-8 Neiva *reg.*
186 D-8 Neiva
134 G-2 Neixiang
68 G-9 Neja *riv.*
68 G-9 Neja
163 P-2 Nejanilini *lake*
95 H-2 Nejo
69 N-5 Nejva *riv.*
69 N-5 Nejvo-Sajtanskij
94 B-7 Nekalagba
95 H-3 Nekemte
78 D-5 Nekob
68 F-9 Nekrasovskoje
123 P-2 Nel'aty
159 J-9 Nelchina
94 G-5 Nelichu *mt*
66 E-2 Nelidovo
169 H-6 Neligh
141 H-5 Nelligere
140 G-7 Nellore
125 M-5 Nel'ma
154 J-4 Nelson *riv.*
156 E-1 Nelson *riv.*
158 E-4 Nelson *isl.*
163 P-6 Nelson *riv.*
201 M-2 Nelson *strt.*
211 M-7 Nelson *cap.*
222 F-7 Nelson *lake*
222 F-6 Nelson *reg.*
162 E-7 Nelson (Canada)
222 G-6 Nelson (Nouvelle Zélande)
52 B-4 Nelson (UK)
222 F-7 Nelson Lake *na.p.*
173 H-1 Nelsonville
105 L-3 Nelspruit
88 E-1 Néma
88 F-1 Néma *hill*
66 A-4 Neman
90 B-8 Nembe
208 E-8 Nembrala
62 F-2 Nembro
68 G-9 Nemda *riv.*
130 E-7 Nemegt *mt*
79 M-3 Nementcha *mt*
188 E-1 Nemete *pte*
66 E-8 Nemirov
164 C-4 Nemiscau
65 P-5 Nemrut *mt*
69 K-4 Nemskaja Vozv. *mt*
125 K-5 Nemta *riv.*
66 B-4 Nemunas *riv.*
136 A-8 Nemuro *strt.*
136 A-8 Nemuro
50 B-4 Nenagh
159 K-8 Nenana
159 K-8 Nenana *riv.*
58 F-9 Nendaz
58 F-9 Nendaz *val.*
53 J-1 Nene *riv.*
146 E-6 Nenggiri *riv.*
102 G-3 Nengo *riv.*
124 E-6 Nenjiang *riv.*
68 D-5 Nenoksa
149 L-1 Nenusa *islds*
195 N-6 Neópolis
169 J-9 Neosho *riv.*
176 C-1 Neosho
164 D-3 Neoskweskau
123 K-1 Nepa *riv.*
142 E-1 Népal *reg.*
118 D-4 Nepal *state*
129 P-2 Nepālganj
189 H-3 Nepeña *riv.*
167 J-8 Nephi
171 P-1 Nepisiguit
165 H-6 Nepisiguit *riv.*
99 P-1 Nepoko *riv.*
60 F-3 Nérac
80 G-7 Nerast *dés*
124 A-3 Nerča *riv.*
124 A-5 Nerčinsk
124 B-5 Nerčinskij *mt*
124 A-4 Nerčinsko-Kuengskij *mt*
67 H-1 Nerekhta
164 E-1 Neret *lake*
64 B-3 Neretva *riv.*
125 K-4 Nergen
57 H-3 Nergena
56 E-7 Nerhoven
102 G-5 Neriquinha
66 C-4 Neris *riv.*
158 E-6 Nerka *lake*
67 H-1 Nerl'
58 A-8 Nernier
122 G-4 Neroj 1-j
69 J-2 Nerojka *mt*
125 N-2 Nerpič'e
123 P-1 Nerpo
63 M-1 Nervesa della Battàglia
62 D-7 Nervi
55 H-2 Nerville-la-Forêt
50 G-5 Nes
68 E-3 Nes'
172 B-2 Nescopeck
172 E-5 Neshaminy
172 E-5 Neshaminy *riv.*
48 C-4 Neskaupstaður
51 L-4 Neskø
54 G-1 Nesles-la-Vallée
48 F-4 Nesna
48 E-4 Nesøya *isl.*
172 C-3 Nesquehonin
168 G-8 Ness City
59 P-2 Nesslau
66 B-7 Nesterov (SSSR)
66 B-4 Nesterov (SSSR)
59 J-7 Nesthorn *mt*
64 E-5 Nestos *riv.*
82 C-2 Netanya
172 F-3 Netcong
56 F-8 Netersel
52 B-6 Nether Stowey
219 K-1 Netherdale
47 D-4 Netherlands *state*
187 H-1 Netherlands Antilles *reg.*
140 A-3 Netrang
59 N-3 Netstal
57 L-5 Netterden
53 H-5 Nettlebed
179 K-7 Netzahualcóyotl *dam.*
51 J-8 Neu Bamberg
59 P-2 Neu Sankt Johann
57 N-9 Neubourg
51 K-5 Neubrandenburg
58 D-4 Neuchâtel *lake*
58 C-3 Neuchâtel *reg.*
61 K-1 Neuchâtel
58 D-3 Neuchâtel (Neuenburg)
59 K-2 Neudorf
59 H-1 Neuendort
58 F-4 Neuenegg
50 G-9 Neufchâteau
50 E-7 Neufchâtel-en-Bray
55 N-4 Neufmontiers-lès-Meaux
55 N-7 Neufmoutiers-en-Brie
58 B-5 Neufs
54 E-1 Neuilly-en-Vexin
55 K-5 Neuilly-Plaisance
55 L-6 Neuilly-sur-Marne
55 H-5 Neuilly-sur-Seine
51 J-8 Neumarkt
51 J-5 Neumünster
145 J-3 Neun *riv.*
50 G-8 Neunkirchen
200 B-3 Neuquén *riv.*
200 C-4 Neuquen
200 C-3 Neuquén *reg.*
191 M-2 Neurara
51 K-6 Neuruppin
58 F-6 Neuschels *pass*
177 M-2 Neuse *riv.*
51 J-5 Neustadt
51 K-5 Neustrelitz
58 E-3 Neuveville
54 F-1 Neuville-Bosc
54 F-3 Neuville-sur-Oise
190 F-1 Nev. Ananea *mt*
68 C-9 Neva *riv.*
170 A-9 Nevada
157 C-3 Nevada *state*
167 J-5 Nevada *state*
200 E-4 Nevada (Argentina) *mt*
60 C-7 Nevada (Spain) *mt*
186 E-7 Nevado *mt*
178 C-5 Nevado de Colima *mt*
178 F-5 Nevado de Toluta *mt*
123 H-2 Nevanka
102 B-3 Neve *mt*
66 D-3 Nevel'
125 N-2 Nevel'Skogo *mt*
125 N-5 Nevel'sk
125 L-1 Nevel'skogo *strt.*
53 M-5 Nevendon
124 D-3 Never
61 H-1 Nevers
221 J-1 Nevertire
63 H-6 Neviano d'Arduini
67 M-9 Nevinnomyssk
181 M-2 Nevis *islds*
65 K-6 Nevşehir
125 N-2 Nevskoje *lake*
69 N-6 Nevyansk
179 N-7 New *riv.*
53 K-4 New
52 F-8 New *ft*
176 F-3 New Albany
52 G-7 New Alresford
192 C-2 New Amsterdam
219 J-7 New Angledool
171 N-5 New Bedford
172 C-5 New Berlinville
177 M-2 New Bern
175 M-5 New Braunfels
171 M-6 New Britain
117 K-7 New Britain *reg.*
211 M-5 New Britain *isl.*
171 L-7 New Brunswick
165 H-6 New Brunswick *state*
53 N-1 New Buckenham
215 L-4 New Caledonia *isl.*
173 J-2 New Canaan
165 H-5 New Carliste
170 F-8 New Castle
171 H-7 New Castle (USA)
170 E-8 New Castle (USA)
53 K-6 New Chapel
173 H-3 New City
173 H-1 New Croton *rés*
118 C-4 New Dehli
139 M-4 New Delhi
172 F-6 New Egypt
168 F-2 New England
219 M-8 New England *mt*
173 J-1 New Fairtlied
158 G-3 New Fort Hamilton
165 K-6 New Glasgow
172 F-7 New Gretna
157 G-3 New Hampshire *state*
164 F-9 New Hampshire *state*
170 B-5 New Hampton
211 M-2 New Hanover (Lavongai) *isl.*
173 K-1 New Haven *reg.*
171 M-6 New Haven
204 G-3 New Hebrides *reg.*
172 B-5 New Holland
172 E-5 New Hope
176 D-6 New Iberia
53 N-7 New Inn Green
211 P-3 New Ireland *isl.*
117 K-7 New Irland *reg.*
201 L-7 New Island *isl.*
171 L-7 New Jersey *state*
157 G-3 New Jersey *state*
176 D-2 New Little Rock
171 M-6 New London
166 E-7 New Meadows
175 H-2 New Mexico *state*
157 D-3 New Mexico *state*
172 F-1 New Milford
52 F-8 New Milton
220 G-9 New Norfolk
176 E-6 New Orleans
172 A-7 New Park
189 H-3 New Pelagatos *mt*
170 G-7 New Philadelphia
223 H-5 New Plymouth
180 F-2 New Providence *isl.*
52 B-2 New Radnor
165 H-5 New Richmond
172 B-3 New Ringgold
192 C-5 New River *riv.*
176 D-5 New Roads
173 H-3 New Rochelle
169 H-2 New Rockford
53 N-7 New Romney
113 N-2 New Siberian *islds*
219 H-8 New South Wales *reg.*
168 F-1 New Town
172 C-3 New Tripoli
170 A-4 New Ulm
170 E-8 New Vernon
172 D-5 New Wales
165 L-5 New Waterford
162 C-6 New Westminster
171 J-5 New York *state*
157 G-2 New York
173 H-3 New York (USA)
171 M-7 New York (USA)
205 H-6 New Zealand *state*
139 L-8 Newaj *riv.*
106 D-7 Newala
50 D-5 Newark (UK)
171 L-6 Newark (USA)
170 G-7 Newark (USA)
170 E-3 Newberry
166 E-4 Newberry Crater *vol.*
52 B-4 Newbridge
52 A-2 Newbridge on Wye
171 L-6 Newburgh
52 G-5 Newbury
221 L-2 Newcastel
105 K-5 Newcastle (South Africa)
214 G-2 Newcastle (Australia) *bay*
210 G-8 Newcastle (Australia) *bay*
165 H-6 Newcastle (Canada)
50 C-3 Newcastle (UK)
168 E-4 Newcastle (USA)
50 E-3 Newcastle upon Tyne
214 A-6 Newcastle Waters
50 A-4 Newcastle West
168 E-4 Newell
163 H-8 Newell *lake*
158 D-5 Newenham *cap.*
52 D-3 Newent
172 E-8 Newfield
172 F-2 Newfoundland
153 N-5 Newfoundland *isl.*
165 M-3 Newfoundland *reg.*
165 M-3 Newfoundland *isl.*
162 C-7 Newhalem
158 F-8 Newhalen
53 K-8 Newhaven
53 M-6 Newington
164 B-7 Newliskeard
212 F-9 Newman *mt*
172 B-5 Newmanstown
164 B-9 Newmarket (Canada)
50 E-5 Newmarket (UK)
177 H-3 Newnan
52 D-4 Newnham (UK)
53 M-6 Newnham (UK)
173 P-1 Newport *bay*
162 E-8 Newport (Canada)
50 D-6 Newport (UK)
171 M-6 Newport (USA)
170 F-8 Newport (USA)
162 A-9 Newport (USA)
164 F-8 Newport (USA)
177 J-1 Newport (USA)
176 E-2 Newport (USA)
167 M-3 Newport Beach
171 K-9 Newport News
53 H-2 Newport Pagnell
213 M-3 Newry (Australia)
50 C-3 Newry (UK)
177 K-2 Newton
53 K-2 Newton (UK)
170 A-6 Newton (USA)
171 M-5 Newton (USA)
176 F-4 Newton (USA)
176 C-5 Newton (USA)
52 A-9 Newton Abbot
172 D-6 Newton Square
50 C-3 Newton Stewart
46 F-1 Newtontoppen
52 D-2 Newtown (UK)
172 A-3 Newtown (USA)
73 P-9 Neyrīz
58 E-5 Neyruz
126 D-1 Neyshābur
141 L-5 Neyyāttinkara
54 A-1 Nézé
54 D-4 Nézel
66 F-6 Nezhin
166 D-7 Nezperce
145 H-2 Nga *riv.*
147 L-9 Ngabang
98 G-5 Ngabé
90 F-2 Ngadda *riv.*
91 L-7 Ngadza
99 J-4 Ngali
91 H-4 Ngam
90 D-8 Ngambé
103 H-8 Ngami *riv.*
102 G-7 Ngamiland *reg.*
103 L-7 Ngamo
94 E-6 Ngangala
144 F-4 Ngao
90 F-6 Ngaoundéré
143 K-7 Ngape
223 K-4 Ngaruawahia
143 K-9 Ngathainggyaung
223 J-5 Ngauruhce *mt*
207 L-6 Ngawi
144 C-5 Ngayok *bay*
101 J-7 Ngerengere
107 J-1 Ngezi *riv.*
145 J-2 Nghia Lo
145 J-3 Ngiap *riv.*
102 C-5 Ngiva
98 G-4 Ngo
145 L-6 Ngoc Linh
98 G-1 Ngok *riv.*
131 N-4 Ngom *riv.*
103 K-5 Ngoma
101 K-5 Ngomeni *cap.*
101 G-3 Ngong
91 L-4 Ngono
100 E-1 Ngora
100 F-5 Ngorongoro *vol.*
86 E-4 Ngoui
98 C-3 Ngounié *riv.*
98 C-3 Ngounié *reg.*
91 P-5 Ngouo *mt*
91 H-2 Ngoura
91 H-1 Ngouri
100 C-4 Ngozi
90 F-8 Nguélémendouka
90 F-1 Nguig
119 J-6 Ngulu *isl.*
145 H-4 Ngum *riv.*
208 D-8 Ngundju *cap.*
223 K-3 Ngunguru *bay*
102 B-1 Ngunza
90 D-2 Nguru
101 H-7 Nguru *mt*
104 G-2 Ngwaketsi *reg.*
103 K-9 Ngwato *reg.*
103 K-6 Ngwesi *riv.*
103 J-6 Ngwezumba *riv.*
129 P-4 Ngyāk
145 M-8 Nha Trang
190 D-8 Nhambiquara
107 H-4 Nhamuabué
192 D-8 Nhamunda
192 C-8 Nhamundá *riv.*
196 F-4 Nhandeara
107 H-3 Nhandugué *riv.*
102 D-1 Nharea
196 B-3 Nhecolândia
102 B-1 Nhia *riv.*
220 E-4 Nhill
214 C-3 Nhulunbuy
100 A-1 Nia-Nia
88 F-3 Niafounké
171 H-5 Niagara Falls (Canada)
171 H-5 Niagara Falls (USA)
87 J-7 Niagassola
147 N-7 Niah
89 L-2 Niakaramandougou
89 H-7 Niamey
88 G-7 Niamey *reg.*
77 C-3 Niamey
89 H-1 Niamina
89 L-6 Niamtougou
87 K-7 Niandan *riv.*
87 J-7 Niandan Koro
94 B-7 Niangara
88 F-4 Niangay *lake*
173 M-1 Niantic
100 E-2 Nianzi
124 E-7 Nianzishan
99 P-1 Niapu
98 D-5 Niari *reg.*
98 E-5 Niari *riv.*
146 B-9 Nias *isl.*
106 E-5 Niassa *reg.*
224 E-5 Niau *isl.*
83 P-5 Nibāk
62 E-5 Nibbiano
146 D-6 Nibong Tebal
69 N-5 Nica *riv.*
157 F-5 Nicaragua *state*
184 G-6 Nicaragua *lake*
64 F-7 Nicaria *isl.*
61 K-4 Nice
62 A-5 Nichelino
170 F-9 Nicholasville
180 E-2 Nicholl's Town
173 K-1 Nichols
213 M-5 Nicholson
214 D-7 Nicholson *riv.*
216 E-3 Nicholson *mt*
192 D-3 Nickerie *riv.*
212 D-7 Nickol *bay*
146 A-3 Nicobar *islds*
146 A-4 Nicobar (Great) *isl.*
146 A-4 Nicobar (little) *isl.*
185 N-8 Nicocli
195 K-2 Nicolau *riv.*
164 E-7 Nicolet
47 G-6 Nicosia
65 K-9 Nicosia
184 G-7 Nicoya
184 G-7 Nicoya *gulf*
184 F-7 Nicoya *pen.*
165 H-6 Nictau
59 N-2 Nied-Urnen

59 L-4 Nieder Bauenstock *mt*
58 G-6 Nieder-Simmen *val.*
51 K-9 Niederbayern *ft*
58 F-6 Niederhorn
59 H-5 Niederried
59 K-7 Niederwald
59 K-1 Niederwil
66 B-6 Niedzyrzec Podlaski
90 D-9 Niéfang
104 F-6 Niekerkshoop
57 M-7 Niel bij As
142 E-1 Nielamu
89 K-2 Niélé
91 J-4 Niellim
100 B-7 Niemba *riv.*
100 B-7 Niemba
66 C-5 Niemen *riv.*
89 J-1 Niéna
51 J-6 Nienburg
87 P-8 Niénokoué *mt*
57 J-1 Niersen
58 G-6 Niesen *mt*
87 P-8 Niete *mt*
104 G-7 Nieu
192 E-3 Nieuw Amsterdam
56 B-5 Nieuw-Beijerland
56 D-7 Nieuw Ginneken
56 D-7 Nieuw Ginneken *reg.*
57 L-1 Nieuw Heeten
56 A-5 Nieuw-Helvoet
56 D-4 Nieuw Lekkerland
56 F-2 Nieuw-Loosdrecht
57 J-2 Nieuw Milligen
192 C-2 Nieuw Nickerie
56 C-1 Nieuw Vennep
56 A-7 Nieuw Vossemeer
56 B-4 Nieuwe Maas *est.*
56 D-5 Nieuwe Merwede *riv.*
56 B-7 Nieuwe Molen
56 A-6 Nieuwe Tonge
56 A-4 Nieuwe Waterweg *est.*
56 C-2 Nieuwe Wetering
56 E-3 Nieuwegein
56 E-5 Nieuwendijk
57 P-8 Nieuwenhagen
56 A-5 Nieuwenhoorn
56 E-2 Nieuwer Ter Aa
56 D-3 Nieuwerbrug
56 C-4 Nieuwerkerk
56 D-2 Nieuwkoop
56 E-4 Nieuwland
56 A-9 Nieuwnamen
104 D-7 Nieuwoudtville
56 D-4 Nieuwpoort
57 N-7 Nieuwstadt
56 D-2 Nieuwveen
188 E-3 Nieva *riv.*
78 B-9 Nieves *mt*
57 H-5 Niftrik
136 A-5 Nigasi-Risiri
65 K-6 Niğde
105 K-4 Nigel
89 J-8 Niger *na.p.*
87 J-8 Niger *riv.*
90 A-3 Niger *reg.*
77 C-3 Niger *state*
77 C-4 Nigeria *state*
170 G-1 Night Hawk *lake*
64 D-5 Nigrita
56 E-1 Nigtevecht
159 L-4 Nigu *riv.*
138 B-3 Nihing *riv.*
224 C-1 Nihoa *isl.*
137 J-8 Nii *isl.*
136 G-6 Niigata
137 K-4 Niihama
224 C-1 Niihau *isl.*
137 K-4 Niimi
136 G-7 Niitu
137 J-8 Niizima-Hon-Son
57 K-1 Nijbroek
56 G-2 Nijkerk
56 G-2 Nijkerkerveen
56 G-1 Nijkernauw *strt.*
57 J-5 Nijmegen
50 G-6 Nijmegen
56 G-7 Nijnsel
57 N-1 Nijstad
57 N-9 Nijswiller
57 M-1 Nijverdal
73 H-5 Nik Pey
48 C-8 Nikel
89 L-8 Nikki
136 G-7 Nikkō
125 K-5 Nikolajevka
125 L-1 Nikolajevsk-an-Amure
67 M-5 Nikolajevskij
64 F-9 Nikólaos
66 F-9 Nikolayev
69 M-8 Nikolo-Ber'ozovka
67 L-2 Nikol'sk (SSSR)
68 G-7 Nikol'sk (SSSR)
120 E-4 Nikol'skij
67 N-6 Nikol'skoje (SSSR)
100 D-5 Nikonga *riv.*
68 D-8 Nikonova Gora
67 H-8 Nikopol'
72 A-4 Niksar
84 A-8 Nīkshahr
64 B-4 Nikšie
127 H-5 Nīl Kowtal *mt*
209 K-5 Nila *isl.*
141 J-4 Nilambūr
69 K-2 Nil'dino
92 G-2 Nile *riv.*
94 E-7 Nile *reg.*
100 D-1 Nile *riv.*
82 B-8 Nile *riv.*
76 F-3 Nile *riv.*
170 E-6 Niles
142 E-6 Nīlgiri
138 K-7 Nīmach
125 H-3 Niman *riv.*
87 M-8 Nimba *mt*
87 N-7 Nimba *reg.*
138 K-7 Nīmbahera
125 J-2 Nimelen *riv.*
61 H-3 Nîmes
125 H-1 Nimi *riv.*
221 J-4 Nimmitabel
162 B-5 Nimpkish *riv.*
72 E-6 Nimrūd *site*
126 C-7 Nīmrūz *reg.*
94 E-7 Nimule
141 K-1 Nine Degree Channel
160 D-9 Ninemile
223 J-1 Ninety Mile Beach
200 E-7 Ninfas *pte*
53 L-8 Ninfield
125 H-9 Ningan
135 N-3 Ningbo
132 G-4 Ningcheng
135 M-6 Ningde
135 K-6 Ningdu
135 M-3 Ningguo
135 N-4 Ninghai
135 K-6 Ninghua
132 E-7 Ningjin
143 N-1 Ningjing
134 A-6 Ninglang
134 E-9 Ningming
134 B-6 Ningnan
134 D-2 Ningqiang
134 D-6 Ningwu
131 H-9 Ningxiahuizu Zizhiqu *reg.*
132 B-8 Ningxian
135 H-5 Ningxiang
135 H-7 Ningyuan
145 K-2 Ninh Binh
145 M-8 Ninh Hoa
211 H-1 Ninigo *islds*
173 P-1 Ninigret Pond *cap.*
86 D-3 Ninijad
158 G-9 Ninilchik
72 E-6 Ninive *site*
179 M-5 Ninúm *pte*
196 C-4 Nioaque
196 B-4 Nioaque *riv.*
168 E-5 Niobrara *riv.*
100 C-1 Nioka
99 H-4 Nioki
87 H-5 Niokolo Koba
87 H-4 Niokolo-Koba *na.p.*
88 G-2 Niono
106 F-6 Niorenge *riv.*
89 J-5 Niorida
86 F-7 Nioro
86 G-2 Nioro du Rip
60 F-1 Niort
140 E-3 Nipāni
163 M-6 Nipawin
163 M-6 Nipawin *na.p.*
180 G-5 Nipe *bay*
170 D-1 Nipigon *lake*
170 D-1 Nipigon
163 K-5 Nipin *riv.*
107 H-6 Nipiodi *riv.*
171 H-3 Nipissing *lake*
72 G-9 Nippur *site*
167 L-5 Nipton
82 C-9 Niqrub al Fawqāni *mt*
194 E-9 Niquelândia
180 F-6 Niquero
190 E-4 Niquiter *riv.*
140 D-4 Nīra *riv.*
187 J-2 Nirgua
140 C-7 Nirmal
64 F-2 Nîrşova
64 C-4 Nis
96 E-4 Nişāb
96 D-2 Nisah *mt*
129 N-3 Nisalgāon
132 B-7 Nisgtiaoliang
158 F-6 Nishilik *lake*
96 C-9 Nishtūn
137 J-3 Nisino *isl.*
137 K-5 Nisinomiya
137 N-3 Nisinoomate
64 G-8 Nisiros *isl.*
137 J-5 Nisiwaki
160 D-3 Nisling *riv.*
56 B-8 Nispen
51 K-3 Nissan *riv.*
57 H-6 Nistelrode
197 K-6 Niterói
137 K-3 Nitihara
137 M-3 Nitinan
52 G-9 Niton
51 M-9 Nitra
51 M-9 Nitra *riv.*
160 E-5 Nitsutlin *plat.*
224 B-5 Niuatobutabu *islds*
224 C-5 Niue *isl.*
124 C-4 Niuerhe *riv.*
129 P-4 Niuku
134 C-7 Niulanjiang *riv.*
147 L-9 Niut *mt*
135 P-4 Niutoushan *isl.*
133 J-4 Niuzhuang
69 J-4 Nivšera
48 D-9 Nivskij
129 H-4 Niyahe *riv.*
131 P-2 Niyanghe *riv.*
122 E-4 Niž Kur'ata
68 E-3 Niž Mgla
69 L-1 Niž. Narykary
121 L-1 Niž'Omka
127 J-4 Niž P'andž
69 P-3 Niz. Rynja
69 N-6 Niž. Sergi
69 P-4 Niž. Tavda
69 M-5 Niž. Tura
51 L-6 Niz Wielkopolska *reg.*
140 D-6 Nizām *lake*
140 D-6 Nizāmabād
126 E-5 Nizgan *riv.*
69 N-5 Nizhniy Tagil
100 C-1 Nizi
51 L-7 Nizina *mt*
65 M-7 Nizip
123 L-1 Nižn'aja Karelina
69 J-3 Nižn'aja Omra
122 G-2 Nižn'aja Pojma
123 L-1 Nizn'aja Tunguska *riv.*
123 H-2 Nižn'aja Zaimka
123 M-3 Nižneangarsk
65 J-1 Nižnegorskij
123 J-2 Nižneilimsk
69 L-9 Nižnekamskij
125 K-3 Nižnetambovskoje
123 H-3 Nižneudinsk
123 P-6 Nižnij Casučej
122 G-2 Nižnij Ingaš
70 B-7 Niž.Oseredok *isl.*
69 J-5 Niž.Voč'
62 C-5 Nizza Monferrato
108 C-3 Njadidja *isl.*
48 C-4 Njardvik
106 C-6 Njenje *riv.*
90 D-6 Njinikom
206 C-1 Njinji *riv.*
101 J-9 Njinjo
103 J-5 Njoko *riv.*
100 F-8 Njombe *riv.*
100 F-9 Njombe
48 D-5 Njunes *mt*
90 D-6 Nkambé
99 J-4 Nkaw
98 E-5 Nkayi
98 F-4 Nkéni *riv.*
106 D-4 Nkhata Bay
98 C-3 Nkomi *riv.*
90 D-7 Nkongsamba
89 M-4 Nkoranza
106 E-4 Nkota Kota
100 E-7 Nkululu *riv.*
105 L-6 Nkwalini
143 M-2 Nmai *riv.*
189 H-9 No Porto
53 L-4 Noak Hill
63 M-2 Noale
173 N-1 Noank
159 K-3 Noatak
159 L-3 Noatak *riv.*
48 D-7 Noavas *mt*
137 M-3 Nobeoka
170 E-8 Noblesville
136 C-6 Noboribetu
218 F-5 Noccundra
62 G-5 Noceto
58 E-2 Nods
51 K-4 Næstved
174 E-3 Nogales
63 J-4 Nogara
137 L-2 Nogata
54 A-9 Nogent-le-Roi
50 E-8 Nogent-le-Rotrou
55 K-6 Nogent-sur-Marne
50 F-8 Nogent-sur-Seine
55 P-2 Nogeon
67 H-2 Noginsk
125 M-1 Nogliki
199 H-5 Nogoyá
199 H-5 Nogoyá *riv.*
139 L-3 Nohar
136 D-7 Nohezi
145 K-5 Noi *riv.*
55 H-2 Nointel
58 A-5 Noir *mt*
201 N-4 Noir *isl.*
78 E-1 Noir *cap.*
50 C-8 Noires *mt*
58 A-7 Noirmont
58 D-2 Noirmont (Le)
50 C-9 Noirmoutier *isl.*
55 L-7 Noiseau
55 L-6 Noisiel
55 L-6 Noisy-le-Grand
55 K-5 Noisy-le-Sec
126 C-8 Nok Kundi
102 G-7 Nokaneng
84 A-8 Nokhowch *mt*
49 J-7 Nokia
208 C-1 Nokilalaki *mt*
163 M-4 Nokomis *lake*
158 G-4 Nokort
91 H-8 Nola
62 C-8 Noli
69 K-8 Nolinsk
102 F-7 Noma Omuramba *riv.*
164 A-4 Nomansland *pte*
179 P-8 Nombre de Dios *mt*
159 H-2 Nome
130 F-9 Nomgon
137 M-2 Nomozaki
130 B-5 Nömrög
224 B-6 Nomuka *islds*
145 H-6 Non Sung
161 M-9 Nonacho *lake*
63 J-6 Nonantola
211 H-5 Nondugl
105 L-5 Nondweni
62 A-5 None
55 M-1 Nonette *riv.*
144 G-6 Nong Bua
145 J-5 Nong Han *lake*
145 H-4 Nong Khai
144 G-5 Nong Phai
133 K-1 Nongan
105 L-5 Nongoma
143 J-3 Nongpoh
89 L-8 Nono *riv.*
133 M-7 Nonsan
144 G-7 Nonthaburi
158 E-8 Nonvianuk *lake*
220 G-5 Noojee
213 J-5 Noonkanbah
56 C-7 Noord Brabant *reg.*
56 C-4 Noord Merwede *riv.*
56 E-4 Noordeloos
56 D-2 Noorden
57 J-9 Noordervaart *cal.*
56 B-2 Noordwijk *reg.*
56 B-2 Noordwijk aan Zee
56 B-2 Noordwijk-Binnen
56 C-1 Noordwijkerhout
159 K-3 Noorvick
56 B-3 Nootdorp
162 A-5 Nootka *strt.*
162 A-5 Nootka *isl.*
98 E-6 Noqui
124 G-3 Nora *riv.*
218 E-1 Noranside
48 C-5 Nord Kvaløy *isl.*
48 G-3 Nord Trøndelag *reg.*
48 C-5 Nordberg
162 G-5 Nordegg
51 H-5 Norden
113 H-2 Nordenšel'da *isl.*
99 L-8 Nordeste
51 J-7 Nordhausen
51 H-6 Nordhorn
48 B-7 Nordkinn *isl.*
48 G-4 Nordli
172 A-1 Nordmont
49 H-1 Nordøyane *isl.*
48 D-2 Nordoyar *islds*
169 H-6 Norfolk
176 D-1 Norfolk *lake*
218 G-5 Norley
172 C-3 Normal
214 F-7 Norman *riv.*
175 N-2 Norman
53 K-1 Norman Cross
161 J-4 Norman Wells
211 N-8 Normanby *isl.*
215 H-5 Normanby *riv.*
180 F-1 Norman's Castle
214 F-7 Normanton
164 B-6 Normetal
216 E-9 Nornalup
200 E-3 Norquinco
48 E-5 Norrbotten *reg.*
51 J-2 Nørresundby
171 L-7 Norristown
172 A-7 Norrisville
51 L-2 Norrköping
51 M-1 Norrtälje
217 H-7 Norseman
124 G-3 Norsk
199 J-8 Norte *pte*
190 C-9 Norte *mt*
186 F-4 Norte de Santander *reg.*
223 J-1 North *cap.*
221 H-7 North *pte*
112 A-2 North *cap.*
165 L-5 North *cap.*
46 D-4 North *sea*
223 L-4 North *isl.*
226 A-6 North *sea*
204 H-5 North (New Zealand) *isl.*
161 L-7 North Arm *strt.*
163 K-6 North Battleford
164 B-8 North Bay
166 D-2 North Bend
53 H-8 North Bersted
50 D-2 North Berwick
172 F-4 North Branch
173 L-1 North Branford
181 J-4 North Caicos *isl.*
168 E-9 North Canadian *riv.*
175 M-1 North Canadian *riv.*
170 F-3 North Channel *cal.*
214 C-4 North East *islds*
172 B-7 North East
162 F-8 North Fork Flathead *riv.*
168 F-3 North Fork Moreau *riv.*
168 D-4 North Fork Powder *riv.*
175 M-2 North Fork Red *riv.*
51 H-4 North Frisian *islds*
173 L-1 North Guilford
173 L-1 North Haven
223 J-3 North Head *cap.*
172 C-4 North Hills *hill*
95 J-7 North Horr
142 C-4 North Koel *riv.*
143 K-2 North Lakhimpur
167 L-5 North Las Vegas
168 G-6 North Loup *riv.*
173 L-1 North Madison
153 H-2 North Magnetic Pole
226 B-3 North Magnetic Pole
161 H-6 North Nahanni *riv.*
224 E-2 North Pacific Ocean
167 K-3 North Palissade *mt*
172 F-4 North Plainfield
168 F-6 North Platte
168 C-5 North Platte *riv.*
165 J-5 North Point *pte*
226 A-1 North Pole
170 F-4 North Pt
144 A-7 North Reef *isl.*
167 L-7 North Rim
162 F-6 North Saskatchewan *riv.*
144 A-8 North Sentinel *isl.*
168 F-8 North Solomon *riv.*
173 H-2 North Tarrytown
52 F-6 North Tidworth
222 B-9 North trap
164 A-3 North Twin *isl.*
50 C-1 North Uist *isl.*
162 C-6 North Vancouver
163 H-1 North Vermillon
168 D-9 North Veta *pass*
212 B-8 North West *cap.*
177 K-1 North Wilkesboro
50 E-4 Northallerton
105 J-3 Northam (South Africa)
216 E-7 Northam (Australia)
216 D-5 Northampton (Australia)
53 H-1 Northampton (UK) *reg.*
53 H-2 Northampton (UK)
172 D-3 Northampton (USA)
172 D-3 Northampton (USA) *reg.*
216 E-9 Northcliffe
181 J-5 Northeast *pte*
158 G-2 Northeast *cap.*
112 A-1 Northeast Land
51 J-6 Northeim
103 H-4 Northern Lueti *riv.*
119 L-5 Northern Marianas *islds*
214 B-6 Northern Territory *reg.*
52 E-1 Northfield (UK)
170 A-4 Northfield (USA)
173 L-1 Northford
53 M-7 Northiam
223 J-2 Northland *reg.*
52 F-3 Northleach
53 J-5 Northolt
170 A-2 Northome
170 E-4 Northport
219 L-1 Northumberland *islds*
220 D-5 Northumberland *cap.*
165 K-6 Northumberland *strt.*
160 D-2 Northway Junction
158 G-1 Northwest *cap.*
161 L-3 Northwest Territories *reg.*
170 A-5 Northwood
159 H-4 Norton *bay*
53 M-2 Norton (UK)
52 E-3 Norton (UK)
177 J-1 Norton (USA)
168 G-7 Norton (USA)
176 G-1 Nortonville
48 F-1 Norvège *sea*
227 M-1 Norvegia *cap.*
170 G-7 Norwalk (USA)
167 M-3 Norwalk (USA)
47 E-3 Norway *state*
46 D-3 Norwegian *sea*
226 A-6 Norwegian *sea*
50 E-5 Norwich (UK)
171 K-5 Norwich (USA)
171 M-6 Norwich (USA)
123 M-4 Nos *mt*
136 A-8 Nosappu *cap.*
122 G-2 Nošino
136 E-6 Nosiro
109 H-7 Nosive *lake*
109 J-5 Nosivolo *riv.*
69 P-3 Noska *riv.*
126 B-6 Noşratābād
104 D-2 Nossob *riv.*
87 H-8 Nossombougou
69 J-6 Nošul'
109 J-2 Nosy Andravoho *isl.*
109 J-2 Nosy Andriamitaroka *isl.*
109 J-2 Nosy Andriangory *isl.*
108 D-8 Nosy Ankao *isl.*
108 D-8 Nosy Ankomba *isl.*
108 D-7 Nosy Bé *isl.*
109 H-7 Nosy Dombala *isl.*
108 C-7 Nosy Hao (Madagascar) *isl.*
109 K-1 Nosy Hao (Madagascar) *isl.*
109 M-2 Nosy Imborona *isl.*
108 G-3 Nosy Lava (Madagascar) *isl.*
108 C-7 Nosy Lava (Madagascar) *isl.*
108 E-6 Nosy Lava (Madagascar) *isl.*
109 M-2 Nosy Manitsa *isl.*
108 G-2 Nosy Marify *isl.*
108 G-2 Nosy Maroanfaly *isl.*
108 G-2 Nosy Mavony *isl.*
108 D-7 Nosy Mitsio *isl.*
109 J-2 Nosy Tania *isl.*
108 G-2 Nosy Vao *isl.*
109 K-6 Nosy-Varika
136 A-5 Nosyappu *cap.*
48 D-8 Nota *riv.*
167 J-7 Notch *mt*
125 K-8 Noto *riv.*
137 H-5 Noto *pen.*
61 N-9 Noto
51 J-1 Notodden
55 L-7 Notre-Dame *ft*
165 M-2 Notre-Dame *bay*
54 A-3 Notre-Dame-de-la-
164 G-6 Notre-Dame-du-Lac
164 D-8 Notre-Dame du Laus
164 B-7 Notre-Dame du Nord
165 N-2 Notre-Dame-Junction
171 H-4 Nottawasaga *bay*
164 B-4 Nottaway *riv.*
156 F-1 Nottingham *isl.*
153 K-5 Nottingham *isl.*
155 K-3 Nottingham (Canada) *isl.*
50 E-5 Nottingham (UK)
172 B-7 Nottingham (USA)
59 J-2 Nottwil
86 A-3 Nouâdhibou *reg.*
86 A-2 Nouâdhibou
86 A-2 Nouâdhibou *cap.*
86 C-3 Nouakchott
77 A-3 Nouakchott
86 B-2 Nouâmghâr
98 D-5 Noumbi *riv.*
215 N-5 Nouméa
78 A-6 Noun *cap.*
98 E-1 Nouna *riv.*
89 H-3 Nouna
104 G-7 Noupoort
164 B-3 Nouveau-Comptoir (Paint Hills)
155 L-4 Nouveau Québec *reg.*
155 M-5 Nouvelle Écosse *reg.*
214 G-1 Nouvelle-Guinée (Papouasie)
193 H-6 Nova *isl.*
195 P-3 Nova Cruz
197 L-6 Nova Friburgo
99 H-9 Nova Gaia
196 G-4 Nova Granada
87 H-3 Nova Lamego
197 K-4 Nova Lima
195 H-3 Nova Lorque
107 K-4 Nova Mambone
62 E-2 Nova Milanese

195 J-4 Nova Olinda riv.
194 C-3 Nova Olinda
192 B-9 Nova Olinda do Norte
64 B-2 Nova Pazova
197 H-5 Nova Resende
195 K-2 Nova Russas
165 K-7 Nova Scotia reg.
87 P-1 Nova Sintra
107 K-3 Nova Sofala
193 K-8 Nova Timboteua
107 J-3 Nova Vanduzi
197 N-3 Nova Venécia
190 B-6 Nova Vida riv.
127 L-3 Novabad
63 N-9 Novafeltria
68 C-9 Novaia Ladoga
66 G-9 Novaja
123 L-6 Novaja Kurba
121 M-5 Novaja Sul'ba
123 J-4 Novaja Uda
61 K-2 Novara
62 C-3 Novara
62 C-2 Novara reg.
167 H-1 Novato
70 A-5 Novaya Kazanka
112 D-2 Novaya Zemlya reg.
63 J-5 Novellara
63 N-2 Noventa di Piave
63 L-3 Noventa Vicentina
66 D-1 Novgorod
66 F-5 Novgorod-Severskij
63 J-5 Novi di Modena
61 L-3 Novi Ligure
69 M-5 Novi Lyalya
64 F-3 Novi Pazar
64 B-2 Novi Sad
63 P-9 Novilara
58 D-7 Noville
194 A-1 Novo riv.
193 H-6 Novo lake
194 E-6 Novo Acordo
197 M-2 Novo Cruzeiro
67 L-9 Novoaleksandrovskaja
70 C-2 Novoaleksejevka
121 P-3 Novoaltajsk
67 L-5 Novoanninskij
67 J-8 Novoazovskoje
70 B-6 Novobogatinskoje
124 G-5 Novoburejskij
67 M-1 Novočeremšansk
67 K-8 Novocherkassk
67 K-5 Novochop'orsk
121 H-4 Novodolinskij
124 F-4 Novogeorgijevka
66 D-7 Novograd-Volynskij
66 C-5 Novogrudok
123 M-6 Novoiljinsk
124 F-3 Novojampol'
125 J-8 Novokačalinsk
71 H-3 Novokazalinsk
124 F-4 Novokijevskij Uval
67 L-9 Novokubansk
125 J-5 Novokurovka
67 N-2 Novokuybyshevsk
122 C-3 Novokuznetsk
227 N-1 Novolazarevskaya
66 C-7 Novolynsk
66 F-8 Novomirgorod
67 H-3 Novomoskovsk (SSSR)
67 H-7 Novomoskovsk (SSSR)
67 H-8 Novonikolajevka
67 K-5 Novonikolajevskij
70 D-1 Novoorsk
123 M-6 Novopavlovka
125 K-7 Novopokrovka
67 L-9 Novopokrovskaja
66 D-3 Novopolock
72 A-1 Novorossiysk
70 A-2 Novosergijevka
67 K-7 Novoshakhtinsk
121 P-2 Novosibirsk
122 B-2 Novosibirsk
67 H-4 Novosil'
66 F-6 Novoska
66 D-3 Novosokol'niki
122 E-3 Novos'olovo
70 C-1 Novotroitsk
66 F-8 Novoukrainka
69 N-6 Novoutkinsk
67 N-4 Novouzensk
121 K-1 Novovaršavka
124 E-4 Novovoskresenovka
69 J-7 Novovyatsk
66 F-5 Novozybkov
66 G-8 Novy Byg
66 F-9 Novy Odessa
125 K-4 Novy Ussura
69 L-9 Novy Zaj
66 G-9 Novy Zburjevka
65 H-1 Novy Zburjevka
68 G-2 Novyj Bor
67 H-6 Novyj Oskol
73 K-4 Now Shahr
126 E-6 Now Zād
51 L-6 Nowa Sól
73 J-6 Nowbarān

73 H-4 Nowdi
143 J-3 Nowgong
159 J-6 Nowitna riv.
168 C-4 Nowood riv.
221 K-3 Nowra
142 B-7 Nowrangapur
127 K-7 Nowshera
66 A-6 Nowy
66 A-8 Nowy Sacz
163 P-1 Nowyak lake
172 B-1 Noxen
60 B-2 Noya
160 B-8 Noyes isl.
130 F-7 Noyon
55 H-9 Nozay
137 J-8 Nozima pte
79 K-5 Nsa riv.
107 H-4 Nsanie
89 N-5 Nsawam
106 E-2 Nsefu
98 G-6 Nsele riv.
89 N-3 Nsinsim
98 D-1 Nsoc
90 B-6 Nsukka
98 C-1 Ntem riv.
90 E-8 Ntui
100 D-2 Ntusi
133 H-4 Nuanchitang
103 N-9 Nuanetsi
103 N-9 Nuanetsi riv.
146 E-7 Nuang mt
149 P-3 Nuangan
89 N-6 Nuatja
93 H-2 Nubian dés
76 F-7 Nubian dés
200 A-2 Nuble riv.
129 P-7 Nubri
62 B-7 Nucetto
130 E-8 Nucgen Chudag lake
72 F-2 Nucha
68 G-5 N'uchca
220 B-1 Nuckey Bluff mt
54 D-1 Nucourt
188 E-5 Nucuray riv.
189 L-8 Nudo Ausangate
189 M-7 Nudo Coropuna
189 L-9 Nudo de Quenamari
189 M-7 Nudo Sarasara
175 L-6 Nueces riv.
154 J-3 Nueltin lake
163 P-2 Nueltin lake
56 G-8 Nuenen
191 N-1 Nuestra Señora bay
201 P-6 Nueva isl.
187 H-5 Nueva Antioquia
191 K-7 Nueva Asuncion reg.
198 C-5 Nueva California
174 G-4 Nueva Casas Grandes
187 L-2 Nueva Esparta reg.
180 B-5 Nueva Gerona
179 M-9 Nueva Ocotepeque
175 K-7 Nueva Rosita
180 F-5 Nuevitas
179 L-4 Nuevo rf
200 E-7 Nuevo gulf
175 L-7 Nuevo Laredo
178 F-1 Nuevo León reg.
191 L-3 Nuevo Mundo mt
188 B-5 Nuevo Rocafuerte
59 P-6 Nufenen
59 L-7 Nufenen pass
97 J-6 Nugāled val.
222 D-9 Nugget pte
138 B-4 Nüh pte
124 E-1 Nujam riv.
93 J-3 Nujaym
131 P-4 Nujiang riv.
68 B-6 N'uk lake
48 F-9 N'uk lake
158 F-9 Nuka isl.
159 M-3 Nuka riv.
92 D-4 Nukhaylah
68 G-7 N'uksenica
224 E-4 Nuku Hiva isl.
225 B-6 Nuku'alofa
211 M-5 Nukuhu
224 B-4 Nukulailai isl.
224 B-4 Nukunono isl.
119 L-6 Nukuoro isl.
71 H-6 Nukus
124 C-1 N'ukža riv.
56 G-6 Nuland
217 N-6 Nularbor
159 J-5 Nulato riv.
56 G-1 Nuldernauw strt.
212 G-7 Nullagine riv.
212 F-8 Nullagine
217 M-6 Nullarbor pl.
204 C-5 Nullarbor pl.
132 G-3 Nuluerhushan mt
148 G-2 Numancia
56 B-6 Numansdorp
141 N-1 Numas riv.
136 G-7 Numata (Japan)
136 B-6 Numata (Japan)
94 B-5 Numatinna riv.

137 J-7 Numazu
209 N-1 Numfoor isl.
172 A-3 Numidia
159 H-1 Nun'amo
158 E-4 Nunavakpak lake
52 G-4 Nuneham Courtenay
87 J-3 Nunez lag.
201 N-3 Nuñez isl.
216 F-6 Nungarin
106 E-6 Nungo
101 J-7 Nungwi cap.
58 G-7 Nünihorn
158 D-3 Nunivak isl.
124 E-6 Nunjiang
124 E-5 Nunjiang riv.
127 N-8 Nunkun mt
48 D-7 Nunnanem
52 D-6 Nunney Catch
52 D-6 Nunney Mallet
58 G-1 Nunningen
130 E-4 Nuomingming-genshamo mt
124 E-6 Nuominhe riv.
87 M-8 Nuon riv.
132 G-1 Nuonayimiao
61 L-6 Nuoro
84 F-9 Nuqdah cap.
83 H-6 Nuqrah
82 C-7 Nuqruş mt
186 C-6 Nuqui
121 H-4 Nura riv.
224 B-5 Nurakita isl.
120 B-9 Nuata
120 B-9 Nuratau mt
62 F-5 Nure riv.
127 K-3 Nurek
172 B-2 Nuremberg
65 M-6 Nurhak mt
93 H-4 Nüri site
187 N-4 Nuria plat.
141 M-1 Nuriwari isl.
67 M-1 Nurlat
48 G-9 Nurmes
51 J-8 Nürnberg
102 E-7 Nurugas
62 A-2 Nus
208 A-7 Nusa Tenggara Barat reg.
208 E-7 Nusa Tenggara Timur reg.
65 P-6 Nusaybin
158 D-6 Nushagak pen.
158 E-7 Nushagak riv.
158 E-6 Nushagak bay
143 N-3 Nushan mt
188 C-4 Nushiño riv.
126 F-9 Nushki
57 N-8 Nuth
53 K-7 Nutley
214 A-5 Nutwood Downs
160 D-2 Nutzotin mt
130 A-3 Nuuruudīn Hotgor mt
141 N-7 Nuwara Eliya
82 C-4 Nuwaybi al Muzayyinah
104 E-8 Nuweveldreeks mt
158 E-6 Nuyakuk lake
220 A-1 Nuyts islds
216 E-9 Nuyts pte
196 B-9 Nuzaingó
140 E-8 Nüzvid
123 P-9 Nvokručininskij
216 F-8 Nyabing
173 H-2 Nyack
103 P-6 Nyadiri riv.
100 E-4 Nyahanga
100 E-6 Nyahua riv.
100 F-4 Nyakabindi
92 C-9 Nyala
100 E-5 Nyalikungu
143 J-1 Nyamjiang riv.
94 B-3 Nyamlell
94 F-3 Nyandina riv.
68 E-7 Nyandoma
98 C-4 Nyanga reg.
98 D-4 Nyanga riv.
100 C-4 Nyanza
100 F-2 Nyanza reg.
100 C-5 Nyanza-Lac
106 D-4 Nyassa lake
143 L-9 Nyaunglebin
107 J-1 Nyazwidzi riv.
49 J-3 Nybergsund
51 J-4 Nyborg
51 L-3 Nybro
129 P-7 Nyenchen Anglha rge
101 G-3 Nyeri
94 E-3 Nyerol
106 C-3 Nyika plat.
129 M-6 Nyima
66 B-9 Nyiregyhaza
101 G-4 Nyiri dés
101 N-1 Nyiru mt
51 K-3 Nykøbing
51 M-1 Nyköping
105 K-3 Nylstroom

221 H-1 Nymagee
51 M-1 Nynäshamn
221 J-1 Nyngan
58 A-7 Nyon
90 E-8 Nyong riv.
61 J-3 Nyons
69 K-4 Nyrob
51 M-7 Nysa
166 E-6 Nyssa
69 L-7 Nytva
136 E-6 Nyudo pte
101 H-5 Nyumba ya Mungu dam.
100 A-7 Nyunzu
94 C-6 Nzara
87 M-7 Nzébéla
106 E-5 Nzega
87 M-7 Nzérékoré
98 E-7 Nzeto
89 N-2 Nzi riv.
101 H-7 Nziha
103 K-1 Nzilo dam.
87 M-8 Nzo riv.
108 C-4 Nzwami mt

# O

137 J-8 O (Japan) isl.
136 D-5 O (Japan) isl.
137 K-6 O (Japan) isl.
201 N-5 O'Brien isl.
213 L-5 O'Donnel riv.
168 E-2 O'Fallon riv.
201 K-3 O'Higgins lake
198 A-7 O'Higgins reg.
191 M-1 O'Higgins
227 M-2 O'Higgins
169 H-6 O'Neill
168 G-4 Oahe lake
224 D-1 Oahu isl.
224 D-2 Oahu
173 J-4 Oak Beach
177 H-1 Oak Ridge
220 E-1 Oakbank
167 J-2 Oakdale
176 D-5 Oakdale (USA)
169 H-3 Oakes
219 M-6 Oakey
164 G-7 Oakfield
167 J-2 Oakland (USA)
52 G-4 Oakley (UK)
168 F-8 Oakley (USA)
219 J-4 Oakwood (Australia)
172 B-7 Oakwood (USA)
53 K-5 Oalders Green
222 E-8 Oamaru
52 F-6 Oare
148 E-4 Oas
167 H-7 Oasis
227 N-6 Oates Coast
221 H-8 Oatlands
179 H-7 Oaxaca reg.
179 H-7 Oaxaca de Juárez
112 F-3 Ob gulf
121 P-2 Ob'
69 M-6 Ob' riv.
59 M-2 Ob
170 F-1 Oba
90 E-8 Obala
137 M-2 Obama (Japan)
137 J-5 Obama (Japan)
90 C-7 Oban hill
222 C-9 Oban (Nouvelle Zélande)
50 C-2 Oban (UK)
136 F-7 Obanazawa
127 J-8 Obashta Tsü Kai mt
57 M-7 Obbicht
67 P-2 Obchtchi syrt mt
162 F-5 Obed
59 L-4 Ober mt
58 F-7 Ober Simmen val.
196 C-9 Oberá
59 K-7 Oberaarhorn mt
59 M-6 Oberalp pass
59 M-5 Oberalpstock mt
61 M-1 Oberbayern mt
58 G-3 Oberburg
58 G-3 Oberdiessbach
58 G-2 Oberdorf
59 H-1 Oberdorf
59 H-5 Oberei
59 K-7 Obergesteln

59 N-5 Oberland val.
176 D-5 Oberlin (USA)
168 F-7 Oberlin (USA)
221 K-2 Oberon
58 F-7 Oberried
59 P-5 Obersaxen
98 C-3 Oberting
59 K-6 Oberwald
58 F-6 Oberwil
59 L-2 Obfelden
209 H-1 Obi strt.
209 H-2 Obi isl.
127 L-3 Obichingou riv.
192 E-8 Obidos
136 B-7 Obihiro
209 H-1 Obilatu isl.
198 F-4 Obispo Trejo
67 J-9 Obitočnaja Kosa isl.
125 L-8 Oblačnaja mt
69 L-6 Oblast' reg.
125 H-5 Obluče
94 A-6 Obo
96 G-2 Obock
67 H-5 Obojan
172 B-4 Obold
125 K-5 Obor
98 G-3 Obouya
68 G-6 Oboz'orskij
174 E-6 Obregón dam.
71 N-5 Obručevo
127 K-1 Obručevol
201 N-7 Observatorio isl.
89 N-4 Obuasi
90 C-6 Obubra
90 C-6 Obudu
59 K-5 Obwalden reg.
186 F-2 Oca mt
66 F-9 Očakov
177 K-6 Ocala
72 C-2 Očamčire
187 L-7 Ocamo riv.
175 J-7 Ocampo
201 N-5 Ocaña (Colombia)
186 E-4 Ocaña (Colombia)
60 D-5 Ocaña (Spain)
62 B-2 Occhieppo Inferiore
63 L-5 Occhiobello
62 C-4 Occimiano
171 L-8 Ocean City
162 B-3 Ocean Falls
172 G-6 Ocean Gate
159 N-2 Océan Glacial Artique
172 G-5 Ocean Grove
172 F-9 Ocean View
174 A-1 Oceanside
172 F-8 Oceanville
69 L-7 Ochanck
169 J-5 Ochedayan mt
57 H-4 Ochten
177 J-4 Ocmulgee riv.
64 C-1 Ocna-mureş
181 K-7 Ocoa bay
179 L-7 Ococingo
189 N-7 Ocoña
189 N-7 Ocoña riv.
177 J-4 Oconee riv.
170 D-4 Oconto
69 L-7 Očor
189 M-8 Ocoruro riv.
184 F-4 Ocotal
184 E-3 Ocotep reg.
184 E-3 Ocotepeque
178 D-4 Ocotlán
58 E-1 Ocourt
177 N-2 Ocracoke Inlet bay
189 L-6 Ocros
113 H-2 October Revolution isl.
172 B-7 Octoraro riv.
185 K-9 Ocú
191 J-4 Ocuri
122 E-4 Ocury
93 K-2 Oda mt
89 N-5 Oda (Ghana)
137 K-3 Oda (Japan)
136 E-7 Odate
137 H-7 Odawara
49 K-1 Odda
60 A-6 Odemira
64 G-7 Odemis
105 H-5 Odendaalsrus
51 J-4 Odense
51 L-6 Oder riv.
63 N-2 Oderzo
51 L-2 Odeshög
66 F-9 Odessa (SSSR)
175 K-4 Odessa (USA)
162 D-9 Odessa (USA)
121 K-1 Odesskoje
93 L-5 Odi riv.
87 L-8 Odienné
53 H-6 Odiham
56 F-3 Odijk
57 H-6 Odiliapeel

98 B-4 Odimba
57 N-4 Oding
94 D-6 Odo mt
145 J-9 Odongk
64 E-1 Odorhei
97 J-4 Odweyne
98 F-2 Odzala na.p.
103 P-7 Odzi riv.
57 J-6 Oeffelt
56 B-2 Oegstgees
195 J-3 Oeiras
57 K-1 Oene
224 F-6 Oeno isl.
214 A-3 Oenpelli Mission
59 H-1 Oensingen
56 G-8 Oerle
56 A-8 Oesterbank lag.
133 L-7 Oeyeon isl.
125 L-8 Ofenhorn mt
59 K-7 Ofenhorn mt
51 H-7 Offenbach
57 K-7 Offenbeek
51 H-9 Offenburg
217 P-3 Officer (The) riv.
98 D-2 Offoué riv.
201 N-5 Ofhidro lake
89 M-8 Ofiki riv.
136 E-6 Oga
97 K-3 Ogaden reg.
137 J-6 Ogaki
168 F-6 Ogallala
206 F-4 Ogan riv.
137 L-4 Ogata
136 D-7 Ogawara lag.
90 A-6 Ogbesse riv.
89 M-9 Ogbomosho
52 F-5 Ogbourne Saint George
160 D-6 Ogden mt
168 A-5 Ogden
172 F-2 Ogdensburg
177 K-4 Ogeechee riv.
62 E-2 Oggiono
136 G-6 Ogi
105 K-4 Ogies
160 F-1 Ogilvie riv.
160 F-1 Ogilvie mt
73 K-1 Oglanly
62 G-1 Oglio riv.
219 L-2 Ogmore (Australia)
52 A-5 Ogmore (UK)
55 N-2 Ognes
149 P-6 Ogoamas mt
125 H-2 Ogodža
90 C-6 Ogoja
86 B-3 Ogol riv.
98 C-3 Ogooué riv.
98 C-3 Ogooué-Haut reg.
98 D-2 Ogooué-Ivindo reg.
98 D-3 Ogooué-Lolo reg.
98 B-3 Ogooué maritime reg.
98 C-3 Ogooué-moyen reg.
89 M-7 Ogou riv.
98 C-3 Ogoulou riv.
66 B-3 Ogre
61 D-2 Ogulin
73 K-2 Ogurčinskij isl.
65 M-7 Oğuzeli
222 C-8 Ohai
223 J-6 Ohakea
223 J-6 Ohakune
79 N-8 Ohanet
136 D-7 Ohata
222 D-7 Ohau lake
170 F-4 Ohaway
57 N-7 Ohe
170 G-7 Ohio state
170 D-9 Ohio riv.
157 F-2 Ohio state
51 K-8 Ohre riv.
64 C-5 Ohrid
64 C-5 Ohridsko lake
105 L-3 Ohrigstad
136 E-8 Ohunato
192 G-4 Oiapoque
56 G-9 Oijen
158 F-8 Oil pte
171 H-6 Oil City
54 D-3 Oinville-sur-Montcient
57 K-7 Oirlo
57 N-8 Oirsbeek
56 F-7 Oirschot
50 F-7 Oise riv.
55 N-1 Oissery
56 F-7 Oisterwijk
137 L-3 Oita
195 K-2 Oiticica
80 F-8 Oiuru riv.
122 E-4 Oja riv.
68 D-8 Ojat' riv.
138 F-9 Ojat riv.
175 H-5 Ojinaga
178 D-3 Ojo Caliente
198 C-1 Ojos del Salado mt
59 K-9 Ojra
120 F-9 Ojtal

178 E-3 Ojuelos de Jalisco
90 A-5 Oka
123 H-5 Oka riv.
210 E-6 Okaba
102 D-9 Okahandja
223 K-2 Okaihau
162 D-7 Okanagan lake
98 D-3 Okanda na.p.
98 D-2 Okano riv.
162 D-7 Okanogan mt
162 D-8 Okanogan
139 L-2 Okāra
73 L-2 Okarem
102 C-7 Okaukuejo
102 F-6 Okavango riv.
76 E-6 Okavango pool
103 H-7 Okavango
137 H-6 Okaya
137 K-4 Okayama
137 J-6 Okazaki
177 L-8 Okeechobee
177 L-8 Okeechobee lake
175 N-1 Okemah
90 A-5 Okene
136 B-7 Oketo
138 F-7 Okha
113 N-4 Okhotsk sea
125 N-1 Okhotsk sea
226 A-1 Okhotsk sea
137 J-3 Oki islds
137 L-8 Oki-no-erabu isl.
104 C-6 Okiep
137 M-8 Okinawa islds
137 L-4 Okino isl.
57 L-1 Okkenbroek
175 N-1 Oklahoma state
157 E-3 Oklahoma state
175 N-1 Oklahoma City
175 P-1 Okmulgee
158 F-5 Oknagamut
66 D-8 Oknica
93 K-2 Oko riv.
159 M-5 Okokmilaga riv.
90 E-8 Okola
94 E-8 Okolo
176 F-3 Okolona
102 D-7 Okomukandi
98 E-3 Okondja
121 L-1 Okonešnikovo
136 A-6 Okoppe
98 F-3 Okoyo
89 L-8 Okpara riv.
159 P-6 Okpilak riv.
48 C-6 Oksfjord
48 F-4 Oksskolten mt
127 N-5 Oksu riv.
66 G-1 Okt'abr'
67 M-2 Okt'abr'sk
124 F-3 Okt'abr'skij'
124 B-6 Okt'abr'skij'
123 H-3 Okt'abr'skij
125 M-3 Okt'abr'skij
70 B-1 Okt'abr'skoje
72 E-3 Oktember'an
69 M-9 Oktyabr'skiy
123 M-1 Okun mt
136 D-5 Okushiri isl.
136 D-5 Okushiri
89 L-8 Okuta
90 B-5 Okwa riv.
48 B-3 Olafsjördur
48 A-1 Olafsvik
184 F-2 Olanchito
184 G-3 Olancho reg.
51 M-3 Oland isl.
220 D-1 Olary
198 G-7 Olascoaga
170 A-8 Olathe
200 A-9 Olavarria
69 K-7 Olazov
61 L-6 Olbia
57 K-3 Olburgen
53 K-1 Old Hurst
172 G-4 Old Bridge
173 K-2 Old Field Point pte
172 C-1 Old Forge
162 D-2 Old Fort
165 L-1 Old Fort Bay
158 E-9 Old Harbor
52 E-1 Old Hill
162 D-1 Old Hogem
173 M-1 Old Lyme
103 M-4 Old Mkushi
173 N-1 Old Mystic
159 N-8 Old Rampart
173 M-1 Old Saybrook
53 H-2 Old Stratford
164 G-8 Old Town
158 G-7 Old Village
163 K-8 Old Wives lake
53 J-6 Old Woking
172 D-4 Old Zionsville
52 E-1 Oldbury
100 G-5 Oldeani
51 H-5 Oldenburg
58 E-8 Oldenhorn mt

57 P-1 Oldenzaal
48 C-6 Olderdalen
50 D-4 Oldham
52 D-5 Oldland Common
162 G-8 Oldman riv.
130 E-9 Oldoho Hiid
124 D-3 Ol'doj riv.
124 D-2 Ol'doj (Bol.) riv.
162 G-6 Olds
132 A-2 Oldzeyte-Suma
130 D-7 Oldziyt
171 J-6 Olean
62 C-2 Oleggio
68 F-4 Olema
68 C-5 Olenij isl.
68 F-2 Olenino
48 D-9 Olenogorsk
70 B-3 Olenty riv.
60 F-1 Oléron isl.
66 D-6 Olevsk
172 C-4 Oley
61 K-1 Olfen
217 N-1 Olga mt
125 L-8 Ol'ga
62 D-2 Olgiate Comasco
62 D-2 Olgiate Olona
125 H-2 Ol'ginsk
130 A-3 Olgiy
104 C-1 Olifants riv.
104 F-5 Olifantshoek
199 K-5 Olimar
199 L-6 Olimar riv.
221 L-6 Olimar (Australia) riv.
119 K-6 Olimarao isl.
64 G-9 Olimbos
196 G-4 Olímpia
125 M-6 Olimpiady isl.
199 M-5 Olimpo
195 P-4 Olinda
195 L-7 Olindina
123 L-7 Olino-Kl'uči
198 F-5 Oliva
198 B-3 Oliva
170 G-9 Olive Hill
197 J-5 Oliveira
195 H-7 Oliveira dos Brejinhos
141 P-2 Olivelifuri isl.
163 M-4 Oliver lake
172 D-8 Olivet
170 A-4 Olivia
59 N-6 Olivone
199 H-6 Olivos
123 L-5 Olkhon isl.
189 L-9 Ollachea
191 K-3 Ollagüe lake
191 K-2 Ollagüe
189 L-7 Ollantaytambo site
198 A-4 Ollita mt
58 D-8 Ollon
60 C-4 Olmedo
62 G-4 Olmeneta
62 F-1 Olmo al Brembo
188 F-2 Olmos
53 H-2 Olney (UK)
170 D-9 Olney (USA)
132 B-3 Olögey Hiid
123 K-5 Oloj
124 B-1 Ol'okma riv.
124 B-3 Ol'okminskij Stanovik mt
51 M-8 Olomouc
130 G-8 Olon Tooroy well
62 D-2 Olona riv.
68 C-8 Olonec
148 D-6 Olongapo
60 F-3 Oloron–Ste–Marie
124 A-6 Olov'annaja
57 K-1 Olst
66 A-5 Olsztyn
198 D-4 Olta
200 F-4 Olte mt
59 H-1 Olten
64 F-3 Oltenița
72 D-3 Oltu
64 C-8 Oltul riv.
135 N-9 Oluanpi
149 J-4 Olutanga isl.
64 D-6 Olympe Or. mt
162 B-8 Olympia
64 D-8 Olympia site
162 B-7 Olympic mt
162 B-7 Olympus na.p.
210 G-3 Om riv.
121 L-1 Om' riv.
93 L-7 Om Hager
144 E-4 Om Koi
136 D-6 Oma
68 F-3 Oma riv.
137 J-7 Omae cap.
136 E-7 Omagari
50 B-3 Omagh
188 E-6 Omaguas
169 J-7 Omaha
125 K-2 Omal'dinskij mt
116 A-4 Oman gulf

118 A-4 Oman state
84 C-7 Oman gulf
84 F-7 Oman state
84 G-7 Oman reg.
102 C-9 Omaruru riv.
189 L-5 Omas
102 D-8 Omatako mt
189 N-9 Omate
208 G-7 Ombai strt.
91 J-7 Ombella-Mpoko reg.
52 E-2 Ombersley
90 C-6 Ombi riv.
82 B-8 Ombos site
98 B-3 Omboué
63 J-9 Ombrone riv.
62 C-1 Omegna
97 L-2 Omein
221 H-5 Omeo
54 C-1 Omerville
184 G-6 Ometepe isl.
178 G-7 Ometepec
137 K-3 Omi isl.
162 D-1 Omineca mt
102 E-9 Omitara
137 H-7 Omiya
160 B-7 Ommaney cap.
130 F-8 Omnögovi reg.
102 E-8 Omuramba Omatako riv.
102 E-8 Omuramba Otjosondjou riv.
137 M-2 Omuta
69 K-7 Omutninsk
122 F-8 Ona riv.
136 F-8 Onagawa
98 C-3 Onangué lake
170 G-2 Onaping lake
169 J-6 Onawa
196 G-5 Onca riv.
164 C-3 Onças riv.
198 E-5 Oncativo
102 C-6 Ondangua
194 G-7 Ondas riv.
57 N-8 Onderbanken reg.
90 A-6 Ondo
130 D-8 Ondör-Onts
130 B-7 Ondör-Ulaan
123 N-9 Ondörhaan
130 A-4 Ondörhangay
130 C-9 Ondorshireet
68 C-6 Ondozero
93 H-6 Ondurman
48 A-1 Ondverđanes cap.
68 E-6 Onega riv.
68 D-5 Onega
68 D-7 Onega lake
62 B-9 Oneglia
171 K-5 Oneida lake
171 K-5 Oneonta
68 C-5 Onezhskaya Guba bay
68 C-5 Onežskij pen.
68 C-7 Onežskoje lake
142 C-6 Ong riv.
104 F-7 Ongers riv.
216 F-8 Ongerup
130 D-8 Ongiin riv.
133 L-6 Ongjin
140 F-7 Ongole
132 D-1 Ongon
121 P-6 Ongudaj
89 N-9 Oni riv.
72 D-2 Oni
108 G-7 Onibe riv.
168 G-4 Onida
109 L-2 Onilahy riv.
90 B-6 Onitsha
109 J-5 Onive riv.
130 C-9 Onjüül
79 M-3 Onk mt
137 H-5 Ono (Japan)
172 A-4 Ono (USA)
123 L-6 Onochoj
187 N-9 Onofre isl.
195 H-8 Onofre isl.
137 K-4 Onomiti
123 M-8 Onon riv.
123 N-8 Onon
125 N-2 Onor
123 J-5 Onot
123 J-5 Onot riv.
104 D-5 Onseepkans
133 M-1 Onseong
59 L-9 Onsernone val.
177 M-2 Onslow bay
212 C-8 Onslow
166 E-6 Ontario state
171 J-5 Ontario lake
156 G-2 Ontario lake

172 C-4 Ontelaunee lake
170 C-3 Ontonagon
186 F-5 Onzaga
98 E-8 Onzo riv.
218 B-5 Oodnadatta
57 K-7 Ooijen
57 L-2 Oolde
217 P-5 Ooldea
175 P-1 Oologah lake
56 B-6 Ooltgensplaat
214 F-9 Oorindi
105 J-8 Oos Londen
57 M-9 Oost
162 C-3 Oosta lake
162 C-3 Oosta L.
56 A-8 Oostdijk
57 F-8 Oostelbeers
50 F-8 Oostende
57 K-8 Oostenrijk
57 J-4 Oosterbeek
56 D-6 Oosterhout
56 A-6 Oosterland
56 A-6 Oostflakkee reg.
56 D-9 Oostmalle
57 K-7 Oostrum
56 A-4 Oostvoorne
141 J-4 Ootacamund
123 K-4 Oousa riv.
99 M-3 Opala
141 N-7 Opanake
94 E-7 Opari
69 H-7 Oparino
51 M-8 Opava
170 F-1 Opazatika lake
177 H-4 Opelika
176 D-5 Opelousas
211 N-4 Open bay
57 L-7 Opglabbeek
163 K-9 Opheim
56 G-5 Ophemert
57 H-4 Opheusden
146 F-8 Ophir mt
57 M-7 Ophoven
212 F-9 Ophtalmia mt
100 A-2 Opienge
56 F-5 Opijnen
164 C-3 Opinaka riv.
164 C-3 Opinaka lake
164 F-2 Opiscotea lake
57 M-7 Opitter
191 K-4 Oploca
57 J-7 Oploo
90 B-8 Opobo
66 D-2 Opočka
57 M-7 Opoeteren
51 M-7 Opole
186 E-5 Opón riv.
66 G-7 Opoš'na
223 L-5 Opotiki isl.
176 G-5 Opp
49 H-3 Oppdal
63 K-3 Oppeano
56 D-4 Opperduit
49 J-2 Oppland reg.
223 H-5 Opunake
70 D-1 Or riv.
80 G-4 Ora
217 H-6 Ora Banda
64 C-1 Oradea
48 C-3 Oraefajökull glac.
139 N-7 Orai
149 J-3 Oramiz
79 H-2 Oran
192 G-3 Orange cap.
221 K-2 Orange (Australia)
61 H-3 Orange (France)
173 K-1 Orange (USA)
172 G-3 Orange (USA)
176 C-6 Orange (USA)
180 E-2 Orange Cay rf
179 N-6 Orange Walk
177 H-5 Orangeburg
172 A-2 Orangeville
87 J-2 Orango isl.
148 D-6 Orani
51 K-6 Oranienburg
192 E-5 Oranje riv.
104 C-3 Oranje riv.
105 H-5 Oranje reg.
104 B-5 Oranjemond
187 H-1 Oranjestad
70 A-7 Orapa
103 J-9 Orapa
148 F-2 Oras
59 M-9 Orasso
64 D-2 Oraștie
64 C-2 Oravita
222 C-8 Orawia
62 C-5 Orba riv.
62 A-8 Orbassano
58 A-6 Orbe riv.
58 B-5 Orbe
61 M-5 Orbetello
221 J-5 Orbost
58 B-2 Orchamps

187 K-1 Orchila isl.
63 P-9 Orciano di Pesaro
213 K-4 Ord mt
213 M-3 Ord riv.
213 M-4 Ord River
121 L-6 Ordatas mt
60 B-2 Ordenes
72 A-4 Ordu
60 E-3 Orduña
168 D-8 Ordway
121 N-2 Ordynskoje
120 D-9 Ordžonikidze
127 K-3 Ordžonikidzeabad
122 D-3 Ordžonikidzevskij
90 A-6 Ore (Nigeria)
53 M-8 Ore (UK)
192 C-3 Orealla
162 B-9 Oregon state
169 J-8 Oregon
157 B-2 Oregon state
162 B-9 Oregon City
49 K-6 Oregrund
67 H-2 Orekhovo-Zuyevo
125 K-1 Orel' lake
66 G-7 Orel riv.
188 E-3 Orellana
168 A-6 Orem
70 B-1 Orenburg
200 B-9 Orense (Argentina)
60 B-3 Orense (Spain)
64 F-5 Orestiás
51 K-3 Oresund riv.
53 P-2 Orford
174 D-2 Organ Pipe Cactus site
192 F-3 Organabo
180 B-4 Organos mt
54 C-6 Orgerus
54 E-5 Orgeval
66 E-9 Orgeyev
63 K-3 Orgiano
132 C-2 Orgön
127 J-7 Orgün
130 B-8 Orhon riv.
69 J-8 Oriči
162 E-8 Orient
173 M-2 Orient pte
173 M-2 Orient (USA)
178 G-5 Oriental
181 L-6 Orientale reg.
200 B-9 Oriente (Argentina)
190 C-5 Oriente (Brazil)
188 D-7 Oriente (Peru)
60 E-7 Orihuela
164 B-9 Orillia
192 B-3 Orinduik
187 K-5 Orinoco riv.
142 C-6 Orissa reg.
61 K-6 Oristano gulf
61 K-6 Oristano
187 K-3 Orituco riv.
49 J-7 Orivesi
68 B-7 Orivesi lake
192 D-8 Oriximiná
196 G-2 Orizona
178 G-6 Orizaba
156 E-5 Orizaba mt
49 H-3 Orkanger
50 E-1 Orkney islds
46 C-4 Orkney islds
227 M-2 Orkney
197 H-4 Orlândia
177 K-7 Orlando
199 P-2 Orleães
164 F-7 Orléans isl.
50 E-9 Orléans
123 H-8 Orlik
123 L-3 Orlingskij mt
102 F-9 Orlogsende
125 N-3 Orlovo
61 L-8 Orlovskij
55 J-7 Orly
138 C-4 Ormāra pte
138 C-4 Ormāra
62 A-8 Ormea
55 L-7 Ormesson-sur-Marne
148 G-3 Ormoc
58 E-8 Ormonts (Les)
54 A-9 Ormoy
58 A-2 Ornans
62 C-1 Ornavasso
49 L-6 Ornö isl.
49 H-6 Ornsköldsvik
133 M-4 Oro
88 F-3 Oro lake
178 E-6 Oro riv.
90 A-5 Oro (Nigeria) riv.
190 E-5 Orobayaya
122 E-6 Orochin-Gol riv.
186 G-6 Orocué
89 K-2 Orodara
166 D-7 Orofino
130 D-7 Orog lake
122 D-6 Orög lake

124 D-2 Orogžan
66 G-4 Or'ol
123 P-2 Oron lake
82 C-3 Oron (Israel)
90 C-7 Oron (Nigeria)
123 P-2 Oron (SSSR)
58 D-6 Oron-la-Ville
187 N-5 Oronato riv.
192 C-5 Oronoque riv.
62 B-2 Oropa
189 L-7 Oropesa riv.
149 J-3 Oroquieta
195 L-3 Oros
64 C-1 Orosháza
185 H-7 Orotina
162 D-7 Oroville (Canada)
166 G-2 Oroville (USA)
189 L-9 Oroya
53 L-6 Orpington
220 D-1 Orroroo
55 K-2 Orry ft
55 K-1 Orry-la-Ville
49 J-4 Orsa
66 E-4 Orša
58 B-2 Orsans
62 G-7 Orsaro mt
54 G-8 Orsay
53 L-5 Orsett
54 G-7 Orsigny
70 D-1 Orsk
49 H-2 Orskog
200 D-2 Orsono
200 D-2 Orsono vol.
49 H-1 Orstavik
62 C-1 Orta lake
62 C-1 Orta San Giulio
128 A-2 Ortasu riv.
186 D-7 Ortega
60 B-2 Ortegal cap.
188 A-5 Orteguaza riv.
60 F-3 Orthez
196 E-7 Ortigueira (Brazil)
60 B-2 Ortigueira (Spain)
187 J-3 Ortíz
128 C-2 Orto-Tokoj
190 C-3 Ortón riv.
169 J-4 Ortonville
72 F-5 Orumiyeh
100 E-1 Orungo
191 H-3 Oruro
191 H-3 Oruro reg.
51 K-2 Orust isl.
126 G-6 Orüzgän reg.
54 B-7 Orval-la-Forêt
61 M-4 Orvieto
54 B-6 Orvilliers
58 E-2 Orvin
53 N-3 Orwell riv.
172 B-3 Orwigsburg
59 P-8 Orza mt
58 C-5 Orzens
62 G-3 Orzinuovi
127 N-2 Oš
49 K-1 Os
123 K-5 Osa
123 K-5 Osa riv.
185 H-8 Osa pen.
170 B-5 Osage
170 A-9 Osage riv.
137 J-5 Osaka
121 H-3 Osakarovka
168 G-8 Osborne
213 K-5 Oscar mt
172 A-9 Osceola (USA)
169 H-7 Osceola (USA)
170 A-7 Osceola (USA)
176 E-2 Osceola (USA)
59 H-7 Oschinen lake
170 F-4 Oscoda
48 G-3 Osen
137 M-2 Oseto
164 C-9 Oshawa (Canada)
171 H-5 Oshawa (Canada)
170 D-5 Oshkosh (USA)
168 F-6 Oshkosh (USA)
72 F-5 Oshnovíyeh
105 L-4 Oshoek
89 M-9 Oshogbo
73 J-7 Oshtorān mt
99 J-5 Oshwe
62 B-7 Osiglia
64 B-2 Osijek
136 F-8 Osika pen.
137 J-8 Osima
136 D-6 Osima pen.
67 N-2 Osinki
122 C-3 Osinniki
66 D-5 Osipoviči
170 B-7 Oskaloosa
51 M-2 Oskarshamn
164 D-6 Oskelaneo
67 J-2 Oskij Zapov. rés
67 J-6 Oskol riv.
49 K-3 Oslo
47 E-3 Oslo
140 D-5 Osmānābād

# P

| | | |
|---|---|---|
| 186 F-3 | Palmira (Vénézuela) | |

186 F-3 Palmira (Vénézuela)
196 A-3 Palmito
224 C-3 Palmyra isl.
170 B-8 Palmyra (USA)
172 E-6 Palmyra (USA)
65 N-8 Palmyre site
141 K-5 Palni
141 K-5 Palni mt
148 G-3 Palo
167 J-1 Palo Alto (USA)
174 E-3 Palo Alto (USA)
191 N-8 Palo Santo
208 D-7 Paloe isl.
147 K-8 Paloh
94 E-2 Paloich
48 D-7 Palojoensuu
190 F-2 Palomani mt
190 G-5 Palometillas riv.
191 N-5 Palomitas
148 G-3 Palompon
208 C-3 Palopo
188 C-3 Palora riv.
60 E-7 Palos cap.
162 D-9 Palouse riv.
189 M-6 Palpa
191 M-5 Palpalá
218 F-3 Palparara
208 G-3 Palpetu cap.
208 C-1 Palu
129 M-5 Palushankou pass
139 M-5 Palwal
91 J-8 Pama riv.
89 K-6 Pama
172 D-1 Pamack
147 K-9 Pamangkat
207 H-5 Pamanukan
108 C-4 Pamanzi isl.
188 C-8 Pamar
129 M-4 Pamar Tsho lake
122 E-2 Pam'ati 13 Barcov
207 M-6 Pamekasan
207 H-6 Pameungpeuk
60 G-3 Pamiers
127 M-4 Pamir reg.
127 M-5 Pamir riv.
177 N-2 Pamlico strt.
187 L-8 Pamoni riv.
197 M-3 Pampá riv.
175 L-1 Pampa
182 C-6 Pampa reg.
200 B-5 Pampa (la) reg.
191 J-3 Pampa Aullagas
191 N-7 Pampa de los Guanacos
201 J-4 Pampa del Asador reg.
200 G-5 Pampa del Castillo reg.
200 G-5 Pampa del Castillo
191 M-3 Pampa del Indio
198 G-1 Pampa del Infierno
191 K-2 Pampa del Tamarugal reg.
191 H-5 Pampa Grande
198 D-7 Pampa Seca pl.
189 M-7 Pampamarca riv.
208 C-4 Pampanua
62 A-7 Pamparato
189 K-6 Pampas
191 H-5 Pampas riv.
199 K-4 Pampeiro
58 B-6 Pampigny
60 E-3 Pamplona
186 F-4 Pamplona pass
104 F-7 Pampoenpoort
131 M-2 Pamuhan
208 A-2 Pamukan bay
170 C-8 Pana
211 P-9 Pana Tinani isl.
211 P-9 Pana Wina isl.
149 J-2 Panabo
170 G-3 Panache lake
211 N-9 Panaete isl.
64 E-4 Panagjurište
206 F-6 Panaitan isl.
140 F-3 Panaji
157 G-6 Panama state
185 L-8 Panama reg.
185 L-8 Panama cal.
185 L-9 Panama gulf
185 L-8 Panama bay
157 G-6 Panama City
177 H-6 Panama City
199 L-2 Panambi
167 K-4 Panamint mt
189 J-5 Panao
148 G-3 Panaon isl.
63 J-6 Panaro riv.
90 D-9 Panavia bay
148 G-5 Panay isl.
148 G-4 Panay gulf
90 C-3 Panbeguwa
62 A-5 Pancalieri
197 M-4 Pancas
64 C-2 Pančevo
142 E-4 Pānchet dam.
103 K-7 Panda ma Tenga
148 E-3 Pandan

206 G-6 Pandeglang
197 K-1 Pandeiros riv.
53 K-4 Panders End
140 D-4 Pandharpur
140 B-7 Pāndhurna
62 F-3 Pandino
131 M-4 Pandit. Tagh mt
206 F-5 Pandjang
147 K-8 Pandjang isl.
146 F-9 Pandjang strt.
199 K-6 Pando
190 C-3 Pando reg.
185 J-8 Pando mt
185 J-7 Pandora
91 K-7 Pandu
142 F-3 Pandua
52 C-3 Pandy
127 K-4 Pandž riv.
127 K-4 P'andž
207 J-1 Panebangan isl.
66 B-3 Panevezys
128 C-4 Panfilov
128 C-3 Panfilova
122 C-2 Panfilovo
143 M-6 Pang riv.
143 N-6 Pāng Yāng
99 P-1 Panga
98 F-5 Pangala
109 J-6 Pangalanes cal.
101 H-5 Pangani riv.
101 J-6 Pangani
148 E-3 Panganiban
90 F-7 Pangar riv.
52 G-5 Pangbourne
129 P-8 Pangduo
129 N-7 Panggehu lake
100 A-5 Pangi
208 E-1 Pangimanan
207 M-6 Pangkah cap.
146 C-7 Pangkalanberandan
207 L-3 Pangkalanbuun
146 C-7 Pangkalansusu
206 G-2 Pangkalpinang
208 F-1 Pangkalsiang cap.
129 K-1 Pangong lake
207 H-6 Pangrango mt
143 L-2 Pangsau pass
143 L-7 Pangtara
200 C-2 Panguipulli
167 K-7 Panguitch
87 L-5 Panguma
146 C-8 Pangururan
149 K-6 Pangutaran isl.
149 K-6 Pangutaran Grande isl.
124 D-3 Pangwuhe riv.
175 L-1 Panhandle
215 M-3 Panié mt
54 A-1 Panilleuse
139 M-4 Pānīpat
59 P-4 Panix
59 P-4 Panixer pass
191 L-3 Panizos mt
127 H-5 Panjāb
138 C-2 Panjgūr
139 J-2 Panjnad riv.
72 G-6 Panjwin
158 A-6 Pankof cap.
90 D-4 Pankshim
133 N-1 Panling mt
134 C-9 Panlongjiang riv.
139 P-8 Panna
57 K-4 Pannerden
57 P-9 Pannesheide
57 K-9 Panningen
207 L-2 Panopah
196 E-5 Panorama
123 J-1 Panovo
133 J-4 Panshan
133 K-2 Panshi
144 C-5 Pantanaw
208 F-6 Pantar isl.
208 F-7 Pante Macassar
61 M-9 Pantelleria isl.
61 M-9 Pantelleria strt.
55 L-5 Pantin
99 J-5 Panu
178 G-3 Pánuco
178 G-3 Pánuco riv.
134 C-7 Panxian
121 P-1 Panyčevo
135 J-9 Panyu
84 A-9 Panzdag mt
99 H-7 Panzi
184 D-2 Panzós
145 H-5 Pao (Thailand) riv.
187 J-3 Pao (Vénézuela) riv.
195 M-6 Pão de açucar
61 P-7 Pàola
172 D-6 Paoli
91 H-6 Paoua
145 H-7 Pàoy Pêt
68 B-5 P'aozero lake
64 A-1 Pápa
197 K-4 Papagaios
184 F-6 Papagayo gulf

198 B-6 Papagayos riv.
140 G-6 Pāpāgni riv.
223 K-4 Papakura
188 B-3 Papallacta
196 F-8 Papanduva
149 L-9 Papar
222 F-6 Paparoa mt
223 K-4 Papatoetoe
56 D-5 Papendrecht
57 M-7 Papenhoven
174 F-5 Papigochic riv.
94 E-5 Papiu
178 G-5 Paplanta
191 N-1 Paposo
211 H-7 Papouasie gulf
63 M-5 Papozze
204 E-2 Papua gulf
205 E-2 Papua New Guinea state
198 A-5 Papudo
64 A-2 Papuk mt
143 M-9 Papun
186 G-8 Papunaua riv.
213 P-9 Papunya
188 A-9 Papuri riv.
191 L-1 Paquica cap.
192 G-9 Paquicama
192 F-9 Para reg.
194 B-2 Pará
193 J-7 Para riv.
192 G-7 Pará (Brazil) isl.
149 M-2 Para (Philippines) isl.
197 K-4 Para de Minas
62 D-2 Parabiago
212 E-8 Paraburdoo
189 L-4 Paracas pen.
197 J-2 Paracatu riv.
197 H-2 Paracatu
145 P-5 Paracel (Xishaqundao) islds
218 D-7 Parachilna
127 J-6 Pārachinār
66 E-1 Parachino-Poddubje
64 C-3 Paracin
195 L-1 Paracuru
193 L-8 Parada
189 N-5 Parada pte
164 C-6 Paradis
172 B-6 Paradise
180 F-2 Paradise isl.
208 B-7 Parado
186 C-7 Parado riv.
176 E-1 Paragould
190 F-7 Paragua riv.
195 K-8 Paraguaçu riv.
196 F-6 Paraguaçu Paulista
196 A-1 Paraguai riv.
186 G-1 Paraguaipoa
187 H-1 Paraguaná pen.
196 B-8 Paraguari reg.
183 E-5 Paraguay state
195 N-5 Paraíba riv.
195 M-4 Paraíba riv.
197 K-5 Paraíba do Sul riv.
194 G-6 Paraim riv.
196 E-2 Paraíso riv.
196 D-3 Paraíso (Brazil)
179 K-6 Paraíso (Mexico)
196 D-6 Paraíso do Norte
197 J-6 Paraisópolis
89 L-8 Parakou
140 C-8 Paralkote
141 L-6 Paramagudi
183 E-2 Paramaribo
195 K-3 Parambu
192 E-3 Paramibo
186 D-5 Paramillo mt
195 H-7 Paramirim riv.
195 J-8 Paramirim
64 C-6 Paramithiá
186 C-5 Paramo Frontino mt
189 J-3 Paramonga
196 D-7 Paraná riv.
194 E-7 Paraná riv.
198 G-4 Paraná (Argentina)
194 E-7 Paraná (Brazil)
189 H-8 Paraná de Ouro riv.
196 G-8 Paranagua bay
196 G-8 Paranagua
196 E-4 Paranaiba
197 H-3 Paranaíba riv.
192 E-3 Paranam
196 E-6 Paranapanema
196 E-6 Paranapanema riv.
196 F-7 Paranapiacaba mt
188 F-4 Paranapura riv.
196 E-6 Paranavaí
207 K-5 Parang isl.
149 K-5 Parang Duyan
94 F-8 Parangaba
195 M-1 Parangaba
196 C-6 Paranhos
127 J-8 Parão
197 J-3 Paraopeba
191 K-6 Parapeti riv.
187 J-6 Paraque mt

197 J-6 Parati
62 G-2 Paratico
197 J-6 Paratinga riv.
195 H-8 Paratinga
194 D-3 Parauapebas riv.
192 F-8 Parauaquara mt
196 F-2 Paraúna
55 J-8 Paray-Vieille-Poste
187 N-7 Paraytequí
139 L-7 Pārbati riv.
140 C-5 Parbhani
196 D-4 Pardo riv.
212 F-7 Pardoo
51 L-8 Pardubice
207 M-6 Pare mt
101 H-5 Pare mt
190 E-8 Parecis mt
198 B-6 Pareditas
175 K-8 Paredón
49 K-7 Pareinen
195 N-3 Parelhas
223 J-1 Parengarenga
164 C-6 Parent lake
164 D-6 Parent
208 C-3 Parepare
198 E-7 Parera
62 C-6 Pareto
68 B-9 Pargolovo
167 L-7 Paria riv.
187 N-2 Paria gulf
187 N-2 Paria pen.
187 L-3 Pariaguán
206 B-1 Pariaman
192 G-9 Pariaxa dam.
66 E-5 Pariči
208 C-1 Parigi
189 L-4 Parinacochas lake
191 H-2 Parinacota mt
188 E-1 Parinas pte
192 D-9 Parintins
55 J-5 Paris
47 D-5 Paris (France)
50 E-8 Paris (France)
164 G-8 Paris (USA)
170 D-8 Paris (USA)
170 F-9 Paris (USA)
176 F-1 Paris (USA)
176 C-2 Paris (USA)
175 P-3 Paris (USA)
46 D-3 Parisien pool
185 L-9 Parita bay
168 C-7 Park mt
169 H-1 Park riv.
52 F-6 Park
170 C-3 Park Falls
170 A-3 Park Rapids
172 G-2 Park Ridge
166 G-8 Park Valley
49 H-7 Parkano
120 D-9 Parkent
216 G-7 Parker mt
174 C-1 Parker (USA)
169 H-5 Parker (USA)
170 G-8 Parkersburg
221 J-2 Parkes
172 B-6 Parkesburg
140 C-8 Parkeston
162 B-6 Parksville
172 A-7 Parkton
142 C-8 Parlakimidi
63 H-5 Parma riv.
62 G-6 Parma reg.
61 L-3 Parma
63 H-5 Parma (Parme)
170 G-7 Parma (USA)
54 G-2 Parmain
187 K-4 Parmana
194 G-6 Parnaguá
194 F-5 Parnaíba riv.
193 P-9 Parnaíba
195 L-4 Parnamirim
195 H-2 Parnarama
64 D-7 Parnassos mt
220 C-3 Parndana
66 B-1 Pärnu
142 G-2 Paro Dzong
218 G-7 Paroo riv.
218 G-8 Paroo strt.
216 G-3 Paros
64 E-8 Páros
167 K-7 Parowan
221 L-3 Parramatta
178 E-1 Parras de la Fuente
62 F-1 Parre
52 C-7 Parrett riv.
177 L-4 Parris isl.
185 H-7 Parrita
165 J-7 Parrsboro
161 L-1 Parry pen.
164 B-8 Parry Sound
139 J-7 Parsad
172 F-3 Parsippany

162 E-3 Parsnip riv.
214 B-3 Parsons mt
146 A-5 Parsons pte
169 J-9 Parsons
138 K-7 Partābgarh
52 A-4 Parth
60 F-1 Parthenay
61 M-8 Partinico
187 K-6 Parú riv.
187 K-7 Parú mt
192 F-8 Paru riv.
192 D-7 Paru de Oeste riv.
141 K-4 Parur
189 L-8 Paruro
207 M-6 Parys
127 J-5 Parvän reg.
142 B-8 Pārvatipuram
64 E-4 Pârvomaj
105 J-4 Parys
46 D-4 Pas-de-Calais strt.
58 D-8 Pas de Morgins pass
175 P-5 Pasadena (USA)
167 M-3 Pasadena (USA)
188 B-1 Pasado cap.
191 N-5 Pasaje (Argentina)
188 D-2 Pasaje (Ecuador)
208 C-1 Pasangkaju
73 N-9 Pasargades site
208 E-4 Pasarwadjo
148 D-6 Pasay
176 F-6 Pascagoula
176 F-5 Pascagoula riv.
66 D-9 Pașcani
189 J-5 Pasco reg.
162 D-9 Pasco
197 N-2 Pascoal mt
182 A-7 Pascua isl.
201 J-3 Pascua riv.
163 M-3 Pasfield lake
126 A-6 Pashūiyeh
63 N-1 Pasiano di Pordenone
148 D-6 Pasig
69 M-6 Pasija
72 C-4 Pasinler
121 P-2 Pašino
179 M-8 Pasión riv.
146 D-9 Pasirpengarajan
125 H-5 Paškovo
72 A-1 Paskovskij
126 B-9 Paskūh
217 J-8 Pasley cap.
138 B-4 Pasni
200 F-4 Paso de Indios
199 J-3 Paso de los Libres
199 K-5 Paso de los Toros
167 K-2 Paso Robles
163 M-7 Pasqua mt
127 M-9 Pasrūr
197 K-6 Passa Vinte
201 L-8 Passage islds
195 H-3 Passagem Franca
172 F-3 Passaic riv.
172 G-3 Passaic
172 G-3 Passaio riv.
51 K-9 Passau
58 G-1 Passwang mt
188 C-3 Pastaza
188 C-8 Pastaza reg.
188 E-4 Pastaza riv.
188 A-3 Pasto vol.
188 A-4 Pasto
159 G-3 Pastol bay
158 G-4 Pastolik
168 A-9 Pastora mt
195 H-3 Pastos Bons
63 J-3 Pastrengo
63 K-2 Pasúbio mt
148 B-6 Pasuquin
207 M-6 Pasūruan
66 B-3 Pasvalys
149 K-5 Pata isl.
190 F-2 Pata (Bolivia)
86 G-3 Pata (Gambia)
191 K-1 Patache pte
182 D-7 Patagonia reg.
201 H-5 Patagonie reg.
142 E-1 Patan
139 H-7 Pātan
190 A-8 Patauá riv.
173 K-3 Patchogue
127 M-4 Patchor mt
223 H-6 Patea
90 A-4 Pategi
104 G-9 Patensie
61 N-8 Paterno
162 D-8 Pateros
222 C-9 Paterson bay
220 G-6 Paterson cap.
171 L-6 Paterson

142 C-5 Pathalgaon
127 M-9 Pathānkot
168 C-5 Pathfinder lake
146 D-2 Pathiu
144 G-7 Pathum Thani
207 L-6 Pati
186 B-8 Patía riv.
139 M-3 Patiāla
66 G-8 P'atichatki
72 C-1 P'atigorsk
181 K-6 Patilla pte
70 A-4 P'atimar
207 L-7 Patjitan
116 E-4 Patkaï Bum rge
143 L-3 Patkai Bum mt
143 L-3 Patkoi mt
64 F-8 Patmos isl.
142 D-3 Patna
142 B-6 Patnāgarh
148 D-5 Patnanongan isl.
72 D-4 Patnos
201 H-3 Pato mt
196 D-8 Pato Branco
143 K-5 Patôlon riv.
113 K-4 Patomskoye mt
195 K-4 Patos
197 H-3 Patos de Minas
64 C-7 Patras
48 A-1 Patreksfjördur (Vatneyri)
201 K-1 Patricio Lynch isl.
197 H-3 Patrocino
101 L-4 Patta isl.
146 E-5 Pattani
54 G-3 Patte-d'Oie (La)
164 G-7 Patten
53 K-4 Patter's Bar
223 N-9 Pattison cap.
139 L-2 Pattoki
141 K-6 Pattukkottai
190 A-8 Patuá riv.
142 G-5 Patuākhāli
184 G-3 Patuca riv.
185 H-2 Patuca pte
207 H-6 Patuha mt
160 D-9 Patullo mt
223 K-5 Paturaru
178 E-5 Pátzcuaro
60 F-3 Pau
194 D-4 Pau d'Arco
195 M-3 Pau dos Ferros
190 A-1 Paucartambo
190 A-1 Pauini riv.
190 A-3 Pauini
143 K-6 Pauk
143 K-8 Paukkaung
143 K-7 Pauksa mt
223 L-5 Paukumara mt
158 B-7 Paul isl.
161 L-2 Paulatuk
184 G-3 Paulaya riv.
172 E-2 Paulins Kill riv.
195 P-4 Paulista
195 K-4 Paulistana
62 E-3 Paullo
188 D-3 Paulo riv.
195 M-5 Paulo Alfonso riv.
195 M-5 Paulo Alfonso
146 F-2 Paulo Wai isl.
158 A-6 Pauloff Hbr
105 L-5 Paulpietersburg
94 B-7 Pauls
175 N-2 Pauls Valley
172 D-7 Paulsboro
143 K-9 Paungde
139 P-3 Pauri
190 G-9 Pauritos
194 G-5 Paus
188 D-2 Paute
186 G-6 Pauto riv.
197 M-2 Pavão
185 N-9 Pavarandocito
72 G-7 Pāveh
62 E-4 Pavia reg.
61 L-3 Pavia
62 E-4 Pavia (Pavie)
69 H-8 Pavino
64 E-3 Pavlikeni
121 L-3 Pavlodar
158 B-6 Pavlof bay
158 B-6 Pavlof vol.
158 B-6 Pavlof islds
67 H-8 Pavlograd
121 K-1 Pavlogradka
67 J-1 Pavlovo
121 N-3 Pavlovsk
67 K-9 Pavlovskaja
123 J-4 Pavlovskij
198 G-6 Pavón riv.
62 A-3 Pavone Canavese
63 J-7 Pavullo nel Frignano
94 B-8 Pawa
207 K-2 Pawan riv.
173 N-1 Pawcatuck
175 P-1 Pawhuska
52 B-6 Pawlett

146 C-3 Phuket mt
142 G-3 Phulchari
145 K-9 Phumi Banam
145 K-8 Phumi Chhlong
145 J-9 Phumi Kus
145 K-9 Phumi Prêk Sândêk
145 J-7 Phumi Puok Chas
145 J-7 Phumi Sâmrong
145 H-7 Phumi Toek Chou
146 D-3 Phun Phin
145 L-8 Phuoc Binh
145 L-9 Phuoc Lê
145 H-6 Phutthaisong
94 A-7 Pia
194 E-4 Piacá
196 F-5 Piacatu
61 L-3 Piacenza
62 F-4 Piacenza
62 F-5 Piacenza reg.
63 L-4 Piacenza d'Adige
63 H-4 Piadena
219 N-4 Pialba
219 K-7 Pian riv.
63 K-8 Pian del Voglio
63 N-9 Pian di Meleto
62 B-7 Piana Crixia
195 M-4 Pianco riv.
195 M-4 Piancó
62 E-5 Pianello val Tidone
62 A-4 Pianezza
129 L-1 Piang
220 F-3 Piangil
63 K-7 Pianoro
61 L-4 Pianosa islds
61 P-5 Pianosa isl.
66 A-6 Piaseczno
195 N-6 Piassabussu
195 J-8 Piatã
64 E-1 Piatra-Neamț
195 H-3 Piau reg.
197 M-2 Piauí riv.
195 J-4 PiauíPiané riv.
63 M-1 Piave riv.
216 E-6 Piawaning
178 B-1 Piaxtla riv.
178 A-2 Piaxtla pte
63 H-8 Piazza al Serchio
61 N-8 Piazza Armerina
62 F-1 Piazza Brembo
201 M-3 Piazzi isl.
63 L-2 Piazzola sul Brenta
94 F-4 Pibor
94 F-4 Pibor Post
210 C-3 Pic Jaya (Sukarno) mt
174 E-2 Picacho pass
174 C-4 Picachos mt
176 E-5 Picayune
189 K-7 Picha riv.
191 J-1 Pichalo pte
191 M-5 Pichanal
200 B-6 Pichi Mahuida
198 A-7 Pichilemu
188 B-3 Pichincha
188 B-2 Pichincha reg.
188 C-2 Pichincha
189 M-7 Pichírhua
189 J-6 Pichis riv.
68 G-6 Pichtovo
188 E-1 Pico pte
191 H-2 Pico Anallacsi mt
185 J-7 Pico Blanco mt
186 G-4 Pico Bolívar mt
196 F-8 Pico Guaricana mt
200 F-3 Pico Negro mt
196 G-7 Pico Tres Pontoes mt
201 H-5 Pico Truncado
188 G-4 Picota
201 N-6 Picton isl.
222 G-7 Picton
220 G-9 Picton mt
165 K-6 Pictou
165 K-6 Pictou
195 N-3 Picuí
200 C-3 Picún Leufú riv.
200 C-4 Picun Leufú
52 D-8 Piddeltrenthide
141 M-7 Pidurutalagala mt
198 C-4 Pie de Palo mt
186 E-5 Piedecuesta
62 B-2 Piedicavallo
62 B-1 Piedimulera
177 H-3 Piedmont
62 A-5 Piedmont reg.
201 H-4 Piedra mt
184 G-6 Piedra
188 D-3 Piedra Blanca mt
200 C-3 Piedra del Aguila
187 K-8 Piedra del Cucuy mt
187 K-8 Piedra Lais
199 K-5 Piedra Sola
185 L-8 Piedras islds
188 D-2 Piedras
199 J-7 Piedras (Argentina) pte
187 L-2 Piedras (Vénézuela) pte
175 L-6 Piedras Negras

49 H-8 Pieksämäki
68 B-7 Pielinen lake
220 G-8 Pieman riv.
62 A-9 Piena
105 J-3 Pienaars riv.
105 K-3 Pienaarsrivier
186 C-8 Piendamó
163 J-5 Pierceland
173 H-2 Piermont
168 G-4 Pierre
58 E-9 Pierre à Voir mt
55 J-4 Pierrefitte-sur-Seine
58 B-2 Pierrefontaine
54 G-3 Pierrelaye
56 B-5 Piershil
51 M-9 Piestany
105 L-4 Piet Retief
48 G-7 Pietarsaari
58 F-2 Pieterlen
105 L-6 Pietermaritzburg
105 K-2 Pietersburg
62 B-8 Pietra Ligure
62 G-9 Pietrasanta
66 C-9 Pietrosu mt
62 D-4 Pieve del Cairo
62 H-1 Pieve di Bono
63 K-6 Pieve di Cento
63 J-1 Pieve di Ledro
62 A-8 Pieve di Teco
62 E-4 Pieve Porto Morone
63 H-8 Pievepelago
64 G-9 Pigádhia
162 G-5 Pigeon lake
213 N-4 Pigeon Hole
170 C-2 Pigeon River
176 E-1 Piggott
105 L-4 Pigg's Peak
62 A-9 Pigna
200 B-8 Pigüe
135 K-2 Pihe riv.
49 J-7 Pihlava
49 H-8 Pihtipudas
179 K-8 Pijijiapan
56 B-3 Pijnacker
184 F-3 Pijol mt
68 D-9 Pikal'ovo
172 E-1 Pike reg.
129 P-5 Pikehu lake
119 K-6 Pikelot isl.
168 D-8 Pikes
104 D-8 Piketberg
170 G-9 Pikeville
98 G-2 Pikounda
163 P-5 Pikwitonei
196 F-1 Piloes riv.
197 H-2 Piloes mt
199 J-7 Pila (Argentina)
51 M-5 Piła (Poland)
195 J-6 Pilão Arcado
198 G-4 Pilar (Argentina)
195 N-6 Pilar (Brazil)
196 G-7 Pilar do Sul
149 K-5 Pilas Grande isl.
59 K-3 Pilatus mt
191 K-5 Pilaya riv.
200 D-3 Pilcaniyeu
196 A-7 Pilcomayo riv.
200 D-4 Pilcui Niyeu plat.
125 K-2 Pil'da riv.
158 F-8 Pile Bay
55 H-8 Pileu (Le)
129 P-1 Pilibhit
52 C-5 Pill
221 H-9 Pillar cap.
188 C-3 Pillaro
219 K-8 Pilliga
58 E-8 Pillon pass
67 K-1 Pil'na
194 E-5 Piloes riv.
178 F-1 Pilón riv.
64 D-8 Pilos
176 F-6 Pilottown
52 D-6 Pilton
143 L-7 Pilu riv.
99 H-5 Pimanga
218 C-8 Pimba
187 N-8 Pimenta riv.
190 D-7 Pimenta Bueno
195 H-5 Pimenteira riv.
195 K-3 Pimenteiras
188 G-2 Pimentel
99 K-1 Pimu
55 L-5 Pin (Le)
174 C-2 Pinacate mt
201 L-3 Pinaculo mt
148 E-5 Pinamalayan
146 D-6 Pinang (Georgetown)
180 B-4 Pinar del Rio
65 L-6 Pinarbaşi
188 D-2 Piñas
63 L-5 Pincara
162 G-8 Pincher Creek
162 D-2 Pinchi lake
195 H-9 Pindaí
194 B-9 Pindaiba riv.
197 J-6 Pindamonhangaba

194 F-1 Pindaré riv.
193 L-9 Pindaré Mirim
127 K-7 Pindi Gheb
149 P-5 Pindjang
188 C-4 Pindo riv.
195 K-6 Pindobaçu
193 J-9 Pindobal
56 B-8 Pindorp
139 J-6 Pindwära
165 P-4 Pine cap.
174 E-1 Pine
177 K-9 Pine islds
177 K-8 Pine isl.
176 D-3 Pine Bluff
180 E-2 Pine Cay rf
170 B-3 Pine City
213 P-2 Pine Creek
163 P-8 Pine Dock
172 A-4 Pine Grove
172 F-1 Pine Island
161 K-8 Pine Point
168 B-4 Pinedale
68 E-5 Pinega riv.
68 E-4 Pinega
216 D-4 Pinegrove
163 L-5 Pinehouse lake
172 D-2 Pines
175 P-3 Pines lake
105 L-6 Pinetown
172 E-5 Pineville
144 F-5 Ping riv.
216 F-7 Pingaring
134 E-3 Pingchang
135 H-1 Pingdingshan
133 H-7 Pingdu
129 P-3 Pingdushankou
119 M-6 Pingelap isl.
216 E-7 Pingelly
135 K-9 Pinghai
135 M-7 Pinghai
135 L-8 Pinghe
135 N-3 Pinghu
135 J-5 Pingjiang
134 G-8 Pingle
132 A-8 Pingliang
132 D-5 Pinglucheng
132 A-6 Pingluo
134 G-8 Pingnan
159 P-5 Pingok isl.
132 G-4 Pingquan
216 F-8 Pingrup
135 J-9 Pingshan
135 M-7 Pingtan
135 N-9 P'ingtung
178 F-4 Pingüicas mt
131 N-9 Pingwu
134 E-9 Pingxiang (China)
135 J-5 Pingxiang (China)
135 N-5 Pingyang
132 D-7 Pingyao
132 G-8 Pingyi
132 F-8 Pingyin
134 C-8 Pingyuan
131 K-7 Pingzhie
132 G-3 Pingzhuang
197 H-6 Pinghal
196 F-7 Pinhalão
195 M-6 Pinhão
193 M-9 Pinheiro
199 L-4 Pinheiro Machado
146 C-9 Pini isl.
216 E-8 Pinjarra
143 L-7 Pinlaung
143 L-4 Pinlebu
222 G-7 Pinnacle mt
220 E-3 Pinnaroo
51 J-5 Pinneberg
53 J-5 Pinner
59 M-9 Pino
200 C-3 Pino Hachado mt
167 L-3 Pinos mt
167 J-1 Pinos pte
178 E-3 Pinos
208 C-3 Pinrang
215 N-5 Pins (Kunié) isl.
89 H-5 Pinsa
66 C-6 Pinsk
112 A-4 Pinsk Marshes lag.
66 C-6 Pinsk Marshes lake
188 G-2 Pinta isl.
191 K-1 Pintados
191 K-1 Pintados lake
54 A-8 Pinthières (Les)
198 F-3 Pinto
69 H-7 Pin'ug
184 B-9 Pinzón isl.
195 K-5 Pio IX
194 G-1 Pio XII
167 K-6 Pioche
59 L-9 Pioda di Crana mt
61 L-4 Piombino
61 L-4 Piombino Dese
168 A-2 Pioneer mt
69 M-3 Pionerskij
210 D-2 Pionierbivak

66 A-7 Pionki
59 M-6 Piora val.
59 N-8 Piota mt
66 A-7 Piotrkow Tryb.
59 M-7 Piotta
63 M-3 Piove di Sacco
63 K-2 Piovene
62 D-5 Piovera
126 A-9 Pip
87 P-3 Pipa pte
198 D-2 Pipanaco lake
139 K-5 Pipār
140 A-7 Piparia
172 D-4 Pipersville
169 J-5 Pipestone
91 M-5 Pipi riv.
164 F-4 Pipmouacane lake
170 F-7 Piqua
195 L-3 Piquet Carneiro
196 D-7 Piquiri riv.
126 A-3 Pir Moral
127 M-8 Pīr Panjāl mt
196 G-2 Piracanjuba
196 G-6 Piracicaba riv.
197 H-6 Piracicaba
195 J-1 Piracuruca
64 E-7 Piraeus
196 F-7 Piraí do Sul
196 F-6 Piraju
191 N-9 Pirané
197 L-5 Piranga riv.
196 E-1 Piranhas
196 E-1 Piranhas riv.
193 L-8 Piranhinha mt
195 H-1 Pirapemas
196 C-8 Pirapo riv.
197 K-2 Pirapora
196 E-5 Pirapózinho
196 C-4 Piraputangas
199 L-6 Pirarajá
192 D-7 Pirarara dam.
197 H-5 Pirassununga
66 F-7 Pir'atin
199 K-2 Piratini riv.
192 C-8 Piratucu riv.
191 H-6 Piray riv.
198 B-5 Pircas mt
196 A-1 Pirenopolis
196 G-2 Pires de Rio
64 C-9 Pirgos
193 L-8 Piria riv.
199 K-7 Piriápolis
195 J-1 Piripiri
195 K-7 Piritiba
187 L-3 Piritu riv.
187 L-2 Piritu islds
196 B-1 Pirizal
51 H-8 Pirmasens
64 D-4 Pirot
209 J-3 Piru
61 L-4 Pisa
222 D-8 Pisa mt
63 H-9 Pisa
191 J-1 Pisagua
209 L-2 Pisang islds
209 J-1 Pisang isl.
62 G-8 Pisanino mt
189 L-8 Pisao
189 L-5 Pisco riv.
189 L-5 Pisco
128 G-2 Pishan
126 C-6 Pishavarah site
138 A-3 Pishūkān pte
69 J-8 Pišnur
87 M-5 Piso lake
190 E-7 Piso Firme
62 G-2 Pisogne
188 G-5 Pisqui riv.
58 D-9 Pissevache
198 B-2 Pissis mt
63 J-8 Pistoia reg.
63 J-8 Pistoia
165 M-1 Pistolet bay
166 F-3 Pit riv.
87 J-5 Pita
164 G-2 Pitaga
186 C-9 Pitalito (Colombia)
188 A-5 Pitalito (Colombia)
196 E-7 Pitanga
196 G-5 Pitangueiras
197 J-4 Pitangui
220 F-2 Pitarpunga lake
224 G-6 Pitcairn islds
48 F-6 Piteå
48 F-5 Piteälven riv.
63 J-8 Piteglio
64 E-2 Pitesti
140 E-9 Pithāpuram
216 E-6 Pithara
50 E-8 Pithiviers
129 N-1 Pithorāgarh
100 E-8 Piti riv.
174 D-4 Pitiquito
68 C-8 Pitk'aranta

50 D-2 Pitlochry
172 E-7 Pitman
78 C-7 Pitones isl.
200 C-2 Pitrufquén
53 M-5 Pitsea
184 C-9 Pitt pte
223 N-9 Pitt strt.
162 B-2 Pitt (Canada) isl.
223 N-9 Pitt (Nouvelle Zélande) isl.
141 J-1 Pitti isl.
177 L-1 Pittsboro
171 H-7 Pittsburgh
171 L-5 Pittsfield
172 C-1 Pittston
219 M-6 Pittsworth
218 D-1 Pituri riv.
63 H-4 Piúbega
197 J-4 Piuí
194 D-6 Pium
194 D-6 Pium riv.
188 F-1 Piura
188 E-1 Piura reg.
188 F-2 Piura riv.
129 P-3 Piuthān
125 K-3 Pivan
186 E-2 Pivijay
131 P-8 Pixian
122 C-5 Piža riv.
190 G-1 Pizacoma
186 B-6 Pizarro
69 J-8 Pižma
68 G-3 Pižma riv.
62 F-4 Pizzighettone
61 P-7 Pizzo
67 K-1 Pjana riv.
48 C-2 Pjorsa riv.
165 P-3 Placentia bay
149 H-2 Placer
168 B-8 Placerville (USA)
159 J-6 Placerville (USA)
180 D-4 Placetas
190 C-3 Plácido de Castro
199 L-5 Placido Rosas
191 P-1 Placilla
58 F-1 Plaffeien
221 H-6 Plage des 90 miles
171 M-3 Plagstaff lair
145 H-6 Plai Mat riv.
54 C-4 Plaigne (La)
55 L-2 Plailly
172 F-4 Plainfield
162 F-9 Plains (USA)
175 K-3 Plains (USA)
170 G-6 Plainsville
175 K-2 Plainview
54 E-6 Plaisir
53 J-7 Plaistow
208 B-7 Plampang
181 H-4 Plana islds
58 D-9 Planachaux
198 B-7 Planchón mt
185 P-8 Planeta Rica
57 H-3 Planken Wambuis ft
169 H-5 Plankinton
58 E-8 Plans (Les)
176 E-6 Plaquemine
60 C-5 Plasencia mt
58 F-5 Plasselb
69 P-7 Plast
165 H-6 Plaster Rock
165 H-6 Plaster Rock Renous mt
125 L-7 Plastun
191 N-1 Plata pte
55 K-2 Plateau (Le)
67 L-2 Plateau de la Volga
158 D-5 Platinum
185 P-7 Plato
122 E-1 Platonovka
168 G-5 Platte
170 A-8 Platte riv.
170 A-8 Plattsburg
164 E-8 Plattsburgh
169 J-7 Plattsmouth
51 K-7 Plauen
66 C-3 Plavinas
67 H-4 Plavsk

58 C-9 Plenay (Le)
223 L-5 Plenty bay
218 B-1 Plenty riv.
168 E-1 Plentywood
68 E-6 Plesetsk
55 N-3 Plessis-aux-Bois (Le)
55 N-2 Plessis-Belleville (Le)
55 J-3 Plessis-Gassot (Le)
55 N-3 Plessis-l'Evêque (Le)
55 K-2 Plessis-Luzarches (Le)
55 J-9 Plessis-Pâté (Le)
55 L-6 Plessis-Trévise (Le)
164 F-7 Plessisville
51 M-6 Pleszew
164 F-3 Pletipi lake
64 E-3 Pleven
64 B-3 Plevlja
64 A-4 Ploce
66 A-6 Plock
64 F-6 Plomárion
221 M-1 Plomer pte
66 A-6 Plonsk
121 P-1 Plotnikovo
103 L-8 Plumtree
173 M-2 Plum isl.
66 A-3 Plungé
66 D-1 Pl'usa riv.
50 C-6 Plymouth (UK)
170 E-7 Plymouth (USA)
181 N-2 Plymouth (USA)
177 N-1 Plymouth (USA)
52 A-1 Plynlimon hill
51 K-8 Plzen
51 M-6 Pniewy
89 K-5 Pô
61 M-3 Pô riv.
62 A-4 Po (Pô) riv.
63 N-5 Po della Pila riv.
63 N-5 Po delle Tolle est.
63 N-5 Po delle Tolle riv.
63 N-5 Po di Goro riv.
63 N-5 Po di Goro e di Gnocca est.
63 L-5 Po di Volano riv.
63 M-5 Po Grande riv.
89 N-8 Pobé
125 N-2 Pobedino
128 D-3 Pobedy mt
112 G-5 Pobedy Peak mt
191 N-7 Población
162 F-5 Pocahontas (Canada)
176 E-1 Pocahontas (USA)
192 E-8 Pocão lake
168 A-4 Pocatello
66 F-5 Počep
122 G-2 Počet
122 G-2 Počet riv.
58 C-3 Poches pass
66 F-4 Počinok
102 E-5 Pôĉô
197 J-1 Poco Fundo dam.
191 J-4 Pocoáta
195 K-9 Poções
52 A-8 Pocombe
172 D-2 Pocono rge
172 D-2 Pocono
172 D-2 Pocono lake
172 D-2 Pocono Lake
197 H-5 Pocos de Caldas
197 M-4 Pocrane
125 K-6 Podchor'onok riv.
67 H-7 Podgorodnoje
131 P-5 Podolatse Kha mt
66 G-3 Podol'sk
112 M-9 Podolskaya mt
66 D-8 Podolskaya Vozv plat.
123 L-1 Podvološino
123 L-2 Podymachino
56 E-5 Poederoijen
56 A-3 Poeldijk
192 E-4 Poeloegoedoe mt
104 D-5 Pofadder
63 J-9 Poggio a Caiano
63 L-5 Póggio Renatico
63 K-5 Póggio Rusco
125 L-1 Pogibi
64 C-5 Pogradec
125 J-3 Pogranicnyj
158 A-5 Pogrommi vol.
196 D-1 Poguba riv.
133 N-6 Pohang
49 H-9 Pohjois Karjala reg.
119 L-6 Pohnpei
139 M-7 Pohri
63 K-3 Poiana Maggiore
64 D-3 Poiana-Mare
54 C-8 Poigny-la-Forêt
55 P-4 Poincy

58 E-3 Prêles
62 E-1 Premana
217 K-6 Premier Downs *hill*
63 L-8 Premilcuore
170 C-4 Prentice
176 E-5 Prentiss
51 K-5 Prenzlau
144 B-6 Preparis *isl.*
51 M-8 Prerov
201 H-2 Pres Rios *lake*
174 D-1 Prescott
168 G-4 Presho
199 H-1 Presidencia de la Plaza
196 E-5 Presidencia Epitácio
190 D-7 Presidencia Hermes
196 D-1 Presidencia Murtinho
197 J-3 Presidencia Olegário
196 E-5 Presidencia Prudente
191 N-8 Presidencia Roca
196 E-5 Presidencia Venceslau
194 G-2 Presidente Dutra
196 A-6 Presidente Hayes *reg.*
178 B-2 Presidio *riv.*
175 J-5 Presidio
55 H-2 Presles
55 M-8 Presles-en-Brie
66 A-8 Prešov
64 C-5 Prespansko *lake*
164 G-6 Presque Isle
195 N-5 Presqueira
89 P-4 Prestea
212 D-8 Preston (Australia)
52 D-3 Preston (UK)
52 D-9 Preston (UK)
168 A-4 Preston (USA)
170 B-5 Preston (USA)
52 G-6 Preston Candover
193 N-9 Preto *riv.*
77 E-8 Pretoria
105 J-3 Pretoria
104 D-1 Pretorius
64 C-7 Preveza
55 P-5 Prévilliers
145 K-9 Prey Vêng
58 D-5 Prez-vers-Noréaz
120 C-3 Priaral'skije Karakumy *dés*
124 B-6 Priargunsk
67 J-8 Priazouskaia Vozv. *mt*
51 K-8 Pribam
158 B-2 Pribilof *islds*
162 A-3 Price *isl.*
168 A-6 Price
159 M-4 Price *riv.*
144 B-7 Price *cap.*
172 C-4 Pricetown
176 F-5 Prichard
57 N-9 Prickart
52 C-6 Priddy
66 A-4 Priekulé
59 J-5 Prienzwiler
62 B-7 Priero
104 F-6 Prieska
162 E-8 Priest *lake*
188 G-2 Prieto *mt*
124 A-5 Priiskovyj
67 M-8 Prijutnoje
69 M-9 Prijutovo
67 N-9 Prikumsk
113 L-3 Prilenskoye *plat.*
64 C-5 Prilep
58 C-6 Prilly
66 F-6 Priluki
193 N-9 Primeira Cruz
198 F-4 Primero *riv.*
201 L-2 Primero *cap.*
163 K-5 Primerose *lake*
63 L-1 Primolano
67 M-5 Primorsk
49 J-9 Primorsk
125 L-6 Primorskij Kraj *reg.*
67 J-9 Primorsko-Akhtarsk
67 J-9 Primorskoje
163 L-6 Prince Albert
163 L-6 Prince Albert *na.p.*
161 N-5 Prince Albert *strt.*
161 N-1 Prince Albert *pen.*
104 E-8 Prince Albert
227 N-3 Prince Charles *rge*
165 K-5 Prince Edouard *reg.*
165 K-5 Prince Edouard *isl.*
165 K-6 Prince Edward *isl.*
162 D-3 Prince George
153 H-1 Prince Gustav Adolf *sea*
214 F-2 Prince of Wales *isl.*
160 C-8 Prince of Wales *isl.*
159 H-1 Prince of Wales *cap.*
147 L-4 Prince of Wales (Guangyatan) *rf*
227 N-2 Prince Olav Coast
153 K-2 Prince Regent *strt.*
162 B-1 Prince Rupert
160 A-1 Prince William *strt.*
53 H-4 Princes Risborough
187 N-2 Princes Town
215 H-4 Princess Charlotte *bay*
227 M-1 Princess Martha Coast *reg.*
227 N-1 Princess Ragnhild Coast *cap.*
162 B-2 Princess Royal *isl.*
52 G-1 Princethorpe
162 D-7 Princeton (Canada)
170 D-9 Princeton (USA)
171 H-9 Princeton (USA)
170 C-7 Princeton (USA)
170 A-7 Princeton (USA)
172 F-5 Princeton Junction
98 A-1 Principe *isl.*
190 D-5 Príncipe da Beira
166 D-4 Prineville
56 D-7 Prinsen Bos *ft*
56 D-7 Prinsenbeek
185 H-4 Prinzapolca *riv.*
185 H-4 Prinzapolca
121 N-4 Priobskoje *plat.*
62 B-7 Priola
220 G-9 Prion *bay*
52 G-6 Priors
68 B-8 Priozersk
128 A-7 Prioz'ornyj
66 C-6 Pripet *riv.*
69 J-2 Pripol'arnyj Ural *reg.*
67 H-5 Pristen'
64 C-4 Priština
51 K-5 Pritzwalk
61 H-3 Privas
67 M-4 Privolzhskaya Vozvyshennost
67 M-4 Privolžskij
64 C-4 Prizren
207 M-6 Probolinggo
72 D-1 Prochladnyj
140 G-6 Proddatūr
51 K-4 Præstø
179 M-4 Progreso
124 G-5 Progress
189 H-8 Progresso
64 B-4 Prokletije *mt*
122 C-3 Prokopjevsk
64 C-4 Prokuplje
122 D-1 Proletarka
127 L-2 Proletarsk
67 L-8 Proletarskaja
67 H-6 Proletarskij
58 D-6 Promasens
143 K-8 Prome
172 E-1 Promised Land *lake*
196 C-2 Promissão (Brazil)
196 F-5 Promissão (Brazil)
122 C-2 Promyšlennaja
133 P-1 Promyslovka
67 A-3 Pron'a *riv.*
125 L-1 Pronge (Niž.)
123 P-1 Pronicha
160 G-9 Prophet River
195 N-5 Propria
70 D-6 Prorva
59 M-6 Prosa *mt*
215 K-9 Proserpine
172 A-6 Prospect
172 D-6 Prospect Park
172 F-5 Prospect Plains
149 H-2 Prosperidad
123 H-1 Prospichino
162 C-9 Prosser
51 M-8 Prostejov
219 M-5 Proston
66 G-3 Protva *riv.*
54 A-8 Prouais
64 F-3 Provadija
222 B-8 Providence *cap.*
171 M-5 Providence
108 A-9 Providence *isl.*
180 F-2 Providence N.E. *strt.*
180 E-1 Providence N.O. *strt.*
185 K-4 Providencia *isl.*
190 C-7 Providência *mt*
190 B-2 Providencia
181 J-4 Providenciales *isl.*
171 N-5 Provincetown
50 F-8 Provins
168 A-6 Provo
163 J-6 Provost
89 M-5 Pru *riv.*
196 E-8 Prudentopolis
63 J-2 Prun
54 B-6 Prunay-le-Temple
109 H-7 Prunes *isl.*
63 J-8 Prunetta
66 A-6 Prusk'ow
64 F-1 Prut *riv.*
66 D-9 Prutul *riv.*
168 C-3 Pryor *mt*
175 P-1 Pryor
66 B-8 Przemysl
128 D-3 Prževal'sk
64 F-7 Psara
72 B-1 Psebaj
72 C-1 Pšiš *mt*
120 D-9 Pskent
66 D-2 Pskov
66 C-1 Pskovskoje *lake*
66 G-7 Ps'ol *riv.*
190 B-3 Pto Acre
196 C-7 Pto Adela
194 B-1 Pto Alegre (Brazil)
196 D-5 Pto Alegre (Brazil)
102 A-5 Pto Alexandre
102 B-1 Pto Amboim
185 J-8 Pto Armuelles
196 A-3 Pto Asperanca
184 B-9 Pto Ayora
201 J-2 Pto Bajo Pisagua
184 E-2 Pto Barrios
196 G-9 Pto Belo *pte*
189 J-6 Pto Bermúdez
186 D-5 Pto Berrío *mt*
201 H-3 Pto Bertrand
190 D-6 Pto Bicentenário
186 D-6 Pto Boyaca
196 A-4 Pto Braga
187 J-2 Pto Cabello
185 J-4 Pto Cabezas
196 D-6 Pto Camargo
188 C-6 Pto Campuya
189 L-9 Pto Carlos (Brazil)
188 D-9 Pto Carranza
187 J-5 Pto Carreño
62 D-1 Pto Ceresio
200 G-3 Pto Cisnes
185 P-7 Pto Colombia
184 F-5 Pto Corinto
187 H-1 Pto Cumarebo
200 D-1 Pto de Corral
187 N-2 Pto de Hierro
194 B-2 Pto de Lontra
192 G-8 Pto de Moz
63 P-2 Pto di Falconera
194 A-7 Pto dos Meinacos
178 G-8 Pto Escondido
185 N-8 Pto Escondido
196 A-1 Pto Espidião
186 G-1 Pto Estrella
188 G-2 Pto Eten
197 H-6 Pto Feliz
187 H-1 Pto Fijo
194 E-3 Pto Franco
192 G-6 Pto Grande
190 G-5 Pto Grether
201 N-6 Pto Harberton
190 D-2 Pto Heath
189 K-8 Pto Honorio
188 B-6 Pto Huitoto
201 H-3 Pto Ibáñez
196 A-2 Pto Isabel
184 G-7 Pto Jesús
179 P-4 Pto Juárez
187 L-2 Pto la Cruz
191 L-6 Pto La Paz
201 H-3 Pto Lago Blanco
200 G-2 Pto Lagunas
188 D-3 Pto Leguía
188 B-5 Pto Leguizamo
188 A-4 Pto Limón (Panama)
186 E-7 Pto Limón (Peru)
186 F-7 Pto López (Colombia)
186 G-1 Pto López (Colombia)
196 C-9 Pto Lucena
63 J-4 Pto Mantovano
184 F-5 Pto Masachapa
188 E-4 Pto Melendes
196 C-7 Pto Mendes
196 A-4 Pto Mihanovich
188 C-9 Pto Miraña
187 P-4 Pto Miranda
78 A-1 Pto Moniz
179 P-5 Pto Morelos
189 H-2 Pto Morin
194 E-6 Pto Nacional
188 C-3 Pto Napo
187 J-6 Pto Nariño
186 D-5 Pto Nino
196 B-2 Pto Novo (Brazil)
187 H-6 Pto Nuevo
200 D-2 Pto Octay
188 B-5 Pto Ospina
187 J-5 Pto Paez
190 D-2 Pto Pardo
191 K-1 Pto Patillos
188 B-6 Pto Piedras
196 A-6 Pto Pinasco
196 D-7 Pto Piquiri
199 H-2 Pto Piracuacito
187 L-3 Pto Piritu
188 B-6 Pto Pizarro
192 E-5 Pto Poet
188 D-4 Pto Prado
185 H-7 Pto Quepos
196 A-2 Pto Quijarro
200 F-3 Pto Ramirez
195 N-6 Pto Real do Colegio
61 N-4 Pto Recanati
181 K-1 Pto Rico *reg.*
196 C-9 Pto Rico (Argentina)
188 A-5 Pto Rico (Colombia)
186 D-8 Pto Rico (Colombia)
188 E-9 Pto Rico (Peru)
186 G-5 Pto Rondón
189 H-8 Pto Rubim
188 D-8 Pto San Augustin
184 F-5 Pto Sandino
192 G-7 Pto Santana (Brazil)
196 D-8 Pto Santana (Brazil)
78 B-1 Pto Santo
78 B-1 Pto Santo *isl.*
196 D-6 Pto Sao José
190 E-6 Pto Saucedo
194 B-3 Pto Seguro *riv.*
197 P-2 Pto Seguro
196 C-7 Pto Sta Helena
201 H-1 Pto Stigh
196 A-3 Pto Suarez
186 C-7 Pto Tejada *mt*
63 N-5 Pto Tolle
61 K-6 Pto Torres
188 D-4 Pto Tunigrama
188 D-5 Pto Ugarte
62 D-1 Pto Valtravaglia
200 E-2 Pto Varas
61 L-5 Pto Vecchio
190 B-5 Pto Velho
185 H-7 Pto Viejo
184 B-9 Pto Villamil
189 H-7 Pto Walter
186 E-4 Pto Wilches
196 A-6 Pto Ybapobó
196 E-5 Pto 15 de Novembro
146 C-4 Pu *isl.*
144 G-3 Pua
200 B-2 Púa
208 E-1 Puah *isl.*
158 D-8 Puale *bay*
200 A-7 Puán
58 B-7 Publier
188 C-1 Puca *riv.*
188 D-5 Puca-Curo *riv.*
188 G-4 Pucacaca
189 H-6 Pucallpa
189 L-9 Pucara *riv.*
188 C-8 Pucauro
67 J-1 Pučež
135 M-5 Pucheng
102 D-5 Pucho *riv.*
148 F-5 Pucio *pte*
172 B-6 Puck
53 K-3 Puckeridge
195 H-2 Pucumã *riv.*
48 F-8 Pudasjärvi
52 D-8 Puddletown
104 G-4 Pudimoe
206 G-5 Pudjut *cap.*
68 D-7 Pudož
134 B-7 Puduhe *riv.*
141 K-6 Pudukkottai
178 G-6 Puebla *reg.*
60 C-3 Puebla de Sanabria
60 B-3 Puebla de Trives
168 D-8 Pueblo
200 E-2 Pueblo *riv.*
191 P-2 Pueblo Hundido
191 M-5 Pueblo Ledesma
187 H-1 Pueblo Nuevo
200 B-6 Puelches
200 B-5 Puelén
200 E-3 Puelo *lake*
60 C-7 Puente Genil
60 B-2 Puentedeume
134 A-9 Puer
185 L-9 Puercos *mt*
129 K-3 Puercuo *lake*
174 D-5 Puerta Baja
187 H-1 Puerta Cardón
184 G-2 Puerta Castilla
188 G-2 Puerta Chicama
189 P-8 Puerta de Bombon
188 G-2 Puerta de Lobos
198 D-3 Puerta de los Llanos
174 C-4 Puerta Prieta
191 L-8 Puerta Rieles
200 C-1 Puerta Saavedra
194 F-7 Puerte Alta do Bom Jesus
196 D-1 Puerte Branca
197 K-3 Puerte de Parauna
190 F-2 Puerto Acosta
200 G-3 Puerto Aisen
190 E-7 Puerto Alegre
188 A-4 Puerto Asís
187 J-6 Puerto Ayacucho
196 A-5 Puerto Casado
189 K-8 Puerto Ceticayo
201 L-5 Puerto Coig
184 F-2 Puerto-Cortès
198 B-2 Puerto de Peña Negra
78 D-9 Puerto del Rosario
201 H-6 Puerto Deseado
190 F-7 Puerto Frey
196 A-5 Puerto Guarani
189 J-7 Puerto Inuya
186 F-8 Puerto la Concordia
185 H-3 Puerto Lempira
174 D-4 Puerto Libertad
200 E-6 Puerto Lobos
200 E-6 Puerto Madryn
174 C-8 Puerto Magdalena
189 K-7 Puerto Mainiqui
190 D-1 Puerto Maldonado
200 E-2 Puerto Montt
196 A-5 Puerto Murtinho
201 M-3 Puerto Natales
185 K-9 Puerto Nutis
187 N-4 Puerto Ordaz
196 A-5 Puerto Palma Chica
174 C-3 Puerto Peñasco
200 E-7 Puerto Pirámides
189 J-7 Puerto Portillo
189 K-6 Puerto Prado
149 H-7 Puerto Princesa
190 C-3 Puerto Rico
201 M-5 Puerto Sara
196 A-5 Puerto Sastre
178 B-4 Puerto Vallarta
190 E-7 Puerto Villazón
60 C-6 Púertollano
201 J-3 Pueyrredòn *lake*
57 P-8 Puffendorf
66 C-9 Pufila
67 N-3 Pugacev
139 K-3 Pūgal
134 B-6 Puge
207 M-7 Puger
172 C-5 Pughtown
58 C-7 Puidoux
57 H-4 Puiflijk
188 F-6 Puinahua *cap.*
55 K-2 Puiseux-en-France
54 F-3 Puiseux-Pontoise
55 P-2 Puisieux
89 K-9 Puissa-Bani
87 M-5 Pujehun
188 C-2 Pujili
222 E-7 Pukaki *lake*
224 F-5 Pukapuka *isl.*
224 F-5 Pukarua *isl.*
223 K-4 Pukekohe
135 L-2 Pukou
68 E-6 Puksoozero
191 K-3 Pulacayo
129 N-2 Pulan
207 N-3 Pulangpisau
119 K-6 Pulap *isl.*
191 M-3 Pular *vol.*
176 G-2 Pulaski (USA)
177 K-1 Pulaski (USA)
171 K-5 Pulaski (USA)
210 E-4 Pulau *riv.*
53 J-7 Pulborough
53 N-1 Pulham
135 N-8 Puli
141 H-7 Pulicat *lake*
141 L-5 Puliyangudi
48 G-8 Pulkkila
162 E-9 Pullman
58 C-7 Pully
141 L-8 Pulmoddai
148 C-6 Pulog *mt*
174 D-7 Púlpito *pte*
66 A-6 Pultusk
119 L-6 Pulusuk *isl.*
119 K-6 Puluwat *isl.*
189 L-7 Pumasillo *mt*
143 H-1 Pumuzhangu *lake*
188 D-2 Puná
191 J-4 Puna
188 D-1 Puná *isl.*
191 N-3 Puna de Argentina *reg.*
142 G-2 Punakha
149 P-9 Punan
191 H-4 Punata
127 M-7 Pünch
140 C-3 Pune
214 C-6 Pungalina
107 J-3 Pungoè *riv.*
133 M-3 Pungsan
99 P-3 Punia
191 N-3 Punilla *riv.*
198 A-3 Punilla *mt*
135 K-8 Puning
198 A-4 Punitaqui
139 M-2 Punjāb *reg.*
139 K-2 Punjab Maidān *reg.*
141 L-7 Punkudutivu *isl.*
189 N-9 Puno
189 M-9 Puno *reg.*
185 M-8 Puno *mt*
142 D-3 Pūnpūn *riv.*
200 B-8 Punta Alta
201 M-4 Punta Arenas
201 M-5 Punta Catalina *pte*
201 M-6 Punta de Arenas *pte*
200 E-7 Punta Delgada
187 J-1 Punta Gavilán *pte*
184 E-2 Punta Gorda
185 H-6 Punta Gorda *riv.*
177 K-8 Punta Gorda (USA)
201 L-5 Punta Loyola *pte*
191 N-2 Punta Negra *lake*
200 E-7 Punta Norte
184 G-7 Puntarenas
185 H-8 Puntarenas *reg.*
191 L-1 Puntillas
180 F-5 Punto Padre
52 B-3 Puntsticill *rés*
158 G-2 Punuk *islds*
48 F-8 Puolanka
135 J-4 Puqi
189 M-6 Puquio
191 K-2 Puquios (Chile)
191 P-2 Puquios (Chile)
186 C-8 Puracé *vol.*
129 P-1 Pūranpur
211 J-6 Purari *riv.*
52 D-9 Purbeck *hill*
175 N-2 Purcell
162 F-8 Purcell (Canada) *mt*
159 K-4 Purcell (USA) *mt*
211 K-3 Purdy *islds*
173 H-1 Purdys
223 J-5 Pureora *mt*
168 D-9 Purgatoire *riv.*
142 D-7 Puri
144 C-5 Purian *pte*
186 D-7 Purificación
53 K-6 Purley
140 B-6 Pūrna *riv.*
142 F-3 Purnea
68 D-5 Purnema
52 E-5 Purton
207 N-1 Puruktjahu
142 E-4 Pūrūlia
187 K-7 Puruname *riv.*
192 B-2 Puruni *riv.*
190 B-3 Purus *riv.*
207 H-6 Purwakarta
207 L-6 Purwodadi
207 J-6 Purwokerto
207 K-6 Purworedio
146 B-6 Pusat Gajo *mt*
68 B-9 Pushkin
141 H-4 Pushpagiri *mt*
72 G-3 Puškino
122 C-4 Pustag *mt*
142 G-5 Pusur *lag.*
198 A-5 Putaendo
191 L-3 Putana *vol.*
143 M-2 Putao
66 B-7 Putawy
57 N-7 Putbroek
55 H-5 Puteaux
57 N-8 Puth
135 M-7 Putian
189 M-9 Putina
207 L-3 Puting *cap.*
66 G-6 Putivl'
178 G-7 Putla de Guerrero
173 H-1 Putnam *reg.*
173 J-1 Putnam
173 J-1 Putnam Lake
113 H-3 Putorana *plat.*
223 K-6 Putorino
66 D-3 Putovška
61 H-1 Putre *mt*
52 B-6 Putsham
147 N-9 Putssibau
141 M-7 Puttalam
56 B-9 Putte
56 B-5 Putten *isl.*
57 H-1 Putten
56 C-5 Puttershoek
51 K-4 Puttgarden
141 H-3 Puttūr
188 A-4 Putumayo *riv.*
188 A-4 Putumayo *reg.*
155 L-4 Puvirnitun
61 H-2 Puy (Le)
61 H-2 Puy de Sancy *mt*
132 E-8 Puyang
200 D-2 Puyehue *lake*
200 D-2 Puyehue
188 C-3 Puyo
222 B-8 Puysegur *pte*
200 G-2 Puyugápi *cap.*
200 G-3 Puyuguapi
100 B-8 Pweto
50 C-4 Pwlheli
144 C-5 Pyamalaw *lag.*
144 C-5 Pyapon
133 L-7 Pyawbwe
158 G-9 Pye *islds*
53 K-8 Pyecombe
133 L-5 Pyeongsan
133 M-6 Pyeongtaeg
133 L-5 Pyeongyang
49 J-7 Pyhäjärvi *lake*
48 G-7 Pyhajoki *riv.*
143 L-8 Pyinmana
52 A-5 Pyle
119 H-3 Pyongyang
175 J-4 Pyote
167 L-5 Pyramid *mt*
166 G-4 Pyramid *lake*
60 F-3 Pyrénées *mt*
212 E-8 Pyrton *mt*
69 H-8 Pyščug

69 P-5 Pyshma riv.
69 P-5 Pyšma
66 C-2 Pytalovo
143 L-9 Pyu
143 L-9 Pyu riv.

# Q

131 L-4 Qabupalong-shankou mt
105 J-6 Qachas Nek
126 F-4 Qādes
82 F-9 Qadimah
85 J-5 Qafa well
96 A-9 Qafa
73 H-5 Qahab
82 E-5 Qal at Akhdar
73 H-9 Qal At Salih
93 K-7 Qala'an Nahl
84 G-4 Qalamat at Tawil well
82 G-2 Qalamat umm Khunsur
65 M-8 Qal'at al Marqab site
96 A-1 Qal'at Bīshah
126 G-7 Qalāt-i-Ghilzai
127 M-5 Qal'eh-e Panj
73 N-4 Qāl'eh Mureh riv.
126 E-7 Qal'eh-ye Best
126 F-4 Qal'eh-ye Nīaz
126 F-4 Qal'eh-ye Now
126 G-8 Qal'eh-ye Rashīd
127 J-6 Qal'eh-ye Sāber
126 G-5 Qal'eh-ye Sang-e Takht
127 H-4 Qal'eh-ye Sarkārī
84 D-9 Qalhāt
96 B-9 Qalib Shinan
93 L-8 Qallābāt
85 K-6 Qamar mt
96 C-9 Qamar bay
105 J-8 Qamata
80 G-2 Qamīnis
96 G-7 Qandala
131 N-9 Qaotianyi
85 K-7 Qara mt
127 K-4 Qara Kūtarma
129 H-2 Qara Qash riv.
72 F-7 Qarah mt
97 H-7 Qardo
72 G-3 Qareh Su riv.
73 J-5 Qareh Tekān
93 N-1 Qarnayt mt
83 L-3 Qaryat al Ulyā
83 J-5 Qaşim reg.
80 G-3 Qasr al Burayqah
138 A-2 Qasr-e-Qand
72 G-7 Qasr-e Shīrīn
81 M-5 Qasr Farāfirah
92 G-1 Qasr Ibrim site
81 M-5 Qaṣṣ Abu Said hill
96 E-3 Qa'tabah
83 P-4 Qatar reg.
118 A-4 Qatar state
81 L-2 Qattārah (Munkhafad al) holl.
80 D-5 Qattūsah dés
93 H-5 Qawz Abū Dulū dés
93 K-6 Qawz Rajab
126 C-3 Qāyen
73 J-5 Qazvīn
172 B-9 Qeen Annes reg.
227 N-4 Qeen Mary Coast
227 M-6 Qeen Maud rge
227 N-1 Qeen Maud Land reg.
94 G-1 Qeissan
82 B-6 Qena
84 B-5 Qeshm reg.
84 B-5 Qeshm
73 K-7 Qeydū
84 C-2 Qeys isl.
126 F-5 Qeysar mt
126 G-3 Qeysār
73 H-5 Qezel Owzan riv.
124 F-9 Qianguoerluosi
134 F-8 Qianjiang
134 F-8 Qianjiang riv.
134 F-4 Qianjiang
131 P-7 Qianning
135 L-5 Qianshan
134 D-6 Qianxi
134 E-1 Qianxian
132 A-9 Qianyang
130 G-4 Qiaoyan
131 N-4 Qiazhe
83 J-4 Qibā

135 N-2 Qidong
131 K-6 Qieji
129 H-6 Qiemo
128 B-6 Qiershankou mt
132 D-3 Qiharigedu
132 F-7 Qihe
134 D-5 Qijiang
130 E-2 Qijiaojing
126 C-9 Qila Lādgasht
126 G-8 Qila Saifullāh
131 H-5 Qilianshanmo mt
129 M-7 Qilinhu lake
135 L-4 Qimen
82 B-6 Qinā riv.
131 L-9 Qinan
131 K-3 Qinchai reg.
124 G-7 Qingan
131 N-9 Qingchuan
134 C-5 Qingfu
124 F-8 Qinggang
130 C-2 Qinggelihe riv.
131 K-6 Qinghai lake
131 K-6 Qinghainanshan mt
125 H-7 Qingheishan mt
134 F-4 Qingjiang riv.
135 K-5 Qingjiang
134 D-7 Qinglong
131 J-6 Qingshiling mt
131 H-6 Qingshui
131 K-9 Qingshuihe riv.
134 F-6 Qingshuijiang riv.
143 N-3 Qingshuilangshan mt
135 N-5 Qingtian
132 D-7 Qingxu
135 L-3 Qingyang
135 H-8 Qingyuan
131 H-8 Qingyuhu lake
132 D-8 Qinhe riv.
133 H-5 Qinhuangdao
132 D-8 Qinshui
132 D-7 Qinxian
135 H-2 Qinyang
132 D-9 Qinyang
145 M-1 Qinzhou
145 N-3 Qionghai
131 P-8 Qionglai
131 P-8 Qionglaishan mt
145 N-3 Qiongzhong
145 N-3 Qiongzhouhaixia strt.
124 E-7 Qiqihaer
81 H-3 Qirdābiyah
82 C-2 Qiryat Gat
134 E-1 Qishan
96 C-8 Qishn
93 N-2 Qishrān isl.
85 J-6 Qitbit riv.
132 D-7 Qixian (China)
132 E-9 Qixian (China)
73 J-8 Qīyād riv.
135 H-6 Qiyang
96 C-1 Qīzān
96 C-1 Qīzān reg.
129 J-2 Qizil Jilga
73 H-5 Qojūr
73 K-6 Qom
127 K-4 Qonduz
73 H-6 Qorveh
72 E-4 Qotur
163 L-8 Qu'Appelle
163 L-8 Qu'Appelle riv.
162 B-5 Quadra isl.
216 F-7 Quairading
172 D-4 Quakertown
126 C-7 Qual'eh-ye Fath
146 G-3 Quan Long
175 M-2 Quanah
145 M-6 Quang Ngai
145 L-5 Quang Tri
145 L-2 Quang Yen
52 B-7 Quantock hill
135 M-7 Quanzhou (China)
134 G-7 Quanzhou (China)
199 J-3 Quaraí riv.
199 K-3 Quaraí
208 C-3 Quarles mt
62 B-2 Quarona
172 B-6 Quarryville
59 P-2 Quarten
63 L-5 Quartesana
63 N-2 Quarto d'Altino
174 C-1 Quartzsite
193 K-7 Quatipuru
162 A-4 Quatsino strt.
52 D-1 Quatt
63 H-6 Quattro Castella
73 N-2 Qūchān
102 C-3 Qué riv.
221 J-4 Quebengevan
155 M-4 Québec reg.
164 F-7 Québec
197 H-3 Quebra-Anzo riv.
195 N-5 Quebrangulo
200 D-1 Quedal cap.
162 C-5 Queen Bess mt
156 A-1 Queen Charlotte islds
162 A-4 Queen Charlotte strt.

162 A-1 Queen Charlotte islds
162 A-1 Queen Charlotte
201 L-8 Queen Charlotte Bay bay
155 J-1 Queen Elizabeth islds
100 C-2 Queen Elizabeth na.p.
153 H-3 Queen Maud gulf
53 M-5 Queenborough
213 M-3 Queens strt.
103 M-8 Queens Mine
220 G-5 Queenscliff
218 G-1 Queensland reg.
105 H-8 Queenstown (South Africa)
222 D-8 Queenstown (Australia)
220 G-8 Queenstown (Australia)
162 B-7 Queets
199 J-5 Queguay
199 J-5 Queguay Grande riv.
191 J-3 Quehua
193 H-7 Queimada isl.
195 L-6 Queimadas
197 H-7 Queimadas islds
98 G-9 Quela
107 H-5 Quelimane
200 F-2 Quellón
186 E-2 Quemado mt
174 G-1 Quemando
102 F-4 Quembo riv.
135 M-7 Quemoy
135 M-7 Quemoy isl.
200 A-7 Quemú Quemú
200 E-2 Quenac isl.
53 L-3 Quendon
172 A-5 Quentin
185 H-4 Quepi
199 H-9 Quequén
189 N-8 Quequeña
189 L-6 Querco
196 D-6 Querencia do Norte
178 E-4 Queretaro
63 L-1 Quero
185 H-7 Quesada
135 J-2 Queshan
162 D-4 Quesnel
162 E-4 Quesnel riv.
162 E-4 Quesnel lake
168 C-9 Questa
191 L-3 Quetena
170 B-2 Quetico Prov. Park reg.
126 F-8 Quetta
54 A-2 Queue-d'Haye (La)
54 C-6 Queue-les-Yvelines (La)
102 C-1 Queve (Cuvo) riv.
188 C-2 Quevedo
184 C-2 Quezaltenango
184 D-3 Quezaltepecque
149 H-8 Quezon
148 D-6 Quezon City
82 B-8 Quffah riv.
96 D-2 Quflat al'Udhr
132 G-8 Qufu
131 K-7 Qugou
145 M-7 Qui Nhon
102 C-1 Quibala
98 F-8 Quibaxe
186 C-5 Quibdó
50 C-8 Quiberon
98 E-9 Quiçama na.p.
160 E-5 Quiet lake
174 D-2 Quijotoa
200 F-1 Quilán isl.
200 F-1 Quilán cap.
78 F-2 Quilatès cap.
102 B-3 Quilengues
191 J-2 Quilhuiri mt
198 A-5 Quilimari
198 E-3 Quilino
163 L-7 Quill lake
189 L-7 Quillabamba
191 H-4 Quillacollo
191 L-2 Quillaga
198 A-4 Quillaicillo
60 G-4 Quillan
198 A-6 Quillota
200 C-2 Quilmes
141 L-4 Quilon
218 G-5 Quilpie
198 A-6 Quilpué
191 P-8 Quiltilipi
191 M-2 Quimal mt
185 N-9 Quimari mt
98 G-7 Quimbele
98 E-8 Quimbumbe
190 G-3 Quime
198 F-1 Quimilí
191 H-7 Quimome riv.
50 B-8 Quimper
50 C-8 Quimperlé
189 K-6 Quimpitirique
148 D-4 Quinalasag isl.
189 L-9 Quince Mil

62 A-2 Quincinetto
171 M-5 Quincy (USA)
170 B-8 Quincy (USA)
177 H-5 Quincy (USA)
162 C-8 Quincy (USA)
166 G-3 Quincy (USA)
55 K-8 Quincy-sur-Seine
55 P-5 Quincy-Voisins
186 D-6 Quindio reg.
198 D-5 Quines
106 G-9 Quinga
132 A-7 Quingshuiying
158 E-5 Quinhagak
148 G-6 Quiniluban Group islds
166 G-5 Quinn riv.
179 N-5 Quintana Roo reg.
60 D-6 Quintanar de la Orden
198 A-6 Quintero
198 E-6 Quinto riv.
59 M-7 Quinto
63 M-2 Quinto di Treviso
63 L-2 Quinto Vicentino
172 D-8 Quinton
62 G-3 Quinzano d'Oglio
106 C-8 Quionga
184 E-2 Quiriga site
200 A-2 Quirihue
106 E-9 Quirimba isl.
196 F-3 Quirinópolis
200 A-1 Quiriquina isl.
187 M-3 Quiriquire
201 J-3 Quiroga lake
198 G-7 Quiroga (Argentina)
191 H-4 Quiroga (Bolivia)
60 B-3 Quiroga (Spain)
186 G-2 Quisiro
106 E-8 Quissanga
63 J-4 Quistello
98 F-8 Quitexe
177 J-5 Quitman (USA)
176 F-4 Quitman (USA)
183 C-3 Quito
188 B-3 Quito
190 C-5 Quixada (Brazil)
195 L-2 Quixadá (Brazil)
106 G-8 Quixaxe
195 L-2 Quixeramobim
195 L-2 Quixeramobim riv.
134 E-3 Qujiang riv.
134 C-7 Qujing
131 L-3 Qumalai
173 L-3 Quogue
213 M-2 Quoin isl.
127 J-4 Quondūz riv.
220 C-1 Quorn
92 D-8 Qurayyāt
84 D-8 Qurdūd
82 B-7 Qūs
96 D-7 Quşay'ir
131 N-8 Qushan
135 P-3 Qushan isl.
72 F-5 Qūshchī
105 J-7 Quthing
81 J-8 Quwayrat ad Dabsh
132 D-8 Quwo
131 K-9 Quwushan mt
134 E-3 Quxian
135 M-4 Quxian

# R

48 G-7 Raahe
82 C-4 Raam mt
56 D-6 Raamsdonksveer
207 N-6 Raas isl.
57 N-8 Raath
208 C-7 Raba
64 A-1 Rába riv.
97 J-6 Rabâble
101 K-5 Rabai
93 H-8 Rabak
78 D-3 Rabat
77 B-1 Rabat
211 P-4 Rabaul
160 F-7 Rabbit riv.
82 F-8 Rābigh
184 D-2 Rabinal
59 N-5 Rabius
142 G-6 Rabnābād isl.
62 A-5 Racconigi
171 N-5 Race pte

165 P-4 Race cap.
146 G-2 Rach Gia
146 G-2 Rach Gia gulf
146 C-4 Racha Noi isl.
146 C-4 Racha Yai isl.
120 E-2 Rachmet
66 C-9 Rachov
170 D-6 Racine
52 A-7 Rackenford
170 A-6 Racoon
96 E-3 Radā
108 E-6 Radama islds
66 D-9 Radauti
58 F-3 Radelfingen
177 K-1 Rādhanpur
139 H-7 Rādhanpur
63 H-8 Radici pass
67 N-2 Radišcevo
164 B-2 Radisson
220 E-1 Radium Hill
162 F-7 Radium Hot Springs
146 B-7 Radja pte
206 G-3 Radjik
53 J-4 Radlett
52 B-1 Radnor ft
66 A-7 Radom
66 A-7 Radomsko
66 E-7 Radomyšl'
220 A-1 Radstock cap.
52 D-6 Radstock
66 B-3 Radviliškis
163 L-9 Radville
82 F-7 Radwā mt
53 L-3 Radwinter
161 M-3 Rae riv.
161 L-7 Rae
142 B-2 Rāe Bareli
57 N-5 Raesfeld
223 J-6 Raetihi
82 F-3 Rāf mt
198 G-4 Rafaela
91 N-7 Rafai
83 H-3 Rafhā
89 H-9 Rafi riv.
73 P-8 Rafsanjan
94 A-3 Raga riv.
94 A-3 Raga
149 J-3 Ragang vol.
180 G-4 Ragged isl.
138 D-2 Rāghai riv.
223 J-4 Raglan (Nouvelle Zélande)
223 J-4 Raglan (port)
52 C-4 Raglan (UK)
175 J-1 Ragland
62 F-6 Ragola mt
173 P-1 Ragueneau
208 E-4 Raha
91 N-3 Rahad al Bardi
82 G-8 Rahaṭ mt
125 K-6 Rahe
96 F-2 Raheite
138 F-6 Rahim Ki Bāzār
139 H-3 Rahīmyār Khān
73 K-6 Rāhjerd
79 H-2 Rahouia
172 G-4 Rahway
146 G-3 Rai isl.
142 F-3 Raiganj
142 C-5 Raigarh
142 F-6 Raimanga lag.
58 F-1 Raimeux (Les) mt
142 F-5 Rainagar
162 G-1 Rainbow Lake
55 K-5 Raincy (Le)
211 H-9 Raine riv.
215 H-2 Raine isl.
53 L-5 Rainham
138 G-3 Raini riv.
162 B-8 Rainier mt
170 B-1 Rainy lake
170 A-1 Rainy River
140 B-9 Raipur
139 M-8 Raisen
170 C-1 Raith
224 E-6 Raivavae isl.
127 L-9 Rāiwind
54 C-2 Raizeux
140 B-9 Rāj Nāndgaon
195 K-5 Rajada
140 E-9 Rājahmundry
91 P-3 Rajaj
147 M-8 Rajang riv.
141 L-5 Rājapālaiyam
139 K-5 Rajasthān reg.
127 M-8 Rājauri
143 K-3 Rājbāri site
124 G-5 Rajčichinsk
69 N-9 Rajevskij
139 L-4 Rājgarh (India)
139 L-8 Rājgarh (India)
142 D-3 Rājgīr

140 B-9 Rājim
138 G-8 Rājkot
142 F-3 Rājmahāl
142 E-3 Rājmahal hill
140 A-3 Rājpīpla
142 F-4 Rajshahi
224 C-4 Rakahanga isl.
222 F-8 Rakaia
83 P-4 Rakan cap.
127 M-6 Rakaposhi mt
206 F-5 Rakata isl.
83 H-9 Rakbah pl.
138 C-2 Rakhshān riv.
222 B-9 Rakiura (Stewart) isl.
70 D-9 Rakušečnyj cap.
70 N-2 Rakvere
145 L-6 Ralao
177 N-2 Raleigh bay
177 M-1 Raleigh
175 L-2 Ralls
221 J-6 Ram cap.
185 H-5 Rama
185 H-5 Rama riv.
198 C-7 Rama Caída
198 B-2 Ramadilla
194 G-9 Ramalho mt
199 H-6 Ramallo
65 J-2 Raman-koš gulf
141 L-6 Rāmanāthapuram
172 G-2 Ramapo
172 G-2 Ramapo riv.
140 F-3 Ramas cap.
82 C-2 Ramat Gan
54 C-9 Rambouillet
54 C-8 Rambouillet ft
54 D-9 Rambouillet na.p.
211 L-2 Rambutyo isl.
140 E-4 Rāmdurg
165 M-4 Ramea islds
142 E-1 Rāmechhāp
108 C-8 Ramena
141 L-6 Rāmeswaram
139 H-4 Ramganga riv.
139 H-4 Rāmgarh
73 K-6 Rāmhormoz
201 M-2 Ramirez isl.
189 L-9 Ramis riv.
62 G-7 Ramiseto
82 C-2 Ramla
96 E-7 Ramlat al Wigh hill
96 F-1 Ramlu mt
97 K-1 Rammis riv.
139 P-4 Rāmnagar
82 C-3 Ramon hill
67 J-5 Ramon
192 F-8 Ramos
178 C-1 Ramos riv.
90 A-7 Ramos strt.
104 E-1 Ramoshwani
159 K-7 Rampart
161 H-3 Ramparts riv.
139 P-4 Rāmpur (India)
139 N-2 Rāmpur (India)
142 F-4 Rāmpur Hāt
139 L-7 Rāmpura
140 B-8 Ramrama
143 J-4 Ramree isl.
143 J-8 Ramree
126 C-7 Ramrud site
73 J-4 Rāmsar
170 F-2 Ramsay lake
53 K-1 Ramsey (UK)
172 G-2 Ramsey (USA)
53 P-6 Ramsgate
211 J-4 Ramu riv.
95 M-6 Ramu
48 F-4 Rana strt.
187 J-7 Rana mt
142 F-5 Rānāghāt
149 K-9 Ranau
206 E-4 Ranau lake
109 N-4 Ranavalona cap.
198 B-6 Rancagua
58 B-5 Rances
196 F-5 Rancharia
186 F-1 Ranchería riv.
142 D-4 Rānchi
198 E-1 Ranchillos
200 D-9 Ranco lake
172 E-6 Rancocas riv.
198 E-7 Rancul
221 H-3 Rand
96 G-2 Randa
51 J-3 Randers
168 A-5 Randolph City
165 P-2 Random isl.
49 J-3 Randsfd. lake
57 H-4 Randwijk
86 F-4 Ranérou
146 E-5 Rangae
143 H-5 Rāngāmāti
208 B-2 Rangasa cap.
223 J-2 Rangaunu bay
168 B-6 Rangely

56 D-7 Rijsbergen
56 F-3 Rijsenburg
57 M-1 Rijssen
56 B-3 Rijswijk (Netherlands)
56 G-4 Rijswijk (Netherlands)
56 E-5 Rijswijk (Netherlands)
83 K-8 Rikā riv.
136 B-7 Rikubetu
136 E-8 Rikuzen-Takata
166 E-5 Riley
56 A-8 Rilland
62 B-1 Rima
90 A-1 Rima riv.
189 K-4 Rimac riv.
188 E-4 Rimachi lake
62 B-1 Rimasco
224 D-6 Rimatara isl.
66 A-9 Rimavska-Sobota
162 G-6 Rimbey
57 P-8 Rimburg
63 N-8 Rimini
64 D-2 Rîminicu-Vîlcea
64 F-2 Rîmnicu-Sarat
164 G-5 Rimouski
59 H-5 Rinagenberg
196 G-5 Rincao
123 H-6 Rinchinlhümbe
174 G-3 Rincon
191 M-3 Rincón mt
191 M-3 Rincon lake
178 D-3 Rincón de Romos
186 E-3 Rincón Hondo
191 L-4 Rinconada
163 M-9 Rinding mt
208 C-7 Rindja isl.
208 A-7 Rindjani mt
221 H-7 Ringarooma bay
51 H-3 Ringkøbing
51 H-3 Ringkøbing fj.
53 L-8 Ringmer
153 H-1 Ringnes isl.
153 J-2 Ringnes islds
172 E-4 Ringoes
51 K-4 Ringsted
172 B-3 Ringtown
139 L-5 Ringus
48 C-5 Ringvassøy isl.
218 B-2 Ringwood (Australia)
52 F-8 Ringwood (UK)
172 G-2 Ringwood (USA)
200 D-2 Rinihue
172 F-1 Rio
196 B-1 Rio Alegre
196 E-8 Rio Azul
190 C-2 Rio Branco (Brazil)
199 L-5 Río Branco (Uruguay)
196 F-8 Rio Branco do Sul
175 H-4 Rio Bravo del Norte riv.
196 C-5 Rio Brilhante
200 D-2 Rio Bueno
201 L-5 Río Callegos
187 M-2 Río Caribe
197 L-4 Rió Casca
201 K-5 Río Chico (Argentina)
187 K-2 Río Chico (Vénézuela)
200 G-3 Río Cisnes
200 G-3 Río Cisnes pte
197 H-6 Río Claro (Brazil)
187 P-2 Río Claro (Vénézuela)
200 C-7 Río Colorado
198 E-5 Río Cuarto
195 J-9 Río de Antonio
197 L-6 Rio de Janeiro reg.
197 K-6 Rio de Janeiro (Guanabara)
199 J-7 Río de la Plata reg.
195 J-8 Rio do Pires
196 F-9 Rio do Sul
199 P-2 Rio Fortuna
201 N-6 Rio Grande
168 C-8 Rio Grande riv.
156 E-4 Rio Grande riv.
199 M-5 Rio Grande (Argentina)
191 K-3 Rio Grande (Bolivia)
178 D-2 Rio Grande (Mexico)
172 E-9 Rio Grande (USA)
175 M-8 Rio Grande City
178 C-3 Rio Grande de Santiago riv.
195 N-2 Rio Grande do Norte reg.
199 L-3 Rio Grande do Sul reg.
185 L-8 Rio Hato
179 N-4 Rio Lagartos
195 N-5 Rio Largo
200 G-4 Rio Mayo
191 J-3 Rio Mulatos
98 C-1 Rio Muni reg.
196 F-8 Rio Negrinho
199 J-5 Rio Negro
200 C-6 Rio Negro riv.
196 B-3 Rio Negro lag.
190 C-4 Rio Negro (Bolivia)
196 F-8 Rio Negro (Brazil)

200 D-2 Rio Negro (Chile)
186 E-4 Río Negro (Colombia)
199 M-3 Rio Pardo
197 L-1 Rio Pardo de Minas
200 F-3 Rio Pico
191 N-5 Rio Piedras
196 A-7 Rio Pilcomayo na.p.
196 F-2 Rio Preto mt
197 K-6 Rio Preto
198 E-4 Río Primero
195 M-7 Rio Real
175 L-7 Río Salado riv.
63 J-5 Rio Saliceto
185 H-6 Rio San Juan reg.
198 E-4 Río Secundo
198 E-5 Río Tercero
188 C-4 Rio Tigre
195 P-3 Rio Tinto
149 J-8 Rio Tuba
178 F-4 Rio Verde riv.
196 F-2 Rio Verde (Brazil)
201 M-4 Rio Verde (Chile)
178 F-3 Río Verde (Mexico)
196 C-3 Rio Verde de Mato Grosso
197 L-3 Rio Vermelho
188 C-3 Riobamba
186 F-1 Riohacha
191 M-1 Rioja (Chile)
188 F-4 Rioja (Peru)
196 F-4 Riolândia
63 L-7 Riolo Terme
61 H-2 Riom
62 F-8 Riomaggiore
162 F-7 Riondel
186 D-5 Rionegro
72 C-2 Rioni riv.
163 M-2 Riou lake
188 A-2 Rioverde
194 B-4 Riozinho riv.
190 B-3 Riozinho
53 J-6 Ripley (UK)
176 F-2 Ripley (USA)
170 G-8 Ripley (USA)
170 D-5 Ripon
55 J-9 Ris-Orangis
186 C-6 Risaralda reg.
52 B-4 Risca
53 J-2 Riseley (UK)
53 H-6 Riseley (UK)
83 J-6 Rishā riv.
139 N-3 Rishikesh
175 M-4 Rising Star
172 B-7 Rising Sun
136 A-5 Risiri isl.
51 J-1 Risør
58 A-6 Risoux mt
48 D-4 Risøyhamn
78 E-5 Rissani
66 A-1 Ristna cap.
172 C-2 Rita
196 D-2 Rita do Araguaia
104 G-5 Ritchie
144 B-8 Ritchie islds
174 B-2 Rito
54 A-5 Ritoire
59 M-6 Ritom lake
59 K-8 Ritter pass
129 K-2 Ritu
59 K-6 Ritzlihorn mt
162 D-9 Ritzville

164 E-7 Rivière-à-Pierre
165 J-4 Rivière-au-Renard
165 H-3 Rivière-aux-Graines
164 G-6 Rivière-Bleue
164 G-6 Rivière-du-Loup
181 P-4 Rivière-Pilote
63 P-1 Rivignano
62 A-4 Rivoli
63 J-2 Rivoli Veronese
62 F-3 Rivolta d'Adda
139 M-8 Rīwa Pathār mt
77 G-2 Riyadh
83 L-6 Riyadh
72 C-3 Rize
73 N-1 Rizeh mt
133 H-8 Rizhao
65 L-8 Rizokárpason
64 A-7 Rizzuto cap.
49 K-2 Rjukan
86 E-3 Rkiz lake
79 N-6 Rmel el Abiod reg.
63 L-5 Ro Ferrarese
181 L-1 Road Town
53 H-2 Roade
168 B-7 Roan plat.
168 B-7 Roan or Brown Cliffs mt
61 H-2 Roanne
177 M-1 Roanoke riv.
177 H-3 Roanoke
177 M-1 Roanoke Rapids
184 F-2 Roatán isl.
184 G-2 Roatán
185 J-8 Robalo
147 M-8 Roban
126 A-2 Robât-e khãn
127 J-4 Robâtak
104 C-9 Robbeneiland isl.
172 A-8 Robbin mt
220 G-7 Robbins isl.
172 F-5 Robbinsville
62 C-3 Robbio
220 D-4 Robe
218 E-8 Robe mt
62 G-4 Robecco d'Oglio
220 D-2 Roberstoune
175 L-4 Robert Lee
198 G-7 Roberts
219 M-6 Roberts (Australia) mt
158 A-8 Roberts (USA) mt
87 N-6 Robertsfield
48 G-6 Robertsfors
142 C-3 Robertsganj
165 K-2 Robertson lake
104 D-9 Robertson
87 M-5 Robertsport
164 E-6 Roberval
172 B-5 Robesomia
95 L-2 Robi
55 H-7 Robinson
214 C-6 Robinson riv.
216 E-2 Robinson (Australia) rge
160 B-3 Robinson (Canada) mt
219 K-4 Robinson Gorge na.p.
60 G-3 Robinson River
220 F-3 Robinvale
163 M-8 Roblin
162 F-4 Robson mt
175 M-7 Robstown
62 A-7 Roburent
175 L-3 Roby (USA)
99 L-1 Roby (Zaïre)
58 B-9 Roc d'Enfer mt
60 A-5 Roca
179 J-6 Roca Partida pte
184 A-8 Roca Redonda isl.
62 C-6 Roçadas
188 B-1 Rocafuerte
62 B-5 Rocca d'Arazzo
62 A-7 Rocca de Baldi
62 B-2 Rocca Pietra
63 L-8 Rocca San Casciano
62 G-3 Roccafranca
62 B-6 Roccaverano
62 D-6 Rocchetta Ligure
199 L-6 Rocha reg.
199 L-6 Rocha
173 H-4 Rochaway Park
58 E-5 Roche (La)
215 P-4 Roche (La)
58 A-1 Roche (Switzerland)
58 D-8 Roche (Switzerland)
58 B-2 Roche de Barchey hill
54 B-2 Roche-Guyon (La)
60 F-1 Roche-sur-Yon (La)
60 G-1 Rochechouart
196 C-3 Rochedo
60 F-1 Rochefort
58 A-5 Rochejean
60 F-1 Rochelle (La)
170 C-6 Rochelle (USA)
161 L-8 Rocher River
58 A-6 Rocheray
164 G-4 Rochers riv.
58 D-7 Rochers de Naye mt

53 M-5 Rochester (UK)
164 G-9 Rochester (USA)
170 E-7 Rochester (USA)
171 J-5 Rochester (USA)
170 B-5 Rochester (USA)
53 M-5 Rochford
160 F-7 Rock riv.
162 B-5 Rock Bay
166 D-6 Rock Creek Butte mt
172 B-7 Rock Glen
172 B-9 Rock Hall
177 K-2 Rock Hill
170 C-7 Rock Island
169 J-7 Rock Port
169 J-5 Rock Rapids
168 D-6 Rock River
180 F-2 Rock Sound
168 B-5 Rock Springs
46 B-4 Rockall (UK) isl.
214 B-8 Rockampton Downs
56 A-4 Rockanje
172 F-3 Rockaway
172 G-9 Rockdale
170 C-6 Rockford
163 K-9 Rockglen
219 L-3 Rockhampton
177 L-2 Rockingham
169 H-1 Rocklake
172 G-2 Rockland mt
164 G-8 Rockland (Canada)
173 L-1 Rockland (USA)
173 H-2 Rockland Lake
220 E-4 Rocklands lake
175 N-7 Rockport
172 A-7 Rocks
175 L-5 Rocksprings
192 C-2 Rockstone
171 K-8 Rockville
173 H-4 Rockville Centre
164 G-7 Rockwood
162 G-9 Rocky mt
163 N-6 Rocky lake
217 J-8 Rocky pte
220 G-7 Rocky cap.
168 C-6 Rocky (USA) mt
159 H-3 Rocky (USA) pte
168 D-8 Rocky Ford
216 F-9 Rocky Gully
172 F-4 Rocky Hill
156 C-2 Rocky Mountains rge
177 M-1 Rocky Mt
162 G-6 Rocky Mtn House
173 K-2 Rocky Point
54 B-2 Roconval
54 F-6 Rocquencourt
49 K-2 Rødberg
62 B-6 Roddi
165 M-1 Roddickton
56 B-4 Rodenrijs
198 B-4 Rodeo (Argentina)
178 C-1 Rodeo (Mexico)
174 F-3 Rodeo (USA)
58 E-8 Rodertsee Heide ft
60 G-3 Rodez
64 G-8 Rodhos
61 P-5 Rodi Garganico
63 H-4 Rodigo
53 L-4 Roding riv.
218 A-3 Rodinga
121 M-3 Rodino
223 K-3 Rodney cap.
112 D-1 Rodolf isl.
188 F-7 Rodrigues
201 M-3 Rodriguez isl.
172 F-6 Roebling
212 D-7 Roebourne
213 J-5 Roebuck Downs
105 K-2 Roedtan
56 C-2 Roelofarendsveen
57 N-6 Roermond
66 E-5 Rogačov
190 E-3 Rogagua lake
51 H-1 Rogaland reg.
53 H-7 Rogate
177 K-1 Rogers mt
176 C-1 Rogers
170 F-4 Rogers City
164 B-2 Roggan riv.
57 J-9 Roggel
104 D-8 Roggeveldberge mt
59 E-4 Roggwil
48 E-4 Rognan
59 H-2 Rohrbach
172 A-6 Rohrerstown
138 G-3 Rohri
172 A-2 Rohrsburg
139 M-4 Rohtak
145 J-5 Roi Et
62 A-9 Roia riv.
55 L-7 Roissy
55 K-3 Roissy-en-France
198 G-6 Rojas
200 G-2 Rojas isl.
179 H-4 Rojo cap.

146 D-9 Rokan riv.
214 G-4 Rokeby
87 L-5 Rokel riv.
127 J-5 Rokheh
66 D-6 Rokitnoje
196 E-6 Rolândia
49 K-1 Røldal
186 C-6 Roldanillo
169 H-1 Rolla
58 B-7 Rolle
54 B-3 Rolleboise
219 K-3 Rolleston
180 G-3 Rolleville
176 E-4 Rolling Fork
63 J-5 Rolo
48 B-6 Rolsvøya isl.
51 H-2 Rom
219 K-5 Roma
63 J-6 Romagna reg.
62 C-2 Romagnano Sesia
62 E-5 Romagnese
177 L-3 Romain cap.
165 J-3 Romaine riv.
58 B-5 Romainmôtier
55 K-5 Romainville
55 N-6 Romainvilliers
64 F-1 Roman
79 M-5 Romane well
62 F-3 Romano di Lombardia
47 F-5 Romania state
54 E-8 Romanie (La)
62 F-3 Romano di Lombardia
123 N-5 Romanovka
61 J-2 Romans-sur-Isère
159 P-7 Romanzof mt
158 F-3 Romanzof cap.
148 F-5 Romblon
148 F-5 Romblon isl.
61 M-5 Rome
47 E-5 Rome
177 H-3 Rome (USA)
171 K-5 Rome (USA)
53 L-5 Romford
50 F-8 Romilly-sur-Seine
78 D-3 Rommani
66 G-6 Rommy
171 J-8 Romney
51 H-4 Rømø
58 D-5 Romont
59 J-3 Romoos
50 E-9 Romorantin-Lanthenay
146 F-8 Rompin riv.
146 F-8 Rompin
52 F-7 Romsey
124 G-4 Romy
140 F-4 Ron
145 K-4 Ron pte
50 E-1 Ronaldsay isl.
162 F-9 Ronan
63 N-2 Roncade
185 L-4 Roncador rf
196 E-7 Roncador
194 B-7 Roncador mt
63 K-1 Roncegno
63 M-7 Ronco riv.
62 A-3 Ronco Canavese
62 D-6 Ronco Scrivia
63 J-4 Roncoferraro
63 N-8 Roncofreddo
63 H-1 Roncone
60 B-7 Ronda
187 N-1 Ronde isl.
187 M-9 Rondon mt
190 C-6 Rondônia reg.
190 C-7 Rondônia
196 C-1 Rondonópolis
143 J-6 Rong Klang
144 G-4 Rong Kwang
134 F-7 Ronge na.p.
119 M-5 Rongelap isl.
119 M-5 Rongerik isl.
129 P-4 Rongga
134 F-7 Rongjiang
134 F-7 Rongjiang riv.
134 C-4 Rongxian
173 K-3 Ronkonkoma lake
173 K-3 Ronkonkoma
51 L-4 Rønne
54 G-1 Ronquerolles
62 B-4 Ronsecco
194 A-7 Ronuro riv.
105 J-4 Roodepoort
168 A-9 Roof Butte mt
102 F-8 Rooibooklaagte riv.
211 K-5 Rooke (Umboi) isl.
139 N-3 Roorkee
50 F-6 Rooselare
56 B-7 Roosendaal
56 B-7 Roosendaal en Nispen reg.
160 F-8 Roosevelt
190 C-8 Roosevelt riv.
227 M-6 Roosevelt isl.

168 A-6 Roosevelt (USA)
174 E-1 Roosevelt (USA)
57 K-8 Rooskenskant
57 N-7 Roosteren
59 L-3 Root
161 H-6 Root riv.
214 B-5 Roper riv.
214 B-4 Roper River Mission
214 A-5 Roper Valley
48 D-6 Ropi
53 H-7 Ropley
193 L-9 Roque
199 H-7 Roque Perez
187 P-6 Roraima mt
187 N-8 Roraima reg.
161 J-2 Rorey lake
163 N-8 Rorketon
49 H-3 Røros
48 G-3 Rørvik
63 L-2 Rosà
184 B-9 Rosa cap.
62 A-1 Rosa mt
61 K-2 Rosa mt
174 E-7 Rosa pte
178 C-3 Rosa Morada mt
188 B-2 Rosa Zarate
67 H-2 Rosal'
148 D-6 Rosales
178 B-3 Rosamorada
191 N-4 Rosaria de Lerma
180 B-4 Rosario mt
180 C-5 Rosario isl.
191 N-4 Rosario riv.
198 G-5 Rosario (Argentina)
191 L-4 Rosario (Argentina)
189 M-9 Rosário (Brazil)
193 M-9 Rosário (Brazil)
191 M-1 Rosário (Chile)
178 B-2 Rosario (Mexico)
174 D-7 Rosario (Mexico)
174 C-5 Rosario (Mexico)
196 B-7 Rosario (Paraguay)
199 J-6 Rosario (Uruguay)
186 F-2 Rosario (Venezuela)
191 N-5 Rosario de la Frontera
199 H-5 Rosario del Tala
199 K-3 Rosário do Sul
174 B-5 Rosarito pte
174 C-5 Rosarito
61 H-4 Rosas gulf
178 A-1 Rosas
54 B-5 Rosay
168 G-3 Roscoe
50 B-7 Roscoff
50 B-3 Roscommon
50 B-4 Roscrea
214 B-4 Rose riv.
224 C-5 Rose isl.
162 A-1 Rose pte
167 H-3 Rose (USA) mt
165 L-4 Rose Blanche
109 P-9 Rose-Hill-Beau-Bassin
162 F-2 Rose Prairie
214 B-4 Rose River Mission
181 N-3 Roseau
157 H-5 Roseau
218 E-4 Roseberth
220 G-8 Rosebery
220 G-5 Rosebud
168 D-2 Rosebud riv.
172 G-3 Roselle
175 P-6 Rosenberg
172 E-8 Rosenhayn
61 M-1 Rosenheim
59 K-5 Rosenlaui
163 K-7 Rosetown
167 H-2 Roseville
55 N-1 Rosières
61 L-4 Rosignamo Marittimo
192 C-2 Rosignol
64 E-3 Roşiorii-de-Vede
51 K-4 Roskilde
66 F-4 Roslavl'
173 H-3 Roslyn
56 G-6 Rosmalen
57 L-9 Rosmeer
54 F-1 Rosnel (Le)
54 B-4 Rosny ft
55 K-5 Rosny-sous-Bois
54 B-3 Rosny-sur-Seine
63 M-4 Rosolina
223 H-7 Ross mt
227 M-6 Ross sea
163 P-6 Ross isl.
160 F-4 Ross riv.
222 E-7 Ross (New Zealand)
52 D-3 Ross (UK)
176 E-4 Ross Barnett lake
86 E-2 Ross Bethio
227 M-6 Ross Ice Shelf glac.
160 F-4 Ross River
59 P-7 Rossa
61 K-5 Rossa pte
59 L-3 Rossberg mt
171 H-4 Rosseau lake

215 N-3 Rossel cap.
62 C-6 Rossiglione
164 D-3 Rossignol lake
58 E-7 Rossinière
86 E-3 Rosso
66 D-3 Rossony
67 J-6 Rossosh
59 M-4 Rostock mt
56 G-5 Rossum
48 F-4 Røssvassbukt
48 E-4 Røst isl.
127 K-4 Rostāq
163 K-7 Rosthern
51 K-5 Rostock
67 H-1 Rostov
67 K-8 Rostov-Na-Donu
48 F-4 Røsvatnet lake
175 J-2 Roswell
145 L-7 Rôtânôkiri reg.
57 M-7 Rotem
51 J-5 Rotenburg
57 P-6 Röthenbach (FRG)
59 H-4 Röthenbach (Switzerland)
59 K-3 Rothenburg
59 M-3 Rothenthurn
53 M-7 Rother riv.
50 D-4 Rotherham
59 L-2 Rothkreuz
59 H-1 Rothrist
59 P-3 Rothhor mt
53 H-1 Rothwell
208 F-8 Roti isl.
208 F-8 Roti strt.
221 H-2 Roto
59 L-6 Rotondo mt
59 P-7 Rotondo pass
51 K-9 Rott riv.
56 C-4 Rotterdam
50 F-6 Rotterdam
53 K-8 Rottingdean
216 D-7 Rottnest isl.
223 K-5 Roturua
63 K-1 Rotzo
50 F-7 Roubaix
50 E-7 Rouen
58 E-7 Rougemont
80 B-9 Roui riv.
79 K-2 Rouiba
210 F-7 Rouku
58 A-1 Roulans
165 L-1 Round lake
109 N-9 Round isl.
219 M-3 Round Hill cap.
219 M-8 Round Mont mt
168 C-2 Roundup
192 G-3 Roura
142 D-5 Rourkela
201 P-5 Rous pen.
54 G-9 Roussigny
55 N-6 Route (La)
55 M-2 Rouvres
105 H-7 Rouxville
164 B-6 Rouyn
48 E-7 Rovaniemi
62 G-2 Rovato
68 F-6 Rovdino
62 E-6 Rovegno
67 K-7 Roven'ki
63 J-4 Roverbella
59 P-8 Roveredo
63 N-1 Roveredo in Piano
63 J-1 Rovereto
145 K-7 Rovieng Tbong
63 L-4 Rovigo reg.
63 L-4 Rovigo
66 D-7 Rovno
106 D-5 Rovuma riv.
73 J-6 Row an
200 G-1 Rowlett isl.
153 L-3 Rowley Hill
212 E-5 Rowley Shoals
87 J-2 Roxa isl.
148 G-7 Roxas (Philippines)
148 F-4 Roxas (Philippines)
177 L-1 Roxboro
218 D-1 Roxborough Downs
172 E-3 Roxburg
222 D-8 Roxburgh
87 H-1 Roxo cap.
53 J-2 Roxton
175 J-1 Roy (USA)
168 A-5 Roy (USA)
212 F-9 Roy Hill
50 B-3 Royal Canal cal.
147 N-4 Royal Charlotte (Huangujiao) rf
52 F-1 Royal Leamington Spa
50 E-6 Royal Tunbridge
53 L-7 Royal Tunbridge Wells
60 F-1 Royan
55 J-1 Royaumont
227 N-6 Royds
172 D-5 Royersford
48 G-4 Røyrvik
53 K-3 Royston

55 P-8 Rozay-en-Brie
121 H-3 Roždestvenka
56 A-4 Rozenburg
57 J-3 Rozendaal
51 M-4 Rozewie cap.
66 A-9 Rožnava
67 J-8 Rozovka
66 B-7 Roztocze mt
67 K-4 Rtishchevo
102 B-6 Ruacana
100 F-8 Ruaha na.p.
223 J-6 Ruahine mt
58 D-9 Ruan mt
223 J-6 Ruapehu
222 C-9 Ruapuke isl.
223 L-6 Ruatoria
80 F-5 Ru'ays riv.
96 A-5 Rub Al Khali dés
100 G-7 Rubeho mt
127 P-8 Ruberung mt
136 B-7 Rubesibe
67 J-7 Rubeznoje
94 A-8 Rubi riv.
194 D-9 Rubiataba
63 J-6 Rubiera
58 G-4 Rubigen
197 N-2 Rubim
196 F-4 Rubinéia
122 D-1 Rubino
186 F-4 Rubio
100 D-4 Rubondo isl.
121 M-4 Rubtsovsk
168 A-2 Ruby riv.
159 J-6 Ruby
160 D-4 Ruby (Canada) mt
167 H-6 Ruby (USA) mt
200 A-6 Rucanelo
135 J-7 Rucheng
68 D-4 Ručji
56 C-7 Rucphen
73 K-5 Rūd-e Shūr riv.
73 J-4 Rūd Sar
142 B-1 Rudauli
126 C-7 Rūdbār
100 G-8 Rudi
138 A-2 Rūdkhaneh-ye Sarbāz riv.
51 J-4 Rudkøbing
67 L-4 Rudn'a (SSSR)
66 E-3 Rudn'a (SSSR)
128 B-4 Rudničnyj
64 E-5 Rudozem
58 D-6 Rue
58 F-5 Rüeggisberg
54 D-3 Rueil
54 G-5 Rueil-Malmaison
54 F-1 Ruel (Le)
107 H-2 Ruenza riv.
59 M-5 Ruèras
93 J-7 Rufa'ah
59 N-2 Rufi
101 H-9 Rufiji riv.
63 L-9 Rufina
198 F-6 Rufino
86 F-1 Rufisque
103 M-4 Rufunsa
103 N-4 Rufunsa riv.
52 F-8 Rufus Stone
135 M-1 Rugao
52 G-1 Rugby (UK)
168 G-4 Rugby (USA)
51 K-4 Rügen isl.
142 F-2 Ruhea
100 C-3 Ruhengeri
66 B-2 Ruhnu isl.
106 B-5 Ruhudji riv.
106 C-4 Ruhuhu riv.
127 J-4 Rūī
195 K-7 Rui Barbosa
135 N-5 Ruian
135 K-7 Ruijin
99 N-3 Ruiki riv.
143 M-5 Ruili
59 P-5 Ruis
78 B-1 Ruivo mt
186 D-6 Ruiz vol.
66 B-2 Rūjiena
99 J-2 Ruki riv.
106 D-3 Rukuru riv.
100 D-8 Rukwa lake
100 D-7 Rukwa reg.
180 G-3 Rum Cay rf
213 N-1 Rum Jungle
93 K-8 Rumaylah
94 D-5 Rumbek
164 G-8 Rumford
198 D-2 Rumi Punco
83 H-6 Rummah riv.
82 D-1 Rummānā mt
136 B-6 Rumoi
106 C-3 Rumpi
90 C-7 Rumpi mt
56 F-4 Rumptë
173 H-5 Rumson
215 J-6 Rumula
100 G-2 Rumuruti

135 J-1 Runan
223 L-5 Runaway isl.
145 H-9 Rung isl.
55 J-7 Rungis
94 B-7 Rungu
100 D-8 Rungwa riv.
100 E-7 Rungwa
172 E-6 Runnemede
102 F-6 Runtu
129 P-5 Ruokazangbuhe riv.
135 K-4 Ruoqi
128 G-8 Ruoqiang
130 G-6 Ruoshut riv.
200 D-2 Rupanco
146 E-8 Rupat isl.
146 E-8 Rupat strt.
164 B-4 Rupert riv.
164 B-4 Rupert bay
166 G-8 Rupert
106 C-7 Ruponda
83 K-2 Ruq'ī
83 K-1 Rurat riv.
190 F-3 Rurrenabaque
224 D-6 Rurutu isl.
127 L-4 Rušan
103 P-7 Rusape
59 L-9 Ruscada mt
64 E-3 Ruse
142 E-3 Rusera
168 E-8 Rush riv.
133 J-7 Rushan
53 J-1 Rushden
172 A-2 Rushtown
168 F-5 Rushville (USA)
170 E-8 Rushville (USA)
170 C-8 Rushville (USA)
175 P-4 Rusk
195 M-2 Russas
161 L-7 Russel lake
160 C-4 Russel Fi.
177 H-1 Russel Springs
163 N-5 Russell lake
217 J-8 Russell mt
223 K-2 Russell (New Zealand)
168 G-8 Russell (USA)
142 C-7 Russellkonda
176 D-2 Russellville (USA)
176 G-1 Russellville (USA)
176 G-3 Russellville (USA)
58 C-2 Russey (Le)
63 M-7 Russi
67 H-4 Russia reg.
131 M-3 Russian geographic society mt
158 F-5 Russian Mission
121 K-1 Russkaja Pol'ana
59 M-9 Russo
72 E-2 Rustavi
105 J-3 Rustenburg
176 D-4 Ruston
100 C-4 Rusumu (chutes)
59 J-3 Ruswil
208 D-7 Ruteng
107 K-1 Rutenga
177 K-2 Rutherfordton
58 F-2 Rüti (Switzerland)
59 N-4 Rüti (Switzerland)
59 N-1 Rüti (Switzerland)
164 F-9 Rutland
144 A-9 Rutland isl.
214 F-5 Rutland Plains
100 B-3 Rutshuru
57 M-3 Ruurlo
84 B-6 Ru'ūs Al Jibal mt
101 J-8 Ruvu riv.
101 J-8 Ruvu
106 D-8 Ruvuma riv.
106 C-5 Ruvuma reg.
100 C-4 Ruvuvu riv.
84 E-3 Ruweis
100 C-2 Ruwenzori mt
106 C-4 Ruwura cap.
106 G-2 Ruya riv.
100 C-5 Ruyigi
58 D-3 Ruz val.
67 K-2 Ruzayevka
66 E-7 Ružin
100 B-4 Ruzizi riv.
77 E-5 Rwanda state
100 B-3 Rwindi
67 H-3 Ryazan
67 J-3 Ryazhsk
48 C-9 Rybačij isl.
128 C-2 Rybačje
124 G-1 Rybalka 3-ja
68 E-9 Rybinsk lake
122 F-3 Rybinskoje
66 E-9 Rybnitsa
67 H-3 Rybnoje
162 F-3 Rycroft
52 G-8 Ryde
53 M-7 Rye (UK)
173 H-2 Rye (USA)
166 G-4 Rye Patch lake
66 G-5 Ryl'sk

221 K-2 Rylstone
70 A-5 Ryn dés
68 B-2 Rynda
136 G-6 Ryōtu
66 D-9 Ryškany
137 M-7 Ryukyu islds
117 H-4 Ryukyu islds
66 B-8 Rzeszów
66 F-2 Ržev

## S

144 G-4 Sa
147 H-2 Sa Dec
73 H-9 Sa Diyah lake
145 M-6 Sa Huynh
73 P-9 Sa Idābad (Sirjan)
73 K-6 Sa je mt
143 L-8 Sa-koi
195 K-7 Sao Cristóvão
196 D-4 Sao Domingos riv.
90 E-8 Saa
84 A-5 Sa'ādatābād
128 E-7 Saaermingshan mt
123 L-7 Saamar
58 E-6 Saane riv.
58 F-7 Saanen (Gessenay)
58 F-7 Saanenmöser
50 G-8 Saar reg.
50 G-8 Saarbrucken
66 A-1 Saaremaa isl.
127 J-3 Saartuz
59 J-9 Saas Amagell
59 J-9 Saas Fee
59 J-9 Saas-Grund
59 H-9 Saastal Saaer Visp reg.
57 N-1 Saasveld
72 G-3 Saatly
200 B-8 Saavedra
181 M-2 Saba isl.
64 B-3 Sabac
60 G-5 Sabadell
149 L-8 Sabah reg.
214 G-1 Sabai isl.
208 E-1 Sabal
208 B-5 Sabalana islds
188 C-7 Sabaloyácu riv.
180 D-4 Sabana islds
181 L-6 Sabana de la Mar
184 F-4 Sabanagrande
185 P-7 Sabanalarga
187 P-4 Sabaneta pte
181 L-6 Sabaneta de Yásica
146 A-5 Sabang
197 K-4 Sabará
140 D-9 Sabari riv.
139 J-7 Sābarmati
95 K-3 Sabata
96 J-3 Sab'atayn dés
191 J-2 Sabaya
93 N-3 Sabāyā isl.
63 H-5 Sabbioneta
93 L-6 Sabderat
126 C-9 Sāberī riv.
83 K-7 Sabhā
80 D-5 Sabhah
80 D-4 Sabhah reg.
107 J-1 Sabi riv.
194 A-3 Sabia riv.
93 L-4 Sabidana mt
105 L-3 Sabie riv.
175 K-7 Sabinas
175 K-7 Sabinas
175 L-8 Sabinas Hidalgo
176 C-5 Sabine riv.
72 G-2 Sabirabad
84 E-4 Sabkat as Salamiyah lag.
80 G-3 Sabkhat al Qunayyin lake
84 E-3 Sabkhat Maţī lag.
148 F-6 Sablayan
165 J-8 Sable isl.
177 K-9 Sable cap.
170 F-4 Sable (Au) rf
50 D-8 Sable-sur-Sarthe
60 F-1 Sables-d'Olonne (Les)
195 L-3 Saboeiro
89 J-8 Sabongari
86 G-2 Saboya
186 E-5 Saboyá mt
80 B-1 Sabrātah
227 N-4 Sabrina Coast
209 L-2 Sabuda isl.

73 H-2 Sabunči
121 H-3 Sabyndy
126 C-1 Sabzevār
191 H-4 Sacaba
191 H-4 Sacaca
198 F-4 Sacanta
72 D-2 Sačchere
63 L-3 Saccolongo
64 E-2 Sacele
125 M-1 Sachalinskaya reg.
198 F-1 Sachayoj
72 H-4 Sachbuz
173 L-1 Sachem pte
127 J-2 Sachrisabž
71 N-5 Sachristan strt.
127 L-2 Sachristan mt
59 K-4 Sachseln
51 K-7 Sachsen
121 H-4 Sachtinks
125 N-3 Sacht'orsk
69 H-9 Sachunja
63 N-1 Sacile
67 J-3 Sack
165 J-6 Sackville
54 G-8 Saclay
168 D-1 Saco
171 N-4 Saco riv.
149 K-4 Sacol isl.
166 G-2 Sacramento val.
166 G-2 Sacramento riv.
175 H-2 Sacramento mt
189 H-5 Sacramento pl.
197 H-4 Sacramento (Brazil)
167 H-2 Sacramento (USA)
60 C-8 Sacratif cap.
190 E-9 Sacre (Timalacia) riv.
190 G-5 Sact riv.
137 L-3 Sada cap.
96 C-2 Sa'dah
208 C-3 Sadang riv.
101 J-7 Sadani
146 D-5 Sadao
96 D-3 Sadd riv.
144 B-7 Saddle Peak hill
159 P-6 Saddlerochit riv.
66 D-9 Sadgora
85 K-7 Sadh
86 F-3 Sadio
139 H-3 Sādiqābād
143 L-2 Sadiya
93 N-1 Sadīyah riv.
82 C-6 Safajah isl.
82 F-6 Safājah mt
172 A-6 Safe Harbor
59 J-1 Safenwil
126 F-2 Saffār Kalay
51 K-1 Säffle
174 F-2 Safford
53 L-3 Saffron Walden
78 B-3 Safi
211 L-8 Safia
88 A-4 Safia dés
127 L-3 Safīd Khers
65 M-9 Sāfitā
68 F-3 Safonovo
65 J-4 Safranbolu
173 M-2 Sag Harbor
211 L-5 Sag Sag
137 L-2 Saga
129 P-4 Saga
87 H-7 Sagabari
136 F-7 Sagae
143 L-4 Sagaing reg.
143 L-6 Sagaing
137 J-8 Sagami gulf
137 H-7 Sagamihara
70 E-4 Sagan riv.
121 L-5 Sagan riv.
120 A-2 Sagan riv.
93 N-6 Saganeiti
146 C-1 Sagaint isl.
142 F-6 Sāgar isl.
140 G-3 Sāgar (India)
159 N-5 Sagavanirktok riv.
168 A-5 Sage
140 F-7 Sagileru riv.
170 F-5 Saginaw
170 F-5 Saginaw bay
70 C-4 Sagiz riv.
70 C-4 Sagiz
155 L-3 Saglouc
122 E-5 Sagonar
60 A-6 Sagres
130 B-2 Sagsayn riv.

180 G-5 Sagua de Tanamo
180 D-4 Sagua la Grande
168 C-8 Saguache
164 F-6 Saguenay riv.
60 E-6 Sagunto
54 E-3 Sagy
128 A-6 Sagymžal mt
84 D-7 Saham
72 G-5 Sahand mt
76 C-2 Sahara dés
86 A-4 Sahara Western reg.
139 N-3 Sahāranpur
142 E-3 Saharsa
139 N-5 Sahaswän
89 H-5 Sahel reg.
142 C-2 Sähibganj
126 B-5 Sahlābād
84 G-6 Saḥmatah
174 F-5 Sahuaripa
178 D-5 Sahuayo de Díaz
83 H-6 Sāḥūq riv.
142 C-2 Sai riv.
146 E-5 Sai Buri
144 F-7 Sai Yok
113 H-4 Saian rge
91 P-5 Said Bundas
79 H-3 Saïda
82 C-1 Saïda
141 H-7 Saidapet
78 G-2 Saïdia
211 K-5 Saidor
142 G-3 Saidpur
127 L-6 Saidu
58 D-1 Saignelégier
137 J-3 Saïgon
145 L-9 Saïgon
130 G-6 Saihantaolai
143 L-2 Saikhoa Ghāt
137 L-3 Saiki
128 C-5 Sailimuhu lake
54 E-3 Saillancourt
58 E-9 Saillon
54 D-3 Sailly
209 L-1 Sailolof
133 K-4 Saima
178 D-2 Saín Alto
61 H-2 St-Agrève
53 J-4 St Albans
50 E-6 St Albans (UK)
164 E-8 St Albans (USA)
170 G-9 St Albans (USA)
164 E-7 St-Alexis-des-Monts
61 H-1 St-Amand-Mont-Rond
108 F-3 St-André cap.
87 M-4 St Ann cap.
222 C-7 St Anne pte
180 F-7 St Ann's Bay
168 A-3 St Anthony
165 M-1 St Anthony
54 A-7 St-Antoine
58 B-5 St-Antoine
220 F-4 St Arnaud
58 C-4 St-Aubin
165 K-1 St-Augustin riv.
109 N-4 St-Augustin bay
165 K-2 St-Augustin-Saguenay
177 K-6 St Augustine
50 B-6 St Austell
181 M-1 St-Barthélémy isl.
222 D-8 St Bathans mt
54 E-8 St-Benoît
109 P-7 St-Benoît
58 D-3 St-Blaise
104 E-9 St Blaize
163 P-9 St Boniface
58 E-1 St-Brais
55 J-3 St-Brice-sous-Forêt
165 P-4 St Bride's
50 C-8 St-Brieuc
171 H-5 St Catharines
52 G-9 St Catherine pte
177 K-4 St Catherines isl.
58 A-7 St-Cergue
170 C-9 St Charles
181 M-2 St Christopher isl.
157 H-5 St Christopher and Nevis state
181 M-2 St Christopher Nevis
170 G-6 St Clair lake
172 B-3 St Clair (USA)
61 J-1 St-Claude
163 P-9 St Cloud
54 G-6 St Cloud
170 A-4 St Cloud (USA)
54 B-7 St-Côme
55 C-5 St-Corentin
108 F-2 St-Cristophe (Juan de Nova) isl.
156 H-5 St Cristopher isl.
181 L-1 St Croix isl.
54 C-3 St-Cyr-en-Arthies
54 F-7 St-Cyr-l'Ecole
50 B-5 St David's cap.
50 E-8 St-Denis

55 J-4 St-Denis
109 P-7 St-Denis
52 C-3 St Devereux
50 G-9 St-Dié
50 F-8 St-Dizier
164 E-7 St-Donat
160 C-3 St Elias *mt*
192 F-3 St-Elie
61 H-2 St-Etienne
164 E-8 St-Eustache
181 M-2 St Eustatius *isl.*
164 E-6 St Félicien
55 P-5 St-Fiacre
91 M-4 St Floris *na.p.*
61 H-2 St-Flour
54 F-8 St-Forget
165 P-2 St Francis *cap.*
168 F-7 St Francis
176 E-1 St Francis *riv.*
104 G-9 St Francis *bay*
176 D-5 St Francisville
61 L-1 St-Gallen
153 N-1 St George *fj.*
158 B-2 St George *isl.*
166 E-2 St George *pte*
219 K-6 St George
211 P-4 St George *cap.*
211 P-4 St George *strt.*
221 K-4 St George *cap.*
177 H-6 St George *cap.*
165 H-7 St George (Canada)
158 B-2 St George (USA)
167 L-6 St George (USA)
172 G-4 St George (USA)
177 L-3 St George (USA)
157 H-5 St George's
165 L-4 St Georges *bay*
192 G-4 St-Georges
187 N-1 St-George's
164 F-7 St-Georges (Canada)
172 C-7 St Georges (USA)
50 B-5 St Georges's *cal.*
54 G-4 St-Germain *ft*
54 E-6 St-Germain-de-la-Grange
54 F-5 St-Germain-en-Laye
55 K-9 St-Germain-lès-Corbeil
55 N-5 St-Germain-sur-Marne
54 C-1 St-Gervais
61 K-2 St-Gervais-les-Bains
58 D-7 St-Gingolph
60 G-4 St-Girons
58 A-3 St-Gorgon
59 L-6 St-Gothard *mt*
55 H-4 St-Gratien
76 B-6 St Helena *isl.*
177 L-4 St Helena *strt.*
104 C-8 St Helena *bay*
50 D-4 St Helens
162 B-9 St Helens *mt*
162 B-9 St Helens
50 C-7 St-Hellier
54 C-9 St-Hilarion
177 M-1 St Hill
58 D-1 St-Hippolyte
54 D-8 St-Hubert-le-Roi
58 F-8 St-Iconard
170 F-3 St Ignace
170 D-1 St Ignace *isl.*
54 A-4 St-Illiers-la-Ville
54 A-4 St-Illiers-le-Bois
58 D-2 St-Imier
58 D-2 St-Imier *val.*
53 K-1 St Ives
162 A-2 St James *cap.*
170 E-3 St James (USA)
170 A-5 St James (USA)
173 K-3 St James (USA)
165 H-3 St Jean *riv.*
164 E-6 St Jean *lake*
164 E-8 St-Jean
60 F-1 St-Jean-d'Angély
58 C-9 St-Jean d'Aulph
54 G-9 St-Jean-de-Beauregard
61 J-2 St-Jean-de-Maurienne
60 E-3 St-Jean-Pied-de-Port
164 F-6 St-Jean-Port-Joli
58 B-9 St-Jeoire
164 E-8 St-Jérôme
162 E-9 St Joe *riv.*
165 J-7 St John
168 G-9 St John
164 G-6 St John *riv.*
165 M-2 St John *cap.*
165 L-2 St John *isl.*
165 L-2 St John *bay*
181 L-1 St John *isl.*
157 H-5 St John's
174 F-1 St Johns
165 P-3 St John's (Canada)
181 N-2 St John's (RU)
170 F-5 St Johns (USA)
164 F-9 St Johnsbury
172 D-9 St Jones
170 F-3 St Joseph *isl.*
176 E-4 St Joseph
170 E-6 St Joseph *riv.*
170 E-6 St Joseph (USA)
170 A-8 St Joseph (USA)
165 P-3 St Joseph's
60 G-1 St-Junien
65 K-1 St Krym
54 F-8 St-Lambert
156 G-2 St-Laurent *riv.*
164 E-7 St Laurent *riv.*
192 E-3 St-Laurent
54 A-8 St-Laurent-la-Gâtine
158 F-1 St Lawrence *isl.*
165 K-4 St Lawrence *gulf*
165 N-4 St Lawrence
164 D-9 St Lawrence *riv.*
219 L-2 St Lawrence (Australia)
52 G-9 St Lawrence (UK)
54 C-8 St-Léger-en-Yvelines
58 D-7 St-Légier
164 G-6 St-Léonard
53 M-8 St Leonards
55 H-3 St-Leu-la-Forêt
58 B-7 St-Livres
50 D-7 St-Lô
109 P-7 St-Louis
163 L-7 St Louis (Canada)
192 G-4 St-Louis (Guyane fr)
86 E-2 St Louis (Senegal)
170 C-9 St Louis (USA)
168 G-7 St Loup *riv.*
54 B-6 St-Lubin-de-la-Haye
58 G-9 St-Luc
157 H-5 St Lucia *state*
156 H-5 St Lucia *isl.*
105 M-6 St Lucia *cap.*
54 B-9 St-Lucien
60 F-1 St-Maixent-l'Ecole
50 C-8 St-Malo
50 C-8 St-Malo *gulf*
55 J-6 St-Mandé
181 J-6 St-Marc
181 J-6 St Marc *cal.*
55 M-3 St-Mard
53 P-6 St Margaret's at Cliffe
162 E-9 St Maries
143 H-7 St Martin *islds*
163 P-8 St Martin *lake*
58 F-9 St-Martin
181 M-1 St-Martin *isl.*
104 C-8 St Martin *cap.*
54 B-9 St-Martin-de-Nigelles
54 C-5 St-Martin-des-Champs
55 J-2 St-Martin-du-Tertre
54 C-3 St-Martin-la-Garenne
165 J-7 St Martins
162 G-8 St Mary *lake*
218 D-8 St Mary *mt*
86 G-1 St Mary *cap.*
165 P-3 St Mary's *bay*
165 P-4 St Mary's *cap.*
165 P-3 St Mary's
53 N-7 St Mary's Bay
50 B-8 St-Mathieu *pte*
158 E-1 St Matthew (USA) *isl.*
211 M-2 St Matthias *islds*
55 K-6 St-Maur-des-Fossés
58 D-9 St-Maurice
171 L-2 St Maurice *riv.*
55 K-6 St-Maurice
50 C-8 St-Méen
52 B-5 St Mellons
55 M-4 St-Mesmes
159 H-4 St Michael
181 J-6 St-Michel de l'Atalaye
164 E-7 St-Michel-des-Saints
55 H-9 St-Michel-sur-Orge
61 L-2 St Moritz
50 C-9 St-Nazaire
53 K-2 St Neots
52 B-5 St Nicholas
50 F-6 St-Niklaas
59 H-9 St Niklaus Barrhorn *mt*
54 F-6 St-Nom-la-Bretèche
50 E-7 St-Omer
53 N-4 St Osyth
55 J-5 St-Ouen
54 G-3 St-Ouen-l'Aumône
54 A-6 St-Ouen-Marchefroy
55 N-2 St-Pathus
158 B-2 St Paul *isl.*
158 B-2 St Paul
168 G-7 St Paul
165 L-1 St Paul *riv.*
164 F-6 St-Paul *bay*
165 L-5 St Paul *isl.*
109 P-7 St-Paul
89 N-6 St Paul *cap.*
163 J-5 St Paul (Canada)
87 M-6 St Paul (Cape Verde) *riv.*
170 B-4 St Paul (USA)
177 J-1 St Paul (USA)
164 G-5 St Paul-du-Nord
52 C-8 St Perrott
51 H-4 St Peter
170 A-4 St Peter
50 C-7 St Peter Port
58 E-3 St-Peters
172 C-5 St Peters
177 K-7 St Petersburg (USA)
52 C-7 St Petherton
165 N-4 St-Pierre *isl.*
164 E-7 St Pierre *lake*
165 N-4 St-Pierre
181 P-4 St-Pierre
109 P-7 St-Pierre (France)
108 A-9 St-Pierre (France) *isl.*
58 E-9 St-Pierre de Clages
55 K-9 St-Pierre-du-Perray
58 B-4 St-Point *lake*
61 H-1 St-Pourçain-sur-Sioule
58 B-7 St-Prex
55 H-3 St-Prix
50 F-7 St-Quentin
165 H-6 St-Quentin
54 E-7 St-Quentin-en-Yvelines
61 J-4 St-Raphaël
54 B-1 St-Rémy
54 D-7 St-Rémy-l'Honoré
54 F-8 St-Rémy-lès-Chevreuse
104 E-9 St Sebastian *bay*
108 C-7 St-Sebastien *cap.*
164 F-6 St-Siméon
58 A-5 St-Sorlin *mt*
55 N-3 St-Soupplets
58 F-7 St-Stephan
165 H-7 St Stephen
58 B-7 St-Sulpice
58 B-4 St-Sulpice
51 L-5 St Szczecinski
160 C-6 St Terese
55 M-5 St-Thibaut-des-Vignes
170 G-5 St Thomas
181 L-1 St Thomas *isl.*
164 E-7 St-Tite
61 J-4 St-Tropez
59 H-2 St Urban
58 E-1 St-Ursanne
62 A-2 St Vincent
220 C-2 St Vincent *gulf*
181 N-8 St Vincent *isl.*
181 N-8 St Vincent *strt.*
187 N-1 St-Vincent *isl.*
109 K-1 St-Vincent *cap.*
157 H-5 St Vincent and the Grenadines *state*
181 N-8 St Vincent Grenadines *reg.*
52 C-3 St Weonards
164 E-8 Ste-Agathe-des-Monts
164 G-4 Ste Anne *lake*
164 F-7 Ste-Anne-de-Beaupré
164 F-6 Ste-Anne-de-la-Pocatière
169 J-1 Ste Anne des Chênes
165 H-4 Ste-Anne-des-Monts
164 D-7 Ste-Anne-du-Lac
165 H-4 Ste-Claire *bay*
58 B-4 Ste-Croix
164 F-7 Ste-Foy
54 E-5 Ste-Gemme
170 C-9 Ste Genevieve (USA)
55 J-9 Ste-Geneviève-des-Bois
54 A-2 Ste-Geneviève-lès-Gasny
221 H-8 Ste Helens *pte*
221 H-8 Ste Helens
164 G-4 Ste Marguerite *riv.*
181 P-4 Ste-Marie
108 G-8 Ste-Marie *isl.*
109 N-2 Ste-Marie *cap.*
221 H-8 Ste Marys
50 F-8 Ste-Menehould
163 N-8 Ste Rose du Lac
161 J-5 Ste Thérèse *lake*
99 M-8 Ste Walburge
60 F-1 Saintes
181 N-3 Saintes *islds*
119 K-5 Saipan Rota
191 L-3 Sairecabur *mt*
137 M-3 Saito
129 H-1 Saitula
137 L-4 Saizyō
206 F-1 Saja *isl.*
128 A-4 Sajak
128 A-4 Sajak Pervyj
191 H-2 Sajama *riv.*
191 H-2 Sajama *mt*
191 H-2 Sajama
126 G-1 Sajat
67 N-5 Sajchin
96 C-1 Sajid *isl.*
85 K-6 Sājir *cap.*
127 N-5 Sajmak
120 E-8 Sajram
104 E-7 Sak *riv.*
138 D-3 Sāka Kalāt
90 A-3 Sakaba *riv.*
137 K-5 Sakai
137 J-4 Sakai-Minato
82 F-3 Sakākā
109 J-5 Sakaleona *riv.*
164 C-2 Sakami *riv.*
164 B-3 Sakami *lake*
103 M-3 Sakania
211 L-4 Sakar *isl.*
126 G-1 Sakar
126 F-1 Sakar-Caga
109 L-2 Sakaraha
64 H-5 Sakarya *riv.*
136 F-7 Sakata
100 B-3 Sake
109 J-4 Sakeny *riv.*
89 N-8 Sakété
125 N-1 Sakhalin *isl.*
113 N-4 Sakhalin *isl.*
126 F-6 Sākhar
65 J-1 Saki
126 G-8 Sakīr *mt*
137 P-6 Sakishima *islds*
70 B-1 Sakmara *riv.*
89 K-6 Sakogu
145 J-5 Sakon Nakhon
104 E-7 Sakrivier
120 B-3 Saksaul'skij
67 M-7 Sal *riv.*
87 N-3 Sal *isl.*
200 D-6 Sal. del Gualicho *lake*
87 N-3 Sal-Rei
51 M-1 Sala
62 G-6 Sala Baganza
208 E-3 Salabangka *islds*
174 B-2 Salada *lag.*
200 F-5 Salada *lake*
198 A-2 Salada *bay*
199 H-2 Saladas
198 D-6 Saladillo
199 H-7 Saladillo
198 E-2 Saladillo *riv.*
198 C-2 Salado (Argentina) *riv.*
174 G-1 Salado (USA) *riv.*
89 M-5 Salaga
101 M-1 Salagle
131 H-4 Salahe *riv.*
122 C-3 Salair
122 B-3 Salairskij Kr'až *mt*
208 D-5 Salajar *strt.*
93 L-2 Salak *bay*
68 E-6 Salakuša
93 K-6 Salalah
85 K-3 Salālah *well*
184 F-3 Salamá
184 D-2 Salamá (Guatémala)
60 C-4 Salamanca
198 A-5 Salamanca (Chile)
178 E-4 Salamanca (Mexico)
171 J-6 Salamanca (USA)
91 L-3 Salamat *reg.*
91 K-4 Salamat *riv.*
186 D-6 Salamina
64 E-7 Salamis
211 K-6 Salamua
127 J-5 Salang *mt*
132 C-5 Salaqi
185 M-9 Salaquí *riv.*
63 K-5 Salara
201 H-2 Salas *isl.*
207 K-6 Salatiga
69 N-9 Salavat
189 H-2 Salaverry
209 K-1 Salawati *isl.*
149 H-3 Salay
138 F-8 Salāya
189 L-7 Salcantay *mt*
181 L-6 Salcedo
159 L-8 Salcha *riv.*
66 C-4 Salčininkai
69 N-5 Salda
104 C-8 Saldanha
86 E-4 Saldé
200 B-8 Saldungaray
66 B-3 Saldus
221 H-5 Sale (Australia)
62 D-5 Sale (Italy)
78 D-2 Salé (Morocco)
149 M-1 Salebabu *isl.*
59 K-8 Salecchio
208 B-7 Saleh *bay*
141 J-6 Salem
162 A-9 Salem (USA)
169 H-5 Salem (USA)
172 D-7 Salem (USA)
172 D-7 Salem (USA) *riv.*
170 B-9 Salem (USA)
171 H-9 Salem (USA)
172 D-7 Salem (USA) *reg.*
50 C-2 Salen
61 N-6 Salerno
58 D-6 Sâles
53 N-4 Sales *pte*
63 L-4 Saletto
50 D-4 Salford
195 M-7 Salgado
58 G-8 Salgesh
66 A-9 Salgótarjan
195 L-4 Salgueiro
140 B-4 Salher *mt*
198 D-1 Salí *riv.*
72 E-1 Sali Martan
62 B-7 Saliceto
168 C-8 Salida
64 G-7 Salihli
106 E-4 Salima
143 K-7 Salin
61 N-7 Salina *isl.*
167 K-8 Salina (USA)
169 H-8 Salina (USA)
200 B-7 Salina Chica *lake*
179 J-8 Salina Cruz
175 H-2 Salinas *mt*
191 K-5 Salinas *riv.*
184 F-6 Salinas *bay*
181 L-7 Salinas *pte*
191 L-5 Salinas (Argentina)
197 L-1 Salinas (Brazil)
191 M-2 Salinas (Chile)
188 C-1 Salinas (Ecuador)
188 A-3 Salinas (Ecuador)
167 J-5 Salinas (USA)
191 J-3 Salinas de Garci Mendoza
178 E-3 Salinas de Hidalgo
200 C-5 Salinas de Trapalcó *lake*
198 E-3 Salinas Grandes *lake*
189 K-3 Salinas ó Lachay *pte*
176 D-3 Saline *riv.*
187 N-1 Saline *pte*
191 N-2 Salinitas
193 K-7 Salinopolis
61 J-1 Salins-le-Bains
155 L-3 Salisbury *isl.*
153 L-3 Salisbury *isl.*
159 N-6 Salisbury *mt*
156 G-1 Salisbury *isl.*
160 C-6 Salisbury *strt.*
217 J-8 Salisbury *isl.*
52 E-6 Salisbury *pl.*
103 N-6 Salisbury (Harare)
50 D-6 Salisbury (UK)
171 L-8 Salisbury (USA)
177 L-2 Salisbury (USA)
162 F-9 Salish *mt*
200 C-7 Salitral *lake*
195 K-6 Salitre *riv.*
63 J-4 Salizzole
72 G-3 Saljany
70 A-3 Salkar *lake*
70 G-1 Salkarteniz
120 D-3 Salkarteniz *lake*
82 D-1 Salkhad
48 E-8 Salla
57 L-1 Salland *reg.*
87 L-4 Sallatouk *pte*
200 A-7 Salliqueló
175 P-1 Sallisaw
81 K-2 Sallūm *gulf*
129 P-2 Sallyāna
46 K-2 Salm *isl.*
68 C-8 Salmi
166 E-8 Salmon
165 L-1 Salmon *riv.*
165 N-3 Salmon *lake*
162 E-6 Salmon Arm
166 E-7 Salmon River *mt*
62 A-6 Salmour
70 B-1 Salmyš *riv.*
49 K-7 Salo
63 H-2 Saló
91 H-9 Salo (Nigeria)
196 B-4 Salobra *riv.*
204 F-2 Salomon *sea*
61 J-3 Salon-de-Provence
99 J-3 Salonga *na.p.*
99 J-2 Salonga *riv.*
64 D-6 Salonica *gulf*
64 D-5 Salonica
64 C-1 Salonta
60 F-5 Salou *cap.*
86 G-3 Saloum *riv.*
86 G-2 Saloum *islds*
86 G-2 Saloum *na.p.*
188 B-2 Saloya *riv.*
198 E-4 Salsacate
192 E-7 Salsal *riv.*
174 C-5 Salsipuedes *strt.*
67 L-8 Sal'sk
68 D-7 Sal'skij
67 M-8 Salsko-Manyčskaja Grada *mt*
62 G-5 Salsomaggiore Terme
166 G-5 Salt *mt*
174 E-1 Salt *riv.*
181 K-5 Salt Cay *isl.*
73 M-5 Salt Desert
175 H-4 Salt Flat
175 L-1 Salt Fork Red *riv.*
168 A-5 Salt Lake City
218 F-7 Salt Lake *lake*
216 G-1 Salt Lakes *lake*
191 N-5 Salta
191 M-6 Salta *reg.*
173 K-4 Saltaire
162 B-6 Saltery Bay
178 E-1 Saltillo
49 K-6 Saltjöbaden
198 G-6 Salto
199 J-4 Salto *reg.*
187 M-4 Salto Arimagua
197 N-1 Salto da Divisa
186 E-8 Salto de Angostura I
186 E-8 Salto de Angostura II
186 G-8 Salto de Angostura III
190 B-5 Salto de Teotonio *riv.*
196 E-4 Salto de Urubupunga *lake*
187 M-5 Salto del Frito
190 B-5 Salto do Jirau *riv.*
188 B-7 Salto Grande *dam.*
187 L-6 Salto Oso
174 B-1 Salton Sea *lake*
192 E-7 Saltopocão *riv.*
181 K-7 Saltrou
51 M-1 Saltsjöbaden
177 K-3 Saluda *riv.*
177 K-3 Saluda
63 P-9 Saludecio
208 F-2 Salue *isl.*
208 F-2 Salue Timpaus *strt.*
62 B-4 Saluggia
142 B-8 Sālūr
62 B-3 Salussola
148 D-7 Salvador *isl.*
195 L-8 Salvador
184 E-4 Salvador *reg.*
157 E-5 Salvador (El) *state*
165 N-2 Salvage
78 C-7 Salvage *islds*
58 D-9 Salvan
178 E-5 Salvatierra
219 J-3 Salvator Rossa *na.p.*
82 B-7 Salwā Baḥrī
83 P-5 Salwah *bay*
143 M-9 Salween *riv.*
131 N-1 Salween (Naquhe) *riv.*
170 G-9 Salyersville
61 N-1 Salzburg
51 J-6 Salzgitter
51 J-6 Salzwedel
145 J-3 Sam *riv.*
139 H-4 Sam
175 P-5 Sam Rayburn *lake*
145 K-3 Sâm Son
189 P-9 Sama *riv.*
60 C-3 Sama de Langreo
122 F-6 Samagaltaj
80 F-4 Samah
191 H-5 Samaipata
208 E-4 Samak
87 H-8 Samakoulou
149 K-2 Samal *isl.*
184 C-3 Samalá *riv.*
127 N-1 Samaldy-Saj
149 K-5 Samales Grande *isl.*
81 N-4 Samālūt
196 D-5 Samambaio *riv.*
123 P-2 Saman *mt*
181 L-6 Samaná *cap.*
139 M-3 Samāna
181 H-3 Samana Cay *rf*
189 H-3 Samanca *bay*
65 L-8 Samandaği
127 J-4 Samāngan
136 C-7 Samani
188 A-3 Samaniego
148 F-2 Samar *isl.*
70 A-2 Samara *riv.*
211 M-8 Samarai
125 L-5 Samarga *riv.*
187 J-6 Samariapo
208 A-1 Samarinda
125 K-8 Samarka
127 J-1 Samarkand
71 N-6 Samarkand
72 F-8 Sāmarra *site*
121 N-6 Samarskoje
142 E-2 Samāstipur
209 L-1 Samate
190 A-8 Samaúma
99 K-2 Samba
207 M-1 Samba *riv.*
98 F-9 Samba Caju
194 G-3 Sambáiba
108 F-4 Sambao *riv.*
207 K-3 Sambar *cap.*
147 K-9 Sambas
147 K-9 Sambas (Singkawang)
108 E-8 Sambava
57 J-6 Sambeek
139 N-4 Sambhal
139 L-5 Sāmbhar *lake*
139 L-5 Sāmbhar
108 D-7 Sambirano *riv.*
149 N-7 Sambit *isl.*
195 J-3 Sambito *riv.*
95 H-4 Sambo
208 A-1 Sambodja

66 B-8 Sambor
199 J-7 Samborombón *bay*
63 J-8 Sambucą Pistojese
101 H-2 Samburu *rés*
133 N-5 Samcheog
133 N-7 Samcheonpo
72 F-2 Samchor
101 H-5 Same
144 G-8 Samet *isl.*
103 M-2 Samfya
64 C-7 Sámi
126 G-7 Sāmī Ghar *mt*
83 H-5 Samirāh
188 E-6 Samiria *riv.*
133 M-2 Samjiyeon
73 M-4 Samnan *reg.*
198 A-4 Samo Alto
68 E-5 Samoded
144 F-3 Samoeng
64 D-4 Samokov
143 L-7 Samon *riv.*
64 F-7 Samos *isl.*
146 C-8 Samosir *isl.*
64 E-5 Samothrace *site*
198 E-6 Sampacho
208 C-2 Sampaga
148 D-7 Sampaloc *pte*
207 M-6 Sampang
89 H-6 Sampelga
207 M-2 Sampit *riv.*
207 M-2 Sampit
207 M-3 Sampit *bay*
100 A-9 Sampwe
145 J-6 Samran *riv.*
93 N-7 Samre
51 J-3 Samsø *isl.*
65 L-4 Samsun
72 C-2 Samtredia
83 J-4 Sāmūdah
141 N-8 Samudra *lake*
214 A-8 Samuel *mt*
198 G-1 Samuhú
146 D-3 Samui *isl.*
122 C-1 Samus'
144 G-7 Samut Prakan
144 F-7 Samut Sakhon
144 F-7 Samut Songkhram
68 F-8 S'amža
89 H-2 San
145 L-7 San *riv.*
60 A-2 San Adrían *cap.*
63 K-5 San Agostino
190 E-4 San Agustín *riv.*
198 E-5 San Agustín (Argentina)
184 D-2 San Agustín (Guatémala)
198 C-4 San Agustín de Valle Fértil
62 A-6 San Albano Stura
63 M-6 San Alberto
189 H-5 San Alejandro
196 E-5 San Anastácio
167 J-3 San Andreas
186 F-5 San Andrés
178 E-5 San Andres *vol.*
175 H-2 San Andres *mt*
190 F-5 San Andrés (Bolivia)
185 K-5 San Andrès (Colombia) *isl.*
185 K-5 San Andrès (Colombia)
184 D-1 San Andrés (Guatémala)
199 H-6 San Andrés de Giles
179 J-6 San Andrés Tuxtla
78 A-8 San Andrés y Sauces
175 L-4 San Angelo
175 L-4 San Angelo *lake*
62 C-4 San Angelo di Lomellina
63 P-9 San Angelo in Lizzola
62 E-4 San Angelo Lodigiano
61 K-7 San Antioco
175 N-7 San Antonio *bay*
175 N-6 San Antonio *riv.*
174 B-4 San Antonio *pte*
174 E-4 San Antonio *mt*
191 M-5 San Antonio (Argentina)
198 D-5 San Antonio (Argentina)
199 J-8 San Antonio (Argentina) *cap.*
198 E-2 San Antonio (Argentina)
190 D-3 San Antonio (Bolivia)
198 A-6 San Antonio (Chile)
186 D-7 San Antonio (Colombia)
180 A-5 San Antonio (Cuba) *cap.*
175 M-6 San Antonio (USA)
175 H-2 San Antonio (USA)
186 G-3 San Antonio (Vénézuela)
187 K-3 San Antonio (Vénézuela)
187 K-7 San Antonio (Vénézuela)
60 F-6 San Antonio Abad
199 H-6 San Antonio de Areco
180 C-4 San Antonio de los Baños
191 M-4 San Antonio de los Cobres
200 D-6 San Antonio Oeste
63 N-8 San Arcangelo di Romagna
149 K-1 San Augustin *cap.*
188 A-4 San Augustín (Colombia)
186 C-8 San Augustín (Colombia)
176 C-5 San Augustine
201 N-7 San Bartolomé *cap.*
59 P-9 San Bartolomeo
63 L-8 San Benedetto *mt*
63 J-4 San Benedetto Po
62 A-4 San Benigno Canavese
174 B-5 San Benito *islds*
185 P-8 San Benito (Colombia)
179 M-7 San Benito (Guatémala)
59 P-7 San Bernardino *pass*
59 P-7 San Bernardino (Switzerland)
167 M-4 San Bernardino (USA)
185 P-8 San Bernardo
185 N-7 San Bernardo *isl.*
63 L-6 San Biagio
63 N-2 San Biagio di Callalta
185 L-8 San Blas *mt*
185 M-7 San Blas *pen.*
185 M-8 San Blas *reg.*
177 H-6 San Blas *cap.*
198 C-2 San Blas (Argentina)
178 B-3 San Blas (Mexico)
175 K-7 San Blas (Mexico)
174 F-7 San Blas (Mexico)
63 K-3 San Bonifácio
174 C-5 San Borias *mt*
190 F-3 San Borja (Bolivia)
190 F-3 San Buenaventura (Bolivia)
175 K-7 San Buenaventura (Mexico)
187 J-3 San Carlos *riv.*
148 D-6 San Carlos
174 E-2 San Carlos *lake*
191 N-4 San Carlos (Argentina)
198 C-6 San Carlos (Argentina)
198 E-4 San Carlos (Argentina)
200 A-2 San Carlos (Chile)
178 G-2 San Carlos (Mexico)
175 L-6 San Carlos (Mexico)
184 G-6 San Carlos (Nicaragua)
185 L-8 San Carlos (Panama)
196 A-5 San Carlos (Paraguay)
148 G-4 San Carlos (Philippines)
199 K-7 San Carlos (Uruguay)
187 J-3 San Carlos (Vénézuela)
187 K-8 San Carlos (Vénézuela)
200 D-3 San Carlos de Bariloche
186 F-3 San Carlos de Zulia
187 K-3 San Casimiro
200 B-9 San Cayetano
63 J-6 San Cesario sul Panaro
60 D-6 San Clemente
174 A-1 San Clemente *isl.*
62 E-7 San Colombano Certenoli
196 A-9 San Cosmé
174 B-6 San Cristobal *bay*
180 B-4 San Cristóbal (Antilles)
181 L-7 San Cristóbal (Antilles)
198 G-3 San Cristóbal (Argentina)
188 C-7 San Cristóbal (Colombia)
184 C-9 San Cristóbal (Ecuador)
186 F-4 San Cristóbal (Vénézuela)
78 B-8 San Cristóbal de la Laguna
179 K-7 San Cristóbal de las Casas
62 B-5 San Damiano d'Asti
201 N-7 San Diego *cap.*
175 M-7 San Diego (Mexico)
174 A-1 San Diego (USA)
87 H-2 San Domingos (Cape Verde)
63 N-2 San Dona di Piave
185 P-7 San Estanislao (Colombia)
196 B-7 San Estanislao (Paraguay)
184 G-3 San Esteban
174 C-5 San Esteban *isl.*
63 K-5 San Felice sul Panaro
174 C-3 San Felipe *pte*
198 A-5 San Felipe (Chile)
178 E-4 San Felipe (Mexico)
174 B-3 San Felipe (Mexico)
188 F-2 San Felipe (Peru)
187 J-2 San Felipe (Vénézuela)
187 K-8 San Felipe (Vénézuela)
181 K-6 San Felipe de Pto. Plata
60 B-7 San Fernando
198 A-7 San Fernando (Chile)
178 G-1 San Fernando (Mexico)
174 B-4 San Fernando (Mexico)
148 C-6 San Fernando (Philippines)
148 D-6 San Fernando (Philippines)
187 N-2 San Fernando (Vénézuela)
187 J-4 San Fernando (Vénézuela)
187 J-7 San Fernando de Atabapo
201 M-5 San Flipe *bay*
191 P-3 San Francisco (Argentina) *mt*
198 C-1 San Francisco (Argentina) *mt*
198 F-4 San Francisco (Argentina)
191 J-6 San Francisco (Bolivia)
188 A-1 San Francisco (Ecuador) *cap.*
167 H-1 San Francisco (USA)
184 E-4 San Francisco de Gotera
181 L-6 San Francisco de Macorís
198 E-3 San Francisco del Chañar
198 D-5 San Francisco del Monte de Oro
174 G-7 San Francisco del Oro
178 D-4 San Francisco del Rincón
186 B-5 San Francisco Solano *pte*
188 A-3 San Gabriel (Ecuador)
200 B-7 San German
181 N-7 San Germán (Antilles)
180 G-5 San German (Antilles)
62 B-3 San Germano Vercellese
186 E-5 San Gil
62 A-3 San Giorgio Canavese
62 D-4 San Giorgio di Lomellina
63 J-4 San Giorgio di Mantova
63 K-6 San Giorgio di Piano
62 F-5 San Giorgio Piacentino
62 F-1 San Giovanni Bianco
63 H-4 San Giovanni in Croce
63 K-6 San Giovanni in Persiceto
63 J-3 San Giovanni Lupatoto
63 M-3 San Giuliano
62 E-3 San Giuliano Milanese
63 H-9 San Giuliano Terme
63 L-9 San Godenzo
167 M-4 San Gorgonio *mt*
199 K-5 San Gregorio
174 D-8 San Hilario
174 B-6 San Hipólito *bay*
174 B-6 San Hipólito *pte*
174 E-8 San Ignacio *isl.*
196 C-9 San Ignacio (Argentina)
190 G-7 San Ignacio (Bolivia)
190 F-4 San Ignacio (Bolivia)
178 B-1 San Ignacio (Mexico)
174 C-6 San Ignacio (Mexico)
196 B-9 San Ignacio (Paraguay)
188 F-2 San Ignacio (Peru)
148 C-5 San Ildefonso *cap.*
148 F-3 San Isidro
175 J-7 San Isidro
198 D-2 San Isidro (Argentina)
199 H-6 San Isidro (Argentina)
148 F-4 San Jacinto
199 H-3 San Javier (Argentina)
196 C-9 San Javier (Argentina)
190 G-6 San Javier (Bolivia)
200 A-2 San Javier (Chile)
188 G-5 San Jeronimo (Peru)
167 K-2 San Joaquim *val.*
167 K-3 San Joaquim *riv.*
190 E-6 San Joaquín *riv.*
190 E-5 San Joaquín
156 B-3 San Joaquin Valley *val.*
175 K-1 San Jon
184 G-6 San Jorge
174 C-3 San Jorge *bay*
191 K-8 San Jorge *mt*
199 J-6 San José *reg.*
200 E-7 San José *gulf*
185 L-8 San José *isl.*
186 B-7 San José *isl.*
148 D-6 San Jose
174 G-1 San Jose *riv.*
191 H-7 San José (Bolivia)
198 D-2 San José (Argentina)
198 D-1 San José (Argentina)
196 C-8 San José (Argentina)
191 P-4 San José (Argentina)
191 H-7 San José (Bolivia) *mt*
187 J-8 San José (Colombia)
185 H-7 San José (Costa-Rica) *reg.*
185 H-7 San José (Costa Rica)
157 F-6 San José (Costa Rica)
179 L-9 San José (Guatémala)
196 B-8 San José (Paraguay)
188 D-6 San José (Peru)
148 F-6 San Jose (Philippines)
148 G-5 San Jose (Philippines)
199 J-4 San José (Uruguay) *mt*
167 J-2 San Jose (USA)
187 P-4 San José de Amacuro
190 F-2 San José de Chupiamonas
199 H-3 San José de Feliciano
198 B-4 San José de Jáchal
198 G-5 San José de la Esquina
200 C-2 San José de la Mariquina
180 C-4 San José de las Lajas
181 K-6 San José de las Matas
198 E-3 San José de las Salinas
199 J-6 San José de Mayo
186 G-7 San José de Ocuné
191 N-6 San José del Boquerón
174 E-9 San José del Cabo
186 F-8 San José del Guaviare
198 B-4 San Juan *reg.*
178 F-1 San Juan *riv.*
168 C-9 San Juan *mt*
168 A-8 San Juan *riv.*
198 C-4 San Juan (Argentina)
198 C-5 San Juan (Argentina) *riv.*
191 H-8 San Juan (Bolivia)
191 K-4 San Juan (Bolivia) *riv.*
181 K-1 San Juan (Caraïbes)
201 N-8 San Juan (Chile) *cap.*
201 N-4 San Juan (Chile)
186 C-6 San Juan (Colombia) *riv.*
188 A-3 San Juan (Colombia) *riv.*
181 K-6 San Juan (Cuba)
98 B-1 San Juan (Gabon) *cap.*
184 E-3 San Juan (Honduras)
179 J-6 San Juan (Mexico) *riv.*
185 H-6 San Juan (Nicaragua) *riv.*
189 L-5 San Juan (Peru)
190 E-1 San Juan (Peru)
189 N-6 San Juan (Peru)
179 N-9 San Juan (El Salvador)
184 E-4 San Juan (San Salvador) *pte*
179 H-6 San Juan B. Tuxtepec
60 F-6 San-Juan-Bautista
196 B-8 San Juan Bautista
186 F-4 San Juan de Colon
178 D-1 San Juan de Guadalupe
187 J-2 San Juan de los Cayos
178 D-4 San Juan de los Lágos
187 J-3 San Juan de los Morros
186 F-2 San Juan del César
185 H-6 San Juan del Norte
185 H-6 San Juan del Norte *bay*
178 F-5 San Juan del Río
184 G-6 San Juan del Sur
185 P-7 San Juan Nepomuceno
174 C-7 San Juanico *pte*
178 A-3 San Juanito *isl.*
201 K-5 San Julian
198 G-4 San Justo
144 G-5 San Khao Phang Hoei *hill*
174 C-8 San Lázaro *cap.*
174 D-9 San Lázaro *mt*
196 A-5 San Lazaro
62 F-4 San Lazzaro
63 K-7 San Lazzaro di Savena
63 N-9 San Leo
201 J-3 San Lorenzo *mt*
178 G-1 San Lorenzo *riv.*
188 B-1 San Lorenzo *cap.*
198 G-5 San Lorenzo (Argentina)
190 D-3 San Lorenzo (Bolivia)
190 F-4 San Lorenzo (Bolivia)
191 K-5 San Lorenzo (Bolivia)
191 H-8 San Lorenzo (Bolivia)
178 A-1 San Lorenzo (Mexico) *riv.*
174 C-5 San Lorenzo (Mexico) *isl.*
190 D-1 San Lorenzo (Peru)
189 K-4 San Lorenzo (Peru) *isl.*
174 G-2 San Lorenzo (USA)
187 L-3 San Lorenzo (Vénézuela)
62 B-9 San Lorenzo al Mare
174 E-9 San Lucas *cap.*
191 J-5 San Lucas (Bolivia)
184 F-4 San Lucas (Honduras)
174 E-9 San Lucas (Mexico)
167 K-2 San Lucas (USA)
174 C-4 San Luis *isl.*
190 E-5 San Luis *lake*
198 D-5 San Luis (Argentina) *mt*
198 D-6 San Luis (Argentina)
201 N-5 San Luis (Chile)
184 D-1 San Luis (Guatémala)
179 M-8 San Luis (Mexico)
187 H-2 San Luis (Vénézuela) *mt*
178 E-4 San Luis de la Paz
196 A-9 San Luis del Palmar
174 C-4 San Luis Gonzaga *bay*
167 L-2 San Luis Obispo
178 E-3 San Luis Potosí *reg.*
178 E-3 San Luis Potosí
174 C-2 San Luis Rio Colorado
63 J-8 San Marcello Pistoiese
174 D-8 San Marcial *pte*
174 D-6 San Marcos *isl.*
198 A-4 San Marcos (Chile)
185 P-8 San Marcos (Colombia)
184 C-2 San Marcos (Guatemala)
178 F-7 San Marcos (Mexico)
61 M-3 San Marino *state*
61 M-4 San Marino
47 E-5 San Marino *state*
47 E-5 San Marino
63 N-8 San Marino *state*
63 N-8 San Marino
201 J-2 San Martín *pen.*
174 A-3 San Martín *isl.*
188 G-4 San Martín *reg.*
190 E-6 San Martín *riv.*
198 D-3 San Martín (Argentina)
198 C-6 San Martín (Argentina)
198 D-5 San Martín (Argentina)
186 E-7 San Martín (Colombia)
200 D-3 San Martín de los Andes
179 J-6 San Martín Pajapan *vol.*
178 G-5 San Martín Texmelucan
63 P-1 San Martino al Tagliamento
63 J-3 San Martino Buon Albergo
63 L-2 San Martino di Lupari
63 L-6 San Martino in Argine
63 J-6 San Martino in Rio
63 K-5 San Martino in Spino
188 D-8 San Mateo
167 J-1 San Mateo (USA)
187 L-3 San Mateo (Vénézuela)
184 C-2 San Mateo Ixtatán
200 D-7 San Matías *gulf*
196 A-1 San Matias
63 N-8 San Mauro Pascoli
62 A-4 San Mauro Torinese
63 J-3 San Michele
63 P-2 San Michele al Tagliamento
198 B-2 San Miguel *mt*
184 E-4 San Miguel *vol.*
149 J-7 San Miguel *isl.*
148 E-3 San Miguel *isl.*
167 M-1 San Miguel *isl.*
174 C-5 San Miguel *cap.*
191 J-8 San Miguel *mt*
196 A-9 San Miguel (Argentina)
198 B-6 San Miguel (Chile)
188 B-4 San Miguel (Ecuador) *riv.*
184 E-4 San Miguel (El Salvador)
174 E-4 San Miguel (USA) *riv.*
178 E-4 San Miguel de Allende
190 F-3 San Miguel de Huachi
188 G-2 San Miguel de Pallaques
198 D-1 San Miguel de Tucumán
199 H-7 San Miguel del Monte
180 C-4 San Miguel del Padron
148 E-5 San Narciso
63 L-1 San Nazario
148 B-6 San Nicolas
167 M-2 San Nicolas *isl.*
189 N-5 San Nicolas *pte*
189 M-5 San Nicolas *bay*
189 M-6 San Nicolas (Peru)
198 G-6 San Nicolás de los Arroyos
63 L-6 San Nicolò Ferrarese
185 P-8 San Onofre
201 N-6 San Pablo
174 B-6 San Pablo *pte*
190 F-6 San Pablo (Bolivia)
186 G-6 San Pablo (Colombia)
196 A-4 San Pablo (Paraguay)
148 E-5 San Pablo (Philippines)
178 G-8 San Pablo Totutepec
148 E-4 San Pascual
200 D-1 San Pedro *bay*
200 F-2 San Pedro *isl.*
87 P-9 San Pédro *riv.*
87 P-9 San Pédro
191 L-2 San Pedro *vol.*
196 B-6 San Pedro *reg.*
199 H-6 San Pedro (Argentina)
198 D-2 San Pedro (Argentina)
191 M-5 San Pedro (Argentina)
196 C-8 San Pedro (Argentina)
190 C-3 San Pedro (Bolivia)
191 H-4 San Pedro (Bolivia)
191 N-1 San Pedro (Chile)
188 E-2 San Pedro (Ecuador)
179 M-7 San Pedro (Mexico) *riv.*
174 D-9 San Pedro (Mexico)
196 B-7 San Pedro (Paraguay)
187 H-3 San Pedro (Vénézuela)
186 F-6 San Pedro de Arimena
191 L-3 San Pedro de Atacama
187 M-5 San Pedro de las Bocas
175 J-8 San Pedro de las Colonias
188 G-2 San Pedro de Lloc
181 L-6 San Pedro de Macorís
178 G-8 San Pedro Juchatenango
174 B-3 San Pedro Mártir *mt*
179 H-8 San Pedro Pochutla
184 E-2 San Pedro Sula
62 F-1 San Pellegrino Terme
62 D-7 San Pier d'Arena
63 K-8 San Piero a Sieve
63 M-9 San Piero in Bagno
61 K-7 San Pietro *isl.*
63 M-1 San Pietro di Feletto
63 K-4 San Pietro di Morùbio
63 J-3 San Pietro in Cariano
63 K-6 San Pietro in Casale
63 L-2 San Pietro in Gu
63 M-7 San Pietro in Vincoli
63 H-6 San Polo d'Enza
63 N-1 San Polo di Piave
63 J-5 San Possidonio
62 E-1 San Primo *mt*
63 J-5 San Prospero
174 B-3 San Quintín
174 B-3 San Quintín *bay*
174 A-3 San Quintín *cap.*
63 N-1 San Quirino
198 C-7 San Rafael (Argentina)
167 H-1 San Rafael (USA)
186 G-2 San Rafael (Vénézuela)
190 E-7 San Ramon *riv.*
190 G-6 San Ramón (Bolivia)
190 E-5 San Ramón (Bolivia)
189 K-5 San Ramón (Peru)
199 K-6 San Ramón (Uruguay)
191 L-5 San Ramón de la Nueva Orán
62 A-9 San Remo
62 F-4 San Rocco al Porto
199 H-2 San Roque
60 B-8 San Roque (Spain)
200 B-2 San Rosendo
175 M-4 San Saba
175 M-5 San Saba *riv.*
184 B-8 San Salvador *isl.*
184 B-8 San Salvador *cal.*
184 D-4 San Salvador
188 C-8 San Salvador
157 E-5 San Salvador
181 H-3 San Salvador (Watling's) *isl.*
191 M-5 San Salvador de Jujuy

193 J-7 São Caetano de Odivelas
197 H-7 São Caetano do Sul
195 N-5 São Caitano
196 D-9 São Carlos (Brazil)
196 G-5 São Carlos (Brazil)
194 F-8 São Domingos
195 L-8 São Estêvão
190 B-7 São Felix riv.
194 E-2 São Felix (Brazil)
194 C-6 São Felix (Brazil)
194 G-3 São Felix do Balsas
194 B-3 São Felix do Xingu
197 L-6 São Fidélis
87 P-1 São Filipe
197 K-1 São Filipe (Brazil) mt
194 A-2 São Francisco riv.
195 J-6 São Francisco mt
187 N-9 São Francisco
196 G-8 São Francisco isl.
197 K-1 São Francisco (Brazil) riv.
199 K-3 São Francisco de Assis
199 N-3 São Francisco de Paula
196 F-4 São Francisco de Sales
195 H-3 São Francisco do Maranhão
196 G-8 São Francisco do Sul
199 L-3 São Gabriel (Brazil)
197 M-4 São Gabriel (Brazil)
197 L-6 São Goncalo
197 J-3 São Goncalo de Abaeté
197 J-3 São Gotardo
100 F-8 Sao Hill
195 H-3 São Jão dos Patos
196 C-2 São Jéronimo mt
196 F-6 São Jeronimo da Serra
193 K-8 São Joachim
193 M-8 São João isl.
195 K-4 São João riv.
197 M-2 São João riv.
190 B-7 São João (Brazil) mt
194 E-9 São João da Aliança
197 H-5 São João da Boa Vista
197 K-1 São João da Ponte
195 N-4 São João de Cariri
197 K-6 São João de Meriti
197 K-5 São João del Rei
197 M-6 São João do Barra
196 E-6 Sao João do Cauia
197 M-1 São Joao do Paraiso
195 J-4 São João do Piauí
197 L-5 Sao João Nepomuceno
199 P-2 São Joaquim
197 H-4 São Joaquim da Barra
193 L-7 São Jorge isl.
87 N-2 São Jorge bay
196 C-1 São José riv.
193 M-8 São José bay
195 P-3 São José de Mipibu
187 N-9 São José do Anauá
195 L-4 São José do Belmonte
195 M-4 São José do Egito
193 L-8 São José do Gurupi
199 M-5 São José do Norte
195 J-4 São José do Peixe
197 H-5 São José do Rio Pardo (Brazil)
196 G-4 São José do Rio Preto
197 J-6 São José dos Campos
196 F-8 São José dos Pinhais
199 N-3 São Leopoldo
195 P-4 São Lorenço da Mata
199 L-2 São Louís Gonzaga
196 B-2 Sao Lourenco lag.
196 C-1 São Lourenço riv.
196 C-1 São Lourenco riv.
197 J-6 São Lourenço (Brazil)
199 M-3 São Lourenço do Sul
193 M-8 São Luis isl.
196 D-3 São Luis riv.
193 M-9 São Luis
190 A-4 São Luis de Cassianã
195 L-1 São Luís do Curu
196 G-6 Sao Manuel
187 J-9 São Marcelino
193 M-8 São Marcos bay
197 N-3 São Mateus
197 L-6 São Mateus mt
197 N-3 São Mateus riv.
196 F-8 São Mateus do Sul
190 D-6 São Miguel (Brazil) riv.
196 D-9 São Miguel d'Oeste
194 C-8 Sao Miguel do Araguaia
195 J-2 Sao Miguel do Tapuio
195 N-6 São Miguel dos Campos
193 H-8 São Miguel dos Macacos
87 N-2 São Nicolau isl.
190 C-7 São Paulo riv.
196 F-5 São Paulo reg.
197 H-7 São Paulo (Brazil)
188 G-6 São Paulo (Brazil)

197 M-1 São Pedro riv.
190 B-6 São Pedro (Brazil)
196 E-6 São Pedro do Avaí
199 L-3 São Pedro do Sul
195 N-3 São Rafael (Brazil)
194 G-3 São Raimundo das Mangabeiras
195 J-5 São Raimundo Nonato
197 K-1 São Romão
197 H-7 São Roque
195 P-2 São Roque cap.
182 G-3 São Roque cap.
195 L-8 São Roque do Paraguai
197 J-7 São Sebastião isl.
187 M-9 Sao Sebastião
197 J-7 São Sebastião (Brazil)
194 B-2 São Sebastião (Brazil)
193 H-8 São Sebastião da Boa Vista
197 H-5 São Sebastião do Paraíso
199 L-3 São Sepé
199 N-4 São Simão pte
197 H-5 São Simão
196 F-3 São Simão (Brazil)
197 K-5 Sao Tiago
87 P-2 São Tiago isl.
197 M-6 São Tomé cap.
77 C-4 São Tomé
98 A-2 São Tomé isl.
98 A-2 São Tomé
77 C-4 São Tomé e Principe state
197 H-7 São Vicente
78 A-1 São Vicente
87 M-1 São Vicente isl.
60 A-4 São Vicente cap.
181 M-7 Saona isl.
61 J-1 Saône riv.
58 A-2 Saône
209 L-1 Saonek
140 B-7 Saoner
78 F-6 Saoura riv.
64 E-5 Sápai
189 K-5 Sapallanga
65 H-5 Sapanca
209 J-3 Saparua isl.
209 J-3 Saparua
192 C-7 Sapateiro dam.
186 E-2 Sapayan lake
195 P-4 Sapé
208 C-7 Sape strt.
208 C-7 Sape
195 L-8 Sapeaçu
90 A-7 Sapele
177 K-5 Sapelo isl.
68 G-1 Sapkina riv.
188 F-4 Saposoa
188 G-4 Saposoa
197 H-4 Sapoucal riv.
168 F-7 Sappa riv.
168 A-1 Sapphire mt
136 C-6 Sapporo
61 P-6 Sapri
122 C-5 Sapšal'skij
196 G-4 Sapucai riv.
197 J-6 Sapucai
192 D-3 Sapucuá lake
207 N-6 Sapudi isl.
207 N-6 Sapudi strt.
175 P-1 Sapulpa
149 L-9 Sapulut
72 G-6 Saqqez
188 B-2 Saquisili
64 C-4 Sar mt
72 F-6 Sar Dasht
127 H-3 Sar-e Pol well
73 N-7 Sar-e Yazd
72 G-5 Sar Eskand Khān
71 P-9 Sar-i-Pul
73 J-8 Sar Kül
89 J-3 Sara
144 G-7 Sara Buri
72 G-4 Sarāb
192 B-9 Saracá lake
91 K-2 Saraf
122 E-3 Saragaš
188 D-2 Saraguro
142 E-5 Saraikela
64 B-3 Sarajevo
126 E-2 Sarakhs
70 C-1 Sarāktaš
192 E-3 Saramacca riv.
143 K-3 Saramati mt
207 L-1 Sarau mt
121 H-4 Saran'
164 E-9 Saranac Lake
123 P-5 Saranakan mt
64 C-6 Sarandë
199 H-3 Sarandi riv.
199 J-4 Sarandi
199 K-6 Sarandi del Yi
142 C-5 Sārangam
149 L-2 Sarangani islds
97 P-2 Saranley

67 K-2 Saransk
69 L-8 Sarapul
125 K-4 Šarapul'skoje
186 G-5 Sarare riv.
177 K-8 Sarasota
120 D-1 Sarat
64 G-1 Sarata
168 C-6 Saratoga
171 L-5 Saratoga Springs
147 M-8 Saratok
67 M-4 Saratov
145 K-6 Saravane
147 N-8 Sarawak reg.
87 H-5 Saraya
188 C-3 Sarayacu
64 G-7 Sarayköy
65 J-6 Sarayönü
138 A-2 Sarbāz
63 J-1 Sarca riv.
55 J-4 Sarcelles
63 J-1 Sarche
198 A-3 Sarco
129 P-1 Sārda riv.
80 A-6 Sardalãs
139 L-4 Sardārshahr
186 F-4 Sardinata riv.
186 F-4 Sardinata
61 K-6 Sardinia isl.
46 D-5 Sardinia isl.
176 E-3 Sardis
59 P-4 Sardona mt
87 H-3 Saré Ndiaye
63 K-3 Sarego
48 E-5 Sarektjåkko mt
207 P-2 Sarempaka mt
86 F-1 Sarēnē pte
59 H-6 Sareten
62 G-2 Sarezzo
61 L-1 Sargans
156 H-3 Sargasso sea
127 K-8 Sargodha
66 E-8 Sargorod
91 K-4 Sarh
127 M-5 Sarhadd
78 D-5 Sarhro mt
73 L-4 Sārī
128 B-7 Sari Emel riv.
64 G-9 Saria isl.
158 A-5 Sarichef cap.
187 J-7 Saridū lake
119 K-5 Sarigan isl.
129 J-2 Sarigh Jilganong lake
72 D-3 Sarikamis
147 M-8 Sarikei
219 L-1 Sarina
174 D-3 Sarir
65 L-5 Sarioğlan
175 M-7 Sarita
133 L-5 Sariweon
83 K-6 Sark dés
128 B-4 Sarkand
65 L-5 Sarkişla
73 L-2 Sarlauk
70 A-1 Sarlyk
62 E-4 Sarmato
99 K-8 Sarmento
210 D-2 Sarmi
201 N-5 Sarmiento mt
199 H-6 Sarmiento
201 L-3 Sarmiento lake
142 C-2 Särnäth site
59 K-4 Sarnen
61 K-1 Sarnent
59 K-4 Sarner lake
170 G-5 Sarnia
62 G-2 Sarnico
66 D-6 Sarny
208 D-2 Saroako
206 D-2 Sarolanguno
136 A-7 Saroma lag.
62 D-2 Saronno
67 N-7 Sarpa
51 K-1 Sarpsborg
92 A-2 Sarra
58 B-6 Sarraz (La)
53 P-6 Sarre
50 G-8 Sarrebourg
50 G-8 Sarreguemines
60 B-3 Sarria
63 M-9 Sarsina
64 G-7 Sart site
61 K-5 Sartène
50 D-8 Sarthe riv.
62 C-4 Sartirana Lomellina
121 M-2 Sartlan lake
54 G-4 Sartrouville
69 L-1 Sartynja
64 G-6 Saruhanli
136 A-6 Saruhutu
126 C-7 Sarutara site
211 K-5 Saruwaged mt
128 A-3 Sary-Lšikotrau riv.
127 N-3 Sary-Taš
120 E-3 Sary-Turgaj riv.
121 K-5 Sarybulak

122 F-6 Saryg-Sep
70 G-8 Sarykamyšskaja lake
127 N-4 Sarykol'skij mt
128 A-2 Sarykomej
120 E-1 Sarykopa lake
120 F-1 Sarymoin lake
128 B-3 Saryozek
120 E-1 Saryozen riv.
122 D-2 Sarypovo
121 H-7 Saryšagan
120 E-5 Sarysu riv.
120 G-4 Sarysu
121 K-5 Sarytau
128 D-4 Saryžaz
62 G-8 Sarzana
84 A-5 Sasabe
97 K-3 Sasabeneh
208 C-7 Sasar cap.
142 C-3 Sasarām
185 N-8 Sasardi islds
137 M-2 Sasebo
105 J-4 Sasolburg
67 J-3 Sasovo
172 C-8 Sassafras
172 B-8 Sassafras riv.
89 P-1 Sassandra
89 P-1 Sassandra riv.
61 K-6 Sassari
62 C-6 Sassello
58 G-9 Sasseneire mt
56 C-2 Sassenheim
51 K-4 Sassnitz
63 K-7 Sasso Marconi
63 N-9 Sassocorvaro
87 P-7 Sasstown
63 J-6 Sassuolo
120 E-8 Sastobe
198 G-4 Sastre
128 A-5 Sasykkol' lake
67 N-6 Sasykoli
137 N-3 Sata
137 N-3 Sata pte
87 H-6 Satadougou-Bafé
140 D-3 Sātāra
91 M-8 Satema
174 G-6 Satevó
189 K-6 Satipo
69 P-7 Satka
142 G-5 Sātkhira
67 K-2 Satki
140 B-4 Satmala mt
139 P-8 Satna
66 B-9 Sátoralja-Ujhely
116 C-4 Satpura rge
140 A-6 Satpura reg.
144 G-8 Sattahip
59 M-3 Sattel
211 K-5 Sattelburg
129 J-1 Satti
66 B-9 Satu-Mare
146 D-5 Satun
137 P-3 Satunan syotō islds
162 C-9 Satus riv.
58 A-6 Saubraz
200 B-8 Sauce riv.
199 H-3 Sauce
220 G-9 Sauce riv.
175 H-6 Saucillo
49 K-1 Sauda
194 A-3 Saudade riv.
48 B-2 Sauðárkrókur
195 J-7 Saudável
195 K-6 Saúde
77 G-2 Saudi Arabia state
190 E-9 Sauêniná riv.
190 E-9 Sauêruiná riv.
173 J-1 Saugatuck rés
198 D-2 Saujil
170 A-3 Sauk Centre
192 F-4 Saül
58 E-1 Saulcy
61 J-1 Saulieu
170 F-3 Sault Sainte Marie
54 B-6 Saulx riv.
55 H-8 Saulx-les-Chartreux
54 D-6 Saulx-Marchais
219 N-2 Saumarez rf
209 L-6 Saumlaki
50 D-9 Saumur
201 L-8 Saunders isl.
67 H-2 Saura
128 B-8 Saur mt
48 B-3 Saurbaer
99 K-9 Saurimo
54 G-1 Sausseron riv.
208 D-1 Sausu
58 C-3 Saut du Doubs mt
102 E-1 Sautar
185 N-9 Sautatá
58 A-8 Sauvergny

61 P-2 Sava riv.
184 G-2 Savá
69 H-8 S'ava
64 B-3 Sava riv.
224 B-5 Savaii
89 M-7 Savalou
180 F-7 Savana la Mar
177 K-3 Savannah riv.
177 K-4 Savannah
145 J-5 Savannakhet
140 F-4 Savanūr
71 J-7 Savat
89 M-7 Savé
60 G-3 Save (France) riv.
107 L-3 Save (Mozambique) riv.
73 J-6 Sāveh
63 K-7 Savena riv.
52 F-5 Savernake ft
51 H-8 Saverne
58 F-8 Savièse
62 A-6 Savigliano
63 N-8 Savignano
63 K-7 Savigno
52 D-6 Savignone
55 J-8 Savigny-sur-Orge
62 B-7 Savona
62 C-7 Savona reg.
61 K-3 Savona
62 C-7 Savona
49 H-9 Savonlinna
158 G-1 Savoonga
66 E-8 Savran'
51 L-2 Sävsjö
204 C-2 Savu sea
48 E-8 Savukoski
143 K-7 Saw
206 C-1 Sawahlunto
209 J-3 Sawai
209 J-3 Sawai bay
139 L-6 Sawai Mādhopur
93 M-3 Sawākin isl.
145 J-4 Sawang Daen Din
144 F-5 Sawankhalok
137 H-8 Sawara
94 E-3 Sawbā riv.
53 L-4 Sawbridgeworth
80 D-7 Sawdah mt
92 F-7 Sawdiri
209 N-1 Saweba cap.
146 D-2 Sawi bay
97 H-6 Sawl Haud plat.
89 L-4 Sawla
161 L-5 Sawmill Bay
85 J-8 Sawqarah
85 J-8 Sawqarah cap.
85 H-8 Sawqirah bay
53 L-2 Sawston
159 K-7 Sawtooth mt
166 F-7 Sawtooth (USA) mt
220 G-7 Sawyer bay
214 G-9 Saxby riv.
59 H-5 Saxeten
129 N-5 Saxikesi
53 P-2 Saxmundham
58 E-9 Saxon
89 H-7 Say
164 G-5 Sayabec
184 D-1 Sayaxché
130 C-9 Sayhan Bayan Suma
132 B-2 Sayhandulaan
96 D-8 Sayhūt
172 D-3 Saylorsburg
132 B-2 Saynshand
146 F-8 Sayong riv.
175 M-1 Sayre
172 G-4 Sayreville
178 C-5 Sayula
96 C-9 Say'ün
173 K-3 Sayville
127 M-4 Sazud reg.
79 N-3 Sbeïtla
148 D-7 Scaborough Shoal (Minzhujiao) isl.
217 H-8 Scaddan
50 D-3 Scaffell Pike mt
158 F-3 Scammon Bay
63 H-6 Scandiano
46 G-3 Scandinavia rge
50 E-4 Scarborough (UK)
187 P-2 Scarborough (Trinidad and Tobago)
172 C-5 Scarlets Mill
62 A-6 Scarnafigi
63 K-8 Scarperia
55 H-7 Sceaux
69 H-1 Sčeljabož
69 H-2 Sčeljajur
161 K-4 Scented Grass hill
121 L-3 Ščerbakty

172 A-5 Schaefferstown
57 N-8 Schaesberg
104 C-1 Schaf riv.
61 L-1 Schaffhausen
56 G-9 Schaft
57 H-5 Schaijk
57 K-1 Schalkhaar
56 F-4 Schalkwijk
165 J-4 Schallop
59 J-1 Schänenwerd
59 H-4 Schangnau
59 N-2 Schänis
56 E-5 Schans
51 K-9 Schärding
59 H-6 Scharze Lütschine
59 H-5 Scharzengg
56 G-5 Schayk
164 F-1 Schefferville
59 M-4 Scherhorn mt
57 P-8 Scherpenseel
56 G-3 Scherpenzeel
58 G-5 Scherzligen
56 A-3 Scheveningen
56 B-4 Schie cal.
56 B-4 Schiedam
59 J-7 Schienhorn mt
58 E-4 Schiffenensee lake
56 C-8 Schijf
56 G-6 Schijndel
57 N-7 Schilberg
59 P-3 Schild mt
62 G-1 Schilpario
59 H-5 Schilthorn mt
59 J-4 Schimberg
57 N-8 Schimmert
57 N-9 Schin op Geul
57 N-8 Schinnen
57 N-8 Schinveld
63 K-2 Schio
56 B-4 Schipluiden
59 N-5 Schlans
51 J-4 Schleswig reg.
51 J-4 Schleswig
59 L-1 Schlieren
59 J-7 Schmadribach
59 N-2 Schmerikon
59 H-1 Schnebelhorn mt
172 C-3 Schnecksville
61 P-1 Schneeberg mt
59 J-1 Schöftland
59 L-2 Schönbrunn
59 G-3 Schönbühl
59 P-1 Schönengrund
105 H-7 Schoombee
56 D-4 Schoonhoven
56 E-4 Schoonrewoerd
56 C-9 Schoten
59 J-2 Schötz
59 J-4 Schrattenfluh mt
59 J-6 Schreckhorn mt
170 D-1 Schreiber
121 H-1 Schuchinsk
175 N-6 Schulenberg
53 F-3 Schüpfen
172 B-3 Schuylkill reg.
172 B-4 Schuylkill Haven
59 L-1 Schwamendingen
207 M-1 Schwaner mt
58 G-7 Schwarenbach
59 H-5 Schwarze Lütschine
59 K-3 Schwarzenbg
58 F-4 Schwarzenburg
59 J-5 Schwarzhorn (Switzerland) mt
59 H-9 Schwarzhorn (Switzerland) mt
104 C-3 Schwarzrand mt
159 L-4 Schwatka mt
58 F-5 Schwefelbergbad
51 J-8 Schweinfurt
105 H-4 Schweizer-Reneke
59 P-1 Schwelbrunn
59 N-4 Schwendi Kaltbad mt
51 K-5 Schwerin
59 M-1 Schwerzenbach
51 J-8 Schw.Hall
61 L-1 Schwyrz
59 M-3 Schwyz
59 M-3 Schwyz reg.
59 H-6 Schynige mt
61 M-8 Sciacca
58 B-8 Sciez
57 H-5 Sčigry
50 B-6 Scilly islds
62 A-4 Sciolze
172 D-2 Sciota
170 G-8 Scioto riv.
67 H-3 Sčokino
168 E-1 Scobey
221 L-1 Scone
62 B-2 Scopa
62 B-2 Scopello

59 N-6 Scopi *mt*
46 A-2 Scoresby *strt.*
66 F-6 Sčors
63 M-2 Scorzè
172 F-3 Scotch Plains
182 F-8 Scotia *sea*
227 M-2 Scotia *sea*
160 D-5 Scotia
50 D-2 Scotland *reg.*
162 A-4 Scott *strt.*
162 A-4 Scott *islds*
166 E-3 Scott *mt*
163 M-1 Scott *lake*
212 G-2 Scott *rf*
227 N-6 Scott *isl.*
213 M-2 Scott *cap.*
227 N-6 Scott
168 F-8 Scott City
105 L-7 Scottburgh
181 N-3 Scotts Head *cap.*
168 E-6 Scottsbluff
176 G-2 Scottsboro
170 E-9 Scottsburg
174 E-1 Scottsdale
221 H-8 Scottsdale
176 G-1 Scottsville
171 K-6 Scranton (USA)
62 D-5 Scrivia *riv.*
66 C-5 Sčučin
50 E-4 Scunthorpe
145 A-6 Se Bai *riv.*
173 H-3 Sea Cliff
172 F-9 Sea Isle City
220 F-3 Sea Lake
201 M-9 Sea Lion Islands *islds*
195 J-7 Seabras
216 G-6 Seabrook *lake*
53 L-8 Seaford
158 C-8 Seal *cap.*
53 L-6 Seal
104 G-9 Sealpunt *pte*
175 N-6 Sealy
59 J-1 Sean
176 D-2 Searcy
162 A-8 Seaside
172 G-6 Seaside Park
52 B-8 Seaton
162 C-8 Seattle
215 J-8 Seaview *mt*
208 E-8 Seba
184 G-4 Sébaco
171 M-4 Sebago *lake*
209 M-3 Sebakor *bay*
121 P-5 Sebalino
207 M-3 Sebangan *bay*
146 G-9 Sebangka *isl.*
174 B-5 Sebastián Vizcaíno *bay*
147 N-7 Sebauh
89 H-6 Sebba
78 G-3 Sebdou
98 E-3 Sébé *riv.*
100 F-1 Sebei *reg.*
67 H-6 Sebekino
87 H-7 Sébékoro
196 D-9 Seberi
123 H-4 Seberta
64 D-2 Sebeş
66 D-3 Sebež
210 G-8 Sebidiro
72 B-4 Sebinkarahisar
70 C-7 Sebir
78 D-2 Sebou *riv.*
177 K-7 Sebring
79 K-5 Sebseb *riv.*
132 C-1 Sebsulin Hudag (puits)
208 A-3 Sebuku *isl.*
103 L-6 Sebungwe *riv.*
125 N-5 Sebunino
194 A-1 Sêca *riv.*
185 J-9 Secas *islds*
63 J-5 Secchia *riv.*
188 F-1 Sechura *bay*
188 F-1 Sechura *dés*
188 F-1 Sechura
184 C-3 Seco *riv.*
87 P-1 Secos *islds*
222 B-7 Secretary *isl.*
140 E-7 Secunderābād
190 G-4 Sécure *riv.*
170 A-9 Sedalia
220 D-2 Sedan (Australia)
50 G-8 Sedan (France)
176 B-1 Sedan (USA)
222 F-6 Seddonville
63 P-1 Sedegliano
52 E-3 Sedgeberrow
52 C-7 Sedgemoor *lake*
87 H-2 Sédhiou
146 G-8 Sedili Besar
53 M-7 Sedlescombe
82 C-3 Sedom
92 F-3 Sedonga *site*
62 D-3 Sedriano
59 M-5 Sedrun
149 P-8 Sedulang
58 G-2 Seeberg

59 M-4 Seedorf
104 C-4 Seeheim
58 F-6 Seehorn *mt*
52 E-6 Seend
59 K-1 Seengen
50 D-8 Sées
59 M-3 Seewen
87 L-6 Sefadu
64 F-7 Seferihisar
86 G-7 Séféto
78 E-3 Sefrou
97 K-2 Segag
86 G-6 Ségala
146 F-8 Segamat
70 C-8 Segendy
68 C-6 Segeža
79 J-5 Seggueur *riv.*
68 G-3 Segmas
59 P-4 Segnes *pass*
89 H-1 Ségou
89 H-1 Ségou *reg.*
60 D-4 Segovia
184 F-6 Segovia *reg.*
68 C-6 Segozero *lake*
60 F-4 Segre *riv.*
50 D-8 Segré
89 M-1 Séguéla
175 M-6 Seguin
60 D-7 Segura *mt*
60 D-7 Segura *riv.*
126 K-4 Seh Darakht *riv.*
127 H-9 Sehän *riv.*
87 P-7 Sehnkwehn *riv.*
139 L-8 Sehore
168 E-8 Seibert
91 M-3 Seïfou
214 C-7 Seigals Creek
164 F-3 Seigneley *riv.*
143 K-7 Seikpyu
48 C-1 Seiland *isl.*
175 M-1 Seiling
50 B-8 Sein *isl.*
54 E-4 Seine *riv.*
50 D-7 Seine *bay*
199 L-4 Seival
67 H-5 Sejm *riv.*
147 L-9 Sekajam *riv.*
206 E-3 Sekaju
105 J-6 Sekakes
206 F-2 Sekanak *bay*
100 F-5 Sekenke
137 L-3 Seki *pte*
89 P-4 Sekondi Takoradi
93 N-8 Sekota
68 C-6 Seküheh
126 C-6 Sekürheh
211 M-5 Sel Apiu *isl.*
113 R-2 Selagkij *cap.*
206 E-1 Selajar *isl.*
122 G-2 Selajevo
207 J-3 Selandu *isl.*
146 E-7 Selangor *reg.*
209 K-6 Selaru *isl.*
208 C-3 Selatan *reg.*
207 N-4 Selatan *isl.*
159 K-4 Selawik
159 K-4 Selawik *riv.*
159 K-3 Selawik *lake*
53 H-7 Selborne
59 N-4 Selbsanft *mt*
168 G-3 Selby
66 F-4 Sel'co
64 G-7 Selcuk
173 K-8 Selden
209 L-1 Sele
123 H-5 Sele *mt*
103 L-9 Selebi Phikwe
100 G-8 Selegu *mt*
124 G-3 Selemdža *riv.*
124 G-3 Selemdžinsk
125 H-2 Selemdžinskij *mt*
123 L-6 Selenduma
123 L-6 Selenga *riv.*
123 L-7 Selenge *reg.*
130 A-9 Selenge (Mongolia)
99 H-4 Selenga (Zaïre)
130 A-7 Selenge Mörön *riv.*
123 L-6 Selenginsk
51 H-9 Sélestat
121 J-2 Selety *riv.*
121 K-2 Seletyteniz *lake*
72 F-8 Seleucie *site*
48 C-1 Selfoss
87 K-5 Seli *riv.*
68 G-4 Selib
86 F-5 Sélibabi
123 K-5 Selichov
67 J-8 Seliger *lake*
66 F-2 Seliger *lake*
167 M-7 Seligman
91 N-7 Selim (Centrafrique)
146 E-7 Selim (Malaysia)
86 G-6 Sélinnkégni
66 F-2 Seližarovo
51 J-1 Seljord
163 P-9 Selkirk

162 F-6 Selkirko *mt*
172 D-5 Sellersville
53 N-7 Sellindge
174 D-3 Sells
176 M-8 Selma
176 F-2 Selmer
66 D-1 Selo *riv.*
208 A-7 Selong
124 B-5 Selopugino
78 F-2 Selouane
101 H-9 Selous *rés*
112 B-3 Selovetskiy *isl.*
62 C-3 Selsa *riv.*
127 J-6 Selseleh-Spin Ghar *mt*
126 F-4 Selseleh-ye Safid *mt*
126 F-4 Selseleh-ye Safid Kuh *rge*
53 H-8 Selsey
53 N-6 Selstead
69 K-8 Selty
209 K-6 Selu *isl.*
207 H-3 Selui *isl.*
103 M-8 Selukwe
198 F-3 Selva
63 K-2 Selva di Progno
78 C-7 Selvagen Grande *isl.*
182 D-3 Selvas *reg.*
63 L-3 Selvazzano Dentro
163 M-2 Selwyn *lake*
214 E-9 Selwyn
214 E-9 Selwyn (Australia) *mt*
160 G-4 Selwyn (Canada) *mt*
58 F-2 Selzach
194 A-1 Sem Tripa
72 G-2 Semacha
208 A-1 Semajang *lake*
73 L-8 Semän
64 B-5 Seman *riv.*
206 F-5 Semangka *bay*
207 K-6 Semarang
147 L-8 Sematan
208 E-8 Semau *isl.*
98 F-1 Sembé
87 M-4 Sembehun
98 E-8 Sembo *riv.*
146 F-8 Sembrong *riv.*
99 H-5 Semendua
59 N-9 Sementina
207 M-7 Semeru *mt*
158 C-8 Semidi *islds*
121 L-4 Semijarka
67 J-5 Semiluki
52 E-6 Semington
168 C-5 Seminoe *lake*
175 K-3 Seminole
59 N-7 Semione
121 M-5 Semipalatinsk
148 F-6 Semirara *islds*
73 L-8 Semirôm *mt*
147 M-9 Semitau
121 J-4 Semizbugy
100 C-2 Semliki *riv.*
97 K-7 Semmade
121 K-1 Semonaicha
69 H-9 Sem'onov
121 H-2 Sem'onovka
69 K-2 šemordan
59 K-2 Sempach
59 K-2 Sempach *lake*
149 L-7 Semporna
207 M-7 Sempu *isl.*
58 D-6 Semsales
207 M-3 Semuda
149 N-8 Semurut
145 J-7 Sên *riv.*
83 P-2 Senã
190 D-3 Sena (Bolivia)
107 H-4 Sena (Mozambique)
190 B-2 Sena Madureira
197 L-3 Senador Mourão
195 L-2 Senador Pompeu
93 N-6 Senafe
149 K-8 Senaja
210 F-6 Senajo
141 N-8 Senanayake *lake*
103 H-5 Senanga
54 B-9 Senantes
55 K-8 Sénart *ft*
176 E-3 Senatobia
188 B-5 Sencella *riv.*
136 F-7 Sendai (Japan)
137 M-3 Sendai (Japan)
95 K-2 Sendefa
89 M-5 Sene *riv.*
146 E-8 Senebui *cap.*
169 J-8 Seneca (USA)
166 E-5 Seneca (USA)
177 J-2 Seneca (USA)
77 A-3 Senegal *state*
86 E-4 Sénégal *riv.*
105 J-5 Senekal
170 E-3 Seney
149 P-8 Sengata
56 G-9 Sengelsbroek
67 M-2 Sengilej
208 C-4 Sengkang

200 G-4 Senguerr *riv.*
103 L-7 Sengwe *riv.*
195 K-6 Senhor de Bonfim
197 L-3 Senhora do Porto
158 C-7 Seniavin *cap.*
61 N-4 Senigallia
200 C-4 Senillosa
184 E-2 Senimlatiu *riv.*
63 L-7 Senio *riv.*
65 H-7 Senirkent
61 N-3 Senj
68 F-6 Senkursk
50 E-8 Senlis
54 E-8 Senlisse
164 C-6 Senneterre
55 N-2 Sennevières
54 C-4 Senneville
67 M-3 Sennoj
52 A-3 Sennybridge
200 G-2 Seno Aisen *bay*
50 F-8 Sens
184 E-3 Sensuntepeque
64 B-2 Senta
122 D-2 Senta *riv.*
67 N-1 Sentala
210 E-2 Sentani *lake*
58 A-6 Sentier (Le)
162 E-3 Sentinel *mt*
196 E-1 Sentinela *mt*
119 L-6 Senyavin *isl.*
91 P-8 Senza
60 G-4 Seo de Urgel
133 M-9 Seogoigo
133 L-5 Seohan-man *bay*
142 B-5 Seonäth *riv.*
133 K-4 Seoncheon
133 M-3 Seongjin
133 N-6 Seonsan
133 M-6 Seosan
133 N-2 Seosura
119 H-3 Seoul
133 M-6 Seoul
207 P-6 Sepandjang *isl.*
222 G-6 Separation *pte*
149 P-8 Sepasu
190 A-4 Sepatini *riv.*
197 K-6 Sepetiba *bay*
66 D-7 Sepetovka
58 E-8 Sépey (Le)
211 H-4 Sepik *riv.*
133 M-5 Sepo
190 A-7 Sepot *riv.*
164 G-4 Sept-Îles
181 K-6 Septentrional *mt*
54 C-5 Septeuil
206 F-5 Seputih
167 K-3 Sequoia *na.p.*
209 L-6 Sera *isl.*
127 J-3 Serabad *riv.*
127 J-3 Serabad
126 E-2 Serachs
67 L-6 Serafimovič
54 D-3 Seraincourt
207 K-6 Seraju *riv.*
209 K-3 Seram *reg.*
117 H-7 Seram *sea*
209 L-3 Seram Laut *islds*
142 F-5 Serampore
206 G-5 Serang
54 D-1 Sérans
147 K-8 Serasan *isl.*
147 K-8 Serasan *strt.*
62 G-8 Seravezza
121 K-1 Serbakul'
146 C-7 Serbeulangit *mt*
64 C-3 Serbia *reg.*
55 P-6 Serbonne
63 H-9 Serchio *riv.*
96 G-1 Serdo
67 L-3 Serdobsk
93 P-7 Sereba
69 M-6 Serebr'anka
121 N-6 Serebr'ansk
66 G-5 Seredina-Buda
65 K-6 Sereflikochisar
62 E-2 Seregno
146 E-8 Serembam
100 F-4 Serengeti *na.p.*
207 K-2 Serengka
106 E-1 Serenje
194 A-4 Sereno *riv.*
66 C-8 Seret *riv.*
122 E-2 Serež *riv.*
67 K-1 Sergač
172 E-4 Sergeantsville
124 F-5 Sergejevka
123 L-9 Sergelen
159 G-9 Sergent *bay*
160 A-1 Sergent Icefield
69 M-1 Serginy
195 M-6 Sergipe *riv.*

195 M-6 Sergipe *reg.*
68 C-3 Sergozero *lake*
147 P-6 Seria
147 L-9 Serian
62 F-1 Seriana *val.*
62 F-2 Seriate
206 G-5 Seribu *cap.*
195 N-3 Serido *riv.*
63 L-7 Serino *isl.*
64 E-8 Serifos *isl.*
190 C-1 Serignal Sacado
146 G-8 Serihuat *islds*
65 J-8 Serik
146 C-1 Serim *riv.*
194 C-3 Seringa *mt*
212 G-2 Seringapatam *rf*
62 G-3 Serpukhov
63 M-9 Serra *mt*
63 H-9 Serra *isl.*
194 F-9 Serra Bonita
197 J-1 Serra das Araras
196 F-8 Serra do Mar *mt*
192 G-6 Serra do Navio *mt*
195 H-8 Serra Dourada
76 D-6 Serra Môco *mt*
195 M-4 Serra Sesia
195 M-4 Serra Talhada
64 D-5 Serrai
63 J-7 Serramazzoni
195 P-5 Serrambi *pte*
188 F-2 Serran
185 L-4 Serrana *rf*
185 L-3 Serranilla *rf*
201 K-2 Serrano *isl.*
196 E-2 Serranópolis
79 N-2 Serrat *cap.*
190 A-3 Seruini *riv.*
207 L-2 Serujan *riv.*
103 L-9 Seruli
207 J-2 Serutu *isl.*
199 L-4 Servásio
54 A-7 Serville
58 B-1 Servin
55 L-8 Servon
124 F-4 Seryševo
149 M-8 Sesajap
100 E-3 Sese *islds*
99 N-1 Sese
103 J-6 Sesheke
92 B-2 Sesia *riv.*
92 F-3 Sesibi *site*
103 M-6 Sessami *riv.*
62 G-7 Sesta Godano
123 K-2 Sestakovo
62 C-2 Sesto Calende
63 K-9 Sesto Fiorentino
62 E-3 Sesto San Giovanni
63 J-7 Sestola
62 D-7 Sestri
62 E-7 Sestri Levante
68 B-9 Sestroretsk
136 C-6 Setana
173 K-2 Setauket
61 H-3 Sète
197 K-4 Sete Lagoas
196 D-6 Sete Quedas *isl.*
196 D-9 Sete Quedas *isl.*
208 A-6 Setengar *isl.*
79 L-2 Setif
102 G-7 Setlekau
137 K-4 Seto Ni (mer)
137 L-9 Setouti
78 C-3 Settat

98 C-4 Setté Cama
62 A-4 Settimo Torinese
62 A-2 Settimo Vittone
214 D-6 Settlement *riv.*
60 A-5 Setúbal
197 L-2 Setubal *riv.*
55 J-2 Seugy
68 F-6 Sev dvina *riv.*
69 L-2 Sev. Sos'va *riv.*
72 E-3 Sevan *lake*
88 G-3 Sévaré
191 J-3 Sevaruyo
65 J-2 Sevastopol
120 B-3 Sevčenko *bay*
70 C-8 Sevčenko
167 K-7 Seveir
216 E-1 Seven Mile *riv.*
162 C-1 Seven Sisters *mt*
52 E-3 Seven Springs
53 L-6 Sevenoaks
57 K-8 Sevenum
191 N-2 Severín
154 J-4 Severn *riv.*
52 C-4 Severn (R.U) *riv.*
172 A-9 Severn (USA) *riv.*
52 E-2 Severn Stoke
172 A-9 Severna Park
113 H-2 Severnaya Zemlya *reg.*
121 M-1 Severnoje
69 K-3 Severnyj Ural *reg.*
123 M-2 Severo Baykal'skoye Nagorye *plat.*
123 N-3 Severo-Mujskij *mt*
48 N-3 Severomorsk
69 M-4 Severoural'sk
62 E-2 Seveso
122 F-5 Sevi
167 K-8 Sevier *riv.*
167 J-7 Sevier *lake*
60 B-7 Seville
186 C-7 Sevilla *pass*
185 J-8 Sevilla *isl.*
124 G-2 Sevli *riv.*
64 E-4 Sevlievo
55 K-4 Sevran
54 G-6 Sèvres
130 E-8 Sevrey
66 G-5 Sevsk
87 L-5 Sewa *riv.*
159 J-2 Seward *pen.*
158 G-9 Seward (USA)
169 H-7 Seward (USA)
198 B-6 Sewell
207 L-7 Sewu *cap.*
108 A-5 Seychelles *islds*
116 A-7 Seychelles *islds*
118 A-7 Seychelles *state*
65 J-7 Seydişehir
48 C-4 Seydisfjördur
72 A-7 Seyhan *riv.*
96 G-2 Seyla'
105 H-8 Seymour (South Africa)
220 A-4 Seymour (Australia)
173 K-1 Seymour (USA)
175 M-3 Seymour (USA)
170 E-8 Seymour (USA)
58 C-8 Seytroux
129 N-7 Seyue
50 F-8 Sézanne
79 P-3 Sfax
64 E-1 Sfîntu-Gheorghe
173 M-2 Sgaponack
100 A-8 Shaba *reg.*
143 H-5 Shābāzpur *lag.*
101 M-1 Shabelle *riv.*
164 G-1 Shabogamo *lake*
100 A-4 Shabunda
96 D-5 Shabwah
227 N-4 Shackleton Ice Shelf *glac.*
131 N-2 Shading
73 M-8 Shādkäm *riv.*
82 C-5 Shadwän *isl.*
167 H-7 Shafter
52 E-7 Shaftesbury
89 N-8 Shagamu
126 B-5 Shāh *mt*
146 E-7 Shah Alam
73 N-2 Shāh Jahän
126 G-9 Shāh Jüy
127 L-9 Shāh Kot
129 P-1 Shāhābād
138 E-6 Shähbandar
126 A-5 Shahdab (saline) *lake*
138 F-3 Shāhdädkot
140 A-9 Shahdol
132 E-6 Shahe *riv.*
125 B-9 Shahestän
142 C-2 Shāhganj
139 N-8 Shāhgarh
73 L-4 Shāhi
126 F-6 Shāhidän
72 G-5 Shāhin Dezh
129 P-1 Shāhjahänpur
140 E-5 Shāhpur

61 K-2 Susa
137 L-4 Susaki
137 K-5 Susami
127 P-1 Susamyr
73 J-9 Süsangerd
125 L-1 Susanino
166 G-3 Susanville
73 J-8 Suse site
63 M-1 Susegana
72 B-4 Suşehri
122 E-4 Sušenkoje
159 J-8 Susitna riv.
159 J-9 Susitna lake
159 H-8 Susitna
69 J-9 Suslonger
122 D-2 Suslovo
199 L-4 Suspiro
171 K-5 Susquehanna riv.
191 M-4 Susques
165 J-7 Sussex (Canada)
53 K-7 Sussex (UK) reg.
172 F-2 Sussex (USA) reg.
172 F-1 Sussex (USA)
59 L-5 Susten pass
59 L-5 Sustenhorn mt
57 N-7 Susteren
57 N-8 Susterseel
63 J-4 Sustinente
72 F-3 Sušu
149 P-7 Susuk
159 J-6 Susulatna riv.
209 N-3 Susunu
124 E-1 Sutam riv.
124 E-1 Sutamo Gonamskij mt
65 J-7 Sütçüler
104 E-8 Sutherland (South Africa)
221 L-3 Sutherland (Australia)
139 J-2 Sutlej riv.
162 B-5 Sutton mt
53 L-1 Sutton (UK)
53 K-6 Sutton (UK)
159 H-9 Sutton (USA)
171 H-8 Sutton (USA)
52 E-5 Sutton Benger
52 G-7 Sutton Scotney
136 C-6 Suttu
158 C-8 Sutwik isl.
125 H-4 Sutyr riv.
225 A-5 Suva
73 H-2 Suvel'an'
66 G-3 Suvorov
66 B-5 Suwalki
177 J-6 Suwannee riv.
137 P-3 Suwanose strt.
137 P-3 Suwanose isl.
224 C-5 Suwarrow isl.
139 L-7 Suwāsra
84 E-9 Suwayḥ
133 M-6 Suweon
135 K-1 Suxian
188 D-2 Suya riv.
172 A-3 Suydertown
121 M-4 Suykbulak
188 E-2 Suyo
120 D-7 Suzak
66 F-5 Suzemka
135 N-2 Suzhou
136 G-6 Suzu
136 G-6 Suzu cap.
137 J-6 Suzuka
121 N-3 Suzun
63 J-5 Suzzara
93 L-3 Svakin
48 E-6 Svappavaara
48 F-4 Svartisen cap.
68 E-1 Sv'atoj Nos cap.
67 J-7 Svatovo
145 K-9 Svay Rieng
49 J-4 Sveg
125 M-6 Sveltaja
67 K-7 Sverdlovsk (SSSR)
71 L-4 Sverdlovsk (SSSR)
69 N-6 Sverdlovsk (SSSR)
120 A-9 Sverdlovsk (SSSR)
112 F-2 Sverdrup isl.
66 A-4 Svetlij
66 E-5 Svetlogorsk
66 A-4 Svetlogorsk
67 M-9 Svetlograd
123 P-1 Svetlyj
67 M-6 Svetlyj Jar
49 J-9 Svetogorsk
64 C-3 Svetozarevo
67 L-1 Svijaga riv.
64 F-4 Sviengrad
127 J-2 Svincovyi Rudnik
68 D-8 Svir riv.
123 J-5 Svirsk
64 E-3 Svištov
51 M-8 Svitavy
124 F-4 Svobodnyj
48 D-4 Svolvaer
219 N-1 Swain rf
224 B-5 Swains isl.

177 K-4 Swainsboro
52 D-5 Swainswick
102 C-9 Swakop riv.
204 G-3 Swallow islds
147 N-4 Swallow (Danwan-jiao) rf
57 P-6 Swalmen
140 F-5 Swāmihalli
162 F-9 Swan riv.
163 M-7 Swan lake
162 F-9 Swan mt
163 M-7 Swan riv.
162 G-4 Swan isl.
216 E-7 Swan (Australia) riv.
180 B-8 Swan (Cisne) isl.
220 F-3 Swan Hill (Australia)
162 G-4 Swan Hills (Canada)
220 D-2 Swan Reach
163 M-8 Swan River
53 M-3 Swan Street Gosfield
52 E-9 Swanage
177 N-1 Swanquarter
165 H-8 Swans isl.
221 H-8 Swansea (Australia)
50 C-5 Swansea (UK)
104 C-7 Swart Doring riv.
104 E-9 Swartberge mt
57 M-6 Swartbroek
153 N-2 Swartenhuk isl.
172 D-6 Swarthmore
102 E-9 Swartnossob riv.
105 J-3 Swartruggens
172 E-2 Swarts Wood
164 B-7 Swastika
127 L-6 Swat reg.
172 A-4 Swatara riv.
105 L-4 Swaziland reg.
77 F-7 Swaziland state
47 E-3 Sweden state
172 D-7 Swedesboro
89 P-5 Swedru
168 C-5 Sweetwater riv.
175 L-3 Sweetwater
104 D-9 Swellendam
52 J-2 Swett pen.
172 B-1 Swett Valley
51 M-7 Swidnica
52 F-5 Swidon
51 L-6 Swiebodzin
159 G-7 Swift riv.
162 B-9 Swift lake
163 J-8 Swift Current
163 J-8 Swiftcurrent riv.
172 D-2 Swiftwater
162 A-3 Swindle isl.
50 D-6 Swindon
51 L-5 Swinoujscie
47 D-5 Switzerland state
57 K-8 Swolgen
52 C-9 Swyre
136 C-6 Syakotan cap.
136 C-6 Syakotan pen.
136 A-7 Syari
66 F-3 Syčovka
51 M-7 Sycow
122 E-3 Syda riv.
71 N-4 Sydarjunskij
224 B-4 Sydney isl.
212 G-8 Sydney mt
165 L-5 Sydney (Canada)
165 L-5 Sydney Mines
69 H-5 Syktyvkar
176 G-4 Sylacauga
143 H-4 Sylhet
51 H-4 Sylt
49 H-2 Sylte
69 M-6 Sylva riv.
69 M-6 Sylva (SSSR)
177 J-2 Sylva (USA)
177 K-4 Sylvania
177 J-5 Sylvester
165 N-3 Sylvester mt
52 D-3 Symond's
137 K-4 Syōbara
137 K-5 Syōdo isl.
173 J-3 Syosset
112 E-5 Syr-Daria riv.
61 P-8 Syracnse
171 K-5 Syracuse (USA)
168 F-9 Syracuse (USA)
120 C-9 Syrdarja
120 C-9 Syrdarjinskij
120 B-4 Syrdarya riv.
120 C-9 Syrdaryinskaya Oblast reg.
47 G-6 Syria state
144 D-5 Syriam
82 E-1 Syrian Desert reg.
69 M-3 Syrkovoje lake
67 J-4 Syrskij
76 D-1 Syrte (Great) gulf
69 P-6 Sysert
122 F-5 Systyg-Chem riv.
122 F-5 Systyg-Chem
67 M-2 Syzran'
51 L-5 Szczecin

51 M-5 Szczecinek
66 A-5 Szczytno
64 B-1 Szeged
64 B-1 Szekszárd
64 B-1 Szentes
64 B-1 Szesfehervár
64 B-1 Szolnok
61 P-1 Szombathely

# T

117 J-2 Taabaeg mt
130 D-7 Taatsiin riv.
191 M-5 Tabacal
148 E-4 Tabaco
188 F-2 Tabaconas riv.
83 H-5 Tābah
190 B-6 Tabajara
186 B-8 Tabaje riv.
211 P-3 Tabar isl.
211 P-3 Tabar islds
79 N-2 Tabarka
126 A-2 Tabas
126 C-4 Tabas
185 K-8 Tabasará riv.
179 K-6 Tabasco reg.
73 M-9 Tābask mt
122 D-4 Tabat
194 G-6 Tabatinga mt
78 E-6 Tabelbala
163 H-8 Taber
185 J-4 Taberis lag.
172 F-6 Tabernacle
129 M-4 Tabihu lake
206 D-2 Tabir riv.
195 M-4 Tabira
89 H-8 Tabla
148 F-5 Tablas strt.
148 F-5 Tablas isl.
149 H-4 Tablas plat.
79 K-2 Tablat
223 L-6 Table cap.
176 C-1 Table Rock lake
213 L-4 Tableland
89 N-7 Tabligbo
194 G-9 Tabocas
194 G-7 Tabocas do Brejo Velho
100 D-6 Tabora reg.
100 E-6 Tabora
87 P-8 Tabou
72 F-4 Tabriz
193 N-9 Tábua lake
195 H-5 Tábua riv.
146 C-9 Tabujung
148 B-6 Tabuk
82 D-4 Tabuk
219 M-7 Tabulam
192 C-8 Tabuleiro dam.
185 M-9 Tacacrcuna mt
192 F-7 Tacaipu mt
192 E-6 Tacalé
178 E-5 Tacambaro de Codallos
179 L-9 Tacana vol.
187 L-2 Tacarigua lag.
187 P-7 Tacatú riv.
66 C-9 T'acév
161 K-6 Tache lake
128 B-6 Tacheng (Chuguchak)
71 H-7 Tachiataš
174 F-8 Tachichilte isl.
186 F-4 Tachira reg.
79 L-3 Tachrirt mt
125 K-1 Tachta
126 F-3 Tachta-Bazar
120 G-1 Tachtabrod
71 H-6 Tachtakupyr
124 D-3 Tachtamygda
148 G-3 Tacloban
189 P-9 Tacna
189 P-9 Tacna reg.
191 N-6 Taco Pozo
54 B-6 Tacoignières
199 K-5 Tacuarembó reg.
199 K-4 Tacuarembó
199 K-4 Tacuarembó riv.
199 L-5 Tacuari riv.
221 L-5 Tacuari riv.
196 B-6 Tacuati
192 B-5 Tacutu riv.
136 G-7 Tadami
196 C-1 Tadarimana riv.
161 K-2 Tadenet lake

215 P-4 Tadine
79 M-8 Tadjentourt reg.
88 C-8 Tadjeraout riv.
96 G-2 Tadjoura bay
96 G-2 Tadjoura
52 G-6 Tadley
53 K-2 Tadlow
52 G-3 Tadmarton
163 P-3 Tadoule lake
164 F-6 Tadoussac
140 G-6 Tādpatri
88 F-7 Tadrak Ararek riv.
114 F-5 Tadzhik rép
127 L-3 Tadžikskaja reg.
133 N-6 Taebaek rge
131 J-2 Taerding
60 E-4 Tafalla
86 B-3 Tafarît cap.
209 N-5 Tafermaar
58 E-5 Tafers
52 B-5 Taff riv.
52 B-5 Taff's Wells
198 D-1 Tafí Viejo
78 E-5 Tafilalt reg.
78 G-2 Tafna riv.
78 B-5 Tafraoute
167 L-2 Taft
126 B-8 Taftān mt
172 E-1 Tafton
85 K-6 Taga
142 G-2 Taga Dzong
149 K-7 Taganak isl.
67 J-8 Taganrog
67 J-8 Taganrogskij zal bay
86 D-7 Tagant reg.
86 D-6 Tagant hill
148 F-3 Tagapula isl.
148 E-6 Tagaytayo
149 H-3 Tagbilaran
60 A-5 Tage riv.
210 G-5 Tagegu
92 E-6 Tagera mt
62 A-9 Taggia
86 B-5 Tagguel val.
78 F-5 Taghit
80 E-4 Taghrîfat
69 N-5 Tagil riv.
160 D-5 Tagish
63 P-2 Tagliamento riv.
63 M-4 Táglio di Po
188 C-9 Tagna
149 H-4 Tagolo pte
78 D-6 Tagounite
186 D-8 Tagua riv.
194 F-7 Taguatinga
149 J-1 Tagubud mt
129 M-4 Taguna mt
122 G-3 Tagul riv.
211 P-9 Tagula isl.
149 J-2 Tagum
122 B-3 T'agun
124 E-4 Tahan mt
222 C-9 Tahakopa
78 E-3 Tahala
146 E-6 Tahan mt
224 E-5 Tahanea isl.
161 P-2 Tahiryuak lake
224 E-5 Tahiti isl.
126 C-8 Tahlāb reg.
175 P-1 Tahlequah
167 H-3 Tahoe lake
167 H-3 Tahoe
175 K-3 Tahoka
162 A-5 Tahsis
81 P-5 Tahţa
160 D-7 Tahtlan
149 H-2 Tahulandang isl.
149 M-2 Tahuna
87 N-8 Taï
87 N-8 Taï na.p.
132 G-8 Taian
134 E-1 Taibaishan mt
135 N-8 T'aichung
222 D-8 Taieri riv.
113 P-3 Taigonos pen.
132 D-7 Taigu
132 E-6 Taihangshan mt
223 J-6 Taihape
135 K-1 Taihe
143 P-4 Taihezhen site
135 M-2 Taihu lake
134 E-6 Taijiang
131 J-2 Taijinaihu lake
132 E-9 Taikang (China)
135 J-1 Taikang (China)
124 E-9 Taikang (Duerbote)
136 B-7 Taiki
143 L-9 Taikkyi
124 E-8 Tailai
220 D-3 Tailem Bend
199 M-5 Taim
50 D-1 Tain

135 N-8 T'ainan
78 E-2 Taineste
199 N-3 Tainhas riv.
196 F-9 Taiö
197 L-1 Taiobeiras
119 H-4 Taipei
135 P-7 T'aipei
135 J-9 Taiping (China)
146 D-6 Taiping (Malaysia)
133 H-3 Taipingfang
132 G-8 Taipingzhen
132 E-4 Taipusiqi
206 D-4 Tais
135 H-9 Taishan
201 H-1 Taitao pen.
128 G-8 Taitemahu lake
135 P-8 T'aitung
48 F-8 Taivalkoski
49 K-7 Taivassalo
119 H-4 Taiwan state
135 N-7 T'aiwan strt.
135 M-2 Taixing
132 D-7 Taiyuan
131 P-1 Taizhao
135 M-1 Taizhou
133 J-3 Taizihe riv.
96 F-2 Taizz
73 H-8 Tājābād
207 K-1 Tajan Barat
193 H-8 Tajapuru riv.
192 G-6 Tajaui riv.
122 C-3 Tajdon riv.
122 C-1 Tajga
68 C-6 Tajginicy
190 E-4 Tajibo
125 H-1 Tajkanskij mt
120 A-5 Tajlakdžegen
69 N-7 Tajmejevo
122 F-2 Tajožnyj
73 K-5 Tajrīsh
122 G-3 Tajšet
207 L-6 Taju
184 C-2 Tajumulco vol.
123 L-3 Tajura riv.
122 C-3 Tajžina
144 F-5 Tak
208 D-5 Taka Bonerate islds
208 D-5 Taka Rewataje isl.
136 G-6 Takada
91 L-4 Takalaou
137 K-4 Takamatsu
137 M-3 Takamori
137 H-6 Takaoka
223 K-4 Takapuna
137 P-2 Takara isl.
137 H-7 Takasaki
208 B-3 Takatalu isl.
101 K-5 Takaungu
137 L-2 Takawa
137 H-6 Takayama
127 K-2 Take isl.
137 N-3 Take isl.
137 J-5 Takehu
128 G-5 Takelamagan-shamo dés
53 L-3 Takeley
129 K-3 Takenake
137 L-2 Takeo
73 L-3 Tākestān
137 L-3 Taketa
145 J-9 Takêv
127 P-9 Takh
127 K-4 Takhār
145 J-9 Takhmau
72 G-5 Takht-e Bālā
90 C-1 Takiéta
136 B-6 Takikawa
146 B-6 Takingeun
161 N-5 Takiyuak lake
162 D-1 Takla riv.
162 D-1 Takla lake
162 D-1 Takla Landing
112 G-6 Takla Makan dés
208 C-2 Takolekadju mt
160 D-6 Taku glac.
160 D-6 Taku riv.
146 C-3 Takua Pa
143 K-2 Takum (India)
90 D-6 Takum (Nigeria)
128 E-1 Takut
187 P-5 Takutu
73 L-9 Tal-e Khosravi
178 C-4 Tala
198 C-4 Talacasto
127 K-8 Talagang
198 A-6 Talagante
141 L-7 Talaimannar
122 G-3 Talaja
125 J-4 Talakan
146 D-9 Talakmau mt
185 H-7 Talamanca mt
206 C-1 Talang mt
184 F-3 Talanga
206 F-3 Talangbetufu
188 E-1 Talara
198 D-4 Talas riv.
120 F-8 Talas riv.

120 F-9 Talas
211 M-4 Talasea
120 F-9 Talasskij Alatau mt
208 E-1 Talatakoh isl.
149 L-1 Talaud islds
196 B-9 Talavera isl.
60 C-5 Talavera de la Reina
94 D-2 Talawdī
163 N-6 Talbot lake
217 L-2 Talbot mt
213 K-2 Talbot cap.
177 H-4 Talbotton
221 K-1 Talbragar riv.
198 A-7 Talca
200 A-2 Talca
198 A-6 Talca pte
198 A-7 Talca reg.
200 A-1 Talcahuano
142 D-6 Tālcher
124 D-3 Taldan
66 G-1 Taldom
214 F-8 Taldora
121 J-5 Taldy riv.
128 B-4 Taldy-Kurgan
127 N-3 Taldyk
97 J-6 Taleh
58 C-5 Talent riv.
91 H-6 Taley
128 C-3 Talgar
52 B-3 Talgarth
212 F-7 Talgatalga
94 D-5 Tali Post
208 F-2 Taliabu isl.
146 C-4 Talibong isl.
69 P-5 Talica
191 K-4 Talina riv.
78 C-5 Taliouine
149 N-7 Talisajan
149 H-3 Talisayan
149 N-2 Talisei isl.
208 A-7 Taliwang
123 J-5 Taljan
159 H-8 Talkeetna
159 J-8 Talkeetna riv.
159 J-9 Talkeetna mt
65 N-7 Tall al Abyad
72 E-6 Tall'afar
177 J-5 Tallahassee
176 G-3 Talledega
216 D-4 Tallering mt
176 E-4 Tallulah
63 P-1 Talmassons
121 P-3 Tal'menka
66 F-8 Tal'noje
140 A-4 Taloda
175 M-1 Taloga
127 K-4 Tāloqān reg.
67 K-5 Talovaja
122 F-1 Talovka
66 B-2 Talsi
121 J-1 Talšik
78 F-4 Talsinnt
123 N-5 Tal'skaja mt
191 N-1 Taltal
191 N-1 Taltal pte
161 M-9 Taltson riv.
149 P-4 Taludaa
206 C-1 Taluk
129 M-4 Talukechi lake
124 C-1 Taluma
128 C-5 Taluokenskankou
48 C-6 Talvik
219 K-6 Talwood
145 M-6 Tam Ky
198 D-4 Tama
143 M-2 Tamai riv.
216 C-3 Tamala
89 L-5 Tamale
65 K-1 Taman'
186 C-6 Tamaná mt
186 C-6 Tamanar
89 H-1 Tamani
137 K-4 Tamano
88 B-7 Tamanrasset riv.
172 B-3 Tamaqua
186 E-4 Tamar riv.
186 E-4 Tamar mt
186 F-6 Tamara
192 E-3 Tamarin
109 H-7 Tamatave (Toamasina)
178 G-2 Tamaulipas reg.
178 G-2 Tamaulipas mt
189 H-6 Tamaya riv.
178 F-4 Tamazunchale
86 G-6 Tamba Oura mt
100 G-2 Tambach
86 G-4 Tambacounda
86 F-6 Tambakara
88 G-6 Tambao
106 G-3 Tambara
147 J-9 Tambelan isl.
147 J-9 Tambelan islds
216 F-8 Tambellup
198 B-4 Tamberías
188 A-3 Tambo
189 K-6 Tambo riv.

108 G-3 Tambohorano
208 C-5 Tambolongang isl.
190 E-1 Tambopata riv.
208 B-7 Tambora mt
195 K-2 Tamboril
188 C-6 Tamboryacu riv.
67 J-4 Tambov
124 F-5 Tambovka
149 L-9 Tambunan
94 B-5 Tambura
195 K-8 Tamburi
86 E-7 Tamchekket
130 C-3 Tamchiyn Dabaa
120 B-7 Tamdybulak
186 F-5 Tame
50 L-2 Tames riv.
79 K-9 Tamesguidat riv.
178 G-3 Tamesi riv.
87 H-5 Tamgué mt
178 G-4 Tamiahua lag.
194 A-7 Tamiloala ou Batois riv.
172 E-2 Tamiment
78 F-4 Tamlelt pl.
142 F-5 Tamlük
49 K-7 Tammisaari
89 J-7 Tamou
177 K-7 Tampa
177 K-7 Tampa bay
178 G-3 Tampico
146 E-8 Tampin
208 E-4 Tampo
192 F-5 Tampoc riv.
109 P-7 Tampon (Le)
146 D-8 Tampulon Andjing mt
209 M-1 Tamrau
124 B-8 Tamsagbulag
66 C-1 Tamsalu
188 E-7 Tamshiyaco
143 K-4 Tamu
190 E-3 Tamupasa
142 F-2 Tamur riv.
221 L-1 Tamworth
145 K-9 Tân An
79 N-9 Tan Emellel
48 C-7 Tana riv.
93 M-8 Tana lake
191 J-1 Tana
137 K-5 Tanabe
196 F-4 Tanabi
87 H-2 Tanaff
146 E-6 Tanah Rata
206 A-1 Tanahbala isl.
208 C-6 Tanahdjampea isl.
208 A-2 Tanahgrogot
206 A-1 Tanahmasa isl.
210 E-5 Tanahmerah (Australia)
149 M-8 Tanahmerah (Borneo)
143 M-3 Tanai riv.
188 A-6 Tanaima isl.
208 C-5 Tanakeke isl.
129 N-1 Tanakpur
88 G-4 Tanal
204 D-3 Tanami dés
213 N-7 Tanami dés
213 M-6 Tanami
159 K-6 Tanana*
159 K-7 Tanana riv.
62 B-6 Tanaro riv.
145 J-7 Tanat riv.
84 B-4 Tanb-e Bozorg isl.
218 F-4 Tanbar
132 G-9 Tancheng
142 C-2 Tânda
88 F-3 Tanda lake
89 M-3 Tanda
149 H-2 Tandag
93 H-8 Tandaltī
102 E-5 Tandaué
200 A-9 Tandil
91 H-4 Tandjilé reg.
207 P-2 Tandjung
146 D-7 Tandjungbalai
207 H-3 Tandjungpandan
146 G-9 Tandjungpinang
146 C-7 Tandjungpura
206 F-3 Tandjungradja
149 N-8 Tandjungredeb
149 N-8 Tandjungselor
138 F-5 Tando Adam
138 F-5 Tando Allāhyār
138 F-5 Tando Muhammad Khān
220 F-1 Tandou lake
140 C-9 Tandula lake
223 K-5 Taneatua
137 N-3 Tanega isl.
137 N-3 Tanegasima strt.
144 E-7 Tanen Taunggyi mt
76 B-2 Tanezrouft dés
88 B-7 Tanezrouft n'Ahenet mt
80 A-6 Tanezzuff riv.
136 A-8 Tanfiljera isl.
101 J-6 Tanga reg.

211 P-3 Tanga islds
101 J-6 Tanga (Tanzania)
123 N-6 Tanga (SSSR)
142 G-4 Tangail
109 L-5 Tangainony
141 N-7 Tangalla
76 F-5 Tanganyika lake
100 C-2 Tanganyika lake
196 E-9 Tangará
130 E-2 Tangchuan mt
131 L-2 Tanggulashan
116 D-3 Tanggulashanmo plat.
129 N-6 Tanggulayumuhu lake
135 H-2 Tanghe
132 E-6 Tanghe riv.
78 E-1 Tangiers
135 J-7 Tangjiang
129 M-9 Tanglashankou mt
129 M-8 Tanglha rge
219 H-1 Tangorin
135 M-3 Tangqi
132 G-5 Tangshan
129 K-1 Tangtse
89 K-7 Tanguiéta
123 J-3 Tanguj
149 M-9 Tangung
125 H-7 Tangwanghe riv.
132 E-6 Tangxian
132 E-8 Tangyin
125 H-7 Tangyuan
145 J-9 Tani
209 L-6 Tanimbar islds
204 D-2 Taninbar islds
58 C-9 Taninges
149 H-4 Tanjay
108 F-4 Tanjona cap.
206 G-5 Tanjungkarang Telukbetung
127 J-8 Tānk
129 N-7 Tankeronghu lake
140 A-4 Tankhala
104 D-8 Tankwa riv.
59 J-5 Tann mt
49 H-4 Tännäs
172 D-2 Tannersville
89 N-4 Tano riv.
149 H-4 Tanon strt.
194 B-7 Tanquro riv.
135 P-7 Tanshui
89 J-3 Tansilla
185 J-3 Tánsin isl.
142 D-1 Tānsing
81 N-2 Tanta
178 G-4 Tantoyuca
162 B-2 Tantsa mt
140 E-9 Tanuku
214 B-6 Tanumbirini
69 M-8 Tanyp riv.
77 F-5 Tanzania state
76 F-5 Tanzania plat.
160 E-7 Tanzilla riv.
146 D-2 Tao isl.
133 H-1 Taoan
124 D-8 Taoerhe riv.
131 L-8 Taohe riv.
109 N-4 Taolagnaro (Fort-Dauphin)
133 K-1 Taolaizhao
132 B-6 Taolimin
119 M-5 Taongi isl.
168 C-9 Taos
88 A-4 Taoudenni
78 E-2 Taounate
78 F-3 Taourirt
78 E-5 Taouz
135 N-7 T'aoyuan
134 G-5 Taoyuang
66 C-1 Tapa
191 H-3 Tapacari
179 K-9 Tapachula
146 E-7 Tapah
192 G-9 Tapaja
192 G-9 Tapajos riv.
146 B-7 Tapaktuan
200 A-9 Tapalquén
206 C-2 Tapan
192 E-4 Tapanahoni riv.
199 J-3 Tapebicuá
199 M-2 Tapejara
199 H-2 Tapenagá riv.
190 E-7 Tapera
191 H-8 Taperas
195 L-8 Taperoa
199 N-4 Tapes pte
199 N-4 Tapes
144 G-5 Taphan Hin
196 A-2 Tapis
149 K-4 Tapiantana Grande isl.
188 F-6 Tapiche riv.
94 B-7 Tapili
211 K-7 Tapini
197 J-4 Tapirai
194 C-6 Tapirapé mt

194 C-6 Tapirapé riv.
187 L-9 Tapirapeco mt
146 F-7 Tapis mt
159 P-3 Tapkaluk islds
89 J-7 Tapoa riv.
91 H-5 Tapol
171 K-9 Tappahannock
173 H-2 Tapparr
136 D-6 Tappi pte
87 N-7 Tappita
122 F-5 Tapsa riv.
69 L-3 Tapsuj riv.
140 A-3 Tāpti riv.
222 G-7 Tapuaeneku mt
194 G-1 Tapuio riv.
149 L-5 Tapul Grande isl.
124 F-6 Taqi
199 N-3 Taquara
199 K-2 Taquarembó riv.
196 B-2 Taquari lag.
196 C-2 Taquari riv.
196 D-2 Taquari
196 D-2 Taquari riv.
196 G-5 Taquaritinga
196 C-4 Taquarucu riv.
200 E-4 Taquetrén mt
201 K-3 Tar lake
177 M-1 Tar riv.
219 L-5 Tara
90 E-5 Taraba riv.
191 J-5 Tarabuco
80 C-1 Tarābulus
191 K-6 Tarairi
149 M-8 Tarakan
149 M-8 Tarakan isl.
64 F-1 Taraklija
126 C-7 Tarakun site
221 K-3 Taralga
137 P-6 Tarama isl.
208 G-6 Taramana
66 A-4 Taran cap.
49 N-6 Taran mt
221 K-2 Tarana
223 H-5 Taranaki reg.
223 J-5 Taranaki bay
223 H-5 Taranaki Bight
60 D-5 Tarancón
139 J-7 Taranga Hill
91 K-4 Tarangara
76 A-6 Taranto gulf
191 J-2 Tarapaca
188 F-4 Tarapoto
123 K-3 Tarasova
123 L-3 Tarasovo
191 H-4 Tarata
188 G-9 Tarauacá riv.
188 G-8 Tarauacá
223 K-5 Tarawera mt
123 L-6 Tarbagataj
128 A-6 Tarbagatay rge
112 G-5 Tarbagatay rge
84 F-8 Tarbān riv.
50 C-1 Tarbert
60 F-3 Tarbes
177 M-1 Tarboro
58 A-2 Tarcenay
65 H-1 Tarchankut cap.
218 A-7 Tarcoola
219 J-7 Tarcoon
221 J-3 Tarcutta
125 L-4 Tardoki-Jani mt
221 M-1 Taree
48 E-7 Tarendø
190 E-3 Tareni riv.
61 P-6 Tarento
82 A-5 Tarfā riv.
96 C-1 Tarfā cap.
81 N-8 Tarfāwi well
92 E-1 Tarfāwi well
78 D-9 Tarfaya
123 H-2 Targiz
78 E-2 Targuist
78 E-5 Tarhbalt riv.
80 C-1 Tarhūnah mt
92 A-2 Tarhūnī mt
130 B-6 Tariat
191 K-6 Tarija reg.
191 K-5 Tarija
140 G-4 Tarikere
210 D-3 Tariku riv.
82 C-5 Tarīm
128 E-4 Tarim riv.
128 F-6 Tarim pool
128 F-7 Tarim riv.
112 G-6 Tarim pool
100 F-3 Tarime
210 E-3 Taritatu riv.
105 H-8 Tarkastad
127 H-4 Tarkhoj
73 J-6 Tarkhowrān
89 P-7 Tarkwa
148 D-6 Tarlac
188 D-8 Tarma
144 A-8 Tarmugli isl.
60 G-3 Tarn riv.
127 M-9 Tarn Tāran

48 F-4 Tärnaby
126 G-7 Tarnak riv.
66 B-7 Tarnobrzeg
68 G-7 Tarnogskij Gorodok
66 A-8 Tarnów
62 G-5 Taro riv.
219 L-4 Taroom
78 B-5 Taroudannt
177 K-7 Tarpon Springs
87 P-2 Tarrafal
60 F-5 Tarragona
220 G-8 Tarraleah
52 E-8 Tarrant Hinton
60 G-5 Tarrasa
173 H-2 Tarrytown
80 F-9 Tarso Emissi mt
123 J-4 Tarsovskij
65 L-7 Tarsus
191 L-5 Tartagal mt
191 L-6 Tartagal riv.
191 L-6 Tartagal
63 J-3 Tartaro riv.
54 B-8 Tartre-Gaudran (La)
66 C-1 Tartu
65 M-8 Tartūş
197 N-4 Tarumirim
137 N-3 Tarumizu
80 C-1 Tarūnah
143 L-2 Tarung riv.
146 D-5 Tarutao isl.
146 C-8 Tarutung
130 B-6 Tarvagatayn mt
190 F-7 Tarv riv.
127 N-1 Tas-Kumyr
122 C-6 Tašanta
121 H-7 Tasaral
121 H-7 Tasaral isl.
80 C-6 Tasāwah
164 B-6 Taschereau
140 A-5 Tasdin mt
122 F-2 Tasejevo
122 F-1 Tasejva riv.
162 C-2 Taseko riv.
162 C-5 Taseko mt
71 H-7 Tashauz
129 M-5 Tashibuhu lake
129 H-5 Tashibulake
143 H-2 Tashigang
127 N-5 Tashiheerhanhe riv.
127 N-5 Tashikuergan
73 N-9 Tashk lake
120 D-9 Tashkent
71 N-4 Tashkent
207 J-6 Tasikmalaja
211 M-2 Tasitel
123 L-5 Taškaj
126 F-2 Taškepri
128 A-5 Taskesken
65 K-4 Taşköprü
211 M-2 Taşkul
70 A-2 Tašla
204 G-5 Tasman sea
204 E-6 Tasman pen.
222 G-6 Tasman bay
221 H-9 Tasman cap.
221 H-9 Tasman pen.
204 E-6 Tasmania reg.
72 A-4 Tašova
86 B-7 Tassârât reg.
88 D-9 Tassili Tin Rerhoh plat.
122 C-4 Taštagol
128 A-6 Tastau mt
122 D-4 Taštyp
78 B-6 Tata
208 G-7 Tata Mailau
64 B-1 Tatabanya
79 P-5 Tatahouine
224 F-5 Tatakoto isl.
131 J-4 Tatalenghe riv.
165 K-6 Tatamagouche
172 D-3 Tatamy
113 N-5 Tatar sea
125 M-2 Tatar strt.
122 F-1 Tatarka
122 F-1 Tatarka riv.
121 L-1 Tatarsk
69 K-9 Tatarskaya ASSR reg.
117 K-2 Tatarskiy strt.
147 N-7 Tatau
147 N-7 Tatau riv.
211 N-3 Tatau isl.
123 L-6 Tataurovo
96 A-2 Tathlīth riv.
96 A-1 Tathlīth
103 L-9 Tati riv.
125 L-6 Tatibe riv.
162 C-4 Tatla Lake
162 C-4 Tatlayoko Lake
112 A-5 Tatry mt
66 A-8 Tatry mt
160 C-4 Tatshenshini riv.

138 E-5 Tatta
196 G-6 Tatui
162 D-3 Tatuk mt
198 B-3 Tatum
175 J-3 Tatum
65 P-5 Tatvan
51 H-1 Tau
195 K-3 Tauá
192 A-9 Tauapeçaçu
192 F-8 Tauaru riv.
197 J-6 Taubate
70 C-8 Taučik
61 N-1 Tauern mt
58 E-3 Täuffelen
190 D-2 Tauhamanu riv.
192 B-6 Tauini riv.
128 A-3 Taukum mt
176 E-1 Taum Sauk mt
223 J-5 Taumarunui
189 H-7 Taumaturgo
196 B-4 Taunay
143 L-7 Taungdwingyi
143 L-7 Taunggyi
143 L-7 Taungtha
143 L-4 Taungthonlon mt
143 K-8 Taungup
143 K-8 Taungup Pass
127 J-9 Taunsa
50 E-7 Taunton
223 J-5 Taupo lake
66 B-4 Tauragé
121 P-5 Taurak
223 K-5 Tauranga
171 K-2 Taureau lake
223 J-5 Tauroa pte
65 K-7 Taurus rge
72 E-2 Tauz
59 P-5 Tavanasa
64 G-7 Tavas
69 P-4 Tavda riv.
69 P-4 Tavda
63 K-3 Tavernelle
62 G-2 Tavernola Bergamo
54 G-3 Taverny
126 D-5 Tavesk
101 H-5 Taveta
59 M-6 Tavetsch val.
179 N-1 Taviche
60 A-7 Tavira
61 L-6 Tavolara isl.
121 L-3 Tavolžan
144 E-7 Tavoy
144 E-7 Tavoy pte
144 E-7 Tavoy riv.
121 K-1 Tavričeskoje
65 H-6 Tavşanli
223 H-7 Tawa
175 P-3 Tawakoni lake
143 M-3 Tawang riv.
146 B-4 Tawar lake
140 F-5 Tāwargeri
170 F-4 Tawas City
149 L-6 Tawi Tawi isl.
149 L-6 Tawi Tawi Grande isl.
82 C-5 Tawilah isl.
93 L-4 Tawkav
127 L-7 Taxila site
216 G-8 Tay lake
145 K-9 Tây Ninh
189 H-4 Tayabamba
97 N-4 Tayegle
129 M-3 Tayepawashankou
158 F-6 Taylor mt
174 G-1 Taylor mt
168 G-6 Taylor (USA)
159 J-2 Taylor (USA)
175 N-5 Taylor (USA)
172 C-1 Taylor (USA)
170 C-8 Taylorville
82 F-5 Taymā'
113 H-2 Taymyr pen.
190 G-4 Tayota riv.
130 C-5 Tayshir
83 J-4 Taysīyah mt
148 G-7 Taytay
126 D-3 Tayyebât
78 A-6 Taza (Morocco)
123 N-3 Taza (SSSR)
86 A-6 Tazadit mt
122 F-4 Tazarama mt
136 E-7 Tazawako
143 L-5 Taze
78 C-5 Tazenakht
81 H-6 Tazerbo (Wāhat)
86 A-4 Tâziâzet reg.
124 E-8 Tazicheng
136 G-7 Tazima
163 L-1 Tazin riv.
163 L-1 Tazin lake
122 D-2 T'ažin riv.
122 D-2 T'ažinskij
160 B-1 Tazlina lake

88 B-6 Tazouikert dés
67 L-9 Tbilisskaia
90 F-5 Tchamba
89 L-7 Tchaourou
126 G-1 Tchardjou
162 D-2 Tchentlo lake
98 C-4 Tchibanga
87 N-8 Tchien
80 D-9 Tchigaï plat.
90 G-5 Tcholliré
159 L-1 Tchoucktchis
79 J-9 Tchouli riv.
51 M-5 Tczew
222 C-8 Te Anau lake
223 J-1 Te Apua
223 K-4 Te Aroha
223 J-5 Te Awamutu
223 J-1 Te Kao
223 J-5 Te Kuiti
86 C-3 Te-n-Dghâmcha lake
223 P-9 Te Whanga Lagoon lag.
218 A-1 Tea Tree
178 B-3 Teacapan
179 K-7 Teapa
79 N-4 Tebaga mt
88 G-9 Tébaram
147 L-9 Tebedu
79 M-3 Tébessa
88 E-7 Tébézas
196 B-8 Tebicuari riv.
146 F-9 Tebingtinggi isl.
146 C-7 Tebingtinggi
206 D-2 Tebo riv.
174 B-1 Tecate
89 M-4 Techiman
200 F-3 Tecka mt
200 E-3 Tecka riv.
200 F-3 Tecka
178 C-5 Tecomán
174 E-5 Tecoripa
178 E-7 Tecpan de Galeana
178 B-3 Tecuala
64 F-1 Tecuci
169 J-7 Tecumseh
97 N-3 Ted'Eidär Dabole
52 A-8 Tedburn Saint Mary
207 P-7 Tedjakula
92 A-9 Tedji
190 C-3 Teduzara
126 E-2 Tedžen riv.
126 E-1 Tedžen
126 E-1 Tedženstroj
50 D-3 Tees riv.
207 J-6 Tegal
123 M-5 Tegda
57 K-9 Tegelen
90 A-4 Tegina
206 F-5 Tegineneng
120 D-7 Tegistyk
219 J-6 Tego
184 F-3 Tegucigalpa
157 F-5 Tegucigalpa
122 D-1 Tegul'det
167 L-3 Tehachapi
167 L-3 Tehachapi mt
109 L-3 Teheza riv.
89 L-3 Téhini
209 K-3 Tehoru
114 D-6 Tehran
73 K-5 Tehrān
139 P-3 Tehri
178 G-6 Tehuacan
179 J-7 Tehuantepec isth.
179 J-8 Tehuantepec gulf
179 H-7 Tehuantepec
156 E-5 Tehuantepec isth.
78 B-8 Teide mt
52 A-9 Teignmouth
195 M-4 Teixeira
87 H-2 Teixeira Pinto
196 F-8 Teixeira Soares
189 H-7 Tejo riv.
167 L-3 Tejon mt
143 L-2 Teju
169 J-6 Tekamah
222 F-5 Tekapo lake
179 M-5 Tekax
121 K-1 Teke lake
128 B-4 Tekeli
128 D-4 Tekes riv.
128 D-5 Tekesike riv.
93 M-7 Tekezze riv.
64 F-5 Tekirdağ
142 C-8 Tekkali
159 K-8 Teklanika riv.
143 H-7 Teknâf
222 F-7 Tekoa mt
88 B-9 Tekouiat riv.
208 F-1 Teku
142 C-6 Tel riv.
82 C-2 Tel Aviv Yafo
184 F-2 Tela

147 H-7 Telaga isl.
78 G-3 Télagh
206 E-2 Telanaipura
159 G-7 Telaquana lake
72 E-2 Telavi
131 M-3 Telaxi
179 M-4 Telchac Puerto
78 C-9 Telde
88 F-3 Télé lake
91 P-9 Tele riv.
98 E-4 Téléb mt
207 L-3 Telegapulang
162 D-4 Telegraph mt
80 B-9 Telei riv.
51 J-1 Telemark reg.
123 N-5 Telemba
188 A-3 Telembi riv.
200 A-6 Telén
167 L-2 Telescope mt
122 D-6 Teli
87 J-4 Télimélé
92 D-7 Teljo mt
159 H-2 Teller
141 J-4 Tellicherry
186 D-7 Tello
59 M-4 Tells-Platte
123 K-5 Tel'ma
130 B-5 Telmen lake
191 L-5 Telmo mt
146 E-7 Telok Anson
69 J-2 Tel'posiz mt
200 E-5 Telsen
66 A-3 Telšiai
149 P-5 Teluk Tomini gulf
149 P-6 Teluk Tomini reg.
206 B-1 Telukbajur
207 K-1 Telukbatang
147 K-6 Telukbutun
146 B-9 Telukdalam
206 D-4 Telukpunggur cap.
149 L-8 Telupid
209 K-3 Teluti bay
94 B-7 Tely
89 P-6 Tema
78 D-3 Temara
224 E-6 Tematagi isl.
179 N-4 Temax
146 F-6 Tembeling riv.
206 D-2 Tembesi riv.
206 E-1 Tembilahan
187 M-3 Temblador
98 D-1 Tembo mt
99 H-8 Tembo Aluma
52 C-1 Teme riv.
146 E-6 Temengor
129 H-9 Temerlik
146 F-7 Temerloh
146 G-9 Temiang isl.
209 L-1 Teminabuan
70 C-3 Temir
71 M-3 Temirlanovka
122 C-4 Temirtau
121 H-4 Temirtau
164 E-3 Temiscamie riv.
164 B-7 Témiscamingue
91 K-3 Temki
220 F-7 Temma
123 K-6 Temnik riv.
67 K-2 Temnikov
221 J-3 Temora
174 F-5 Temosachic
208 C-4 Tempe lake
174 E-2 Tempe
217 P-1 Tempe Downs
206 E-2 Temping
184 G-6 Tempisque riv.
214 G-3 Temple bay
54 E-3 Temple (Le)
172 C-4 Temple (USA)
175 N-5 Temple (USA)
52 D-7 Temple Combe
53 P-6 Temple Ewell
214 D-9 Templeton riv.
172 C-9 Templeville
65 L-1 Temr'uk
200 C-2 Temuco
222 E-8 Temuka
177 K-9 Ten Thousand islds
188 B-3 Tena
94 C-7 Tena mt
179 M-5 Tenabo
160 C-5 Tenakee Springs
140 F-8 Tenäli
178 F-6 Tenango del Aire
144 E-7 Tenasserim reg.
146 C-1 Tenasserim
144 F-8 Tenasserim (Great) riv.
52 D-1 Tenbury
211 N-2 Tench isl.
62 A-8 Tenda pass
93 P-8 Tendaho
62 A-8 Tende
78 F-4 Tendrara
58 A-6 Tendre mt
53 N-3 Tendring Weeley
72 D-4 Tendürük mt

87 J-5 Téné riv.
80 A-9 Ténéré du Tafas sasset mt
78 B-8 Tenerife isl.
79 J-2 Ténès
143 M-7 Teng riv.
208 B-6 Tenga islds
133 J-4 Tengaobao
143 N-4 Tengchong
208 A-1 Tenggarong
131 H-9 Tenggelishamo mt
146 G-6 Tenggol isl.
120 G-3 Tengiz lake
120 G-3 Tengiz-Kurgal'džinskaja Vpadina reg.
134 B-9 Tengtiaohe riv.
122 D-1 Tenguly
134 G-9 Tengxian
191 L-8 Teniente F. Delgado
227 M-3 Teniente Matienzo
79 J-2 Teniet el Had
59 N-5 Tenigerbad
141 L-5 Tenkäsi
103 K-1 Tenke
89 J-5 Tenkogodo
214 A-8 Tennant Creek
172 G-5 Tennent
157 E-3 Tennessee state
176 F-2 Tennessee riv.
176 G-2 Tennessee state
58 D-9 Tenneverge pass
78 B-4 Tennsitt riv.
198 A-7 Teno
198 B-7 Teno riv.
48 C-7 Tenojoki riv.
149 L-9 Tenom
179 L-7 Tenosique de Pino Suárez
201 H-1 Tenquehuén isl.
137 K-5 Tenri
137 J-6 Tenryū riv.
137 J-7 Tenryū
219 M-7 Tent Hill mt
53 M-7 Tenterden
219 M-7 Tenterfield
149 P-5 Tentolomatinan mt
178 D-4 Teocaltiche
63 M-8 Teodorano
197 M-3 Téofilo Otoni
178 E-7 Teotepec
178 F-5 Teotihuacan site
178 G-6 Teotitlán del Camino
209 K-6 Tepa
178 D-5 Tepalcatepec
178 D-4 Tepatitlán de Morelos
178 G-6 Tepeaca
178 B-1 Tepehuanes
64 C-6 Tepelenë
187 N-7 Tepequem mt
178 C-3 Tepic
51 K-7 Teplice
174 C-4 Tepoca cap.
174 C-4 Tepoca bay
178 C-4 Tequila
178 F-4 Tequisquiapan
60 C-5 Ter riv.
56 D-2 Ter Aar
89 H-6 Téra
94 E-5 Terakeka
61 N-5 Teramo
57 L-4 Terborg
86 A-3 Tercat mt
198 F-5 Tercero riv.
122 F-7 Tere-Chol' lake
72 D-1 Terek riv.
120 E-9 Terek-Saj
70 A-9 Terekli-Mektet
121 P-6 Terektinskij mt
191 M-7 Terenganu (see Teuco)
165 N-3 Terenceville
67 M-2 Teren'ga
196 C-4 Terenos
120 C-5 Terenuzek
196 E-7 Teresa Cristina
195 J-2 Teresina
67 M-3 Tereška riv.
197 L-6 Teresópolis
146 A-4 Teressa isl.
192 G-6 Terezinha
56 D-6 Terheijden
146 B-7 Teripa riv.
57 N-9 Terlinden
72 A-4 Terme
86 F-8 Termessa reg.
65 H-8 Termessus site
127 J-3 Termez
217 H-8 Termination isl.
61 N-8 Termini
61 L-6 Terminos lag.
61 N-5 Termoli
57 M-9 Ternaaien
149 P-1 Ternate
125 L-7 Ternej
61 M-4 Terni

66 C-8 Ternopol'
66 G-8 Terny
89 L-7 Térou riv.
56 E-8 Terover
220 D-1 Terowie
125 N-3 Terpenija bay
125 P-2 Terpenija pen.
125 P-3 Terpenija cap.
197 L-2 Terra Branca
104 F-3 Terra Firma
162 C-1 Terrace
61 M-5 Terracina
61 K-6 Terralba
155 L-3 Terre de Baffin reg.
46 F-1 Terre du Nord-Est (Norway) isl.
46 F-2 Terre du Roi Karl isl.
154 E-3 Terre du Yukon reg.
170 D-8 Terre Haute
172 B-5 Terre Hill
155 M-4 Terre Neuve reg.
175 N-3 Terrel
58 E-1 Terri mt
59 N-6 Terri pass
58 D-7 Territet
218 B-2 Territoire du Nord reg.
154 H-3 Territoires du Nord-Ouest (Canada) reg.
168 E-2 Terry
122 C-3 Ters' riv.
120 G-2 Tersakkan riv.
56 G-2 Terschuure
91 J-2 Tersef
128 D-2 Terskej Alatau mt
68 C-4 Terskij Bereg reg.
54 B-4 Tertre-Saint-Denis (Le)
60 E-5 Teruel
57 K-1 Terwolde
122 E-6 Tes
122 F-6 Tes-Chem riv.
93 L-6 Teseney
159 N-4 Teshekput lake
89 L-9 Teshi riv.
136 B-8 Tesikaga
136 A-6 Tesio
136 A-6 Tesio mt
130 A-5 Tesiyn riv.
160 E-6 Teslin lake
160 E-5 Teslin
160 E-5 Teslin riv.
100 E-1 Teso reg.
196 D-1 Tesouro
88 C-7 Tessalit
54 E-3 Tessancourt-sur-Aubette
90 C-1 Tessaoua
52 F-7 Test riv.
61 K-5 Testa cap.
191 M-1 Tetas pte
52 E-4 Tetbury
103 P-5 Tete reg.
106 G-3 Tete
58 D-3 Tête de Rang mt
66 E-7 Teterev riv.
56 D-7 Teteringen
125 L-8 Tetioukhe
125 L-8 Tetioukhe-Pristan
191 J-2 Tetivilla mt
160 D-1 Tetlin lake
160 D-1 Tetlin
160 D-1 Tetlin Junction
162 G-9 Teton riv.
78 E-2 Tétouan
64 C-4 Tetovo
68 D-4 Tetrino
53 H-4 Tetsworth
142 G-6 Tetulia lag.
67 M-1 Tet'uš
191 M-7 Teuco
57 K-2 Teuge
190 A-3 Teuini
61 K-7 Teulada cap.
209 J-5 Teun isl.
136 B-6 Teuri isl.
184 G-5 Teustepe
61 M-5 Tevere riv.
52 E-3 Tewkesbury
162 B-6 Texada isl.
176 C-3 Texarkana
157 D-3 Texas state
175 M-4 Texas state
175 P-6 Texas City
50 G-5 Texel isl.
175 N-2 Texoma lake
105 J-6 Teyateyaneng
64 D-8 Teyea site
67 H-1 Teykovo
126 F-5 Teyvareh
178 G-5 Teziutlán
143 J-2 Tezpur
63 L-1 Tezze
63 L-2 Tezze san Bretta
162 D-2 Tezzeron lake
88 A-3 Tghâza
144 G-2 Tha riv.
145 H-4 Tha Bo

144 G-4 Tha Li
144 G-4 Tha Pla
144 E-5 Tha Song Yang
145 J-6 Tha Tum
144 F-8 Tha Yang
105 H-6 Thaba Nchu
105 K-6 Thabana Ntlenyana mt
105 J-2 Thabazimbi
143 L-5 Thabeikkyin
145 K-2 Thai Binh
145 K-2 Thai Nguyên
118 F-5 Thailand state
144 G-9 Thailand gulf
127 J-7 Thal
79 N-3 Thala
146 C-4 Thalang
219 K-6 Thallon
59 L-1 Thalwil
80 F-6 Thamad Bu Hashishah
103 H-7 Thamalakane riv.
85 K-6 Thamarïd
144 C-5 Thamihla isl.
96 B-7 Thamūd
146 C-2 Than isl.
145 J-1 Than Uyen
140 C-3 Thāna
144 E-5 Thanbyuzayat
143 L-8 Thandaung
219 M-6 Thane
139 M-3 Thānesar
53 P-5 Thanet isl.
213 H-5 Thangoo
145 K-3 Thanh Hoa
141 K-6 Thanjävür
138 F-5 Thāno Bula Khān
146 D-1 Thap Sakae
145 J-6 Thap Than riv.
116 C-4 Thar dés
139 H-4 Tharäd
218 G-5 Thargomindah
143 L-9 Tharrawaddy
64 E-5 Thasos isl.
64 E-5 Thasos
145 J-5 That Phanom
52 G-5 Thatcham
144 E-5 Thaton
162 C-2 Thatsa lake
129 M-7 Thau Tsho lake
144 E-5 Thaungyin riv.
53 L-3 Thaxted
146 C-1 Thayawthadangyi isl.
176 D-1 Thayer
162 D-7 Thayetchaung
143 K-8 Thayetmyo
143 L-7 Thazi
180 G-3 The Bight
162 B-9 The Dalles
56 A-3 The Hague
163 N-6 The Pas
181 M-1 The Valley
50 E-5 The Wash gulf
53 H-8 The Witterings
82 B-7 Thebes (Egypt) site
168 G-6 Thedford
219 M-5 Theebine
161 M-9 Thekulthili lake
52 A-8 Thelbridge
161 P-8 Thelon riv.
54 E-2 Thémericourt
219 L-4 Theodore
146 E-5 Thepha
59 J-8 Thermen
168 C-4 Thermopolis
55 N-2 Thérouanne
170 F-3 Thessalon
53 M-1 Thet riv.
53 M-1 Thetford
164 F-7 Thetford Mines
145 J-4 Theun (Kading) riv.
105 H-5 Theunissen
54 F-1 Theuville
55 J-1 Thève riv.
212 C-8 Thevenard isl.
55 J-7 Thiais
176 E-6 Thibodaux
169 J-2 Thief River Falls
58 C-5 Thièle riv.
166 E-3 Thielsen mt
63 K-2 Thiene
58 G-5 Thierachern
58 C-5 Thierrens
61 H-2 Thiers
55 J-1 Thiers-sur-Thève
86 F-1 Thiés
86 F-1 Thiès
55 M-3 Thieux
101 G-3 Thika
55 K-3 Thillay (Le)

86 F-2 Thilmakha
142 G-2 Thimbu
118 E-4 Thimphu
215 N-4 Thio
50 G-8 Thionville
54 B-7 Thionville-sur-Opton
64 F-8 Thíra
54 A-4 Thiron
51 J-2 Thisted
48 B-4 Thistilfjördur bay
220 B-3 Thistle isl.
147 N-2 Thitu (Zhongyedao) rf
64 D-7 Thívai site
54 E-6 Thiverval-Grignon
146 G-3 Thô Châu isl.
163 L-1 Thoa riv.
144 F-4 Thoen
144 F-3 Thoeng
105 L-1 Thohoyandou
54 D-6 Thoiry
54 D-6 Thoiry (Réserve africaine na.p.
56 A-7 Tholen isl.
56 A-7 Tholen
58 C-7 Thollon
218 D-3 Thomas lake
177 H-4 Thomaston
176 G-4 Thomasville
177 J-5 Thomasville
214 G-3 Thompson mt
163 P-5 Thompson (Canada)
170 A-7 Thompson (USA) riv.
166 F-2 Thompson (USA) mt
162 F-9 Thompson Falls
161 M-7 Thompson Landing
218 G-3 Thomson (Australia) riv.
216 C-1 Thomson (Australia) mt
177 K-3 Thomson (USA)
100 G-2 Thomson's Falls
144 G-7 Thon Buri
144 D-5 Thongwa
58 B-8 Thonon-les-Bains
58 G-3 Thorberg
55 M-5 Thorigny-sur-Marne
54 F-4 Thörishaus
57 N-6 Thorn
52 D-7 Thornbury
53 H-1 Thornby
172 C-2 Thornhurst
53 N-3 Thorpe le Socken
60 F-1 Thouars
143 K-4 Thoubāl
164 D-9 Thousand islds
101 J-3 Thowa riv.
64 E-5 Thráki reg.
53 J-1 Thrapston
217 J-3 Thrassell lake
162 D-7 Three Pinnacles mt
172 E-4 Three Bridges
168 B-2 Three Forks
162 G-3 Three Hills
220 G-7 Three Hummock isl.
223 J-1 Three Kings isl.
204 G-5 Three Kings islds
89 P-4 Three Points cap.
175 M-6 Three Rivers
166 D-4 Three Sisters mt
104 F-7 Three Sisters
175 M-3 Throckmorton
172 C-1 Throop
212 G-8 Throssel mt
145 M-6 Thu Bôn riv.
161 L-8 Thubun riv.
146 A-4 Thuillier mt
138 G-3 Thul
222 E-7 Thumbs (The) mt
58 G-5 Thun lake
58 G-5 Thun
61 K-1 Thun
170 C-2 Thunder Bay
59 H-5 Thuner See
146 D-4 Thung Song
51 J-7 Thüringen Wald ft
50 B-4 Thurles
227 M-4 Thurston isl.
160 E-9 Thutade lake
53 N-1 Thwaite
218 A-4 Thylungra
58 F-9 Thyon
88 D-7 Ti-N-Zaouatene
190 G-2 Tiahuanacu
135 K-4 Tianban
130 K-4 Tiancang
134 E-8 Tiandong
134 D-8 Tianlin
135 H-3 Tianmushan mt
135 M-3 Tianmushan mt
131 L-9 Tianshui

131 L-9 Tianshuizhen
131 K-8 Tiantangsi
131 K-7 Tiantangsi
134 E-8 Tianyang
132 E-5 Tianzhen
134 F-6 Tianzhu
79 J-2 Tiaret
63 H-1 Tiarno
89 N-2 Tiassalé
137 H-8 Tiba
196 F-7 Tibaji riv.
196 F-7 Tibaji
80 E-7 Tibasti dés
90 F-6 Tibati
95 J-3 Tibbè
163 H-9 Tiber lake
82 C-1 Tiberias
76 D-2 Tibesti dés
80 E-9 Tibesti reg.
129 K-5 Tibet plat.
196 F-5 Tibirica riv.
192 D-3 Tibiti riv.
65 P-7 Tibnī
218 F-6 Tibooburra
129 P-3 Tibrikot
186 B-5 Tibuga gulf
137 J-3 Tiburi isl.
185 M-8 Tiburón cap.
174 D-5 Tiburón isl.
148 F-4 Ticao isl.
184 E-3 Ticatuyo riv.
53 L-7 Ticehurst
52 G-8 Tichfield
86 D-8 Tichît hill
86 D-8 Tichît
95 K-3 Ticho mt
93 P-6 Ticho
123 K-5 Tichonovka
62 D-3 Ticino riv.
59 M-8 Ticino (Tessin) reg.
163 P-5 Ticket Portage
164 E-9 Ticonderoga
189 L-5 Ticrapo
179 M-5 Ticul
143 J-5 Tiddim
80 F-9 Tideli riv.
79 H-9 Tidikelt reg.
78 E-2 Tidirhine mt
86 D-6 Tidijkja
62 E-5 Tidone riv.
62 E-5 Tidone
149 P-1 Tidore isl.
86 B-5 Tïdra isl.
89 M-2 Tiébissou
128 D-5 Tieersikeshan mt
128 F-8 Tieganlike
86 F-3 Tiel
56 F-5 Tielerwaard reg.
124 G-7 Tieli
128 F-1 Tieliekezhuang
129 N-5 Tielinanmuhu lake
133 J-3 Tieling
87 L-9 Tiemba riv.
131 L-3 Tiemiankuzhu
128 E-7 Tien Shan reg.
112 F-5 Tien Shan rge
145 L-2 Tiên Yên
56 B-6 Tiengemeten
56 E-4 Tienhoven
57 K-7 Tienray
91 K-3 Tiéou
79 N-6 Tieret
49 K-5 Tierp
185 N-9 Tierra Alta
168 C-9 Tierra Amarilla
188 F-5 Tierra Blanca
200 E-5 Tierra Colorada bay
182 D-8 Tierra del Fuego isl.
201 N-5 Tierra del Fuego isl.
201 N-6 Tierra del Fuego reg.
196 G-6 Tiete riv.
196 F-4 Tietê riv.
218 A-4 Tieyon
170 G-7 Tiffin
72 E-2 Tiflis
149 P-1 Tifore isl.
177 J-5 Tifton
209 H-3 Tifu
147 P-5 Tiga isl.
148 G-5 Tigbauan
55 P-6 Tigeaux
162 E-8 Tiger
55 K-9 Tigery
56 C-7 Tiggelt
79 H-2 Tighennif
121 N-5 Tigireckij mt
62 B-5 Tigliole
90 F-6 Tignère
165 J-6 Tignish
93 N-7 Tigray reg.
188 D-6 Tigre riv.
191 L-1 Tigre
179 M-7 Tigre (Guatémala) lag.
188 E-6 Tigrillo riv.
72 E-6 Tigris riv.

218 C-7 Torrens *lake*
215 H-9 Torrens Creek
58 G-9 Torrent *pass*
58 G-8 Torrenthorn *mt*
178 D-1 Torreón
214 F-1 Torres *strt.*
204 G-3 Torres *islds*
204 E-2 Torres *strt.*
199 P-3 Tôrres
210 G-8 Torres *strt.*
60 E-7 Torrevieja
167 K-8 Torrey
63 H-2 Torri del Benaco
63 L-3 Torri di Quart
62 E-6 Torriglia
162 G-6 Torrington
168 E-5 Torrington (USA)
189 J-7 Torro *riv.*
218 E-8 Torrowangee
49 K-4 Torsby
48 D-1 Tórshavn
120 D-8 Tortkol'
181 L-1 Tortola *isl.*
62 D-5 Tortona
60 F-7 Tortosa *cap.*
60 F-5 Tortosa
181 J-5 Tortue *isl.*
174 D-6 Tortuga (Mexico) *isl.*
187 K-2 Tortuga (Vénézuela) *isl.*
198 G-5 Tortugas
185 H-6 Tortuguero
187 N-4 Tortula *isl.*
72 C-4 Tortum
146 C-8 Toru *riv.*
73 M-4 Torūd
128 E-1 Torugart Dayan *pass*
51 M-6 Torun
187 H-4 Torunos
50 B-2 Tory *isl.*
66 F-2 Torzhok
137 L-4 Tosa
137 L-4 Tosa *bay*
67 J-2 T'oša
67 K-2 T'oša *riv.*
137 L-4 Tosa-Simizu
133 M-5 Tosan
61 L-3 Toscany *reg.*
63 D-2 Toscolano
48 F-4 Tosen
130 B-6 Tosontsengel
88 F-6 Tossaye *val.*
208 C-8 Tossi
63 L-7 Tossignano
130 E-7 Tost *mt*
198 G-3 Tostado
137 L-2 Tōsu
65 K-4 Tosya
186 F-6 Tota *lake*
103 H-8 Toteng
97 N-3 Totias
192 D-3 Totness
98 F-7 Toto
184 C-2 Totonicapán
191 H-4 Totora
221 J-1 Tottenham
172 G-4 Tottenville
52 F-8 Totton
137 J-4 Tottori
89 H-4 Tou
78 G-8 Touat *reg.*
86 F-2 Touba
78 C-5 Toubkal *mt*
86 F-4 Toueïrja *riv.*
89 H-4 Tougan
79 L-4 Touggourt
172 C-6 Toughkenamon
89 H-5 Tougouri
87 J-5 Tougué
215 M-3 Touho
79 J-3 Touil *riv.*
87 H-7 Toukoto
50 G-8 Toul
87 N-8 Toulépleu
61 J-4 Toulon
60 G-3 Toulouse
80 C-8 Toummo
89 N-2 Toumodi
143 L-8 Toungoo
50 E-7 Touquet-Paris-Plage (Le)
58 D-8 Tour d'Ai *mt*
58 D-7 Tour de Peilz (La)
58 E-6 Tour de Trême (La)
61 J-2 Tour-du-Pin (La)
58 D-9 Tour Sallière *mt*
87 M-8 Toura *mt*
71 H-5 Touran *holl.*
91 H-2 Tourba
50 F-7 Tourcoing
60 A-2 Touriñan *cap.*
55 N-7 Tournan-en-Brie
189 H-6 Tournavista
80 A-8 Tourndo *riv.*
61 H-2 Tournon
54 A-1 Tourny

195 P-2 Touros
50 D-9 Tours
76 D-2 Toussidé *mt*
91 N-4 Toussoro *mt*
54 G-7 Toussus-le-Noble
104 D-8 Touwsrivier
130 C-9 Töv *reg.*
67 H-3 Tovarkovskij
136 D-7 Towada *lake*
136 D-7 Towada
192 B-2 Towakaima
171 K-6 Towanda
53 H-2 Towcester
170 B-2 Tower
172 A-4 Tower City
217 J-8 Tower Peak *mt*
126 G-7 Towkhī Selam
172 B-8 Town Point
168 G-1 Towner
173 H-1 Towners
214 B-5 Towns *riv.*
168 B-1 Townsend
219 M-2 Townshend *cap.*
219 M-2 Townshend *isl.*
215 J-8 Townsville
94 G-5 Towot
127 K-6 Towr Kham
126 F-8 Towrzī
171 K-8 Towson
208 D-3 Towuti *lake*
52 A-2 Towy *riv.*
136 C-6 Toya *lake*
175 J-4 Toyahvale
137 H-6 Toyama *gulf*
137 H-6 Toyama
137 L-5 Tōyō
137 J-6 Toyohasi
137 J-5 Toyonaka
137 J-6 Toyota
79 M-4 Tozeur
159 K-6 Tozitna *riv.*
64 E-3 Tr. Magurele
147 H-3 Tra Cu
145 M-4 Tra Khuc *riv.*
165 J-5 Tracadie
59 H-5 Trachsellauenen
59 H-3 Trachselwald
167 J-2 Tracy
62 D-2 Tradate
60 B-8 Trafalgar *cap.*
109 M-4 Trafonaomby *mt*
200 D-3 Traful *lake*
200 D-3 Traful *riv.*
200 B-2 Traiguén
200 G-2 Traiguén *isl.*
162 E-8 Trail
166 E-3 Trail (USA)
195 N-6 Traipu
194 D-9 Trairas *riv.*
194 E-8 Trairas *mt*
195 L-1 Trairi
50 A-4 Tralee
51 L-2 Tranas
191 P-5 Trancas
51 J-3 Tranebjerg
146 D-4 Trang
209 N-5 Trangan *isl.*
221 J-1 Trangie
141 K-7 Tranquebar
200 F-2 Tranqui *isl.*
72 G-6 Trānshah
198 A-3 Trânsito
200 G-8 Trânsito *isl.*
105 J-8 Transkei *reg.*
105 K-2 Transvaal *reg.*
112 A-5 Transylvania *reg.*
64 D-3 Transylvanian Alps *rge*
61 M-8 Trapani
179 L-8 Trapichillo *riv.*
62 B-8 Trappe
172 D-5 Trappe
54 F-7 Trappes
221 H-5 Traralgon
86 D-4 Trarza *reg.*
61 M-4 Trasimeno *lake*
59 K-9 Trasquera
63 H-8 Trassilico
145 H-8 Trat
193 L-7 Trauira *isl.*
62 G-3 Travagliato
161 J-1 Travaillant *lake*
220 F-2 Travellers *isl.*
194 B-3 Travenão de Urubu *riv.*
58 C-4 Travers *val.*
58 C-4 Travers
159 J-4 Traverse *mt*
170 E-4 Traverse City
59 P-5 Travesasch
198 C-6 Travesía del Tunuyán *reg.*
198 D-6 Travesía Puntana *reg.*
194 D-3 Travessão de Correão *riv.*

194 E-6 Travessão Jacare *riv.*
192 D-7 Travia *dam.*
62 F-5 Travo
72 B-3 Trazbon
63 H-8 Tre Potenze *mt*
62 F-1 Tre Signori *mt*
62 E-5 Trebbia *riv.*
62 E-5 Trebecco *lake*
52 A-3 Trecastle
62 D-3 Trecate
148 E-6 Trece Martires
63 K-4 Trecenta
52 B-4 Tredegar
63 J-2 Tredici Comuni *reg.*
52 F-2 Tredington
63 L-8 Tredozio
57 N-8 Treebeek
63 K-3 Tregnago
215 M-7 Tregrosse *islds*
59 L-3 Treib
199 L-5 Treinta-y-Tres
199 L-5 Treinta-y-Tres *reg.*
214 E-9 Trekelano
200 E-6 Trelew
58 A-7 Trélex
51 K-4 Trelleborg
52 C-4 Trellech
55 L-4 Tremblay-lès-Gonesse
54 E-7 Tremblay-sur-Marne
197 M-1 Tremedal
61 P-5 Tremiti *isl.*
172 A-4 Tremont
60 F-4 Tremp
51 M-9 Trencin
198 E-7 Trenel
196 D-9 Trenente Portela
146 F-6 Trengganu *reg.*
200 A-7 Trente de Agosto
61 M-2 Trentino Alto Adige *reg.*
63 J-1 Trento
164 C-9 Trenton (Canada)
170 A-8 Trenton (USA)
168 F-7 Trenton (USA)
171 L-7 Trenton (USA)
62 G-3 Trenzano
199 J-5 Tres Arboles
200 B-9 Tres Arroyos
188 F-9 Tres Bocas
190 A-6 Tres Casas
201 J-5 Tres Cerros
197 J-5 Tres Coracoes
198 A-3 Tres Cruces
188 A-5 Tres Esquinas
196 F-3 Tres Fronteiras
190 B-4 Tres Irmãos *mt*
196 B-2 Tres Irmãos
191 P-8 Tres Isletas
196 E-4 Tres Lagoas
201 K-4 Tres Lagos
197 J-3 Tres Marias *dam.*
201 H-2 Tres Montes *gulf*
201 J-1 Tres Montes *pen.*
196 C-9 Tres Passos
194 E-3 Tres Pedras
200 B-8 Tres Picos *mt*
200 E-3 Tres Picos *mt*
200 C-5 Tres Picos *lag.*
197 J-5 Tres Pontas
198 A-2 Tres Puentes
184 E-2 Tres Puntas *cap.*
197 H-3 Tres Ranchos
197 K-6 Tres Rios
188 E-5 Tres Unidos
174 C-6 Tres Virgenes *vol.*
62 F-2 Tresara
62 F-2 Trescore Balneario
54 E-5 Tressancourt
58 D-9 Trétien (Le)
121 M-5 Tretjakovo
62 B-3 Tretower
200 F-3 Trevelin
62 F-3 Treviglio
63 M-2 Trevignano
58 D-1 Trévillers
63 M-2 Treviso
63 M-1 Treviso *reg.*
61 M-2 Treviso
172 A-3 Trevorton
172 C-4 Trexler
172 C-4 Trexlertown
58 D-5 Trey
62 D-3 Treyvaux
62 G-2 Trezzano san Naviglio
62 F-2 Trezzo sull'Adda
146 E-8 Tri Tôn
221 H-9 Triabunna
122 A-3 Triangul'atorov *mt*
179 L-4 Triángulos *rf*
191 K-5 Trias *riv.*
168 F-8 Tribune
62 C-4 Tricerro
56 F-4 Tricht

141 K-4 Trichür
52 E-8 Trickett's Cross
166 G-5 Trident *mt*
54 F-4 Triel-sur-Seine
59 J-2 Triengen
50 G-8 Trier
61 N-2 Trieste
62 F-3 Trigolo
64 C-6 Trikkala
210 D-4 Trikora *site*
55 N-4 Trilbardou
55 P-4 Trilport
50 B-4 Trim
59 H-1 Trimbach
53 P-3 Trimley
174 D-4 Trincheras
141 L-8 Trincomalee
196 G-1 Trindade
53 J-4 Tring
201 L-2 Trinidad *cal.*
200 C-8 Trinidad *isl.*
156 H-5 Trinidad *isl.*
190 F-6 Trinidad (Bolivia)
186 F-6 Trinidad (Colombia)
180 D-5 Trinidad (Cuba)
196 B-9 Trinidad (Paraguay)
199 J-6 Trinidad (Uruguay)
166 F-1 Trinidad (USA)
157 H-5 Trinidad and Tobago *state*
62 A-6 Trinità
187 P-2 Trinité *isl.*
192 F-3 Trinité *mt*
158 D-9 Trinity *islds*
165 P-3 Trinity *bay*
175 P-5 Trinity *riv.*
146 A-4 Trinity *mt*
93 L-3 Trinkitat
62 C-9 Trino
62 A-8 Triora
142 D-1 Trisúli *riv.*
145 P-6 Triton *isl.*
194 B-3 Triunfo *riv.*
141 L-4 Trivandrum
62 B-2 Trivero
51 M-9 Trnava
211 N-7 Trobriand *islds*
54 C-7 Troche (La)
55 L-5 Trocy-en-Marne
62 A-5 Trofarello
48 F-4 Trofors
122 F-1 Troick
69 P-5 Troickij
69 J-3 Troicko-Pecorsk
121 P-4 Troickoje
78 F-2 Trois Fourches *cap.*
164 G-6 Trois-Pistoles
164 E-7 Trois-Rivières
58 D-9 Troisitorrents
64 E-4 Trojan
51 K-2 Trollhättan
195 L-9 Tromba Grande *cap.*
192 D-8 Trombetas *riv.*
62 D-4 Tromello
200 C-3 Tromen *lake*
200 B-3 Tromen *mt*
62 A-5 Trompia *val.*
105 H-6 Trompsburg
48 D-6 Troms *reg.*
48 C-5 Tromsø
200 D-3 Tronador *mt*
146 E-6 Tronoh
59 K-9 Tronom
62 B-3 Tronzano Vercellese
65 K-9 Tróodos *mt*
194 E-7 Tropejo *riv.*
194 G-9 Tropeiros *mt*
162 E-5 Trost'anec
66 G-6 Trost'anec
154 J-4 Trout *lake*
161 H-8 Trout *lake*
161 J-7 Trout *riv.*
168 B-3 Trout *mt*
165 L-3 Trout River
52 E-6 Trowbridge
220 G-7 Trowutta
64 F-6 Troy *site*
167 J-6 Troy *mt*
170 C-8 Troy (USA)
177 H-4 Troy (USA)
50 F-8 Troyes
210 C-9 Truant *isl.*
214 C-2 Truant *islds*
66 D-8 Trubčevsk

59 H-4 Trubschachen
59 L-5 Trübsee
147 H-2 Truc Giang
162 F-1 Trucht
84 D-4 Trucial Coast *reg.*
167 H-3 Truckee
70 A-7 Trudfront
68 F-4 Trufanogorskaja
186 G-3 Trujillo
189 H-2 Trujillo *site*
60 C-5 Trujillo (Spain)
184 G-2 Trujillo (Honduras)
186 G-3 Trujillo (Vénézuela) *reg.*
119 L-6 Truk *isl.*
167 L-7 Trumbull *mt*
173 K-1 Trumbull
59 J-6 Trümmelbach (Falls)
59 N-5 Trun
59 H-4 Trut
174 G-2 Truth or Consequences (Hot Springs)
130 F-6 Tsagaan Bogd *mt*
123 J-6 Tsagaan-Hüryee
130 A-6 Tsagaan-Uür
132 A-1 Tsagaandelger
130 A-4 Tsagaanhayrhan
130 A-2 Tsagaannuur
130 A-1 Tsagan *riv.*
130 C-7 Tserserleg
104 C-3 Tses
130 C-3 Tsetseg
58 F-8 Tseuzier *lake*
89 N-6 Tsévié
104 F-3 Tshabong
104 F-2 Tshane
103 L-1 Tshangalele *lake*
98 E-6 Tshela
99 K-5 Tshikapa
99 K-7 Tshikapa *riv.*
99 N-6 Tshofa
99 N-2 Tshopo *riv.*
99 K-2 Tshuapa *riv.*
98 G-4 Tshumbiri
109 H-5 Tsiafajavona *mt*
109 H-6 Tsiazompaniry *lake*
109 N-3 Tsihombe
109 L-3 Tsikoriky *mt*
109 L-2 Tsimanampetsotsa *lake*
132 F-7 Tsinan
133 H-8 Tsingtao
109 J-5 Tsinjoarivo
109 H-3 Tsiribihina *riv.*
109 H-4 Tsiroanomandidy
109 K-4 Tsitondroina
105 K-7 Tsitsa *riv.*
162 C-3 Tsitsutl *mt*
109 M-3 Tsivory
72 D-7 Tskhinvali
132 A-3 Tsogdor Uula *mt*
161 L-9 Tsu *lake*
136 D-6 Tsugaru *strt.*
113 N-5 Tsugaru *strt.*
102 E-7 Tsumeb
104 C-2 Tsumis Park
135 J-9 Tsun Wan *bay*
113 L-6 Tsushina *strt.*
102 G-9 Tswane
48 G-2 Tsyp Navolok
137 J-6 Tu
206 G-5 Tua *cap.*
98 G-5 Tua
209 M-4 Tual
50 A-3 Tuam
224 E-5 Tuamotu *islds*
146 C-9 Tuan *pte*
145 J-2 Tuan Giao
146 B-8 Tuangku *isl.*
133 H-6 Tuaojidao *isl.*
72 A-1 Tuapse
149 N-2 Tuaran
70 A-8 T'ub-Karachan *cap.*
122 E-4 Tuba *riv.*
123 J-2 Tuba
82 G-1 Tubal *riv.*
199 P-2 Tubarao

195 N-2 Tubarão *pte*
149 H-6 Tubbataha *rf*
51 H-9 Tübingen
82 F-6 Tubjah *riv.*
149 J-3 Tubod
224 E-6 Tubuai *isl.*
69 P-6 T'ubuk
148 G-3 Tuburan
187 J-2 Tucacas
188 B-9 Tucano *dam.*
195 L-6 Tucano
200 B-1 Tucapel *pte*
191 H-6 Tucavaca *riv.*
135 P-7 Tuchang
160 F-9 Tuchodi *riv.*
122 D-2 T'uchtet
173 H-2 Tuckahoe
172 G-2 Tuckerton
174 E-3 Tucson
201 J-3 Tucu Tucu
186 F-3 Tucuco *riv.*
198 D-1 Tucumán *reg.*
175 J-1 Tucumcari
198 C-4 Tucunuco
187 N-3 Tucupita
193 H-9 Tucurui
192 G-9 Tucurui *riv.*
211 L-7 Tufi
97 J-5 Tug Der *riv.*
170 G-9 Tug Fork *riv.*
136 D-6 Tugaru *pen.*
105 L-6 Tugela *riv.*
158 D-9 Tugidak *isl.*
152 C-4 Tugidak *isl.*
149 K-1 Tugubun *pte*
148 B-5 Tuguegarao
125 J-1 Tugur
125 J-1 Tugur *riv.*
125 J-1 Tugurskij *mt*
132 C-3 Tuhamumiao
89 J-3 Tui *riv.*
190 F-2 Tuichi *riv.*
78 C-9 Tuineje
105 K-3 Tuinplaas
194 E-3 Tuitizinho *riv.*
69 M-7 Tuj *riv.*
130 D-7 Tujin *riv.*
125 H-4 Tuka *mt*
95 H-3 Tuka *mt*
69 P-9 Tukan
208 F-5 Tukangbesi *islds*
164 B-1 Tukarak *isl.*
129 N-3 Tuksum
66 B-3 Tukums
124 E-2 Tukuringra *rge*
100 E-9 Tukuyu
82 C-2 Tül Karm
101 J-3 Tula *riv.*
178 F-3 Tula (Mexico)
67 H-3 Tula (SSSR)
178 F-5 Tula de Allende
163 M-6 Tulabi Lake
126 F-4 Tūlak
178 G-5 Tulancingo
206 F-4 Tulangbawang *riv.*
167 K-3 Tulare
175 H-2 Tularosa
140 D-9 Tulasi *mt*
188 A-3 Tulcán
64 G-2 Tulcea
172 A-9 Tulchester Beach
66 H-2 Tul'čin
166 F-3 Tulelake
73 H-4 T'ulenij *pte*
125 P-3 T'ulenij *isl.*
70 C-7 T'ulenij (O-va) *islds*
70 B-1 Tul'gan
105 J-1 Tuli *reg.*
103 M-9 Tuli *riv.*
175 K-2 Tulia
149 L-9 Tulid
133 H-1 Tuliemaodu
120 E-8 T'ul'kubas
176 G-2 Tullahoma
221 J-1 Tullamore (Australia)
50 B-4 Tullamore (UK)
60 G-2 Tulle
95 L-4 Tullu Michire
95 K-2 Tullumilki
91 P-3 Tullus
215 J-7 Tully
172 E-5 Tullytown
175 P-1 Tulsa
149 L-8 Tulto
188 B-4 Tulu
187 M-9 Tulu Tuloi *mt*

# U

66 F-5 Uneča
130 D-5 Uneen Us
186 F-6 Unete riv.
158 B-7 Unga isl.
158 B-7 Unga
159 H-4 Ungalik
159 J-4 Ungalik riv.
221 H-2 Ungarie
155 L-4 Ungava pen.
156 G-1 Ungava pen.
123 M-2 Ungdar mt
66 E-9 Ungeny
133 N-2 Ungigi bay
133 N-2 Ungigi
143 J-8 Unguan isl.
93 K-5 Ungwatiri
69 K-7 Uni
195 J-2 União
196 E-8 União da Vitória
195 N-5 União dos Palmares
158 A-5 Unimak
158 A-5 Unimak isl.
189 J-6 Unini
200 C-8 Unión bay
172 E-8 Union lake
174 D-1 Union mt
172 G-3 Union reg.
162 A-5 Union (Canada) isl.
187 N-1 Union (Grenada) isl.
170 B-9 Union (USA)
177 K-2 Union (USA)
172 G-3 Union (USA)
172 G-4 Union Beach
176 F-1 Union City (USA)
172 G-3 Union City (USA)
180 C-4 Union dé Reyes
178 C-5 Unión de Tula
177 H-4 Union Springs
104 F-9 Uniondale
171 H-7 Uniontown
172 C-6 Unionville (USA)
172 F-1 Unionville (USA)
170 A-7 Unionville (USA)
118 A-4 United Arab Emirates state
47 C-4 United Kingdom state
157 G-3 United States state
163 J-7 Unity
139 P-6 Unnão
87 J-2 Uno isl.
133 L-3 Unsong
59 L-2 Unt-Ageri
59 K-6 Unteraar glac.
59 H-5 Unterseen
59 K-4 Unterwalden reg.
59 K-6 Unterwasser
69 M-1 Untor lake
187 L-9 Unturán mt
160 D-8 Unuk riv.
72 A-4 Unye
68 G-8 Unza riv.
122 G-6 Unžej-Aksy
123 N-3 Uojan
137 N-5 Uoturi isl.
137 H-6 Uozu
187 N-4 Upata
100 A-9 Upemba na.p.
99 P-8 Upemba lake
52 G-7 Upham
149 K-3 Upi
186 F-6 Upía riv.
104 E-5 Upington
138 F-8 Upleta
53 L-5 Upminster
158 F-6 Upnuk lake
224 B-5 Upolu isl.
52 B-8 Upottery
162 E-7 Upper Arrow lake
172 E-4 Upper Black Edc
52 A-2 Upper Chapel
165 L-3 Upper Humber ri
166 E-3 Upper Klamath lake
160 E-4 Upper Laberge
166 F-4 Upper Lake lake
172 C-2 Upper Lehigh
170 B-1 Upper Manitou lake
165 K-7 Upper Musquodoboit
170 A-2 Upper Red lake
170 F-7 Upper Sandusky
52 D-2 Upper Stapey
53 J-8 Upper Waltham
51 M-1 Uppsala
158 D-1 Upright cap.
129 K-1 Upshi
215 K-8 Upstart cap.
53 N-6 Upstreet
52 E-2 Upton (UK)
172 F-6 Upton (USA)
52 E-1 Upton Warren
83 H-6 Uqlat aş Suqūr
83 J-1 Ur site
127 L-2 Ura-T'ube
187 N-3 Uracoa
136 B-7 Urahoro
69 N-3 Uraj
136 C-7 Urakawa

112 D-4 Ural rge
69 P-8 Ural riv.
69 M-5 Ural mt
219 L-8 Uralla
70 A-3 Ural'sk
221 H-3 Urana
218 D-1 Urandangi
195 H-9 Urandí
163 L-2 Uranium City
187 N-7 Uraricão riv.
187 M-7 Uraricoera riv.
187 P-7 Uraricoera
137 H-7 Urawa
170 D-8 Urbana
193 N-9 Urbano Santos
62 C-6 Urbe
63 N-9 Urbino
52 E-6 Urchfont
189 L-8 Urcos
67 N-5 Urda
199 H-5 Urdinarrain
69 H-5 Urdoma
128 A-6 Urđžar
69 H-9 Uren'
191 P-5 Ureña riv.
174 E-5 Ures
223 K-5 Urewera na.p.
65 N-6 Urfa
130 B-4 Urgamal
71 J-7 Urgench
65 K-6 Urgup
127 J-2 Urgut
130 G-8 Uri riv.
187 M-4 Uri dam.
59 M-5 Uri
59 L-4 Uri Rotstock mt
186 F-4 Uribante riv.
186 E-7 Uribe
186 F-1 Uribia
123 H-5 Urik riv.
187 N-6 Urimán
67 L-1 Urimary
218 G-6 Urimbin
191 K-5 Uriondo
174 F-6 Urique riv.
188 E-5 Urituyacu riv.
193 H-9 Uriuaná
124 C-3 Urka riv.
124 E-3 Urkan riv.
124 D-2 Urkan (Bol.) riv.
64 F-7 Urla
123 L-7 Urluk
125 J-4 Urmi riv.
57 M-8 Urmond
59 P-1 Urnäsch
59 N-4 Urner Boden riv.
64 C-4 Urosevac
186 C-5 Urrao
200 B-6 Urre Lauquen lag.
59 H-2 Ursenbach
59 L-6 Urseren val.
121 P-5 Ursul riv.
193 H-9 Uruá dam.
194 D-9 Uruaçu
196 G-1 Uruana
178 D-5 Uruapán
192 F-9 Uruará riv.
189 L-7 Urubamba
189 L-7 Urubamba riv.
194 D-6 Urubu riv.
192 C-8 Urucará
195 L-9 Uruçuca
194 G-5 Uruçui mt
194 G-3 Uruçui
194 G-4 Uruçui-Prêto riv.
197 J-1 Urucuia riv.
192 F-8 Urucuituba riv.
192 C-9 Urucurituba
199 M-1 Uruguai (Brazil) riv.
199 J-3 Uruguaiana
183 E-6 Uruguay state
83 J-1 Uruk site
187 H-2 Urumaco
128 D-8 Urumchi
124 B-5 Ur'umkan riv.
124 B-5 Ur'umkanskij mt
211 K-7 Urun
195 L-1 Uruoca
122 D-2 Ur'up riv.
72 B-1 Urup
190 C-6 Urupá riv.
192 G-8 Urutai isl.
187 N-6 Uruyén
67 K-5 Uruypinsk
210 D-2 Urville cap.
121 P-7 Uryl'
69 K-8 Urzhum
64 F-2 Urziceni
122 E-5 Us riv.
122 G-6 Uš-Bel'dir
122 D-3 Usa riv.
65 H-6 Uşak

102 C-9 Usakos
124 E-4 Uškovo
125 K-1 Usalgin
101 J-6 Usambara mt
130 B-3 Usan Hötöl Dabaa mt
120 E-7 Usaral
201 L-9 Usborne mt
62 E-7 Uscio
93 M-1 Usfan
82 G-9 Ushin
83 K-5 Ushayrah
132 B-6 Ushin
128 B-3 Ushtobe
201 N-6 Ushuaia
137 M-2 Usibuka
66 D-8 Ušica
52 C-4 Usk
52 C-4 Usk riv.
125 M-3 Us'ka-Oročinskaja
123 L-4 Uškannijo (bol.) mt
185 J-3 Uskira lag.
125 K-3 Usman
62 E-2 Usmate Velate
123 J-5 Usolje-Sibirskoje
122 G-2 Usolka riv.
69 L-5 Usol'ye
121 H-5 Uspenskij
121 J-2 Uspenskoje
60 G-2 Ussel
125 K-7 Ussuri riv.
133 N-1 Ussurijskij
125 K-9 Ussuriysk
68 G-2 Ust'-Cil'ma
123 N-4 Ust'Džilinda
69 H-2 Ust'-Ižma
123 J-4 Ust'-Kada
122 G-1 Ust'-Kajtym
121 N-4 Ust' Kalmanka
121 N-6 Ust-Kamenogorsk
122 G-1 Ust'-Karabula
124 A-3 Ust'-Karenga
124 B-4 Ust'-Karsk
69 N-8 Ust'-Katav
123 H-4 Ust'-Kirej
121 P-6 Ust' Koksa
69 J-5 Ust'-Kulom
123 K-2 Ust'-Kut
67 K-9 Ust'-Labinsk
123 J-1 Ust'-Ilimsk
69 K-3 Ust'-Ilyč
49 K-9 Ust'-Luga
122 C-4 Ust'-Majra
123 P-2 Ust'-Muja
69 J-4 Ust'-Nem
125 H-3 Ust'Niman
124 C-1 Ust'-N'ukža
123 K-5 Ust'-Ordynskij
123 J-5 Ust-Ordynskiy Buratskiy National Okrug reg.
69 J-2 Ust'-Ščugor
121 L-1 Ust'Tarka
124 F-3 Ust'Tygda
123 J-4 Ust'-Uda
122 C-6 Ust' Ulagan
69 L-4 Ust'-Uls
125 H-3 Ust'Umal'ta
124 C-2 Ust'-Urkima
124 C-4 Ust'-Urov
112 D-5 Ust Urt plat.
70 F-7 Ust'-Urt plat.
69 H-1 Ust'-Usa
130 C-9 Ust Uul mt
123 N-5 Ust'Zaza
122 E-4 Ust'abakan
191 J-7 Ustares mt
123 M-5 Ust'barguzin
59 M-1 Uster
51 L-7 Usti
61 M-7 Ustica isl.
122 F-1 Ustje
123 J-1 Ustje Ilima
51 M-4 Ustka
124 F-2 Ust'unja
68 E-9 Ust'užna
123 P-5 Usugli
137 L-3 Usuki
159 N-3 Usutuk riv.
184 E-4 Usulután
179 L-9 Usumachinta riv.
184 C-1 Usumacinta riv.
105 L-4 Usutu riv.
167 J-7 Utah state
167 J-8 Utah lake
157 C-3 Utah state
201 H-2 Utarupa cap.
136 B-6 Utasinai
123 J-6 Utata
188 F-3 Utcubamba riv.
175 K-1 Ute riv.
102 G-5 Utembo riv.
101 J-8 Utenge lake

101 J-8 Utete
144 F-6 Uthai Thani
138 E-4 Uthal
190 E-9 Utiariti
171 K-5 Utica
60 E-6 Utiel
163 H-3 Utikuma lake
184 F-2 Utila isl.
184 F-2 Utila
195 K-7 Utinga
195 K-7 Utinga riv.
137 N-3 Utinoura
119 N-5 Utirik isl.
136 C-6 Utiura gulf
127 K-7 Utmānzai
49 L-6 Utö isl.
137 M-3 Uto
218 A-1 Utopia
142 C-1 Utraula
47 D-5 Utrecht reg.
56 E-2 Utrecht reg.
105 L-5 Utrecht (South Africa)
56 F-3 Utrecht (Pays-bas)
60 B-7 Utreta
48 C-7 Utsjoki
67 N-7 Utta
139 N-5 Uttar Pradesh reg.
144 F-4 Uttaradit
139 P-3 Uttarkāshi
181 J-1 Utuado
124 E-1 Utugej riv.
159 M-4 Utukok riv.
136 G-7 Utunomiya
70 B-3 Utva riv.
49 J-1 Utvik
58 G-2 Utzensdorf
130 C-4 Uulaiin Dabaa mt
132 C-1 Uulbayan
130 A-8 Uür riv.
49 H-7 Uusikaarlepyy
49 J-7 Uusikaupunki
49 K-8 Uusimaa
186 G-7 Uvá riv.
186 G-7 Uvá lake
69 K-8 Uva
70 F-7 Uval Karabaur mt
175 L-6 Uvalde
67 K-4 Uvarovo
69 P-2 Uvat
69 P-7 Uvel'ka riv.
100 C-6 Uvinza
100 B-5 Uvira
122 E-6 Uvs lake
146 B-6 Uwak
84 E-7 Uwayfiyah
94 B-3 Uwayl
92 C-2 Uwaynât mt
147 J-9 Uwi isl.
210 F-5 Uwimmerah riv.
53 J-5 Uxbridge
179 M-5 Uxmal site
158 E-9 Uyak bay
130 C-3 Uyench
130 A-1 Uygar riv.
143 L-4 Uyu riv.
191 K-3 Uyuni
191 K-3 Uyuni lake
66 G-7 Už riv.
67 L-3 Uza riv.
71 M-1 Užaral
114 E-5 Uzbekistan rép
120 A-7 Uzbekskaya rép
70 D-2 Uzen'
127 N-2 Uzgen
66 B-9 Užgorod
137 N-2 Uzi islds
66 E-7 Uzin
67 H-3 Uzlovaya
59 N-2 Uznach
66 B-8 Užokskij strt.
72 B-1 Uzst'-Džegulinskaja
128 C-2 Uzunagač
64 F-5 Uzunköprü
122 D-2 Užur

# V

105 J-4 Vaal dam.
105 H-5 Vaal riv.
48 G-8 Vaala
105 J-2 Vaalwater
57 H-8 Vaarsel
49 H-7 Vaasa reg.
49 H-6 Vaasa
57 J-1 Vaassen

120 A-9 Vabkent
66 A-9 Vac
199 L-3 Vacacaí riv.
189 J-7 Vacapista riv.
196 C-5 Vacaria riv.
197 L-1 Vacaria riv.
199 N-2 Vacaria
127 M-5 Vachanski mt
181 J-7 Vache isl.
58 C-8 Vacheresse
54 A-9 Vacheresses-les-Basses
125 N-3 Vachrušev
127 J-3 Vachš riv.
58 B-2 Vachtan
69 H-8 Vachtan
109 P-9 Vacoas-Phoenix
62 C-7 Vado cap.
62 C-7 Vado
48 C-8 Vadsø
61 L-1 Vaduz
47 D-5 Vaduz
48 E-4 Vaerøy isl.
48 E-1 Våg
48 F-7 Vaga riv.
63 K-9 Vaglia
48 D-1 Vågø
48 D-5 Vagsfd bay
49 H-1 Vågsøy isl.
51 M-9 Váh riv.
141 K-6 Vaigai riv.
62 F-3 Vailate
58 B-8 Vailly
172 G-1 Vails Gate
59 J-9 Vaira val.
58 A-1 Vaire-le-Grand
55 L-5 Vaires-sur-Marne
55 L-5 Vaires-sur-Marne
91 M-4 Vakaga riv.
91 M-4 Vakaga reg.
138 G-6 Väkrio
125 K-7 Vaku riv.
125 M-1 Val
54 B-9 Val (Le)
54 G-7 Val d'Albian (Le)
164 C-6 Val-d'Or
163 J-9 Val Marie
57 M-9 Val-Meer
62 D-6 Val Noci lake
69 L-8 Vala riv.
68 B-8 Valaam isl.
197 L-3 Valadares
58 D-3 Valangin
66 E-1 Valdagno
58 B-2 Valdahon
112 B-4 Valdayskaya mt
51 M-2 Valdemarsvik
60 D-6 Valdepeñas
198 G-7 Valdés
160 B-1 Valdez
200 D-2 Valdivia
63 N-1 Valdobbiadene
177 J-5 Valdosta
63 J-2 Valdritta mt
166 E-6 Vale
49 J-3 Válebru
54 C-1 Valécourt
63 J-3 Valeggio sul Mincio
197 K-6 Valenca
195 L-8 Valença
60 B-3 Valença (Spain)
195 J-3 Valença do Piaui
61 J-2 Valence (France)
60 E-6 Valencia
60 E-6 Valencia reg.
187 J-2 Valencia (Vénézuela)
60 C-3 Valencia de Don Juan
50 F-7 Valenciennes
59 P-5 Valendas
195 L-7 Valente
195 H-2 Valentim mt
168 G-5 Valentine
59 N-7 Valentino
62 C-4 Valenza
186 G-3 Valera
194 E-7 Valerio riv.
61 N-9 Valette
66 C-2 Vålga
173 H-2 Valhalla
54 F-2 Valhermeil (Le)
185 K-8 Valiente pen.
210 G-3 Valif isl.
64 B-3 Valjevo
66 C-2 Valka
49 J-8 Valkeakoski
56 G-2 Valkenburg
56 G-9 Valkenswaard
104 D-9 Valker Baai riv.
60 C-3 Valladolid (Spain)
179 N-5 Valladolid (Mexico)
54 G-1 Vallangoujard

63 J-1 Vallarsa riv.
63 K-2 Vallarsa Raossi
184 F-4 Valle reg.
178 B-4 Valle de Banderas
189 J-7 Valle de la Pascua
187 K-3 Valle de la Pascua
178 E-4 Valle de Santiago
186 C-7 Valle del Cauca reg.
174 G-7 Valle del Rosario
198 C-3 Valle Fértil mt
191 H-5 Valle Grande
178 G-1 Valle Hermoso
62 B-2 Valle Mosso
186 E-2 Valledupar
164 F-7 Vallée-Jonction
167 H-2 Vallejo
198 A-2 Vallenar
47 E-6 Valletta
169 H-2 Valley City
166 F-4 Valley Falls
172 D-6 Valley Forge
173 H-3 Valley Stream
172 A-3 Valley View
164 E-8 Valleyfield
162 G-3 Valleyview
49 H-6 Vallgrund isl.
63 K-2 Valli del Pasúbio
198 A-6 Vallimanca riv.
63 L-9 Vallombrosa
58 B-5 Vallorbe
60 F-5 Valls
105 J-5 Vals riv.
210 C-7 Vals cap.
58 E-6 Valsainte
104 C-9 Valsbaai bay
59 P-6 Valser val.
48 G-4 Valsjön
63 L-1 Valstagna
48 E-8 Valtavaara mt
62 A-1 Valtournanche
67 J-6 Valujki
78 A-9 Valverde (Spain)
181 K-6 Valverde (République Dominicaine)
60 B-7 Valverde del Camino
63 H-2 Valvestino lake
161 N-6 Vamba lake
106 D-9 Vamizi isl.
49 J-7 Vammala
194 E-4 Vamos Ver
142 C-7 Vamsadhāra riv.
72 D-5 Van lake
72 E-5 Van
192 D-4 Van Asch van Wijck mt
192 E-3 Van Blommestein lake
176 E-1 Van Buren
209 M-4 Van Der Bosch cap.
209 L-9 Van Diemen cap.
214 E-6 Van Diemen cap.
145 M-8 Van Fong bay
172 G-5 Van Hiseville
175 H-4 Van Horn
145 M-8 Van Ninh
210 D-2 Van Rees mt
170 F-7 Van Wert
145 J-2 Van Yên
224 E-6 Vanavana isl.
127 L-3 Vanč
125 L-9 Vancin riv.
168 B-8 Vancorum
162 C-6 Vancouver
156 B-2 Vancouver isl.
158 E-3 Vancouver cap.
160 C-3 Vancouver
162 B-5 Vancouver Island mt
162 A-5 Vancouver Island pen.
227 N-6 Vanda
170 C-8 Vandalia
105 J-4 Vanderbijlpark
162 D-3 Vanderhoot
214 C-5 Vanderlin isl.
69 M-1 Vandmtor lake
51 K-1 Vänern lake
51 K-2 Vänesborg
109 M-5 Vangaindrano
53 M-5 Vange
147 L-4 Vanguard (Wanantan) rf
58 E-7 Vanil Noir mt
210 F-2 Vanimo
125 M-3 Vanino
140 G-4 Vānīvilās Sāgara lake
141 H-6 Vāniyambādi
48 C-5 Vanna isl.
48 G-6 Vännäs
50 C-8 Vannes

104 D-7 Vanrhynsdorp
214 F-6 Vanrook
49 K-4 Vansbro
213 K-2 Vansittart *bay*
66 A-3 V'anta *riv.*
224 B-5 Vanua Levu *isl.*
205 G-3 Vanuatu *state*
55 H-6 Vanves
104 E-6 Vanwyksvlei
69 L-1 Vanzetur
62 B-1 Vanzone
215 N-5 Vao
62 F-2 Vaprio d'Adda
61 K-3 Var *riv.*
62 F-8 Vara *riv.*
61 P-2 Varazdin
140 F-4 Varada *riv.*
89 L-3 Varalé
62 C-2 Varallo Pombia
62 B-1 Varallo Sésia
142 C-2 Vārānasi (Benares)
112 A-2 Varanger *isl.*
48 C-8 Varangerfd. *fj.*
48 C-8 Varangerhalvoya *pen.*
62 G-6 Varano de Melegari
62 C-7 Varazze
51 K-3 Varberg
127 H-6 Vardak *reg.*
64 D-5 Vardar *riv.*
51 H-3 Varde
48 C-8 Vardø
87 H-1 Varela *pte*
58 G-8 Varen
66 C-4 Varèna
62 E-1 Varenna
55 K-7 Varenne (La)
55 L-8 Varennes-Jarcy
62 D-1 Varese *lake*
62 D-2 Varese *reg.*
62 D-1 Varese
62 F-7 Varese Ligure
125 K-8 Varfolomejevka
51 K-2 Vargarda
193 M-9 Vargem Grande
197 J-5 Varginha
195 L-5 Varguem *riv.*
56 G-5 Varik
191 M-1 Varillas
196 G-2 Varjão
126 G-5 Varkhān *riv.*
51 K-1 Värmland *reg.*
63 P-1 Varmo
64 F-3 Varna
51 L-3 Värnamo
69 H-9 Varnavino
55 P-3 Varreddes
62 F-6 Varsi
57 M-4 Varsseveld
72 D-4 Varto
127 L-2 Varuch
196 D-9 Várzea *riv.*
199 M-1 Várzea *riv.*
195 L-3 Varzea Alegre
197 E-2 Várzea da Palma
197 K-1 Varzelândia
62 E-5 Varzi
68 C-2 Varzino
59 K-9 Varzo
68 C-4 Varzuga *riv.*
68 G-4 Vašca *riv.*
60 E-3 Vascongadas *reg.*
126 E-6 Vāshīr
66 E-6 Vasilevići
67 H-8 Vasiljevka
66 E-7 Vasil'kov
67 H-8 Vasil'kovka
64 F-1 Vaslui
91 K-5 Vassako *riv.*
48 E-5 Vastenjaure *lake*
51 L-1 Västeras
48 G-5 Västerbotten *reg.*
49 J-4 Västerdalalven *riv.*
49 H-5 Västernorrland *reg.*
51 M-2 Västervik
51 L-1 Västmanland *reg.*
61 N-5 Vasto
47 E-5 Vatican *state*
61 M-5 Vatican City
61 P-7 Vaticano *cap.*
48 C-3 Vatnajökull *glac.*
48 A-1 Vatneyri (Patreksfjördur)
108 G-6 Vatoloha *mt*
109 J-6 Vatomandry
69 J-8 V'atskij uval *mt*
51 L-2 Vättern *lake*
54 A-9 Vaubrun
54 C-4 Vaucouleurs *riv.*
55 P-5 Vaucourtois
58 D-6 Vauderens
170 A-1 Vaugh
213 N-8 Vaughan Springs
175 J-1 Vaughn
54 G-9 Vaugrigneuse
54 G-7 Vauhallan
55 L-5 Vaujours
58 B-5 Vaulion *mt*
58 B-5 Vaulion
58 D-6 Vaulruz
54 C-1 Vaumion
188 A-8 Vaupés *riv.*
188 A-8 Vaupes *reg.*
54 F-3 Vauréal
215 P-4 Vauvilliers *isl.*
58 A-4 Vaux
54 E-8 Vaux de Cernay (Les) *site*
54 E-3 Vaux-sur-Seine
108 G-7 Vavatenina
224 B-5 Vavau *islds*
89 M-1 Vavoua
141 L-7 Vavuniya
51 L-3 Växjö
195 L-6 Vaza-Barris *riv.*
197 H-2 Vazante
125 K-6 V'azemskij
67 J-1 V'azniki
109 H-5 Vazobe *mt*
63 N-1 Vazzola
63 H-9 Vecchiano
64 E-3 Vedea *riv.*
63 M-2 Vedelago
198 G-6 Vedia
90 F-3 Vedseram *riv.*
57 H-3 Veenendaal
175 K-1 Vega
48 F-3 Vega *isl.*
49 K-2 Veggli
57 H-6 Veghel
163 H-5 Vegreville
58 A-8 Veigy
192 G-8 Veiros
51 J-3 Vejle
184 G-6 Velas *cap.*
199 L-6 Velasquez
67 H-9 Vel.Beloz'orka
104 C-8 Velddrif
57 K-8 Velden
57 L-2 Veldhoek
56 G-8 Veldhoven
57 M-9 Veldwezelt
61 N-3 Velebit *mt*
186 E-5 Vélez
66 D-2 Velikaia *riv.*
125 M-7 Velikaja Kema
68 G-6 Velikiy Ustyug
66 E-3 Velikiye Luki
64 E-4 Veliko Târnovo
140 G-7 Velikonda *mt*
68 G-1 Velikovisočnoje
189 L-8 Velille *riv.*
86 F-3 Velingara
64 D-4 Velingrad
66 E-3 Veliž
54 G-7 Vélizy-Villacoublay
63 J-9 Vellano
141 J-6 Vellār *riv.*
141 H-7 Vellore
63 J-2 Velo Veronese
57 J-4 Velp
68 F-7 Vel'sk
57 L-3 Velswijk
57 J-7 Veltum
57 H-9 Veluwe *lake*
168 G-1 Velva
55 L-2 Vémars
141 K-4 Vembanāo *lake*
214 F-7 Vena Park
185 H-5 Venado *isl.*
198 F-6 Venado Tuerto
187 P-5 Venamo *riv.*
187 N-6 Venamo *mt*
62 A-4 Venaria
125 J-6 Vencelevo
196 F-7 Venceslau Braz
105 L-1 Venda *reg.*
63 L-3 Venda *hill*
50 E-9 Vendôme
63 M-3 Veneta *lag.*
61 M-2 Venetia *reg.*
63 L-2 Venetia *reg.*
195 L-4 Veneza
63 N-2 Venezia *reg.*
183 D-2 Venezuela *state*
156 G-5 Venezuela *gulf*
121 M-1 Vengerovo
140 E-3 Vengurla
57 H-7 Venhorst
158 C-7 Veniaminof *mt*
61 M-2 Venice
63 N-3 Venice
63 N-3 Venice *gulf*
140 D-8 Venkatāpuram
57 K-8 Venlo
48 F-3 Vennesund
51 P-2 Venta *riv.*
174 E-9 Ventana *pte*
200 B-8 Ventana *mt*
105 J-5 Ventersburg
105 J-4 Ventersdorp
105 H-7 Venterstad
62 A-9 Ventimiglia
200 E-3 Ventisquero
52 G-9 Ventnor (UK)
172 F-8 Ventnor (USA)
61 M-6 Ventotène *isl.*
61 J-3 Ventoux *mt*
66 A-2 Ventspils (Windaw)
187 K-7 Ventuari *riv.*
167 M-2 Ventura
220 G-6 Venus *bay*
55 M-2 Ver-sur-Laurette
196 A-8 Verá *lake*
200 F-6 Vera *bay*
198 G-3 Vera (Argentina)
60 D-7 Vera (Spain)
196 F-5 Vera Cruz
184 E-3 Veracruz
179 H-5 Veracruz *reg.*
179 H-6 Veracruz Llave
185 K-8 Veraguas *reg.*
62 B-4 Veralengo
140 A-1 Verāval
62 C-1 Verbania
58 E-9 Verbier
58 B-2 Vercel-Villedieu-le-Camp
62 B-2 Vercelli *reg.*
62 C-3 Vercelli
61 K-2 Vercelli
68 F-4 Verch. Bereznickoje
69 N-7 Verch. Kigi
69 N-6 Verch. Pyshma
69 N-6 Verch. Tagil
69 M-5 Verch. Tura
69 P-6 Verch. Ufalej
69 K-9 Verch. Ulson
58 C-9 Verchaix
67 N-6 Verch.Baskunčak
66 D-3 Verchenedvinsk
123 M-3 Verchn'aja Angara *riv.*
121 M-3 Verchn'aja Cumanka
121 N-2 Verchn'aja Irmen'
123 M-3 Verchn'aja Zaimka
123 M-3 Verchneangarskij *mt*
121 M-5 Verchneber'ozovskij
66 G-8 Verchnedneprovsk
69 K-6 Verchnekamskaja Vozv. *mt*
122 E-5 Verchneusinskoje
123 K-4 Vercholensk
69 M-5 Verchoturje
122 G-1 Verchoturovo
66 G-8 Vérchovceco
67 H-4 Verchovje
121 N-5 Verchubinka
48 G-3 Verdalsøra
190 E-8 Verde *riv.*
200 C-8 Verde *pen.*
196 E-2 Verde (Brazil) *riv.*
191 L-8 Verde (Paraguay) *riv.*
167 M-7 Verde (USA) *riv.*
174 E-1 Verde (USA) *riv.*
195 H-9 Verde Pequeno *riv.*
62 F-2 Verdello
169 H-9 Verdigris *riv.*
196 E-2 Verdinho *mt*
61 J-3 Verdon *riv.*
60 F-1 Verdon-sur-Mer (Le)
56 A-9 Verdronken Land van Saeftinge *lag.*
56 A-8 Verdronken Land van Zuid-Beveland *lag.*
153 J-1 Verdrup *islds*
164 E-8 Verdun
50 G-8 Verdun-sur-Marne
174 F-8 Verdura
197 M-1 Vereda do Paraiso
105 J-4 Vereeniging
164 C-7 Vérendrye *na.p.*
69 L-7 Vereshchagino
87 K-3 Verga *cap.*
199 L-5 Vergara
63 K-7 Vergato
59 M-9 Vergeletto
218 G-2 Vergemont *riv.*
218 G-2 Vergemont
63 M-9 Verghereto
62 D-2 Vergiate
60 B-3 Verin
97 K-8 Verissimo
69 P-8 Verkhneural'sk
113 K-3 Verkhoyansk *rge*
68 F-5 Verkola
58 F-8 Vermala
195 H-5 Vermelha *mt*
87 N-2 Vermelharia *pte*
194 D-3 Vermelho *riv.*
194 F-4 Vermelhos
170 B-2 Vermillon *lake*
163 J-6 Vermillon (Canada)
169 H-5 Vermillon (USA)
170 B-1 Vermillon Bay
163 J-2 Vermillon
157 G-3 Vermont *state*
164 F-9 Vermont *state*
168 B-6 Vernal
62 F-5 Vernasca
58 D-8 Vernaz *pass*
62 F-8 Vernazza
55 N-9 Verneuil-l'Etang
54 E-4 Verneuil-sur-Seine
104 E-6 Verneukpan *lake*
58 A-2 Vernierfontaine
63 K-8 Vernio
216 E-1 Vernon *mt*
162 E-6 Vernon (Canada)
54 A-2 Vernon (France)
175 M-2 Vernon (USA)
54 A-2 Vernonnet
54 E-4 Vernouillet
177 L-7 Vero Beach
64 D-5 Veroia
62 G-3 Verolanuova
63 J-3 Verona *reg.*
61 M-2 Verona
63 J-3 Verona (Vérone)
199 J-7 Verónica
173 H-1 Verplanck
56 A-9 Verrebroek
57 H-7 Verreheide
62 A-2 Verrés
181 J-6 Verrettes
54 E-7 Verrière (La)
58 B-4 Verrières (Les)
55 H-7 Verrières-le-Buisson
54 F-6 Versailles
50 E-8 Versailles (France)
170 F-8 Versailles (USA)
190 D-6 Versalles
59 M-9 Verscio
55 N-1 Versigny
123 P-5 Veršino-Darasunskij
124 B-5 Veršino-Sachtaminskij
58 A-8 Versoix *riv.*
58 A-8 Versoix
54 C-4 Vert
165 M-2 Verte *bay*
194 C-6 Vertentes *riv.*
180 E-5 Vertientes
62 F-1 Vertova
63 N-8 Verucchio
50 G-7 Verviers
50 F-7 Vervins
52 E-8 Verwood
59 M-8 Verzasca *val.*
66 F-9 Vesélinovo
121 M-2 Veselovskoje
58 A-8 Vésenaz
67 K-6 Vešenskaja
54 B-7 Vesgre *riv.*
54 G-5 Vésinet (Le)
189 H-3 Vesique
68 E-9 Vesjegonsk
67 L-2 Veškajma
125 J-2 Ves'olaja Gorka
124 D-2 Ves'olyj
121 M-4 Ves'olyj Jar
61 K-1 Vesoul
62 C-3 Vespolate
56 F-8 Vessem
51 H-1 Vest Agder *reg.*
48 D-4 Vestågøy *isl.*
196 E-4 Véstea
63 K-2 Vestenanuova
48 D-4 Vesteralen *islds*
48 E-4 Vestfjorden *strt.*
51 J-1 Vestfold *reg.*
48 D-1 Vestmanhavn
48 C-1 Vestmannaeyjar
48 C-1 Vestmannaeyjar *islds*
63 H-2 Vestone
61 N-6 Vesuvio *vol.*
64 A-1 Veszprem
105 H-5 Vet *riv.*
159 L-9 Veta *mt*
54 C-3 Vétheuil
51 L-2 Vetlanda
69 H-9 Vetluga
58 F-9 Vétroz
63 H-7 Vetto
94 F-5 Veveno'Khwar *riv.*
58 D-7 Vevey
58 F-9 Vex
54 D-1 Vexin *reg.*
58 A-9 Veyrier
58 D-7 Veytaux
60 G-2 Vézère *riv.*
65 K-4 Vezirköprü
62 F-8 Vezzano Ligure
61 P-4 Viski *cap.*
87 M-7 Via *riv.*
190 G-2 Viacha
125 M-1 Viachtu
63 H-5 Viadana (Italy)
98 B-7 Viadana (Zaïre)
198 F-6 Viamonte
198 G-7 Viamonte
193 M-9 Viana
60 A-3 Viana do Castelo
56 E-4 Vianen
63 H-6 Viano
196 G-2 Vianópolis
62 G-9 Viareggio
62 C-5 Viarigi
55 J-2 Viarmes
63 K-9 Vicchio
190 F-8 Vicente *mt*
178 C-2 Vicente Guerrero
61 M-2 Vicenza
63 K-2 Vicenza *reg.*
63 L-2 Vicenza (Vicence)
60 G-4 Vich
187 H-6 Vichada *reg.*
187 J-6 Vichada *riv.*
199 L-4 Vichadero
123 J-3 Vichorevka
198 A-7 Vichuquén
61 H-1 Vichy
176 E-4 Vicksburg
62 A-7 Vicoforte
63 H-9 Vicopisano
197 L-5 Vicosa (Brazil)
195 N-5 Viçosa (Brazil)
193 P-9 Vicosa do Ceara
54 D-6 Vicq
55 L-1 Victoire
188 D-9 Victoiria de Rio Branco
210 F-4 Victor Emmanuel *mt*
220 D-3 Victor Harbour
153 P-1 Victoria *fj.*
118 A-7 Victoria
143 K-6 Victoria *mt*
211 K-7 Victoria (Australia) *mt*
220 F-1 Victoria (Australia) *lake*
220 G-5 Victoria (Australia) *reg.*
213 N-3 Victoria (Australia) *riv.*
184 E-1 Victoria (Belize) *mt*
161 N-2 Victoria (Canada) *isl.*
162 B-5 Victoria (Canada) *mt*
171 J-2 Victoria (Canada) *lake*
200 B-2 Victoria (Chile)
200 G-2 Victoria (Chile) *isl.*
76 E-6 Victoria (Falls)
204 C-4 Victoria (Great) *dés*
217 M-3 Victoria (Great) *dés*
90 C-8 Victoria (Limbé)
100 E-3 Victoria (Uganda) *lake*
149 H-7 Victoria (Philippines) *mt*
107 K-1 Victoria (Rhodesie) *reg.*
76 F-5 Victoria (Tanzania) *lake*
175 N-6 Victoria (USA)
135 J-9 Victoria (Xianggang)
163 P-9 Victoria Beach
178 C-2 Victoria de Durango
180 F-5 Victoria de las Tunas
215 J-9 Victoria Downs
103 K-6 Victoria Falls
103 K-6 Victoria Falls
227 N-6 Victoria Land
213 N-4 Victoria River Downs
104 F-7 Victoria West
164 F-7 Victoriaville
200 A-6 Victorica
187 J-8 Victorino
167 M-4 Victorville
67 H-1 Vičuga
198 A-3 Vicuña
198 E-6 Vicuña Mackenna
174 C-1 Vidal
201 M-2 Vidal Gormaz *isl.*
201 J-3 Videau *pen.*
196 E-9 Videira
48 D-2 Viderø *islds*
123 J-2 Vidim
64 D-3 Vidin
139 M-8 Vidisha
68 C-8 Vidlica
63 M-1 Vidor
66 C-2 Vidzemes Augst. *mt*
201 K-3 Viedma *lake*
200 D-7 Viedma
54 D-9 Vieille-Eglise-en-Yvelines
200 A-1 Vieja *pte*
188 E-2 Viejo *mt*
181 L-6 Viejo Francés *cap.*
51 M-9 Vienna
47 E-5 Vienna
176 F-1 Vienna (USA)
61 J-2 Vienne
60 G-1 Vienne *riv.*
54 C-2 Vienne-en-Arthies
145 H-4 Vientiane
118 F-5 Vientiane
200 A-3 Viento *mt*
181 K-1 Vieques
181 K-1 Vieques *isl.*
105 H-4 Vierfontein
57 J-1 Vierhouten
57 K-7 Vierlingsbeek
56 A-4 Vierpolders
59 L-3 Vierwald Statter *lake*
61 H-1 Vierzon
178 D-1 Viesca
61 P-5 Vieste
118 F-5 Vietnam *state*
181 N-8 Vieux Fort
58 B-5 Vieux-les-Hôpitaux
148 B-6 Vigan
61 H-3 Vigan (Le)
63 L-5 Vigarano Mainarda
63 J-3 Vigásio
62 D-3 Vigevano
59 L-9 Vigezzo *val.*
193 J-7 Vigia
201 J-6 Vigia *cap.*
179 N-5 Vigia Chico
62 C-4 Vignale Monferrato
62 E-3 Vignate
55 N-4 Vignely
54 A-7 Vignes (Les)
55 J-8 Vigneux-sur-Seine
63 J-7 Vignola
54 E-2 Vigny
60 B-3 Vigo
63 K-1 Vigolo Vattaro
62 D-5 Viguzzolo
139 K-2 Vihāri
48 G-5 Vihelmina
49 H-9 Viinijarvi
140 E-2 Vijayadurg
140 F-8 Vijayawāda
56 D-1 Vijfhuizen
57 N-9 Vijlen
49 J-1 Vik
163 H-6 Viking
48 G-3 Vikna *isl.*
205 G-3 Vila
107 H-6 Vila da Maganja
103 P-7 Vila de Manica
107 N-2 Vila do Chibuto
107 J-3 Vila do Dondo
106 F-3 Vila Gamilo
107 J-3 Vila Machado
102 C-2 Vila Nova
60 A-4 Vila Nova de Gaia
60 B-3 Vila Pouca de Aquiar
60 B-4 Vila Real
209 H-7 Vila Salazar
106 F-2 Vila Vasco da Gama
103 P-4 Vila Vasco da Gama
192 G-4 Vila Velha
197 M-5 Vila Velha (Espirito Santo)
50 C-8 Vilaine *riv.*
107 L-4 Vilanculos
181 K-3 Vilavila
55 P-8 Vilbert
189 L-7 Vilcabamba *site*
189 K-7 Vilcabamba *mt*
189 L-8 Vilcanota *mt*
189 M-8 Vilcanota *riv.*
69 H-6 Viled' *riv.*
66 C-4 Vilejka
190 D-8 Vilhena
66 C-4 Vilija *riv.*
66 B-1 Viljandi
105 J-4 Viljoenskroon
112 F-2 Vil'kickogo *isl.*
113 J-2 Vilkitskogo *strt.*
64 G-2 Vilkovo
178 B-2 Villa Unión
174 G-4 Villa Ahumada
198 D-1 Villa Alberdi
198 E-4 Villa Allende
198 G-1 Villa Angela
191 P-8 Villa Angela
198 E-2 Villa Atimisqui
198 C-7 Villa Atuel
63 K-4 Villa Bartolomea
190 C-4 Villa Bella
198 G-1 Villa Berthet
191 P-8 Villa Berthet
198 C-3 Villa Bustos
198 G-6 Villa Cañás
198 E-4 Villa Carlos Paz
198 C-3 Villa Castelli
198 C-4 Villa Colón
198 G-5 Villa Constitución
175 H-7 Villa Coronado
198 E-4 Villa Cura Brochero
62 F-2 Villa d'Almè
187 J-3 Villa de Cura
198 E-3 Villa de María
198 F-4 Villa del Rosario
198 C-4 Villa del Salvador
198 G-5 Villa Diego
198 D-2 Villa el Alto
63 L-4 Villa Estense
198 E-1 Villa Figueroa
179 K-8 Villa Flores
196 B-8 Villa Florida
175 K-7 Villa Frontera
198 E-4 Villa Gal. Mitre
198 D-5 Villa General Roca
199 H-2 Villa Guillermina
196 A-7 Villa Hayes
178 E-3 Villa Hidalgo
198 E-7 Villa Huidobro

198 C-5 Villa Kraus
63 J-1 Villa Lagarina
198 F-5 Villa María
199 H-4 Villa María Grande
198 D-2 Villa Mazán
198 G-2 Villa Minetti
191 K-6 Villa Montes
190 C-4 Villa Murtinho
198 C-5 Villa Nueva
199 H-2 Villa Ocampo (Argentina)
175 H-7 Villa Ocampo (Mexico)
198 E-3 Villa Ojo de Agua
196 B-8 Villa Pastoreo
198 G-5 Villa Ramírez
200 C-5 Villa Regina
198 C-4 Villa San Isidro
198 E-2 Villa San Martín
198 C-5 Villa Santa Rosa
198 E-3 Villa Tulumba
198 C-3 Villa Unión (Argentina)
198 F-3 Villa Unión (Argentina)
175 L-6 Villa Unión (Mexico)
198 E-6 Villa Valeria
61 N-2 Villach
62 B-4 Villadeati
62 A-6 Villafalletto
62 B-5 Villafranca d'Asti
60 C-3 Villafranca del Berzio
63 J-3 Villafranca di Verona
62 G-7 Villafranca in Lunigiana
63 L-3 Villafranca Padovana
62 A-5 Villafranca Piemonte
63 L-3 Villaga
199 H-4 Villaguay
60 D-6 Villahermosa (Spain)
179 K-7 Villahermosa (Mexico)
55 J-2 Villaines-sous-Bois
60 B-2 Villalba
175 L-8 Villaldama
60 C-4 Villalpando
62 D-5 Villalvernia
162 A-9 Villamette riv.
63 H-7 Villaminozzo
188 C-4 Villano riv.
62 B-8 Villanova d'Albenga
62 B-5 Villanova d'Asti
63 M-5 Villanova March
62 A-7 Villanova Mondovi
62 C-4 Villanova Monferrato
62 A-6 Villanova Solaro
62 E-4 Villanterio
178 D-3 Villanueva
60 G-5 Villanueva y Geltrú
63 H-2 Villanuova sul Clisi
54 C-2 Villarceaux
58 B-9 Villard
60 F-6 Villareal
196 B-8 Villarica
200 D-6 Villarino pte
55 M-9 Villaroche
54 F-7 Villaroy
200 C-2 Villarrica
200 C-2 Villarrica lake
60 D-6 Villarrobledo
58 E-8 Villars
172 E-9 Villas
62 A-5 Villastellone
63 K-2 Villaverla
186 E-7 Villavicencio
58 D-5 Villaz-Saint-Pierre
54 G-6 Ville-d'Avray
55 H-9 Ville-du-Bois (La)
58 B-3 Ville-du-Pont
54 A-6 Ville-l'Evêque (La)
164 B-7 Ville-Marie
176 D-5 Ville Platte
55 H-8 Villebon-sur-Yvette
55 H-9 Villebouzin
55 K-8 Villecresnes
60 G-3 Villefranche-de-Rouergue
61 J-2 Villefranche-sur-Saône
54 A-3 Villegats
55 J-7 Villejuif
55 H-8 Villejust
60 E-6 Villena
54 C-2 Villeneuve (France)
54 D-4 Villeneuve (La) (France)
54 B-9 Villeneuve (La) (France)
54 D-9 Villeneuve (La) (France)
58 D-7 Villeneuve (Switzerland)
54 A-3 Villeneuve-en-Chevrie (La)
55 N-6 Villeneuve-le-Comte
55 N-6 Villeneuve-Saint-Denis
54 E-2 Villeneuve-Saint-Martin (La)

55 L-3 Villeneuve-sous-Dammartin
55 K-7 Villeneuve-St-Georges
60 G-2 Villeneuve-sur-Lot
54 E-4 Villennes-sur-Seine
55 P-4 Villenoy
55 L-4 Villeparisis
55 K-4 Villepinte
54 F-6 Villepreux
54 G-7 Villeras
55 L-3 Villeron
55 N-4 Villeroy
54 C-2 Villers-en-Arthies
55 P-1 Villers-Saint-Genest
54 C-5 Villette
58 E-6 Villette (La)
61 J-2 Villeurbanne
55 M-5 Villevaudé
54 A-3 Villez
54 G-8 Villeziers
198 C-4 Villicún mt
105 K-4 Villiers
55 H-3 Villiers-Adam
54 A-4 Villiers-en-Désoeuvre
54 G-8 Villiers-le-Bâcle
55 J-3 Villiers-le-Bel
54 C-6 Villiers-le-Mahieu
54 A-9 Villiers-le-Mornier
55 J-2 Villiers-le-Sec
54 D-6 Villiers-Saint-Frédéric
55 L-6 Villiers-sur-Marne
55 P-6 Villiers-sur-Marne
55 H-9 Villiers-sur-Orge
104 D-9 Villiersdorp
51 H-9 Villingen im Sch.
178 D-6 Villita dam.
59 K-1 Villmergen
141 J-7 Villupuram
62 G-1 Vilminore di Scalve
66 C-4 Vilnius
189 N-8 Vilor riv.
57 N-9 Vilt
113 J-3 Vilyuyskoye plat.
62 E-2 Vimercate
51 L-2 Vimmerby
90 G-5 Vina riv.
198 A-6 Viña del Mar
55 M-3 Vinantes
60 F-5 Vinaroz
55 J-6 Vincennes
170 D-9 Vincennes (USA)
172 F-6 Vincentown
188 C-2 Vinces
188 C-2 Vinces riv.
198 C-3 Vinchina
198 C-2 Vinchina riv.
63 J-9 Vinci
54 F-3 Vincourt
55 P-2 Vincy-Manoeuvre
48 G-6 Vindeln
116 C-4 Vindhya rge
172 E-8 Vineland (USA)
171 L-7 Vineland (USA)
145 K-4 Vinh
145 L-5 Vinh Linh
147 H-2 Vinh Long
145 K-2 Vinh Yên
175 P-1 Vinita
49 H-2 Vinjeøra
56 G-6 Vinkel
56 E-2 Vinkeveen
56 E-2 Vinkeveen en Waverveen reg.
64 B-2 Vinkovci
66 E-8 Vinnitsa
66 B-9 Vinogradov
62 A-5 Vinovo
227 M-3 Vinson mt
49 J-2 Vinstra
170 B-6 Vinton
140 F-7 Vinukonda
172 C-9 Viola
58 D-8 Vionnaz
54 E-2 Viosne riv.
213 L-3 Viotti mt
106 D-3 Vipya mt
209 H-7 Viqueque
59 N-9 Vira
59 N-9 Vira-Gambarogno
148 E-3 Virac
139 H-8 Viramgām
68 C-6 Virandozero
65 N-6 Viranşehir
196 B-9 Virasoro
163 M-9 Virden
50 D-8 Vire
191 L-1 Vireira mt
197 L-2 Virgem da Lapa
201 M-6 Virgenes (Argentina) cap.
174 D-6 Virgenes (USA) cap.
63 J-4 Virgilio
156 H-5 Virgin islds
167 L-6 Virgin riv.
181 L-1 Virgin (UK) islds
181 L-1 Virgin (USA) islds

181 L-1 Virgin Gorda isl.
157 G-3 Virginia state
177 L-1 Virginia state
170 C-8 Virginia (USA)
170 B-2 Virginia (USA)
157 G-3 Virginia (West) state
171 H-8 Virginia (West) state
171 K-9 Virginia Beach
168 A-2 Virginia City
197 L-3 Virginópolis
197 L-3 Virgolândia
48 E-5 Virihaure lake
145 L-7 Virôchey
54 G-7 Viroflay
170 C-5 Viroqua
64 A-2 Virovitica
49 H-7 Virrat
189 H-3 Virú
189 H-3 Virú riv.
141 K-5 Virudunagar
100 B-3 Virunga na.p.
55 J-8 Viry-Chatillon
61 P-4 Vis isl.
104 C-4 Vis riv.
167 K-3 Visalia
63 H-3 Visano
140 A-1 Visavadar
148 F-4 Visayan sea
49 M-6 Visby
197 L-5 Visconde do Rio Branco
112 F-2 Vise isl.
64 B-3 Višegrad
69 L-4 Višera riv.
63 N-8 Viserba
193 L-8 Viseu
60 B-4 Viseu (Portugal)
66 C-9 Viseu-de-Sus
142 B-8 Vishakhapatnam
69 L-2 Visim riv.
69 M-6 Visimo-Utkinsk
59 H-7 Visnagar
121 H-3 Višn'ovka
61 K-3 Viso mt
59 H-8 Visp
59 H-8 Visperterminen
58 G-9 Vissoie
174 A-1 Vista
196 B-3 Vista Alegre
66 A-7 Vistule riv.
55 P-8 Visy
66 E-3 Vitebsk
61 M-5 Viterbo
64 D-8 Víthion
224 B-5 Viti Levu isl.
211 K-5 Vitiaz strt.
191 K-4 Vitichi
60 B-4 Vitigudino
124 A-3 Vitim riv.
123 N-4 Vitimkan riv.
123 N-1 Vitimskij
123 P-4 Vitimskoje Ploskogorje plat.
196 A-3 Vitiones lake
197 M-5 Vitória (Brazil)
60 E-3 Vitoria (Spain)
197 M-1 Vitória da Conquista
193 M-9 Vitoria de Mearim
195 P-4 Vitória de sto Antão
50 D-8 Vitré
54 A-5 Vitre
50 F-8 Vitry-le-François
55 J-7 Vitry-sur-Seine
48 E-6 Vittangi
61 N-9 Vittória
63 M-1 Vittorio Veneto
211 M-4 Vitu islds
124 D-5 Vitulihe
59 L-3 Vitznau
58 B-9 Viuz-en-Sallaz
187 L-6 Vive riv.
60 B-2 Vivero
62 B-3 Viverone lake
105 K-1 Vivo
220 C-3 Vivonne bay
199 J-9 Vivoratá
49 H-5 Vivsta
69 L-3 Vižaj
69 E-3 Vižas
174 B-6 Vizcaíno mt
174 C-6 Vizcaíno dés
68 B-5 Vize
142 B-8 Vizianagaram
69 H-6 Vizinga
66 C-9 Vižnica
64 B-6 Vjosë riv.
121 P-2 Vjuny
46 D-4 Vlaanderen reg.
56 B-4 Vlaardingen
67 H-1 Vladimir
66 C-7 Vladimir-Volynskij
66 C-6 Vladimirec
123 H-4 Vladimirovka
125 N-2 Vladimirovo
124 F-1 Vladimirovskij

66 F-3 Vladimirskij-Tupik
133 N-1 Vladivostok
56 E-3 Vleuten
56 E-3 Vleuten de Meern reg.
57 H-8 Vlierden
56 B-3 Vliet cal.
56 F-6 Vlijmen
56 D-9 Vlimmeren
56 D-4 Vlist
57 P-7 Vlodrop
64 B-6 Vlorë
51 L-8 Vltava riv.
145 L-9 Vo Dat
63 H-2 Vobarno
62 D-6 Vobbia
69 H-8 Vochma
61 N-1 Vöcklabruck
68 D-7 Vodla riv.
68 D-7 Vodlozero lake
69 H-7 Vodolaga
66 G-8 Vody
57 N-9 Voerendaal
90 E-5 Vogel mt
62 D-5 Voghera
63 L-5 Voghiera
62 C-1 Vogogna
59 N-9 Vogorno mt
59 N-9 Vogorno
59 N-9 Vogorno lake
69 L-1 Vogulka riv.
69 L-4 Vogul'skij Kamen' mt
215 M-3 Voh
108 D-8 Vohimarina
109 M-3 Vohimena mt
109 L-5 Vohipeno
109 H-6 Vohitra riv.
101 K-5 Voi
101 J-5 Voi
87 L-7 Voinjama
61 J-2 Voiron
58 B-8 Voirons mt
55 P-5 Voisins
54 F-7 Voisins-le-Bretonneux
69 J-4 Voj-Vož
64 B-2 Vojvodina reg.
211 H-3 Vokeo isl.
90 F-5 Vokré mt
198 A-4 Volcán mt
184 G-6 Volcanica mt
117 K-4 Volcano foss
67 H-6 Volčansk
66 E-1 Volchon riv.
121 M-4 Volčicha
66 G-1 Volga riv.
66 G-1 Volga
112 C-4 Volga plat.
67 L-7 Volgodonsk
67 M-6 Volgograd
69 K-2 Volja riv.
57 H-6 Volkel
66 C-9 Volkhov
66 C-5 Volkovysk
105 K-5 Volksrust
121 J-1 Vol'noje
67 J-3 Voločajevka 2-ja
66 D-8 Voločisk
70 A-7 Volodarskij
68 F-8 Vologda
66 G-2 Volokolamsk
67 J-6 Volokonovka
76 D-6 Vólos
63 M-2 Volpago del Montello
62 A-4 Volpiano
133 N-1 Vol'po-Nadeždinskoje
67 M-3 Vol'sk
89 N-9 Volta riv.
89 L-5 Volta Blanche riv.
63 H-3 Volta Mantovana
89 L-4 Volta Noire riv.
89 J-3 Volta noire reg.
197 K-6 Volta Redonda
89 K-5 Volta Rouge riv.
62 D-6 Voltággio
62 D-7 Voltri
78 E-3 Volubilis site
66 C-7 Volynskaya reg.
69 K-9 Volzhsk
66 M-6 Volzhskiy
159 J-6 Von Frank mt
194 B-5 Von Martius riv.
109 L-4 Vondrozo
68 B-5 Von'ga riv.
64 B-2 Vónitsa
56 B-3 Voorburg
56 C-2 Voorhout
56 A-4 Voorne isl.
56 A-4 Voorns cal.
56 B-2 Voorschoten
57 K-2 Voorst
56 F-7 Voort
57 H-2 Voorthuizen
48 B-4 Vopnafjördur bay
48 B-4 Vopnafjördur
59 P-4 Vorab mt

59 N-3 Vorauen
57 L-3 Vorden
59 N-5 Vorderrhein
59 N-2 Vorderthal
51 K-4 Vordingborg
66 A-1 Vormsi isl.
123 J-2 Vorobjovo
67 K-4 Vorona riv.
123 N-1 Voroncovka
57 J-4 Voronež riv.
67 J-5 Voronezh
67 J-5 Voronežskij Zapov rés
68 B-3 Voronja riv.
68 D-3 Voronov cap.
67 K-7 Voroshilovgrad
67 K-1 Vorotynec
66 G-6 Vorožba
66 G-7 Vorskla riv.
67 J-1 Vorsma
57 H-6 Vorstenbosch
66 C-1 Vortsjarv riv.
57 K-6 Vortum Mullen
66 C-2 Võru
104 F-7 Vosburg
127 K-3 Vose
67 H-2 Voskresensk
49 J-1 Voss
56 D-9 Vosselaar
121 N-6 Vostochno-Kazakhstanskaya oblast reg.
68 C-2 Vostochnaja Lica
69 N-4 Vostočnyj
125 M-2 Vostočnyj mt
125 N-3 Vostočnyj
122 E-6 Vostočnyj Tannu-Ola mt
224 D-5 Vostok isl.
227 N-4 Vostok
69 L-7 Votkinsk
145 J-7 Vôtt Bantéay Srei site
196 F-4 Votuporanga
55 P-6 Voulangis
58 D-8 Vouvry
50 F-8 Vouziers
91 P-6 Vovodo riv.
69 H-4 Vožajel
68 C-8 Voze
68 F-8 Vožega
68 G-4 Vožgora
68 D-8 Voznesenje
121 H-2 Voznesenka
66 F-9 Voznesensk
70 G-5 Vozroždenija isl.
126 F-3 Vozv Karabil' mt
57 M-3 Vragender
64 C-4 Vranje
64 B-2 Vrbas
64 A-3 Vrbas riv.
51 L-8 Vrchovina mt
57 J-7 Vrede lake
105 K-5 Vrede
105 J-4 Vredefort
104 C-8 Vredenburg
104 C-7 Vredendal
192 B-2 Vreed en Hoop
56 E-2 Vreeland
56 E-6 Vrijhoeve Capelle
59 P-6 Vrin
57 M-9 Vroenhoven
64 C-2 Vršac
104 G-4 Vryburg
105 L-5 Vryheid
68 B-9 Vsevoložsk
58 E-6 Vuadens
58 E-6 Vuarrens
94 B-8 Vube
57 M-8 Vucht
58 B-6 Vufflens
56 F-7 Vught
58 A-3 Vuillafans
58 C-5 Vuissens
58 D-6 Vuisternens
58 B-5 Vuiteboeuf
64 B-2 Vukovar
162 G-7 Vulcan (Canada)
64 D-2 Vulcan (Romania)
61 N-7 Vulcano isl.
58 E-4 Vully mt
66 F-4 Vya
69 K-9 Vyatskiye Polyany
66 F-3 Vyaz'ma
49 J-9 Vyborg
69 H-5 Vyčegda riv.
123 K-6 Vydrino
68 D-6 Vyg riv.
68 C-6 Vygozero lake
67 J-2 Vym riv.
69 H-4 Vym riv.
68 B-9 Vyrica

67 K-9 Vyselki
66 F-1 Vyshniy Volochek
66 F-5 Vyškov
49 J-9 Vysock
125 L-6 Vysokaja mt
125 L-3 Vysokogornyj
66 G-2 Vysokovsk
68 D-8 Vytegra
125 N-4 Vzmorje

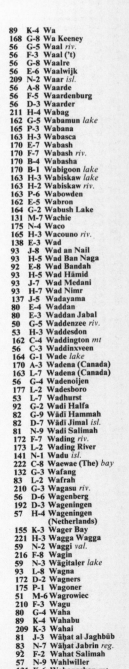

89 K-4 Wa
168 G-8 Wa Keeney
56 G-5 Waal riv.
56 F-3 Waal ('t)
56 G-8 Waalre
56 E-6 Waalwijk
209 N-2 Waar isl.
56 A-8 Waarde
56 F-5 Waardenburg
56 D-3 Waarder
211 H-4 Wabag
162 G-5 Wabamun lake
165 P-3 Wabana
163 H-3 Wabasca
170 E-7 Wabash
170 F-7 Wabash riv.
170 B-1 Wabigoon lake
163 H-3 Wabiskaw lake
163 H-2 Wabiskaw riv.
163 P-6 Wabowden
164 G-2 Wabush Lake
131 M-7 Wachie
175 N-4 Waco
165 H-3 Wacouno riv.
138 E-3 Wad
93 J-8 Wad an Nail
93 H-5 Wad Ban Naga
92 E-8 Wad Bandah
93 H-5 Wad Hāmid
93 J-7 Wad Medani
93 H-7 Wad Nimr
137 J-5 Wadayama
80 E-4 Waddan
80 E-3 Waddan Jabal
50 G-5 Waddenzee riv.
53 H-3 Waddesdon
162 C-4 Waddington mt
56 C-3 Waddinxveen
164 G-1 Wade lake
170 A-3 Wadena (Canada)
163 L-7 Wadena (Canada)
56 C-3 Wadenoijen
177 L-2 Wadesboro
53 L-7 Wadhurst
92 G-2 Wadi Halfa
82 G-9 Wādī Hammah
82 D-7 Wādī Jimal isl.
81 N-9 Wadi Salimah
172 F-7 Wading riv.
173 L-2 Wading River
141 N-1 Wadu isl.
222 C-8 Waewae (The) bay
132 G-3 Wafang
83 L-2 Wafrah
210 G-3 Wagasu riv.
56 D-6 Wagenberg
192 D-3 Wageningen
57 H-4 Wageningen (Netherlands)
155 K-3 Wager Bay
221 H-3 Wagga Wagga
59 N-2 Waggi val.
216 F-8 Wagin
59 N-3 Wägitaler lake
93 L-8 Wagna
172 D-2 Wagners
175 P-1 Wagoner
51 M-6 Wagrowiec
210 F-9 Wagu
80 G-4 Waha
89 K-4 Wahabu
209 K-3 Wahai
81 J-3 Wāḥat al Jaghbūb
83 N-7 Wāḥat Jabrin reg.
92 F-2 Wahat Salimah
57 N-9 Wahlwiller
131 K-6 Wahongshan mt
169 H-7 Waho
169 J-3 Wahpeton
222 G-7 Waiau

320 □ Wai-Wes


222 F-7 Waiau *riv.*
134 G-1 Waifangshan *mt*
209 L-1 Waigeo *isl.*
223 K-4 Waihi
208 C-8 Waikabubak
223 K-6 Waikaremoana *lake*
223 J-4 Waikato *riv.*
220 D-2 Waikerie
223 K-4 Wailkare *lake*
222 F-8 Waimakariri *riv.*
222 E-8 Waimate
140 A-8 Wainganga *riv.*
208 D-8 Waingapu
159 N-3 Wainwright (USA)
163 J-6 Wainwright (USA)
223 J-6 Waiouru
222 F-7 Waipara *mt*
223 J-6 Waipukurau
222 G-7 Wairau *riv.*
223 K-6 Wairoa
222 E-8 Waitaki *riv.*
223 N-9 Waitangi
223 H-5 Waitara
162 D-9 Waitsburg
223 J-4 Waiuku
208 E-7 Waiwerang
82 D-6 Wajh
97 N-3 Wājid
101 K-1 Wajir
99 K-2 Waka
137 J-5 Wakasa *bay*
163 L-7 Wakaw
137 K-5 Wakayama
136 F-7 Wakayanagi
172 B-7 Wakefield (USA)
173 P-1 Wakefield (USA)
192 C-2 Wakenaam *isl.*
53 M-3 Wakes Colne
136 A-5 Wakkanai
105 L-5 Wakkerstroom
215 L-2 Wala
126 E-5 Wāla *mt*
100 D-6 Wala *riv.*
51 L-7 Wałbrzych
221 L-1 Walcha
59 L-3 Walchwil *mt*
168 C-5 Walcott
51 M-5 Wałcz
59 N-1 Wald
168 C-6 Walden
59 H-1 Waldenburg
57 H-3 Walderveen
176 C-2 Waldron
59 P-1 Waldstatt
208 E-1 Waleabahi *isl.*
208 E-1 Waleakodi *isl.*
59 P-2 Walensee *lake*
59 P-2 Walenstadt *reg.*
50 C-5 Wales *reg.*
159 J-1 Wales
89 K-5 Walewale
219 J-7 Walgett
227 M-4 Walgreen Coast *reg.*
221 H-5 Walhalla
100 B-3 Walikale
161 N-1 Walker *bay*
170 A-2 Walker
167 J-4 Walker *lake*
180 E-1 Walker Cay *isl.*
53 K-3 Walkern
58 G-4 Walkringen
212 D-9 Wall *mt*
168 F-4 Wall
166 D-6 Walla-Walla
216 C-5 Wallabi *islds*
214 F-5 Wallaby *isl.*
164 C-8 Wallace
170 G-6 Wallaceburg
212 G-7 Wallal
220 C-2 Wallaroo Snowtown
50 D-4 Wallasey
161 N-2 Wallaston *pen.*
172 D-1 Wallenpaupack *lake*
52 G-5 Wallingford (UK)
173 L-1 Wallingford (USA)
224 B-5 Wallis *isl.*
172 G-1 Wallkill *riv.*
219 L-4 Walloon
166 D-6 Wallowa *mt*
53 P-6 Walmer
161 N-7 Walmsley *lake*
172 C-3 Walnutport
215 P-6 Walpole *isl.*
53 P-1 Walpole
50 D-5 Walsall
57 J-8 Walsberg
168 D-9 Walsenburg
215 H-6 Walsh *riv.*
215 H-6 Walsh
172 D-2 Walter *rés*
177 H-4 Walter F. George *lake*
177 L-4 Walterboro
175 M-2 Walters
53 K-4 Waltham Abbey
53 K-4 Waltham Cross
53 J-6 Walton
53 P-3 Walton on The Naze
76 C-7 Walvis *foss*
102 B-9 Walvis *bay*
102 B-9 Walvis Bay
104 A-1 Walvisbaai *bay*
94 A-7 Wamani
98 G-6 Wamba *riv.*
100 A-1 Wamba
211 N-8 Wamea *isl.*
56 G-4 Wamel
101 J-7 Wami *riv.*
185 H-3 Wampusirpi
210 D-6 Wan
125 P-7 Wan *bay*
133 M-8 Wan *isl.*
143 M-7 Wān-Yin
127 J-7 Wāna
218 G-7 Wanaaring
222 D-8 Wanaka *lake*
172 C-3 Wanamakers
164 B-8 Wanapitei *lake*
172 G-2 Wanaque *rés*
172 G-2 Wanaque
196 C-8 Wanda
125 K-6 Wandashan *mt*
153 S-1 Wandel *sea*
133 M-8 Wando (South Korea)
219 L-5 Wandoan
144 F-4 Wang *riv.*
144 F-3 Wang Nua
144 G-5 Wang Saphung
90 D-6 Wanga *mt*
220 G-3 Wanganella
223 J-6 Wanganui
223 J-6 Wanganui *riv.*
221 H-4 Wangaratta
220 B-2 Wangary
134 D-2 Wangcang
142 G-2 Wangdu
59 H-1 Wangen (Switzerland)
58 G-2 Wangen (Switzerland)
58 F-4 Wangen (Switzerland)
208 D-8 Wanggameti *mt*
101 L-4 Wangi
208 F-4 Wangiwangi *isl.*
124 F-8 Wangkui
89 L-3 Wango-Fitini
133 M-1 Wangqing
99 N-2 Wanie-Rukula
138 G-8 Wānkāner
103 K-7 Wankie *na.p.*
103 K-7 Wankie
97 P-4 Wanleweyn
59 J-7 Wannehorn *mt*
172 D-2 Wannertown
145 N-3 Wanning
145 J-4 Wanon Niwat
57 J-6 Wanroij
57 J-6 Wanroyse *lake*
215 M-9 Wansfell *rf*
134 E-5 Wanshengchang
57 K-3 Wanssum
52 D-6 Wanstrow
52 G-5 Wantage
173 J-3 Wantagh
134 E-3 Wanxian
134 E-2 Wanyuan
135 J-5 Wanzai
135 L-3 Wanzhizhen
170 F-7 Wapakoneta
163 M-5 Wapawekka *lake*
170 B-7 Wapello
211 H-5 Wapenamanda
162 F-3 Wapiti *riv.*
210 C-3 Wapoga *riv.*
172 B-2 Wapwallopen *riv.*
94 D-8 War
220 G-4 Waranga *lake*
140 D-7 Warangal
220 G-6 Waratah *bay*
53 K-1 Warboys
218 G-3 Warbreccan
220 G-5 Warburton
217 L-2 Warburton *mt*
218 D-5 Warburton (the) *riv.*
217 L-2 Warburton Mission
219 H-4 Ward *riv.*
211 M-8 Ward Hunt *strt.*
211 L-6 Ward Hunt *cap.*
220 C-2 Wardang *isl.*
105 K-5 Warden
140 B-7 Wardha
140 B-7 Wardha *riv.*
52 G-2 Wardington
160 F-9 Ware (Canada)
53 K-4 Ware (UK)
52 E-9 Wareham
210 C-2 Waren (Australia)
51 K-5 Waren (GDR)
218 E-1 Warenda
209 N-2 Wareno
172 G-7 Waretown
53 H-5 Wargrave
211 N-9 Wari *isl.*
83 L-3 Wari'ah
219 L-7 Warialda
97 J-5 Waridad
209 N-4 Warilau *isl.*
145 J-6 Warin Chamrap
159 K-4 Waring *mt*
223 K-3 Warkworth
53 K-6 Warlingham
158 D-6 Warlus *islds*
167 J-5 Warm Springs
209 M-1 Warmandi
105 K-3 Warmbad (South Africa)
104 D-5 Warmbad (South Africa)
52 G-2 Warmington
66 A-5 Warminski
52 E-6 Warminster
56 C-2 Warmond
52 D-9 Warmwell
51 K-5 Warnemünde
166 F-4 Warner *mt*
191 H-6 Warnes
52 G-7 Warnford
53 J-7 Warnham
57 L-2 Warnsveld
140 C-7 Warora
219 L-5 Warra
220 F-4 Warracknabeal
221 K-3 Warragamba *lake*
220 G-5 Warragul
218 C-5 Warrandirinna *lake*
212 G-7 Warrawagine
219 H-6 Warrego *riv.*
219 J-3 Warrego *mt*
216 E-9 Warren *riv.*
160 B-8 Warren *isl.*
172 E-3 Warren *reg.*
169 J-2 Warren (USA)
171 H-7 Warren (USA)
170 G-6 Warren (USA)
176 D-3 Warren (USA)
172 G-7 Warren Grove
170 A-9 Warrensburg
104 G-5 Warrenton (South Africa)
170 B-9 Warrenton (USA)
171 J-8 Warrenton (USA)
90 A-7 Warri
218 B-5 Warrina
220 F-5 Warrnambool
170 A-1 Warroad
221 J-1 Warrumbungle *na.p.*
140 B-8 Warsa
47 E-4 Warsaw
66 A-6 Warsaw
170 E-7 Warsaw (USA)
170 A-9 Warsaw (USA)
171 J-5 Warsaw (USA)
97 P-5 Warshikh
51 M-6 Warta *riv.*
53 L-8 Wartling
209 K-3 Waru
210 E-3 Waruta *riv.*
52 F-2 Warwick *reg.*
219 M-6 Warwick (Australia)
52 F-2 Warwick (UK)
171 M-5 Warwick (USA)
214 C-4 Warwick Chan *strt.*
90 A-3 Wasagu
168 A-5 Wasatch *mt*
167 L-3 Wasco
90 D-4 Wase *riv.*
59 H-3 Wasen
168 G-2 Washburn
52 B-6 Washford
165 K-3 Washikuti
224 D-3 Washington *isl.*
162 C-8 Washington *reg.*
157 G-3 Washington *state*
164 F-9 Washington *mt*
171 K-8 Washington (D.C.)
53 J-8 Washington (UK)
170 E-9 Washington (USA)
169 H-8 Washington (USA)
170 E-4 Washington (USA) *isl.*
170 B-7 Washington (USA)
171 H-7 Washington (USA)
172 E-3 Washington (USA)
177 J-3 Washington (USA)
172 A-6 Washington (USA)
170 F-8 Washington (USA)
177 M-1 Washington (USA)
172 E-5 Washington Crossing
172 G-1 Washingtonville (USA)
172 A-2 Washingtonville (USA)
175 N-2 Washita *riv.*
129 H-7 Washixia
209 M-2 Wasian
210 A-2 Wasian *riv.*
209 M-2 Wasian *riv.*
101 K-6 Wasin *isl.*
209 N-2 Wasior
209 N-4 Wasir *isl.*
73 H-9 Wasit *site*
163 L-6 Waskesiu Lake
158 E-6 Waskey *mt*
185 H-3 Waspan
56 E-6 Waspic
136 B-6 Wassamu
59 M-5 Wassen
56 B-2 Wassenaar
57 P-7 Wassenberg
211 K-5 Wasu
211 M-5 Wasum
164 C-5 Waswanipi
164 C-5 Waswanipi *lake*
164 A-4 Wataboahegan *riv.*
211 H-3 Watam
208 C-4 Watampone
208 C-4 Watansoppeng
173 N-1 Watch Hill
52 B-6 Watchet
180 E-3 Water Cays *rf*
173 M-2 Water Mill
53 L-2 Waterbeach
102 D-8 Waterberg
163 M-3 Waterbury *lake*
171 L-6 Waterbury
177 K-2 Wateree *riv.*
53 J-4 Waterend
160 B-8 Waterfall
50 B-4 Waterford (UK)
173 M-1 Waterford (USA)
172 E-7 Waterford Works
163 N-8 Waterhen *lake*
214 A-4 Waterhouse *riv.*
56 B-3 Wateringen
213 M-4 Waterloo (Australia)
87 L-4 Waterloo (Sierra Leone)
170 B-6 Waterloo (USA)
52 B-8 Waterloo Cross
53 H-8 Waterloo Ville
201 P-5 Waterman *isl.*
105 L-1 Waterpoort
170 C-3 Watersmeet
162 G-8 Waterton Park
169 H-4 Watertown (USA)
170 D-5 Watertown (USA)
164 G-8 Waterville (USA)
171 K-5 Waterville (USA)
163 J-3 Waterways
162 D-8 Watewille
53 J-4 Watford
168 F-1 Watford City
94 E-3 Wa'th
53 J-3 Wathing *hill*
162 G-3 Watino
181 H-3 Watling's (San Salvador)
53 H-4 Watlington
211 N-4 Watom *isl.*
175 M-1 Watonga
163 L-7 Watrous
94 D-7 Watsa
170 D-7 Watseka
99 K-3 Watsi Kengo
217 P-5 Watson (Australia)
163 L-7 Watson (Canada)
160 F-6 Watson Lake
167 J-2 Watsonville
217 L-3 Watt *mt*
163 H-1 Watt (Canada) *mt*
58 G-5 Wattenwil
53 K-3 Watton at Stone
59 P-1 Wattwil
209 L-4 Watubela *islds*
208 C-2 Watukama
211 K-6 Wau
221 M-1 Wauchope
177 K-7 Wauchula
213 H-7 Waukarlycarly *lake*
170 D-6 Waukegan
170 D-6 Waukesha
175 N-2 Waurika
170 C-4 Wausau
59 J-3 Wauwil
213 N-4 Wave Hill
170 B-6 Waverly (USA)
176 F-1 Waverly (USA)
56 D-2 Waverveen
143 L-9 Waw (Birman)
80 E-6 Wāw al Kabir
80 E-7 Wāw an Nāmūs
81 B-4 Wāw Nahr *riv.*
89 P-9 Wawa
92 F-3 Wawa
211 M-7 Wawiwa *isl.*
208 D-3 Wawo
210 G-6 Wawoi *riv.*
208 E-3 Wawotobi
175 N-4 Waxahachie
216 G-3 Way *lake*
177 K-5 Waycross
171 J-5 Wayland
169 H-6 Wayne
176 F-5 Waynesboro (USA)
171 J-7 Waynesboro (USA)
171 J-9 Waynesboro (USA)
177 K-3 Waynesboro (USA)
176 G-2 Waynesboro (USA)
171 H-7 Waynesburg
170 B-9 Waynesville (USA)
177 J-2 Waynesville (USA)
90 G-3 Waza *na.p.*
127 J-7 Wazay
136 G-5 Wazima
127 L-8 Wazīrābād
50 D-5 W.Bromwich
215 N-4 Wé
53 L-7 Weald *reg.*
172 C-2 Weatherly
166 F-2 Weaverville
162 C-1 Weber *mt*
169 H-4 Webster
170 A-6 Webster City
56 D-9 Wechelderzande
161 M-6 Wecho *lake*
201 L-7 Weddel Island *isl.*
227 M-2 Weddell *sea*
51 J-5 Wedel
216 D-6 Wedge
220 B-1 Wedge (Australia) *mt*
162 C-6 Wedge (Canada) *mt*
52 C-6 Wedmore
56 F-9 Weebosch
166 F-3 Weed
52 G-2 Weedon Beck
209 K-2 Weeim *isl.*
172 F-7 Weekstown
56 E-8 Weelde
105 K-6 Weenen
57 N-1 Weerselo
57 H-9 Weert
59 P-2 Weesen
56 E-1 Weesp
53 M-1 Weeting
57 M-2 Wegdam
59 L-3 Weggis
146 A-5 Weh *isl.*
57 L-4 Wehl
132 F-3 Weichang *mt*
132 F-3 Weichang
51 K-8 Weiden
133 H-7 Weifang
133 J-6 Weihai
132 E-8 Weihe (China) *riv.*
132 A-9 Weihe (China) *riv.*
133 H-7 Weihe (China) *riv.*
51 J-7 Weimar
132 B-9 Weinan
134 C-6 Weining
214 F-3 Weipa
219 L-6 Weir *riv.*
53 M-5 Weir
171 H-7 Weirton
166 E-6 Weiser
134 A-7 Weishan
132 E-9 Weishi
58 F-6 Weissenburg
51 K-7 Weissenfels
58 G-2 Weissenstein (Switzerland) *mt*
59 P-6 Weissenstein (Switzerland) *mt*
59 H-9 Weisshorn *mt*
59 J-9 Weissmies *mt*
143 N-2 Weixi
132 E-7 Weixian
134 D-5 Weixin
131 L-8 Weiyuan
132 A-7 Weizhou
145 M-2 Weizhoudao *isl.*
163 N-6 Wekusko
163 N-6 Wekusko *lake*
218 A-5 Welbourn Hill
93 N-8 Weldiya
94 G-2 Welega *reg.*
218 G-3 Welford (Australia)
52 G-5 Welford (UK)
53 H-1 Welford (UK)
141 N-7 Weligama
95 J-3 Welkite
105 H-5 Welkom
57 K-7 Well
171 H-5 Welland
141 N-8 Wellawaya
57 K-7 Wellerlooi
52 F-2 Wellesbourne Hastings
56 F-8 Welleseind
214 E-6 Wellesey *islds*
214 E-6 Wellesley *islds*
160 D-2 Wellesley *lake*
168 F-7 Wellfleet
53 H-1 Wellingborough
223 J-6 Wellington *reg.*
201 K-2 Wellington *isl.*
205 H-6 Wellington
104 D-9 Wellington (South Africa)
221 K-2 Wellington (Australia)
223 H-7 Wellington (New Zealand)
52 B-7 Wellington (UK)
169 H-9 Wellington (USA)
175 L-2 Wellington (USA)
217 J-3 Wells *lake*
52 C-6 Wells
162 E-5 Wells Gray *na.p.*
171 J-6 Wellsboro
223 K-3 Wellsford
171 J-6 Wellsville
174 C-2 Wellton
95 L-5 Welmel *riv.*
61 N-1 Wels
58 G-1 Welschenrohr
50 D-5 Welshpool
57 K-1 Welsum
57 N-9 Welten
53 K-4 Welwyn
53 K-4 Welwyn Garden City
99 L-3 Wema
100 F-6 Wembere *riv.*
53 K-5 Wemblay
162 C-8 Wenatchee
162 C-8 Wenatchee *mt*
145 N-3 Wenchang
89 M-4 Wenchi
95 K-2 Wenchit *riv.*
133 J-7 Wendeng
53 L-3 Wendens Ambo
209 N-2 Wendesi
52 G-3 Wendlebury
95 K-4 Wendo
53 H-4 Wendover (UK)
167 H-7 Wendover (USA)
134 E-6 Weng'an
129 N-6 Wengbo
59 H-5 Wengen
132 G-3 Wengniuteqi
135 J-8 Wengyuan
135 N-4 Wenling
214 G-3 Wenlock *riv.*
184 A-7 Wenman *isl.*
172 E-7 Wenonah
131 P-8 Wenquan (China)
128 C-5 Wenquan (China)
134 C-9 Wenshan
132 F-8 Wenshang
220 E-2 Wentworth
52 B-5 Wenvoe
131 M-9 Wenxian
128 E-4 Wenxu
135 N-5 Wenzhou
133 M-4 Weonsan
105 H-6 Wepener
104 F-3 Werda
97 L-4 Werder
209 M-3 Weri
56 D-5 Werkendam
56 F-3 Werkhoven
160 F-2 Wernecke *mt*
172 B-5 Wernersville
56 C-8 Wernhout
51 J-7 Werra *riv.*
220 G-5 Werribee
221 L-1 Werris Creek
59 J-3 Werthenstein
172 C-4 Wescosville
51 J-5 Weser *riv.*
95 H-5 Weska Weka
165 N-2 Wesleyville
89 K-9 Wessa *riv.*
214 C-2 Wessel *cap.*
57 H-2 Wessel
214 C-2 Wessel Islands *islds*
105 H-5 Wesselbron
57 N-6 Wessem
169 H-4 Wessington Springs
72 E-4 West Azerbaijan *reg.*
213 M-4 West Baines *riv.*
144 A-9 West Bay *bay*
180 C-6 West Bay (Antilles)
52 C-8 West Bay (UK)
170 D-5 West Bend
170 F-5 West Branch
173 H-1 West Branch *rés*
171 J-6 West Branch Susquehanna *riv.*
181 J-4 West Caicos *isl.*
216 F-9 West Cape Howe
172 C-6 West Chester
175 P-6 West Columbia
172 D-6 West Conshohocken
172 G-7 West Creek
180 E-1 West End
175 M-3 West Fork Trinity *riv.*
50 G-5 West Frisian *islds*
162 F-9 West Glacier
172 C-7 West Grove
53 H-1 West Haddon
50 E-3 West Hartlepool
56 C-4 West IJsselmonde
214 C-5 West Island *isl.*
52 E-6 West Lavington
172 G-5 West Long Branch
103 J-2 West Lunga *riv.*
53 L-6 West Malling
176 E-2 West Memphis
52 G-7 West Meon
53 N-4 West Mersea
172 F-2 West Milford
52 E-8 West Moors
172 B-1 West Nanticoke
103 M-9 West Nicholson

172 C-1 West Pittston
176 D-1 West Plains
159 L-8 West Point *mt*
176 F-3 West Point (USA)
169 H-6 West Point (USA)
172 E-3 West Portal
172 B-5 West Reading
162 D-4 West Road *riv.*
173 K-3 West Sayville
69 M-3 West Siberian Plain *reg.*
165 L-1 West St Modeste
168 A-6 West Tavaputs *plat.*
50 G-5 West-Terschelling
172 E-5 West Trenton
170 B-6 West Union (USA)
171 H-8 West Union (USA)
173 K-1 West Waven
168 B-3 West Yellowstone
147 P-2 West York (Xiyuedao) *rf*
220 A-1 Westall *pte*
56 F-2 Westbroek
173 M-1 Westbrook
52 D-4 Westbury (UK)
52 E-6 Westbury (UK)
173 J-3 Westbury (USA)
173 H-2 Westchester *reg.*
168 D-8 Westcliffe
56 D-1 Westeinder Plassen *lake*
57 J-7 Westerbeek
53 L-6 Westerham
56 G-9 Westerhoven
51 H-4 Westerland
173 N-1 Westerly
211 J-2 Western *isl.*
220 G-6 Western Port *bay*
62 C-8 Western Riviera
225 B-5 Western Samoa *state*
122 E-5 Western Sayan *rge*
57 J-4 Westervoort
53 M-8 Westfield (U.K.)
172 G-4 Westfield (USA)
219 H-5 Westgate
53 P-5 Westgate on Sea
173 L-3 Westhampton
222 E-7 Westland (New Zealand) *reg.*
56 A-3 Westland (Netherlands) *reg.*
53 P-1 Westleton
56 C-5 Westmaas
56 C-9 Westmalle
53 K-8 Westmeston
171 K-8 Westminster (USA)
214 D-6 Westmoreland
171 H-8 Weston
52 G-3 Weston on the Green
52 C-6 Weston Super Mare
222 F-6 Westport (New Zealand)
50 A-3 Westport (UK)
173 J-2 Westport (USA)
164 A-7 Westree
172 F-1 Westtown
172 E-6 Westville
56 A-4 Westvoorne
219 L-3 Westwood (Australia)
166 G-3 Westwood (USA)
164 A-1 Wetailtok *bay*
209 H-6 Wetar *isl.*
163 H-6 Wetaskiwin
101 K-6 Wete
59 J-6 Wetterhorn *mt*
61 K-1 Wettingen
176 G-4 Wetumpka
59 M-1 Wetzikon
51 H-7 Wetzlar
57 J-5 Weurt
177 H-6 Wewahitchka
211 H-3 Wewak
175 N-2 Wewoka
50 B-4 Wexford
53 J-6 Wey *riv.*
53 J-6 Weybridge
163 L-9 Weyburn
52 F-6 Weyhill
52 D-9 Weymouth *bay*
215 H-3 Weymouth *cap.*
50 C-6 Weymouth
165 J-8 Weymouth (Canada)
52 D-9 Weymouth (UK)
57 K-1 Wezepe
223 K-5 Whakatane
144 E-9 Whale (Birman) *bay*
160 B-7 Whale (USA) *bay*
201 L-9 Whale Point
223 K-3 Whangarei
223 K-2 Whangaruru
175 N-6 Wharton (USA)
172 F-3 Wharton (USA)
222 E-7 Whataroa
175 N-3 Wheatherford
168 D-5 Wheatland
169 J-3 Wheaton
52 A-7 Wheddon Cross
163 M-3 Wheeler *riv.*
175 L-1 Wheeler
167 J-6 Wheeler (USA) *mt*
168 D-9 Wheeler (USA) *mt*
171 H-8 Wheeling
57 N-8 Wher
52 G-6 Wherwell
220 A-2 Whidbey *islds*
220 B-2 Whidbey *pte*
52 A-8 Whimple
217 N-2 Whinham *mt*
172 F-3 Whippany
53 J-3 Whipsnade
50 E-4 Whitby
52 C-3 Whitchurch (UK)
52 G-6 Whitchurch (UK)
52 B-5 Whitchurch (UK)
52 D-5 Whitchurch (UK)
53 H-3 Whitchurch (UK)
165 M-2 White *bay*
68 E-8 White *lake*
223 L-5 White *isl.*
226 A-5 White *sea*
46 G-3 White *sea*
213 M-7 White *lake*
159 L-8 White *mt*
160 D-2 White (Canada) *riv.*
170 E-8 White (USA) *riv.*
176 D-2 White (USA) *riv.*
165 M-4 White Bear *lake*
168 F-3 White Butte *mt*
218 F-7 White Cliffs
170 E-5 White Cloud
172 C-2 White Haven
159 N-5 White Hills *mt*
52 F-5 White Horse *hill*
172 E-4 White House Station
176 D-6 White Lake *lake*
167 J-4 White Mountain (USA) *mt*
159 H-3 White Mountain (USA)
76 F-4 White Nile *riv.*
171 L-6 White Plains (USA)
170 E-1 White River (Canada)
168 G-5 White River (USA)
164 F-9 White River Junction
175 H-3 White Sands *site*
168 B-1 White Sulphur Springs
162 C-5 Whitecap *mt*
162 G-4 Whitecourt
162 F-9 Whitefish
170 E-3 Whitefish *bay*
161 N-8 Whitefish *lake*
172 A-7 Whiteford
50 D-3 Whitehaven
160 D-5 Whitehorse
221 H-7 Whitemark
52 F-7 Whiteparish
162 C-2 Whitesail *lake*
201 N-5 Whiteside *strt.*
160 F-1 Whitestone *riv.*
172 G-6 Whitesville
177 M-2 Whiteville
174 F-2 Whitewater Baldy *mt*
163 M-9 Whitewood
52 D-9 Whithcombe
50 C-3 Whithorn
172 G-6 Whiting
163 H-9 Whitlash
164 C-8 Whitney
167 K-3 Whitney *mt*
52 B-2 Whitney (UK)
53 N-5 Whitstable
215 L-9 Whitsunday *isl.*
53 H-2 Whittlebury
105 H-8 Whittlesea
52 B-1 Whitton
52 G-6 Whitway
163 N-1 Wholdaia *lake*
220 C-1 Whyalla
53 K-7 Whych Cross
218 F-7 Whyjonta
133 M-7 Wi *isl.*
164 A-9 Wiarton
89 K-5 Wiasi
89 N-4 Wiawso
168 E-2 Wibaux
144 G-6 Wichian Buri
169 H-9 Wichita
175 M-2 Wichita *riv.*
175 M-2 Wichita *mt*
175 M-2 Wichita Falls
57 L-3 Wichmond
58 G-4 Wichtrach
50 E-1 Wick
172 G-5 Wickatunk
174 D-1 Wickenburg
216 F-8 Wickepin
53 M-4 Wickford
52 G-8 Wickham
220 F-6 Wickham *cap.*
53 P-2 Wickham Market
53 M-2 Wickhambrook
166 E-3 Wickiup *lake*
50 B-4 Wicklow
52 D-5 Wickwar
211 P-4 Wide (Australia) *bay*
158 D-8 Wide (USA) *bay*
54 E-5 Wideville
217 H-6 Widgiemooltha
209 J-1 Widi *islds*
82 F-1 Widyād *mt*
58 G-2 Wiedlisbach
51 M-7 Wielun
61 P-1 Wiener Neustadt
66 B-6 Wieprz *riv.*
57 M-1 Wierden
51 H-7 Wiesbaden
59 H-4 Wiggen
59 J-2 Wigger *riv.*
176 F-5 Wiggings
50 D-6 Wight *isl.*
52 C-1 Wigmore
57 H-5 Wijchen
56 F-5 Wijk (Netherlands)
57 M-9 Wijk (Netherlands)
57 N-9 Wijlre
57 N-8 Wijnandsrade
56 D-5 Wijngaarden
57 L-7 Wijshagen
169 H-7 Wilber
214 C-2 Wilber force *cap.*
162 D-8 Wilbur
53 L-1 Wilburton (UK)
175 P-2 Wilburton (USA)
53 H-1 Wilby (UK)
53 N-1 Wilby (UK)
218 F-8 Wilcannia
112 E-1 Wilczek *isl.*
169 J-2 Wild Rice *riv.*
162 F-4 Wilderness *na.p.*
59 H-5 Wilderswil
59 H-6 Wilderwil
58 F-8 Wildhorn *mt*
162 G-5 Wildwood
105 K-5 Wilge *riv.*
211 H-5 Wilhelm *mt*
56 E-7 Wilhelmina *cal.*
192 D-4 Wilhelmina *mt*
51 H-5 Wilhelmshaven
102 D-9 Wilhemstal
171 K-6 Wilkes Barre
227 N-3 Wilkes Land *reg.*
163 J-7 Wilkie
217 P-5 Wilkinson *lake*
160 E-8 Will *mt*
162 A-8 Willapa *bay*
175 H-1 Willard
220 F-5 Willaura
187 H-1 Willemstad (Antilles)
56 B-6 Willemstad (Netherlands)
213 P-3 Willeroo
52 C-2 Willersley
56 D-3 Willeskop
163 L-2 William *riv.*
163 P-6 William *lake*
220 F-4 William *mt*
218 B-6 William Creek
216 C-1 Williambury
214 F-9 Williams *riv.*
180 E-3 Williams *isl.*
216 E-8 Williams (Australia)
167 M-7 Williams (USA)
167 H-2 Williams (USA)
162 D-5 Williams Lake
177 H-1 Williamsburg
170 G-9 Williamson
171 K-6 Williamsport
177 M-1 Williamston
170 F-9 Williamstown
172 E-6 Willingboro
53 L-8 Willingdon
53 K-1 Willingham
215 M-6 Willis Group *rf*
59 J-2 Willisau
104 E-7 Williston (South Africa)
168 F-1 Williston (USA)
177 K-6 Williston (USA)
52 B-6 Williton
166 G-1 Willits
170 A-4 Willmar
218 C-8 Willochra *riv.*
220 C-4 Willoughby *cap.*
162 E-3 Willow *riv.*
161 J-7 Willow *lake*
159 H-8 Willow
172 E-5 Willow Grove
172 A-6 Willow Street
161 J-6 Willowlake *riv.*
104 F-8 Willowmore
166 G-2 Willows
176 D-1 Willows Springs
220 D-3 Willunga
53 L-8 Wilmington
220 C-1 Wilmington (Australia)
170 F-8 Wilmington (USA)
177 M-2 Wilmington (USA)
56 E-2 Wilnis
57 K-2 Wilp
218 D-8 Wilpena *riv.*
220 G-5 Wilson *na.p.*
52 E-5 Wilson *pte*
184 E-1 Wilson (Honduras) *mt*
168 B-8 Wilson (USA) *mt*
177 M-1 Wilson (USA)
172 D-3 Wilson (USA)
217 M-6 Wilson Bluff *mt*
221 H-6 Wilson's Promontory *cap.*
58 G-7 Wilstrubel *mt*
214 A-4 Wilton *riv.*
215 H-5 Wilton (Australia)
52 E-7 Wilton (UK)
173 J-2 Wilton (USA)
52 E-5 Wiltshire *reg.*
216 G-3 Wiluna
171 L-8 Wilwood
53 K-5 Wimbledon
53 K-1 Wimblington
58 G-5 Wimmis
105 J-5 Winburg
52 D-7 Wincanton
52 E-3 Winchcombe
53 M-7 Winchelsea
52 G-7 Winchester
50 D-6 Winchester (UK)
170 F-7 Winchester (USA)
170 F-9 Winchester (USA)
170 C-8 Winchester (USA)
176 G-2 Winchester (USA)
171 J-8 Winchester (USA)
160 G-2 Wind (Canada) *riv.*
159 M-6 Wind (USA) *riv.*
172 D-3 Wind Gap
168 B-4 Wind River *mt*
66 A-2 Windaw (Ventspils)
52 E-8 Windborne Minster
53 K-4 Windford
59 M-5 Windgälle *mt*
59 M-4 Windgälle
77 D-7 Windhoek
102 D-9 Windhoek
170 A-5 Windom
218 F-4 Windorah
52 F-3 Windrush *riv.*
165 M-3 Windsor (Canada)
165 K-7 Windsor (Canada)
53 J-5 Windsor (UK)
170 G-6 Windsor (USA)
172 A-6 Windsor (USA)
224 D-5 Windward *islds*
181 H-6 Windward *strt.*
181 N-9 Windward *islds*
159 H-7 Windy Fork *riv.*
169 H-9 Winfield
53 H-3 Wing
213 N-2 Wingate *mt*
221 M-1 Wingham (Australia)
53 N-6 Wingham (UK)
168 C-1 Winifred
200 A-6 Winifreda
155 K-4 Winisk
53 H-5 Winkfield
89 P-5 Winneba
170 D-5 Winnebago *lake*
213 N-5 Winnecke *riv.*
163 K-4 Winnefred *lake*
166 G-5 Winnemucca
168 G-5 Winner
168 C-1 Winnett
176 D-4 Winnfield
216 C-1 Winning Pool
163 P-8 Winnipeg *lake*
163 P-9 Winnipeg
152 H-4 Winnipeg *lake*
163 N-7 Winnipegosis *lake*
163 N-8 Winnipegosis
171 M-4 Winnipesaukee *lake*
176 D-4 Winnsboro
170 B-5 Winona (USA)
176 E-3 Winona (USA)
52 A-7 Winsford
53 H-3 Winslow (UK)
167 M-8 Winslow (USA)
177 L-1 Winston-Salem
56 G-8 Wintelre
177 K-7 Winter Haven
162 A-4 Winter Hbr
105 H-8 Winterberge *mt*
52 D-8 Winterborne Abbas
52 D-8 Winterborne Whithchurch
52 E-6 Winterbourne Stoke
175 L-4 Winters
170 A-7 Winterset
172 A-6 Winterstown
57 N-4 Winterswijk
61 L-1 Winterthun
218 A-5 Wintinna
218 G-1 Winton (Australia)
222 C-8 Winton (New Zealand)
52 E-8 Winton (UK)
177 M-1 Winton (USA)
53 J-1 Winwick
220 A-1 Wirrulla
164 G-9 Wiscasset
57 M-4 Wisch *reg.*
170 B-4 Wisconsin *state*
170 C-5 Wisconsin *riv.*
157 E-2 Wisconsin *state*
170 C-5 Wisconsin Dells
170 C-5 Wisconsin Rapids
53 J-7 Wishborough Green
168 G-3 Wishek
51 K-5 Wismar
172 G-1 Wisner
55 J-8 Wissous
49 P-6 Wista *riv.*
103 L-1 Wiswila *riv.*
105 K-3 Witbank
57 K-8 Witbroek
53 M-4 Witham
52 A-8 Witheridge
53 L-2 Withersfield
52 A-8 Withleigh
105 K-5 Witkoppies *mt*
52 F-4 Witney
104 B-4 Witputs
104 E-9 Witsand
57 N-9 Wittem
51 K-6 Wittenberg (GDR)
170 C-4 Wittenberg (USA)
51 K-5 Wittenberge
212 E-8 Wittenoom
53 M-7 Wittersham
101 K-4 Witu
102 E-9 Witvlei
105 H-3 Witwatersrand *reg.*
52 B-7 Wivelicombe
53 N-3 Wivenhoe
53 N-3 Wix
49 N-6 Władystawowo
207 M-7 Wlingi
51 M-6 Włocławek
53 J-3 Woburn
221 H-4 Wodonga
56 B-8 Woensdrecht
56 G-8 Woensel
56 D-3 Woerden
57 J-3 Woeste Hoeve
58 F-3 Wohlen
58 F-3 Wohlensee *lake*
227 N-1 Wohlthat *rge*
146 A-6 Wojla *riv.*
209 N-5 Wokam *isl.*
125 H-7 Wokenhe *riv.*
50 D-6 Woking
53 H-5 Wokingham
218 G-3 Wokingham *riv.*
98 D-1 Woleu-Ntem *reg.*
170 D-4 Wolf *riv.*
160 E-5 Wolf *lake*
184 A-8 Wolf *vol.*
168 B-1 Wolf Creek
168 E-1 Wolf Point
59 L-4 Wolfenschiessen
57 J-3 Wolfheeze
51 J-6 Wolfsburg
59 H-1 Wolfwill
51 K-5 Wolgast
59 J-3 Wolhusen
91 N-9 Wolikombo
51 L-5 Wolin *pen.*
95 J-3 Woliso
53 J-2 Wollaston
163 N-3 Wollaston *lake*
201 P-6 Wollaston *islds*
161 M-1 Wollaston *cap.*
163 M-3 Wollaston Lake Post
59 M-2 Wollerau
214 D-6 Wollogorang
221 L-3 Wollongong
105 H-4 Wolmaransstad
163 L-9 Wolseley
169 H-4 Wolsey
50 D-5 Wolverhampton
53 H-2 Wolverton (UK)
52 G-6 Wolverton (UK)
52 G-1 Wolvey
172 B-5 Womelsdorf
219 M-5 Wondai
220 A-1 Wondoma *cap.*
216 E-6 Wongan Hills
95 K-3 Wonji
133 M-6 Wonju
90 E-5 Wonka *hill*
207 K-6 Wonoboso
207 K-7 Wonosario
209 H-6 Wonreli
220 G-6 Wonthaggi
210 C-2 Wonti
216 F-2 Wonyulgunna *mt*
218 C-8 Woocalla
163 K-9 Wood *mt*
168 G-5 Wood
201 P-5 Wood *isl.*
159 K-8 Wood *riv.*
156 E-2 Wood *lake*
163 J-1 Wood Buffalo *na.p.*
214 C-4 Woodah *isl.*
172 A-7 Woodbine (USA)
172 E-9 Woodbine (USA)
53 P-2 Woodbridge (UK)
172 G-4 Woodbridge (USA)
173 K-1 Woodbridge (USA)
53 P-3 Woodbridge Haven
52 A-9 Woodbury (UK)
172 E-7 Woodbury (USA)
159 L-9 Woodchopper
53 M-7 Woodchurch
214 A-8 Woodcock *mt*
219 M-6 Woodenbong
219 N-5 Woodford
184 B-9 Woodford *isl.*
218 A-1 Woodgreen
167 H-2 Woodland
211 P-7 Woodlark *isl.*
162 D-3 Woodpecker
217 P-2 Woodroffe *mt*
214 A-7 Woods *lake*
170 A-1 Woods *lake*
172 C-9 Woodside
215 J-8 Woodstock (Australia)
165 H-7 Woodstock (Canada)
171 H-5 Woodstock (Canada)
52 G-3 Woodstock (UK)
170 D-6 Woodstock (USA)
172 D-7 Woodstown
164 F-9 Woodsville (USA)
223 J-6 Woodville (New Zealand)
175 P-5 Woodville (USA)
176 E-5 Woodville (USA)
131 M-3 Woodville Rockhill *mt*
175 M-1 Woodward
52 E-7 Woodyates
52 C-1 Woofferton
52 D-9 Wool
57 N-4 Woold *reg.*
214 G-8 Woolgar
164 D-4 Woollett *lake*
53 N-2 Woolpit
218 D-7 Wooltana
52 D-6 Woolverton
53 L-5 Woolwich
218 C-8 Woomera
169 H-5 Woonsocket
216 C-3 Wooramel
216 D-3 Wooramel *riv.*
219 H-6 Wooroorooka
170 G-7 Wooster
52 E-5 Wootton Bassett
58 G-4 Worb
58 F-3 Worben
104 D-9 Worcester (South Africa)
50 D-5 Worcester (UK)
171 M-5 Worcester (USA)
209 N-5 Workai *isl.*
50 D-3 Workington
168 C-4 Worland
52 C-6 Worle
53 K-4 Wormley
51 H-8 Worms
56 D-8 Wortel
53 J-8 Worthing
169 J-5 Worthington
172 B-9 Worton
209 J-1 Wosi
119 M-5 Wotho *isl.*
119 N-6 Wotje *isl.*
52 D-4 Wotton under Edge
56 C-2 Woubrugge
56 G-3 Woudenberg
56 E-5 Woudrichem
80 D-9 Wour
90 D-8 Wouri *riv.*
56 B-7 Wouw
56 B-7 Wouwse Hil
56 B-8 Wouwse Plantage *reg.*
219 L-3 Wowan
208 F-3 Wowoni *isl.*
113 R-2 Wrangel *isl.*
160 C-2 Wrangell *mt*
160 C-8 Wrangell
160 C-8 Wrangell *isl.*
50 D-1 Wrath *cap.*
168 E-7 Wray
184 C-9 Wreck *pte*
50 D-4 Wrexham
174 E-3 Wrightson *mt*
172 F-6 Wrightstown
177 J-4 Wrightsville
161 J-5 Wrigley
53 L-4 Writtle
51 M-7 Wrocław
53 L-6 Wrotham
53 L-6 Wrotham Heart
52 G-2 Wroxton
51 M-6 Wrzesnia
216 E-6 Wubin
132 B-4 Wubulangkou
124 G-9 Wuchang
135 M-7 Wuchiu Hsu *isl.*
145 N-2 Wuchuan (China)
132 C-4 Wuchuan (China)

96 C-4 Wuday'ah
90 C-2 Wudil
134 B-7 Wuding
132 C-7 Wudinghe *riv.*
131 M-9 Wudu
128 B-7 Wuergasaershan *mt*
132 G-2 Wuerjimulunhe *riv.*
124 B-7 Wuershunhe *riv.*
134 G-4 Wufeng
134 G-6 Wugang
135 J-6 Wugongshan *mt*
135 J-3 Wuhan
135 L-1 Wuhe
135 L-2 Wuhu
132 A-4 Wujiahe *riv.*
134 E-5 Wujiang *riv.*
90 D-5 Wukari
131 K-5 Wulan
131 H-3 Wulandabanshan *mt*
124 D-9 Wulanhaote
132 D-3 Wulanhe Duojia
129 L-9 Wulanmulunhe *riv.*
131 L-1 Wulanmulunhe (Yangtse) *riv.*
129 L-9 Wulanshan *mt*
128 D-7 Wulanwusu
127 M-7 Wular *lake*
128 E-7 Wulasitaishui *riv.*
133 J-7 Wuleidaowan *bay*
134 C-5 Wulianfeng *mt*
143 P-1 Wuliang *riv.*
134 A-8 Wuliangshan *mt*
132 B-4 Wuliangsuhai *lake*
209 L-6 Wuliaru *isl.*
124 C-9 Wuliluojihe *riv.*
134 F-5 Wulingshan *mt*
129 J-7 Wulukemushiling *mt*
128 B-9 Wulunguhe *riv.*
128 B-8 Wulunguhu *lake*
209 J-6 Wulur
90 D-6 Wum
124 C-4 Wuma
134 C-6 Wumengshan *mt*
134 E-9 Wuming
94 C-3 Wun Rog
94 E-3 Wunagak
143 L-7 Wundwin
58 F-4 Wünnewil
143 L-5 Wuntho
128 E-1 Wupa
51 H-7 Wuppertal
132 B-7 Wuqi
127 P-3 Wuqia
132 F-5 Wuqing
216 E-4 Wurarga
57 P-9 Würselen
51 J-8 Würzburg
51 K-7 Wurzen
131 L-9 Wushan
128 E-3 Wushi
134 F-6 Wushui *riv.*
129 J-5 Wusidengshan *mt*
135 N-2 Wusong
128 C-7 Wusu
132 D-6 Wutaishan *mt*
83 K-6 Wuthaythiyah
125 H-6 Wutonghe *riv.*
134 C-4 Wutongqiao
56 C-8 Wuustwezel
210 G-2 Wuvulu *isl.*
131 J-8 Wuwei (China)
134 E-9 Wuwei (China)
135 L-3 Wuwei (China)
135 M-2 Wuxi
134 F-8 Wuxuan
135 L-4 Wuyang
124 G-6 Wuying
135 K-6 Wuyishan *mt*
132 B-4 Wuyuan
124 G-5 Wuyun
132 D-6 Wuzhai
124 F-8 Wuzhan
145 N-3 Wuzhishan *mt*
132 A-7 Wuzhong
134 G-8 Wuzhou
54 D-2 Wy-dit-Joli-Village
216 E-6 Wyalkatchem
221 H-2 Wyalong
219 H-5 Wyandra
221 K-3 Wyangala *lake*
218 G-6 Wyara *lake*
220 F-4 Wycheproof
53 H-4 Wycombe
53 N-6 Wye
52 A-1 Wye *riv.*
216 F-4 Wyemandoo
57 J-5 Wyler
212 D-9 Wyloo
52 E-7 Wylye
213 L-3 Wyndham
52 D-2 Wynds Point
58 G-3 Wynigen
176 E-2 Wynne
161 P-1 Wynniatt *bay*
219 N-6 Wynnum
220 G-7 Wynyard (Australia)
163 L-8 Wynyard (USA)
168 B-4 Wyoming *mt*
168 C-4 Wyoming *state*
157 D-2 Wyoming *state*
172 B-5 Wyomissing
220 E-3 Wyperfield *na.p.*
177 K-1 Wytheville


## X


145 J-3 Xai Lai Leng *mt*
107 N-2 Xai-Xai
144 G-3 Xaignabouri
145 J-2 Xam Nua
194 E-3 Xambioa
196 D-7 Xambré *riv.*
64 E-5 Xánthi
196 D-9 Xanxere
190 C-2 Xapuri
194 B-3 Xateturu *riv.*
194 B-6 Xavantinho *riv.*
179 N-4 Xcán
145 K-6 Xêdôn
145 H-2 Xeng *riv.*
170 F-8 Xenia
145 K-5 Xénô
145 K-5 Xepon
132 G-4 Xiabancheng
125 J-8 Xiachengzi
145 P-1 Xiachuandao *isl.*
128 E-2 Xiadengcao
134 A-7 Xiaguan
131 L-7 Xiahe
135 M-7 Xiamen (Amoy)
132 B-9 Xian
134 F-4 Xianfeng
145 H-3 Xiang Khoang *plat.*
135 H-1 Xiangcheng
135 H-2 Xiangfan
135 H-6 Xiangjiang *riv.*
145 J-3 Xiangkhoang
131 K-5 Xiangride
135 H-5 Xiangtan
135 K-5 Xiangtang
135 H-5 Xiangxiang
135 H-5 Xiangyin
134 A-7 Xiangyun
135 N-4 Xianju
135 J-4 Xianning
131 P-7 Xianshuihe *riv.*
132 F-6 Xianxian
134 F-1 Xianyang
135 M-7 Xianyou
124 G-7 Xiaobai
133 L-2 Xiaobuchaihekou
134 F-9 Xiaodong
135 J-3 Xiaogan
132 G-3 Xiaohe *riv.*
124 C-6 Xiaohezi
131 P-7 Xiaojin
135 J-9 Xiaolan
132 G-7 Xiaoqinghe *riv.*
135 M-3 Xiaoshan
132 G-9 Xiaoxian
179 N-5 Xiatil
133 H-3 Xiawa
134 B-5 Xichang
134 C-9 Xichou
134 G-2 Xichuan
129 P-8 Xideqing
131 M-4 Xidi
187 J-9 Xié *riv.*
129 M-3 Xielipuke
131 P-6 Xieluo
135 K-1 Xifeihe *riv.*
134 D-6 Xifeng
124 C-6 Xiguituqi
131 M-9 Xihanshui *riv.*
131 H-8 Xihe *riv.*
132 E-5 Xiheying
135 J-1 Xihua
135 H-9 Xijiang *riv.*
135 J-4 Xilianghu *lake*
132 G-2 Xiliaohe *riv.*
133 J-2 Xiliaohe *riv.*
142 F-1 Xilin
132 E-2 Xilinhaoté
132 D-3 Xilinhuduga
129 P-7 Xilintuo
135 J-3 Ximakou
133 N-6 Ximeng
135 M-4 Xinanjiang *lake*
107 N-2 Xinavane
133 K-3 Xinbin
135 J-2 Xincai
125 H-7 Xinchengzhen
132 G-3 Xindi
124 G-8 Xindian
135 H-8 Xindu
134 G-7 Xing'an
124 E-4 Xinganlingzhan
133 H-4 Xingcheng
128 F-8 Xingdi
135 K-7 Xingfeng
135 K-6 Xingguo
135 M-1 Xinghua
134 B-4 Xingjing
124 G-8 Xinglongzhen
134 E-1 Xingping
134 D-7 Xingren
134 G-3 Xingshan
132 E-7 Xingtai
194 B-2 Xingu *riv.*
132 C-6 Xingxian
130 F-4 Xingxingxia
134 C-7 Xingyi
133 H-9 Xinhailian
132 E-7 Xinhe
134 F-2 Xinhe *riv.*
134 G-5 Xinhua
134 F-6 Xinhuang
135 H-9 Xinhui
131 K-7 Xining
132 C-8 Xinjiang
135 L-5 Xinjiang *riv.*
133 J-5 Xinjin
133 H-2 Xinkaihe *riv.*
133 J-3 Xinlitun
131 P-6 Xinlong
133 J-3 Xinmin
132 G-8 Xintai
135 J-4 Xintanpu
132 D-6 Xinxian
132 E-8 Xinxiang
135 J-2 Xinyang
135 H-2 Xinye
132 G-9 Xinyi
133 H-9 Xinyihe *riv.*
131 K-9 Xinying
135 J-5 Xinyu
128 D-5 Xinyuan
133 L-1 Xinzhan
132 B-6 Xinzhao
135 H-1 Xinzheng
135 J-3 Xinzhou
132 G-1 Xiongershan *mt*
133 J-4 Xiongyuecheng
190 C-2 Xipamanu *riv.*
135 J-1 Xiping (China)
134 G-1 Xiping (China)
131 L-7 Xiqingshan *mt*
195 J-6 Xique-Xique
192 D-8 Xiriri *lake*
190 A-2 Xiruá *riv.*
145 P-5 Xishaqundao (Paracel) *islds*
129 M-6 Xitai
134 F-5 Xiushan
135 J-4 Xiushui
132 E-9 Xiuwu
133 J-4 Xiuyan
133 H-2 Xiwushijiazi
132 F-2 Xiwuzhumuqinqi
134 E-2 Xixiang
145 H-4 Xong *riv.*
145 L-9 Xuân Lôc
135 L-3 Xuancheng
145 H-3 Xuang *riv.*
132 E-5 Xuanhua
134 C-7 Xuanwei
135 H-1 Xuchang
132 G-9 Xuecheng
134 G-6 Xuefengshan *mt*
128 F-2 Xuemaner
134 B-7 Xundian
124 F-5 Xunhe *riv.*
124 G-5 Xunhe
131 L-7 Xunhua
124 G-5 Xunke
135 K-7 Xunwu
145 N-2 Xuwen
134 D-5 Xuyong
132 G-9 Xuzhou


## Y


219 L-2 Yaamba
134 B-4 Yaan
90 D-8 Yabassi
95 K-6 Yabelo
123 P-5 Yablonovyy *rge*
125 H-9 Yabuluoni
185 H-4 Yacaltara
196 A-5 Yacare *riv.*
134 D-6 Yachihe *riv.*
196 B-9 Yacireta *isl.*
221 H-4 Yackandandaft
191 L-6 Yacuiba
190 E-4 Yacuma *riv.*
140 E-5 Yādgīr
142 G-2 Yadong
137 P-5 Yaeyamata *islds*
80 C-2 Yafran
129 M-8 Yagemu
136 B-6 Yagisiri *isl.*
91 H-3 Yagoua
188 C-2 Yaguachi
187 M-2 Yaguaraparo
199 K-4 Yaguari *riv.*
199 L-5 Yaguaron *riv.*
221 L-5 Yaguaron *riv.*
188 D-9 Yaguas *riv.*
143 J-1 Yaguhu *lake*
146 E-5 Yaha
99 M-1 Yahila
162 F-8 Yahk
178 D-4 Yahualica de G. Gallo
99 M-1 Yahuma
65 L-6 Yahyali
146 D-5 Yai *riv.*
145 M-4 Yaichengzhen
78 D-8 Yaisa
137 J-7 Yaizu
131 P-6 Yajiang
129 K-7 Yakehu *lake*
162 C-9 Yakima *mt*
162 C-8 Yakima *lake*
162 C-9 Yakima
126 D-9 Yakmach
89 H-4 Yako
160 B-6 Yakobi *isl.*
91 M-8 Yakoma
91 N-7 Yakosi
137 N-3 Yaku
137 N-3 Yaku *isl.*
94 C-6 Yakuluku
136 C-6 Yakumo
160 C-4 Yakutat *bay*
89 K-4 Yala (Ghana)
146 E-5 Yala (Thailand)
162 B-9 Yale *lake*
216 E-4 Yalgoo
91 N-6 Yalinga
219 H-3 Yalleroi
91 J-7 Yaloké
129 P-6 Yalong
134 B-6 Yalongjiang *riv.*
64 G-5 Yalova
65 J-2 Yalta
124 D-7 Yalu
124 D-7 Yaluhe *riv.*
133 K-3 Yalujiang *riv.*
65 J-6 Yalvac
96 C-3 Yam *dés*
136 F-7 Yamagata
137 L-3 Yamaguti
112 E-2 Yamal *pen.*
84 B-7 Yamāsūr
131 H-4 Yamatengwumulu
95 H-3 Yamba
220 F-6 Yambacoona
91 L-5 Yambala
94 C-6 Yambio
64 F-4 Yambol
99 N-1 Yambuya
143 L-7 Yamethin
218 F-4 Yamma Yamma *lake*
77 B-4 Yamoussoukro
89 N-2 Yamoussoukro (Côte d'Ivoire)
168 B-6 Yampa *riv.*
213 H-4 Yampi Sound
142 B-2 Yamuna *riv.*
139 N-3 Yamunanagār
141 M-7 Yan *riv.*
144 D-5 Yan-gon (Rangoon)
188 D-5 Yana-Yacu
211 N-7 Yanaba *isl.*
220 E-4 Yanac
140 F-9 Yanam
132 B-8 Yanan
189 M-8 Yanaoca
65 P-5 Yanarsu
134 A-6 Yanbian
82 F-7 Yanbu
135 M-1 Yancheng
216 D-7 Yanchep
132 A-7 Yanchi
132 C-7 Yanchuan
219 H-7 Yanda
219 H-8 Yanda *riv.*
215 L-2 Yandé *isl.*
99 H-3 Yandja
130 F-3 Yandun
87 J-8 Yanfolila
145 J-5 Yang *riv.*
99 M-2 Yangambi
80 G-9 Yangara *riv.*
135 H-9 Yangchun
133 L-4 Yangdeog
132 D-5 Yanggao
132 E-5 Yanghe *riv.*
145 P-1 Yangjiang
132 G-7 Yangjiaogou
133 H-4 Yangjiazhangzi
134 B-7 Yanglin
132 F-5 Yangliuqing
135 H-8 Yangshan
134 G-8 Yangshuo
131 M-4 Yangtse (Tongtianhe) *riv.*
131 L-1 Yangtse (Wulanmulunhe) *riv.*
135 J-3 Yangtze (Changjiang) *riv.*
135 N-3 Yanguan
128 E-6 Yangxia
134 E-2 Yangxian
132 E-5 Yangyuan
135 M-2 Yangzhou
143 H-1 Yangzhuoyonghu *lake*
134 E-5 Yanhe
89 M-1 Yani *riv.*
133 M-1 Yanji
134 C-5 Yanjing
90 D-4 Yankari Game *rés*
221 H-3 Yanko *riv.*
169 H-5 Yankton
99 N-2 Yanonge
128 E-7 Yanqi (China)
134 G-5 Yanqi (China)
134 C-8 Yanshan
132 G-5 Yanshan *hill*
124 G-8 Yanshou
132 C-8 Yanshui *riv.*
219 H-7 Yantabulla
133 J-6 Yantai
218 F-7 Yantara *lake*
131 P-9 Yanting
134 A-6 Yanyuan
132 F-8 Yanzhou
91 J-2 Yao
91 K-7 Yao Malikidza
146 C-4 Yao Noi *isl.*
146 C-4 Yao Yai *isl.*
134 A-7 Yaoan
99 L-1 Yaolumbu
90 E-8 Yaoundé
77 D-4 Yaoundé
132 B-9 Yaoxian
124 E-5 Yaozhan
119 J-6 Yap *isl.*
187 K-7 Yapacana *mt*
190 G-5 Yapacani *riv.*
220 E-3 Yapeet
173 K-3 Yaphank
214 F-7 Yappar *riv.*
65 K-4 Yaprakli
174 E-6 Yaqui *riv.*
187 H-2 Yaracuy *reg.*
218 G-3 Yaraka
73 K-5 Yaramin
52 B-8 Yarcombe
172 E-5 Yardley
53 H-2 Yardley Gobion
53 H-2 Yardley Hastings
172 F-5 Yardville
119 M-7 Yaren
201 N-5 Yarfou
140 E-4 Yargatti
188 A-6 Yari *pl.*
188 A-6 Yari *riv.*
96 E-3 Yarīm
187 H-2 Yaritagua
127 M-5 Yarkhūn *riv.*
217 N-5 Yarles *lake*
165 J-8 Yarmouth (Canada)
52 F-9 Yarmouth (UK)
192 F-5 Yaro *mt*
69 N-7 Yaroslavka
67 H-1 Yaroslavl
216 D-5 Yarra *riv.*
216 D-5 Yarra *lake*
214 G-4 Yarraden
212 D-8 Yarraloola
221 H-6 Yarram
219 M-5 Yarraman
221 H-4 Yarrawonga
219 H-5 Yarronvale
143 J-1 Yartotra La
187 L-5 Yarua *riv.*
186 D-5 Yarumal
191 J-2 Yarvicoya
131 L-3 Yasha
129 M-2 Yashan
96 E-5 Yashbum
127 M-5 Yāsīn
145 J-6 Yasokhon
221 J-3 Yass
72 A-4 Yasun *pte*
188 B-4 Yasuní *riv.*
52 D-3 Yat
190 E-3 Yata
190 E-3 Yata *riv.*
200 E-2 Yate *mt*
215 N-5 Yaté
161 K-9 Yates *riv.*
169 J-9 Yates Center
152 H-3 Yathkyed *lake*
99 N-2 Yatolema
101 G-4 Yatta *plat.*
52 C-5 Yatton
52 E-5 Yatton Keynell
187 K-9 Yatua *riv.*
137 M-3 Yatusiro
189 M-6 Yauca
188 D-4 Yauchari *riv.*
181 J-2 Yauco
189 K-5 Yauli
188 D-3 Yaupi (Ecuador)
189 J-5 Yaupi (Peru)
189 K-5 Yauyos
188 E-7 Yavari *riv.*
188 E-7 Yavari Mirim *riv.*
187 K-7 Yavero *riv.*
187 K-6 Yavi *mt*
143 K-6 Yaw *riv.*
137 L-4 Yawatahama
143 L-7 Yawnghwe
87 L-4 Yawri *bay*
129 J-3 Yaxier *lake*
131 H-4 Yayahu
133 L-3 Yayuan
126 A-2 Yazd *reg.*
73 N-7 Yazd
73 M-8 Yazd-e Khvāst
126 D-4 Yazdān
176 E-4 Yazoo *riv.*
176 E-4 Yazoo City
98 E-1 Yé *riv.*
144 E-6 Ye
143 J-8 Ye Kyun *isl.*
143 L-5 Ye-u
80 E-9 Yébbigué *riv.*
55 N-9 Yèbles
128 G-1 Yecheng
60 E-6 Yecla
97 N-2 Yed
143 L-8 Yedashe
213 H-5 Yeeda River
129 M-8 Yeernuozhahu *lake*
128 F-3 Yeerqianghe *riv.*
67 H-4 Yefremov
131 P-2 Yegelanghe *riv.*
196 B-8 Yegros
93 M-7 Yeha *site*
201 N-6 Yehuin *lake*
94 D-6 Yei
211 P-9 Yeina *isl.*
95 H-4 Yeki
99 K-1 Yekokora *riv.*
69 L-9 Yelabuga
219 L-6 Yelarbon
227 M-3 Yelcho
200 F-3 Yelcho *lake*
87 L-5 Yele
67 H-4 Yelets
94 F-2 Yelgu
86 F-6 Yelimané
140 E-8 Yellandlapād
140 F-3 Yellāpur
133 K-7 Yellow *sea*
117 J-2 Yellow *sea*
116 G-3 Yellow *riv.*
113 L-6 Yellow *sea*
176 G-5 Yellow *riv.*
131 K-8 Yellow river (Huanghe) *riv.*
161 L-6 Yellowknife *rés*
161 L-7 Yellowknife (Canada)
168 B-3 Yellowstone *na.p.*
168 B-3 Yellowstone *lake*
168 B-2 Yellowstone *riv.*
168 C-3 Yellowtail *lake*
185 H-3 Yeluca *mt*
131 L-1 Yelusuhu *lake*
214 D-8 Yelvertoft
90 A-3 Yelwa
128 D-5 Yemadu
130 F-5 Yemajing
69 P-7 Yemanzhelinsk
131 H-4 Yemashan *mt*
131 L-5 Yematan
77 G-3 Yemen *state*
146 D-5 Yen
145 J-1 Yên Bay
90 B-7 Yenagoa
143 K-7 Yenangyaung
143 K-8 Yenanma
89 L-6 Yendi
91 M-8 Yengazewe
99 K-3 Yenge *riv.*
73 H-5 Yengī Kand
65 H-5 Yenişehir
112 G-2 Yenisey *bay*
122 F-1 Yenisey *riv.*

| Abbr. | Term | Language | Meaning |
|---|---|---|---|
| | Ab | afghan | River |
| | Adlar | turkish | Archipelago |
| | Adrar | arabic | Mountain peak |
| Akr. | Akra | greek | Cape |
| | Ao | thai | Bay |
| | Ar | hindi | River |
| Arch. | Archipelag | russian | Archipelago |
| Arch° | Archipelago | english | |
| Arch° | Archipelago | spanish | Archipelago |
| Arr. | Arrecife | spanish | Reef |
| | Aw | burmese | Bay |
| B. | Bahia | spanish | Bay |
| B. | Baie | french | Bay |
| B. | Bay | english | |
| B. | Bught | danish | Bay |
| | Baai | afrikaans | Bay |
| | Baixos | spanish | Reef |
| | Band | afghan | Mountain range |
| | Bandao | chinese | Peninsula |
| | Bar | hindi | Great |
| | Batang | indonesian | River |
| | Berg(e) | afrikaans | Mountain(s) |
| Bin | Basin | english | |
| | Bir | arabic | Well |
| Bj. | Bjerg | danish | Mountain |
| Bk. | Bank | english | |
| | Bo | chinese | Lake |
| | Bois | french | Woods |
| | Bœng | khmer | Lake |
| Boğ | Boğazi | turkish | Strait |
| Bol. | Bol'šoj | russian | Great |
| Bt | Buhayrat | arabic | Lake |
| Bü | Büyük | turkish | Great |
| Buch. | Buchta | russian | Bay |
| | Bulag | mongolian | Well |
| | Bum | burmese | Mount |
| Bur. | Burun | turkish | Cape |
| C. | Cabo | spanish | Cape |
| | Canal | french | Channel |
| C. | Cap | french | Cape |
| C. | Cape | english | |
| C. | Cove | english | |
| Cach. | Cachorara | portuguese | Waterfall |
| Ch. | Chott | arabic | Salt lake |
| | Chãh | afghan | Well |
| Chan. | Channel | english | |
| | Chhâk | khmer | Bay |
| | Chhotã | hindi | Little |
| | Chong | thai | Strait |
| | Chott | arabic | Salt lake |
| Chr. | Chrebet | russian | Mountain range |
| | Chrouy | khmer | Point |
| | Chuŏr Phnum. | khmer | Mountain range |
| Ck | Creek | english | |
| C° | Cerro(s) | spanish | Mountain(s) |
| Cord. | Cordillera | spanish, english | |
| | Cu Lao | vietnamese | Island |
| D. | Dağ, Daği | turkish | Mountain |
| D. | Dake | japanese | Mount |
| D. | Danau | indonesian | Lake |
| | Dãgh | persian | Mountain |
| Dagl. | Dağlari | turkish | Mountain range |
| | Dakshin | hindi | Southern |
| | Dao | chinese | Island(s) |
| | Daryã | afghan | River |
| | Daryãcheh | persian | Lake |
| | Dasht | afghan | Depression |
| | Dasht | persian | Plain |
| | Davãn | afghan | Neck |
| | Détroit | french | Strait |
| Dj. | Djebel | arabic | Mount |
| | Do | korean | Island(s) |
| | Do | vietnamese | River |
| | Doi | thai | Mount |
| | Dvip | hindi | Island(s) |
| E. | East | english | |
| Ent. | Entrance | english | Estuary |
| | Erg | arabic | Sand desert |
| | Forêt | french | Forest |
| F. | Fork | english | |
| Fd. | Fjord | norwegian | Fjord |
| Fin | Fortin | spanish | Fort |
| For. | Forest | english | |
| G. | Gang | korean | River |
| G. | Gawa | japanese | River |
| G. | Göl, Gölü | turkish | Lake |
| G. | Golfe | french | Gulf |
| G. | Golfo | spanish | Gulf |
| G. | Gora | russian | Mountain |
| G. | Gulf | english | |
| G. | Gunong | malay | Mountain |
| G. | Gunung | indonesian | Mount |
| | Gara | arabic | Mount |
| Geb. | Gebirge | german | Mountain chain |
| | Ghar | afghan | Mountain |
| | Ghãt | hindi | Neck |
| Gl. | Gleitscher | danish | Glacier |
| | Gol | mongolian | River |
| | Govi | mongolian | Depression |
| | Gowd | afghan | Depression |
| Gr. | Group | english | |
| Gr. | Gross | german | Great |
| | Groot | afrikaans | Great |
| Gt | Great | english | |
| Gub. | Guba | russian | Bay |
| | Haehyeop | korean | Strait |
| | Hai | chinese | Lake |
| | Haixia | chinese | Island(s) |
| | Hamada | arabic | Steppes |
| | Hâmũn | afghan | Lake |
| | Hassi | arabic | Well |
| Hbr. | Harbour | english | |
| | He | chinese | River |
| | Hka | burmese | River |
| | Hon | vietnamese | Island |
| | Honhor | mongolian | Depression |
| Ht | Height | english | |
| | Hu | chinese | Lake |
| | Hudãg | mongolian | Well |
| I.Is. | Island(s) | english | |
| | Isla(s) | spanish | Island(s) |
| Ia | Ilha(s) | portuguese | Island(s) |
| Is. | Ile(s) | french | Island(s) |
| | Idehan | arabic | Sand desert |
| If. | Icefield | english | |
| In. | Inlet | english | |
| J. | Jabál | arabic | Mount |
| J. | Jazirat | arabic | Island(s) |
| | Jedo | korean | Archipelago |
| | Jehil | afghan | Lake |
| | Jhil | hindi | Reservoir |
| | Jiang | chinese | River |
| | Jiao | chinese | Cape |
| Junc. | Junction | english | |
| K. | Kap | danish | Cape |
| K. | Kapp | norwegian | Cape |
| K. | Kolpos | greek | Bay, gulf |
| K. | Kyun | burmese | Island |
| Kan. | Kaap | afrikaans | Cape |
| | Kanal | russian | Channel |
| | Kandao | pakistani | Neck |
| | Kaôh | khmer | Island(s) |
| | Karoo | afrikaans | Steppe |
| | Kaur | pakistani | River |
| Kep. | Kepulauan | indonesian, malay | Archipelago |
| | Khalij | arabic | Bay |
| | Khao | thai | Mount |
| | Khor | pakistani | Bay |
| | Klang | burmese | Mountain |
| | Klein | afrikaans | Little |
| | Ko | thai | Island |
| Kō | Kaikyō | japanese | Strait |
| | Koh | pakistani | Mountain |
| Kör | Körfez | turkish | Bay |
| | Körfezi | turkish | Gulf |
| | Kotal | persian | Neck |
| | Kowtal | afghan | Neck |
| | Krueng | indonesian | River |
| | Kũh | afghan, persian | Mountain |
| | Kũhhã | persian | Mountain range |
| | Kyunzu | burmese | Archipelago |
| L. | Lac | french | Lake |
| L. | Lake | english | |
| L. | Lago | spanish | Lake |
| L. | Laut | indonesian | Lake |
| | Lã | hindi | Neck |
| | Laem | thai | Cape |
| Lag. | Laguna | spanish | Lagoon |
| Lagn | Lagoon | english | |
| | Liedao | chinese | Archipelago |
| | Ling | chinese | Mountain |
| Lit. | Little | english | |
| M. | Mys | russian | Cape |
| | Madhya | hindi | Middle |
| | Mae | thai | River |
| | Maidãn | hindi | Plain |
| Mal. | Malyj | russian | Little |
| | Man | korean | Bay |
| | Massif | french | Mountains |
| | Maw | burmese | Point |
| | Mer | french | Sea |
| Mi. | Misaki | japanese | Cape |
| | Mörön | mongolian | River |
| Mt | Mont | french | Mount |
| Mt | Mount | english | |
| Mte | Monte | spanish | Mount |
| Mts | Montagnes | french | Mountains |
| Mtes | Montes | spanish | Mounts |
| Mtns | Mountains | english | |
| | Mul | vietnamese | Cape |
| | Mu Ko | thai | Archipelago |
| N. | Norden | danish | North |
| N. | Nørdre | norwegian | Northern |
| N. | North | english | |
| Na. | Nada | japanese | Gulf |
| Nac. | Nacional | spanish | National |
| | Nadī | hindi | River |
| | Nam | burmese, thai | River |
| Nev. | Nevada | spanish | Snowy summit |
| Ni. | Naikal | japanese | Inland sea |
| | Nižnij | russian | Lower |
| | Norte | spanish | Northern |
| Nov. | Novyj | russian | New |
| | Nuruu | mongolian | Mountain range |
| | Nuur | mongolian | Lake |
| Nva | Nueva | spanish | New |
| Nvo | Nuevo | spanish | New |
| O. | Ostrov | russian | Island |
| O. | Oued | arabic | Seasonal river |
| Ø. | Øy, Øya | norwegian | Island(s) |
| Or. | Oro, Ori | greek | Mountain |
| O-va | Ostrova | russian | Island |
| Oz | Ozero | russian | Lake |
| P. | Parvat | hindi | Range (mount.) |
| P. | Phou | laotian | Mountain |
| P. | Pulau | indonesian, malay | Island(s) |
| | Pahãriyãn | hindi | Mount |
| | Pashehim | hindi | Western |
| | Pathãr | hindi | Plateau |
| Peg. | Pegunungan | indonesian | Range (mount.) |
| Pen. | Peninsula | english, spanish | |
| Per. | Pereval | russian | Neck |
| | Pingyuan | chinese | Plain |
| | Pintu | indonesian | Channel |
| Pk. | Pik | russian | Peak |
| | Plato | afrikaans | Plateau |
| Po | Paso | spanish | Neck |
| P-ov | Poluostrov | russian | Peninsula |
| Pr. | Proliv | russian | Strait |
| | Prêk | khmer | River |
| Pres. | Preserve | english | |
| Pt | Point | english | |
| Pta | Punta | spanish | Point |
| Pte | Ponte | portuguese | Point |
| Plo | Portezuelo | spanish | Neck |
| Pto | Pórto | portuguese | Port |
| | Purva | hindi | Eastern |
| Q | Qelay | arabic | Lake |
| | Qarãt | arabic | Hill(s) |
| | Ql | chinese | River |
| | Qolleh | afghan | Mount |
| | Qolleh | persian | Peak |
| | Qundao | chinese | Archipelago |
| | Qunjiao | chinese | Bank |
| | Quwayrat | arabic | Hill(s) |
| R. | River | english | |
| Ra. | Range | english | |
| | Ramlat | arabic | Sand desert |
| | Rãs | arabic | Cape |
| | Reka | russian | River |
| | Reshteh | persian | Range (mount.) |
| | Riviere | french | River |
| Rō | Rettō | japanese | Archipelago |
| | Rowd | afghan | River |
| | Rũd | afghan, persian | River |
| S. | San | korean, japanese | Mount |
| S. | San | spanish | Saint |
| S. | Sao | portuguese | Saint |
| S. | Søndre | norwegian | Southern |
| S. | South | english | |
| S. | Sul | portuguese | Southern |
| Sa. | Sima | japanese | Island |
| Sa | Serra | portuguese | Mountains |
| Sa | Sierra | spanish | Mountains |
| | Sahrã | arabic | Desert |
| Sal. | Salar | spanish | Salt flat |
| | Sanmaeg | korean | Range (mount.) |
| | Saridag | mongolian | Range (mount.) |
| | Sarir | arabic | Desert |
| Sd | Sound | english | |
| Sd | Sund | danish | Sound |
| | Sebkha | arabic | Salt Lake |
| Sel. | Selat | indonesian | Strait |
| Sem. | Semandjung | indonesian | Peninsula |
| Semp. | Sempitan | indonesian | Strait |
| | Sha | chinese | High ground |
| Ser. | Serrania | spanish | Mountains |
| Sh. | Shoal | english | |
| | Shan | chinese | Mount |
| | Shankou | chinese | Neck |
| | Shanmo | chinese | Range (mount.) |
| | Shelleh | afghan | River |
| | Shũr | persian | River |
| Si. | Saki | japanese | Cape, Point |
| Sō | Syotō | japanese | Archipelago |
| So. | Seno | spanish | Gulf |
| | Solončak | russian | Salt lake |
| | Sõng | vietnamese | River |
| Sr. | Srednij | russian | Middle |
| St | Saint | english | |
| Sta | Santa | spanish | Saint |
| | Stad | afrikaans | City |
| Sto | Santo | spanish | Saint |
| | Stœng | khmer | River |
| Str. | Strait | english | |
| | Su | japanese | High ground |
| Su. | Senmyaku | japanese | Range (mount.) |
| | Sungai | indonesian | River |
| | Tal | mongolian | Plain |
| Tanj. | Tanjong | malay | Cape |
| | Tassill | arabic | Steppes |
| | Taungdan | burmese | Range (mount.) |
| | Taunggyl | thai | Range (mount.) |
| | Tayga | mongolian | Range (mount.) |
| Tel. | Teluk | indonesian | Bay |
| Tg. | Tandjung | indonesian | Cape |
| | Tsũkai | pakistani | Peak |
| U. | Udjung | indonesian | Peak |
| Up. | Upper | english | |
| | Upar | hindi | High |
| | Uttar | hindi | Northern |
| | Uul | mongolian | Mount |
| Va | Villa | spanish | City |
| Va | Vila | portuguese | City |
| Vdchr. | Vodochranilišče | russian | Reservoir |
| Vel. | Velikij | russian | Great |
| | Veld | afrikaans | Country |
| Verch. | Verchnij | russian | Upper |
| | Vinh | vietnamese | Bay |
| Vol. | Volcano | spanish, english | |
| Vost. | Vostočnys | russian | Eastern |
| Vozv. | Vozvišennost | russian | High |
| | Vung | vietnamese | Bay |
| W. | Wadi, Wabi | arabic | Seasonal river |
| W. | Wan | japanese | Bay |
| W. | West | english | |
| | Wan | chinese | Bay |
| | Wãng | burmese | River |
| | Xé | laotian | River |
| | Xu | chinese | Island(s) |
| | Yoma | burmese | Range (mount.) |
| Za. | Zima | japanese | Island |
| Zal. | Zalif | russian | Bay |
| Zap. | Zapadnyj | russian | Western |
| | Zapovednik | russian | State reservation |

The transliteration of the Cyrillic alphabet conforms to the International System.
The Chinese transcription follows the Pinyin System for mainland China.
The Japanese transcription follows the Kunreisiki System.
The transliteration of the Arabic, Greek, and Persian alphabets follows the system used by the United States Board on Geographic Names (BGN).

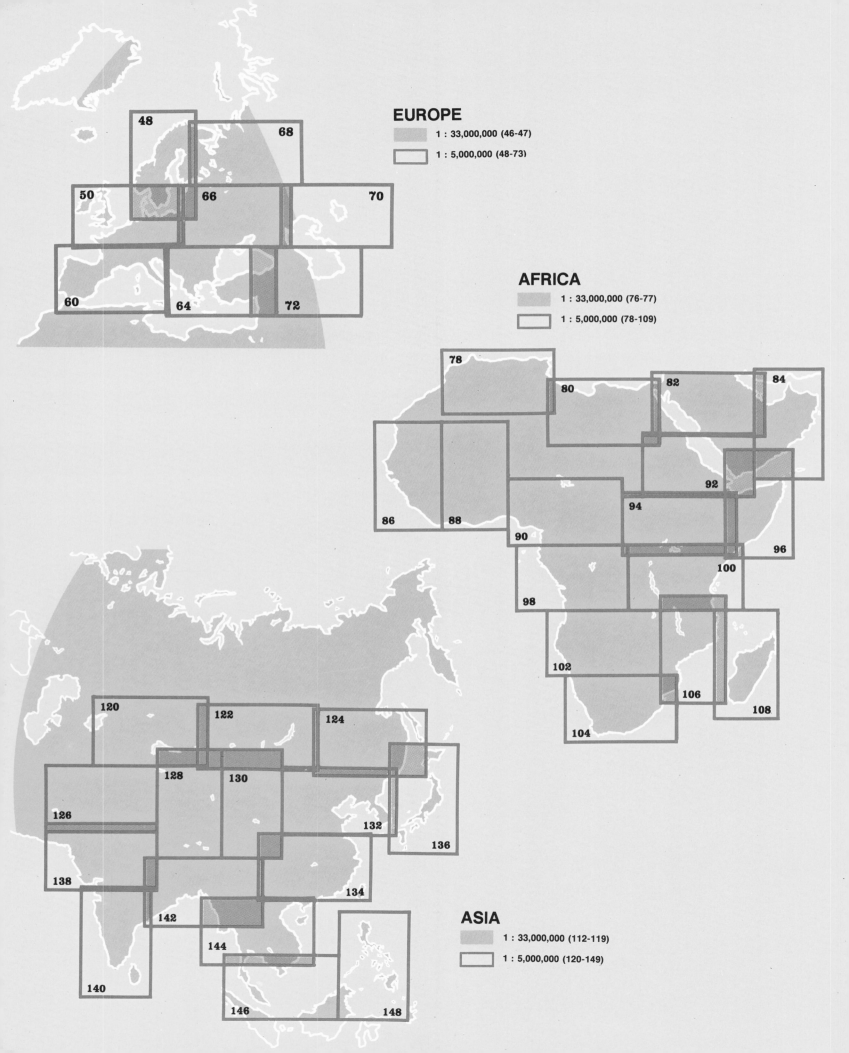

## EUROPE

1 : 33,000,000 (46-47)

1 : 5,000,000 (48-73)

## AFRICA

1 : 33,000,000 (76-77)

1 : 5,000,000 (78-109)

## ASIA

1 : 33,000,000 (112-119)

1 : 5,000,000 (120-149)